Southern Living®
ANNUAL RECIPES
MASTER INDEX

1979-1995

Oxmoor House®

Library of Congress Catalog Number: 79-88364
ISBN: 0-8487-1459-8
ISSN: 0272-2003

Manufactured in the United States of America
First Printing 1996

Oxmoor House, Inc.
    Editor-in-Chief: Nancy Fitzpatrick Wyatt
    Senior Foods Editor: Susan Carlisle Payne
    Senior Editor, Editorial Services: Olivia Kindig Wells
    Art Director: James Boone

Southern Living®
    Foods Editor: Dana Adkins Campbell

Southern Living® *Annual Recipes Master Index 1979-1995*
    Editor: Whitney Wheeler Pickering
    Copy Editor: Donna Baldone
    Editorial Assistant: Stacey Geary
    Production and Distribution Director: Phillip Lee
    Associate Production Manager: Theresa L. Beste
    Production Coordinator: Marianne Jordan Wilson
    Production Assistant: Valerie L. Heard
    Indexer: Mary Ann Laurens
    Designer and Illustrator: Carol Middleton

INTRODUCTION

Many readers call us asking for help in finding recipes that have appeared in *Southern Living*® magazine over the years, and this *Southern Living*® *Annual Recipes Master Index* is what we use to answer every inquiry. With this valuable guide – a true cook's companion – thousands of kitchen-tested recipes are at your fingertips.

To help you use the index, we've cross-referenced every single recipe we've printed in the magazine since 1979 by the type of dish and one or more ingredients in it. The page numbers of all microwave recipes are preceded by an "M." To quickly locate recipes, just look for the alphabetized guide word at the bottom of each page.

If you enjoy our delicious light recipes, you'll find them under the "Living Light" category. Although the name of our light section has changed over time, you can find every light recipe from previous columns called "On the Light Side" and "Cooking Light" now under the new heading.

Occasionally, you'll find that the same recipe has appeared in different volumes of *Southern Living*® *Annual Recipes*. There's a simple reason why: A recipe may appear in the magazine edition for one state before it appears in another state. To make sure you can find the recipes you seek, this index gives all of the page references to those bonus recipes that have appeared in more than one edition of the magazine – and *Southern Living*® *Annual Recipes* cookbooks.

To meet the demand of today's cooks, we've reworked and updated the index this year, adding new categories like "Grilling," "Salsas," and "Cheesecakes." We've added more topics to and expanded the reader-favorite, "From Our Kitchen to Yours." And we've made the index more reader-friendly by adding more subcategories and cross-referencing even more recipes.

We hope you're pleased with this index of our recipes. With it, you know that the recipe you're searching for is just seconds away.

Dana Adkins Campbell

MASTER INDEX

All recipes are listed by their complete titles under a specific food category and ingredient. The volume is indicated in boldface, followed by the page number. Microwave recipe page numbers are preceded by an "M."

ALMONDS

Appetizers
Cheese, Almond, '88 173
Cheese Ball, Fruit-and-Nut, '91 251
Cheese Ball, Pinecone, '93 288
Chicken Almondette Fingers, '93 12
Chicken Nut Puffs, '81 260
Crostini, Almond-Bacon-Cheese, '94 318
Dip, Almond Delight, '90 226
Dip with Strawberries, Almond Cream, '92 164
Nippy Nuts, '93 301
Olives, Almond-Stuffed, '88 95
Pastry Cups, Mushroom-Almond, '88 210
Pesto-Spiced Nuts, '95 173
Rollups, Almond-Ham, '89 284
Braid, Almond, '89 86
Bread, Cocoa-Nut Swirl, '80 257
Caramelized Almonds, '92 303
Coffee Cake, Almond-Blueberry, '85 152
Coffee Cake, Apricot-Almond, '93 26
Coffee Cake Twist, Almond, '91 22
Coffee, Chocolate-Almond, '84 54
Coffee Delight, Almond-, '84 115
Coleslaw with Grapes and Almonds, '83 59
Cream, Peaches 'n' Almond, '86 229
Curried Almonds, '82 297
Danish, Almond, '87 301
Desserts
Apricot-Almond Squares, '95 272
Balls, Coconut-Almond, '84 256
Balls, Toasted Almond Chip, '84 240
Bars, Almond-Chocolate, '83 304
Biscotti, Almond, '91 108
Biscotti, Almond-Anise, '93 266
Biscuits, Raspberry-Almond, '93 160
Brickle Treats, Almond, '95 321
Brie, Almond-Raspberry, '94 M89
Brownies, Date-and-Almond, '88 217
Butter-Nut Strips, '82 167
Cake, Almond-Butter, '86 107
Cake, Almond-Butter Wedding, '86 106
Cake, Almond Legend, '82 8
Cake, Almond Whipping Cream, '80 295
Cake, Chocolate-Almond, '91 248
Cake, Peach-Almond Pound, '89 86
Cake, Peachy Almond-Butter, '90 107
Cake Squares, Almond, '79 111
Cake with Cherry Filling, Chocolate-Almond, '84 225
Candied Nuts, '81 261
Candy, Almond Brittle, '80 255
Cheesecake, Chocolate-Almond, '93 53
Chocolate-Almond Dessert, '82 306

Chocolate Almond Velvet, '81 148
Cinnamon Stars, Swiss, '87 293
Cobbler, Blackberry-Almond, '81 132
Combs, Almond, '84 136
Confections, Almond Cream, '87 198; '90 310
Cookies, Almond, '83 22, 181; '91 51; '92 176
Cookies, Almond Butter, '79 52
Cookies, Almond Spritz, '82 306
Cookies, Chocolate-Almond Surprise, '88 M45
Cookies, Double Chocolate Chunk-Almond, '95 178
Cookies, Light Almond, '83 151
Cookies, Swedish Almond, '85 312
Cookies, Texan-Size Almond Crunch, '91 236
Cream, Chocolate-Almond, '91 108
Cream, Peach Almond, '82 108
Cream with Fresh Strawberries, Almond, '87 93
Crème Brûlée, Almond, '95 323
Crêpes Gelée Amandine, '83 126
Crunch, Almond Butter, '80 301
Crunch, Vanilla Almond, '93 243
Custard with Raspberries, Almond Crème, '88 174
Drops, Cherry-Almond, '81 20
Drops, Chocolate-Coconut Almond, '87 223
Filling, Almond Cream, '85 320; '91 248
Filling, Ground Almond, '87 14
Filling, Nut, '91 35
Float, Nutmeg-Almond, '84 106
Frosting, Almond-Butter, '86 107
Frosting, Chocolate-Almond, '83 241
Frozen Almond Crunch, '94 283
Fudge, Creamy Almond, '95 51
Glaze, Honey-Nut, '87 15
Ice Cream, Almond-Fudge, '93 205
Ice Cream Balls, Almond, '86 315
Ice Cream, Peach-Almond, '89 156
Leaves, Almond Holly, '86 319
Meringue Fingers, Chocolate-Almond, '84 158
Mocha-Almond Dessert, '80 289; '81 62
Mousse, Chocolate-Almond, '93 316
Pastry, Almond, '85 177; '89 317; '92 30
Pears, Almond-Stuffed, '83 207
Petits Fours, Chocolate-Almond, '93 255
Pie Amandine, Chocolate, '83 300
Pie, Apple-Amandine, '89 215
Pie, Creamy Chocolate-Almond, '85 102

Pie, Toasted Almond, '86 163
Pineapple-Almond Delight, '85 96
Praline Sauce, '93 214
Pudding, Chocolate-Almond, '82 142; '88 24
Pudding, Mandarin-Almond, '85 M12
Roca, Almond, '86 49
Sauce, Almond-Vanilla Custard, '88 M177
Sauce, Angel Food Cake with Amaretto-Almond, '90 199
Snaps, Almond, '92 273
Sour Cream-Almond Dessert, '92 120
Spread, Almond Cheese, '87 292
Squares, Cream Cheese-Almond, '85 68
Tart, Almond, '89 232
Tarts, Almond Tea, '85 120
Tassies, Lucky Almond, '91 13
Toffee Crunch, Almond-, '88 285
Topping, Almond, '86 200
Tortoni, Coffee-Almond, '81 30
Truffles, Almond, '83 298
Wafers, Almond-Filled, '88 120
Filling, Almond, '87 301
French Toast, Almond, '88 62
Fruit, Almond-Curried, '83 261
Liqueur, Almond-Flavored, '81 287
Main Dishes
Casserole, Chicken-Almond, '94 199
Catfish Amandine, Mandarin, '84 183
Catfish Amandine, Spicy, '89 52
Chicken and Vegetables, Almond, '86 21
Chicken, Creamy Almond, '89 281
Chicken in Orange-Almond Sauce, '79 219; '80 13
Chicken, Spicy Almond, '88 150
Fish, Almond Baked, '88 270; '89 203
Fish Amandine, '85 179
Fish Amandine, Fillet of, '80 M54
Flounder Amandine, '89 M196
Orange Lake Amandine, '80 99
Pollo Almendrado, '81 193
Quiche, Almond-Topped Crab, '79 127
Muffins, Almond, '90 87
Muffins, Banana-Honey-Nut, '88 62
Muffins, Peachy-Almond, '86 301
Phyllo Nests, Nutty, '87 277
Rice, Almond, '81 195; '85 M112; '89 100; '91 291
Rice, Almond Wild, '86 50
Rice with Almonds, Curried, '83 M285
Rolls, Almond Crescent, '90 283
Rolls, Cherry-Almond, '84 M198
Salad Amandine, Chicken, '81 37
Salad, Cheesy Fruit-'n'-Nut, '87 56

ALMONDS *(continued)*

Salad, Chicken-Almond, '81 133
Salad, Cucumber-Almond, '86 147
Salad Dressing, Almond, '81 37
Salad, Sesame-Almond, '89 123
Salad Shanghai, Almond-Chicken, '90 160
Sandwiches, Chicken-Almond Pocket,
    '81 240; '83 69
Sauce, Mandarin-Almond Cream, '84 183
Sauce, Shrimp-and-Almond, '87 282
Slaw, Pineapple-Almond, '92 171
Snack Balls, Orange-Almond, '95 214
Soup, Almond, '79 48
Soup, Chicken-Almond Cream, '92 21
Spoons, Dipped Chocolate-Almond,
    '95 M277
Streusel, Almond-Garlic, '95 159
Sunburst, Almond, '94 245
Syrup, Almond, '82 47
Tea, Almond, '85 43; '86 329; '89 212
Tea, Almond-Lemonade, '86 229
Tea, Ginger-Almond, '94 131
Toast Amandine, Baked, '82 47
Topping, Almond, '85 152; '86 200
Vegetables
    Asparagus, Almond, '83 86
    Asparagus with Almond Butter, '84 85
    Asparagus with Almond Sauce, '91 117
    Broccoli Casserole, Almond-, '88 62
    Broccoli with Almonds, Glazed, '80 12
    Brussels Sprouts Amandine, '79 213
    Cabbage with Almonds, Creamed, '79 4
    Cauliflower and Peas with Curried
        Almonds, '79 221; '80 82
    Cauliflower with Almond Sauce, '82 270
    Celery Almondine, '85 116
    Celery Amandine, Buttered, '82 98
    Eggplant with Almonds, '79 179
    Green Beans Amandine, '79 276;
        '82 M20
    Green Beans with Almonds, '84 253
    Green Beans with Almonds, Italian,
        '81 207
    Peas with Almonds, Curried, '88 M294
    Potatoes, Almond-Fried, '82 25
    Potatoes, Broccoli-and-Almond-Topped,
        '83 3
    Stir-Fry, Almond-Vegetable, '86 222
AMBROSIA
Anytime Ambrosia, '86 182
Baked Ambrosia, '83 303
Bowl, Ambrosia, '80 138; '84 313
Brunch, Ambrosia, '83 57
Cake, Ambrosia, '79 229
Cake Royale, Ambrosia, '89 335
Carrot-Marshmallow Ambrosia, '80 5
Chicken Salad Ambrosia, '85 216
Citrus Ambrosia, '82 287
Cookies, Ambrosia, '81 301; '82 110;
    '86 313
Cups, Sherbet Ambrosia, '82 159
Custard Sauce Ambrosia, '84 256
Easy Ambrosia, '92 45
Fantastic Ambrosia, '91 277
Fruit Ambrosia, Fresh, '88 184
Fruit Ambrosia, Mixed, '83 10
Grandma's Ambrosia, '90 254
Honey Bee Ambrosia, '83 267
Layered Ambrosia, '88 304
Mold, Ambrosia, '79 241
Mold, Ambrosia Cream Cheese, '79 249

Old-Fashioned Ambrosia, '80 5
Orange Ambrosia Supreme, '79 37
Pancakes with Orange Syrup, Ambrosia,
    '89 254
Peach Ambrosia, '83 53
Pie, Ambrosia, '79 284
Pie, Orange Ambrosia, '80 237
Pineapple-Orange Ambrosia, '88 252
Rhubarb Ambrosia, '88 93
Salad, Ambrosia, '83 231; '94 271
Salad, Carrot-Ambrosia, '81 252
Sauce, Hot Ambrosia, '89 335
Sherried Ambrosia, '84 324; '86 317
Spread, Ambrosia, '92 50
Tropical Ambrosia, '79 74
ANCHOVIES
Appetizers, Zesty Anchovy, '83 93
Mayonnaise, Anchovy, '86 179
Tapenade, '92 194

APPETIZERS. *See also* **PÂTÉS.**
Almond-Ham Rollups, '89 284
Almonds, Curried, '82 297
Anchovy Appetizers, Zesty, '83 93
Antipasto, Easy, '92 24
Antipasto Relish, '86 327
Apple-Phyllo Rolls, '88 213
Apple Quarters, Honey-Baked, '86 93
Artichoke-and-Shrimp Appetizer, '93 271
Artichoke Appetizer Frittata, '92 58
Artichoke Appetizer, Zesty, '80 146
Artichoke-Caviar Mold, '87 239
Artichoke-Cheese Bottoms, Baked, '94 61
Artichoke-Parmesan Phyllo Bites, '87 54
Artichokes, Marinated, '87 250
Artichokes, Spring, '86 62
Asparagus Croquettes, '85 265
Asparagus, Prosciutto-Wrapped, '91 98
Asparagus Rolls, '79 296; '80 31
Asparagus Rolls, Hot, '93 329
Asparagus Rollups, '79 63
Asparagus Roll-Ups, '84 270
Asparagus with Garlic Cream, '95 83
Avocado-Crabmeat Cocktail, Sherried, '87 95
Bacon Appetizers, Hot, '80 248
Bacon-Chestnut Wraps, '84 M216
Bacon-Jalapeño-Tomato Quesadillas, '95 240
Bacon-Onion Appetizers, '94 290
Bacon Rolls, '84 270; '93 330
Bacon Rollups, '79 34
Bacon Swirls, '89 214
Bacon-Wrapped Crackers, '93 280
Bacon-Wrapped Pineapple Chunks, '84 25
Bacon-Wrapped Water Chestnuts, '79 63
Bagel Chips, '91 138
Bagel Chips, Cinnamon-and-Sugar, '91 139
Bagel Chips, Garlic, '91 139
Bagel Chips, Lemon-and-Herb, '91 139
Bagel Crisps, '86 278

Bean Burrito Appetizers, '94 226
Beef on a Stick, Marinated, '85 234
Beef Sticks, '93 331
Beefy Party Snacks, '80 249
Beets, Blue Cheese-Stuffed, '88 211
Black Bean Appetizer, '83 50
Black Bean Cakes with Greens and Apple
    Dressing, '92 216
Black-Eyed Pea Pinwheels, '85 300; '86 18
Broccoli-Cheese Appetizer, '92 265
Broccoli, Cocktail, '80 192
Broccoli Soup, Mock Cream of, '85 288
Brussels Sprouts, Marinated, '88 265
Burgers, Saucy Cocktail, '83 217
Burrito Rollups, '90 119
Burritos, Chinese, '87 181
Buzzard's Nests, '93 244
Canapés
    Bread, Canapé, '89 292
    Bread, Rye Canapé, '89 293
    Bread, Whole Wheat Canapé, '89 293
    Crab Canapés, '93 130
    Crab Canapés, Cheesy, '86 262
    Crab Canapés, Hot, '86 70; '87 239
    Crabmeat Canapés, '88 150
    Cucumber Canapés, '95 88
    Fruit-Topped Canapés, '85 80
    Green Onion Canapés, '84 M216
    Lemon-Cheese Canapés, '87 93
    Mushroom Canapés, '80 285
    Party Canapés, '86 128
    Shrimp-and-Cucumber Canapés, '93 164
    Shrimp Canapés, '84 116
    Swiss Canapés, Hot, '83 259
    Vegetable Canapés, '91 252
Caponata, '87 166
Caramel Corn, Oven-Made, '91 233
Caramel Good Stuff, Baked, '80 284
Caraway Wafers, '81 261
Carrots, Dilled Baby, '84 80
Carrots, Dill-Spiced, '87 200
Carrots, Pickled, '93 12
Catfish Appetizer, Layered, '92 209
Cauliflower, Crispy Fried, '80 220
Cauliflower, Dilled, '83 93
Cauliflower, French-Fried, '86 211
Cauliflower, Golden Fried, '82 78
Cauliflower, Pickled, '94 183
Cauliflower with Cheese Sauce, Fried, '87 231
Caviar Crown, '83 78
Caviar Pie, '79 154
Caviar Potatoes, '84 80
Caviar Potatoes, Appetizer, '86 223
Caviar, Texas, '86 218
Caviar Tomatoes, '91 12
Celery, Creamy Stuffed, '82 102
Celery, Jalapeño Stuffed, '79 70
Celery, Stuffed, '82 98
Celery Trunks, Stuffed, '85 115
Cereal Bites, Buttery, '89 97
Cereal Nibblers, Great, '82 297
Cereal Snack, Toasted, '85 215
Ceviche (Marinated Raw Fish), '80 194
Ceviche, Mexican-Style, '88 115
Cheese. *See also* Appetizers/Dips, Spreads
    and Fillings.
    Bagel Chips, Parmesan Cheese, '91 138
    Bake, Appetizer Cheese, '92 209
    Ball, Blue Cheese, '80 259; '84 221
    Ball, Blue Cheese-Olive, '82 248
    Ball, Bourbon Cheese, '81 57
    Ball, Brandied Blue Cheese, '85 283
    Ball, Carrot-Cheese, '86 325

Ball, Cheese, '82 161; '91 200
Ball, Cheese and Chutney, '87 247
Ball, Cheese 'n' Beef, '83 230
Ball, Chicken-Cheese, '93 216
Ball, Chicken-Curry Cheese, '85 118
Ball, Cocktail Cheese, '83 174
Ball, Curried Shrimp Cheese, '86 135
Ball, Deviled Pecan, '80 258
Ball, Festive Cheese, '79 44; '94 279
Ball, Fruit-and-Nut Cheese, '91 251
Ball, Herbed Cheese, '89 246
Ball, Holiday Cheese, '79 285
Ball, Olive Cheese, '80 258
Ball, Parmesan-Cream Cheese, '89 246
Ball, Party Cheese, '84 258
Ball, Party Pecan Cheese, '81 235
Ball, Peanut Butter-Cheese, '86 136
Ball, Pecan Cheese, '83 127
Ball, Peppered Cheese, '79 100; '94 118
Ball, Pimiento Cheese, '80 258
Ball, Pineapple Cheese, '81 160
Ball, Pineapple-Cheese, '84 26
Ball, Pinecone Cheese, '93 288
Balls, Bite-Size Cheese, '92 321
Balls, Cheese and Mushroom, '79 63
Balls, Fried Cheese, '89 181
Ball, Shrimp-Cheese, '85 208
Ball, Smoky Salmon Cheese, '82 247
Balls, Olive-Cheese, '84 206
Balls with Sun-Dried Tomatoes, Cheese, '94 317
Ball, Tangy Cheese, '81 263, 287
Bar, Savory Cheese, '91 98
Bars, Bacon-Cheese Toast, '79 36
Bars, Camembert, '86 58
Bear Claws, '81 161
Biscuits, Cheese, '79 296; '80 31
Biscuits, Cheesy Sausage, '80 78
Biscuits, Petite Ham and Cheese, '79 193
Biscuits, Tiny Cheese, '80 192
Bites, Benne Cheese, '80 121
Bites, Cheese, '93 329
Bites, Cheesy Pecan, '82 248
Bites, Curried Swiss, '85 220
Bites, Lemon-Cheese Party, '95 160
Bit-of-Brie Appetizer, '88 M8
Bonbons, Cheese, '87 93
Brie, Chutney-Bacon, '90 M292
Brie, Honey-Mustard, '91 252
Brie in Rye, Raspberry, '93 252
Brie, Kahlúa-Pecan, '92 289
Brie, Parmesan-Coated, '95 286
Brie, Tropical Breeze, '94 M18
Brie with Fresh Fruit, Caramel, '90 266
Brie, Wrapped, '92 126
Brie Wrapped in Phyllo, '93 173
Caraway Cheese, '89 246
Caraway-Cheese Crisps, '95 284
Chiles-Rellenos Squares, '91 161
Cracker Nibbles, Cheese, '84 328
Crackers, Cheddar, '84 236
Cream Cheese Appetizer, Baked, '92 58
Cream Cheese Round, Pesto-and-, '90 242
Crème Brûlée, Roquefort-and-Black Pepper, '95 324
Crispies, Cheese-Bacon, '84 270
Crispies, Pecan-Cheese, '87 168
Croquettes, Hot Cheese, '89 182
Crostini, Almond-Bacon-Cheese, '94 318

Crostini, Mozzarella, '94 319
Crostini, Swiss-Blue Cheese, '94 318
Cucumber Slices, Cheesy, '84 80
Cups, Cottage Cheese-Spinach, '87 190
Cutouts, Sesame-Cheese, '82 296
Feta Cheesecakes, Little, '86 277
Fiesta Cheesecake, '93 273
Flaming Cheese, '84 187
Fondue, Cheese, '81 40
Fondue, Nacho, '95 35
Fondue, Party Cheese, '92 20
Fondue, Pub, '95 35
Fondue, Swiss Cheese, '91 48
Fried Cheddar Cheese, '89 182
Fried Cheese Bites, '82 77
Fried Cheese, Italian-Style, '83 250; '89 182
Garnished Cheese, '91 98
Goat Cheese, Peppered, '94 128
Goat Cheese Rosemary, '89 270
Goat Cheese with Sun-Dried Tomatoes and Rosemary, '93 319
Grapes, Blue Cheese-Pecan, '95 48
Herb Cheese, Pot-of-, '85 210
Herbed Cheese, '88 152
Kabobs, Peppered Cheese, '91 279
Little Bits, '79 196
Log, Cheesy Surprise, '82 247
Log, Garlic Cheese, '85 21
Log, Hawaiian Cheese, '89 246
Log, Roquefort Pecan, '89 247
Logs, Black Pepper Cheese, '90 61
Logs, East Indian Cheese, '88 173
Log, Toasted Pecan Cheese, '86 M288
Marinated Cheese, '90 244; '95 21
Meat-and-Cheese Appetizers, '87 7
Mexicali Appetizer, Cheesy, '82 108
Mold, Blue Cheese, '85 210
Mold, Cheese-and-Wine, '84 197
Mold, Cream Cheese-Crabmeat, '90 71
Mold, Garlic-Chive Cheese, '85 210
Mousse, Roquefort, '82 71
Nuggets, Cheesy Ham, '81 290
Olive Appetizers, Cheesy, '85 113
Olive Appetizers, Cheesy-, '87 246
Olive Snack, Open-Faced Cheese-and-, '89 97
Pasta Bites, Pesto-Cheese, '87 251
Pastries, Cream Cheese, '80 250
Pastries, Date-Filled Cheese, '83 259
Pastry, Brie Wrapped in, '80 241
Pastry, Sausage Balls in Cheese, '80 248
Pastry Shells, Miniature Cream Cheese, '87 190
Patty, Lemon-Pepper Cheese, '84 117
Patty Shells, Cream Cheese, '82 249
Peachy Cream Cheese, '92 289
Pepper-Cheese Stacks, '87 80
Peppers, Cheesy Jalapeño, '80 195
Phyllo-Cheese Triangles, '87 246
Phyllo Cheese Triangles, '93 329
Phyllo Triangles, Cheese-Filled, '83 259
Pie, Cheesy Hors d'Oeuvre, '88 91
Pinwheels, Mexican, '95 21
Pinwheels, Santa's, '91 275
Potato Skins, Cheesy, '82 78
Puffs, Bavarian Cheese, '80 191
Puffs, Cheese, '79 110
Puffs, Cheese-and-Spinach, '87 246
Puffs, Cream Cheese, '84 151
Puffs, Gouda-Shrimp, '79 234
Puffs, Ham-and-Cheese, '86 277
Puffs, Mexican Cheese, '87 8

Puffs, Oregano Cheese, '95 21
Puffs, Surprise Cheese, '79 295; '80 31
Quesadillas, Green Chile, '90 121
Queso Blanco, '93 322
Quiches, Miniature Bacon-Cheese, '83 93
Quiches, Miniature Cheese, '80 150
Quick Cheese Snack, '89 98
Ring, Cheese, '81 261
Ring, Strawberry-Cheese, '86 14
Roll, Chili-Cheese, '84 114
Roll, Ham-and-Cheese, '79 234
Rollups, Ham-and-Swiss, '85 113
Round, Brie Appetizer, '82 41
Round, Herbed Cheese, '84 300
Rounds, Cheese, '86 262
Rounds, Parmesan, '85 131
Rounds, Parmesan Party, '82 248
Salami-Cheese Snacks, '88 96
Sandwiches, Cheese Tea, '92 276
Sandwiches, Cheshire Claret Cheese-and-Ham Striped Tea, '94 16
Sesame Cheese Bites, '89 24
Soufflé, Blue Cheese, '91 244
Sour Cream Appetizer, Cheesy, '84 51
Spinach-Cheese Bites, '94 23
Squares, Cream Cheese-Almond, '85 68
Squares, Green Chile-Cottage Cheese, '86 85
Squares, Jalapeño Cheese, '80 195
Squares, Quick Cheese, '84 191
Sticks, Parmesan, '82 297
Sticks, Parmesan Sesame, '81 39
Sticks, Peppery Cheese, '81 M289
Straws, Brie Cheese, '94 216
Straws, Cheese, '80 150; '82 137; '88 77
Straws, Chili-Cheese, '94 216
Straws, Easy-as-Pie Cheese, '94 216
Straws, Italian Cheese, '94 217
Straws, Parmesan Cheese, '94 216
Tartlets, Cheese, '88 211
Tarts, Blue Cheese Appetizer, '85 300; '86 18
Terrine, Italian Cheese, '93 64
Three-Cheese Appetizer, '80 174
Toast Treats, Cheese, '83 100
Turnovers, Cheesy Sesame Seed, '91 252
Twists, Double Cheese, '85 131
Wafers, Cheese, '80 151; '95 174
Wafers, Hope Farm Cheese, '93 282
Wafers, Pecan-Cheese, '81 119
Wafers, Sage-Pecan Cheese, '93 12
Wedges, Cheesy Party, '84 84
Wonton Chips, Parmesan Cheese, '91 138
Wonton Envelopes, Fried, '95 96
Wontons with Hot Sauce, Cheese, '83 74
Cherries, Stuffed, '85 81
Chicken. *See also* Appetizers/Dips, Spreads and Fillings.
Balls, Coconut Curried Chicken, '91 165
Balls, Curried Chicken, '91 98
Bites, Curried Chicken, '85 40
Bites, French-Fried Chicken, '85 160
Bites, Savory Chicken, '92 209
Deep-Fried Walnut Chicken, '87 175
Drummettes, Down-Home Chicken, '93 157
Drummettes, Ginger-Garlic Appetizer, '93 157
Drummettes, Orange-Pecan Chicken, '93 158

APPETIZERS, Chicken (continued)

Drummettes, Southwestern Chicken, '93 158
Fingers, Chicken Almondette, '93 12
Fingers, Chicken Little, '80 249
Liver and Bacon Roll-Ups, Chicken, '80 200; '81 57
Livers, Party Chicken, '83 242
Liver Turnovers, Chicken, '79 141
Log, Chicken-Pecan, '81 290
Mushroom Appetizers, Chicken-, '88 210
Nuggets, Baked Chicken, '81 149
Nuggets, Lemon-Chicken, '87 283
Nuggets Supreme, Chicken, '85 160
Nuggets with Pineapple Sauce, Chicken, '84 236
Puffs, Appetizer Chicken, '85 72
Puffs, Chicken Nut, '81 260
Quesadillas, Spicy Chicken, '95 42
Salad, Old-Fashioned Chicken, '83 79
Sesame Chicken Appetizers, '89 61
Tarts, Chicken Salad, '84 257
Tarts, Deviled Chicken, '94 14
Tempura Delight, Chicken, '85 66
Terrine, Vegetable-Chicken, '83 224
Wings, Broiled Chicken, '80 149
Wings, Honey-Glazed Chicken, '91 251
Wings, Spicy Buffalo, '95 239
Wings, Sweet-and-Sour Chicken, '90 206
Wings, Teriyaki Chicken, '85 300; '86 18
Chile-Sausage Squares, '86 297
Chiles Rellenos, Bite-Size, '87 246
Chiles Rellenos, Roasted, '95 64
Chili in Pastry Cups, '90 68
Chips with Guacamole Spread, Homemade Texas, '90 119
Chocolate-Almond Cream, '91 108
Chocolate Bites, Snowy, '90 47
Chocolate-Dipped Horns, '93 197
Chocolate-Peanut Butter Snacks, '90 226
Chocolate-Sesame Sticks, '91 316
Chutney Roll, '83 259
Chutney with Cream Cheese, Cranberry-Amaretto, '87 244
Cinnamon Sticks, '95 244
Cinnamon Wafers, '84 324
Clam Crisps, '80 151
Clam Puffs, '90 60
Clams Casino, '81 125
Clams Oreganata, '85 104
Cocktail Puffs, '91 106
Confetti Appetizers, '84 191
Corn Salsa, Spicy, '93 322
Crab. See also Appetizers/Dips, Spreads and Fillings.
Balls, Crabmeat, '88 150
Bites, Crab-Zucchini, '84 M216
Bites, Spicy Crab, '91 165
Broiled Crab Meltaways, '93 287
Casserole, Easy Crab, '93 270
Chafing Dish Crabmeat, '89 284
Crisps, Crab, '79 63
Deviled Crab, Devilish, '85 264
Hors d'Oeuvre, Crabmeat, '94 236
Mold, Crab, '85 318
Oysters, Crabmeat Stuffed, '94 328
Puffs, Crab, '80 20; '84 269
Rémoulade, Crabmeat, '93 280
Snacks, Crab, '83 93
Topping, Crabmeat, '91 64

Cracker Bread, Sesame, '87 2
Crackers, Critter, '93 193
Crackers, Easy Bisque, '93 252
Crackers, Fennel-Rye, '87 2
Crackers, Florida, '86 179
Crackers, Hot Nut, '90 206
Cracker Snackers, '86 229; '93 197
Crackers, Oatmeal-Wheat Germ, '84 236
Crackers, Olive-Rye Snack, '84 191
Crawfish on Eggplant, Soft-Shell, '88 222
Crème Brûlée, Onion, '95 324
Crème Brûlée, Roasted Garlic, '95 324
Crème Brûlées, Savory, '95 324
Crostini, Christmas, '94 318
Crostini, Hot Artichoke, '94 319
Crostini, Mexican, '95 142
Crunchy Munchies, '94 196
Cucumber Delights, '84 117
Cucumber Fingers, Fried, '86 146
Cucumber Rounds, '88 78
Cucumber Sandwiches, '94 14
Cucumber Vichyssoise, '94 90
Date-Nut Ball, '92 326
Dates, Apricot-Stuffed, '80 250
Dips. See also Appetizers/Fondue.
Almond Cream Dip with Strawberries, '92 164
Almond Delight Dip, '90 226
Antipasto Dip, '93 313
Apple Dip, '93 205
Apricot Dip, '86 178
Artichoke Dip, Baked, '95 239
Artichoke Dip, Deluxe, '80 87
Artichoke Dip in a Bread Basket, '93 13
Artichoke Dip, Mexican, '90 292
Artichoke Dip, Seasoned Mayonnaise, '80 87
Artichoke-Seafood Dip, Hot, '80 241
Artichoke Seafood Dip, Hot, '85 M212
Avocado Dip, '80 285; '81 57, 306
Avocado Dip, "Bring-Home-the-Bacon," '92 80
Avocado Dip, Zippy, '82 9; '83 69
Bacon-and-Tomato Dip, '90 147
Bacon Dip, '82 197
Bacon Dip, Zesty, '92 156
Bacon-Guacamole Dip, '85 25
Basket, Dips and Dippers in a, '83 171
Bean Dip, '89 97
Bean Dip, Hotshot, '87 195
Bean Dip, Prairie Fire, '80 195
Beau Monde Dip in Rye Bread, Party, '83 127
Beef Dip, Chipped, '88 M8
Beef Dip, Hot Cheesy, '80 85
Black Bean Dip, '95 93
Black-Eyed Pea Dip, '81 8
Blue Cheese Dip, '80 285; '83 169; '93 313
Braunschweiger-and-Beer Dip, '85 69
Broccoli Dip, Cheesy, '83 92
Broccoli-Garlic Dip, '82 59
Brown Sugar Dip with Fruit, Buttery, '90 243
Cabbage, Dock Dip in, '86 179
Cheddar-Bacon Dip, '89 M119
Cheese-and-Chile Dip, '83 31
Cheese and Crab Dip, Hot, '81 261
Cheese-Bean Dip, '85 208
Cheese-Crab Dip, '91 200
Cheese Dip, Hot, '91 171
Cheese Dip, Meaty, '82 59; '92 160
Cheese Dip, Seaside, '85 284

Cheese Dunk, Deviled, '80 265
Cheese-Garlic Dip, '80 192
Cheese-Herb Dip, '89 20
Chicken Dip, Hot, '80 86
Chile-Beef Dip, Hot, '83 218
Chile-Cheese Dip, '87 173
Chile con Queso, '80 194; '81 195
Chile con Queso Supreme, '80 265
Chile Dip, Hot, '82 248
Chile Sauce, Hot, '92 156
Chili-and-Black-Eyed Pea Dip, '92 155
Chili-and-Cheese Dip, '89 328
Chili-Cheese Dip, '90 225
Chili con Queso Dip, '86 81
Chili Dip, '82 161; '88 218; '89 47; '91 143
Chili Dip, Cheesy, '80 150
Chive-Cheese Dip, '94 62
Christmas Confetti Dip, '92 279
Clam Dip, '79 151; '80 265
Clam Dip, Hot, '82 59; '89 48
Clam Dip, Zesty, '92 25
Confetti Snack Dip, '79 107
Corn-and-Avocado Dip, Roasted, '91 279
Cottage Cheese Sun-Dried Tomato Dip, '93 13
Crab-and-Cheese Dip, Hot, '94 282
Crab Dip, Creamy, '80 M135
Crab Dip, Festive, '92 285
Crab Dip, Hot, '93 269
Crab Dip, Oven-Baked, '82 59
Crab Dip, Tangy, '83 5
Crab Dip, Trawler, '93 238
Crabmeat Dip, Hot, '95 154
Cranberry Fruit Dip, '89 60
Cranberry-Horseradish Dip, '85 65
Cream Cheese Dip, Fruited, '88 261
Cream Cheese-Onion Dip, '79 236
Creamy Texas Dip, '94 161
Crudité Dip, '86 105
Crudité Platter with Dip, '84 139
Cucumber Dipping Sauce, '94 47
Curried Dip, '81 262
Curry Dip, '80 84; '81 9; '85 132; '86 184; '87 25
Curry Dip and Vegetable Platter, '89 327
Curry Dip, Creamy, '84 206
Curry-Onion Dip, '93 313
Deviled Dip, '87 25
Dill Dip, '80 265; '93 330
Dilled Garden Dip, '84 324
Egg Dip, Festive, '79 285
Fiesta Dip, '81 206; '92 263
Fish Dip, Smoked, '84 46
Fruit Dip, Coconut-Honey, '84 171
Fruit Dip, Creamy, '84 51
Fruit Dip, Fresh, '80 265; '95 94
Fruit Dip, Heavenly, '81 160
Fruit Dip, Marshmallow, '84 171
Fruit Dip, Quick, '90 110
Fruit Dip, Sweet, '89 328
Garbanzo Dip, '93 94
Gazpacho Dip, '95 243
Ginger Dip, '94 12, 19
Grand Marnier Dip, '86 142
Green Goddess Dip, '84 159
Guacamole, '79 185; '80 74; '83 179; '91 161
Guacamole, Black Bean, '94 277
Guacamole, Creamy, '79 91; '83 174
Guacamole Dip, '86 4; '95 96
Guacamole in Shells, '86 74

Ham Dip, Creamy, '93 125
Herbal Dip, '86 14
Holiday Dip, '83 321; '84 289
Horseradish Dip, Creamy, '94 122
Hummas, '92 155
Hummus, Black-Eyed Pea, '94 123
Hummus, Creamy Dried Tomato, '95 284
Hummus, Quick, '95 93
Leek Dip, Creamy, '86 77
Lime-Dill Dip, '92 65
Mexican Appetizer, Chilled, '87 197
Mint Dip with Fresh Fruit, '87 146
Monster Mash Dip, '93 244
Mushroom Dip, Hot, '89 48
Nacho Dip, '83 239; '93 M330
Nacho Dip, Layered, '81 261
Nacho Dip, Quick, '90 168
Olive-Relish Dip, '84 205
Onion Dip, '94 21
Onion Dip, Cheesy, '83 145
Onion Dip, Chunky, '84 257
Orange Cream, '90 126
Orange Dip, Creamy, '84 117; '87 247
Orange Dip, Spicy, '85 230
Orange Sour Cream Dip, '79 208
Oyster Dip, Smoked, '79 233
Parsley-Dill Dip with Fresh Vegetables, '85 79
Peach Dip, Creole, '80 142
Peachy Dip, '92 179
Peanut Butter Dip, '86 135
Peanut Butter-Honey Dip, '85 19
Peanut Butter Lovers' Dip, '93 162
Peas, Passion, '89 17
Pepperoncini-Cream Cheese Dip, '91 252
Pesto Dip, '95 93
Pineapple Dip, Cheesy, '80 249
Pineapple-Ginger Dip, '86 104
Plantain Dip, '92 158
Quick Fiesta Dip, '95 M237
Ranch Dip, Skinny, '93 96
Ranch-Style Dip, '90 138; '92 148
Salsa, Chunky, '90 206
Salsa Cruda, '87 180
Salsa, Fresh Summer, '87 89
Salsa Picante, '84 108
Seafood Dip, '79 3
Seafood Dip, Hot Cheesy, '84 221
Seafood Dip, Super, '90 292
Shrimp Dip, '86 84; '88 M261
Shrimp Dip, Hot, '87 190
Shrimp Dip, Quick, '79 153
Shrimp Dip, Zesty, '80 150
Six-Layer Dip, '81 160
Skinny Dip, Santa Fe, '94 137
Sour Cream Dip, '86 278
South-of-the-Border Dip, '81 235
Spinach-Cheese Dip, Hot, '89 48
Spinach con Queso, Easy, '88 101
Spinach Dip, '80 86; '86 159; '87 25, 214; '93 324
Spinach Dip, Cheesy, '82 59
Spinach Dip, Creamy, '88 132
Spinach Dip, Hot, '80 249
Spinach Dip in Cabbage, '82 155
Sugar Snap Dip, '88 91
Summer Dip, '94 157
Swiss-Onion Dip, '95 93

Taco Dip, Hot, '93 238
Tarragon Dip, '83 78
Tennessee Sin, '95 218
Tequila Dip, '91 166
Thick-and-Creamy Dip, '90 271
Tofu Dip, '86 109
Tostada Dip, '84 206
Tropical Dip for Fruit, '91 252
Tuna-Curry Dip, '84 31
Tuna Dip, Low-Cal, '87 25
Turnip Green Dip, '91 13
Turnip Green Dip with Jalapeño-Corn Muffins, Hot, '93 164
Vegetable Dip, '79 52; '82 161
Vegetable Dip, Creamy, '82 132; '83 99, 180
Vegetable Dip, Cucumber-Cheese, '83 128
Vegetable Dip, Fresh, '80 249
Vegetable Dip, Herb, '89 269
Vegetable Dip, Starburst, '82 248
Vegetable Dip, Tangy, '87 196
Vegetable Dip, Zippy, '84 256
Vegetable Garden Dip, '85 215
Water Chestnut Dip, '80 86; '86 183
Yellow Squash-Zucchini Dip, '89 48
Yogurt Dip, '94 21
Yogurt Dip, Fruited, '84 171
Yogurt Herring Dip, '80 232
Zesty Party Dip, '83 259
Eggplant Appetizer, '83 187
Eggplant Appetizer, Grilled, '95 198
Eggplant Caviar, '88 262
Eggplant, Cheesy Fried, '90 75
Eggplant, Fried Parmesan, '87 166
Eggplant Sticks, Ned's, '95 309
Egg Rolls, '86 81
Egg Rolls, Chiles Rellenos, '86 296
Eggrolls, Shrimp and Pork, '82 240; '83 18
Egg Rolls, Vegetarian, '86 148
Empanadas, '92 156
Endive Boats, '84 80
Endive with Caviar, '93 118
Escargots Provençal, '82 238; '83 156
Eye-of-Round, Burgundy, '90 243
Fast Goodies, '84 206
Filet Mignon, Cajun Blackened, '95 85
Firecrackers, Texas, '95 96
Flank Steak, Marinated, '83 258; '88 262
Flank Steak, Red Wine-Marinated, '95 283
Fondue, Fruitcake, '84 258
Fondue, Nacho, '94 332
Fondue, Peppermint, '95 35
Fondue, Pub, '94 332
Frankfurter Appetizers, Bourbon, '85 207
Franks, Pickled Party, '83 174
Franks, Saucy Appetizer, '84 M12
Franks, Tipsy, '85 52
Frog Legs, Crispy, '80 99
Fruit and Cheese Tray, '83 171
Fruit Bowl, Sparkling Fresh, '80 146
Fruit Cascade, '86 104
Fruit Cup, Appetizer, '86 131
Fruit Kabobs, '86 181
Fruit Kabobs with Coconut Dressing, '87 251
Fruit with Curried Rum Sauce, Tropical, '91 164
Fruit with Dressing, Chilled, '85 222
Fruit with Honey-Sour Cream Dip, Fresh, '90 180
Gorp, Elf, '90 270
Gorp, Fancy, '89 253
Granola, '93 197

Granola, Fabulous, '92 213
Granola Gorp, '89 59
Granola, Nutty, '90 95
Green Onion Teasers, '82 42
Guacamole, Easy, '95 94
Guacamole Mold, '86 184
Ham-and-Cheese Balls, Fried, '84 221
Ham Appetillas, '93 63
Ham-Filled Party Puffs, '84 116
Ham-Pineapple Nibbles, '95 283
Ham Rolls, '79 153
Ham Rolls, Party, '85 318
Ham Tapas, Garlic-, '92 175
Ham Turnovers, Chile-, '88 64
Ham Turnovers, Party, '82 39
Ham Twists, Deviled, '82 86
Hawaiian Dream Boats, '86 151
Hazelnuts, Curried, '93 301
Honey-and-Spice Crunch, '94 290
Horseradish Squares, Baked, '92 24
Hot Munch, Oriental, '87 8
Jalapeño Peppers, Fried Stuffed, '95 22
Jalapeños, Fiery Fried Stuffed, '90 118
Jalapeños, Shrimp-Stuffed, '88 115
Jezebel Sauce, '93 331
June Bugs, '85 11
Lettuce Folds, Thai, '94 47
Links, Cocktail Smoky, '90 168
Meatballs
    Bacon-Wrapped Meatballs, '79 81
    Brandied Meatballs, '83 78
    Burgundy-Bacon Meatballs, '80 283
    Chafing Dish Meatballs, '81 260
    Chestnut Meatballs, '79 110
    Cocktail Meatballs, '79 63, 207
    Flavorful Meatballs, '84 206
    German Meatballs, Crisp, '92 326
    Ham Balls, '86 256
    Ham Balls, Appetizer, '82 39
    Polynesian Meatballs, '80 207
    Saucy Party Meatballs, '80 149
    Sauerkraut Meatballs, '86 257
    Spiced Meatballs, '79 284
    Sweet-and-Sour Meatballs, '82 247
    Sweet-and-Sour Party Meatballs, '79 233
    Tamale Meatballs, '80 194
    Venison Sausage Balls, '80 42
    Zesty Meatballs, '80 250
Melon Balls, Minted, '87 162
Melon, Berry-Filled, '86 93
Mints, Party, '81 119
Mirliton Balls, '90 217
Mixes
    Bunny Trail Mix, '95 101
    Cereal Snack Mix, '93 129
    Creole Snack Mix, '91 171
    Crunchy Snack Mix, '93 94
    Dried Fruit Mix, '92 22
    Granola Snack Mix, '86 229
    Mexicali Snack Mix, '86 230
    Nutty Snack Mix, '92 22
    Party Mix, '87 257
    Quick Party Mix, '83 92
    Raisin-Nut Party Mix, '83 60
    Rice Mix, Crunchy, '85 327
    Sea-and-Ski Cocktail Mix, '90 319
    Snack-Attack Party Mix, '84 328
    Snack Mix, '89 19
    Spicy Party Mix, '81 M138
Monster Mouths, '95 274
Mousses
    Catfish Mousse, '92 327
    Caviar Mousse, '82 71; '83 258; '85 86

APPENDIX, Mousses (continued)

Chicken Mousse, Curried, '95 328
Crabmeat Mousse, '90 190; '91 244
Crab Mousse, '79 117; '95 327
Ham Mousse Pitas, '95 328
Horseradish Mousse, '84 126
Mustard Mousse, '84 127; '86 184;
  '95 328
Oyster Mousse, '81 245
Salmon Dill Mousse, '81 21
Salmon Mousse, '83 79
Salmon Mousse, Irresistible, '79 284
Shrimp Mousse, '87 196, 251
Smoked Oyster Mousse, '84 320
Tuna Mousse, '80 275
Munchies, Reindeer, '91 276
Mushrooms
Drunk Mushrooms, '83 174
French-Fried Mushrooms, '82 78
French-Fried Mushrooms with Tartar
  Sauce, '86 233
Logs, Mushroom, '84 206
Marinated Herb Mushrooms, '86 327
Marinated Mushroom Caps, '83 128
Marinated Mushrooms, '80 82, 270;
  '86 135; '91 306; '92 328
Marinated Mushrooms, Easy, '86 217
Pastry Cups, Mushroom-Almond,
  '88 210
Rollups, Mushroom, '85 318
Stems, Mushrooms with, '86 258
Stuffed Mushroom Appetizers, '88 210
Stuffed Mushroom Caps, Crab-, '84 160
Stuffed Mushroom Delight, '87 281
Stuffed Mushrooms, '79 212; '81 239;
  '83 13, 66, 126, 136; '93 172
Stuffed Mushrooms, Black Olive-,
  '86 258
Stuffed Mushrooms, Cheese 'n' Bacon-,
  '86 258
Stuffed Mushrooms, Crab-, '81 190
Stuffed Mushrooms, Crawfish-, '86 258
Stuffed Mushrooms, Elegant Cheese-,
  '81 57
Stuffed Mushrooms, Flavor-, '85 288
Stuffed Mushrooms, Italian Sausage-,
  '83 127
Stuffed Mushrooms, Parmesan, '83 115
Stuffed Mushrooms, Pâté-, '85 118
Stuffed Mushrooms, Pecan-, '84 261
Stuffed Mushrooms, Pesto-, '86 150
Stuffed Mushrooms, Pistachio-, '86 141
Stuffed Mushrooms, Ricotta-, '85 20
Stuffed Mushrooms, Sausage-, '80 248;
  '91 164
Stuffed Mushrooms, Seasoned, '84 206
Stuffed Mushrooms, Shrimp-, '80 M135
Stuffed with Crab, Mushrooms, '82 249
Stuffed Mushrooms, Spinach-, '86 81;
  '88 131, M261; '89 M133
Tapas, Majorcan Mushroom, '95 159
Tarts, Hot Sherried Mushroom, '83 78
Tarts, Mushroom, '88 161
Tipsy Mushrooms, '84 M216
Vegetable Mushroom Caps, '81 246
Nachos, Best-Ever, '79 91
Nachos, Chicken, '84 244
Nachos, Commissary Barbecue, '91 171
Nachos, Easy, '84 30
Nachos, Make-Ahead, '80 M135
Nachos, South Texas, '93 321

Nachos Supreme, '81 306
Nachos, Texas Oyster, '87 39
Nachos, Tex-Mex, '89 97
Nachos, Tuna, '95 127
Nachos, Turkey, '90 118
Nachos, Vegetable, '91 17
Nectarine Cocktail, '85 107
New Potatoes, Ham-Stuffed, '88 211
Nibbles, Party, '90 249
Nuts, Chesapeake, '93 269
Nuts, Deviled, '93 118
Nuts, Hot Chili, '81 254
Nuts, Nippy, '93 301
Nuts, Pesto-Spiced, '95 173
Nuts, Sherry-Orange, '86 M289
Nuts, Spiced, '84 257; '91 M316
Nuts, Spicy, '82 161
Nuts, Spicy Curried, '82 250
Olive Quiche Appetizers, '86 159
Olives, Caliente Marinated, '95 177
Olives, Herb-Marinated, '92 176
Olives, Lemon-Garlic, '94 118
Onion Blossom, '94 226
Onion Crescent Crunch Sticks, '90 206
Orange-Almond Snack Balls, '95 214
Orange-Berry Appetizer, '85 81
Orange Halves, Broiled, '85 288
Oyster Nachos, Texas, '87 39
Oysters à la Casino, '80 296
Oysters Annapolis, '89 195
Oysters, Barbecued, '82 247
Oysters Bienville, Baked, '90 27
Oysters Buccaneer, '87 40
Oysters Chesapeake, '92 254
Oysters, Creamed, '92 254
Oysters in Patty Shells, '85 257
Oysters Italiano, Baked, '89 97
Pasta Bites, Pesto-Cheese, '87 251
Pastry, Processor, '87 67
Peanuts, Sugared, '82 249
Pears, Pineapple-Honey, '86 94
Pecans
Barbecued Pecans, '83 222
Christmas Eve Pecans, '91 276
Coffee 'n' Spice Pecans, '88 256
Curried Pecans, '91 208
Hot-and-Spicy Pecans, '89 161
Hot Pepper Pecans, '85 4
Orange Pecans, '87 292
Pepper Pecans, '87 137; '93 79
Salted Pecans, Southern, '80 285
Savory Southern Pecans, '95 240
Spiced Pecans, '79 296; '80 31
Spicy Pecans, '93 279
Sugar and Spice Pecans, '82 297
Sugar-and-Spice Pecans, '86 121
Sweet-and-Spicy Pecans, '92 321
Toasted Chili Pecans, '85 154
Toasted Pecans, '84 321; '86 229
Toasted Pecans, Buttery, '88 77
Pepper Feet, '93 258
Pepperoni Rolls, Ground-, '83 244
Peppers, Marinated Roasted, '92 176
Peppers with Balsamic Vinaigrette, Roasted,
  '94 128
Pesto Rounds, Toasted, '94 289
Pickles, French-Fried, '82 77
Pickles, Fried Dill, '84 206
Pineapple and Strawberries, Skewered, '84 251
Pineapple Delight, Fresh, '79 111
Pineapple Spritz, '86 94
Piroshki, '92 84
Pita Bread Triangles, '88 211

Pita Chips, '89 19; '91 138
Pita Pizza Snack, '94 193
Pita Wedges, Garlic, '93 98
Pizza Bites, '95 244
Pizza-Burger Snacks, '84 30
Pizza Horns, '89 214
Pizza Party Snacks, '86 262
Pizzas, Appetizer, '89 M118
Pizzas, Cocktail, '79 110
Pizza Slices, '84 269
Pizza Snacks, Tasty Little, '79 248
Pizzas, Pita, '89 19
Pizza Squares, '87 168
Pizzas, Quick Little, '88 227
Pizza Turnovers, Little, '85 327
Pizzettes, Party, '80 192
Plantain Chips, '95 M203
(Plantain Chips), Tostones de Plátano, '92 158
Pork Rounds, Sesame, '89 122
Pork Strips, Marinated, '92 219
Potato-Pea Soup, '94 90
Potato Shell Appetizers, '89 M119
Potato Skins, Baked, '86 81
Potato Skin Snack, '91 18
Puff Nibbles, '84 191
Puffs, Cajun Hot, '94 277
Quiche, South-of-the-Border, '93 321
Quiche Squares, '84 222
Quiches, Tarragon Cocktail, '84 127
Raisin-Granola Treats, '92 22
Raspberry Party Puffs, '90 170
Ravioli, St. Louis Toasted, '95 117
Ravioli, Sweet, '91 107
Relish Tree, Christmas, '84 257
Reubens, Party, '90 61
Riblets, Sweet-and-Sour, '85 276
Rice Balls, '81 51
Rosettes, Savory, '91 107
Rumaki, '80 136
Rye Appetizers, Party, '86 262
Salami Rollups, '90 226
Salmon Ball, '80 149; '86 262
Salmon, Drizzled Smoked, '88 91
Salmon Log, '81 22
Salmon Party Roll, '83 127
Samosas, '89 266
Samurai 'shrooms, '93 258
Sandwiches, Apple Party, '92 234
Sandwiches, Asparagus Spear, '84 165
Sandwiches, Bread Basket of, '86 126
Sandwiches, Calla Lily, '91 106
Sandwiches, Cucumber, '90 81
Sandwiches, Curried Tea, '91 314
Sandwiches, Dainty Cucumber, '81 119
Sandwiches, Double-Filled Party, '93 159
Sandwiches, Stacking, '86 127
Sandwiches, Victoria, '94 16
Sandwiches, Watercress, '90 82
Sandwich Wreath, Festive, '86 333
Sausage-Apple Balls, '90 85
Sausage-Bacon Rollups, '88 51
Sausage-Mushroom-Phyllo Bites, '89 284
Sausage Party Ryes, '89 315
Sausage Pinwheels, '80 209; '93 238
Sausage Quesadillas, '90 118
Sausage, Sweet-and-Sour, '88 296
Sausages with Mustard Sauce, Smoked, '81 56
Scallop Appetizer, '86 155
Scallop Appetizers, Flaky, '86 327
Scallops, Bacon-Wrapped, '87 94
Seafood Appetizer, Layered, '88 2
Seafood Mold, Chilled, '86 70
Seafood Tartlets, '87 247

Sesame Bites, '88 67
Seviche Cocktail, '83 258
Shrimp. *See also* Appetizers/Dips, Spreads
  and Fillings.
    Balls, Curried Shrimp, '94 180
    Bayou, Shrimp, '88 261
    Boiled Shrimp, Spicy, '84 289
    Boiled Shrimp with Cocktail Sauce,
     '79 151
    Cocktail Shrimp, '87 173
    Coconut-Beer Shrimp, '85 230
    Dilled Shrimp, '88 150
    Dippers, Shrimp, '84 324
    Herbed Jalapeño Cheese, Shrimp with,
     '87 112
    Kabobs, Appetizer Shrimp, '91 251
    Kabobs, Shrimp, '80 150
    Key West Shrimp, '94 278
    Manale, Shrimp, '86 268
    Marinated Shrimp and Cucumber,
     '91 166
    Marinated Shrimp, Icy, '84 215
    Marinated Shrimp, Zesty, '87 173
    Miniquiches, Shrimp, '87 146
    Mold, Shrimp, '87 94
    Mold with Asparagus, Shrimp, '93 214
    Pickled Shrimp, '94 182
    Pickle, Shrimp-in-a-, '86 326
    Pineapple Appetizer, Shrimp-, '85 80
    Pizza Wedges, Shrimp, '89 158
    Rémoulade, Shrimp, '83 173
    Rock Shrimp Conga, '80 2
    Salsa Picante with Shrimp, '92 210
    Sesame Shrimp, '95 92
    Sherried Garlic Shrimp, '92 175
    Smoked Shrimp, Citrus-Marinated,
     '95 114
    Toast, Shrimp, '86 91
    Tortilla Bites, '95 42
    Tostadas, Shrimp-and-Black Bean,
     '93 204
    Tree, Shrimp, '83 320; '84 288; '85 318
Snackwiches, '88 172
Snow Peas and Dip, Crunchy, '86 62
Snow Peas, Crab-Stuffed, '85 288
Snow Peas, Stuffed, '84 80
Spinach-Artichoke-Tomato Puffs, '95 284
Spinach-Filled Phyllo Triangles, '84 52
Spinach Madeleine in Chafing Dish, '85 319
Spinach-Mushroom Cheesecake, '92 326
Spinach Puffs, '95 316
Spinach Quichelets, '87 67
Spinach Quiches, Miniature, '82 38
Spinach-Ricotta Phyllo Triangles, '88 212
Spinach Squares, '88 131
Spinach Strudels, '93 249
Spinach Supreme, Layered, '82 38
Spinach Tarts, '82 249
Spinach Triangles, Phyllo-, '87 53
Spreads and Fillings
    Aloha Spread, '83 93
    Antipasto Spread, '81 25
    Apple-Date Spread, '91 231; '92 67
    Apricot Brie Spread, '86 275
    Apricot-Cream Cheese Spread, '82 161;
     '87 158
    Artichoke-Crab Spread, Hot, '85 81
    Artichoke Hearts with Caviar, '79 142
    Artichoke-Parmesan Spread, '92 95
    Artichoke Spread, Chunky, '89 98

Artichoke Spread, Hot, '79 110
Beef Spread, Hot, '83 50; '84 M216
Beer Cheese Spread, '81 160; '94 123
Beer-Cheese Spread, '85 69
Black-Eyed Pea Spread, '86 77
Blue Cheese Spread, '90 215; '95 92
Boursin Cheese Spread, Buttery, '94 301
Boursin Cheese Spread, Garlic, '94 301
Braunschweiger-Onion Spread, '79 82
Broccamoli Curry Spread, '88 55
Caraway Spread, '85 276
Carrot Spread, Nutty, '94 123
Caviar-Artichoke Mound, '91 244
Caviar-Cream Cheese Spread, '84 256
Caviar Spread, Creamy, '92 58
Cheese-and-Orange Filling, '93 159
Cheese-Horseradish Spread, '84 222
Cheese-Olive Spread, '79 82
Cheese Spread, '86 135
Cheese Spread, Confetti, '84 256
Cheese Spread, Creamy Sweet, '79 264
Cheese Spread, German, '79 82
Cheese Spread, Hawaiian, '87 158
Cheese Spread, Make-Ahead, '93 324
Cheese Spread, Mexican, '90 119
Cheese Spread, Tipsy, '80 150
Cheese Spread, Zippy, '85 4
Cheesy Beer Spread, '87 196
Chicken Salad Party Spread, '88 M8
Chicken Spread, Festive, '87 158
Chicken Spread, Tasty, '84 193
Chili Cheese Spread, '93 242
Chive-Mustard Spread, '91 12
Chocolate Chip Cheese Loaves, '91 299
Chutney Spread, Curried, '89 283
Clam Spread, Creamy, '91 274
Coconut-Cranberry Cheese Spread,
  '92 328
Corned Beef Spread, '87 196
Crabmeat-Horseradish Spread, '90 292
Crabmeat Spread, '79 81
Crabmeat Spread, Layered, '83 127
Crab Soufflé Spread, '85 4
Crab Spread, '93 167
Crab Spread, Baked, '80 86
Crab Spread, Superb, '81 235
Cream Cheese Filling, '90 170
Cream Cheese Spread, Deviled, '81 235
Cream Cheese Spread, Fruited, '91 306;
  '93 79
Cream Cheese Spread, Nutty, '89 327
Cucumber Spread, '79 295; '80 31
Dried Tomato-Cheese Spread, '90 204
Edam-Sherry Spread, '84 257
Egg Mound, Frosted, '79 33
Eggplant-Mushroom Spread, '92 156
Egg, Sour Cream, and Caviar Spread,
  '85 279
Fruit and Cheese Spread, '81 245
Fruit-and-Cheese Spread, Nutty, '87 246
Fruit Spread, '85 135
Garden Spread, '86 135
Garlic Spread, '85 111
Gouda Cheese Spread, '90 36
Green Onion-Cheese Spread, '92 24
Gruyère-Apple Spread, '81 160
Guacamole Spread, '90 119
Ham and Pimiento Spread, '80 285;
  '81 56
Ham Spread, Buttery, '95 93
Ham Spread, Cold, '82 248
Ham Spread, Country, '87 8
Hearts of Palm Spread, '90 293

Herb-Cheese Spread, '91 124
Herb-Cream Cheese Spread, '83 24
Honey-Nut Spread, '87 157
Horseradish Spread, '90 243
Italian Spread, '85 135
Jalapeño-Cheese Spread, '82 248
Liver Spread, '89 161
Liver Spread, Sherried, '80 86
Mullet Spread, '94 159
Mushroom Spread, Hot, '81 190
Olive Spread, Creamy, '81 290
Olive Spread, Tomatoes with, '85 114
Oyster Spread, Smoked, '91 64
Party Bread Spread, '82 161
Peanut Butter Spread, '92 21
Pear-Cream Cheese Spread, '93 80
Pepper Spread, Roasted, '94 123
Pimiento Cheese, Hot, '87 173
Radish Spread, Fresh, '84 166
Raisin Spread, Creamy, '90 36
Salmon-and-Horseradish Spread, '87 146
Salmon Spread, '81 149
Salmon Spread, Smoked, '84 324
Seafood Spread, '86 M58; '87 146
Shrimp Spread, '81 306; '85 135;
  '87 111; '93 205
Shrimp Spread, Chunky, '85 300; '86 18
Shrimp Spread, Curried, '87 158
Shrimp Spread, Tempting, '79 57
Shrimp Spread, Zippy, '90 36
Smoked Fish Spread, '92 305
Smoked Whitefish Spread, '92 58
Sombrero Spread, '87 111
Spinach-Bacon Spread, '92 M310
Spinach Spread, '88 132
Spinach Spread, Savory, '82 180
Sweet 'n' Sour Spread, '86 184
Swiss Cheese Spread, '90 60
Tomato-Cheese Spread, '81 157
Tomato-Cheese Spread, Fiery, '87 196
Tomato Spread, '94 123
Tuna Spread, '91 305
Tuna Spread, Chunky, '89 147
Tuna Tapenade, '95 127
Turkey Party Spread, '83 282
Turkey Spread, Curried, '92 16
Vegetable Party Spread, '84 166
Vegetable Sandwich Spread, '85 135
Vegetable Spread, '90 144
Vegetable Spread, Garden, '93 184
Watercress Spread, '88 103
White Bean Spread, '95 279
Squash Nosh, '90 147
Stalks, Splendid, '93 258
Steak-and-Chestnut Appetizers, Marinated,
  '84 323
Strawberries with Chocolate Cream, '85 81
Strawberries with Lemon Cream, '90 170
Strawberries with Walnuts, Stuffed, '85 122
Sugar Peas with Dip, '86 170
Sugar Plums, '92 281
Sugar Snap Pea Appetizers, '86 115
Swamp Sticks, '95 274
Sweet Potato Chips, '91 138; '93 332;
  '95 M202
Sweet Potato Chips with Blue Cheese, '93 290
Tabbouleh, '88 211
Taco Appetizer, Layered, '84 206
Tamale Balls, Tangy, '89 60
Tamales, Miniature, '85 154
Tarts, Party, '95 90
Toasted Appetizers, '94 167
Toast Points, '93 270

APPETIZERS (continued)

Toast Strips, Seasoned, '93 98
Tomato Appetizers, Oven-Baked, '95 172
Tomato Bites, '84 80
Tomatoes, Cucumber-Stuffed Cherry, '88 262
Tomatoes, Stuffed Cherry, '84 160;
  '88 95, 212; '92 25
Tomatoes, Tuna-Stuffed Cherry, '89 214
Tomato Soup, Appetizer, '86 258
Tomato Soup, Savory, '94 91
Tortilla Appetizers, Tex-Mex, '86 297
Tortilla Chips, '91 137
Tortilla Chips, Corn, '91 17
Tortilla Chips, Light, '91 257
Tortilla Dippers, Rolled, '86 4
Tortilla Española, '92 175
Tortilla Snacks, Pesto, '89 19
Tortilla Snack, Two-Cheese, '90 119
Tostados, Hot Chile Salsa with Homemade,
  '88 115
Tuna Mound, '80 276
Tuna Nachos, '95 127
Tuna-Pecan Ball, '87 94
Turkey Appetizers, '91 314
Turkey, Country-Fried Wild, '94 306
Turkey Sausage Turnovers, '95 239
Turnovers, Meat, '86 326
Vegetable Appetizer, Tarragon, '83 277
Vegetable Juice Appetizer, Hot, '93 324
Vegetable Nachos, '91 17
Vegetable Party Tray, Fresh, '82 122
Vegetables Italian, Marinated, '90 242
Vegetables, Marinated, '94 183
Veggie Bites, '91 171
Venison Tenderloin Appetizers, '88 249
Walnuts, Chinese Fried, '81 254
Wings, Hot Buffalo, '87 176
Wings, Satan's, '87 214
Wonton Chips, Baked, '91 138
Wonton Chips, Cinnamon-and-Sugar, '91 138
Wonton Chips, Garlic, '91 138
Wonton Chips, Lemon-and-Herb, '91 138
Wonton Nibbles, '85 287
Zucchini Bites, Scalloped, '91 165
Zucchini Caviar, '88 212
Zucchini French Fries, '82 78
Zucchini Fries, '90 147
Zucchini Hors d'Oeuvres, '80 151
Zucchini Pizzas, '88 212
Zucchini-Shrimp Appetizers, '89 311
Zucchini with Cocktail Sauce, French Fried,
  '86 146

APPLES
Acorn Squash, Apple-Stuffed, '83 296;
  '84 285
Baked. *See also* Apples/Desserts.
  à l'Orange, Baked Apples, '90 280
  Apples, Baked, '79 276; '86 40
  Carrot Bake, Apple-, '93 304
  Cheese Bake, Apple-, '92 225
  Easy Baked Apples, '82 22, 238
  Ham and Apples, Baked, '82 M237
  Honey-Baked Apple Quarters, '86 93
  Honey-Baked Apples, '83 234; '84 244
  Imperial Baked Apples, '82 273
  Maple Baked Apples, '85 232
  Mincemeat-Filled Apples, Baked,
    '80 276
  Orange-Pecan Baked Apples, '85 45
  Orange Sauce, Baked Apples with,
    '84 314

Squash and Apple Bake, '79 210
Stuffed Baked Apples, '89 217
Sweet Potato-Apple Bake, '83 25;
  '86 282
Balls, Sausage-Apple, '90 85
Beets and Apples, '80 137; '88 155
Beverages
  Berry Sparkler, Apple-, '93 104
  Berry Sparkler, Apple, '94 100
  Cider, Apple, '95 198
  Cider, Apple-Orange, '92 20
  Cider, December, '91 260
  Cider, Holiday, '82 264
  Cider, Hot Apple, '90 21, 225
  Cider, Hot Mexican, '87 213
  Cider, Hot Mulled, '79 205; '84 323
  Cider, Hot Spiced Apple, '84 318
  Cider Ice, '83 162
  Cider, Mulled, '91 209; '94 227
  Cider, Mulled Apple, '92 208
  Cider Nog, Hot Apple, '84 42
  Cider, Red Apple, '80 259
  Cider, Sparkling Apple, '88 276
  Cooler, Apple, '90 14
  Cooler, Minted Apple, '88 169
  Juice, Hot Apple, '86 270
  Juice, Perky Cinnamon-Apple, '90 22
  Juice, Sparkling Apple, '95 141
  Julep, Apple, '86 103, 215
  Lemonade, Apple, '89 212
  Limeade, Pink Apple, '89 46
  Punch, Apple-Tea, '85 82
  Punch, Hot Apple, '84 324
  Punch, Hot Spiced, '80 250
  Shrub, Shenandoah Apple Juice, '79 282
  Tea, Cranberry-Apple, '88 169
  Tea, Hot Apple-Cinnamon, '87 57
  Tea, Johnny Appleseed, '85 23
Breads
  Apple Bread, '79 205; '80 226
  Banana-Apple Bread, '85 250
  Blue Cheese-Apple Sunburst, '94 245
  Butter Bread, Apple, '84 49; '86 69
  Danish, Deep-Dish Apple, '86 161
  Date-Nut Ring, Apple-, '90 212
  Loaf, Fresh Apple, '82 206
  Loaf, Spiced Apple, '79 215
  Muffins, Apple, '83 96; '84 193; '87 23
  Muffins, Apple-Bran, '85 M89
  Muffins, Apple-Carrot, '91 213
  Muffins, Apple-Cinnamon Oat Bran,
    '89 106
  Muffins, Fresh Apple, '84 264
  Muffins, Spiced Apple, '79 60
  Muffins, Spicy Apple-Oat, '86 45
  Nut Bread, Apple-, '79 12; '85 281
  Nut Bread, Fresh Apple-, '87 256
  Pinwheel, Quick Apple, '85 42
  Pull-Apart Bread, Apple, '86 330
  Swirl Bread, Apple, '85 4
  Zucchini-Apple Bread, '87 255
Breakfast Delight, '93 195
Burgers, Apple, '86 137
Butter, Apple, '79 200; '81 217; '92 311
Butter, Half-Hour Apple, '81 203
Butternut Squash, Apple-Stuffed, '81 232
Cabbage with Apples and Franks, '87 42
Casserole, Apple-Cheese, '84 287
Casserole, Apple-Egg, '85 44
Casserole, Apple Ham, '79 213
Casserole, Cranberry-Apple, '83 311
Casserole, Squash and Apple, '79 209
Casserole, Sweet Potato-and-Apple, '94 280

Casserole, Sweet Potatoes-and-Apple, '90 228
Chicken, Apple, '85 57
Chutney, Apple, '92 309
Chutney, Pear-Apple, '89 141
Chutney, Tomato-Apple, '84 180
Cider Sauce, '87 224
Cinnamon Apples, Rosy, '87 M37
Coffee Cake, Apple, '81 249
Coffee Cake, Apple-Pecan, '84 242
Coffee Cake, Fresh Apple, '92 32
Conserve, Apple-Cranberry, '82 308
Cooked Apples, '93 338
Curried Apples, '93 252
Desserts
  Baked Alaska, Apple, '80 226
  Baked Apples with Cookie Crumbs,
    Orange, '95 271
  Bars, Apple Butter, '84 153
  Betty, Apple Brown, '83 213
  Betty, Pineapple-Apple, '85 46
  Brandied Apples, '81 248
  Brandied Apples and Cream, '82 M237
  Brownies, Frosted Apple, '86 216
  Cake, Apple, '83 312; '84 262
  Cake, Apple Cider Pound, '84 10
  Cake, Apple Coconut, '80 226
  Cake, Apple-Ginger Upside-Down,
    '94 180
  Cake, Apple-Nut, '87 76
  Cake, Apple-Pecan, '92 167
  Cake, Apple Pie, '82 226; '86 301
  Cake, Apple Slice, '85 93
  Cake, Apple Spice, '94 225
  Cake, Apple-Walnut, '94 242
  Cake, Covered Apple, '89 317
  Cake, Dried-Apple, '79 13
  Cake, Dried Apple Stack, '85 242
  Cake, Fresh Apple-Date, '83 300
  Cake, Golden Apple-Oatmeal, '86 301
  Cake Squares, Apple-Date Dream, '85 10
  Cake Squares, Apple-Orange, '84 150
  Candied Red Apples, '81 217
  Candy Apple Creations, '94 256
  Candy Apples, '84 243
  Caramel Apples, '79 220; '89 M231
  Caramel Apples, Old English, '85 231
  Caramel-Peanut Apples, '93 M244
  Cheesecake, Dieter's Apple, '86 318
  Chimichangas, Apple, '95 43
  Cinnamon Apples with Brandied Date
    Conserve, '85 315
  Cobbler, Apple-Pecan, '84 M198
  Cobbler, Apple Walnut, '79 154
  Cobbler, Apple-Walnut, '81 248
  Cobbler, Cranberry-and-Apple, '84 306;
    '90 294
  Cobbler, Easy Apple, '83 174
  Cobbler for Two, Apple, '85 261
  Cobbler, New-Fashioned Apple, '91 221
  Cookies, Apple Butter Spice, '79 291
  Cookies, Apple-Filled, '92 311
  Cookies, Apple-Nut, '80 228
  Cookies, Apple-Oatmeal, '85 215;
    '90 218
  Cookies, Fresh Apple, '84 36
  Cranberry Apple Dessert, '80 253
  Crisp, Apple, '84 122
  Crisp, Apple-Cheese, '92 235
  Crisp, Delicious Apple, '82 303
  Crisp, Granola Apple, '85 78
  Crisp, Oatmeal Cherry-Apple, '90 M16
  Crisp, Orange-Apple, '80 295
  Crisp, Tart Apple, '92 226

APPLES, Desserts (continued)

Crumble, Whole Wheat-Apple, '90 M213

Crunch, Apple-Cranberry, '86 300; '87 178

Crunch, Apple-Nut, '82 M238

Cupcakes, Apple-Nut, '82 279

Delight, Apple, '80 109

Dumplings, Apple, '82 273

Dumplings, Old-Fashioned Apple, '84 226

Dumplings with Maple-Cider Sauce, Apple, '95 288

Dumplings with Orange Hard Sauce, Apple, '88 224

Dutch Apple Dessert, Creamy, '91 19

Filling, Apple-Date, '83 301

Filling, Dried Apple, '85 242; '87 229

Flambé, Hot Apples and Rum, '92 88

Flan, Apple, '81 309

Foldovers, Apple, '84 136

Fritter Rings, Apple, '88 44

Fritters, Apple, '81 105; '82 273; '85 14

Fritters, Apple Holiday, '86 314

Goblins, Apple, '94 256

Honey-Baked Apple Dessert, '90 M213

Ice, Cranberry-Apple, '82 290

Kuchen, Apple, '79 24

Melting Apples, '88 19

Mousse, Cran-Apple, '93 255

Pie, American Apple, '91 197

Pie, Apple-Amandine, '89 215

Pie, Apple-Bourbon, '95 302

Pie, Apple-Cheese, '85 284

Pie, Apple Cider, '84 227

Pie, Apple-Cream Cheese, '81 247

Pie, Apple Custard, '88 236

Pie, Apple-Lemon Chess, '86 220

Pie, Apple-Mincemeat, '85 316

Pie, Apple-Pear, '83 249

Pie, Apple-Raisin Brandy, '89 58

Pie, Autumn Apple, '79 205

Pie, Berry-Apple, '88 251

Pie, Blackberry-Apple, '87 130

Pie, Brandy-Apple, '86 301

Pie, Brandy Raisin-Apple, '83 192

Pie, Caramel-Pecan Apple, '85 247

Pie, Cornbread-Sausage-Apple, '87 171

Pie, Cran-Apple, '92 304

Pie, Cranberry-Apple, '79 264

Pie, Cranberry-Apple Holiday, '81 M269

Pie, Dutch Apple, '81 105; '82 273

Pie, Easy-Crust Apple, '87 11

Pie Filling in a Jar, Apple, '95 251

Pie, Fresh Apple, '84 178

Pie, Grandmother's Apple, '87 212

Pie, Grated Apple, '83 304

Pie, Holiday Apple, '87 260

Pie, Mexican Apple, '94 97

Pie, Natural Pear-Apple, '88 226

Pie, No-Crust Apple, '88 204

Pie, Old-Fashioned Apple, '82 M299; '88 94

Pie, Red Apple, '79 282

Pies, Delicious Fried, '83 84

Pies, Fried Apple, '81 217; '86 302; '88 112, 225; '94 61

Pie, Tart Lemon-Apple, '80 100

Pie, Upside-Down Southern Apple, '88 226

Pie with Hot Cinnamon Sauce, Apple, '88 210

Poached Apples, Spicy, '90 M141

Pudding, Apple-Raisin Bread, '88 175

Pudding, Apple Rice, '91 217

Pudding with Hot Rum Sauce, Apple-Nut, '79 86

Rings, Apple, '85 232

Roll, Apple, '82 178

Rolls, Luscious Apple, '88 225

Sauce, Apple Ambrosia, '89 95

Sauce, Apple-Cinnamon, '93 42

Sauce, Apple Dessert, '87 M165

Sauce, Spicy Apple Dessert, '82 177

Shortcake, Quick Apple, '93 42

Sorbet, Cran-Apple Spice, '93 153

Squares, Apple, '92 311

Squares, Sour Cream Apple, '82 262

Strudel, Apple, '85 259; '89 267; '92 269

Sugar-Crusted Apples in Walnut-Phyllo Baskets, '93 210

Sundae, Hot Apple Spice, '92 239

Sundaes, Spicy Apple Ice Cream, '86 M195

Tart, Apple Cream, '84 207

Tart, Apricot-Apple Crumb, '94 60

Tart, Creamed Apple, '94 17

Tart, Deluxe Apple, '84 227

Tarte aux Pommes, La, '80 125

Tarts, Apple-Pecan, '80 282

Tart with Cheese Pastry, Apple, '88 225

Topping, Apple-Nut, '93 162

Topping, Spicy Apple, '87 125

Turnovers, Baked Apple, '93 338

Turnovers, Delicious Apple, '86 25

Turnovers, Fried Apple, '81 161

Turnovers, Puffy Apple, '87 276

Dip, Apple, '93 205

Dressing, Apple, '92 216

Dressing, Sausage-Apple, '93 305; '94 296

Dried Apple Side Dish, '92 226

Dried Lady Apple Slices, '95 263

Fillets, Apple-Carrot Stuffed, '88 M192

Filling, Apple, '85 5

Glazed Apples, Honey-, '90 125

Glazed Apples, Orange-, '82 51

Golden Apples, '82 254

Honey-Yogurt Apples, '92 46

Jelly, Apple, '82 149

Jelly, Apple-Mint, '87 134

Jelly, Crabapple, '79 120; '81 217

Jelly, Spiced Apple, '95 251

Juice, Nectarines in Apple, '83 183

Marmalade, Apple, '79 120

Monster Mouths, '95 274

Muesli, '89 208

Omelet Stack, Apple, '94 50

Pancake, Apple-Filled, '86 96

Pancakes, Apple-Topped, '93 339

Pancakes with Cider Sauce, Spicy Apple, '87 224

Piggy Apple, '94 194

Poached Lemon Apples, Chilled, '86 182

Pork Chops and Apples, Baked, '81 10

Pork Chops, Apple, '91 198

Pork Chops, Apple-Crumb Stuffed, '81 234; '82 26

Pork Chops, Apple-Glazed, '84 212; '87 35

Pork Chops, Apple-Kraut, '84 50

Pork Chops, Apple-Stuffed, '79 125

Pork Chops, Glazed Apple, '86 300

Pork Chops, Sherry-Apple, '88 40

Pork Chops, Spicy Apple, '87 230

Pork Chops with Apples, Parmesan, '93 338

Pork Chops with Crabapple Peaches, Broiled, '81 83

Pork Cutlets, Apple-Glazed, '92 181

Pork Loin with Apples and Mushrooms, Roast, '92 218

Pork Tenderloin, Apple-Ginger, '86 75

Pork Tenderloin, Apple-Mushroom, '95 53

Pork Tenderloin with Apples, Celery, and Potatoes, Grilled, '95 161

Pot Roast, Spicy Apple, '83 7

Quiche, Crustless Sausage-Apple, '87 70

Red Cabbage and Apples, '85 32

Relish, Apple-Celery, '89 141

Relish, Cran-Apple, '84 300

Relish, Spicy Apple, '84 M323

Ribs, Apple Barbecued, '80 111

Rice, Apple-Cinnamon, '86 249

Rings, Cinnamon Apple, '82 M237; '90 250

Rings, Cinnamon-Apple, '85 107

Rings, Fried Apple, '81 209

Rings, Honey Apple, '80 243

Rolls, Apple-Phyllo, '88 213

Salads

Apple Salad, '87 233

Apricot Salad, Apple-, '88 121

Aspic, Sunshine Apple, '81 73

Beet Salad, Apple-, '91 237

Blue Cheese Dressing, Apple Salad with, '87 103

Blue Cheese-Pear-Apple Salad, '81 224

Carrot Salad, Apple-, '85 22

Cheesy Apple Salad, '86 301

Cherry-Apple Salad, '86 31

Chicken-Apple Salad, '90 216

Cider Salad, Apple, '83 123

Coleslaw, Apple, '89 315

Congealed Apple Salad, '85 252

Crunch Salad, Apple, '84 232; '86 331

Crunchy Apple Salad, '80 138

Curried Apple-Raisin Salad, '80 24

Double Apple Salad, '84 227

English Pea-and-Apple Salad, '87 24

Fresh Apple Salad, '81 207

Frozen Apple-Cream Salad, '82 80

Grapefruit-Apple Salad, '89 41

Greens with Apple and Brie Salad, '93 241

Ham-and-Apple Salad, '88 139

Lemony Apple-Bran Salad, '86 223

Mold, Apple Cider Salad, '85 54

Mold, Cranberry-Apple, '89 277

Nut Salad, Apple-, '80 226

Peanut-Apple Salad, '80 5

Poppyseed Dressing, Apple Wedges with, '86 131

Sesame-Apple Toss, '88 21

Slaw, Apple-Carrot, '92 243

Slaw, Apple-Pineapple, '79 241

Slaw, Fresh Apple, '81 63

Slaw, Nutty Apple, '88 216

Slaw, Red Cabbage-and-Apple, '87 31; '91 309

Snow Salad, Apple, '81 224

Spicy Apple Salad, '85 215

Spinach-Apple Salad, '90 89; '92 13

Stuffed Apple Ring Salad, '91 198

Stuffed Apple Salad, '92 266

Summer Apple Salad, '80 149

Swiss-Apple Salad, '84 81

Triple Apple Salad, '88 122

Turkey-Apple Salad, '88 123; '90 181

APPLES, Salads *(continued)*

Waldorf Salad, '89 278
Waldorf Salad, Congealed, '82 80
Waldorf Salad, Creamy, '87 311
Waldorf Salad, Deluxe, '83 81
Waldorf Salad, Frozen, '79 126; '82 145
Waldorf Salad, Jiffy, '88 100
Waldorf Salad, New Wave, '92 36
Waldorf Salad, Old-Fashioned, '81 295
Waldorf Salad, Pineapple, '92 97
Waldorf Salad, Southern Classic, '92 36
Waldorf Salad, Tropical, '89 12
Wild Rice-Green Apple Salad, '92 90
Sandwiches, Apple, '79 164; '80 130
Sandwiches, Apple Breakfast, '92 332
Sandwiches, Apple-Cinnamon Breakfast,
  '85 298
Sandwiches, Apple Party, '92 234
Sauce, Apple-Horseradish, '82 229
Sauce, Cranberry-Apple, '92 203
Sausage Patties, Apples on, '82 120
Sautéed Apples, Onions, and Pears over
  Spinach, '94 212
Scalloped Apples, '84 70; '87 156
Scallop, Yam-and-Apple, '91 199
Shells, Sweet Potatoes in Apple, '85 206
Soup, Creamed Butternut-and-Apple, '88 228
Spareribs, Apple-Barbecue, '90 160
Spiced Apples, '93 123
Spiced Apple Slices, '83 289
Spiced Apples, Skillet, '83 234; '84 244
Spread, Apple-Date, '91 231; '92 67
Spread, Gruyère-Apple, '81 160
Squash, Apple-and-Pecan-Filled, '88 228
Squash, Apple-Stuffed, '85 206
Stir-Fry, Apple-Sesame-Chicken, '92 226
Stuffed Apples, Peanutty, '85 25
Stuffing, Apple-Crumb, '81 234; '82 26;
  '83 39
Stuffing, Apple-Walnut, '95 289
Sweet Potatoes, Apple-Glazed, '82 303
Sweet Potatoes, Apple-Stuffed, '88 207
Sweet Potatoes, Cinnamon-Apple, '95 M23
Sweet Potatoes Stuffed with Apples, '82 228
Syrup, Spiced Apple, '79 114
Toast, Apple, '81 278
Topping, Apple, '89 107
Veal Chops, Apple, '87 220
Vinaigrette, Spinach Salad with Apple-Onion,
  '94 276

APPLESAUCE

Applesauce, '90 255
Bread, Applesauce-Honey Nut, '87 300
Bread, Applesauce Nut, '81 305
Bread, Applesauce-Pecan, '90 66
Bread, Bran-Applesauce, '84 229
Butter, Half-Hour Apple, '81 203
Cake, Applesauce, '80 270
Cake, Applesauce Carrot, '81 202
Cake, Applesauce-Oatmeal, '92 119
Cake, Applesauce-Spice, '83 42
Cake, Applesauce Spice, '89 296
Cake, My Favorite Applesauce, '87 263
Cakes, Applesauce Snack, '88 215; '89 20
Cake Squares, Applesauce, '86 8
Cake with Bourbon Frosting, Applesauce,
  '88 236
Doughnuts, Applesauce, '81 203
Doughnuts, Applesauce Drop, '90 70
Dressing, Apple, '83 181
Fluff, Applesauce, '91 173

Fruitcake, Applesauce, '83 258
Gingerbread, Applesauce, '94 179
Loaf, Brandy Applesauce, '81 263
Muffins, Applesauce, '84 284; '91 141
Muffins, Applesauce Spice, '88 236
Muffins, Bite-Size Applesauce, '82 104
Oatmeal, Applesauce, '89 108
Pancakes, Applesauce, '79 114
Pudding, Applesauce-Graham Cracker, '81 34
Ribs, Apple Barbecued, '80 111
Spicy Applesauce, '82 296
Squares, Applesauce-Spice, '86 248
Sweet Potatoes, Applesauce, '91 292; '92 256

APRICOTS

Bake, Sweet Potato-Apricot, '85 206
Beverages
  Cooler, Apricot, '81 100
  Cooler, Apricot Mint, '90 165
  Fruit Flip, Apricot, '91 18
  Nectar, Hot Apricot, '81 265
  Nectar, Mulled Apricot, '86 229
  Punch, Apricot Spiced, '80 269
  Shake, Apricot, '84 115
  Slush, Apricot, '93 205
  Slush, Apricot Brandy, '91 278
  Slush, Apricot-Citrus, '88 82
  Tea, Hot Spiced Apricot, '88 248
  Wassail, Pineapple-Apricot, '83 275
Bread, Apricot-Nut, '79 24
Bread, Apricot-Orange, '92 285
Bread, Pineapple-Apricot, '84 7
Bread, Tangy Apricot, '81 249
Butter, Apricot, '82 308
Carrots, Apricot, '84 6
Carrots, Apricot Glazed, '80 89
Coffee Cake, Apricot-Almond, '93 26
Coffee Cake, Apricot Lattice, '94 48
Curried Apricots, '91 315
Dates, Apricot-Stuffed, '80 250
Delight, Apricot, '81 42
Desserts
  Almond Squares, Apricot-, '95 272
  Baked Apricots, Delicious, '82 10
  Balls, Apricot, '79 274
  Balls, Crunchy Apricot, '89 307
  Bars, Apricot, '81 247
  Bars, Apricot-Oatmeal, '86 216
  Bars, Apricot-Raisin, '87 32
  Cake, Apricot Brandy Pound, '83 267
  Cobble Up, Apricot, '82 138
  Cookie Rolls, Apricot, '80 282
  Cookies, Apricot, '95 322
  Cookies, Frosted Apricot, '81 192
  Cream, Peachy-Apricot, '86 163
  Crescents, Apricot, '90 181
  Divinity, Apricot, '83 297
  Filling, Apricot, '83 84; '86 107; '93 316
  Filling, Lemon-Apricot, '90 105
  Freeze, Apricot, '82 10
  Frosting, Apricot, '81 192
  Frozen Apricot Fluff, '86 242
  Glaze, Apricot, '82 8
  Glaze, Apricot-Kirsch, '87 14
  Glaze, Sweet Apricot, '82 304
  Ice, Apricot Yogurt, '81 177
  Kolaches, Apricot, '83 84; '94 291
  Mousse, Apricot, '82 72; '91 297
  Noodle Kugel, Apricot, '92 251
  Pastries, Apricot, '83 297
  Pie, Apricot Surprise, '88 99
  Pie, Dried Fruit, '83 249
  Pies, Apricot Fried, '86 269
  Pies, Fried Apricot, '95 215

Pies, Special Apricot, '94 60
Pie, Yogurt-Apricot, '85 132
Pinwheels, Apricot, '87 276
Pudding, Apricot Bread, '85 24
Sauce, Apricot, '82 212
Sauce, Apricot Ice Cream, '91 57
Sauce, Apricot-Walnut Hard, '88 153
Sherbet, Apricot, '81 177; '92 164
Soufflé, Baked Apricot, '88 267
Tart, Apricot-Apple Crumb, '94 60
Tarts, Apricot, '79 282; '88 281
Tea Cakes, Brandied Apricot, '91 241
Torte, Apricot-Filled Chocolate, '90 107
Torte, Apricot Sponge, '90 59
Torte, Lucy's Apricot Praline, '95 243
Tortoni, Apricot-Yogurt, '95 124
Turnovers, Fried Apricot, '86 24
Wonders, Apricot, '93 316
Dip, Apricot, '86 178
Dressing, Honeydew Salad with Apricot
  Cream, '84 191
Glaze, Apricot, '80 280; '82 8; '86 197
Glaze for Ham, Apricot, '85 256
Glaze, Sweet Potatoes with Apricot,
  '89 331
Jam, Golden Apricot, '80 31
Loaf, Apricot-Cranberry, '79 235
Loaf, Apricot-Nut, '81 8
Loaf, Tasty Apricot-Nut, '82 10
Main Dishes
  Chicken, Apricot, '92 12
  Chicken Breasts, Apricot, '88 301
  Cornish Hens, Apricot-Glazed, '80 84;
    '87 306
  Cornish Hens, Apricot-Stuffed, '84 6
  Ham and Apricots, '90 53
  Ham, Apricot Baked, '84 160
  Ham Slice, Apricot-Glazed, '93 252
  Pork Chops, Apricot-Mushroom Stuffed,
    '95 287
  Pork Chops, Apricot-Sauced, '85 22
  Pork Chops, Apricot-Stuffed, '86 76;
    '92 219
  Pork Chops, Curried Apricot, '89 191
  Pork Chops, Mustard-Apricot, '89 225
  Pork Chops with Apricot Glaze, Stuffed,
    '89 M36
  Pork Loin, Apricot-Pecan Stuffed,
    '94 274
  Sausage-Apricot Breakfast Dish, '82 10
Rolls, Cheese-Apricot Sweet, '90 195
Salad, Apple-Apricot, '88 121
Salad, Apricot, '81 251; '83 123
Salad, Apricot Fruit, '82 132
Salad, Apricot Nectar, '83 218; '87 236
Salad, Creamy Apricot, '85 263
Salad, Frosted Apricot, '80 248
Salad, Spinach-Apricot, '94 63
Sauce, Apricot, '82 212; '87 172
Sauce, Fresh Cranberry-Apricot, '87 243
Spread, Apricot Brie, '86 275
Spread, Apricot-Cream Cheese, '82 161;
  '87 158
Sweet Potatoes, Apricot, '82 228
Sweet Potatoes, Apricot-Glazed, '81 295
Syrup, Apricot Fruit, '82 10

ARTICHOKES

Appetizers
  Baked Artichoke-Cheese Bottoms, '94 61
  Caviar, Artichoke Hearts with, '79 142
  Crostini, Hot Artichoke, '94 319
  Dip, Baked Artichoke, '95 239
  Dip, Deluxe Artichoke, '80 87

ARTICHOKES, Appetizers (continued)

Dip, Hot Artichoke-Seafood, '80 241
Dip, Hot Artichoke Seafood, '85 M212
Dip in a Bread Basket, Artichoke, '93 13
Dip, Mexican Artichoke, '90 292
Dip, Seasoned Mayonnaise Artichoke,
 '80 87
Frittata, Artichoke Appetizer, '92 58
Marinated Artichoke Hearts, '88 95
Marinated Artichokes, '87 250
Mold, Artichoke-Caviar, '87 239
Mound, Caviar-Artichoke, '91 244
Phyllo Bites, Artichoke-Parmesan,
 '87 54
Puffs, Spinach-Artichoke-Tomato,
 '95 284
Shrimp Appetizer, Artichoke-and-,
 '93 271
Spread, Antipasto, '81 25
Spread, Artichoke-Parmesan, '92 95
Spread, Chunky Artichoke, '89 98
Spread, Hot Artichoke, '79 110
Spread, Hot Artichoke-Crab, '85 81
Zesty Artichoke Appetizer, '80 146
Artichokes, '92 107
au Gratin, Crab, Shrimp, and Artichoke,
 '90 240
Baked Chicken and Artichoke Hearts,
 '82 260
Bake, Spinach-Artichoke, '95 48
Bake, Tomato-and-Artichoke Heart, '85 81
Beef with Tomatoes and Artichokes, '92 282
Bread, Artichoke, '93 140
Casserole, Alii Artichoke, '93 294
Casserole, Asparagus-Artichoke, '86 279
Casserole, Brussels Sprouts-and-Artichoke,
 '94 279
Casserole, Italian Green Bean-and-Artichoke,
 '85 81
Casserole, Mushroom-Artichoke, '87 241
Casserole, Spinach and Artichoke, '81 103
Casserole, Spinach-Artichoke, '88 252; '93 44
Chicken and Artichokes, Italian, '95 68
Chicken, Artichoke, '81 97
Chicken with Artichoke Hearts, '88 54
Chicken with Artichokes and Mushrooms,
 '90 35
Chicken with Artichokes, Sherried, '87 143
Chilled Artichokes with Lemon-Pepper
 Dressing, '87 55
Crabmeat with Artichoke Hearts, Creamed,
 '93 26
Dressing, Artichoke, '84 126
Dried Beef with Artichokes, Creamed, '85 81
Eggs Sardou, '92 93
Herb-Mayonnaise Dip, Artichokes with,
 '84 67
Lemon, Artichoke Hearts with, '90 98
Linguine, Artichoke and Shrimp, '95 210
Marinated Artichoke Hearts, '95 66
Marinated Artichokes, '87 250; '88 41
Marinated Cucumbers and Artichokes,
 '82 111
Pasta with Artichoke Hearts, '86 209
Pasta with Catfish and Artichokes, '90 123
Pie, Artichoke, '79 25
Pizza with Artichoke and Prosciutto,
 '87 182
Quiche, Artichoke, '91 71
Ragout, Veal-and-Artichoke, '94 43
Relish, Jerusalem Artichoke, '89 197

Salads
 Artichoke Salad, '86 333
 Asparagus-Artichoke Salad, '85 162
 Aspic, Tomato-Artichoke, '84 320;
  '86 92
 Avocado Acapulco, '83 2
 Chicken-Rice Salad, Artichoke-, '94 132
 Chicken Salad with Artichokes, '86 186
 Italian Salad, '87 145
 Marinated Artichoke Salad, '83 241;
  '95 66
 Marinated Cucumbers and Artichokes,
  '82 111
 Orzo Salad, Artichokes with, '88 M193
 Pasta Salad, Artichoke-, '94 180
 Rice Salad, Artichoke-, '80 178; '81 41;
  '85 81
 Rice Salad with Artichoke Hearts,
  '80 232
 Stuffed Tomato Salad, Artichoke-,
  '82 101
 Tomato Salad, Artichoke-, '82 239
 Zucchini-Artichoke Salad, '91 229
Soup, Artichoke, '89 269
Soup, Artichoke Cream, '94 62
Soup, Chicken, Artichoke, and Mushroom,
 '92 324
Soup, Cream of Artichoke, '82 232
Soup, Louisiana Oyster-and-Artichoke, '92 81
Spring Artichokes, '86 62
Steamed Artichokes, '81 59
Strata, Artichoke-Cheese, '90 236
Stuffed Artichokes, '79 76; '82 92; '91 117
Stuffed Artichokes, Ham-Mushroom-,
 '95 228
Stuffed Artichokes, Shrimp-, '84 67; '87 55
Stuffed Artichokes, Shrimp, '94 62
Stuffed with Shrimp and Scallops, Artichokes,
 '84 174
Veal with Artichoke Hearts, Lemon, '87 219
Vinaigrette, Artichokes, '88 101
Whole Cooked Artichokes, '94 61

ASPARAGUS
Almond Asparagus, '83 86
Almond Butter, Asparagus with, '84 85
Almond Sauce, Asparagus with, '91 117
Basil Butter, Asparagus with, '85 40
Basil Sauce, Asparagus with, '86 33
Beef with Asparagus, '90 100
Caesar, Asparagus, '88 133
Cashew Butter, Asparagus with, '87 56
Casseroles
 Artichoke Casserole, Asparagus-, '86 279
 Cheesy Asparagus Casserole, '82 281;
  '83 32
 Chicken-Asparagus Casserole, '83 76;
  '84 71
 Creamy Asparagus Casserole, '80 76
 Easy Asparagus Casserole, '83 255
 English Pea Casserole, Asparagus-
  and-, '86 324
 Pea Casserole, Asparagus-, '88 M294
 Peas Casserole, Asparagus and, '80 152
 Spaghetti Casserole, Asparagus-, '80 77
 Turkey-Asparagus Casserole, '86 284
Cheesecake, Ham-and-Asparagus, '90 174
Company Asparagus, '85 82
Creamed Asparagus on Toast, '95 61
Cream Sauce, Asparagus with, '90 291
Croquettes, Asparagus, '85 265
Curry Sauce, Asparagus with, '90 17
Cutlets, Asparagus, '80 147
Delight, Asparagus, '82 269
Delight, Ham-Asparagus, '86 48
Dilly Asparagus, '88 180
Dinner, Ham-Asparagus, '80 M10
Eggs à la Asparagus, Creamed, '81 201
en Papillote, Shrimp with Asparagus,
 '86 145
Fettuccine, Ham-and-Asparagus, '94 84
Fish-Asparagus Divan, '87 128
French-Fried Asparagus, '79 66; '83 46
Garlic Cream, Asparagus with, '95 83
Goat Cheese Sauce, Asparagus with, '93 116
Goldenrod, Asparagus, '79 66
Guacamole, Mock, '93 36
Ham Rolls, Asparagus, '91 117
Holiday Asparagus, '85 260
Jeweled Asparagus, '80 42
Lemon Butter, Asparagus in, '80 M123
Lemon Butter, Asparagus with, '87 M151
Lemon Sauce, Asparagus with, '86 62
Lemon-Sesame Asparagus, '91 31
Loaf, Asparagus-Pimiento, '84 86
Marinated Asparagus, '81 108; '83 46;
 '84 67, 86; '86 92; '87 74
Marinated Asparagus, Easy, '81 148
Marinated Asparagus Spears, '88 130
Marinated Asparagus with Prosciutto, '95 83
Mayonnaise, Asparagus with Hot Wine, '81 83
Meringue, Asparagus, '88 131
Mushrooms, Asparagus and, '85 108
Orange Butter Sauce, Asparagus with, '85 43
Orange Sauce, Asparagus with, '83 46
Pasta with Asparagus, Tomatoes, and Shrimp,
 Garlicky, '95 82
Pasta with Shrimp and Asparagus, Angel Hair,
 '92 100
Pickled Asparagus, '83 46
Pilaf, Turkey-Asparagus, '88 200
Pork Arlo, '87 229
Prosciutto-Wrapped Asparagus, '91 98
Quiche, Asparagus-Tomato, '88 198
Quiche, Springtime, '83 122
Rarebit, Uptown Welsh, '87 279
Rice and Asparagus, '93 324
Rolls, Asparagus, '79 296; '80 31
Rolls, Chicken-Asparagus, '86 M211
Rolls, Ham-Asparagus, '79 41
Rolls, Hot Asparagus, '93 329
Rollups, Asparagus, '79 63
Roll-Ups, Asparagus, '84 270
Roulade, Asparagus, '86 102
Salads
 Artichoke Salad, Asparagus-, '85 162
 Asparagus Salad, '88 121; '94 67
 Chicken Salad, Asparagus-, '89 83
 Chicken Salad with Asparagus, Curried,
  '81 36
 Congealed Asparagus Salad, '83 260
 Crab-and-Asparagus Salad, '92 141
 Crabmeat-and-Asparagus, Congealed
  Salad with, '84 86
 Cups, Asparagus Salad, '83 47

ASPARAGUS, Salads *(continued)*

Easy Asparagus Salad, '88 131
Egg Salad, Asparagus-and-, '86 305
Horseradish Salad, Asparagus-, '87 80
Lemon-Asparagus Salad, Creamy, '93 116
Marinated Asparagus, '83 46; '84 67, 86; '86 92
Marinated Asparagus and Hearts of Palm, '90 91
Marinated Asparagus Medley, '91 105
Marinated Asparagus Salad, '79 20
Marinated Asparagus with Prosciutto, '95 83
Mold, Asparagus, '80 104
Mold, Asparagus-Cucumber, '85 252
Mousse Salad, Asparagus, '86 252
Mustard Sauce, Chilled Asparagus in, '88 130
New Potato Salad, Asparagus-and-, '86 69
Peas-and-Asparagus Salad, '83 141
Tarragon Marinade, Asparagus with, '83 47
Tart Asparagus Salad, '81 203
Tomato-Asparagus Salad, '92 79
Vinaigrette, Asparagus, '80 77; '90 138
Vinaigrette, Asparagus Salad, '88 56
Vinaigrette, Light Asparagus, '82 50
Yogurt Dressing, Asparagus with, '79 66
Sandwiches, Asparagus-and-Ham Melt, '88 M96
Sandwiches, Asparagus Grill, '79 164; '80 130
Sandwiches, Asparagus Spear, '84 165
Sauce, Asparagus White, '80 147
Sauté, Asparagus-and-Mushroom, '93 115
Sautéed Asparagus, '79 66
Shrimp Mold with Asparagus, '93 214
Soufflé, Asparagus, '79 66; '83 265; '89 89
Soup, Asparagus, '84 67
Soup, Asparagus-Potato, '85 23
Soup, Cream of Asparagus, '84 111
Soup, Creamy Asparagus, '94 225
Soup, Creamy Asparagus-and-Chicken, '95 82
Sour Cream, Asparagus with, '83 46
Squares, Asparagus, '79 161
Squash Rings, Asparagus in, '87 68
Steamed Asparagus, '92 211
Stir-Fried Asparagus, '87 52
Stir-Fry, Asparagus, '95 83
Stir-Fry Beef and Asparagus, '91 124
Supreme, Asparagus, '80 77; '89 245
Supreme, Cauliflower and Asparagus, '79 287; '80 35
Sweet-and-Sour Asparagus, '89 159
Tangy Asparagus, '84 86
Tomatoes, Fresh Asparagus and, '94 162
Tomato Sauce, Asparagus with, '83 46
Toss, Asparagus-Carrot-Squash, '91 45
Vinaigrette, Asparagus, '80 77; '90 82, 138; '93 174

ASPIC
Apple Aspic, Sunshine, '81 73
Basic Aspic for Garnishing, '84 189
Beet Aspic, '90 123
Chicken Salad, Aspic-Topped, '88 88
Coating, White Aspic, '85 151
Cucumber-Curry Dressing, Aspic with, '89 178
Fish Aspic, '84 190
Fish 'n Aspic, '84 190
Gazpacho Aspic, '89 179
Grapefruit Aspic, '80 297; '82 112; '83 153
Madeira Aspic, '86 65
Orange-and-Carrot Aspic, '86 199
Shrimp-Coleslaw Aspic, '79 88
Shrimp-Cucumber Aspic, '83 108
Sunshine Aspic, '80 103
Three-Layer Aspic, '88 120
Tomato
Artichoke Aspic, Tomato-, '84 320; '86 92
Bloody Mary-Tomato Aspic, '81 77
Chicken in Tomato Aspic, '84 190
Chili Sauce Tomato Aspic, '85 252
Classic Tomato Aspic, '91 229
Crab Aspic, Tomato-, '85 287
Herbed Tomato Aspic, '81 73
Layered Tomato Aspic, '90 99
Light Tomato Aspic, '85 83
Ranch Tomato Aspic, '83 218
Shrimp, Tomato Aspic with, '79 241
Spicy Tomato Aspic, '81 40; '89 288
Tangy Tomato Aspic, '83 124
Two, Aspic for, '83 209
Vegetable Aspic, Cheesy, '81 73
Vegetable Aspic with Horseradish Dressing, Crisp, '87 152

AVOCADOS
Baked Avocado-and-Crabmeat, '84 119
Broiled Crab and Avocado, '79 116
Chicken, Orange-Avocado, '80 38
Cocktail, Sherried Avocado-Crabmeat, '87 95
Crabmeat, Avocado with, '86 119
Cream, Avocado, '92 158
Dip, Avocado, '80 285; '81 57, 306
Dip, "Bring-Home-the-Bacon" Avocado, '92 80
Dip, Gazpacho, '95 243
Dip, Roasted Corn-and-Avocado, '91 279
Dip, Six-Layer, '81 160
Dip, Zippy Avocado, '82 9; '83 69
Dressing, Avocado, '80 15; '92 321
Dressing, Avocado Fruit Salad, '82 93
Filled Avocados, Shrimp-, '83 2
Guacamole
Coleslaw, Guacamole Mexican, '82 302
Creamy Guacamole, '79 91; '83 174
Dip, Bacon-Guacamole, '85 25
Dip, Guacamole, '86 4; '95 96
Dressing, Guacamole, '92 64
Easy Guacamole, '95 94
Guacamole, '79 185; '80 74; '83 179; '89 226; '90 205; '91 161; '94 116
Mold, Guacamole, '86 184
Salad, Guacamole, '80 14; '87 181
Salad, Guacamole-Tomato, '81 302
Sandwiches, Guacamole, '82 9; '83 68
Shells, Guacamole in, '86 74
Spicy Guacamole, '93 218
Spread, Guacamole, '90 119
Subs, Guacamole, '84 293
Ice, Avocado, '83 179
Kabobs, Chicken-Avocado, '82 9; '83 68
Omelet, Yogurt-Avocado, '81 33
Pie, Mexican Cheese, '83 69
Potatoes, Avocado-Topped, '83 3
Relish, Avocado, '87 120

Salads
Acapulco, Avocado, '83 2
Avocado Salad, '81 195; '82 9; '83 69; '92 246
Chicken-Avocado Salad, '80 139
Chicken-Avocado Salad, Fruited, '82 101
Chicken-Avocado Salad Platter, '83 2
Chicken-Avocado Salad, Tossed, '80 4
Chicken Salad, Avocado-, '87 107
Chicken Salad in Avocados, '85 216
Chicken Salad in Avocados, Fruited, '87 41
Citrus-Avocado Salad, '82 265
Congealed Avocado Crunch Salad, '85 26
Congealed Avocado Salad, '84 266
Congealed Avocado Salads, '87 42
Crab-Avocado Salad, '81 114
Dude Ranch Salad, '80 15
Endive Salad, Avocado-, '94 88
Fruit Salad, Avocado, '87 41
Fruit Salad with Honey-Yogurt Dressing, Avocado-, '93 172
Garbanzo Salad, Avocado-, '81 33
Grapefruit-Avocado Salad, '83 316; '84 16; '89 41
Grapefruit Salad, Avocado-, '85 26; '93 282
Melon Salad, Avocado-, '82 164
Mexican Salad Supper, '82 9; '83 68
Orange Salad, Avocado-, '91 44
Rice-and-Avocado Salad, '89 146
Romaine Salad, Tangy, '80 155
Shrimp and Avocado Salad, '80 266
Shrimp Salad, Avocado Stuffed with, '82 207
Shrimp Salad on the Half Shell, '86 73
Spanish Avocado Salad, '87 41
Spinach Salad, Green, '79 142
Tomato-Avocado Salad, '86 74
Tomatoes, Avocado-Stuffed, '82 101
Zucchini Salad, Creamy Avocado and, '79 208
Salsa, Avocado, '91 182
Salsa, Avocado-Corn, '94 201
Salsa, Tomato-Avocado, '94 83
Sandwiches, Avocado, Bacon, and Cheese, '87 279
Sandwiches, Avocado-Crabmeat, '83 2
Sauce, Avocado, '80 198; '83 200
Sauce, Avocado-Tomatillo, '95 206
Shells, Ceviche in Avocado, '81 33
Sherbet, Avocado, '83 162
Sherbet, Mexican, '79 155
Sorbet, Avocado, '88 117
Soup, Avocado, '88 160
Soup, Avocado-Banana-Yogurt, '80 78
Soup, Chilled Avocado, '81 34; '87 37; '93 108
Soup, Creamy Avocado, '79 107
Soup, Creamy Avocado-Mushroom, '85 25
Soup, Sherried Avocado, '84 181
Stuffed Avocados, Crab-, '86 73
Stuffed Avocados, Salmon-, '86 74
Stuffed Broiled Avocados, '88 246
Tomatoes, Crab-and-Avocado Stuffed, '94 141
Topping, Avocado, '93 309; '94 96
Tostadas, Crispy, '83 2
Whip, Avocado, '79 107

Bacon

Appetizers
Brie, Chutney-Bacon, '90 M292
Cheese-Bacon Crispies, '84 270
Chestnut Wraps, Bacon-, '84 M216
Crackers, Bacon-Wrapped, '93 280
Crostini, Almond-Bacon-Cheese, '94 318
Dip, Bacon, '82 197
Dip, Bacon-and-Tomato, '90 147
Dip, Bacon-Guacamole, '85 25
Dip, "Bring-Home-the-Bacon" Avocado, '92 80
Dip, Cheddar-Bacon, '89 M119
Dip, Zesty Bacon, '92 156
Hot Bacon Appetizers, '80 248
Meatballs, Burgundy-Bacon, '80 283
Mushrooms, Cheese 'n' Bacon-Stuffed, '86 258
Onion Appetizers, Bacon-, '94 290
Oysters in Bacon, '83 211
Pineapple Chunks, Bacon-Wrapped, '84 25
Popcorn, Bacon-Cheese, '86 74
Quesadillas, Bacon-Jalapeño-Tomato, '95 240
Quiches, Miniature Bacon-Cheese, '83 93
Rolls, Bacon, '84 270; '93 330
Rollups, Bacon, '79 34
Roll-Ups, Chicken Liver and Bacon, '80 200; '81 57
Rollups, Sausage-Bacon, '88 51
Rumaki, '80 M136
Scallops, Bacon-Wrapped, '87 94
Spread, Bacon-Cheese, '83 241
Swirls, Bacon, '89 214
Water Chestnuts, Bacon-Wrapped, '79 63
Bagels, Meal-in-One, '88 159
Bake, Lima-Bacon, '86 9
Bars, Bacon-Cheese Toast, '79 36
Beef-and-Bacon Twirls, '91 163
Biscuits, Bacon-Cheese, '88 84
Biscuits, Potato-Bacon, '94 214
Bread, Bacon-and-Cheese, '83 255
Bread, Bacon-Cheese French, '92 54
Bread, Bacon Monkey, '94 283
Breakfast Bake, '85 45
Breakfast Eye-Openers, '82 231
Breakfast, Farmer's, '81 44
Broccoli with Bacon, '92 302
Bundles, Bean, '80 246
Burgers, Cheesy Bacon, '81 29
Butternut and Bacon, Skillet, '85 9
Canadian Bacon, Lima Beans with, '83 219; '84 245
Canadian-Style Bacon, Glazed, '82 197
Carrots with Bacon and Onion, Glazed, '87 200
Casserole, Bacon and Egg, '81 225
Casserole, Egg-and-Bacon, '85 248
Champignons au Vin, '79 47
Chicken Bundles with Bacon Ribbons, '87 68
Chowder, Fresh Corn and Bacon, '93 203
Coleslaw, Bacon, '83 58
Cookies, Take-Along Breakfast, '84 59
Cornbread, Cowboy, '81 188
Delight, Bacon-and-Egg, '85 143
Dressing, Green Beans with Bacon, '85 147
Dressing, Hot Bacon, '84 12
Dressing, Potatoes with Hot Bacon, '88 M294
Dressing, Sweet Bacon, '93 108
Egg Salad, Bacon-Horseradish, '94 181

Eggs, and Hominy, Bacon, '85 143
Eggs, Bacon Deviled, '86 136
Eggs Benedict, Bacon-and-Tomato, '87 195
Flank Steak, Bacon-Wrapped, '85 59
Franks, Bacon-Wrapped, '81 202
Frittata, Potato-Bacon, '95 269
Green Beans, Bacon-Topped, '80 M123
Green Beans, Mushroom-Bacon, '91 291; '92 255
Green Beans with Bacon and Mushrooms, '92 13
Hush Puppies, Bacon, '91 201
Kabobs, Scallop-Bacon, '81 111
Linguine Carbonara, '87 108
Meatballs, Bacon-Wrapped, '79 81
Muffins, Bacon-and-Cheese, '89 205
Mushrooms with Bacon, Stir-Fried, '80 123
Oysters, Bacon-Baked, '86 132
Pancake, Maple-Bacon Oven, '89 255
Peas and Bacon, Sautéed, '89 331
Pie, Country Breakfast, '93 M328
Pizza, The King Henry, '95 267
Popcorn, Bacon-Cheese, '86 74
Pork Tenderloin, Spinach-and-Bacon Stuffed, '94 81
Potatoes, Bacon-Stuffed, '86 193
Potatoes, Bacon-Topped Blue Cheese, '79 46
Potatoes, Cheesy Bacon-Stuffed, '81 M61
Quiche, Bacon, '85 60
Quiche Lorraine, '80 M108
Quiche Lorraine, Classic, '81 131
Quiche Lorraine, Mushroom-, '86 242
Quiche Lorraine, Peppery, '81 228
Rice, Bacon-Chive, '83 129
Rice, Bacon Fried, '80 115
Rutabaga with Bacon, '83 243
Salad, Bacon-Topped Potato, '85 59
Salad, BLT Chicken, '87 144
Salad, Endive, Bacon, and Pecan, '89 12
Salad, Escarole-and-Bacon, '84 85
Salad, Hot Bacon and Black-Eyed, '85 7
Salad, Spinach and Bacon, '81 143
Salad, Wilted Bacon-and-Lettuce, '85 69
Salad with Bacon, Rice, '79 52
Sandwiches
Avocado, Bacon, and Cheese Sandwiches, '87 279
Bagel, Breakfast on a, '94 66
Breakfast Sandwiches, '82 M123; '89 M230
Breakfast Sandwiches, Open-Faced, '92 140
Cheese, and Tomato Sandwiches, Bacon, '84 14
Cheesy BLT's, '85 92
Croissants, BLT, '93 158
Curried BLT Sandwiches, '93 158
Grilled Bacon-Cheese Sandwiches, '83 242
Hoagies, Bacon, Pimiento, and Cheese, '90 144
Open-Faced Cheesy Bacon Sandwiches, '80 78
Pita Pockets, BLT in, '93 158
Poor Boys, Oyster-and-Bacon, '87 40
Welsh Rarebit with Tomatoes and Bacon, '92 M159
Scramble, Bacon-and-Eggs, '80 M267
Soup, Bacon-Beer Cheese, '87 M7
Soup, Bacon, Lettuce, and Tomato, '91 207
Soup, Bacon-Topped Cheese, '80 M224
Soup, Bean and Bacon, '83 26
Soup, Potato-Bacon, '84 M38

Spaghetti, Bacon, '86 213; '87 82
Spoonbread, Corn and Bacon, '81 129
Spread, Spinach-Bacon, '92 M310
Squash, Bacon-Flavored, '82 158
Supper Supreme, Sunday, '79 76
Sweet Potatoes, Bacon-Stuffed, '86 224
Tomatoes, Bacon-and-Egg-Stuffed, '80 162
Tomatoes with Bacon, Saucy Fried, '81 210
Vegetable-Bacon Bowl, Marinated, '79 191

BANANAS

Alaskas, Banana Split, '87 10
Baked Bananas, '79 103
Baked Bananas, Honey-, '81 268
Baked Bananas with Orange Sauce, '79 115
Bars, Banana Breakfast, '79 124
Beverages
Banana Smoothie, '87 160; '93 95
Berry Flip, Banana-, '88 215; '89 20
Blueberry Smoothie, Banana-, '90 104
"Concrete," All Shook Up, '94 114
Coolers, Banana, '91 308
Crush, Banana, '80 88; '83 142
Flip, Banana, '83 303
Float, Strawberry-Banana, '87 160
Frostee, Banana, '91 66
Honey-Banana Smoothie, '89 144
Kabana, Banana, '86 316
Malt, Banana-Chocolate, '89 170
Milkshake, Banana, '85 47; '90 179
Milk Shake, Banana-Pineapple, '84 59
Milk Shake, Chocolate-Banana, '94 113
Nog, Banana, '82 290
Orange-Banana Flip, '82 48
Orange-Banana Whip, '95 244
Orange Slush, Banana-, '80 48; '81 155
Pineapple-Banana Slush, '90 14
Pineapple Smoothie, Quick Banana-, '93 195
Shake, Pineapple-Banana, '85 215
Shake, Raspberry-and-Banana, '89 183
Shake, Strawberry-Banana, '89 35
Slush, Banana, '83 56
Strawberry-Banana Smoothie, '81 59
Strawberry Frost, Banana-, '87 199
Tropical Delight, '89 182
Tropical Smoothie, '81 50
Bisque, Banana-Raspberry, '93 161
Boats, Banana, '82 50
Breads
Apple Bread, Banana-, '85 250
Banana Bread, '87 72
Blueberry Bread, Banana-, '81 163
Butterscotch Bread, Banana, '79 116
Chocolate Chip-Banana Bread, '90 267
Chocolate Chip-Banana Loaf, '85 115
Cranberry-Banana Bread, '80 281; '90 294
Date-Banana Loaves, Tropical, '95 143
Fruity Banana Bread, '95 78
Hawaiian Loaf, '80 225
Honey-Banana Bread, '91 68
Jam Bread, Banana-, '84 73
Muffins, Banana, '80 88; '84 75
Muffins, Banana Bran, '83 48
Muffins, Banana-Chocolate, '94 197
Muffins, Banana-Honey-Nut, '88 62
Muffins, Banana-Nut, '93 140
Muffins, Banana-Oat, '87 188
Muffins, Banana Oat Bran, '89 106
Muffins, Banana-Oatmeal, '84 20
Muffins, Banana-Orange, '84 148
Muffins, Banana-Poppyseed, '89 205
Muffins, Banana-Raisin, '89 218

BANANAS, Breads *(continued)*

Muffins, Banana Surprise, '82 105
Muffins, Jumbo Banana-Chocolate Chip, '93 339
Muffins, Oat Bran-Banana, '91 18
Nut Bread, Banana-, '86 8, 70
Nut Bread, Hawaiian Banana, '79 235
Nut-Raisin Bread, Banana-, '81 59
Oat Tea Loaf, Banana-, '87 256
Roll, Banana-Nut, '85 112
Sour Cream-Banana Bread, '79 190
Wheat Bread, Banana, '81 14
Whole Wheat Banana Bread, '80 88
Whole Wheat-Banana Nut Bread, '84 50
Zucchini Bread, Banana-, '85 326
Breakfast-in-a-Bowl, '89 87
Broiled Bananas with Honey, '84 175
Brownies, Chocolate-Banana, '80 160
Cake, Banana, '84 151
Cake, Banana-Blueberry, '86 247
Cake, Banana-Coconut, '93 154
Cake, Banana-Nut, '92 204
Cake, Bananas Foster Crunch, '93 339
Cake, Banana Waldorf, '85 118
Cake, Chocolate-Banana, '86 138
Cake, Deluxe Light Banana, '84 314
Cake, Marvelous Banana, '79 115
Cake, Peanut Butter-Banana, '80 87
Candied Bananas, '83 179
Casserole, Sweet Potato-Banana, '86 276
Coffee Cake, Banana, '81 288
Coffee Cake, Banana Cream, '85 46
Coffee Cake, Banana-Sour Cream, '80 186
Cookies, Banana Oatmeal, '79 217
Crêpes Flambé, Banana, '84 262
Cupcakes, Banana-Cocoa, '80 130
Curried Bananas, Fillets with Horseradish Sauce and, '85 230
Dessert, Banana Cream, '81 180
Doughnuts, Banana, '86 137
Fish, Caribbean Banana, '95 202
Flambé, Banana-Peach, '85 316
Foster, Bananas, '79 18; '83 M114; '86 139
Foster, Elegant Bananas, '81 59
Foster for Two, Bananas, '80 115
Foster, Orange-Glazed Bananas, '91 91
Foster, Tropical Bananas, '79 231
Fritters, Banana, '79 213
Frosting, Banana-Nut, '79 115
Green Bananas Escabeche (Pickled Green Bananas), '92 169
Hawaiian, Bananas, '89 94
Ice Cream, Banana-Graham, '91 56
Ice Cream, Banana Split, '80 176
Ice Cream, Straw-Ba-Nut, '80 177
Ice Cream, Strawberry-Banana-Nut, '88 203
Ice Milk, Banana Yogurt, '89 199
Jam, Banana, '82 296
Jam, Rosy Peach-Banana, '80 142
Nutty Bananas, '79 251
Pancakes, Island, '87 225
Pancakes, Wheat Germ-Banana, '79 114
Pie, Banana Cream, '84 48; '87 207
Pie, Blueberry-Banana, '93 115
Pie, Caramel-Banana, '86 M165
Pie, Chocolate-Banana-Pecan Cream, '94 210
Pie, Hawaiian Banana Cream, '90 105
Pie, Layered Banana Split, '83 189
Pie, Luscious Caramel Banana, '79 115
Pie, Strawberry-Banana Glazed, '81 181

Pie, White Chocolate-Banana Cream, '94 314
Pie with Hot Buttered Rum Sauce, Banana, '88 204
Pops, Banana, '83 60; '84 44
Pops, Orange-Banana, '82 129
Praline Bananas, '84 313
Pudding, Almost Banana, '88 174
Pudding, Banana, '82 53; '84 94; '85 255; '88 16, 32
Pudding, Banana-Mallow, '86 139
Pudding, Basic Banana, '81 59
Pudding, Creamy Banana, '89 M130
Pudding, Delicious Banana, '80 9
Pudding, No-Bake Banana, '91 172
Pudding, Old-Fashioned Banana, '92 94
Pudding, Peanut Butter-Banana, '93 340
Pudding, Surprise Banana, '86 7
Regal Bananas, '85 46
Salad, Banana, '87 80
Salad, Banana-Mixed Fruit, '79 270
Salad, Banana Split, '91 58
Salad, Frozen Banana, '82 80, 132
Salad with Celery Seed Dressing, Grapefruit-Banana, '91 237
Salsa, Banana Rum, '94 97
Sauce, Banana-Pineapple, '83 48
Sauce, Banana Sundae, '84 275
Sauce, Strawberry-Banana, '81 41
Sherbet, Banana-Orange, '83 162
Shortcake, Banana-Pecan, '93 43
Slaw, Banana-Nut, '86 250
Sorbet, Banana-Orange, '88 117
Soufflé, Banana Daiquiri, '84 317
Soup, Avocado-Banana-Yogurt, '80 78
Soup, Strawberry-Banana, '86 181
Splits, Cottage Cheese-Banana, '87 56
Supreme, Banana-Berry, '81 205
Supreme, Bananas, '84 256
Topping, Pound Cake with Strawberry-Banana, '89 200
Topping, Strawberry-Banana, '87 125
Waffles, Banana-Ginger, '86 96
Waffles, Banana-Oatmeal, '94 206
Waffles, Banana Split, '89 205
BARBECUE. *See also* **GRILLED.**
Beans, Barbecued, '94 248
Beans, Barbecued Green, '86 252
Beans, Barbecued Lima, '82 2
Beans, Barbecued Pork and, '79 100
Beans, Commissary Barbecue, '90 120
Beans, Skillet Barbecued, '93 217
Beef. *See also* Barbecue/Ribs.
Barbecued Beef, '81 18
Bourbon Barbecue, '88 129
Brisket, Barbecued, '86 154; '88 218
Brisket, Barbecued Beef, '83 11
Brisket, Denton, Texas, Barbecued Beef, '81 55
Brisket with Sauce, Barbecued Beef, '86 153
Burgers, Barbecued, '82 168; '89 164
Corned Beef Sandwiches, Barbecued, '83 130
Cups, Barbecue, '79 129
Kabobs, Barbecued Steak, '79 89
Liver, Barbecued, '85 219
Loaves, Individual Barbecued Beef, '95 242
Meatballs, Oven Barbecued, '82 233
Meat Loaf, Barbecued, '80 60; '81 275; '87 216
Pot Roast, Barbecued, '79 17; '83 319
Rib Roast, Barbecued, '86 152

Roast Barbecue, Beef, '79 159
Roast, Barbecued Beef, '82 96; '83 103
Sandwiches, Barbecued Beef, '81 25; '82 31; '83 34
Saucy Barbecued Beef, '82 156
Steak, Barbecued Flank, '79 89
Steak, Marinated Barbecued Chuck, '80 156
Steak, Saucy Oven-Barbecued, '83 10
Tenderloin, Barbecued Beef, '94 26
Cabrito, Barbecued, '86 153
Corn on the Cob, Barbecued, '81 128
Dressing, Barbecue Salad, '80 74
Fish. *See also* Barbecue/Seafood.
Catfish, Barbecued, '80 157
Catfish, Lemon Barbecued, '89 202
Fillets, Barbecued Fish, '86 182
Salmon, Barbecued, '81 181
Tacos, Barbecued Fish, '95 339
Tuna, Barbecued, '80 275
Frank Barbecue, Tangy, '79 63
Frankfurters, Barbecued, '83 144
Frankfurters, Oven-Barbecued, '83 11
Franks, Barbecued, '85 192
Lamb, Barbecued, '79 58
Lamb Chops, Barbecued, '79 89
Lamb Shanks, Barbecued, '92 128; '93 113
Outdoor Cooking, '82 109
Popcorn, Cheesy Barbecue, '95 239
Pork. *See also* Barbecue/Ribs.
Bannister's Barbecue, '92 166
Barbecued Pork, '80 72
Chops, Barbecued Pork, '81 10
Chops, Marinated Barbecued Pork, '79 90
Chops, Oven-Barbecued Pork, '81 234; '82 26; '83 40
Ham Slices, Barbecued, '81 110
Home-Style Barbecue, '88 145
Nachos, Commissary Barbecue, '91 171
Roast, Barbecued Pork Loin, '93 34
Roast Barbecue, Pork, '82 97; '83 104
Roast, Berry Barbecued Pork, '80 288
Shoulder, Barbecued Pork, '81 111; '82 11
Spicy Barbecued Pork, '84 296
Potatoes, Barbecued, '91 311; '92 26
Poultry
Chicken Bake, Barbecued, '81 97
Chicken, Barbecue, '86 122
Chicken, Barbecued, '82 97, 106; '83 103; '85 144; '86 153; '89 167
Chicken, Barbecued Cranberry, '83 178
Chicken, Carambola-Glazed Barbecued, '92 246
Chicken, Golden Barbecued, '83 136
Chicken, Grilled Barbecued, '81 154
Chicken Legs and Thighs, Barbecued, '94 94
Chicken, Lemon Barbecued, '93 215
Chicken, Marinated Barbecued, '79 90
Chicken, Old South Barbecued, '82 97; '83 103
Chicken, Orange Barbecued, '88 123
Chicken, Oven-Barbecued Cranberry, '93 332
Chicken, Saucy Barbecued, '83 11
Chicken, Tangy Barbecued, '86 186
Chicken, Zesty Barbecued, '80 M76
Chicken, Zippy Barbecued, '83 213
Turkey Barbecue, '90 158

Rabbit, Hickory Barbecued, '82 216
Ribs
    Apple Barbecued Ribs, '80 111
    Apple-Barbecue Spareribs, '90 160
    Barbecued Ribs, '80 111; '85 159;
        '91 205
    Barbecued Spareribs, '81 112; '82 12;
        '86 232; '95 236
    Beef Short Ribs, Barbecued, '83 178
    Country-Style Barbecued Ribs, '79 42
    Country-Style Ribs, Barbecued, '95 237
    Country-Style Spareribs, Barbecued,
        '80 73
    Easy Barbecued Spareribs, '82 97;
        '83 104
    Herbed Barbecued Ribs, '86 185
    Oven-Barbecued Pork Ribs, '88 132
    Saucy Barbecued Spareribs, '79 14
    Short Ribs, Barbecued, '90 148
    Smoky Barbecued Ribs, '80 111
    Southern Barbecued Spareribs, '79 90
    Spicy Barbecued Spareribs, '84 93
    Tangy Barbecued Ribs, '83 160
    Tangy Barbecued Spareribs, '82 106
Salad, Barbecue Macaroni, '82 276
Sauces
    Bannister's Barbecue Sauce, '92 166
    Barbecue Sauce, '84 172; '86 153;
        '88 218; '91 16, 205; '93 129; '94 27
    Barbecue Sauce, Baked Fish with, '84 92
    Basting Sauce, '90 120
    Beef Marinade, Tangy, '86 113
    Beer Barbecue Sauce, '84 173
    Blender Barbecue Sauce, Ribs with,
        '90 12
    Bourbon Barbecue Sauce, '85 90
    Brisket with Barbecue Sauce, Smoked,
        '85 144
    Dressed-Up Barbecue Sauce, '84 173
    Eastern-Style Barbecue Sauce, '88 145
    Easy Barbecue Sauce, '79 90; '82 178
    John Wills's Barbecue Sauce, '92 255
    Lemon Barbecue Sauce, Herbed,
        '94 154
    Lemony Barbecue Sauce, '88 M177;
        '95 31
    Maple Syrup Barbecue Sauce, '94 154
    Mustard Barbecue Sauce, '84 173
    Orange Barbecue Sauce, Spareribs with,
        '83 11
    Oven Barbecue Sauce, '82 233
    Paprika Barbecue Sauce, '79 90
    Peanut Butter Barbecue Sauce, '81 233
    Piquant Barbecue Sauce, '79 159
    Savory Barbecue Sauce, '86 153
    Special Barbecue Sauce, '82 177
    Spicy Southwest Barbecue Sauce,
        '94 154
    Sweet-and-Sour Marinade, '86 113
    Sweet Sauce, '90 120
    Teriyaki Marinade, '86 114
    Thick and Robust Barbecue Sauce, '94 95
    Thick and Sweet Barbecue Sauce, '94 95
    Thin and Tasty Barbecue Sauce, '94 95
    Tomato Barbecue Sauce, Fresh, '84 172
    Western-Style Barbecue Sauce, '88 145
    White Barbecue Sauce, '94 95
    White Barbecue Sauce, Chicken with,
        '89 M84
    Zippy Barbecue Sauce, '92 166

Sausage, Barbecued, '86 153
Seafood. *See also* Barbecue/Fish.
    Oysters, Barbecued, '82 247
    Shrimp, Barbecued, '82 74; '84 93;
        '90 28
    Shrimp, Cajun Barbecued, '87 95

BARLEY
Baked Barley, '91 133
Casserole, Barley, '84 281
Pilaf, Barley-Vegetable, '91 33
Rolls, Wine-Sauced Beef-and-Barley, '87 269
Salad, Barley, '92 212
Salad, Barley-Broccoli, '90 135
Salad, Black Bean-and-Barley, '94 174
Soup, Hearty Bean-and-Barley, '86 304
Soup, Turkey-Barley, '91 312
Vegetables, Barley and, '91 81

BEANS. See also LENTILS.
Anasazi Beans with Mushrooms, Stewed,
    '95 226
Bake, Cheesy Beef-and-Bean, '82 89
Baked
    Barbecued Beans, '94 248
    Barbecued Pork and Beans, '79 100
    Beefy Baked Beans, '80 136; '84 149;
        '85 142
    Bourbon Baked Beans, '95 182
    Chuckwagon Beans, '81 188
    Crowd-Pleasing Baked Beans, '82 127
    Easy Baked Beans, '85 141
    Favorite Baked Beans, '86 210
    Franks, Beans and, '85 142
    Franks, Beany Kraut and, '79 64
    Franks, Hawaiian Baked Beans and,
        '80 136
    Genuine Baked Beans, '83 26
    Ham, Baked Beans with, '80 136
    Hamburger-Bean Bake, '95 121
    Hawaiian-Style Baked Beans, '86 210
    Maple Heights Baked Beans, '91 223
    Meat Baked Beans, Three-, '86 210
    Medley, Baked Bean, '80 100
    Mixed Baked Beans, '87 92
    Molasses Baked Beans, '82 139; '84 327;
        '86 20
    More Beans, Baked Beans and, '92 173
    Old-Fashioned Baked Beans, '84 25
    Picnic Baked Beans, '83 143; '85 142
    Polynesian Beans-and-Franks, '84 M11
    Pork Chops with Baked Beans, '93 18
    Quick Baked Beans, '80 136
    Quintet, Baked Beans, '93 105; '94 100
    Rum-Laced Bean Bake, '82 283; '83 72
    Smoked Baked Beans, '79 150
    Spiced Baked Beans, '85 142
    Three-Bean Bake, '81 155
    White Bean Bake, Turnip Greens and,
        '94 246
Barbecue Beans, Commissary, '90 120
Barbecued Beans, Skillet, '93 217
Beefy Beans, '82 59
Black. *See also* Beans/Salads, Soups.
    Appetizer, Black Bean, '83 50
    Black Beans, '93 28
    Broth with Black Beans and Cilantro,
        Southwestern Scallop, '87 123
    Cakes with Greens and Apple Dressing,
        Black Bean, '92 216
    Casserole of Black Beans, '95 27
    Chicken with Black Beans and Salsa,
        Poached, '87 217
    Chili Goes Southwest, Basic, '93 326
    Chili Marsala, Black Bean, '95 16

Cuban Black Beans, '88 196
Dip, Black Bean, '95 93
Frijoles con Cerveza (Beans with Beer),
    '81 66
Guacamole, Black Bean, '94 277
Marinated Black Beans, '93 131
Pancakes with Gazpacho Butter, Black
    Bean, '92 86
Relish, Black Bean-Tomatillo, '87 121
Rice, Black Beans and, '80 222; '89 178;
    '91 82; '95 309
Salsa, Black Bean, '93 155; '94 161
Salsa, Black Bean-and-Corn, '94 80
Sauce, Black Bean, '93 59
Spaghetti, Black Bean, '92 217
Spanish Black Beans, '84 327
Terrine with Fresh Tomato Coulis and
    Jalapeño Sauce, Black Bean, '93 230
Terrine with Goat Cheese, Black Bean,
    '87 120
Tostadas, Shrimp-and-Black Bean,
    '93 204
Yellow Rice, Black Beans and, '95 126
Yellow Rice, Black Beans with, '82 2
Yellow Rice, Easy Black Beans and,
    '92 308
Burrito Appetizers, Bean, '94 226
Burritos, Meat-and-Bean, '81 194
Butterbeans, '90 166
Cannellini Beans, Rosemary, '95 213
Casserole, Bean-and-Cornbread, '92 243
Casserole, Chuck Wagon Bean, '93 198
Casserole, Spicy Mexican Bean, '84 114
Casserole, Three-Bean, '88 56
Chili and Beans, Ranch, '79 270; '80 11
Chili Bean Roast, '87 268; '88 102
Chili, Mom's, '93 292
Chili Surprise, '82 229
Chili, Turkey-Bean, '88 M213
Chili, White, '91 284
Chili with Beans, Easy, '92 262
Chili with Beans, Meaty, '85 250
Chimichangas (Fried Burritos), '81 196
Creole Beans and Rice, '80 223
Crostini, Mexican, '95 142
Dip, Bean, '89 97
Dip, Cheese-Bean, '85 208
Dip, Hotshot Bean, '87 195
Dip, Layered Nacho, '81 261
Dip, Prairie Fire Bean, '80 195
Dip, South-of-the-Border, '81 235
Enchiladas, Three-Bean, '91 133
Franks, Jiffy Beans and, '91 M172
Franks 'n' Beans, Stove-Top, '88 201
Garbanzo Dinner, Beef-and-, '84 31
Garbanzo Dip, '93 94
Green. *See also* Beans/Salads, Soups.
    Almonds, Green Beans with, '84 253
    Amandine, Green Beans, '79 276;
        '82 M20; '85 156
    Appalachian Green Beans, '81 215
    au Gratin, Green Beans, '80 116
    Bacon and Mushrooms, Green Beans
        with, '92 13
    Bacon Dressing, Green Beans with,
        '85 147
    Bacon-Topped Green Beans, '80 M123
    Baked Green Beans, '91 159
    Barbecued Green Beans, '86 252
    Basil Beans and Tomatoes, '83 172
    Basil, Green Beans with, '82 96
    Blue Cheese, Green Beans with, '88 57
    Bow-Tie Green Beans, '94 320

BEANS, Green *(continued)*

Buffet Green Beans, '93 325
Bundles, Bean, '80 246; '83 67
Bundles, Green Bean, '83 180; '87 118
Buttered Green Beans, '92 54
Caramelized Onions, Green Beans with, '95 288
Cashews, Green Beans with, '89 202
Casserole, Chicken-Green Bean, '85 296
Casserole, Corn-and-Bean, '90 208
Casserole, Easy Green Bean, '87 284
Casserole, Green Bean, '79 106; '84 145
Casserole, Green Bean-and-Corn, '88 123
Casserole, Italian Green Bean-and-Artichoke, '85 81
Celery, Green Beans and Braised, '84 254
Cheese-Topped Green Beans, '79 100
Cheesy Green Beans, '80 157
Creamed Green Beans, French-Style, '88 252
Cumin Green Beans, '82 90
Dilled Green Beans, '82 106; '86 157; '88 101; '89 203; '93 279
Dill Green Beans, '93 136
Dilly Green Beans, '80 116
Excellent, Green Beans, '94 321
French Green Beans, '90 208
French Quarter Green Beans, '80 298; '81 26
Fresh Green Beans, '79 122
Garlic Green Beans, '91 159; '94 273
Goldenrod Beans, '83 111
Greek Green Beans, '94 165
Green Beans, '80 126; '87 M151
Herbed Green Beans, '83 M147, 177; '88 M190
Herb Green Beans, '89 321
Herbs, Green Beans with, '82 90
Indian-Style Green Beans, '88 265
Italian Green Beans, '85 147; '90 164; '92 183
Italian, Green Beans, '87 10
Italian Green Beans, Sesame, '82 174
Italian Green Beans with Almonds, '81 207
Italiano, Green Bean, '94 248
Italiano, Green Beans, '86 144
Lemon Green Beans, '89 275
Lemon-Walnut Green Beans, '93 304
Lemony Green Beans, '85 190
Marinated Beets, Green Beans, and Carrots, '88 162
Marinated Green Beans, '83 145
Marinated Italian Beans, '86 M226
Marinated Vegetables, '81 239
Marjoram, Fresh Green Beans with, '91 159
Mediterranean-Style Green Beans, '79 100
Medley, Green Bean, '85 108
Medley, Peppery Green Bean, '93 181
Minted Green Beans, '84 104
Mushroom-Bacon Green Beans, '91 291; '92 255
Mushroom Sauce, Green Beans in Sherried, '93 206
Mushrooms, Green Beans with, '82 21; '93 89
Mustard, Green Beans and Tomatoes with, '87 83

New Potatoes, Green Beans with, '87 164
Nutty Green Beans, '88 M187
Oriental Green Beans, '88 43
Oriental, Green Beans, '91 158
Pecans, Green Beans with Buttered, '92 61
Pepper Strips, Green Beans and, '86 170
Pickled Beans, Dressed-Up, '86 251
Pole Beans, Old-Fashioned, '80 100
Potatoes, Down-Home Beans and, '85 254
Potatoes, Green Beans and, '91 221
Provençal, Green Beans, '81 182; '91 158
Red Peppers and Pearl Onions, Green Beans with Roasted, '93 260
Saucy Green Beans, '83 206
Savory Green Beans, '89 70, 235
Seasoned Green Beans, '88 304
Shuck Beans, '81 216
Simple Green Beans, '92 100
Snap Beans, '86 218
Snap Beans, Simple, '85 148
Snap, or Wax Beans, Green, '85 105
Sour Cream, Green Beans in, '80 116
Sour Cream, Green Beans with, '82 90
Southern-Style Green Beans, '79 283
Spanish Green Beans, '80 116
Spanish-Style Green Beans, '84 128
Special Green Beans, '90 268
Squash, Beans, and Tomatoes, '83 148
Stir-Fried Green Beans, '85 148; '86 305
Surprise, Green Bean, '86 9
Sweet-and-Sour Beans, '87 197
Sweet-and-Sour Green Beans, '79 184; '81 158; '82 90; '91 250
Sweet-and-Sour Green Beans and Carrots, '83 6
Sweet-and-Sour Snap Beans, '89 173
Tangy Green Beans, '85 M142; '89 314, 332
Tarragon Dressing, Green Beans with Creamy, '93 191
Tomatoes, Bean-Stuffed, '84 34
Tomatoes, Green Beans with, '85 137
Tomatoes, Green Beans with Cherry, '86 177
Tomato Skillet, Bean-and-, '90 316
Vegetable-Herb Trio, '83 172
Vinaigrette, Green Beans, '93 120; '94 90
Vinaigrette, Kentucky Wonder Green Beans, '94 158
Walnut Dressing, Green Beans with, '94 279
Zucchini, Green Beans with, '84 128
Hot Dogs, Beany, '82 190
Hummas, '92 155
Hummus, Quick, '95 93
Kidney Bean Casserole, '90 136
Kidney Beans, Mexican, '90 205
Lasagna, Spinach-Bean, '92 96
Legumes, Marinated, '90 197
Lemon-Mint Beans, '88 22
Lima. *See also* Beans/Salads, Soups.
Bake, Lima-Bacon, '86 9
Barbecued Lima Beans, '82 2
Beans, Lima, '80 127
Beef-and-Lima Bean Dinner, '84 292
Canadian Bacon, Lima Beans with, '83 219; '84 245
Casserole, Ham and Lima, '79 192

Casserole, Lima Bean, '79 189; '83 313; '86 225; '87 284; '95 132
Casserole, Lima Bean Garden, '83 218; '84 246
Casserole, Spicy Lima Bean, '79 189
Casserole, Swiss Lima Bean, '80 191
Cheese and Limas in Onion Shells, '81 86
Cheese Limas, Spanish, '86 225
Chilly Lima Beans, '81 206
Combo, Hot Lima and Tomato, '83 219
Creole, Lima Beans, '80 191; '85 137
Deluxe, Lima Beans, '79 289; '80 26
Fresh Lima Beans and Scallions, '82 133
Marinated Limas, '86 225
Medley, Carrot-Lima-Squash, '80 123
Rancho Lima Beans, '80 191
Savory Lima Beans, '83 219; '84 246
Savory Sauce, Lima Beans and Carrots with, '84 196
Sour Cream, Lima Beans in, '79 189; '88 41
Spanish-Style Lima Beans, '83 25
Succotash, Easy, '80 165
Super Lima Beans, '79 189
Supper, Sausage-Bean, '86 52
Mogumbo, '93 32
Nachos, Best-Ever, '79 91
Nachos, Easy, '84 30
Nachos, Make-Ahead, '80 M135
Pinto. *See also* Beans/Salads, Soups.
Beef-and-Bean Supper, '82 2
Chalupa, Bean, '80 223
Chalupas, Bean, '83 313
Chalupas, Pork, '83 160
Chili, Tex-Mex, '83 26
Cow Camp Pinto Beans, '94 28
Enchiladas, Spicy Bean, '88 18
Frijoles Rancheros, '88 148
Mexican Pinto Beans, '93 69; '94 30
Pie, Pinto Bean, '80 40
Pinto Beans, '87 303
Ranch Beans, Laredo, '81 75
Ranch Beans, Texas, '90 198
Razorback Beans, '84 328
Refried Beans, '79 185
Rice, South Texas Beans and, '85 252
Sandwiches, Bean Salad, '81 243
Sausage, Hearty Pintos and, '88 296
Southwestern Beans, '89 16
Spicy-Hot Beans, '89 17
Spicy Hot Pintos, '83 26
Sweet-Hot Pinto Beans, '86 114
Trailride Pinto Beans, '85 154
Red Beans and Rice, '80 58; '83 89; '84 37; '87 45; '90 27
Red Beans and Rice, Cajun, '83 26
Red Beans and Rice, Easy, '90 220
Refried Beans, '79 185
Salads
Black Bean-and-Barley Salad, '94 174
Black Bean-and-Cheese Salad, '92 217
Black Bean Salad, '89 217
Black Bean Salad, Caribbean Shrimp-and-, '93 143
Cannellini Bean Salad, Tuna-and-, '86 143
Chilled Bean Salad, '80 178
Cucumber-Bean Salad, '83 81
Five-Bean Salad, Hot, '81 149
Four-Bean Salad, '79 20; '84 82
Full o' Beans Salad, '81 38
Garbanzo Salad, '82 2
Garbanzo Salad, Avocado-, '81 33

Garden Medley Salad, '80 122
Green Bean-and-Tomato Salad, '86 180
Green Bean-Peanut Salad, '86 117
Green Bean-Potato Salad, '83 80
Green Bean Salad, '87 90
Green Bean Salad, Cold, '84 106
Green Bean Salad, Crispy, '82 239
Green Bean Salad, German, '92 169
Green Bean Salad, Hot, '86 298; '87 176
Green Bean Salad, Lettuce and, '80 79
Green Bean Salad, Molded, '85 252
Green Bean Salad, Paprika-, '86 191
Green Bean Salad, Pickled, '82 239
Green Bean Salad, Speedy, '84 283
Green Beans-and-Cheese Salad, '91 159
Green Bean Slaw, '95 108
Green Beans Vinaigrette, '83 25
Hominy-Bean Salad, '88 266
Hot German-Style Bean Salad, '91 314
Kidney Bean-Salami Pasta Toss, '85 165
Layered Salad, '86 35
Lima Bean-Tomato Salad, '85 137
Marinated Bean-and-Rice Salad, '87 152
Marinated Bean-Pasta Salad, '94 167
Marinated Bean Salad, '85 137, 296;
    '89 314; '93 312; '94 167
Marinated Bean Salad, Crunchy, '84 197
Marinated Combo Salad, '82 267
Marinated Corn-Bean Salad, '87 9
Mexican Salad, '94 202
Mexican Tossed Salad, '81 280
Mixed Bean Salad, '83 217
Niçoise, Salad, '86 35
Overnight Fiesta Salad, '83 80
Pinto Salad, '86 169
Pole Bean-Potato Salad, Hot, '79 74
Pork-'n'-Bean Salad, '87 83
Potato-Bean Salad, '82 301
Quick Bean Salad, '89 128
Red Bean Slaw, '79 247
Rice-and-Bean Salad, '85 22
Rice Salad, Beans-and-, '91 44
Saucy Bean Salad, '84 18
Sausage Salad, Bean-and-, '91 313
Six-Bean Salad, Colorful, '87 82
Southwest Salad, '81 113
Sprout Salad, Bean, '82 113
Supreme Bean Salad, '91 202
Sweet-and-Sour Bean Salad, '85 198;
    '86 147
Sweet-and-Sour Beans with Sprouts,
    '86 32
Sweet-and-Sour Vegetable Salad, '81 25
Sauce, Pork-and-Onions with Bean, '85 76
Sausage-and-Bean Dinner, '95 108
Sausage, Beans, and Rice, Texas, '84 296
Sauté, Vegetarian, '95 69
Shuck Beans, '81 216
Soups
    Bacon Soup, Bean and, '83 26
    Barley Soup, Hearty Bean-and-, '86 304
    "Bean Counter" Soup, '92 80
    Beanolla Soup, '94 248
    Bean Soup, '80 25
    Black Bean Soup, '88 30, 266; '89 28;
        '93 231
    Black Bean Soup, Carolina, '92 139
    Capitol Hill Bean Soup, '80 222
    Chill-Chaser Soup, '87 282
    Drunken Bean Soup, '87 283

French Market Soup, '92 49; '94 317
French Market Soup Mix, '94 317
Green Bean Soup, Cream of, '84 111
Guadalajara Soup, '88 30
Ham-and-Bean Soup, '84 4
Ham-and-Bean Soup, Spicy, '94 322
Hominy Soup, Bean-and-, '95 23
Leafy Bean Soup, '86 223
Minestrone Soup, '91 258
Minestrone Soup Mix, '91 258
Navy Bean Soup, '84 280
Navy Bean Soup, Chunky, '83 291
Navy Bean Soup, Savory, '87 282
Pasta Soup, Bean and, '94 220
Sausage-Bean Chowder, '83 20
Sausage-Bean Soup, '85 88
Sausage-Bean Soup, Spicy, '83 229
Three-Bean Soup, '89 17
Three-Bean Soup, Spicy, '91 28
Turkey Soup, Bean-and-, '93 319
Vegetable-Bean Soup, '83 317
White Bean Soup, '83 229; '90 201
White Bean Soup, Spicy, '94 225
Tacos, Chicken-and-Bean, '93 293
White Bean Pot, '86 194
White Bean Relish, '93 229
White Beans, Caesar Salad with, '93 30
White Bean Spread, '93 30; '95 279

BEEF. *See also* **GRILLED/BEEF.**

Appetizers, Meat-and-Cheese, '87 7
Asparagus, Beef with, '90 100
Ball, Cheese 'n' Beef, '83 230
Barbecue, Bourbon, '88 129
Barbecued Beef, Saucy, '82 156
Bouilli, '80 58
Bourguignon, Beef, '79 104; '82 288
Bourguignon, Royal Beef, '80 106
Brisket, Barbecued, '86 154; '88 218
Brisket, Barbecued Beef, '83 11
Brisket, Denton, Texas, Barbecued Beef,
    '81 55
Brisket, Heavenly Smoked, '95 114
Brisket, Home-Style, '87 303
Brisket in Beer, Beef, '93 63
Brisket, Marinated, '86 129
Brisket, Passover, '95 102
Brisket, Smoke-at-Home, '93 192
Brisket, Smoked, '89 168
Brisket with Barbecue Sauce, Smoked,
    '85 144
Brisket with Sauce, Barbecued Beef, '86 153
Broccoli, Quick Beef and, '91 123
Broccoli with Chive Gravy, Beef and, '88 214
Burgoo, Five-Meat, '87 3
Burgoo, Kentucky, '88 235
Burgoo, Old-Fashioned, '87 3
Burgundy, Beef, '82 259; '83 125, 281;
    '88 25; '95 69
Burgundy, Simple Beef, '90 234
Burgundy with Pearl Onions, Beef, '81 108
Burritos, Carne Guisada, '95 43
Burritos, Cheesy Beef, '85 193
Burritos, Meat-and-Bean, '81 194
Caldo de Rez (Mexican Beef Stew), '89 276
Carne Guisada, '93 68
Chalupa, Bean, '80 223
Chili, Bodacious, '95 14
Chili, Chuck Wagon, '81 282; '82 57
Chili, Chunky, '82 M282; '86 3
Chili con Carne, '82 310; '83 30; '86 2
Chili, Cowboy, '86 2
Chili, Firestarter, '93 34
Chili Marsala, Black Bean, '95 16

Chili, North Texas Red, '87 303
Chili, Out West, '95 15
Chili, Red, '93 108
Chili, South-of-the-Border, '83 283;
    '91 283
Chili, Texas Championship, '81 54
Chili Verde, '95 14
Chili, Zippy, '87 110
Chimichangas (Fried Burritos), '85 244;
    '86 114
Chimichangas, Oven-Fried Beef, '92 124
Chinese-Style Beef, '87 50
Chipped Beef and Toast, Creamy, '79 180
Corned Beef
    Birming "Ham," '94 229
    Brunch Bake, Corned Beef, '82 44
    Cabbage au Gratin, Corned Beef and,
        '83 16
    Cabbage, Corned Beef and, '83 104;
        '93 64
    Cabbage, Corned Beef Squares and,
        '82 86
    Cabbage, Quick Corned Beef and, '79 54
    Dijon Glaze, Corned Beef with, '87 54
    Dinner, Corned Beef, '87 54
    Hash, Corned Beef, '95 262
    Hash, Red Flannel, '79 191
    Reuben Buns, '88 298
    Reuben Casserole, '90 240
    Reuben Cheesecake, '90 175
    Reuben Loaf, '95 338
    Reuben Meat Pie, '80 189
    Reuben Sandwiches, '80 M201
    Reuben Sandwiches, Broiled, '81 240
    Reuben Sandwiches, Crispy, '85 299
    Reuben Sandwiches, Grilled, '81 206
    Reuben Sandwiches, Open-Face, '91 199
    Reubens, Party, '90 61
    Reuben Turnovers, '94 253
    Roll, Corned Beef, '85 66
    Salad, Corned Beef, '80 104
    Salad, Corned Beef-Cauliflower, '83 16
    Salad, Corned Beef-Potato, '85 213
    Salad, Molded Corned Beef, '82 86
    Salad, Potato-Corned Beef, '81 36
    Salad, Vegetable-Corned Beef, '80 148
    Sandwich, Corned Beef and Cheese,
        '79 214
    Sandwiches, Barbecued Corned Beef,
        '83 130
    Sandwiches, Corned Beef, '83 291;
        '85 242; '92 23
    Sandwiches, Grilled Corned Beef,
        '87 54
    Sandwiches, Meal-in-One, '80 218
    Soup, Corned Beef, '83 16
    Soup, French Onion-Beef, '87 54
    Spread, Corned Beef, '87 196
Creamed Beef and Chicken-Topped Potatoes,
    '83 210
Creamed Chipped Beef, '92 42
Creamed Dried Beef with Artichokes, '85 81
Cubes in Wine Sauce, Beef, '79 264
Curried Beef Dinner, '83 4
Dip, Chipped Beef, '88 M8
Dip, Hot Cheesy Beef, '80 85
Élégante, Beef, '80 125
en Daube, Beef, '79 163
Fajitas, Beef, '88 233
Fajitas, Favorite, '86 114
Filet Mignon, Cajun Blackened, '95 85
Fillet of Beef with Blue Cheese Sauce, Pan-
    Roasted, '94 320

BEEF *(continued)*

Goulash, Beef, '83 231
Goulash, Hungarian, '81 227; '92 227
Green Peppers, Beef and, '79 104
Grillades and Grits, '89 47; '93 62
Gumbo, Texas Ranch-Style, '82 226
Gumbo z'Herbes, '94 239
Hash, Beef, '95 24
Hash with Cabbage Salad, Austrian, '95 262
Jerky, Beef, '80 269; '81 26
Kabobs
    Barbecued Steak Kabobs, '79 89
    Beef Kabobs, '85 110
    Chile-Beef Kabobs, '94 251
    Deluxe, Beef Kabobs, '82 182
    Hot-and-Spicy Kabobs, '87 193
    Liver Kabobs, '80 185
    Marinated Beef Kabobs, '82 105; '85 159
    Marinated Beef Kabobs with Rice, '84 32
    Marinated Beef on a Stick, '85 234
    Marinated Sirloin Kabobs, '82 162
    Marinated Steak Kabobs, '80 184
    Pineapple-Beef Kabobs, '83 212
    Saucy Beef Kabobs, '83 109
    Shrimp Kabobs, Steak-and-, '80 184
    Spirited Beef Kabobs, '87 142
    Steak Kabobs, '82 4; '93 95
    Steak on a Stick, '83 109
    Steak with Vegetables, Skewered, '81 124
    Teriyaki Beef Kabobs, '80 207
    Vegetable Kabobs, Beef-and-, '91 148
    Vegetables, Beef Kabobs with, '90 148
Liver
    Creamy Liver and Noodle Dinner, '80 11
    Creole Sauce, Liver in, '87 33
    French-Style Liver, '80 10
    Gravy, Liver and, '80 10
    Herbs, Liver with, '81 277
    Kabobs, Liver, '80 185
    Patties, Beef Liver, '81 277
    Saucy Liver, '81 277
    Sauté, Liver, '81 277
    Spanish-Style Liver, '80 11
    Stroganoff, Liver, '79 54
    Sweet-and-Sour Liver, '81 277
    Tasty Liver, '83 29
Mango-Beef and Rice, '88 138
Meatballs, Quick Processor, '87 111
Medaillons, Italian Beef, '87 305
Medaillons of Beef with Ancho Chile Sauce, '87 122
Medaillons of Beef with Horseradish Cream, '90 96
Mongolian Beef, '85 2, 75
Oriental, Beef and Cauliflower, '80 220
Oriental Beef and Snow Peas, '79 105
Oriental Beef with Pea Pods, '86 M328
Pastichio, '85 194
Pies, Carry-Along Beef, '80 224; '81 56
Pie, Shepherd's, '92 168
Pot Pie, Oriental Beef, '92 253
Pot Pies with Yorkshire Pudding Topping, Beef, '93 45
Ribs
    Barbecued Beef Short Ribs, '83 178
    Barbecued Short Ribs, '90 148
    Hearty Beef Shortribs, '79 14
    Supreme, Beef Shortribs, '79 14
Rice, Beef and Cauliflower over, '93 94

Roasts
    Barbecue, Beef Roast, '79 159
    Barbecued Beef Roast, '82 96; '83 103
    Beer-and-Onion Sauce, Roast in, '80 124
    Brisket Roast, Peppery, '83 319
    Burgundy Gravy, Beef Roast with, '95 263
    Burgundy Roast, Beef, '85 291
    Chili Bean Roast, '87 268; '88 102; '89 68
    Chuck Roast, Fruited, '91 289
    Chuck Roast in Sauce, '91 47
    Chuck Roast, Marinated, '80 59
    Chuck Roast, Orange Marinated, '85 179
    Cola Roast, '81 298
    Deli-Style Roast Beef, '93 15
    Diablo, Beef, '79 17
    Easy Beef Roast, '89 M65
    Easy Oven Roast, '93 64
    Eye-of-Round, Burgundy, '90 243
    Eye-of-Round, Grilled Beef, '82 91
    Eye-of-Round Roast with Rice Gravy, Seasoned, '89 118
    Eye Round Roast, Mexican, '89 190
    French-Style Beef Roast, '89 32
    Grillades and Grits, '88 126
    Grilled Marinated Beef Roast, '93 141
    Grilled Pepper Roast, '81 110
    Herbed Roast, '91 288
    Java Roast, '83 319
    Marengo, Beef, '82 284; '83 14
    Marinated Roast, '85 3
    Marinated Roast, Dijon Wine-, '91 289
    New York Strip Roast, Spicy, '93 131
    Patio Steak, '87 141
    Pot Pie, Beef Roast, '88 296
    Pot Roast, All-Seasons, '86 89
    Pot Roast and Gravy, '89 234
    Pot Roast and Gravy, Country-Style, '94 308
    Pot Roast, Autumn Gold, '83 7
    Pot Roast, Barbecued, '79 17; '83 319
    Pot Roast, Basic, '81 M208
    Pot Roast, Bavarian-Style, '79 17
    Pot Roast, Beef Brisket, '93 20
    Pot Roast, Bloody Mary, '86 47
    Pot Roast, Cardamom, '79 12
    Pot Roast, Company, '79 162; '88 M14
    Pot Roast, Country, '87 216
    Pot Roast, Dillicious, '81 187
    Pot Roast, Easy Oven, '86 52
    Pot Roast, Favorite, '89 118
    Pot Roast, Fruited, '90 211
    Pot Roast, Hawaiian, '81 298
    Pot Roast, Indian, '87 215
    Pot Roast in Red Sauce, '87 215
    Pot Roast in Sour Cream, '89 117
    Pot Roast in White Wine Gravy, '81 299
    Pot Roast, Italian, '81 299; '87 95
    Pot Roast, Marinated, '85 21
    Pot Roast Medley, Vegetable-, '83 319
    Pot Roast, Mushroom, '79 17
    Pot Roast, Peppered, '87 215
    Pot Roast, Perfect, '83 7
    Pot Roast, Polynesian, '80 59
    Pot Roast, Regal, '79 17
    Pot Roast, Spicy Apple, '83 7
    Pot Roast, Swedish, '80 59
    Pot Roast, Sweet-and-Sour, '83 8
    Pot Roast with Gravy, '81 298
    Pot Roast with Herbed Red Sauce, '88 29
    Pot Roast with Sour Cream Gravy, '79 17
    Pot Roast with Spaghetti, '80 59

    Pot Roast with Vegetables, '80 59; '81 M208
    Pot Roast with Vegetables, Marinated, '88 M52
    Pot Roast, Zesty, '81 206
    Pressure-Cooker Roast, '91 289
    Rib-Eye Beef, Spicy, '84 259
    Rib-Eye Roast, Marinated, '90 318
    Rib Roast, Barbecued, '86 152
    Rib Roast, Standing, '80 246; '84 187; '95 28
    Rib Roast with Yorkshire Pudding, Standing, '80 252
    Rump Roast, Easy, '93 217
    Sauerbraten Beef, Marinated, '93 16
    Sauerbraten, Quick, '80 139
    Simple Roast, '81 298
    Sirloin Roast, Canary, '89 117
    Sirloin Tip Roast with Mustard Cream Sauce, Herbed, '88 61
    Supreme, Roast Beef, '83 8
    Vegetables, Company Beef and, '88 234
    Wellington, Beef, '83 319
Rolls, Stuffed Sherried Beef, '79 105
Rolls, Wine-Sauced Beef-and-Barley, '87 269
Roll-Ups, Mexican Beef, '90 176
Rollups with Rice, Royal Beef, '79 105
Roulades, Beef, '83 47
Roulades, Roquefort Beef, '88 215
Salads. *See also* Beef/Corned Beef.
    Broccoli Salad, Beef-and-, '87 187
    Cucumber-Roast Beef Salad, '89 162
    Fajita Salad, Beef, '91 70
    Gingered Beef Salad, '88 61
    Greek Steak Salad, '92 107
    Peking Beef Salad, '88 60
    Roast Beef Salad, '80 223; '81 56; '90 318
    Sirloin Salad, Grilled, '94 129
    Tangy Beef Salad, '87 M218
    Vinaigrette Salad, Beef, '95 177
    Western-Style Beef Salad, '93 321
    Zesty Beef Salad, '79 56
Sandwich, Beef-and-Kraut, '91 167
Sandwiches, Beef and Pork Tenderloin, '80 175
Sandwiches, Beef Salad Pocket, '83 267
Sandwiches, Dried Beef Pita, '86 160
Sandwiches, Wake-Up, '84 58
Sandwich, Roast Beef Hero, '91 167
Sandwich, Saucy Beef Pocket, '80 92
Seasoning Blend, Meat, '88 29
Shredded Beef over Rice Noodles, '85 74
Soup, Beefy Lentil, '87 282
Soup, Hearty Vegetable-Beef, '84 102
Soup, Vegetable-Beef, '88 296
Spaghetti, Meaty, '82 19
Spread, Hot Beef, '83 50; '84 M216
Steaks. *See also* Beef/Kabobs, Salads.
    American Steakhouse Beef, '93 15
    Appetizers, Marinated Steak-and-Chestnut, '84 323
    au Poivre, Steak, '88 232
    Bacon Twirls, Beef-and-, '91 163
    Barbecued Beef, '81 18
    Barbecued Steak, Saucy Oven-, '83 10
    Bean Sprouts, Beef and, '82 281; '83 42
    Benedict for Two, Steaks, '85 295
    Blackened 'n' Peppered Steak, '95 174
    Blue Cheese Steaks, '84 171
    Blue Cheese-Walnut Stuffed Fillets, '95 327
    Bourbon Steak, '90 148

Braised Steaks, Beer-, '87 96
Broiled Oriental Steaks, '83 110
Carne Guisada, '94 219
Carpetbagger Steak, '84 87
Chicken-Fried Steak, '92 214
Chicken-Fried Steaks, '88 110
Chuck Steak, Marinated Barbecued, '80 156
Continental, Steak, '83 178
Country-Fried Steak and Cream Gravy, '84 8
Country-Fried Steak, Mock, '87 163
Crêpes, Special Steak, '91 24
Curried Beef Steak, '88 60
Cutlets, Lemon-Flavored, '79 105
de Burgo, Steak, '84 117
Diane Flambé, Steak, '79 103
Diane, Steak, '82 275; '92 306
Dianne, Steak, '83 47
Fajita Crêpes, '94 116
Fajitas, '84 233
Fajitas, Plum Good, '94 115
Filet Mignon, Marinated, '84 171
Filet Mignons with Shiitake Madeira Sauce, '95 265
Filet Mignon Tarragon, '94 46
Filet Mignon with Horseradish Gravy, '92 262
Filet Mignon with Mushroom Sauce, '94 250
Fillets au Vin, Beef, '79 137
Fillets with Horseradish Sauce and Curried Bananas, '85 230
Fingers, Golden Steak, '85 110
Flank Steak and Mushrooms, '87 61
Flank Steak-and-Spinach Pinwheels, '95 56
Flank Steak, Bacon-Wrapped, '85 59
Flank Steak, Barbecued, '79 89
Flank Steak, Beer-Marinated, '87 35
Flank Steak, Ginger-Marinated, '89 25
Flank Steak, Grilled, '80 152; '89 168; '91 80; '92 166
Flank Steak, Herbed, '92 127
Flank Steak, Herb-Marinated, '85 275
Flank Steak, Lemon-Lime, '95 55
Flank Steak, Marinated, '82 162; '83 35, 258; '85 86; '88 262; '95 237
Flank Steak, Oriental, '83 178
Flank Steak Pinwheels, '87 141
Flank Steak, Red Wine-Marinated, '95 283
Flank Steaks, Delicious Marinated, '83 110
Flank Steak Sukiyaki, '88 233
Flank Steak, Tangy, '86 184
Flank Steak, Tenderized, '82 105
Flank Steak Teriyaki, '81 110
Flank Steak, Texas, '86 185
Flank Steak with Black Bean-and-Corn Salsa, Grilled, '94 80
Flank Steak with Noodles, Stuffed, '90 101
Flank Steak with Sweet Peppers, Grilled, '90 138
French Quarter Steak, '81 17
Garlic Steak, '84 8
Greek Pocket Steaks, '81 262
Grillades and Baked Cheese Grits, '94 240

Grilled Black Pepper Steak, '86 184
Grilled Steaks, Mesquite-, '85 154
Grilled Steaks with Green Chiles, '85 144
Grill, Steak Brunch, '82 44
Ham-and-Mushroom Sauce, Steak with, '83 109
Horseradish Steak, '88 39
Korean Steak, '89 190
Lemon-Butter Steak with Brandy Sauce, '85 78
lo Mein, Steak, '90 100
London Broil, Grilled, '92 59
London Broil, Marinated, '87 32
London Broil, Peppercorn, '88 60
London Broil, Teriyaki, '92 282
Marinated Bourbon Steak, '95 91
Marinated Steak, '88 233
Marinated Steak, Mexican, '88 148
Mesquite-Ginger Beef with Fresh Fruit Relish, '95 158
Mexican Steak, '84 76
Mushroom Sauce, Steak with, '83 212
Mush, Steak and Gravy with, '81 215
Oriental Beef, '85 20
Parmesan, Steak, '93 41
Parmigiana, Beef, '84 8; '85 234
Pepper-Beef Steak, '85 21
Pepper Cream, Steak in, '94 117
Pepper Steak, '81 273; '85 57; '88 113
Pepper Steak and Rice, '81 17
Pepper Steak, Chinese, '82 236
Pepper Steak, Cold, '91 208
Pepper Steak, Cracked, '83 109
Pepper Steak Salad Cups, '86 206
Pepper Stir-Fry Steak, '81 240
Pies, Cornish Meat, '84 23
Pirate Steak, '79 89
Red Wine Marinade, Beef with, '91 46
Rib-Eye Steaks with Roquefort Glaze, '89 310
Ropa Vieja, '93 28
Roulades, Beef, '85 234
Round Steak, Braised, '87 35
Round Steak over Rice, Burgundy, '90 M33
Round Steak, Parmesan, '80 106
Round Steak, Red Pepper, '88 214
Round Steak, Savory Stuffed, '81 18
Round Steak, Skillet, '83 29
Round Steak, Tangy, '82 284; '83 14
Round Steak, Tender Grilled, '85 3
Saltillo, Beef (Beef with Tomatillos), '82 219
Shrimp, Steak and, '88 123
Sirloin, Mustard Marinated, '94 41
Sirloin Steak, Secret, '81 110
Sirloin Supreme, Shrimp and, '81 131
Skillet Steak in Red Wine Sauce, '85 21
Skillet Steak 'n Potatoes, '81 18
Smothered Beef and Onions, '85 293
Smothered Steak, '79 212
Smothered Steak, Onion-, '87 M189
Stir-Fried Beef, '84 26
Stir-Fried Steak, Fast-and-Easy, '87 50
Stir-Fry, Beef-and-Vegetable, '87 22
Stir-Fry, Beef-and-Vegetables, '84 141
Stir-Fry, Pepper Steak, '89 191
Stir-Fry, Steak-and-Vegetable, '84 8
Stuffed Steak, Italian-, '88 232
Stuffed Steak Rolls, '82 135
Stuffed Steaks, Cheese-, '81 17
Sweet-and-Sour Marinated Steaks, '83 110

Swiss Steak Cheese Skillet, '80 106
Swiss Steak, Deviled, '80 107
Swiss Steak, Oven, '85 234
Swiss Steak Surprise, '81 17
Swiss Steak with Vegetables, '81 273
Tabasco Steak, '95 207
Tartare, Steak, '83 78
Teriyaki Beef Broil, '92 56
Teriyaki, Marinated Steak, '84 50
Tomatoes and Artichokes, Beef with, '92 282
Tournedos Mouton, '83 262
Vegetables, Beef with Chinese, '81 211
Vegetables, Beef with Oriental, '84 140
Wellingtons, Individual Beef, '82 259
Zippy Steak and Gravy, '90 35
Stews
Beef Stew, '86 51; '90 230
Brown Stew, '85 239
Brunswick Stew, Bama, '87 4
Brunswick Stew, Easy, '92 280
Brunswick Stew, Georgian, '92 35
Brunswick Stew, Virginia Ramsey's Favorite, '91 16
Burgundy Beef Stew, '88 234
Burgundy Stew with Drop Dumplings, '83 125
Company Beef Stew, '83 85
Dumplings, Beef Stew with, '84 3
Dumplings, Beef Stew with Parsley, '81 76; '82 13; '85 M246
Emerald Isle Stew, '95 71
Hungarian Stew with Noodles, '80 263
Irish Stew, '90 64
Mexican Stew, '82 231
Mexican Stew Olé, '86 296
Onion Stew, Beef-and-, '87 18
Oven Beef Stew, '79 222; '80 64
Quick Beef Stew, '92 71
Red Chili Stew, '95 226
Spicy Beef Stew, '86 228
Sweet-and-Sour Beef and Vegetable Stew, '85 87
Vegetable-Beef Stew, '94 323
Vegetable-Beef Stew, Shortcut, '89 218
White Wine Stew, '82 228
Stir-Fried Beef and Vegetables, '88 301
Stir-Fry Beef and Asparagus, '91 124
Stir-Fry Beef and Broccoli, '79 47
Stir-Fry, Beef-and-Broccoli, '91 46
Stir-Fry Beef and Pea Pods, '80 19
Stir-Fry, Beef-and-Shrimp, '93 32
Stir-Fry, Beef and Snow Pea, '82 98
Stir-Fry, Beef and Snow Peas, '83 22
Stir-Fry, Beef-and-Vegetable, '81 211
Stir-Fry Broccoli and Beef, '83 110
Stir-Fry, Chinese Beef, '83 151
Stir-Fry, Hungarian, '93 64
Stir-Fry, Indian, '92 126
Stir-Fry, Lime-Ginger Beef, '92 65
Stir-Fry, Mongolian Beef, '89 25
Stir-Fry, Peanutty Beef, '95 157
Stir-Fry, Teriyaki, '83 110
Stock, Beef, '95 17
Stock, Brown Meat, '90 31
Stroganoff, Beef, '79 163; '81 179; '91 134; '93 18
Stroganoff, Beef Burgundy, '85 31
Stroganoff, Light Beef, '86 36
Stroganoff, Liver, '79 54
Stroganoff, Quick Beef, '92 20
Stroganoff Sandwiches, Steak, '85 110
Stroganoff, Sirloin, '81 297

BEEF *(continued)*

Stroganoff with Parslied Noodles, Steak,
  '85 31
Tacos al Carbón, '86 19
Tacos al Carbón, Tailgate, '79 185
Tamales, '80 195
Tempting Twosome, '81 240
Tenderloin, Barbecued Beef, '94 26
Tenderloin Bundles, Peppered Beef, '89 272
Tenderloin, Chutneyed Beef, '94 270
Tenderloin Deluxe, Beef, '85 109
Tenderloin, Easy Beef, '90 268
Tenderloin, Elegant Beef, '88 244
Tenderloin for Two, Beef, '90 295
Tenderloin, Grilled, '91 166
Tenderloin, Herb Marinated, '83 109
Tenderloin, Lobster-Stuffed Beef, '87 248
Tenderloin, Marinated, '80 146
Tenderloin, Marinated Beef, '81 246; '85 302;
  '93 215
Tenderloin Picnic Sandwiches, Beef, '90 91
Tenderloin, Spicy Beef, '88 29
Tenderloin, Spicy Marinated Beef, '83 262
Tenderloin, Spinach-Stuffed, '89 311
Tenderloin, Stuffed, '86 323; '88 50
Tenderloin with Mushroom Sauce, Beef,
  '88 3
Tenderloin with Mushrooms, Beef,
  '87 115
Tenderloin with Mushroom-Sherry Sauce,
  Beef, '87 306
Tenderloin with Peppercorns, Beef, '91 246
Tips and Noodles, Beef, '86 293
Tips on Rice, Beef, '85 87
Tournedos Diables, '87 60
Turnovers, Roast Beef, '88 273; '89 180
Tzimmes, Sweet Potato-Beef, '92 234
Tzimmes with Brisket, Mixed Fruit, '93 114
Vegetables in a Noodle Ring, Beef and,
  '85 285
Vegetables, Savory Beef and, '79 163
Wellington, Beef, '93 288

BEEF, GROUND

Acorn Squash, Stuffed, '83 15
Appetizer, Cheesy Mexicali, '82 108
Barbecue Cups, '79 129
Bean Bake, Cheesy Beef-and-, '82 89
Bean Medley, Baked, '80 100
Beans, Beefy, '82 59
Beans, Beefy Baked, '80 136; '84 149;
  '85 142
Beans, Rancho Lima, '80 191
Beans, Three-Meat Baked, '86 210
Brunswick Stew, Breeden Liles's, '91 14
Burger Boat, '95 70
Burgoo, Harry Young's, '87 3
Burritos, Chinese, '87 181
Burritos, Fiesta, '86 114

Cabbage-and-Beef Rolls, Easy, '88 49
Cabbage, Italian Stuffed, '84 294
Cabbage Rolls, '83 104
Cabbage Rolls, Beef Stuffed, '81 87; '82 7
Cabbage Rolls, Fried, '95 270
Cabbage Rolls, Hungarian, '94 47
Cabbage Rolls, Spicy, '84 2
Cabbage Rolls, Stuffed, '84 217
Cabbage Rollups, Beef-and-, '80 63
Cabbage, Stuffed, '84 282
Casseroles. *See also Beef, Ground/Lasagna.*
  Bean Bake, Hamburger-, '95 121
  Biscuit Casserole, Beef-and-, '83 75
  Cabbage Beef Bake, Zesty, '80 300
  Cavatini, '94 214
  Cheeseburger Casserole, '95 255
  Cheesy Ground Beef Casserole, '79 44
  Cheesy Mexican Casserole, '82 224
  Chili-Rice Casserole, '79 54
  Cornbread Casserole, '81 91
  Cornbread Skillet Casserole, '83 243;
    '84 101
  County Fair Casserole, '79 130
  Creamy Ground Beef Casserole, '81 142
  Crusty Beef Casserole, '82 88
  Easy Beef Casserole, '86 M58
  El Dorado Casserole, '81 140
  Enchilada Casserole, '87 287
  Enchilada Casserole, Firecracker,
    '80 260
  Enchilada Casserole, Sour Cream,
    '82 113
  Five-Layer Meal, '81 140
  Grits Italiano, '92 43
  Hamburger Casserole, '95 210
  Italian Cabbage Casserole, '87 42
  Italian Casserole, '80 81
  Layered Beef Casserole, '82 M203
  Layered Grecian Bake, '82 119
  Macaroni Bake, Beef-, '94 255
  Macaroni-Cheese-Beef Casserole,
    '95 125
  Macaroni Combo, Beef-, '79 194
  Matador Mania, '86 19
  Mexican Casserole, '92 M22
  Mexican Casserole, Microwave,
    '90 M231
  Mexi Casserole, '83 M87
  Moussaka Casserole, '79 179
  Noodle Bake, Hamburger-, '81 140
  Noodles Casserole, Beef-and-, '84 72
  Pastitsio, '87 12; '88 11
  Pizza Casserole, '88 273; '89 181
  Pizza Casserole, Microwave, '89 M248
  Pizza Casserole, Quick, '83 266
  Sausage Casserole, Ground Beef and,
    '80 260
  Seashell-Provolone Casserole, '80 189
  Sour Cream-Noodle Bake, '79 55
  Spaghetti and Beef Casserole, '79 129
  Spaghetti, Casserole, '95 132
  Spinach and Beef Casserole, '79 192
  Spinach-Beef-Macaroni Casserole,
    '83 313
  Taco Beef-Noodle Bake, '81 141
  Taco Casserole, '80 33
  Taco Squares, Deep-Dish, '91 88
  Tamale, Mozzarella, '95 70
  Tortilla Bake, Texas, '94 285
  Vegetable Casserole, Beefy, '79 248
  Vegetable Chow Mein Casserole, Beef-
    and-, '83 313
  Zucchini-Beef Bake, '86 146

Chiles Rellenos Egg Rolls, '86 296
Chili
  Basic Chili, '82 M11; '93 326
  Basic Chili Embellished, '93 327
  Basic Chili Goes Southwest, '93 326
  Before-and-After Burner, Roy's, '89 316
  Cheese-Topped Chili, '82 M11
  Cheesy Chili, '82 310
  Chili, '87 17; '89 143; '93 89
  Choo-Choo Chili, '89 316
  Company Chili, '82 311; '83 30
  con Carne, Beef and Sausage Chili,
    '83 284
  con Carne, Chili, '84 72
  con Carne, Favorite Chili, '86 293
  con Carne, Quick-and-Easy Chili, '86 2
  Dip, Chili, '89 47
  Double-Meat Chili, '79 269; '80 12
  Easy Chili, '82 310; '83 30
  Easy Texas Chili, '90 201
  Five-Ingredient Chili, '95 212
  Friday Night Chili, '86 228
  Greek Chili, '95 16
  Hominy Bake, Chili, '81 282; '82 58
  Hot Texas Chili, '80 222; '81 77
  Hotto Lotto Chili, '89 316
  I-Cious, Chili-, '89 315
  "In-the-Red" Chili over "Rolling-in-
    Dough" Biscuits, '92 80
  Kielbasa Chili, Hearty, '91 28
  Lolly's Pop Chili, '89 316
  Lunchtime Chili, '81 230
  Meaty Chili, '81 282; '82 58
  Meaty Chili with Beans, '85 250
  Mexican Chili, '89 18
  Noodles, Chili with, '81 282; '82 57
  Now, Thatsa Chili, '95 16
  Pastry Cups, Chili in, '90 68
  Potato Chili, Savory, '83 284
  Potatoes, Chili-Topped, '83 3
  Quick-and-Easy Chili, '92 20
  Quick and Simple Chili, '81 282; '82 58
  Quick Chili, '83 283
  Ranch Chili and Beans, '79 270;
    '80 11
  Rice, Chili with, '82 M11
  Roundup Chili, '79 269; '80 12
  Sauce, Chili Meat, '83 4
  Sausage-Beef Chili, '86 232
  Sausage Chili, Beefy, '82 M11
  Simple Chili, '79 269; '80 11
  Speedy Chili, '92 66
  Spiced Chili, Hot, '83 214
  Spicy Chili, Old-Fashioned, '79 269;
    '80 11
  Texas-Style Chili, '82 311; '83 30
  Tex-Mex Chili, '83 26
  Tree-Hunt Chili, '87 292
Cornbread, Beefy Jalapeño, '82 142
Cornbread, Cheesy Beef, '81 242
Cornbread Tamale Bake, '79 163
Crêpes, Italian, '90 157
Crêpes, Sherried Beef, '85 M29
Curried Beef and Rice, '88 164
Dinner, Beef-and-Garbanzo, '84 31
Dinner, Beef-and-Lima Bean, '84 292
Dinner, Beef-Cabbage, '81 179
Dinner, Beefy Sausage, '80 M9
Dinner, Black-Eyed Pea Skillet, '86 6
Dinner, Fiesta, '85 110
Dinner, Ground Beef Skillet, '82 60
Dinner, Mexican Beef-and-Rice, '88 199
Dip, Hot Chile-Beef, '83 218

Dip, Meaty Cheese, '82 59; '92 160
Dip, Quick Nacho, '90 168
Dip, Tostada, '84 206
Eggplant, Baked Stuffed, '81 133
Eggplant, Beefy Stuffed, '81 204
Eggplant, Cheesy Stuffed, '79 188
Empanadas, '92 156
Enchiladas, American, '81 170
Enchiladas, Hot and Saucy, '81 141; '82 6
Enchiladas, Skillet, '82 89
Enchiladas, Sour Cream, '87 37
Enchiladas, Weeknight, '93 63
Fiesta, '87 180
Filet Mignon, Mock, '80 81
Filet Mignon Patties, Mock, '82 M68
Fillets, Poor Boy, '82 106
Filling, Beef, '80 81
Flips, Pea, '80 7
Green Peppers, Beefy Stuffed, '81 86
Green Peppers, Mexican, '80 65
Gumbo, Carolina, '95 70
Gumbo, Ground Beef, '87 283
Gumbo Joes, '88 158
Hamburgers
  Apple Burgers, '86 137
  au Poivre Blanc, Burgers, '87 186
  Bacon Burgers, Cheesy, '81 29
  Barbecued Burgers, '82 168; '89 164
  Beefburger on Buns, '84 71
  Beerburgers, '79 129
  Blue Cheese Burgers, '89 M66
  Brie-Mushroom Burgers, '95 128
  Burgundy Burgers, '80 156
  Cheeseburger Biscuits, '79 194
  Cheeseburger Loaves, '86 19
  Cheeseburgers, Fried Green Tomato,
    '94 138
  Cheesy Beef Burgers, '83 217
  Chili Burgers, Open-Face, '81 24;
    '82 31; '83 33
  Cocktail Burgers, Saucy, '83 217
  Cracked Pepper Patties, '89 M131
  Deluxe, Burgers, '84 125
  Favorite Burgers, '89 165
  Glorified Hamburgers, '81 73
  Grilled Hamburgers, '93 198
  Grilled Hamburgers, Flavorful, '81 110
  Hawaiian, Beefburgers, '86 137
  Mexicali Beef Patties, '86 137
  Mexicali, Hamburgers, '93 217
  Mushroom Burgers, '89 164
  Nutty Burgers, '87 185
  Old-Fashioned Hamburgers, '79 149
  Oven Burgers, '83 130
  Party Burgers, '83 164; '84 39
  Patties, Deviled-Beef, '87 22
  Patties, Hamburger, '82 M172
  Pineapple Burgers, '82 169
  Pizza Burger, '87 185
  Pizza Burgers, '80 M201; '81 73
  Pizza Burgers, All-American, '92 148
  Pizza Burgers, Easy, '82 190
  Sauce, Hamburgers with Tomato, '81 73
  Saucy Burgers, '80 93
  Saucy Hamburgers, Quick, '82 60
  Sausage Burgers, '83 212
  Seasoned Burgers, '85 158
  Seasoned Hamburgers, '84 230
  Seasoned Stuffed Burgers, '86 136
  Sour Cream Burgers, Grilled, '87 287

Spirals, Burger, '94 139
Sprouts, Burgers with, '89 164
Steak-House Burgers, '87 186
Steaks, Company Hamburger, '82 169
Steaks with Mustard Sauce, Hamburger,
  '84 230
Stuffed Burgers, '85 159
Superburgers, '79 89
Super Hamburgers, '79 129
Super Supper Burgers, '82 110
Surprise Burgers, '82 169
Sweet-and-Sour Burgers, '90 128
Tahiti Burgers, '85 179
Teriyaki Burgers, '81 72
Teriyaki, Hamburgers, '89 309
Teriyaki Hamburgers, '94 138
Tortilla Burgers, '94 138
Triple-Layer Burgers, '89 165
Vegetable Burgers, '89 164
Vegetable Burgers, Beef-and-, '84 125
Venison Burgers, '87 304
Kheema, Indian, '81 226
Kielbasa, '92 242
Lasagna, '82 119; '83 M6
Lasagna, Beefy, '80 81
Lasagna, Cheesy, '82 224; '88 299
Lasagna, Cheesy Spinach, '83 204
Lasagna, Easy, '92 M197; '93 M24
Lasagna for Two, '81 91
Lasagna in a Bun, '90 176
Lasagna, Light, '95 212
Lasagna, Lots of Noodles, '91 M127
Lasagna, Mexican, '89 63
Lasagna, Quick, '84 220
Lasagna, Quick 'n Easy, '80 M10
Lasagna, Simple, '81 188
Lasagna, South-of-the-Border, '84 31
Lasagna Supreme, '92 198; '93 24
Lasagna, Vintage, '79 194
Log, Stuffed Beef, '79 71
Macaroni, Ground Beef and, '85 218
Macaroni, Skillet Beef and, '82 130
Madras, Beef, '87 284
Manicotti, Quick, '79 6
Manicotti, Saucy Stuffed, '83 288
Manicotti, Special, '88 50
Meatballs
  Bacon-Wrapped Meatballs, '79 81
  Barbecued Meatballs, Oven, '82 233
  Brandied Meatballs, '83 78
  Burgundy-Bacon Meatballs, '80 283
  Chafing Dish Meatballs, '81 260
  Charleston Press Club Meatballs, '93 129
  Chestnut Meatballs, '79 110
  Chinese Meatballs, '83 116; '87 194
  Cocktail Meatballs, '79 63, 207
  Creole, Meatball-Okra, '83 156
  Creole, Meatballs, '82 233
  Español, Meatballs, '82 110
  Flavorful Meatballs, '84 206
  Golden Nugget Meatballs, '82 233
  Gravy, Meatballs in, '79 136
  Hawaiian Meatballs, '85 86
  Hawaiian Meatballs, Tangy, '79 129
  Heidelberg, Beef Balls, '83 164; '84 39
  Horseradish Dressing, Meatballs and
    Vegetables with, '91 32
  Kabobs, Meatball, '95 192
  Meatballs, '89 237
  Paprikash with Rice, Meatballs, '85 31
  Pineapple and Peppers, Meatballs with,
    '90 145
  Pizza Meatballs, '85 86

Polynesian Meatballs, '80 207
Red Delicious Meatballs, '85 85
Royal Meatballs, '87 268; '88 102;
  '89 67
Sandwich, Giant Meatball, '92 196
Saucy Meatballs, '85 68; '90 122
Saucy Party Meatballs, '80 149
Sauerbraten Meatballs, '85 85
Spaghetti-and-Herb Meatballs, '84 75
Spaghetti with Meatballs, '81 38
Spiced Meatballs, '79 284
Spicy Meatballs and Sausage, '79 163
Stew, Meatball, '79 198
Stroganoff, Meatball, '81 297
Stroganoff, Mushroom-Meatball, '85 85
Swedish Meatballs, '80 80; '86 256
Sweet-and-Sour Meatballs, '82 233;
  '86 240
Sweet-and-Sour Party Meatballs, '79 233
Tamale Balls, Tangy, '89 60
Tamale Meatballs, '80 194
Zesty Meatballs, '80 250
Meat Loaf
  All-American Meat Loaf, '92 341; '93 46
  Barbecued Beef Loaves, Individual,
    '95 242
  Barbecued Meat Loaf, '80 60; '81 275;
    '84 50; '87 216
  Basic Meat Loaf, '88 M14
  Blue Cheese Meat Loaf Roll, '93 247
  Cheeseburger Loaf, '81 236, 276
  Cheesy Meat Roll, '82 136
  Chili Meat Loaf, '81 275
  Corny Meat Loaf, '86 68
  Crunchy Meat Loaf Oriental, '79 212
  Curried Meat Loaf, '86 43
  Easy Meat Loaf, '88 M214; '95 125
  Elegant Meat Loaf, '89 243
  Family-Style Meat Loaf, '93 18
  Fennel Meat Loaf, '88 46
  German Meat Loaf, '87 216
  Glazed Beef Loaf, '86 19
  Hurry-Up Meat Loaf, '82 21
  Hurry-Up Meat Loaves, '88 15
  Individual Meat Loaves, '81 279; '82 24;
    '83 154; '92 229
  Italian Meat Loaf, '79 187
  Meat Loaf, '81 170; '89 109
  Mexicali Meat Loaf, '81 275
  Mexican Meat Loaf, '87 217
  Miniature Meat Loaves, '85 24
  Mini-Teriyaki Meat Loaf, '90 69
  Mozzarella-Layered Meat Loaf, '79 71
  My-Ami's Meat Loaf, '94 229
  Oriental Meat Loaf, '81 M122;
    '83 M194
  Parsleyed Meat Loaf, '83 35
  Parsley Meat Loaf, '87 22
  Pineapple Loaves, Individual, '81 M121
  Pizza Meat Loaf, Cheesy, '81 M121
  Roll, Meat Loaf, '79 129
  Saucy Meat Loaves, '79 186
  Savory Meat Loaf, '87 216
  Southwestern Meat Loaf, '93 248
  Special Meat Loaf, '89 70
  Spicy Meat Loaf, '79 71
  Sprout Meat Loaf, '85 51
  Stuffed Beef Log, '79 71
  Stuffed Meat Loaf, '79 187
  Stuffed Meat Loaf, Rolled, '80 80
  Sun-Dried Tomatoes and Herbs, Meat
    Loaf with, '92 192
  Supreme, Meat Loaf, '92 33

BEEF, GROUND, Meat Loaf (continued)

Swedish Meat Loaf, '81 M121
Tasty Meat Loaf, '83 213
Tex-Mex Meat Loaf for Two, '90 234
Tomato Sauce, Meat Loaf with Chunky, '95 264
Triple Meat Loaf, '79 186
Vegetable Loaf, Beef-, '79 164
Vegetable Meat Loaf, '85 M29
Wellington, Meat Loaf, '79 186; '87 284
Wrap, Meat Loaf in a, '89 122
Mexican Stack-Up, '95 69
Mix, Ground Beef, '84 71
Mix, Ground Meat, '89 143
Moussaka, '87 166; '90 68
Moussaka, Corn, '87 190
Mushrooms, Stuffed, '83 13
Noodle Dinner, Beefy, '81 179
Noodles, Easy Beef and, '83 288
Omelet, Beefy Vegetable, '83 188
Omelet con Carne, Tex-Mex, '81 209
Patties, Foo Yong, '80 223
Peppers, Beefed-Up, '82 186
Peppers, Beef-Stuffed, '84 154; '85 146; '91 M127
Peppers for Two, Stuffed, '80 84
Peppers, Stuffed, '81 239; '83 66
Peppers Stuffed with Beef, '84 72
Picadillo II, '93 72
Picadillo (Spanish Hash), '91 87
Picadillo (Spicy Beef over Rice), '80 193; '84 118; '85 57
Picadillo Tarts, '91 279
Pies
Broccoli-Beef Pie, '83 196
Burrito Pie, Mexican, '87 287
Cheese-Beef Pie, '85 33
Cheeseburger Pie, '89 121
Continental Meat Pie, '95 256
Corn Burger Pie, '83 156
Country Pie, '83 155
Enchilada Pie, '83 155
Hamburger Pie, '81 92; '84 13
Mexicali Meat Pie, '81 194
Natchitoches Meat Pies, '84 21; '91 241
Old-Fashioned Meat Pie, '82 110
Potato Pie, Meat-and-, '84 23
Shepherd Pie, '83 116
Sombrero Pie, '81 140
Spaghetti Pie, '81 32
Spaghetti Pie, Weeknight, '95 312
Taco Pie, '88 256
Taco Pie, Crescent, '80 80
Taco Pie, Double-Crust, '88 272; '89 180
Taco Pies, Individual, '82 M282
Vegetable-Beef Pies, '80 286
Pitas, Curried Beef, '85 220
Pizza, Best Ever Homemade, '80 233
Pizza-Burger Snacks, '84 30
Pizza Cups, '81 215
Pizza, Double Cheesy Beef-and-Sausage, '86 77
Pizza Horns, '89 214
Pizza, Quick Hamburger, '85 243
Pizza Supreme, '81 214
Pizza, Tostada, '81 16; '82 13
Pizza, Upside-Down, '91 185
Potatoes, Taco-Topped, '93 M18
Quiche, Green Chile, '83 31
Ravioli, Homemade, '87 230

Rice, Arabic, '94 200
Rice, Spanish, '81 51
Rice, Spiced Beef and, '84 285
Rice, Spicy Beef and, '83 231
Rolls, Italian Meat, '86 137
Rolls, Spicy Beef, '85 110
Roulades, Beef, '80 80
Salad Cups, Taco, '85 M29
Salad, Dude Ranch, '80 15
Salad in a Shell, Mexican, '86 4
Salad, Mexican, '81 36
Salad, Mexican Chef, '85 84; '92 64
Salad, Mexican Olive, '85 84
Salad, Mexi-Pea, '81 7
Salad, Spicy Chili, '86 71
Salad, Spicy Taco, '87 287
Salad Supper, Mexican, '82 9; '83 68
Salad, Taco, '79 56; '83 145; '84 221; '85 84; '90 20
Salisbury Steak Deluxe, '81 170
Sandwiches, Barbecued Beef, '81 25; '82 31; '83 34
Sandwiches, Bavarian Pita, '83 31
Sandwiches, Beef-Eater, '86 72
Sandwiches, Hearty Pocket, '80 93
Sandwiches, Hot Pita, '83 217; '87 M6
Sandwiches, Open-Face Pizza, '82 3
Sauce, Italian, '90 67
Sauce, Italian Meat, '83 193
Shells, Cheesy Beef-Stuffed, '83 217
Shells, Mexican Stuffed, '91 87
Skillet, Vegetable-Beef, '86 172
Slice, French Beef, '79 125
Sloppy Joe Dogs, '85 192
Sloppy Joe Pocket Sandwiches, '81 200
Sloppy Joes, '81 279; '82 24; '83 153; '89 143; '91 172
Sloppy Joes, Easy, '82 31, 278; '83 34
Sloppy Joes, Pocket, '85 M328
Sloppy Joes, Simple, '82 130
Sloppy Joes, Super, '83 130
Snacks, Beefy Party, '80 249
Soup, Beef-and-Barley Vegetable, '89 31
Soup, Beefy Black-Eyed, '85 6
Soup, Beefy Vegetable, '79 113; '84 M38
Soup, Hamburger, '80 263
Soup, Quick Beefy Vegetable, '80 25
Soup, Spicy Vegetable-Beef, '88 11
Soup, Taco, '94 225
Soup, Tamale, '95 213
Soup, Vegetable-Burger, '82 6
Spaghetti. See also Beef, Ground/Casseroles, Meatballs, Pies.
Black-Eyed Pea Spaghetti, '81 7
Easy Spaghetti, '83 M317; '84 72; '92 66
Italian Spaghetti, Real, '81 233
Meaty Spaghetti, '82 19
Mushrooms, Spicy Spaghetti with, '85 2
Pepperoni Spaghetti, Quick, '88 40
Pizzazz, Spaghetti with, '80 85
Sauce, Beer Spaghetti, '85 13
Sauce for 4, Easy Spaghetti Meat, '92 244
Sauce for 25, Easy Spaghetti Meat, '92 245
Sauce, Herbed Spaghetti, '85 13
Sauce, Quick Spaghetti and Meat, '94 64
Sauce, Thick Spaghetti, '84 118
Thick-and-Spicy Spaghetti, '83 287
Zucchini Spaghetti, '83 160
Squash, Beef-Stuffed, '83 134
Steak, Spanish, '80 80
Stew, Campeche Bay Rib-Tickling, '89 317

Stew, Hamburger Oven, '84 4
Stew, Mixed Vegetable, '84 13
Stew, Quick Beef, '86 302
Sticks, Beef, '93 331
Stroganoff, Easy Hamburger, '79 208
Stroganoff, Ground Beef, '84 71
Stroganoff, Hamburger, '82 108, 110
Stroganoff, Quickie, '81 200
Stromboli, '87 283
Supper, Beef-and-Bean, '82 2
Supper, Beef-and-Eggplant, '84 291
Supper, Oriental Beef, '79 192
Supper, Quick Skillet, '84 69
Supreme, Beef, '83 196
Taco Joes, '91 167
Tacoritos, '90 133
Taco Rolls, Chinese, '95 339
Tacos, '80 196
Tacos, Basic, '83 199
Tacos, Corn Chip, '81 67
Tacos, Jiffy, '83 M318
Tacos, Microwave, '88 M213
Tacos, Soft Beef, '91 88
Taco Tassies, '95 339
Texas Straw Hat, '85 293
Torta Mexican Style, '89 122
Tostada Compuestas, '81 194
Tostadas, Crispy, '83 2
Tostadas, Super, '83 199
Turnovers, Meat, '86 326
Wontons, Tex-Mex, '87 196
Zucchini, Beef-Stuffed, '86 M139

BEETS
Apples, Beets and, '80 137; '88 155
Aspic, Beet, '90 123
Borscht, Crawfish, '92 84
Borscht, Ruby Red, '83 176
Cake, Chocolate Beet, '80 40
Cake with Almond Topping, Beet, '86 200
Chilled Beets and Cauliflower, '80 137
Creamy Beets, '80 136
Deviled Beets, '84 217; '86 252
Glazed Beets, Ginger-Marmalade, '93 35
Glazed Beets, Orange-, '81 167; '85 289; '86 187
Glazed Beets, Strawberry-, '83 234
Glazed Fresh Beets, '81 167
Greens, Beets 'n', '95 179
Harvard Beets, '83 M195
Ivy League Beets, '84 122
Marinated Beets, Green Beans, and Carrots, '88 162
Orange Beets, '91 219
Orange Beets, Spicy, '94 280
Orange-Ginger Beets, '80 137
Pickled Beets, '79 276; '81 216; '87 163
Pickled Beets, Easy, '80 137
Pickles, Beet, '81 210
Pineapple, Beets with, '79 249; '82 204
Relish, Beet, '84 179
Relish, Colorful Beet, '85 136
Rice Ring with Beets, '79 225
Salad, Apple-Beet, '91 237
Salad, Beet-Nut, '79 74
Salad, Marinated Beet, '83 216
Salad Mold, Beet, '82 267
Salad, Orange-and-Beet, '88 43
Salad, Pickled Beet, '83 234
Salad, Red-and-Green, '90 55
Salad, Tangy Beet, '86 199
Slaw, "Think Pink," '94 247
Soup, Potato-Beet, '88 156
Sour Cream Dressing, Beets with, '88 M295

BEETS *(continued)*

Spiced Beets, '79 22
Stuffed Beets, '88 155
Stuffed Beets, Blue Cheese-, '88 211
Stuffed Beets, Potato-, '83 234
Sweet-and-Sour Beets, '81 167; '82 22;
　'89 314
BEVERAGES. *See also* COFFEE, TEA.
Alcoholic
　Almond-Flavored Liqueur, '81 287
　Amaretto, '90 272
　Amaretto Breeze, '83 172
　Amaretto Slush, '90 322; '95 90
　Apricot Brandy Slush, '91 278
　Apricot Slush, '93 205
　Banana Flip, '83 303
　Banana Kabana, '86 316
　Bay Bloodies, '93 268
　Bellinis, '88 77
　Bellini Spritzers, '90 110
　Bloody Mary, '80 221
　Bloody Mary, Easy, '84 115
　Bloody Marys, '79 33, 38; '80 51
　Bloody Marys, Eye-Opener, '82 48
　Bloody Marys, Overnight, '81 270
　Bloody Marys, Pitcher, '81 198
　Bloody Marys, Spicy, '87 173; '90 207
　Blueberry Cordial, '95 142
　Blue Woo-Woo, '94 226
　Bourbon Blizzard, '92 287
　Bourbon Slush, '84 58
　Bourbon Slush, Summertime, '81 101
　Brandy Alexander, '92 283
　Brandy Cream, '84 312
　Brandy Slush, '89 110
　Brandy Velvet, '89 170
　Burgundy Bowl, Sparkling, '83 276
　Champagne Delight, '83 304
　Champagne Fruit Slush, '90 322
　Champagne with Orange Juice, '91 71
　Chocolate, Flaming Brandied, '80 M290
　Chocolate, Hot Laced Marshmallow,
　　'93 53
　Cider, Cinnamon Winter, '95 337
　Cider, December, '91 260
　Cider, Hot Mexican, '87 213
　Cider, Hot Mulled, '84 323
　Cider, Red Apple, '80 259
　Clam Diggers, '91 63
　Coconut Frost, Pink, '79 174; '80 128
　Coconut Nog, '83 275
　Coconut-Pineapple Drink, '83 172
　Cranapple Glogg, Hot, '90 22
　Cranapple Wine, '90 272
　Cranberry Cooler, '86 229
　Cranberry-Rum Slush, '84 259
　Cranberry Spritzer, '91 66; '92 265
　Cranberry Spritzers, '89 213
　Cranberry-Vodka Refresher, '91 210
　Cranberry Wine Cup, '85 23
　Cricket, '89 289
　Daiquiris, Cranberry, '81 245
　Daiquiris, Creamy Strawberry, '91 66
　Daiquiris, Freezer Lime, '79 141
　Daiquiris, Mint, '89 157
　Daiquiris, Peach, '90 322
　Daiquiris, Strawberry, '90 125
　Daiquiri, Strawberry, '81 156
　Daiquiritas, '82 160
　Daiquiri, Watermelon, '95 143
　Dessert, After Dinner-Drink, '82 100

Dessert Drink, Creamy, '86 131
Dessert Drink, Simply Super, '83 303
Eggnog, Blender, '93 341
Eggnog, Christmas, '87 242
Eggnog, Creamy, '80 259; '83 303
Eggnog Deluxe, Holiday, '79 232
Eggnog, Easy, '91 305
Eggnog, Edenton, '84 251
Eggnog, Thick and Creamy, '80 261
Frosty Sours, '81 156
Fruit 'ritas, '94 157
Fuzz Buzz, '82 160
Game-Cocktails, '93 214
Gin Cooler, Sparkling, '90 272
Ginger Beer, '84 159
Golden Dream, '82 100
Grapefruit Drink, '95 238
Holiday Brew, '81 265
Hot Chocolate Deluxe, '90 272
Kahlúa Hummer, '91 176
Kahlúa Smoothie, '87 242
Kahlúa Velvet Frosty, '82 244
King Alfonso, '80 259
Lemonade, Claret, '93 72
Lemonade, Hot Buttered, '88 208
Lemon Cooler, '82 48
Lime Fizz, '81 172
Liqueur Sampler, Miniature, '95 332
Magnolia Blossoms, '87 72
Magnolias, '82 196
Margaritas, '92 210; '93 273
Margaritas, Frosted, '84 115
Margaritas, Frosty, '83 172
Margaritas, Lemon-Lime, '94 227
Margaritas, Pitcher, '83 175
Margaritas Supreme, Frozen, '80 160
Margaritas, Tart, '85 153
Melon Ball Cooler, '86 131
Mimosa Hawaiian, '85 44
Mimosas, '86 91
Minted Delight, '87 107
Mint Juleps, '81 155; '82 41; '85 40;
　'90 81
Mix, Bloody Mary, '89 110
Mix, Hot Wine, '81 287
Mix, Mulled Wine Spice, '85 266
Mocha Chocolate Fluff, '89 170
Mocha Deluxe Hot Drink, '82 289
Mocha Polka, '89 171
Mocha, Spirited Hot, '91 M260
New Orleans, Mr. Funk of, '95 57
Oklahoma Sunrise, '87 67
Old-Fashioneds, '86 270
Old-Fashioned Slush, '93 340
Orange Blossom Flips, '80 51
Orange-Champagne Cocktail, '79 39
Orange Liqueur, '81 287
Orange Milk Shake, '84 166
Peach Frosty, '81 156
Peach Petals, '90 104
Peach Smash, '88 161
Peppermint Flip, Hot, '86 329
Piña Coladas, '95 203
Piña Coladas, Frosty, '83 176
Piña Coladas, Luscious, '81 134
Piña Colada Slush, '95 90
Pineapple-Strawberry Slush, '94 227
Pink Palace, '93 293
Plum Slush, '84 139
Punch, Amaretto, '91 277
Punch, Anytime Wine, '79 232
Punch, Bourbon, '92 208
Punch, Bourbon-Citrus, '94 227

Punch, Bourbon-Tea, '87 57
Punch, Brandy Milk, '85 44; '88 83
Punch, Brandy Slush, '87 72
Punch, Caribbean, '95 173
Punch, Champagne, '85 153, 257;
　'86 101
Punch, Champagne Blossom, '81 50
Punch, Chatham Artillery, '80 121
Punch, Cranapple-Vodka, '87 72
Punch, Cranberry, '85 90
Punch, Cranberry Percolator, '88 248
Punch, Extra-Kick, '91 209
Punch, Festive, '94 289
Punch, Frozen Margarita, '95 91
Punch, Fruit, '83 52
Punch, Fruit Juicy Rum, '91 175
Punch, Gin, '80 160
Punch, Golden Gin, '79 233
Punch, Golden Spiked, '79 285
Punch, Health-Kick, '80 174
Punch, Hot Cranberry, '84 41
Punch, Hot Molasses-Milk, '86 329
Punch, Hot Pineapple, '82 264
Punch, Hot Wine, '85 265
Punch, Irish Coffee-Eggnog, '95 314
Punch, Jefferson County, '86 267
Punch, Lemonade-Bourbon, '95 287
Punch, Lemon Champagne, '94 176
Punch, Lime, '84 58
Punch, Milk, '79 38
Punch, Mixed Fruit, '95 239
Punch, Mulled Wine, '95 337
Punch, New Orleans Milk, '81 50
Punch, Orange-Lime, '82 160
Punch, Party, '81 265
Punch, Perky Rum, '85 116
Punch, Pimms, '92 167
Punch, Piña Colada, '89 212
Punch, Pineapple, '79 174; '80 128
Punch, Pineapple-Gin, '95 140
Punch, Raspberry-Rosé, '87 242
Punch, Red Velvet, '89 289
Punch, Refreshing Champagne, '84 259
Punch, Rum, '85 265
Punch, Southern Fruit, '95 238
Punch, Sparkling Champagne, '84 58
Punch, Sparkling Holiday, '81 290
Punch, Spiked Tea, '86 101
Punch, Spirited Fruit, '81 100
Punch, Stormy Petrel Rum Thunder,
　'93 269
Punch, Strawberry Champagne, '90 315
Punch, Streetcar Champagne, '88 82
Punch, Tropical Fruit, '83 176
Punch, Vodka, '85 265
Punch, Wedding, '86 107
Punch, Whiskey, '90 64; '91 175
Punch, Whiskey Sour, '91 209
Punch, Wine, '93 331
Punch, Yacht Club Milk, '89 86
Raspberry Kir, '86 183
Red Roosters, '87 147
Red Ruby, '92 209
Rum, Hot Buttered, '80 259; '82 244;
　'88 247
Rum Slush, Easy, '79 174; '80 129
Sangría, '79 186; '81 67, 196; '82 121;
　'86 214
Sangría, Cranberry, '95 238
Sangría, Easy Citrus, '80 218
Sangría, Easy Frozen, '92 208
Sangría, Grapefruit, '89 92
Sangría, Orange, '81 237

BEVERAGES, Alcoholic (continued)

Sangría, Pineapple, '91 176
Sangría, Punchy, '80 160
Sangría, Quick, '81 156
Sangría Slush, White, '90 322
Sangría, Spanish, '83 81
Sangría, Teaberry, '87 147
Sangría, Three-Fruit, '89 212
Sangría, White, '83 180; '94 289
Screwdrivers, '79 33
Sea Mist, '93 167
Sherry Sour, '87 74
Sipper, Sunshine, '86 179
Slush, Mexican, '83 176
Slush with a Punch, '90 322
Spritzers, Citrus, '91 231; '92 67
Spritzers, Spiced, '86 229
Strawberry-Banana Smoothie, '81 59
Strawberry Mimosa, Sparkling, '88 169
Sunny Morning, '93 295
Sunrise, St. Pete, '94 227
Syllabub, '81 265; '84 319
Tart Caribbean Cooler, '81 134
Tequila Slush, '83 176
Tequila Sunrise, '83 175
Toddy, Molasses Rum, '91 36
Tomato Bouillon, New Year's, '94 24
Tomato-Orange Juice Cocktail, '83 169
Tomato Sipper, Peppy, '94 227
Vodka, Frozen Pink, '89 170
Vodka-Orange Slush, '89 92
Vodka Slush, '88 82
Wassail, '83 311
Wassail, Bourbon, '86 270
Wassail, Four-Fruit, '90 22
Whiskey Sours, Frozen, '93 176
Whiskey Sours, Frozen Orange-, '92 67
Whisky Sour Slush, '86 183
Whispers, '86 317
Wine, Christmas Dreams in, '91 260
Wine Cooler, '82 41
Wine Cooler, Fruited, '86 176
Wine, Hot Mulled, '83 251
Wine, Hot Spiced, '84 41
Wine Spritzers, '81 94
Wine Tasting, '95 332
Wine Welcomer, '81 100
Yellow Birds, '90 103
Apple-Berry Sparkler, '93 104
Apple Berry Sparkler, '94 100
Apple Cooler, '90 14
Apple Cooler, Minted, '88 169
Apple Juice, Hot, '86 270
Apple Juice, Perky Cinnamon-, '90 22
Apple Juice Shrub, Shenandoah, '79 282
Apple Juice, Sparkling, '95 141
Apple Julep, '86 103, 215
Apricot-Citrus Slush, '88 82
Apricot Cooler, '81 100
Apricot Fruit Flip, '91 18
Apricot Mint Cooler, '90 165
Apricot Nectar, Hot, '81 265
Apricot Nectar, Mulled, '86 229
Banana-Berry Flip, '88 215; '89 20
Banana-Blueberry Smoothie, '90 104
Banana-Chocolate Malt, '89 170
Banana Coolers, '91 308
Banana Crush, '80 88; '83 142
Banana Frostee, '91 66
Banana Nog, '82 290
Banana-Orange Slush, '80 48; '81 155

Banana-Pineapple Smoothie, Quick, '93 195
Banana Slush, '83 56
Banana Smoothie, '87 160; '93 95
Banana-Strawberry Frost, '87 199
Berry Shrub, '95 29
Black Russian, Mock, '92 322
Bloodless Mary, '80 146
Breakfast Eye-Opener, '87 199
Brew, Beach, '91 177
Brew, Holiday, '90 272
Brew, Quilter's, '85 43
Brew, Witch's, '93 244
Bullshots, '86 91
Carambola-Yogurt Calypso, '90 169
Caribbean Cooler, '95 203
Carrot Cooler, '89 35
Champagne, Mock Pink, '89 46
Chocolate Malt, '86 183
Chocolate, Mexican-Style, '81 187
Chocolate Milk, French, '79 38
Chocolate-Mint Smoothie, '84 166
Chocolate Sipper, '88 83
Cider, Apple, '95 198
Cider, Apple-Orange, '92 20
Cider, Cherry, '94 288
Cider, Holiday, '82 264
Cider, Hot Apple, '90 21, 225
Cider, Hot Mulled, '79 205
Cider, Hot Spiced, '82 290
Cider, Hot Spiced Apple, '84 318
Cider, Hot Spicy, '84 265
Cider, Mulled, '91 209; '94 227
Cider, Mulled Apple, '92 208
Cider Nog, Hot Apple, '84 42
Cider, Sparkling Apple, '88 276
Cider, Spiced Apple, '85 256
Cider, Spiced Cranberry, '84 261
Citrus Cooler, '82 160; '93 105
Citrus Float, '89 171
Citrus Slush, '93 198
Cocoa, Mocha, '83 318
Coco-Berry Calypso, '89 171
Cooler, Spring, '86 214
Cranberry Cocktail, Hot, '89 310
Cranberry Drink, Mulled, '92 12
Cranberry Frappé, '82 263
Cranberry Juice, Sparkling, '88 275
Cranberry-Orange Soda, '79 148
Cranberry Smoothie, '86 183; '91 307
Cubes, Berry-Good, '95 201
Cubes, Cranberry, '95 201
Cubes, Florida, '95 201
Cubes, Lemonade, '95 201
Cubes, Lemon-Mint, '95 201
Eggnog, '83 318
Eggnog, Cooked Custard, '91 305
Eggnog, Sparkling, '79 232
Eggnog with Orange and Nutmeg, Mock, '92 323
Espresso, Italian Mocha, '82 254
Float, Frosty Fruit, '87 159
Float, Nutmeg-Almond, '84 106
Float, Pineapple Sherbet, '79 148
Floats, Maple-Coffee, '86 195
Float, Sparkling Cranberry, '86 195
Float, Strawberry-Banana, '87 160
Frappé, Hootenanny, '89 110
Fruit Beverage, Blender, '83 318
Fruit Cooler, Four-, '86 101
Fruit Drink, Three-, '79 38; '80 50; '87 199
Fruit Drink, Tropical, '85 43
Fruit Juice Cooler, '92 67
Fruit Juicy, Breakfast, '86 176

Fruit Refresher, '91 203
Fruit Refresher, Four-, '79 174; '80 129
Fruit Slush, Refreshing, '82 35
Fruit Slushy, '80 146
Fruit Smoothie, '89 87
Fruit Smoothie, Two-, '89 182
Fruit Whisper, Tropical, '89 212
Funshine Fizz, '91 66
Ginger-Mint Cooler, '89 92
Grapefruit Cooler, '88 81
Grapefruit Drink, '90 84; '95 238
Grapefruit-Orange Refresher, '82 174
Grapefruit Refresher, '88 85
Grape Juice, Mulled, '90 21
Grape Juice, Spiced White, '92 320
Grape-Lime Cooler, '94 227
Hawaiian Crush, '91 66
Honey-Banana Smoothie, '89 144
Honey-Yogurt Smoothie, Fruited, '88 231; '89 23
Hot Chocolate, '94 290
Hot Chocolate, Creole, '80 M290
Hot Chocolate, Favorite, '83 55
Hot Chocolate, French, '86 328
Hot Chocolate, Old-Fashioned, '85 23
Hot Chocolate, Special, '82 5
Hot Chocolate, Spiced, '80 50
Hot Chocolate, Spicy, '85 278
Hot Chocolate, Sugar-and-Spice, '95 34
Hot Cocoa, Quick, '82 5
Ice Bowl, '83 152
Ice Cream Ginger Fizz, '83 303
Ice Mold, Strawberry, '91 278
Ice Ring, '95 140
Ice Ring, Strawberry, '94 176
Jogger's Sunrise, '93 213
Kid's Cooler, '90 95
Kona Luscious, '84 54
Lemonade, Apple, '89 212
Lemonade, Berry Delicious, '93 205
Lemonade Concentrate, '89 110
Lemonade, Fresh Squeezed, '81 172
Lemonade, Front Porch, '90 156
Lemonade, Hot Buttered, '94 18
Lemonade, Pineapple, '93 194
Lemonade Slush, Pink, '80 151
Lemonade, Strawberry, '80 160
Lemonade with Frozen Tea Cubes, '85 161
Lemon Frappé, '92 44
Lemon Velvet, '90 15
Limeade, Pink Apple, '89 46
Lime Cooler, '87 160
Lime Fizz, Frosty, '90 104
Malt Special, '85 198
Mango Frappé, '86 216
Mango-Orange Smoothie, '86 216
Margaritas, Mock, '88 209
Melon Julep, Rainbow, '80 183
Milk, Santa Claus, '92 281
Mix, Beetle Cider, '82 308
Mix, Bloody Mary, '89 110
Mix, Cappuccino, '90 87
Mix, Deluxe Hot Chocolate, '80 M290
Mix, Hot Cocoa, '81 287
Mix, Hot Mocha-Cocoa, '82 296
Mix, Hot Spiced Cider, '84 42
Mix, Instant Cocoa, '86 332
Mix, Minted Hot Cocoa, '91 316
Mix, Mocha-Flavored Hot Cocoa, '91 316
Mix, Spicy-Hot Chocolate, '85 278
Mocha Espresso, Italian, '82 254
Mocha Frosty, '92 44
Mocha, Hot, '84 60

BEVERAGES (continued)

Mocha, Mexican, '93 M341
Mocha, Quick Viennese, '79 232
Mocha, Swiss-Style, '82 253
Nog, Speedy Breakfast, '82 47
Orange-Banana Flip, '82 48
Orange-Banana Whip, '95 244
Orange Blush, '80 51
Orange Frosty, '86 101
Orange Juicy, '90 178
Orange-Lemon Mist, '79 288; '80 35
Orange Pick-Me-Up, '80 232
Orange-Pineapple Drink, '89 35
Orange Slush, '82 49
Orange Spiced Nog, '82 48
Patio Blush, '92 43
Peach Cooler, '85 198
Peaches 'n' Almond Cream, '86 229
Peach Frost, '89 155
Peach Frosty, '83 318
Peach Pick-Me-Up, '89 183
Peach Refresher, '86 103
Peanut Butter Cooler, '84 115
Piña Colada, Mock, '92 322
Piña Colada, Parson's, '89 46
Pineapple-Banana Slush, '90 14
Pineapple Cooler, '90 207
Pineapple Drink, Hot Buttered, '91 260
Pineapple Nectar, Hot, '90 21
Pineapple Slush, '88 82
Pineapple Soda, '90 179
Pineapple Sparkle, Spiced, '92 322
Pineapple-Yogurt Whirl, '91 132
Pink Soda, Blushing, '90 104
Punch. See also Beverages/Alcoholic.
    Apple Punch, Hot, '84 324
    Apple-Tea Punch, '85 82
    Apricot Spiced Punch, '80 269
    Autumn Punch, '88 209
    Berry Punch, '92 67
    Bubbling Jade Punch, '79 174;
      '80 129
    Bunch, Punch for a, '95 90
    Cantaloupe Punch, '81 147
    Caribbean Punch, '95 173
    Children's Punch, '85 322
    Christmas Eve Punch, '86 314
    Christmas Punch, '84 259; '89 330
    Cider Punch, Hot, '95 238
    Cider Punch, Spiced, '84 258
    Citrus Party Punch, '83 141; '92 289
    Citrus Punch, '85 319; '93 99
    Citrus Punch, Budget, '82 121
    Citrus Punch, Fresh, '85 154
    Citrus Punch, Party, '84 117
    Citrus Punch, Sparkling, '95 337
    Cola Punch, '91 144
    Cranapple Punch, '83 142
    Cranberry-Cherry Punch, '91 176
    Cranberry-Cinnamon Punch, '86 270
    Cranberry Punch, '83 275
    Cranberry Punch, Holiday, '85 265
    Cranberry Punch, Hot, '80 288;
      '84 319; '85 265
    Cranberry Punch, Sparkling, '85 277;
      '95 101
    Cranberry Punch, Spiced, '89 290
    Cranberry Punch, Tart, '83 318
    Cran-Grape-Tea Punch, '92 209
    Eggnog Punch, Holiday, '86 281
    False-Kick Punch, '82 121

    Frozen Punch Ring, '83 152
    Fruit Punch, Can-Can, '94 122
    Fruit Punch, Florida, '92 247
    Fruit Punch, Golden, '80 299; '83 56
    Fruit Punch, Holiday, '79 232
    Fruit Punch, Holiday Hot, '92 286
    Fruit Punch, Hot, '83 33
    Fruit Punch, Mixed, '90 207; '95 239
    Fruit Punch, Party, '82 137
    Fruit Punch, Passion, '90 169
    Fruit Punch, Spiced, '82 2
    Fruit Punch, Summertime, '80 160
    Fruit Punch, Tropical, '80 51; '90 169
    Fruit Slush Punch, '91 278
    Fruity Witches' Brew, '95 273
    Ginger Ale-Nectar Punch, '92 171
    Goblin Punch, '88 228
    Golden Punch, '85 207
    Grape Punch, Sparkling, '82 48
    Holiday Punch, '87 252
    Irish Coffee-Eggnog Punch, '95 314
    Lemonade Punch, Sparkling, '88 276
    Lemon Balm Punch, '80 42
    Lime-Pineapple Punch, '83 142
    Lime Punch, Calypso Presbyterian
      Church Women's, '95 141
    Lime Punch, Foamy, '82 264
    Lime Slush Punch, '90 273
    Merry Christmas Punch, '79 285
    Mocha Punch, '84 58, 166; '86 270;
      '95 141
    Mock Champagne Punch, '93 340
    Morning Punch, '88 82
    Nectar Punch, '93 283
    Orange Blossom Punch, '83 142
    Orange-Mint Punch, '82 121
    Orange Punch, Refreshing, '81 39
    Orange Sherbet Party Punch, '83 142
    Orange Soda Punch, '83 214
    Parsonage Punch, '79 148
    Party Punch, '91 106, 278
    Party Punch in a Pail, '94 289
    Party Punch, Special, '81 119
    Peppermint-Eggnog Punch, '90 273
    Percolator Punch, '91 306
    Percolator Punch, Hot, '81 288
    Pineapple-Mint Punch, '88 209
    Pineapple-Orange Punch, '85 236
    Pineapple Punch, '79 174
    Pineapple Punch, Frosty, '91 66
    Pineapple Punch, Spiced, '83 33; '92 66
    Pineapple Sherbet Punch, '95 141
    Pink Lady Punch, '81 100
    Polka Dot Punch, '95 178
    Ponche de Piña, '84 58
    Raspberry Sherbet Punch, '95 141
    Raspberry Sparkle Punch, '84 57
    Rum Punch, Spiced, '86 179
    Sherbet Punch, Double, '79 232
    Spiced Punch, Hot, '80 250
    Strawberry-Lemonade Punch, '85 116;
      '91 175
    Strawberry Punch, '90 273
    Strawberry Punch, Creamy, '86 195
    Tangy Punch, '83 142
    Tea Party Punch, '87 147
    Tea Punch, '90 143, 207
    Tea Punch, Citrus-, '85 116
    Traders' Punch, '87 94
    Tropical Punch, '90 207
    Vegetable Punch, Hot, '93 12
    Watermelon Punch, '89 204; '92 190
    White Grape Punch, '90 15

Raspberry Cooler, '89 171
Raspberry Fizz, Rosy, '90 179
Sangría, Southern, '88 170
Sangría, Virgin, '89 46
Scarlet Sipper, '90 198
Shakes
    Apricot Shake, '84 115
    Banana Milkshake, '85 47; '90 179
    Banana-Pineapple Milk Shake, '84 59
    Chocolate-Banana Milk Shake, '94 113
    Chocolate Mint Shake, '89 170
    "Concrete," Abaco Mocha, '94 114
    "Concrete," All Shook Up, '94 114
    "Concrete," Cardinal Sin, '94 113
    "Concrete," Foxtreat, '94 113
    Cranberry Shake, '83 171
    Date Shake, '92 44
    Fruit Shake, Frosty, '87 23
    Fruit Shake, Tangy, '95 129
    Mocha Milkshake, '89 35
    Orange Milk Shake, '84 166
    Orange Shake, Peachy, '81 156
    Papaya Shake, '90 169
    PBJ Shake, '93 292
    Peach Melba Sundae Shake, '93 134
    Peanut Butter Milkshakes, '85 198
    Peanut Butter Shake, '82 48
    Pep Shake, '79 38
    Pineapple-Banana Shake, '85 215
    Pineapple Milkshake, '87 199
    Pineapple Milk Shake, '94 113
    Raisin Shake, Amazin', '86 195
    Raspberry-and-Banana Shake,
      '89 183
    Raspberry Milk Shakes, '95 238
    Strawberry-Banana Shake, '89 35
    Strawberry-Cheesecake Shake,
      '92 44
    Strawberry Milk Shake, '94 113
    Strawberry Milkshake, Fresh,
      '82 113
    Strawberry-Orange Breakfast Shake,
      '87 186
    Strawberry-Pear Shake, '92 139
    Strawberry-Pineapple Shake,
      '84 166
    Strawberry-Yogurt Shake, '87 199
    Summer Shake, '82 161
    Sunshine Shake, '79 53
    Tropical Shake, '87 200; '93 212
Slush, Santa's, '90 271
Spiced Brew, Hot, '91 36
Spices, Barclay House Mulling, '86 289
Strawberry Cooler, '83 56; '84 51
Strawberry Coolers, '92 67
Strawberry-Mint Cooler, '84 57
Strawberry-Orange Slush, '83 172
Strawberry-Peach Smoothie, '89 182
Strawberry Refresher, Frozen, '93 213
Strawberry Slurp, '81 96
Strawberry Smoothie, '86 183
Strawberry Soda, '84 115
Strawberry Soda, Old-Fashioned,
  '79 49
Strawberry Spritzer, '90 14
Sunrise Smoothie, '93 139
Sunshine Fizz, '92 44
Syllabub, Plantation, '79 233
Syrup, Mint, '90 89
Tahitian Flower, '87 159
Toddy, Jolly, '86 229
Toddy, Tasty, '88 82
Tofruitti Breakfast Drink, '88 26

BEVERAGES (continued)

Tomato Bouillon, '83 8
Tomato-Clam Cocktail, '87 252
Tomato Cocktail, '83 M203
Tomato Juice Cocktail, '79 212; '83 230;
    '90 12
Tomato Juice Cocktail, Zesty, '83 289
Tomato Juice, Homemade, '81 50
Tomato Juice, Spicy, '85 189
Tomato Refresher, '83 318
Tomato Sipper, Peppy, '94 227
Tomato Sipper, Spicy, '86 229
Tomato Warm-Up, Spicy, '95 328
Tropical Cooler, '84 120
Tropical Delight, '89 182
Tropical Ice, '79 174; '80 129
Tropical Refresher, '85 198
Tropical Smoothie, '81 50; '90 169
Vanilla Frosty, French, '79 148
Vegetable Cocktail, Fresh, '82 165
Vegetable Juice Delight, '84 58
Virgin Mary, Spicy, '92 323
Wassail, '84 259, 318; '88 248; '90 273
Wassail, Christmas, '93 295
Wassail, Cranberry, '88 289
Wassail, Holiday, '89 289; '91 260
Wassail, Pineapple-Apricot, '83 275
Watermelon-Berry Slush, '90 137
Zippy Red Eye, '91 209

BISCUITS

Angel Biscuits, '80 49; '90 28; '93 270
Angel Biscuits, Ham-Filled, '80 159
Baking Powder Biscuits, '82 195; '89 144
Basil Biscuits, '93 160
Beaten Biscuits, '86 54
Benne Seed Biscuits, '79 38
Biscuits, '92 31
Blueberry Buttermilk Biscuits, '89 210
Bran Biscuits, '85 228
Bread, Biscuit, '84 284
Buttermilk Biscuits, '83 208; '85 255, 321
Buttermilk Biscuits, Basic, '94 214
Buttermilk Biscuits, Deluxe, '82 130
Buttermilk Biscuits, Favorite, '81 191
Buttermilk Biscuits, Fluffy, '84 102
Buttermilk Biscuits, Old-Fashioned, '80 77
Buttermilk Biscuits, Quick, '83 311; '88 15;
    '92 269
Buttermilk-Raisin Biscuits, '92 338
Caramel Dessert Biscuits, '95 36
Casserole, Beef-and-Biscuit, '83 75
Casserole, Biscuit-Topped Tuna, '79 113
Cheese
    Angel Biscuits, Cheese, '89 211
    Bacon-Cheese Biscuits, '88 84
    Beer-and-Cheese Biscuits, '94 215
    Blue Cheese Biscuits, '88 83
    Butter Cheese Dips, '80 46
    Cheese Biscuits, '79 296; '80 31;
        '81 288; '83 253; '85 32; '87 78
    Cheeseburger Biscuits, '79 194
    Chive Biscuits, Cheese-, '94 324
    Easy Cheese Biscuits, '81 99
    Ham and Cheese Biscuits, Petite, '79 193
    Hot Cheesy Biscuits, '80 186
    Lightnin' Cheese Biscuits, '90 283
    Onion Biscuits, Cheesy, '95 98
    Pepper-Cheese Biscuit Fingers, '88 283
    Roquefort Biscuits, Herbed, '84 95
    Sausage Biscuits, Cheesy, '80 78
    Tiny Cheese Biscuits, '80 192

Chicken in a Biscuit, '79 263
Cinnamon-Raisin Breakfast Biscuits, '93 159
Cloud Biscuits, '87 15
Coconut Biscuits, Yummy, '95 99
Cornmeal Biscuits, '85 228; '95 98
Cornmeal-Jalapeño Biscuits, '94 214
Country Ham Biscuits, '94 215
Country Ham, Biscuits with, '90 93
Daisy Biscuits, '90 86
Dressing, Cornbread-Biscuit, '79 296
Elgin Biscuits, '93 281
Feather Biscuits, '80 78
Feather Light Biscuits, '80 246
Flaky Biscuits, '84 228
Grapefruit Juice Biscuits, '83 10
Ham and Biscuits, Southern, '91 12
Ham 'n' Angel Biscuits, Kentucky, '90 83
Heart Biscuits, Country Ham in, '86 105
Heart Biscuits with Sausage, Angel, '87 156
Hearty Biscuits, '83 121
Herb Biscuits, Easy, '90 283
Herbed Biscuit Ring, '95 161
Herbed Biscuits, '85 228; '93 67
Honey Angel Biscuits, '95 138
Hot Biscuits, '86 269
Light Biscuits, '89 53
Marmalade Biscuits, Carolina, '85 42
Marmalade Biscuit Squares, '79 193
Mile-High Biscuits, '85 41
Nannie's Biscuits, '82 156
Nutty Tea Biscuits, '89 210
Oatmeal Biscuits, '89 108
One-Step Biscuits, '82 173
Orange Biscuits, '88 85
Orange Puffs, Upside-Down, '83 57
Parker House-Style Biscuits, '79 162
Pepperoni Biscuits, '84 95
Potato-Bacon Biscuits, '94 214
Processor Biscuits, Easy, '84 218
Pudding, Biscuit, '79 86; '93 51
Pudding, Chocolate Biscuit Bread, '94 215
Pull-Apart Biscuits, Surprise, '95 46
Quick Biscuits, '89 30
Raised Biscuits, Southern, '82 94
Raisin Biscuits, Glazed, '89 210
Raspberry-Almond Biscuits, '93 160
Rise-and-Shine Biscuits, '89 211
"Rolling-in-Dough" Biscuits, '92 80
Rosemary Biscuits, '95 91
Rye Biscuits, '84 96
Sausage and Biscuits, Southern, '82 43
Sausage Biscuit Bites, '84 95
Sausage Gravy, Biscuits and, '92 270; '94 20
Scones, Breakfast Drop, '88 83
Scones, Currant, '84 117
Snowflake Biscuits, '90 158
Sour Cream Biscuits, '79 128
Sour Cream Biscuits, Soft-as-a-Cloud, '86 138
Sourdough Biscuits, '82 201
Spoon Biscuits, Mexican Fiesta, '95 161
Sweetened Biscuits, '80 42
Sweet Little Biscuits, '85 305
Sweet Potato Angel Biscuits, '93 312
Sweet Potato Biscuits, '80 287; '84 140;
    '89 210
Taco Biscuit Bites, '91 89
Tomato Biscuits, '86 72
Tomato-Eggplant Biscuit Cakes, '95 170
Tomato-Herb Biscuits, '94 215
Topping, Biscuit, '86 157, 265
Up-and-Down Biscuits, '88 263
Velvet Cream Biscuits, '92 303
Wheat Bran Biscuits, '81 49

Wheat Germ Biscuits, '86 261
Wheat Quick Biscuits, '85 278
Whipping Cream Biscuits, '80 77
Whole Wheat Biscuits, '83 18; '84 60, 268;
    '85 227; '88 83; '91 222
Yeast Biscuits, '87 71, 301
Yeast Biscuits, Refrigerator, '85 48

BLACKBERRIES

Bars, Blackberry, '87 130
Bars, Blackberry-Filled, '79 124
Bars, Blackberry Jam, '82 M185
Berry Shrub, '95 29
Cake, Fresh Blackberry, '81 132
Cobbler, Blackberry, '82 139; '83 175
Cobbler, Blackberry-Almond, '81 132
Cobbler, Deep-Dish Blackberry, '80 186
Cobbler, Deluxe Blackberry, '81 132
Cobbler, Juicy Blackberry, '89 137
Cobbler, New-Fashioned Blackberry,
    '87 164
Cobbler, Southern Blackberry, '81 132
Crème Brûlée, Berry, '95 323
Dumplings, Blackberries and, '86 196
Flan, Blackberry, '79 182
Jam, Berry Refrigerator, '89 139
Jam, Blackberry, '82 149; '89 138
Jam, Freezer Blackberry, '84 M181
Jelly, Blackberry, '82 149
Napoleons, Berry, '94 120
Parfait, Blackberries-and-Cream, '87 129
Pie, Berry-Apple, '88 251
Pie, Blackberry, '84 141; '86 152
Pie, Blackberry-Apple, '87 130
Pie, Blackberry Cream, '81 132
Pie, Creamy Blackberry, '88 179
Pie, Peach-and-Blackberry, '89 136
Roll, Blackberry, '82 178
Sauce, Berry, '94 130
Sauce, Blackberry, '86 152; '94 232
Sauce, Ducklings with Blackberry, '82 251
Tamales, Blackberry Dessert, '94 190
Tart, Cherry and Blackberry, '83 225
Tart, Pick-a-Berry, '91 118
Tarts, Berry Good Lemon, '91 119
Tarts, Blackberry Pudding, '93 200

BLUEBERRIES

à la Frederick, Blueberries, '93 123
Appetizer, Orange-Berry, '85 81
Basket, Summer Berry, '84 158
Berry Tartlets, Fresh, '91 98
Breads
    Banana-Blueberry Bread, '81 163
    Biscuits, Blueberry Buttermilk, '89 210
    Buns, Deluxe Blueberry, '81 164
    Hot Blueberry Bread, '81 164
    Lemon Bread, Blueberry-, '85 190
    Muffins, Blueberry, '80 143;
        '91 140, 203
    Muffins, Blueberry-Bran, '89 23
    Muffins, Blueberry Buttermilk, '80 16
    Muffins, Blueberry-Cream Cheese,
        '86 14
    Muffins, Blueberry Ice Cream, '82 143
    Muffins, Blueberry-Lemon, '79 7
    Muffins, Blueberry-Oat, '92 119
    Muffins, Blueberry Oat Bran, '89 106
    Muffins, Blueberry-Oatmeal, '87 24
    Muffins, Blueberry Streusel, '80 46
    Muffins, Easy Blueberry, '81 197
    Muffins, Golden Blueberry, '79 235
    Muffins, Old-Fashioned Blueberry,
        '86 161
    Muffins, Speedy Blueberry, '95 135

BLUEBERRIES, Breads (continued)

Muffins with Streusel Topping, Blueberry, '88 129
Oatmeal Bread, Blueberry-, '83 139
Orange Bread, Blueberry-, '87 140
Orange Nut Bread Blueberry-, '84 141
Pinwheels, Blueberry, '82 205
Buckle, Blueberry, '85 30
Cake, Banana-Blueberry, '86 247
Cake, Blueberry Brunch, '83 183
Cake, Blueberry-Sour Cream, '90 140
Cake, Blueberry Streusel, '92 144
Cheesecake, Blueberries 'n' Cream, '87 140
Cheesecake, Blueberry Chiffon, '87 76
Chutney, Blueberry, '95 190
Cobbler, Blueberry, '83 175
Cobbler, Blueberry Pinwheel, '87 140
Cobbler, Easy Blueberry, '83 183
Cobbler, Fresh Blueberry, '80 144
Cobbler, No-Dough Blueberry-Peach, '86 177
Cobbler, Peachy Blueberry, '80 143
Coffee Cake, Almond-Blueberry, '85 152
Coffee Cake, Blueberry, '82 206; '85 326; '88 263
Coffee Cake, Blueberry Streusel, '88 154
Coffee Cake, Fresh Blueberry, '81 164
Cointreau, Blueberries and, '82 100
Compote, Berry-Peach, '82 133
Compote, Peach-Berry, '89 112
Conserve, Blueberry, '82 149
Cordial, Blueberry, '95 142
Cream, Lemon-Blueberry, '92 153
Crisp, Blueberry, '84 177
Crumble, Blueberry, '81 84
Crunch, Fresh Blueberry, '82 143
Dessert, Easy Blueberry, '89 M130
Dessert, Peach-Blueberry, '92 184
Dessert Squares, Chocolate-Blueberry, '87 299
Dream, Blueberry, '88 94
Fritters, Blueberry, '85 152
Glaze, Blueberry, '83 143
Huckle-Buckle Blueberry, '86 151
Ice Cream, Blueberry, '88 203
Jam, Blueberry, '79 120; '85 130
Jam, Blueberry Refrigerator, '89 139
Kuchen, Blueberry, '80 143
Lemon Curd with Berries, '90 102
Napoleons, Blueberry-Lemon, '94 122
Pancakes, Blueberry, '85 152; '89 138
Pancakes, Blueberry Buttermilk, '79 114
Pancakes, Blue Cornmeal-Blueberry, '94 115
Pancakes, Sour Cream Blueberry, '81 164
Pie, Blueberry-Banana, '93 115
Pie, Blueberry Cream, '84 142
Pie, Blueberry-Cream Cheese, '88 154
Pie, Blueberry-Peach, '94 158
Pie, Blueberry-Sour Cream, '83 183
Pie, Chilled Blueberry, '89 136
Pie, Fresh Blueberry, '83 183; '85 152
Pie, Fresh Blueberry Cream, '80 144
Pie, Fresh Blueberry Streusel, '89 137
Pie, Old-Fashioned Blueberry, '89 136
Pudding, Blueberry Bread, '88 154
Puree, Grapefruit with Pear-Berry, '89 213
Quick Blueberry Slump, '91 20
Raspberry Custard Sauce, Fresh Berries with, '88 163
Salad, Layered Berry, '79 173

Salad, Melon-Berry, '90 180
Sauce, Berry, '94 130; '95 103
Sauce, Blueberry, '80 144; '86 248; '88 155; '89 M130; '94 122; '95 135
Sauce, Cinnamon-Blueberry, '86 11
Sauce, Melon Wedges with Berry, '86 178
Sauce, Peach-Berry, '87 M165
Sauce, Peach-Blueberry, '81 170
Sauce, Peach-Blueberry Pancake, '82 177
Smoothie, Banana-Blueberry, '90 104
Snow, Berries on, '82 227
Sorbet, Blueberry-Kirsch, '83 120
Squares, Blueberry-Amaretto, '83 220
Tart, Pick-a-Berry, '91 118
Tarts, Berry Good Lemon, '91 119
Topping, Blueberry, '87 125
Trifle, Lemon-Blueberry, '88 210

BOK CHOY
Stir-Fry, Bok Choy-Broccoli, '84 2

BOYSENBERRIES
Cobbler, Boysenberry, '82 133
Compote, Berry-Peach, '82 133
Cream Mold, Peachy Berry, '83 130
Cream Supreme, Boysenberries and, '82 133
Crisp, Berry, '83 130
Pie, Boysenberry, '82 133

BRAN
Biscuits, Bran, '85 228
Biscuits, Wheat Bran, '81 49
Bread, Bran-Applesauce, '84 229
Bread, Honey-Oat, '93 232
Bread, Wheat-and-Oat Bran, '92 102
Bread, Whole Wheat Bran, '79 58
Chocolate-Bran Raisin Jumbos, '91 142
Crêpes, Bran, '83 70; '86 44
Cupcakes, Carrot-Bran, '82 16
Eggplant, Ratatouille-Bran Stuffed, '86 44
Muesli, Bran-and-Fruit, '91 134
Muffins
All-Bran Oat Bran Muffins, '91 134
Apple-Bran Muffins, '85 M89
Apple-Cinnamon Oat Bran Muffins, '89 106
Banana Bran Muffins, '83 48
Banana Oat Bran Muffins, '89 106
Big Batch Moist Bran Muffins, '95 214
Blueberry-Bran Muffins, '89 23
Blueberry Oat Bran Muffins, '89 106
Bran Muffins, '84 53
Buttermilk Muffins, Bran-, '85 7
Cranberry Bran Muffins, '89 107
Easy Bran Muffins, '83 55
Ever-Ready Bran Muffins, '81 106
Freezer Bran Muffins, '91 141
High-Fiber Muffins, '85 250
Honey Bran Muffins, '88 171
Honey-Bran Muffins, '89 250
Made of Bran Muffins, '86 103
Maple-Bran Muffins, '90 66
Oat Bran-Banana Muffins, '91 18
Oat Bran Muffins, '89 106
Oatmeal Bran Muffins, '81 236
Oatmeal-Bran Muffins, '91 83
Quick Bran Muffins, '86 85
Raisin Oat Bran Muffins, '89 106
Refrigerator Bran Muffins, '79 6
Sour Cream-Bran Muffins, '87 98
Spiced Bran Muffins, '84 229
Two, Bran Muffins for, '84 211
Whole Wheat Bran Muffins, '88 M274

Pancakes with Cinnamon Syrup, Bran, '91 315
Rolls, Bran, '85 145
Rolls, Bran Yeast, '87 116
Salad, Lemony Apple-Bran, '86 223
Waffles, Oat Bran, '92 139

BREADS. *See also* **BISCUITS; CAKES/COFFEE CAKES; CORNBREADS; CROUTONS; FRENCH TOAST; MUFFINS; PIES AND PASTRIES/PASTRIES; ROLLS AND BUNS.**
Apple Bread, '79 205; '80 226
Apple Butter Bread, '84 49; '86 69
Apple Loaf, Fresh, '82 206
Apple Loaf, Spiced, '79 215
Apple-Nut Bread, '79 12; '85 281
Apple-Nut Bread, Fresh, '87 256
Applesauce-Honey Nut Bread, '87 300
Applesauce Loaf, Brandy, '81 263
Applesauce Nut Bread, '81 305
Applesauce-Pecan Bread, '90 66
Apple Toast, '81 278
Apricot Bread, Tangy, '81 249
Apricot-Cranberry Loaf, '79 235
Apricot-Nut Bread, '79 24
Apricot-Nut Loaf, '81 8
Apricot-Nut Loaf, Tasty, '82 10
Apricot-Orange Bread, '92 285
Artichoke Bread, '93 140
Asparagus Squares, '79 161
Bacon-and-Cheese Bread, '83 255
Bacon-Cheese Toast Bars, '79 36
Banana-Apple Bread, '85 250
Banana-Blueberry Bread, '81 163
Banana Bread, '87 72
Banana Bread, Fruity, '95 78
Banana Bread, Sour Cream-, '79 190
Banana Bread, Whole Wheat, '80 88
Banana Butterscotch Bread, '79 116
Banana-Jam Bread, '84 73
Banana-Nut Bread, '86 8, 70
Banana Nut Bread, Hawaiian, '79 235
Banana Nut Bread, Whole Wheat-, '84 50
Banana-Nut-Raisin Bread, '81 59
Banana-Nut Roll, '85 112
Banana-Oat Tea Loaf, '87 256
Banana Wheat Bread, '81 14
Banana-Zucchini Bread, '85 326
Batter Bread, Soft, '84 253
Batter, Primary, '89 192
Beer Bread, Easy, '79 213; '84 160
Biscuit Bread, '84 284
Blueberry Bread, Hot, '81 164
Blueberry-Lemon Bread, '85 190
Blueberry-Oatmeal Bread, '83 139
Blueberry-Orange Bread, '87 140
Blueberry-Orange Nut Bread, '84 141
Blue Cheese-Apple Sunburst, '94 245
Bourbon-Pecan Bread, '93 308
Bran-Applesauce Bread, '84 229
Breakfast Bread, Crunchy, '93 327
Breakfast Bread, Easy, '83 289
Brie Bread, '87 143
Brie Cheese Bake, '87 117
Brown Bread, '84 242; '88 63
Brown Bread, Eighteenth-Century, '79 72
Brown Bread, Steamed Buttermilk, '86 261
Buttermilk-Cheese Loaf, '91 52
Butternut-Raisin Bread, '79 25
Butternut Spice Loaf, '92 235
Calas, Easy, '92 89
Carrot Bread, '89 143
Carrot Bread, Tasty, '84 328
Carrot-Nut Loaf, '83 117
Carrot-Pineapple Bread, '82 210

BREADS (continued)

Carrot Puffs, '87 200
Carrot-Walnut Bread, '88 284
Cheddar-Nut Bread, '85 41
Cheese Bread, '82 174
Cheese Bread, Dilly, '83 5
Cheese Bread, Easy, '82 74; '86 17
Cheese Bread, Quick, '83 9
Cheese Breadsticks, Italian, '95 126
Cheese Delights, Toasted, '79 37
Cheese-Herb Bread, '85 283
Cheese Loaf, '87 92; '90 93
Cheese Loaves, Little, '86 213
Cheese-Olive Bread, Spicy, '84 150
Cheese Puffs, Bavarian, '80 191
Cheesy Twists, '84 284
Cherry Nut Bread, '81 306; '82 36
Cherry Nut Bread, Maraschino, '79 234
Cherry-Nut Bread, Quick, '85 55
Chocolate Chip-Banana Bread, '90 267
Chocolate Date-Nut Bread, '81 284
Chocolate-Zucchini Bread, '93 308
Cinnamon Puffs, '81 209
Cinnamon Sticks, '95 244
Cinnamon Toast, Buttery Skillet, '79 36
Citrus-Nut Bread, '83 294
Coconut Bread, '83 140
Cranberry-Banana Bread, '80 281; '90 294
Cranberry Bread, '79 242
Cranberry Fruit-Nut Bread, '79 275
Cranberry-Orange Bread, '87 244
Cranberry-Orange Nut Bread, '80 288
Date-Banana Loaves, Tropical, '95 143
Date-Nut Bread, '85 306
Date-Nut Loaf, '85 10
Date-Walnut Loaf, Blue Ribbon, '80 15
Easy Bread, '87 168
Egg Bread, '95 121
Eggnog Bread, '83 294
Feta Cheese-Spinach Roll, '91 22
Flatbread, Mexican, '80 197
Focaccia, Mustard-and-Onion, '90 321;
   '92 97
French Bread, Bacon-Cheese, '92 54
French Bread Bowls, '95 58
French Bread, Cheesy, '88 172; '95 218
French Bread, Chive-Garlic, '89 29
French Bread, Herbed, '82 174; '93 283
French Bread, Herb-Seasoned, '83 198
French Bread, Hot Garlic, '81 83
French Bread, Onion-Cheese, '89 29
French Loaf, Herbed, '87 243
Fruit-Nut Bread, Kahlúa, '79 235
Fruit-Nut Twists, '82 253
Fry Bread, '84 140; '85 155
Fry Bread, Indian, '81 56
Garlic Bread, '82 19; '89 282; '91 204;
   '95 218
Garlic Bread, Cheesy, '84 150
Garlic Bread, Dilly, '95 218
Garlic Bread, Quick, '90 283
Garlic Breadsticks, '79 70
Garlic-Stuffed Bread, Cheesy, '95 176
Gingerbread Loaf, '82 14
Gingerbread, Mocha, '81 207; '82 14
Gingerbread, Molasses, '88 203
Gingerbread, Old English, '79 265
Gingerbread, Old-Fashioned, '81 157, 207;
   '82 14; '91 240
Gingerbread, Refrigerator, '80 52
Gingerbread, Spicy, '84 263

Gingerbread Squares, '84 16
Gingerbread, Very Moist, '86 261
Greek Bread, '89 200
Greek Sunburst, '94 245
Ham-and-Cheese Bread, '86 213
Hawaiian Loaf, '80 225
Herb-and-Cheese Pull Aparts, '87 143
Herb Bread, '86 17
Herb Loaf, Toasted, '84 150
Herbs-and-Cheese Bread, '93 56
Herb Sticks, '83 252
Herb-Vegetable-Cheese Bread, '88 172
Hobo Bread, '86 86
Honey-Banana Bread, '91 68
Irish Soda Bread, '90 214; '95 71
Jam-and-Cheese Loaf, '89 246
Koulourakia, '90 193
Lahvosh Cracker Bread Bowls, '95 58
Lemon Bread, '79 275; '87 256
Lemon-Cream Tea Loaf, '84 50
Lemon-Nut Bread, '79 24
Lemon-Pecan Bread, '83 54
Lemon Tea Bread, '92 268; '93 183
Mayonnaise Bread, '89 29
Mix, Quick Bread, '81 90; '86 8
Molasses-Nut Bread, '84 24
Monkey Bread, Bacon, '94 283
Monkey Bread, Cheese-Filled, '91 21
Monkey Bread, Quick, '81 306; '82 36
Mustard-Rye Ovals, '84 149
Nautical Knots, '93 168
Oatmeal Bread, '81 236, 300
Oatmeal Raisin Bread, '81 14
Onion Bread, Easy, '81 162
Onion-Cheese Bread, '79 180; '81 8
Onion-Cheese Supper Bread, '83 112
Onion-Herb Bread, Toasted, '83 266
Onion-Parmesan Bread, '84 284
Orange, Baba au, '86 138
Orange-Cranberry Bread, '85 266
Orange-Cream Cheese Bread, '82 210
Orange-Nut Bread, '82 75
Orange Nut Loaf, '80 226
Orange-Pecan Bread, '79 148
Orange-Pecan Bread, Glazed, '81 250
Orange-Pecan Loaves, '79 215
Orange Praline Toast, '79 36
Orange Puffs, Upside-Down, '83 57
Orange-Pumpkin Bread, '87 300
Orange Tea Bread, '79 234
Pane Cunsado (Fixed Bread), '95 218
Papaya Bread, '88 138
Parmesan Herb Bread, '82 235; '83 41
Parmesan Rounds, '79 170
Parmesan Sesame Sticks, '81 39
Parmesan Twists, '82 239
Peach Bread, '82 170
Peach Bread, Georgia, '79 161
Peanut Bread, '87 184
Peanut Butter Bread, '88 64
Pear Bread, '80 218
Pecan-Cornmeal Rounds, '95 99
Pepper Bread, '85 156
Persimmon Bread, '80 228
Persimmon Date-Nut Bread, '82 218
Pineapple-Apricot Bread, '84 7
Pineapple Bread, '83 139
Pineapple-Carrot Bread, '79 106
Pineapple-Nut Bread, '79 215
Pineapple-Pecan Loaf Bread, '87 256
Pita Bread Salad, '95 86
Pita Triangles, Cheesy, '93 70
Pizza Sunburst, '94 245

Popovers
   Blender Popovers, Perfect, '79 53
   Cheddar Cheese Popovers, '85 41
   Cheese Popover Puffs, '85 6
   Cinnamon Popovers, '90 66
   Good Old Southern Popovers, '79 138
   Jumbo Popovers, '83 225
   Muffin Tin Popovers, '79 138
   Parmesan Popovers, '90 66
   Pecan Popovers, Giant, '83 208
   Pimiento Popovers, '79 138
   Popovers, '94 43
   Ring, Cheesy Popover, '80 45
   Seasoned Popovers, '86 86
   Two, Popovers for, '81 304
   Whole Wheat Popovers, '90 66
Poppy Seed Bread, '83 140
Poppy Seed Loaf, Quick, '82 75
Poppy Seed-Swiss Cheese Bread, '91 52
Prune-Nut Bread, '87 255; '91 55
Puddings
   Amish Bread Pudding, '80 8
   Apple-Raisin Bread Pudding, '88 175
   Apricot Bread Pudding, '85 24
   Blueberry Bread Pudding, '88 154
   Bread Pudding, '89 M130; '90 219
   Buttermilk Bread Pudding with Butter-
      Rum Sauce, '95 134
   Cheesy Bread Pudding, '83 68
   Chocolate Bread Pudding, '80 8
   French Bread Pudding, '85 231
   Lemon Bread Pudding, Old-Fashioned,
      '88 95
   Old-Fashioned Bread Pudding, '83 213;
      '88 175
   Old-Fashioned Bread Pudding with
      Bourbon Custard Sauce, '95 271
   Old-Fashioned Bread Pudding with Rum
      Sauce, '88 32
   Peachy Bread Pudding, '88 175
   Raisin Bread Pudding, '94 215
   Soufflé, Creole Bread Pudding, '92 87
   Spiced Bread Pudding, '93 52
   Sweet Potato Bread Pudding, '94 241
   Tennessee Bread Pudding with Bourbon
      Sauce, '93 51
   Whiskey Sauce, Bread Pudding with,
      '80 58; '90 230; '92 93
Pumpkin Bread, '81 8
Pumpkin Bread, Harvest, '90 M215
Pumpkin Bread, Moist, '80 245
Pumpkin Bread, Spiced, '91 233
Pumpkin Bread with Cream Cheese and
   Preserves, '84 264
Pumpkin-Coconut Bread, '87 255
Pumpkin Loaf, Harvest, '85 232
Pumpkin-Nut Bread, '83 294
Pumpkin-Oatmeal Loaf, '81 49
Pumpkin-Pecan Bread, '87 221
Raisin-Cranberry Bread, '81 305; '82 36
Saffron Tea Bread, '85 26
Sally Lunn, Quick, '87 16
Salt-Rising Bread, '79 145
Santa Gertrudis Pan de Campo, '94 27
Sausage-Onion Squares, '83 112
Scones, Breakfast, '88 231; '89 22
Scones, Cranberry, '95 283
Scones, Currant, '84 117; '92 332
Scones, Hazelnut, '94 16
Scones, Lemon-Raisin, '87 69
Scones, Orange-Pecan, '94 215
Seasoned Breadsticks, '81 84
Sesame Bread Twists, '84 283

Sesame-Cheddar Sticks, '81 150
Sesame Sticks, '83 9
Sesame Wheat Crisps, '81 106
Shortbread, '85 266
Shrimp Toast, '86 91
Sourdough Dill Bread, '89 192
Sourdough Starter, '89 192
Sourdough Wedges, '90 199
Spinach Bread, '83 121; '87 144
Spoonbreads
    Cheddar Spoonbread, '82 196
    Cheese Spoonbread, '86 261
    Corn and Bacon Spoonbread, '81 129
    Corn-Cheese Spoonbread, '88 9
    Dressing, Southwestern-Style
      Spoonbread, '94 273
    Garlic Spoonbread, '79 269; '80 14
    Golden Spoonbread, '83 286; '84 17
    Grits Spoonbread, '79 38
    Memmie's Spoonbread, '95 27
    Old Virginia Spoonbread, '84 102
    Spoonbread, '80 43; '81 138; '90 200;
      '95 156
Squash Bread, '79 210
Squash Bread, Spicy, '83 121
Stars, Bread, '93 286
Starter Food, '94 324; '95 77
Stollen, '86 291
Strawberry Bread, '81 250; '83 140;
  '84 49
Strawberry Jam Bread, '79 216
Strawberry-Nut Bread, '79 24
Tacos, Navajo, '84 246
Tennessee Sin, '95 218
Three-C Bread, '81 284
Toast Points, '93 270
Toast Strips, Seasoned, '93 98
Tomato-Cheese Bread, Herbed, '88 143
Tortillas, Flour, '81 303
Tortillas, Never-Fail Flour, '80 198
Vegetable Bread, Breakaway, '82 74
Wampus Bread, '81 305
Wheat Loaf, Nutty, '90 65
Whole Wheat Cardamom Bread, '86 223
Whole Wheat Coffee Can Bread, Molasses-,
  '85 111
Whole Wheat Orange Bread, '85 5
Whole Wheat Quick Bread, '82 65
Wine-Date Nut Bread, '82 253
Yeast
    Almond Braid, '89 86
    Almond Danish, '87 301
    Anise-Orange Bread, '83 295
    Apple Danish, Deep-Dish, '86 161
    Apple-Date-Nut Ring, '90 212
    Apple Pull-Apart Bread, '86 330
    Apple Swirl Bread, '85 4
    Armenian Thin Bread, '94 108
    Austrian Sweet Bread, '83 294
    Austrian Twists, '80 45
    Bagels, '89 266
    Bagels, Whole Wheat, '84 20
    Baguettes, '85 70
    Beer Bread, Best-Ever, '82 129
    Beer Bread, Hearty, '87 226; '88 133
    Beignets, '84 56
    Beignets, French Market, '92 88;
      '93 219; '94 319; '95 80
    Binning Bread, '80 68
    Braided Bread, '88 76

Braided Loaf, '82 17
Braids, Festive, '87 297
Braids, Holiday, '83 295
Braid, Sweet Yeast, '90 46
Break-Away Bread, '86 56
Brioche, '81 122; '89 90
Brioche Chicken Curry, '88 124
Brioche Loaves, Vienna, '87 300
Brown Bread, Light-, '84 268
Bubble Bread, '81 107
Bunny Bread, Glazed, '92 102
Butter-Egg Bread, '85 269
Butterhorns, '84 267
Cake Bread, Golden, '84 269
Canapé Bread, '89 292
Caramel Bread, '82 75
Caramel-Orange Coffee Ring, '80 45
Caraway Breadsticks, '89 239
Caraway Puffs, '82 174
Caraway Seed Bread, Dark, '80 256
Challah, '92 62
Cheddar Cheese Bread, '84 268
Cheese Bread, '83 208; '87 11
Cheese Bread, Crusty, '86 233
Cheese-Caraway Batter Bread, '85 33
Cheese Crescents, '82 18
Cheese-Herb Bread, '84 M144
Cheese Loaf, Jalapeño-, '84 76
Cheese-Wine Bread, '87 254
Chocolate Loaf Bread, '88 M188
Chocolate Pinwheel Loaf, '80 256
Christmas Bread, '87 296; '88 288
Christmas Bread, Norwegian, '79 234
Christmas Wreath, '80 280
Cinnamon Loaf, '82 18; '85 55
Cinnamon-Nut Bubble Bread, '80 22
Cinnamon-Oat Bread, '90 135
Cinnamon Raisin Bread, '80 22
Cinnamon Swirl Loaf, '79 23
Cinnamon Twists, '83 53
Cocoa-Nut Swirl Bread, '80 257
Coffee Ring, Filled, '82 18
Coffee Ring, Sugarplum, '83 M37
Cornmeal Yeast Bread, '89 54
Cottage Cheese-Dill Bread, '83 154
Cracker Bread, Sesame, '87 2
Cream Cheese Braids, '82 243
Cream Cheese Loaves, Processor,
  '85 48
Crescents, Festive, '80 281
Croissants, '83 54; '84 188
Croissants, Flaky Butter, '85 42
Crust Bread, Country, '80 225
Dill-Oat Bread, '91 95
Dough, Basic Yeast, '88 74
Easter Bread, Golden, '91 54
Easter Egg Bread, '84 94
Easy Yeast Bread, '79 147
Egg Bread, County Fair, '87 68
Elephant Ears, '84 18
English Muffin Bread, '95 M79
English Muffin Loaf, '82 96
English Muffin Loaves, '85 42
Figure-8 Bread, '79 171
Flat Bread, Italian-Style, '82 235; '83 41
Focaccia, Dried Tomato, '94 65
Focaccia, Onion, '93 77
Focaccia, Rosemary, '95 190
French Bread, '79 158; '87 227;
  '89 54
French Bread, Easy, '88 299
French Bread, Glazed, '88 75
French Bread, Herbed, '85 222; '86 166

French Bread, New Orleans, '80 212
French Bread, Whole Wheat, '88 63
French Loaves, Crusty, '85 37
French Onion Bread, '91 90
Fruit-and-Cheese Braid, '86 214
Gingerbread Men, Yeast, '92 312
Golden Bread, '90 47
Gouda Bread, '91 52
Grittibanz (Swiss Bread Figure),
  '93 265
Ham Bread with Herb Butter, Country,
  '86 255
Heartland Loaves, '89 287
Herb Bread, '84 268
Herb Bread, No-Knead, '81 217
Herb-Cheese Bread, '85 70
Herbed Bread, '89 34
Herb Loaf, Butterflake, '86 261
Herb-Sour Cream Bread, '85 268
Herman Food, '82 200
Holiday Wreath, '81 284
Honey-Cinnamon Swirl Bread,
  '88 287
Honey-Curry Bread, '89 250
Honey-Granola Bread, '86 56
Honey Loaves, Hint o', '81 104
Honey-Oat Bread, '89 107; '93 232
Honey Oatmeal Bread, '80 60
Honey Twist, '79 80
Honey-Walnut Swirl, '80 21
Honey Wheat Bread, '85 18, 268
Honey-Wheat Bread, '91 223
Italian Bread, '82 297
Kolecz (Polish Bread), '80 29
Lightbread, Coffee Can, '79 59
Light Yeast Bread, '81 299
Loaf Bread, Hospitality, '86 299
Loaf Bread, Old-Fashioned, '88 75
Loaves, Sweet-Filled Yeast, '90 46
Mandelkrantz, '92 32
Marble Loaf, '80 230
Monkey Bread, '82 243; '95 174
Monkey Bread, Easy, '90 214
Multi-Grain Bread, '86 236
Oat Bread, Caraway-Raisin, '86 44
Oatmeal Bread, '81 300; '92 212
Oatmeal Bread, Round, '84 20
Oatmeal-Raisin Bread, '83 59
Oat-Molasses Bread, '82 139
Old-Fashioned Yeast Bread, '79 284
Olive Bread, '93 78
Olive-Dill Casserole Bread, '92 16
Onion-Dill Bread, Easy, '85 5
Onion-Herb Bread, '90 165
Onion Twist Loaves, '84 300
Pandoro, '93 267
Panettone, '93 266
Parmesan Bread, '92 19; '93 231
Party Bread, '86 218
Peanut Butter Bread, '86 171
Peanut Lover's Bread, '93 211
Pimiento-Cheese Bread, '85 223;
  '86 166
Pizza Batter Bread, '85 56
Pocket Bread, '79 58
Poppy Seed Loaf, '83 254
Portuguese Round Bread, '83 295
Potato Bread, '85 56
Potato Bread, Old-Fashioned, '86 57
Potato Lightbread, '80 225
Potato Loaves, '86 162
Pull-Apart Yeast Bread, '94 132
Raisin Batter Bread, Salt-Free, '86 33

BREADS, Yeast *(continued)*

Raisin Bread, Curried Chicken Salad on,
'85 96
Raisin Bread, Homemade, '87 300
Raisin Bread, Round, '89 230
Raisin-Whole Wheat Bread, '93 77
Refrigerator Bread, No-Knead,
'83 155
Roasted Red Bell Pepper Bread,
'95 241
Rounds, Individual Bread, '83 159
Rye Bread, '84 21
Rye Bread, Swedish Orange-, '85 111
Rye Canapé Bread, '89 293
Rye Sandwich Bread, '82 65
Sally Lunn, '81 157; '88 163; '94 233
Sandwiches, Stacking, '86 127
Savarin, Holiday, '80 280
Sesame-Wheat Breadsticks, '93 114
Soft Breadsticks, '83 115
Sopaipillas, '80 197
Sour Cream Bread, '79 59
Sour Cream-Cheese Bread, '85 33
Sourdough Bread, '82 201
Sourdough Bread Dough, Potato,
'94 324; '95 77
Sourdough Bread, Potato, '94 325;
'95 77
Sourdough Starter, Herman, '82 200
Sourdough Starter, Potato, '94 324;
'95 77
"Sponge," '93 267
Squares, Yeast Bread, '83 155
Starter Food, '94 324
Sugar Plum Bread, '80 256
Sweet Bread Wreath, Glazed, '90 192
Sweet Christmas Loaf, '84 278
Swiss Cheese Bread, '79 60
Swiss Cheese Loaves, Mini, '95 80
Techniques of Breadmaking, '82 17
Trinity Feast Bread, '82 92; '83 83
Walnut Bread, '93 77
Wheat-and-Oat Bran Bread, '92 102
Wheat Bread, Buttermilk, '86 236
Wheat Bread, Pull-Apart Maple, '85 222;
'86 166
White Bread, '79 275
White Bread, Cardamom, '82 236;
'83 41
White Bread, Old-Fashioned, '81 285
White Bread, Special, '86 57
Whole Wheat Bran Bread, '79 58
Whole Wheat Bread, '83 17
Whole Wheat Bread and Rolls, Hearty,
'79 92
Whole Wheat Bread, Anise-, '93 36
Whole Wheat Bread, Quick, '92 25
Whole Wheat Breadsticks, '84 228
Whole Wheat Canapé Bread, '89 293
Whole Wheat Honey Bread, '82 65;
'83 106
Whole Wheat-Oatmeal Bread, '87 85
Whole Wheat-Rye Bread, '83 M37
Whole Wheat-White Bread, '82 130
Yellow Squash Bread, '84 140
Zucchini-Apple Bread, '87 255
Zucchini Bread, '85 111; '86 93
Zucchini Bread, Spiced, '79 161; '86 162
Zucchini Bread, Spicy, '81 305; '82 36
Zucchini-Carrot Bread, '83 190
Zucchini-Honey Bread, '89 143

BROCCOLI
Appetizer, Broccoli-Cheese, '92 265
au Gratin, Broccoli, '82 M20
Bacon, Broccoli with, '92 302
Bake, Broccoli, '81 246; '89 279
Beef and Broccoli, Quick, '91 123
Beef and Broccoli with Chive Gravy, '88 214
Burritos, Broccoli, '83 200
Carnival Broccoli, '81 2
Casseroles
Almond-Broccoli Casserole, '88 62
au Gratin, Broccoli-and-Eggs, '85 289
au Gratin, Broccoli-Ham, '90 239
Bake, Broccoli, '89 279
Blue Cheese Casserole, Broccoli-,
'85 260
Broccoli Casserole, '87 284;
'88 M146, 265
Cheese Casserole, Broccoli-, '82 269;
'84 9; '94 132
Cheesy Broccoli Bake, '83 255
Cheesy Broccoli Casserole, '84 293;
'92 342; '95 M191
Cheesy Italian Broccoli Bake, '83 5
Chicken-Broccoli Casserole, '79 48;
'91 315
Chicken Casserole, Broccoli-, '82 33
Company Broccoli Bake, '83 279
Corn Casserole, Broccoli-, '83 313
Crabmeat-Broccoli Casserole, '84 232
Divan Casserole, Chicken, '82 M203
Divan, Chicken, '80 10; '87 M218
Divan, Creamy Turkey, '90 M34
Divan, Curried Chicken, '80 83
Divan, Easy Chicken, '94 310
Divan, Gourmet Chicken, '82 83
Divan, Overnight Chicken, '83 198
Divan Quiche, Chicken, '88 M125
Divan, Quick Turkey, '89 178
Divan, Sherried Chicken, '80 38
Divan, Turkey, '82 268
Egg Casserole, Broccoli-and-, '86 324
English Walnut Broccoli, '89 68
Garden Surprise, '83 112
Ham and Broccoli Casserole, '81 133
Ham and Broccoli Strata, '80 261
Ham-Broccoli Casserole, Quick, '82 40
Italian Broccoli Casserole, '82 6, 280;
'83 32
Onion Deluxe, Broccoli-, '81 75
Potato-Broccoli-Cheese Bake, '80 114
Rice Casserole, Broccoli-, '81 101
Sausage and Broccoli Casserole, '80 33
Stuffing, Broccoli with, '95 341
Supreme, Broccoli, '85 68
Swiss Cheese Casserole, Broccoli-,
'83 322; '85 M211
Tuna-Broccoli Casserole, Tangy, '83 75
Turkey-and-Broccoli Casserole, '86 332
Winter Broccoli Casserole, '94 280
Cheese Sauce, Broccoli with, '82 107
Chinese Broccoli, '85 M12
Chowder, Broccoli, '79 16
Chowder, Swiss-Broccoli, '80 73
Cocktail Broccoli, '80 192
Crêpes, Royal Brunch, '81 44
Dip, Broccoli-Garlic, '82 59
Dip, Cheesy Broccoli, '83 92
Dip, Santa Fe Skinny, '94 137
Eggs, Broccoli and Creamed, '83 84
Elegant, Broccoli, '81 267
Fettuccine, Broccoli-Parmesan, '93 55
Fettuccine with Broccoli, '90 97

Filling, Broccoli, '81 44
French Sauce, Broccoli with, '81 295
Frittata, Broccoli-Cheese, '81 243
Fritters, Cheesy Broccoli, '79 53
Garlic Broccoli, '93 35; '95 54
Glazed Broccoli with Almonds, '80 12
Herbed Broccoli, '88 101
Hollandaise Sauce, Broccoli with,
'79 244, 276
Hollandaise Sauce, Broccoli with Mock,
'82 272
Horseradish Sauce, Broccoli with, '81 2;
'83 206; '84 33
Horseradish Sauce, Carrots and Broccoli with,
'91 246
Italian-Style Broccoli, '88 41
Italienne, Broccoli, '82 300
Jade-Green Broccoli, '80 12
Lemon Broccoli, '88 119; '95 53
Lemon-Broccoli Goldenrod, '84 M89
Lemon Cream, Broccoli with, '89 245
Lemon Dressing, Chilled Broccoli with,
'88 270
Lemon Sauce and Pecans, Broccoli with,
'86 71
Lemon Sauce, Broccoli with, '91 292; '92 256
Marinated Broccoli, '80 79; '81 40; '85 207;
'86 157; '88 255
Marinated Fresh Broccoli, '81 M139
Medley, Cauliflower-Broccoli, '81 69
Olive-Butter Sauce, Broccoli with,
'83 118
Omelet, Broccoli-Mushroom, '85 45
Onions, Broccoli-Stuffed, '84 154
Orange Broccoli, Easy, '85 267
Orange Sauce, Broccoli with, '80 243
Pasta, Broccoli, '84 176
Pasta, Chicken-and-Broccoli, '87 286
Pasta with Broccoli and Sausage, '87 109
Pasta with Peppers and Broccoli, '91 69
Pickled Broccoli, '81 308
Pie, Broccoli-and-Turkey Pasta, '88 269
Pie, Broccoli-Beef, '83 196
Pie, Broccoli-Cheese, '84 235
Pimiento Broccoli, '86 268
Polonaise, Broccoli, '86 55
Potatoes and Broccoli, Creamy, '92 61
Potatoes, Broccoli-and-Almond-Topped, '83 3
Potatoes, Broccoli-Shrimp Stuffed, '92 M228
Potatoes, Broccoli-Topped Baked, '86 17
Puff, Broccoli, '81 94; '82 95
Quiche, Broccoli-Rice, '81 228
Quiche, Easy Broccoli, '82 34
Quiche, Italian Broccoli, '85 45
Quick-and-Easy Broccoli, '86 55
Rice, Holiday Broccoli with, '87 252
Rolls, Broccoli-Cheddar, '91 21
Rolls, Ham-and-Broccoli, '86 212; '87 82
Salads
Barley-Broccoli Salad, '90 135
Beef-and-Broccoli Salad, '87 187
Broccoli Salad, '82 24; '85 249; '90 292;
'95 95
Cauliflower-Broccoli Crunch, '88 216
Cauliflower-Broccoli Salad, '79 20
Cauliflower-Broccoli Toss, '82 54
Cauliflower Salad, Broccoli-, '92 97
Cauliflower Salad, Broccoli and, '81 280
Cauliflower Salad, Broccoli 'n', '90 32
Cauliflower Salad, Creamy Broccoli and,
'81 23
Cauliflower Toss, Crunchy Broccoli,
'83 25

Broccoli 33

BROCCOLI, Salads *(continued)*

Chicken Salad, Broccoli-, '90 129
Congealed Broccoli Salad, '84 124
Corn Salad, Broccoli-, '87 24
Creamy Broccoli Salad, '79 143
Crunchy Broccoli Salad, '83 39
Curried Broccoli Salad, '86 225
Fresh Broccoli Salad, '82 34; '87 103
Mandarin Salad, Broccoli-, '93 325
Marinated Broccoli, '80 79
Marinated Broccoli Salad, '83 240
Marinated Broccoli, Tangy, '80 284
Medley, Broccoli, '81 206
Orange Salad, Broccoli-, '94 281
Pasta Salad, Broccoli-Cauliflower,
    '88 269
Peanut Salad, Broccoli-, '92 35
Pepperoni-and-Broccoli Salad, '83 216
Potato Salad, Hot Broccoli-, '85 23
Raisin Salad, Creamy Broccoli-, '92 106
Red Pepper Salad, Broccoli and, '83 224
Red, White, and Green Salad, '90 18
Slaw, Zesty Broccoli, '93 246
Supreme, Broccoli Salad, '83 260
Warm Broccoli Salad, '92 35
Sauce, Broccoli, '91 85
Sauté, Broccoli and Walnut, '95 52
Sautéed Broccoli, '79 246
Savory Broccoli, '79 268; '80 14
Sesame Broccoli, '84 69; '85 8
Sesame, Broccoli with, '80 13
Sesame Seeds, Broccoli with, '82 34
Shrimp Sauce, Broccoli and Cauliflower
    with, '84 248
Soufflé, Broccoli, '81 24
Soufflé, Golden Broccoli, '84 283
Soup, Broccoli, '86 161, M194; '87 288
Soup, Broccoli-and-Chicken, '90 202
Soup, Broccoli-Swiss, '86 6
Soup, Cheese-and-Broccoli, '89 276
Soup, Cheesy-Broccoli, '86 258
Soup, Creamed Broccoli, '85 24
Soup, Cream of Broccoli, '79 130;
    '80 188, M225; '82 314; '83 66; '86 259
Soup, Cream-of-Broccoli, '88 56
Soup, Creamy Broccoli, '81 75; '82 13;
    '83 99; '91 307
Soup, Easy Broccoli, '81 307
Soup, Fresh Broccoli, '91 86
Soup, Hot Broccoli, '81 235; '83 44
Soup, Light Cream of Broccoli, '93 17
Soup, Mock Cream of Broccoli, '85 288
Sour Cream Sauce, Broccoli with, '87 127
Spears, Saucy Broccoli, '84 35
Spears, Zesty Broccoli, '79 152
Spread, Broccamoli Curry, '88 55
Stack-Ups, Jiffy Tomato, '80 161
Steamed Broccoli, '80 122
Steamed Broccoli with Tangy Chive Sauce,
    '83 101
Stew, Oyster-Broccoli, '89 242
Stir-Fried Broccoli, '83 227
Stir-Fry Beef and Broccoli, '79 47
Stir-Fry, Beef-and-Broccoli, '91 46
Stir-Fry, Bok Choy-Broccoli, '84 2
Stir-Fry Broccoli, '80 19
Stir-Fry Broccoli and Beef, '83 110
Stir-Fry, Chicken-Broccoli, '82 33
Stir-Fry, Turkey-Broccoli, '91 62
Stroganoff, Chicken-and-Broccoli, '89 M248
Sunshine Sauce, Broccoli with, '84 248

Supreme, Broccoli, '82 34; '85 68
Supreme, Broccoli-Carrot, '89 331
Supreme, Creamy Broccoli, '82 287
Tomatoes, Broccoli-Stuffed, '83 136;
    '93 216
Toss, Broccoli, '86 294
Toss, Italian Cauliflower-Broccoli, '88 269
Vinaigrette, Potato-Broccoli, '85 84
White Wine, Broccoli with, '80 12
Wine Sauce, Broccoli with, '84 187
Ziti with Sausage and Broccoli, '95 340
BROWNIES. *See also* **COOKIES/BARS AND SQUARES.**
Alaskas, Brownie, '83 299
Amaretto Brownies, '86 246
Apple Brownies, Frosted, '86 216
Biscuit Mix Brownies, '94 M51
Blonde Brownies, Nutty, '81 64
Blonde Brownies with Chocolate Chunks,
    '91 271
Buttermilk Brownies, '85 249
Buttermilk Cake Brownies, '87 198
Butterscotch Brownies, '85 248
Candy Bar Brownies, '92 204
Cheesecake Brownies, '85 249
Chocolate-Banana Brownies, '80 160
Chocolate Chip Brownies, '81 162
Chocolate Chip-Peanut Butter Brownies,
    '84 73
Chocolate Ice Cream Brownies, '89 124
Chocolate-Kahlúa Brownies, '93 99
Chocolate-Mint Brownies, '85 M294;
    '88 80
Chocolate-Mint Brownies, Southern, '93 216
Chocolate-Nut Brownies, '81 129
Chocolate-Peanut Butter Chip Brownies,
    '91 306
Chocolate-Pecan Brownies, '81 64
Chocolate-Peppermint Brownies, '88 262
Chocolate Tea Brownies, '83 79
Chocolate-Walnut Brownies, '89 325
Choco-Mallow Brownies, '87 198; '90 309
Cinnamon Brownie Bars, '81 230
Cocoa Brownies, Nutty, '81 64
Cookies, Brownie Chip, '90 320
Cream Cheese Swirl Brownies, '79 51
Crème de Menthe Brownies, '83 244
Crunch-Crust Brownies, '87 198
Date-and-Almond Brownies, '88 217
Derby Brownies, Special, '90 94
Easy Brownies, '83 245
Favorite Brownies, '86 158
Fudge Brownies, Nutty, '80 M171
German Cream Cheese Brownies, '80 269
Heavenly Hash Brownies, '83 245
Honey Brownies, Heavenly, '79 83
Macadamia-Fudge Designer Brownies, '94 51
Marshmallow Brownies, Chewy, '83 306
Mint Dessert, Brownie-, '82 227
Mint Julep Brownies, '93 165
Mississippi Mud Brownies, '89 M25
Mix, Brownie, '82 6
Mocha Brownies, '87 93
Mocha Frosting, Brownies with, '94 292
Mother's Brownies, '93 239
Muffins, Fudge Brownie, '95 M50
No-Bake Brownies, '94 330
Oat Brownies, '89 59
Oatmeal Brownies, '87 199
Oat 'n' Crunch Brownies, '91 233
Peanut Butter Brownies, '87 199
Peanut Butter Brownies, Frosted,
    '92 272
Pistachio-Mint Brownies, '94 50

Praline Brownies, '93 243
Pretzel Brownies, Saucepan, '85 171
Quick and Easy Brownies, '82 6
Quick Brownies, '87 M302
Raspberry Brownies, '92 274
Rich Brownies, '95 84
Rocky Road Brownies, '86 320
Triple Decker Brownies, '92 319
Walnut-Cream Cheese Brownies, '84 240
White Chocolate Brownies, '89 169

BRUSSELS SPROUTS
Amandine, Brussels Sprouts, '79 213
Beer, Brussels Sprouts in, '85 69
Brussels Sprouts, '89 278
Carrots and Brussels Sprouts, '82 300
Cashews, Brussels Sprouts with, '81 2
Casserole, Brussels Sprouts-and-Artichoke,
    '94 279
Casserole of Brussels Sprouts, '86 294
Celery, Brussels Sprouts and, '79 21
Cheese Sauce, Brussels Sprouts with, '79 246
Citrus Brussels Sprouts, Calico, '85 303
Creamed Brussels Sprouts and Celery, '83 322
Creamy Brussels Sprouts, '79 212
Deviled Brussels Sprouts, '84 248
Dilled Brussels Sprouts, '88 180
Fried Brussels Sprouts, '81 308
Glorified Brussels Sprouts, '86 282
Lemon Sauce, Brussels Sprouts in, '82 269
Lemon Sprouts, '85 288
Lemony Brussels Sprouts with Celery, '85 25
Marinated Brussels Sprouts, '88 265
Medley, Brussels Sprouts, '79 212; '85 267
Mustard Sauce, Brussels Sprouts in, '87 253;
    '90 228
Onion Sauce, Brussels Sprouts in, '81 308
Orange Brussels Sprouts, '84 34
Orange Sauce, Brussels Sprouts in, '86 55
Pierre, Brussels Sprouts, '84 248
Polonaise, Brussels Sprouts, '85 79
Rice, Brussels Sprouts and, '79 288; '80 26
Salad, Brussels Sprouts, '87 233
Salad, Cauliflower-Brussels Sprouts, '83 240
Sesame Brussels Sprouts, '86 55
Shallots and Mustard, Brussels Sprouts with,
    '85 258
Stir-Fry, Brussels Sprouts, '81 308
Tangy Brussels Sprouts, '88 40
Tarragon Brussels Sprouts, '83 291
Wine Butter, Brussels Sprouts in, '86 327
BULGUR
Tabbouleh, '93 70
Tabbouleh Salad, '92 212; '94 174
Wild Rice Bulgur, '91 83
BURRITOS
Bean Burrito Appetizers, '94 226
Beef Burritos, Cheesy, '85 193
Breakfast Burritos, '84 57; '90 192

BURRITOS *(continued)*

Broccoli Burritos, '83 200
Brunch Burritos, '91 77
Burritos, '80 196
Carne Guisada Burritos, '95 43
Chimichangas (Fried Burritos), '81 196;
　'85 244; '86 114
Chinese Burritos, '87 181
Egg Burritos, Tex-Mex, '95 34
Fiesta Burritos, '86 114
Meat-and-Bean Burritos, '81 194
Monterey Burritos, '84 292
Pie, Mexican Burrito, '87 287
Rollups, Burrito, '90 119
Vegetable Burritos, '80 197; '90 134; '92 138
Vegetable Burritos with Avocado Sauce,
　'83 200
Vegetarian Burritos, '93 319

BUTTER

Acorn Squash-and-Bourbon Butter, '94 266
Apple Butter, '79 200; '81 217; '92 311
Apple Butter, Half-Hour, '81 203
Apricot Butter, '82 308
Balls, Butter, '82 189; '89 90
Basil Butter, '87 171
Basil Butter, Asparagus with, '85 40
Cashew Butter, Asparagus with, '87 56
Cheese Butter, '84 114
Chervil Butter, '83 129
Chervil Butter, Swordfish Steak with, '91 147
Chili Butter, '82 219
Cinnamon Butter, '92 319
Cinnamon-Honey Butter, '89 281
Clarified Butter, '81 59
Clarifying Butter, '82 189
Curls, Butter, '82 51, 189; '89 90
Garlic Butter, '83 193; '84 108; '95 89
Gazpacho Butter, '92 86
Ginger Butter, '91 26
Green Peppercorn Butter, '88 60; '90 117
Herb Butter, '86 128, 255, 261, 306
Herb Butter, Cauliflower with, '81 2
Herb Butter, Corn-on-the-Cob with, '84 160
Herbed Caper Butter, '94 62
Herbed Unsalted Butter, '82 67
Honey Butter, '93 309; '94 206; '95 139
Honey-Orange Butter, '79 36; '85 19
Horseradish-Chive Butter, '86 277
Lemon Butter, '95 32
Lemon Butter, Asparagus with, '87 M151
Lime Butter, Chicken with, '84 68
Maple-Flavored Butter, Whipped, '79 36
Molds, Butter, '89 90
Nectarine Butter, '79 175
Olive Butter, '91 295
Onion Butter, '86 253
Onion Butter, Sweet, '93 124
Orange Butter, '81 8, 42; '90 323; '92 319;
　'94 115
Orange-Pecan Butter, '84 75
Peach Butter, '82 308
Peach Butter, Golden, '91 178
Pear Butter, '85 130
Pear Butter, Spiced, '80 218
Plum Butter, '88 152
Prune-Orange Butter, '92 49
Raisin Butter, '81 272
Roasted Red Bell Pepper Butter, '95 242
Sauce, Brown Butter, '91 65
Sauce, Butter-Rum, '95 134
Sauce, Garlic Buerre Blanc, '88 222

Sauce, Garlic-Butter, '95 327
Sauce, Garlic-Ginger Butter, '94 89
Sauce, Pecan-Butter, '91 65
Sauce, White Butter, '92 107
Shrimp Butter, '92 91
Southwestern Butter, '92 320
Strawberry Butter, '79 36; '81 286; '91 71
Sweet Potato Butter, '95 M290
Tomato Butter, '86 128
Tomato-Curry-Orange Butter, '93 159

BUTTERSCOTCH

Bars, Butterscotch, '82 209; '83 297
Bars, Chocolate-Butterscotch, '81 197
Bread, Banana Butterscotch, '79 116
Brownies, Butterscotch, '85 248
Cake, Butterscotch, '91 270
Cake, Butterscotch-Pecan Pound, '92 153
Cheesecake, Butterscotch, '86 188
Cookies, Butterscotch, '87 58
Cookies, Butterscotch-Pecan, '84 36
Fantastic, Butterscotch, '83 76
Filling, Butterscotch, '91 271
Fudge, Butterscotch Rum, '88 256
Fudge, Four Chips, '92 318
Fudge Scotch Ring, '79 273
Mousse, Butterscotch, '93 254
Pie, Butterscotch Cream, '84 48; '87 207
Pie, Butterscotch Meringue, '83 158
Pinwheels, Butterscotch, '90 49
Pralines, Butterscotch, '81 253
Sauce, Butterscotch-Pecan, '82 212
Trail Mix, Bunny, '95 101

C

CABBAGE. *See also* **SLAWS, SAUERKRAUT.**

Apples and Franks, Cabbage with, '87 42
au Gratin, Cabbage, '83 279
Bake, Zesty Cabbage Beef, '80 300
Beef-Cabbage Dinner, '81 179
Braised Red Cabbage, '95 343
Bubbling Cabbage, '84 2
Caraway Cabbage, '85 32, 289
Caraway, Cabbage with, '93 181
Casserole, Cheesy Cabbage, '79 4
Casserole, Creamy Cabbage, '80 63
Casserole, Italian Cabbage, '87 42
Casserole, Savory Cabbage, '82 168
Chop Suey, Cabbage, '81 101
Chow-Chow, '82 196
Chowchow, '87 150
Chowder, Hearty Cabbage, '80 25
Colcannon, '90 64
Corned Beef and Cabbage, '83 104; '93 64
Corned Beef and Cabbage au Gratin, '83 16
Corned Beef and Cabbage, Quick, '79 54
Corned Beef Squares and Cabbage, '82 86
Country-Style Cabbage, '81 271
Creamed Cabbage with Almonds, '79 4
Creole Cabbage, '87 189
Frankfurter-Cabbage Skillet, '80 166
Hot Cabbage Creole, '87 42
Kielbasa and Cabbage, '85 67; '89 M196
Kielbasa, Cabbage, '87 42
Lemon-Butter Cabbage, '88 156
Medley, Cabbage, '80 64; '83 104
Piccalilli, Kentucky, '81 216
Quick Cooked Cabbage, '95 270
Red Cabbage and Apples, '85 32
Red Cabbage, German, '94 254
Red Cabbage, German-Style, '84 2
Red Cabbage, Pickled, '81 271
Red Cabbage, Sweet-Sour, '79 5

Relish, Cabbage, '83 260
Relish, Spanish Cabbage, '95 270
Rolls, Beef Stuffed Cabbage, '81 87; '82 7
Rolls, Cabbage, '83 104
Rolls, Crunchy Cabbage-Rice, '85 32
Rolls, Easy Cabbage-and-Beef, '88 49
Rolls, Fried Cabbage, '95 270
Rolls, Hot-and-Spicy Cabbage, '84 249
Rolls, Hungarian Cabbage, '94 47
Rolls, Spicy Cabbage, '84 2
Rolls, Stuffed Cabbage, '84 217; '88 18;
　'92 251
Rolls, Vegetarian Cabbage, '91 86
Rollups, Beef-and-Cabbage, '80 63
Salad, Austrian Hash with Cabbage, '95 262
Salad, Cabbage, '87 120, 233
Salad, Cabbage and Fruit, '79 286
Salad, Chinese Cabbage, '81 271
Salad, Chinese Green, '88 48
Salad, Garden Cabbage, '81 210
Salad, Nutty Cabbage, '87 42
Salad, Overnight Cabbage, '79 83
Salad, Red Cabbage Citrus, '94 72
Salad, Tangy Cabbage, '82 55
Salad, Wilted Cabbage, '94 281
Sausage, Cabbage with Polish, '83 104
Sausage-Sauced Cabbage, '81 271
Sausage Surprise, '83 245; '84 42
Scalloped Cabbage, '82 269
Scalloped Cabbage, Cheese, '81 87; '82 7
Skillet Cabbage, '89 314; '90 229
Skillet, Cabbage-and-Tomato, '86 110
Soup, Cabbage, '83 291
Soup, Sweet-and-Sour Cabbage, '89 314
Spinach Dip in Cabbage, '82 155
Stir-Fried Cabbage, '81 75, 271; '85 109
Stuffed Cabbage, '84 282
Stuffed Cabbage, Italian, '84 294
Supper, Cabbage, '89 314
Supreme, Cabbage, '79 4; '83 206
Sweet-and-Sour Cabbage, '86 295;
　'87 189
Tex-Mex Cabbage, '80 63
Tomatoes, Cabbage and, '83 104
Tomatoes, Tasty Cabbage and, '86 72
Wedges, Saucy Cabbage, '83 86
Wedges, Smothered Cabbage, '81 87; '82 7
Wilted Cabbage, '80 64; '88 229

CAKES. *See also* **BREADS, CHEESECAKES.**

Almond-Butter Cake, '86 107
Almond-Butter Cake, Peachy, '90 107
Almond-Butter Wedding Cake, '86 106
Almond Legend Cake, '82 8
Almond Whipping Cream Cake, '80 295
Amaretto Cake, Easy, '85 79
Ambrosia Cake, '79 229
Ambrosia Cake Royale, '89 335
Angel Food
　Amaretto-Almond Sauce, Angel Food
　　Cake with, '90 199
　Chocolate Angel Cake, '88 128
　Chocolate Angel Food Cake, '87 21;
　　'90 111; '91 55
　Chocolate Angel Food Cake with Custard
　　Sauce, '88 259
　Coconut Angel Cake, Spiked, '85 279
　Deluxe Angel Food Cake, '86 121
　Ice Cream Angel Cake, '83 23
　Ice-Cream Angel Dessert, Triple Mint,
　　'93 86
　Lemon Angel Cake, '80 147
　Orange-Coconut Angel Food Cake,
　　'94 294

Pineapple-Orange Sauce, Angel Cake with, '84 14
Surprise, Angel Cake, '93 86
Trifle, Pineapple Angel Food, '93 86
Apple Cake, '83 312; '84 262
Apple Cake, Dried-, '79 13
Apple-Date Cake, Fresh, '83 300
Apple-Ginger Upside-Down Cake, '94 180
Apple-Nut Cake, '87 76
Apple-Oatmeal Cake, Golden, '86 301
Apple-Pecan Cake, '92 167
Apple Pie Cake, '86 301
Applesauce Cake, '80 270
Applesauce Cake, My Favorite, '87 263
Applesauce Cake with Bourbon Frosting, '88 236
Applesauce Carrot Cake, '81 202
Applesauce-Oatmeal Cake, '92 119
Applesauce Snack Cakes, '88 215; '89 20
Applesauce-Spice Cake, '83 42
Applesauce Spice Cake, '89 296
Apple Shortcake, Quick, '93 42
Apple Slice Cake, '85 93
Apple Spice Cake, '92 225
Apple Stack Cake, Dried, '85 242
Apple-Walnut Cake, '94 242
Banana-Blueberry Cake, '86 247
Banana Cake, '84 151
Banana Cake, Deluxe Light, '84 314
Banana Cake, Marvelous, '79 115
Banana-Coconut Cake, '93 154
Banana-Nut Cake, '92 120
Banana-Pecan Shortcake, '93 43
Bananas Foster Crunch Cake, '93 339
Banana Waldorf Cake, '85 118
Bars and Squares
  Almond Cake Squares, '79 111
  Apple-Date Dream Cake Squares, '85 10
  Apple-Orange Cake Squares, '84 150
  Applesauce Cake Squares, '86 8
  Applesauce-Spice Squares, '86 248
  Carrot-Lemon Squares, Golden, '80 40
  Carrot Squares, '79 256
  Cinnamon Cake Squares, '87 222
  Cream Cheese Cake Squares, '84 321
  Crumb Cake, Calico, '87 261
  Gingerbread Squares, '84 16
  Ginger Cake, '87 222
  Honey Cake Squares, '89 250
  Honey-Oatmeal Cake, '87 222
  Jam Squares, '81 M289
  Orange Cake Squares, '81 34
  Orange-Pumpkin Cake Squares, '83 242
  Pecan Squares, Easy, '81 230
  Pumpkin Cake Bars, '80 245
  Rhubarb Squares, '92 129
  Strawberry Shortcake Squares, '85 122; '86 124
  Zucchini-Carrot Cake, '93 20
Beet Cake with Almond Topping, '86 200
Birdhouse Cake, '93 284
Birthday Cake, Clowning Around, '94 52
Blackberry Cake, Fresh, '81 132
Blackberry Flan, '79 182
Black Walnut Cake, '80 253; '84 316; '90 308
Blueberry-Sour Cream Cake, '90 140
Blueberry Streusel Cake, '92 144
Boston Cream Pie, '83 220
Bourbon-Pecan Cake, '84 25
Brown Mountain Cake, '84 39

Brown Sugar Meringue Cake, '81 70
Bûche de Noël, '84 304; '87 241
Bûche de Noël Cake, '82 262
Bunny Cake, '94 98
Butter Brickle Cake, '85 118
Butter Pecan Cake, '80 229
Butter Pecan Cake, Caramel-Filled, '88 278
Butterscotch, '91 270
Cajun Cake, '87 138
Candy Bar Cake, '92 204
Caramel Cake, '89 55; '90 307
Caramel Layer Cake, Creamy, '81 71
Carolina Dream Cake, '88 278
Carrot Cake, '79 45; '82 137; '84 315
Carrot Cake, Applesauce, '81 202
Carrot Cake, Blue Ribbon, '81 70
Carrot Cake, Coconut-Pecan, '84 322
Carrot Cake, Easy, '83 215
Carrot Cake, Fresh Coconut-, '80 299
Carrot Cake, Frosted, '92 19
Carrot Cake, Old-Fashioned, '83 M232
Carrot Cake, Old-South, '80 120
Carrot Cake, Quick-and-Easy, '84 150
Carrot Cakes, Miniature, '90 94
Carrot Cake, Spiced, '87 296
Carrot Cake, Spicy Fruited, '85 117
Carrot Pudding Cake, '83 24
Carrot Snack Cake, Easy, '82 235
Chart, Cake Failure, '81 72
Cherry Bourbon Cake, '82 287
Cherry Cake, '79 165
Cherry Cake, Quick, '81 238
Cherry Upside-Down Cake, '82 56
Chocolate
  Almond Cake, Chocolate-, '91 248
  Almond Cake with Cherry Filling, Chocolate-, '84 225
  Banana Cake, Chocolate-, '86 138
  Banana Loaf, Chocolate Chip-, '85 115
  Beet Cake, Chocolate, '80 40
  Birthday Cake, Fishin'-for-Fun, '93 194
  Black Forest Cake, '81 126; '92 174
  Black Forest Cake, Six-Layer, '85 125
  Black Forest Cherry Cake, '83 302
  Black Forest Dump Cake, '85 13
  Brownie Baked Alaska, '80 66
  Brownie Delight, Chocolate, '87 224
  Buttercream Cake, Chocolate, '90 108
  Buttermilk Chocolate Cake, '79 13
  Cameo Cake, '94 58
  Candy Cake, Chocolate, '81 238
  Caramel-Nut Cake, Chocolate-, '83 23
  Carrot Cake, Brownie, '92 120
  Cherry Cake, Chocolate-, '84 200; '86 239
  Chiffon Cake with Coffee Buttercream, Chocolate, '95 277
  Cinnamon Cake, Chocolate-, '93 154
  Cocoa Crown Cake, '90 107
  Coconut Cake, Chocolate-, '83 23
  Cola Cake, Quick Chocolate, '95 56
  Cookies-and-Cream Cake, '92 163
  Custard Cake, Chocolate, '88 175
  Decadent Chocolate Cake, '86 142
  Easy Chocolate Cake, '80 140
  Father's Day Cake, '92 134
  Frosting, Chocolate Cake with Double, '86 314
  Fudge Cake, '94 M293
  Fudge Cake, Best, '83 301
  Fudge Cake, Brown Sugar, '86 316
  Fudge Cake, Chocolate, '80 279
  Fudge Cake for Two, '81 205

  Fudge Cake, One-Foot-in-the-Fire, '90 252
  Fudge Frosting, Chocolate Cake with, '89 56
  German Chocolate Cake, '81 296; '83 M233
  German Chocolate Chip Cake, '86 247
  Grandma's Chocolate Cake, '94 133
  Kahlúa Cake, Chocolate, '91 298
  Kahlúa Chocolate Cake, '81 303
  Marbled Cake, Cocoa, '82 265
  Marshmallow Cake, No-Egg Chocolate, '87 M97
  Mayonnaise Cake, Chocolate, '83 99
  Mocha Cake, Belgian, '84 316
  Mocha Cake, Double, '84 311
  Mocha-Chocolate Cake, Dark, '84 311
  Mousse Cake, Chocolate, '87 264
  Nut Cake, Rich Chocolate-, '86 8
  Pastry Cake, Chocolate, '91 196
  Peanut Butter Cake, Chocolate-, '84 240
  Peanut Butter Cake, Fudgy, '85 91
  Peanut Cluster Cake, Chocolate-, '87 184
  Perfect Chocolate Cake, '82 244; '90 307
  Pound Cake. See Cakes/Pound.
  Pudding Cake, Hot Fudge, '88 255
  Pudding, Chocolate Cake, '81 99
  Pudding, Hot Fudge Sundae Cake, '88 167
  Queen's Chocolate Cake, '89 271
  Raspberry Cake, Chocolate-, '92 173
  Rich Chocolate Cake, '89 43
  Rocky Road Cake, '81 178
  Roll, Chocolate Cream, '85 317
  Roll, Chocolate-Frosted Ice Cream, '84 200
  Roll, Chocolate-Mocha Cream, '84 304
  Roll, Chocolate Mousse, '83 290; '88 280
  Roll, Chocolate-Orange, '87 21
  Roll, Make-Ahead Chocolate-Mint Cake, '95 220
  Rolls, Chocolate Cake, '94 312
  Royal, Chocolate Cake, '86 239
  Rum Cake, Chocolate, '79 67
  Sachertorte, '84 253
  Shortcake, Chocolate-Raspberry, '95 99
  Snack Cake, Black Widow, '93 245
  Snack Cake, Frosted Chocolate, '90 194
  Sour Cream Cake, Chocolate-, '87 222
  Sour Cream Cake, Chocolate Chip-, '85 115
  Sour Cream Chocolate Cake, '79 282
  Strawberry Shortcake, Chocolate-, '89 216
  Swiss Chocolate Chip Cake, '87 85
  Tic-Tac-Toe Cake, '94 52
  Tiered Cameo Cake, '94 125
  Toffee Cake, Chocolate-, '89 335
  Triangle Cake, Chocolate, '85 126
  Truffle Cake, Chocolate, '89 43
  Wedding Cake, Cameo, '94 124
  Wedding Cake, Double Chocolate, '91 100
  Whipped Cream Cake, Chocolate-Mint, '90 265
  White Chocolate-Cherry Cake, '88 268
  White Chocolate Mousse Cake, '89 160
  Yule Log, '79 281; '82 289
  Zucchini Cake, Chocolate, '85 156

CAKES *(continued)*

Cinnamon Crumb Cake, '85 290
Cinnamon Streusel Cake, '84 151
Coconut
  Apple Coconut Cake, '80 226
  Cake, Coconut, '92 120
  Carrot Cake, Coconut-Pecan, '84 322
  Carrot Cake, Fresh Coconut-, '80 299
  Chocolate-Coconut Cake, '83 23
  Christmas Coconut Cake, '82 262
  Cream Cake, Coconut, '81 179; '91 269
  Creamy Coconut Cake, '84 43
  Fresh Coconut Cake, '80 289; '82 52;
    '85 281
  Holiday Coconut Cake, '90 308
  Layer Cake, Coconut-Pineapple, '80 140
  Layer Cake, Stately Coconut, '81 70
  Lemon Cake, Coconut-, '95 319
  Lemon-Coconut Cream Cake, '81 179
  Lemon-Coconut Sheet Cake, '85 117
  Pineapple Cake, Coconut-, '89 56
  Pineapple Cake Roll, Coconut-, '84 304
  Regal Coconut Cake, '83 299
  Rum-Orange Coconut Cake, '88 224
  Spice Cake, Coconut-, '84 255; '87 296
  Toasted Coconut Cake, '86 60
  Unforgettable Coconut Cake, '90 104
  White Chocolate-Coconut Cake, '87 263
Coffee Cakes
  Almond-Blueberry Coffee Cake, '85 152
  Almond Coffee Cake Twist, '91 22
  Almond Sunburst, '94 245
  Apple Coffee Cake, '81 249
  Apple Coffee Cake, Fresh, '92 32
  Apple Loaf, Spiced, '79 215
  Apple-Pecan Coffee Cake, '84 242
  Apricot-Almond Coffee Cake, '93 26
  Apricot Lattice Coffee Cake, '94 48
  Banana Coffee Cake, '81 288
  Banana Cream Coffee Cake, '85 46
  Banana-Sour Cream Coffee Cake,
    '80 186
  Blueberry Brunch Cake, '83 183
  Blueberry Coffee Cake, '82 206;
    '85 326; '88 263
  Blueberry Coffee Cake, Fresh, '81 164
  Blueberry Streusel Coffee Cake, '88 154
  Braid Coffee Cake, Daisy, '82 197
  Breakfast Pullapart, '81 278
  Butterflake Coffee Ring, '79 216
  Buttermilk Coffee Cake, '89 50
  Buttermilk Crumb Cake, '79 72
  Caramel Bread, '82 75
  Caramel Breakfast Rolls, '79 193
  Caramel-Orange Coffee Ring, '80 45
  Caramel Ring, Easy, '85 M89
  Cardamom Coffee Cake, '83 246; '84 17
  Cheesecake Coffee Cake, Deep-Dish,
    '90 50
  Cherry Blossom Coffee Cake, '80 21
  Cherry Coffee Cake, '94 49
  Chocolate-Chip Coffee Cake, '79 249
  Chocolate Chip Coffee Cake, '83 231
  Christmas-Tree Coffee Cakes, '87 298
  Christmas Wreath, '80 280
  Cinnamon-Buttermilk Coffee Cake,
    '80 45
  Cinnamon Coffee Cake, '83 M203
  Cinnamon Crisps, '81 113
  Cinnamon-Nut Bubble Bread, '80 22
  Cinnamon-Pecan Coffee Cake, '87 69

  Cinnamon-Raisin Coffee Cake, '93 180
  Cinnamon Twist Coffee Cake, '84 322
  Cinnamon Upside-Down Coffee Cake,
    '85 256
  Coffee Cake, '94 167
  Cora's Coffee Cake, '91 186
  Cowboy Coffee Cake, '95 84
  Cranberry-Coconut Coffee Cake,
    '93 332
  Cranberry Coffee Cake, '81 14; '90 159
  Cranberry-Nut Coffee Cake, '81 250
  Cranberry-Orange Coffee Cake, '82 283
  Cream Cheese Coffee Cake, '86 290
  Crescent Coffee Cake, '81 229
  Danish Coffee Ring, '80 20
  Fig Coffee Cake, Easy, '80 116
  Holiday Coffee Cake, '84 284
  Holiday Wreath, '81 284
  Honey Twist, '79 80
  Lemon Coffee Cake, Lightly, '81 14
  Macadamia Ring Coffee Cake, '85 326
  Maple-Nut Coffee Twist, '86 290
  Marbled Coffee Cake, '86 9
  Mix, Quick, '94 167
  Muffins, Coffee Cake, '79 7
  Oatmeal-Coconut Coffee Cake, '83 312
  Orange Breakfast Ring, '81 229
  Orange Butter Coffee Cake, '89 229
  Orange Coffee Cake, '85 M88
  Orange Coffee Cake, Nutty, '95 160
  Orange Marmalade Swirl Coffee Cake,
    '81 107
  Orange-Pecan Coffee Cake, '86 86
  Overnight Coffee Cake, '80 52; '92 213
  Peach Flip, '79 217
  Pecan-Topped Coffee Cake, '81 41
  Pineapple-Coconut Coffee Cake, '94 49
  Raisin Coffee Cake, Spicy, '88 63
  Raspberry Coffee Cake, '83 112
  Raspberry Tea Cake, '91 271
  Ring, Coffee Cake, '85 M89
  Savarin, Holiday, '80 280
  Snack Cake, Coffee, '86 247
  Sour Cream Coffee Cake, '81 270;
    '93 154
  Sour Cream-Walnut Coffee Cake,
    '79 209
  Special Coffee Cake, Mama Cle's,
    '94 287
  Strawberry Coffee Cake, '85 46
  St. Timothy's Coffee Cake, '91 54
  Sugar Cake, Moravian, '87 228
  Sugar Cake, Polish, '89 267
  Sugarplum Coffee Ring, '79 235;
    '83 M37
  Sweet Roll Dough, '79 80
  Tropical Coffee Cake, '80 232; '90 323
  Walnut Coffee Cake, '93 124
  Whole Wheat Coffee Cake, Crunchy-
    Topped, '79 93
Cola Cake, '81 238
Compromise Cake, The, '90 253
Cranberry Upside-Down Cake, '87 8
Cream Cheese Cake, Regal, '80 140
Cream Cheese Loaf Cake, '84 151
Crème de Menthe Cake, '81 178
Cupcakes
  Apple-Nut Cupcakes, '82 279
  A Tisket, a Tasket, '92 15
  Banana-Cocoa Cupcakes, '80 130
  Birthday Balloon Cakes, '92 15
  Black Bottom Cups, '82 279
  Brownie Cupcakes, '82 280

  Carrot-Bran Cupcakes, '82 16
  Chocolate Chip Cupcakes, Marble,
    '81 239
  Chocolate Cupcakes, '92 14
  Chocolate Surprise Cupcakes, '85 91
  Cinnamon-Chocolate Cupcakes,
    '81 M139
  Confetti Cupcakes, New Year's, '92 15
  Cream Cheese Party Cupcakes, '82 279
  Date Cupcakes, '84 7
  Graveyard Grumblings, '92 15
  Happy Day Cupcakes, '80 129
  Ice-Cream Cone Cakes, Fourth-of-July,
    '92 15
  Lemon Moist Cupcakes, '82 112;
    '83 153
  Mocha Cupcakes, '85 250
  Pumpkin Cupcakes, '85 121
  Self-Filled Cupcakes, '80 129
  Sweetheart Cupcakes, '92 15
  Tannenbaum Temptations, '92 14
  Turkey Talk, '92 15
  Vanilla Cupcakes, '92 14
  Vanilla Cupcakes, Golden, '85 121
  Yellow Cupcakes, Easy, '83 241
Daffodil Cake, '84 161
Date Nut Cake, '79 176; '80 5
Date-Nut Cake Roll, '89 94
Decorating Techniques, Cake, '83 72, 240;
  '84 224
Easter Egg Cake, '94 98
Easter Rabbit Cake, '94 99
Éclair Cake, '93 42
Fig Cake, '79 32
Fig Preserve Cake, '79 140; '84 316
Fig Preserves Cake, '89 335
Friendship Cake, '82 250
Fruit-and-Cereal Brunch Cake, '88 263
Fruit-and-Nut Cake, Stately, '84 226
Fruitcakes
  Applesauce Fruitcake, '83 258
  Aronowitz Fruitcake, '86 285
  Bourbon Fruitcake, '85 315
  Brandy Fruitcake, '82 261
  Burgundy Fruitcake, '85 292
  Cake Mix Fruit Cake, '95 248
  Chocolate Fruitcakes, '95 250
  Classic Fruitcake, '91 258
  Favorite Fruitcake, Family, '88 284
  Fondue, Fruitcake, '84 258
  Grandmother's Fruitcake, '95 248
  Japanese Fruitcake, '83 268; '90 252
  Jeweled Fruitcake, '88 260
  Jill's Fruitcake, '95 249
  Kentucky Fruitcake, '86 266
  Layered Fruitcake, '87 265
  Lemon Fruitcake, '83 258
  Light Fruitcake, '90 309
  Mom's Fruitcake, '85 321
  No-Bake Fruitcake, '95 249
  Old-South Fruitcake, '79 289
  Regal Fruitcake, '83 257
  Sherry-Nut Fruitcake, '84 266
  Spice Cake, Fruit and, '87 M97
  White Fruitcake, '80 280; '85 316
  Zucchini Fruitcake, '88 284
Funnel Cakes, '83 250
Funnel Cakes, Nutty, '91 233
Gingerbread, Applesauce, '94 179
Gingerbread Cake Roll, '89 214
Gingerbread Mix, '92 312
Gingerbread, No-Molasses, '92 313
Gingerbread, Old English, '79 265

Gingerbread, Old-Fashioned, '91 240
Gingerbread, Refrigerator, '80 52
Gingerbread, Spicy, '84 263
Gingerbread with Caramel Sauce, Pumpkin, '93 235
Ginger Shortcakes, '94 179
Graham Cracker Cake, '79 13
Grapefruit Cake, Fresh, '89 308
Holiday Cake, Favorite, '81 264
Honey Bun Cake, '91 214
Honey Cake, '92 250
Honey Cake, Southern, '89 251
Hummingbird Cake, '82 244; '90 305
Ice Cream Cake, '86 321; '89 71
Ice Cream Cake for Grown-Ups, '88 M192
Ice Cream Cake, Fruity, '87 110
Ice Cream Yule Log, '83 253
Jam Cake, Spicy, '89 236
Jellyroll, Easy, '82 176
Jellyroll Layer Cake, '85 125
Jellyroll, Spiced, '82 176
Key Lime Cake, '91 214
King Cake, '90 20
Lady Baltimore Cake, '90 45
Lane Cake, '80 121; '83 269
Lane Cake, Nanny's, '89 55
Lemon Cake, Easy, '83 24
Lemon Cake, Glazed, '86 70
Lemon Cake, Luscious, '93 81
Lemon Cake Pudding, '92 96
Lemon Cake Roll, '89 312
Lemon Cake Roll, Elegant, '80 70
Lemon-Cheese Cake, Tart, '88 7
Lemon Gold Cake, '83 301
Lemon Layer Cake, Luscious, '86 61
Lemon Layer Cake, Old-Fashioned, '85 191
Lemon Meringue Cake, '89 296
Lemon-Pineapple Cake, '86 60, 239
Lemon-Poppy Seed Cake, '93 154
Lemon Pudding Cake, '83 106
Lemon-Raspberry Cake, '91 247
Lemon Roll, Snow-Capped, '79 68
Lemon Sponge Cups, '83 10
Light Cake, Basic, '90 107
Lime Layer Loaf, '85 96
Lord Baltimore Cake, '90 45
Mandarin-Rum Cake, '84 150
Mango Cake, '83 150
Maraschino Nut Cake, '83 268
Mincemeat Spice Cake, '79 246
Molasses Snack Cake, '86 20
Moravian Sugar Cake, '95 304
Neapolitan Cake, '88 168
Nutmeg Feather Cake, '81 238
Nutty Cakes, '89 50
Oatmeal Cake, Dutch, '83 95
Orange Butter Cake, '95 46
Orange Cake, '86 61; '95 320
Orange Cake, Fresh, '83 300
Orange Cake, Mandarin, '83 24
Orange Cake, Williamsburg, '81 120; '82 23
Orange Chiffon Cake, '91 56
Orange Chiffon Cake, Fresh, '88 179
Orange-Cranberry Cake, '85 314
Orange-Date Cake, '94 60
Orange-Lemon Cake, General Robert E. Lee, '88 92
Orange Liqueur Cake, '87 84
Orange Marmalade Cake, '85 53
Orange Meringue Cake, '86 336; '87 84

Orange-Nut Butter Cake, '80 254
Orange Nut Cake, '80 70
Orange-Pecan Crunch Cake, '83 10
Orange Rum Cake, '79 2
Orange Shortcake, Fresh, '80 100
Orange-Slice Cake, '81 264
Orange Streusel Cake, '88 10
Peach Cake, Fresh, '85 178
Peaches and Cream Cake, '80 142
Peach Shortcakes, Spicy, '89 154
Peach Upside-Down Cake, '87 8
Peachy Picnic Cake, '79 178
Peanut Butter-and-Jelly Cake, '85 34
Peanut Butter-Banana Cake, '80 87
Peanut Butter Cake, '79 51; '83 M233
Peanut Butter Swirl Cake, '86 109
Peanutty Layer Cake, Super, '83 222
Pear Cake with Caramel Drizzle, '86 247
Pear Preserve Cake, '85 52
Pecan Cake, Kentucky, '84 263
Pecan Cake with Praline Glaze, '82 196
Pecan-Cornmeal Rounds, '95 99
Pecan Roulade, '87 183
Peppermint Candy Cake, '89 254
Persimmon Cake, '79 205
Petit Fours, Simple, '92 277
Petits Fours, '79 117
Petits Fours, Chocolate-Almond, '93 255
Petits Fours, Teatime, '85 119
Pineapple Cake, Heavenly, '83 303
Pineapple-Pecan Upside-Down Cake, '84 25
Pineapple Upside-Down Cake, '80 102; '88 10
Pineapple Upside-Down Cake, Skillet, '85 242
Pineapple Upside-Down Cake, Stacked, '86 239
Popcorn-Gumdrop Cake, '87 262
Poppy Seed Cake, '92 174; '95 63
Poppy Seed Cake, Lemon-, '93 154
Poppy Seed Cake, Plantation, '79 13
Poppy Seed Loaf Cake, '81 63
Poppy Seed Loaf, Quick, '82 75
Pound
   Apple Cider Pound Cake, '84 10
   Apricot Brandy Pound Cake, '83 267
   Black Walnut Pound Cake, '92 16
   Bourbon-Pecan Pound Cake, '91 270
   Brandied Pound Cake, '89 292
   Brown Sugar Pound Cake, '82 135
   Buttermilk Pound Cake, '79 285; '85 255
   Buttermilk Pound Cake, Old-Fashioned, '82 52
   Buttermilk Pound Cake, Spiced, '84 73
   Butter-Nut Pound Cake, '86 235
   Butternut Pound Cake with Caramel Sauce, Betty's, '95 308
   Butterscotch-Pecan Pound Cake, '92 153
   Caramel Frosting, Pound Cake with, '87 39
   Carrot Pound Cake, '87 41
   Cherry Pound Cake, Cute-as-a-Button, '95 139
   Chocolate Chip Pound Cake, '86 178; '93 105; '94 100
   Chocolate Marble Pound Cake, '88 16
   Chocolate-Orange Pound Cake, '89 94
   Chocolate Pound Cake, '82 88; '84 10; '89 325; '94 288
   Chocolate Pound Cake with Frosting, '90 284
   Chocolate Pound Cake with Fudge Frosting, '87 296

   Chocolate-Sour Cream Pound Cake, '83 239; '92 153
   Coconut-Cream Cheese Pound Cake, '85 297; '90 305
   Coconut Cream Pound Cake, '84 10
   Coconut Pound Cake, '82 87; '91 224
   Cream Cheese Pound Cake, '81 290; '86 287; '95 304
   Cream Cheese Pound Cake, Crusty, '89 124
   Croutons, Cinnamon Pound Cake, '93 161
   Daiquiri Pound Cake, '93 83
   Eggnog-Pecan Pound Cake, '95 313
   Eggnog Pound Cake, '90 253
   Favorite Pound Cake, '81 132; '92 171
   Five-Flavor Pound Cake, '87 264
   Four-Flavor Pound Cake, '91 136
   Fruited Pound Cake, '81 265
   Glazed Pound Cake, '89 207
   Golden Pound Cake, '90 284
   I Remember Pound Cake, '86 180
   Irish Cream-and-Coffee Pound Cake, '92 287
   Lemon Pound Cake, '82 88
   Lemon-Sour Cream Pound Cake, '87 38
   Loaf, Pound Cake, '85 306
   Mahogany Pound Cake, '89 207
   Marbled Pecan Pound Cake, '93 313
   Marble Pound Cake, '95 29
   Milk Chocolate Pound Cake, '90 306
   Million Dollar Pound Cake, '90 306
   Mini Pound Cakes, '86 148
   Old-Fashioned Buttermilk Pound Cake, '88 16
   Old-Fashioned Pound Cake, '80 279; '82 88; '93 120
   Orange-Pecan Pound Cake, '93 13
   Orange Pound Cake, '87 84, 221; '92 69
   Peach-Almond Pound Cake, '89 86
   Pineapple Pound Cake, '79 148
   Pound Cake, '92 94
   Praline Pound Cake, '82 88
   Problems to Avoid Chart, '84 319
   Pumpkin Pound Cake, '92 235
   Rose-Geranium Pound Cake, Mrs. Willoughby's, '84 318
   Rum Pound Cake, Buttered, '83 220
   Sandwich, Grilled Pound Cake Dessert, '94 171
   Sour Cream-Orange Pecan Pound Cake, '89 207
   Sour Cream Pound Cake, '89 56; '92 153
   Sour Cream Pound Cake, Cinnamon-Topped, '82 43
   Sour Cream Pound Cake, Elegant, '83 79
   Southern Pound Cake, Smoothest, '93 237
   Strawberry-Banana Topping, Pound Cake with, '89 200
   Sweet Potato Pound Cake, '83 85
   Whipping Cream Pound Cake, '90 284
   White Chocolate Pound Cake, '91 101
   Yogurt Pound Cake, '84 10
Praline Cake, '81 162
Praline Ice Cream Cake, '80 84
Prune Cake, '85 223
Prune Cake and Sauce, '85 118
Prune Cake, Spicy, '79 136
Pudding Cake, Danish, '91 269

CAKES *(continued)*

Pudding Cake with Blueberry Sauce, Buttermilk-Lemon, '95 135
Pumpkin Cake, '81 272; '93 303
Pumpkin Date Cake, '79 251
Pumpkin Kahlúa Cake, '86 292
Pumpkin Layer Cake, '80 245
Pumpkin Roll, '79 206; '91 297
Queen Bee Cake, '81 237
Raisin Layer Cake, Spicy, '79 230
Red Velvet Cake, '93 318
Satin Ribbon Cake, '92 68
Sauerkraut Cake, '94 254
Savarin, '79 171
Shortcake, Orange-Strawberry, '95 100
Shortcakes, Cheesy Chicken, '95 98
Sorghum Cake, '85 239
Sorghum Tea Cakes, '85 239
Spice Cake, '81 162
Spice Cake, Buttermilk, '81 211
Spice Cake, Dark, '82 314; '83 43
Spice Cake, Old South, '84 263
Spice Cake, Sugar 'n, '84 226
Spice Cake with Caramel Frosting, '82 314; '83 42
Spice Cake with Chocolate-Coffee Frosting, '88 268
Spice Cake, Yule Log, '85 314
Spice Layer Cake with Coffee Frosting, '94 86
Sponge
    Burnt Sugar Sponge Cake with Berry Sauce, '95 103
    Chocolaty Sponge Cake, '86 60
    Coffee Sponge Cake, '83 229; '91 55
    Coffee Sponge Cake, Two-Day, '86 75
    Daffodil Sponge Cake, '79 175; '80 6; '84 315
    Passover Sponge Cake, '90 106
    Strawberries 'n Cream Sponge Cake Roll, '81 95
    Yellow Sponge Cake, '80 250
Squash Cake, '86 200
Stack Cake, Favorite, '87 228
Stack Cake, Old-Fashioned, '81 216
Strawberry Cake Roll, '79 49; '83 129; '84 305; '85 172
Strawberry Cream Cake, '86 61
Strawberry Crispy Shortcakes, '93 42
Strawberry Crunch Cake, '79 288; '80 35
Strawberry Delight Cake, '85 30
Strawberry Ice Cream Roll, '84 105
Strawberry Meringue Cake, '86 240
Strawberry Pinwheel Shortcake, '89 112
Strawberry Roll, '82 120
Strawberry Roll, Heavenly, '82 176
Strawberry Shortcake, '81 96; '83 122; '92 184; '94 162
Strawberry Shortcake, A Favorite, '88 136
Strawberry Shortcake, Elegant, '88 37
Strawberry Shortcake Jubilee, '88 209
Strawberry Shortcake Shells, '88 196
Strawberry Yogurt Layer Cake, '94 85
Sweet Potato Cake, '79 207; '89 295
Sweet Potato Loaf Cake, '81 224
Sweet Potato Log Roll, '82 227
Sweet Potato Surprise Cake, '80 287
Tea Cake, Lemon, '82 169
Tea Cakes, Mexican, '81 196
Teacakes, Old-Fashioned, '84 43
Teddy Bear Cakes, '92 278
Tipsy Squire, '85 41

Tortes
    Amaretto Torte, '82 303
    Apricot Praline Torte, Lucy's, '95 243
    Apricot Sponge Torte, '90 59
    Black Forest Torte, '88 209
    Black Forrest Cherry Torte, '88 178
    Carob-Pecan Torte, '85 218
    Chocolate Mint Torte, '94 86
    Chocolate-Pecan Torte, '89 42
    Chocolate Praline Torte, '84 165
    Chocolate-Strawberry Ice Cream Torte, '79 7
    Chocolate Torte, Apricot-Filled, '90 107
    Chocolate Torte, Double-, '79 67
    Chocolate Torte Royale, '82 263
    Chocolate Velvet Torte, '86 316
    Hazelnut Torte, '91 248
    Lemon Meringue Torte with Raspberry Sauce, '93 82
    Mocha Brownie Torte, '85 102
    Mocha-Pecan Torte, '86 26
    Mocha Velvet Torte, '92 318
    Passover Linzer Torte, '90 106
    Pecan, Torte Heavenly, '81 266
    Spring Torte, '91 57
    Strawberry Meringue Torte, '88 136
    Sugar Cookie Torte, '79 68
    Toffee Meringue Torte, '87 118
Twelfth Night Cake, '93 337
Upside Down Cake, Quick, '90 219
Upside-Down Sunburst Cake, '87 9
Vanilla Chiffon Cake, '79 266
Walnut Cream Roll, '84 192
White Cake, Buttermilk, '86 235
White Cake with Strawberries and Chocolate Glaze, '87 76
White Cake with Strawberry Frosting, Rich, '89 184
Yogurt-Lemon-Nut Cake, '89 169
Zucchini Cake, '79 24
Zucchini-Pineapple Cake, '95 160
Zuppa Inglese, '85 229

CANDIES
Almond Brittle Candy, '80 255
Almond Butter Crunch, '80 301
Almond Roca, '86 49
Almond-Toffee Crunch, '88 285
Apples, Candied Red, '81 217
Apples, Candy, '84 243
Apricot Balls, '79 274
Balls, No-Cook Candy, '85 14
Bourbon Balls, '81 254; '83 315; '90 83
Bourbon Balls, Chocolate, '84 298
Brandy Balls, '86 319
Brittle with Crushed Peanuts, '87 184
Buckeyes, '85 321
Butter Creams, '80 302
Buttermilk Candy, '80 302
Caramel Corn Candy, '84 243
Caramel Good Stuff, Baked, '80 284
Caramel-Peanut Squares, '85 247
Chocolate Brittle, '83 315
Chocolate Brittle, Quick, '82 114
Chocolate Caramels, '91 35
Chocolate-Coconut Almond Drops, '87 223
Chocolate-Covered Cherries, '81 286; '84 298
Chocolate-Covered Pecan Fritters, '79 205
Chocolate-Covered Pretzels, '82 295
Chocolate Drops, '84 111
Chocolate Greeting Card, '83 40
Chocolate-Marshmallow Squares, '92 M50

Chocolate-Nut Log Candy, '86 335
Chocolate Nut Teasers, '91 35
Chocolate-Peanut Butter Balls, '80 87
Chocolate-Peanut Butter Bites, '92 M317
Chocolate-Peanut Butter Drops, '92 322
Chocolate-Peanut Clusters, '81 16
Chocolate Peanutty Swirls, '94 M330
Chocolate Rum Balls, '80 302
Chocolate-Rum Balls, '88 285
Chocolates, Liqueur Cream-Filled, '87 258
Chocolate Spiders, '85 236
Chocolates, Spirited, '86 278
Chocolate, Tempered, '91 35
Chocolate Velvets, '84 298
Coconut-Almond Balls, '84 256
Coconut-Black Walnut Bonbons, '82 307
Coconut Candy, '79 272; '80 250
Corn Brittle, Crunchy, '85 208
Crème de Cacao Balls, '86 266
Crème de Menthe Chocolates, '91 36
Crystal Candy, '84 299
Date Candy, '89 308
Date Loaf Candy, '80 302
Date Logs, '79 274
Divinity, Apricot, '83 297
Divinity, Christmas, '81 286
Divinity Ghosts, '95 273
Divinity, Peanut, '85 233; '87 M278
Divinity, Pink, '86 49
Divinity, Strawberry, '91 272
Frosting, Chocolate Candy, '81 238
Fruit Balls, '82 296; '84 299
Fudge
    Almond Fudge, Creamy, '95 51
    Buttermilk Fudge, '95 52
    Butterscotch Rum Fudge, '88 256
    Caramel Fudge, '91 273
    Cherry Nut Fudge, '83 315
    Chocolate Fudge, '82 20
    Chocolate Fudge, Five Pounds of, '95 51
    Chocolate-Peanut Butter Fudge, '87 257; '90 311
    Coffee-Chip Fudge, '86 74
    Cream Cheese Fudge, '84 111
    Creamy Dark Fudge, '82 295
    Creamy Fudge, '81 218
    Diamond Fudge, '92 193
    Double-Good Fudge, '79 M263; '95 M50
    Double Good Fudge, '87 M278
    Fast Fudge, '79 274
    Four Chips Fudge, '92 318
    Fudge, '86 266
    Microwave Chocolate Fudge, '92 M50
    Microwave Fudge, '91 M92
    Mint Fudge, '95 50
    Mint Fudge, Dinner, '88 285
    Mocha Fudge, Creamy, '95 51
    Mocha Fudge, Holiday, '84 298
    Nut Fudge, Quick, '83 316
    Nutty White Fudge, '81 253
    Orange-Walnut Fudge, '92 288
    Peanut Butter Fudge, '80 302; '89 307; '95 51
    Peanut Butter Fudge, Creamy, '92 240
    Peanut Butter Fudge, Marbled, '88 65
    Peanut-Fudge Bites, '91 M231; '92 M68
    Peanut Fudge, Double, '85 91
    Pecan Fudge, Creamy, '84 321
    Penuche, '79 272
    Pistachio Fudge, '83 298
    Quick-and-Easy Fudge, '88 M190

CANDIES, Fudge (continued)

Scotch Ring, Fudge, '79 273
Sour Cream Fudge, '95 52
Strawberry Fudge Balls, '93 80
Tiger Butter, '86 48
White Chocolate-Coffee Fudge, '94 232
White Chocolate Fudge, '92 317; '95 51
Kentucky Colonels, '79 273
Lollipops, Colorful Molded, '81 218
Marzipan, '83 306
Millionaires, '79 M262
Mints, Cream Cheese, '93 79
Mints, Dinner, '88 66
Mints, Easy Holiday, '84 299
Mints, Party, '79 273; '81 119
Mint Twists, '86 106
Molded Candies, '84 40
Nut Clusters, '81 254
Nuts, Candied, '81 261
Orange Balls, '94 331
Orange Peel, Candied, '81 286
Peanut Brittle, '79 M263; '80 87; '84 298; '92 240
Peanut Brittle, Golden, '83 223
Peanut Brittle, Never-Fail, '79 273
Peanut Brittle, Orange, '80 302
Peanut Butter Candy, '93 166
Peanut Butter-Chocolate Balls, '80 269
Peanut Butter-Chocolate Candy Squares, '82 56
Peanut Butter Creams, '79 273
Peanut Butter Easter Eggs, '87 86
Peanut Butter Temptations, '84 29
Peanut Butter Yummies, '83 223
Peanut Clusters, '87 184; '92 288
Peanutty Clusters, '83 143
Pecan Brittle, '91 272
Pecan Clusters, '81 266
Pecan Clusters, Roasted, '85 233; '90 310
Pecan-Coconut Clusters, '86 M251
Pecan Rolls, '79 285
Pecans, Brown Sugar, '81 266
Pecans, Glazed, '81 254
Pecans, Honeycomb, '84 300
Pecans, Orange, '84 299
Pecans, Spiced, '79 296; '81 286
Pecans, Spicy, '81 289
Pecans, Sugar-and-Honey, '86 319
Peppermint Patties, '86 278
Potato Candy, '79 273
Pralines
    Basic Pralines, '92 313; '93 50
    Bourbon Pralines, '92 313; '93 51
    Butterscotch Pralines, '81 253
    Café au Lait Pralines, '92 313; '93 51
    Chocolate-Mint Pralines, '92 313; '93 51
    Chocolate-Peanut Butter Pralines, '92 313; '93 51
    Chocolate Pralines, '92 313; '93 51
    Coffee Pralines, Plantation, '86 241
    Creamy Pralines, '80 198; '92 289
    Dark Praline Clusters, '86 313
    Dark Pralines, '83 52
    Hot Spicy Pralines, '92 313; '93 51
    Maple-Pecan Pralines, '83 222
    Mocha Pralines, '92 313; '93 51
    New Orleans-Style Pralines, '86 335
    Old-Fashioned Pralines, '89 318
    Orange Pralines, '92 313; '93 51
    Peanut Butter Pralines, '92 313; '93 51
    Pecan Pralines, Original, '81 11

    Pralines, '79 272; '86 M288; '89 60; '90 48
    Southern Pralines, '79 M263
    Spicy Praline Delights, '84 299
    Texas-Size Pralines, '79 186
    Vanilla Pralines, '92 313; '93 51
Quemada (Burnt-Sugar Candy), '87 38
Raisin Candy, Mixed, '84 111
Raspberry Cream Chocolates, '91 36
Red Rock Candy, '92 240
Rocky Road, '84 298
Rum Balls, '93 314
Strawberries, Christmas, '94 331
Taffy, Old-Fashioned, '80 302
Toffee, English, '79 273
Toffee, Microwave, '92 M317
Toffee, Nutty, '79 M263
Truffles, Almond, '83 298
Truffles, Amaretto Dessert, '86 319
Truffles, Bittersweet, '94 330
Truffles, Chocolate, '85 114; '89 43; '91 108
Truffles, Chocolate-Kahlúa, '92 285
Truffles, Orange-Pecan, '95 92
Truffles, White Chocolate, '87 45
Truffles, Yule Street, '90 242
Turtle Candies, '93 M41
White Chocolate Salties, '92 50
White Chocolate Surprises, '91 36

CANNING AND PRESERVING
Apple Rings, Cinnamon, '85 107
Asparagus, Pickled, '83 46
Beets, Pickled, '81 216
Berries (except Strawberries), '80 128
Black-Eyed, Field, and Crowder Peas, '80 126
Catsup, Homemade, '85 188
Catsup, Spicy Tomato, '83 182
Chili Sauce, '81 175
Chili Sauce, Chunky, '85 188
Chow-Chow, '82 196
Confit, Roasted Shallot-Garlic, '94 303
Corn, Cold-Pack, '81 216
Corn, Cream-Style, '80 127; '85 106
Corn, Whole Kernel, '85 106
Cranberry Conserve, '83 279
Fruit Juices, '85 107
Fruit, Unsweetened Mixed, '83 182
Green Beans, '80 126
Green Bean Salad, Pickled, '82 239
Green Beans, Appalachian, '81 215
Green Beans, Dill, '93 136
Green, Snap, or Wax Beans, '85 105
Lima Beans, '80 127
Mincemeat, Homemade, '79 245
Nectarines in Apple Juice, '83 183
Okra, '80 127
Peaches, '80 128
Peaches and Pears, '85 106
Peaches, Honey-Sweet, '85 107
Pear Mincemeat, '79 196
Piccalilli, Kentucky, '81 216
Sauerkraut, Homemade, '81 216
Squash, Summer, '80 127; '85 105
Succotash, '85 106
Tomatoes, '80 128; '85 106
Tomatoes, Canned Flavored, '95 217
Tomatoes, Stewed, '83 182
Tomatoes with Okra, '85 106
Tomato Juice, Spicy, '85 189
Tomato Puree, Seasoned, '83 182
Vegetable Soup, '80 128; '85 106

CARAMEL
Apples, Caramel, '79 220; '89 M231
Apples, Caramel-Peanut, '93 M244

Apples, Old English Caramel, '85 231
Baked Caramel Good Stuff, '80 284
Bars, Oatmeal-Caramel, '85 247
Bars, Yummy, '92 171
Biscuits, Caramel Dessert, '95 36
Bombe, Caramel-Toffee, '93 214
Bread, Caramel, '82 75
Brie with Fresh Fruit, Caramel, '90 266
Cake, Caramel, '89 55; '90 307
Cake, Caramel-Filled Butter Pecan, '88 278
Cake, Chocolate-Caramel-Nut, '83 23
Cake, Creamy Caramel Layer, '81 71
Candy, Caramel Corn, '84 243
Cheesecake, Chocolate-Caramel-Pecan, '91 197
Chocolate Caramels, '91 35
Cobbler, Peach-Caramel, '86 300; '87 178
Cookies, Caramel-Filled Chocolate, '92 319
Corn, Baked Caramel, '81 218
Corn, Caramel, '88 64
Corn, Nutty Caramel, '92 317
Corn, Oven-Made Caramel, '91 233
Crème d'Ange, '83 91
Crunch, Caramel, '95 165
Dessert, Coconut-Caramel, '92 44
Drizzle, Caramel, '86 247
Filling, Caramel, '88 278
Flans, Caramel-Crowned, '90 227
Flan with Caramel, Baked, '92 231
Fondue, Caramel, '94 331; '95 35
Frosting, Caramel, '81 278, M289; '82 314; '83 43; '84 39, 263; '86 239; '87 265; '89 55, 236; '90 307
Frosting, Creamy Caramel, '81 71
Frosting, Easy Caramel, '87 39
Frosting, Favorite Caramel, '83 106
Fudge, Caramel, '91 273
Helado, Caramel-Vanilla (Caramel-Vanilla Ice Cream), '81 67
Ice Cream Dessert, Caramel, '95 36
Millionaires, '79 M262
Peaches, Caramel, '93 134
Pie, Burnt Caramel, '82 53
Pie, Caramel-Banana, '86 M165
Pie, Caramel Ice Cream, '82 181
Pie, Caramel-Nut Crunch, '94 244
Pie, Caramel-Peanut, '86 259
Pie, Caramel-Pecan, '88 282
Pie, Caramel-Pecan Apple, '85 247
Pie, Luscious Caramel Banana, '79 115
Pies, Coconut-Caramel, '87 260
Popcorn, Caramel, '79 219; '86 M212
Popcorn, Crispy Caramel, '85 247
Ring, Caramel-Orange Coffee, '80 45
Ring, Easy Caramel, '85 M89
Rolls, Caramel Breakfast, '79 193
Rolls, Caramel-Nut, '86 312
Rolls, Easy Caramel, '90 195
Sauce, Caramel, '79 79; '91 56, 180; '93 210, 235, 296; '94 234; '95 308
Sauce, Caramel-Raisin, '88 127
Sauce, Easy Caramel, '87 38
Sauce, Pears with Orange-Caramel, '95 281
Sauce, Toffee-Fudge, '89 95
Sauce, White Caramel, '92 195
Squares, Caramel-Peanut, '85 247
Squares, Chocolate-Caramel Layer, '79 83
Sticky Buns, Easy Caramel-Chocolate, '95 36
Surprise, Caramel, '88 202
Syrup, Caramel, '82 43
Tart, Caramel Turtle Truffle, '93 M131
Tarts, Caramel, '82 43

CARROTS

Aloha Carrots, '85 261
Ambrosia, Carrot-Marshmallow, '80 5
Apricot Carrots, '84 6
Aspic, Orange-and-Carrot, '86 199
Baby Carrots, Zucchini with, '88 24
Bake, Apple-Carrot, '93 304
Bake, Creamy Carrot, '85 67
Ball, Carrot-Cheese, '86 325
Balls, Carrot, '79 178
Bourbonnaise, Baby Carrots, '85 89
Braised Carrots and Celery, '86 327
Brandied Carrots, '87 253
Brandy Sauce, Carrots in, '83 86
Breads
    Carrot Bread, '89 143
    Cornbread, Carrot, '80 89; '81 163
    Muffins, Apple-Carrot, '91 213
    Muffins, Carrot-and-Raisin, '87 24
    Muffins, Carrot-Date-Nut, '86 262
    Muffins, Carrot-Pineapple, '81 6
    Muffins, Carrot-Wheat, '88 9
    Muffins, Morning Glory, '93 327
    Pineapple Bread, Carrot-, '82 210
    Pineapple-Carrot Bread, '79 106
    Tasty Carrot Bread, '84 328
    Three-C Bread, '81 284
    Walnut Bread, Carrot-, '88 284
    Zucchini-Carrot Bread, '83 190
Brussels Sprouts, Carrots and, '82 300
Buttered Carrots and Celery, '89 44
Caprice, Carrots, '84 6
Cardamom Carrots, '89 271
Casserole, Carrot, '86 279; '87 285
Casserole, Carrot and Zucchini, '83 256
Casserole, Carrot-Pecan, '93 44
Casserole, Cauliflower-and-Carrot, '83 280
Casserole, Scrumptious Carrot, '84 328
Casserole, Squash-Carrot, '81 157
Celeriac and Carrots, '91 219
Chowchow, Carrot, '93 218
Classy Carrots, '94 36
Combo, Carrot, '79 45
Cooler, Carrot, '89 35
Curried Carrots and Pineapple, '90 228
Desserts
    Cake, Applesauce Carrot, '81 202
    Cake, Blue Ribbon Carrot, '81 70
    Cake, Brownie Carrot, '92 120
    Cake, Carrot, '79 45; '82 137; '84 315
    Cake, Carrot Pound, '87 41
    Cake, Carrot Pudding, '83 24
    Cake, Coconut-Pecan Carrot, '84 322
    Cake, Easy Carrot, '83 215
    Cake, Easy Carrot Snack, '82 235
    Cake, Fresh Coconut-Carrot, '80 299
    Cake, Frosted Carrot, '92 19
    Cake, Old-Fashioned Carrot, '83 M232
    Cake, Old-South Carrot, '80 120
    Cake, Quick-and-Easy Carrot, '84 150
    Cakes, Miniature Carrot, '90 94
    Cake, Spiced Carrot, '87 296
    Cake, Spicy Fruited Carrot, '85 117
    Cake, Zucchini-Carrot, '93 20
    Cookies, Carrot, '82 137
    Cookies, Carrot-Orange, '83 149
    Cookies, Frosted Carrot, '81 7
    Cupcakes, Carrot-Bran, '82 16
    Pie, Carrot Custard, '79 45
    Pie, Carrot Ice Cream, '86 200
Deviled Carrots, '83 322
Dilled Baby Carrots, '84 80; '92 145
Dilled Carrots, '85 24; '90 17

Dill-Spiced Carrots, '87 200
Dilly Carrots, '85 85
Fillets, Apple-Carrot Stuffed, '88 M192
Fried Carrot Balls, '82 16
Fried Carrots, Crispy, '94 36
Garden Surprise, '83 112
Ginger Carrots, '83 9; '85 139
Gingered Carrots, '85 95; '92 302
Glazed
    Apricot Glazed Carrots, '80 89
    Baby Carrots, Glazed, '91 291; '92 256
    Baby Carrots, Mint-Glazed, '89 102
    Bacon and Onion, Glazed Carrots with,
        '87 200
    Candied Carrots, '82 269; '83 225
    Ginger Carrots, '83 9
    Ginger-Cinnamon Carrots, '93 168
    Gingered Carrots, '85 95
    Ginger-Glazed Carrots, '87 68
    Glazed Carrots, '81 304; '83 117;
        '85 258; '88 304; '89 106, 235
    Golden Carrots, '85 267
    Grapes, Glazed Carrots with, '82 287
    Harvard Carrots, '83 117
    Honey-Glazed Carrots, '80 115;
        '84 121; '85 18; '92 229
    Honey-Kissed Carrots, '84 122
    Horseradish Glaze, Carrots with, '85 66
    Lemon-Glazed Carrots, '84 16
    Light Glazed Carrots, '92 227
    Mint-Glazed Carrots and Peas, '90 291
    Onions, Glazed Carrots and, '83 25;
        '87 128
    Orange-Glazed Carrots, '79 12;
        '81 M165; '90 M98
    Orange-Raisin Carrots, '80 24
    Peach-Glazed Carrots, '90 13
    Pineapple Carrots, '83 198
    Spice-Glazed Carrots, '83 M58
    Sunshine Carrots, '82 16
Herbed Carrots and Onions, '87 31
Horseradish Sauce, Carrots and Broccoli with,
    '91 246
Julienne Carrots, How to Prepare, '84 120
Julienne Carrots, Sautéed, '82 91
Julienne Carrots with Walnuts, '84 188
Julienne, Tarragon Carrots, '84 329
Julienne, Turnips and Carrots, '86 295
Julienne Zucchini and Carrots, '90 14
Lemon-Carrot Bundles, '91 80
Lemon Carrots, '82 300; '83 111
Loaf, Carrot-Nut, '83 117
Madeira, Carrots, '80 125; '83 281
Marinated Beets, Green Beans, and Carrots,
    '88 162
Marinated Carrots, '86 108, 111; '91 103
Marinated Carrots, Creamy, '87 200
Marinated Carrots, Crispy, '81 7
Marinated Carrot Strips, '88 176
Marmalade, Carrot-Citrus, '81 148
Marsala, Carrots, '83 56
Medley, Carrot-and-Leek, '88 102
Medley, Carrot-Lima-Squash, '80 123
Minted Carrots, '81 101
Minted Carrots, Saucy, '82 252
Orange Carrots and Turnips, Sunset, '94 213
Orange-Fennel Carrots, '92 133
Orange Sauce, Carrots in, '82 107
Orange-Spiced Carrots, '88 18
Orangy Carrot Strips, '89 312
Parsleyed Turnips and Carrots, '79 253
Patties, Carrot, '80 89
Pecans, Carrots and Celery with, '84 254

Pickled Carrots, '93 12
Pie, Carrot, '83 117
Pie, Cauliflower-Carrot, '82 191
Polynesian, Carrots, '79 45
Pudding, Carrot-Potato, '94 279
Puff, Carrot, '84 328; '89 89
Puffs, Carrot, '87 200
Puree, Carrot-and-Sweet Potato, '94 56
Puree, Carrot-Sweet Potato, '92 90
Ring, Festive Carrot, '82 16
Ring, Rice-Carrot, '79 246
Roasted Carrots, '92 340
Roasted Potatoes, Carrots, and Leeks, '94 276
Rosemary Carrots, '91 219
Salad, Apple-Carrot, '85 22
Salad, Carrot, '82 137
Salad, Carrot-Ambrosia, '81 252
Salad, Carrot-and-Zucchini, '83 240
Salad, Carrot-Caraway, '89 105
Salad, Carrot-Pineapple, '91 83
Salad, Carrot-Raisin, '83 117; '84 174; '87 10
Salad, Carrot-Tangerine, '83 316; '84 16
Salad, Creamy Carrot-Nut, '86 331
Salad, Favorite Carrot, '80 33
Salad, Fruity Carrot-and-Seed, '86 223
Salad, Harvest Carrot, '89 128
Salad, Honey-Sweet Carrot, '89 161
Salad, Lime-Carrot, '92 65
Salad, Orange-Carrot, '80 89; '84 325
Salad, Shredded Carrot, '80 178
Salad, Simple Carrot, '82 101; '84 152
Salad, Sunshine Carrot, '82 132
Salad, Turkey-Carrot, '86 283
Salad, Turnip-and-Carrot, '91 212
Saucy Carrots, '87 41
Sauté, Carrot-Turnip, '93 241
Sautéed Zucchini and Carrots, '92 62, 99
Savory Sauce, Lima Beans and Carrots with,
    '84 196
Scalloped Carrots, '81 6
Scalloped Carrots-and-Celery, '84 M112
Scalloped Carrots, Cheese, '94 36
Slaw, Apple-Carrot, '92 243
Soufflé, Carrot, '79 73
Soufflé, Carrots, '83 265
Soup, Carrot, '80 88; '89 146
Soup, Carrot Cream, '90 210
Soup, Carrot-Leek, '86 34
Soup, Carrot-Orange, '79 172
Soup, Cheesy Carrot, '81 262
Soup, Chilled Carrot-Mint, '90 M168
Soup, Cream of Carrot, '81 307; '88 46;
    '91 69
Soup, Cream of Carrot-and-Tomato,
    '94 176
Soup, Creamy Carrot, '92 218
Soup, Curried Carrot, '82 157
Soup, Potato-Carrot, '88 297
Soup, Savory Carrot, '84 107
Special Carrots, '81 108; '84 6
Spiced Carrots Polynesian, '88 85
Spread, Nutty Carrot, '94 123
Squares, Carrot, '79 256
Squares, Golden Carrot-Lemon, '80 40
Steamed Carrots, Lemon-Dill, '93 180
Sticks, Carrot, '89 106
Stuffed Carrots, '86 324; '87 40
Sugar Snaps and Carrots, Creamed,
    '93 139
Sunshine Carrots, '82 16; '83 25
Supreme, Broccoli-Carrot, '89 331
Swamp Sticks, '95 274
Sweet-and-Sour Carrots, '82 137

CARROTS *(continued)*

Sweet-and-Sour Green Beans and Carrots,
'83 6
Tarragon Carrots, '83 173
Tipsy Carrots, '87 40
Toss, Asparagus-Carrot-Squash, '91 45
Toss, Carrot-Fruit, '82 235
Tropical Carrots, '84 34
Veal and Carrots, Company, '85 22
Veal and Carrots in Wine Sauce, '81 31;
'86 M139
White Wine, Carrots in, '81 109
Wine Sauce, Carrots in, '80 88
Zesty Carrots, '84 5
Zucchini and Carrots, Buttered, '83 252
Zucchini, Carrots and, '84 262

CASSEROLES. *See also* **LASAGNA.**
Apple-Cheese Casserole, '84 287
Barley, Baked, '91 133
Barley Casserole, '84 281
Bean
　Baked Bean Medley, '80 100
　Baked Beans, Hawaiian-Style, '86 210
　Baked Beans, Maple Heights, '91 223
　Baked Beans Quintet, '94 100
　Baked Beans, Three-Meat, '86 210
　Baked Beans with Ham, '80 136
　Beef-and-Bean Bake, Cheesy, '82 89
　Black Beans, Casserole of, '95 27
　Chuck Wagon Bean Casserole, '93 198
　Cornbread Casserole, Bean-and-, '92 243
　Green Bean and Artichoke Casserole,
　　Italian, '85 81
　Green Bean-and-Corn Casserole, '88 123
　Green Bean Casserole, '79 106; '84 145
　Green Bean Casserole, Easy, '87 284
　Green Bean Italiano, '94 248
　Green Bean Salad, Hot, '86 298
　Green Beans au Gratin, '80 116
　Green Beans, French Quarter, '80 298;
　　'81 26
　Green Beans in Sour Cream, '80 116
　Green Beans, Italian, '85 147
　Green Beans Italian, '87 10
　Green Bean Surprise, '86 9
　Green Beans with Sour Cream, '82 90
　Kidney Bean Casserole, '90 136
　Lentils with Cheese, Baked, '84 113
　Lima-Bacon Bake, '86 9
　Lima Bean Casserole, '79 189; '83 313;
　　'86 225; '87 284; '95 132
　Lima Bean Casserole, Spicy, '79 189
　Lima Bean Casserole, Swiss, '80 191
　Lima Bean Garden Casserole, '83 218;
　　'84 246
　Lima Beans Deluxe, '79 289; '80 26
　Lima Beans, Savory, '83 219; '84 246
　Lima Beans, Super, '79 189

Lima Beans with Canadian Bacon,
　'83 219; '84 245
Lima Casserole, Ham and, '79 192
Limas, Spanish Cheese, '86 225
Mexican Bean Casserole, Spicy, '84 114
Three-Bean Bake, '81 155
Three-Bean Casserole, '88 56
White Bean Bake, Turnip Greens and,
　'94 246
Breakfast and Brunch
　Apple-Egg Casserole, '85 44
　Bacon and Egg Casserole, '81 225
　Bacon-and-Eggs Scramble, '80 M267
　Breakfast Casserole, '91 285
　Brunch Casserole, '82 124
　Bunch, Brunch for a, '88 57
　Cheese Blintz Casserole, '92 251
　Cheesy Breakfast Casserole, '85 247
　Cheesy Brunch Casserole, Easy, '92 91
　Chile-Hominy Casserole, '81 29
　Chile 'n' Cheese Breakfast Casserole,
　　'88 57
　Corned Beef Brunch Bake, '82 44
　Cornmeal Puff, '82 42
　Cranberry-Apple Casserole, '83 311
　Egg-and-Bacon Casserole, '85 248
　Egg-and-Cheese Casserole, '84 293
　Egg-and-Cheese Puff, '85 45
　Egg Casserole, '83 311
　Egg Casserole, Brunch, '86 329
　Egg Casserole, Cheesy, '81 244; '86 15
　Egg Casserole, Scrambled, '80 51;
　　'86 241
　Egg Casserole, Sunday, '95 100
　Egg-Mushroom Casserole, '83 49
　Eggs Bel-Mar, '90 92
　Eggs, Bruncheon, '83 83
　Eggs, Chile, '88 80
　Eggs, Creole, '82 42
　Egg Soufflé Casserole, '83 55
　Fruit Bake, Hot, '81 270
　Grits, Baked Cheese-and-Garlic, '83 292
　Grits Casserole, Cheesy, '81 270
　Grits Casserole, Garlic, '81 47
　Grits, Orange, '81 47
　Grits-Sausage Casserole, '84 75; '86 241
　Grits, Swiss-and-Cheddar Baked, '91 71
　Ham and Egg Casserole, Breakfast,
　　'79 253
　Hash Brown Cheese Bake, '82 50
　Hash Brown Potato Casserole, '81 40
　Hominy, Gold Coast, '83 52
　Huevos Rancheros, '82 197
　Potato Breakfast Casserole, '80 52
　Sausage-and-Egg Casserole, '94 284
　Sausage Breakfast Casserole, '81 270
　Sausage Brunch, Italian, '88 57
　Sausage Casserole, Hawaiian, '85 42
　Sausage Casserole, Swiss, '80 209
　Sausage-Cheese Bake, '88 58
　Sausage, Country Grits and, '83 54
　Sausage Egg Bake, '81 225
　Sausage-Egg Bake, Smoked, '85 248
　Sausage-Mushroom Breakfast Casserole,
　　'86 95
　Sausage Strata, '83 243
Broccoli-Ham au Gratin, '90 239
Brown Rice Casserole, '87 118
Cannelloni, '92 17
Cheese Bake, Continental, '81 89
Cheese Casserole, Feather-Light, '79 84
Cheese Casserole, Four, '92 170
Chile-Cheese Casserole, '82 90

Chiles Rellenos Casserole, '79 84; '92 18
Chili Casserole, '90 176
Chili-Rice Casserole, '79 54
Chili-Tamale Pie, '83 68
Egg and Rice Bake, '83 119
Egg Casserole, Saucy Scrambled, '89 213
Eggplant-and-Oyster Louisiane, '95 196
Eggplant-Sausage-Pasta Casserole, Freezer,
　'95 197
Enchilada Casserole, '87 287
Enchilada Casserole, Green, '79 76
Franks, Mexican, '93 78
Fruit Casserole, Sherried, '80 284
Fruit, Gingered Baked, '81 232
Grits, Garlic-Cheese, '86 180
Grits, Garlicky Ham-and-Spinach, '94 177
Grits Italiano, '92 43
Grits with Green Chiles, Cheese, '95 208
Hominy Casserole, Cheesy, '83 170
Hominy-Chili Casserole, '86 255
Hominy, Hot Cheese, '84 77
Hominy, Jalapeño, '82 51
Hominy with Chiles and Cheese, '86 78
Italian Casserole, '90 238
Kale, Scalloped, '86 224
Lentils-and-Rice Casserole, '93 301
Macaroni and Blue Cheese, '93 248
Macaroni and Cheese, Creamy, '93 249
Macaroni and Cheese, Old-Fashioned,
　'92 215
Macaroni and Cheese, Thick-and-Rich,
　'84 329
Macaroni Bake, Jack-in-the-, '93 249
Macaroni Casserole, '84 220; '87 154
Macaroni, Glorious, '84 76
Macaroni-Mushroom Bake, Cheesy, '81 243
Meat. *See also* Casseroles/Pork.
　Beef-and-Bean Bake, Cheesy, '82 89
　Beef-and-Biscuit Casserole, '83 75
　Beef-and-Noodles Casserole, '84 72
　Beef-and-Vegetable Chow Mein
　　Casserole, '83 313
　Beef Bake, Zesty Cabbage, '80 300
　Beef Bake, Zucchini, '86 146
　Beef Casserole, Crusty, '82 88
　Beef Casserole, Macaroni-Cheese-,
　　'95 125
　Beef Casserole, Spinach and, '79 192
　Beef-Macaroni Bake, '94 255
　Beef-Macaroni Combo, '79 194
　Beef-Noodle Bake, Taco, '81 141
　Beef Supreme, '83 196
　Beefy Vegetable Casserole, '79 248
　Cavatini, '94 214
　Cheeseburger Casserole, '95 255
　Cheesy Mexican Casserole, '82 224
　Chiles Rellenos Casserole, '79 84;
　　'84 31, 234; '92 18
　Chili Hominy Bake, '81 282; '82 58
　Cornbread Casserole, '81 91
　Cornbread Skillet Casserole, '83 243;
　　'84 101
　Cornbread Tamale Bake, '79 163
　Corned Beef and Cabbage au Gratin,
　　'83 16
　County Fair Casserole, '79 130
　El Dorado Casserole, '81 140
　Enchilada Casserole, Firecracker, '80 260
　Enchilada Casserole, Sour Cream,
　　'82 113
　Five-Layer Meal, '81 140
　Frankaroni Potluck Dish, '88 201
　Franks 'n' Beans, Stove-Top, '88 201

CASSEROLES, Meat *(continued)*

Ground Beef and Sausage Casserole, '80 260
Ground Beef Casserole, Cheesy, '79 44
Ground Beef Casserole, Creamy, '81 142
Hamburger-Bean Bake, '95 121
Hamburger Casserole, '95 210
Hamburger-Noodle Bake, '81 140
Hamburger Pie, '81 92
Hot Doggie Casserole, '88 200
Italian Casserole, '80 81
Layered Grecian Bake, '82 119
Matador Mania, '86 19
Moussaka, '87 166; '90 68
Moussaka Casserole, '79 179
Moussaka, Corn, '87 190
Pastichio, '85 194
Pastitsio, '87 12; '88 11
Pizza Casserole, '88 273; '89 181
Pizza Casserole, Quick, '83 266
Sour Cream-Noodle Bake, '79 55
Spaghetti and Beef Casserole, '79 129
Spaghetti Casserole, '84 241
Spinach and Beef Casserole, '79 192
Spinach-Beef-Macaroni Casserole, '83 313
Taco Beef-Noodle Bake, '81 141
Taco Casserole, '80 33
Taco Squares, Deep-Dish, '91 88
Tamale, Mozzarella, '95 70
Tortilla Bake, Texas, '94 285
Veal and Wild Rice Casserole, '79 180
Veal Cutlet Casserole, '79 109
Venison-Vegetable Bake, '87 304
Ziti, Baked, '94 65
Microwave
Asparagus-Pea Casserole, '88 M294
Beans-and-Franks, Polynesian, '84 M11
Beef Casserole, Easy, '86 M58
Beef Casserole, Layered, '82 M203
Beefy Sausage Dinner, '80 M9
Broccoli Casserole, '88 M146
Broccoli-Swiss Cheese Casserole, '85 M211
Carrots-and-Celery, Scalloped, '84 M112
Chicken Divan, '80 M10
Chicken Divan Casserole, '82 M203
Chicken Mexicana, '91 M127
Chicken Tetrazzini, Cheesy, '83 M87
Green Beans, Herbed, '83 M147
Ham-and-Potato Casserole, '83 M87
Ham-Asparagus Dinner, '80 M10
Ham Roll Casserole, '91 M127
Macaroni-Ham Casserole, '81 M177
Mexican Casserole, '92 M22
Mexican Casserole, Microwave, '90 M231
Mexi Casserole, '83 M87
Okra and Tomatoes, Fresh, '81 M165
Onion-Potato Bake, '83 M195
Pineapple, Scalloped, '84 M323
Pizza Casserole, Microwave, '89 M248
Pork Casserole, Cheesy, '81 M74
Potato Casserole, Creamy, '84 M113
Potatoes, Parmesan, '90 M62
Sausage and Rice Casserole, Oriental, '82 M123
Sausage Casserole, Easy, '87 M189
Sausage-Egg Casserole, '86 M12
Sausage Jambalaya Casserole, '82 M203
Spinach Delight, '84 M144

Squash Bake, Cheddar-, '84 M113
Squash Casserole, Cheesy, '82 M21
Squash Casserole, Jiffy, '81 M144
Squash Medley, Fresh, '81 M165
Tuna Casserole, Easy, '82 M203
Turkey Casserole, Crunchy, '89 M282
Zucchini-Egg Casserole, '84 M113
Zucchini, Italian, '83 M147
Paella Casserole, '95 254
Pineapple Bake, '79 251
Pineapple, Baked, '84 287
Pineapple, Scalloped, '79 106
Pork
Casserole, Pork, '83 116
Chop Casserole, Peppered Pork, '81 235; '82 25; '83 39
Chop Casserole, Pork, '94 255
Chops and Potato Scallop, Pork, '82 114
Chops Italiano, Pork, '80 72
Chop-Vegetable Casserole, Pork, '90 208
Fiesta Pork Bake, '79 265
Frankfurter Casserole, Layered, '79 64
Franks, Family-Style, '79 54
Ham and Broccoli Casserole, '81 133
Ham and Broccoli Strata, '80 261
Ham-and-Cheese Casserole, '87 78
Ham and Lima Casserole, '79 192
Ham and Noodle Casserole, '80 300
Ham-and-Potato Casserole, Cheesy, '84 326
Ham-and-Rice Casserole, '84 75
Ham and Turkey Bake, Layered, '79 252
Ham Bake, Harvest, '79 210
Ham-Broccoli Casserole, Quick, '82 40
Ham Casserole, Apple, '79 213
Ham Casserole, Golden, '82 119
Ham Casserole, Macaroni-, '83 283
Ham Casserole, Vegetable-and-, '84 91
Ham Medley, Creamy, '84 90
Ham Pie, Golden, '87 78
Ham-Rice-Tomato Bake, '87 78
Ham Strata, '95 308
Ham Strata, Baked, '83 283
Ham Tetrazzini, '84 241
Salami-Corn Casserole, '80 209
Sausage and Broccoli Casserole, '80 33
Sausage and Noodle Casserole, '82 123
Sausage-and-Noodle Casserole, '95 255
Sausage-and-Rice Bake, Creole, '88 58
Sausage and Wild Rice Casserole, '83 196
Sausage Bake, Eggplant, '85 221
Sausage Bake, Hominy-, '88 51
Sausage-Bean Supper, '86 52
Sausage Casserole, '81 112; '82 12
Sausage Casserole, Cheesy, '82 124
Sausage Casserole, Country, '79 192
Sausage Casserole, Crunchy, '81 288
Sausage Casserole, Eggplant-, '84 215
Sausage Casserole, Ground Beef and, '80 260
Sausage-Chile Rellenos Casserole, '88 52
Sausage Grits, '86 92
Sausage-Lasagna Rollups, '80 236
Sausage-Noodle Bake, '81 92
Sausage-Potato Casserole, '86 217
Sausage-Rice Casserole, '82 50; '83 75
Sausages, Baked Zucchini and, '80 300
Sausage, Wild Rice and, '86 268
Sausage-Wild Rice Casserole, '84 250
Spaghetti Bake, Pork, '81 11
Strata, Christmas Morning, '95 282
Supper Supreme, Sunday, '79 76
Vegetable-Pork Combo, '85 113

Poultry
Chicken à la Russell, '95 175
Chicken-Almond Casserole, '94 199
Chicken-and-Chiles Casserole, '93 107
Chicken-and-Dressing Casserole, '81 263
Chicken and Green Noodle Casserole, '80 32
Chicken and Grits, '95 263
Chicken and Rice, '95 54
Chicken and Rice Casserole, '80 260
Chicken-and-Shrimp Florentine, '89 64
Chicken-and-Spinach Enchiladas, '91 222
Chicken and Wild Rice, '79 248
Chicken-Asparagus Casserole, '83 76; '84 71
Chicken Bake, Company, '80 301
Chicken Bake, Spicy, '85 251
Chicken Bake with Sweet Bacon Dressing, Vegetable-, '93 108
Chicken-Broccoli Casserole, '79 48; '91 315
Chicken-Brown Rice Bake, '91 314
Chicken Casserole, Broccoli-, '82 33
Chicken Casserole, Cheesy, '85 34
Chicken Casserole, Macaroni and, '80 260
Chicken Casserole, Make-Ahead, '84 241
Chicken Casserole, Mexi-, '93 69; '94 30
Chicken Casserole, Mexican, '82 143
Chicken Casserole, Pesto-, '94 231
Chicken Casserole, Quick, '81 91
Chicken Casserole, Rice-and-, '87 154
Chicken Casserole, Simply Good, '95 255
Chicken Casserole, Sunday, '83 290
Chicken Casserole, Swiss, '90 67
Chicken Chili Bake, '93 302
Chicken Chimichangas, '93 68
Chicken Dinner, Hot-and-Spicy, '94 M94
Chicken Divan, '80 M10
Chicken Divan, Curried, '80 83
Chicken Divan, Easy, '94 310
Chicken Divan, Gourmet, '82 83
Chicken Divan, Overnight, '83 198
Chicken Divan, Sherried, '80 38
Chicken-Eggplant Parmigiana, '82 212
Chicken Enchiladas, '80 301
Chicken Enchiladas, Easy, '82 89
Chicken Florentine, '93 107
Chicken, Fontina-Baked, '90 64
Chicken, French Herbed, '86 89
Chicken, Garlic-Spinach, '92 56
Chicken-Green Bean Casserole, '85 296
Chicken, King Ranch, '95 193
Chicken Lasagna Bake, '95 55
Chicken-Macaroni Casserole, '85 219
Chicken-Noodle Casserole, '94 286
Chicken Parmigiana, '80 190
Chicken-Rice Casserole, '86 52
Chicken Salad, Baked, '86 297
Chicken, Scarborough, '80 38
Chicken Skillet Casserole, Spaghetti Squash and, '94 134
Chicken-Spaghetti Casserole, '84 15
Chicken, Spicy Mexican, '82 89
Chicken-Squash Casserole, '95 121
Chicken Superb Casserole, '89 83
Chicken Supreme Casserole, '84 219
Chicken Supreme, Hot, '81 76
Chicken, Swiss, '95 54
Chicken Tetrazzini, '79 268; '80 M75
Chicken Thighs, Swiss, '94 282
Chicken Tortilla Bake, '82 89

CASSEROLES, Poultry *(continued)*

Chicken Tortilla Casserole, '81 166
Chicken-Wild Rice Casserole, '84 241;
  '85 65
Chicken-Wild Rice Supreme, '79 77
Cornish Hens-and-Rice Casserole,
  '92 267
Crêpes Divan, Elegant, '81 91
Duck and Wild Rice Casserole, '79 224
Pollo, Chilaquiles con (Tortillas with
  Chicken), '81 66
Rice Casserole, Mexican, '83 31
Turkey-and-Broccoli Casserole, '86 332
Turkey-and-Shrimp Florentine Casserole,
  '92 122
Turkey-Asparagus Casserole, '86 284
Turkey Bake, Layered Ham and, '79 252
Turkey Casserole, '84 327
Turkey Casserole, Golden, '80 271
Turkey Casserole, Stuffed, '88 246
Turkey Florentine, '88 264
Turkey Noodle Bake, '93 243
Turkey-Noodle-Poppyseed Casserole,
  '90 239
Turkey-Olive Casserole, '87 268
Turkey Parmigiana, '87 193
Turkey Salad Bake, '79 253
Turkey Salad, Hot, '86 297
Turkey-Spinach Casserole, '84 71
Turkey-Swiss Casserole, '86 283
Turkey Tetrazzini, Herbed, '86 47
Provolone Casserole, Seashell-, '80 189
Quiche Casserole, '95 33
Ravioli, Mediterranean, '93 301
Reuben Casserole, '90 240
Rice-and-Cheese con Chiles, '89 99
Rice and Green Chiles, '83 152
Rice au Gratin Supreme, '86 78
Rice, Baked, '94 270
Rice Bake, Green, '79 43
Rice Casserole, '87 45
Rice Casserole, Chili-, '79 54
Rice Casserole, Colorful, '82 199
Rice Casserole, Green, '95 181
Rice Casserole, Jalapeño, '81 66
Rice Casserole, Spanish, '79 192
Rice Chantilly, '86 82
Rice, Easy Mushroom, '89 286
Rice, Fiesta, '84 76
Rice, Hot Pepper, '92 310
Rice Mélange, '87 240
Rice, Mexican, '85 147
Rice Pilaf, '86 82
Rice, Savannah Red, '95 27
Rice, Spanish, '81 51; '90 183
Rice, Spicy, '85 256
Rotini Romano, '87 193
Seafood
  Crab-and-Mushroom Casserole, '89 96
  Crab-and-Shrimp Casserole, '84 71
  Crab and Spinach Casserole, Creamy,
    '80 3
  Crab Bake, Quick, '87 192
  Crab Casserole, '79 228
  Crab Casserole, Deviled, '91 238; '92 27
  Crab Casserole, Easy, '93 270
  Crab, Dressed, '82 276
  Crab-Egg Casserole, '80 260
  Crab Imperial, '79 82, 116
  Crab Imperial, Elegant, '83 245
  Crabmeat-Broccoli Casserole, '84 232

Crabmeat Imperial, '82 311
Crabmeat with Artichoke Hearts,
  Creamed, '93 26
Crab Puff, '79 116
Crab, Shrimp, and Artichoke au Gratin,
  '90 240
Crawfish Lasagna, '91 89
Fish and Potato Bake, Herbed, '79 287;
  '80 34
Fish Casserole, Green Chile-and-, '84 32
Miss Hannah's Casserole, '92 236
Oyster-and-Corn Bake, '83 34; '84 44
Oyster-and-Spinach Casserole, '83 34;
  '84 44
Oyster-and-Wild Rice Casserole, '83 34;
  '84 44
Oyster Casserole, '79 228
Oyster Casserole, Wild Rice-, '86 256
Oysters Johnny Reb, '82 42
Oysters, Scalloped, '79 225; '84 213;
  '86 132; '95 318
Salmon Casserole, '81 22
Salmon Florentine, '83 43
Scallop Casserole, '79 228
Seafood Casserole, '87 109; '89 63
Shrimp-and-Chicken Casserole, '91 102
Shrimp-and-Noodle Casserole, '90 240
Shrimp and Rice Casserole, '79 228
Shrimp-and-Rice Casserole, '94 328
Shrimp au Gratin, '85 79
Shrimp Casserole, '85 240
Shrimp Casserole, Chayotes and, '80 230
Shrimp-Crab Puff, '79 57
Shrimp Delight, '79 192
Shrimp Florentine Casserole, Turkey-
  and-, '92 122
Tuna and Peas in Wine Sauce, Baked,
  '83 196
Tuna-Broccoli Casserole, Tangy, '83 75
Tuna Casserole, '82 119
Tuna Casserole, Biscuit-Topped, '79 113
Tuna Casserole, Nippy, '84 241
Tuna Casserole with Cheese Swirls,
  '88 256
Tuna Chopsticks, '94 255
Tuna-Macaroni Treat, '82 131
Tuna Vegetable Casserole, '81 135
Shells, Southwestern Stuffed, '93 234
Spaghetti, Casserole, '95 132
Tamale Casserole, Quick, '94 255
Vegetable
  Artichoke Casserole, Alii, '93 294
  Asparagus-and-English Pea Casserole,
    '86 324
  Asparagus and Peas Casserole, '80 152
  Asparagus-Artichoke Casserole, '86 279
  Asparagus Casserole, Cheesy, '82 281;
    '83 32
  Asparagus Casserole, Creamy, '80 76
  Asparagus Casserole, Easy, '83 255
  Asparagus Delight, '82 269
  Asparagus, Holiday, '85 260
  Asparagus-Pea Casserole, '88 M294
  Asparagus-Pimiento Loaf, '84 86
  Asparagus-Spaghetti Casserole, '80 77
  Asparagus Supreme, '89 245
  Black-Eyed Peas with Rice, '83 12
  Broccoli-and-Egg Casserole, '86 324
  Broccoli-and-Eggs au Gratin, '85 289
  Broccoli Bake, '81 246; '89 279
  Broccoli Bake, Cheesy, '83 255
  Broccoli Bake, Cheesy Italian, '83 5
  Broccoli Bake, Company, '83 279

Broccoli-Blue Cheese Casserole, '85 260
Broccoli Casserole, '87 284;
  '88 M146, 265
Broccoli Casserole, Almond-, '88 62
Broccoli Casserole, Cheesy, '84 293;
  '92 342; '95 M191
Broccoli Casserole, Italian, '82 6, 280;
  '83 32
Broccoli Casserole, Winter, '94 280
Broccoli-Cheese Casserole, '82 269;
  '84 9; '94 132
Broccoli-Corn Casserole, '83 313
Broccoli Elegant, '81 267
Broccoli, English Walnut, '89 68
Broccoli-Onion Deluxe, '81 75
Broccoli Puff, '82 95
Broccoli-Rice Casserole, '81 101
Broccoli Supreme, '82 34; '85 68
Broccoli-Swiss Cheese Casserole,
  '83 322; '85 M211
Broccoli with Lemon Cream, '89 245
Broccoli with Rice, Holiday, '87 252
Broccoli with Stuffing, '95 341
Brussels Sprouts-and-Artichoke
  Casserole, '94 279
Brussels Sprouts, Casserole of, '86 294
Butternut Casserole, '83 280
Butternut Casserole, Sweet, '83 256
Butternut Squash Casserole, '79 210
Butternut Squash Puff, '85 205
Cabbage au Gratin, '83 279
Cabbage, Caraway, '85 32, 289
Cabbage Casserole, Cheesy, '79 4
Cabbage Casserole, Creamy, '80 63
Cabbage Casserole, Italian, '87 42
Cabbage Casserole, Savory, '82 168
Cabbage, Cheese Scalloped, '81 87;
  '82 7
Cabbage, Scalloped, '82 269
Cabbage Wedges, Smothered, '81 87;
  '82 7
Cabbage with Apples and Franks, '87 42
Calabaza Mexicano (Mexican Squash),
  '81 196
Carrot and Zucchini Casserole, '83 256
Carrot Bake, Creamy, '85 67
Carrot Casserole, '86 279; '87 285
Carrot Casserole, Scrumptious, '84 328
Carrot-Pecan Casserole, '93 44
Carrot Puff, '84 328
Carrots, Scalloped, '81 6
Carrots, Zesty, '84 5
Cashew Casserole, '95 166
Cauliflower and Asparagus Supreme,
  '79 287; '80 35
Cauliflower-and-Carrot Casserole,
  '83 280
Cauliflower and Peas with Curried
  Almonds, '80 82
Cauliflower Bake, '95 342
Cauliflower Casserole, '86 10, 279
Cauliflower Casserole, Easy, '82 204
Cauliflower Casserole, Festive, '87 232
Cauliflower Casserole, Herbed, '79 221
Cauliflower, Curried, '91 315
Cauliflower Italiano, Cheesy, '82 300
Cauliflower, Main-Dish, '79 221; '80 83
Cauliflower Medley, '80 220
Cauliflower 'n' Chiles Casserole, '87 285
Cauliflower-Pea Casserole, '85 260
Cauliflower Scallop, '88 270
Cauliflower, Spanish-Style, '79 21
Celery and Cheese Casserole, '79 178

CASEROLES, Vegetable (continued)

Celery au Gratin, '83 38
Celery, Baked, '82 98
Celery Casserole, '80 246
Celery Casserole, Creamy, '82 98;
 '83 255
Celery, Creamed, '79 247
Celery, Exotic, '83 280
Celery Oriental, '83 206; '85 116
Celery, Saucy, '83 39
Chayote-Cheese Bake, '80 230
Cheesy Vegetable Casserole, '81 103
Chilaquiles, '82 220
Collards Casserole, Parmesan-, '95 233
Corn-and-Bean Casserole, '90 208
Corn and Cheese Casserole, '81 128
Corn-and-Green Chile Casserole, '89 68
Corn and Tomato Casserole, '81 127
Corn-and-Tomato Casserole, '84 145
Corn, Baked Scalloped, '85 290
Corn Casserole, '79 247; '89 126;
 '93 141
Corn Casserole, Chili-, '88 266
Corn Casserole, Fresh, '80 165
Corn Casserole, Jalapeño-, '83 256
Corn, Creamy Baked, '90 60
Corn, Elegant Scalloped, '86 268
Corn Pudding, '86 192
Corn, Scalloped, '80 164; '81 128;
 '86 111; '88 218
Corn with Sour Cream, Baked, '86 170
Corn-Zucchini Bake, '79 178
Curry Casserole, Vegetable-, '91 286;
 '92 27
Eggplant and Noodle Casserole, '82 230
Eggplant and Squash, '83 187
Eggplant-and-Tomato Casserole, '83 187
Eggplant and Zucchini, Italian-Style,
 '79 289; '80 26
Eggplant Bake, '80 82
Eggplant Cakes, '95 196
Eggplant Casserole, '81 205; '84 217;
 '93 44; '94 214
Eggplant Casserole, Easy, '80 202
Eggplant Casserole, Elegant, '82 168
Eggplant Casserole, Flavorful, '79 92
Eggplant Casserole, Spicy Hot, '93 92
Eggplant Casserole, Super, '80 202
Eggplant Chiles Rellenos, '91 86
Eggplant Creole, '86 110
Eggplant, Heavenly, '79 293
Eggplant, Italian, '84 216
Eggplant Italiano, '91 212
Eggplant, Lebanese, '81 24
Eggplant, Mexican, '83 187
Eggplant Parmesan, '83 186; '84 215;
 '92 18; '95 84
Eggplant Parmigiana, '81 19; '95 197
Eggplant, Rolled Stuffed, '80 63
Eggplant, Scalloped, '91 223
Eggplant Supreme, '79 188; '86 170
English Pea Casserole, Cheesy, '83 216
English Pea Casserole, Quick Fresh,
 '84 145
English Pea-Pimiento Casserole, '83 207
Fresh Vegetable Casserole, '82 225
Garden Casserole, '82 168; '88 122
Garden Surprise, '83 112
Green-and-Gold Scallop, '81 159
Green Beans, Baked, '91 159
Greens Dinner Bake, Grits 'n, '84 281

Green Vegetable Medley, '79 287; '80 34
Hash Brown Cheese Bake, '82 50
Hominy, Mexican, '91 133, 162
Hubbard Squash, Tart, '80 214
Lasagna Casserole, Vegetable, '92 198;
 '93 25
Layered Vegetable Casserole, '91 286;
 '92 27
Lentils with Cheese, Baked, '84 113
Medley, Baked Vegetable, '81 75
Medley Bake, Vegetable, '81 268
Mixed Vegetable Casserole, '83 208, 256;
 '86 327
Mixed-Vegetable Casserole, '87 154
Mixed Vegetables, Scalloped, '83 5
Mushroom-Artichoke Casserole, '87 241
Mushroom Bake, Windsor, '88 132
Mushroom Casserole, '95 211
Mushroom-Cheese Casserole, '83 216
Mushroom-Macaroni Casserole, '95 180
Mushrooms Supreme, '84 214
New Potatoes, Cheesy, '85 156
Noodle Casserole, Vegetable, '91 30
Okra Casserole, '79 160
Okra-Tomato Bake, '80 298; '81 26
Onion Bake, Four, '93 304
Onion Casserole, Cheesy, '79 101
Onion Casserole, French, '95 26
Onions, Baked Sweet, '91 79
Pea Casserole, Curry, '87 154
Pea Casserole, Reunion, '87 11
Pea Casserole Supreme, '82 281; '83 32
Peas and Rice, '88 97
Peas, Cajun, '88 3
Peas, Chinese-Style Baked, '86 305
Peas, Mexi-, '88 3
Peas, Party, '79 102
Peas, Sweet-and-Sour, '88 3
Potato Bake, '83 209
Potato Bake, Creamy, '82 201
Potato-Broccoli-Cheese Bake, '80 114
Potato Casserole, '87 190
Potato Casserole, Cheesy, '80 244;
 '83 53; '92 229
Potato Casserole, Easy, '80 114
Potato Casserole, Fluffy, '80 268
Potato Casserole, Hash Brown, '81 40
Potato Casserole, Holiday, '92 302
Potato Casserole, Irish, '81 263
Potato Casserole, Mashed, '85 296
Potato Casserole, Mushroom-, '84 5
Potato Casserole, Peppery, '95 182
Potato Casserole, Processor, '86 159
Potato Casserole, Saucy, '81 276
Potato-Cheese Casserole, '79 101
Potato-Egg Casserole, Cheesy, '84 5
Potato-Eggplant Casserole, '87 166
Potatoes and Eggs au Gratin, '79 107
Potatoes and Turnips, Scalloped, '85 235
Potatoes-and-Zucchini au Gratin, '84 5
Potatoes au Gratin, Shredded, '89 69
Potatoes, Cheesy Scalloped, '83 82
Potatoes, Christmas, '88 252
Potatoes, Cottage, '89 69
Potatoes, Double-Cheese, '86 6
Potatoes, Easy Oven-Baked, '82 202
Potatoes, Fix-Ahead Mashed, '89 70
Potatoes, Fluffy, '84 296; '85 196
Potatoes for Company, Saucy, '82 202
Potatoes, Garlic, '84 296; '85 196
Potatoes Gourmet, '80 114
Potatoes, Gruyère, '83 193
Potatoes, Hot Deviled, '84 296; '85 196

Potatoes, Italian-Style, '89 69
Potatoes, Jalapeño, '84 39
Potatoes, Jazzy Mashed, '87 192
Potatoes, Lemon and Nutmeg, '80 36
Potatoes, Light Scalloped, '89 311
Potatoes Lorraine, '87 190
Potatoes, Mexican-Style, '91 78
Potatoes, Missy, '85 259
Potatoes Moussaka, '93 44
Potatoes, Mushroom Scalloped, '87 191
Potatoes, Olive, '80 114
Potatoes, Parmesan, '82 270; '90 M62
Potatoes, Party Scalloped, '87 191
Potatoes, Scalloped, '82 300; '83 211;
 '92 48
Potatoes, Sour Cream, '84 39
Potatoes, Special Scalloped, '88 162
Potatoes, Two-Cheese, '80 114
Potatoes, Wayside Scalloped, '79 283
Potatoes with Feta Cheese, '84 295;
 '85 196
Potatoes with Ham Bits, Creamy, '87 191
Potatoes with Sweet Marjoram and
 Parmesan Cheese, Scalloped, '91 246
Potato-Tomato Bake, '86 17
Potato-Tomato Casserole, Saucy, '79 46
Potato Tuna Bake, Shoestring, '82 211
Pumpkin, Baked, '82 217
Spinach and Artichoke Casserole, '81 103
Spinach-and-Celery Casserole, '84 294
Spinach and Egg Casserole, '82 270
Spinach-Artichoke Bake, '95 48
Spinach-Artichoke Casserole, '88 252;
 '93 44
Spinach Bake, Creamy, '89 68
Spinach Casserole, '79 265; '91 31
Spinach Casserole, Cheesy, '81 263
Spinach Casserole, Cottage Cheese-and-,
 '84 77
Spinach Casserole, Creamy, '86 111
Spinach-Cheese Bake, '88 10
Spinach-Cheese Casserole, '83 216;
 '89 64
Spinach-Cheese Puff, '84 96
Spinach, Cheesy Topped, '84 85
Spinach, Company, '89 280
Spinach, Creamy Lemon, '82 302
Spinach Fantastic, '93 173
Spinach, Gourmet Baked, '82 180
Spinach Parmesan, '93 72
Spinach-Parmesan Casserole, '82 281;
 '83 32
Spinach Rice, '85 146
Spinach Supreme, '84 77
Spinach Surprise, '82 42
Spinach with Cheese, Scalloped, '79 8
Squash and Apple Casserole, '79 209
Squash and Egg Casserole, '80 146
Squash and Tomato Bake, '95 180
Squash, Bacon-Flavored, '82 158
Squash Bake, '82 107
Squash Bake, Cheddar-, '84 128
Squash Bake, Cheesy, '80 183
Squash-Carrot Casserole, '81 157
Squash Casserole, '87 163; '89 159;
 '90 161; '92 342
Squash Casserole, Baked, '83 149
Squash Casserole, Blender, '81 212
Squash Casserole, Calico, '90 290
Squash Casserole, Cheesy, '79 123
Squash Casserole, Company, '81 183
Squash Casserole, Creamy Rice and,
 '95 26

CASSEROLES, Vegetable (continued)

Squash Casserole, Crunchy, '84 293
Squash Casserole, Fresh, '82 204
Squash Casserole, Jiffy, '81 M144
Squash Casserole, Summer,
   '81 102, 184
Squash Casserole, Two-, '79 101
Squash Casserole, Zippy, '80 183
Squash, Country Club, '88 M16
Squash, Greek-Style, '91 285; '92 26
Squash, Mexican, '83 31
Squash Nicholas, '94 236
Squash, Posh, '81 159
Squash, South-of-the-Border, '89 148
Sweet Potato-and-Apple Casserole,
   '94 280
Sweet Potato-Apple Bake, '83 25
Sweet Potato-Apricot Bake, '85 206
Sweet Potato Bake, '80 287
Sweet Potato Bake, Holiday, '90 291
Sweet Potato-Banana Casserole,
   '86 276
Sweet Potato Casserole, '79 289; '80 26;
   '85 256; '89 279
Sweet Potato Casserole, Glazed,
   '90 250
Sweet Potato Cassserole, Pear-, '86 280
Sweet Potato Delight, '86 335
Sweet Potato-Eggnog Casserole, '95 291
Sweet Potatoes-and-Apple Casserole,
   '90 228
Sweet Potatoes-and-Berries Casserole,
   '84 231
Sweet Potatoes, Bourbon, '86 324;
   '87 280
Sweet Potatoes, Candied, '86 111;
   '88 207
Sweet Potatoes Royale, '91 250
Sweet Potatoes with Sherry and Walnuts,
   '86 286
Sweet Potato-Rum Casserole, '84 231
Sweet Potato Supreme, '94 196
Sweet Potato Surprise, '81 267
Swiss Vegetable Medley, '95 26
Tomato-and-Artichoke Heart Bake,
   '85 81
Tomato Casserole, Scalloped, '88 144
Tomatoes, Herbed, '81 102
Tomatoes, Italian-Sauced Green,
   '85 214
Tomatoes, Scalloped, '84 142
Torta, Mexican, '88 149
Turnip Casserole, '83 242; '84 229
Turnip Casserole, Baked, '82 274
Turnips au Gratin, '84 229
Turnips, Scalloped, '79 254
Veggies Casserole, '88 123
Vidalia Deep Dish, '89 120
Wine Sauce Casserole, Vegetables in,
   '95 133
Yam-and-Apple Scallop, '91 199
Yams, Brandied, '94 273
Yellow Squash Casserole, '79 179;
   '85 135; '88 166
Zucchini and Tomato Bake, '82 158
Zucchini-and-Tomato Casserole,
   '88 265
Zucchini, Baked, '83 209
Zucchini Casserole, '79 157; '87 154
Zucchini Casserole, Cheese-Egg-,
   '84 114

Zucchini Casserole, Cheesy, '82 168;
   '84 145
Zucchini Casserole, Italian, '85 59
Zucchini-Jack Casserole, '85 296
Zucchini-Rice Casserole Italiano, '89 146
Wild Rice Casserole, '82 199; '95 176

CAULIFLOWER
Almond Sauce, Cauliflower with, '82 270
au Gratin, Cauliflower, '82 204
Bake, Cauliflower, '95 342
Baked Swiss Cauliflower, '79 100
Beef and Cauliflower Oriental, '80 220
Beef and Cauliflower over Rice, '93 94
Beets and Cauliflower, Chilled, '80 137
Casserole, Cauliflower, '86 10, 279
Casserole, Cauliflower-and-Carrot, '83 280
Casserole, Cauliflower 'n' Chiles, '87 285
Casserole, Cauliflower-Pea, '85 260
Casserole, Easy Cauliflower, '82 204
Casserole, Festive Cauliflower, '87 232
Casserole, Herbed Cauliflower, '79 221
Cheese-Frosted Cauliflower, '85 68
Cheese Sauce, Cauliflower with, '81 101
Cheesy Cauliflower Italiano, '82 300
Curried Cauliflower, '91 315
Dilled Cauliflower, '83 93
Festive Cauliflower, '84 34
French-Fried Cauliflower, '86 211
French-Fried Cauliflower au Gratin, '79 221;
   '80 82
Fried Cauliflower, '83 5; '84 248; '90 18
Fried Cauliflower, Crispy, '80 220
Fried Cauliflower, Golden, '82 78
Fried Cauliflower with Cheese Sauce, '87 231
Garden Surprise, '83 112
Goldenrod, Cauliflower, '79 21
Gratin, Cauliflower with Chinese Mustard,
   '94 45
Herb Butter, Cauliflower with, '81 2
Italian-Style Cauliflower, '92 36
Lemon Cauliflower, Easy, '83 322
Main-Dish Cauliflower, '79 221; '80 83
Medley, Cauliflower, '80 220
Medley, Cauliflower-Broccoli, '81 69
Medley, Cauliflower-Snow Pea, '87 305
Oriental Cauliflower, '81 75
Peas and Cauliflower, '82 288
Peas with Curried Almonds, Cauliflower and,
   '79 221; '80 82
Pickled Cauliflower, '94 183
Pie, Cauliflower-Carrot, '82 191
Pimiento Sauce, Cauliflower with, '87 232
Quiche, Cauliflower, '83 86
Salads
   Broccoli and Cauliflower Salad, '81 280
   Broccoli and Cauliflower Salad, Creamy,
      '81 23
   Broccoli and Cauliflower Toss, Crunchy,
      '83 25
   Broccoli-Cauliflower Pasta Salad, '88 269
   Broccoli-Cauliflower Salad, '92 97
   Broccoli Crunch, Cauliflower-, '88 216
   Broccoli 'n' Cauliflower Salad, '90 32
   Broccoli Salad, Cauliflower-, '79 20
   Broccoli Toss, Cauliflower-, '82 54
   Broccoli Toss, Italian Cauliflower-,
      '88 269
   Brussels Sprouts Salad, Cauliflower-,
      '83 240
   Cauliflower Salad, '79 221; '80 83;
      '81 225; '84 291; '85 240, 279;
      '92 36
   Celery-and-Cauliflower Salad, '83 39

Corned Beef-Cauliflower Salad, '83 16
Creamy Cauliflower Salad, '82 102
Crunchy Cauliflower Salad, '80 4; '82 75
English Pea Salad, Cauliflower-, '95 66
Green Salad, Crunchy, '89 321
Layered Cauliflower Salad, '83 240
Lemon Salad, Cauliflower-, '81 23
Marinated Cauliflower Salad, '82 303;
   '84 232
Orange-Cauliflower Salad, '82 266
Pea Salad, Cauliflower-, '87 231
Pea Salad, Savory Cauliflower and, '81 280
Red, White, and Green Salad, '90 18
Slaw, Cauliflower, '92 167
Sweet-and-Sour Cauliflower Salad, '81 2
Vegetable Salad, Cauliflower-, '85 158
Sauté, Cauliflower, '94 67
Scallop, Cauliflower, '88 270
Shrimp Sauce, Broccoli and Cauliflower with,
   '84 248
Soufflé, Cauliflower, '82 76; '89 279; '90 17
Soup, Cauliflower, '90 211
Soup, Cauliflower and Caraway, '82 264
Soup, Cream of Cauliflower, '87 M7; '88 12
Soup, Cream of Cauliflower and Watercress,
   '83 126
Soup, Creamy Cauliflower, '82 76
Soup, Fresh Cauliflower, '84 279
Spanish-Style Cauliflower, '79 21
Supreme, Cauliflower and Asparagus, '79 287;
   '80 35
Toss, Cauliflower, '85 289
Toss, Cauliflower-Olive, '85 198; '86 147

CAVIAR
Artichoke Hearts with Caviar, '79 142
Crown, Caviar, '83 78
Eggplant Caviar, '88 262
Eggplant Caviar with Tapenade, '92 194
Endive with Caviar, '93 118
Homemade Cowboy Caviar, '94 64
Mold, Artichoke-Caviar, '87 239
Mound, Caviar-Artichoke, '91 244
Mousse, Caviar, '82 71; '83 258; '85 86;
   '92 83
Pie, Caviar, '79 154
Potatoes, Appetizer Caviar, '86 223
Potatoes, Caviar, '84 80
Spread, Caviar-Cream Cheese, '84 256
Spread, Creamy Caviar, '92 58
Spread, Egg, Sour Cream, and Caviar, '85 279
Texas Caviar, '86 218
Tomatoes, Caviar, '91 12
Zucchini Caviar, '88 212

CELERY
Almondine, Celery, '85 116
Amandine, Buttered Celery, '82 98
Ants on a Float, '91 177
au Gratin, Celery, '83 38
Baked Celery, '82 98
Braised Carrots and Celery, '86 327
Braised Celery, Green Beans and, '84 254
Brussels Sprouts and Celery, '79 21
Brussels Sprouts with Celery, Lemony, '85 25
Buttered Carrots and Celery, '89 44
Carrots and Celery with Pecans, '84 254
Casserole, Celery, '80 246
Casserole, Celery and Cheese, '79 178
Casserole, Creamy Celery, '82 98; '83 255
Casserole, Spinach-and-Celery, '84 294
Chicken-and-Celery Skillet, '88 6
Creamed Brussels Sprouts and Celery, '83 322
Creamed Celery, '79 247
Croutons, Celery, '79 16

CELERY (continued)

Curried Corn and Celery, '86 192
Dressing, Celery-Honey, '80 42
Dressing, Watermelon Salad with Celery-Nut, '80 182
Exotic Celery, '83 280
Orange Sauce, Celery in, '79 70
Oriental, Celery, '83 206; '85 116
Peas and Celery, '93 289
Peas and Celery, Deluxe, '81 267
Pork Tenderloin with Apples, Celery, and Potatoes, Grilled, '95 161
Potatoes, Whipped Celery, '94 305
Potato Puffs, Celeried, '89 279
Relish, Apple-Celery, '89 141
Salad, Celery, '79 70
Salad, Celery-and-Cauliflower, '83 39
Salad, Chicken-Celery, '81 187
Salad, Overnight Alfalfa-Celery, '82 97
Salad, Pear-and-Celery, '87 56
Salad, Pineapple-Celery, '85 95
Sauce, Baked Fillets in Lemon-Celery, '84 91
Saucy Celery, '83 39
Scalloped Carrots-and-Celery, '84 M112
Snow Peas with Celery, Skillet, '84 123
Soup, Burnet-Celery, '84 107
Soup, Celery-and-Potato, '84 279
Soup, Cream of Celery, '79 71; '90 210
Soup, Light Cream-of-Celery, '82 279
Soup, Tomato-Celery, '83 M58
Splendid Stalks, '93 258
Stuffed Celery, '82 98; '86 324
Stuffed Celery, Creamy, '82 102
Stuffed Celery, Jalapeño, '79 70
Stuffed Celery Trunks, '85 115
Toss, Celery-Parmesan, '84 34

CHAYOTES

Bake, Chayote-Cheese, '80 230
Casserole, Chayotes and Shrimp, '80 230
Fried Chayotes, '80 230
Pickles, Chayote Squash, '89 197
Sautéed Chayote Squash with Cilantro, '95 227
Stuffed Chayote, '92 247

CHEESE. See also APPETIZERS/CHEESE; CHEESECAKES.

Almond Cheese, '88 173
Apple-Cheese Bake, '92 225
Bake, Brie Cheese, '87 117
Bake, Chicken, Ham, and Cheese, '87 217
Baked Brie, Walnut-, '93 241
Bake, Pineapple-Cheese, '79 106
Bake, Spinach-Ricotta, '88 97
Beef Parmigiana, '85 234
Beef Roulades, Roquefort, '88 215
Blintzes, Cheese, '82 146; '83 71; '92 84
Blue Cheese, Creamy, '88 173
Bobolis, Easy Cheesy, '92 278

Breads

Bacon-and-Cheese Bread, '83 255
Bacon-Cheese Toast Bars, '79 36
Batter Bread, Cheese-Caraway, '85 33
Biscuit Fingers, Pepper-Cheese, '88 283
Biscuits, Bacon-Cheese, '88 84
Biscuits, Beer-and-Cheese, '94 215
Biscuits, Blue Cheese, '88 83
Biscuits, Cheese, '81 288; '83 253; '85 32; '87 78
Biscuits, Cheese Angel, '89 211
Biscuits, Cheeseburger, '79 194
Biscuits, Cheese-Chive, '94 324
Biscuits, Cheesy Onion, '95 98
Biscuits, Easy Cheese, '81 99
Biscuits, Herbed Roquefort, '84 95
Biscuits, Hot Cheesy, '80 186
Biscuits, Lightnin' Cheese, '90 283
Biscuits, Mexican Fiesta Spoon, '95 161
Biscuits, Petite Ham and Cheese, '79 193
Biscuits, Surprise Pull-Apart, '95 46
Biscuits, Tiny Cheese, '80 192
Blue Cheese-Apple Sunburst, '94 245
Bobolis, Easy Cheesy, '92 278
Breadsticks, Italian Cheese, '95 126
Brie Bread, '87 143
Buns, Cheesy Onion, '85 5
Buns, Hurry-Up Cheese, '81 300
Buns, Onion-Cheese, '88 218
Butter Cheese Dips, '80 46
Buttermilk-Cheese Loaf, '91 52
Cheddar Cheese Bread, '84 268
Cheddar-Nut Bread, '85 41
Cheese Bread, '82 174; '83 208; '87 11
Cornbread, Cheddar, '83 285; '84 17
Cornbread, Cheddar-Jalapeño, '85 3
Cornbread, Cheesy Beef, '81 242
Cornbread, Chile-Cheese, '87 171
Cornbread, Cottage Cheese, '80 90
Cornbread, Swiss Cheese, '79 60
Cottage Cheese-Dill Bread, '83 154
Cream Cheese Braids, '82 243
Cream Cheese Loaves, Processor, '85 48
Cream Cheese Pinches, '87 85
Crescents, Cheese, '82 18
Croissants, Cream Cheese, '92 159
Crusty Cheese Bread, '86 233
Dilly Cheese Bread, '83 5
Easy Cheese Bread, '82 74; '86 17
French Bread, Bacon-Cheese, '92 54
French Bread, Cheesy, '88 172; '95 218
French Bread, Onion-Cheese, '89 29
French Toast au Fromage, '88 288
French Toast, Cottage-Topped, '85 49
French Toast, Three Cheese Stuffed, '93 122
Fruit-and-Cheese Braid, '86 214
Garlic Bread, Cheesy, '84 150
Garlic-Stuffed Bread, Cheesy, '95 176
Gouda Bread, '91 52
Ham-and-Cheese Bread, '86 213
Herb-and-Cheese Pull Aparts, '87 143
Herb Bread, Cheese-, '84 M144; '85 283
Herb-Cheese Bread, '85 70
Herbs-and-Cheese Bread, '93 56
Herb-Vegetable-Cheese Bread, '88 172
Jalapeño-Cheese Loaf, '84 76
Jam-and-Cheese Loaf, '89 246
Lemon-Cream Tea Loaf, '84 50
Little Cheese Loaves, '86 213

Loaf, Cheese, '90 93
Monkey Bread, Cheese-Filled, '91 21
Muffin Mix, Cheese-and-Pepper, '89 330
Muffins, Bacon-and-Cheese, '89 205
Muffins, Blueberry-Cream Cheese, '86 14
Muffins, Caraway-Cheese, '91 213
Muffins, Cheddar, '89 15
Muffins, Cheddar-Raisin, '91 51
Muffins, Cheese-and-Pepper, '84 139
Muffins, Cheesy Cornbread, '88 M275
Muffins, Cheesy Sausage, '92 252; '93 144
Muffins, Dilly Cheese, '95 245
Muffins, Ham-and-Cheese, '92 252; '93 144
Muffins, Marvelous Cheese, '83 96
Muffins, Sausage-Cheese, '86 213
Muffins, Sesame-Cheese, '86 16
Olive Bread, Spicy Cheese-, '84 150
Onion-Cheese Bread, '79 180; '81 8
Onion-Cheese Supper Bread, '83 112
Onion-Parmesan Bread, '84 284
Orange-Cream Cheese Bread, '82 210
Pane Cunsado (Fixed Bread), '95 218
Parmesan Bread, '92 19; '93 231
Parmesan Herb Bread, '82 235; '83 41
Parmesan Sesame Sticks, '81 39
Parmesan Twists, '83 239
Pimiento-Cheese Bread, '85 223; '86 166
Pita Triangles, Cheesy, '93 70
Popover Puffs, Cheese, '85 6
Popover Ring, Cheesy, '80 45
Popovers, Cheddar Cheese, '85 41
Popovers, Parmesan, '90 66
Poppy Seed-Swiss Cheese Bread, '91 52
Quick Cheese Bread, '83 9
Roll, Feta Cheese-Spinach, '91 22
Rolls, Broccoli-Cheddar, '91 21
Rolls, Cheese, '80 286
Rolls, Cheese-Apricot Sweet, '90 195
Rolls, Cottage Cheese, '81 78
Rolls, Ham-and-Cheese, '82 3
Rolls, Parmesan, '79 181
Rolls, Romano Sesame, '87 144
Sesame-Cheddar Sticks, '81 150
Sour Cream-Cheese Bread, '85 33
Spinach Bread, '87 144
Spoonbread, Cheddar, '82 196
Spoonbread, Cheese, '86 261
Spoonbread, Corn-Cheese, '88 9
Swiss Cheese Bread, '79 60
Swiss Cheese Bread, Poppy Seed-, '91 52
Swiss Cheese Loaves, Mini, '95 80
Toasted Cheese Delights, '79 37
Tomato-Cheese Bread, Herbed, '88 143
Twists, Cheesy, '84 284
Wine Bread, Cheese-, '87 254
Bugs in a Rug, '95 178
Burgers, Blue Cheese, '89 M66
Burgers, Brie-Mushroom, '95 128
Burgers, Cheesy Bacon, '81 29
Burgers, Cheesy Beef, '83 217
Burritos, Breakfast, '90 192
Burritos, Cheesy Beef, '85 193
Butter, Cheese, '84 114
Calzones, Spinach-and-Cheese, '95 310

Casseroles

Apple-Cheese Casserole, '84 287
Asparagus Casserole, Cheesy, '82 281;
    '83 32
Beef-and-Bean Bake, Cheesy, '82 89
Blintz Casserole, Cheese, '92 251
Breakfast Casserole, '91 285
Breakfast Casserole, Cheesy, '85 247
Broccoli Bake, Cheesy, '83 255
Broccoli-Blue Cheese Casserole, '85 260
Broccoli Casserole, Cheesy, '84 293;
    '92 342; '95 M191
Broccoli-Cheese Casserole, '82 269;
    '84 9; '94 132
Broccoli-Ham au Gratin, '90 239
Broccoli-Swiss Cheese Casserole,
    '83 322; '85 M211
Brunch Casserole, '82 124
Brunch Casserole, Easy Cheesy,
    '92 91
Brunch for a Bunch, '88 57
Cabbage au Gratin, '83 279
Cabbage Casserole, Cheesy, '79 4
Carrots, Cheese Scalloped, '94 36
Celery and Cheese Casserole, '79 178
Celery au Gratin, '83 38
Chayote-Cheese Bake, '80 230
Cheeseburger Casserole, '95 255
Chicken Casserole, Cheesy, '85 34
Chicken Casserole, Swiss, '90 67
Chicken, Fontina-Baked, '90 64
Chicken, Swiss, '95 54
Chicken Tetrazzini, Cheesy, '83 M87
Chicken Thighs, Swiss, '94 282
Chilaquiles, '82 220
Chile-Cheese Casserole, '82 90
Chile 'n' Cheese Breakfast Casserole,
    '88 57
Chiles Rellenos Casserole, '79 84;
    '84 31, 234; '92 18
Collards Casserole, Parmesan-, '95 233
Continental Cheese Bake, '81 89
Corn and Cheese Casserole, '81 128
Corned Beef and Cabbage au Gratin,
    '83 16
Crab, Shrimp, and Artichoke au Gratin,
    '90 240
Egg-and-Cheese Casserole, '84 293
Egg Casserole, Cheesy, '81 244; '86 15
Eggplant Parmesan, '83 186; '84 215;
    '86 53; '95 84
Eggplant Parmigiana, '81 19
English Pea Casserole, Cheesy, '83 216
Feather-Light Cheese Casserole, '79 84
Florentine Bake, Cheesy, '95 131
Four Cheese Casserole, '92 170
Grits, Baked Cheese, '80 49, 99; '83 311;
    '85 41
Grits, Baked Cheese-and-Garlic, '83 292;
    '84 78
Grits Casserole, Cheesy, '81 270
Grits, Cheese, '86 242
Grits, Garlic-Cheese, '80 47; '81 197;
    '86 180
Grits, Swiss-and-Cheddar Baked, '91 71
Ground Beef Casserole, Cheesy, '79 44
Ham-and-Cheese Casserole, '87 78
Hominy Casserole, Cheesy, '83 170
Hominy with Chiles and Cheese, '86 78
Lasagna, Cheesy, '82 224; '88 299

Lasagna, Cheesy Spinach, '80 32;
    '83 204
Lasagna, Cheesy Vegetable, '79 84
Lasagna Maria, '90 191
Lentils with Cheese, Baked, '84 113
Lima Bean Casserole, Swiss, '80 191
Limas, Spanish Cheese, '86 225
Macaroni and Blue Cheese, '93 248;
    '94 44
Macaroni and Cheese, '83 M7;
    '88 M147, M190; '90 30
Macaroni and Cheese, Baked, '82 199
Macaroni and Cheese, Creamy, '93 249;
    '94 45
Macaroni-and-Cheese Deluxe, '79 84
Macaroni and Cheese Deluxe, '80 236
Macaroni and Cheese, Old-Fashioned,
    '92 215
Macaroni and Cheese, Tasty, '83 288
Macaroni and Cheese, Thick-and-Rich,
    '84 329
Macaroni-and-Cheese with Wine, '86 78
Macaroni Bake, Jack-in-the-, '93 249;
    '94 45
Macaroni, Cheese, and Tomatoes,
    '95 213
Macaroni-Cheese-Beef Casserole,
    '95 125
Macaroni, Double Cheese, '82 224
Macaroni-Mushroom Bake, Cheesy,
    '81 243
Manicotti, Cheesy, '83 216
Manicotti, Special, '88 50
Manicotti, Stuffed, '83 M6
Mexican Casserole, Cheesy, '82 224
Mexican Casserole, Microwave,
    '90 M231
Mushroom-Cheese Casserole, '83 216
Mushrooms au Gratin, '81 108
Onion Casserole, Cheesy, '79 101
Parmigiana, Eggplant, '95 197
Pineapple-Cheese Bake, '79 106
Pork Casserole, Cheesy, '81 M74
Pork Parmigiana, Easy, '94 57
Potato Casserole, Cheesy, '80 244;
    '83 53; '92 229
Potato-Cheese Casserole, '79 101
Potato-Cheese Dream, '91 307
Potato-Egg Casserole, Cheesy, '84 5
Potatoes and Eggs au Gratin, '79 107
Potatoes au Gratin, Shredded, '89 69
Potatoes, Cheesy Scalloped, '83 82
Potatoes, Cottage, '89 69
Potatoes, Double-Cheese, '86 6
Potatoes Gourmet, '80 114
Potatoes, Gruyère, '83 193
Potatoes, Mushroom Scalloped, '87 191
Potatoes, Scalloped, '83 211
Potatoes, Special Scalloped, '88 162
Reuben Casserole, '90 240
Rice-and-Cheese con Chiles, '89 99
Rice au Gratin, '83 129
Rice au Gratin Supreme, '86 78
Rice, Cheese-Parslied, '89 99
Rice Strata, Cheese-, '81 176
Sausage Brunch, Italian, '88 57
Sausage Casserole, Cheesy, '82 124
Sausage Casserole, Swiss, '80 209
Sausage-Cheese Bake, '88 58
Sausage-Chile Rellenos Casserole, '88 52
Seashell-Provolone Casserole, '80 189
Spinach Casserole, Cheesy,
    '81 263

Spinach Casserole, Cottage Cheese-and-,
    '84 77
Spinach-Cheese Bake, '88 10
Spinach-Cheese Casserole, '83 216;
    '89 64
Spinach-Parmesan Casserole, '82 281;
    '83 32
Spinach Ring au Fromage, '79 8
Squash Bake, Cheddar-, '84 M113, 128
Squash Casserole, Cheesy, '79 123;
    '82 M21
Tamale, Mozzarella, '95 70
Tuna Casserole with Cheese Swirls,
    '88 256
Turkey Parmigiana, '87 193
Turkey-Swiss Casserole, '86 283
Vegetable Casserole, Cheesy, '81 103
Vegetable Medley, Swiss, '95 26
Zucchini Casserole, Cheese-Egg-,
    '84 114
Zucchini Casserole, Cheesy, '82 168;
    '84 145
Zucchini-Jack Casserole, '85 296
Catfish Parmesan, '79 184; '86 210
Catfish, Parmesan, '92 309
Chicken Alouette, '91 295
Chicken, Baked Parmesan, '83 320
Chicken Breasts, Celebrity, '95 60
Chicken Breasts, Cream Cheese, '90 234
Chicken Breasts Gruyère, '80 189
Chicken Breasts Romano, '79 218
Chicken Cordon Bleu, '81 304; '82 83;
    '86 37
Chicken, Crispy Parmesan, '80 M76
Chicken Fiesta, Breast-of-, '88 151
Chicken Monterey, '82 275
Chicken-Mozzarella Melt, Italian, '95 153
Chicken, Oven-Fried Parmesan, '81 97;
    '82 148
Chicken Parmesan, '83 184; '95 210
Chicken Parmesan, Baked, '83 137
Chicken Provolone, '93 323
Chicken Rollups, Cheesy, '82 44
Chicken, Roquefort, '89 320
Chicken Skillet, Cheesy, '80 115
Chiles Rellenos, '88 116; '89 226
Chiles Rellenos, Roasted, '95 64
Chiles Rellenos with Walnut Cream Sauce,
    Havarti-and-Corn-Stuffed, '93 M275
Chili-Cheese Dogs, '81 M176
Chili, Cheese-Topped, '82 M11
Chili, Cheesy, '82 310
Chunky Cream Cheese, '85 306
Chutney with Cream Cheese, Cranberry-
    Amaretto, '87 244
Coffee Cake, Cream Cheese, '86 290
Coffee Cake, Deep-Dish Cheesecake, '90 50
Corn on the Cob, Parmesan, '88 M187
Country Ham Puff, Cheesy, '90 88
Crab Bake, Quick, '87 192
Crabmeat au Gratin, '86 154
Crackers, Hot Nut, '90 206
Cream Puffs with Chicken Salad, Cheesy,
    '86 260
Cream-Style Cheese, '85 209
Crème Brûlée, Roquefort-and-Black Pepper,
    '95 324
Crêpe Cups, Florentine, '89 44
Crêpes, Cheese and Mushroom, '81 88
Crêpes, Cheesy Sausage, '82 240; '83 71
Crêpes, Mushroom-Cheese, '87 289; '88 135
Crêpes, Spinach-Ricotta, '81 52
Crostini, Feta-Tomato, '92 159

CHEESE (continued)

Crust, Cheese, '80 286; '86 264
Crust, Cheesy Crumb, '88 86
Crust, Chicken Pot Pie with Cheese, '86 264
Crust, Parmesan, '94 304
Crust, Parmesan Pizza, '93 58
Desserts
  Almond-Raspberry Brie, '94 M89
  Bites, Starlight Cheese, '95 329
  Blintzes, Cheese, '82 146
  Brownies, Cream Cheese Swirl, '79 51
  Brownies, German Cream Cheese,
    '80 269
  Brownies, Walnut-Cream Cheese,
    '84 240
  Cake, Coconut-Cream Cheese Pound,
    '85 297; '90 305
  Cake, Cream Cheese Loaf, '84 151
  Cake, Cream Cheese Pound, '81 290;
    '86 287; '95 304
  Cake, Crusty Cream Cheese Pound,
    '89 124
  Cake, Poppy Seed, '95 63
  Cake, Regal Cream Cheese, '80 140
  Cake Squares, Cream Cheese, '84 321
  Cake, Tart Lemon-Cheese, '88 7
  Cannoli, '91 20
  Chocolate-Cheese Cups, '91 142
  Cookies, Cream Cheese, '80 282
  Cottage Cheese Dessert, Creamy,
    '87 191
  Crackers, Taco-Cheese Animal, '94 197
  Cream Cheese Frills, '79 291
  Crisp, Apple-Cheese, '92 235
  Cupcakes, Cream Cheese Party, '82 279
  Date-Cream Cheese Rollups, '83 298
  Date Dessert Cheese, Nutty, '87 299
  Frosting, Coconut Cream Cheese, '86 60
  Frosting, Cream Cheese, '79 45;
    '80 140, 253, 299; '82 135, 244;
    '83 105, 215, M233;
    '84 201, 255, 315, 316; '85 118, 121;
    '86 217, 337; '87 58; '90 305, 308;
    '92 120; '93 20; '94 254; '95 139
  Frosting, Deluxe Cream Cheese, '80 120
  Frosting, Fluffy Cream Cheese, '80 245
  Frosting, Lemon-Cream Cheese, '81 157
  Frosting, Nutty Cream Cheese, '85 117
  Frosting, Orange Cream, '82 14
  Frosting, Orange-Cream Cheese, '81 70;
    '82 16; '92 19
  Frosting, Pineapple-Cream Cheese,
    '95 160
  Frosting, White Chocolate-Cream
    Cheese, '94 58
  Frosting, White Chocolate-Cream Cheese
    Tiered Cake, '94 125
  Fruit, Cheese, and Nuts, '93 324
  Fruited Cream Cheese, '85 306
  Fruit with Cheese, Luscious Fresh,
    '79 153
  Fudge, Cream Cheese, '84 111
  Ginger Cheese, '92 163
  Glaze, Cream Cheese, '84 150; '94 242
  Kuchen, Cheese, '86 84
  Lemon-Cream Cheese Dessert, '84 95
  Loaves, Chocolate Chip Cheese, '91 299;
    '92 264
  Mints, Cream Cheese, '93 79
  Molds, Heavenly Dessert Cheese,
    '85 209

Pastries, Cream Cheese, '80 250
Pastries, German, '86 78
Pastry, Apple Tart with Cheese, '88 225
Pastry, Cheddar, '86 206
Pastry, Cheddar Cheese, '80 219;
  '82 194
Pastry, Cream Cheese, '86 78; '89 136
Pastry Shell, Cheese, '85 284
Pastry Shells, Cheese, '86 13
Patty Shells, Cream Cheese, '81 266
Pear-Blue Cheese Gratin, '93 328
Pecan-Cheese Crispies, '87 168
Pie, Apple-Cheese, '85 284
Pie, Apple-Cream Cheese, '81 247
Pie, Blueberry-Cream Cheese, '88 154
Pie, Chocolate-Cream Cheese, '80 69
Pie, Chocolate Cream Cheese, '92 240
Pie, Cottage Cheese, '82 85
Pie, Fruited Cheese, '92 228
Pie, Lemon Cheese, '81 136; '82 146
Pie, Lemon-Cottage Cheese, '79 44
Pie, Lemon Cottage Cheese, '81 143
Pie, Yogurt-Cheese, '82 121
Soufflé, Blintz, '88 155
Soufflé, Cream Cheese, '88 11
Spread, Chocolate Cheese, '87 292
Spread, Orange Cheese, '87 292
Squares, Lemony Cream Cheese, '82 159
Strawberry Cheese Delight, '79 50
Strawberry-Cream Cheese Dessert,
  '83 123
Tarts, Cranberry-Cream Cheese, '80 154
Tarts, Cream Cheese, '84 74; '90 312
Tarts, Lemon-Cheese, '79 2
Tiramisù, '91 21; '94 295
Wafers, Hope Farm Cheese, '93 282
Dressing, Blue Cheese, '79 69; '82 166;
  '86 233; '90 286
Dressing, Blue Cheese Salad, '82 94
Dressing, Cheese Fluff, '91 256
Dressing, Cheesy Barbecue Salad, '92 255
Dressing, Creamy, '95 66
Dressing, Creamy Blue Cheese, '81 150;
  '91 307
Dressing, Creamy Blue Cheese Salad, '86 123
Dressing, Creamy Roquefort, '84 12
Dressing, Garden Salad with Tomato-Cream
  Cheese, '79 173
Dressing, Parmesan, '86 192
Dressing, Romano, '80 174
Dressing, Roquefort, '79 85; '80 74; '93 128
Dressing, Special Blue Cheese, '80 74
Dressing, Tangy Blue Cheese, '87 81
Dressing, Zesty Blue Cheese, '79 104
Dumplings, Chicken Ragout with Cheddar,
  '94 44
Egg Medley, Cheddary, '81 M176
Eggs and Cheese, '95 165
Eggs, Blue Cheese Stuffed, '93 87
Eggs, Cheddar, '94 M141
Eggs, Cheese-Chive Scrambled, '95 34
Eggs, Chile-Cheese Deviled, '93 87
Eggs, Cottage, '85 44
Eggs, Cottage Cheese Scrambled, '81 142
Eggs, Cottage-Scrambled, '80 49
Eggs, Cream Cheese Scrambled, '81 287
Enchiladas, Cheese, '81 194; '85 154;
  '95 311
Enchiladas, Cheesy Sour Cream, '79 25
Enchiladas, Meatless, '93 106
Enchiladas, Saucy Cheese, '84 220
Enchiladas, Vegetable-Cheese, '94 42
Fettuccine, Broccoli-Parmesan, '93 55

Fillets, Blue Cheese-Walnut Stuffed, '95 327
Fillets, Parmesan, '86 M112
Fillings
  Blintz Filling, '92 84
  Cheese Filling, '89 91
  Chocolate-Cheese Filling, '90 47
  Cinnamon-Cheese Filling, '90 46
  Cream Cheese Filling, '90 170
  Lemon-Cheese Filling, '79 68; '88 7
  Orange-Cheese Filling, '90 47
  Orange Filling, Cheese-and-, '93 159
  Ricotta Filling, '80 58
  Spinach-Ricotta Filling, '81 53
Flounder au Fromage, Baked, '86 234
Flounder, Cheesy Broiled, '84 69
Fondue, Nacho, '94 332
Fondue, Pub, '94 332
Fowl, Fancy, '81 76
Fried Brie, Walnut-, '86 244
Frittata, Broccoli-Cheese, '81 243
Fritters, Cheesy Zucchini, '88 44
Frosting. See Cheese/Desserts.
Goat Cheese and Greens, '90 54
Grits, Baked Cheese, '94 240
Grits, Cheese, '90 102
Grits, Garlic-and-Herb Cheese, '95 122
Grits, Garlic-Cheese, '88 126; '89 47
Grits, Good Morning, '87 156
Grits, Grilllades and Baked Cheese, '94 240
Grits, Gruyère Cheese, '81 47
Grits, Jalapeño Cheese, '85 43
Grits, Quick Cheese, '83 M203
Grits, Sausage-Cheese, '90 238
Grits, Sliced Cheese, '84 75
Grits with Green Chiles, Cheese, '95 208
Ham-and-Cheese Bundles, '93 63
Ham-and-Cheese Flips, '92 46
Ham and Eggs on Toast with Cheese
  Sauce, '81 43
Ham-Cheese Chips, '82 34
Ham Dinner, Cheesy, '84 90
Ham, Frosted, '89 71
Ham Towers, Cheesy, '82 M77
Hominy, Hot Cheese, '84 77
Hush Puppies, Cheesy Mexican, '91 201
Kabobs, Swiss-Ham, '81 124
Little Bits, '79 196
Loaf, Cheese, '87 92
Loaf, Cheeseburger, '81 236, 276
Loaf, Pepperoni and Cheese, '82 32
Loaves, Sausage-Cheese, '88 235
Marinated Cheese, '90 244
Mayonnaise, Parmesan, '86 79
Meatballs, Golden Nugget, '82 233
Meatballs, Mock, '81 243
Meat Loaf, Mozzarella-Layered, '79 71
Meat Loaf Roll, Blue Cheese, '93 247
Noodles and Mushrooms, Cheesy, '79 84
Noodles, Cheesy Parmesan, '83 M7
Noodles, Ham and Swiss on, '87 108
Noodles, Parmesan, '83 118
Omelet, Cheddar-Vegetable, '83 205
Omelet, Cheesy Picante, '86 95
Omelet, Cheesy Vegetable, '85 49
Omelet, Dill-Cheese-Ham, '95 33
Omelet, Golden Cheese-Shiitake, '95 265
Omelet, Ham and Cheese, '79 262; '80 123
Omelet, Herbed Cheese, '93 47
Omelet, Puffed Cheese, '89 227
Omelets, George's, '80 68
Omelet, Shrimp-and-Cheddar, '84 57
Omelet, Shrimp-and-Cheese, '94 31
Omelet, Spinach-Cheese, '83 119

CHEESE (continued)

Omelet, Swiss Oven, '80 189
Omelet, Zippy Cheese, '87 287
Orange Cream Cheese, '91 177
Pancakes, Cottage Cheese, '79 115
Pasta, Mamma Mia, '95 25
Pasta Stuffed with Five Cheeses, '88 197
Pastry, Cheese, '88 56
Pastry, Cream Cheese, '82 39; '86 78;
    '89 136
Pastry Shells, Miniature Cream Cheese,
    '87 190
Pastry Tart Shells, Cheese, '85 216
Pâté, Cream Cheese, '80 154
Pâté, Liver-Cheese, '85 276
Patty Shells, Cream Cheese, '81 266; '82 249
Pears, Cheese-Filled, '81 268
Pears Stuffed with Cheese, '82 290
Peppers, Macaroni-and-Cheese-Stuffed,
    '80 65
Perch, Parmesan-Crusted, '93 91
Pie, Breakfast, '86 242
Pie, Broccoli-Cheese, '84 235
Pie, Cheese-Beef, '85 33
Pie, Cheesy Mexican Chicken, '82 142
Pie, Green Chile-Cheese, '84 234
Pie, Ham-and-Cheese, '95 256
Pie, Mexican Cheese, '82 9; '83 69
Pie, Mincemeat-Cheese, '80 253
Pie, Onion-Cheese, '88 86
Pie, Quick and Cheesy Corn, '82 191
Pie, Tortilla, '85 M211
Pie, Turkey-Cheese, '88 264
Pie, Zucchini-Ham-Cheese, '80 272
Pimiento Cheese, Chunky, '88 91
Pineapple Gratin, '93 328
Pizza, Breakfast, '88 288
Pizza, Cheese-and-Mushroom, '83 226
Pizza, Double Cheesy Beef-and-Sausage,
    '86 77
Pizza, Gruyère-Chicken, '87 182
Polenta Squares, Skillet, '94 22
Popcorn, Bacon-Cheese, '86 74
Popcorn, Cheesy Barbecue, '95 239
Popcorn, Sesame-Cheese, '79 220
Pork Chops, Cheese-Stuffed, '84 81
Pork Chops with Apples, Parmesan, '93 338
Pork Tenderloin with Blue Cheese, '86 76
Preserves, Cream Cheese and Peach, '84 264
Pudding, Baked Cheese, '86 78
Pudding, Cheesy Bread, '83 68
Pudding, Corn-Cheese, '80 244
Puff, Egg-and-Cheese, '85 45
Puff, Macaroni and Cheese, '79 5
Puffs, Bavarian Cheese, '80 191
Puffs, Turkey-Cheese, '87 301
Quesadillas, Quick, '89 87
Quesadillas, Sausage, '90 118
Quesadillas with Shrimp and Brie, '94 173
Quiches
    Bacon-Cheese Quiches, Miniature,
        '83 93
    Benedict Quiche, '80 M107
    Blue Cheese Quiche, '84 52
    Cheddar-Leek Quiche, '88 198
    Eggless Quiche, '87 220
    Green Onion Quiche, Cheesy, '83 194;
        '84 42
    Ham-Cheese Quiche, '79 26
    Ham Quiche, Cheesy, '79 127
    Jalapeño Quiche, Cheesy, '84 31

Lorraine, Perfect Quiche, '79 127
Lorraine, Quiche, '79 40; '80 M108
Miniature Cheese Quiches, '80 150
Sausage-Cheddar Quiche, '79 26
Sausage Quiche, Spicy, '80 M108
South-of-the-Border Quiche, '93 321
Spinach Quiche, Cheesy, '81 228
Squares, Cheesy Hot Quiche, '79 124
Swiss Alpine Quiche, '90 18
Swiss-Zucchini Quiche, '82 49
Tasty Quiche, '82 264
Vegetable Quiche, Cheese-, '81 228
Zucchini Quiche, Cheesy, '83 312
Ramekins, Three-Cheese, '79 26
Rarebit, Cheese, '86 78
Rarebit, Tangy Welsh, '88 159
Rarebit, Uptown Welsh, '87 279
Raspberry Brie in Rye, '93 252
Rice, Chili-Cheesy, '79 43
Roll, Cheesy Meat, '82 136
Rolls, Ham-and-Cheese Lettuce, '89 217
Rounds, Parmesan, '79 170
Rounds, Turkey-Mozzarella, '82 3
Salads
    Apple Salad, Cheesy, '86 301
    Apple Salad, Swiss-, '84 81
    Aspic, Cheesy Vegetable, '81 73
    Banana Splits, Cottage Cheese-, '87 56
    Black Bean-and-Cheese Salad, '92 217
    Blue Cheese Chicken Salad, '94 81
    Blue Cheese Salad, '88 48
    Blue Cheese Tossed Salad, '84 195
    Cantaloupe-Cheese Salad, '88 184
    Citrus-Blue Cheese Salad, '92 220
    Coleslaw, Blue Cheese, '89 13; '95 270
    Coleslaw, Cottage, '80 64
    Cottage Cheese Salad, Different, '85 328;
        '86 22
    Cottage Cheese Salad, Out-of-This-
        World, '79 44
    Cranberry-Cheese Ribbon Salad, '79 241
    Crunchy-Creamy Salad, '88 100
    Freeze Salad, Party, '82 145
    Fruit-'n'-Nut Salad, Cheesy, '87 56
    Fruit Salad, Cottage Cheese-and-, '86 16
    Goat Cheese and Black-Eyed Pea Salad,
        Fearrington House, '95 60
    Green Beans-and-Cheese Salad, '91 159
    Greens with Parmesan Walnuts, Mixed,
        '95 301
    Ham-and-Cheese Salad, '88 138
    Ham-Pecan-Blue Cheese Pasta Salad,
        '90 62
    Layered Salad, Cheesy, '81 37
    Lemon-Cheese Salad, '85 240
    Lettuce, Cheesy Stuffed, '79 175
    Lettuce Salad, Blue Cheese-Stuffed,
        '94 202
    Lime-Cheese Salad, Frosted, '79 286
    Macaroni-Cheese Salad, Dilled,
        '86 208
    Marinated Tomato and Brie Salad, '95 95
    Mexican Salad, '81 36
    Mold, Ambrosia Cream Cheese, '79 249
    Mold, Cheesy Lemon, '79 241
    Mold, Creamy Tuna-Cheese, '81 135
    Molds, Snowcap Cheese, '79 242
    Mushroom Salad, Quick Cheesy-,
        '89 128
    Orange-Cottage Cheese Salad, '79 44
    Pear-Apple Salad, Blue Cheese-, '81 224
    Pear-Swiss Cheese Salad, '91 237
    Pea Salad, Cheddar-, '84 82

    Pepper Toss, Parmesan, '93 208
    "Pig in the Garden" Salad, '92 255
    Potato Salad, Blue Cheese-, '91 208
    Potato Salad, Cottage Cheese-,
        '79 147, 285
    Potato Salad, Hot Parmesan, '79 78
    Roquefort Salad, Creamy, '79 73
    Spinach-Blue Cheese Salad, '82 166
    Spinach Salad with the Blues, '95 66
    Tomato-Basil-Mozzarella Salad, '95 171
    Tomato-Basil Salad, Fresh Mozzarella-,
        '93 131
    Tomatoes, Cottage Cheese Salad in,
        '86 208
    Tomato-Feta Salad, '81 246; '91 168
    Tomato-Mozzarella Salad, '89 220
    Tomato Salad, Cottage-, '85 163
    Tuna Salad, Cheese-Sauced, '87 M124
    Tuna Salad, Swiss, '86 186
    Vegetable Congealed Salad, Cheesy-,
        '86 199
    Ziti-Cheddar Salad, '85 165
Salmon Patties, Cheesy, '89 99
Sandwiches
    Avocado, Bacon, and Cheese Sandwiches,
        '87 279
    Bacon, Cheese, and Tomato Sandwiches,
        '84 14
    Bacon-Cheese Sandwiches, Grilled,
        '83 242
    Bacon, Pimiento, and Cheese Hoagies,
        '90 144
    Bacon Sandwiches, Open-Faced Cheesy,
        '80 78
    BLT's, Cheesy, '85 92
    Breakfast Sandwiches, '80 52
    Breakfast Sandwiches, Cheesy, '90 140
    Brown Bread-Cream Cheese Sandwiches,
        '87 M6
    Buns, Snack, '87 279
    Chicken-and-Cheese Sandwiches,
        Toasted, '85 242
    Chicken Parmigiana Sandwich, '94 65
    Chicken Sandwiches, Cheesy, '82 190
    Christmas Tree Sandwiches, '92 279
    Corned Beef and Cheese Sandwich,
        '79 214
    Crab-and-Cheese Sandwiches, Hot,
        '87 279
    Egg Sandwiches, Open-Faced Cheesy,
        '86 67
    Fruit-and-Cheese Breakfast Sandwiches,
        '89 M21
    Gingered Tea Sandwiches, '84 116
    Grilled Cheese Sandwiches, '82 M172;
        '94 167
    Grilled Cheese Sandwich, Mexican,
        '92 63
    Grilled Sandwiches, Tasty, '84 30
    Ham-and-Cheese Pita Pockets,
        '90 271
    Ham-and-Cheese Pita Sandwiches,
        '87 202; '88 44
    Ham-and-Cheese Sandwiches, Hot,
        '85 299
    Ham-and-Cheese Sandwich Round,
        '94 326
    Ham-and-Cheese Sandwich, Tex-Mex,
        '86 4
    Ham and Swiss in the Pocket, '83 31
    Ham-and-Swiss Sandwiches, Tangy,
        '85 164
    Ham-and-Turkey Specials, Cheesy, '84 14

CHEESE, Sandwiches *(continued)*

Ham 'n' Cheese Chicken, Sandwich, '95 153
Ham Sandwiches, Creamy Blue Cheese-, '87 279
Hot French Cheese Sandwiches, '82 3
Lasagna in a Bun, '90 176
Leafy Cheese Sandwiches, '90 56
"Muffy" Sandwich, Fertitta's, '94 34
Peanut-Cheese-Raisin Sandwiches, '88 140
Pimiento Cheese Sandwiches, '82 278
Pita, Stuffed, '89 87
Sausage-Cheese Muffin Sandwiches, '92 M212
Sebastian, The, '94 184
Shrimp-Cheese Sandwiches, '85 242
Tea Sandwiches, Cheese, '92 276
Tortilla Stack-Ups, '92 196
Tuna Cheesies, '82 191
Yummy Sandwiches, '81 229
Sauces
Blue Cheese Sauce, '90 142; '94 320
Cheddar Cheese Sauce, '91 286
Cheese Sauce, '79 M156;
  '81 43, 44, 225; '82 M123;
  '83 49, 138, 188; '84 57; '85 92;
  '86 241; '88 78, 272; '89 181, 229;
  '90 235; '93 48
Cottage Cheese Sauce, '87 232
Cream Sauce, Cheesy, '82 79
Devonshire Sauce, Processor, '86 337
Easy Cheese Sauce, '79 22
Garlic-Cheese Sauce, '84 M70
Guilt-Free Cheese Sauce, '93 M95
Lemon-Cheese Sauce, '91 24
Lemony Cheese Sauce, '84 183
Monterey Jack Sauce, '84 293
Mornay Sauce, '80 120; '81 90; '89 195
Mushroom-Cheese Sauce, '83 190;
  '86 48
Parmesan Cheese Sauce, '79 165;
  '80 162; '85 143
Parmesan Sauce, '92 17
Rich Cheese Sauce, '81 89
Roquefort Sauce, '89 321
Seafood Cheese Sauce, '89 240
Swiss Cheese Sauce, '79 35; '87 289;
  '88 135
Swiss Sauce, '83 M195
Swiss Sauce, Creamy, '80 M53
Topper, Vegetable-Cheese Potato, '86 6
Vegetable-Cheese Sauce, '85 M152
Vegetable Sauce, Cheesy, '92 M134
Scallops, Baked Gruyère, '92 57
Scallops, Chip and Cheese, '80 301
Scallops Mornay, '80 164
Schnitzel, Swiss, '80 189
Shake, Strawberry-Cheesecake, '92 44
Shell, Rice-Cheese, '82 49
Shells, Cheesy Beef-Stuffed, '83 217
Shells, Cream Cheese, '79 2
Shortcakes, Cheesy Chicken, '95 98
Shrimp au Gratin, '85 79
Shrimp, Parmesan-Stuffed, '85 103
Soufflé, Blue Cheese, '91 244
Soufflé, Cheese, '79 72, 261; '94 116
Soufflé, Cheesy Spinach, '81 53
Soufflé, Corn-and-Cheese, '88 122
Soufflé Cups, Hot, '85 284
Soufflé for Two, Cheese, '81 226

Soufflé, Rice-Cheese, '79 270
Soufflé, Rolled Cheese, '89 13
Soufflés, Individual, '80 190
Soufflés, Individual Frozen, '80 52
Soufflé, Three-Egg Cheese, '87 234
Soups
Anytime Soup, Cheesy, '81 307; '82 314;
  '83 66
Bacon-Beer Cheese Soup, '87 M7
Bacon-Topped Cheese Soup, '80 M224
Beer-Cheese Soup, '84 246
Bell Pepper-Cheese Chowder, '95 240
Broccoli Soup, Cheese-and-, '89 276
Broccoli Soup, Cheesy-, '86 258
Broccoli-Swiss Soup, '86 6
Carrot Soup, Cheesy, '81 262
Cheddar Chowder, Hearty, '79 16
Chicken Chowder, Cheesy, '92 21
Corn and Cheese Chowder, '80 228
Cream of Cheese Soup, '83 99
Cream with Greens Soup, '94 277
Favorite Cheese Soup, Uncle Ed's, '94 228
Gazebo Cheese Soup, '90 158
Gazpacho, Shrimp-Cream Cheese, '94 137
Golden Cheese Chowder, '80 73
Ham-and-Cheese Chowder, '89 15
Ham 'n Cheese Chowder, '79 199
Hearty Cheese Soup, '84 4
Hot Cheese Chowder, '89 16
Macaroni and Cheese Soup, '95 264
Monterey Jack Cheese Soup, '81 112;
  '85 M211
Onion Cheese Soup, '87 81
Onion Soup, Double-Cheese, '85 227
Onion Soup, Double Cheese-Topped, '79 49
Oyster-Cheese Soup, '84 213
Potato-and-Wild Rice Soup, Cheesy, '89 16
Roquefort Vichyssoise, Velvety, '83 223
Swiss-Broccoli Chowder, '80 73
Tomato Soup with Parmesan Cheese, Cream of, '86 161
Vegetable-Cheese Soup, '89 15
Vegetable-Cheese Soup, Creamy, '81 244
Vegetable Cheese Soup, Creamy, '83 230
Vegetable Chowder, Cheesy, '80 25;
  '83 20
Vegetable Soup, Cheesy, '80 73
Velvet Soup, Cheese, '80 74; '92 193
Spaghetti, Three-Cheese, '83 105
Spanakópita, '86 58
Spreads
Almond Cheese Spread, '87 292
Aloha Spread, '83 93
Apricot Brie Spread, '86 275
Apricot-Cream Cheese Spread, '82 161;
  '87 158
Artichoke-Parmesan Spread, '92 95
Bacon-Cheese Spread, '83 241
Beer Cheese Spread, '81 160; '85 69
Beer Spread, Cheesy, '87 196
Blue Cheese Spread, '90 215; '95 79, 92
Boursin Cheese Spread, Buttery, '94 301
Boursin Cheese Spread, Garlic, '94 301
Caviar-Cream Cheese Spread, '84 256
Chile-and-Cheese Spread, '86 297
Chili Cheese Spread, '93 242
Chocolate Cheese Spread, '87 292

Coconut-Cranberry Cheese Spread, '92 328
Confetti Cheese Spread, '84 256
Cottage Cheese Spread, '87 107
Cottage-Egg Salad Spread, '82 146
Cream Cheese-Olive Spread, '82 35
Cream Cheese Spread, Deviled, '81 235
Cream Cheese Spread, Fruited, '91 306;
  '93 79
Cream Cheese Spread, Peachy, '90 M215
Cream Cheese Spread, Pear-, '93 80
Cucumber and Cream Cheese Spread, '82 140
Edam-Sherry Spread, '84 257
Fruit and Cheese Spread, '81 245
Fruit-and-Cheese Spread, Nutty, '87 246
Garlic Pimiento Cheese Spread, '79 58
German Cheese Spread, '79 82
Gouda Cheese Spread, '90 36
Green Onion-Cheese Spread, '92 24
Gruyère-Apple Spread, '81 160
Ham and Pimiento Spread, '80 285
Hawaiian Cheese Spread, '87 158
Herb-Cream Cheese Spread, '83 24
Herbed Cheese Spread, '87 247
Horseradish Spread, Cheese-, '84 222
Jalapeño-Cheese Spread, '82 248
Make-Ahead Cheese Spread, '93 324
Mexican Cheese Spread, '90 119
Olive Spread, Cheese-, '79 82
Orange Cheese Spread, '87 292
Parmesan-Spinach Spread, '93 55
Pimiento and Three Cheeses, '86 296
Pimiento Cheese, Chunky, '86 295
Pimiento Cheese, Creamy, '86 296
Pimiento Cheese Spread, '82 35; '83 93;
  '86 127
Pimiento Cheese Spread, Creamy, '92 159
Pimiento Cheese Spread, Low-Calorie, '85 215
Pimiento Cheese, West Texas, '84 9
Pineapple-Cheese Spread, '86 126;
  '91 167
Pineapple-Cream Cheese Spread, '82 35
Sandwich Spread, Benedictine, '80 299
Swiss Cheese Spread, '90 60
Tomato-Cheese Spread, '81 157
Tomato-Cheese Spread, Fiery, '87 196
Tropical Cheese Spread, '95 46
Vegetable Sandwich Spread, '83 174
Waldorf Cheese Spread, '88 173
Zesty Cheese Spread, '82 140
Zippy Cheese Spread, '85 4
Steak Cheese Skillet, Swiss, '80 106
Steak Parmesan, '93 41
Steak, Parmesan Round, '80 106
Steaks, Blue Cheese, '84 171
Steaks, Cheese-Stuffed, '81 17
Strata, Artichoke-Cheese, '90 236
Strata, Tomato-Cheese, '81 209
Stromboli, '88 272; '89 181
Stuffing, Catfish with Cream Cheese, '89 52
Supper Supreme, Sunday, '79 76
Sweet Potato Chips with Blue Cheese, '93 290
Tart, Dried Tomato-Cheese, '90 203
Tart, Ham-and-Cheese, '92 332
Tart, Herb-Cheese, '87 98
Tart Milan, '87 70
Tart Shells, Cheese, '88 88
Tarts, Sausage 'n' Cheese, '88 51
Terrine, Italian Cheese, '93 64

CHEESE *(continued)*

Terrine with Goat Cheese, Black Bean,
  '87 120
Tomato, Basil, and Cheese, '95 165
Topping, Blue Cheese Burger, '93 218
Topping, Cheese, '86 233
Topping, Yogurt-Cheese, '88 55
Tortellini with Rosemary-Parmesan Sauce,
  '92 284
Tortillas, Cheesy, '81 62
Tortilla Snack, Two-Cheese, '90 119
Tortilla Stack, Cheesy Chicken-, '86 3
Toss, Ham and Cheese, '79 55
Trout Florentine, Cheesy, '85 53
Turkey Parmesan, '82 268
Turnovers, Sausage-Cheese, '88 231; '89 22
Twists, Cheese, '92 125
Veal Parmigiana, '81 227
Vegetables
  Artichoke-Cheese Bottoms, Baked,
    '94 61
  Asparagus on Toast, Creamed, '95 61
  Asparagus with Goat Cheese Sauce,
    '93 116
  Broccoli-and-Eggs au Gratin, '85 289
  Broccoli au Gratin, '82 M20
  Broccoli Fritters, Cheesy, '79 53
  Broccoli with Cheese Sauce, '82 107
  Brussels Sprouts with Cheese Sauce,
    '79 246
  Cabbage, Cheese Scalloped, '81 87;
    '82 7
  Cauliflower au Gratin, '82 204
  Cauliflower au Gratin, French-Fried,
    '79 221; '80 82
  Cauliflower, Baked Swiss, '79 100
  Cauliflower, Cheese-Frosted, '85 68
  Cauliflower Italiano, Cheesy, '82 300
  Cauliflower with Cheese Sauce, '81 101
  Cherry Tomatoes, Cheesy, '83 135
  Chiles Rellenos (Stuffed Chiles), '82 220;
    '83 150
  Corn-and-Swiss Cheese Bake, '92 133
  Corn, Grilled Parmesan, '82 127
  Eggplant, Cheesy Fried, '90 75
  Eggplant, Cheesy Stuffed, '79 188;
    '82 208
  Eggplant, Fried Parmesan, '87 166
  Eggplant Parmesan, '82 230; '92 18
  Eggplant, Parmesan Fried, '79 189
  Eggplant Parmesan, No-Fry, '92 172
  Eggplant, Scalloped, '91 223
  Fries, Cheesy Oven, '91 187
  Green Beans au Gratin, '80 116
  Green Beans, Cheese-Topped, '79 100
  Green Beans, Cheesy, '80 157
  Green Beans with Blue Cheese, '88 57
  Hash Brown Cheese Bake, '82 50
  Lentils with Cheese, Baked, '84 113
  Limas in Onion Shells, Cheese and,
    '81 86
  Loaf, Pureed Vegetable-Cheese, '85 297
  Mushrooms, Parmesan Stuffed, '83 115
  Mushrooms, Ricotta-Stuffed, '85 20
  New Potatoes, Cheesy, '85 156
  Okra with Cheese, '80 185
  Onion Bake, Cheese, '82 32
  Onion Bake, Romano, '90 98
  Onions, Cheese-Stuffed, '90 34
  Onions, Parmesan, '93 170
  Onions, Sherried Cheese, '82 32

Potato-Broccoli-Cheese Bake, '80 114
Potato-Cheese Puff, '95 269
Potato Croquettes, Parmesan, '84 210
Potatoes Alfredo, '89 204
Potatoes-and-Zucchini au Gratin, '84 5
Potatoes au Gratin, '93 90, 217
Potatoes, Bacon-Topped Blue Cheese,
  '79 46
Potatoes, Basil-Cheese, '90 M316
Potatoes, Blue Cheese Mashed, '92 330
Potatoes, Blue Cheese Stuffed, '81 276;
  '92 M228
Potatoes, Blue Cheese-Stuffed, '89 69
Potatoes, Cheesy, '82 211
Potatoes, Cheesy Bacon-Stuffed, '81 61
Potatoes, Cheesy Caraway, '86 17
Potatoes, Cheesy Chive, '79 46
Potatoes, Cheesy Chive-Stuffed,
  '91 128
Potatoes, Cheesy Crab-Stuffed, '86 17
Potatoes, Cheesy Frank-Topped, '83 3
Potatoes, Chicken-Cheese Stuffed,
  '86 55
Potatoes, Chili-Cheese, '90 M62
Potatoes, Chive-Cream Cheese Mashed,
  '92 330
Potatoes, Creamy Cheese, '88 M146
Potatoes, Feta Mashed, '92 330
Potatoes, Parmesan, '82 270; '90 M62;
  '92 M341; '93 M46
Potatoes Roquefort, '79 211
Potatoes, Two-Cheese, '80 114
Potatoes with Cheese Sauce, Baked,
  '83 239
Potatoes with Cheese Sauce, Stuffed,
  '87 192
Potatoes with Feta Cheese, '84 295;
  '85 196
Potatoes with Sweet Marjoram and
  Parmesan Cheese, Scalloped, '91 246
Potato Fans, Parmesan-, '88 M190
Potato Gratin, Dual, '93 328
Potato Skins, Cheese, '84 M239
Potato Soufflé, Cheesy, '89 332
Potato Wedges, Parmesan, '95 181
Rice au Gratin, '83 129
Rutabaga au Gratin, '79 254
Spinach-Cheese Puff, '84 96
Spinach, Cheesy Topped, '84 85
Spinach Parmesan, '93 72
Spinach Pie with Muenster Crust,
  '95 48
Spinach, Savory Parmesan, '85 68
Spinach with Cheese, Scalloped, '79 8
Spinach with Feta, Lemon, '85 190
Squash and Tomato Bake, '95 180
Squash Bake, Cheesy, '80 183
Squash Boats, Parmesan-Stuffed,
  '79 156
Squash, Cheesy Stuffed, '82 134
Squash, Greek-Style, '92 26
Squash Soufflé, Cheesy, '82 146
Stalks, Splendid, '93 258
Summer Vegetables, Cheesy, '94 119
Sweet Potato Blues, Stacked, '95 290
Swiss Chard Bundles, '94 48
Tomato Cheese Puffs, '81 48
Tomatoes, Baked Cheddar, '85 43
Tomatoes, Cheese Herbed-Topped,
  '86 108
Tomatoes, Cheese-Stuffed, '91 69
Tomatoes, Cheese-Topped, '81 160
Tomatoes, Cheesy Grilled, '79 150

Tomatoes, Cheesy Puff-Top, '86 187
Tomatoes, Cheesy Stuffed, '80 161
Tomatoes, Chile-Cheese Stuffed,
  '94 141
Tomatoes, Parmesan, '80 161
Tomatoes, Parmesan-Stuffed, '92 182
Tomatoes, Romano Broiled, '80 42
Tomatoes with Cheese Sauce over Toast,
  '88 159
Turnip au Gratin, '79 289
Turnips au Gratin, '88 229; '89 244
Turnips in Cheese Sauce, '84 229
Yellow Squash with Cheese Sauce,
  Stuffed, '80 162
Zucchini and Tomato au Gratin,
  '82 208
Zucchini Fries, Parmesan-, '95 129
Zucchini, Ham and Cheese Stuffed,
  '79 157
Zucchini Parmesan, '81 108; '82 103
Zucchini, Parmesan, '81 234
Zucchini Pie, Cheesy, '82 103
Zucchini with Feta, Greek Grilled,
  '95 190
Vermicelli, Shrimp and Feta Cheese on,
  '87 108
Vinaigrette, Blue Cheese, '90 55, 280
Vinaigrette, Garlic-Blue Cheese, '92 57
Wafers, Cheese, '95 174
Wafers, Hope Farm Cheese, '93 282
Wafers, Italian, '87 36
Wafers, Sage-Pecan Cheese, '93 12
Walnut-Baked Brie, '93 241

CHEESECAKES

Amaretto Cheesecake, '81 150
Amaretto-Irish Cream Cheesecake, '90 266
Apple Cheesecake, Dieter's, '86 318
Black Forest Cheesecake, '84 74; '89 93;
  '94 21
Blueberries 'n' Cream Cheesecake, '87 140
Blueberry Chiffon Cheesecake, '87 76
Brownies, Cheesecake, '85 249
Brown Sugar-and-Spice Cheesecake, '89 93
Butter Pecan Cheesecake, '86 61
Butterscotch Cheesecake, '86 188
Candy Bar Cheesecake, '85 298; '86 120
Cherry Cheesecake, '79 50
Cherry-Topped Cheesecake, '80 23
Chicken Cheesecake, Curried, '90 174
Chicken-Chile Cheesecake, '92 42
Chocolate-Almond Cheesecake, '93 53
Chocolate-Amaretto Cheesecake, '85 M294;
  '93 97
Chocolate-Caramel-Pecan Cheesecake,
  '91 197
Chocolate Cheesecake, '81 16; '82 305
Chocolate Cheesecake, Rich, '84 74; '85 38

CHEESECAKES (continued)

Chocolate Cheesecakes, Tiny, '92 288
Chocolate Cheesecake with Whipped Cream Frosting, '89 42
Chocolate Chip Cheesecake, '85 114
Chocolate Cookie Cheesecake, '91 298
Chocolate Marble Cheesecake, '89 93
Chocolate-Mint Baked Alaska Cheesecake, '94 142
Chocolate-Mint Cheesecake, '91 104
Chocolate-Raspberry Truffle Cheesecake, '91 270
Chocolate Swirl Cheesecake, '84 295; '85 26
Coffee Cake, Deep-Dish Cheesecake, '90 50
Cottage Cheese Cheesecake, '80 24
Cream Cheesecake, Rich, '83 270
Crème de Menthe Cheesecake, '82 263; '89 93
Daiquiri Chiffon Cheesecake, '88 66
Deluxe Cheesecake, '80 23
Feta Cheesecakes, Little, '86 277
Fiesta Cheesecake, '93 273
Frozen Cheesecake with Raspberry Sauce, '84 73
Fruit-Glazed Cheesecake, '80 24; '90 162
German Chocolate Cheesecake, '87 265
Glazed Cheesecake, '83 142
Grasshopper Cheesecake, '80 191
Ham-and-Asparagus Cheesecake, '90 174
Individual Cheesecakes, So Easy, '85 30
Kahlúa Cheesecake, Heavenly, '83 48
Lemon Cheesecake, '86 194; '91 308; '92 24
Lemon Cheesecake, Luscious, '90 M196
Lemon Cheesecake with Orange-Pineapple Glaze, '81 60
Lemon Delight Cheesecake, '95 219
Light-and-Easy Cheesecake, '88 55
Make-Ahead Cheesecake Pie, '81 233
Marbled Cheesecake, '87 261
Marble Mint Cheesecake, '84 152
Margarita Cheesecake, '92 211; '94 142
Mile-High Cheesecake, '86 334
Miniature Cheesecakes, '82 305; '90 170
Mocha-Chocolate Cheesecake, '88 258
Mocha Swirl Cheesecake, '87 262
Orange Cheesecake, '81 84; '85 38
Passover Cheesecake, '91 53
Peaches 'n' Cream Cheesecake, '88 137
Peanut Butter Cheesecake, '94 142
Pear-Berry Cheesecake, '82 M141
Pear-Glazed Cheesecake, '79 67
Pecan Cheesecake, '85 38
Peppermint Cheesecake, Frozen, '94 143
Petite Cheesecakes, Holiday, '86 321
Phyllo Cheesecakes, Little, '87 275
Piña Colada Cheesecake, '92 70
Pineapple Cheesecake, '81 32
Pineapple Cheesecake, Ultimate, '85 38
Praline Cheesecake, '83 270; '89 93
Pumpkin Cheesecake, '80 254; '85 280
Raspberry Sauce, Cheesecake with, '87 116
Reuben Cheesecake, '90 175
Ricotta Cheesecake, Italian, '95 303
Shrimp-and-Gruyère Cheesecake, '92 57
Sour Cream Cheesecake, '86 320
Spinach-Mushroom Cheesecake, '92 326
Spinach Pesto Cheesecake, '90 175
Squares, Cheesecake, '84 151

Strawberry Cheesecake, Almost, '86 32
Sweet Potato Cheesecake, '80 287
Tarts, Cream Cheese, '84 74
Triple-Layer Cheesecake, Chocolate-Glazed, '86 315; '90 310
Vanilla Cheesecake, Creamy, '89 93
Vegetable Cheesecake, Layered, '91 62; '92 51
White Chocolate Cheesecake, '87 44; '88 267; '94 180
Yam Cheesecake, '81 224

CHERRIES

à la Mode, Cherries, '88 202
Bars, Delightful Cherry, '86 217
Bread, Cherry Nut, '81 306; '82 36
Bread, Maraschino Cherry Nut, '79 234
Bread, Quick Cherry-Nut, '85 55
Cake, Black Forest Cherry, '83 302
Cake, Cherry, '79 165
Cake, Cherry Bourbon, '82 287
Cake, Cherry Upside-Down, '82 56
Cake, Chocolate-Cherry, '84 200; '86 239
Cake, Cute-as-a-Button Cherry Pound, '95 139
Cake, Maraschino Nut, '83 268
Cake, Quick Cherry, '81 238
Cake, Upside-Down Sunburst, '87 9
Cake, White Chocolate-Cherry, '88 268
Cheesecake, Black Forest, '89 93; '94 21
Cheesecake, Cherry, '79 50
Cheesecake, Cherry-Topped, '80 23
Chocolate-Covered Cherries, '81 286; '84 298
Chocolates, Cherry, '95 321
Cider, Cherry, '94 288
Cloud, Cherry-Berry on a, '79 94
Cobbler, Berry-Cherry, '83 270
Cobbler, Cherry, '82 91, 139
Cobbler, Colossal Cherry, '89 137
Cobbler, Fresh Cherry, '84 178
Cobbler, Raspberry-Cherry, '93 230
Coffee Cake, Cherry, '94 49
Coffee Cake, Cherry Blossom, '80 21
Compote, Cherry, '83 139
Compote, Watermelon-Cherry, '90 180
"Concrete," Cardinal Sin, '94 113
Cookies, Cherry Bonbon, '93 52
Cookies, Cherry Pecan, '82 136
Cookies, Chocolate-Cherry, '85 324
Cookies, Christmas Cherry, '88 282
Cookies, Coconut-Cherry, '79 292
Cookies, Frosted Chocolate-Cherry, '89 294
Cream, Maraschino Russian, '79 231
Crêpes, Cherry, '91 67
Crêpes Flambé, Cherry, '79 18
Crisp, Cherry, '91 20
Crisp, Oatmeal Cherry-Apple, '90 M16
Crowns, Cherry, '92 275
Dessert, Cherry Cordial, '84 312
Dessert, Holiday Cherry, '80 255
Drops, Cherry-Almond, '81 20
Filling, Cherry, '83 302; '84 225; '88 178
Frosting, Cherry, '86 217
Frosting, Chocolate-Cherry, '89 294
Fudge, Cherry Nut, '83 315
Glaze, Cherry, '83 143; '93 52
Ice Cream, Black Forest, '88 203
Ice Cream, Cherry, '84 184
Ice Cream, Cherry-Nut, '86 129
Ice Cream, Cherry-Pecan, '88 203
Jubilee, Cherries, '79 18; '83 139
Jubilee, Quick Cherries, '82 M100

Jubilite, Cherries, '86 317
Kirsch, Melon Balls and Cherries in, '91 91
Muffins, Cherry, '82 105
Muffins, Cherry-Nut, '90 87
Muffins, Dried Cherry, '94 59
Nuggets, Cherry Nut, '81 286
Pies
    Berry Pie, Cherry-, '92 316
    Coconut Crumb Cherry Pie, '92 30
    Cranberry-Cherry Pie, Tart, '87 299
    Cream Pie with Almond Pastry, Cherry, '92 30
    Easy Cherry Pie, '82 M299
    Fresh Cherry Pie, '88 178
    Lemony Cherry Pie, '92 30
    No-Bake Cherry Confetti Pie, '93 114
    Pecan Pie, Cherry-, '92 30
    Prize-Winning Cherry Pie, '82 57
    Red Cherry Pie, '83 192
    Scrumptious Cherry Pie, '83 250
Pork Roast, Cherry-Glazed, '91 84
Punch, Cranberry-Cherry, '91 176
Rolls, Cherry-Almond, '84 M198
Sabayon, Cherries, '88 178
Salads
    Apple Salad, Cherry-, '86 31
    Best Cherry Salad, '82 302
    Cola Salad, Cherry, '80 104
    Cola Salad, Cherry-, '91 224; '95 94
    Congealed Cherry Salad, '89 278
    Festive Cherry Salad, '84 265
    Fresh Cherry Salad, '83 120
    Frozen Black Cherry Salad, '89 163
    Frozen Cherry Salad, '79 126
    Frozen Cherry Salad, Delicious, '81 252
    Fruit Salad, Cherry, '87 236
    Honey-Lime Dressing, Cherry Salad with, '83 139
    Orange Salad, Cherry-, '79 74; '82 56
    Port Wine-Cherry Salad, '86 11
    Sherry Dressing, Cherry Salad with, '79 165
    Sweet Cherry Salad, '89 326
    Wine Salad, Elegant Cherry-, '82 56
Sauce, Cherry, '79 91; '83 276; '84 91; '91 67
Sauce, Cherry-Wine, '95 285
Sauce, Chocolate-Cherry, '85 189
Sauce, Chocolate Cherry, '87 M165
Sauce, Elegant Cherry, '79 M156
Sauce, Ham Balls with Spiced Cherry, '81 112; '82 12
Sauce, Roast Ducklings with Cherry, '86 312
Sauce, Roast Pork with Spiced Cherry, '89 324
Sauce, Royal Cherry, '85 224; '86 83
Sauce, Spicy Cherry, '83 244
Sherried Cherries, '93 289
Slump, Cherry, '83 139
Snow, Berries on, '82 227
Spread, Cherry, '93 309
Squares, Surprise Cherry, '82 57
Stuffed Cherries, '85 81
Syrup, Cherry-Lemonade, '86 214
Tart, Cherry and Blackberry, '83 225
Tarts, Cheery Cherry, '80 238
Topping, Cherry-Pineapple, '87 126
Torte, Black Forest Cherry, '88 178

CHICKEN

Acapulco, Chicken, '84 32
à la King, Chicken, '79 218; '83 137;
   '87 197; '94 41
à la King, Easy Chicken, '93 14
Almond Chicken and Vegetables, '86 21
Almond Chicken, Creamy, '89 281
Almond Chicken, Spicy, '88 150
à l'Orange, Chicken, '84 277
Alouette, Chicken, '91 295
Andalusia, Chicken, '87 103
Appetizers, Chicken-Mushroom, '88 210
Appetizers, Sesame Chicken, '89 61
Apple Chicken, '85 57
Apricot Chicken, '92 12
Apricot Chicken Breasts, '88 301
Ariosto, Shrimp and Chicken, '79 31
Artichoke Chicken, '81 97
Artichoke Hearts, Chicken with, '88 54
Artichokes and Mushrooms, Chicken with,
   '90 35
Artichokes, Italian Chicken and, '95 68
Bag, Chicken in a, '86 M57; '87 23
Bake, Chicken, Ham, and Cheese, '87 217
Bake, Chicken-Italian Dressing, '91 199
Bake, Chicken-Tomato, '83 35
Bake, Crispy Chicken, '83 115
Baked Breast of Chicken with Marinated
   Bermuda Onions, '92 194
Baked Chicken and Artichoke Hearts, '82 260
Baked Chicken and Dressing, '79 296
Baked Chicken, Breaded, '81 76
Baked Chicken Breasts, Sherried, '79 83
Baked Chicken Breasts, Wine-, '83 177
Baked Chicken, Citrus Herb, '85 303
Baked Chicken, Fancy, '79 85
Baked Chicken, Herb-, '82 229
Baked Chicken in Wine, '81 109
Baked Chicken, Italian, '82 84
Baked Chicken Parmesan, '83 137
Baked Chicken, Tomato-, '81 281; '82 30
Baked Chicken with Tarragon Sauce, '94 126
Baked Chicken with Wine-Soaked Vegetables,
   '84 277
Baked Hen with Cranberry Pan Gravy,
   '94 308
Baked Italian Chicken, '83 184
Baked Lemon Chicken, '85 190
Baked Mustard Chicken, '87 10
Baked Parmesan Chicken, '83 320
Bake, Herb Chicken, '82 186
Bake, Individual Chicken, '90 279
Bake, Mushroom-Chicken, '89 147
Bake, Parslied Chicken, '90 65
Bake, Pineapple Chicken, '82 120
Bake, Saucy Chicken, '84 220
Bake, Seasoned Chicken, '94 278
Ball, Chicken-Cheese, '93 216
Ball, Chicken-Curry Cheese, '85 118
Balls, Coconut Curried Chicken, '91 165
Balls, Curried Chicken, '91 98
Barbecued
   Bake, Barbecued Chicken, '81 97
   Bundles, Chicken-Mushroom, '80 157
   Chicken, Barbecue, '86 122
   Chicken, Barbecued, '82 97, 106;
      '83 103; '85 144; '86 153; '89 167
   Cranberry Chicken, Barbecued,
      '83 178
   Glazed Barbecue Chicken, Carambola-,
      '92 246
   Golden Barbecued Chicken, '83 136
   Grilled Barbecued Chicken, '81 154

Legs and Thighs, Barbecued Chicken,
   '94 94
Lemon Barbecued Chicken, '93 215
Marinated Barbecued Chicken, '79 90
Old South Barbecued Chicken, '82 97;
   '83 103
Orange Barbecued Chicken, '88 123
Oven-Barbecued Cranberry Chicken,
   '93 332
Saucy Barbecued Chicken, '83 11
Tangy Barbecued Chicken, '86 186
White Barbecue Sauce, Chicken with,
   '89 M84
Zesty Barbecued Chicken, '80 M76
Zippy Barbecued Chicken, '83 213
Basil Chicken, '87 171
Bengalese Chicken, '79 12
Bird's-Nest Chicken, '88 152
Birds of Paradise, '82 224
Biscuit, Chicken in a, '79 263; '80 30
Bites, Curried Chicken, '85 40
Bites, Savory Chicken, '92 209
Bourbon Chicken with Gravy, '94 252
Bourbon-Purple Onion Relish, Chicken with,
   '95 253
Braised Bourbon Chicken, '86 51
Braised Chicken Breast in Lemon Cream
   Sauce, '94 184
Brandado, Chicken, '84 195
Breaded Chicken Breasts, '89 M196
Breast of Chicken, Herbed, '79 100
Breasts, Celebrity Chicken, '95 60
Breasts, Greek Chicken, '95 170
Breasts, Island Chicken, '84 68
Breasts Lombardy, Chicken, '82 242
Breasts, Salsa-Topped Chicken, '94 144
Breasts, Saucy Chicken, '83 184; '87 167
Breasts with Herb Butter, Chicken, '89 120
Brioche Chicken Curry, '88 124
Broiled Chicken Breast Tarragon, '89 310
Broiled Chicken, Island, '84 288
Broth, Easy Microwave Chicken, '90 M167
Bundles, Cheesy Chicken-and-Ham, '84 261
Bundles, San Antonio-Style Chicken, '85 251
Bundles with Bacon Ribbons, Chicken, '87 68
Burgers, Open-Faced Chicken-Onion, '94 139
Burgoo, Five-Meat, '87 3
Burgoo, Harry Young's, '87 3
Burgoo, Old-Fashioned, '87 3
Buttermilk-Pecan Chicken, '89 166
Cajun Chicken over Rice, '87 268; '88 102;
   '89 67
Cashew Chicken, '79 255; '80 8; '83 21
Cashew, Chicken, '88 38
Cashews, Chicken with, '79 207
Casseroles
   à la Russell, Chicken, '95 175
   Almond Casserole, Chicken-, '94 199
   Asparagus Casserole, Chicken-, '83 76;
      '84 71
   Breast-of-Chicken Fiesta, '88 151
   Breasts, Creamy Baked Chicken, '83 24
   Broccoli Casserole, Chicken-, '79 48;
      '91 315
   Broccoli-Chicken Casserole, '82 33
   Brown Rice Bake, Chicken-, '91 314
   Cacciatore, Chicken, '80 39; '83 118;
      '84 9; '86 42
   Cacciatore, Quick Chicken-and-Rice,
      '88 38
   Cheesy Chicken Casserole, '85 34
   Chilaquiles con Pollo (Tortillas with
      Chicken), '81 66

Chile Chicken with Salsa, Baked, '88 147
Chiles Casserole, Chicken-and-, '93 107
Chili Bake, Chicken, '93 302
Chimichangas, Chicken, '93 68; '94 30
Company Chicken Bake, '80 301
Countryside Chicken Bake, '88 39
Dilly Chicken, '90 65
Divan Casserole, Chicken, '82 M203
Divan, Chicken, '80 M10; '87 M218
Divan, Curried Chicken, '80 83
Divan, Easy Chicken, '94 310
Divan, Elegant Crêpes, '81 91
Divan, Gourmet Chicken, '82 83
Divan, Overnight Chicken, '83 198
Divan, Sherried Chicken, '80 38
Dressing Casserole, Chicken-and-,
   '81 263
Enchiladas, Chicken, '80 301; '86 296;
   '90 121
Enchiladas, Chicken-and-Spinach,
   '91 222
Enchiladas, Easy Chicken, '82 89;
   '86 231
Enchiladas with Tomatillo Sauce,
   Chicken, '95 206
Florentine, Chicken, '93 107
Florentine, Chicken-and-Shrimp, '89 64
Fontina-Baked Chicken, '90 64
Garlic-Spinach Chicken, '92 56
Good Chicken Casserole, Simply, '95 255
Green Bean Casserole, Chicken-, '85 296
Green Noodle Casserole, Chicken and,
   '80 32
Grits, Chicken and, '95 263
Herbed Chicken, French, '86 89
Hot-and-Spicy Chicken Dinner, '94 M94
King Ranch Chicken, '95 193
Lasagna Bake, Chicken, '95 55
Lasagna, Chicken, '87 M302; '88 90;
   '92 197; '93 25
Lasagna, Creamy Ham-and-Chicken,
   '95 88
Lasagna Florentine, Chicken, '95 158
Macaroni and Chicken Casserole, '80 260
Macaroni Casserole, Chicken-, '85 219
Make-Ahead Chicken Casserole, '84 241
Manicotti, Creamy Chicken, '85 60
Mexicana, Chicken, '91 M127
Mexican Chicken Casserole, '82 143
Mexican Chicken, Spicy, '82 89
Mexi-Chicken Casserole, '93 69; '94 30
Noodle Casserole, Chicken-, '94 286
Paella Casserole, '95 254
Parmigiana, Chicken, '80 190
Parmigiana, Chicken-Eggplant, '82 212
Pesto-Chicken Casserole, '94 231
Quick Chicken Casserole, '81 91
Rice-and-Chicken Casserole, '87 154
Rice Casserole, Chicken-, '86 52
Rice Casserole, Chicken and, '80 260
Rice, Chicken and, '95 54
Salad, Baked Chicken, '86 297; '87 176
Scarborough Chicken, '80 38
Shrimp-and-Chicken Casserole, '91 102
Spaghetti Casserole, Chicken-, '84 15
Spaghetti Squash and Chicken Skillet
   Casserole, '94 134
Spicy Chicken Bake, '85 251
Squash Casserole, Chicken-, '95 121
Sunday Chicken Casserole, '83 290
Superb Casserole, Chicken, '89 83
Supreme Casserole, Chicken, '84 219
Supreme, Hot Chicken, '81 76

CHICKEN, Casseroles (continued)

Swiss Chicken, '95 54
Swiss Chicken Casserole, '90 67
Swiss Chicken Thighs, '94 282
Tangy Chicken, '85 251
Tetrazzini, Cheesy Chicken, '83 M87
Tetrazzini, Chicken, '79 268; '80 M75;
  '83 288
Tortilla Bake, Chicken, '82 89
Tortilla Casserole, Chicken, '81 166
Vegetable-Chicken Bake with Sweet
  Bacon Dressing, '93 108
Wild Rice Casserole, Chicken-, '84 241;
  '85 65
Wild Rice, Chicken and, '79 248
Wild Rice Supreme, Chicken-, '79 77
Celery Skillet, Chicken-and-, '88 6
Chafing Dish Chicken, '82 284
Chalupas, Chicken, '79 185
Chalupas, Chicken-Olive, '81 227
Champagne Chicken, '85 251
Champagne Sauce, Chicken Breasts with,
  '86 49
Charcoal Broiled Chicken, '79 90
Charlemagne, Chicken, '86 293
Cheesecake, Chicken-Chile, '92 42
Cheesecake, Curried Chicken, '90 174
Chili, White, '91 284
Chili, White Lightning Texas, '92 321
Chimichangas, Oven-Fried Chicken, '90 175
Chinese, Chicken, '94 33
Chinese Chicken and Vegetables, '81 212
Chinese Chicken, Lazy Day, '81 3
Chinese-Style Chicken Dinner, '89 247
Chinese-Style Dinner, '84 26
Chop Suey, Chicken, '81 227
Chowder, Cheesy Chicken, '92 21
Chowder, Chicken, '83 20
Chowder, Creamy Chicken-Vegetable, '92 20
Chowder, Curried Chicken-and-Corn, '92 21
Chow Mein, Chicken, '90 68
Chutney Chicken, '86 249
Coconut Chicken with Fresh Fruit, '93 294
Company Chicken, '80 39; '83 125
Continental, Chicken, '82 274
Cordon Bleu, Chicken, '81 304; '82 83;
  '86 37; '93 126
Cordon Bleu, Company Chicken, '82 274
Cordon Bleu in Mushroom Sauce, Chicken,
  '86 198
Corn Flake Chicken, '91 172
Country Captain Chicken, '94 252
Country Poulet, '86 292
Crabmeat Stuffing, Chicken Breasts with,
  '85 302
Cracked Wheat, "Fried," '89 31
Cream Cheese Chicken Breasts, '90 234
Creamed Chicken, '82 49, 284; '83 14
Creamed Chicken and Vegetables, '91 90
Creamed Chicken, Company, '82 84
Creamed Chicken in a Shell, '79 138
Creamed Chicken in Patty Shells, '86 123
Creamed Chicken over Confetti Rice Squares,
  '81 282; '82 31
Creamed Chicken over Cornbread, '86 231
Creamed Ham and Chicken, '81 M74
Creole, Chicken, '86 231; '89 33; '90 146
Creole Chicken, '94 93; '95 261
Creole Chicken and Rice, '92 262
Crêpes, Chicken, '80 39
Crêpes, Chicken-Vegetable, '83 70

Crêpes, Creamy Chicken, '81 200
Crispy Chicken, '84 152
Croissants, Chutney-Chicken, '92 22
Croquettes and Mushroom Sauce, Chicken,
  '91 220
Croquettes, Chicken, '81 133
Croquettes, Crispy Chicken, '88 206
Curried Chicken, '86 43
Curried Chicken, Quick, '89 219
Curried Chicken, Regal, '84 110
Curry, Chicken, '84 110; '85 220; '86 21;
  '89 219
Curry, Turban Chicken, '94 266
Cutlets with Lemon, Chicken, '85 8
Dante's Chicken, '88 25
Deviled Chicken, Zesty, '90 232
Dijon Chicken, '81 156
Dijon Chicken with Pasta, '90 318
Dijon-Herb Chicken, '89 120
Dilled Chicken Paprika, '86 41
Dinner, Chicken-Mushroom, '81 3
Dinner, Chicken Peach, '79 77
Dinner, Curried Chicken Skillet, '95 47
Dinner, Healthful Chicken, '83 232
Dip, Hot Chicken, '80 86
Dixie Manor, Chicken à la, '85 3
Dressing, Chicken and Rice, '79 288
Dressing, Chicken Cornbread, '90 159
Dressing, Tipsy Chicken and, '88 151
Drummettes, Down-Home Chicken, '93 157
Drummettes, Ginger-Garlic Appetizer,
  '93 157
Drummettes, Orange-Pecan Chicken, '93 158
Drummettes, Southwestern Chicken, '93 158
Drumsticks, Cajun-Style, '87 159
Dumplings, Country Chicken and, '85 254
Dumplings, Easy Chicken and, '86 21
Dumplings, Old-Fashioned Chicken and,
  '79 55; '83 228; '93 302
Dumplings, Quick Chicken and, '95 125
Dumplings with Herbed Broth, Chicken
  and, '95 338
Dumplings with Vegetables, Chicken and,
  '85 M56
Easy Chicken, '89 M129
Egg Bread, Chicken on, '95 120
Empanadas, '92 156
Enchiladas, Creamy, '93 174
Enchiladas Terrificas, '84 32
Enchiladas Verde, Chicken, '93 274
Enchiladas with Spicy Sauce, Chicken, '84 76
Enchiladas with Tomatillo Sauce, Chicken,
  '94 231
English Muffin Delight, '82 45
en Papillote, Chicken and Vegetables, '86 145
Fajita Fettuccine, '94 84
Fajita in a Pita, '90 177
Fajitas, Chicken, '88 231; '89 100; '90 204
Fancy Fowl, '81 76; '82 13
Fettuccine, Chicken-and-Tomatoes over,
  '90 204
Fettuccine, Chicken-Pecan, '86 52
Fiesta Chicken, Spicy, '84 234
Filling, Chicken, '81 200
Filling, Chicken Divan, '81 91
Filling, Chicken-Olive, '81 227
Filling, Curried Chicken, '88 125
Filling Luau, Chicken, '79 81
Fingers, Buttermilk-Pecan Chicken, '93 165
Fingers, Chicken Little, '80 249
Fingers, Herb-Baked Chicken, '86 249
Fingers, No-Fry-Pan Chicken, '91 120
Fingers, Spicy Chicken, '91 162

Firecrackers, Texas, '95 96
Flautas, '83 199
Flautas with Guacamole, Chicken, '89 226
Florentine with Mushroom Sauce, Chicken,
  '87 250
Foil, Chicken in, '91 134; '94 93
Fried
  Beaumont Fried Chicken, '88 92
  Best Ever Sunday Chicken, '89 234
  Bites, French-Fried Chicken, '85 160
  Buttermilk Fried Chicken, Company,
    '86 177
  Cheese-Stuffed Chicken Thighs, Fried,
    '88 206
  Cream Gravy, Fried Chicken with,
    '85 241
  Crispy Fried Chicken Breasts, '80 155
  Curried Fried Chicken, '85 160
  Delicious Fried Chicken, '86 156
  Dixie Fried Chicken, '88 14
  Drummettes with Horseradish Sauce,
    Fried Chicken, '88 207
  Drumsticks, Buttermilk, '87 175
  Fingers, Chicken Almondette, '93 12
  Garlic-Flavored Fried Chicken, '79 147
  Garlic Fried Chicken, '82 148
  Gravy, Fried Chicken, '95 235
  Herbed Fried Chicken, '87 91
  Herb-Seasoned Fried Chicken, '80 8
  Kudzu Fried Chicken, '95 198
  Lemon-Fried Chicken, '79 77
  Lemon Fried Chicken, '82 275
  Mandarin Chicken, Crispy, '86 119
  Mexican Fried Chicken, '81 166; '87 176
  Nuggets, Golden Chicken, '80 159
  Nuggets, Lemon-Chicken, '87 283
  Oven-Fried Chicken, '84 118; '93 90;
    '95 236
  Oven-Fried Chicken, Crisp, '94 220
  Oven-Fried Chicken, Crunchy, '87 163
  Oven-Fried Chicken, Crusty, '79 77
  Oven-Fried Chicken, Golden-Brown,
    '86 21
  Oven-Fried Chicken Legs, Jalapeño,
    '94 94
  Oven-Fried Chicken, Nutty, '85 160
  Oven-Fried Chicken, Southern, '86 37
  Oven-Fried Chicken with Honey-Butter
    Sauce, '85 18
  Oven-Fried Parmesan Chicken, '81 97;
    '82 148
  Oven-Fried Pecan Chicken, '84 288
  Oven-Fried Sesame Chicken, '79 77
  Sesame Chicken, '82 148
  Southern Fried Chicken, Our Best,
    '95 235
  Special Fried Chicken, '88 220
  Spicy Country-Fried Chicken, '82 148
  Spicy Fried Chicken, '83 5; '88 129;
    '94 162
  Spinach-Stuffed Chicken Breasts, Fried,
    '88 206
  Sunday Dinner Fried Chicken, '88 110
  Super Fried Chicken, '82 148
  Traditional Fried Chicken, '82 148
  Walnut Chicken, Deep-Fried, '87 175
  Wings, Hot Buffalo, '87 176
Fruited Chicken en Crème, '83 264
Garden, Chicken-in-a-, '80 18
Garlic Chicken, Forty-Cloves-of-, '95 261
Ginger Chicken and Cashews, '85 M11
Ginger-Nut Chicken, '90 M33
Glazed Chicken, Fruit-, '80 211

CHICKEN (continued)

Gold Nugget Chicken, '95 120
Greek Lemon Chicken, '90 65
Grilled Basil Chicken, '93 201
Grilled Chicken, '89 200; '92 170; '94 167
Grilled Chicken Breasts, '84 172
Grilled Chicken, Garlic-, '87 180
Grilled Chicken, Lemon-Herb, '95 87
Grilled Chicken, Smoky, '85 160
Grilled Chicken with Dill Sauce, '88 162
Grilled Chicken with Tabbouleh Salad, '91 70
Grilled Chicken with Vegetables Vinaigrette, '91 26
Grilled Cumin Chicken, '87 142
Grilled Ginger-Orange Chicken, '91 26
Grilled Jalapeño Chicken, '93 213
Grilled Lime-Jalapeño Chicken, '91 87
Grilled Teriyaki Chicken, '92 59
Grilled Yogurt-Lemon Chicken, '81 111
Gruyère, Chicken Breasts, '80 189
Gumbo, Chicken, '79 199; '90 26
Gumbo, Chicken and Oyster, '81 198
Gumbo, Chicken-and-Sausage, '89 275; '90 256; '94 20
Gumbo, Chicken-Ham-Seafood, '81 6
Gumbo, Combo, '81 198
Gumbo, Easy Chicken, '83 156
Gumbo, The Gullah House, '92 237
Gumbo, Wild Game, '91 290
Gumbo with Smoked Sausage, Chicken, '81 199
Gumbo Ya Ya, '87 210
Hawaiian Chicken, '82 274
Hawaiian, Chicken, '84 88
Herb Chicken, Smoky, '95 116
Herbed Chicken, Sunny, '86 156
Herbed Chicken, Tangy, '87 M302
Herb-Seasoned Chicken Breasts, '93 M325
Honey Chicken, '82 55; '88 67
Honey-Curry Chicken, '87 36
Honey Sauce, Chicken in, '89 82
Honolulu Chicken, '85 52
Imperial Chicken, '81 238
Italian Chicken, '86 122; '91 206
Italian Chicken Cutlets, '89 82
Italian Chicken-Mozzarella Melt, '95 153
Jalapeño, Easy Chicken, '92 310
Jambalaya, '90 26
Jambalaya, Chicken-and-Sausage, '88 200; '91 216
Jambalaya, Red Rice, '91 18
Kabobs, Chicken, '87 141
Kabobs, Chicken-Avocado, '82 9; '83 68
Kabobs, Good-and-Easy Chicken, '85 87
Kabobs, Hawaiian, '85 157
Kabobs, Marinated Chicken, '84 M144
Kabobs, Oriental Chicken, '95 193
Kabobs, Pineapple-Chicken, '86 M328
Kabobs, Sesame Chicken, '82 165
Kabobs, Soy-Chicken, '86 156
Kabobs Supreme, Chicken, '81 124
Kiev, Chicken, '80 39
Kiev, Cranberry Chicken, '87 250
Kiev, Oven-Baked Chicken, '86 37
Kiev, Oven Chicken, '82 83
King Ranch Chicken, '94 26
la France, Chicken, '86 248
Lemonade Chicken, '82 163
Lemon and Wine, Chicken in, '83 281
Lemon Chicken, '81 M138; '86 173
Lemon Chicken and Vegetables, '88 118

Lemon Chicken Breasts, '89 18
Lemon Chicken, Sweet, '79 218
Lemon-Chicken, Sweet, '84 69
Lemon-Dill Chicken, '93 19
Lemon-Dill Chicken Sauté, '91 186
Lemon-Frosted Chicken, '88 170
Lemon-Garlic Chicken, '89 M132; '90 35
Lemon-Herb Chicken, '85 127
Lemon-Pepper Chicken, '89 104
Lemon-Rosemary Chicken, '94 201
Lime Butter, Chicken with, '84 68
Livers
  Bits and Livers, Chicken, '84 222
  en Brochette, Chicken Livers, '84 222
  Italian Sauce, Chicken Livers in, '83 117
  Kabobs, Rumaki, '82 182
  Mushrooms, Chicken Livers with, '81 133
  Omelet, Chicken Liver, '82 44
  Orange Sauce, Chicken Livers in, '82 218
  Party Chicken Livers, '83 242
  Pâté, Chicken Liver, '79 153; '81 235; '83 108; '84 205; '88 M132
  Pâté Maison, '84 222
  Potatoes, Chicken Livers and, '82 218
  Rice, Chicken Livers with, '80 200; '81 58; '84 292
  Rice Dish, Chicken Livers and, '82 218
  Risotto, Chicken Livers, '82 218
  Roll-Ups, Chicken Liver and Bacon, '80 200; '81 57
  Rumaki, '80 M136
  Sautéed Chicken Livers, '80 200; '81 57
  Scrumptious Chicken Livers, '84 230
  Spread, Sherried Liver, '80 86
  Stroganoff, Chicken Livers, '80 200; '81 57
  Supreme, Chicken Livers, '81 298
  Turnovers, Chicken Liver, '79 141
  Wine Sauce, Chicken Livers in, '81 104
  Wine Sauce, Chicken Livers with Marsala, '81 76
Log, Chicken-Pecan, '81 290
Luzianne, Poulet, '86 197
Marengo, Chicken, '92 70
Marinara, Chicken, '86 77
Marinated Breast of Chicken, '87 123
Marinated Chicken, '87 61
Marinated Chicken Breasts, '90 54
Marinated Chicken Strips and Vegetables, '90 110
Marsala, Chicken, '83 137; '89 237
Medaillons in Pepper Pesto, Chicken-Rice, '90 97
Mediterranean Chicken, '91 27; '94 72
Medley, Creamy Ham-and-Chicken, '92 272
Mexican Chicken, '80 124
Milano, Chicken, '84 220
Minted Chicken, '81 102
Mole, Chicken, '81 193
Mole Sauce, Chicken with, '93 34
Monterey, Chicken, '82 275
Mornay Sauce, Chicken Breasts in, '81 273
Mousse, Curried Chicken, '95 328
Murphy, Chicken, '89 82
Mushrooms, Chicken-Stuffed, '80 162
Mustard Chicken, '80 222; '86 293; '93 239
Mustard Cream Sauce, Chicken in, '92 181
Nachos, Chicken, '84 244
Nuggets, Baked Chicken, '81 149; '89 18
Nuggets, Golden Chicken, '80 159; '81 237
Nuggets, Lemon-Chicken, '86 337
Nuggets Supreme, Chicken, '85 160

Nuggets with Pineapple Sauce, Chicken, '84 236
Onion-Crusted Chicken, '88 40
Orange-Almond Sauce, Chicken in, '79 219; '80 13
Orange-Avocado Chicken, '80 38
Orange Chicken, '83 278; '86 M140
Orange Chicken Breasts with Parslied Rice, '87 242
Orange, Lime, and Ginger Sauce, Chicken with, '92 123
Orange Sauce, Chicken Breasts with, '79 77
Orange Sauce, Chicken in, '83 8
Orange Sauce, Skillet Chicken in, '94 252
Oregano Chicken, '95 84
Oriental Chicken, '80 40, 208; '82 131
Oriental Chicken with Peanuts, '82 236
Oriental Chicken with Pineapple, '86 42
Oriental Stuffed Pockets, '79 14
Paella, Chicken-Pork-Shrimp, '82 245
Paella, Chicken-Seafood, '88 68
Paella, Shrimp-and-Chicken, '94 168
Paella, Spanish, '85 26
Paella Valenciana, '82 246
Paprika Chicken, '95 125
Parmesan, Chicken, '83 184; '95 210
Parmesan Chicken, Crispy, '80 M76
Pasquale, Chicken, '83 67
Pasta and Chicken, Taste-of-Texas, '92 78
Pasta and Garden Vegetables, '87 192
Pasta, Chicken-and-Broccoli, '87 286
Pasta Platter, Cold, '88 42
Pasta, Quick Chicken and, '93 14
Pastry, Chicken in, '86 122
Pâté, Vegetable-Chicken, '86 66
Peachy Chicken, '90 212
Peanut Butter-Marmalade Chicken, '81 282; '82 30
Pecan Chicken, '90 54
Pecan-Rice Dressing, Chicken with, '85 M57
Pecan-Sausage Stuffing, Chicken Breasts with, '94 212
Peppers, Chicken Breasts with Curried, '90 227
Peppers, Curried Chicken-Stuffed, '87 19
Peppers, Devilish Chicken, '80 65
Pesto Chicken and Pasta, '89 M132
Pesto Chicken with Basil Cream, '89 158
Phyllo, Chicken in, '87 286
Phyllo Pastry, Chicken Breasts in, '91 105
Piccata, Chicken, '83 35; '84 230
Piccata, Herbed Chicken, '88 28
Pie, Biscuit-Topped Chicken, '86 157, 264
Pie, Cheesy Mexican Chicken, '82 142
Pie, Chicken, '81 281; '82 31
Pie, Chicken Dumpling, '95 245
Pie, Chicken Pot, '81 210; '82 114; '84 21; '94 21; '95 54, 256
Pie, Chicken-Vegetable Pot, '81 281; '82 30
Pie, Deluxe Chicken, '88 298
Pie, Double-Crust Chicken, '87 111
Pie, Double-Crust Chicken Pot, '90 220
Pie, Easy Chicken Pot, '83 156; '89 218
Pie, Egg-Stra Special Chicken, '86 264
Pie, Greek Chicken Phyllo, '92 328
Pie, Montezuma Tortilla, '83 199
Pie, Nana's Chicken, '90 25
Pie, Old-Fashioned Chicken Pot, '92 271
Pie, Savory Southern Chicken, '90 24
Pie, Thick 'n' Crusty Chicken Pot, '87 267; '88 102; '89 67
Pie with Cheese Crust, Chicken Pot, '86 264
Pilaf, Chicken, '82 246

CHICKEN *(continued)*

Piña Colada Chicken, '86 21
Pineapple Chicken, '83 M194; '85 3
Pineapple, Chicken and, '81 281; '82 30
Pineapple Chicken, Oriental, '84 288
Piquant Chicken, '86 76
Piquant, Chicken, '94 19
Pita, Oriental Chicken, '89 216
Pita, Peppery Chicken in, '93 62
Pitas, Acadian Stuffed, '90 177
Pizza, Chicken, '94 218
Pizza, Gruyère-Chicken, '87 182
Pizza, Southwest Deluxe, '95 268
Plum Sauce, Chicken with, '82 236
Poached Chicken Breast in Wine, '91 184
Poached Chicken Breasts, Wine-, '85 58
Poached Chicken Breast with Turned
   Vegetables and Chive Sauce, '94 309
Poached Chicken with Black Beans and Salsa,
   '87 217
Poached Chicken with Creamy Mustard Sauce,
   Champagne-, '94 24
Pollo Almendrado (Chicken in Almond
   Sauce), '81 193
Pollo con Calabacita (Mexican Chicken with
   Zucchini), '82 219
Pollo en Mole de Cacahuate (Chicken with
   Peanut Mole Sauce), '80 194
Pollo en Pipián, Mexican, '88 31
Poppy Seed Chicken, '94 108
Potatoes, Chicken-Cheese Stuffed, '86 55
Potatoes, Creamed Beef and Chicken-Topped,
   '83 210
Potatoes, Gumbo, '95 22
Potatoes, Sweet-and-Sour-Topped, '83 4
Pot, Chicken in a, '81 3
Pretzel-Crusted Chicken, '94 252
Primavera, Chicken-Pasta, '91 72
Princess Chicken, '86 122
Provolone, Chicken, '93 323
Puffs, Appetizer Chicken, '85 72
Puffs, Chicken Nut, '81 260
Quesadillas, Spicy Chicken, '95 42
Quiche, Chicken Divan, '88 M125
Quiche, Chicken-Pecan, '91 206
Quiche Noël, '82 310
Quick Chicken, '90 117
Ragout with Cheddar Dumplings, Chicken,
   '94 44
Rice, Chicken Caruso and, '89 177
Rice Pilaf, Chicken Breasts with Fruited,
   '92 307
Rice, Shortcut Chicken and, '90 220
Rice, Spicy Chicken and, '88 200
Roast Chicken, '93 14
Roast Chicken and Brown Rice, '83 268
Roast Chicken and Vegetables, '81 3
Roast Chicken with Pineapple-Mustard Glaze,
   '89 83
Roast Chicken with Rice, '95 261
Roasted Chicken, Herb-, '87 155
Roasted Chicken, Lemon-, '95 24
Roasted Chicken, Rice-Stuffed, '88 38
Rockefeller Chicken, '79 219
Rolls à la Swiss, Chicken-and-Ham, '92 42
Rolls, Chicken-Asparagus, '86 M211
Rolls, Crispy Chicken, '84 288
Rolls Élégante, Chicken, '80 210
Rolls, Hearts of Palm Chicken, '89 201
Rolls, Hearty Salad, '81 206
Rolls Jubilee, Chicken, '87 118

Rolls, Mexican Chicken, '93 242
Rolls, Pesto-Stuffed Chicken, '93 82
Rollups, Cheesy Chicken, '82 44
Rollups, Chicken, '85 179; '88 38
Rollups, Chicken and Spinach, '80 90;
   '82 M68
Rollups, Imperial Chicken, '80 217
Rollups in Gravy, Chicken, '83 184
Rollups, Sunshine Chicken, '85 251
Romano, Chicken alla, '83 M58
Romano, Chicken Breasts, '79 218
Romanoff, Chicken, '84 292
Roquefort Chicken, '89 320
Rotelle, Chicken and Tomato with, '87 108
Salads
   Almond-Chicken Salad Shanghai,
      '90 160
   Almond Salad, Chicken-, '81 133
   Aloha Chicken Salad, '80 297
   Amandine, Chicken Salad, '81 37
   Ambrosia, Chicken Salad, '85 216
   Apple Salad, Chicken-, '90 216
   Artichoke-Chicken-Rice Salad, '94 132
   Artichokes, Chicken Salad with, '86 186
   Asparagus-Chicken Salad, '89 83
   Aspic-Topped Chicken Salad, '88 88
   Avocado-Chicken Salad, '87 107
   Avocado Salad, Chicken-, '80 139
   Avocado Salad, Fruited Chicken-,
      '82 101
   Avocado Salad Platter, Chicken-, '83 2
   Avocado Salad, Tossed Chicken-, '80 4
   Avocados, Chicken Salad in, '85 216
   Baked Chicken Salad, '86 297; '87 176
   Basil-Chicken-Vegetable Salad, '92 162
   BLT Chicken Salad, '87 144
   Blue Cheese Chicken Salad, '94 81
   Broccoli-Chicken Salad, '90 129
   Celery Salad, Chicken-, '81 187
   Chicken Salad, '86 232, 261
   Chop Suey Salad, '81 37
   Chutney-Chicken Salad, '87 74
   Chutney Salad, Chicken, '82 108
   Coleslaw, Chicken, '84 2
   Cream Puff Bowl, Chicken Salad in,
      '86 232
   Crisp Salad, Crunchy, '95 28
   Crunchy Chicken Salad, '86 157, 207
   Curried Chicken-and-Orange Salad,
      '87 144
   Curried Chicken-Rice Salad, '92 190
   Curried Chicken Salad, '79 219; '84 66;
      '85 96; '86 131; '89 176
   Curried Chicken Salad with Asparagus,
      '81 36
   Dilled Chicken Salad, '91 212
   Exotic Luncheon Salad, '83 210
   Fancy Chicken Salad, '79 55
   Filling, Chicken Salad, '87 106
   Fruit, Chicken Salad with, '82 171
   Fruited Chicken Salad, '84 25, 290;
      '88 88; '90 318
   Fruited Chicken Salad in Avocados,
      '87 41
   Fruit Salad, Chicken-, '82 79; '90 234
   Fruity Chicken Salad, '83 157
   Ginger Salad, Fried Chicken, '93 290
   Grapes, Chicken Salad with, '86 117
   Green Salad with Chicken, Mixed, '80 54
   Grilled Chicken Salad, Moroccan,
      '95 231
   Grilled Chicken Salad with Raspberry
      Dressing, '95 202

Hot Chicken Salad, '81 201; '83 196
Hot Chicken Salad, Country Club-Style,
   '86 10
Hot Chicken Salad, Crunchy, '80 138
Hot Chicken Salad Pinwheel, '80 139
Italian, Chicken Salad, '89 18
Layered Chicken Salad, '89 162
Macadamia Chicken Salad, '80 138
Macaroni-Chicken Salad, '85 296;
   '86 302
Macaroni-Chicken Salad, Dilled, '92 142
Mama Hudson's Chicken Salad, '93 238
Mandarin Chicken, Carousel, '79 88
Mango, Chicken Salad with, '86 215
Marinated Chicken-Grape Salad, '85 74
Marinated Chicken-Raspberry Salad,
   '93 190
Mexican Chicken Salad, '85 84; '88 272
Minted Chicken Salad, '92 104
Mold, Chicken-Cucumber, '80 175
Mold, Chicken Salad, '83 80; '84 163
Nectarine Chicken Salad, '79 175
Noodle Salad, Chicken, '95 25
Old-Fashioned Chicken Salad, '83 79
Oriental Chicken Salad, '85 216;
   '88 271; '91 43
Oriental, Chicken Salad, '90 146
Pasta-Chicken Salad, Tarragon, '87 155
Pasta Salad, Chicken, '88 89
Pasta Salad, Grilled Chicken-, '94 64
Pea Salad, Chicken-, '83 218
Persian Chicken Salad, '81 12
Pineapple-Chicken Salad Pie, '80 138
Pineapple-Nut Chicken Salad, '83 80
Pocket, Chicken Salad in a, '88 139
Polynesian Chicken Salad, '88 272
Poulet Rémoulade, '87 144
Rice Salad, Chicken-, '81 203
Rice Salad, Hot Chicken-and-, '83 22
Rice Salad, Nutty Chicken-, '83 157
Ring, Chicken Salad, '90 123
Ring Salad, Chicken Jewel, '83 282
Roasted Chicken Salad, '93 14
Rolls, Hearty Salad, '81 206
Sandwiches, Chicken-Salad Finger,
   '85 119
Southwestern Chicken Salad, '88 88
Spaghetti Salad, Chicken-, '90 146
Special Chicken Salad, '85 82; '87 183;
   '88 M193
Spinach Tossed Salad, Chicken-and-,
   '83 157
Spread, Chicken Salad Party, '88 M8
Stack-Up Salad, Chicken, '83 80
Summer Chicken Salad, '83 145
Summery Chicken Salad, '95 138
Super Chicken Salad, '82 174
Supreme, Chicken Salad, '79 107, 152;
   '89 176
Taco Salad, Chicken, '94 M136
Tahitian Chicken Salad, '84 120
Tarragon Chicken Salad, '90 199
Tarts, Chicken Salad, '84 257
Thai Chicken Salad, '95 177
Tortellini Salad, Chicken, '87 288
Tortilla Salads, Mexican Chicken, '95 129
Tropical Chicken Boats for Two, '82 186
Tropical Chicken Salad, '85 216
Twist, Chicken Salad with a, '84 221
Vegetable-Chicken Salad, '91 287
Vegetable-Chicken Vinaigrette Salad,
   '86 135
Walnut-Chicken Salad, '89 14

Walnut Salad, Sunburst Chicken-and-, '93 91
Wild Rice-Chicken Salad, '83 146
Saltimbocca alla Romana, Chicken, '80 212
San Antonio-Style Chicken, '81 166
Sandwich, Chicken Parmigiana, '94 65
Sandwich, Crispy Chicken, '81 114
Sandwiches, Baked Chicken, '79 164; '80 130; '84 165
Sandwiches, Cheesy Chicken, '82 190
Sandwiches, Chicken-Almond Pocket, '81 240; '83 69
Sandwiches, Chicken Club, '86 160
Sandwiches, Hot Brown, '80 202
Sandwiches, Hot Chicken, '83 291
Sandwiches, Marinated Chicken, '86 M45
Sandwiches, Puffed Chicken, '82 35
Sandwiches, Toasted Chicken-and-Cheese, '85 242
Sandwich, Ham 'n' Cheese Chicken, '95 153
Sandwich, Jamaican Chicken, '95 153
Sandwich, Marinated Chicken in a, '86 185
Sauce, Chicken Curry, '90 117
Sauce, Creamy Chicken, '81 91
Sauce, Curry, '95 18
Saucy, Chick-Wiches, '81 25; '82 31; '83 34
Sautéed Chicken Breasts, '87 36
Sauté, Savory Chicken, '88 254; '89 120
Sauté, Sherry-Chicken, '87 218
Sauté, Sweet Pepper-Chicken, '89 104
Scallopini with Lemon Sauce, Chicken, '86 156
Scallopini with Peppers, Chicken, '85 78
Scotch Cream, Chicken in, '88 42
Seasoned Browned Chicken, '85 25
Seasoned Chicken, Crunchy, '87 217
Seasoning Blend, Poultry, '88 28
Sesame Chicken, '85 252; '86 122
Sesame Chicken, Hawaiian, '81 106
Sesame Chicken with Noodles, '88 M125
Sherried Chicken, '79 214
Sherried Chicken with Artichokes, '87 143
Sherry Chicken with Rice, '81 97
Shortcakes, Cheesy Chicken, '95 98
Skillet, Cheesy Chicken, '80 115
Skillet Chicken, '81 180
Skillet Chicken Dinner, '86 249; '89 247
Skillet Chicken, Spicy, '94 220
Skillet Company Chicken, '82 60
Snow Peas, Chicken with, '83 187
Soufflé, Chicken-Chestnut, '79 107
Soups
    Artichoke, and Mushroom Soup, Chicken, '92 324
    Asparagus-and-Chicken Soup, Creamy, '95 82
    Broccoli-and-Chicken Soup, '90 202
    Chicken Soup, '81 98
    Chowder Sauterne, Chicken, '84 235
    Chunky Chicken-Noodle Soup, '88 12
    Cream of Chicken Soup, '85 243
    Cream Soup, Chicken-Almond, '92 21
    Curried Chicken Soup, '86 34
    Enchilada Soup, Chicken, '86 22
    Ham, and Oyster Soup, Chicken, '79 198
    Homemade Chicken Soup, '82 34
    Lime Soup, '88 31
    Mexican Chicken Soup, '84 234
    Noodle Soup, Chicken, '80 264; '95 45

Pepper-and-Chicken Soup, Roasted, '90 58
Quick Chicken Soup, '86 M72
Rice Soup, Chicken-and-, '88 236
Sopa de Lima, '79 211
Stock, Chicken, '95 18
Vegetable Soup, Chicken-, '88 18
Soy and Wine, Chicken in, '84 26
Spaghetti, Chicken, '83 105; '87 221
Spaghetti, Chicken-Vegetable, '92 281
Special Occasion Chicken, '91 206
Spiced Chicken, Crunchy, '85 M57
Spiced Fruited Chicken with Almond Rice, '81 195
Spicy Chicken Dish, '87 267; '88 103; '89 66
Spinach Fettuccine, Easy Chicken with, '88 89
Spinach Noodles, Chicken and, '82 19
Spread, Festive Chicken, '87 158
Spread, Low-Fat Chicken, '82 290
Spread, Tasty Chicken, '84 193
Steamed Dinner, Easy, '83 M314
Stew and Dumplings, Chicken, '84 4
Stew, Bama Brunswick, '87 4.
Stew, Breeden Liles's Brunswick, '91 14
Stew, Brunswick, '80 264
Stew, Brunswick Chicken, '87 4
Stew, Chili-Chicken, '90 319
Stew, Dan Dickerson's Brunswick, '91 16
Stew, Gay Neale's Brunswick, '91 17
Stew, Georgian Brunswick, '92 35
Stew, Jeff Daniel's Brunswick, '91 16
Stew, Sonny Frye's Brunswick, '87 4
Stew, Strader, '89 28
Stew, Van Doyle's Family-Size Brunswick, '91 14
Stew, Virginian Brunswick, '92 34
Stew, Virginia Ramsey's Favorite Brunswick, '91 16
Stir-Fried Chicken Curry, '87 51
Stir-Fried Chicken, Zesty, '83 82
Stir-Fry, Apple-Sesame-Chicken, '92 226
Stir-Fry Chicken à l'Orange, '83 82
Stir-Fry, Chicken and Snow Pea, '95 157
Stir-Fry, Chicken and Vegetable, '82 237
Stir-Fry Chicken and Vegetables, '86 249
Stir-Fry, Chicken-and-Vegetables, '86 68
Stir-Fry, Chicken-Broccoli, '82 33
Stir-Fry, Chicken-Vegetable, '83 151; '84 13, 141
Stir-Fry, Chicken-Zucchini, '84 50
Stir-Fry, Chinese Chicken, '90 100
Stir-Fry, Easy Chicken, '91 124
Stir-Fry, Herb-Chicken, '89 177
Stir-Fry, Hurry-Up Chicken, '91 124
Stir-Fry, Kyoto Orange-Chicken, '87 96
Stir-Fry, Mexican, '92 126
Stir-Fry, Orange-Chicken, '84 68
Stir-Fry, Pineapple-Chicken, '89 176
Stir-Fry, Shiitake-Chicken, '89 61
Stir-Fry Vegetables with Chicken, '84 195
Stock, Light Poultry, '90 31
Strips, Zippy Chicken, '84 205
Stroganoff, Chicken-and-Broccoli, '89 M248
Stuffed Chicken Breasts, '85 291; '82 36; '88 50; '89 274
Stuffed Chicken Breasts, Peach-, '79 177
Stuffed Chicken Breasts Sardou, '87 269
Stuffed Chicken Breasts, Walnut-, '85 293
Stuffed Chicken Breasts with White Grape Sauce, '80 38
Stuffed Chicken, Crab-, '84 101
Stuffed Chicken in Puff Pastry, Spinach-, '92 125

Stuffed Chicken, Rice-, '81 4
Stuffed Chicken Rolls, Spinach-, '86 248
Stuffed Chicken Thighs, '82 84
Stuffed Chicken, Vegetable-, '89 M65
Stuffed Chicken, Wild Rice-, '79 219
Stuffed Chicken with Sautéed Peppers and Mushrooms, Herb-, '91 26
Stuffed Chicken with Tomato-Basil Pasta, Basil-, '94 M204
Sunday Chicken, '95 228
Sunshiny Chicken, '81 309
Suprêmes de Volaille à Blanc (Chicken Breasts in Cream Sauce), '82 83
Sweet-and-Sour Chicken, '79 106; '83 184; '84 218; '86 217, 240; '90 161; '91 202
Sweet-and-Sour Chicken Nuggets, '90 168
Sweet-and-Sour Chicken Wings, '90 206
Sweet-and-Sour Lemon Chicken, '84 93
Sweet-and-Sour Shrimp and Chicken, '87 267; '88 103; '89 66
Szechwan Chicken, '83 85
Szechwan Chicken with Cashews, '81 212
Tacos, Chicken-and-Bean, '93 293
Tacos, Pizza-Flavored Chicken, '95 340
Tahitian Chicken, '84 68
Tamales, Chicken, '88 151
Tangy Chicken, '85 251; '86 292; '87 35
Tarragon Chicken, '86 231
Tarts, Deviled Chicken, '94 14
Tempura Delight, Chicken, '85 66
Teriyaki, Chicken, '80 M76
Teriyaki Chicken, '91 163
Teriyaki Chicken Wings, '85 300; '86 18
Terrine, Chicken-Vegetable, '84 131
Terrine, Cold Chicken-Leek, '92 145
Terrine Ring, Chicken, '84 132
Terrine, Vegetable-Chicken, '83 224
Tomato Aspic, Chicken in, '84 190
Tortilla Stack, Cheesy Chicken-, '86 3
Toss, Quick Chicken, '87 M124
Tostadas, Chicken, '93 204; '95 122
Valencia, Chicken-and-Rice, '85 113
Vegetable Platter, Chicken-and-, '88 M52
Vegetables, Chicken and, '88 165
Vegetables with Ginger-Soy Sauce, Chicken and, '91 32
Vermouth, Chicken and Vegetables, '87 M37
Véronique, Chicken, '84 260; '85 302
Waffles, Southern Chicken-Pecan, '82 231
Walnut Chicken, '85 126
Walnut Chicken and Vegetables, '85 194
Walnut Chicken, Crispy, '90 89
Wellington, Chicken Breasts, '84 22
White Wine, Chicken in, '81 97
Wild Rice, Chicken-Fried, '89 24; '91 132
Wild Rice, Elegant Chicken with, '80 M76
Wine Sauce, Chicken and Mushrooms in, '81 109
Wine Sauce, Chicken in, '80 8
Wings, Broiled Chicken, '80 149
Wings, Honey-Glazed Chicken, '91 251
Wings, Satan's, '87 214
Wings, Spicy Buffalo, '95 239
Wontons, Chicken, '92 284
Yogurt Chicken, Savory, '91 238; '92 28
Yogurt-Sesame Chicken, '90 216

CHILI
Bake, Chili Hominy, '81 282; '82 58
Basic Chili, '82 M11; '93 326
Basic Chili Embellished, '93 327
Basic Chili Goes Southwest, '93 326
Before-and-After Burner, Roy's, '89 316
Black Bean Chili Marsala, '95 16

CHILI (continued)

Bodacious Chili, '95 14
Burgers, Open-Face Chili, '82 31; '83 33
Casserole, Chili, '90 176
Casserole, Chili-Rice, '79 54
Casserole, Hominy-Chili, '86 255
Cheese-Topped Chili, '82 M11
Cheesy Chili, '82 310
Chili, '87 17; '93 89
Choo-Choo Chili, '89 316
Chuck Wagon Chili, '81 282; '82 57
Chunky Chili, '82 M282; '86 3
Company Chili, '82 311; '83 30
con Carne, Beef and Sausage Chili, '83 284
con Carne, Chili, '82 310; '83 30; '84 72;
   '86 2
con Carne, Favorite Chili, '86 293
con Carne, Quick-and-Easy Chili, '86 2
Cowboy Chili, '86 2
Dip, Cheesy Chili, '80 150
Dip, Chili, '82 161; '88 218; '89 47; '91 143
Dip, Chili-and-Cheese, '89 328
Dog, Dinglewood Pharmacy's Scrambled,
   '95 118
Dogs, Chili-Cheese, '81 M176
Double-Meat Chili, '79 269; '80 12
Easy Chili, '82 310; '83 30
Easy Chili with Beans, '92 262
Easy Texas Chili, '90 201
Eggplant Chili, '85 88
Firestarter Chili, '93 34
Five-Ingredient Chili, '95 212
Friday Night Chili, '86 228
Greek Chili, '95 16
Hot Spiced Chili, '83 214
Hotto Lotto Chili, '89 316
I-Cious, Chili-, '89 315
"In-the-Red" Chili over "Rolling-in-Dough"
   Biscuits, '92 80
Kielbasa Chili, Hearty, '91 28
Lolly's Pop Chili, '89 316
Lunchtime Chili, '81 230
Manicotti, Chili, '89 247
Meat Loaf, Chili, '81 275
Meaty Chili, '81 282; '82 58
Meaty Chili with Beans, '85 250
Mexican Chili, '89 18
Microwave Chili, '91 M232
Mom's Chili, '93 292
Noodles, Chili with, '81 282; '82 57
Now, Thatsa Chili, '95 16
Out West Chili, '95 15
Pastry Cups, Chili in, '90 68
Pie, Chili-Tamale, '82 9; '83 68
Potato Chili, Savory, '83 284
Potatoes, Chili-Topped, '83 3
Potatoes, South-of-the-Border Stuffed, '86 54
Quick-and-Easy Chili, '92 20
Quick and Simple Chili, '81 282; '82 58
Quick Chili, '83 283
Ranch Chili and Beans, '79 270; '80 11
Red Chili, '93 108
Red Chili, North Texas, '87 303
Rice, Chili with, '82 M11
Roundup Chili, '79 269; '80 12
Salad, Spicy Chili, '86 71
Sauce, Chili, '81 175; '94 287
Sauce, Chili Meat, '83 4
Sauce, Chunky Chili, '85 188
Sauce, Spicy Chili, '87 127
Sausage-Beef Chili, '86 232

Sausage Chili, Beefy, '82 M11
Simple Chili, '79 269; '80 11
Soup, Chili Vegetable, '94 120
South-of-the-Border Chili, '83 283; '91 283
Southwestern Chili, '91 284
Spaghetti, Herbed Chili-, '84 222
Speedy Chili, '92 66
Spicy Chili, Old-Fashioned, '79 269; '80 11
Stew, Red Chili, '95 226
Surprise, Chili, '82 229
Texas Championship Chili, '81 54
Texas Chili, Hot, '80 222; '81 77
Texas-Style Chili, '82 311; '83 30
Tex-Mex Chili, '83 26
Topping, Chili, '84 246; '94 22
Tree-Hunt Chili, '87 292
Turkey-Bean Chili, '88 M213
Vegetable Chili, '91 28
Vegetarian Chili, '84 280, 327; '91 284
Venison Chili, '82 216; '86 3; '87 304
Venison Chili, Hot, '91 283
Verde, Chili, '95 14
White Chili, '91 284
White Lightning Texas Chili, '92 321
Zippy Chili, '87 110

CHOCOLATE. *See also* **BROWNIES.**
Bags, Chocolate-Raspberry, '95 97
Banana Pops, '84 44
Bars and Cookies
   Almond Chip Balls, Toasted, '84 240
   Almond-Chocolate Bars, '83 304
   Almond Cream Confections, '87 198;
      '90 310
   Almond Surprise Cookies, Chocolate-,
      '88 M45
   Biscotti, Chocolate-Hazelnut, '95 80
   Biscotti Cioccolata, '93 268
   Blond Nut Squares, '82 156
   Bonbons, Chocolate-Filled, '89 162
   Bran Raisin Jumbos, Chocolate-, '91 142
   Brazil Squares, '82 306
   Brownie Alaskas, '83 299
   Brownie Bars, Cinnamon, '81 230
   Brownie Chip Cookies, '90 320
   Brownie-Mint Dessert, '82 227
   Brownie Waffle Cookies, '86 245
   Butter Cookies, Chocolate-Tipped,
      '84 258; '90 312
   Butter Pecan Turtle Bars, '90 70
   Butterscotch Bars, Chocolate-, '81 197
   By-Cracky Bars, '84 212
   Caramel-Filled Chocolate Cookies,
      '92 319
   Caramel Layer Squares, Chocolate-,
      '79 83
   Cherry Chocolates, '95 321
   Cherry Cookies, Chocolate-, '85 324
   Chess Squares, Chocolate, '92 45
   Chewies, Chocolate, '93 216
   Chewies, Easy Chocolate, '93 296;
      '94 234
   Chewy Chocolate Chip Squares, '91 175
   Chewy Chocolate Cookies, '80 208
   Chip Bars, Chocolate, '81 130
   Chip Cookies, '84 120
   Chip Cookies, Chocolate, '86 245;
      '90 193
   Chip Cookies, Chocolate-Chocolate,
      '82 35
   Chip Cookies, Mom Ford's Chocolate,
      '94 287
   Chippers, Chocolate, '92 206
   Chips Cookies, Loaded-with-, '87 223

   Chip Squares, Chocolate, '83 170;
      '89 143
   Cinnamon Bars, Chocolate, '82 209
   Cocoa Drop Cookies, '80 217
   Cocoa Kiss Cookies, '85 171
   Coconut Squares, Chocolate-, '90 70
   Crème de Menthe Bars, Chocolate-,
      '86 245
   Crème de Menthe Bites, Chocolate,
      '88 285
   Crème de Menthe Squares, '93 256
   Crispies, Chocolate-Peanut, '93 80
   Crispy Cookies, Chocolate, '85 115
   Crumble Bars, Choco-, '79 292
   Crunch Cookies, Chocolate, '91 316
   Crunchies, Chocolate, '92 50
   Date-Nut Chocolate Chip Cookies, Rich,
      '92 207
   Deluxe Chocolate Chip Cookies, '79 216
   Devil Doggies, '84 37
   Different Chocolate Chip Cookies,
      '83 114
   Double Chip Cookies, '81 301
   Double Chocolate Chip Cookies, '79 217
   Double Chocolate Chunk-Almond
      Cookies, '95 178
   Double-Chocolate Cookies, '95 272
   Doubly-Good Chocolate Cookies,
      '82 M185
   Dream Bars, Chocolate, '79 256; '82 298
   Drop Cookies, Chocolate, '84 36
   Fibber McGee Cookies, '95 72
   Forget 'em Cookies, '83 256
   Frosted Chocolate-Cherry Cookies,
      '89 294
   Fudge Bars, '86 93
   Fudge Bars, Yummy, '87 158
   Fudge-Pecan Chewies, Alabama, '95 143
   Fudge Puddles, '94 292
   German Chocolate Chess Squares, '94 51
   Giant Chocolate Chip Cookies, '84 119
   Gingerbread Cookies, Chocolate-,
      '94 293
   Jumbo Chocolate Chip Cookies, '82 110
   Keyboard Cookies, '94 M330
   Kissy Cookies, '93 331
   Light Chocolate Chip Cookies, '86 46
   Log Cookies, Chocolate-Tipped, '87 294
   Lollapalooza, '94 194
   Macaroon Cookies, Chocolate, '88 217
   Macaroons, Chocolate, '83 300; '87 57
   Meltaways, Chocolate, '81 302
   Melt-Aways, Chocolate Chip, '84 118
   Meringue-Chocolate Chip Bars, '84 118
   Meringue Kiss Cookies, '86 121
   Mint Chip Cookies, Chocolate-,
      '86 245
   Mint Cookies, Chocolate-, '92 206
   Mint Snaps, Chocolate-, '83 103; '84 96
   Monster Cookies, '84 36
   Nugget Cookies, '79 291
   Nut Chews, Chocolate-, '81 92
   Nut Freezer Cookies, Chocolate-,
      '88 217
   Nutty Choco Snacks, '83 305
   Nutty Oatmeal-Chocolate Chip Cookies,
      '82 M185
   Oatmeal Bars, Chocolate-Topped,
      '86 110
   Oatmeal-Chocolate Chippers, '90 218
   Oatmeal-Chocolate Morsel Cookies,
      '95 46
   Oatmeal Cookies, Chocolate-, '80 105

CHOCOLATE, Bars and Cookies *(continued)*

Oatmeal Cookies, Chocolate Chip-,
   '84 119
Oatmeal-Peanut Butter Chocolate Chip
   Cookies, '92 207
Oatmeal-Toffee Lizzies, Crispy, '95 136
Orange-Chocolate Cookies, '83 113
Orange Delights, Chocolate-, '93 52
Peanut Blossom Cookies, '95 245
Peanut Butter and Chocolate Chunk
   Cookies, '94 169
Peanut Butter-and-Fudge Bars,
   '80 M172
Peanut Butter Bars, '84 243
Peanut Butter-Chocolate Chip Cookies,
   Freezer, '86 230
Peanut Butter-Chocolate Kiss Cookies,
   '86 49
Peanut Butter Cones, Chocolate-, '85 14
Peanut Butter Cookies, Chocolate-,
   '85 90
Peanut Butter Cups, Chocolate-, '85 14
Peanut Butter Fingers, '79 256
Peanut Butter Squares, Chocolate Chip-,
   '84 118
Peanut Chip Cookies, Choco-, '92 318
Peanut Cookies, Chocolate-, '83 223
Peppermint Squares, Chocolate-, '81 119
Pinwheel Cookies, '93 316
Pinwheel Cookies, Chocolate, '86 245
Pinwheels, '95 321
Polka Dots, '95 272
Pudding Cookies, Chocolate Chip-,
   '93 21
Pumpkin-Chocolate Chip Cookies,
   '93 235
Raisin Oatmeal Cookies, Chocolate-,
   '95 136
Sandwich Cookies, Chocolate, '81 192
Sandwich Cookies, Choco-Nut, '84 200
Sandwiches, Chocolate Cookie Ice
   Cream, '87 147
Seashells, Chocolate, '91 178
Shortbread Wafers, Cocoa, '88 243
Snappers, Jumbo Chocolate, '81 218
Snowball Cookies, Chocolate, '82 295
Snowflake Cookies, Chocolate, '89 329
Sugar-Coated Chocolate Cookies,
   '92 274
Sugar Cookies, Double-Chocolate,
   '92 206
Super Chocolate Chunk Cookies,
   '88 217
Surprise Bonbon Cookies, '88 119
Surprise Cookies, Choco, '80 60
Teasers, Chocolate, '87 44
Toffee Treats, '89 330
White Chocolate Cookies, Chunky
   Macadamia Nut, '92 207
White Chocolate-Macadamia Nut
   Cookies, '94 315
Whoopie Pies, '86 246
Yummy Bars, '92 171
Baskets with Berry Cream, Chocolate, '92 118
Beverages
Brandied Chocolate, Flaming, '80 M290
Café au Lait, German Chocolate, '92 264
Café Colombian Royal, '80 M290
Café Mexicano, '92 208
Cappuccino, Chocolate Castle, '84 53
Cocoa Mix, Instant, '86 332

Coffee, Chocolate, '82 43
Coffee, Chocolate-Almond, '84 54
Coffee, Cocoa-, '83 55
Coffee, Mexican, '83 175, 275; '88 247;
   '91 78; '93 310; '94 97
"Concrete," Abaco Mocha, '94 114
"Concrete," Cardinal Sin, '94 113
"Concrete," Foxtreat, '94 113
Hot Chocolate, '94 290
Hot Chocolate, Creole, '80 M290
Hot Chocolate Deluxe, '90 272
Hot Chocolate, Favorite, '83 55
Hot Chocolate, French, '86 328
Hot Chocolate Mix, Deluxe, '80 M290
Hot Chocolate Mix, Spicy, '85 278
Hot Chocolate, Old-Fashioned, '85 23
Hot Chocolate, Special, '82 5
Hot Chocolate, Spiced, '80 50
Hot Chocolate, Spicy, '85 278
Hot Chocolate, Sugar-and-Spice, '95 34
Hot Cocoa Mix, '81 287
Hot Cocoa Mix, Minted, '91 316
Hot Cocoa Mix, Mocha-Flavored,
   '91 316
Hot Cocoa, Quick, '82 5
King Alfonso, '80 259
Malt, Banana-Chocolate, '89 170
Malt, Chocolate, '86 183
Marshmallow Chocolate, Hot Laced,
   '93 53
Mexican-Style Chocolate, '81 187
Milk, French Chocolate, '79 38
Milk Shake, Chocolate-Banana, '94 113
Mocha Blend, '95 276
Mocha Chocolate Fluff, '89 170
Mocha Cocoa, '83 318
Mocha-Cocoa Mix, Hot, '82 296
Mocha Coffee, '85 M329
Mocha Cream, Café, '84 54
Mocha Deluxe Hot Drink, '82 289
Mocha Espresso, Italian, '82 254
Mocha Frosty, '92 44
Mocha, Hot, '84 60
Mocha, Mexican, '93 M341
Mocha Polka, '89 171
Mocha Punch, '84 58, 166; '95 141
Mocha, Quick Viennese, '79 232
Mocha, Spirited Hot, '91 M260
Shake, Chocolate Mint, '89 170
Sipper, Chocolate, '88 83
Smoothie, Chocolate-Mint, '84 166
Bites, Snowy Chocolate, '90 47
Black-Bottom Goodies, '89 251
Bread, Chocolate Chip-Banana, '90 267
Bread, Chocolate Date-Nut, '81 284
Bread, Chocolate Loaf, '88 M188
Bread, Chocolate-Zucchini, '93 308
Bread, Cocoa-Nut Swirl, '80 257
Brickle Squares, Chocolate, '94 290
Buns, Chocolate-Cinnamon, '85 5
Buns, Chocolate Sticky, '81 300; '82 124
Cakes and Tortes
Almond Cake, Chocolate-, '91 248
Almond Cake with Cherry Filling,
   Chocolate-, '84 225
Angel Cake, Chocolate, '88 128
Angel Food Cake, Chocolate, '87 21;
   '90 111; '91 55
Angel Food Cake with Custard Sauce,
   Chocolate, '88 259
Apricot-Filled Chocolate Torte, '90 107
Banana Cake, Chocolate-, '86 138
Banana-Cocoa Cupcakes, '80 130

Banana Loaf, Chocolate Chip-, '85 115
Beet Cake, Chocolate, '80 40
Birthday Balloon Cakes, '92 15
Birthday Cake, Fishin'-for-Fun, '93 194
Black Bottom Cups, '82 279
Black Forest Cake, '81 126; '92 174
Black Forest Torte, '88 209
Brownie Cupcakes, '82 280
Brownie Delight, Chocolate, '87 224
Brown Mountain Cake, '84 39
Bûche de Noël, '84 304; '87 241
Bûche de Noël Cake, '82 262
Buttercream Cake, Chocolate, '90 108
Buttermilk Chocolate Cake, '79 13
Candy Cake, Chocolate, '81 238
Caramel-Nut Cake, Chocolate-, '83 23
Carrot Cake, Brownie, '92 120
Cheesecake, Black Forest, '84 74; '89 93;
   '94 21
Cheesecake, Candy Bar, '86 120
Cheesecake, Chocolate, '81 16; '82 305
Cheesecake, Chocolate-Almond, '93 53
Cheesecake, Chocolate-Amaretto,
   '85 M294; '93 97
Cheesecake, Chocolate-Caramel-Pecan,
   '91 197
Cheesecake, Chocolate Chip, '85 114
Cheesecake, Chocolate Cookie, '91 298
Cheesecake, Chocolate-Glazed Triple-
   Layer, '86 315; '90 310
Cheesecake, Chocolate Marble, '89 93
Cheesecake, Chocolate-Mint, '91 104
Cheesecake, Chocolate-Mint Baked
   Alaska, '94 142
Cheesecake, Chocolate-Raspberry
   Truffle, '91 270
Cheesecake, Chocolate Swirl, '84 295;
   '85 26
Cheesecake, German Chocolate, '87 265
Cheesecake, Marbled, '87 261
Cheesecake, Marble Mint, '84 152
Cheesecake, Mocha-Chocolate, '88 258
Cheesecake, Mocha Swirl, '87 262
Cheesecake, Rich Chocolate, '84 74;
   '85 38
Cheesecakes, Tiny Chocolate, '92 288
Cheesecake, White Chocolate, '87 44;
   '88 267; '94 180
Cheesecake with Whipped Cream
   Frosting, Chocolate, '89 42
Cherry Cake, Chocolate-, '84 200;
   '86 239
Chiffon Cake with Coffee Buttercream,
   Chocolate, '95 277
Cinnamon Cake, Chocolate-, '93 154
Cinnamon-Chocolate Cupcakes,
   '81 M139
Cocoa Crown Cake, '90 107
Coconut Cake, Chocolate-, '83 23
Coconut Cake, White Chocolate-,
   '87 263
Coffee Cake, Chocolate-Chip, '79 249
Coffee Cake, Chocolate Chip, '83 231
Cola Cake, Quick Chocolate, '95 56
Crumb Cake, Calico, '87 261
Cupcakes, Chocolate, '92 14
Custard Cake, Chocolate, '88 175
Decadent Chocolate Cake, '86 142
Double-Chocolate Torte, '79 67
Easy Chocolate Cake, '80 140
Father's Day Cake, '92 134
Frosting, Chocolate Cake with Double,
   '86 314

CHOCOLATE, Cakes and Tortes (continued)

Fruitcakes, Chocolate, '95 250
Fudge Cake, '94 M293
Fudge Cake, Best, '83 301
Fudge Cake, Brown Sugar, '86 316
Fudge Cake, Chocolate, '80 279
Fudge Cake for Two, '81 205
Fudge Cake, One-Foot-in-the-Fire, '90 252
Fudge Frosting, Chocolate Cake with, '89 56
German Chocolate Cake, '81 296; '83 M233
German Chocolate Chip Cake, '86 247
Grandma's Chocolate Cake, '94 133
Graveyard Grumblings, '92 15
Kahlúa Cake, Chocolate, '91 298
Kahlúa Chocolate Cake, '81 303
Marble Chocolate Chip Cupcakes, '81 239
Marbled Cake, Cocoa, '82 265
Marshmallow Cake, No-Egg Chocolate, '87 M97
Mayonnaise Cake, Chocolate, '83 99
Mint Torte, Chocolate, '94 86
Mocha Brownie Torte, '85 102
Mocha Cake, Belgian, '84 316
Mocha Cake, Double, '84 311
Mocha-Chocolate Cake, Dark, '84 311
Mocha Cream Roll, Chocolate-, '84 304
Mocha Cupcakes, '85 250
Mocha-Pecan Torte, '86 26
Mocha Velvet Torte, '92 318
Mousse Cake, Chocolate, '87 264
Mousse Roll, Chocolate, '88 280
Nut Cake, Rich Chocolate-, '86 8
Pastry Cake, Chocolate, '91 196
Peanut Butter Cake, Chocolate-, '84 240
Peanut Butter Cake, Fudgy, '85 91
Peanut Cluster Cake, Chocolate-, '87 184
Pecan Torte, Chocolate-, '89 42
Perfect Chocolate Cake, '82 244; '90 307
Petits Fours, Chocolate-Almond, '93 255
Pound Cake, Chocolate, '82 88; '84 10; '89 325; '94 288
Pound Cake, Chocolate Chip, '86 178; '93 105; '94 100
Pound Cake, Chocolate Marble, '88 16
Pound Cake, Chocolate-Orange, '89 94
Pound Cake, Chocolate-Sour Cream, '83 239; '92 153
Pound Cake, Mahogany, '89 207
Pound Cake, Marble, '95 29
Pound Cake, Marbled Pecan, '93 313
Pound Cake, Milk Chocolate, '90 306
Pound Cake, White Chocolate, '91 101
Pound Cake with Frosting, Chocolate, '90 284
Pound Cake with Fudge Frosting, Chocolate, '87 296
Praline Torte, Chocolate, '84 165
Pudding Cake, Hot Fudge, '88 255
Pudding Cake, Warm Chocolate, '92 324
Pudding, Chocolate Cake, '81 99
Queen's Chocolate Cake, '89 271
Raspberry Cake, Chocolate-, '92 173
Rich Chocolate Cake, '89 43
Rocky Road Cake, '81 178
Roll, Chocolate Cream, '85 317

Roll, Chocolate-Frosted Ice Cream, '84 200
Roll, Chocolate Mousse, '83 290
Roll, Chocolate-Orange, '87 21
Roll, Make-Ahead Chocolate-Mint Cake, '95 220
Rolls, Chocolate Cake, '94 312
Roulage, Chocolate-Cranberry, '94 313
Roulage, Chocolate-Orange, '94 314
Roulage, Mint-Chocolate, '94 314
Royal, Chocolate Cake, '86 239
Royale, Chocolate Torte, '82 263
Rum Cake, Chocolate, '79 67
Sachertorte, '84 253
Self-Filled Cupcakes, '80 129
Shortcake, Chocolate-Raspberry, '95 99
Snack Cake, Black Widow, '93 245
Snack Cake, Frosted Chocolate, '90 194
Sour Cream Cake, Chocolate-, '87 222
Sour Cream Cake, Chocolate Chip-, '85 115
Sour Cream Chocolate Cake, '79 282
Sponge Cake, Chocolaty, '86 60
Strawberry Ice Cream Torte, Chocolate-, '79 7
Strawberry Shortcake, Chocolate-, '89 216
Sugar Cookie Torte, '79 68
Surprise Cupcakes, Chocolate, '85 91
Swiss Chocolate Chip Cake, '87 85
Tannenbaum Temptations, '92 14
Toffee Cake, Chocolate-, '89 335
Triangle Cake, Chocolate, '85 126
Truffle Cake, Chocolate, '89 43
Turkey Talk, '92 15
Velvet Torte, Chocolate, '86 316
Wedding Cake, Double Chocolate, '91 100
Whipped Cream Cake, Chocolate-Mint, '90 265
White Chocolate-Cherry Cake, '88 268
White Chocolate Mousse Cake, '89 160
Yule Log, '79 281; '82 289
Zucchini Cake, Chocolate-, '85 156
Candies
Almond Roca, '86 49
Bourbon Balls, '83 315; '90 83
Bourbon Balls, Chocolate, '84 298
Brittle, Chocolate, '83 315
Brittle, Quick Chocolate, '82 114
Butter Creams, '80 302
Caramels, Chocolate, '91 35
Cherries, Chocolate-Covered, '81 286; '84 298
Coconut Almond Drops, Chocolate-, '87 223
Cream-Filled Chocolates, Liqueur, '87 258
Crème de Cacao Balls, '86 266
Crème de Menthe Chocolates, '91 36
Drops, Chocolate, '84 111
Fudge, '86 266
Fudge Balls, Strawberry, '93 80
Fudge Bites, Peanut-, '91 M231; '92 M68
Fudge, Cherry Nut, '83 315
Fudge, Chocolate, '82 20
Fudge, Chocolate-Peanut Butter, '87 257; '90 311
Fudge, Coffee-Chip, '86 74
Fudge, Cream Cheese, '84 111
Fudge, Creamy, '81 218
Fudge, Creamy Almond, '95 51

Fudge, Creamy Dark, '82 295
Fudge, Creamy Mocha, '95 51
Fudge, Creamy Pecan, '84 321
Fudge, Diamond, '92 193
Fudge, Dinner Mint, '88 285
Fudge, Double-Good, '79 M263; '95 M50
Fudge, Double Good, '87 M278
Fudge, Double Peanut, '85 91
Fudge, Fast, '79 274
Fudge, Five Pounds of Chocolate, '95 51
Fudge, Four Chips, '92 318
Fudge, Holiday Mocha, '84 298
Fudge, Marbled Peanut Butter, '88 65
Fudge, Microwave Chocolate, '92 M50
Fudge, Mint, '95 50
Fudge, Orange-Walnut, '92 288
Fudge, Peanut Butter, '89 307
Fudge, Pistachio, '83 298
Fudge, Quick-and-Easy, '88 M190
Fudge, Quick Nut, '83 316
Fudge Scotch Ring, '79 273
Fudge, White Chocolate, '92 317; '95 51
Fudge, White Chocolate-Coffee, '94 232
Greeting Card, Chocolate, '83 40
Kentucky Colonels, '79 273
Marshmallow Squares, Chocolate-, '92 M50
Millionaires, '79 M262
Mints, Dinner, '88 66
Molded Candies, '84 40
Nut Clusters, '81 254
Nut Log Candy, Chocolate-, '86 335
Nut Teasers, Chocolate, '91 35
Peanut Butter Balls, Chocolate-, '80 87
Peanut Butter Bites, Chocolate-, '92 M317
Peanut Butter-Chocolate Balls, '80 269
Peanut Butter-Chocolate Candy Squares, '82 56
Peanut Butter Creams, '79 273
Peanut Butter Drops, Chocolate-, '92 322
Peanut Clusters, '92 288
Peanut Clusters, Chocolate-, '81 16
Peanutty Clusters, '83 143
Peanutty Swirls, Chocolate, '94 M330
Pecan Clusters, Roasted, '90 310
Pecan Fritters, Chocolate-Covered, '79 205
Pralines, Chocolate, '92 313; '93 51
Pralines, Chocolate-Mint, '92 313; '93 51
Pralines, Chocolate-Peanut Butter, '92 313; '93 51
Pralines, Mocha, '92 313; '93 51
Pretzels, Chocolate-Covered, '82 295
Raspberry Cream Chocolates, '91 36
Rocky Road, '84 298
Rum Balls, Chocolate, '80 302
Rum Balls, Chocolate-, '88 285
Spiders, Chocolate, '85 236
Spirited Chocolates, '86 278
Tempered Chocolate, '91 35
Tiger Butter, '86 48
Toffee, English, '79 273
Toffee, Microwave, '92 M317
Toffee, Nutty, '79 M263
Truffles, Almond, '83 298
Truffles, Amaretto Dessert, '86 319
Truffles, Bittersweet, '94 330
Truffles, Chocolate, '85 114; '89 43; '91 108

CHOCOLATE, Candies (continued)

Truffles, Chocolate-Kahlúa, '92 285
Truffles, Orange-Pecan, '95 92
Truffles, White Chocolate, '87 45
Truffles, Yule Street, '90 242
Turtle Candies, '93 M41
Velvets, Chocolate, '84 298
White Chocolate Salties, '92 50
White Chocolate Surprises, '91 36
Cannoli, '80 58
Charlotte Russe, Chocolate, '87 74
Cheese Cups, Chocolate-, '91 142
Cinnamon-Chocolate Cream, '94 199
Cocoa to Chocolate Equivalents, '84 200
Combo, Strawberry-Chocolate, '85 96
Cream, Chocolate-Almond, '91 108
Cream, Heavenly Chocolate, '88 128
Cream, Strawberries with Chocolate, '85 81
Crème Brûlée, Chocolate, '95 323
Crème Brûlée, White Chocolate-Macadamia
    Nut, '95 323
Crêpes, Chocolate, '86 164
Crêpes, Chocolate Chantilly, '82 183
Crêpes, Chocolate Dessert, '84 84; '85 262
Crêpes, Chocolate Dream, '86 164
Crêpes, Chocolate-Orange, '85 263
Crêpes, Fruit-Filled Chocolate, '89 325
Crust, Chocolate, '87 264; '90 M15
Crust, Chocolate-Coconut, '87 261
Crust, Chocolate Crumb, '87 261
Crust, Chocolate Wafer, '89 42, 93
Cups, Chocolate, '80 207
Cups, Chocolate Crinkle, '93 270
Cups, Chocolate Lace, '87 133
Cups, Chocolate-Mint, '80 71
Cups, Chocolate-Walnut, '85 213
Cups, Miniature Chocolate, '87 132
Custard, Chocolate, '88 258
Custard, Chocolate-Topped Amaretto,
    '87 M37
Date-Nut Delight, Chocolate, '88 168
Decadence, Chocolate, '89 183
Dessert, Chilled Chocolate, '83 177
Dessert, Chocolate-Almond, '82 306
Dessert, Chocolate-Coffee Frozen, '85 172
Dessert, Chocolate Dream, '83 198
Dessert, Chocolate Ladyfinger, '86 162
Dessert, Chocolate-Mint, '82 100
Dessert, Chocolate-Rum, '81 247
Dessert, Chocolate Truffle, '88 281
Dessert, Choco-Maple Frozen, '86 300;
    '87 178
Dessert, Cool Chocolate-Mint, '80 109
Dessert, Easy Chocolate, '79 75
Dessert, Frozen Chocolate, '83 76
Dessert, Fudge-Peanut Ice Cream, '88 167
Dessert, Hello Dolly, '95 168
Dessert, Layered Ice Cream, '83 189
Dessert, Nutty Fudgy Frozen, '94 28
Dessert, Peanut-Chocolate, '80 86
Dessert Squares, Chocolate-Blueberry,
    '87 299
Dessert, Triple Cream, '94 244
Dessert with Kahlúa Cream, Fudge, '91 197
Dip, Chocolate, '92 50
Doughnuts, Chocolate, '83 95
Doughnuts, Chocolate-Covered, '84 55
Doughnuts, Chocolate-Glazed Potato, '85 6
Flan, Layered, '89 45
Fondue, Brandied Chocolate, '93 162
Fondue, Chocolate, '91 142

Fondue, Dessert, '89 281
Fondue, White Chocolate, '92 287
Frostings, Fillings, and Toppings
    Almond Frosting, Chocolate-, '83 241
    Buttercream, Chocolate, '84 156
    Butter Frosting, Chocolate, '89 271
    Candy Frosting, Chocolate, '81 238
    Cheese Filling, Chocolate-, '90 47
    Cherry Frosting, Chocolate-, '89 294
    Chocolate Frosting, '80 M171;
        '81 265; '82 262; '83 79, 99, M233,
        253; '84 200; '85 323;
        '86 8, 93, 138, 239, 314;
        '87 M97,198, 199, 293; '89 M25;
        '90 194, 252, 265, 284, 309; '91 248;
        '92 319; '93 239; '94 133
    Cocoa Frosting, '86 60
    Coconut Chocolate Frosting, '79 13
    Coffee Frosting, Chocolate-, '84 36;
        '88 269
    Cola Frosting, Chocolate-, '95 56
    Cream, Chocolate, '94 57
    Creamy Chocolate Frosting, '85 314;
        '86 316; '87 241
    Creamy Chocolate Glaze, '82 88
    Fluffy Chocolate Frosting, '86 336;
        '87 58
    Fudge Filling, '94 292
    Fudge Frosting, '81 303; '87 296;
        '89 56; '94 51
    Fudge Frosting, Chocolate, '83 105
    Fudge Frosting, Quick, '81 278
    Ganache, Chocolate, '93 255
    Ganache Cream, '92 318
    Glaze, Chocolate, '81 119; '83 220;
        '84 10, 55, 253; '85 6; '86 315, 316;
        '89 325; '90 310; '91 M296;
        '93 52
    Glaze, White Cake with Strawberries and
        Chocolate, '87 76
    Honey Chocolate Frosting, '79 83
    Honey Glaze, Chocolate-, '82 306
    Kahlúa Frosting, Chocolate, '91 298
    Marshmallow Frosting, Chocolate-,
        '83 245
    Mocha Butter Cream Frosting, '79 281
    Mocha-Buttercream Frosting, '86 26
    Mocha Cream, '94 47
    Mocha Cream Filling, '84 305
    Mocha Frosting, '83 301; '84 316;
        '87 224; '94 292
    Mocha Frosting, Creamy, '82 289;
        '84 311; '91 248
    Nut Frosting, Chocolate, '80 140
    Peanut Butter Frosting, Chocolate-,
        '84 240; '87 222
    Peanut Butter-Fudge Frosting, '87 184
    Peanut Topping, Chocolate-, '79 222
    Perfect Chocolate Frosting, '90 307
    Rich Chocolate Filling, '79 68
    Rich Chocolate Frosting, '84 304
    Rum Frosting, Chocolate, '79 67
    Satiny Chocolate Frosting, '85 126;
        '89 43
    Truffle Filling, Chocolate, '87 69
    Whipped Cream Frosting, '89 43
    White Chocolate-Cream Cheese Frosting,
        '94 58
    White Chocolate-Cream Cheese Tiered
        Cake Frosting, '94 125
    White Chocolate Filling, '89 160
    White Chocolate Frosting, '88 280;
        '91 101

Garnishes, Chocolate, '85 16
Garnishes, Lacy Chocolate, '89 43
Gâteau Panache, '83 269
Granola with Chocolate Morsels, '86 69
Grapefruit, Chocolate-Topped, '89 88
Horns, Chocolate-Dipped, '93 197
Ice Cream, Almond-Fudge, '93 205
Ice Cream Balls, Easy, '84 106
Ice Cream Balls, Nutty, '89 72
Ice Cream, Chocolate, '80 176; '86 129
Ice Cream, Chocolate Chunk-Peanut Butter,
    '85 297; '86 120
Ice Cream, Chocolate Cookie, '95 245
Ice Cream, Chocolate-Covered Peanut,
    '88 203
Ice Cream, Double-Chocolate, '88 203
Ice Cream, Mexican Chocolate, '91 162
Ice Cream, Mint-Chocolate Chip, '88 202
Ice Cream, Mocha, '88 202
Ice Cream Party Squares, '91 214
Ice Cream Sandwiches, Chocolate, '89 72
Ice Cream Squares, Mint-Chocolate Chip,
    '94 245
Kahlúa Delight, '83 67
Leaves, Chocolate, '88 281; '89 42
Loaf, Chocolate Pinwheel, '80 256
Loaves, Chocolate Chip Cheese, '91 299;
    '92 264
Log, Chocolate Cream, '94 220
Meringue Acorns, '93 284
Meringue Fingers, Chocolate-Almond,
    '84 158
Mexican Fiesta Confection, '82 223
Mint Freeze, Chocolate, '88 167
Mocha Alaska Dessert, '84 191
Mocha Chiffon, '86 75
Mocha Dessert, Frozen, '84 311
Mocha Freeze, Royal, '84 53
Mocha-Mallow Parfaits, '80 219
Mocha Squares, Frozen, '81 187
Mousse, Amaretto-Chocolate, '86 50
Mousse au Grand Marnier, Chocolate, '91 296
Mousse Baked Alaska, Chocolate, '85 195
Mousse, Blender Chocolate, '82 71
Mousse, Blender-Quick Chocolate, '80 269
Mousse, Brandy-Chocolate, '85 102
Mousse, Chocolate, '88 280
Mousse, Chocolate-Almond, '93 316
Mousse, Chocolate-Orange, '81 16, 205
Mousse, Chocolate Rum, '86 189
Mousse, Creamy Chocolate, '87 133
Mousse, Elegant Amaretto-Chocolate,
    '86 337
Mousse, Honeyed Chocolate, '87 223
Mousse, Kid-Pleasin' Chocolate, '90 271
Mousse, Quick Chocolate, '85 87
Mousse, White Chocolate, '91 247; '93 315
Mousse with Raspberry Sauce, Chocolate
    Truffle, '95 327
Muffins, Banana-Chocolate, '94 197
Muffins, Chocolate Chip, '90 87
Muffins, Fudge Brownie, '95 M50
Muffins, Jumbo Banana-Chocolate Chip,
    '93 339
Muffins, Peanut Butter-Chocolate Chip,
    '94 167
Napoleons, Coffee, '95 276
Napoleons, Peanut Butter-and-Chocolate,
    '94 121
Parfait, Bodacious Peanut, '95 167
Parfait, Chocolate Mousse, '94 90
Parfaits, Chocolate-Crème de Menthe,
    '85 161

CHOCOLATE *(continued)*

Parfaits, Chocolate-Mint, '90 M15
Parfaits, Chocolate-Peppermint, '88 65
Parfaits, Speedy, '83 76
Parfait, White Chocolate-Raspberry Swirl,
'93 315
Pies and Tarts
Almond Pie, Creamy Chocolate-, '85 102
Amandine, Chocolate Pie, '83 300
Amaretto Heavenly Tarts, Chocolate-,
'88 4
Amaretto Mousse Pie, Chocolate-,
'80 180; '81 30
Banana-Pecan Cream Pie, Chocolate-,
'94 210
Bavarian Pie, Chocolate, '89 326
Berry Pie, Heavenly Chocolate-, '85 102
Best-Ever Chocolate Pie, '88 M45
Black Bottom Mocha-Cream Tart,
'92 304
Black Bottom Pie, '82 53
Bluegrass Chocolate Tarts, '90 84
Bourbon Pie, Chocolate, '88 99
Brownie Pie, Crustless, '82 33
Caramel Turtle Truffle Tart, '93 M131
Chess Pie, Chocolate, '81 161; '86 220;
'92 13
Chess Tarts, Chocolate, '92 214
Chilled Chocolate Pie, '88 99
Chip Pie, Chocolate, '85 114
Cream Cheese Pie, Chocolate-, '80 69
Cream Cheese Pie, Chocolate, '92 240
Cream Pie, Chocolate, '83 192; '84 49;
'87 208; '94 208
Creamy Chocolate Pie, '85 298; '86 119
Double Chocolate Pie, '82 M282
Easy Chocolate Pie, '83 158
French Silk Pie, '80 247
French Silk Tarts, '79 236
Frozen Chocolate Pie, '80 154
Frozen Chocolate Pie with Pecan Crust,
'89 291
Fudge Pie, '87 168; '89 252
Fudge Pie, Sweetheart, '86 316; '90 313
German Chocolate Pie, '93 129
Heavenly Chocolate Pie, '87 260
Ice Cream Pie, Chocolate-, '87 224
Ice Cream Pie, Chocolate, '91 56
Ice Cream Pie, Chocolate-Mint, '81 144
Ice Cream Sundae Pie, '94 244
Kahlúa Pie, '83 191
Kentucky Derby Tarts, '79 102
Meringue Pie, Chocolate, '80 238;
'82 206; '83 158; '92 216
Meringue Pie, Chocolate-Filled, '86 121
Microwave Chocolate Pie, '90 M15
Midnight Delights, '95 278
Mocha Crunch Pie, Chocolate-, '81 136
Mocha Meringue Pie, '80 242
Mocha Pie, '94 168
Mousse Pie, Chocolate, '81 136
Mud Pie, Decadent, '89 252
Mud Pie, Mississippi, '89 26
Mud Pie, Tipsy, '80 255
Party Tarts, '95 90
Peanut Butter Pie, Chocolate-, '85 91
Peanut Butter Swirl Pie, Chocolate-,
'87 262
Peanut Butter Tarts, Chocolate-, '92 277
Pecan Chess Pie, Chocolate-, '93 251
Pecan Pie, Choco-, '82 86

Pecan Pie, Chocolate, '80 237; '83 12;
'90 184
Pecan Pie, Chocolate-, '91 272
Pecan Tart with Caramel Sauce,
Chocolate-, '93 296; '94 234
Praline Pie, Chocolate-, '86 259
Silk Pie, Chocolate, '88 67
Strawberry-Chocolate Truffle Pie,
'89 112
Tin Roof Pie, '85 91
Turtle Pecan Pie, '93 250
Whipped Cream Pie, Chocolate, '79 124
White Chocolate-Banana Cream Pie,
'94 314
White Chocolate Chess Tart, '95 303
Pineapple with Raspberry Sauce, Chocolate-
Drizzled, '90 57
Pizza, Chocolate, '91 298
Plunge, Chocolate, '94 332; '95 35
Pots de Chocolat, Petits, '82 272
Pots de Crème, '81 15; '84 M145
Pots de Crème au Chocolate, '93 53
Pots de Crème, Chocolate, '93 296; '94 234
Pots de Crème for Two, '89 275
Pots de Crème, Mocha, '88 M45
Pots de Crème, Rum-Flavored, '85 102
Pots de Crème with Orange Meringues,
Chocolate, '95 318
Pudding, Brownie, '79 265; '80 295
Pudding, Chocolate-Almond, '82 142; '88 24
Pudding, Chocolate Biscuit Bread, '94 215
Pudding, Chocolate Bread, '80 8
Pudding, Creamy Chocolate, '83 106
Pudding, Hot Fudge, '81 208
Pudding, Hot Fudge Sundae Cake, '88 167
Pudding with Lemon Meringue, Chocolate,
'88 258
Roulage, '90 266
Roulage, Chocolate-Mocha, '80 216
Roulage, Frozen Chocolate, '90 56
Roulage, White Chocolate, '92 230
Sack, Large Chocolate, '93 314
Sack, Small Chocolate, '93 314
Sauces
Amaretto-Chocolate Sauce, '92 154
Bittersweet Chocolate Sauce, '92 319
Cherry Sauce, Chocolate-, '85 189
Cherry Sauce, Chocolate, '87 M165
Chocolate Sauce, '83 189;
'84 208, 313; '86 322; '90 57;
'91 56, 57; '93 276; '94 121
Cinnamon-Fudge Sauce, '85 141
Classic Chocolate Sauce, '85 207
Creamy Chocolate Sauce, '88 M177
Dark Chocolate Sauce, '93 296;
'94 234, 283
Dark Chocolate Sauce, Poached Pears
with, '90 M141
Double Chocolate Sauce, '83 79
Easy Chocolate Sauce, '92 148
Fudge Sauce, '91 174
Fudge Sauce, Easy Hot, '94 194
Heavenly Chocolate Sauce, '79 79;
'82 167
Honey-Chocolate Sauce, '89 251
Hot Fudge Sauce, '82 181, 295; '84 143
Hot Fudge Sauce, Easy, '84 69
Hot Fudge Sauce, Quick, '82 212
Kahlúa Chocolate Sauce, '85 155
Mint Sauce, Chocolate-, '93 86; '94 314
Mint Sauce, Quick Chocolate, '86 M58
Orange Sauce, Chocolate-, '86 165;
'94 314

Peanut Butter Sauce, Chocolate-,
'79 91, M156
Peppermint Sauce, Chocolate-, '94 205
Praline Sauce, Chocolate-, '85 M295
Supreme, Chocolate Sauce, '85 189
Toffee-Fudge Sauce, '89 95
White Chocolate Sauce, '92 164
Shavings, Chocolate Hearts and, '86 26
Shell, Chocolate-Coconut Pie, '82 210;
'83 100
Shell, Chocolate Pastry, '87 262
Shells with Kahlúa Cream, Chocolate, '88 195
Snacks, Chocolate-Peanut Butter, '90 226
Soufflé au Chocolat Cointreau, '94 56
Soufflé, Chocolate, '84 317; '94 46
Soufflé, Chocolate Mint, '81 16
Soufflé, Light Chocolate, '83 278
Spoons, Dipped Chocolate-Almond,
'95 M277
Spread, Chocolate Cheese, '87 292
Sticks, Chocolate-Sesame, '91 316
Sticky Buns, Easy Caramel-Chocolate, '95 36
Strawberries Dipped in White Chocolate,
'90 83
Sundae Dessert, Hot Fudge, '84 313; '86 322
Sundaes, Cocoa-Kahlúa, '83 M58
Supreme, Chocolate, '84 94
Torte, Frozen Viennese, '93 171
Trifle, Chocolate, '88 258; '93 326
Velvet, Chocolate Almond, '81 148
Waffles, Fudge, '94 205
Waffles with Strawberry Cream, Chocolate,
'88 153
Whip, Chocolate, '89 326
Yogurt, Mocha Sauce with Chocolate, '92 243

CHOP SUEY
Cabbage Chop Suey, '81 101
Chicken Chop Suey, '81 227
Salad, Chop Suey, '81 37

CHOWDERS. *See also* **GUMBOS, SOUPS.**
Bell Pepper-Cheese Chowder, '95 240
Bluefish Chowder, '84 282
Broccoli Chowder, '79 16
Cabbage Chowder, Hearty, '80 25
Cheddar Chowder, Hearty, '79 16
Cheese Chowder, Golden, '80 73
Cheese Chowder, Hot, '89 16
Chicken-and-Corn Chowder, Curried, '92 21
Chicken Chowder, '83 20
Chicken Chowder, Cheesy, '92 21
Chicken Chowder Sauterne, '84 235
Chicken-Vegetable Chowder, Creamy, '92 20
Clam-and-Sausage Chowder, '94 104
Clam Chowder, '79 182; '81 32; '85 9;
'86 36; '89 95; '90 202
Clam Chowder, New England, '86 M72
Clam Chowder, Ocracoke, '79 31
Clam Chowder, Tomato-, '84 251
Corn and Bacon Chowder, Fresh, '93 203
Corn and Cheese Chowder, '80 228
Corn Chowder, '81 128; '83 20; '84 M38;
'85 10; '90 202; '91 132
Corn Chowder, Delicious, '82 279
Fish Chowder, '79 152; '84 M38
Fish Chowder, Basque, '86 36
Fish Chowder, Chunky, '92 331
Fish Chowder, Creamy, '79 16
Fish Chowder, Tasty, '80 188
Ham-and-Cheese Chowder, '89 15
Ham and Corn Chowder, '79 16
Ham-and-Corn Chowder, '82 40
Ham Chowder, Creamy, '88 M53
Ham 'n Cheese Chowder, '79 199

CHOWDERS *(continued)*

Harvest Chowder, '83 317
Mushroom Chowder, '79 16
Mushroom-Potato Chowder, '92 331
Okra Chowder, Quick, '80 185
Oyster Chowder, '83 229
Oyster-Corn Chowder, '83 211
Potato-Corn Chowder, '94 66
Red Snapper Chowder, '85 217
Sausage-Bean Chowder, '83 20
Seafood Chowder, '85 9; '92 122
Seafood Chowder, Curried, '94 103
Seafood Chowder, Southern, '83 20
Shrimp and Corn Chowder, '79 199
Shrimp Chowder, '89 218
Swiss-Broccoli Chowder, '80 73
Turkey Chowder, '85 10; '91 312
Turkey-Corn Chowder, '81 98
Vegetable Chowder, Cheesy, '80 25; '83 20
Vegetable Chowder, Hearty, '88 56
Vegetable Chowder, Oven-Roasted,
'95 229

CHOW MEIN
Beef-and-Vegetable Chow Mein Casserole,
'83 313
Chicken Chow Mein, '90 68
Noodles, Chow Mein over Crispy,
'85 286
Pork Chow Mein, '80 208; '90 101
Shrimp Chow Mein, '82 30

CHRISTMAS. *See also* **COOKIES/CHRISTMAS**.
Beverages
Milk, Santa Claus, '92 281
Punch, Christmas, '84 259; '89 330
Punch, Christmas Eve, '86 314
Punch, Merry Christmas, '79 285
Tea, Christmas Fruit, '83 275
Wassail, Christmas, '93 295
Bread, Christmas, '87 296; '88 288
Bread, Norwegian Christmas, '79 234
Bread Stars, '93 286
Cake, Christmas Coconut, '82 262
Candy Canes and Wreaths, Braided, '92 276
Cinnamon Ornaments, '85 284
Coeur à la Crème, Christmas, '86 278
Coffee Cakes, Christmas-Tree, '87 298
Cookie Advent Calendar, '85 325
Cookie Cards, Christmas, '84 302
Cookie, Elf, '80 279, 303
Cookie, Mrs. Claus, '80 279, 303
Cookie, Rudolph, '80 279, 303
Cookie, Santa Claus, '80 278, 303
Cookies, Christmas Cherry, '88 282
Cookies, Christmas Date, '88 287
Cookies, Christmas Tree, '93 286
Cookies, Easy Santa, '95 321
Cookies, Eggnog Christmas, '79 255
Cookies, Gingerbread, '80 278

Cookies, Jolly Reindeer, '91 273
Cookie, Sleigh, '80 279, 303
Cookies, Moravian Christmas, '91 282
Cookies, Painted, '86 322
Cookies, Spiced Christmas, '87 294
Cookies, Swedish Christmas, '79 290
Corn, Christmas, '93 325
Cottage, Quick-Fix Christmas, '91 280
Cottage, Sugarplum, '88 309
Cranberry Hearts, '93 286
Crostini, Christmas, '94 318
Custard, Boiled Christmas, '95 329
Dessert, White Christmas, '82 261
Dip, Christmas Confetti, '92 279
Divinity, Christmas, '81 286
Doughnuts, Snowy, '93 286
Fruit Squares, Christmas, '88 282
Gingerbread Bowl, Christmas, '93 266
Grittibanz (Swiss Bread Figure), '93 265
Jam, Christmas, '88 288
Jam, Christmas Brunch, '81 286
Jammies, Christmas, '95 322
Jelly, Christmas Freezer, '86 M288
Lizzies, Christmas, '87 257
Loaf, Sweet Christmas, '84 278
Munchies, Reindeer, '91 276
Orange Baskets, '93 286
Ornaments, Edible, '94 316
Pandoro, '93 267
Panettone, '93 266
Peanut Butter Elf Bites, '91 275
Pecans, Christmas Eve, '91 276
Pie, White Christmas, '88 281; '93 289
Pinecones, Peanut Butter-Suet, '93 286
Pinwheels, Santa's, '91 275
Potatoes, Christmas, '88 252
Potpourri, Christmas, '94 317
Pretzel Garlands, '93 286
Pudding with Brandy Sauce, Baked Christmas,
'88 279
Reindeer Nibbles, '92 280
Relish Tree, Christmas, '84 257
Salad, Christmas, '88 249
Salad, Christmas Snow, '82 266
Salad, Cranberry Christmas, '79 243
Salad, Eggnog Christmas, '86 281
Sandwiches, Christmas Tree, '92 279
Sandwich Wreath, Festive, '86 333
Santa's Hat, '92 279
Santa's Whiskers, '85 323
Scent, Christmas, '84 325
Spices, Barclay House Mulling, '86 289
Strata, Christmas Morning, '95 282
Strawberries, Christmas, '87 293; '94 331
Sugar Plums, '92 281
Sugarplum Sticks, '95 321
Tannenbaum Temptations, '92 14
Trees, Christmas, '89 294
Wine, Christmas Dreams in, '91 260
Wreath, Christmas, '80 280
Wreath, Della Robbia Fruit, '87 294

CHUTNEYS. *See also* **PESTOS, RELISHES, SALSAS,
TOPPINGS**.
Apple Chutney, '92 309
Blueberry Chutney, '95 190
Commander's Chutney, '87 245
Cranberry-Amaretto Chutney with Cream
Cheese, '87 244
Cranberry Chutney, '80 243; '83 260;
'84 265
Cranberry-Orange Chutney, '79 292
Fruit Chutney, Autumn, '88 M230
Kiwifruit-Onion Chutney, '93 125

Mango Chutney, '89 141
Orange-Cranberry Chutney, '86 266
Pâté, Chutney-Cheese, '84 152
Peach Chutney, '84 179
Pear-Apple Chutney, '89 141
Pear Chutney, '95 251
Pepper Chutney, Jeweled, '94 316
Plum Chutney, '84 179
Rhubarb Chutney, '87 245
Roll, Chutney, '83 259
Rosy Chutney, '80 120
Sauce, Chutney-Mustard, '89 242
Tomato-Apple Chutney, '84 180

CLAMS
Backyard Clambake, '81 92
Bisque, Clam, '86 228
Casino, Clams, '81 125
Casino, Maryland Clams, '89 196
Chase, Clams, '79 85
Chowder, Clam, '79 182; '81 32; '85 9;
'86 36; '89 95; '90 202
Chowder, Clam-and-Sausage, '94 104
Chowder, New England Clam, '86 M72
Chowder, Ocracoke Clam, '79 31
Chowder, Tomato-Clam, '84 251
Cocktail, Tomato-Clam, '87 252
Crisps, Clam, '80 151
Dip, Clam, '79 151; '80 265
Dip, Hot Clam, '82 59; '89 48
Dip, Zesty Clam, '92 25
Fritters, Clam, '79 151; '86 71
Linguine, Clam, '95 212
Linguine, Quick Clam, '90 233
Oreganata, Clams, '85 104
Pizza, Baby Clam, '87 182
Puffs, Clam, '90 60
Quiche, Clam, '83 215
Sauce, Linguine in Clam, '81 83
Sauce, Linguine with Clam, '84 124; '88 90;
'89 178
Sauce, Pasta with Clam, '84 291
Sauce, Tricolor Pasta with Clam, '93 272
Sauce, Vermicelli and Sprouts with Red Clam,
'86 143
Sauce, Vermicelli with Clam, '85 295
Sauce with Linguine, Clam, '84 9
Shells, Baked Clam, '87 94
Soup, Clam Florentine, '85 23
Spread, Creamy Clam, '91 274
Steamed Clams Chesapeake, '89 196

COCONUT. *See also* **AMBROSIA**.
Balls, Coconut-Almond, '84 256
Bars, Coconut Granola, '85 202
Biscuits, Yummy Coconut, '95 99
Bonbons, Coconut-Black Walnut, '82 307
Bread, Coconut, '83 140
Bread, Pumpkin-Coconut, '87 255
Cakes
Angel Cake, Spiked Coconut, '85 279
Apple Coconut Cake, '80 226
Banana-Coconut Cake, '93 154
Carrot Cake, Fresh Coconut-, '80 299
Chocolate-Coconut Cake, '83 23
Christmas Coconut Cake, '82 262
Coconut Cake, '92 120
Coffee Cake, Cranberry-Coconut,
'93 332
Coffee Cake, Oatmeal-Coconut, '83 312
Coffee Cake, Pineapple-Coconut, '94 49
Cream Cake, Coconut, '81 179; '91 269
Creamy Coconut Cake, '84 43
Fresh Coconut Cake, '80 289; '82 52;
'85 281

COCONUT, Cakes *(continued)*

Holiday Coconut Cake, '90 308
Layer Cake, Stately Coconut, '81 70
Lemon Cake, Coconut-, '95 319
Lemon-Coconut Cream Cake, '81 179
Lemon-Coconut Sheet Cake, '85 117
Orange-Coconut Angel Food Cake, '94 294
Pineapple Cake, Coconut-, '89 56
Pineapple Layer Cake, Coconut-, '80 140
Pound Cake, Coconut, '82 87; '91 224
Pound Cake, Coconut Cream, '84 10
Pound Cake, Coconut-Cream Cheese, '85 297; '90 305
Regal Coconut Cake, '83 299
Roll, Coconut-Pineapple Cake, '84 304
Rum-Orange Coconut Cake, '88 224
Spice Cake, Coconut-, '84 255; '87 296
Toasted Coconut Cake, '86 60
Unforgettable Coconut Cake, '90 104
White Chocolate-Coconut Cake, '87 263
Calypso, Coco-Berry, '89 171
Candy, Coconut, '79 272; '80 250
Chicken Balls, Coconut Curried, '91 165
Chicken with Fresh Fruit, Coconut, '93 294
Cloud, Coconut, '80 70
Clusters, Pecan-Coconut, '86 M251
Cookies
Bars, Golden, '84 255
Bars, Hawaiian, '84 153
Cherry Cookies, Coconut-, '79 292
Chocolate Macaroon Cookies, '88 217
Crinkle Sunflower Cookies, '83 149
Crisp Coconut Cookies, '89 162
English Cherubs, '83 257
Kisses, Coconut, '90 106
Macaroons, Chewy Peanut Butter, '95 214
Macaroons, Chocolate, '83 300
Macaroons, Coconut, '79 52
Oatmeal-Coconut Cookies, '80 218
Oatmeal Cookies, Crispy Coconut-, '93 80
Peanut Butter-Coconut Cookies, '83 113
Shortbread Cookies, Coconut, '93 316
Squares, Chocolate-Coconut, '90 70
Cream, Orange-Coconut, '84 24
Crust, Chocolate-Coconut, '87 261
Crust, Coconut, '89 160
Custard, Coconut, '86 109
Dessert, Chilled Coconut, '83 116
Dessert, Coconut-Caramel, '92 44
Dessert, Macaroon-Sherbet Frozen, '79 212
Dip, Coconut-Honey Fruit, '84 171
Dressing, Coconut, '87 251
Dressing, Orange-Coconut, '80 158
Dressing, Tangy Coconut-Fruit, '84 171
Drink, Coconut-Pineapple, '83 172
Drops, Chocolate-Coconut Almond, '87 223
Filling, Coconut, '81 265
Filling, Coconut Cream, '84 200
Filling, Sour Cream-Coconut, '92 120
Frosting, Coconut, '82 262; '91 269
Frosting, Coconut Chocolate, '79 13
Frosting, Coconut Cream Cheese, '86 60
Frosting, Coconut-Pecan, '81 296; '83 M233; '84 43, 322
Frosting, Creamy Coconut, '80 287
Frosting, Lemon-Coconut, '90 253
Frosting, Nutty Coconut, '86 8
Frost, Pink Coconut, '79 174; '80 128

Fruit Bowl, Coconut, '83 111
Ice Cream, Coconut Fried, '85 141
Ice Cream, Fresh Coconut, '79 166
Macaroon Charlotte, '81 296
Macaroon-Stuffed Peaches, '79 178
Mousse, Coconut-Pineapple, '94 198
Muffins, Coconut, '95 214
Muffins, Coconut-Molasses, '82 210
Nests, Strawberry Coconut, '88 136
Nog, Coconut, '83 275
Pears, Spicy Coconut, '83 207
Pecan Coils, Coconut-, '90 196
Pies
Blender Coconut Pie, '84 236
Buttermilk-Coconut Pie, '94 246
Caramel Pies, Coconut-, '87 260
Cherry Pie, Coconut Crumb, '92 30
Chess Pie, Coconut, '86 220
Coconut Pie, '93 115
Cream Pie, Coconut, '80 238; '81 136; '82 85; '84 49; '87 207; '89 236; '90 312
Cream Pie, Fresh Coconut, '80 289
Cream Pie, Surprise Coconut, '92 43
Crunch Pie, Coconut, '90 105
Custard Pie, Coconut, '82 33
French Coconut Pie, '90 162
Macaroon Pie, Coconut, '88 204
Magic Coconut Pie, '79 53
Mock Coconut Pie, '86 200
Orange Chess Pie, Coconut-, '89 169
Orange-Coconut Cream Pie, '94 208
Orange-Coconut Pie, '90 90
Pecan Chess Pie, Coconut-, '81 248
Pecan Pie, Coconut, '81 161
Pineapple-Coconut Chess Pie, '92 214
Pineapple Pie, Coconut-, '84 256
Quick Coconut Pie, '83 115
Shell, Chocolate-Coconut Pie, '82 210; '83 100
Toasted Coconut Pie, '90 105
Puffs, Coconut, '87 277
Salad, Chunky Fruit-and-Coconut, '84 24
Sauce, Coconut-Orange, '85 189
Sauce, Creamy Light Coconut, '82 177
Shrimp, Coconut-Beer, '85 230; '89 23
Soufflé, Coconut, '79 73; '85 212
Spread, Coconut-Cranberry Cheese, '92 328
Spread, Coconut-Pineapple, '93 309
Sweet Potatoes, Coconut-Broiled, '84 231
Sweet Potatoes, Coconut-Orange, '84 252
Sweet Potatoes, Coconut-Stuffed, '82 204
Tropical Snow, '86 34

COFFEE
Beverages
After-Dinner Coffee, '81 262
Almond-Coffee Delight, '84 115
Blends, Coffee, '95 276
Brandied Coffee, '81 244
Cappuccino, Café, '82 253
Cappuccino, Chocolate Castle, '84 53
Cappuccino Coffee Dessert, '92 264
Cappuccino, Flaming, '79 293
Chocolate-Almond Coffee, '84 54
Chocolate Coffee, '82 43
Cocoa-Coffee, '83 55
Colombian Royal, Café, '80 M290
Colonial Coffee, '89 290
"Concrete," Abaco Mocha, '94 114
Cream, Café, '82 312
Cream, Icy Rum Coffee, '83 172
Creamy Coffee, '81 244
Dessert Drink, Simply Super, '83 303

Dessert, Light Coffee, '88 260
Diablo, Café, '80 259
Espresso, Amaretto, '92 263
Floats, Maple-Coffee, '86 195
Frosted Coffee, '81 244
German Chocolate Café au Lait, '92 264
Hazelnut-Coffee Ice, '94 233
Holiday Coffee, '90 273
Irish Coffee, Creamy, '79 232
Irish Coffee, Flaming, '79 293
Irish Coffee Nog, '84 258; '93 340
Irish Cream Nog, '82 312
Kahlúa Delight, Make-Ahead, '84 M89
Kona Luscious, '84 54
Liqueur, Coffee-Flavored, '86 266
Mexican Coffee, '83 175, 275; '88 247; '91 78; '93 310; '94 97
Mexicano, Café, '92 208
Mix, Cappucino, '90 87
Mix, Fireside Coffee, '87 241
Mix, Hot Mocha-Cocoa, '82 296
Mix, Mocha-Flavored Hot Cocoa, '91 316
Mocha Blend, '95 276
Mocha Chocolate Fluff, '89 170
Mocha Cocoa, '83 318
Mocha Coffee, '85 M329
Mocha Cream, Café, '84 54
Mocha Deluxe Hot Drink, '82 289
Mocha Espresso, Italian, '82 254
Mocha Frosty, '92 44
Mocha, Hot, '84 60
Mocha, Mexican, '93 M341
Mocha Milkshake, '89 35
Mocha Polka, '89 171
Mocha, Quick Viennese, '79 232
Mocha, Spirited Hot, '91 M260
Mocha, Swiss-Style, '82 253
Nog, Brandied Coffee, '86 329
Orange Blend, '95 276
Orange Coffee, Viennese, '84 54
Pontalba, Cafe, '92 83
Praline-Flavored Coffee, '87 69
Punch, Coffee, '80 50; '83 275; '88 83
Punch, Coffee-and-Cream, '85 116
Punch, Coffee-Eggnog, '86 281
Punch, Coffee Eggnog, '92 264
Punch, Creamy Coffee, '81 50
Punch, "Eye-Opener" Coffee, '92 80
Punch, Irish Coffee-Eggnog, '95 314
Punch, Mocha, '84 58, 166; '86 270; '95 141
Punch, Rich-and-Creamy Coffee, '82 121
Refresher, Velvet Coffee, '79 149
Royal, Café, '80 259
Shake, Peach-Coffee Milk, '84 284
Spiced Brew, Hot, '91 36
Spiced Coffee, Special, '84 284
Spiced-Up Coffee, '89 92
Vienna Blend, '95 276
Viennese, Café, '82 254
Buttercream, Coffee, '95 277
Cake, Coffee Sponge, '83 229; '91 55
Cake, Two-Day Coffee Sponge, '86 75
Cookies, Java Shortbread, '94 233
Cream Puffs, Java, '81 187
Crème Brûlée, Coffee, '95 323
Crêpes, Coffee Ice Cream, '84 85
Dessert, Chocolate-Coffee Frozen, '85 172
Frosting, Chocolate-Coffee, '84 36; '88 269
Frosting, Coffee, '94 86
Fudge, Coffee-Chip, '86 74

COFFEE *(continued)*

Fudge, White Chocolate-Coffee, '94 232
Granita, Coffee-Kahlúa, '88 118
Ice Cream, Coffee, '88 202
Ice Cream Crunch, Coffee, '82 182
Mallow, Coffee, '80 109
Meringues with Butterscotch Mousse, Coffee, '93 254
Mocha
    Blend, Mocha, '95 276
    Brownies, Mocha, '87 93
    Buttercream, Mocha, '89 42
    Cake, Belgian Mocha, '84 316
    Cake, Dark Mocha-Chocolate, '84 311
    Cake, Double Mocha, '84 311
    Cheesecake, Mocha-Chocolate, '88 258
    Cheesecake, Mocha Swirl, '87 262
    Chiffon, Mocha, '86 75
    "Concrete," Abaco Mocha, '94 114
    Cupcakes, Mocha, '85 250
    Dessert, Frozen Mocha, '84 311
    Dessert, Mocha Alaska, '84 191
    Dessert, Mocha-Almond, '80 289; '81 62
    Filling, Mocha, '80 55; '82 262
    Filling, Mocha Cream, '81 187; '84 305
    Freeze, Royal Mocha, '84 53
    Frosting, Creamy Mocha, '82 289; '84 311; '91 248
    Frosting, Mocha, '83 301; '84 316; '87 224; '94 292
    Frosting, Mocha Butter Cream, '79 281
    Frosting, Mocha-Buttercream, '86 26
    Frozen Mocha Squares, '81 187
    Fudge, Creamy Mocha, '95 51
    Gingerbread, Mocha, '81 207; '82 14
    Ice Cream, Mocha, '88 202
    Parfaits, Mocha-Mallow, '80 219
    Pie, Chocolate-Mocha Crunch, '81 136
    Pie, Mocha, '94 168
    Pie, Mocha Meringue, '80 242; '88 163
    Pots de Crème, Mocha, '88 M45
    Pralines, Mocha, '92 313; '93 51
    Pudding, Pecan-Mocha, '89 M130
    Punch, Mocha, '95 141
    Roll, Chocolate Mocha Cream, '84 304
    Roulage, Chocolate-Mocha, '80 216
    Sauce with Chocolate Yogurt Mocha, '92 243
    Tart, Black Bottom Mocha-Cream, '92 304
    Torte, Mocha Brownie, '85 102
    Torte, Mocha Velvet, '92 318
Mousse, Coffee, '84 126
Mousse, Coffee-Nut, '86 319
Mousse, Quick-as-a-Wink, '84 311
Napoleons, Coffee, '95 276
Nuggets, Coffee, '95 278
Parfaits, Coffee Crunch, '82 159
Pecans, Coffee 'n' Spice, '88 256
Pie, Coffee Cream, '94 209
Pie, Coffee Ice Cream, '79 231
Pie, Coffee Pecan, '82 74
Pie, Decadent Mud, '89 252
Pralines, Café au Lait, '92 313; '93 51
Pralines, Plantation Coffee, '86 241
Tortoni, Coffee-Almond, '81 30
Tortoni, Creamy Coffee, '88 268
COLESLAW. *See* **SLAWS.**

COOKIES. *See also* **BROWNIES.**
Almond-Anise Biscotti, '93 266
Almond Biscotti, '91 108
Almond Butter Cookies, '79 52
Almond Chip Balls, Toasted, '84 240
Almond Cookies, '83 22, 181; '91 51; '92 176
Almond Cookies, Light, '83 151
Almond Cookies, Swedish, '85 312
Almond Snaps, '92 273
Almond Spritz Cookies, '82 306
Apple-Filled Cookies, '92 311
Apricot Cookies, '95 322
Bars and Squares
    Almond Brickle Treats, '95 321
    Almond Cake Squares, '79 111
    Almond-Chocolate Bars, '83 304
    Almond Cream Confections, '87 198; '90 310
    Apple Butter Bars, '84 153
    Apple Kuchen, '79 24
    Apricot-Almond Squares, '95 272
    Apricot Bars, '81 247
    Apricot-Oatmeal Bars, '86 216
    Apricot-Raisin Bars, '87 32
    Banana Breakfast Bars, '79 124
    Blackberry Bars, '87 130
    Blackberry-Filled Bars, '79 124
    Blackberry Jam Bars, '82 M185
    Blondie Swirls, '85 248
    Blond Nut Squares, '82 156
    Brazil Squares, '82 306
    Brownie Alaskas, '83 299
    Brownie-Mint Dessert, '82 227
    Butter Pecan Pie Squares, '81 262
    Butter Pecan Turtle Bars, '90 70
    Butterscotch Bars, '82 209; '83 297
    By-Cracky Bars, '84 212
    Carrot-Lemon Squares, Golden, '80 40
    Carrot Squares, '79 256
    Cherry Bars, Delightful, '86 217
    Cherry Squares, Surprise, '82 57
    Choco-Crumble Bars, '79 292
    Chocolate-Butterscotch Bars, '81 197
    Chocolate-Caramel Layer Squares, '79 83
    Chocolate Chess Squares, '92 45
    Chocolate Chip Bars, '81 130
    Chocolate Chip-Peanut Butter Squares, '84 118
    Chocolate Chip Squares, '83 170; '89 143
    Chocolate Chip Squares, Chewy, '91 175
    Chocolate Cinnamon Bars, '82 209
    Chocolate-Coconut Squares, '90 70
    Chocolate-Crème de Menthe Bars, '86 245
    Chocolate Crème de Menthe Bites, '88 285
    Chocolate Dream Bars, '79 256; '82 298
    Chocolate-Peanut Crispies, '93 80
    Chocolate-Peppermint Squares, '81 119
    Cinnamon Chews, '84 110
    Cinnamon Sand Bars, '91 178
    Coconut Granola Bars, '85 202
    Coffee Bars, Frosted, '79 256
    Crème de Menthe Squares, '93 256
    Date Bars, '84 313; '95 322
    Date Bars, No-Bake, '79 256
    Date Bars, Nutty, '84 153
    Date-Nut Bars, '80 166
    Date-Oat Bars, '80 M172
    English Cherubs, '83 257
    Fudge Bars, '86 93

Fudge Bars, Yummy, '87 158
German Chocolate Chess Squares, '94 51
Golden Bars, '84 255
Granola Bars, '83 305; '95 214
Granola Bars, Fruit and Nut, '81 49
Hawaiian Bars, '84 153
Honey Cake Squares, '89 250
Jam-It Bars, '87 159
Jam Squares, '81 M289
Janhagel Cookies, '86 195
Layer Squares, Novelty, '90 70
Lemon Bars Deluxe, '79 35
Lemon Bars, Tangy, '86 217
Lemon-Pecan Squares, '89 124
Lemon Squares, '81 197
Lemon Yogurt Wheat Bars, '79 93
Lime Squares, '79 2
Marmalade Biscuit Squares, '79 193
Meringue-Chocolate Chip Bars, '84 118
Mincemeat-Spice Bars, '88 231; '89 22
Mystery Bars, '93 239
Nutmeg Logs, Frosted, '85 324
Nutty Choco Snacks, '83 305
Oatmeal Bars, Chocolate-Topped, '86 110
Oatmeal-Caramel Bars, '85 247
Oatmeal-Date Bars, Layered, '85 10
Peanut Bars, '89 307
Peanut Bars, Chewy, '80 M172
Peanut Butter-and-Fudge Bars, '80 M172
Peanut Butter Bars, '84 243; '93 166
Peanut Butter Fingers, '79 256
Peanut Butter Frosts, '84 153
Peanut Butter-Jam Bars, '94 291
Peanut Butter Logs, No-Bake, '84 211
Peanut Butter 'n' Jelly Bars, '83 305
Peanut Butter Squares, '83 116
Pecan Bars, '82 209
Pecan Bars, Gooey, '94 133
Pecan Squares, '79 205; '90 69
Pecan Squares, Easy, '81 230
Pecan Squares, Twice-Baked, '79 291
Pumpkin Bars, '80 40
Pumpkin Nut Bars, '82 217
Raisin Bars, '94 228
Raspberry Bars, '82 209; '84 212
Rhubarb Squares, '91 146
Rhubarb Squares, Rosy, '79 111
Shortbread, Orange, '91 272
Strawberry Bars, '81 301
Toffee Treats, '89 330
Tropical Bars, '80 284
Wheat Germ Squares, Spicy, '80 44
Yummy Bars, '92 171
Zucchini Bars, '85 77
Bird's Nest Cookies, '93 284
Biscotti Cioccolata, '93 268
Bonbon Cookies, Surprise, '88 119
Bourbon Balls, '81 254
Bourbon Dunkers, Crunchy, '85 90
Brutti Ma Buoni (Ugly but Good), '93 267
Butter Cookies, '85 322
Butter Cookies, Chocolate-Tipped, '84 258; '90 312
Butter Cookies, Holiday, '92 317
Butter Cookies, Melt-Away, '81 20
Butter-Nut Strips, '82 167
Butter Pecan Cookies, '82 139
Cheesecake Cookies, Chewy, '82 109
Cheese Straws, '88 77
Cherry Bonbon Cookies, '93 52
Cherry Crowns, '92 275

COOKIES (continued)

Cherry Nut Nuggets, '81 286
Chocolate-Cherry Cookies, Frosted, '89 294
Chocolate Chewies, Easy, '93 296; '94 234
Chocolate Chip Cookies, Giant, '84 119
Chocolate Chip Melt-Aways, '84 118
Chocolate Cookies, Caramel-Filled, '92 319
Chocolate Cookies, Sugar-Coated, '92 274
Chocolate Crunch Cookies, '91 316
Chocolate-Filled Bonbons, '89 162
Chocolate-Mint Snaps, '83 103; '84 96
Chocolate-Peanut Butter Cones, '85 14
Chocolate-Peanut Butter Cookies, '85 90
Chocolate-Peanut Butter Cups, '85 14
Chocolate Seashells, '91 178
Chocolate Snappers, Jumbo, '81 218
Chocolate Snowflake Cookies, '89 329
Chocolate-Tipped Log Cookies, '87 294
Choco-Nut Sandwich Cookies, '84 200
Christmas
    Calendar, Cookie Advent, '85 325
    Candy Canes and Wreaths, Braided, '92 276
    Cards, Christmas Cookie, '84 302
    Cherry Cookies, Christmas, '88 282
    Date Cookies, Christmas, '88 287
    Eggnog Christmas Cookies, '79 255
    Elf Cookie, '80 279, 303
    Fruit Squares, Christmas, '88 282
    Gingerbread Bowl, Christmas, '93 266
    Gingerbread Cookies, '80 278
    Jammies, Christmas, '95 322
    Lizzies, Christmas, '87 257
    Moravian Christmas Cookies, '91 282
    Mrs. Claus Cookie, '80 279, 303
    Painted Cookies, '86 322
    Reindeer Cookies, Jolly, '91 273
    Rudolph Cookie, '80 279, 303
    Santa Claus Cookie, '80 278, 303
    Santa Cookies, Easy, '95 321
    Santa's Whiskers, '85 323
    Sleigh Cookie, '80 279, 303
    Spiced Christmas Cookies, '87 294
    Strawberries, Christmas, '87 293
    Sugarplum Sticks, '95 321
    Swedish Christmas Cookies, '79 290
    Tree Cookies, Christmas, '93 286
    Trees, Christmas, '89 294
Cinnamon Balls, '79 23
Cinnamon Sticks, Italian, '93 204
Cinnamon Wafers, '81 192
Cocoa Kiss Cookies, '85 171
Coconut Cookies, Crisp, '89 162
Coconut-Oatmeal Cookies, Crispy, '93 80
Curled Cookies, French, '87 16
Drop
    Ambrosia Cookies, '81 301; '82 110; '86 313
    Apple Butter Spice Cookies, '79 291
    Apple Cookies, Fresh, '84 36
    Apple-Nut Cookies, '80 228
    Apple Oatmeal Cookies, '85 215
    Apple-Oatmeal Cookies, '90 218
    Apricot Cookies, Frosted, '81 192
    Banana Oatmeal Cookies, '79 217
    Benne Seed Cookies, '84 318
    Breakfast Cookies, Take-Along, '84 59
    Brownie Chip Cookies, '90 320
    Butterscotch Cookies, '87 58
    Butterscotch-Pecan Cookies, '84 36
    Candy Bit Cookies, '81 192

Carrot Cookies, '82 137
Carrot Cookies, Frosted, '81 7
Carrot-Orange Cookies, '83 149
Cashew Crunch Cookies, '92 17
Cherry-Almond Drops, '81 20
Chip Cookies, Double, '81 301
Chips Cookies, Loaded-with-, '87 223
Chocolate-Bran Raisin Jumbos, '91 142
Chocolate Chewies, '93 216
Chocolate Chip Cookies, '84 120; '86 245; '90 193
Chocolate Chip Cookies, Deluxe, '79 216
Chocolate Chip Cookies, Different, '83 114
Chocolate Chip Cookies, Double, '79 217
Chocolate Chip Cookies, Jumbo, '82 110
Chocolate Chip Cookies, Light, '86 46
Chocolate Chip Cookies, Mom Ford's, '94 287
Chocolate Chip Cookies, Nutty Oatmeal-, '82 M185
Chocolate Chip-Oatmeal Cookies, '84 119
Chocolate Chippers, '92 206
Chocolate Chip-Pudding Cookies, '93 21
Chocolate-Chocolate Chip Cookies, '82 35
Chocolate Chunk-Almond Cookies, Double, '95 178
Chocolate Chunk Cookies, Super, '88 217
Chocolate Cookies, Double-, '95 272
Chocolate Cookies, Doubly-Good, '82 M185
Chocolate Crispy Cookies, '85 115
Chocolate Drop Cookies, '84 36
Chocolate Macaroon Cookies, '88 217
Chocolate Macaroons, '83 300; '87 57
Chocolate-Mint Chip Cookies, '86 245
Chocolate-Mint Cookies, '92 206
Chocolate-Nut Chews, '81 92
Chocolate-Oatmeal Cookies, '80 105
Chocolate-Orange Delights, '93 52
Chocolate-Peanut Cookies, '83 223
Chocolate-Raisin Oatmeal Cookies, '95 136
Chocolate Sandwich Cookies, '81 192
Choco-Peanut Chip Cookies, '92 318
Cocoa Drop Cookies, '80 217
Coconut-Cherry Cookies, '79 292
Coconut Kisses, '90 106
Coconut Macaroons, '79 52
Cream Cheese Cookies, '80 282
Date-Nut Chocolate Chip Cookies, Rich, '92 207
Devil Doggies, '84 37
Fibber McGee Cookies, '95 72
Forget 'em Cookies, '83 256
Fruitcake Cookies, '79 291; '86 320; '88 286
Fruitcake Cookies, Holiday, '81 301
Fruitcake Drop Cookies, '92 275
Fruit Cookies, Bourbon, '86 334
Fruit Cookies, Spicy Holiday, '83 298
Fruit Drops, Candied, '89 329
Fudge-Pecan Chewies, Alabama, '95 143
Gumdrop Cookies, '79 292
Jack-o'-Lantern Cookies, '87 214
Lace Cookies, '86 8
Lemonade Cookies, '79 51
Lemon Yummies, '81 301

Macadamia Nut White Chocolate Cookies, Chunky, '92 207
Melting Moments, '85 191
Meringue Kiss Cookies, '86 121
Meringue Surprise Cookies, '86 320
Mincemeat Drop Cookies, '79 246
Molasses Cookies, Chewy, '87 257
Molasses Cookies, Crispy-Chewy, '90 218
Monster Cookies, '84 36
Nugget Cookies, '79 291
Oatmeal-Chocolate Chippers, '90 218
Oatmeal-Chocolate Morsel Cookies, '95 46
Oatmeal Cookies, '92 82
Oatmeal Cookies, Cinnamon, '84 72
Oatmeal Cookies, Crunchy, '85 202
Oatmeal Cookies, Easy, '80 105
Oatmeal Cookies, Nutty, '81 130
Oatmeal Cookies, Old-Fashioned, '80 106; '85 250
Oatmeal Cookies, Orange-Glazed, '80 60
Oatmeal Cookies, Peanutty, '80 106; '83 95
Oatmeal Cookies, Spicy, '81 197
Oatmeal Cookies, Toasted, '92 273; '95 136
Oatmeal-Date Cookies, '82 109
Oatmeal Krispies, '85 115
Oatmeal-Peanut Butter Chocolate Chip Cookies, '92 207
Oatmeal-Peanut Butter Cookies, '85 171
Oatmeal-Raisin Cookies, '87 221; '93 127
Oatmeal-Raisin Cookies, Frosted, '79 290
Oatmeal-Spice Cookies, Giant, '80 105
Oatmeal Sunshine Cookies, '89 59
Oats-and-Peanut Cookies, '89 60
Orange-Chocolate Cookies, '83 113
Orange Cookies, Frosted, '83 114
Orange Crinkles, '95 272
Peanut Butter Cookies, No-Bake, '94 197
Peanut Butter Macaroons, Chewy, '95 214
Peanut Butter-Oatmeal Cookies, '81 218
Peanut Cookies, Salted, '87 92
Persimmon-Raisin Cookies, '85 232
Pineapple Cookies, '79 216
Polka Dots, '95 272
Potato Chip Cookies, '86 93
Praline Cookies, '91 271
Pumpkin-Chocolate Chip Cookies, '93 235
Pumpkin Drop Cookies, '79 206
Pumpkin-Walnut Cookies, Frosted, '82 217
Rainy Day Cookies, '94 168
Raisin Cookies, Alltime Favorite, '80 24
Raisin-Granola Treats, '92 22
Sour Cream Cookies, Southern, '83 113
Sour Cream-Nutmeg Cookies, '85 171
Sugar Cookies, Nutmeg, '79 136
Sugar Cookies, Stir-and-Drop, '92 174
Sunflower Cookies, Crinkle, '83 149
Tea Cakes, Dropped, '90 156
Toffee Crunch Cookies, '93 80
Walnut Spice Kisses, '89 295
White Chocolate-Macadamia Nut Cookies, '94 315

Cookies   67

COOKIES *(continued)*

Easter Basket and Eggs, '95 101
Eggnog Logs, '92 274
Ginger Cookies, '85 306
Ginger Crinkles, '83 149
Gingersnaps, '79 146; '91 299; '92 264
Gingersnaps, Best-Ever, '79 208
Hazelnut Cookies, '84 111
Hazelnut-Lemon Logs, '84 117
Heavenly Delights, '85 324
Keyboard Cookies, '94 M330
Kissy Cookies, '93 331
Lace Cookies, Florentine, '88 120
Lemon Cookies, Sunshine, '86 69
Lemon Crinkle Cookies, '81 287
Lemon Crisps, '95 272
Lemon Zephers, '81 172
Lollipop Cookies, '94 196
Macadamia-Oat Snowballs, '92 274
Madeleines, Snow-Capped, '85 120
Mailing Cookies, Tips on, '83 305
Miracle Cookies, '83 149
Mix, Quick, '94 167
Molasses Crinkles, '92 276
Oat Cookies, Crispy, '88 203; '90 311
Oatmeal Cookies, Special, '81 236
Orange Fingers, '87 57
Peanut Blossom Cookies, '95 245
Peanut Butter and Chocolate Chunk Cookies, '94 169
Peanut Butter-Chocolate Kiss Cookies, '86 49
Peanut Butter-Cinnamon Cookies, '84 30
Peanut Butter Cookies, '82 56
Peanut Butter Cookies, Double-Chip, '89 169
Peanut Butter Cookies, Easy, '92 272
Peanut Butter Cookies, Quick, '86 109
Peanut Butter-Oatmeal Cookies, '84 72
Peanut Butter Temptations, '84 29
Peanut-Date Balls, '81 92
Peanut Truffle Cookies, '93 212
Pecan-Butter Cookies, '83 113
Pecan Crescent Cookies, '85 324
Pecan Pie Cookies, '92 289
Peppermint Candy Cookies, '88 286
Peppermint Sandwich Cookies, '92 277
Peppermint Wreaths, Melt-Away, '85 324
Pizzelles, '83 298
Pumpkin Cookies, Peppy, '89 253
Refrigerator
    Almond Crunch Cookies, Texan-Size, '91 236
    Apricot Kolaches, '83 84
    Biscotti, Chocolate-Hazelnut, '95 80
    Biscotti, Light, '91 310
    Brown Sugar-Pecan Cookies, '91 236
    Buckin' Bronco Cookies, '90 95
    Butter Cookie Dough, Basic, '95 320
    Butter Cookies, Valentine, '81 20
    Cardamom Cookies, '79 12
    Cheese Wafers, Hope Farm, '93 282
    Cherry Chocolates, '95 321
    Cherry Pecan Cookies, '82 136
    Chocolate-Almond Surprise Cookies, '88 M45
    Chocolate-Cherry Cookies, '85 324
    Chocolate-Gingerbread Cookies, '94 293
    Chocolate Meltaways, '81 302
    Chocolate-Nut Freezer Cookies, '88 217
    Chocolate Pinwheel Cookies, '86 245
    Chocolate Snowball Cookies, '82 295

Chocolate Teasers, '87 44
Choco Surprise Cookies, '80 60
Coffee Nuggets, '95 278
Crème de Menthe Cookies, '86 230
Crescents, '85 321
Date-Cream Cheese Rollups, '83 298
Date Nut Roll, '79 249
Fudge Puddles, '94 292
Gingerbirds, '93 283
Gingerbread Men, '84 299
Gingerbread Men, Miniature, '84 318
Ginger Icebox Cookies, '93 205
Gingersnaps, Raisin, '85 324
Holiday Garland Cookies, '83 299
Holiday Riches, '83 257
Jack-o'-Lantern Cookies, '95 273
Lollipop Cookies, '95 322
Memory Book Cookies, '92 45
Molasses Cookies, '86 20
Oatmeal Cookies, Crispy, '89 328
Oatmeal-Date Sandwich Cookies, '83 257
Oatmeal-Toffee Lizzies, Crispy, '95 136
Orange Crispies, '84 205
Orange Refrigerator Cookies, '86 230
Orange-Slice Cookies, '89 294
Peanut Butter-Chocolate Chip Cookies, Freezer, '86 230
Peanut Butter-Coconut Cookies, '83 113
Peanut Butter Cookie Ice Cream Sandwiches, '93 199
Peanut Butter Cookies, '87 58
Peanut Butter Crisps, '79 50
Peanut Butter Slice-and-Bakes, '82 M185
Peanut Butter Snaps, '81 237
Pecan-Cheese Wafers, '81 119
Pecan Crisps, Sugar, '86 230
Peppermint Rounds, '94 19
Pinwheel Cookies, '93 316
Raspberry Sandwich Cookies, '82 306
Ravioli, Sweet, '91 107
Ribbon Cookies, '87 293
Sandwich Cookies, Grandmother's, '82 306
Sesame-Cheese Cutouts, '82 296
Shortbread Cookie Crumbs, '83 298
Shortbread Cookies, '87 58
Shortbread Cookies, Crispy, '83 113
Snowball Surprises, '93 315
Sour Cream Cookies, Dutch, '83 149
Spice Cookies, Slice-of-, '79 290
Spice-Molasses Cookies, '89 289
Spooky Eyes, '95 273
Springerle, '81 251
Sugar Cookies, Crisp, '84 243
Sugar Cookies, Golden, '88 286
Sugar Cookies, Molasses, '80 270
Sugar Cookies, Red-, '81 21
Sugar Cookies, Symbol, '91 282
Sugar Cookies, Valentine, '82 20
Sugar 'n Spice Cookies, '81 21
Swedish Cookies, '82 306
Taco-Cheese Animal Crackers, '94 197
Tea Cakes, Old-Fashioned, '91 72
Tea Cookies, '83 170
Vanilla Crescents, '82 307
Vanilla Slice-and-Bake Cookies, '85 171
Wafers, Italian, '87 36
Walnut Cookies, '81 301
Watermelon Cookies, '92 179
Rolled
    Almond-Filled Wafers, '88 120
    Almond Holly Leaves, '86 319

Apricot Cookie Rolls, '80 282
Apricot Kolaches, '94 291
Apricot Wonders, '93 316
Bears, Red-Bellied, '92 277
Biscochitos, '92 230
Cheese Bites, Starlight, '95 329
Cheese Straws, '82 137
Chocolate Cookies, Chewy, '80 208
Cinnamon Stars, Swiss, '87 293
Cream Cheese Frills, '79 291
Crème de Menthe Cookies, '80 282
Cutout Cookies, Old-Fashioned, '92 273
Date-Filled Cookies, '91 95
Frosted Cutout Cookies, '85 236
Fruit Cookies, Rolled, '80 15
Fruit-Nut Twists, '82 253
Gingerbread Animal Cookies, '86 70
Gingerbread Cookies, '80 278; '92 343
Gingerbread Man Cookies, '88 227
Gingerbread Men, '85 259
Gingerbread Men Cookies, '85 319
Gingerbread People, '92 312
Ginger Cookies, Swedish, '85 323
Grandmother's Cookies, '85 319
Ice Box Filled Cookies, '79 112
Lemon Pecan Dainties, '80 208
Lemony Cutout Cookies, '85 323
Maple Sandwich Cookies, '85 322
Mincemeat Cookies, '79 51
Mincemeat Sweetheart Cookies, '87 293
Oat Crispies, '83 96
Oatmeal-Coconut Cookies, '80 218
Oatmeal Cookies, Date-Filled, '86 314
Oatmeal Cookies, Slice-and-Bake, '80 105
Oatmeal Nut Crispies, '80 208
Orange-Pecan Cookies, '88 119
Ornaments, Edible, '94 316
Peanut Butter Cookies, Double, '80 209
Peanuttiest Cookies, Crisp, '88 65
Pear Mincemeat Cookies, '84 264
Pecan Cookies, Easy, '80 208
Peppermint Cookies, '95 322
Pinwheels, '95 321
Pueblo Indian Cookies, '95 228
Pumpkin Cookies, Great, '91 234
Raspberry Swirl Cookies, '90 111
Rugelach, '92 252
Scones, Currant, '84 117
Sherry Snaps, '87 94
Shortbread Cookies, Butter Pecan, '80 282
Shortbread Cookies, Coconut, '93 316
Shortbread, Easy Roll-Out, '81 21
Shortbread Sugarplums, Pecan-, '83 298
Snowflake Cookies, '92 278
Snow Flurries, '92 275
Strawberry Cookie Tarts, '89 112
Sugar Cookies, '94 271
Sugar Cookies, Crescent, '87 294
Sugar Cookies, Molasses, '80 270
Sugar Cookies, Moravian, '85 321
Sugar Cookies, Old-Fashioned, '86 313
Sugar Cookies, Orange, '89 329
Sugar Cookies, Rolled, '79 291
Sweetheart Cookies, '93 53
Tea Cakes, Back-Home, '90 156
Teacakes, Currant, '80 88
Tea Cakes, Decorative, '90 156
Tea Cakes, Grandma's, '90 156
Teacakes, Old-Fashioned, '84 43
Tea Cakes, Sorghum, '85 239

COOKIES (continued)

Sandwich Cookies, Viennese, '87 293
Sesame Cookies, Italian, '85 311
Shortbread, Brown Sugar, '93 331
Shortbread Cookie, Old-Fashioned, '88 242
Shortbread Cookies, Java, '94 233
Shortbread Cookies, Praline, '88 242
Shortbread Cookies, Spiced, '88 242
Shortbread Madeleines, Orange, '88 242
Shortbread, Peanut Butter, '95 321
Shortbread, Scottish, '94 242; '95 34
Shortbread Wafers, Cocoa, '88 243
Spice Cookies, '87 M278
Spice Thins, '95 322
Spider Cookies, '93 M166
Spritz Cookies, Butter, '91 175
Spritz Hearts, '91 107
Sugar Cookies, Cinnamon, '84 73
Sugar Cookies, Double-Chocolate, '92 206
Sugar Cookies, Molasses, '82 140
Sugar Cookies, Sour Cream, '79 51
Swedish Heirloom Cookies, '81 129; '90 311
Tea Cakes, Brandied Apricot, '91 241
Tea Cakes, Mexican, '81 196
Thumbprint Cookies, Childhood, '85 323
Thumbprint Cookies, Praline, '89 328
Turkey Treats, '93 256
Turtle Cookies, Snappin', '85 323
Waffle Cookies, Brownie, '86 245
Walnut Cookies, Simply, '91 236
Wedding Cookies, '82 M185
Whoopie Pies, '86 246
COOKING LIGHT. See **LIVING LIGHT.**
CORN
Bake, Corn-and-Swiss Cheese, '92 133
Baked Corn, Creamy, '90 60
Balls, Zesty Corn Dressing, '82 307
Casseroles
    Bean Casserole, Corn-and-, '90 208
    Broccoli-Corn Casserole, '83 313
    Cheese Casserole, Corn and, '81 128
    Chili-Corn Casserole, '88 266
    Corn Casserole, '79 247; '89 126;
      '93 141
    Creamy Corn, '79 213; '90 207
    Escalloped Corn, '79 251
    Fresh Corn Casserole, '80 165
    Green Bean-and-Corn Casserole, '88 123
    Green Chile Casserole, Corn-and-, '89 68
    Jalapeño-Corn Casserole, '83 256
    Moussaka, Corn, '87 190
    Oyster-and-Corn Bake, '83 34; '84 44
    Salami-Corn Casserole, '80 209
    Scalloped Corn, '80 164; '81 128;
      '86 111; '88 218
    Scalloped Corn, Baked, '85 290
    Scalloped Corn, Elegant, '86 268
    Scalloped Corn for Two, '82 208
    Sour Cream, Baked Corn with, '86 170
    Tomato Casserole, Corn and, '81 127
    Tomato Casserole, Corn-and-, '84 145
    Zucchini Bake, Corn-, '79 178
Chiles Rellenos with Walnut Cream Sauce,
  Havarti-and-Corn-Stuffed, '93 M275
Christmas Corn, '93 325
Cob
    Baked Corn on the Cob, Seasoned,
      '82 134
    Barbecued Corn on the Cob, '81 128
    Corn on the Cob, '79 122
    Foil-Baked Corn on the Cob, '81 128

Foiled Corn on the Cob, '80 165
Grill, Corn on the, '94 161
Grilled Corn-on-the-Cob, '90 166
Grilled Parmesan Corn, '82 127
Herb Butter, Corn-on-the-Cob with,
  '84 160
Herb Butter Sauce, Corn with, '79 150
Hickory-Smoked Corn, '85 145
Lemony Corn on the Cob, '89 200
Microwaved Corn on the Cob, '80 M122
Parmesan Corn on the Cob, '88 M187
Parslied Corn, '90 155
Roasted Red Pepper Corn, '91 122
Spicy Corn-on-the-Cob, '84 149
Spicy Corn on the Cob, '87 M151
Cold-Pack Corn, '81 216
Combo, Zucchini-Corn, '86 218
Creamed Corn, Southern-Style, '81 M165;
  '92 201
Creamed Fresh Corn, '82 158
Cream-Style Corn, '80 127; '85 106
Creamy Corn, '79 213; '90 207
Creole Corn, '81 128
Creole, Corn-and-Okra, '89 127
Creole, Okra-Corn, '83 157
Curried Corn and Celery, '86 192
Curried Corn and Sweet Red Peppers, '95 47
Custard, Fresh Corn, '89 127
Deviled Corn, '86 192
Dinner, Corn-and-Ham Skillet, '83 190
Dip, Roasted Corn-and-Avocado, '91 279
Flan, Corn-Chive, '94 172
Fresh Corn, Seasoned, '83 M147
Fried Corn, '89 127; '94 158
Fried Corn, Skillet, '83 190
Frittata, Corn-and-Squash, '89 144
Frittata, Skillet Corn, '87 90
Fritters, Corn, '86 192; '94 22
Fritters, Golden Corn, '80 165; '81 128
Fritters, Skillet-Fried Corn, '85 14
Hush Puppies with Corn, '83 286; '84 17
Limping Susan, '90 155
Macque Choux (Smothered Corn), '94 236
Meat Loaf, Corny, '86 68
Medley, Okra-Corn-Tomato, '81 159
Medley, Peas-and-Corn, '85 138
Medley, Skillet Corn, '86 192
Medley, Summer Garden, '84 158
Medley, Zucchini-and-Corn, '80 298; '81 25
Mexican Corn, '80 157, 165
Mexican Corn, Spicy, '93 90
Mexi-Corn, '82 M21
Muffins, Corn-Oat, '89 108
Muffins, Tex-Mex Corn, '92 253; '93 144
Okra and Corn in Cream, '79 160
Okra, Corn, and Peppers, '87 M151
Okra, Corn, and Tomatoes, '95 203
Pancakes, Corn, '93 43
Peppers, Corn-Stuffed, '84 104
Peppers, Ham-and-Corn Stuffed, '81 87
Pie, Quick and Cheesy Corn, '82 191
Pie with Fresh Tomato Salsa, Buttercrust
  Corn, '95 181
Posole, '95 226
Pudding, Baked Corn, '83 314
Pudding, Corn, '79 276; '81 128; '86 192;
  '90 219
Pudding, Corn-Cheese, '80 244
Pudding, Creamy Corn, '81 267
Pudding, Easy Corn, '83 280
Pudding, Fresh Corn, '80 157, 165; '89 172
Pudding, Tee's Corn, '95 318
Quiche, Jalapeño-Corn, '85 122

Quick Corn Fix-Up, '81 M4
Relish, Corn, '81 129, 175; '83 189; '84 107;
  '85 136; '87 120, 245; '92 241
Relish Dogs, Corn, '85 192
Relish, Easy Corn, '83 260
Relish, Quick Corn, '90 13
Relish, Summer Corn, '89 127
Relish, Sweet Corn, '93 119
Relish, Virginia Corn, '79 283
Salads
    Broccoli-Corn Salad, '87 24
    Chilled Corn Salad, '79 20
    Corn Salad, '80 247; '81 139; '85 236;
      '91 27; '95 214
    Festive Corn Salad, '92 263
    Fresh Corn Salad, '91 126; '94 162
    Garden Medley Salad, '80 122
    Marinated Corn-Bean Salad, '87 9
    Marinated Corn Salad, '89 126
    Pea Salad, Corn-and-, '90 181
    Shoepeg Corn Salad, '81 23
    Shuck Salad, Corn-in-the-, '93 236
    Slaw, Corn and Cabbage, '79 135
    Tangy Corn Salad, '88 176
    Tasty Corn Salad, '84 289
    Wheat Berry-and-Roasted Corn Salad,
      '94 175
Salsa, Avocado-Corn, '94 201
Salsa, Black Bean-and-Corn, '94 80
Salsa, Mexi-Corn, '91 182
Salsa, Spicy Corn, '93 322
Salsa, Sweet Corn, '95 156
Salsa, Yellowfin Tuna with Corn, Pepper, and
  Tomato, '94 164
Sauté, Corn, '80 165
Sautéed Corn and Okra, '84 158
Soufflé, Corn-and-Cheese, '88 122
Soufflé, Zucchini-and-Corn, '83 265
Soups
    Bisque, Crab-and-Corn, '87 137
    Bourbon Soup, Corn-and-, '92 194
    Chowder, Corn, '81 128; '83 20;
      '84 M38; '85 10; '90 202; '91 132
    Chowder, Corn and Cheese, '80 228
    Chowder, Curried Chicken-and-Corn,
      '92 21
    Chowder, Delicious Corn, '82 279
    Chowder, Fresh Corn and Bacon,
      '93 203
    Chowder, Ham and Corn, '79 16
    Chowder, Ham-and-Corn, '82 40
    Chowder, Oyster-Corn, '83 211
    Chowder, Potato-Corn, '94 66
    Chowder, Shrimp and Corn, '79 199
    Chowder, Turkey-Corn, '81 98
    Corn Soup, '80 56; '85 243; '87 156
    Crab Soup, Fresh Corn-and-, '92 183
    Cream of Corn Soup, '90 210
    Favorite Corn Soup, '85 155
    Grilled Corn Soup, '87 121
    Pimiento-Corn Soup, '89 126
    Pumpkin-Corn Soup with Ginger-Lime
      Cream, '95 227
    Shrimp-and-Corn Soup, '84 88
Spoonbread, Corn and Bacon, '81 129
Spoonbread, Corn-Cheese, '88 9
Succotash, Easy, '80 165
Timbales, Corn-and-Zucchini, '92 100
Tomatoes-and-Corn, Creole-Style, '84 142
Tomatoes, Corn-Stuffed, '82 270
Tomatoes with Corn, Baked, '80 161
Vinaigrette, Okra-Corn-and-Tomato, '90 173
Waffles, Corn-Chile, '94 206

Whole Kernel Corn, '85 106
Zucchini and Corn, '86 177
Zucchini and Corn, Dilled, '83 173
Zucchini, Corn and, '83 190

CORNBREADS. *See also* **HUSH PUPPIES.**
Bake, Cornbread Tamale, '79 163
Beef Cornbread, Cheesy, '81 242
Biscuits, Cornmeal-Jalapeño, '94 214
Bites, Corn Dog, '85 245
Bowls, Cornbread, '95 58
Buttermilk Cornbread, '79 34; '82 70
Carrot Cornbread, '80 89; '81 163
Casserole, Bean-and-Cornbread, '92 243
Casserole, Cornbread, '81 91
Casserole, Cornbread Skillet, '83 243; '84 101
Cheddar Cornbread, '83 285; '84 17
Cheddar-Jalapeño Cornbread, '85 3
Chicken over Cornbread, Creamed, '86 231
Chile-Cheese Cornbread, '87 171
Chile Cornbread, '86 254
Confetti Cornbread, '94 170
Cornbread, '80 272; '86 231; '87 197;
   '92 324; '93 122
Cornish Hens, Cranberry-Cornbread Stuffed,
   '95 325
Cottage Cheese Cornbread, '80 90
Cowboy Cornbread, '81 188
Cracklin' Cornbread, '92 216
Cracklin' Cornbread, Southern, '80 119
Crackling Cornbread, '85 200
Crackling Cowboy Cornbread, '82 114
Crispy Cornbread, '92 340
Croutons, Cornbread, '93 192
Croutons, Honeyed Cornbread, '94 106
Crust, Turkey and Peppers in Cornbread,
   '95 312
Crusty Cornbread, '85 255
Dieter's Cornbread, '87 164
Dressings
   Biscuit Dressing, Cornbread-, '79 296
   Chicken Cornbread Dressing, '90 159
   Cornbread Dressing, '86 286; '88 254;
      '92 267
   Fruited Cornbread Dressing, '80 262
   Green Chile-Cornbread Dressing,
      '93 306; '94 296
   Herb-Seasoned Cornbread Dressing,
      '83 315
   Kentucky Cornbread Dressing, '86 281
   Light Cornbread Dressing, '92 324
   Nannie's Cornbread Dressing, '95 306
   Old-Fashioned Cornbread Dressing,
      '84 321
   Quail Stuffed with Cornbread Dressing,
      '93 280
   Roast Turkey and Cornbread Dressing,
      '89 324
   Sage-Cornbread Dressing, '84 283
   Sage Dressing, Cornbread-, '80 262
   Sausage-Cornbread Dressing, '95 289
   Sausage-Cornbread Dressing, Turkey
      with, '83 287
   Sausage Dressing, Cornbread-, '82 307;
      '85 280
   Sausage Dressing, Cornbread-and-,
      '83 213
   Savory Cornbread Dressing, '88 303
   Spoonbread Dressing, Southwestern-
      Style, '94 273
   Texas Cornbread Dressing, '82 243

Easy Cornbread, '94 158
Fresh Cornbread, '80 165
Green Chile Cornbread, '82 134
Herbed Cornbread, '90 214
Hoecake, Hot Water, '81 56
Hoecakes, Green Onion, '88 112
Honey Cornbread, '83 286; '84 17
Hot Water Cornbread, '88 92
Jalapeño Cornbread, '85 200; '94 78
Jalapeño Cornbread, Beefy, '82 142
Jalapeño Pepper Bread, '83 121
Lacy Corncakes, '81 242
Lightbread, Corn, '81 137
Light Cornbread, Old Southern, '81 242
Loaf, Cornbread, '85 200
Menfolks' Cornbread, '82 156
Mexican Cornbread, '80 198; '81 137;
   '84 140, 242; '93 182
Mexican Cornbread, Hot, '83 286; '84 17
Mexican Cornbread, Quick, '81 242
Mexican Flatbread, '80 197
Muffins
   Blue Corn Muffins, '89 145; '92 52;
      '94 114
   Cheesy Cornbread Muffins, '88 M275
   Cornmeal Muffins, '80 90; '88 92
   Corn Muffins, '82 M282; '84 16
   Four-Grain Muffins, '80 46
   Jalapeño-Corn Muffins, '93 164
   Miniature Cornmeal Muffins, '93 119
   Quick Corn Muffins, '88 15
   Sage-Corn Muffins, '83 207
   Sour Cream Corn Muffins, '95 176
   Southern Cornbread Muffins, '85 201
   Spicy Cornbread Muffins, '90 59
   Tex-Mex Corn Muffins, '93 144
   Tomato Corn Muffins, '81 137
   Yeast Muffins, Cornmeal, '92 49
Mush, '81 215
Old-Fashioned Cornbread, '81 242
Onion Cornbread, '88 283
Onion-Topped Cornbread, '84 153
Oysters Casino on Cornbread, '79 34
Paprika Cornbread, '90 213
Pastry, Cornmeal, '81 140
Pecan Cornbread, '94 169
Picante Cornbread, '94 169
Pie, Cornbread-Sausage-Apple, '87 171
Pie, Cornbread-Tamale, '92 123
Pie, Sausage-and-Cornbread, '90 25
Puff, Cornmeal, '82 42
Quick-and-Easy Cornbread, '83 9
Quick Cornsticks, '81 192
Salad, Cornbread, '87 172
Salad, Mexican Cornbread, '95 210
Seasoned Cornbread, '90 320
Serrano Chile Blue Cornbread, '94 114
Skillet Cornbread, '81 31; '84 102; '85 200;
   '90 13
Sour Cream Cornbread, '81 137
Southern Cornbread, '79 123; '81 56; '83 12
Southern Corncakes, '88 166
Spinach Cornbread, '95 49
Spoonbread, '81 138
Spoonbread, Cheddar, '82 196
Spoonbread, Golden, '83 286; '84 17
Spoonbread, Old Virginia, '84 102
Spoonbread, Ozark, '85 202
Sticks, Angel Corn, '84 20
Sticks, Blue Ribbon Corn, '84 102
Sticks, Buttermilk Corn, '80 120
Sticks, Corn, '79 275; '89 54; '90 214
Sticks, Cornbread, '87 15

Sticks, Favorite Corn, '85 202
Sticks, Firecracker Corn, '85 241
Sticks, Garlic-Thyme Corn, '93 242
Sticks, Golden Cornbread, '94 213
Sticks, Old-Fashioned Corn, '90 232
Sticks, Quick Corn, '81 192; '88 15
Sticks, Savory Corn, '93 33
Sticks, Southern Corn, '81 242
Stuffing, Cornbread, '94 305
Supreme, Cornbread, '93 67
Swiss Cheese Cornbread, '79 60
Toasted Cornbread, '82 174
Ultimate Cornbread, '80 90
Waffles, Cornbread, '79 265; '91 90
Waffles, Cornmeal, '85 201
Wampus Bread, '81 305; '82 36

CORNISH HENS
à l'Orange, Cornish Hens, '95 325
Brandied Cornish Hens, '81 259
Brown Rice, Cornish Hens with, '82 275
Buttered Cornish Hens, Brandy-, '79 292;
   '80 32
Cajun-Fried Cornish Hens, '95 326
Casserole, Cornish Hens-and-Rice, '92 267
Chutney-Mustard Glaze, Game Hens with,
   '93 66
Company Cornish Hens, '83 263
Cranberry Cornish Hens, '86 303
Cranberry-Orange Sauce, Cornish Hens with,
   '86 119
Cranberry Sauce, Cornish Hens with, '79 180
Elegant Cornish Hens, '80 227; '81 52
Flambé, Cornish Hens, '80 227; '81 52
Fruited Stuffing, Cornish Hens with, '90 191
Glazed Cornish Hens, Apricot-, '80 84;
   '87 306
Glazed Cornish Hens, Jelly-, '89 193; '93 251
Glazed Cornish Hens, Orange-, '83 267
Glazed Stuffed Cornish Hens, Orange-,
   '84 M89
Grilled Cornish Hens, '88 243; '92 59
Grilled Cornish Hens, Orange-Glazed,
   '86 250
Herbed Cornish Hens, '82 271
Marinated Cornish Hens, Sherry-, '91 148
Mesquite-Smoked Cornish Hens, '92 144
Orange Glaze, Cornish Hens with, '79 244
Port and Sour Cream, Cornish Hens in,
   '86 323
Roast Cornish Hens, '86 89
Roasted Cornish Hens, Herb-, '88 29
Roasted Cornish Hens, Lemon, '82 260
Roasted Cornish Hens with Vegetables,
   Tarragon, '94 79
Roasted Rock Cornish Hens, '82 66
Smoked Cornish Hens, '86 142, 154; '88 168
Stuffed Cornish Hens, '85 261
Stuffed Cornish Hens, Apricot-, '84 6
Stuffed Cornish Hens, Cranberry-Cornbread,
   '95 325
Stuffed Cornish Hens, Rice-, '82 302
Tarragon, Cornish Hens, '95 326
Tarragon, Cornish Hens with, '83 143
Teriyaki Cornish Hens, '86 198
Texas-Style Game Hens, '87 61
Vermouth, Cornish Hens in, '86 33
Wild Rice Stuffing, Cornish Hens with,
   '79 222; '80 64; '82 136

COUSCOUS
Fruit, Couscous with Mixed, '95 232
Salad, Basil-and-Tomato Couscous, '94 175
Salad, Curried Couscous, '91 44
Tabbouleh Salad, '91 70

CRAB

Appetizers
  Balls, Crabmeat, '88 150
  Bites, Crab-Zucchini, '84 M216
  Bites, Spicy Crab, '91 165
  Broiled Crab Meltaways, '93 287
  Canapés, Cheesy Crab, '86 262
  Canapés, Crab, '93 130
  Canapés, Crabmeat, '88 150
  Canapés, Hot Crab, '86 70; '87 239
  Chafing Dish Crabmeat, '89 284
  Cherry Tomatoes, Crab-Stuffed, '82 289;
    '88 78
  Cocktail Puffs, '91 106
  Cocktail, Sherried Avocado-Crabmeat,
    '87 95
  Deviled Crab, Devilish, '85 264
  Dip, Cheese-Crab, '91 200
  Dip, Creamy Crab, '80 M135
  Dip, Festive Crab, '92 285
  Dip, Hot Cheese and Crab, '81 261
  Dip, Hot Crab, '93 269
  Dip, Hot Crab-and-Cheese, '94 282
  Dip, Hot Crabmeat, '95 154
  Dip, Oven-Baked Crab, '82 59
  Dip, Tangy Crab, '83 5
  Dip, Trawler Crab, '93 238
  Hors d'Oeuvre, Crabmeat, '94 236
  Mold, Crab, '85 318
  Mousse, Crab, '79 117; '95 327
  Mousse, Crabmeat, '90 190; '91 244;
    '94 159
  Mushroom Caps, Crab-Stuffed, '84 160
  Mushrooms, Crab-Stuffed, '81 190
  Mushrooms Stuffed with Crab, '82 249
  Oysters, Crabmeat Stuffed, '94 328
  Pâté, Crab, '79 233
  Puffs, Crab, '80 20; '84 269
  Sauce, Stone Crab Mustard, '80 3
  Sauce, Tangy Stone Crab, '80 3
  Snacks, Crab, '83 93
  Snow Peas, Crab-Stuffed, '85 288
  Spread, Baked Crab, '80 86
  Spread, Crab, '93 167
  Spread, Crabmeat-Horseradish, '90 292
  Spread, Crab Soufflé, '85 4
  Spread, Hot Artichoke-Crab, '85 81
  Spread, Layered Crabmeat, '83 127
  Spread, Superb Crab, '81 235
  Topping, Crabmeat, '91 64
au Gratin, Crabmeat, '86 154
au Gratin, Crab, Shrimp, and Artichoke,
  '90 240
Baked Avocado-and-Crabmeat, '84 119
Bake, Easy Crab, '95 209
Bake, Quick Crab, '87 192
Benedict, Crab, '92 63
Benedict, Lion, '93 121
Blue Crabs, Festive, '85 103
Blue Crabs, Spicy Steamed, '84 162
Blue Crabs, Steamed, '89 195
Broiled Crab and Avocado, '79 116
Brunch Scramble, Crabmeat, '95 32
Burgers, Potato-Crusted Crab, '94 139
Cakes, Baltimore Crab, '92 117
Cakes, Chesapeake Bay Crab, '89 194;
  '95 155
Cakes, Country Crab, '95 20
Cakes, Crab, '81 125; '90 71; '91 122
Cakes, Crispy Fried Crab, '80 119
Cakes, Down-East Crab, '79 151
Cakes, Gulf Coast Crab, '94 71
Cakes, Mock Crab, '95 159

Cakes, Victoria Crab, '92 195
Cakes with Tomato Cream, Crab, '94 70
Casserole, Crab, '79 228
Casserole, Crab-and-Mushroom, '89 96
Casserole, Crab-and-Shrimp, '84 71
Casserole, Crab-Egg, '80 260
Casserole, Crabmeat-Broccoli, '84 232
Casserole, Creamy Crab and Spinach, '80 3
Casserole, Deviled Crab, '91 238; '92 27
Casserole, Easy Crab, '93 270
Chicken, Crab-Stuffed, '84 101
Cornbread, Crab with Chile, '86 254
Creamed Crabmeat with Artichoke Hearts,
  '93 26
Crêpes, Crab, '79 165
Crêpes, Sautéed Crab, '84 84
Crisps, Crab, '79 63
Delight, Crab-and-Egg, '84 261
Deviled Crab, '85 104; '92 117
Dressed Crab, '82 276
Eggs New Orleans, Crabmeat and, '82 45
Eggs, Shrimp and Crab Scrambled, '79 261
Étouffée, Crab-and-Shrimp, '89 96
Filling, Crab, '89 13
Flounder, Crab-Stuffed, '80 120
Fresh Crab, Preparing, '82 127
Fried Soft-Shell Crabs, '95 154
Imperial, Crab, '79 82, 116; '89 194; '95 155
Imperial, Crabmeat, '82 311; '83 72
Imperial, Easy Crab, '93 128
Imperial, Elegant Crab, '83 245
Imperial, Pineapple-Crab, '84 M286
Imperial, Speedy Crabmeat, '90 M112
Karen, Crabmeat, '93 49
Lobster Tails, Crab-Stuffed, '95 326
Meunière, Soft-Shell Crab, '80 57
Mold, Cream Cheese-Crabmeat, '90 71
Mushrooms on Toast Points, Crabmeat and,
  '82 M91
Oysters and Crabmeat, Creamy, '83 211
Potatoes, Cheesy Crab-Stuffed, '86 17
Potatoes, Crabmeat-Topped, '83 3; '95 22
Potatoes, Crab-Stuffed, '91 311; '92 26
Puff, Crab, '79 116
Puff, Shrimp-Crab, '79 57
Quiche, Almond-Topped Crab, '79 127
Quiche, Crab, '82 M122, 243
Quiche, Quick Crab, '84 96
Quiche, Sherried Crab, '83 180
Quiche, Simple Crab, '85 207
Ravigote, Crabmeat, '82 250; '92 329
Salads
  Asparagus Salad, Crab-and-, '92 141
  Avocado Salad, Crab-, '81 114
  Avocados, Crab-Stuffed, '86 73
  Avocado with Crabmeat, '86 119
  Chesapeake Crab Salad, '89 195
  Congealed Salad with Crabmeat-and-
    Asparagus, '84 86
  Crabmeat Salad, '91 169
  Delightful Crab Salad, '87 145
  Louis, Crab, '95 94
  Luncheon Salad, Crabmeat, '82 207
  Macaroni-Crabmeat Salad, '81 153
  Marinated Crab-and-Endive Salad, '93 22
  Rémoulade, Crabmeat, '93 280
  Shrimp Pasta Salad, Crabmeat-, '86 208
  Tomato Salad, Crab-Stuffed, '80 148
  Wild Rice Salad, Crab-, '86 207
  Wild Rice Salad, Crab and, '79 116
Sandwiches, Avocado-Crabmeat, '83 2
Sandwiches, Crabmeat, '84 285
Sandwiches, Deluxe Crabmeat, '81 M74

Sandwiches, Hot Crab-and-Cheese, '87 279
Sandwiches, Open-Face Crab Tomato, '81 29
Sandwiches, Open-Faced Crab, '87 106
Sandwiches, Puffy Crab, '83 291
Sauce Piquante, Crab and Shrimp, '83 92
Sauce, Quick Crab Marinara, '85 M151
Sautéed Crabmeat, Roussos', '84 88
Shrimp Bundles, Crab-Stuffed, '81 176
Shrimp, Crab-Stuffed, '84 259
Soft-Shell Crabs, Chesapeake, '89 194
Soups
  Beaufort Crab Soup, '92 238
  Bisque, Crab, '88 251
  Bisque, Crab-and-Corn, '87 137
  Bisque, Crab-and-Leek, '94 104
  Corn-and-Crab Soup, Fresh, '92 183
  Crabmeat Soup, '84 123
  Cream of Crab Soup, '88 302
  Cream of Crab Soup, Steamboat's,
    '81 127
  Creamy Crab Soup, '80 M224
  Elegant Crab Soup, '80 188
  Gumbo, Crab and Shrimp, '81 200
  Gumbo with Whole Crabs, Seafood,
    '85 2
  Old-Fashioned Crab Soup, '90 71
  Plantation Crab Soup, '92 237
  Quick Crab Soup, '84 279
  She-Crab Soup with Marigold, '79 32
Spread, Crabmeat, '79 81
Stroganoff, Crab, '79 116
Stuffed Soft-Shell Crabs, '83 91
Stuffed Soft-Shell Crabs, Steamboat's, '81 127
Stuffing, Chicken Breasts with Crabmeat,
  '85 302
Stuffing, Crabmeat, '94 68
Supreme, Crab, '79 181
Tomatoes, Crab-and-Avocado Stuffed,
  '94 141
Tostadas, Crab, '93 203
Veal with Crabmeat, New Orleans, '86 94

CRACKERS
Bacon-Wrapped Crackers, '93 280
Bread, Sesame Cracker, '87 2
Cheddar Crackers, '84 236
Cheese Cracker Nibbles, '84 328
Dessert Crackers, '87 3
Fennel-Rye Crackers, '87 2
Florida Crackers, '86 179
Hot Nut Crackers, '90 206
Hush Puppies, Cracker, '80 99
Oatmeal-Wheat Germ Crackers, '84 236
Olive-Rye Snack Crackers, '84 191
Pie, Cracker, '79 113
Snackers, Cracker, '86 229; '93 197

CRANBERRIES
Acorn Squash, Cranberry-Filled, '81 M231
Beverages
  Apple-Berry Sparkler, '93 104
  Apple Berry Sparkler, '94 100
  Beach Brew, '91 177

CRANBERRIES, Beverages *(continued)*

Cider, Spiced Cranberry, '84 261
Cooler, Cranberry, '86 229
Cubes, Cranberry, '95 201
Daiquiris, Cranberry, '81 245
Float, Sparkling Cranberry, '86 195
Frappé, Cranberry, '82 263
Juice, Sparkling Cranberry, '88 275
Lemonade, Spiced Cranberry, '87 292
Mulled Cranberry Drink, '92 12
New Orleans, Mr. Funk of, '95 57
Punch, Cranberry, '83 275; '85 90
Punch, Cranberry-Cherry, '91 176
Punch, Cranberry-Cinnamon, '86 270
Punch, Cranberry Percolator, '88 248
Punch, Cran-Grape-Tea, '92 209
Punch, Holiday Cranberry, '85 265
Punch, Hot Cranberry, '80 288; '84 41,
    319; '85 265
Punch, Hot Spiced, '80 250
Punch, Pink Lady, '81 100
Punch, Sparkling Cranberry, '85 277;
    '95 101
Punch, Spiced Cranberry, '89 290
Punch, Tart Cranberry, '83 318
Red Roosters, '87 147
Refresher, Cranberry-Vodka, '91 210
Sangría, Cranberry, '95 238
Shake, Cranberry, '83 171
Slush, Cranberry-Rum, '84 259
Smoothie, Cranberry, '86 183; '91 307
Soda, Cranberry-Orange, '79 148
Spritzer, Cranberry, '91 66; '92 265
Spritzers, Cranberry, '89 213
Tea, Cranberry, '94 131
Tea, Cranberry-Apple, '88 169
Tea, Pink Sangría, '95 200
Wassail, Cranberry, '88 289
Wine Cup, Cranberry, '85 23
Brandied Cranberries, '86 269; '95 306
Bread, Cranberry, '79 242
Bread, Cranberry-Banana, '80 281; '90 294
Bread, Cranberry Fruit-Nut, '79 275
Bread, Cranberry-Orange, '87 244
Bread, Cranberry-Orange Nut, '80 288
Bread, Orange-Cranberry, '85 266
Bread, Raisin-Cranberry, '81 305; '82 36
Casserole, Cranberry-Apple, '83 311
Casserole, Sweet Potatoes-and-Berries,
    '84 231
Chicken, Barbecued Cranberry, '83 178
Chicken Kiev, Cranberry, '87 250
Chicken, Oven-Barbecued Cranberry, '93 332
Chutney, Cranberry, '80 243; '83 260;
    '84 265
Chutney, Cranberry-Orange, '79 292
Chutney, Orange-Cranberry, '86 266
Chutney with Cream Cheese, Cranberry-
    Amaretto, '87 244
Cocktail, Hot Cranberry, '89 310
Coffee Cake, Cranberry, '81 14; '90 159
Coffee Cake, Cranberry-Coconut, '93 332
Coffee Cake, Cranberry-Nut, '81 250
Coffee Cake, Cranberry-Orange, '82 283
Conserve, Apple-Cranberry, '82 308
Conserve, Cranberry, '79 243; '83 279;
    '85 266
Cornish Hens, Cranberry, '86 303
Cornish Hens, Cranberry-Cornbread Stuffed,
    '95 325
Cream, Cranberry, '90 66

Desserts
Apple Dessert, Cranberry, '80 253
Bake, Hot Cranberry, '91 250
Cake, Cranberry Upside-Down, '87 8
Cake, Orange-Cranberry, '85 314
Cloud, Cranberry, '90 287
Cobbler, Cranberry, '81 275
Cobbler, Cranberry-and-Apple, '84 306;
    '90 294
Cobbler, Cranberry-Peach, '92 322
Cobbler, Easy Cranberry, '86 260
Cobbler Roll, Cranberry, '80 288;
    '81 248
Compote, Berry, '81 275
Crêpes, Cranberry, '85 262
Crisp, Cranberry-Pear, '83 207
Crunch, Apple-Cranberry, '86 300;
    '87 178
Glaze, Cranberry, '84 306
Ice, Cranberry-Apple, '82 290
Ice, Tangy Cranberry, '87 305
Ice, Tart Cranberry-Orange, '86 317
Jubilee, Cranberries, '85 312; '90 293
Jubilee, Tasty Cranberry, '84 305;
    '85 189
Mousse, Cran-Apple, '93 255
Orange Surprise, Cran-, '94 143
Pie, Autumn Apple, '79 205
Pie, Berry-Apple, '88 251
Pie, Cran-Apple, '92 304
Pie, Cranberry-Apple, '79 264
Pie, Cranberry-Apple Holiday, '81 M269
Pie, Cranberry-Pecan, '92 316
Pie, Cranberry-Raisin, '80 283; '85 316
Pie, Cran-Raspberry, '87 244
Pie, Festive Cranberry Freezer, '84 306
Pie, Frosty Cranberry, '79 249
Pie, Nutty Cranberry, '82 M298
Pie, Peach-Cranberry, '83 249
Pie, Tart Cranberry-Cherry, '87 299
Pie, Walnut-Cranberry, '87 259
Pudding, Cranberry, '84 306
Roulage, Chocolate-Cranberry, '94 313
Sherbet, Cranberry, '88 280
Sorbet, Cranberry, '82 251
Sorbet, Cranberry Juice, '85 259
Soufflé, Cranberry-Topped Holiday,
    '84 306
Supreme, Cranberry, '85 280
Surprise Dessert, Cranberry, '79 242
Tart, Cranberry-Nut, '84 305
Tartlets, Fresh Cranberry, '87 244
Tarts, Cranberry-Cream Cheese, '80 154
Tarts, Cranberry Holiday, '83 279
Tarts, Cran-Raspberry Meringue, '92 286
Dip, Cranberry Fruit, '90 60
Dip, Cranberry-Horseradish, '85 65
Dressing, Cranberry-Orange, '91 287
Dressing, Orange Salad with Honey-Berry,
    '89 250
Frosted Cranberries, '82 280
Fruit Bake, Cranberry-Mustard, '90 287
Glaze, Cranberry, '84 306; '86 171; '88 244
Glaze, Cranberry-Honey, '89 273
Gravy, Baked Hen with Cranberry Pan,
    '94 308
Ham, Cranberry Broiled, '88 301
Ham, Cranberry Glazed, '81 274
Ham, Cranberry-Orange Glazed, '81 295
Hearts, Cranberry, '93 286
Jam, Christmas, '88 288
Jam, Christmas Brunch, '81 286
Jelly, Cranberry-Wine, '81 290

Lamb, Cranberry Leg of, '90 52
Loaf, Apricot-Cranberry, '79 235
Loaf, Cranberry-Ham, '82 M77
Mexican Cranberries, '94 273
Muffins, Cranberry, '81 249
Muffins, Cranberry Oat Bran, '89 107
Muffins, Cranberry-Pecan, '84 269
Muffins, Cranberry Streusel Cake, '88 M274
Muffins, Miniature Cranberry, '90 294
Orange Delight, Cranberry-, '90 168
Pork Chops, Cranberry, '80 288; '90 53
Pork Chops, Orange-Cranberry, '86 335;
    '87 84
Pork, Cranberry, '90 293
Pork Roast, Berry Barbecued, '80 288
Relish, Cran-Apple, '84 300
Relish, Cranberry, '81 275; '83 144;
    '85 258, 264; '86 283; '87 245; '91 257;
    '92 341; '95 318
Relish, Cranberry-Nut, '86 275
Relish, Cranberry-Orange, '81 M289; '88 254
Relish, Cranberry-Pear, '85 232
Relish, Frozen Cranberry, '95 302
Relish, Holiday Cranberry, '88 304
Relish, Lemony Cranberry, '79 243
Relish, Old-Fashioned Cranberry, '82 297
Relish, Tipsy Cranberry, '92 M310
Ring, Cranberry, '90 291
Rolls, Cranberry-Pineapple, '86 275
Salads
Cheese Ribbon Salad, Cranberry-,
    '79 241
Christmas Salad, Cranberry, '79 243
Congealed Cranberry Salad, '90 124
Congealed Salad, Cranberry, '91 296
Congealed Salad, Lemon-Cranberry,
    '87 311
Cranberry Salad, '88 250
Cup, Berry Grapefruit, '79 242
Festive Cranberry Salad, '81 264, 296
Frosted Cranberry Salad, '90 288
Frozen Cranberry-Pineapple Salad,
    '91 237
Green Salad, Cranberry-Topped, '87 311
Holiday Cranberry Salad, '82 266, 288;
    '95 301
Holiday Jewel Salad, '81 252
Holiday Salad, Cranberry, '89 277
Jellied Cranberry Salad, '83 279; '85 281
Layered Cranberry Salad, '84 322;
    '86 325
Mold, Cranberry, '79 250
Mold, Cranberry-Apple, '89 277
Mold, Cranberry Gelatin, '92 271
Oriental, Cranberry, '79 126
Ring, Cranberry Salad, '80 247
Ring, Spicy Peach-Cranberry, '85 264
Tart Cranberry Salad, '79 286
Whipped Cream Salad, Cranberry-,
    '83 261
Sauces
Apple Sauce, Cranberry-, '92 203
Apricot Sauce, Fresh Cranberry-, '87 243
Baked Cranberry Sauce, '88 257
Cranberry Sauce, '86 278; '88 280;
    '92 269
Dried Cranberry Sauce, Pork Medaillons
    with Port Wine and, '95 330
Fresh Cranberry Sauce, '79 283; '84 275
Jalapeño-Cranberry Sauce, '92 310
Juice Sauce, Cranberry, '85 224; '86 83
Orange Sauce, Cornish Hens with
    Cranberry-, '86 119

CRANBERRIES, Sauces *(continued)*

Raisin Sauce, Baked Ham with Cranberry-, '88 244
Salsa, Grilled Turkey Breast with Cranberry, '95 252
Salsa with Sweet Potato Chips, Cranberry, '93 332
Tart Cranberry Sauce, '83 261
Wine Sauce, Cranberry, '83 276
Scones, Cranberry, '95 283
Spiced Cranberries, '82 254, 287
Spread, Coconut-Cranberry Cheese, '92 328
Stuffing, Crown Roast of Pork with Cranberry-Sausage, '88 49
Turkey Loaf, Cranberry-Glazed, '86 171
Vinegar, Cranberry, '91 288
Wild Rice, Cranberry-Pear, '83 279

CRAWFISH. *See* **FISH.**

CRÈME FRAÎCHE

Fraîche, Crème, '85 39; '91 99
Sauce, Crème Fraîche, '79 281; '93 135

CRÊPES

Basic Crêpes, '84 83; '86 38
Beef Crêpes, Sherried, '85 M29
Beef Roulades, '80 80
Blintzes, Cheese, '92 84
Bran Crêpes, '83 70; '86 44
Breakfast Crêpes, Country-Style, '79 22
Brunch Crêpes, Nutritious, '80 44
Brunch Crêpes, Royal, '81 44
Cannelloni Crêpes, '86 143
Cheese and Mushroom Crêpes, '81 88
Cheese Blintzes, '82 146; '83 71
Cheesy Party Wedges, '84 84
Cherry Crêpes, '91 67
Chicken Crêpes, '80 39
Chicken Crêpes, Creamy, '81 200
Chicken-Vegetable Crêpes, '83 70
Coquilles St. Jacques Crêpes, '83 13
Cornmeal Sombreros, '93 277
Crab Crêpes, '79 165
Crab Crêpes, Sautéed, '84 84
Crêpes, '82 38, 46, 146, 240;
    '83 13, 71, 122, 127, 205, 282;
    '84 186; '86 216; '87 126; '88 295;
    '89 44; '90 157; '91 24; '92 41, 88;
    '93 123; '94 116
Cups, Florentine Crêpe, '89 44
Desserts
    Amandine, Crêpes Gelée, '83 126
    Amaretto-and-Orange Crêpes, '86 260
    Banana Crêpes Flambé, '84 262
    Basic Dessert Crêpes, '82 183; '85 262; '86 275
    Cheese Blintzes, '82 146
    Cherry Crêpes Flambé, '79 18
    Chocolate Chantilly Crêpes, '82 183
    Chocolate Crêpes, '86 164
    Chocolate Crêpes, Fruit-Filled, '89 325
    Chocolate Dessert Crêpes, '84 84; '85 262
    Chocolate Dream Crêpes, '86 164
    Chocolate-Orange Crêpes, '85 263
    Coffee Ice Cream Crêpes, '84 85

Cranberry Crêpes, '85 262
Dessert Crêpes, '84 84; '86 260; '87 290; '88 134
Dixie Dessert Crêpes, '79 222
Fruit Crêpes, Tropical, '87 77
Fruit Filling, Crêpes with, '81 96
Low-Calorie Crêpes, '87 77
Mango-Pineapple Crêpes, '86 216
Orange Dream Crêpes, '82 183
Peach Crêpes, '82 184
Peach Crêpes, Fresh, '84 186
Plain Crêpes, '83 70
Processor Crêpes, Basic, '87 289; '88 135
Raspberry Crêpes, '87 126
Spicy Dessert Crêpes, '84 262
Strawberry Dessert Crêpes, '83 122
Strawberry Ice Cream Crêpes, '87 290; '88 135
Suzette, Raspberry Crêpes, '84 84
Suzettes, Light Crêpes, '83 71
Tropical Crêpes, '86 275
Whole Wheat Crêpes, '83 70
Divan, Elegant Crêpes, '81 91
Entrée Crêpes, '79 264
Fajita Crêpes, '94 116
Florentine Crêpe Pie, '79 34
Florentine, Crêpes, '80 190
Ham-and-Egg Crêpes, '83 204
Ham-and-Egg Crêpes with Mushroom Sauce, '82 46
Italian Crêpes, '90 157
Lemon Crêpes with Fruit Filling, '82 46
Light Crêpes, '86 143
Mushroom-Cheese Crêpes, '87 289; '88 135
Plain Crêpes, '83 70
Processor Crêpes, Basic, '87 289; '88 135
Raspberry Crêpes with Yogurt Filling, Fresh, '93 123
Sausage Crêpes, '88 295
Sausage Crêpes, Cheesy, '82 240; '83 71
Sausage-Filled Crêpes, '79 39
Spinach-Ricotta Crêpes, '81 52
Steak Crêpes, Special, '91 24
Turkey Crêpes, '92 41
Turkey Crêpes, Elegant, '83 282
Virginia Crêpes, '79 264
Whole Wheat Crêpes, '80 44; '83 70
Zucchini Crêpes, '79 157

CROUTONS

Bagel Croutons, '93 192
Bourbon Croutons, '93 234
Bread Croutons, Hawaiian, '94 107
Bread, Quick Crouton, '90 138
Celery Croutons, '79 16
Cinnamon Pound Cake Croutons, '93 161
Cornbread Croutons, '93 192
Cornbread Croutons, Honeyed, '94 106
Crispy Italian Croutons, '84 126
Crostini, '92 56
Croûtes, Croutons and, '93 30
Croutons, '86 M288
Dilled Croutons, '93 161
Egg Roll Fan, Sesame, '94 107
Garlic Croutons, '92 71
Garlic-Flavored Croutons, '86 47
Herb Croutons, '81 150
Microwave Croutons, '86 M227
Pita Croutons, '93 192
Pumpernickel Croutons, '94 62
Tortilla Triangles, '94 107
Vegetable-Flavored Croutons, '84 148

CUCUMBERS

Bisque, Shrimp-Cucumber, '79 172
Canapés, Cucumber, '95 88
Canapés, Shrimp-and-Cucumber, '93 164
Chips, Cucumber, '85 176
Combo, Cucumber-and-Pepper, '88 176
Cool Cucumbers, '84 152
Creamy Cucumbers, '92 62
Delights, Cucumber, '84 117
Dills, Lazy Wife, '87 149
Dip, Cucumber-Cheese Vegetable, '83 128
Dressing, Creamy Cucumber Salad, '82 79
Dressing, Cucumber, '80 74; '90 144
Dressing, Cucumber-Curry, '89 179
Dressing, Cucumber-Mint, '87 153
Dressing, Tomato, Onion, and Cucumber in Italian, '81 83
Fried Cucumber Fingers, '86 146
Gazpacho-Stuffed Endive, '95 287
Lemony Cucumbers, '89 102
Marinated Cucumbers and Artichokes, '82 111
Marinated Cucumbers and Squash, '86 146
Marinated Shrimp and Cucumber, '91 166
Mold, Chicken-Cucumber, '80 175
Mold, Lemon-Cucumber, '87 90
Pickled Cucumber Rounds, Easy, '90 143
Pickles, Cucumber Sandwich, '81 174
Pickles, Dill, '81 174
Pickles, Mixed, '81 174
Pickles, Quick Sweet, '87 149
Pickles, Sour Cucumber, '85 176
Pickles, Sweet Icicle, '85 176
Red Snapper Rolls, Cucumber-Stuffed, '83 176
Relish, Cucumber, '85 176
Rounds, Cucumber, '88 78
Salads
    Almond Salad, Cucumber-, '86 147
    Aspic, Shrimp-Cucumber, '83 108
    Bean Salad, Cucumber-, '83 81
    Congealed Salad, Pineapple-Cucumber, '83 118
    Cooler, Simple Cucumber, '86 147
    Creamy Cucumber Salad, '86 147; '92 97
    Dilled Cucumber and Tomato Salad, '81 153
    Dilled Cucumber on Tomatoes, '84 142
    Dilled Cucumber Salad, '82 229; '92 72; '93 65
    Grapefruit-Cucumber Salad, '80 100
    Marinated Cucumber Salad, '82 111
    Marinated Tomato-and-Cucumber Salad, '92 216
    Mold, Asparagus-Cucumber, '85 252
    Mold, Creamy Cucumber, '84 164
    Mold, Cucumber Salad, '82 111; '83 81, 253
    Mousse, Cucumber, '79 11; '88 121
    Mousse with Dill Sauce, Cucumber, '95 216
    Pineapple Salad, Cucumber-, '84 124
    Roast Beef Salad, Cucumber-, '89 162
    Scallions, Cukes and, '91 168
    Slaw, Creamy Cucumber, '89 49
    Sour Cream, Cucumbers in, '79 52; '80 178
    Tomato-and-Cucumber Summer Salad, '93 141
    Tomato-Cucumber-Onion Salad, '81 239
    Tomato-Cucumber Salad, '86 218; '92 199

CUCUMBERS, Salads (continued)

Tomato-Cucumber Salad with Yogurt-
Herb Dressing, '92 96
Tomato Salad, Cucumber-, '90 144
Tuna Boats, Cucumber, '83 136
Vinaigrette Oriental, Cucumber-,
'85 198; '86 147
Yogurt-Cucumber Salad, '82 122
Yogurt Salad, Cucumber-, '87 33
Salsa, Cucumber, '95 131
Salsa, Cucumber-Dill, '95 107
Sandwiches, Cucumber, '88 159; '90 81;
'94 14
Sandwiches, Cucumber Pinwheel, '85 120
Sandwiches, Dainty Cucumber, '81 119
Sauce, Cucumber, '82 111; '84 M286; '92 41
Sauce, Cucumber Cream, '92 33
Sauce, Cucumber-Dill, '86 5; '91 62; '92 51
Sauce, Cucumber Dipping, '94 47
Sauce, Lemony Cucumber, '89 245
Sesame Cucumbers, '85 85
Slices, Cheesy Cucumber, '84 80
Slices, Fresh Cucumber, '86 177
Soup, Chilled Cucumber, '79 144
Soup, Chilled Cucumber-Buttermilk, '95 134
Soup, Cold Cucumber, '79 130; '81 130
Soup, Cold Minted Cucumber, '86 34
Soup, Cold Potato-Cucumber, '88 160
Soup, Cream of Cucumber, '81 98
Soup, Creamy Cucumber, '80 171
Soup, Cucumber-Yogurt, '82 157; '83 205
Soup, Dilled Cucumber, '90 M167
Sour Cream, Cucumber and Onion in, '81 69
Sour Cream, Cucumbers and, '93 203
Spread, Cucumber, '79 295; '80 31; '93 158
Spread, Cucumber and Cream Cheese,
'82 140
Spread, Shrimp-Cucumber, '79 81
Stuffed Cucumbers, '81 237
Tartlets, Smoked Salmon and Cucumber,
'95 216
Tomatoes, Cucumber-Stuffed Cherry, '88 262
Topping, Lamb Pockets with Dilled
Cucumber, '87 104
Vichyssoise, Cucumber, '94 90
CURRANTS. See RAISINS.
CURRY
Almonds, Cauliflower and Peas with Curried,
'79 221
Almonds, Curried, '82 297
Appetizers
Bites, Curried Swiss, '85 220
Cheese Ball, Chicken-Curry, '85 118
Cheese Ball, Curried Shrimp, '86 135
Chicken Balls, Coconut Curried, '91 165
Chicken Balls, Curried, '91 98
Chicken Bites, Curried, '85 40
Dip and Vegetable Platter, Curry, '89 327
Dip, Curried, '81 262
Dip, Curry, '80 84; '81 9; '85 132;
'86 184; '87 25
Dip, Tuna-Curry, '84 31
Hazelnuts, Curried, '93 301
Pecans, Curried, '91 208
Popcorn Mix, Curried, '86 326
Sandwiches, Curried Tea, '91 314
Sauce, Curry, '94 54
Shrimp Balls, Curried, '94 180
Spread, Broccamoli Curry, '88 55
Spread, Curried Chutney, '89 283
Spread, Curried Shrimp, '87 158

Apples, Curried, '93 252
Apricots, Curried, '91 315
Bananas, Fillets with Horseradish Sauce and
Curried, '85 230
Beef and Rice, Curried, '88 164
Beef Dinner, Curried, '83 4
Beef Pitas, Curried, '85 220
Beef Steak, Curried, '88 60
Bread, Honey-Curry, '89 250
Butter, Tomato-Curry-Orange, '93 159
Carrots and Pineapple, Curried, '90 228
Casserole, Curry Pea, '87 154
Casserole, Vegetable-Curry, '91 286; '92 27
Cauliflower, Curried, '91 315
Chicken
Brioche, Chicken Curry, '88 124
Cheesecake, Curried Chicken, '90 174
Country Captain Chicken, '94 252
Curried Chicken, '86 43
Curried Chicken Divan, '80 83
Curry, Chicken, '84 110; '85 220;
'86 21; '89 219
Dinner, Curried Chicken Skillet, '95 47
Filling, Curried Chicken, '88 125
Fried Chicken, Curried, '85 160
Honey-Curry Chicken, '87 36
Mousse, Curried Chicken, '95 328
Peppers, Chicken Breasts with Curried,
'90 227
Peppers, Curried Chicken-Stuffed, '87 19
Quick Curried Chicken, '89 219
Regal Curried Chicken, '84 110
Sauce, Chicken Curry, '90 117
Soup, Curried Chicken, '86 34
Stir-Fried Chicken Curry, '87 51
Turban Chicken Curry, '94 266
Chops, Pineapple-Curry Glazed, '82 106
Chowder, Curried Chicken-and-Corn, '92 21
Chowder, Curried Seafood, '94 103
Corn and Celery, Curried, '86 192
Corn and Sweet Red Peppers, Curried, '95 47
Dip, Curry-Onion, '93 313
Dressing, Cucumber-Curry, '89 179
Dressing, Curried, '84 115
Dressing, Curry, '80 242; '82 78
Eggs, Curried Deviled, '93 87
Eggs, Saucy Shrimp-Curried, '84 143
Fish, Curried Baked, '87 5
Fish, Curry-Baked, '91 196
Fruit, Almond-Curried, '83 261
Fruit Bake, Curried, '87 241
Fruit, Hot Curried, '79 225; '81 264;
'84 287; '95 72
Fruit Medley, Curried, '95 329
Ham and Peaches, Curried, '82 60
Ham Steak, Curried, '82 120
Ham with Rice, Curried, '80 111
Hurry Curry, '79 103
Kheema, Indian, '81 226
Lamb Curry with Rice, '80 83; '81 10
Lamb with Rice Mold, Curried, '85 36
Mayonnaise, Curry, '95 66
Meat Loaf, Curried, '86 43
Mushrooms, Curried, '84 214
Nuts, Spicy Curried, '82 250
Onions, Curried, '90 34
Peas with Almonds, Curried, '88 M294
Pecans, Curried, '91 208
Pork Chops, Curried Apricot, '89 191
Pork Tenderloin, Curried, '86 76
Rice and Shrimp, Curried, '83 231
Rice, Curried, '90 183
Rice, Curry-Spiced, '86 M226

Rice Mix, Fruited Curry-, '86 326
Rice Mold, Curried, '85 36
Rice, Quick Curried, '86 81
Rice with Almonds, Curried, '83 M285
Rice with Curry, Raisin, '85 83
Rice with Pineapple, Curried, '79 142
Salads
Apple-Raisin Salad, Curried, '80 24
Broccoli Salad, Curried, '86 225
Chicken-and-Orange Salad, Curried,
'87 144
Chicken-Rice Salad, Curried, '92 190
Chicken Salad, Curried, '79 219; '84 66;
'85 96; '86 131; '89 176
Chicken Salad with Asparagus, Curried,
'81 36
Coleslaw, Curried, '85 139
Coleslaw, Curried Pineapple, '88 172
Couscous Salad, Curried, '91 44
Indian Curry Salad, Hot, '83 23
Rice Salad, Curried, '80 84;
'85 147, 220
Rice Salad, Curry, '89 146
Shrimp Salad, Aloha, '95 46
Spinach Salad, Curry, '80 242
Tuna Salad, Curried, '86 208
Tuna Salad with Grapes, Curried, '87 201
Turkey Salad, Curried, '88 140
Sandwiches, Curried BLT, '93 158
Sauce, Asparagus with Curry, '90 17
Sauce, Curried Rum, '91 164
Sauce, Curried Sour Cream, '90 174
Sauce, Curry, '79 156; '83 138; '84 M71;
'95 18
Sauce, Halibut with Orange-Curry, '87 91
Sauce, Pineapple-Curry, '79 252
Sauce, Turkey Slices with Curried Cream,
'91 60
Shrimp, Curried, '84 110
Shrimp Curry, Creamy, '90 145
Shrimp Curry, Polynesian, '89 23
Shrimp Curry, Sour Cream, '80 83
Shrimp Curry, Sour Cream and, '81 10
Shrimp Malai Curry, '84 110
Shrimp, Quick Curried, '84 M198
Snapper, Honey-Curried, '85 181
Soup, Cold Curried Pea, '91 120
Soup, Curried, '81 130
Soup, Curried Carrot, '82 157
Soup, Curried Chicken, '86 34
Soup, Curried Mushroom, '84 M89
Soup, Curried Turkey, '86 332
Spread, Curried Shrimp, '87 158
Spread, Curried Turkey, '92 16
Spread, Curry, '93 159
Stir-Fry, Indian, '92 126
Tomatoes, Curried Green, '93 138
Tuna Melts, Curried, '95 46
Turkey Pie, Crumb-Crust Curried, '86 265
Vegetables, Curried, '89 219
Vegetables with Curry, Stir-Fried, '87 51
Vinaigrette, Warm Curry, '93 107
CUSTARDS. See also PUDDINGS.
Acorn Squash, Custard-Filled, '86 334
Almond Crème Custard with Raspberries,
'88 174
Amaretto Custard, Chocolate-Topped,
'87 M37
Amaretto Custard, Range-Top, '87 77
Amaretto Custard with Raspberries, '86 152
Ambrosia, Custard Sauce, '84 256
Baked Custard, '80 219
Baked Custard, Creamy, '86 7

74   Cucumbers

CUSTARDS *(continued)*

Baked Custard, Easy, '85 52
Baked Vanilla Custard, '82 129
Boiled Christmas Custard, '95 329
Boiled Custard, Favorite, '81 181
Boiled Custard, Perfect, '81 34
Cake, Chocolate Custard, '88 175
Chocolate Custard, '88 258
Citrus Custard with Fresh Fruit, '93 70
Coconut Custard, '86 109
Corn Custard, Fresh, '89 127
Crema, '80 175
Crème Brûlée, Almond, '95 323
Crème Brûlée, Basic, '95 323
Crème Brûlée, Berry, '95 323
Crème Brûlée, Chocolate, '95 323
Crème Brûlée, Coffee, '95 323
Crème Brûlée, Double Raspberry, '95 323
Crème Brûlée, Ginger, '95 323
Crème Brûlée, Onion, '95 324
Crème Brûlée, Orange, '95 323
Crème Brûlée, Peppermint, '95 323
Crème Brûlée, Roasted Garlic, '95 324
Crème Brûlée, Roquefort-and-Black Pepper, '95 324
Crème Brûlées, Savory, '95 324
Crème Brûlée, White Chocolate-Macadamia Nut, '95 323
Crème Patissière, '84 207
Easy Custard with Nutmeg, '90 316
Filling, Creamy Custard, '81 180
Filling, Custard, '82 52, 298; '85 281
Filling, Egg Custard, '87 14
Flans
　　Almendra, Flan, '80 199
　　Baked Flan with Caramel, '92 231
　　Blackberry Flan, '79 182
　　Caramel-Crowned Flans, '90 227
　　Corn-Chive Flan, '94 172
　　de Leche (Flan with Milk), Flan, '92 169
　　de Queso, Flan, '95 303
　　Flaming Flan, '85 313
　　Flan, '88 247
　　Individual Flans, '85 52
　　Layered Flan, '89 45
　　Luscious Flan, '90 56
　　Orange Flan, '84 95
　　Pumpkin Flan, '82 217
　　Spanish Flan, '85 51, 311
　　Sweet Potato Flan, '95 291
Lemon-Buttermilk Custards, '89 49
Lemon Custard in Meringue Cups, '80 295; '81 172
Mexican Custard, Light, '88 149
Napoleon Cream, '84 138
Orange Custard Pudding, '88 174
Peach Custard Dessert, Fresh, '86 162
Pears in Custard, Poached, '88 20
Pie, Apple Custard, '88 236
Pie, Carrot Custard, '79 45
Pie, Coconut Custard, '82 33
Pie, Custard Pecan, '87 184
Pie, Old-Fashioned Egg Custard, '82 261
Pie, Perfect Custard, '82 92
Pumpkin Custard, '88 148
Rice Custard, Baked, '92 308
Sauce, Bourbon Custard, '95 271
Sauce, Custard, '85 41; '88 154, 251, 259; '89 291
Sauce, Fresh Berries with Raspberry Custard, '88 163

Stirred Custard, '92 45
Stirred Custard, Old-Fashioned, '85 52
Stirred Custard over Fruit, '84 83
Tocino del Cielo, '93 29
Vanilla Cream, '83 M115

Dates

Ball, Date-Nut, '92 326
Bars and Cookies
　　Balls, Date-Nut, '85 10
　　Balls, Peanut-Date, '81 92
　　Brownies, Date-and-Almond, '88 217
　　Chocolate Chip Cookies, Rich Date-Nut, '92 207
　　Christmas Date Cookies, '88 287
　　Date Bars, '84 313; '95 322
　　Filled Cookies, Date-, '91 95
　　Fruit Cookies, Rolled, '80 15
　　No-Bake Date Bars, '79 256
　　Nut Bars, Date-, '80 166
　　Nutty Date Bars, '84 153
　　Oat Bars, Date-, '80 M172
　　Oatmeal-Date Bars, Layered, '85 10
　　Oatmeal-Date Cookies, '82 109
　　Oatmeal-Date Sandwich Cookies, '83 257
Breads
　　Apple-Date-Nut Ring, '90 212
　　Banana Loaves, Tropical Date-, '95 143
　　Chocolate Date-Nut Bread, '81 284
　　Muffins, Carrot-Date-Nut, '86 262
　　Muffins, Date, '79 142
　　Muffins, Date-Nut, '84 75
　　Muffins, Orange-Date, '92 119
　　Muffins, Surprise Date, '79 216
　　Nut Bread, Date-, '85 306
　　Nut Loaf, Date-, '85 10
　　Persimmon Date-Nut Bread, '82 218
　　Walnut Loaf, Blue Ribbon Date-, '80 15
　　Wine-Date Nut Bread, '82 253
Cake, Date Nut, '79 176; '80 5
Cake, Fresh Apple-Date, '83 300
Cake, Orange-Date, '94 60
Cake, Pumpkin Date, '79 251
Cake, Queen Bee, '81 237
Cake Roll, Date-Nut, '89 94
Cake Squares, Apple-Date Dream, '85 10
Candy, Date, '89 308
Candy, Date Loaf, '80 302
Cheese, Nutty Date Dessert, '87 299
Chocolate Date-Nut Delight, '88 168
Conserve, Brandied Date, '85 315
Cupcakes, Date, '84 7
Dessert Squares, Date, '89 255
Dressing, Date, '87 57
Filling, Apple-Date, '83 301
Filling, Date, '80 15; '83 257; '86 314
Filling, Date Cream, '81 303
June Bugs, '85 11
Logs, Date, '79 274
Pastries, Date-Filled Cheese, '83 259
Pie, Date-Pecan, '80 15
Pie, Dried Fruit, '83 249
Pudding, Steamed Date, '79 86
Roll, Date Nut, '79 249
Rollups, Date-Cream Cheese, '83 298
Salad, Festive Fruit, '80 16
Sandwich, Date-Nut Lettuce, '94 202
Sauce, Date-Nut Sundae, '82 167
Spread, Apple-Date, '91 231; '92 67

Spread, Breakfast Date, '84 7
Spread, Date-Walnut, '87 292
Squares, Date, '90 49
Stuffed Dates, Apricot-, '80 250
DESSERTS. *See also* **BROWNIES, CAKES, CHEESECAKES, COOKIES, CUSTARDS, ICE CREAMS, MOUSSES, PIES AND PASTRIES, PUDDINGS, SHERBETS.**
Alaska, Peachy Melba, '88 266
Alaskas, Brownie, '83 299
Almond Dessert, Sour Cream-, '92 120
Amaretto Cream Tortoni, '85 161
Ambrosia, Baked, '83 303
Ambrosia, Brunch, '83 57
Ambrosia, Easy, '92 45
Ambrosia, Honey Bee, '83 267
Ambrosia, Layered, '88 304
Apple
　　Baked Alaska, Apple, '80 226
　　Baked Apples, Imperial, '82 273
　　Baked Apples, Orange-Pecan, '85 45
　　Baked Apples with Orange Sauce, '84 314
　　Baked Mincemeat-Filled Apples, '80 276
　　Brandied Apples, '81 248
　　Brandied Apples and Cream, '82 M237
　　Brown Betty, Apple, '83 213
　　Caramel Apples, Old English, '85 231
　　Cheese Crisp, Apple-, '92 235
　　Cinnamon Apples with Brandied Date Conserve, '85 315
　　Cooked Apples, '93 338
　　Cranberry Apple Dessert, '80 253
　　Cranberry Crunch, Apple-, '86 300; '87 178
　　Crisp, Delicious Apple, '82 303
　　Crisp, Granola Apple, '85 78
　　Crumble, Whole Wheat-Apple, '90 M213
　　Delight, Apple, '80 109
　　Dumplings, Apple, '82 273
　　Dumplings with Orange Hard Sauce, Apple, '88 224
　　Dutch Apple Dessert, Creamy, '91 19
　　Flambé, Hot Apples and Rum, '92 88
　　Flan, Apple, '81 309
　　Fritters, Apple, '82 273
　　Golden Apples, '82 254
　　Honey-Baked Apple Dessert, '90 M213
　　Kuchen, Apple, '79 24
　　Melting Apples, '88 19
　　Nut Crunch, Apple-, '82 M238
　　Oatmeal Cherry-Apple Crisp, '90 M16
　　Orange-Apple Crisp, '80 295
　　Poached Lemon Apples, Chilled, '86 182
　　Rings, Apple, '85 232
　　Rings, Cinnamon Apple, '82 M237
　　Sour Cream Apple Squares, '82 262
　　Sundae, Hot Apple Spice, '92 239
Apricot Cream, Peachy-, '86 163
Avocado Whip, '79 107
Banana
　　Alaska, Banana Split, '87 10
　　Baked Bananas with Orange Sauce, '79 115
　　Berry Supreme, Banana-, '81 205
　　Candied Bananas, '83 179
　　Cream Dessert, Banana, '81 180
　　Flambé, Banana-Peach, '85 316
　　Flip, Banana, '83 303
　　Foster, Bananas, '79 18; '83 M114; '86 139; '88 20
　　Foster, Elegant Bananas, '81 59

DESSERTS, Banana (continued)

Foster for Two, Bananas, '80 115
Foster, Tropical Bananas, '79 231
Pie, Layered Banana Split, '83 189
Pops, Banana, '83 60; '84 44
Pops, Orange-Banana, '82 129
Praline Bananas, '84 313
Regal Bananas, '85 46
Soufflé, Banana Daiquiri, '84 317
Supreme, Bananas, '84 256
Bavarian Cream with Fresh Fruit, '88 137
Bavarian Cream with Raspberry Sauce,
'91 180
Bavarian Dessert, Light, '86 6
Berried Treasure, '89 124
Berries on Snow, '82 227
Berries with Raspberry Custard Sauce, Fresh,
'88 163
Berry Basket, Summer, '84 158
Berry Compote, '81 275
Berry Grapefruit Cup, '79 242
Beverages
Brandy Alexander, '92 283
Brandy Float, Blazing, '85 314
Cappuccino Coffee Dessert, '92 264
Champagne Delight, '83 304
Creamy Dessert Drink, '86 131
Golden Dream, '82 100
Ice Cream Ginger Fizz, '83 303
Super Dessert Drink, Simply, '83 303
Biscotti, Light, '91 310
Biscuits, Sweet Little, '85 305
Blackberries and Dumplings, '86 196
Blackberry Dessert Tamales, '94 190
Blackberry Flan, '79 182
Blueberries and Cointreau, '82 100
Blueberry-Amaretto Squares, '83 220
Blueberry Crumble, '81 84
Blueberry Crunch, Fresh, '82 143
Blueberry Dessert, Easy, '89 M130
Blueberry Dream, '88 94
Boysenberries and Cream Supreme, '82 133
Bread, Fry, '85 155
Brie, Almond-Raspberry, '94 M89
Brownie Ice Cream Sandwich Shells, '88 195
Brûlé, Petit, '93 219
Buñuelos, '80 199
Buñuelos, King-Size, '86 5
Butter-Nut Strips, '82 167
Butterscotch Fantastic, '83 76
Cakes, Funnel, '83 250
Cakes, Spanish Wind, '84 157
Cannoli, '80 58; '91 20
Cantaloupe Compote, '81 147
Cantaloupe Cream Delight, '82 179
Cantaloupe Delight, '89 204
Caramel Dessert Biscuits, '95 36
Caramel Fondue, '94 331; '95 35
Caramel Surprise, '88 202
Charlotte, Macaroon, '81 296
Charlotte, Peach, '79 68
Charlotte, Pineapple, '90 288
Charlotte Russe, '80 71; '82 M142; '90 288
Charlotte Russe, Fresh Lemon, '80 13
Charlotte Russe, Lemon, '84 192
Charlotte Russe, Wine Jelly and, '82 305
Charlotte Russe with Strawberry Sauce, '92 85
Cheese Blintzes, '82 146; '83 71
Cheese Kuchen, '86 84
Cheese Molds, Heavenly Dessert, '85 209
Cheese, Nutty Date Dessert, '87 299

Cherries à la Mode, '88 202
Cherries Jubilee, '79 18; '83 139
Cherries Jubilee, Quick, '82 M100
Cherries Jubilite, '86 317
Cherries Sabayon, '88 178
Cherries, Sherried, '93 289
Cherry-Berry on a Cloud, '79 94
Cherry Compote, '83 139
Cherry Dessert, Holiday, '80 255
Chocolate. See also Desserts/Frozen, Sauces.
Almond Dessert, Chocolate-, '82 306
Almond Meringue Fingers, Chocolate-,
'84 158
Bags, Chocolate-Raspberry, '95 97
Baskets with Berry Cream, Chocolate,
'92 118
Black-Bottom Goodies, '89 251
Brickle Squares, Chocolate, '94 290
Brownie-Mint Dessert, '82 227
Buttercream, Chocolate, '84 156
Charlotte Russe, Chocolate, '87 74
Chilled Chocolate Dessert, '83 177
Cinnamon-Chocolate Cream, '94 199
Coffee Mallow, '80 109
Cream, Heavenly Chocolate, '88 128
Crêpes, Chocolate Dream, '86 164
Crêpes, Fruit-Filled Chocolate, '89 325
Cups, Chocolate, '80 207
Cups, Chocolate Crinkle, '93 270
Cups, Chocolate Lace, '87 133
Cups, Chocolate-Mint, '80 71
Cups, Miniature Chocolate, '87 132
Date-Nut Delight, Chocolate, '88 168
Decadence, Chocolate, '89 183
Dip, Chocolate, '92 50
Dream Dessert, Chocolate, '83 198
Easy Chocolate Dessert, '79 75
Fondue, Dessert, '89 281
Fondue, White Chocolate, '92 287
Fudge Dessert with Kahlúa Cream,
'91 197
Hello Dolly Dessert, '95 168
Ladyfinger Dessert, Chocolate, '86 162
Loaves, Chocolate Chip Cheese, '91 299;
'92 264
Log, Chocolate Cream, '94 220
Midnight Delights, '95 278
Mint Dessert, Chocolate-, '82 100
Mint Dessert, Cool Chocolate-, '80 109
Peanut-Chocolate Dessert, '80 86
Pizza, Chocolate, '91 298
Plunge, Chocolate, '94 332; '95 35
Pots de Chocolat, Petits, '82 272
Pots de Crème, '81 15; '84 M145
Pots de Crème au Chocolate, '93 53
Pots de Crème, Chocolate, '93 296;
'94 234
Pots de Crème for Two, '89 275
Pots de Crème, Mocha, '88 M45
Pots de Crème, Rum-Flavored, '85 102
Pots de Crème with Orange Meringues,
Chocolate, '95 318
Roll, Chocolate Cream, '85 317
Roll, Chocolate Mousse, '83 290
Roulage, '90 266
Roulage, Chocolate-Cranberry,
'94 313
Roulage, Chocolate-Mocha, '80 216
Roulage, Chocolate-Orange, '94 314
Roulage, Mint-Chocolate, '94 314
Roulage, White Chocolate, '92 230
Rum Dessert, Chocolate-, '81 247
Sack, Large Chocolate, '93 314

Sack, Small Chocolate, '93 314
Shells with Kahlúa Cream, Chocolate,
'88 195
Squares, Chocolate-Blueberry Dessert,
'87 299
Strawberry-Chocolate Combo, '85 96
Sundae Dessert, Hot Fudge, '84 313
Supreme, Chocolate, '84 94
Trifle, Chocolate, '88 258; '93 326
Truffle Dessert, Chocolate, '88 281
Waffles with Strawberry Cream,
Chocolate, '88 153
Cinnamon Crisps, '93 106
Coconut Cloud, '80 70
Coconut Dessert, Chilled, '83 116
Coeur à la Crème, Christmas, '86 278
Coffee-Almond Tortoni, '81 30
Cottage Cheese Dessert, Creamy, '87 191
Crackers, Dessert, '87 3
Cranberries, Brandied, '86 269
Cranberries Jubilee, '85 312; '90 293
Cranberry Apple Dessert, '80 253
Cranberry Bake, Hot, '91 250
Cranberry Jubilee, Tasty, '84 305
Cranberry Supreme, '85 280
Cranberry Surprise Dessert, '79 242
Cream, Bavarian, '86 M165
Cream Cheese, Chunky, '85 306
Cream Cheese, Fruited, '85 306
Cream Cheese Squares, Lemony, '82 159
Cream, Molded French, '85 311
Cream Puffs, Captivating, '81 180
Cream Puffs, Java, '81 187
Cream Puffs, Strawberry, '81 95
Cream Puffs, Tutti-Frutti, '79 231
Crème Celeste, '88 94
Crème d'Ange, '83 91
Crème Patissière, '84 207
Crêpes, Basic Dessert, '82 157; '86 275
Crêpes, Dessert, '86 260; '87 290; '88 134
Crêpes, Dixie Dessert, '79 222
Crêpes Flambé, Cherry, '79 18
Crêpes, Strawberry Dessert, '83 122
Crêpes Suzettes, Light, '83 71
Date Dessert Squares, '89 255
Date-Nut Balls, '85 10
De-Light-Ful Dessert, '95 220
Doughnuts, Orange Spiced, '79 136
Éclair Cake, '93 42
Éclairs, Miniature Orange, '95 92
Éclairs, Minted Miniature, '88 66
Éclairs, Pistachio-Cream, '91 296
Éclairs with Pecan Sauce, '83 219
Eggnog Dessert, '95 314
Flan de Leche (Flan with Milk), '92 169
Frozen
After Dinner-Drink Dessert, '82 100
Almond Crunch, Frozen, '94 283
Amaretto Chantilly, '89 14
Amaretto Freeze, '82 182
Amber Bombe, '80 255
Applesauce Fluff, '91 173
Apricot Fluff, Frozen, '86 242
Apricot Freeze, '82 10
Baked Alaska, '84 105; '85 295
Baked Alaska, Apple, '80 226
Baked Alaska, Brownie, '80 66
Baked Alaska, Chocolate Mousse,
'85 195
Banana Pops, '83 60; '84 44
Banana Split Alaskas, '87 10
Banana Split Pie, Layered, '83 189
Bombe, Ice Cream, '90 269

DESSERTS, Frozen *(continued)*

Bombe with Raspberry Sauce, Creamy, '89 322
Cantaloupe Cream, Frozen, '82 159
Cantaloupe Whip, '89 198
Caramel-Toffee Bombe, '93 214
Charlotte, Spumoni, '90 193
Cherry Cordial Dessert, '84 312
Chocolate Almond Velvet, '81 148
Chocolate-Coffee Frozen Dessert, '85 172
Chocolate Dessert, Frozen, '83 76
Chocolate Mint Freeze, '88 167
Chocolate Roulage, Frozen, '90 56
Chocolate-Walnut Cups, '85 213
Chocolate Whip, '89 326
Choco-Maple Frozen Dessert, '86 300; '87 178
Cinnamon Ice Cream Sombreros, '93 276
Citrus Cup, Snowball, '79 2
Coconut-Caramel Dessert, '92 44
Coffee Dessert, Light, '88 260
Coffee Ice Cream Crunch, '82 182
Coffee Tortoni, Creamy, '88 268
Cookies 'n' Cream Dessert, Gold-Dusted, '94 271
Cream, Betty's Holiday, '95 303
Cream Dessert, Triple, '94 244
Elegant Ending, '86 145
Frappé, Hawaiian, '81 178
Fruit Cream Freeze, '82 144
Fruit Cups, Frozen, '93 197
Fruit Freeze, Holiday, '88 283
Fruit Ice, Mixed, '88 85
Fruit Pops, '87 168
Fudge-Peanut Ice Cream Dessert, '88 167
Fudgy Frozen Dessert, Nutty, '94 28
Grand Marnier Cream, '84 312
Grapefruit Freeze, '93 242
Grasshopper Freeze, Creamy, '81 180
Ice-Cream Angel Dessert, Triple Mint, '93 86
Ice Cream Bombe, '82 305
Ice Cream Delight, '80 69
Ice Cream Dessert, Caramel, '95 36
Ice Cream Dessert, Decadent, '91 56
Ice Cream Dessert, Layered, '83 189; '84 94, 105; '86 163
Ice Cream Dessert, Mint, '88 66
Ice Cream Party Squares, '91 214
Ice Cream Sandwiches, Chocolate Cookie, '87 147
Ice Cream Treats, Crunchy, '86 300; '87 178
Ice, Hazelnut-Coffee, '94 233
Ice, Mimosa, '94 24
Lemon-Chiffon Frozen Yogurt, '85 54
Lemon Cream, Frozen, '83 118
Lime-Mint Refresher, '82 144
Lime Whip, '89 199
Little Bits, '79 196
Macaroon-Sherbet Frozen Dessert, '79 212
Mint Patty Alaska, '80 219
Mocha Alaska Dessert, '84 191
Mocha Dessert, Frozen, '84 311
Mocha Freeze, Royal, '84 53
Mocha Squares, Frozen, '81 187
Orange Alaska, '83 177

Orange Dessert, Frozen, '92 44
Oranges Grand Marnier, '92 82
Ozark Pudding, Frozen, '88 127
Peach Freeze, Creamy, '82 144
Peach Torte, Frozen, '93 135
Peanut Butter Delight, Frozen, '88 137
Pineapple Delight, Fresh, '79 111
Pineapple-Orange Bars, '82 129
Pops, Deep Blue Sea, '94 143
Pops, Hawaiian Orange-Pineapple, '94 143
Pops, Orange-Banana, '82 129
Pops, Pineapple-Yogurt, '91 173
Popsicles, Smoothie Strawberry, '82 112
Praline Freeze, '89 60
Pumpkin Dessert, Frozen, '88 167
Rainbow Delight, Frozen, '84 105
Raspberry Dessert, Frozen, '84 192
Raspberry Fluff, '89 198
Sherbet Ambrosia Cups, '82 159
Sherbet Dessert, Layered, '87 109
Strawberry Cups, Frozen, '91 173
Strawberry Delight, Frozen, '82 112, 174
Strawberry Frost, '82 24; '83 154
Strawberry Puff, '82 5
Strawberry Whip, '89 198
Texas Tornadoes for Grown-Ups, '94 143
Toffee Ice Cream Dessert, '87 110
Torte, Frozen Viennese, '93 171
Tortoni, Apricot-Yogurt, '95 124
Vanilla Almond Crunch, '93 243
Vanilla Frozen Yogurt, '87 125
Vanilla Soufflé, Frozen, '79 230; '82 173
Watermelon Frost, '86 196
Fruit
Amaretto Crème on Fresh Fruit, '93 176
Bake, Nutty Fruit, '83 127
Bowl, Fresh Fruit, '89 137
Caribbean Fruit Dessert, '84 314
Cheese, and Nuts, Fruit, '93 324
Cheese, Luscious Fresh Fruit with, '79 153
Chilled Fruit with Dressing, '85 222
Combo, Fresh Fruit, '86 178
Compote, Baked Fruit, '80 276; '84 314
Compote, Baked Mustard Fruit, '85 47
Compote, Champagne Fruit, '81 309; '82 124
Compote, Chilled Fruit, '83 123
Compote, Fresh Fruit, '79 162; '82 197, 272; '84 82; '94 190
Compote, Fruit, '86 330
Compote, Gingered Fruit, '88 184
Compote, Hot Fruit, '81 203; '83 53
Compote, Jicama-Fruit, '92 49
Compote, Mixed Fruit, '93 123
Compote, Warm Praline Fruit, '85 260
Compote, Wine Fruit, '81 272
Crisp, Fruit, '94 168
Cup, Fruit, '81 141; '91 202
Cup with Rum, Fruit, '83 55
Curried Fruit, Hot, '95 72
Flame, Sherried Fruit, '85 313
Flaming Fruit Dessert, '83 302
Fondue, Fruitcake, '84 258
Gazpacho, Tropical, '95 204
Gingered Fruit, '83 151
Glazed Fruit, '85 83
Hot Fruit Delight, '83 281
Kabobs with Mint Marinade, '82 157
Lemon Curd, Fresh Fruit with, '88 21

Medley, Chinese Fruit, '83 22
Medley, Fancy Fruit, '84 82
Medley, Fresh Fruit, '81 141
Medley, Frosty Fruit, '82 226
Medley of Fruit, Tropical, '86 53
Meringue Shells, Fruited, '87 32
Mint-Balsamic Tea, Fresh Fruit with, '95 232
Orange, Fruit Dessert, '84 314
Planter's Punch Dessert, '95 175
Rainbow Fruit Dessert, '85 108
Soup Dessert, Fruit, '79 172
Spiced Fruit Delight, '82 229
Spiced Fruit Dessert, '82 50
Tequila, Fruit in, '82 223
Trifle, Tropical, '95 204
Turnovers, Fruit, '79 150
Gâteau Panache, '83 269
Glacé, Sabayon, '89 306
Grahams, Praline, '92 239
Grape Juice-Fruit Refresher, '86 182
Honeydew-Berry Dessert, '83 120
Honeydew Melon with Grapes, '91 91
Kahlúa Cream, '87 134
Kahlúa Delight, '83 67
Kahlúa Delight, Make-Ahead, '84 M89
Kahlúa Velvet Dessert, '85 M294
Kiwi and Cream in Meringue Cups, '81 279
Kiwi-and-Orange Dessert, '93 295
Kiwi-Berry Pizza, '86 198
Kiwifruit Pizza, '89 306
Kiwi Jubilee, '83 120
Kugel, Apricot Noodle, '92 251
Kugel, Sweet, '90 254
Lemon Angel Rolls with Raspberry Sauce, '94 294
Lemon-Cream Cheese Dessert, '84 95
Lemon Cups, Baked, '87 128
Lemon Curd, '89 334
Lemon Curd with Berries, '90 102
Lemon Delight, '82 227
Lemon Dessert, Layered, '88 134
Lemon Solid, '93 279
Little Nothings, '79 135
Lollapalooza, '94 194
Madeleines, '88 79
Mango Dessert Tamales, '94 190
Mango Pan Dowdy, '83 150
Maple Nut Dessert, '81 84
Maraschino Russian Cream, '79 231
Melon Ball Compote, '85 157
Melon Balls and Cherries in Kirsch, '91 91
Melon Balls in Watermelon Sauce, '79 177
Melon-Mint Julep, '86 196
Melons in Mint Sauce, '85 164
Melon Wedges with Berry Sauce, '86 178
Meringue Cream Cups, Lemon, '84 23
Meringue Flowers, '84 156
Meringue, Piping, '84 156
Meringues, Baked Pear, '85 232
Meringues, Strawberry, '84 188
Mocha-Almond Dessert, '80 289; '81 62
Mocha Chiffon, '86 75
Nectarines Royale, '85 132
Oatmeal Cherry-Apple Crisp, '90 M16
Orange. *See also* Desserts/Frozen.
  Baked Apples, Orange-Pecan, '85 45
  Baked Orange Elegance, '80 13
  Baskets, Orange, '81 308
  Champagne Oranges, '93 83
  Chiffon Dessert, Orange, '93 295
  Cream Dessert, Orange, '80 254; '84 165

DESSERTS, Orange (continued)

Cream, Orange, '81 12
Cream, Orange Chantilly, '84 156
Cream, Orange-Coconut, '84 24
Crisp, Orange-Apple, '80 295
Delight, Pumpkin-Orange, '86 321
Dip, Creamy Orange, '84 117
Doughnuts, Orange Spiced, '79 136
Éclairs, Miniature Orange, '95 92
Flambé, Dessert Orange, '85 313
Frosted Oranges, '83 270
Fruit Dessert Orange, '84 314
Grand Marnier, Oranges, '92 82
Kiwi-and-Orange Dessert, '93 295
Molded Dessert, Orange, '83 302
Parfaits, Chilled Orange, '80 219
Parfaits, Orange Cream, '94 198
Pears Flambé, Orange-Poached, '85 313
Poached Oranges, Wine-, '84 M323
Rice Cream with Mandarin Oranges,
    '85 317
Slices, Burgundy-Spiced Orange, '93 294
Soufflé, Chilled Orange, '84 317;
    '86 189
Soufflé, Frozen Orange, '79 211
Soufflé, Orange Dessert, '83 206
Strawberries with Brandied Orange Juice,
    '82 160
Tapioca Crème, Orange-, '82 M283
Tapioca Fluff, Orange, '87 31
Pancakes, Dessert Ginger, '88 153
Pancakes, Luau Dessert, '88 154
Parfaits
    Blackberries-and-Cream Parfait, '87 129
    Chocolate-Crème de Menthe Parfaits,
        '85 161
    Chocolate-Mint Parfaits, '90 M15
    Chocolate Mousse Parfait, '94 90
    Chocolate-Peppermint Parfaits, '88 65
    Coffee Crunch Parfaits, '82 159
    Eggnog Bavarian Parfait, '79 255
    Family, Parfait, '94 130
    Kiwi Parfait, '86 199; '87 55
    Lime Parfaits, '80 153
    Mocha-Mallow Parfaits, '80 219
    Orange Cream Parfaits, '94 198
    Orange Parfaits, Chilled, '80 219
    Peach Parfait, '82 166
    Peanut Butter Parfaits, Crunchy, '79 176;
        '80 6
    Peppermint Parfait, '93 315
    Pineapple Parfait, '84 83
    Speedy Parfaits, '83 76
    Strawberry-Lemon Parfaits, '84 198
    Strawberry Parfait, '79 99
    Strawberry Parfaits, Frosty, '85 213
    Strawberry Parfait, Surprise, '86 151
    Strawberry-Yogurt Parfait, Crunchy,
        '79 124
    Surf-and-Sand Parfaits, '93 169
    Tropical Trilogy Parfait, '92 247
    White Chocolate-Raspberry Swirl Parfait,
        '93 315
Pavlova, '92 101
Peach. See also Desserts/Frozen, Sauces.
    Baked Peaches, '92 179
    Blueberry Dessert, Peach-, '92 184
    Brandy Peaches, '85 275
    Caramel Peaches, '93 134
    Cardinale, Peach, '89 155
    Champagne, Peaches, '79 146

Charlotte, Peach, '79 68
Compote, Berry-Peach, '82 133
Compote, Peach-Berry, '89 112
Cream, Bavarian Peach, '82 171
Cream, Peach Almond, '82 108
Cream, Peaches and, '95 196
Cream, Peachy-Apricot, '86 163
Crisp, Peach, '92 13
Custard Dessert, Fresh Peach, '86 162
Dumplings, Peach, '85 177
Foster, Peaches, '86 240
Ginger Peaches with Rum, '84 M323
Gingersnap Peaches, '85 M329
Honeyed Peaches 'n' Cream, '93 134
Layered Peach Dessert, '95 196
Marinated Peaches, '91 91
Melba, Peach, '81 83; '83 M114
Melt-Away Dessert, Peachy, '87 298
Oven-Baked Peaches with Ginger,
    '82 170
Parfait, Peach, '82 166
Quick Peach Dessert, '85 178
Sherbet Cooler, Peachy, '91 187
Spiced Peach Dessert, '83 9
Spiced Peaches with Nutty Dumplings,
    '87 164
Split, Peach, '85 277
Strawberry Sauce, Peaches with, '85 8
Stuffed Peaches, Macaroon-, '79 178
Stuffed Peach Halves, '86 196
Sundaes Flambé, Peach, '81 88
Trifle, Peach, '92 179
Wine Sauce, Peaches in, '79 184
Peanut Butter Dessert, '92 164
Peanut-Buttery Dessert, Crunchy, '92 204
Pear. See also Desserts/Sauces.
    Amaretto Pears with Meringue, '90 M58
    Baked Pears à la Mode, '95 129
    Baked Pears Elegant, '91 48
    Belle Helene, Pears, '86 164
    Coconut Pears, Spicy, '83 207
    Crème Chantilly, Holiday Pears with,
        '91 297
    Crème de Menthe Pears, '94 50
    Crisp, Raspberry-Pear, '89 109
    Flaming Pears, '84 313
    Gratin, Pear-Blue Cheese, '93 328
    Maple-Sugared Pears, '81 232
    Meringues, Baked Pear, '85 232
    Orange-Caramel Sauce, Pears with,
        '95 281
    Poached in Red Wine, Pears, '83 302
    Poached Pear Fans with Raspberry-
        Orange Sauce, '88 22
    Poached Pears Flambé, Orange-, '85 313
    Poached Pears in Custard, '88 20
    Poached Pears in Wine, '82 194
    Poached Pears, Lemon, '82 74
    Poached Pears, Vanilla, '90 57
    Poached Pears with Berry Sauce, Wine-,
        '86 144
    Poached Pears with Dark Chocolate
        Sauce, '90 M141
    Poached Pears with Honey-Yogurt Sauce,
        '92 306
    Poached Pears with Raspberry Sauce,
        '84 213; '87 69; '88 223
    Red Wine, Pears in, '82 254
    Stuffed Pears, Almond-, '83 207
    Sundaes, Quick Pear, '86 71
Pecans, Sugared, '82 167
Peppermint Bavarian, '80 153
Peppermint Fondue, '94 332

Peppermint Wafer Dessert, '79 176; '80 7
Pineapple-Almond Delight, '85 96
Pineapple Dessert Chimichangas, '86 4
Pineapple, Meringue-Topped, '84 178
Pineapple 'n' Cream, '88 202
Pineapple, Scalloped, '79 106; '82 254
Pineapple with Natillas Sauce, Baked, '83 179
Pineapple with Raspberry Sauce, Chocolate-
    Drizzled, '90 57
Pizzelles, '83 298
Plum Crunch, Layered, '86 174
Port Wine Jelly with Whipped Cream, '84 254
Pots de Crème, Easy, '93 281
Profiteroles, '84 208
Prune Bavarian, '86 223
Pumpkin Chiffon, '82 216; '86 283; '88 260
Pumpkin Chiffon Dessert, '88 128
Pumpkin Mold, '82 311
Pumpkin-Orange Delight, '86 321
Pumpkin Swirl, Easy, '93 234
Raspberry Dream, '83 108
Raspberry-Jellyroll Dessert, '85 95
Raspberry Jellyrolls, '93 M255
Raspberry-Pear Crisp, '89 109
Raspberry Prunes, '82 124
Raspberry-Strawberry Bavarian, '89 15
Rhubarb Crisp, '91 146; '92 130
Rhubarb-Strawberry Bavarian, '86 140
Rhubarb Whip, '79 112
Rice Cream with Mandarin Oranges, '85 317
Roulage, Toffee-Pecan, '94 312
Rum Balls, '93 314
Sabayon, '93 272
Santa's Hat, '92 279
Sauces
    Almond-Vanilla Custard Sauce,
        '88 M177
    Amaretto-Chocolate Sauce, '92 154
    Amaretto-Cinnamon Sauce, '93 171
    Amaretto-Strawberry Sauce, '87 M165
    Ambrosia Sauce, Hot, '89 335
    Apple Ambrosia Sauce, '89 95
    Apple-Cinnamon Sauce, '93 42
    Apple Dessert Sauce, '87 M165
    Apple Dessert Sauce, Spicy, '82 177
    Apple Topping, Spicy, '87 125
    Apricot Ice Cream Sauce, '91 57
    Apricot Sauce, '82 212
    Apricot-Walnut Hard Sauce, '88 153
    Banana-Pineapple Sauce, '83 48
    Banana Sundae Sauce, '84 275
    Berry Mimosa Sauce, '90 315
    Berry Sauce, '87 290; '88 135; '94 130;
        '95 103
    Bittersweet Chocolate Sauce, '92 319
    Blackberry Sauce, '86 152; '94 232
    Blueberry Sauce, '88 155; '89 M130;
        '94 122; '95 135
    Blueberry Topping, '87 125
    Bourbon Praline Sauce, '81 170
    Bourbon Sauce, '93 51
    Brandied Hard Sauce, '80 264; '83 250;
        '85 313
    Brandy-Butter Sauce, '79 230
    Brandy-Macadamia Sauce, '82 311
    Brandy Sauce, '88 279
    Brown Sugar Sauce, '90 314
    Buttered Rum Sauce, '83 249
    Buttered Rum Sauce, Hot, '88 204
    Buttermilk Sauce, '95 183
    Butter Pecan Sauce, '91 174
    Butter-Rum Sauce, '95 134
    Butterscotch-Pecan Sauce, '82 212

DESSERTS, Sauces (continued)

Caramel-Raisin Sauce, '88 127
Caramel Sauce, '79 79; '91 56, 180;
    '93 210, 235, 296; '94 234; '95 308
Caramel Sauce, Easy, '87 38
Caramel Sauce, White, '92 195
Cherry-Pineapple Topping, '87 126
Cherry Sauce, '79 91
Cherry Sauce, Elegant, '79 M156
Chocolate-Cherry Sauce, '85 189
Chocolate Cherry Sauce, '87 M165
Chocolate-Mint Sauce, '93 86; '94 314
Chocolate Mint Sauce, Quick, '86 M58
Chocolate-Orange Sauce, '86 165;
    '94 314
Chocolate-Peanut Butter Sauce,
    '79 91, M156
Chocolate-Peppermint Sauce, '94 205
Chocolate-Praline Sauce, '85 M295
Chocolate Sauce, '83 189;
    '84 208, 313; '86 322; '90 57;
    '91 56, 57; '93 276; '94 121
Chocolate Sauce, Classic, '85 207
Chocolate Sauce, Creamy, '88 M177
Chocolate Sauce, Dark, '93 296;
    '94 234, 283
Chocolate Sauce, Double, '83 79
Chocolate Sauce, Easy, '92 148
Chocolate Sauce, Heavenly, '79 79;
    '82 167
Chocolate Sauce Supreme, '85 189
Cinnamon-Blueberry Sauce, '86 11
Cinnamon-Fudge Sauce, '85 141
Cinnamon Sauce, Apple Pie with Hot,
    '88 210
Coconut-Orange Sauce, '85 189
Coconut Sauce, Creamy Light, '82 177
Cranberry Jubilee, Tasty, '85 189
Cranberry Sauce, '86 278; '88 280
Crème Anglaise, '92 164
Crème Fraîche Sauce, '79 281; '93 135
Custard Sauce, '85 41; '88 154, 251, 259;
    '89 291
Date-Nut Sundae Sauce, '82 167
Fig Sauce, '79 140
Fruit Dessert Sauce, Hot, '87 299
Fruit Puree, '94 190
Fruit Sauce, Golden, '89 281
Fruit Sauce, Quick, '82 212
Fudge Sauce, '91 174
Fudge Sauce, Easy Hot, '84 69; '94 194
Fudge Sauce, Hot, '82 181, 295; '84 143
Fudge Sauce, Quick Hot, '82 212
Golden Sauce, '88 267
Hard Sauce, '80 265; '82 14
Hard Sauce, Special, '86 318
Honey-Chocolate Sauce, '89 251
Honey-Orange Sauce, '85 108
Honeyscotch Sundae Sauce, '82 167
Honey-Yogurt Sauce, '92 307
Kahlúa Chocolate Sauce, '85 155
Lemon Cream Sauce, '93 200
Lemon Dessert Sauce, '87 M165
Lemon Sauce, '84 258, 306; '85 77, 190;
    '91 240
Lemon Sauce, Tart, '85 191
Mandarin Dressing, '89 137
Mandarin Orange Sauce, '89 204
Mango Sauce, '83 120
Marshmallow Sauce, '91 91
Melba Sauce, '87 77

Mint Sauce, Party, '82 212
Orange Dessert Sauce, '86 337; '87 58
Orange Hard Sauce, '88 225
Orange Sauce, Fresh, '85 209
Peach-Berry Sauce, '87 M165
Peach-Blueberry Pancake Sauce, '82 177
Peach Blueberry Sauce, '81 170
Peach-Praline Sauce, '85 161
Peach Sauce, '84 144
Peach Sauce, Creamy, '85 189
Peach Sauce, Fresh, '87 167
Peanut Butter Ice Cream Sauce, '84 30
Peanut Dessert Sauce, '86 M251
Pear Sauce, '92 164
Pecan Sauce, '83 219
Piña Colada Topping, Chunky, '87 125
Pineapple Ice Cream Sauce, '81 M289
Pineapple-Rhubarb Sauce, '88 94
Pineapple-Rum Sauce, '84 275
Plum Sauce, Fresh, '94 129
Praline Ice Cream Sauce, '85 189
Praline Ice Cream Sauce, Southern,
    '86 M227
Praline Sauce, '83 25; '84 143; '89 95;
    '92 282; '93 214; '94 206, 312
Raspberry-Amaretto Sauce, '88 130
Raspberry-Orange Sauce, '88 22;
    '92 154
Raspberry-Peach Topping, '87 126
Raspberry Sauce, '82 289; '83 108;
    '84 73, 213; '87 69, 117, 183;
    '88 267; '89 183, 322;
    '91 96, 180, 270; '92 130;
    '93 82, 99, 315; '94 295;
    '95 327
Raspberry Sauce, Crimson, '79 91;
    '85 30
Raspberry Sauce Dessert, '80 147
Raspberry Sauce Flambé, '84 142
Raspberry Sauce, Fresh, '93 120
Rhubarb Sauce, Chilled, '88 94
Rum-Butter Sauce, '86 301
Rum-Fruit Sauce, '84 312
Rum-Raisin Sauce, '84 7; '94 295
Rum Sauce, '88 32; '94 241
Rum Sauce, Brown Sugar-, '85 231
Rum Sauce, Hot, '79 86
Rum Sundae Sauce, '93 162
Sherry Sauce, '84 109
Spicy Sauce, '93 52
Strawberries Arnaud Sauce, '93 50
Strawberry-Banana Topping, '87 125
Strawberry-Peach Sauce, '92 154
Strawberry Sauce, '84 144;
    '87 93, 198; '92 85; '94 121
Strawberry Sauce, Brandied, '88 196
Strawberry Sauce, Fresh, '82 177
Strawberry Sauce, Old-Fashioned,
    '94 130
Strawberry Sauce, Peaches with, '85 8
Strawberry Sauce with Crunchy Topping,
    '81 170
Strawberry Sauce with Dumplings,
    '84 314
Taffy Dessert Sauce, '86 20
Tea-Berry Sauce, '94 130
Toffee-Fudge Sauce, '89 95
Toffee Sauce, '94 72
Vanilla Crème Sauce, '94 243
Watermelon Sauce, Melon Balls in,
    '79 177
Whiskey Sauce, '90 230; '92 87, 93
White Chocolate Sauce, '92 164

Savarin, '79 171
Sherbet-Cantaloupe Surprise, '91 105
Sopaipillas, '80 197; '88 112; '91 78
Sopaipillas, Pineapple, '83 179
Soufflés
    Banana Daiquiri Soufflé, '84 317
    Brandy Alexander Soufflé, '82 173;
        '83 M114
    Chocolate-Mint Soufflé, '81 16
    Chocolate Soufflé, Light, '83 278
    Coconut Soufflé, '85 212
    Daiquiri Soufflé, Elegant, '80 69
    Devonshire Soufflé, Chilled, '88 279
    Grand Marnier Soufflé, '79 281
    Grasshopper Soufflé, '81 248; '86 188
    Kahlúa Soufflé, '82 173
    Lemon-Lime Soufflé, Cold, '84 24
    Lemon Soufflé, '82 170
    Lemon Soufflé, Tart, '85 82
    Orange Dessert Soufflé, '83 206
    Orange Soufflé, Chilled, '84 317;
        '86 189
    Orange Soufflé, Frozen, '79 211
    Pineapple Dessert Soufflé, '80 153
    Raspberry Soufflé, '86 188
    Raspberry-Topped Soufflé, '85 317
    Vanilla Soufflé, Frozen, '79 230;
        '82 173
Soup, Sherry-Berry Dessert, '91 180
Spumoni and Berries, '91 204
Strawberry. See also Desserts/Frozen,
    Parfaits, Sauces.
    Almond Cream with Fresh Strawberries,
        '87 93
    Arnaud, Strawberries, '93 50
    Banana-Berry Supreme, '81 205
    Bavarian, Raspberry-Strawberry, '89 15
    Bavarian, Rhubarb-Strawberry, '86 140
    Brandied Orange Juice, Strawberries with,
        '82 160
    Carousel, Strawberry, '91 247
    Charlotte Russe with Strawberry Sauce,
        '92 85
    Cheese Delight, Strawberry, '79 50
    Cherry-Berry on a Cloud, '79 94
    Chilled Strawberry Dessert, '84 164
    Chocolate Combo, Strawberry-, '85 96
    Coconut Nests, Strawberry, '88 136
    Compote, Peach-Berry, '89 112
    Cream Cheese Dessert, Strawberry-,
        '83 123
    Cream Puffs, Strawberry, '81 95
    Cream, Strawberries and, '82 100
    Cream, Strawberries 'n', '90 30
    Cream, Strawberries with Strawberry,
        '84 108
    Crêpes, Strawberry Dessert, '83 122
    Deep-Fried Strawberries, '84 109
    Delight, Strawberry, '81 85
    Dipped Strawberries, '94 17
    French Cream, Strawberries with, '83 191
    Frost, Strawberry, '81 279; '82 24;
        '83 154
    Glazed Strawberry Dessert, '84 33
    Honeydew-Berry Dessert, '83 120
    Jamaica, Strawberries, '85 161; '93 239
    Juliet, Strawberries, '84 82
    Lemon Dessert, Strawberry-, '86 162
    Marsala, Strawberries, '88 171
    Meringues, Strawberry, '84 188
    Napoleons, Strawberry, '81 126
    Pizza, Kiwi-Berry, '86 198
    Pizza, Strawberry, '79 94

DESSERTS, Strawberry *(continued)*

Raspberry Custard Sauce, Fresh Berries with, '88 163
Rock Cream with Strawberries, Old-Fashioned, '90 125
Romanoff, Strawberries, '84 108; '88 95; '91 126
Ruby Strawberries, '82 100
Sabayon, Strawberries, '79 94
Shortcake Squares, Strawberry, '85 122
Soup, Sherry-Berry Dessert, '91 180
Spumoni and Berries, '91 204
Strawberry Dessert, '83 123
Stuffed Strawberries with Walnuts, '85 122; '86 124
Summer Strawberry Dessert, '92 143
Sweet-and-Sour Strawberry Dessert, '92 54
Swirl, Strawberry, '84 108
Trifle, Easy Strawberry, '88 201
Yogurt Delight, Strawberry, '85 77
Yogurt Dessert, Strawberry-, '90 295
Zabaglione, Strawberries, '81 95
Sundaes
Apple Spice Sundae, Hot, '92 239
Cantaloupe Sundae, '89 166
Cocoa-Kahlúa Sundaes, '83 M58
Hot Fudge Sundae Dessert, '86 322
Mauna Loa Sundaes, '80 126
Peach Sundaes Flambé, '81 88
Pear Sundaes, Quick, '86 71
Strawberry Sundaes, Hot, '81 M5
Tiramisù, '91 21; '94 295
Toffee Dessert, English, '88 136
Tortilla Baskets, '94 97
Trifle, All Seasons Lemon, '95 219
Trifle, Angel Food, '91 184
Trifle, Easy Strawberry, '88 201
Trifle, English, '93 289
Trifle, Island, '92 238
Trifle, Lemon-Blueberry, '88 210
Trifle, Olde English, '95 331
Trifle, Pineapple Angel Food, '93 86
Trifle, Raspberry, '88 259
Trifle, Rum, '86 322
Trifle, Savannah, '80 121
Trifles, Easy Individual, '92 239
Trifle, Toffee, '94 168
Tropical Snow, '86 34
Vacherin Moka, '80 55
Vanilla Cream, '83 M115
Vanilla Sherry Dessert, Glorified, '81 85
Waffles, Banana Split, '89 205
Waffles with Mandarin Orange Sauce, Dessert Pumpkin, '89 204
Waffle, Whole Wheat Dessert, '79 92
White Christmas Dessert, '82 261
Wine Jelly, Rosy, '85 306
Yule Log, '79 281; '82 289
DOUGHNUTS
Applesauce Doughnuts, '81 203
Applesauce Drop Doughnuts, '90 70
Banana Doughnuts, '86 137
Beignets, '84 56
Cake Doughnuts, Quick, '82 226
Chocolate-Covered Doughnuts, '84 55
Chocolate Doughnuts, '83 95
Cinnamon Puffs, '81 209
Dutch Doughnuts, '81 50
Fry Bread, '84 140
Glazed Doughnuts, '83 94

Jelly-Filled Doughnuts, '84 55
Orange Spiced Doughnuts, '79 136
Pineapple Drop Doughnuts, '83 95
Potato Doughnuts, Chocolate-Glazed, '85 6
Potato Doughnuts, Old-Fashioned, '84 56
Puffs, Doughnut, '86 85
Puffs, Wheat Quick Doughnut, '85 278
Pumpkin Doughnut Drops, '90 323
Snowy Doughnuts, '93 286
Spice Doughnuts, '84 56
Sufganiyot (Jelly-Filled Doughnuts), '90 255
Whole Wheat Doughnuts, '84 56

DOVE. *See* **GAME.**
DRESSINGS. *See also* **SALAD DRESSINGS, STUFFINGS.**
Cajun Dressing, '82 307
Chicken and Dressing, Baked, '79 296
Cornbread
Biscuit Dressing, Cornbread-, '79 296
Chicken Cornbread Dressing, '90 159
Cornbread Dressing, '86 286; '88 254; '92 267
Fruited Cornbread Dressing, '80 262
Green Chile-Cornbread Dressing, '93 306; '94 296
Herb-Seasoned Cornbread Dressing, '83 315
Kentucky Cornbread Dressing, '86 281
Light Cornbread Dressing, '92 324
Nannie's Cornbread Dressing, '95 306
Old-Fashioned Cornbread Dressing, '84 321
Quail Stuffed with Cornbread Dressing, '93 280
Sage-Cornbread Dressing, '84 283
Sage Dressing, Cornbread-, '80 262
Sausage-Cornbread Dressing, '95 289
Sausage-Cornbread Dressing, Turkey with, '83 287
Sausage Dressing, Cornbread-, '82 307; '85 280
Sausage Dressing, Cornbread-and-, '83 213
Savory Cornbread Dressing, '88 303
Texas Cornbread Dressing, '82 243
Turkey and Cornbread Dressing, Roast, '89 324
Corn Dressing Balls, Zesty, '82 307
Crawfish Dressing, Louisiana, '90 103
Creole Dressing, '95 289
Eggplant Dressing, '90 236
Fruit-and-Pecan Dressing, '84 252
Fruit Dressing, Baked, '87 253
Giblet Dressing, '91 255
Grandmother's Dressing, '91 254
Grits Dressing, '93 306; '94 296
Oyster Bread Dressing, '82 251
Oyster Dressing, '79 250
Peanut Dressing, Roast Turkey with, '79 283

Pecan-Rice Dressing, Chicken with, '85 M57
Pecan-Sage Dressing, '80 262
Pretzel Dressing, '86 280
Rice Dressing, '91 217
Rice Dressing, Chicken and, '79 288
Rice Dressing, Mexican, '87 253
Rice Dressing, Roast Turkey with, '82 286
Sausage-Apple Dressing, '93 305; '94 296
Sausage Dressing, '86 280
Sausage Dressing, Harvest, '88 254
Seasoned Dressing, Stuffed Turkey Breast with, '83 320; '84 128
Spoonbread Dressing, Southwestern-Style, '94 273
Squash Dressing, '83 315; '86 280; '95 290
Squash Dressing, Turkey with, '87 248
Turkey and Dressing, Easy, '79 296
Turkey-and-Dressing Pie, '84 326
Turkey Dressing, '85 298
Whole Wheat-Mushroom Dressing, '84 283
Zucchini Dressing, '86 282
DUCK AND DUCKLING. *See* **GAME.**
DUMPLINGS
Apple Dumplings, '82 273
Apple Dumplings, Old-Fashioned, '84 226
Apple Dumplings with Maple-Cider Sauce, '95 288
Apple Dumplings with Orange Hard Sauce, '88 224
Beef Stew with Dumplings, '84 3
Blackberries and Dumplings, '86 196
Cheddar Dumplings, Chicken Ragout with, '94 44
Chicken and Dumplings, Country, '85 254
Chicken and Dumplings, Easy, '86 21
Chicken and Dumplings, Old-Fashioned, '79 55; '83 228; '93 302
Chicken and Dumplings, Quick, '95 125
Chicken and Dumplings with Herbed Broth, '95 338
Chicken and Dumplings with Vegetables, '85 M56
Chicken Stew and Dumplings, '84 4
Cornmeal Dumplings, Turnip Greens with, '82 211
Drop Dumplings, Burgundy Stew with, '83 125
Green Peas and Dumplings, '80 102
Old-Fashioned Dumplings, '81 191
Parsley Dumplings, Beef Stew with, '81 76; '82 13; '85 M246
Peach Dumplings, '80 143; '85 177
Potato Dumplings, Venison Stew with, '87 304
Shrimp with Dumplings, Stewed, '79 31
Strawberry Sauce with Dumplings, '84 314
Tomato Dumplings, '88 144

EGGNOG
Beverages
Blender Eggnog, '93 341
Breakfast Nog, Speedy, '82 47
Christmas Eggnog, '87 242
Coconut Nog, '83 275
Coffee Nog, Brandied, '86 329
Cooked Custard Eggnog, '91 305
Creamy Eggnog, '80 259; '83 303; '85 300
Easy Eggnog, '91 305
Edenton Eggnog, '84 251
Eggnog, '83 318

EGGNOG, Beverages *(continued)*

Holiday Brew, '81 265
Holiday Eggnog Deluxe, '79 232
Irish Coffee Nog, '84 258; '93 340
Irish Cream Nog, '82 312
Mock Eggnog with Orange and Nutmeg,
  '92 323
Orange Spiced Nog, '82 48
Punch, Coffee-Eggnog, '86 281
Punch, Coffee Eggnog, '92 264
Punch, Holiday Eggnog, '86 281
Punch, Irish Coffee-Eggnog, '95 314
Punch, Peppermint-Eggnog, '90 273
Sparkling Eggnog, '79 232
Thick and Creamy Eggnog, '80 261
Bread, Eggnog, '83 294
Cake, Eggnog-Pecan Pound, '95 313
Cake, Eggnog Pound, '90 253
Casserole, Sweet Potato-Eggnog, '95 291
Cookies, Eggnog Christmas, '79 255
Dessert, Eggnog, '95 314
French Toast, Eggnog, '95 313
Parfait, Eggnog Bavarian, '79 255
Pie, Eggnog, '80 254; '83 205; '86 317;
  '87 295
Pie, Eggnog Chiffon, '86 281
Pie, Fluffy Eggnog, '81 M269
Salad, Eggnog Christmas, '86 281
Tarts, Creamy Eggnog, '79 255

EGGPLANT

Almonds, Eggplant with, '79 179
Appetizer, Eggplant, '83 187
Appetizer, Grilled Eggplant, '95 198
Balsamic-Flavored Eggplant, '95 342
Biscuit Cakes, Tomato-Eggplant, '95 170
Cakes, Eggplant, '95 196
Caponata, '87 166
Casseroles
  Bake, Eggplant, '80 82
  Cakes, Eggplant, '95 196
  Chiles Rellenos, Eggplant, '91 86
  Creole Eggplant, '86 110
  Easy Eggplant Casserole, '80 202
  Eggplant Casserole, '81 205; '84 217;
    '93 44; '94 214
  Elegant Eggplant Casserole, '82 168
  Flavorful Eggplant Casserole, '79 92
  Frittata, Fresh Vegetable, '93 140
  Heavenly Eggplant, '93 293
  Italian Eggplant, '84 216
  Italian-Style Eggplant and Zucchini,
    '79 289; '80 26
  Lebanese Eggplant, '81 24
  Mexican Eggplant, '83 187
  Moussaka, '87 166; '90 68
  Moussaka Casserole, '79 179
  Moussaka, Potatoes, '93 44
  Noodle Casserole, Eggplant and, '82 230
  Oyster Louisiane, Eggplant-and-, '95 196
  Parmesan, Eggplant, '82 230; '83 186;
    '84 215; '86 53; '92 18; '95 84
  Parmesan, No-Fry Eggplant, '92 172
  Parmigiana, Eggplant, '81 19; '82 186;
    '95 197
  Potato-Eggplant Casserole, '87 166
  Sausage Bake, Eggplant-, '85 221
  Sausage Casserole, Eggplant-, '84 215
  Sausage-Pasta Casserole, Freezer
    Eggplant-, '95 197
  Scalloped Eggplant, '91 223
  Spanish Eggplant, '79 21

Spicy Hot Eggplant Casserole, '93 92
Super Eggplant Casserole, '80 202
Supreme, Eggplant, '79 188; '86 170
Tomato Casserole, Eggplant-and-,
  '83 187
Caviar, Eggplant, '88 262
Caviar, Homemade Cowboy, '94 64
Caviar with Tapenade, Eggplant, '92 194
Crawfish on Eggplant, Soft-Shell, '88 222
Creole, Eggplant, '82 107; '83 86; '86 110
Dressing, Eggplant, '90 236
Easy Eggplant, '87 M151
French-Fried Eggplant, '81 204
Fried Eggplant, '79 178; '83 187; '88 111
Fried Eggplant, Cheesy, '90 75
Fried Eggplant, Parmesan, '79 189
Fried Parmesan Eggplant, '87 166
Fritters, Eggplant, '91 211
Gravy, Roast Duck with Sweet Potato-
  Eggplant, '83 90
Grilled Eggplant, '80 202; '89 174
Italiano, Eggplant, '91 212
Jackstraw Eggplant, '82 230
Julienne, Eggplant, '85 221
Main Dish, Sausage-Eggplant, '80 211
Medley, Eggplant-Shrimp, '79 188
Mexicano, Eggplant à la, '82 229
Oven-Fried Eggplant, '91 187
Parmigiana, Chicken-Eggplant, '82 212
Patties, Eggplant, '83 186
Pizza, Eggplant, '85 221
Provençal, Eggplant, '92 82
Ratatouille, Eggplant-Zucchini, '81 205
Relish, Eggplant, '95 342
Salad, Eggplant, '90 99
Sandwiches, Baked Eggplant, '82 230
Sandwiches, Open-Face Eggplant, '95 124
Sautéed Eggplant and Zucchini, '82 96
Slices, Quick Eggplant, '90 75
Soup, Eggplant Supper, '85 221
Soup, Herbed Eggplant, '90 173
Spaghetti Squash with Sesame Eggplant,
  '92 252
Spread, Eggplant, '86 278
Spread, Eggplant-Mushroom, '92 156
Squash, Eggplant and, '83 187
Stacks, Eggplant, '91 211
Sticks, Ned's Eggplant, '95 309
Stuffed
  Baked Stuffed Eggplant, '81 133
  Beefy Stuffed Eggplant, '81 204
  Cheesy Stuffed Eggplant, '79 188;
    '82 208
  Creole Stuffed Eggplant, '82 230
  Eggplant, Stuffed, '80 158
  Ham-Stuffed Eggplant, '80 162
  Italian-Stuffed Eggplant, '90 74
  Mushroom-Stuffed Eggplant, '83 136
  Ratatouille-Bran Stuffed Eggplant, '86 44
  Ratatouille-Stuffed Eggplant, '83 187
  Rolled Stuffed Eggplant, '80 63
  Sausage Stuffed Eggplant, '81 204
  Sausage-Stuffed Eggplant, '91 211
  Seafood Stuffed Eggplant, '79 187
  Shrimp-Stuffed Eggplant, '92 99
  Tophats, Eggplant, '79 188
Supper, Beef-and-Eggplant, '84 291
Tophats, Eggplant, '79 188

EGGS

Baked Egg Crisps, '83 57
Baked Eggs Florentine, '86 M12
Baked Eggs in Spinach Nests, '82 70
Baked in Mushroom Sauce, Eggs, '93 47
Bake, Egg and Rice, '83 119

Bedeviled Eggs, '86 67
Benedict, Bacon-and-Tomato Eggs, '87 195
Benedict, Easy Eggs, '80 M268
Benedict, Eggs, '79 40, 254; '85 49
Benedict, Light Eggs, '93 M68
Benedict, Lion, '93 121
Benedict with Cheese Sauce, Eggs, '81 225
Brandied Cream Sauce, Eggs in, '82 70
Bread, Butter-Egg, '85 269
Bread, County Fair Egg, '87 68
Bread, Easter Egg, '84 94
Breakfast Eye-Openers, '82 231
Breakfast, Farmer's, '81 44
Brunch Eggs, '85 44
Brunch, Texas, '82 70
Bunwiches, '80 92
Burritos, Brunch, '91 77
Burritos, Tex-Mex Egg, '95 34
Casseroles
  Apple-Egg Casserole, '85 44
  Bacon and Egg Casserole, '81 225
  Bacon Casserole, Egg-and-, '85 248
  Bel-Mar, Eggs, '90 92
  Breakfast Bake, '85 45
  Broccoli-and-Egg Casserole, '86 324
  Broccoli-and-Eggs au Gratin, '85 289
  Brunch Egg Casserole, '86 329
  Bruncheon Eggs, '83 83
  Cheese Casserole, Egg-and-, '84 293
  Cheese-Egg-Zucchini Casserole, '84 114
  Cheesy Egg Casserole, '81 244; '86 15
  Chile Eggs, '88 80
  Crab-Egg Casserole, '80 260
  Creole Eggs, '82 42
  Egg Casserole, '83 311
  Frittata, Fresh Vegetable, '93 140
  Ham and Egg Casserole, Breakfast,
    '79 253
  Mushroom Casserole, Egg-, '83 49
  Potato-Egg Casserole, Cheesy, '84 5
  Potatoes and Eggs au Gratin, '79 107
  Sausage-and-Egg Casserole, '94 284
  Sausage Breakfast Casserole, '81 270
  Sausage Egg Bake, '81 225
  Sausage-Egg Bake, Smoked, '85 248
  Sausage-Egg Casserole, '86 M12
  Scrambled Egg Casserole, Saucy, '89 213
  Soufflé Casserole, Egg, '83 55
  Spinach and Egg Casserole, '82 270
  Squash and Egg Casserole, '80 146
  Strata, Cheese-Rice, '81 176
  Strata, Sausage, '84 101
  Strata, Tomato-Cheese, '81 209
  Sunday Egg Casserole, '95 100
  Zucchini-Egg Casserole, '84 M113
Cheddar Eggs, '94 M141
Cheese, Eggs and, '95 165
Cottage Eggs, '85 44
Crabmeat and Eggs New Orleans, '82 45
Creamed Eggs à la Asparagus, '81 201
Creamed Eggs, Broccoli and, '83 84
Creamed Eggs in Patty Shells, '80 M267
Creamed Eggs in Toast Cups, '83 83
Creole, Eggs, '92 86
Creole, Skillet Eggs, '85 143
Crêpes, Ham-and-Egg, '83 204
Crêpes with Mushroom Sauce, Ham-and-Egg,
  '82 46
Croissant Eggwiches, '91 160
Croquettes, Tuna-Egg, '80 275
Delight, Bacon-and-Egg, '85 143
Delight, Crab-and-Egg, '84 261
Delight, Mushroom-Egg, '83 14

Dip, Festive Egg, '79 285
Dressing, Egg, '86 79
Featherbed Eggs, '93 122
Florentine, Eggs, '79 39; '83 56
Florentine-Style Eggs, '82 38
Foo Yong, Egg, '80 19; '86 232
Foo Yong Patties, '80 223
Foo Yong, Shrimp Egg, '83 22
Frittata, Broccoli-Cheese, '81 243
Frittata, Corn-and-Squash, '89 144
Frittata, Firecracker Pasta, '94 230
Frittata, Potato, '89 145
Frittata, Potato-Bacon, '95 269
Frittata, Spinach, '81 53
Frittata, Vegetable, '92 48; '93 183
Ham and Eggs à la Swiss, '88 158
Ham and Eggs, Creamed, '82 40
Ham and Eggs, Creamy, '87 286
Ham and Eggs on Toast with Cheese Sauce,
    '81 43
Ham and Eggs, Savory, '82 231
Hard-Cooked Eggs (garnish), '82 280
Hash Brown Skillet Breakfast, '82 5
Herb Sauce, Eggs in, '88 80
Hominy, Bacon, Eggs, and, '85 143
Huevos Rancheros, '82 197; '91 77
Medley, Cheddar Egg, '81 M176
Mexicana, Eggs, '82 146
Mound, Frosted Egg, '79 33
Mushroom Eggs, Sherried, '83 49
Mushrooms and Eggs in Patty Shells, '85 143;
    '88 197
Mushrooms and Eggs, Saucy, '79 138
Nests, Fluffy Egg, '79 128
Omelets
    Apple Omelet Stack, '94 50
    Baked Omelets, '94 50
    Broccoli-Mushroom Omelet, '85 45
    Cheese Omelet, Herbed, '93 47
    Cheese Omelet, Puffed, '89 227
    Cheese Omelet, Zippy, '87 287
    Cheese-Shiitake Omelet, Golden, '95 265
    Cheesy Picante Omelet, '86 95
    Chicken Liver Omelet, '82 44
    Country Omelets, '91 128
    Creole Sauce, Omelets with, '89 228
    Dill-Cheese-Ham Omelet, '95 33
    Fines Herbes, Omelette aux, '92 82
    Fluffy Omelet, '84 56
    George's Omelets, '80 68
    Ham and Cheese Omelet, '79 262;
        '80 123
    Italian Omelet, '92 47
    Mexican Omelet, '79 128; '81 225
    Mexican Omelet, Easy, '88 114
    Mushroom Omelet, Rolled, '82 70
    Mushroom Sauce, Puffy Omelets with,
        '85 40
    Olé Omelet, '87 M124
    Olé, Omelet, '94 31
    Oyster Omelets, Smoked, '84 96
    Potato Omelet, Family-Size, '94 31
    Potato-Sprout Omelet, '79 128
    Primavera, Omelet, '87 71
    Rising Sun Omelet, '82 281; '83 42
    Rolled Omelet, '89 228
    Sandwich, Omelet, '86 95
    Sausage Filling, Omelet with, '81 43
    Sausage Omelet, Puffy, '80 M268
    Shrimp-and-Cheddar Omelet, '84 57
    Shrimp-and-Cheese Omelet, '94 31
    Sour Cream-Ham Omelet, '79 261
    Spanish Omelet, '81 201; '83 243;
        '84 101
    Spanish-Style Omelets, '83 188
    Spinach-Cheese Omelet, '83 119
    Strawberry-Sour Cream Omelet, '89 229
    Sunrise Omelet, '83 289
    Swiss Oven Omelet, '80 189
    Tarragon Omelet, '89 144
    Tex-Mex Omelet con Carne, '81 209
    Vegetable Omelet, Beefy, '83 188
    Vegetable Omelet, Cheddar-, '83 205
    Vegetable Omelet, Cheesy, '85 49
    Vegetable Omelet, Fresh, '84 211
    Vegetable Omelet, Golden, '82 M123
    Vegetable Omelet, Puffy, '83 188
    Vegetarian Omelet, '84 114
    White Wine Omelet, '79 103
    Yogurt-Avocado Omelet, '81 33
    Zucchini Omelet, '81 99
Paint, Egg Yolk, '86 322
Peanut Butter Easter Eggs, '87 86
Pickled Eggs, Beet, '84 287
Pickled Eggs, Rosy, '86 68
Pickled Eggs, Spiced, '84 288
Pie, Country Breakfast, '93 M328
Pie, Egg-Stra Special Chicken, '86 264
Pie, Old-Fashioned Egg Custard, '82 261
Pillows, Egg, '92 332
Pizza, Breakfast, '85 44
Pizza, Ham-and-Eggs Crescent, '93 47
Poached Eggs, '92 87, 93; '93 121
Poached Eggs, Basic, '82 58
Poached Eggs, French-Style, '82 58
Potatoes with Eggs and Meat, '91 311; '92 25
Potato Nests, Mashed, '94 141
Puff, Egg-and-Cheese, '85 45
Rancheros, Easy Eggs, '88 81
Rice, Egg Fried, '79 252; '80 19
Roll-Ups, Spicy Egg, '90 140
Roulade with Mushroom Filling, Egg, '88 84
Salads
    Asparagus-and-Egg Salad, '86 305
    Bacon-Horseradish Egg Salad, '94 181
    Deviled Egg Salad, '83 124
    Ham-and-Egg Potato Salad, '86 84
    Ham 'n Egg Salad, '81 36
    Rice Salad, Egg-, '84 18; '86 169
    Shrimp-and-Egg Salad Sandwiches,
        '94 182
    Shrimp-Egg Salad, Tossed, '80 4
    Spread, Cottage-Egg Salad, '82 146
    Spread, Egg Salad, '86 127
    Tacos, Mexican Egg Salad, '94 181
    Tuna-Egg Salad, '81 135
    Vegetable and Egg Salad, Green, '79 191
    Yolkless Egg Salad, '94 181
Sandwiches, Breakfast, '82 M123; '89 M230
Sandwiches, Confetti, '79 236
Sandwiches, Eggsclusive, '79 164; '80 130
Sandwiches, Eggs-Tra Special, '81 240; '83 69
Sandwiches, Open-Faced Cheesy Egg, '86 67
Sandwiches, Open-Face Egg, '83 292; '84 78;
    '86 160
Sandwiches, Saucy Egg, '91 160
Sardou, Eggs, '92 93
Saucy Eggs, '83 84
Saucy Eggs on Toast, '81 209
Scotch Eggs, '79 261; '83 289
Scrambled
    Bacon-and-Eggs Scramble, '80 M267
    Buttermilk Scrambled Eggs, '79 72
    Casserole, Scrambled Egg, '80 51;
        '86 241
    Cheese-Chive Scrambled Eggs, '95 34
    Cottage Cheese Scrambled Eggs, '81 142
    Cottage-Scrambled Eggs, '80 49
    Country Eggs, '86 330
    Country-Style Scrambled Eggs, '79 22
    Crabmeat Brunch Scramble, '95 32
    Cream Cheese Scrambled Eggs, '81 287
    Creamy Scrambled Eggs, '90 82
    Home-Style Scrambled Eggs, '84 66
    Mexican-Style Scrambled Eggs, '85 50
    Migas, '87 180; '94 26
    Onion Scrambled Eggs, Creamy,
        '83 M203
    Shrimp and Crab Scrambled Eggs,
        '79 261
    Sonora, Eggs, '80 196
    Spanish Scrambled Eggs, '83 49; '84 60
    Special Scrambled Eggs, '81 103
    Supreme, Scrambled Eggs, '79 39
    Tostadas, Scrambled Egg, '86 95
    Wild Rice, Scrambled Eggs with, '80 42
Soufflés, Little Egg, '83 57
Soufflé, Three-Egg Cheese, '87 234
Soup, Egg Drop, '83 21; '86 16
Soup, Egg-Drop, '85 M12
Soup, Egg Flower, '81 307; '82 313; '83 65
Soup, Lemon-Egg Drop, '93 81
Spread, Cottage-Egg Salad, '82 146
Spread, Egg Salad, '86 127
Spread, Egg, Sour Cream, and Caviar, '85 279
Spread, Ham-and-Egg, '79 59
Spread, Vegetable-Egg, '87 106
Stuffed
    Blue Cheese Stuffed Eggs, '93 87
    Creamed Eggs, '86 67
    Creamy Stuffed Eggs, '84 143
    Crunchy Stuffed Eggs, '86 67
    Deluxe, Eggs, '82 79
    Deviled Eggs, '86 176; '94 161
    Deviled Eggs, Bacon, '86 136
    Deviled Eggs, Best, '80 159
    Deviled Eggs, Chile-Cheese, '93 87
    Deviled Eggs, Creamed, '82 79
    Deviled Eggs, Curried, '93 87
    Deviled Eggs, Easy, '82 127
    Deviled Eggs, Nippy, '80 217
    Deviled Eggs, Pimiento-, '84 143
    Deviled Eggs, Saucy, '82 80
    Deviled Eggs Surprise, '79 83
    Deviled Eggs, Sweet, '93 88
    Deviled Eggs with Smoked Oysters,
        '84 161
    Deviled Eggs, Zesty, '84 205
    Devil's Island Eggs, '82 79
    Eggs, Stuffed, '80 155; '88 95
    Ham Devils, '93 88
    Herb-Sour Cream Stuffed Eggs, '93 87
    Mustard Eggs, Spicy, '84 143
    Pecan-Stuffed Eggs, '80 78
    Shrimp-Curried Eggs, Saucy, '84 143
    Stuffed Eggs, Easy, '93 87
    Tomato Slices, Stuffed Eggs-and-,
        '84 152
    Tuna-Stuffed Eggs, '83 83
Substitute, Homemade Egg, '92 47
Sunny-Side-Up Eggs, '79 38
Tacos, Breakfast, '80 43
Tomatoes, Bacon-and-Egg-Stuffed, '80 162
Tortillas, Chorizo and Egg, '81 193
Tortillas, Egg-and-Sausage, '83 246; '84 42
Tulsa Eggs, '87 95

ENCHILADAS
American Enchiladas, '81 170
Bean Enchiladas, Spicy, '88 18
Bean Enchiladas, Three-, '91 133
Casserole, Enchilada, '87 287
Casserole, Firecracker Enchilada, '80 260
Casserole, Green Enchilada, '79 76
Casserole, Sour Cream Enchilada, '82 113
Cheese Enchiladas, '81 194; '85 154; '95 311
Cheese Enchiladas, Saucy, '84 220
Chicken-and-Spinach Enchiladas, '91 222
Chicken Enchiladas, '80 301; '86 296;
    '90 121
Chicken Enchiladas, Easy, '82 89; '86 231
Chicken Enchiladas Verde, '93 274
Chicken Enchiladas with Spicy Sauce, '84 76
Chicken Enchiladas with Tomatillo Sauce,
    '94 231; '95 206
Creamy Enchiladas, '93 174
Dove Enchiladas, '85 270
Duck Enchiladas with Red Pepper-Sour
    Cream, Smoked, '87 121
Green Chile-Sour Cream Enchiladas, '84 234
Hot and Saucy Enchiladas, '81 141; '82 6
Meatless Enchiladas, '93 106
New Mexican Flat Enchiladas, '85 244
Pie, Enchilada, '83 155
Sauce, Enchilada, '81 194
Sauce, Red Chile Enchilada, '85 245
Shrimp Enchiladas in Tomatillo Sauce, '95 310
Skillet Enchiladas, '82 89
Soup, Chicken Enchilada, '86 22
Soup, Shrimp Enchilada, '94 103
Sour Cream Enchiladas, '83 200; '87 37
Sour Cream Enchiladas, Cheesy, '79 25
Spinach Enchiladas, '83 60; '84 14
Terríficas, Enchiladas, '84 32
Weeknight Enchiladas, '93 63
ESCARGOTS
Provençal, Escargots, '82 238; '83 156
ESCAROLE
Cooked Escarole, Easy, '84 85
Salad, Escarole-and-Bacon, '84 85

Fajitas

Beef Fajitas, '88 233
Beef Fajita Salad, '91 70
Chicken Fajitas, '88 231; '89 100; '90 204
Crêpes, Fajita, '94 116
Fajitas, '84 233
Favorite Fajitas, '86 114
Fettuccine, Fajita, '94 84
Pita, Fajita in a, '90 177
Plum Good Fajitas, '94 115
FETTUCCINE
Alfredo, Fettuccine, '80 236; '86 158
Broccoli, Fettuccine with, '90 97
Broccoli-Parmesan Fettuccine, '93 55
Chicken and Pasta, Pesto, '89 M132
Chicken-and-Tomatoes over Fettuccine,
    '90 204
Chicken-Pecan Fettuccine, '86 52
Chicken with Pasta, Dijon, '90 318
Creamy Fettuccine, '92 283
Fajita Fettuccine, '94 84
Greens, Pasta with, '95 211
Ham-and-Asparagus Fettuccine, '94 84
Parsley, Fettuccine with, '83 115
Peas and Pasta, '93 139
Pepper Pasta, '89 321
Poppy Seeds, Fettuccine with, '91 48

Primavera, Fettuccine, '89 238; '94 85
Prosciutto, Party Pasta with, '94 176
Salmon Fettuccine, '90 123
Shrimp Élégante, '83 48
Shrimp Fettuccine, '94 84
Shrimp with Dried Tomato Pesto, Fettuccine
    and, '94 249
Spinach Fettuccine, '82 179
Spinach, Fettuccine and, '88 90
Spinach Fettuccine, Easy Chicken with, '88 89
Spinach Fettuccine, Fresh, '83 60
Spinach Fettuccine with Mustard Greens,
    '94 247
Spinach Sauce, Fettuccine with, '84 329
Supreme, Fettuccine, '83 288; '86 333
Tomato-Olive Pasta Toss, '86 209
Vegetable Fettuccine, '83 312
FIGS
Cake, Fig, '79 32
Cake, Fig Preserve, '79 140; '84 316
Cake, Fig Preserves, '89 335
Cobbler, Cajun Fig, '94 196
Cobbler, Fig, '79 140
Cobbler, Super Fig, '86 206
Coffee Cake, Easy Fig, '80 116
Ice Cream, Fig, '87 139
Jam, Fig, '86 206
Muffins, Fig, '86 206
Pickled Figs, '79 140
Preserves, Fig, '79 140; '82 150; '89 140
Sauce, Fig, '79 140
Snacks, Sliced Fig, '86 206
FILLINGS
Savory
    Beef Filling, '80 81
    Blintz Filling, '92 84
    Broccoli Filling, '81 44
    Cheese-and-Orange Filling, '93 159
    Chicken Divan Filling, '81 91
    Chicken Filling, '81 200
    Chicken Filling, Curried, '88 125
    Chicken Filling Luau, '79 81
    Chicken-Olive Filling, '81 227
    Chicken Salad Filling, '87 106
    Crab Filling, '89 13
    Fruit Filling, '94 245
    Mushroom Filling, '81 89; '88 84
    Omelet Filling, Greek, '80 68
    Omelet Filling, Spanish, '80 68
    Peanut Filling, '93 211
    Pesto, '89 158
    Shrimp Filling, '89 320
    Shrimp Salad Filling, '87 106
    Spinach Filling, '95 316
    Spinach-Mushroom Filling, '80 215
    Spinach-Ricotta Filling, '81 53
Sweet
    Almond Cream Filling, '85 320; '91 248
    Almond Filling, '87 301
    Almond Filling, Ground, '87 14
    Amaretto Filling, '87 241
    Apple-Date Filling, '83 301
    Apple Filling, '85 5
    Apple Filling, Dried, '85 242; '87 229
    Apricot Filling, '83 84; '86 107;
        '93 316
    Butterscotch Filling, '91 271
    Caramel Filling, '88 278
    Chantilly Crème, '80 280
    Cheese Filling, '89 91
    Cherry Filling, '83 302; '84 225;
        '88 178
    Chocolate Buttercream, '84 156

Chocolate-Cheese Filling, '90 47
Chocolate Filling, Rich, '79 68
Chocolate Truffle Filling, '87 69
Cinnamon-Cheese Filling, '90 46
Coconut Cream Filling, '84 200
Coconut Filling, '81 265
Cran-Apple Mousse, '93 255
Cream Cheese Filling, '90 170
Cream Filling, '83 220; '84 37; '87 198;
    '90 311
Crème Fraîche, '91 99
Custard Filling, '82 52, 298; '85 281
Custard Filling, Creamy, '81 180
Custard Filling, Egg, '87 14
Date Cream Filling, '81 303
Date Filling, '80 15; '83 257; '86 314
Fluffy Filling, '81 192; '86 246
Fluffy White Filling, '90 252
Fruit-Nut Filling, '80 289
Fudge Filling, '94 292
Honey Filling, '88 287
Honey-Walnut Filling, '80 21
Lane Cake Filling, '89 55
Lemon-Apricot Filling, '90 105
Lemon-Cheese Filling, '79 68; '88 7
Lemon Cream, '91 119
Lemon Cream Filling, '84 23; '87 14
Lemon Filling, '81 172; '84 137;
    '85 191; '86 235; '87 293; '89 312;
    '90 308; '94 122; '95 319
Lemon Filling, Creamy, '80 70
Lemon-Orange Filling, '81 71
Mocha Cream Filling, '81 187;
    '84 305
Mocha Filling, '80 55; '82 262
Napoleon Cream, '84 138
Nut-and-Fruit Filling, '84 263
Nut Filling, '91 35
Orange-Cheese Filling, '90 47
Orange Filling, '79 229; '86 336; '87 84;
    '88 224; '89 287
Pastry Cream, Luscious, '82 304
Peach Filling, '89 154; '90 107
Peach Pie Filling, Fresh, '95 195
Peppermint Filling, '81 119; '89 254
Pineapple Filling, '80 140; '83 179;
    '84 153; '89 57
Praline Buttercream, '95 243
Praline Filling, '89 328
Raisin Filling, '90 86
Raspberry Filling, '90 111
Ricotta Filling, '80 58
Sour Cream-Coconut Filling, '92 120
Whipped Cream Filling, '90 265, 307
White Chocolate Cream Filling, '92 230
White Chocolate Filling, '89 160
FISH. *See also* **CLAMS, CRAB, LOBSTER, OYSTERS,
    SALMON, SCALLOPS, SEAFOOD, SHRIMP, TUNA.**
Amandine, Fillet of Fish, '80 M54
Amberjack Sandwiches, Grilled, '91 195
Asparagus Divan, Fish-, '87 128
Baked
    Almond Baked Fish, '88 270; '89 203
    Barbecue Sauce, Baked Fish with,
        '84 92
    Creamy Baked Fillets, '84 91
    Creamy Baked Fish Fillets, '85 217
    Crunchy Baked Fish Fillets, '85 217
    Curried Baked Fish, '87 5
    Curry-Baked Fish, '91 196
    Fast Fish Bake, '85 218
    Herbed Fish and Potato Bake, '79 287;
        '80 34

FISH, Baked (continued)

Lemon-Celery Sauce, Baked Fillets in, '84 91
Saucy Fish Bake, '79 75
Southern Baked Fish, '82 73
Beer-Batter Fish, '85 68
Bluefish Chowder, '84 282
Broiled Fish Fillets Piquante, '84 91
Broiled Herb Fish Fillets, '79 99
Cakes, Fish, '85 54
Caper Sauce, Fish in, '95 209
Catfish
Amandine, Mandarin Catfish, '84 183
Amandine, Spicy Catfish, '89 52
Appetizer, Layered Catfish, '92 209
Baked Catfish, '94 67
Barbecued Catfish, '80 157
Barbecued Catfish, Lemon, '88 271;
'89 202
Breaded Catfish with Creole Sauce,
'90 28
Breaded Herbed Fish Fillets, '91 121
Broiled Manchac, Catfish, Middendorf's,
'84 183
Cakes, Catfish, '94 70
Cream Cheese Stuffing, Catfish with,
'89 52
Eldorado de Colorado, Catfish, '84 183
Fingers, Crackermeal Catfish, '89 53
Fried Catfish, '82 135; '83 169
Fried Catfish, Crisp, '82 242
Fried Catfish, Crisp-, '88 110
Fried Catfish, Golden, '80 99
Fry, Burk's Farm-Raised Catfish, '95 158
Fry, Catfish, '84 184
Grilled Catfish Cajun-Style, '90 129
Grilled Catfish with Red Salsa, '90 172
Grilled Catfish with Relish, '92 54
Grilled Fish with Heather Sauce, Catfish
Inn's, '84 182
Gumbo, Catfish, '90 278; '91 216
Kiev-Style, Catfish, '84 184
Louisiana, Catfish, '93 291
Meunière, Catfish, '80 57
Microwave Catfish, '89 M52
Mousse, Catfish, '92 327
Oven-Fried Catfish, '95 106
Oven-Fried Catfish, Southern, '87 163
Parmesan, Catfish, '79 184; '86 210
Parmesan Catfish, '92 309
Pasta with Catfish and Artichokes,
'90 123
Pecan, Catfish, '85 53
Pilaf, Catfish, '94 171
Sesame, Catfish, '81 106
Smoked Catfish, '84 47
Spicy-Seasoned Catfish, '89 M66
Stew, Cajun-Style Catfish, '88 12
Stir, Catfish, '84 184
Stuffed Catfish, Crown Room's
Shrimp-, '84 182
Stuffed Catfish, Soufflé-, '84 183
Ceviche in Avocado Shells, '81 33
Ceviche (Marinated Raw Fish), '80 194;
'82 220
Ceviche, Mexican-Style, '88 115
Chart, Fat and Lean Fish, '85 180
Chowder, Basque Fish, '86 36
Chowder, Chunky Fish, '92 331
Chowder, Creamy Fish, '79 16
Chowder, Fish, '79 152; '84 M38

Chowder, Tasty Fish, '80 188
Corned Fish, '79 32
Crawfish Borscht, '92 84
Crawfish Dressing, Louisiana, '90 103
Crawfish Étouffée, '83 91; '86 156; '90 103;
'94 239
Crawfish Lasagna, '91 89
Crawfish on Eggplant, Soft-Shell, '88 222
Crawfish Salad, Dilled, '83 126
Crawfish Spaghetti, '85 104
Crawfish Stroganoff, '91 89
Crawfish-Stuffed Mushrooms, '86 258
Dinner, Fish-and-Vegetable, '91 196
Dinner, Jollof Rice, '91 230; '92 325
Dip, Smoked Fish, '84 46
en Papillote, Fish with Snow Peas, '86 144
Fillet of Fish à l'Orange, '89 180
Fillets, Apple-Carrot Stuffed, '88 M192
Fillets, Lemon-Coated, '80 M53
Fillets, Pan-Fried Fish, '91 196
Fillets Tomatillo, '94 135
Florentine, Fish, '86 35
Florentine in Parchment, Fish, '87 22
Flounder
Amandine, Flounder, '89 M196
Ambassador, Flounder, '86 234
Aspic, Fish 'n, '84 190
Baked Flounder, '79 31; '90 316
Baked Flounder au Fromage, '86 234
Baked Flounder Supreme, '79 75
Broiled Flounder, '88 28; '89 310
Broiled Flounder, Cheesy, '84 69
Broiled Flounder, Pesto, '86 150
Broil, Flounder-Grapefruit, '85 53
Caesar's Fish, '90 76
Casserole, Green Chile-and-Fish, '84 32
Creole-Style Flounder, '85 180
Crunchy Flounder, Quick, '90 76
Crust, Fish in a, '84 294
Delight, Fish, '86 M212
Dijon, Flounder, '85 95
Fried Fish, '79 151
Fried Fish, Crispy, '84 92
Fried Flounder, Crispy, '84 93
Fried Flounder, Seasoned, '79 214
Grilled Flounder Fillets, '83 213
Hollandaise-Shrimp Sauce, Flounder
with, '86 234
Monterey, Fish, '84 293
Nicole, Flounder, '85 217
Oven-Fried Fish Fillets, '79 75
Papillote, Ocean, '84 M287
Rolls, Vegetable-Filled Fish, '86 M251
Rollups, Shrimp-Stuffed, '82 234
Royal Flounder Fillets, '91 128
Sesame Flounder, '89 33
Shrimp Sauce, Flounder Fillets in,
'83 227
Stuffed Flounder, Crab-, '80 120;
'81 176
Stuffed Flounder Fillets, '86 234
Stuffed Flounder, Grand Lagoon, '94 68
Stuffed Flounder Rolls, Vegetable-, '87 6
Stuffed Flounder Rolls with Citrus Sauce,
'85 180
Stuffed with Shrimp, Flounder, '88 51
Thermidor, Flounder, '85 190
Vegetable Medley, Flounder-, '85 217
Wine Sauce, Fillet of Flounder in,
'80 179; '81 30
Fresh Fish, Preparing, '82 127
Fried Fish, Golden, '82 134
Fried Fish, Southern, '92 168

Greek Fish with Vegetable Sauce, '82 72
Grilled Fish and Vegetables, '89 179
Grilled Fish, Easy, '91 194
Grill Fish, How to Charcoal-, '84 48
Grouper
Baked Grouper, Creamy, '85 292
Breaded Grouper Fillets, '89 M36
Creole Fish, '87 M79
Gourmet Fish, '86 71
Grilled Grouper, '86 185
Grilled Marinated Grouper, '90 166
Herb-Coated Fish, '86 M112
Hot Spicy Grouper, '94 78
Macadamia, Grouper, '85 127
Marinated Grouper, Garlic-Basil, '94 160
Pan-Fried Grouper with Vanilla Wine
Sauce, '94 241
Parmesan Fillets, '86 M112
Sauté, Shrimp-and-Grouper, '87 91
Spectacular, Grouper, '84 163
Vegetables, Grouper with Confetti,
'88 M189
Vegetables, Grouper with Sautéed,
'90 M233
Gumbo, Easy Fish, '81 6
Haddock, Baked, '80 179; '81 30
Haddock Fillets in White Wine, '90 76
Haddock Fillets with Zucchini Stuffing,
'88 M191
Haddock Italiano, '81 M4
Halibut, Chinese-Style Fried, '80 179; '81 30
Halibut Steaks Italiano, '88 M191
Halibut Steak, Wine-Herb, '94 171
Halibut with Champagne Sauce, Baked,
'90 29
Halibut with Cider, '79 182
Halibut with Orange-Curry Sauce, '87 91
Halibut with Swiss Sauce, '83 M195
Hash, Smoked Fish, '92 306
Heroes, Neptune, '84 281
Herring Dip, Yogurt, '80 232
Italian Fish, '88 270; '89 203
Italian Fish, Easy, '86 M112
Mackerel Creole, '80 126
Mackerel, Lemon-Baked, '79 182
Mackerel, Rosemary-Garlic, '92 200
Mackerel, Smoked Salmon or, '84 46
Mahimahi in Grape Sauce, '91 218
Mahi Mahi, Macadamia, '88 164
Marinated Beer-Battered Fish, '86 180
Monkfish, Greek-Style, '87 M79
Mullet, Festive, '79 75
Mullet, Smoked, '84 47
Mullet Spread, '94 159
Orange Roughy-and-Vegetable Stir-Fry,
'91 50
Orange Roughy Fillets with Herb Sauce,
'91 29
Orange Roughy, Kiwi, '87 193
Orange Roughy, Vegetable-Topped, '93 67
Orange Roughy with Herbs, Steamed, '95 189
Orange Roughy with Spinach Pesto,
'88 M192
Orange Roughy with Vegetables, Basil-,
'92 98
Oven-Fried Fish, '91 172; '94 172
Oven-Fried Fish, Mexi-Style, '90 76
Perch Fillets, Buttery Baked, '81 134
Perch, Parmesan-Crusted, '93 91
Poached Fish in Creamy Swiss Sauce, '80 M53
Poached Fish with Greek Sauce, '91 M183
Pollock with Summer Squash Relish, '92 200
Potatoes, Fish-Stuffed, '92 306

84 Fish

FISH (continued)

Potato Platter, Fish-and-, '89 M248
Redfish Court Bouillon, '83 290; '84 93
Roughy with Brown Butter Sauce, Pecan, '91 64
Salad, Smoked Fish-Potato, '84 233
Salad, Smoky Seafood, '84 46
Sautéed Seafood Platter, '83 89
Scamp, Tangy Broiled, '87 5
Seasoning Blend, Fish-and-Seafood, '88 28
Seviche Cocktail, '83 258
Shad Roe with Lemon-Butter Sauce, Baked, '84 252
Shark, Marinated, '79 151
Skillet Fish Dinner, '88 199
Smoked Fish, '92 305
Smoked Fish Log, '85 144
Snapper
    Baked Snapper à l'Orange, '85 181
    Baked Snapper and Stuffing, '82 72
    Baked Snapper with Tarragon Stuffing, '82 136
    Banana Fish, Caribbean, '95 202
    Blackened Red Snapper, '90 27
    Captain's Spicy One, '81 125
    Caribbean Banana Fish, '95 202
    Caribbean Snapper, '87 5
    Chowder, Red Snapper, '85 217
    Company Red Snapper, '82 72
    Destin, Snapper, '88 222
    Dill, Snapper with, '84 190
    Gumbo, Savannah Snapper, '94 105
    Honey-Curried Snapper, '85 181
    Huachinango à la Veracruzana (Veracruz-Style Red Snapper), '80 193
    Louisiane, Red Snapper, '85 217
    Orangy Snapper, '88 23
    Oven-Fried Snapper, '90 75
    Peppered Snapper with Creamy Dill Sauce, '94 42
    Poached Fish with Vegetables, '89 332; '90 18
    Poached Red Snapper, '85 127
    Poached Snapper, '83 101
    Provençal, Snapper, '91 M170
    Rome, Fillet of Snapper, '80 57
    Southwestern Snapper, '91 195
    Spanish-Style Fillets, '86 M112
    Spicy Snapper, '89 179
    Stuffed Red Snapper Rolls, Cucumber-, '83 176
    Stuffed Red Snapper with Lime, '83 246
    Stuffed Snapper, '87 138
    Vegetables, Yellowtail Snapper with Julienne, '93 31
    Veracruz, Red Snapper, '88 149; '92 142
    Wine Sauce, Red Snapper in, '85 138
Sole Divan, '87 21
Sole Fillets, Herbed, '82 21
Sole Fillets in Wine Sauce, '81 109
Sole in Papillote, '82 22
Sole Provençal, Fillet of, '85 78
Sole Royale, '89 104
Sole, Saucy, '82 M68
Sole Véronique, '85 181
Sole with Cucumber Sauce, '84 M286
Soup with Garlic Mayonnaise, Rich Fish, '92 56
Sour Cream, Fish with, '89 180
Spread, Smoked Fish, '92 305
Steaks, Soy Fish, '86 M112

Steamed Fish and Vegetables, '91 32
Stew, Fish-and-Vegetable, '87 220
Stock, Fish, '95 19
Stock, Homemade Fish, '92 237
Surprise, Fish, '84 231
Sweet-and-Sour Fish, '80 M54
Swordfish, Foil-Baked, '87 5
Swordfish, Skewered, '86 256
Swordfish Steaks, Orange-Ginger Marinated, '93 271
Swordfish Steak with Chervil Butter, '91 147
Swordfish with Caper Sauce, Grilled, '95 230
Tacos, Barbecued Fish, '95 339
Tomato Sauce, Fish in, '85 75
Trout
    Amandine, Fish, '85 179
    Amandine, Orange Lake, '80 99
    Baked Trout, '95 106
    Cakes with Lemon-Butter Sauce, Mountain Trout, '92 337
    Delmonico, Trout, '80 57
    Fillets with Capers, Trout, '95 252
    Florentine, Cheesy Trout, '85 53
    Grilled Trout, '95 106
    Grilled Trout with Ginger and Soy Sauce, '85 228
    Laurie, Trout, '88 270; '89 202
    Poached Trout, '95 106
    Smoked Trout, '84 47
    Spread, Smoked Trout, '84 47
    Stuffed Rainbow Trout, '93 121
    Sunshine Trout, '84 M286
    Wine Sauce, Trout in, '80 180; '81 31
Two, Fish for, '92 60
Vegetables, Cheesy Fish and, '94 254
Veracruz Fish with Shrimp, '86 130
Whitefish Spread, Smoked, '92 58

FRANKFURTERS

Appetizer Franks, Saucy, '84 M12
Appetizers, Bourbon Frankfurter, '85 207
Bacon-Wrapped Franks, '81 202
Barbecued Frankfurters, '83 144; '84 M12
Barbecued Frankfurters, Oven-, '83 11
Barbecued Franks, '85 192
Barbecue, Tangy Frank, '79 63
Beans and Franks, '85 142
Beans and Franks, Hawaiian Baked, '80 136
Beans and Franks, Jiffy, '91 M172
Beans-and-Franks, Polynesian, '84 M11
Beans, Stove-Top Franks 'n', '88 201
Beany Hot Dogs, '82 190
Cabbage with Apples and Franks, '87 42
Casserole, Hot Doggie, '88 200
Casserole, Layered Frankfurter, '79 64
Chafing Dish Franks, '83 143
Chili-Cheese Dogs, '81 M176
Corn Dog Bites, '85 245; '93 79
Corn Dogs, Favorite, '83 144
Corn Relish Dogs, '85 192
Crusty Franks, '80 166
Delicious, Hot Dogs, '81 202
Family-Style Franks, '79 54
Grilled Stuffed Franks, '82 163
Hash Browns, Franks and, '80 166
Hawaiian Franks, '81 202
Jubilee, Hot Dog, '81 113
Kraut and Franks, Beany, '79 64
Mexicali Hot Dogs, '82 131
Mexican Franks, '93 78
Pickled Party Franks, '83 174
Pigs in a Blanket, '95 178
Pizzas, Hot Dog, '93 78
Potatoes, Cheesy Frank-Topped, '83 3

Potatoes, Frank-Filled, '84 M11
Potluck Dish, Frankaroni, '88 201
Sandwiches, Frankfurter, '84 M11
Sauce, Hot Diggity Dog, '93 198
Saucy Franks, '88 201
Scrambled Dog, Dinglewood Pharmacy's, '95 118
Skillet Dinner, Frankfurter, '80 166
Skillet, Frankfurter-Cabbage, '80 166
Skillet, Hot Dog and Spaghetti, '83 144
Sloppy Joe Dogs, '85 192
Soup, Split Pea and Frankfurter, '79 64
Spanish Frankfurters, '80 166
Spicy Frankfurters, '81 202
Stuffed Franks and Potatoes, '81 202
Supper, Hot Dog, '93 78
Tipsy Franks, '85 52

FRENCH TOAST

Almond French Toast, '88 62
Amandine, Baked Toast, '82 47
au Fromage, French Toast, '88 288
Caribbean French Toast, '92 46
Cinnamon French Toast, '84 211
Cottage-Topped French Toast, '85 49
Easy French Toast, '82 M172
Eggnog French Toast, '95 313
Grand Marnier Fruit Sauce, French Toast with, '90 93
Macadamia French Toast, '86 96
Macadamia Nut French Toast, '95 282
Orange Butter, French Toast with, '81 42
Orange French Toast, '83 292; '84 78; '86 329
Orange Sauce, French Toast with, '82 47
Oven-Baked French Toast, '82 47; '90 192
Oven-Baked French Toast, Easy, '93 195
Overnight French Toast, '89 227
Overnight French Toast Deluxe, '79 216
Pain-Perdu Po-Boy, '93 291
Peanut Butter French Toast, '93 166
Potato-Crusted Texas Toast, '94 142
Sandwiches, Strawberry-French Toast, '91 160
Slender French Toast, '86 103
Stuffed French Toast, Three Cheese, '93 122
Waffled French Toast, '82 47

FRITTERS

Apple Fritter Rings, '88 44
Apple Fritters, '81 105; '82 273; '85 14
Apple Holiday Fritters, '86 314
Banana Fritters, '79 213
Blueberry Fritters, '85 152
Broccoli Fritters, Cheesy, '79 53
Buñuelos, '93 29
Clam Fritters, '79 151; '86 71
Corn Fritters, '86 192; '94 22
Corn Fritters, Golden, '80 165; '81 128
Corn Fritters, Skillet-Fried, '85 14
Eggplant Fritters, '91 211
Ham Fritters, '82 39
Ham Fritters with Creamy Sauce, '81 105
Okra, Fritter-Fried, '86 218
Okra Fritters, '79 160
Orange Fritters, Puffy, '81 169
Oyster Fritters, '79 31
Pear Fritters, Ol' Timey, '86 51
Pecan Fritters, Chocolate-Covered, '79 205
Pineapple Fritters, '88 112
Squash Fritters, '89 68
Sweet Potato Fritters, '88 44
Sweet Potato Fritters, Golden, '79 9
Zucchini Fritters, '81 163
Zucchini Fritters, Cheesy, '88 44

FROG LEGS
Crispy Frog Legs, '80 99
Fried Frog Legs, '88 110
FROM OUR KITCHEN TO YOURS (FOKTY)
Alcohol
substituting in recipes, '92 314
Apples, '84 227, 228
amounts to buy, '84 228
preventing browning after cutting,
'84 228
selecting for cooking, '84 227, 228
selecting for eating, '84 227, 228
storing, '84 228
Appliances, kitchen. See FOKTY/Kitchen,
Dishwasher, Food processor, Freezer,
Microwave oven, Oven, Refrigerator.
Arrowroot, as a thickening agent, '83 147
Barbecue, '94 155. See also FOKTY/Grilling.
chicken, '94 155
Bay leaves, removing from soups, '95 314
Beans, dried, '88 4
buying, '88 4
cooking, '88 4
soaking, '88 4
storing, '88 4
Beef, '83 38; '92 65, 66; '94 140
browning, '83 38
buying, '83 38; '90 276; '92 65
cooking methods, '83 38
fat content of, '92 65, 66; '94 140
handling properly, '87 208; '94 140
making gravy from pan drippings,
'83 38
storing, '94 140
tenderizing, '83 38
Beverages, '83 191; '90 276, 277. See also
FOKTY/Alcohol, Buttermilk, Eggnog, Ice,
Tea, Wines.
determining amounts to buy for
entertaining, '90 276, 277
freezing, '92 314
ice molds, '86 331
placement of in basic table setting,
'90 182
placement of when entertaining,
'90 277
substituting for alcohol in recipes,
'92 314
Biscuits, '89 211, 212; '92 52. See also
FOKTY/Breads, Rolls, Yeast.
baking, '89 211, 212
cutting dough, '89 211; '95 30
freezing, '89 212
kneading, '92 52
making dough for, '89 211;
'92 52
reheating, '89 212
storing leftovers, '89 212
using food processor to make,
'89 211, 212
Breads, '82 198; '84 92; '89 268; '92 52,
102, 314; '93 183. See also
FOKTY/Biscuits, Rolls, Yeast.
cutting, '91 144, 145
doubling recipes, '91 22
freezing, '89 268; '90 315; '91 95;
'92 102
as gifts, '91 95
metal dough scraper, '90 126; '92 52
microwave oven, '89 268
quick breads, '84 92; '89 268
rising procedures, '87 12; '89 268
testing for doneness, '84 92; '92 314

yeast breads, '84 92; '87 12; '89 268;
'92 314
yeast rolls, '83 323
Broccoli, '84 249
cutting, '93 132
preparing, '84 249
selecting, '84 249
Broths. See FOKTY/Soups.
Brussels Sprouts, '84 249
preparing, '84 249
selecting, '84 249
Butter, '82 189; '95 314
availability of, '82 189
balls, how to make, '82 189
clarifying, '82 189
curls, how to make, '82 189
fat content of, '82 189
storing, '82 189
substituting for in baked goods,
'90 314
Buttermilk, freezing, '92 314
Cactus (Nopales), '94 29
cooking, '94 29
selecting, '94 29
storing, '94 29
Cakes, '89 57, 58; '91 144, 200, 201;
'92 154, 155, 314; '94 59
baking techniques, '89 57
cheesecakes, eliminating cracks in,
'91 300
cooling, '92 155
cutting, '91 144; '92 314; '95 30
decorating, '94 59
dry ingredients, '87 12; '92 155
freezing, '89 58; '90 314, 315
frosting, '89 57, 58
greasing pans, '92 314
jellyroll cakes, '92 314
mixing procedures, '89 57; '92 154, 155
pan sizes, '92 154, 314
pound cakes, '84 92, 319 (baking tips
chart); '92 154, 155
as snacks, '91 200, 201
storing, '89 57, 58; '92 155
substituting flours, '92 155
testing for doneness, '84 92; '92 155
Campsite cooking, '86 172
cleaning up, '86 172
making lists, '86 172
packing, '86 172
planning, '86 172
Canning fruits and vegetables, '84 180;
'89 141, 142; '93 136, 137. See also
FOKTY/Paraffin.
boiling water bath, '84 180; '89 141,
142; '91 300; '93 136, 137
equipment, '93 137
packing, '84 180; '89 141, 142
safety, '84 180; '89 141, 142; '91 300;
'93 137
steam pressure method of, '84 180;
'89 141, 142
Casseroles
doubling recipes, '91 22, 23, 96
freezing, '90 314; '91 96
preventing spoilage of, '87 208
Cast-iron cookware, '93 33
caring for, '93 33
seasoning, '93 33
Cauliflower, '84 249
cutting, '93 132
preparing, '84 249
selecting, '84 249

Centerpieces, '90 205
Champagne. See FOKTY/Wines.
Cheese, '82 109
buying, '85 210; '90 276
cooking with, '85 210; '87 12
freezing, '82 109; '85 211
handling properly, '87 208
serving, '85 210, 211
shredding, '95 31 (illustration)
as snacks, '91 200, 201
storing, '85 210
Cheesecakes. See FOKTY/Cakes.
Chicken, '87 12; '88 39; '94 155, 253
barbecuing, '94 155
boning, '88 39
cooking, '87 12; '88 39; '95 246
cutting up, '94 253
handling properly, '87 208
microwaving, '88 39
packaging of, '88 39
preparing for stir-frying, '91 160
Children. in the kitchen, '91 92; '92 102, 207
China, '88 301
removing marks from, '88 301
storing, '88 301
washing, '88 301
Chinese cooking, '85 76
equipment, '85 76
garnishing, '85 76
preparing food for, '85 76
Chocolate, '86 246, 247; '92 314; '93 317
dipping, '86 330, 331
garnishing with, '86 247; '93 317;
'94 59
illustrations for chocolate sacks, '93 317
kinds of, '86 246, 247
melting, '92 314; '93 317
substitutions, '86 246, 247
white chocolate, '86 246, 247; '94 59
Cholesterol, '90 72
and food labels, '90 72
Cookies, '91 234; '92 207, 208; '95 30
baking, '92 208
cooling, '92 208
crushing, '95 30
equipment, '92 208
freezing, '90 314; '92 207, 208;
as gifts, '91 95
mixing procedures, '92 207
storing, '92 208
testing for doneness, '84 92
Cooking directions, basic, '87 12, 208.
See also FOKTY/Handling food properly,
Recipe preparation.
chicken, '87 12
shrimp, '87 12
Cooking spray. See FOKTY/Vegetable cooking
spray.
Cookware, '85 329; '86 227; '90 50;
'93 33, 183, 220. See also FOKTY/
Cast-iron cookware.
caring for, '85 329; '93 33, 183
for microwave, '86 227
selecting, '85 329; '86 227; '93 220
Cornbread, '87 16
cornmeal, '87 16
ingredients in, '87 16
making cornbread, '87 16
Cornmeal, '87 16
making cornbread, '87 16
understanding the label, '87 16
Cornstarch, '83 146, 147
as a thickening agent, '83 146, 147

Crab, cracking, '95 156
Cranberries
    buying, '92 314
    freezing, '92 314
    frosted cranberries (garnish), '82 280
Crystal, '88 300, 301
    removing discolorations and stains,
      '88 300, 301
    repairing chips, '88 300
    storing, '88 300
    washing, '88 300, 301
Custards
    preparing and storing properly (chart),
      '87 208
    testing for doneness, '84 92
    thickening, '83 147
Cutting boards, '87 208
    acrylic, '87 208
    cleaning, '87 208
    and food safety, '87 208
    wooden, '87 208
Dishwasher, '87 130
Drying foods, '93 23
    cherry tomatoes, '93 23
    equipment, '93 23
    safety, '93 23
    uses for, '93 23
Eggnog, freezing, '92 314
Eggs, '83 147, 214; '89 26. *See also*
    FOKTY/Meringue.
    cooking methods, '83 214
    handling properly (chart), '87 208
    pasteurized egg substitute, '89 26
    preventing curdling, '82 198; '83 147
    using raw egg whites, '91 300
    using raw egg yolks, '89 26
    yolks, thick and lemon colored, '83 214
Entertaining, '84 122, 123; '88 276;
    '90 182, 276, 277; '91 300; '94 17, 18
    determining amounts of food to buy,
      '90 276 (chart)
    determining traffic flow, '84 122, 123;
      '86 191; '90 276, 277
    making preparations for, '84 122;
      '86 191; '94 17, 18
    outdoors, '86 191
    presenting food, '84 122; '88 276
    selecting menus for, '84 122; '86 191;
      '88 276; '90 276
    serving food safely, '91 300
    setting up a bar for, '90 277
    table setting, '90 182 (illustration), 276
Equivalents of ingredients, '91 22, 23
Etiquette, '90 225
    basic manners at the table, '90 225
Fat, dietary, '82 189; '90 72; '91 200, 201;
    '92 65, 66; '93 207
    in beef, '92 65, 66
    in butter, '82 189; '90 314
    eliminating in snacks, '91 200, 201
    and food labels, '90 72; '92 65; '93 207
    in margarine, '82 189; '90 314
    storing, '82 189
Fish, '84 48; '87 79, 80; '90 130;
    '94 105, 106. *See also* FOKTY/Seafood,
    Shrimp, Surimi.
    buying, '84 48; '87 79, 80; '90 130;
      '94 106
    cooking, '87 80
    eliminating odors on hands, '82 109

fat fish, '87 79
freezing, '87 80
grilling, '84 48; '92 52
handling properly, '87 208
lean fish, '87 79
market forms of, '87 79
selecting fish for grilling, '84 48;
    '90 130
storing, '87 80; '90 130; '94 105, 106
substituting, '90 130
thawing, '87 80; '90 130
transporting fresh, '94 105, 106
Flour, '82 197, 198
    all purpose, '82 197, 198; '87 12
    cake flour, '82 197, 198; '87 12
    cracked wheat, '82 197, 198
    sifting, '82 197, 198; '87 12
    storing, '82 197, 198
    types of, '82 197, 198
Flowers, edible, '94 59
    crystallizing, '94 59
Food processor, '82 109; '86 13
    chopping nuts, '92 314; '95 208
Food safety. *See* FOKTY/Handling food
    properly.
Freezer, '83 14, 15; '86 50, 51; '87 112, 208;
    '93 83, 84
    amount of food to store in, '87 112
    casseroles in, '87 112
    cleaning, '84 11; '87 112
    constant freezer temperature, '86 50
    defrosting, '87 112
    foods that freeze well, '86 50; '87 112;
      '90 314, 315
    fruits in, '87 112
    labeling foods in, '84 11; '86 51;
      '87 112
    leftovers, freezing safely, '87 112
    organizing foods in, '87 112
    and power loss, '83 14, 15; '93 83, 84
    preventing sogginess of particular foods
      to be frozen, '87 112
    refreezing foods, '83 15; '93 83, 84
    reheating frozen foods, '87 112
    sausage, '87 238
    vegetables in, '87 112
    wraps and containers for freezing foods,
      '86 50, 51; '87 112
Fruitcakes, '83 285; '86 331; '95 343
    storing, '83 285; '86 331
    purchasing candied fruit for, '92 314
Fruits, '83 94; '85 233; '89 141, 142;
    '92 248, 249, 250. *See also* FOKTY/Apples,
    Kiwifruit, Mangoes, Melons, Pears.
    canning, '84 180; '89 141, 142
    in centerpieces, '90 205
    exotic fruits, '92 248, 249, 250
    fall fruits, '85 233
    freezing, '87 112
    nutritive values of, '92 248, 249, 250
    preparing, '92 248, 249, 250
    selecting, '84 186, 187;
      '92 248, 249, 250
    as snacks, '91 200, 201
    storing, '83 94; '92 248, 249, 250
Frying foods, '84 211; '88 112, 113
    cooking fat to use, '88 113
    equipment, '88 113
    safety, '90 22
    techniques, '88 113
Garlic, '93 182
    baker, '94 332
    press, '94 332

Garnishes, '82 138, 280; '89 100; '90 108;
    '93 317; '94 59
    chocolate sacks, '93 317
    curling garnishes, '89 100
    eggs, hard-cooked, '82 280
    flowers, crystallized edible, '94 59
    fruit garnishes, '82 280
    illustrations, '89 100; '90 108; '93 317
    making ahead, '89 100
    piped garnishes, '82 280; '86 330;
      '90 108
    utensils for creating, '89 100; '90 108
    vegetable garnishes, '82 280;
      '89 100, 243; '95 343
    whipped cream, '86 330
Gelatin, '83 124, 125; '91 300
    chilling, '83 124; '86 13
    molds, determining size of, '82 313
    softening, '91 300
    unmolding, '83 124, 125; '86 330
    using fresh fruits and vegetables in,
      '91 300
Gifts of food, '86 289; '91 95, 96; '95 343
    containers for, '86 289; '91 95, 96
    freezing, '91 95, 96
    mailing, '86 289
    storing, '91 95, 96
    wrapping, '86 289
Gingerroot, '94 29
    cooking with, '92 314; '94 29
    selecting, '94 29
    in stir-frying, '92 314
    storing, '92 314
Grating citrus rind, '95 314
Gravies, '83 38; '86 330
    serving and storing properly (chart),
      '87 208
Grilling, '82 109; '83 191; '84 48; '86 172;
    '88 145, 146; '92 202; '93 103, 104. *See
    also* FOKTY/Smoking (cooking method).
    avoiding flare-ups, '88 145; '92 202
    basting, '82 109; '88 146; '93 103
    charcoal, '82 109; '93 103, 104
    cleanup, '93 104
    cooking times, '95 194 (chart)
    direct/indirect cooking methods,
      '88 145; '93 103, 104; '95 194
    equipment, '82 109; '88 146; '92 52;
      '93 103; '95 274
    flavoring with wood chips, '88 145;
      '93 103
    kabobs, '88 146; '93 103
    temperature of fire, '82 109;
      '88 145, 146; '95 195
    thermometer, '93 103, 104; '95 195
Grocery shopping, '84 11; '91 187, 188
    best time for, '84 11
    comparative shopping, '91 188
    determining best values (chart), '91 188
    making lists for, '82 312; '83 284; '84 11
    planning menus, '82 312; '83 284;
      '84 11
    saving time and money, '91 187, 188
    stocking up, '91 188
    using coupons, '91 188
Ham, '89 333, 334; '90 276
    cooking in microwave oven, '89 333, 334
    determining amount to buy for
      entertaining, '90 276
    freezing, '89 334
    preparing, '89 333, 334
    selecting, '89 333
    storing, '89 334

Handling food properly, '87 208; '89 26;
  '91 300; '92 202; '93 23, 83, 84.
  See also FOKTY/Beef, Canning, Chicken,
  Eggs, Fish, Turkey.
    chart, '87 208
    egg whites, raw, '91 300
    egg yolks, raw, '89 26
    when entertaining, '91 300
Herbs, '85 58; '89 121. *See also*
  FOKTY/Seasonings, Spices.
    amounts to use, '89 121; '95 30
    chart, '89 121
    cooking with, '85 58
    drying, '85 58
    freezing, '85 58
    gathering fresh, '85 58; '89 121
    storing, '85 58; '89 121
Ice
    dry ice, '83 14, 15
    molds, '86 331
Ice cream, '82 171; '86 215
    adding fresh fruit to homemade, '82 171
    homemade, '82 171
    varieties of, '86 215
Kitchen, '83 191; '84 10, 11, 148, 149;
  '90 22, 50; '93 220; '94 332
    appliances, '87 130
    basic equipment, '90 50; '93 220;
      '94 332
    cookware, '85 329; '90 50; '93 220
    countertops, '84 148, 149
    gadgets, '86 13; '90 126; '94 332;
      '95 343
    keeping cool in summer, '83 191
    knives, '91 144, 145
    organizing, '84 10, 11
    safety in, '84 37; '90 22
    shears, '91 160; '92 52
Kiwifruit, peeling, '95 31 (illustration)
Knives, '84 11; '91 144, 145
    buying, '91 144, 145
    sharpening, '91 144, 145
    storing, '84 11
    using properly, '86 13; '91 144, 145
    varieties of, '91 144, 145 (illustration)
Labels, food, '90 72; '93 207; '94 140
    chart, '90 72
    sample label, '93 207
    understanding, '90 72; '93 207
Lamb, '88 59
    buying, '88 59
    cooking, '88 59; '95 105 (chart)
    seasoning, '95 105
    selecting, '88 59
    storing, '88 59; '95 105 (chart)
Leftovers, '82 313; '87 112, 208; '92 314;
  '95 30, 274
    bread slices, '82 313
    buns, '82 313
    freezing, '87 112, 208; '92 314
Lettuce, '86 80; '95 67
    coring, '86 80
    selecting, '86 80
    storing, '86 80
    types of (illustration), '86 80
    yields, '86 80
List making, '82 312; '83 284; '84 11, 122;
  '86 172
    and grocery shopping, '88 165;
      '91 188

and meal planning, '82 312; '83 284;
  '84 11; '91 188
    telephone numbers for emergencies,
      '84 37
Mailing food, '86 289
Mangoes, '94 192
Manners. *See* FOKTY/Etiquette.
Margarine, '82 189
    availability of, '82 189
    diet margarine, '82 189
    fat content of, '82 189; '90 314
    storing, '82 189
    substituting in baked goods, '90 314
Marinating, '88 165; '95 30
    containers to use, '87 208
Masa harina, '94 192
Meal planning, '82 312, 313; '83 191, 284;
  '84 122, 123; '86 13; '88 165, 276.
  See also FOKTY/Snacks.
    advance planning, '82 312, 313; '86 172
    for a crowd, '82 313; '86 191
    for holidays, '83 284
    making lists, '82 312; '83 284;
      '84 11, 122; '86 172
    party menus, '82 313; '84 122, 123;
      '86 191; '88 276
Measuring, '85 192, 193; '86 13
    butter, '85 192, 193
    determining cup measurement of dish,
      '85 193
    dry measuring utensils, '85 192, 193
    how to measure accurately, '85 192, 193
    liquid measuring utensils, '85 192, 193
    sifting ingredients for, '82 197, 198;
      '85 192, 193; '87 12
    solid shortening, '85 192, 193
Meats, '89 191, 192; '91 300; '92 202. *See
  also* FOKTY/Beef.
    handling properly, '87 208
    meat-cure mix, '91 300
    serving safely, '87 208; '91 300
    standing time, '89 192
    suggested cooking temperatures,
      '89 191, 192; '92 202
    using a meat thermometer, '89 191, 192;
      '92 202
Melons, '88 183
    cantaloupe, '88 183
    honeydew, '88 183
    selecting, '88 183
    storing, '88 183
    watermelon, '88 183
Meringue, '83 214
    baking, '83 214
    equipment, '83 214
    humidity, effects of, '83 214
    making, '83 214
    powder, '92 314
    preventing weeping, '83 214; '95 246
Microwave oven, '83 191; '84 211;
  '86 113, 227; '87 130; '92 176
    cleaning, '87 130
    cookware for, '86 227
    features, '86 113
    recipe, Microwave Fudge, '91 92
    roasting peppers in, '92 176
    safety when using, '91 92
    sizes, '86 113
    variations of, '86 113
    wattage, '86 113
Mushrooms
    as garnish, '82 280
    storing, '92 314

Nopales. *See* FOKTY/Cactus.
Nutrition, '90 72; '91 200, 201;
  '92 65
    food labels, '90 72; '92 65
    snacks, '91 200, 201
Olive oil, '89 175
    flavored, '89 175
    selecting, '89 175
    storing, '89 175
    varieties of, '89 175
Onions, '88 87; '95 30
    chopping, '92 314; '95 246
    cooking with, '88 87
    eliminating odor on hands, '82 109;
      '94 332
    extracting onion juice, '88 87
    grating, '92 314; '95 30
    selecting, '88 87
    varieties of (illustrations), '88 87
Outdoor cooking. *See* FOKTY/Campsite
  cooking, Grilling, Smoking (cooking
  method).
Ovens, '83 191; '84 211; '86 113; '87 130
    cleaning, '87 130
    convection, '86 113
    conventional, '86 113
    microwave, '83 191; '84 211; '86 113;
      '87 130
    preheating, '86 13
Paraffin, '89 244
    as a seal in canning, '84 180; '89 142;
      '91 300
Pastas, '87 177
    basic categories, '87 177
    cooking, '87 177; '95 30
    measuring, '87 177
    reheating, '87 177; '95 31
    storing, '87 177
    substituting, '87 177
Pastry. *See* FOKTY/Piecrust.
Peanuts, '83 228, 229
    boiling, '83 228
    chopping, '83 229
    roasting, '83 228
Pears, '85 233
    cooking, '85 233
    peeling, '85 233
    ripening, '85 233
    selecting, '85 233
Peas, dried, '88 4
    buying, '88 4
    cooking, '88 4
    soaking, '88 4
    storing, '88 4
Pecans, '83 228, 229; '94 59
    chopping, '83 229; '95 208
    as garnish, '94 59
    toasting, '83 228
Peppers, '85 4; '92 176; '94 29; '95 30, 208
    freezing, '85 4
    as garnish, '82 280; '89 100
    removing skins of, '85 4
    roasting, '92 176
    selecting, '94 29
    storing, '94 29
    substituting, '85 4
    types of, '85 4
    working with hot peppers, '85 4; '94 29;
      '95 208
Persimmons, '85 233
    freezing, '85 233
    preparing, '85 233
    selecting, '85 233

Pickles, '87 150
  pickling vegetables, '87 150
  spoilage, '87 150
Piecrust, '82 234, 235; '92 52, 314; '94 210;
  '95 246
  equipment, '82 234; '94 332; '95 208
  finishing, '82 234
  glazing, '82 235
  mixing, '82 234; '92 52; '95 246
  preventing overbrowning, '92 314;
    '95 30
  preventing sogginess, '86 330; '91 300;
    '92 314
  recipe, Water-Whipped Baked Pastry
    Shell, '95 246
  rolling, '82 234; '92 314
  variations of, '82 234, 235
Planning meals. See FOKTY/Meal planning.
Poaching, '85 127
  eggs, '85 127
  equipment, '85 127
  fish, '85 127
  fruits, '85 127
  liquid to use, '85 127
Pork, cooking, '95 246
Potatoes, '84 210, 211. See also
  FOKTY/Sweet Potatoes.
  preparing, '84 210, 211
  selecting, '84 210, 211
  storing, '84 211
Poultry. See FOKTY/Chicken, Turkey.
Pound cakes. See FOKTY/Cakes.
Puddings, '86 330. See also FOKTY/Custards.
  preventing "skin" from forming, '86 330
Pumpkins, '85 233
  preparing for cooking, '85 233
  selecting, '85 233
  storing, '85 233
Raspberries, making sauce, '92 314
Recipe preparation, '86 13; '91 22, 23;
  '93 235. See also FOKTY/Cooking
  directions, Handling food properly,
  Substitutions.
  cleaning up, '86 13; '95 31 (illustration)
  determining solutions to problems,
    '93 235
  doubling recipes, '91 22, 23; '92 66;
    '95 30
  equipment, '86 13
  measuring, '86 13; '95 274
  planning menus, '86 13
  preparing ingredients, '86 13; '95 30, 31
    (illustration), 208
  substitutions, '92 314, 344
  utensils, '86 13
Recycling, '92 28
  items to be recycled, '92 28
  packaging of products, '92 28
  setting up home recycling center, '92 28
  the three Rs, '92 28
Refrigerator, '83 94; '87 130
  canned foods (opened), '83 94
  cleaning, '84 11; '87 130
  dairy products, '83 94
  food storage chart, '83 94
  meats, '83 94
Rice, '87 46
  cooking, '95 30
  flavoring, '87 46
  forms of, '87 46

preparing, '87 46
  reheating, '87 46
  storing, '87 46
  types of, '87 46
Rolls, '83 323. See also FOKTY/Biscuits,
  Breads, Yeast.
  glazing, '83 323
  variations of, '83 323
  yeast, '83 323
Roux, '87 211, 212
  color of, '87 211, 212
  cooking temperature, '87 211
  cooking times, '87 211
  ingredient amounts, '87 211
  microwave roux, '87 211, 212
  oven roux, '87 211
  reducing fat in roux, '87 212
  utensils to use, '87 212
Safety, '84 37, 180; '90 22; '91 92, 300.
  See also FOKTY/Handling food properly.
  canning fruits and vegetables, '84 180;
    '91 300
  first aid for burns, '90 22
  in the kitchen, '84 37; '90 22
  preventing burns in the kitchen, '84 37;
    '90 22
  when serving food, '91 300
  when using the microwave, '91 92
Salads, '82 313; '95 67
  congealed, '82 313; '91 300
  equipment, '94 332
Sauces, '83 146, 147; '92 314; '94 274;
  '95 30
  chilling quickly, '86 13
  reduction sauces, '94 274
  thickening, '83 146, 147
Sausage, '87 238
  classifications of, '87 238
  freezing, '87 238
  meat-cure mix, '91 300
Seafood, '90 130. See also FOKTY/Crab, Fish,
  Shellfish, Shrimp, Surimi.
Seasonings, '92 121, 344; '93 182. See also
  FOKTY/Herbs, Spices.
  in recipes, '91 22
  recipes for seasoning blends, '92 121
  storing, '82 198; '84 11; '92 121
  substitutions, '92 344
Shellfish, '94 105, 106
  buying, '94 106
  transporting fresh, '94 105, 106
Shelf life, '83 65
  of canned foods, '83 65
  chart, '83 65
  of packaged mixes, '83 65
  of staples, '83 65
Shopping. See FOKTY/Grocery shopping.
Shrimp, '87 12; '94 105, 106
  cooking, '87 12
  deveining, '92 52
  grilling, '92 52
  selecting, '94 106
  transporting fresh, '94 105
Sifting, '82 197, 198; '85 192, 193; '87 12
  flour, '82 197, 198; '87 12
  powdered sugar, '85 192; '87 12
Silver, '88 300
  avoiding spotting and pitting, '88 300
  cleaning, '88 300
  removing tarnish, '88 300
  storing, '88 300
Smoking (cooking method), '95 116
  adding the food, '95 116

cleaning the smoker, '95 117
  filling the water pan, '95 116
  maintaining the temperature, '95 116
  soaking the wood, '95 116
  starting the fire, '95 116
Snacks, '91 200, 201
  nutritious, '91 200 201
  planning, '91 200, 201
  recipes for, '91 200, 201
Sodium, '90 72
  content of in surimi, '90 130
  and food labels, '90 72
Soufflés, '84 92
  testing for doneness, '84 92
Soups, '89 30; '95 274
  broths, '89 30
  freezing, '89 30
  as gifts, '91 95
  reheating, '89 30
  removing bay leaf, '95 314
  stocks, '89 30; '95 30
  storing, '89 30
Spices, '87 297. See also FOKTY/Herbs,
  Seasonings.
  amounts to use, '87 297
  buying, '87 297
  checking for freshness, '84 11; '87 297
  grinding your own, '87 297
  storing, '82 198; '84 11; '87 297
  substituting, '87 297
  whole spices, '87 297
Squash, winter, '88 229, 230
  cooking, '88 229, 230
  determining amount to buy, '88 229
  selecting, '88 229, 230
  storing, '88 229, 230
  types of, '88 229, 230
Stir frying, '95 30
Stocks. See FOKTY/Soups.
Strawberries, '82 109
  buying, '82 109
  as garnish, '82 138
Substitutions, '92 344
  alcohol, '92 314
  emergency substitutions (chart),
    '92 344
Sugar, '85 19
  making colored sugar, '86 331
  measuring, '85 19; '87 12
  powdered sugar, '87 12
  preventing brown sugar from drying out,
    '85 19
  sifting powdered sugar, '85 192; '87 12
  substitutions, '85 19
  types of, '85 19
Surimi, '90 130
Sweet potatoes, '88 208. See also
  FOKTY/Potatoes.
  cooking, '88 208
  handling, '88 208
  selecting, '88 208
  storing, '88 208
  substituting canned for fresh, '88 208
  yams, '88 208
Table setting, '90 182, 225
  centerpieces, '90 205
  for formal entertaining, '90 182
  illustration, '90 182
Tamales, '94 192. See also FOKTY/
  Masa harina.
  making tamale dough, '94 192
Tapioca, as a thickening agent, '83 147
Tarts, '95 274

Tea, '85 120, 121
    brewing, '85 120, 121
    storing, '85 121
    types of, '85 120, 121
Thawing food, '83 14, 15; '86 330; '87 208;
    '88 165
    turkey, '83 284; '86 330
Thermometers, '89 191, 192; '92 202;
    '93 103, 104
    deep-fat frying, '84 37
    instant-read, '89 191, 192; '92 202, 314;
        '93 104
    meat, '89 191, 192; '92 202
    storing, '89 192; '92 202
    testing for accuracy, '89 192; '92 202
Thickening agents, '83 146, 147.
    See also FOKTY/Arrowroot, Cornstarch,
    Eggs, Tapioca.
Tomatoes, '85 181, 182; '93 23; '95 30
    drying cherry tomatoes, '93 23
    as garnish, '82 280; '89 100
    peeling large amount of, '82 138;
        '85 181, 182
    recipe, Marinated Dried Cherry
        Tomatoes, '93 23
    ripening, '85 181
    seeding, '85 182
    selecting, '85 181
    slicing, '85 181, 182
    storing, '85 181
    stuffing, '85 182
Tortillas, '95 44
    equipment, '95 44
    how to cook, '95 44
    how to shape, '95 44
    recipe, Flour Tortillas '95 44
    reheating, '95 44
    storing, '95 44
Turkey, '83 284, 285; '93 306, 307
    carving, '93 306, 307
    chart, '83 285
    cooking, '83 284, 285; '86 330
    determining amounts to buy for
        entertaining, '90 276
    handling properly, '87 208
    leftovers, storing, '83 285
    stuffing, '83 284
    thawing, '83 284; '86 330
U.S. Department of Agriculture (USDA),
    '89 142; '90 72; '92 65, 202; '93 83
Vegetable cooking spray, '92 208
    cleanup, easy, '82 198, 314; '84 48;
        '92 314; '93 104; '95 31
Vegetable oil, '82 189; '84 211; '88 112, 113
    deep-fat frying thermometer, '84 37;
        '88 113
    preventing fire, '84 37; '88 112, 113
Vegetables, '82 138; '83 94; '84 180, 211,
    249; '86 140, 141; '89 243, 244;
    '92 344; '93 132; '94 29, 92; '95 30.
    See also FOKTY/Broccoli, Brussels sprouts,
    Canning, Cauliflower, Garnishes, Lettuce,
    Mushrooms, Onions, Peas, Peppers,
    Potatoes, Pumpkins, Squash, Sweet
    Potatoes, Tomatoes.
    basic cooking methods, '82 138;
        '84 249; '94 29, 92 (chart)
    canning, '84 180; '93 136, 137
    cutting, '86 13; '92 52; '93 132;
        '94 29

determining amounts to buy for
    entertaining, '90 276
freezing, '87 112
grilling, '83 191; '92 52; '95 274
microwaving, '82 138; '83 191
preparing, '86 140, 141; '89 243, 244
seasoning (chart), '94 92
selecting, '84 249; '86 140, 141;
    '89 243, 244; '94 29
stir-frying, '82 138; '83 191
storing, '83 94; '84 211; '86 140, 141;
    '89 243, 244; '94 29
substitutions, '92 344
winter vegetables, '84 249; '88 229
White chocolate. *See* FOKTY/Chocolate.
Wines, '85 292, 293
    champagne, '85 293
    selecting, '85 292
    serving, '85 292, 293
    storing, '85 292
Wok cooking, '85 76
    equipment, '85 76
    preparing food for, '85 76
Yams. *See* FOKTY/Sweet Potatoes.
Yeast, '89 268. *See also* FOKTY/Biscuits,
    Breads, Rolls.
    kinds of, '89 268

FROSTINGS. *See also* **FILLINGS, GLAZES, TOPPINGS.**
Almond-Butter Frosting, '86 107
Amaretto Frosting, '86 246
Apricot Frosting, '81 192
Banana-Nut Frosting, '79 115
Boiled Frosting, '90 45; '92 14; '93 318
Bourbon Frosting, '88 236
Brandy Cream Frosting, '86 239
Brown Sugar Frosting, '79 13; '87 296;
    '91 236
Brown Sugar Meringue Frosting, '81 70
Buttercream Frosting, '85 322; '92 230;
    '93 53, 285
Butter Cream Frosting, '88 279
Buttercream Frosting, White, '93 337
Buttercream Icing, '83 73
Butter Frosting, '80 129
Butter Frosting, Browned, '86 248
Butter Frosting, Williamsburg, '81 120;
    '82 23
Buttermilk Frosting, '85 249
Butter Pecan Frosting, '80 229
Caramel Frosting, '81 278, M289; '82 314;
    '83 43; '84 39, 263; '86 239; '87 265;
    '89 55, 236; '90 307
Caramel Frosting, Creamy, '81 71
Caramel Frosting, Easy, '87 39
Caramel Frosting, Favorite, '83 106
Carob Frosting, '85 218
Carolina Dream Frosting, '88 278
Cheese Spread, Tropical, '95 46
Cherry Frosting, '86 217
Chocolate
    Almond Frosting, Chocolate-, '83 241
    Butter Frosting, Chocolate, '89 271
    Candy Frosting, Chocolate, '81 238
    Cherry Frosting, Chocolate-, '89 294
    Chocolate Frosting, '80 M171 '81 265;
        '82 262; '83 79, 99, M233, 253;
        '84 200; '85 323;
        '86 8, 93, 138, 239, 314;
        '87 M97, 198, 199, 293; '89 M25;
        '90 194, 252, 265, 284, 309; '91 248;
        '92 319; '93 239; '94 133
    Cocoa Frosting, '86 60
    Coconut Chocolate Frosting, '79 13

Coffee Frosting, Chocolate-, '84 36;
    '88 269
Cola Frosting, Chocolate-, '95 56
Creamy Chocolate Frosting, '85 314;
    '86 316; '87 241
Fluffy Chocolate Frosting, '86 336;
    '87 58
Fudge Frosting, '81 303; '87 296;
    '89 56; '94 51
Fudge Frosting, Chocolate, '83 105
Fudge Frosting, Quick, '81 278
Ganache, Chocolate, '93 255
Honey Chocolate Frosting, '79 83
Kahlúa Frosting, Chocolate, '91 298
Marshmallow Frosting, Chocolate-,
    '83 245
Mocha Buttercream, '89 42
Mocha Butter Cream Frosting,
    '79 281
Mocha-Buttercream Frosting, '86 26
Mocha Frosting, '83 301; '84 316;
    '87 224; '94 292
Mocha Frosting, Creamy, '82 289;
    '84 311; '91 248
Nut Frosting, Chocolate, '80 140
Peanut Butter Frosting, Chocolate-,
    '84 240; '87 222
Peanut Butter-Fudge Frosting,
    '87 184
Perfect Chocolate Frosting, '90 307
Rich Chocolate Frosting, '84 304
Rum Frosting, Chocolate, '79 67
Satiny Chocolate Frosting, '85 126;
    '89 43
White Chocolate Frosting, '88 280;
    '91 101
Cinnamon-Cream Frosting, '84 311
Cinnamon Frosting, Buttery, '81 M139
Coconut Cream Cheese Frosting, '86 60
Coconut Frosting, '82 262; '91 269
Coconut Frosting, Creamy, '80 287
Coconut Frosting, Nutty, '86 8
Coconut-Pecan Frosting, '81 296; '83 M233;
    '84 43, 322
Coffee Buttercream, '95 277
Coffee Frosting, '94 86
Cola Frosting, '81 238
Colored Frostings, '90 21
Cream Cheese Frosting, '79 45;
    '80 140, 253, 299; '82 135, 244;
    '83 105, 215, M233;
    '84 201, 255, 315, 316;
    '85 118, 121; '86 217, 337;
    '87 58; '90 305, 308; '92 120;
    '93 20; '94 254; '95 139
Cream Cheese Frosting, Deluxe, '80 120
Cream Cheese Frosting, Fluffy, '80 245
Cream Cheese Frosting, Nutty, '85 117
Crème Chantilly, '87 9; '91 297
Crème de Menthe Frosting, '86 245;
    '93 256
Decorating Techniques, Cake, '83 72, 240
Decorator Frosting, '82 20, 307; '83 106;
    '87 86; '91 282; '93 285
Decorator Frosting, Creamy, '79 117
Decorator Frosting, Green, '93 286
Decorator Frosting, Yellow, '93 283
Divinity Frosting, '79 229
Fluffy Frosting, '79 246; '86 235; '88 268;
    '89 254; '90 308
Fluffy White Frosting, '90 105; '95 319
Fondant, Rolled, '92 69
Ganache Cream, '92 318

FROSTINGS *(continued)*

Grapefruit Frosting, '89 308
Heavenly Frosting, '80 140
Lemon
　Buttercream Frosting, Lemon, '83 301;
　　'86 61; '91 247
　Butter Cream Frosting, Lemon-,
　　'85 117
　Coconut Frosting, Lemon-, '90 253
　Cream Cheese Frosting, Lemon-,
　　'81 157
　Creamy Lemon Frosting, '79 93
　Lemon Frosting, '85 191; '86 217;
　　'93 81
　Orange-Lemon Frosting, '88 92
　White Frosting, Lemony, '88 7
Maple Frosting, '82 217; '85 322
Meringue Frosting, '86 336; '87 84
Mint Cream Frosting, '93 216
Mint Frosting, '88 80
Never Fail Frosting, '86 314
Orange
　Buttercream Frosting, Orange, '80 70
　Butter Frosting, Orange, '83 300
　Cream Cheese Frosting, Orange, '81 70;
　　'82 16; '92 19
　Cream Frosting, Orange, '81 207;
　　'82 14
　Creamy Orange Frosting, '83 24, 241
　Lemon Frosting, Orange-, '88 92
　Orange Frosting, '81 7; '86 61; '88 119
Panocha Frosting, '89 296
Peanut Butter Frosting, '83 223; '84 153;
　'85 34
Peanut Butter Swirl Frosting, '86 109
Peanut Frosting, Creamy, '80 87
Pecan Frosting, '86 86
Peppermint Birthday Cake Frosting, Pink,
　'92 269
Pineapple-Cream Cheese Frosting, '95 160
Piping Icing, '92 69
Piping Icing, Tips for, '84 302
Quick Pour Frosting, '85 119
Royal Icing, '80 278; '81 21; '83 73;
　'84 303; '85 323; '87 295; '88 309;
　'91 281
Rum Cream, '88 154, 224
Sea Foam Frosting, '81 211; '91 271
Seven-Minute Double Boiler Frosting,
　'81 278
Seven-Minute Frosting, '80 289;
　'83 299, 301; '87 296; '89 55, 57;
　'94 98, 99
Snow Peak Frosting, '82 53; '85 281
Spiced Buttercream, '84 226
Spiced Cream, '89 215
Strawberry Frosting, '89 184
Toffee Frosting, English, '85 125
Vanilla Buttercream Frosting, '92 239;
　'94 99
Vanilla Frosting, '84 36; '85 236; '92 14, 274
Vanilla-Rum Frosting, '85 324
Whipped Cream Frosting, '83 229; '85 125;
　'87 263; '89 43; '93 86
White Chocolate-Cream Cheese Frosting,
　'94 58
White Chocolate-Cream Cheese Tiered Cake
　Frosting, '94 125
White Frosting, '83 268
White Frosting, Fluffy, '81 278
White Frosting, Luscious, '81 71

FRUIT. *See also specific types.*
Acorn Squash, Fruited, '85 235
Acorn Squash, Fruit-Stuffed, '81 295
Amaretto Crème on Fresh Fruit, '93 176
Appetizers
　Bowl, Sparkling Fresh Fruit, '80 146
　Brie, Tropical Breeze, '94 M18
　Brown Sugar Dip with Fruit, Buttery,
　　'90 243
　Canapés, Fruit-Topped, '85 80
　Cascade, Fruit, '86 104
　Cheese Ball, Fruit-and-Nut, '91 251
　Cup, Appetizer Fruit, '86 131
　Curried Rum Sauce, Tropical Fruit with,
　　'91 164
　Fresh Fruit, Mint Dip with, '87 146
　Fresh Fruit with Lemon Sauce, '82 290
　Kabobs with Coconut Dressing, Fruit,
　　'87 251
　Soup, Cold Fresh Fruit, '87 157
　Soup, Swedish Fruit, '82 313; '83 65
　Spread, Fruit and Cheese, '81 245
　Spread, Fruited Cream Cheese, '91 306
　Spread, Nutty Fruit-and-Cheese, '87 246
Bake, Cranberry-Mustard Fruit, '90 287
Baked Fruit, Gingered, '81 232
Baked Fruit, Ginger-Orange, '93 313
Baked Spiced Fruit, '89 305
Bake, Hot Fruit, '81 270
Bake, Mustard Fruit, '90 291
Bake, Nutty Fruit, '83 127
Bars, Fruit and Nut Granola, '81 49
Beverages
　Apricot Fruit Flip, '91 18
　Blender Fruit Beverage, '83 318
　Breakfast Fruit Juicy, '86 176
　Brew, Fruity Witches', '95 273
　Champagne Fruit Slush, '90 322
　Cooler, Four-Fruit, '86 101
　Cooler, Fruited Wine, '86 176
　Cooler, Fruit Juice, '92 67
　Float, Frosty Fruit, '87 159
　Four-Fruit Refresher, '79 174
　Frappé, Hootenanny, '89 110
　Honey-Yogurt Smoothie, Fruited,
　　'88 231; '89 23
　Ice Tropical, '79 174
　Punch, Can-Can Fruit, '94 122
　Punch, Caribbean, '95 173
　Punch, Florida Fruit, '92 247
　Punch for a Bunch, '95 90
　Punch, Fruit, '83 52
　Punch, Fruit Juicy Rum, '91 175
　Punch, Fruit Slush, '91 278
　Punch, Golden Fruit, '80 299; '83 56
　Punch, Holiday Fruit, '79 232
　Punch, Holiday Hot Fruit, '92 286
　Punch, Hot Fruit, '83 33
　Punch, Mixed Fruit, '90 207; '95 239
　Punch, Party Fruit, '82 137
　Punch, Passion Fruit, '90 169
　Punch, Polka Dot, '95 178
　Punch, Southern Fruit, '95 238
　Punch, Spiced Fruit, '88 2
　Punch, Spirited Fruit, '81 100
　Punch, Summertime Fruit, '80 160
　Punch, Tropical Fruit, '81 51; '83 176;
　　'90 169
　Refresher, Fruit, '91 203
　'ritas, Fruit, '94 157
　Sangría, Three-Fruit, '89 212
　Shake, Frosty Fruit, '87 23
　Shake, Tangy Fruit, '95 129

Shake, Tropical, '93 212
Slushy, Fruit, '80 146
Smoothie, Fruit, '89 87
Tea, Christmas Fruit, '83 275
Tea Cooler, Fruited, '94 131
Tea, Fruited Mint, '88 79; '91 81
Tea, Hot Spiced Fruit, '87 242
Tea-Ser, Tropical, '95 200
Three-Fruit Drink, '79 38; '80 50;
　'87 199
Tropical Fruit Drink, '85 43
Tropical Fruit Whisper, '89 212
Two-Fruit Smoothie, '89 182
Boats, Honeydew Fruit, '81 147
Braid, Fruit-and-Cheese, '86 214
Brandied Fruit, Hot, '80 48
Bread, Cranberry Fruit-Nut, '79 275
Bread, Fruity Banana, '95 78
Bread, Kahlúa Fruit-Nut, '79 235
Canning and Preserving
　Apple Rings, Cinnamon, '85 107
　Berries (except Strawberries), '80 128
　Conserve, Dried Fruit, '82 308
　Dehydration Chart, Fruit and Vegetable,
　　'84 147
　Freezing Chart, Fruit, '85 187
　Juices, Fruit, '85 107
　Mixed Fruit, Unsweetened, '83 182
　Peaches, '80 128
　Peaches and Pears, '85 106
　Peaches, Honey-Sweet, '85 107
　Syrup, Fruit, '86 176
Chafing Dish Fruit, '89 305
Chilled Fruit with Dressing, '85 222
Chutney, Autumn Fruit, '88 M230
Combo, Fresh Fruit, '86 178
Compotes
　Amaretto-Hot Fruit Compote, '90 250
　Baked Fruit Compote, '80 276; '84 314;
　　'87 228
　Baked Mustard Fruit Compote, '85 47
　Champagne Fruit Compote, '81 309;
　　'82 124
　Chilled Fruit Compote, '83 123
　Festive Fruit Compote, '94 279
　Fresh Fruit Compote, '79 162; '82 197,
　　272; '84 82; '94 190
　Fruit Compote, '86 330
　Gingered Fruit Compote, '88 184
　Hot Fruit Compote, '81 203; '83 53;
　　'86 324; '90 124
　Jicama-Fruit Compote, '92 49
　Mixed Fruit Compote, '93 123
　Praline Fruit Compote, Warm, '85 260
　Pudding Compote, Fresh Fruit, '86 151
　Raspberry Puree, Fruit Compote with,
　　'88 81
　Wine Fruit Compote, '81 272
Couscous with Mixed Fruit, '95 232
Cup, Fruit, '81 141; '91 202
Cup, Mixed Fruit, '94 60
Cups, Honeydew Fruit, '82 179
Cup, Tipsy Fruit, '81 268
Curried Fruit, Almond-, '83 261
Curried Fruit Bake, '87 241
Curried Fruit, Hot, '79 225; '81 264;
　'84 287; '95 72
Delight, Fruit, '86 131
Delight, Winter Fruit, '80 243
Desserts. *See also Fruit/Fruitcakes.*
　Balls, Fruit, '82 296; '84 299
　Bavarian Cream with Fresh Fruit, '88 137
　Brandied Fruit Starter, '82 249

FRUIT, Desserts (continued)

Brie with Fresh Fruit, Caramel, '90 266
Cake, Fruit-and-Cereal Brunch, '88 263
Cake, Fruit and Spice, '87 M97
Cake, Fruited Pound, '81 265
Cake, Fruity Ice Cream, '87 110
Cake, Spicy Fruited Carrot, '85 117
Cake, Stately Fruit-and-Nut, '84 226
Caribbean Fruit Dessert, '84 314
Cheese, and Nuts, Fruit, '93 324
Cheesecake, Fruit-Glazed, '80 24;
  '90 162
Cobbler, Quick Fruit, '91 20
Cookies, Bourbon Fruit, '86 334
Cookies, Fruitcake, '79 291; '86 320;
  '88 286
Cookies, Fruitcake Drop, '92 275
Cookies, Holiday Fruitcake, '81 301
Cookies, Rolled Fruit, '80 15
Cookies, Spicy Holiday Fruit, '83 298
Cream Cheese, Fruited, '85 306
Cream Freeze, Fruit, '82 144
Cream Puffs, Tutti-Frutti, '79 231
Crêpes, Fruit-Filled Chocolate, '89 325
Crêpes, Tropical, '86 275
Crêpes, Tropical Fruit, '87 77
Crisp, Fruit, '94 168
Cup, Fruit, '81 141
Cup, Snowball Citrus, '79 2
Cup, Vanilla Fruit, '80 183
Curried Fruit, Hot, '95 72
Custard over Fruit, Stirred, '84 83
Custard with Fresh Fruit, Citrus, '93 70
Drops, Candied Fruit, '89 329
Elegant Fruit, '91 91
Filling, Crêpes with Fruit, '81 96
Filling, Fruit-Nut, '80 289
Filling, Tutti-Frutti, '79 231
Flaming Fruit Dessert, '83 302
Freeze, Holiday Fruit, '88 283
Fresh Fruit with Cheese, Luscious,
  '79 153
Frozen Fruit Cream, '94 129
Frozen Fruit Cups, '93 197
Glazed Fruit, '85 83
Ice Cream, Tutti-Frutti, '86 129
Ice, Fruit, '86 176
Ice, Mixed Fruit, '81 178; '88 85
Kabobs, Fruit, '86 181
Kabobs with Mint Marinade, Fruit,
  '82 157
Lemon Curd, Fresh Fruit with, '88 21
Marinated Fruit Bowl, '80 297
Meringue Shells, Fruit-Filled, '86 151
Parfait, Tropical Trilogy, '92 247
Pie, Crispy-Crust Fruit, '88 68
Pie, Fruitcake, '80 237
Pie, Fruited Cheese, '92 228
Pie, Fruit-Topped Vanilla Cream, '84 49
Pie, Japanese Fruit, '80 238
Pies, Baked Fruit, '84 7
Pizza, Peanut Butter-Fruit, '94 60
Planter's Punch Dessert, '95 175
Pops, Fruit, '87 168
Pudding, Fruited Rice, '86 95
Puff, Giant Fruit, '85 72
Puff Pastry Baskets, Tropical, '93 177
Puree, Fruit, '94 190
Rainbow Fruit Dessert, '85 108
Refresher, Grape Juice-Fruit, '86 182
Rumtopf, '95 142

Sauce, Fruit, '81 177
Sauce, Golden Fruit, '89 281
Sauce, Hot Fruit Dessert, '87 299
Sauce, Quick Fruit, '82 212
Sauce, Rum-Fruit, '84 312
Shells, Fruited Meringue, '87 32
Sherbet, Freezer Fruit, '86 334
Sherbet, Frozen Fruit, '79 155
Sherbet, Fruit Punch, '86 129
Sherbet, Instant Fruit, '85 158
Sherried Fruit Flame, '85 313
Slush, Refreshing Fruit, '82 35
Soup Dessert, Fruit, '79 172
Spiced Fruit Dessert, '82 50
Squares, Christmas Fruit, '88 282
Sugarplum Sticks, '95 321
Tart, Fancy Fruit, '82 128; '91 119
Tart, Fresh Fruit, '84 178; '90 58
Tartlets, Fresh Fruit, '93 96
Tart, Open-Face Fruit, '84 207
Tart, Rainbow Fruit, '82 304
Tarts, Bowl-Me-Over Fresh Fruit,
  '93 200
Tequila, Fruit in, '82 223
Topping, Fruity Dessert, '82 167
Trifle, Olde English, '95 331
Turnovers, Fruit, '79 150
Winter Fruit with Custard Sauce, '88 251
Dips
  Coconut-Honey Fruit Dip, '84 171
  Cranberry Fruit Dip, '89 60
  Cream Cheese Dip, Fruited, '88 261
  Fresh Fruit Dip, '80 265; '95 94
  Heavenly Fruit Dip, '81 160
  Marshmallow Fruit Dip, '84 171
  Quick Fruit Dip, '90 110
  Sweet Fruit Dip, '89 328
  Tropical Dip for Fruit, '91 252
  Yogurt Dip, Fruited, '84 171
Dressings
  Avocado Fruit Salad Dressing, '82 93
  Baked Fruit Dressing, '87 253
  Coconut-Fruit Dressing, Tangy, '84 171
  Cornbread Dressing, Fruited, '80 262
  Fluffy Fruit Dressing, '79 69
  Fresh Fruit Dressing, '87 134
  Lime-Honey Fruit Salad Dressing, '87 81
  Marmalade-Fruit Dressing, '84 171
  Nutty Fruit Dressing, '88 68
  Pecan Dressing, Fruit-and-, '84 252
  Salad Dressing for Fruit, '86 40
  Salad, Dressing for Fruit, '87 81
  Salad Dressing, Fruit, '79 69; '93 184
  Whipped Cream Fruit Dressing, '79 270
Filling, Fruit, '94 245
Filling, Lemon Crêpes with Fruit, '82 46
Fresh Fruit with Lemon-Yogurt Dressing,
  '93 17
Fruitcakes
  Applesauce Fruitcake, '83 258
  Aronowitz Fruitcake, '86 285
  Bourbon Fruitcake, '85 315
  Brandy Fruitcake, '82 261
  Burgundy Fruitcake, '85 292
  Cake Mix Fruit Cake, '95 248
  Chocolate Fruitcakes, '95 250
  Classic Fruitcake, '91 258
  Favorite Fruitcake, Family, '88 284
  Fondue, Fruitcake, '84 258
  Grandmother's Fruitcake, '95 248
  Japanese Fruitcake, '83 268; '90 252
  Jeweled Fruitcake, '88 260
  Jill's Fruitcake, '95 249

  Kentucky Fruitcake, '86 266
  Layered Fruitcake, '87 265
  Lemon Fruitcake, '83 258
  Light Fruitcake, '90 309
  Mom's Fruitcake, '85 321
  No-Bake Fruitcake, '95 249
  Old-South Fruitcake, '79 289
  Regal Fruitcake, '83 257
  Sherry-Nut Fruitcake, '84 266
  White Fruitcake, '80 280; '85 316
  Zucchini Fruitcake, '88 284
Garnishes, '82 280; '85 339
Gingered Fruit, '83 151
Granola, Fruity, '84 148
Grilled Fruit with Honey Yogurt, '95 87
Hawaiian Fruit Dish, '82 112
Honey-Sour Cream Dip, Fresh Fruit with,
  '90 180
Hot Fruit Delight, '83 281
Kabobs, Fruit, '86 181; '89 85
Kabobs, Fruity Mermaid, '91 177
Kabobs, Winter Fruit, '89 34
Main Dishes
  Brisket, Mixed Fruit Tzimmes with,
    '93 114
  Chicken Breasts with Fruited Rice Pilaf,
    '92 307
  Chicken en Crème, Fruited, '83 264
  Chicken, Fruit-Glazed, '80 211
  Chicken with Almond Rice, Spiced
    Fruited, '81 195
  Chicken with Fresh Fruit, Coconut,
    '93 294
  Chuck Roast, Fruited, '91 289
  Cornish Hens with Fruited Stuffing,
    '90 191
  Goose, Fruit- and Pecan-Stuffed, '83 268
  Goose, Fruited Stuffed Wild, '88 248
  Goose, Fruit Stuffed, '83 320
  Ham Slice, Fruited, '83 M317
  Pork Chops, Fruited, '87 194
  Pork Chops, Fruited Stuffed, '86 197
  Pork Chops, Fruit-Stuffed, '82 136
  Pork Chops, Fruit-Topped, '94 41
  Pork Chops with Rice, Fruit-Glazed,
    '82 73
  Pork Loin, Fruitcake-Stuffed, '95 250
  Pork Pilaf, Fruited, '82 246
  Pork Tenderloins, Fruit-Stuffed, '87 270
  Pot Roast, Fruited, '90 211
  Salad, Main Dish Fruit, '83 119
  Spareribs, Fruit-Stuffed, '79 14
  Turkey-and-Fruit Kabobs, '88 140
Marinated Fruit, '91 67
Marinated Fruit, Minted, '92 138
Marmalade, Delicious Fruit, '81 285
Medleys
  Baked Fruit Medley, '81 297
  Chilled Fruit Medley, '84 60
  Chinese Fruit Medley, '83 22
  Cup Medley, Fruit, '85 47
  Curried Fruit Medley, '95 329
  Fancy Fruit Medley, '84 82
  Fresh Fruit Medley, '81 141
  Frosty Fruit Medley, '82 226
  Fruit Medley, '89 235
  Midsummer Fruit Medley, '88 182
  Minted Fruit Medley, '80 182
  Tropical Medley of Fruit, '86 53
Mélange, Fruit, '88 M295
Mélange, Melon, '84 139
Mint-Balsamic Tea, Fresh Fruit with, '95 232
Mix, Dried Fruit, '92 22

FRUIT (continued)

Muesli, Bran-and-Fruit, '91 134
Muesli, Homestyle, '91 315
Muffins, Fruited Wheat, '79 93
Nuggets, Dried Fruit, '86 326
Oatmeal, Fruited, '88 19
Pick, Fruit-on-a-, '90 179
Relish, Fresh Fruit, '95 158
Rhapsody, Fruit, '80 158
Rice, Far East Fruited, '81 175
Rice Mix, Fruited, '90 267
Rice Mix, Fruited Curry-, '86 326
Rice Pilaf, Fruit-and-Vegetable, '84 196
Salads
    Apricot Fruit Salad, '82 132
    Avocado Fruit Salad, '87 41
    Avocado-Fruit Salad with Honey-Yogurt
      Dressing, '93 172
    Banana-Mixed Fruit Salad, '79 270
    Berry-Citrus Twist, '95 100
    Bowl, Fresh Fruit, '89 137
    Cabbage and Fruit Salad, '79 286
    Cantaloupe, Fruit-Filled, '83 120
    Carrot-and-Seed Salad, Fruity, '86 223
    Carrot-Fruit Toss, '82 235
    Chef Salad, Fruited, '85 222
    Chef's Fruit Salad, '86 35
    Cherry Fruit Salad, '87 236
    Chicken-Avocado Salad, Fruited, '82 101
    Chicken-Fruit Salad, '82 79
    Chicken Fruit Salad, '90 234
    Chicken Salad, Fruited, '84 25, 290;
      '88 88; '90 318
    Chicken Salad, Fruity, '83 157
    Chicken Salad in Avocados, Fruited,
      '87 41
    Chicken Salad, Summery, '95 138
    Chicken Salad with Fruit, '82 171
    Citrus-Cilantro Dressing, Fruit Salad
      with, '93 310; '94 97
    Citrus Dressing, Fruit Salad with, '88 6
    Coconut Fruit Bowl, '83 111
    Coconut Salad, Chunky Fruit-and-,
      '84 24
    Coleslaw, Fruited, '83 209; '85 139
    Coleslaw, Three-Fruit, '86 250
    Colorful Fruit Bowl, '91 58
    Colorful Fruit Salad, '82 113
    Congealed Fresh Fruit, Jeweled, '95 89
    Cottage Cheese-and-Fruit Salad, '86 16
    Cottage-Fruit Split, '86 169
    Cream Dressing, Fruit Salad with,
      '89 277
    Creamy Fruit Salad, '84 265
    Creamy Holiday Fruit Salad, '90 251
    Cups, Royal Fruit, '81 146
    Curried Fruit Salad, '85 107
    Date Dressing, Fruit Salad with, '87 57
    Dressed-Up Fruit, '82 5
    Easy Fruit Salad, '80 221
    Easy Patio Fruit Salad, '88 184
    Fall Salad with Ginger Dressing, '82 194
    Festive Fruit Salad, '80 16
    Freeze, Fruity Lemon, '82 145
    Fresh Fruit Cup with Mint Dressing,
      '80 183
    Fresh Fruit Salad, '82 165
    Fresh Fruit Salad with Celery-Honey
      Dressing, '80 42
    Fresh Fruit Salad with Poppy Seed
      Dressing, '91 168

Frisky Fruit Salad, '85 46
Frozen Fruit Salad, '83 110
Frozen Fruit Salad, Dreamy, '79 126
Frozen Fruit Salad, Luscious, '81 204
Frozen Fruit Salad, Summertime, '89 111
Frozen Salad Christmas Wreath, '79 241
Fruit Salad, '83 209; '89 277
Gingered Fruit Salad, '95 95
Glazed Fruit Salad, '83 48; '84 290
Green Fruit Salad with Honey-Lime
    Dressing, '93 71
Ham Salad, Fruited, '81 36, 146
Heavenly Salad, '81 252
Holiday Fruit Salad, '87 236
Honeydew Fruit Bowl, '84 186
Honey Dressing, Fruit Salad with,
    '87 129
Honey Fruit Salad, '80 276
Honey-Lemon Dressing, Fruit Salad with,
    '93 21
Hurry-Up Fruit Salad, '87 236
Jicama-Fruit Salad, '86 83
Layered Fruit Salad, '84 290; '89 277;
    '91 58
Lemonade Fruit Salad, '84 24
Lettuce and Fruit Salad with Poppy Seed
    Dressing, '80 152
Main Dish Fruit Salad, '83 119
Marinated Fruit Deluxe, '81 146
Mélange Delight, Fruit, '81 302
Melon-Citrus Mingle, '79 177
Mint-Gin Fruit Salad, '92 92
Mint Sauce, Fruit Salad with, '88 M96
Mixed Fruit Cup, '87 233
Mold, Sherried Fruit, '90 124
Multi-Fruit Salad, '93 184
Nut Salad, Cheesy Fruit-'n'-, '87 56
Old-Fashioned Fruit Salad, '82 80
Orange Cream, Fresh Fruit Salad with,
    '90 126
Orange Fruit Cup, '91 277
Oriental Dressing, Fruit Salad with,
    '91 277
Pasta Salad, Fruited, '92 108
Peachy Fruit Salad, '89 206
Persimmon Fruit Salad, '79 206
Picks, Fruit on, '80 159
Pineapple Cream Dressing, Fruit Cups
    with, '83 81
Pineapple Dressing, Fruit Salad with,
    '85 207
Pineapple-Fruit Salad, Icy, '87 9
Platter, Fresh Fruit Salad, '92 213
Platter, Fruit Salad, '83 261
Poppy Seed Dressing, Fruit Salad with,
    '88 78
Potato Salad, Fruity, '85 214
Quick-and-Easy Fruit Salad, '81 99
Raspberry Fruit Mounds, '79 35
Refreshing Fruit Salad, '85 92
Rum, Fruit Cup with, '83 55
Sangría Fruit Cups, '89 34
Shrimp Salad, Fruited, '86 156
Sour Cream Fruit Salad, '80 138
Sparkling Fruit Salad, '82 266
Spiced Autumn Fruit Salad, '87 228
Springtime Fruit Salad, '81 96
Summer Fruit Salad, '82 164; '92 171
Summer Salad, Favorite, '80 158
Sunny Fruit Salad, '91 58
Sweet-and-Sour Fruit Salad, '80 13;
    '84 125
Tossed Fruit Salad, '92 106

Tropical Fruit Salad, '89 306
Tropical Fruit Salad with Fresh Mint
    Dressing, '84 126
Turkey-Fruit Salad, '79 56
Turkey Fruit Salad, '83 233; '84 244
Turkey Salad, Fruit-and-, '89 176
Turkey Salad, Fruit-and-Spice, '94 325
Turkey Salad, Fruitful, '84 197
Watermelon Fruit Basket, '84 161
Winter Fruit Salad, '80 248; '82 23
Wreath, Della Robbia Fruit, '87 294
Yogurt Fruit Salad, '81 114
Yogurt-Granola Fruit Medley, '91 58
Sandwiches, Fruit-and-Cheese Breakfast,
    '89 M21
Sandwiches, Glazed Breakfast Fruit, '93 178
Sauce for Fruit, Tangy, '90 161
Sauce, Grand Marnier Fruit, '90 93
Sherried Fruit Casserole, '80 284
Sherried Fruit Mélange, '80 158
Soup, Chilled Fresh Fruit, '88 160
Soup, Dried Fruit, '79 23
Soup, Fruit, '87 98
Soup, Yogurt Fruit, '86 176
Spiced Fruit, '79 23
Spiced Fruit, Cold, '90 269
Spiced Fruit Delight, '82 229
Spiced Fruit, Warm, '86 39
Spiced Winter Fruit, '83 262
Spread, Fruit, '85 135
Spread, Fruited Cream Cheese, '91 306;
    '93 79
Spread, Sugarless Fruit, '84 60
Strudel, Fruit Basket, '87 276
Stuffing Mix, Fruited, '89 331
Summer Fruit Fantasy, '91 178
Syrup, Apricot Fruit, '82 10
Topping, Fruit, '81 42; '87 225; '89 50
Tropical Fruit Fluff, '88 68
Tropical Fruit Tray, '93 72
Twists, Fruit-Nut, '82 253
White Wine, Fruit in, '81 48
Wontons, Fruit-Filled, '85 287

Game

Birds in Wine Marinade, Game, '94 306
Chili, Double-Meat, '79 269; '80 12
Dove and Sausage Gumbo, '81 199
Dove au Vin, '95 309
Dove Enchiladas, '85 270
Doves, Pan-Roasted, '87 240
Doves, Sherried, '91 290
Duck and Wild Rice Casserole, '79 224
Duck Breasts, Blackened, '93 259
Duck Breasts, Charcoaled Marinated, '79 226
Duck Breasts, Smoked, '87 121
Duck Breasts with Raspberry Sauce, '87 240
Duck, Buffet Wild, '86 268
Duck, Chafing Dish Orange, '79 226
Duck Enchiladas with Red Pepper-Sour
    Cream, Smoked, '87 121
Duck, Foxfire, '89 241
Duck Kabobs with Almond Rice, Grilled,
    '91 291
Duckling, Holiday, '80 251
Duckling, Roast Long Island, '84 87
Ducklings with Blackberry Sauce, '82 251
Ducklings with Cherry Sauce, Roast, '86 312
Duckling with Orange Sauce, Roast, '81 125
Duckling with Tangerine Stuffing, Roast,
    '90 16

GAME *(continued)*

Duckling with Wine Jelly, Roast, '88 243
Duck Liver Pâté, '79 227
Duck, Oyster, and Sausage Gumbo, '79 226
Duck Pâté, '79 226
Duck, Sherried Baked, '79 224
Duck with Orange Gravy, '81 259
Duck with Orange Gravy, Roast Wild, '89 323
Duck with Orange Sauce, Grilled, '94 305
Duck with Pecan Stuffing, Wild, '85 269
Duck with Sweet Potato-Eggplant Gravy, Roast, '83 90
Goose, Fruit- and Pecan-Stuffed, '83 268
Goose, Fruited Stuffed Wild, '88 248
Goose, Fruit-Stuffed, '83 320
Goose with Currant Sauce, Wild, '87 240
Gumbo, Wild Game, '91 290
Gumbo Ya Ya, '87 210
Mallard, Prairie Wings, '83 252
Pepper Feet, '93 258
Pheasant Muscatel, '85 269
Pheasants with Port Wine Sauce, '84 252
Pot Pie with Parmesan Crust, Game, '94 304
Quail Breasts, Southern, '85 270
Quail, Foxfire, '89 240
Quail, Fried, '82 45
Quail, Grilled, '92 90
Quail, Grilled Breakfast, '88 220
Quail, Hatcreek, '89 270
Quail, Hawkeye-Stuffed, '89 241
Quail, J.W., '89 240
Quail, Magnificent, '82 214
Quail, Marinated, '80 221
Quail, Seasoned Fried, '88 220
Quail, Smoked, '93 236
Quail Stuffed with Cornbread Dressing, '93 280
Quail Superb, '81 303
Quail with Cornbread Stuffing, Baked, '94 305
Quail with Currant Jelly Sauce, '86 94
Quail with Gravy, Georgia, '87 240
Quail with Mushroom Gravy, Baked, '89 273
Quail with Mushrooms, '85 138
Quail with Mushrooms, Baked, '81 259
Quail with Onion Gravy, Fried, '82 214
Quail with Orange Sauce in Potato Baskets, '86 193
Quail with Red Plum Sauce, '80 48
Rabbit, Hickory Barbecued, '87 216
Rabbit, Santa Fe Spanish, '94 307
Squab, Baked Stuffed, '82 260
Stew, Hunter's, '85 270
Turkey, Country-Fried Wild, '94 306
Venison and Tomatoes, '85 270
Venison Burgers, '87 304
Venison Chili, '82 216; '86 3; '87 304
Venison Chili, Hot, '91 283
Venison, Country-Fried, '81 233
Venison Kabobs, '82 215; '88 249
Venison Loin, Mushroom-Crusted, '94 302
Venison Reduction Sauce, '94 303
Venison Roast, '82 226
Venison Roast, Grilled, '93 278
Venison Roast, Lillie Bell's, '89 242
Venison Roast with Red Wine Gravy, '85 270
Venison Sausage Balls, '80 42
Venison Sausage Stew, '87 238
Venison Soup, '82 216
Venison Steak, Country-Fried, '83 262
Venison Steaks, Country-Style, '82 215

Venison Steaks, Grilled, '82 215
Venison Stew, '86 294
Venison Stew with Potato Dumplings, '87 304
Venison Stock, '94 302
Venison Tenderloin Appetizers, '88 249
Venison-Vegetable Bake, '87 304
Venison with Chutney-Mustard Sauce, Bostick, '89 242

GARNISHES
Butter
    Balls, Butter, '82 189; '89 90
    Curls, Butter, '82 51, 189; '89 90
    Molds, Butter, '89 90
Chocolate
    Cups, Chocolate, '80 207
    Cups, Chocolate Crinkle, '93 270
    Cups, Miniature Chocolate, '87 132
    Curls, Chocolate, '85 338
    Hearts and Shavings, Chocolate, '86 26
    Lacy Chocolate Garnishes, '89 43
    Leaves, Chocolate, '88 281; '89 42
    Sack, Large Chocolate, '93 314
    Sack, Small Chocolate, '93 314
Eggs, Hard-Cooked, '82 280
Fruit
    Citrus Cups, '85 339
    Citrus Cups, Notched, '82 280
    Cranberries, Frosted, '82 280; '85 339
    Grapes, Frosted, '82 51; '85 339
    Lemon Peel, Candied, '94 199
    Lemon Roses, '82 280; '85 338
    Lemon Slices, Fluted, '82 51
    Orange Rose, '85 338
    Orange Zest, Candied, '95 320
    Vegetable and Fruit Garnishes, '82 280
Guide, Garnishing, '82 138
Marinade, Dill, '87 115
Marinade, Garlic-and-Oregano, '87 115
Marinade, Sweet-and-Sour, '87 115
Piped Garnishes, '82 280
Vegetable
    Broccoli Bouquet, '87 115
    Carrot Curls, '85 338
    Carrot Flowers, '85 338
    Celery Fans, '85 338
    Fruit Garnishes, Vegetable and, '82 280
    Green Onion Fans, '85 339
    Green Pepper Cups, '85 339
    Mushrooms, Aztec, '82 51
    Mushrooms, Fluted, '82 280; '85 338
    Onion Mum, '85 339
    Onion Rose, '85 339
    Radish Rose, '85 339
    Squash Buttercup, '87 114
    Tomato Cups, '85 339
    Tomato Flower, Marinated Pasta in, '87 115
    Tomato Rose, '82 51; '85 338
    Zucchini Fan, '87 114

GIFTS
Gadgets, Off-the-Wall, '95 332
Gifts That Measure Up, '95 332
Hot Handlers, '95 332
Miniature Liqueur Sampler, '95 332
Wine Tasting, '95 332

GLAZES. *See also* FROSTINGS, TOPPINGS.
Apricot Glaze, '80 280; '82 8; '86 197
Apricot Glaze for Ham, '85 256
Apricot Glaze, Sweet, '82 304
Apricot-Kirsch Glaze, '87 14
Berry Glaze, '83 225
Blueberry Glaze, '83 143
Brandy Glaze, Powdered Sugar-, '86 291

Brown Sugar Glaze, '83 312
Buttermilk Glaze, '79 140; '81 70; '84 316
Caramel Glaze, '85 320
Cherry Glaze, '83 143; '93 52
Chocolate Glaze, '81 119; '83 220; '84 10, 55, 253; '85 6; '86 315, 316; '89 325; '90 310; '91 M296; '93 52
Chocolate Glaze, Creamy, '82 88
Chocolate-Honey Glaze, '82 306
Cinnamon Glaze, '88 83
Citrus Glaze, '82 128; '89 205
Cranberry Glaze, '84 306; '86 171; '88 244
Cranberry-Honey Glaze, '89 273
Cream Cheese Glaze, '84 150; '94 242
Daiquiri Glaze, '93 83
Dijon Glaze, '87 54
Drizzle Glaze, '87 94
Drizzling Icing, '91 35
Honey Glaze, '88 287
Honey-Nut Glaze, '87 15
Irish Cream Glaze, '92 287
Kahlúa Glaze, '86 292
Lemon Glaze, '79 285; '86 194; '87 41; '92 269; '93 154, 183
Orange Butter Glaze, '90 194
Orange Glaze, '79 2; '80 257; '81 34, 107; '82 75, 206; '83 33, 114, 140, 267; '84 161; '86 298; '92 263; '95 320
Orange Glaze, Nutty, '80 45
Orange-Pineapple Glaze, '81 60
Paint, Egg Yolk, '86 322
Pineapple Glaze, '83 143; '85 38
Powdered Sugar Glaze, '79 24; '82 92, 283; '83 83, 295; '85 55; '90 95
Praline Glaze, '82 196
Rum Glaze, Buttered, '83 220
Snowy Glaze, '82 295
Strawberry Glaze, '80 35; '83 142
Sugar Glaze, '86 161; '90 47
Teriyaki Glaze, '94 82
Topping Glaze, '87 69
Vanilla Glaze, '85 M89; '89 211

GOOSE. *See* GAME.
GRANOLA
Apple Crisp, Granola, '85 78
Bars, Coconut Granola, '85 202
Bars, Fruit and Nut Granola, '81 49
Bars, Granola, '83 305; '95 214
Bread, Honey-Granola, '86 56
Chocolate Morsels, Granola with, '86 69
Crunchy Granola, '81 218; '84 144
Easy Granola, '81 49
Fabulous Granola, '92 213
Fruit Medley, Yogurt-Granola, '91 58
Fruity Granola, '84 148
Gorp, Granola, '89 59
Granola, '79 190; '93 197
Homemade Granola, '84 58
Mix, Granola, '94 168
Mix, Granola Snack, '86 229
Muffins, Granola, '95 78
Nutty Granola, '90 95
Orange Granola, Sunny, '84 212
Pancakes, Granola-Squash, '94 267
Peanut Butter Granola, '82 296
Peanut Granola, Crunchy, '90 48
Raisin-Granola Treats, '92 22
Reindeer Nibbles, '92 280
Sunshine Granola, '79 37
Toasty Granola, '79 37
Trail Mix, Bunny, '95 101
Whole Wheat Granola, '82 167

GRAPEFRUIT

Beverages
Cooler, Grapefruit, '88 81
Freeze, Grapefruit, '93 242
Grapefruit Drink, '90 84; '95 238
Refresher, Grapefruit, '88 85
Refresher, Grapefruit-Orange, '82 174
Sangría, Grapefruit, '89 92
Tea, Grapefruit, '92 67
Three-Fruit Drink, '80 50
Biscuits, Grapefruit Juice, '83 10
Broiled Grapefruit, '85 7
Broiled Grapefruit, Holiday, '88 251
Broiled Grapefruit, Sherried, '80 50
Broil, Flounder-Grapefruit, '85 53
Cake, Fresh Grapefruit, '89 308
Chocolate-Topped Grapefruit, '89 88
Compote, Spicy Grapefruit-Berry, '91 19
Cup, Berry Grapefruit, '79 242
Delight, Winter Fruit, '80 243
Dressing, Grapefruit French, '80 101
Dressing, Grapefruit Salad, '84 262
Frosting, Grapefruit, '89 308
Ice, Grapefruit, '91 122
Ice, Pink Grapefruit, '85 304
Marmalade, Combination Citrus, '80 50
Marmalade, Grapefruit, '82 308
Minted Grapefruit, '88 81
Pear-Berry Puree, Grapefruit with, '89 213
Salads
Apple Salad, Grapefruit-, '89 41
Aspic, Grapefruit, '80 297; '82 112; '83 153
Avocado-Grapefruit Salad, '85 26; '93 282
Avocado Salad, Grapefruit-, '83 316; '84 16; '89 41
Banana Salad with Celery Seed Dressing, Grapefruit-, '91 237
Combo Salad, Grapefruit, '80 50
Congealed Grapefruit Salad, '84 325; '85 279
Congealed Salad, Grapefruit, '83 190
Cucumber Salad, Grapefruit-, '80 100
Grapefruit Salad, '83 124; '84 325; '88 122
Greens and Grapefruit Salad, '95 301
Orange-Grapefruit Salad, '93 294
Orange Salad, Grapefruit-, '91 276
Shrimp Salad, Grapefruit-and-, '88 5
Winter Salad, Grapefruit, '84 24
Sorbet, Grapefruit-Mint, '93 153
Sorbet, Pink Grapefruit and Tarragon, '95 163
Supreme, Grapefruit, '80 50

GRAPES

Beverages
Cooler, Grape-Lime, '94 227
Mulled Grape Juice, '90 21
Punch, Sparkling Grape, '82 48
Punch, White Grape, '90 15
Tea, White Grape Juice, '87 57
Blue Cheese-Pecan Grapes, '95 48
Caribbean Grapes, '95 48
Carrots with Grapes, Glazed, '82 287
Chicken Véronique, '84 260; '85 302
Desserts
Granita, Grape, '88 118
Ice Cream, Scuppernong, '88 216
Ice, Grape, '83 162
Ice, Muscadine, '82 202
Pie, Grape, '85 212
Pie, Grape Juice, '79 123
Pie, Muscadine, '82 202

Pie, Scuppernong, '88 216
Refresher, Grape Juice-Fruit, '86 182
Tart, Green Grape, '87 77
Frosted Grapes, '82 51; '85 339
Green Grapes Supreme, '88 81
Ham Véronique, '85 90
Honeydew Melon with Grapes, '91 91
Honeyed Grapes, '95 47
Jelly, Grape, '89 140
Jelly, Grape-Burgundy Freezer, '85 130
Jelly, Quick Grape, '89 M156
Jelly, Thyme-Grape, '89 193
Jelly, Wild Muscadine, '79 32
Mold, Double Grape-Cantaloupe, '79 173
Salad, Marinated Chicken-Grape, '85 74
Salad Mold, Grape, '83 120
Salad Véronique, Macaroni, '85 164
Salad with Grapes, Chicken, '86 117
Salad with Grapes, Curried Tuna, '87 201
Sauce, Pears in Muscadine, '88 216
Sauce, White Grape, '80 38
Scallops Véronique, '83 144
Slaw, Grape-Poppy Seed, '86 225
Sole Véronique, '85 181
Wild Rice with Grapes, '95 48

GRAVIES. *See also* **SAUCES.**

Black-Eyed Pea Gravy, '87 12
Burgundy Gravy, Beef Roast with, '95 263
Chive Gravy, Beef and Broccoli with, '88 214
Cranberry Pan Gravy, Baked Hen with, '94 308
Cream Gravy, '88 15
Cream Gravy, Country-Fried Steak with, '84 8
Cream Gravy, Fried Chicken with, '85 241
Currant Gravy, '83 276
Dill-Cream Gravy, Pork Chops with, '84 81
Fried Chicken Gravy, '95 235
Fried Ripe Tomatoes with Gravy, '82 180
Giblet Gravy, '79 283; '88 253
Giblet Gravy, Roast Turkey and, '94 308
Gravy, '88 303
Ham with Gravy, Virginia, '86 15
Horseradish Gravy, Filet Mignon with, '92 262
Mushroom Gravy, Baked Quail with, '89 273
Onion Gravy, Fried Quail with, '82 214
Orange Gravy, '81 259; '89 323
Red-Eye Gravy, Country Ham with, '79 37
Redeye Gravy, Country Ham with, '86 254
Red-Eye Gravy, Ham and, '88 221
Red Wine Gravy, Venison Roast with, '85 270
Sausage Gravy, '92 271; '94 20
Sour Cream Gravy, '92 301
Sour Cream Gravy, Pot Roast with, '79 17
Sweet Potato-Eggplant Gravy, Roast Duck with, '83 90
Tasso Gravy, '92 236
Tomato Gravy, '93 18
Tomato Gravy, Spicy, '95 172
Turkey Gravy, '91 255; '94 306
White Wine Gravy, '89 322
White Wine Gravy, Pot Roast in, '81 299

GREENS

Bake, Grits 'n Greens Dinner, '84 281
Beets 'n' Greens, '95 179
Chard, Buttered, '83 36
Collard Greens, '95 233
Collard Greens, Seasoned, '82 211
Collards, '79 32
Collards and Sausage, Pasta with, '94 230
Collards Casserole, Parmesan-, '95 233
Collards, Southern-Style, '82 107
Collards, Uptown, '92 23

Escarole-and-Bacon Salad, '84 85
Escarole, Easy Cooked, '84 85
Grits and Greens, '95 233
Gumbo z'Herbes, '94 239
Kale, Scalloped, '86 224
Kale, Sweet-and-Sour, '80 298
Kale with Salsa, Southwest, '94 246
Kale with Tomato and Onion, '92 244
Mustard Greens and Potatoes, '86 224
Mustard Green Soup, Cream of, '93 280
Mustard Greens, Spinach Fettuccine with, '94 247
Pasta with Greens, '95 211
Stewed Tomatoes and Greens, '95 234
Stir-Fried Greens, '94 33
Swiss Chard with Tomatoes, '83 36
Turnip-and-Carrot Salad, '91 212
Turnip-and-Collard Greens, '92 215
Turnip Green Dip, '91 13
Turnip Green Dip with Jalapeño-Corn Muffins, Hot, '93 164
Turnip Greens, '90 13, 232; '95 306
Turnip Greens and Ham Hock, Southern, '80 119
Turnip Greens and White Bean Bake, '94 246
Turnip Greens, Fresh, '92 339
Turnip Greens, Old-Fashioned, '85 255
Turnip Greens, Saucy, '83 12
Turnip Greens with Cornmeal Dumplings, '82 211
Turnip Greens with Turnips, '84 230
Watercress-and-Mushroom Salad, '88 104
Watercress Mousse, '88 104
Watercress Soup, '88 104
Watercress Spread, '88 103

GRILLED. *See also* **BARBECUE.**

Beef
Burgers, All-American Pizza, '92 148
Burgers, Burgundy, '80 156
Burgers, Favorite, '89 165
Burgers, Grilled Sour Cream, '87 287
Burgers, Mushroom, '89 164
Burgers, Nutty, '87 185
Burgers, Party, '83 164; '84 39
Burgers, Sausage, '83 212
Burgers, Seasoned, '85 158
Burger Spirals, '94 139
Burgers, Steak-House, '87 186
Burgers, Stuffed, '85 159
Burgers, Sweet-and-Sour, '90 128
Burgers, Tortilla, '94 138
Burgers, Triple-Layer, '89 165
Burgers with Sprouts, '89 164
Cheeseburgers, Fried Green Tomato, '94 138
Eye of Round, Grilled Beef, '82 91
Fajita Salad, Beef, '91 70
Fajitas, Favorite, '86 114
Fajitas, Plum Good, '94 115

GRILLED, Beef *(continued)*

Filet Mignon, Marinated, '84 171
Flank Steak and Mushrooms, '87 61
Flank Steak, Ginger-Marinated, '89 25
Flank Steak, Grilled, '80 152; '89 168;
   '91 80; '92 166
Flank Steak, Lemon-Lime, '95 55
Flank Steak, Marinated, '82 162; '83 35;
   '85 86; '95 237
Flank Steak, Oriental, '83 178
Flank Steak Pinwheels, '87 141
Flank Steaks, Delicious Marinated,
   '83 110
Flank Steak, Tangy, '86 184
Flank Steak, Tenderized, '82 105
Flank Steak Teriyaki, '81 110
Flank Steak, Texas, '86 185
Flank Steak with Black Bean-and-Corn
   Salsa, Grilled, '94 80
Flank Steak with Sweet Peppers, Grilled,
   '90 138
Hamburgers, Flavorful Grilled, '81 110
Hamburgers, Grilled, '93 198
Hamburgers, Old-Fashioned, '79 149
Hamburgers, Teriyaki, '94 138
Kabobs, Beef, '85 110
Kabobs, Beef-and-Vegetable, '91 148
Kabobs Deluxe, Beef, '82 182
Kabobs, Marinated Beef, '82 105;
   '85 159
Kabobs, Meatball, '95 192
Kabobs, Pineapple-Beef, '83 212
Kabobs, Saucy Beef, '83 109
Kabobs, Spirited Beef, '87 142
Kabobs, Teriyaki Beef, '80 207
Kabobs with Rice, Marinated Beef, '84 32
Kabobs with Vegetables, Beef, '90 148
London Broil, Teriyaki, '92 282
Marinated Beef on a Stick, '85 234
Medaillons of Beef with Horseradish
   Cream, '90 96
Poor Boy Fillets, '82 106
Red Wine Marinade, Beef with, '91 46
Roast, Grilled Marinated Beef, '93 141
Roast, Grilled Pepper, '81 110
Round Steak, Tender Grilled, '85 3
Salad, Beef Vinaigrette, '95 177
Sirloin Kabobs, Marinated, '82 162
Sirloin Salad, Grilled, '94 129
Sirloin Steak, Secret, '81 110
Steak-and-Shrimp Kabobs, '80 184
Steak, Bourbon, '90 148
Steak Continental, '83 178
Steak, Curried Beef, '88 60
Steak, Grilled Black Pepper, '86 184
Steakhouse Beef, American, '93 15
Steak Kabobs, '93 95
Steak Kabobs, Marinated, '80 184
Steak, Marinated Bourbon, '95 91
Steak, Mesquite-Grilled, '85 154
Steak on a Stick, '83 109
Steak, Patio, '87 141
Steak, Pirate, '79 89
Steaks, Blue Cheese, '84 171
Steaks, Sweet-and-Sour Marinated,
   '83 110
Steaks with Green Chiles, Grilled,
   '85 144
Steak, Tabasco, '95 207
Steak with Ham-and-Mushroom Sauce,
   '83 109
Steak with Mushroom Sauce, '83 212
Steak with Vegetables, Skewered, '81 124
Superburgers, '79 89
Tacos al Carbón, '86 19
Tacos al Carbón, Tailgate, '79 185
Tenderloin, Grilled, '91 166
Tenderloin, Herb Marinated, '83 109
Tenderloin, Marinated Beef, '93 215
Tenderloin with Mushrooms, Beef,
   '87 115
Tomatoes and Artichokes, Beef with,
   '92 282
Tournedos Diables, '87 60
Bratwurst, Grilled, '94 253
Bread, Greek, '89 200
Burgers, Pizza, '89 165
Cantaloupe Wedges, Grilled, '87 162
Chicken
   Barbecued Chicken, Grilled, '81 154
   Basil Chicken, Grilled, '93 201
   Basil-Stuffed Chicken with Tomato-Basil
      Pasta, '94 204
   Breast of Chicken, Marinated, '87 123
   Breasts, Grilled Chicken, '84 172
   Bundles with Bacon Ribbons, Chicken,
      '87 168
   Burgers, Open-Faced Chicken-Onion,
      '94 139
   Charcoal Broiled Chicken, '79 90
   Cumin Chicken, Grilled, '87 142
   Dill Sauce, Grilled Chicken with, '88 162
   Garlic-Grilled Chicken, '87 180
   Ginger-Orange Chicken, Grilled, '91 26
   Grilled Chicken, '89 200; '92 170
   Jalapeño Chicken, Grilled, '93 213
   Kabobs, Chicken, '87 141
   Kabobs, Hawaiian, '85 157
   Kabobs, Oriental Chicken, '95 193
   Kabobs, Sesame Chicken, '82 165
   Kabobs, Soy-Chicken, '86 156
   Kabobs Supreme, Chicken, '81 124
   Lemonade Chicken, '82 163
   Lemon-Herb Grilled Chicken, '95 87
   Lime-Jalapeño Chicken, Grilled, '91 87
   Marinated Chicken, '87 61
   Marinated Chicken Breasts, '90 54
   Marinated Chicken in a Sandwich,
      '86 185
   Mushroom Bundles, Chicken-, '80 157
   Orange, Lime, and Ginger Sauce,
      Chicken with, '92 123
   Pesto Chicken with Basil Cream, '89 158
   Provolone, Chicken, '93 323
   Rumaki Kabobs, '82 182
   Salad, Grilled Chicken-Pasta, '94 64
   Salad, Moroccan Grilled Chicken,
      '95 231
   Salad, Thai Chicken, '95 177
   Salad with Raspberry Dressing, Grilled
      Chicken, '95 202
   Sandwich, Ham 'n' Cheese Chicken,
      '95 153
   Sandwich Jamaican Chicken, '95 153
   Smoky Grilled Chicken, '85 160
   Tabbouleh Salad, Grilled Chicken with,
      '91 70
   Teriyaki Chicken, '91 163
   Teriyaki Chicken, Grilled, '92 59
   Vegetables Vinaigrette, Grilled Chicken
      and, '91 26
   Yogurt-Lemon Chicken, Grilled, '81 111
Cornish Hens, Grilled, '88 243; '92 59
Cornish Hens, Jelly-Glazed, '93 251
Cornish Hens, Orange-Glazed Grilled,
   '86 250
Cornish Hens, Sherry-Marinated, '91 148
Duck Breasts, Charcoal Marinated, '79 226
Duck Kabobs with Almond Rice, Grilled,
   '91 291
Duck with Orange Sauce, Grilled, '94 305
Fennel and Radicchio with Orange
   Vinaigrette, Grilled, '95 253
Fish
   Amberjack Sandwiches, Grilled, '91 195
   Catfish Cajun-Style, Grilled, '90 129
   Catfish with Red Salsa, Grilled, '90 172
   Catfish with Relish, Grilled, '92 54
   Easy Grilled Fish, '91 194
   Fillets Tomatillo, '94 135
   Flounder Fillets, Grilled, '83 213
   Grouper, Garlic-Basil Marinated, '94 160
   Grouper, Grilled, '86 185
   Grouper, Grilled Marinated, '90 166
   Grouper, Hot Spicy, '94 78
   Heather Sauce, Catfish Inn's Grilled Fish
      with, '84 182
   Salmon Fillets with Sweet Corn Relish,
      '93 119
   Salmon Quesadilla with Cucumber Salsa,
      Grilled, '95 131
   Salmon Steaks, Grilled, '94 278
   Salmon Steaks, Grilled Herbed, '93 176
   Salmon Steaks with Tarragon Butter,
      '87 155
   Swordfish, Skewered, '86 256
   Swordfish Steaks, Orange-Ginger
      Marinated, '93 271
   Swordfish Steak with Chervil Butter,
      '91 147
   Swordfish with Caper Sauce, Grilled,
      '95 230
   Trout, Grilled, '95 106
   Tuna, Grilled Florida, '93 128
   Tuna Steaks, Grilled, '90 129
   Tuna Steaks on Mixed Greens with
      Lemon-Basil Vinaigrette, Seared,
      '94 205
   Tuna with Poblano Salsa, Grilled,
      '91 135
   Yellowfin Tuna with Corn, Pepper, and
      Tomato Salsa, '94 164
Franks, Grilled Stuffed, '82 163
Fruit with Honey Yogurt, Grilled, '95 87
Game Hens, Texas-Style, '87 61
Lamb
   Burgers, Mesquite-Grilled Lamb, '88 59
   Chops, Grilled Lamb, '91 163
   Chops, Peppercorn-Crusted Lamb,
      '92 142
   Chops, Teriyaki Lamb, '87 60
   Chops with Shrimp, Lamb, '88 58
   Kabobs, Lamb, '85 159; '95 192
   Kabobs, Lamb Shish, '93 70
   Kabobs, Overnight Shish, '81 124
   Kabobs, Rosemary Marinated Lamb,
      '93 203
   Kabobs, Saucy Lamb, '89 167
   Kabobs, Savory Lamb, '80 184
   Kabobs, Shish, '82 182
   Kabobs, Teriyaki Shish, '85 37
   Leg of Lamb, Greek-Style, '93 170
   Mango Salsa, Grilled Lamb with, '95 104
   Steaks with Béarnaise Sauce, Lamb,
      '85 37
   Sweet Pepper Relish, Grilled Lamb with,
      '95 104

GRILLED *(continued)*

Liver Kabobs, '80 185
Melon Salad with Orange-Raspberry
   Vinaigrette, Grilled, '95 144
Pizzas, Grilled, '93 178
Polenta with Black Bean Salsa, Grilled,
   '93 155
Pork
    Burgers, Hearty Sauced Pork, '84 125
    Burgers, Sausage, '83 212
    Chops, Apricot-Stuffed Pork, '92 219
    Chops, Country Pride Pork, '79 159
    Chops, Glazed Pork, '86 185
    Chops, Grilled Pork, '88 113
    Chops, Hawaiian Grilled Pork, '85 159
    Chops, Lemon-Herb Pork, '84 81
    Chops, Marinated Grilled Pork, '81 110
    Chops, Pineapple-Curry Glazed, '82 106
    Chops with Ancho Cream Sauce,
      Boneless Pork, '95 205
    Ham, Easy Grilled, '92 134
    Ham, Golden Grilled, '79 90
    Ham, Hickory-Grilled, '92 81
    Ham Kabobs, Honey, '80 156
    Ham Kabobs, Swiss-, '81 124
    Ham 'n' Cheese Chicken Sandwich,
      '95 153
    Ham Slice, Apricot-Glazed, '93 252
    Honey-and-Herb Grilled Pork, '90 148
    Kabobs, Spicy Pork, '82 182
    Loin, Honey-Grilled Pork, '92 219
    Medaillons, Grilled Pork, '93 229
    Ribs, Adams', '95 236
    Ribs, Lemon Grilled, '81 154
    Ribs, Smoky, '84 172
    Salsa, Grilled Pork with, '90 128
    Spareribs, Honey-Glazed, '82 163
    Spareribs, Peach-Glazed, '86 14
    Spareribs, Spicy, '89 168
    Steaks, Glazed Pork, '83 178
    Superburgers, '79 89
    Tenderloin, Garlic Grilled Pork, '90 172
    Tenderloin, Grilled Marinated Pork,
      '91 199
    Tenderloin, Grilled Pork, '91 163; '94 88
    Tenderloin, Marinated Pork, '84 175
    Tenderloins, Grilled Pork, '88 98;
      '94 158
    Tenderloins, Honey-Grilled, '92 199
    Tenderloin Towers, Pork, '86 75
    Tenderloin with Apples, Celery, and
      Potatoes, Grilled Pork, '95 161
    Tenderloin with Brown Sauce, Grilled
      Pork, '89 32
Quail, Grilled, '92 90
Quail, Grilled Breakfast, '88 220
Quail, Marinated, '80 221
Seafood
    Brochette, Seafood, '87 96
    Oysters Mornay, Grilled, '89 195
    Oysters Supreme, Smoky, '87 60
    Scallop-Bacon Kabobs, '81 111
    Scallop Kabobs, Grilled, '83 101
    Scallops, Marinated Grilled, '84 171
    Scallop Kabobs, Sea, '82 162
    Scallops Tostada, Grilled, '87 120
    Scallops with Cilantro-Lime Vinaigrette,
      Grilled Orange, '94 77
    Shrimp-and-Scallop Kabobs, Grilled,
      '92 210
    Shrimp, Grilled, '85 103

Shrimp, Grilled Marinated, '87 173
Shrimp Kabobs, Marinated, '85 158
Shrimp Kabobs, Steak-and-, '80 184
Shrimp, Marinated and Grilled, '87 141
Tortilla Bites, '95 42
Turkey-and-Fruit Kabobs, '88 140
Turkey Breast, Citrus-Marinated, '94 272
Turkey Breast, Smoky, '89 323
Turkey Breast with Cranberry Salsa, Grilled,
   '95 252
Turkey Burgers, Grilled, '91 61
Turkey Drumsticks, Grilled, '89 168
Turkey Steaks, Grilled Marinated, '93 170
Turkey Tenderloins, Lime-Buttered, '92 127
Vegetables
    à la Grill, Vegetables, '88 130
    Burgers, Vegetable, '89 164
    Corn, Grilled Parmesan, '82 127
    Corn-on-the-Cob, Grilled, '90 166
    Corn on the Cob, Lemony, '89 200
    Corn on the Grill, '94 161
    Corn Soup, Grilled, '87 121
    Corn with Herb Butter Sauce, '79 150
    Eggplant Appetizer, Grilled, '95 198
    Eggplant, Balsamic-Flavored, '95 342
    Eggplant, Grilled, '80 202
    Grilled Vegetables, '84 172; '92 124
    Italian-Style Grilled Vegetables, '92 143
    Kabobs, Beef-and-Vegetable, '91 148
    Kabobs, Fresh Vegetable, '92 101
    Kabobs, Grilled Vegetable, '93 170
    Kabobs, Tangy Marinated Vegetable,
      '88 142
    Kabobs, Vegetable, '87 116
    Marinated Grilled Vegetables, '95 162
    Onions, Grilled Stuffed, '95 180
    Pepper Kabobs, Pretty, '90 166
    Pepper Tacos, Grilled, '95 340
    Portabello Mushrooms, Grilled,
      '95 123
    Potatoes, Grilled Herb, '84 172
    Salad, Grilled Vegetable, '94 203
    Shiitakes, Grilled, '95 265
    Skewers, Grilled Vegetable, '94 160
    Squash and Onion, Grilled, '79 150
    Squash-and-Pepper Kabobs, Summery,
      '95 193
    Sweet Potatoes, Grilled, '93 213
    Tomatoes, Cheesy Grilled, '79 150
    Tomatoes, Grilled, '85 158
    Zucchini Fans, Grilled, '89 200
    Zucchini with Feta, Greek Grilled,
      '95 190
Venison Kabobs, '82 215; '88 249
Venison Roast, Grilled, '93 278
Venison Steaks, Grilled, '82 215
GRITS
Bake, Grits 'n Greens Dinner, '84 281
Cakes, Southwestern Grits, '93 61
Casserole, Garlic Grits, '81 47
Casserole, Grits-Sausage, '84 75; '86 241
Cheese
    Baked Cheese-and-Garlic Grits, '83 292;
      '84 78
    Baked Cheese Grits, '80 49, 99; '83 311;
      '85 41; '94 240
    Baked Cheese Grits, Grillades and,
      '94 240
    Baked Grits, Swiss-and-Cheddar, '91 71
    Casserole, Cheesy Grits, '81 270
    Cheese Grits, '86 242; '90 102
    Garlic-and-Herb Cheese Grits, '95 122
    Garlic Cheese Grits, '80 47; '81 197

    Garlic-Cheese Grits, '86 180; '88 126;
      '89 47
    Green Chiles, Cheese Grits with, '95 208
    Gruyère Cheese Grits, '81 47
    Jalapeño Cheese Grits, '85 43
    Quick Cheese Grits, '83 M203
    Sausage-Cheese Grits, '90 238
    Sliced Cheese Grits, '84 75
Chicken and Grits, '95 263
Country Grits and Sausage, '83 54
Creamy Grits, '92 237, 238; '93 60
Dressing, Grits, '93 306; '94 296
Eggs Creole, '92 86
Fried Grits, '83 292; '84 78
Good Morning Grits, '87 156
Greens, Grits and, '95 233
Grillades and Grits, '88 126; '89 47; '93 62
Ham-and-Spinach Grits, Garlicky, '94 177
Italiano, Grits, '92 43
Nassau Grits, '81 47
Orange Grits, '81 47
Pan-Fried Grits, '93 62
Patties, Grits, '83 52
Pie, Crustless Grits-and-Ham, '86 103
Pie, Grits Fiesta, '92 43
Quiche, Ham-and-Grits Crustless, '94 89
Sausage Grits, '86 92
Scrambled Grits, '80 48
Shrimp Stew and Grits, '80 118
Shrimp Stew over Grits, '89 47
Soufflé, Grits, '80 30
Soufflé, Mexican Grits, '79 55
Spoonbread, Grits, '79 38
Stew over Grits, Shrimp, '88 126
Timbales, Chives-Grits, '90 172
Timbales, Grits, '88 223
Tomato Grits, Hot, '95 171
GUMBOS. *See also* **CHOWDERS, JAMBALAYAS,
SOUPS, STEWS.**
Carolina Gumbo, '95 70
Chicken
    Chicken Gumbo, '79 199; '90 26
    Easy Chicken Gumbo, '83 156
    Gullah House Gumbo, The, '92 237
    Ham-Seafood Gumbo, Chicken-, '81 6
    Oyster Gumbo, Chicken and, '81 198
    Sausage Gumbo, Chicken-and-, '89 275;
      '90 256; '94 20
    Smoked Sausage, Chicken Gumbo with,
      '81 199
    Ya Ya, Gumbo, '87 210
Dove and Sausage Gumbo, '81 199
Duck, Oyster, and Sausage Gumbo, '79 226
Fish
    Catfish Gumbo, '90 278; '91 216
    Easy Fish Gumbo, '81 6
    Snapper Gumbo, Savannah, '94 105
Ground Beef Gumbo, '87 283
Mogumbo, '93 32
Okra Gumbo, '86 210; '91 206
Okra Gumbo, Deep South, '79 48
Okra Gumbo Freezer Mix, '86 210
Seafood
    Cajun Seafood Gumbo, '94 238
    Champion Seafood Gumbo, '86 293
    Chicken-Ham-Seafood Gumbo, '81 6
    Combo Gumbo, '81 198
    Crab and Shrimp Gumbo, '81 200
    Creole Gumbo, '86 228
    Creole Gumbo, Quick, '82 87
    Creole Seafood Gumbo, '82 278
    Ham and Seafood Gumbo, '81 199
    Okra Gumbo, Light Seafood-, '86 155

GUMBOS, Seafood *(continued)*

Oyster Gumbo, Chicken and, '81 198
Seafood Gumbo, '79 198, 286; '80 34;
'81 5; '83 90; '84 87, 92; '87 210;
'90 154
Shrimp Gumbo, '81 199
Shrimp Gumbo, Quick, '86 71
Southern Gumbo, '82 242
Spicy Seafood Gumbo, '91 207
Whole Crabs, Seafood Gumbo with,
'85 2
Texas Ranch-Style Gumbo, '82 226
Turkey Gumbo, '82 268; '85 258
Wild Game Gumbo, '91 290
z'Herbes, Gumbo, '94 239

HAM. *See also* PORK.

Acorn Squash, Ham-Stuffed, '81 239; '83 66
Appetizers
Appetillas, Ham, '93 63
Balls, Appetizer Ham, '82 39
Balls, Fried Ham-and-Cheese, '84 221
Balls, Ham, '86 256
Biscuits, Country Ham in Heart, '86 105
Biscuits, Cured Ham and, '85 320
Biscuits, Kentucky Ham 'n' Angel,
'90 83
Biscuits, Petite Ham and Cheese, '79 193
Biscuits, Southern Ham and, '91 12
Biscuits with Country Ham, '90 93
Deviled Ham Twists, '82 86
Dip, Creamy Ham, '93 125
Meat-and-Cheese Appetizers, '87 7
Mousse Pitas, Ham, '95 328
New Potatoes, Ham-Stuffed, '88 211
Nibbles, Ham-Pineapple, '95 283
Nuggets, Cheesy Ham, '81 290
Pâté, Ham, '85 279
Prosciutto-Wrapped Asparagus, '91 98
Puffs, Ham-and-Cheese, '86 277
Puffs, Ham-Filled Party, '84 116
Roll, Ham-and-Cheese, '79 234
Rolls, Ham, '79 153
Rollups, Almond-Ham, '89 284
Rollups, Ham-and-Swiss, '85 113
Spread, Buttery Ham, '95 93
Spread, Cold Ham, '82 248
Spread, Country Ham, '87 8
Spread, Ham and Pimiento, '80 285;
'81 56
Tapas, Garlic-Ham, '92 175
Tennessee Sin, '95 218
Turnovers, Chile-Ham, '88 64
Turnovers, Party Ham, '82 39
Apricots, Ham and, '90 53
Artichokes, Ham-Mushroom-Stuffed, '95 228
Baked
Apricot Baked Ham, '84 160
Burgundy Ham, Baked, '94 326
Cranberry-Raisin Sauce, Baked Ham
with, '88 244
Festive Baked Ham, '83 263
Maple-Raisin Sauce, Baked Ham with,
'83 215
Marinated Baked Ham, '86 94; '88 133
Orange-Honey Glaze, Baked Ham with,
'90 53
Orange Sauce, Baked Ham with, '86 294
Pineapple-Baked Ham, '86 48

Plum Ham, '80 110
Royale, Ham, '84 260
Slice, Baked Ham, '83 12
Balls, Ham, '84 91; '86 256
Balls with Spiced Cherry Sauce, Ham,
'81 112; '82 12
Barbecued Ham Slices, '81 110
Birming "Ham," '94 229
Biscuits, Country Ham, '94 215
Biscuits, Ham-Filled Angel, '80 159
Biscuits, Surprise Pull-Apart, '95 46
Black-Eyed Peas with Ham Hocks, '79 122
Bread, Ham-and-Cheese, '86 213
Broiled Ham, Cranberry, '88 301
Bundles, Ham-and-Cheese, '93 63
Cakes, Hawaiian Ham, '79 252
Casseroles
Apple Ham Casserole, '79 213
Apples, Baked Ham and, '82 M237
Asparagus Dinner, Ham-, '80 M10
Asparagus Ham Rolls, '91 117
au Gratin, Broccoli-Ham, '90 239
Beans with Ham, Baked, '80 136
Breakfast Casserole, '91 285
Broccoli Casserole, Ham and, '81 133
Broccoli Casserole, Quick Ham-, '82 40
Cheese Casserole, Ham-and-, '87 78
Chicken, Ham, and Cheese Bake,
'87 217
Creamy Ham Medley, '84 90
Egg Casserole, Breakfast Ham and,
'79 253
Golden Ham Casserole, '82 119
Harvest Ham Bake, '79 210
Lasagna, Creamy Ham-and-Chicken,
'95 88
Lima Casserole, Ham and, '79 192
Macaroni-Ham Casserole, '81 M177;
'83 283
Noodle Casserole, Ham and, '80 300
Potato Casserole, Cheesy Ham-and-,
'84 326
Potato Casserole, Ham-and-, '83 M87
Potatoes with Ham Bits, Creamy, '87 191
Potato-Pineapple Bake, Ham-, '93 302
Quiche Casserole, '95 33
Rice Casserole, Ham-and-, '84 75
Rice-Stuffed Ham Rolls, '83 190
Rice-Tomato Bake, Ham-, '87 78
Roll Casserole, Ham, '91 M127
Spaghetti, Ham-and-Turkey, '95 19
Spinach-and-Ham Rollups, '86 84
Spinach-Ham Rolls, '88 78
Spinach Roll-Ups, Ham and, '81 143
Strata, Baked Ham, '83 283
Strata, Ham, '95 308
Strata, Ham and Broccoli, '80 261
Tetrazzini, Ham, '82 M77; '84 241
Turkey Bake, Layered Ham and, '79 252
Vegetable-and-Ham Casserole, '84 91
Cheesecake, Ham-and-Asparagus, '90 174
Cheese Chips, Ham-, '82 34
Cheesy Chicken-and-Ham Bundles, '84 261
Cheesy Ham Dinner, '84 90
Cheesy Ham Towers, '82 M77
Chowder, Creamy Ham, '88 M53
Chowder, Ham-and-Cheese, '89 15
Chowder, Ham and Corn, '79 16
Chowder, Ham-and-Corn, '82 40
Chowder, Ham 'n Cheese, '79 199
Citrus-and-Spice Ham, '88 40
Cordon Bleu, Chicken, '81 304; '82 83;
'93 126

Cordon Bleu, Company Chicken, '82 274
Cordon Bleu, Veal, '87 219
Country Ham
Biscuits, Country Ham in Heart,
'86 105
Biscuits with Country Ham, '90 93
Bread with Herb Butter, Country Ham,
'86 255
Brown Sugar Coating, Country Ham
with, '90 88
Chips, Country Ham, '92 338
Cider-Baked Country Ham, '82 195
Cider, Country Ham in Apple, '80 251
Cornbread, Crab with Chile, '86 254
Kentucky Hot Brown, '86 254
Kentucky Jack, '86 254
Oven-Braised Country Ham, '90 87
Oysters and Ham, Edwards', '86 253
Puff, Cheesy Country Ham, '90 88
Quiche, Country Ham, '87 287
Red-Eye Gravy, Country Ham with,
'79 37
Redeye Gravy, Country Ham with,
'86 254
Roasted Country Ham, Edwards',
'86 253
Sauce, Country Ham, '90 117
Sotterley Plantation Country Ham,
'93 270
Stuffed Country Ham, '90 317
Stuffed Country Ham, Maryland,
'88 49
Swirls, Veal-and-Smithfield Ham,
'86 253
Virginia Ham with Gravy, '86 15
Wine, Country Ham in, '81 260
Creamed Ham and Chicken, '81 M74
Creamed Ham and Eggs, '82 40
Creamy Ham Towers, '79 138
Crêpes, Ham-and-Egg, '83 204
Crêpes with Mushroom Sauce, Ham-and-Egg,
'82 46
Croquettes, Ham, '82 119
Curried Ham and Peaches, '82 60
Curried Ham Steak, '82 120
Curried Ham with Rice, '80 111
Deviled Delight, '83 130
Devils, Ham, '93 88
Dinner, Corn-and-Ham Skillet, '83 190
Dinner, Ham Skillet, '85 179
Eggplant, Ham-Stuffed, '80 162
Eggs, Creamy Ham and, '87 286
Eggs on Toast with Cheese Sauce, Ham and,
'81 43
Eggs, Savory Ham and, '82 231
Fettuccine, Ham-and-Asparagus, '94 84
Flips, Ham-and-Cheese, '92 46
Fritters, Ham, '82 39
Fritters with Creamy Sauce, Ham, '81 105
Frosted Ham, '89 71
Glazed
Apricot-Glazed Ham Slice, '93 252
Brown Sugar Glaze, Smithfield Ham
with, '86 253
Cranberry Glazed Ham, '81 274
Cranberry-Honey Glaze, Baked Ham
with, '89 273
Cranberry-Orange Glazed Ham,
'81 295
Currant-Glazed Ham, '91 249
Fruited Ham Slice, '83 M317
Honey-Glazed Ham Slice, '81 104
Honey-Orange Glazed Ham, '83 320

HAM, Glazed *(continued)*

Marmalade-Glazed Ham, '89 M196
Molasses-Glazed Ham, '84 24
Orange-Glazed Ham, '89 324
Steak, Glazed Ham, '91 13
Strawberry-Glazed Ham, '91 84
Stuffed Ham, Glazed, '84 321
Sunshine-Glazed Ham, '84 252
Sweet-and-Sour Glazed Ham, '88 M15
Sweet-Sour Glazed Ham, '83 311
Green Peppers, Ham-Stuffed, '80 65
Griddle Cakes, Ham, '89 255
Grilled Ham, Easy, '92 134
Grilled Ham, Golden, '79 90
Grilled Ham, Hickory-, '92 81
Grits, Garlicky Ham-and-Spinach, '94 177
Gumbo, Chicken-Ham-Seafood, '81 6
Gumbo, Combo, '81 198
Gumbo, Ham and Seafood, '81 199
Hash Brown Bake, '95 281
Hopping John with Ham, '81 7
Jambalaya, Creole, '87 210
Jambalaya de Covington, '87 211
Kabobs, Honey Ham, '80 156
Kabobs, Swiss-Ham, '81 124
Loaves
Chili-Sauced Ham Ring, '81 M122
Country Ham Loaves, '86 255
Cranberry-Ham Loaf, '82 M77
Glazed Ham Loaf, '79 187; '90 212
Ham Loaf, '79 180; '80 272
Ham Loaves, '90 235
Hawaiian Ham Loaf, '79 71
Pineapple Upside-Down Ham Loaf, '79 253
Ring, Ham, '84 91
Saucy Ham Loaf, '86 M328
Spicy Ham Loaf, '80 110
Supreme Ham Loaf, '79 242
Upside-Down Ham Loaf, '82 40
Medley, Creamy Ham-and-Chicken, '92 272
Muffins, Ham-and-Cheese, '92 252; '93 144
Noodles, Ham and Swiss on, '87 108
Omelet, Dill-Cheese-Ham, '95 33
Omelet, Ham and Cheese, '79 262; '80 123
Omelet, Rolled, '89 228
Omelet, Sour Cream-Ham, '79 261
Omelets with Creole Sauce, '89 228
Patties, Ham, '81 99
Patties, Ham-Sprout, '85 51
Patties, Pineapple-Ham, '80 110
Patties, Spicy Ham, '90 235
Peas and Ham, Southern, '85 138
Peppers, Ham-and-Corn Stuffed, '81 87
Peppers with Rice and Ham, Stuffed, '82 131
Pie, Crustless Grits-and-Ham, '86 103
Pie, Golden Ham, '87 78
Pie, Ham-and-Cheese, '95 256
Pie, Ham Pot, '90 25
Pie, Spaghetti-Ham, '93 19
Pie with Cheese Crust, Ham, '80 286
Pie, Zucchini-Ham-Cheese, '80 272
Pineapple-Flavored Ham, '87 160
Pinwheels, Ham, '90 235
Pizza, Ham-and-Eggs Crescent, '93 47
Pizza, Southern Classic, '95 268
Po-Boy, Pain-Perdu, '93 291
Potatoes, Ham Stuffed, '79 210
Potatoes, Jalapeño-Ham Stuffed, '81 M61

Praline Ham, '85 302
Prosciutto, Party Pasta with, '94 176
Prosciutto, Pizza with Artichoke and, '87 182
Quiches
Cheese Quiche, Ham-, '79 26
Cheesy Ham Quiche, '79 127
Crustless Ham Quiche, '84 235
Grits Crustless Quiche, Ham-and-, '94 89
Ham Quiche, '80 110
Jalapeño Quiche, Cheesy, '84 31
Mushroom Quiche, Ham-and-, '81 11
Vegetable Quiche, Ham-and-, '84 326
Raisin Ham, '80 124
Raisin Sauce, Ham with, '82 M76
Red-Eye Gravy, Ham and, '88 221
Rice, Savannah Red, '80 119
Roast, Peachy Ham, '86 118
Rolls à la Swiss, Chicken-and-Ham, '92 42
Rolls, Ham-and-Broccoli, '86 212; '87 82
Rolls, Ham-and-Cheese, '82 3
Rolls, Ham-and-Cheese Lettuce, '89 217
Rolls, Ham-Asparagus, '79 41
Salads
Apple Salad, Ham-and-, '88 139
Asparagus with Prosciutto, Marinated, '95 83
Baked Ham Salad, Crunchy, '83 23
Boats, Salad, '80 93
Cheese Salad, Ham-and-, '88 138
Cheese Toss, Ham and, '79 55
Coleslaw, Ham, '84 195
Congealed Ham Salad, '81 36
Egg Salad, Ham 'n, '81 36
Fruited Ham Salad, '81 36, 146
Hearty Ham Salad, '82 40
Italian Ham Salad, Spicy, '85 74
Macaroni-Ham Salad, '85 218
Macaroni Salad, Ham and, '79 220
Mandarin Ham-and-Rice Salad, '87 145
Noodle Salad, Ham-, '85 249
Pasta Salad, Ham-and-, '90 128
Pasta Salad, Ham-Dijon, '92 191
Pasta Salad, Ham-Pecan-Blue Cheese, '90 62
Pasta Salad with Ham, '92 108
Pilaf Mold, Ham, '86 222
Potato Salad, Ham and, '80 272
Potato Salad, Ham-and-, '95 94
Potato Salad, Ham-and-Egg, '86 84
Prosciutto Salad, Melon-and-, '92 191
Rice Salad, Colorful Ham-and-, '90 319
Rice Toss, Ham-, '82 40
Rolls, Hearty Salad, '81 206
Spread, Ham Salad, '87 92
Sweet Potato Salad, Hawaiian Ham-, '82 232
Tropical Ham Salad, '89 175
Sandwiches
Asparagus-and-Ham Melt Sandwiches, '88 M96
Asparagus Delight, Ham-, '86 48
Baked Ham Sandwiches, '81 29
Blue Cheese-Ham Sandwiches, Creamy, '87 279
Cheese-and-Ham Striped Tea Sandwiches, Cheshire Claret, '94 16
Cheese Chicken Sandwich, Ham 'n', '95 153
Cheese Sandwiches, Hot Ham-and-, '85 299

Cheese Sandwich Round, Ham-and-, '94 326
Cheese Sandwich, Tex-Mex Ham-and-, '86 4
Club Sandwiches, Double-Decker, '91 231; '92 68
Croissant Sandwiches, '89 161
Eggs à la Swiss, Ham and, '88 158
Hideaways, Ham, '81 29
Hot Ham Sandwiches, '79 214
Hot Rods, Ham, '86 136
Meal-in-One Sandwiches, '80 218
Monte Cristo Sandwiches, '83 134
Muffuletta, Doodles, '94 35
Open-Faced Sandwiches, '79 214
Open-Face Ham Sandwiches, '82 40; '85 8
Pineapple-Ham Sandwich Loaf, '91 167
Pita Pockets, Ham-and-Cheese, '90 271
Pita Sandwiches, Denver, '86 M12
Pita Sandwiches, Ham-and-Cheese, '87 202; '88 44
Pita, Stuffed, '89 87
Pocket, Ham and Swiss in the, '83 31
Sebastian, The, '94 184
Stroganoff on Cheesy Onion Biscuits, Ham, '95 98
Swiss Sandwiches, Tangy Ham-and-, '85 164
Tangy Ham Salad Sandwich, '80 272
Turkey Specials, Cheesy Ham-and-, '84 14
Virginia Ham Sandwiches, '80 155
Yummy Sandwiches, '81 229
Sauce, Steak with Ham-and-Mushroom, '83 109
Skillet Ham-and-Vegetables, '84 90
Skillet, Ham-Noodle, '87 78
Skillet, Ham Spaghetti, '83 283
Slice with Cinnamon Apple Rings, Holiday Ham, '90 250
Smoked Ham, '86 92
Soufflé, Virginia Ham Breakfast, '93 121
Soufflé with Cucumber Sauce, Ham, '92 41
Soup, Chicken, Ham, and Oyster, '79 198
Soup, Ham-and-Bean, '84 4
Soup, Hearty Ham, '82 4
Soup, Spicy Ham-and-Bean, '94 322
Spread, Deviled Ham, '79 81
Spread, Ham, '86 126
Spread, Ham-and-Egg, '79 59
Spread, Ham Salad, '87 92
Spread, Hawaiian Ham, '87 106
Spread, Horseradish-Ham, '91 167
Stew, Blakely Brunswick, '87 4
Stew, Ham-and-Black-Eyed Pea, '93 20
Stir-Fry, Easy Ham, '86 332
Stir-Fry, Ham and Zucchini, '79 47
Stroganoff, Ham, '82 40
Stromboli, '88 272; '89 181
Stuffed Ham, '86 323
Superburgers, '79 89
Supper, Top-of-Stove, '86 332
Tart, Ham-and-Cheese, '92 332
Tart Milan, '87 70
Tart, Supreme Ham, '84 22
Tennessee Ham, '95 263
Turnip Greens and Ham Hock, Southern, '80 119
Véronique, Ham, '85 90
Waffles, Ham, '80 44
Zucchini, Ham and Cheese Stuffed, '79 157

HEARTS OF PALM
Chicken Rolls, Hearts of Palm, '89 201
Marinated Asparagus and Hearts of Palm, '90 91
Salad, Different Vegetable, '82 143
Salad, Hearts of Palm, '81 252; '89 276
Salad, Hearts-of-Palm, '87 138
Salad with Basil-and-Garlic Dressing, Hearts of Palm, '94 55
Sandwich, Hearts of Palm, '92 191
Spread, Hearts of Palm, '90 293

HOMINY
Bacon, Eggs, and Hominy, '85 143
Bake, Chili Hominy, '81 282; '82 58
Bake, Hominy-Sausage, '88 51
Casserole, Cheesy Hominy, '83 170
Casserole, Chile-Hominy, '81 29
Casserole, Hominy-Chili, '86 255
Caviar, Texas, '86 218
Cheese Hominy, Hot, '84 77
Chiles and Cheese, Hominy with, '86 78
Gold Coast Hominy, '83 52
Jalapeño Hominy, '82 51
Mexican Hominy, '86 255; '91 133, 162
Salad, Hominy-Bean, '88 266
Skillet, Hominy-Sausage, '81 29
Soup, Bean-and-Hominy, '95 23
Soup, Black, White, and Red All Over, '95 126
Soup, Southwest, '86 255

HONEY
Ambrosia, Honey Bee, '83 267
Apple Quarters, Honey-Baked, '86 93
Apples, Honey-Baked, '83 234; '84 244
Apples, Honey-Yogurt, '92 46
Bananas, Honey-Baked, '81 268
Breads
    Applesauce-Honey Nut Bread, '87 300
    Banana Bread, Honey-, '91 68
    Biscuits, Honey Angel, '95 138
    Cinnamon Swirl Bread, Honey-, '88 287
    Curry Bread, Honey-, '89 250
    Granola Bread, Honey-, '86 56
    Muffins, Banana-Honey-Nut, '88 62
    Muffins, Honey Bran, '88 171
    Muffins, Honey-Bran, '89 250
    Muffins, Honey-Oatmeal, '84 229
    Muffins, Honey-Wheat, '83 96; '88 263
    Muffins, Oatmeal-Honey, '83 95
    Muffins, Orange-Honey, '88 284
    Muffins, Peanut Butter-Honey, '82 56
    Oat Bread, Honey-, '89 107; '93 232
    Oatmeal Bread, Honey, '80 60
    Rolls, Dilled Honey-Wheat, '83 254
    Rolls, Honey Wheat, '83 278
    Rolls, Super Honey, '80 115
    Wheat Bread, Honey, '85 18, 268
    Wheat Bread, Honey-, '91 223
    Whole Wheat Honey Bread, '82 65; '83 106
    Zucchini-Honey Bread, '89 143
Brie, Honey-Mustard, '91 252
Brownies, Heavenly Honey, '79 83
Buns, Honey Oatmeal, '83 154
Butter, Cinnamon-Honey, '89 281
Butter, Honey, '93 309; '94 206; '95 139
Butter, Honey-Orange, '79 36; '85 19
Cake, Honey, '92 250
Cake, Honey-Oatmeal, '87 222
Cake, Southern Honey, '89 251
Cake Squares, Honey, '89 250
Carrots, Honey-Glazed, '80 115; '84 121; '85 18

Carrots, Honey-Kissed, '84 122
Chicken, Honey, '82 55; '88 67
Chicken, Honey-Curry, '87 36
Chicken Wings, Honey-Glazed, '91 251
Cornbread, Honey, '83 286; '84 17
Crunch, Honey-and-Spice, '94 290
Dip, Coconut-Honey Fruit, '84 171
Dip, Peanut Butter-Honey, '85 19
Dressings
    Berry Dressing, Orange Salad with Honey-, '89 250
    Celery-Honey Dressing, '80 42
    Dijon-Honey Dressing, '89 45
    French Dressing, Honey, '87 81
    Honey Dressing, '79 242; '83 146; '87 129
    Lemon Dressing, Fruit Salad with Honey-, '93 21
    Lemon Dressing, Honey-, '95 133
    Lime Dressing, Honey-, '83 139; '93 71
    Lime-Honey Dressing, '92 213
    Lime-Honey Fruit Salad Dressing, '87 81
    Mustard Dressing, Honey-, '90 55, 111, 146
    Orange Salad with Honey Dressing, '89 14
    Spinach Salad with Honey Dressing, '90 16
    Tomato-Honey French Dressing, '81 105
    Vinaigrette, Honey-Mustard, '94 249
    Vinaigrette, Honey-Orange, '91 255
    Walnut Dressing, Honey-, '93 107
    Yogurt Dressing, Honey-, '93 172
Filling, Honey, '88 287
Filling, Honey-Walnut, '80 21
Frosting, Honey Chocolate, '79 83
Glaze, Chocolate-Honey, '82 306
Glaze, Cranberry-Honey, '89 273
Glaze, Honey, '88 287
Glaze, Honey-Nut, '87 15
Grapes, Honeyed, '95 47
Ham, Honey-Orange Glazed, '83 320
Ham Slice, Honey-Glazed, '81 104
Ice Cream, Honey-Vanilla, '95 178
Kabobs, Honey Ham, '80 156
Leeks, Honey-Glazed, '86 62
Lemon Honey, '94 16
Loaves, Hint o' Honey, '81 104
Marinade, Garlic-Honey, '93 102
Marinade, Honey-Mustard, '93 103
Mousse, Honeyed Chocolate, '87 223
Mustard, Hot Honey, '93 240
Mustard, Peppered Honey, '95 312
Onions, Honey, '81 86
Onions, Honey-Paprika Sweet, '92 52
Pancakes, Honey, '91 139
Peaches, Honey-Sweet, '85 107
Peaches 'n' Cream, Honeyed, '93 134
Pear Honey, '90 159
Pears, Honey-Baked, '93 47
Pears, Pineapple-Honey, '86 94
Pecans, Honeycomb, '84 300
Pecans, Sugar-and-Honey, '86 319
Pork Chops, Honey-Lime, '91 33
Pork Tenderloin, Honey-Mustard, '95 52
Preserves, Honeyed Peach, '85 130
Rice, Honey, '85 83
Rings, Honey Apple, '80 243
Rutabaga, Honey, '91 220
Salad, Honey Fruit, '80 276

Sauces
    Butter Sauce, Honey-, '85 18
    Chicken in Honey Sauce, '89 82
    Chocolate Sauce, Honey-, '89 251
    Cinnamon-Pecan-Honey Pancake Sauce, '88 46
    Lemon Mustard Sauce, Honey-, '84 275
    Lime Sauce, Honey-, '82 85
    Mustard Sauce, Honey-, '85 13
    Mustard Sauce, Smoked Ribs with Honey-, '92 168
    Orange Sauce, Honey-, '85 108
    Poppy Seed Sauce, Honey-, '93 13
    Sundae Sauce, Honeyscotch, '82 167
    Yogurt Sauce, Honey-, '92 307
Shrimp, Tangy Honeyed, '94 32
Smoothie, Fruited Honey-Yogurt, '88 231; '89 23
Smoothie, Honey-Banana, '89 144
Snapper, Honey-Curried, '85 181
Spareribs, Honey-Glazed, '82 163
Spread, Honey, '81 229
Spread, Honey-Nut, '87 157
Stir-Fry, Honey-Butternut, '93 184
Swirl, Honey-Walnut, '80 21
Syrup, Maple-Honey-Cinnamon, '85 19
Tea, Honey, '81 105
Topping, Honey, '83 154
Turkey Salad, Honey-Mustard, '92 309
Twist, Honey, '79 80
Vegetables, Honey-Mustard Marinated, '93 236
Whip, Peaches with Honey-Lime, '85 108
Yogurt, Orange Slices with Honey, '91 68

HONEYDEW. *See* **MELONS.**

HORS D'OEUVRES. *See* **APPETIZERS.**

HOT DOGS. *See* **FRANKFURTERS.**

HUSH PUPPIES
Acorn Squash Puppies, '94 268
Aunt Jenny's Hush Puppies, '84 88
Bacon Hush Puppies, '91 201
Baked Hush Puppies, '89 53; '95 108
Beer Hush Puppies, Fiery, '86 233
Corn, Hush Puppies with, '83 286; '84 17
Cracker Hush Puppies, '80 99
Easy Hush Puppies, '81 191; '85 14
Golden Hush Puppies, '82 135
Hush Puppies, '84 102; '87 15; '92 168
Mexican Hush Puppies, '90 214
Mexican Hush Puppies, Cheesy, '91 201
Onion Hush Puppies, '85 14
Peppery Hush Puppies, '80 221; '88 111
Tomato-Onion Hush Puppies, '91 201
Topsail Island Hush Puppies, '79 152

ICE CREAMS. *See also* SHERBETS.
Alaska, Apple Baked, '80 226
Alaska, Baked, '84 105; '85 295
Alaska, Brownie Baked, '80 66
Alaska, Mint Patty, '80 219
Alaskas, Banana Split, '87 10
Almond-Fudge Ice Cream, '93 205
Amaretto Freeze, '82 182
Balls, Almond Ice Cream, '86 315
Balls, Easy Ice Cream, '84 106
Balls, Nutty Ice Cream, '89 72
Banana-Graham Ice Cream, '91 56
Bananas Foster, Elegant, '81 59
Banana Split Ice Cream, '80 176
Banana Split Pie, Layered, '83 189

ICE CREAMS (*continued*)

Beverages
    Almond Float, Nutmeg-, **'84** 106
    Amaretto Breeze, **'83** 172
    Apple Juice Shrub, Shenandoah, **'79** 282
    Banana Flip, **'83** 303
    Banana-Pineapple Milk Shake, **'84** 59
    Banana Smoothie, **'87** 160
    Brandy Cream, **'84** 312
    Champagne Delight, **'83** 304
    Chocolate-Mint Smoothie, **'84** 166
    Coffee Floats, Maple-, **'86** 195
    Coffee Punch, Creamy, **'81** 50
    Coffee Refresher, Velvet, **'79** 149
    Cranberry Float, Sparkling, **'86** 195
    Cranberry-Orange Soda, **'79** 148
    Cranberry Shake, **'83** 171
    Fruit Float, Frosty, **'87** 159
    Ginger Fizz, Ice Cream, **'83** 303
    Golden Dream, **'82** 100
    Kahlúa Velvet Frosty, **'82** 244
    Lime Cooler, **'87** 160
    Lime Fizz, **'81** 172
    Lime-Pineapple Punch, **'83** 142
    Mocha Punch, **'84** 166
    Orange Milk Shake, **'84** 166
    Orange Shake, Peachy, **'81** 156
    Peach Frosty, **'81** 156
    Peanut Butter Milkshakes, **'85** 198
    Peanut Butter Shake, **'82** 48
    Pineapple Soda, **'90** 179
    Pink Soda, Blushing, **'90** 104
    Punch, Parsonage, **'79** 148
    Raisin Shake, Amazin', **'86** 195
    Raspberry Fizz, Rosy, **'90** 179
    Rum Coffee Cream, Icy, **'83** 172
    Shake, Pep, **'79** 38
    Strawberry-Banana Float, **'87** 160
    Strawberry Milkshake, Fresh, **'82** 113
    Strawberry-Pineapple Shake, **'84** 166
    Strawberry Punch, Creamy, **'86** 195
    Strawberry Smoothie, **'86** 183
    Strawberry Soda, Old-Fashioned, **'79** 149
    Tahitian Flower, **'87** 159
    Vanilla Frosty, French, **'79** 148
    Whispers, **'86** 317
Black Forest Ice Cream, **'88** 203
Blueberry Ice Cream, **'88** 203
Bombe, Amber, **'80** 255
Bombe, Ice Cream, **'82** 305; **'90** 269
Bombe with Raspberry Sauce, Creamy, **'89** 322
Bourbon Ice Cream, **'87** 139
Brownie Dessert, Special-Occasion, **'87** 139
Brownies, Chocolate Ice Cream, **'89** 124
Butter Crisp Ice Cream, **'92** 132
Butter Pecan Ice Cream, **'80** 176; **'86** 129; **'88** 202
Cake for Grown-Ups, Ice Cream, **'88** M192
Cake, Fruity Ice Cream, **'87** 110
Cake, Ice Cream, **'86** 321; **'89** 71
Cake, Ice Cream Angel, **'83** 23
Cake, Praline Ice Cream, **'80** 84
Candy Crunch Ice Cream, **'79** 166
Cantaloupe Ice Cream, **'79** 177
Caramel Ice Cream Dessert, **'95** 36
Caramel-Vanilla Helado (Caramel-Vanilla Ice Cream), **'81** 67
Cherry Ice Cream, **'84** 184
Cherry-Nut Ice Cream, **'86** 129

Cherry-Pecan Ice Cream, **'88** 203
Chocolate Chunk-Peanut Butter Ice Cream, **'85** 297; **'86** 120
Chocolate Cookie Ice Cream, **'95** 245
Chocolate-Covered Peanut Ice Cream, **'88** 203
Chocolate Ice Cream, **'80** 176; **'86** 129
Chocolate Ice Cream, Mexican, **'91** 162
Cinnamon Ice Cream, **'95** 126
Cinnamon Ice Cream Sombreros, **'93** 276
Coconut Ice Cream, Fresh, **'79** 166
Coffee Ice Cream, **'88** 202
Coffee Ice Cream Crunch, **'82** 182
Cookies and Cream Ice Cream, **'88** 203
Crêpes, Coffee Ice Cream, **'84** 85
Crêpes, Strawberry Ice Cream, **'87** 290
Delight, Ice Cream, **'80** 69
Dessert, Decadent Ice Cream, **'91** 56
Dessert, Layered Ice Cream, **'83** 189; **'84** 94, 105; **'86** 163
Double-Chocolate Ice Cream, **'88** 203
Fennel Ice Cream, **'95** 281
Fig Ice Cream, **'87** 139
Frangelica Cream, **'89** 291
French-Fried Ice Cream, **'85** 141
Fried Ice Cream, Coconut, **'85** 141
Fried Ice Cream Puffs, **'85** 141
Fruit Cream, Frozen, **'94** 129
Fudge-Peanut Ice Cream Dessert, **'88** 167
Galore and More, Ice Cream, **'91** 144
Granitas
    Coffee-Kahlúa Granita, **'88** 118
    Grape Granita, **'88** 118
    Honeydew Granita, **'87** 162
    Mint Tea Granita, **'88** 117
    Orange Granita, **'88** 118
    Raspberry Liqueur Granita, **'88** 117
Hawaiian Frappé, **'81** 178
Honey-Vanilla Ice Cream, **'95** 178
Ice Milks
    Banana Yogurt Ice Milk, **'89** 199
    Strawberry Ice Milk, Fresh, **'92** 94
Ices
    Apricot Yogurt Ice, **'81** 177
    Avocado Ice, **'83** 179
    Champagne Ice, **'90** 315
    Cider Ice, **'83** 162
    Cranberry-Apple Ice, **'82** 290
    Cranberry Ice, Tangy, **'87** 305
    Cranberry-Orange Ice, Tart, **'86** 317
    Fruit Ice, **'86** 176
    Fruit Ice, Mixed, **'81** 178
    Grapefruit Ice, **'91** 122
    Grape Ice, **'83** 162
    Kiwi Ice, **'84** 315
    Merlot Ice, **'93** 323
    Muscadine Ice, **'82** 202
    Peach Ice, **'81** 178
    Peach-Yogurt Ice, **'84** 83
    Pink Grapefruit Ice, **'85** 304
    Raspberry Ice, **'92** 268
    Strawberry Ice, **'84** 175; **'85** 108
    Strawberry-Orange Ice, **'86** 196
    Watermelon Ice, **'91** 173
    Wine Ice, **'83** 163
Italian-Style Ice Cream, **'79** 245
Lemonade Ice Cream, **'88** 202
Lemon Ice Cream, **'79** 142; **'83** 170; **'91** 65
Lemon Ice Cream Tarts, **'80** 152
Loaf, Pink Lemonade Ice Cream, **'88** 202
Log, Ice Cream Yule, **'83** 253
Making Ice Cream, About, **'82** 171

Mango Ice Cream, **'86** 216
Mint-Chocolate Chip Ice Cream, **'88** 202
Mint-Chocolate Chip Ice Cream Squares, **'94** 245
Mint Ice-Cream Angel Dessert, Triple, **'93** 86
Mint Ice Cream Dessert, **'88** 66
Mocha Ice Cream, **'88** 202
Orange-Pineapple Ice Cream, **'86** 117
Parfaits, Chocolate-Crème de Menthe, **'85** 161
Parfaits, Coffee Crunch, **'82** 159
Parfait, Strawberry, **'79** 99
Parfait, Surprise Strawberry, **'86** 151
Peach-Almond Ice Cream, **'89** 156
Peach Ice Cream, **'81** 184; **'82** 171; **'83** 159; **'86** 15; **'93** 135
Peach Ice Cream, Creamy, **'85** 177
Peach Ice Cream, Deluxe, **'80** 176; **'90** 314
Peach Ice Cream, Fresh, **'95** 195
Peanut Butter Ice Cream, **'81** 103; **'88** 64, 203
Peanut Ice Cream, **'92** 132
Peppermint Ice Cream, **'80** 176; **'86** 129
Pies
    Banana Split Pie, Layered, **'83** 189
    Caramel Ice Cream Pie, **'82** 181
    Carrot Ice Cream Pie, **'86** 200
    Chocolate-Ice Cream Pie, **'87** 224
    Chocolate Ice Cream Pie, **'91** 56
    Chocolate-Mint Ice Cream Pie, **'81** 144
    Coffee Ice Cream Pie, **'79** 231
    Divine Ice Cream Pie, Absolutely, **'82** 181
    Double-Delight Ice Cream Pie, **'89** 72
    Heavenly Ice Cream Pie, **'82** 181
    Kona Ice Cream Pie, **'83** 189
    Lemon Ice Cream Pie, **'80** 70
    Meringue-Pecan Crust, Ice Cream Pie with, **'88** 127
    Nutty Ice Cream Pie, **'91** 180
    Peanutty Ice Cream Pie, **'82** 56
    Peppermint Candy-Ice Cream Pie, **'87** 260
    Pumpkin Ice Cream Pie, **'81** 272
    Pumpkin-Ice Cream Pie, **'87** 243
    Rum-Fruit Sauce, Ice Cream Pie with, **'84** 312
    Spectacular, Ice-Cream Pie, **'90** 314
    Sundae Pie, Ice Cream, **'94** 244
Piña Colada Ice Cream, **'91** 181
Pineapple-Mint Ice Cream, **'84** 186
Praline Freeze, **'90** 48
Praline Ice Cream, **'89** 318
Pralines and Cream Ice Cream, **'82** 184; **'83** 159
Rainbow Candy Ice Cream, **'88** 202
Raspberry Ice Cream, **'80** 176
Raspberry Ice Cream, Fresh, **'86** 152
Roll, Chocolate-Frosted Ice Cream, **'84** 200
Roll, Strawberry Ice Cream, **'84** 105
Salad, Ice Cream, **'79** 126
Sandwiches, Chocolate Cookie Ice Cream, **'87** 147
Sandwiches, Chocolate Ice Cream, **'89** 72
Sandwiches, Oatmeal Crispy Ice Cream, **'93** 199
Sandwiches, Peanut Butter Cookie Ice Cream, **'93** 199
Sandwich Shells, Brownie Ice Cream, **'88** 195
Scuppernong Ice Cream, **'88** 216
Snow Ice Cream, **'88** 10

ICE CREAMS (continued)

Sorbets
    Avocado Sorbet, '88 117
    Banana-Orange Sorbet, '88 117
    Berry Sorbet, Very, '90 85
    Blueberry-Kirsch Sorbet, '83 120
    Cran-Apple Spice Sorbet, '93 153
    Cranberry Juice Sorbet, '85 259
    Cranberry Sorbet, '82 251
    Grapefruit-Mint Sorbet, '93 153
    Lemon Sorbet, '93 153
    Mango Sorbet, '86 196
    Orange Sorbet, Fresh, '92 143
    Peach Sorbet, '93 153
    Pear-Lemon Sorbet, '88 116
    Pink Grapefruit and Tarragon Sorbet,
      '95 163
    Strawberry-Champagne Sorbet, '83 162;
      '95 20
    Strawberry Margarita Sorbet, '89 111
    Strawberry Sorbet, '88 117; '93 153
    Watermelon Sorbet, '92 190
Squares, Ice Cream Party, '91 214
Straw-Ba-Nut Ice Cream, '80 177
Strawberries and Cream, '92 132
Strawberry-Banana-Nut Ice Cream, '88 203
Strawberry Ice Cream, '80 177
Strawberry Ice Cream Crêpes, '88 135
Strawberry Ice Cream, Fresh, '89 111
Strawberry Ice Cream, Homemade, '84 184
Strawberry Ice Cream, Old-Fashioned, '79 94
Strawberry Ice Cream, Very, '81 155
Sundaes
    Apple Ice Cream Sundaes, Spicy,
      '86 M195
    Cocoa-Kahlúa Sundaes, '83 M58
    Hot Fudge Sundae Dessert, '84 313
    Mauna Loa Sundaes, '80 126
    Peach Sundaes Flambé, '81 88
    Pear Sundaes, Quick, '86 71
    Strawberry Sundaes, Hot, '81 M5
Toffee Ice Cream, '88 202
Toffee Ice Cream Dessert, '87 110
Treats, Crunchy Ice Cream, '86 300; '87 178
Tropical Paradise, Frozen, '89 206
Tutti-Frutti Ice Cream, '86 129
Vanilla Custard Ice Cream, '92 148
Vanilla Ice Cream, '80 176; '86 129; '91 174
Vanilla Ice Cream, Basic, '88 202
Vanilla Ice Cream, Country, '82 143
Vanilla Ice Cream Spectacular, '82 166
ICINGS. *See* **FROSTINGS.**

J
AMBALAYAS
Black-Eyed Pea Jambalaya, '92 70
Chicken-and-Sausage Jambalaya, '88 200;
  '91 216
Creole Jambalaya, '81 51; '87 210
de Covington, Jambalaya, '87 211
Good Luck Jambalaya, '87 11
Jambalaya, '84 282
Oven Jambalaya, '84 44
Red Rice Jambalaya, '91 18
Sausage Jambalaya, '80 210; '84 249
Seafood Jambalaya, Three-, '82 126
Shrimp Jambalaya, Creole, '92 99
Smoked Sausage Jambalaya, '79 42
Trail Jambalaya, '93 179
Tuna Jambalaya, '83 44

JAMS AND JELLIES
Apple Jelly, '82 149
Apple Jelly, Spiced, '95 251
Apple-Mint Jelly, '87 134
Apricot Jam, Golden, '80 31
Banana Jam, '82 296
Basil Jelly, '82 301
Blackberry Jam, '82 149; '89 138
Blackberry Jelly, '82 149
Blueberry Jam, '79 120; '85 130
Cantaloupe-Peach Jam, '95 143
Champagne Jelly, '90 248
Chile Piquín Jelly, '94 28
Christmas Brunch Jam, '81 286
Christmas Jam, '88 288
Conserves
    Apple-Cranberry Conserve, '82 308
    Blueberry Conserve, '82 149
    Cranberry Conserve, '79 243; '85 266
    Fruit Conserve, Dried, '82 308
    Peach Conserve, '79 120
Crabapple Jelly, '79 120; '81 217; '89 139
Cranberry-Wine Jelly, '81 290
Di-Calcium Phosphate Solution, '89 138
Fig Jam, '86 206
Freezer
    Blackberry Jam, Freezer, '84 M181
    Christmas Freezer Jelly, '86 M288
    Grape-Burgundy Freezer Jelly,
      '85 130
    Peach Jam, Freezer, '83 182; '84 M182
    Peach-Plum Freezer Jam, '85 130
    Plum Jam, Freezer, '89 M156
    Raspberry Freezer Jam, '84 M181
    Strawberry Freezer Jam, '84 M182
    Strawberry Preserves, Freezer, '82 112
Grape Jelly, '89 140
Grape Jelly, Quick, '89 M156
Grape Jelly, Thyme-, '89 193
Green Pepper Jelly, Unusual, '82 132
Green Tomato Jam, '79 121
Jalapeño Jelly, '92 230
Kudzu Blossom Jelly, '95 198
Lime Jelly, '94 23
Marmalades
    Apple Marmalade, '79 120
    Carrot-Citrus Marmalade, '81 148
    Citrus Marmalade, '80 101
    Citrus Marmalade, Combination,
      '80 50
    Citrus Marmalade, Mixed, '81 43
    Fruit Marmalade, Delicious, '81 285
    Grapefruit Marmalade, '82 308
    Kumquat Marmalade, '90 48
    Orange Marmalade, '81 42
    Orange-Pineapple Marmalade, '82 150;
      '89 M156
    Peach-Orange Marmalade, '82 150
    Pear Marmalade, '79 196
    Strawberry-Pineapple Marmalade,
      '85 130
Mint Jelly, '79 121; '82 301
Muscadine Jelly, Wild, '79 32
Onion Jelly, '93 135
Peach-Banana Jam, Rosy, '80 142
Peach Jam, '93 135
Pear Jam, Paradise, '84 300
Pepper Jelly, '79 121
Pineapple Jam, '81 147
Pineapple-Orange Mint Jelly, '92 105
Plum Jelly, '82 150
Port Wine Jelly with Whipped Cream,
  '84 254

Preserves
    Fig Preserves, '79 140; '82 150; '89 140
    Mango-Pineapple Preserves, '79 137
    Peach Preserves, '81 147; '89 140
    Peach Preserves, Honeyed, '85 130
    Peach Preserves, Old-Fashioned, '82 150
    Pear Preserves, '82 195
    Strawberry Preserves, '79 120; '81 96
    Strawberry Preserves Deluxe, '82 150
    Watermelon Preserves, '79 120
Red Bell Pepper Jam, '95 242
Red Pepper Jelly, '89 M156
Refrigerator
    Berry Refrigerator Jam, '89 139
    Blueberry Refrigerator Jam, '89 139
    Plum Refrigerator Jam, '89 139
Rose Geranium Jelly, '82 301
Rosemary Jelly, '82 301
Sage Jelly, '82 301
Sangría Jelly, '93 341
Strawberry Jam, '89 138
Strawberry Jelly, '81 147
Thyme Jelly, '82 301
Wine Jelly, '88 243
Wine Jelly, Rosy, '85 306

JICAMA
Compote, Jicama-Fruit, '92 49
French-Fried Jicama, '81 88
Parsleyed Jicama, '81 88
Salad, Jicama, '87 123
Salad, Jicama-and-Orange, '88 246
Salad, Jicama-Fruit, '86 83
Salad, Jicama-Orange, '86 83; '90 122
Tomatillo Soup with Crunchy Jicama, '92 245

K
ABOBS
Antipasto Kabobs, '94 144
Beef
    Beef Kabobs, '85 110
    Chile-Beef Kabobs, '94 251
    Deluxe Beef Kabobs, '82 182
    Hot-and-Spicy Kabobs, '87 193
    Marinated Beef Kabobs, '82 105;
      '85 159
    Marinated Beef Kabobs with Rice, '84 32
    Meatball Kabobs, '95 192
    Pineapple-Beef Kabobs, '83 212
    Saucy Beef Kabobs, '83 109
    Sirloin Kabobs, Marinated, '82 162
    Spirited Beef Kabobs, '87 142
    Steak-and-Shrimp Kabobs, '80 184
    Steak Kabobs, '82 4; '93 95
    Steak Kabobs, Barbecued, '79 89
    Steak Kabobs, Marinated, '80 184

KABOBS, Beef (continued)

Steak on a Stick, '83 109
Steak with Vegetables, Skewered, '81 124
Teriyaki Beef Kabobs, '80 207
Vegetable Kabobs, Beef-and-, '91 148
Vegetables, Beef Kabobs with, '90 148
Cantaloupe Wedges, Grilled, '87 162
Cheese Kabobs, Peppered, '91 279
Fruit Kabobs, '86 181; '89 85
Fruit Kabobs, Winter, '89 34
Fruit Kabobs with Coconut Dressing, '87 251
Fruit Kabobs with Mint Marinade, '82 157
Fruity Mermaid Kabobs, '91 177
Ham Kabobs, Honey, '80 156
Ham Kabobs, Swiss-, '81 124
Lamb Kabobs, '85 159; '86 90; '92 129;
'95 192
Lamb Kabobs, Rosemary Marinated, '93 203
Lamb Kabobs, Saucy, '89 167
Lamb Kabobs, Savory, '80 184
Lamb Shish Kabobs, '79 142; '93 70
Liver Kabobs, '80 185
Oysters Brochette, '80 56
Pepper Kabobs, Pretty, '90 166
Pork Kabobs, Spicy, '82 182
Poultry
Chicken-Avocado Kabobs, '82 9; '83 68
Chicken, Garlic-Grilled, '87 180
Chicken Kabobs, '87 141
Chicken Kabobs, Good-and-Easy, '85 87
Chicken Kabobs, Marinated, '84 M144
Chicken Kabobs, Oriental, '95 193
Chicken Kabobs, Pineapple-, '86 M328
Chicken Kabobs, Sesame, '82 165
Chicken Kabobs, Soy-, '86 156
Chicken Kabobs Supreme, '81 124
Chicken Livers en Brochette, '84 222
Duck Kabobs with Almond Rice, Grilled,
'91 291
Hawaiian Kabobs, '85 157
Turkey-and-Fruit Kabobs, '88 140
Rumaki Kabobs, '82 182
Salmon Kabobs, '81 182
Scallop-Bacon Kabobs, '81 111
Scallop Kabobs, Grilled, '83 101
Scallop Kabobs, Sea, '82 162
Scallops en Brochette with Vegetables, '80 163
Seafood Brochette, '87 96
Shish Kabobs, '82 182; '85 M112
Shish Kabobs, Overnight, '81 124
Shish Kabobs Teriyaki, '85 37
Shrimp
Appetizer Shrimp Kabobs, '91 251
Barbecued Shrimp, '90 28
Marinated and Grilled Shrimp, '87 141
Marinated Shrimp, Grilled, '87 173
Marinated Shrimp Kabobs, '84 276;
'85 158
Scallop Kabobs, Grilled Shrimp-and-,
'92 210
Shrimp Kabobs, '80 150, 184
Steak-and-Shrimp Kabobs, '80 184
Squash-and-Pepper Kabobs, Summery,
'95 193
Vegetable Kabobs, Fresh, '81 158; '92 101
Vegetable Kabobs, Grilled, '93 170
Vegetable Kabobs, Marinated, '83 M195
Vegetable Kabobs, Tangy Marinated, '88 142
Vegetable Skewers, Grilled, '94 160
Venison Kabobs, '82 215; '88 249
Watermelon, Sherried, '92 117

KIWIFRUIT

Chutney, Kiwifruit-Onion, '93 125
Dessert, Kiwi-and-Orange, '93 295
Glacé, Sabayon, '89 306
Ice, Kiwi, '84 315
Jubilee, Kiwi, '83 120
Meringue Cups, Kiwi and Cream in, '81 279
Muffins, Kiwifruit, '87 255
Orange Roughy, Kiwi, '87 193
Parfait, Kiwi, '86 199; '87 55
Pizza, Kiwi-Berry, '86 198; '87 55
Pizza, Kiwifruit, '89 306
Salad, Peach-and-Kiwi, '90 180
Salad, Spinach-Kiwifruit, '87 305
Salsa, Hot Kiwifruit, '94 82
Tart, Kiwifruit, '89 232
Tart, Kiwifruit-Peach, '88 20

LAMB

Barbecued Lamb, '79 58
Burgers, Mesquite-Grilled Lamb, '88 59
Burgoo, Five-Meat, '87 3
Casserole, Moussaka, '79 179
Chops
Barbecued Lamb Chops, '79 89
Broiled Lamb Chops, '85 22
Dijonaise, Gourmet Lamb Chops,
'82 93
Dijon Lamb Chops, '84 277
Dijon-Rosemary Lamb Chops, '95 285
Grilled Lamb Chops, '91 163
Herbs, Lamb Chops with, '90 164
Orange Lamb Chops, '83 35
Peppercorn-Crusted Lamb Chops,
'92 142
Shrimp, Lamb Chops with, '88 58
Teriyaki, Lamb Chops, '85 109
Teriyaki Lamb Chops, '87 60
Curried Lamb with Rice, '82 93
Curried Lamb with Rice Mold, '85 36
Curry with Rice, Lamb, '80 83; '81 10
Fillets of Lamb with Vegetables, '85 36
Grape Leaves, Stuffed, '94 48
Grilled Lamb with Sweet Pepper Relish,
'95 104
Kabobs
Lamb Kabobs, '85 159; '86 90; '92 129;
'95 192
Marinated Lamb Kabobs, Rosemary,
'93 203
Saucy Lamb Kabobs, '89 167
Savory Lamb Kabobs, '80 184
Shish Kabobs, '82 182; '85 M112
Shish Kabobs, Lamb, '79 142; '93 70
Shish Kabobs, Overnight, '81 124
Shish Kabobs Teriyaki, '85 37
Leg of Lamb
Cranberry Leg of Lamb, '90 52
Glazed Lamb, Honey-Mustard, '90 52
Glazed Leg of Lamb, '86 90
Greek-Style Leg of Lamb, '93 170
Grilled Lamb with Mango Salsa, '95 104
Half of Leg of Lamb, '86 90
Hawaii, Lamb, '81 58
Hunter Sauce, Leg of Lamb with,
'95 317
Leg of Lamb, '86 90; '95 285
Mustard Sauce, Leg of Lamb with,
'89 71
Roasted Lamb Rosemary, '88 244
Roasted Rosemary Lamb, '86 89

Roast, Garlic-Rolled Lamb, '92 128;
'93 113
Roast Leg of Lamb, '87 96
Stuffed Leg of Lamb, '82 93; '87 248
Meatballs with Yogurt Sauce, Lamb, '85 132
Meat Loaf, Minted Lamb, '93 248
Moussaka, '87 166
Pie, Lamb, '90 26
Pilaf, Hearty Lamb, '83 101
Pockets with Dilled Cucumber Topping,
Lamb, '87 104
Quenelles, Veal-Vermicelli Soup with, '94 14
Rack of Lamb, '89 270
Rack of Lamb, Marinated, '94 55
Rack of Lamb with Cherry-Wine Sauce,
Hazelnut-Crusted, '95 284
Rack of Lamb with Herb Mustard Glaze,
'81 260
Roast of Lamb, Crown, '81 58
Roast, Rolled Lamb, '95 285
Salad, Spinach-Lamb, '85 58
Shanks, Barbecued Lamb, '92 128; '93 113
Shanks Milanaise, Lamb, '82 93
Steak, Destin Lamb, '92 129; '93 113
Steaks with Béarnaise Sauce, Lamb, '85 37
Stewed Lamb with Five Spices, '92 72
Stew, Emerald Isle, '95 71
Stew-in-a-Loaf, Lamb, '85 37
Stew, Lamb, '79 293; '88 58
Stew with Popovers, Lamb, '94 43
Stir-Fry, Indian, '92 126

LASAGNA

Beefy Lasagna, '80 81
Bun, Lasagna in a, '90 176
Cheesy Lasagna, '82 224; '88 299
Chicken Lasagna, '87 M302; '88 90; '92 197;
'93 25
Chicken Lasagna Bake, '95 55
Chicken Lasagna Florentine, '95 158
Crawfish Lasagna, '91 89
Easy Lasagna, '92 M197; '93 M24
Ham-and-Chicken Lasagna, Creamy, '95 88
Lasagna, '82 119; '83 M6
Lean Lasagna, '86 37
Light Lasagna, '95 212
Maria, Lasagna, '90 191
Mexican Lasagna, '89 63
Noodles Lasagna, Lots of, '91 M127
One-Step Lasagna, '89 M129
Pizza, Lasagna, '85 285
Quick Lasagna, '84 220
Quick 'n Easy Lasagna, '80 M10
Rolls, Pepper-Topped Lasagna, '89 M36
Sausage Lasagna, '83 288
Sausage-Lasagna Rollups, '80 236
Sausage Pinwheels, Lasagna, '79 6
Simple Lasagna, '81 188
South-of-the-Border Lasagna, '84 31
Supreme, Lasagna, '92 198; '93 24
Tofu Lasagna, '83 312
Tuna Lasagna, '83 44; '84 123
Turkey Lasagna, '83 239; '91 130
Two, Lasagna for, '81 91
Vegetable
Casserole, Vegetable Lasagna, '92 198;
'93 25
Cheesy Vegetable Lasagna, '79 84
Colorful Vegetable Lasagna, '87 19
Florentine, Creamy Lasagna, '91 94
Florentine, Lasagna, '88 196
Garden Lasagna, '83 119
Spaghetti Squash Lasagna, '84 127
Spinach-Bean Lasagna, '92 96

LASAGNA, Vegetable *(continued)*

Spinach Lasagna, '79 25; '81 243
Spinach Lasagna, Cheesy, '80 32;
'83 204
Vegetable Lasagna, '84 201; '93 320;
'95 211
Zucchini Lasagna, '85 194
Vintage Lasagna, '79 194
Zesty Lasagna, '87 M188

LEEKS
Bisque, Crab-and-Leek, '94 104
Dilled Lemon-Butter, Leeks in, '90 M98
Dilly Leek Combo, '82 26
Dip, Creamy Leek, '86 77
Glazed Leeks, '82 26
Glazed Leeks, Honey-, '86 62
Medley, Carrot-and-Leek, '88 102
Orange Sauce, Leeks in, '88 86
Quiche, Cheddar-Leek, '88 198
Roasted Potatoes, Carrots, and Leeks,
'94 276
Soup, Carrot-Leek, '86 34
Soup, Leek-and-Potato, '84 112
Soup, Leek-Vegetable, '86 304
Soup, Watercress-and-Leek, '86 161
Tarragon Leeks, '84 66
Terrine, Cold Chicken-Leek, '92 145

LEMON
Apples, Chilled Poached Lemon, '86 182
Artichoke Hearts with Lemon, '90 98
Asparagus, Lemon-Sesame, '91 31
Bagel Chips, Lemon-and-Herb, '91 139
Beans, Lemon-Mint, '88 22
Beverages
Apple Lemonade, '89 212
Berry Delicious Lemonade, '93 205
Caribbean Cooler, '95 203
Claret Lemonade, '93 72
Concentrate, Lemonade, '89 110
Cooler, Lemon, '82 48
Cranberry Lemonade, Spiced, '87 292
Cubes, Lemonade, '95 201
Cubes, Lemon-Mint, '95 201
Frappé, Lemon, '92 44
Fresh Squeezed Lemonade, '81 172
Front Porch Lemonade, '90 156
Hot Buttered Lemonade, '88 208;
'94 18
Margaritas, Lemon-Lime, '94 227
Mist, Orange-Lemon, '79 288; '80 35
Orange-Mint Lemonade, '88 82
Piña Coladas, '95 203
Pineapple Lemonade, '93 194
Punch, Lemonade-Bourbon, '95 287
Punch, Lemon Balm, '80 42
Punch, Lemon Champagne, '94 176
Punch, Sparkling Lemonade, '88 276
Punch, Strawberry-Lemonade, '85 116;
'91 175
Sipper, Sunshine, '86 179
Slush, Pink Lemonade, '80 151
Strawberry Lemonade, '80 160
Sweetened Preserved Lemons, '95 141
Syrup, Cherry-Lemonade, '86 214
Tea, Almond-Lemonade, '86 229
Tea Cubes, Lemonade with Frozen,
'85 161
Tea, Lemon, '82 156
Tea, Lemon-Mint, '85 162
Tea Tingler, Lemon, '95 200
Velvet, Lemon, '90 15

Breads
Blueberry-Lemon Bread, '85 190
French Lemon Spirals, '81 94
Lemon Bread, '79 275; '87 256
Muffins, Blueberry-Lemon, '79 7
Muffins, Fresh Lemon, '79 161
Muffins, Lemon, '88 119, M275
Muffins, Lemon-Raspberry, '92 119
Nut Bread, Lemon-, '79 24
Pecan Bread, Lemon-, '83 54
Scones, Lemon-Raisin, '87 69
Tea Bread, Lemon, '92 268; '93 183
Tea Loaf, Lemon-Cream, '84 50
Broccoli Goldenrod, Lemon-, '84 M89
Broccoli, Lemon, '88 119; '95 53
Brussels Sprouts with Celery, Lemony, '85 25
Butter, Asparagus in Lemon, '80 M123
Butter, Asparagus with Lemon, '87 M151
Butter, Lemon, '95 32
Cabbage, Lemon-Butter, '88 156
Canapés, Lemon-Cheese, '87 93
Carrot Bundles, Lemon-, '91 80
Carrots, Lemon, '82 300; '83 111
Carrots, Lemon-Dill Steamed, '93 180
Carrots, Lemon-Glazed, '84 16
Cauliflower, Easy Lemon, '83 322
Cheese Party Bites, Lemon-, '95 160
Cheese Patty, Lemon-Pepper, '84 117
Corn on the Cob, Lemony, '89 200
Cream, Broccoli with Lemon, '89 245
Cream, Strawberries 'n Lemon, '85 120
Crêpes with Fruit Filling, Lemon, '82 46
Cucumbers, Lemony, '89 102
Curd, Lemon, '94 315
Desserts
Apples, Chilled Poached Lemon, '86 182
Bars Deluxe, Lemon, '79 35
Bars, Lemon Yogurt Wheat, '79 93
Bars, Tangy Lemon, '86 217
Cake, Coconut-Lemon, '95 319
Cake, Easy Lemon, '83 24
Cake, General Robert E. Lee Orange-
Lemon, '88 92
Cake, Glazed Lemon, '86 70
Cake, Lemon Angel, '80 147
Cake, Lemon-Coconut Cream, '81 179
Cake, Lemon-Coconut Sheet, '85 117
Cake, Lemon Gold, '83 301
Cake, Lemon Meringue, '89 296
Cake, Lemon-Pineapple, '86 60, 239
Cake, Lemon-Poppy Seed, '93 154
Cake, Lemon Pound, '82 88
Cake, Lemon Pudding, '83 106
Cake, Lemon-Raspberry, '91 247
Cake, Lemon-Sour Cream Pound, '87 38
Cake, Lemon Tea, '82 169
Cake, Lightly Lemon Coffee, '81 14
Cake, Luscious Lemon, '93 81
Cake, Luscious Lemon Layer, '86 61
Cake, Old-Fashioned Lemon Layer,
'85 191
Cake Roll, Elegant Lemon, '80 70
Cake Roll, Lemon, '89 312
Cake, Tart Lemon-Cheese, '88 7
Cake with Blueberry Sauce, Buttermilk-
Lemon Pudding, '95 135
Cake, Yogurt-Lemon-Nut, '89 169
Candied Lemon Peel, '94 199
Charlotte Russe, Fresh Lemon, '80 13
Charlotte Russe, Lemon, '84 192
Cheesecake, Lemon, '86 194; '91 308;
'92 24
Cheesecake, Lemon Delight, '95 219

Cheesecake, Luscious Lemon, '90 M196
Cheesecake with Orange-Pineapple Glaze,
Lemon, '81 60
Cookies, Lemonade, '79 51
Cookies, Lemon Crinkle, '81 287
Cookies, Lemony Cutout, '85 323
Cookies, Sunshine Lemon, '86 69
Cream Cheese Dessert, Lemon-, '84 95
Cream, Frozen Lemon, '83 118
Cream, Lemon, '82 237; '91 119
Cream, Lemon-Blueberry, '92 153
Cream Puffs, Lemon, '93 254
Cream Puffs, Strawberry-Lemon, '87 75
Cream, Strawberries with Lemon,
'90 170
Crisps, Lemon, '95 272
Cupcakes, Lemon Moist, '82 112;
'83 153
Cups, Baked Lemon, '87 128
Curd, Fresh Fruit with Lemon, '88 21
Curd, Lemon, '87 139; '89 334
Curd with Berries, Lemon, '90 102
Custard in Meringue Cups, Lemon,
'80 295; '81 172
Custards, Lemon-Buttermilk, '89 49
Dainties, Lemon Pecan, '80 208
Delight, Lemon, '82 227
Filling, Creamy Lemon, '80 70
Filling, Lemon, '81 172; '84 137;
'85 191; '86 235; '87 293; '89 312;
'90 308; '94 122; '95 319
Filling, Lemon-Apricot, '90 105
Filling, Lemon-Cheese, '79 68; '88 7
Filling, Lemon Cream, '84 23; '87 14
Filling, Lemon-Orange, '81 71
Frosting, Creamy Lemon, '79 93
Frosting, Lemon, '85 191; '86 217;
'93 81
Frosting, Lemon Buttercream, '83 301;
'86 61; '91 247
Frosting, Lemon-Butter Cream, '85 117
Frosting, Lemon-Coconut, '90 253
Frosting, Lemon-Cream Cheese, '81 157
Frosting, Lemony White, '88 7
Frosting, Orange-Lemon, '88 92
Fruitcake, Lemon, '83 258
Glaze, Lemon, '79 285; '86 194; '87 41;
'92 269; '93 154, 183
Ice Cream, Lemon, '79 142; '83 170;
'91 65
Ice Cream, Lemonade, '88 202
Layered Lemon Dessert, '88 134
Logs, Hazelnut-Lemon, '84 117
Melting Moments, '85 191
Meringue, Chocolate Pudding with
Lemon, '88 258
Meringue Cream Cups, Lemon, '84 23
Mousse, Lemon Cloud, '90 90
Mousse, Strawberry-Lemon, '82 128
Mousse with Raspberry Sauce, Lemon,
'91 96; '92 130
Napoleons, Blueberry-Lemon, '94 122
Parfaits, Strawberry-Lemon, '84 198
Pastry Shell, Lemon in, '84 137
Pears, Lemon Poached, '82 74
Pie, Angel, '79 123
Pie, Apple-Lemon Chess, '86 220
Pie, Best-Ever Lemon Meringue, '94 208
Pie, Buttermilk Lemon, '81 120; '82 23
Pie, Buttermilk-Lemon, '88 297
Pie, Buttermilk-Lemon Cream, '88 99
Pie, Deluxe Lemon Meringue, '81 172;
'90 313

LEMON, Desserts *(continued)*

Pie, Frozen Lemonade, '92 101
Pie, Frozen Lemon Cream, '82 86
Pie, Lemonade, '91 42
Pie, Lemon-Buttermilk, '91 272
Pie, Lemon Cheese, '81 136; '82 146
Pie, Lemon Chess, '79 32; '82 196
Pie, Lemon-Cottage Cheese, '79 44
Pie, Lemon Cottage Cheese, '81 143
Pie, Lemon Fluff, '92 342; '93 46
Pie, Lemon Ice Cream, '80 70
Pie, Lemon Meringue, '85 M112;
'86 130
Pie, Lemon-Orange, '85 172
Pie, Lemon Parfait, '94 310
Pie, Lemon-Pecan, '93 251
Pie, Lemon-Sour Cream, '82 169
Pie, Lemon Sponge, '83 192
Pie, Lemon-Strawberry, '88 127
Pie, Lemon Twirl, '84 94
Pie, Lemony Cherry, '92 30
Pie, Slice of Lemon, '84 23
Pie, Tart Lemon, '91 275
Pie, Tart Lemon-Apple, '80 100
Pie, Whipped Lemon, '79 124
Pops, Deep Blue Sea, '94 143
Pudding, Layered Lemon, '82 128
Pudding, Lemon, '79 86; '81 99
Pudding, Lemon Cake, '92 96
Pudding, Lemon Fluff, '85 304
Pudding, Old-Fashioned Lemon Bread,
'88 95
Roll, Snow-Capped Lemon, '79 68
Rolls with Raspberry Sauce, Lemon
Angel, '94 294
Sauce, Lemon, '84 258, 306;
'85 77, 190; '91 240
Sauce, Lemon Cream, '93 200
Sauce, Lemon Dessert, '87 M165
Sauce, Tart Lemon, '85 191
Sherbet, Lemon, '91 309
Sherbet, Lemon Cream, '79 114
Solid, Lemon, '93 279
Sorbet, Lemon, '93 153
Sorbet, Pear-Lemon, '88 116
Soufflé, Cold Lemon-Lime, '84 24
Soufflé, Lemon, '82 170, 252; '94 199
Soufflés, Quick Lemon Sauce, '88 43
Soufflé, Tart Lemon, '85 82
Soufflé with Raspberry-Amaretto Sauce,
Frozen Lemon, '88 130
Sponge Cups, Lemon, '83 10
Squares, Golden Carrot-Lemon, '80 40
Squares, Lemon, '81 197
Squares, Lemon-Pecan, '89 124
Squares, Lemony Cream Cheese, '82 159
Strawberry-Lemon Dessert, '86 162
Tarts, Berry Good Lemon, '91 119
Tarts, Dainty Lemon, '82 304
Tarts, Golden Lemon, '85 191
Tart Shells, Lemon, '88 195
Tarts, Lemon, '82 156; '83 79
Tarts, Lemon-Cheese, '79 2
Tarts, Lemon Ice Cream, '80 152
Tarts, Lemon-Sour Cream, '81 304
Tart, Strawberry-Lemon, '89 111
Topping, Lemon-Pineapple, '86 60
Torte with Raspberry Sauce, Lemon
Meringue, '93 82
Trifle, All Seasons Lemon, '95 219
Trifle, Lemon-Blueberry, '88 210

Yogurt, Lemon-Chiffon Frozen, '85 54
Yummies, Lemon, '81 301
Zephers, Lemon, '81 172
Dressing, Chilled Broccoli with Lemon,
'88 270
Dressing, Creamy Lemon, '88 M193
Dressing, Fruit Salad with Honey-Lemon,
'93 21
Dressing, Green Salad with Lemony French,
'85 67
Dressing, Honey-Lemon, '95 133
Dressing, Lemon-and-Herb, '92 108
Dressing, Lemon Herb, '82 170
Dressing, Lemon-Herb Salad, '82 67
Dressing, Lemon-Pepper, '87 55
Dressing, Lemon Salad, '79 8
Dressing, Lemon-Yogurt, '93 17
Dressing, Lemon-Yogurt Slaw or Salad, '88 54
Dressing, Tomato Slices with Lemon, '87 167
Green Beans, Lemon, '89 275
Green Beans, Lemon-Walnut, '93 304
Green Beans, Lemony, '85 190
Honey, Lemon, '94 16
Knots, Glazed Lemon, '86 290
Main Dishes
Catfish, Lemon Barbecued, '88 271;
'89 202
Chicken and Vegetables, Lemon, '88 118
Chicken, Baked Lemon, '85 190
Chicken Breasts, Lemon, '89 18
Chicken Cutlets with Lemon, '85 8
Chicken, Greek Lemon, '90 65
Chicken, Grilled Yogurt-Lemon, '81 111
Chicken in Lemon and Wine, '83 281
Chicken, Lemon, '81 M138; '86 173
Chicken, Lemonade, '82 163
Chicken, Lemon Barbecued, '93 215
Chicken, Lemon-Dill, '93 19
Chicken, Lemon-Fried, '79 77
Chicken, Lemon Fried, '82 275
Chicken, Lemon-Frosted, '88 170
Chicken, Lemon-Garlic, '89 M132;
'90 35
Chicken, Lemon-Herb, '85 127
Chicken, Lemon-Herb Grilled, '95 87
Chicken, Lemon-Pepper, '89 104
Chicken, Lemon-Roasted, '95 24
Chicken, Lemon-Rosemary, '94 201
Chicken Nuggets, Lemon-, '86 337;
'87 283
Chicken Piccata, Herbed, '88 28
Chicken Sauté, Lemon-Dill, '91 186
Chicken, Sweet-and-Sour Lemon, '84 93
Chicken, Sweet Lemon, '79 218
Chicken, Sweet Lemon-, '84 69
Cornish Hens, Lemon Roasted, '82 260
Cutlets, Lemon-Flavored, '79 105
Fillets, Lemon-Coated, '80 M53
Flank Steak, Lemon-Lime, '95 55
Flounder Thermidor, '85 190
Linguine with Garlic and Lemon, '88 91
Mackerel, Lemon-Baked, '79 182
Pork Chops, Lemon-Herb, '84 81;
'89 M132
Pork Chops, Lemony, '88 118
Pork Piccata, '94 57
Ribs, Lemon Baked, '81 166
Ribs, Lemon Grilled, '81 154
Shrimp in Lemon Butter, '84 163
Shrimp, Lemon-Garlic Broiled, '82 29;
'86 182
Shrimp, Luscious Lemon, '88 150
Spareribs, Lemony Sweet, '80 73

Steak with Brandy Sauce, Lemon-Butter,
'85 78
Turkey Piccata, '91 137
Veal, Lemon, '93 35
Veal Piccata, '92 181
Veal Piccata, Lemon, '86 118
Veal with Artichoke Hearts, Lemon,
'87 219
Marinade, Lemon-Soy, '91 194
Marmalade, Citrus, '80 101
Mayonnaise, Lemon, '95 32
Mayonnaise, Lemon-Cream, '85 264
Mold, Cheesy Lemon, '79 241
Mold, Lemon-Cucumber, '87 90
New Potatoes, Lemon-Buttered, '84 149;
'90 268
New Potatoes, Lemony, '82 158
Olive Oil, Lemon-Infused, '95 231
Olives, Lemon-Garlic, '94 118
Pasta, Lemon-Garlic, '95 181
Potatoes, Herbed Lemon Mashed, '93 208
Potatoes, Lemon and Nutmeg, '80 36
Potatoes, Lemon-Herb Stuffed, '83 173
Potatoes, Lemon-Steamed, '86 177
Potatoes, Oregano-and-Lemon Skillet, '93 54
Potato Wedges, Lemon, '88 21
Potato Wedges, Lemony, '90 M61
Relish, Lemony Cranberry, '79 243
Rice, Lemon, '89 166
Roses, Lemon, '82 280
Salads
Apple-Bran Salad, Lemony, '86 223
Asparagus Salad, Creamy Lemon-,
'93 116
Cauliflower-Lemon Salad, '81 23
Cheese Salad, Lemon-, '85 240
Congealed Lemon-Tomato Salad,
'89 178
Congealed Salad, Lemon-Cranberry,
'87 311
Congealed Salad, Lemon-Vegetable,
'85 22
Cream Salad, Lemon-, '88 250
Freeze, Fruity Lemon, '82 145
Fruit Salad, Lemonade, '84 24
Onion Salad, Lemon-, '85 252
Sauces
Asparagus with Lemon Sauce, '86 62
Barbecue Sauce, Herbed Lemon, '94 154
Barbecue Sauce, Lemony, '88 M177;
'95 31
Basting Sauce, Lemon, '95 32
Broccoli with Lemon Sauce, '91 292;
'92 256
Broccoli with Lemon Sauce and Pecans,
'86 71
Brussels Sprouts in Lemon Sauce,
'82 269
Butter Sauce, Lemon-, '84 252; '92 337
Celery Sauce, Baked Fillets in Lemon-,
'84 91
Cheese Sauce, Lemon-, '91 24
Cheese Sauce, Lemony, '84 183
Cream Sauce, Braised Chicken Breast in
Lemon, '94 184
Cucumber Sauce, Lemony, '89 245
Garlic Sauce, Shrimp in Lemon, '83 67
Honey-Lemon Mustard Sauce, '84 275
Hot Lemon-Herb Sauce, '91 286
Lemon Sauce, '82 290
Meunière Sauce, Lemon, '88 222
New Potatoes with Lemon Sauce,
'86 130

LEMON, Sauces (continued)

Parsley Sauce, Lemon, '81 106
Parsley Sauce, Lemon-, '93 48
Tartar Sauce, Lemony, '95 32
Slices, Fluted Lemon, '82 51
Soup, Lemon-Egg Drop, '93 81
Spinach, Creamy Lemon, '82 302
Spinach with Feta, Lemon, '85 190
Sprouts, Lemon, '85 288
Squeezers, Lemon, '95 32
Sugar, Lemon-Mint, '95 32
Sugar Snap Peas with Basil and Lemon, '93 66
Sweetened Preserved Lemons, '95 141
Vegetables, Lemon, '93 83
Vermicelli, Lemon, '84 329
Vinaigrette, Lemon, '95 31
Vinaigrette, Lemon-Basil, '94 205
Vinegar, Lemon, '95 31
Vinegar, Lemon-Mint, '85 124
Vinegar, Raspberry-Lemon, '87 134
Vinegar, Spicy Oregano-Lemon, '85 124
Wild Rice, Pecan-Lemon, '92 211
Wonton Chips, Lemon-and-Herb, '91 138
Zucchini, Lemon-Garlic, '89 226

LENTILS
Baked Lentils with Cheese, '84 113
Burgers, Lentil, '95 123
Casserole, Lentils-and-Rice, '93 301
Pilaf, Rice-and-Lentil, '88 17
Salad, Lentils-and-Rice, '90 197
Sauce, Lentil Spaghetti, '90 198
Soup, Beefy Lentil, '87 282
Soup, Lentil, '83 292; '86 304; '91 28
Stew, Lentil-Rice, '82 232
Supper, Lentil-and-Rice, '84 202
Tacos, Lentil, '88 197

LIME
Beverages
Apple Limeade, Pink, '89 46
Cooler, Grape-Lime, '94 227
Cooler, Lime, '87 160
Daiquiris, Freezer Lime, '79 141
Fizz, Frosty Lime, '90 104
Fizz, Lime, '81 172
Fuzz Buzz, '82 160
Margaritas, Frosted, '84 115
Margaritas, Frosty, '83 172
Margaritas, Lemon-Lime, '94 227
Margaritas, Pitcher, '83 175
Punch, Calypso Presbyterian Church
    Women's Lime, '95 141
Punch, Foamy Lime, '82 264
Punch, Lime, '84 58
Punch, Lime-Pineapple, '83 142
Punch, Lime Slush, '90 273
Punch, Orange-Lime, '82 160
Candied Lime Strips, '94 137
Cream, Ginger-Lime, '95 227
Desserts
Cake, Key Lime, '91 214
Cream, Lime-Rum, '93 169
Loaf, Lime Layer, '85 96
Mousse Freeze, Luscious Lime, '81 173
Parfaits, Lime, '80 153
Parfaits, Surf-and-Sand, '93 169
Pie, Key Lime, '91 42
Pie, Lime Chiffon, '86 130
Pie, Lime Fluff, '84 43
Pie, Manny and Isa's Key Lime, '95 118
Pies, Key Lime, '95 86
Pies, Lime Party, '92 65

Refresher, Lime-Mint, '82 144
Sherbet, Creamy Lime, '84 165
Sherbet, Lime, '82 159; '89 202
Soufflé, Cold Lemon-Lime, '84 24
Squares, Lime, '79 2
Tart in Coconut Crust, Key Lime,
    '89 160
Tart, Lime-Pineapple, '88 6
Tornadoes for Grown-Ups, Texas,
    '94 143
Whip, Lime, '89 199
Dip, Lime-Dill, '92 65
Dressing, Honey-Lime, '83 139; '93 71
Dressing, Lime, '79 2; '83 120
Dressing, Lime-Honey, '92 213
Dressing, Lime-Honey Fruit Salad, '87 81
Dressing, Lime-Parsley, '85 131
Dressing, Lime Sherbet, '80 221
Dressing, Spinach Salad with Chili-Lime,
    '94 63
Jelly, Lime, '94 23
Main Dishes
Beef Stir-Fry, Lime-Ginger, '92 65
Chicken, Grilled Lime-Jalapeño, '91 87
Chicken with Lime Butter, '84 68
Chicken with Orange, Lime, and Ginger
    Sauce, '92 123
Flank Steak, Lemon-Lime, '95 55
Pork Chops, Honey-Lime, '91 33
Red Snapper with Lime, Stuffed, '83 246
Turkey Tenderloins, Lime-Buttered,
    '92 127
Veal, Amaretto-Lime, '93 54
Marmalade, Citrus, '80 101
Muffins, Key Lime, '95 50
Mustard, Key Lime, '94 278
Rice, Lime-Flavored, '84 175
Salad, Emerald, '81 143
Salad, Frosted Lime-Cheese, '79 286
Salad, Lime-Carrot, '92 65
Salad, Pear-Lime, '84 152
Salad, Pineapple-Lime, '84 320
Salad, Snowy Emerald, '87 311
Sauce, Honey-Lime, '82 85
Sauce, Lime Hollandaise, '93 121
Sauce, Lime-Saffron, '94 71
Sauce, Sour Cream-Lime, '91 286
Sopa de Lima, '79 211
Soup, Lime, '88 31
Vinaigrette, Cilantro-Lime, '94 77
Whip, Peaches with Honey-Lime, '85 108

LINGUINE
Artichoke and Shrimp Linguine, '95 210
Artichoke Hearts, Pasta with, '86 209
Basil Pasta, Fresh Tomato Sauce over, '93 176
Carbonara, Linguine, '87 108
Chicken, Taste-of-Texas Pasta and, '92 78
Clam Linguine, '95 212
Clam Linguine, Quick, '90 233
Clam Sauce, Linguine in, '81 83
Clam Sauce, Linguine with, '84 124; '88 90;
    '89 178
Clam Sauce with Linguine, '84 9
Favorite Pasta, My, '95 213
Garlic and Lemon, Linguine with, '88 91
Mussels Linguine, '90 M112
Pasta Verde, '84 201
Pesto and Pasta, '92 98
Pesto Pasta, Asian, '95 189
Red Pepper Sauce, Linguine with, '93 127
Salad, Pasta, '84 139
Salad Pasta, Caesar, '95 230
Seafood Delight, '86 208

Seafood Linguine, '79 227
Seafood Sauce, Linguine with, '83 232
Shrimp and Linguine, Spicy, '92 34
Shrimp and Pasta, Mediterranean, '95 286
Shrimp Marinara, '84 233
Spinach, Linguine with, '91 30
Tomato-Cream Sauce, Linguine with,
    '86 158
Vegetables, Traveling Linguine with Roasted,
    '93 178
Verde, Pasta, '84 201
Whole Wheat Linguine, '84 177

LIVER
Appetizers
Chicken Liver and Bacon Roll-Ups,
    '80 200; '81 57
Chicken Livers, Party, '83 242
Chicken Liver Turnovers, '79 141
Pâté, Chicken Liver, '79 153; '81 235;
    '83 108; '84 205
Pâté, Country, '86 66
Pâté, Duck Liver, '79 227
Pâté, Liver-Cheese, '85 276
Pâté with Cognac, '86 159
Pâté with Madeira Sauce, Liver,
    '93 323
Rumaki, '80 M136
Spread, Liver, '89 161
Spread, Sherried Liver, '80 86
Barbecued Liver, '85 219
Beef Liver Patties, '81 277
Calf's Liver with Vegetables, '85 219
Chicken
en Brochette, Chicken Livers, '84 222
Italian Sauce, Chicken Livers in, '83 117
Marsala Wine Sauce, Chicken Livers with,
    '81 76
Mushrooms, Chicken Livers with,
    '81 133
Omelet, Chicken Liver, '82 44
Orange Sauce, Chicken Livers in, '82 218
Party Chicken Livers, '83 242
Pâté, Chicken Liver, '79 153; '81 235;
    '83 108; '84 205
Potatoes, Chicken Livers and, '82 218
Rice, Chicken Livers with, '80 200;
    '81 58; '84 292
Rice Dish, Chicken Livers and, '82 218
Risotto, Chicken Livers, '82 218
Roll-Ups, Chicken Liver and Bacon,
    '80 200; '81 57
Rumaki Kabobs, '82 182
Sautéed Chicken Livers, '80 200; '81 57
Scrumptious Chicken Livers, '84 230
Stroganoff, Chicken Livers, '80 200;
    '81 57
Supreme, Chicken Livers, '81 298
Turnovers, Chicken Liver, '79 141
Wine Sauce, Chicken Livers in, '81 104
Creamy Liver and Noodle Dinner, '80 11
Creole Liver, '85 219; '86 108
Creole Sauce, Liver in, '87 33
French-Style Liver, '80 10
Gravy, Liver and, '80 10
Herbs, Liver with, '81 277
Italiano, Liver, '85 219
Kabobs, Liver, '80 185
Loaf, Skillet Liver, '80 11
Saucy Liver, '81 277
Sauté, Liver, '81 277
Spanish-Style Liver, '80 11
Stroganoff, Liver, '79 54
Sweet-and-Sour Liver, '81 277

LIVING LIGHT
Andouille, '92 242
Appetizers
 Ambrosia, Sherried, '84 324
 Apple-Phyllo Rolls, '88 213
 Artichokes, Marinated, '87 250
 Artichokes with Herb-Mayonnaise Dip,
  '84 67
 Beets, Blue Cheese-Stuffed, '88 211
 Buzzard's Nests, '93 244
 Carrot-Cheese Ball, '86 325
 Cheese Tartlets, '88 211
 Chicken-Mushroom Appetizers, '88 210
 Chicken Wontons, '92 284
 Chips, Bagel, '91 138
 Chips, Baked Wonton, '91 138
 Chips, Cinnamon-and-Sugar Bagel,
  '91 139
 Chips, Cinnamon-and-Sugar Wonton,
  '91 138
 Chips, Corn Tortilla, '91 17
 Chips, Garlic Bagel, '91 139
 Chips, Garlic Wonton, '91 138
 Chips, Lemon-and-Herb Bagel, '91 139
 Chips, Lemon-and-Herb Wonton,
  '91 138
 Chips, Light Tortilla, '90 278; '91 257
 Chips, Parmesan Cheese Bagel, '91 138
 Chips, Parmesan Cheese Wonton,
  '91 138
 Chips, Pita, '89 19; '91 138
 Chips, Sweet Potato, '91 138
 Chips, Tortilla, '91 137
 Crudité Platter with Dip, '84 139
 Dip, Cheese-Herb, '89 20
 Dip, Creamy Ham, '93 125
 Dip, Curry, '87 25
 Dip, Deviled, '87 25
 Dip, Dilled Garden, '84 324
 Dip, Festive Crab, '92 285
 Dip, Garbanzo, '93 94
 Dip, Low-Cal Tuna, '87 25
 Dip, Monster Mash, '93 244
 Dip, Quick Fruit, '90 110
 Dip, Ranch-Style, '90 138
 Dip, Santa Fe Skinny, '94 137
 Dip, Skinny Ranch, '93 96
 Dip, Spinach, '87 25
 Dip, Tofu, '86 109
 Dip, Vegetable Garden, '85 215
 Eggplant Appetizer, Grilled, '95 198
 Fruit Kabobs with Coconut Dressing,
  '87 251
 Fruit with Lemon Sauce, Fresh, '82 290
 Mix, Crunchy Snack, '93 94
 Mix, Snack, '89 19
 Mousse, Shrimp, '87 251
 Mushroom-Almond Pastry Cups,
  '88 210
 Mushroom Appetizers, Stuffed, '88 210
 Mushrooms, Spinach-Stuffed, '89 M133
 Nectarine Cocktail, '85 107
 New Potatoes, Ham-Stuffed, '88 211
 Orange Halves, Broiled, '85 288
 Oysters Bienville, Baked, '90 27
 Oysters Italiano, Baked, '89 97
 Pasta Bites, Pesto-Cheese, '87 251
 Pâté, Black-Eyed Pea, '93 97
 Pâté, Lentil, '92 285
 Pâté, Mock, '87 251
 Pears Stuffed with Cheese, '82 290
 Pita Bread Triangles, '88 211
 Pita Wedges, Garlic, '93 98

Pizzas, Pita, '89 19
Plantain Chips, '95 M203
Popcorn, Chili, '91 17
Popcorn Mix, Curried, '86 326
Popcorn with Pizzazz, '93 245
Potato Skin Snack, '91 18
Pretzels, Whole Wheat, '89 20
Quesadillas, Green Chile, '90 121
Scallop Appetizer, '86 155
Shrimp Dippers, '84 324
Snow Peas, Crab-Stuffed, '85 288
Spinach-Ricotta Phyllo Triangles, '88 212
Spread, Artichoke-Parmesan, '92 95
Spread, Broccamoli Curry, '88 55
Spread, Low-Fat Chicken, '82 290
Spread, Smoked Salmon, '84 324
Steak-and-Chestnut Appetizers,
 Marinated, '84 323
Sweet Potato Chips, '95 M203
Tabbouleh, '88 211
Tomatoes, Crab-Stuffed Cherry, '82 289
Tomatoes, Stuffed Cherry, '88 212
Tortilla Snacks, Pesto, '89 19
Vegetable Appetizer, Tarragon, '83 277
Vegetable Nachos, '91 17
Zucchini Caviar, '88 212
Zucchini Pizzas, '88 212
Zucchini-Shrimp Appetizers, '89 311
Apple-Cheese Bake, '92 225
Apples, Baked, '86 40
Apple Side Dish, Dried, '92 226
Apples, Stuffed Baked, '89 217
Apples with Orange Sauce, Baked, '84 314
Barley, Baked, '91 133
Beverages
 Apple Cooler, '90 14
 Apple Julep, '86 103
 Apricot Fruit Flip, '91 18
 Apricot Mint Cooler, '90 165
 Banana Coolers, '91 308
 Banana Nog, '82 290
 Banana Smoothie, '93 95
 Bellini Spritzers, '90 110
 Black Russian, Mock, '92 322
 Bourbon Blizzard, '92 287
 Brew, Witch's, '93 244
 Caribbean Cooler, '95 203
 Carrot Cooler, '89 35
 Cider, Hot Spiced, '82 290
 Cocoa, Mocha, '83 318
 Cranberry Cocktail, Hot, '89 310
 Cranberry Smoothie, '91 307
 Eggnog, '83 318
 Eggnog with Orange and Nutmeg, Mock,
  '92 323
 Fruit Beverage, Blender, '83 318
 Fruit Refresher, '91 203
 Fruit Shake, Frosty, '87 23
 Fruit Smoothie, '89 87
 Grapefruit Refresher, '88 85
 Lemon Velvet, '90 15
 Milkshake, Mocha, '89 35
 Mocha, Hot, '84 60
 Orange Juicy, '90 178
 Orange-Pineapple Drink, '89 35
 Orange Slush, '82 49
 Peach Cooler, '86 6
 Peach Frosty, '83 318
 Peach Refresher, '86 103
 Piña Colada, Mock, '92 322
 Piña Coladas, '95 203
 Pineapple-Banana Slush, '90 14
 Pineapple Sparkle, Spiced, '92 322

 Pineapple-Yogurt Whirl, '91 132
 Punch, Apple-Tea, '85 82
 Punch, Citrus, '93 99
 Punch, Holiday, '87 252
 Punch, Holiday Hot Fruit, '92 286
 Punch, Hot Apple, '84 324
 Punch, Tart Cranberry, '83 318
 Punch, White Grape, '90 15
 Scarlet Sipper, '90 198
 Shake, Strawberry-Banana, '89 35
 Shake, Strawberry-Orange Breakfast,
  '87 186
 Shake, Strawberry-Pear, '92 139
 Strawberry Cooler, '83 56
 Strawberry Spritzer, '90 14
 Tea Mix, Spiced, '86 32
 Tea Mix, Sugar-Free Spiced, '91 258
 Tofruitti Breakfast Drink, '88 26
 Tomato-Clam Cocktail, '87 252
 Tomato Refresher, '83 318
 Vegetable Cocktail, Fresh, '82 165
 Virgin Mary, Spicy, '92 323
 Watermelon-Berry Slush, '90 137
Breads
 Apricot-Orange Bread, '92 285
 Banana Bread, '87 72
 Banana Bread, Fruity, '95 78
 Biscuits and Sausage Gravy, '94 20
 Biscuits, Angel, '90 28
 Biscuits, Cheese-Chive, '94 324
 Biscuits, Herbed, '93 67
 Biscuits, Light, '89 53
 Biscuits, Oatmeal, '89 108
 Biscuits, Orange, '88 85
 Biscuits, Whole Wheat, '84 60; '91 222
 Biscuits, Yeast, '87 71
 Caraway Breadsticks, '89 239
 Cinnamon-Oat Bread, '90 135
 Cornbread, '92 324
 Cornbread, Dieter's, '87 164
 Cornbread, Jalapeño, '94 78
 Cornbread, Mexican, '93 182
 Cornbread Supreme, '93 67
 Cornmeal Yeast Bread, '89 54
 Corn Sticks, '89 54
 Cranberry-Banana Bread, '90 294
 Crouton Bread, Quick, '90 138
 English Muffin Bread, '95 M79
 Focaccia, Rosemary, '95 190
 French Bread, '89 54
 French Toast, Cottage-Topped, '85 49
 French Toast, Slender, '86 103
 Garlic Bread, '82 19; '91 204
 Herbed Bread, '89 34
 Honey-Oat Bread, '89 107
 Hush Puppies, Baked, '89 53; '95 108
 Muffins, All-Bran Oat Bran, '91 134
 Muffins, Apple, '84 193
 Muffins, Applesauce, '91 141
 Muffins, Banana-Oat, '87 188
 Muffins, Banana-Raisin, '89 218
 Muffins, Blueberry, '91 140, 203
 Muffins, Bran-Buttermilk, '85 7
 Muffins, Cornmeal, '91 19
 Muffins, Cornmeal Yeast, '92 49
 Muffins, Corn-Oat, '89 108
 Muffins, Freezer Bran, '91 141
 Muffins, Granola, '95 78
 Muffins, Honey Bran, '88 171
 Muffins Made of Bran, '86 103
 Muffins, Miniature Cranberry, '90 294
 Muffins, Oat Bran, '89 106
 Muffins, Oat Bran-Banana, '91 18

Muffins, Oatmeal-Bran, '91 83
Muffins, Spicy Apple-Oat, '86 45
Muffins, Spicy Cornbread, '90 59
Muffins, Yogurt, '88 55
Oat Bread, Caraway-Raisin, '86 44
Onion-Herb Bread, '90 165
Pumpkin-Pecan Bread, '87 221
Rolls, Dinner, '89 312
Rolls, Honey Wheat, '83 278
Rolls, Old-Fashioned Cinnamon, '92 226
Rolls, Parsley-Garlic, '93 319
Rolls, Vegetable Salad, '82 278
Rolls, Whole Wheat, '90 111
Rolls, Yogurt Crescent, '91 123
Sourdough Wedges, '90 199
Spoonbread, '90 200
Swiss Cheese Loaves, Mini, '95 80
Toast Strips, Seasoned, '93 98
Whole Wheat Cardamom Bread, '86 223
Breakfast-in-a-Bowl, '89 87
Chorizo, '92 241
Chutney, Blueberry, '95 190
Couscous with Mixed Fruit, '95 232
Crab Cakes, Country, '95 20
Crêpes, Basic, '86 38
Crêpes, Bran, '83 70; '86 44
Crêpes, Ham-and-Egg, '83 204
Crêpes, Light, '86 143
Crêpes, Low-Calorie, '87 77
Crêpes, Plain, '83 70
Crêpes Suzettes, Light, '83 71
Crêpes, Whole Wheat, '83 70
Croutons, Bagel, '93 192
Croutons, Cornbread, '93 192
Croutons, Garlic, '92 71
Croutons, Pita, '93 192
Crust, Whole Wheat, '94 78
Desserts
Alaska, Orange, '83 177
Alaska, Peachy Melba, '88 266
Ambrosia, Baked, '83 303
Ambrosia, Layered, '88 304
Apple Crisp, Tart, '92 226
Apples à l'Orange, Baked, '90 280
Applesauce Fluff, '91 173
Apples, Caramel-Peanut, '93 M244
Apples, Melting, '88 19
Bananas Foster, '88 20
Bananas with Honey, Broiled, '84 175
Bars, Apricot-Raisin, '87 32
Bars, Pineapple-Orange, '82 129
Bavarian Dessert, Light, '86 6
Biscotti, Chocolate-Hazelnut, '95 80
Biscotti, Light, '91 310
Blackberries and Dumplings, '86 196
Blintzes, Cheese, '83 71
Blueberry Crisp, '84 177
Brownies, Chocolate-Kahlúa, '93 99
Brownies, Chocolate-Walnut, '89 325
Cake, Apple-Nut, '87 76
Cake, Apple Spice, '92 225
Cake, Banana-Coconut, '93 154
Cake, Black Widow Snack, '93 245
Cake, Blueberry Streusel, '92 144
Cake, Chocolate Angel Food, '87 21; '90 111
Cake, Chocolate-Cinnamon, '93 154
Cake, Chocolate Custard, '88 175

Cake, Chocolate Pound, '89 325
Cake, Deluxe Light Banana, '84 314
Cake, Four-Flavor Pound, '91 136
Cake, Frosted Carrot, '92 19
Cake, Heavenly Pineapple, '83 303
Cake, Lemon-Poppy Seed, '93 154
Cake, Orange-Coconut Angel Food, '94 294
Cake, Orange Pound, '87 221
Cake, Pound, '92 94
Cake, Pumpkin, '93 303
Cake, Red Velvet, '93 318
Cake Roll, Lemon, '89 312
Cake Roll, Make-Ahead Chocolate-Mint, '95 220
Cake, Strawberry Yogurt Layer, '94 85
Cake, Warm Chocolate Pudding, '92 324
Cake with Amaretto-Almond Sauce, Angel Food, '90 199
Cake with Coffee Frosting, Spice Layer, '94 86
Cake with Custard Sauce, Chocolate Angel Food, '88 259
Cake with Pineapple-Orange Sauce, Angel, '84 14
Cake with Strawberries and Chocolate Glaze, White, '87 76
Cantaloupe Whip, '89 198
Cheesecake, Almost Strawberry, '86 32
Cheesecake, Black Forest, '94 21
Cheesecake, Blueberry Chiffon, '87 76
Cheesecake, Chocolate-Amaretto, '93 97
Cheesecake, Dieter's Apple, '86 318
Cheesecake, Lemon, '91 308
Cheesecake, Lemon Delight, '95 219
Cheesecake, Light-and-Easy, '88 55
Cherries Jubilee, '86 317
Chocolate-Bran Raisin Jumbos, '91 142
Chocolate-Cheese Cups, '91 142
Chocolate Cream Log, '94 220
Chocolate Cream Roll, '85 317
Chocolate Fondue, '91 142
Chocolate Glaze, '89 325
Chocolate-Orange Roll, '87 21
Chocolate Whip, '89 326
Chocolat, Petits Pots de, '82 272
Cobbler, Cranberry-and-Apple, '90 294
Cobbler, Fresh Cherry, '84 178
Cobbler, New-Fashioned Apple, '91 221
Cobbler, New-Fashioned Blackberry, '87 164
Cobbler, Peach, '84 178
Cobbler, Raspberry-Cherry, '93 230
Coffee Cake, Sour Cream, '93 154
Coffee Dessert, Light, '88 260
Compote, Baked Fruit, '84 314
Compote, Fresh Fruit, '82 272; '84 82
Compote, Jicama-Fruit, '92 49
Compote, Melon Ball, '85 157
Compote, Spicy Grapefruit-Berry, '91 19
Cookies, Almond, '91 51
Cookies, Apple-Oatmeal, '85 215
Cookies, Light Almond, '83 151
Cookies, Light Chocolate Chip, '86 46
Cookies, Oatmeal-Raisin, '87 221; '93 127
Cranberries Jubilee, '90 293
Cream Puffs, Strawberry-Lemon, '87 75
Crêpes, Fruit-Filled Chocolate, '89 325
Crêpes, Tropical Fruit, '87 77
Crust, Gingersnap, '90 296
Crust, Graham Cracker, '86 32; '88 55; '91 308
Crust, Lattice, '90 294

Custard, Baked Rice, '92 308
Custard, Baked Vanilla, '82 129
Custard, Coconut, '86 109
Custard, Light Mexican, '88 149
Custard over Fruit, Stirred, '84 83
Custard, Range-Top Amaretto, '87 77
Custard with Raspberries, Almond Crème, '88 174
De-Light-Ful Dessert, '95 220
Filling, Lemon, '89 312
Flambé, Banana-Peach, '85 316
Flan, Luscious, '90 56
Frosting, Boiled, '93 318
Frosting, Coffee, '94 86
Frosting, Orange-Cream Cheese, '92 19
Fruitcake, Classic, '91 258
Fruitcake, Jeweled, '88 260
Fruit Cup, '91 202
Fruit Dessert, Caribbean, '84 314
Fruit Dessert, Flaming, '83 302
Fruit Dessert Orange, '84 314
Fruit Dessert, Rainbow, '85 108
Fruit Dessert, Spiced, '82 50
Fruit, Gingered, '83 151
Fruit, Glazed, '85 83
Fruit Medley, Fancy, '84 82
Fruit with Lemon Curd, Fresh, '88 21
Fruit with Mint-Balsamic Tea, Fresh, '95 232
Glaze, Lemon, '93 154
Honeydew-Berry Dessert, '83 120
Ice, Cranberry-Apple, '82 290
Ice, Grapefruit, '91 122
Ice, Kiwi, '84 315
Ice Milk, Banana Yogurt, '89 199
Ice Milk, Fresh Strawberry, '92 94
Ice, Mixed Fruit, '88 85
Ice, Peach-Yogurt, '84 83
Ice, Strawberry, '84 175; '85 108
Ice, Strawberry-Orange, '86 196
Ice, Tangy Cranberry, '87 305
Ice, Tart Cranberry-Orange, '86 317
Ice, Watermelon, '91 173
Kiwi Jubilee, '83 120
Lemon Angel Rolls with Raspberry Sauce, '94 294
Lemon Curd with Berries, '90 102
Lime Strips, Candied, '94 137
Lime Whip, '89 199
Melon Mélange, '84 139
Melon-Mint Julep, '86 196
Meringue Shells, Fruited, '87 32
Meringues, Peach Melba, '87 76
Mocha Sauce with Chocolate Yogurt, '92 243
Mousse, Coffee-Nut, '86 319
Mousse, Peach, '85 54
Mousse, Strawberry-Lemon, '82 128
Orange-Mallow Cream, '94 295
Orange Molded Dessert, '83 302
Oranges and Pineapple, Glazed, '86 318
Parfait, Peach, '82 166
Parfait, Pineapple, '84 83
Pastry, Light, '92 95
Peach-Blueberry Dessert, '92 184
Peach Dessert, Spiced, '83 9
Peaches with Honey-Lime Whip, '85 108
Peaches with Nutty Dumplings, Spiced, '87 164
Peaches with Strawberry Sauce, '85 8
Peach Halves, Stuffed, '86 196
Pear Fans with Raspberry-Orange Sauce, Poached, '88 22

LIVING LIGHT, Desserts (continued)

Pears in Custard, Poached, '88 20
Pears in Orange Sauce, Poached, '82 19
Pears Poached in Red Wine, '83 302
Pears, Vanilla Poached, '90 57
Pears with Berry Sauce, Wine-Poached,
    '86 144
Pears with Honey-Yogurt Sauce,
    Poached, '92 306
Pears with Meringue, Amaretto, '90 M58
Pie, Buttermilk, '92 95
Pie, Chocolate Bavarian, '89 326
Pie, Eggnog, '83 205
Pie, Fresh Apple, '84 178
Pie, Fruited Cheese, '92 228
Pie, New-Fashioned Pumpkin, '90 296
Pineapple, Meringue-Topped, '84 178
Pineapple with Raspberry Sauce,
    Chocolate-Drizzled, '90 57
Plum Slush, '84 139
Pops, Orange-Banana, '82 129
Pops, Pineapple-Yogurt, '91 173
Prune Bavarian, '86 223
Pudding, Almost Banana, '88 174
Pudding, Apple-Raisin Bread, '88 175
Pudding, Layered Lemon, '82 128
Pudding, Lemon Cake, '92 96
Pudding, Light Plum, '86 318
Pudding, Old-Fashioned Banana, '92 94
Pudding, Old-Fashioned Bread, '88 175
Pudding, Orange Custard, '88 174
Pudding, Peachy Bread, '88 175
Pudding, Raisin-Pumpkin, '84 315
Pudding with Whiskey Sauce, Bread,
    '90 230
Pumpkin Chiffon, '86 283; '88 260
Raspberry Fluff, '89 198
Raspberry-Pear Crisp, '89 109
Rice Cream with Mandarin Oranges,
    '85 317
Roulage, Frozen Chocolate, '90 56
Sauce, Chocolate, '90 57
Sauce, Creamy Light Coconut, '82 177
Sauce, Custard, '88 259
Sauce, Golden, '88 267
Sauce, Honey-Orange, '85 108
Sauce, Honey-Yogurt, '92 307
Sauce, Mango, '83 120
Sauce, Melba, '87 77
Sauce, Pineapple-Orange, '84 14
Sauce, Raspberry, '88 267; '93 99;
    '94 295
Sauce, Raspberry-Orange, '88 22
Sauce, Rum-Raisin, '94 295
Sauce, Special Hard, '86 318
Sauce, Spicy Apple Dessert, '82 177
Sauce, Whiskey, '90 230
Sherbet, Easy Pineapple, '92 199
Sherbet, Fresh Mint, '88 23
Sherbet, Instant Fruit, '85 158
Sherbet, Lemon, '91 309
Sherbet, Nectarine, '89 199
Sherbet, Peach, '90 179
Sherbet, Pineapple, '84 83; '89 199
Sherbet, Watermelon, '92 124
Shortcake, Strawberry, '92 184
Sorbet, Blueberry-Kirsch, '83 120
Sorbet, Fresh Orange, '92 143
Sorbet, Mango, '86 196
Sorbet, Pink Grapefruit and Tarragon,
    '95 163

Sorbet, Strawberry-Champagne, '95 20
Soufflé, Baked Apricot, '88 267
Soufflé, Light Chocolate, '83 278
Soufflé, Orange Dessert, '83 206
Soufflé, Raspberry-Topped, '85 317
Soufflé, Tart Lemon, '85 82
Spumoni and Berries, '91 204
Strawberries Juliet, '84 82
Strawberries Marsala, '88 171
Strawberries 'n' Cream, '90 30
Strawberry Cups, Frozen, '91 173
Strawberry Dessert, Glazed, '84 33
Strawberry Dessert, Summer, '92 143
Strawberry Puff, '82 5
Strawberry Whip, '89 198
Strawberry-Yogurt Dessert, '90 295
Tapioca Fluff, Orange, '87 31
Tart, Fancy Fruit, '82 128
Tart, Fresh Fruit, '84 178; '90 58
Tart, Green Grape, '87 77
Tart, Kiwifruit-Peach, '88 20
Tartlets, Fresh Fruit, '93 96
Tart, Pear, '92 72
Tarts, Cran-Raspberry Meringue, '92 286
Tart Shell, '87 77; '88 20
Tiramisù, '94 295
Topping, Blueberry, '87 125
Topping, Cherry-Pineapple, '87 126
Topping, Chunky Piña Colada, '87 125
Topping, Raspberry, '85 317
Topping, Raspberry-Peach, '87 126
Topping, Reduced-Calorie Whipped,
    '85 55
Topping, Spicy Apple, '87 125
Topping, Strawberry, '86 32
Topping, Strawberry-Banana, '87 125
Torte, Apricot Sponge, '90 59
Torte, Chocolate Mint, '94 86
Tortoni, Apricot-Yogurt, '95 124
Trifle, All Seasons Lemon, '95 219
Trifle, Angel Food, '91 184
Trifle, Olde English, '95 331
Trifle, Raspberry, '88 259
Trifle, Tropical, '95 204
Truffles, Chocolate-Kahlúa, '92 285
Wafers, Cinnamon, '84 324
Watermelon Frost, '86 196
Yogurt, Frozen Fresh Peach, '90 139
Yogurt, Lemon-Chiffon Frozen, '85 54
Yogurt, Vanilla Frozen, '87 125
Di-Calcium Phosphate Solution, '89 138
Dressing, Light Cornbread, '92 324
Dressing, Savory Cornbread, '88 303
Eggs and Omelets
    Benedict, Eggs, '85 49
    Benedict, Light Eggs, '93 M68
    Cheddar-Vegetable Omelet, '83 205
    Florentine, Eggs, '83 56
    Italian Omelet, '92 47
    Primavera, Omelet, '87 71
    Roulade with Mushroom Filling, Egg,
        '88 84
    Scrambled Eggs, Mexican-Style, '85 50
    Scrambled Eggs, Spanish, '84 60
    Substitute, Homemade Egg, '92 47
    Vegetable Omelet, Cheesy, '85 49
Enchiladas, Three-Bean, '91 133
Fettuccine and Spinach, '88 90
Fettuccine Primavera, '89 238
Filling, Chicken Salad, '87 106
Filling, Mushroom, '88 84
Filling, Shrimp Salad, '87 106
Fruit Kabobs, Winter, '89 34

Fruit Medley, Chilled, '84 60
Fruit, Minted Marinated, '92 138
Fruit Nuggets, Dried, '86 326
Fruit-on-a-Pick, '90 179
Fruit, Warm Spiced, '86 39
Fruit with Lemon-Yogurt Dressing, Fresh,
    '93 17
Glaze, Cranberry-Honey, '89 273
Glaze, Teriyaki, '94 82
Grapefruit, Broiled, '85 7
Grits, Cheese, '90 102
Grits, Garlic-and-Herb Cheese, '95 122
Guacamole, Mock, '93 36
Ham-and-Cheese Lettuce Rolls, '89 217
Jam, Berry Refrigerator, '89 139
Jam, Blackberry, '89 138
Jam, Blueberry Refrigerator, '89 139
Jam, Plum Refrigerator, '89 139
Jam, Strawberry, '89 138
Jelly, Crabapple, '89 139
Jelly, Grape, '89 140
Kielbasa, '92 242
Linguine with Garlic and Lemon, '88 91
Linguine with Red Pepper Sauce, '93 127
Low Sodium
    Applesauce, Spicy, '82 296
    Asparagus with Basil Sauce, '86 33
    Beef and Rice, Spicy, '83 231
    Beef Burgundy, '83 281
    Beef Goulash, '83 231
    Beef Roast, French-Style, '89 32
    Biscuits, Flaky, '84 228
    Bread, Bran-Applesauce, '84 229
    Bread, Salt-Free Raisin Batter, '86 33
    Breadsticks, Whole Wheat, '84 228
    Brussels Sprouts, Calico Citrus, '85 303
    Butter, Herbed Unsalted, '82 67
    Carrots Madeira, '83 281
    Catsup, Spicy Tomato, '83 182
    Cereal Snack, Toasted, '85 215
    Chicken à l'Orange, '84 277
    Chicken-and-Vegetables, Stir-Fry, '86 68
    Chicken, Citrus-Herb Baked, '85 303
    Chicken, Creole, '89 33
    Chicken Dinner, Healthful, '83 232
    Chicken, Herb-Baked, '82 229
    Chicken in Lemon and Wine, '83 281
    Chicken Piccata, '83 35
    Chicken-Tomato Bake, '83 35
    Chicken with Wine-Soaked Vegetables,
        Baked, '84 277
    Chili Surprise, '82 229
    Cookies, Sunshine Lemon, '86 69
    Cornish Hens in Vermouth, '86 33
    Cornish Hens, Roasted Rock, '82 66
    Dressing, Basil, '88 24
    Dressing, Lemon-Herb Salad, '82 67
    Dressing, Orange-Yogurt, '85 304
    Fish, Curried Baked, '87 5
    Flank Steak, Marinated, '83 35
    Flounder Rolls, Vegetable-Stuffed, '87 6
    Flounder, Sesame, '89 33
    Fruit Delight, Hot, '83 281
    Fruit Delight, Spiced, '82 229
    Fruit, Unsweetened Mixed, '83 182
    Green Beans, Minted, '84 104
    Ice, Pink Grapefruit, '85 304
    Jam, Banana, '82 296
    Jam, Freezer Peach, '83 182
    Lamb Chops, Dijon, '84 277
    Lamb Chops, Orange, '83 35
    Linguine with Seafood Sauce, '83 232
    Meat Loaf, Corny, '86 68

LIVING LIGHT, Low Sodium (continued)

Meat Loaf, Parsleyed, '83 35
Mocha-Cocoa Mix, Hot, '82 296
Mousse, Orange, '86 69
Muffins, Honey-Oatmeal, '84 229
Muffins, Spiced Bran, '84 229
Mustard, Lower Sodium Horseradish, '86 325
Nectarines in Apple Juice, '83 183
Onions, Glazed, '84 104
Orange Scampi, '85 303
Pastry Shell, Sesame, '82 67
Peppers, Corn Stuffed, '84 104
Pie, Nutty Pumpkin, '82 67
Pork, Roast Loin of, '84 276
Pork Tenderloin with Brown Sauce, Grilled, '89 32
Potato Bake, Chive-, '82 229
Potatoes, Yogurt-Stuffed, '88 24
Pretzels with Lower Sodium Horseradish Mustard, Herb, '86 325
Pudding, Chocolate-Almond, '88 24
Pudding, Lemon Fluff, '85 304
Ratatouille, '84 105
Rice and Shrimp, Curried, '83 231
Rice, Calico Brown, '86 33
Rolls, Low-Sodium Refrigerator, '82 67
Rolls, Low-Sodium Yeast, '84 228
Salad, Asparagus-and-New Potato, '86 69
Salad, Citrus Green, '85 304
Salad, Dilled Cucumber, '82 229
Salad Mold, Golden Citrus, '85 303
Salad, Mushroom-and-Pepper, '86 68
Salad, Sesame-Citrus Green, '86 33
Salmon, Poached, '83 35
Salmon Steaks, Marinated, '87 6
Sauce, Apple-Horseradish, '82 229
Sauce, Brown, '89 32
Sauce, Green Herb, '83 36
Sauce, Seafood, '83 36
Scallops, Sherried, '83 281
Scamp, Tangy Broiled, '87 5
Seasoning Blend, '82 296
Shake, Pineapple-Banana, '85 215
Shrimp Kabobs, Marinated, '84 276
Shrimp, Special Boiled, '83 36
Snapper, Caribbean, '87 5
Snapper, Orangy, '88 23
Soup, Chunky Chicken-Noodle, '88 12
Soup, Chunky Mushroom, '88 12
Soup, Cream of Cauliflower, '88 12
Soup, Spicy Vegetable-Beef, '88 11
Squash Sauté, '82 67
Squash, Vegetable-Stuffed, '84 104
Stew, Cajun-Style Catfish, '88 12
Stew, White Wine, '82 228
Stuffing, Low-Sodium, '82 66
Swordfish, Foil-Baked, '87 5
Tomatoes, Stewed, '83 182
Tomato Puree, Seasoned, '83 182
Tropical Snow, '86 34
Veal, Savory, '83 281
Veal Spaghetti, '84 276
Vegetable Stir-Fry, '84 104
Waffles, Whole Wheat, '84 228
Zucchini, Herbed, '84 104
Zucchini with Baby Carrots, '88 24
Macaroni and Cheese, Baked, '82 199
Macaroni with Pesto, Whole Wheat, '89 238

Main Dishes

Asparagus Roulade, '86 102
Beans and Rice, Red, '90 27
Beef, American Steakhouse, '93 15
Beef-and-Barley Rolls, Wine-Sauced, '87 269
Beef and Cauliflower over Rice, '93 94
Beef-and-Rice Dinner, Mexican, '88 199
Beef and Vegetables, Company, '88 234
Beef-and-Vegetable Stir-Fry, '87 22
Beef Burgundy, '88 25
Beef Chimichangas, Oven-Fried, '92 124
Beef, Chinese-Style, '87 50
Beef Fajitas, '88 233
Beef Hash, '95 24
Beef Kabobs, Chile-, '94 251
Beef Kabobs, Spirited, '87 142
Beef Kabobs with Rice, Marinated, '84 32
Beef, Marinated Sauerbraten, '93 16
Beef Medaillons, Italian, '87 305
Beef Patties, Deviled-, '87 22
Beef Stir-Fry, Chinese, '83 151
Beef Stroganoff, '91 134
Beef Stroganoff, Light, '86 36
Beef Tenderloin Bundles, Peppered, '89 272
Beef Tenderloin for Two, '90 295
Beef with Asparagus, '90 100
Black Beans and Rice, '91 82
Black Beans and Yellow Rice, Easy, '92 308
Burgers, Barbecued, '89 164
Burgers, Favorite, '89 165
Burgers, Lentil, '95 123
Burgers, Mushroom, '89 164
Burgers, Pizza, '89 165
Burgers, Seasoned, '85 158
Burgers, Triple-Layer, '89 165
Burgers, Vegetable, '89 164
Burgers, Walnut, '89 163
Burgers with Sprouts, '89 164
Burritos, Cheesy Beef, '85 193
Cabbage Rolls, Stuffed, '88 18
Cannelloni, '92 17
Carne Guisada, '94 219
Casserole, Bean-and-Cornbread, '92 243
Casserole, Breakfast, '91 285
Casserole, Chiles Rellenos, '92 18
Casserole, Crab-and-Mushroom, '89 96
Casserole, Freezer Eggplant-Sausage-Pasta, '95 197
Casserole, Turkey-and-Shrimp Florentine, '92 122
Catfish, Baked, '94 67
Catfish, Oven-Fried, '95 106
Catfish, Parmesan, '92 309
Catfish, Southern Oven-Fried, '87 163
Catfish with Creole Sauce, Breaded, '90 28
Chicken à la King, '94 41
Chicken and Dumplings, Old-Fashioned, '93 302
Chicken and Rice, Spicy, '88 200
Chicken-and-Sausage Jambalaya, '88 200
Chicken and Spinach Noodles, '82 19
Chicken and Vegetables, Stir-Fry, '86 249
Chicken and Vegetables, Walnut, '85 194
Chicken and Vegetables with Ginger-Soy Sauce, '91 32
Chicken Bake, Individual, '90 279
Chicken Breast in Wine, Poached, '91 184
Chicken Breasts Sardou, Stuffed, '87 269

Chicken Breasts, Wine-Baked, '83 177
Chicken Breasts with Fruited Rice Pilaf, '92 307
Chicken Cacciatore, '86 42
Chicken Chili Bake, '93 302
Chicken, Chutney, '86 249
Chicken Cordon Bleu, '86 37; '93 126
Chicken, Creamed, '82 49
Chicken Croquettes and Mushroom Sauce, '91 220
Chicken, Crunchy Oven-Fried, '87 163
Chicken, Curried, '86 43
Chicken Curry, Stir-Fried, '87 51
Chicken Cutlets with Lemon, '85 8
Chicken, Dante's, '88 25
Chicken Dinner, Skillet, '86 249
Chicken Enchiladas, '90 121
Chicken Fingers, Herb-Baked, '86 249
Chicken Fingers, No-Fry-Pan, '91 120
Chicken-Fried Wild Rice, '91 132
Chicken Gumbo, '90 26
Chicken in a Bag, '87 23
Chicken in Foil, '91 134
Chicken in Orange Sauce, '83 8
Chicken Kabobs, Sesame, '82 165
Chicken Kiev, Oven-Baked, '86 37
Chicken la France, '86 248
Chicken Lasagna, '88 90
Chicken-Leek Terrine, Cold, '92 145
Chicken, Lemon-Frosted, '88 170
Chicken, Lemon-Roasted, '95 24
Chicken Marengo, '92 70
Chicken Marsala, '89 237
Chicken, Orange, '83 278
Chicken, Oven-Fried, '93 90
Chicken Paprika, Dilled, '86 41
Chicken, Pineapple, '83 M194
Chicken Pot Pie, '94 21
Chicken Rolls, Spinach-Stuffed, '86 248
Chicken, Southern Oven-Fried, '86 37
Chicken Spaghetti, '87 221
Chicken Stir-Fry, Apple-Sesame-, '92 226
Chicken Stir-Fry, Chinese, '90 100
Chicken Strips and Vegetables, Marinated, '90 110
Chicken, Sweet-and-Sour, '91 202
Chicken Tostadas, '95 122
Chicken-Vegetable Stir-Fry, '83 151; '84 13
Chicken with Artichoke Hearts, '88 54
Chicken with Artichokes, Sherried, '87 143
Chicken with Mole Sauce, '93 34
Chicken with Orange, Lime, and Ginger Sauce, '92 123
Chicken with Pineapple, Oriental, '86 42
Chicken with Salsa, Baked Chile, '88 147
Chicken with Spinach Fettuccine, Easy, '88 89
Chicken with Tabbouleh Salad, Grilled, '91 70
Chicken with Tomato-Basil Pasta, Basil-Stuffed, '94 M204
Chiles Rellenos, Light, '93 156
Chiles Rellenos with Tomatillo Sauce, Roasted, '94 203
Chile Verde, Light, '88 148
Chili, '93 89
Chili, Firestarter, '93 34
Chili, Hot Venison, '91 283
Chili, South-of-the-Border, '91 283
Chili, Southwestern, '91 284
Chili, Vegetarian, '91 284

LIVING LIGHT, Main Dishes *(continued)*

Chili, White, '91 284
Cornbread-Tamale Pie, '92 123
Cornish Hens, Herbed, '82 271
Cornish Hens, Mesquite-Smoked,
   '92 144
Cornish Hens, Orange-Glazed Grilled,
   '86 250
Cornish Hens with Vegetables, Tarragon
   Roasted, '94 79
Crab-and-Shrimp Étouffée, '89 96
Crab Cakes, '91 122
Crabmeat au Gratin, '86 154
Cracked Wheat, "Fried," '89 31
Crawfish Étouffée, '86 156
Crêpes, Cannelloni, '86 143
Crêpes, Chicken-Vegetable, '83 70
Eggplant Parmesan, '92 18
Enchiladas, Spicy Bean, '88 18
Fajita Fettuccine, '94 84
Fajita in a Pita, '90 177
Fettuccine and Shrimp with Dried
   Tomato Pesto, '94 249
Fettuccine, Ham-and-Asparagus, '94 84
Fettuccine Primavera, '94 85
Fettuccine, Shrimp, '94 84
Filet Mignon with Mushroom Sauce,
   '94 250
Fillets, Apple-Carrot Stuffed, '88 M192
Fillets Tomatillo, '94 135
Fish and Vegetables, Steamed, '91 32
Fish, Caribbean Banana, '95 202
Fish Dinner, Skillet, '88 199
Fish Fillets, Breaded Herbed, '91 121
Fish Florentine, '86 35
Fish Florentine in Parchment, '87 22
Fish with Greek Sauce, Poached,
   '91 M183
Flank Steak Sukiyaki, '88 233
Flank Steak with Black Bean-and-Corn
   Salsa, Grilled, '94 80
Flank Steak with Noodles, Stuffed,
   '90 101
Flank Steak with Sweet Peppers, Grilled,
   '90 138
Flounder, Creole-Style, '85 180
Flounder Rolls with Citrus Sauce, Stuffed,
   '85 180
Frijoles Rancheros, '88 148
Frittata, Vegetable, '92 48
Game Hens with Chutney-Mustard
   Glaze, '93 66
Goulash, Hungarian, '92 227
Grits-and-Ham Pie, Crustless, '86 103
Grouper, Grilled Marinated, '90 166
Grouper, Hot Spicy, '94 78
Haddock Fillets with Zucchini Stuffing,
   '88 M191
Halibut Steaks Italiano, '88 M191
Halibut with Champagne Sauce, Baked,
   '90 29
Halibut with Swiss Sauce, '83 M195
Hamburger Pie, '84 13
Ham-Potato-Pineapple Bake, '93 302
Ham with Cranberry-Honey Glaze,
   Baked, '89 273
Hopping John with Grilled Pork
   Medaillons, '93 229
Jambalaya, '90 26
Jambalaya, Black-Eyed Pea, '92 70
Jambalaya, Red Rice, '91 18

Kabobs, Hawaiian, '85 157
Lamb Chops, Broiled, '85 22
Lamb Chops, Peppercorn-Crusted,
   '92 142
Lamb Chops with Herbs, '90 164
Lamb with Five Spices, Stewed, '92 72
Lasagna, Cheesy Spinach, '83 204
Lasagna, Creamy Ham-and-Chicken,
   '95 88
Lasagna in a Bun, '90 176
Lasagna, Lean, '86 37
Lasagna, Light, '95 212
Lasagna, Spinach-Bean, '92 96
Lasagna, Vegetable, '84 201
Lasagna, Zucchini, '85 194
Lentil-and-Rice Supper, '84 202
Lentils-and-Rice Casserole, '93 301
Linguine with Clam Sauce, '88 90
Liver, Creole, '86 108
Liver in Creole Sauce, '87 33
Lobster Tails with Spiced Orange Sauce,
   '86 155
London Broil, Marinated, '87 32
Mackerel, Rosemary-Garlic, '92 200
Manicotti, Spinach, '82 199
Meatballs and Vegetables with
   Horseradish Dressing, '91 32
Meat Loaf, '89 109
Meat Loaf, Curried, '86 43
Meat Loaf, Oriental, '83 M194
Meat Loaf, Parsley, '87 22
Orange Roughy-and-Vegetable Stir-Fry,
   '91 50
Orange Roughy, Vegetable-Topped,
   '93 67
Orange Roughy with Herbs, Steamed,
   '95 189
Orange Roughy with Spinach Pesto,
   '88 M192
Pasta, Creamy Turkey-Basil, '89 216
Pasta, Mamma Mia, '95 25
Pasta Primavera, Almost, '86 38
Pasta Salad, Main-Dish, '82 199
Pasta Verde, '84 201
Pasta with Peanut Sauce, '95 252
Pastichio, '85 194
Pear Breakfast Treat, '87 72
Peppers Stuffed with Shrimp-and-Orzo
   Salad, '91 203
Perch, Parmesan-Crusted, '93 91
Pie, Italian Meat, '89 109
Pizza, Breakfast, '90 178
Pizza, Garden, '89 108
Pizza, Turkey-Vegetable, '90 139
Pizza, Vegetable, '94 218
Pizza, Veggie, '94 78
Pizza, Whole Wheat, '84 33
Polenta with Black Bean Salsa, Grilled,
   '93 155
Pollock with Summer Squash Relish,
   '92 200
Pork-and-Noodles Skillet Dinner,
   '88 199
Pork, Chinese Roast, '91 308
Pork Chop Dinner, '88 25
Pork Chops, Apricot-Sauced, '85 22
Pork Chops, Creole-Style, '91 49
Pork Chops, Fruit-Topped, '94 41
Pork Chops, Honey-Lime, '91 33
Pork Chops in Gravy, '91 137
Pork Chow Mein, '90 101
Pork, Cranberry, '90 293
Pork Loin Roast, Barbecued, '93 34

Pork Medaillons, Grilled, '93 229
Pork Medaillons with Port Wine and
   Dried Cranberry Sauce, '95 330
Pork Roast, Oven-Barbecued, '91 50
Pork Roast, Stuffed Crown, '89 272
Pork, Stir-Fried, '87 51
Pork, Sweet-and-Sour, '85 34, 194
Pork Tenderloin, Apple-Mushroom,
   '95 53
Pork Tenderloin, Honey-Mustard,
   '95 52
Pork Tenderloin, Marinated, '84 175
Pork Tenderloin, Sesame, '95 53
Pork Tenderloins, Fruit-Stuffed,
   '87 270
Pork Tenderloin, Spinach-and-Bacon
   Stuffed, '94 81
Pork Tenderloin with Apples, Celery, and
   Potatoes, Grilled, '95 161
Pork Tenderloin with Orange Marmalade,
   '91 49
Pot Roast, Marinated, '85 21
Quail with Mushroom Gravy, Baked,
   '89 273
Quesadillas, Quick, '89 87
Quiche, Eggless, '87 220
Quiche, Fiesta, '92 47
Quiches, Individual Spinach, '86 38
Quiche, Spinach, '85 49; '91 204
Quiche, Swiss-Zucchini, '82 49
Ravioli, Mediterranean, '93 301
Red Snapper, Blackened, '90 27
Red Snapper Rolls, Cucumber-Stuffed,
   '83 176
Red Snapper Veracruz, '88 149;
   '92 142
Rice-and-Lentil Pilaf, '88 17
Roast Beef, Deli-Style, '93 15
Salmon Burgers, '95 24
Salmon Fillets with Red Wine Garlic
   Sauce, '94 250
Salmon in Parchment, '95 311
Salmon Loaf with Cucumber-Dill Sauce,
   '86 5
Salmon-Pesto Vermicelli, '92 200
Salmon with Ginger Vinaigrette, Sesame-
   Crusted, '95 162
Salmon with Horseradish Sauce, Poached,
   '91 183
Sausage, Dieters' Spicy, '85 49
Scallop Kabobs, Grilled, '83 101
Scallops in Vegetable Nests, '91 70
Scallops with Cilantro-Lime Vinaigrette,
   Grilled Orange, '94 77
Scallops with Tomato-Mango Salsa,
   Seared, '95 122
Shrimp, Barbecued, '90 28
Shrimp, Beer-Broiled, '87 142
Shrimp Cancun en Papillote, '91 136
Shrimp Enchiladas in Tomatillo Sauce,
   '95 310
Shrimp Étouffée, '90 229
Shrimp Skillet, Quick, '87 50
Shrimp, Sweet-and-Sour, '83 278
Shrimp with Peanut Sauce, '93 303
Sirloin, Mustard Marinated, '94 41
Snapper à l'Orange, Baked, '85 181
Snapper, Honey-Curried, '85 181
Snapper, Poached, '83 101
Snapper with Creamy Dill Sauce,
   Peppered, '94 42
Snow Peas and Red Pepper, Sesame,
   '84 175

LIVING LIGHT, Main Dishes (continued)

Sole Divan, '87 21
Sole Véronique, '85 181
Spaghetti, Meaty, '82 19
Spinach-and-Cheese Calzones, '95 310
Steak au Poivre, '88 232
Steak Diane, '92 306
Steak, Fast-and-Easy Stir-Fried, '87 50
Steak in Red Wine Sauce, Skillet, '85 21
Steak, Italian-Stuffed, '88 232
Steak Kabobs, '82 4; '93 95
Steak lo Mein, '90 100
Steak, Marinated, '88 233
Steak, Mexican Marinated, '88 148
Steak, Mock Country-Fried, '87 163
Steak, Pepper-Beef, '85 21
Stew, Burgundy Beef, '88 234
Swordfish with Caper Sauce, Grilled,
    '95 230
Tacoritos, '90 133
Tenderloins, Honey-Grilled, '92 199
Tenderloin, Spinach-Stuffed, '89 311
Tofu, Stroganoff, '84 202
Tomato with Tuna Pasta, Stuffed, '88 54
Trout, Baked, '95 106
Trout Fillets with Capers, '95 252
Trout, Grilled, '95 106
Trout, Poached, '95 106
Tuna Croquettes with Parsley Sauce,
    '86 108
Tuna Steaks on Mixed Greens with
    Lemon-Basil Vinaigrette, Seared,
    '94 205
Tuna with Poblano Salsa, Grilled, '91 135
Tuna with Rosemary, Broiled, '93 127
Tuna with Tangy Mustard Sauce, '92 201
Turkey-Asparagus Pilaf, '88 200
Turkey Breast and Gravy, Roast, '88 303
Turkey Breast, Stuffed, '87 270
Turkey Breast with Cranberry Salsa,
    Grilled, '95 252
Turkey Breast with Special Gravy, Roast,
    '86 282
Turkey Cutlets, Oven-Fried, '91 121
Turkey Cutlets with Pepper Salsa, Spicy,
    '88 26
Turkey Lasagna, '91 130
Turkey, Lazy Day, '93 93
Turkey Piccata, '91 137
Veal and Carrots, Company, '85 22
Veal, Lemon, '93 35
Veal Marsala, '91 310
Veal Picante, '87 31
Veal Piccata with Capers, '87 142
Veal Scallopini, '83 8
Vegetarian Supper, '86 222
Vermicelli and Sprouts with Red Clam
    Sauce, '86 143
Vermicelli, Scallop-Vegetable, '87 143
Zucchini Frittata, '86 103
Meatballs, '89 237
Meatballs, Turkey, '89 237
Meat Mixture, Basic, '92 241
Muesli, Bran-and-Fruit, '91 134
Oatmeal, Applesauce, '89 108
Oatmeal, Fruited, '88 19
Olive Oil, Basil-Infused, '95 231
Olive Oil, Lemon-Infused, '95 231
Pancakes, Honey, '91 139
Pancakes, Oatmeal, '89 107
Pancakes, Shredded Wheat, '84 59

Pancakes, Whole Wheat-Oat, '93 16
Pasta, Asian Pesto, '95 189
Pasta-Basil Toss, '87 33
Pasta, Caesar Salad, '95 230
Pasta, Garden, '82 199
Pasta Provençale, '88 90
Pasta, Tomato-Basil, '94 204
Peaches, Spicy Baked, '86 39
Pizza Crust, Special, '90 139
Pizza Crusts, Skillet, '94 218
Pizza on a Bagel, '93 M94
Preserves, Fig, '89 140
Preserves, Peach, '89 140
Relish, Cranberry, '86 283; '91 257
Relish, Holiday Cranberry, '88 304
Relish, Papaya-Basil, '94 82
Relish, White Bean, '93 229
Rice
    Apple-Cinnamon Rice, '86 249
    Black-Eyed Peas, Rice with, '93 66
    Casserole, Colorful Rice, '82 199
    Herb Rice, '91 257
    Lime-Flavored Rice, '84 175
    Mexican Rice, Spicy, '88 149
    Mix, Fruited Curry-Rice, '86 326
    Onion Rice, Seasoned, '82 166
    Orange Rice, '82 200
    Peppered Rice, '82 4
    Pilaf, Browned Rice, '87 305
    Pilaf, Brown Rice, '90 136; '91 82
    Shell, Rice-Cheese, '82 49
    Southwestern Rice, '90 121
    Spanish Rice with Tofu, '88 26
    Tomatoes and Basil, Rice with,
        '95 232
    Wild Rice and Mushrooms, '83 278
    Wild Rice Bulgur, '91 83
    Yellow Rice, '91 136
Salad Dressings
    Blue Cheese Dressing, '82 166
    Blue Cheese Dressing, Creamy,
        '91 307
    Blue Cheese Vinaigrette, '90 280
    Caper Vinaigrette, '91 310
    Cilantro-Lime Vinaigrette, '94 77
    Coconut Dressing, '87 251
    Creamy Dressing, '93 318
    Cucumber-Mint Dressing, '87 153
    Cucumber Salad Dressing, Creamy,
        '82 79
    Curry Dressing, '82 78
    French Dressing, Miracle, '82 79
    Fruit, Salad Dressing for, '86 40
    Herb Salad Dressing, '86 40
    Honey-Mustard Dressing, '90 111
    Horseradish Dressing, '87 152; '91 32
    Lemon-Basil Vinaigrette, '94 205
    Lemon-Yogurt Dressing, '93 17
    Lemon-Yogurt Slaw or Salad Dressing,
        '88 54
    Lime Dressing, '83 120
    Orange-Poppy Seed Dressing, '87 187
    Papaya Seed Dressing, '95 204
    Pineapple-Poppy Seed Dressing, '85 55
    Raspberry Dressing, '87 153; '95 202
    Soy-Sesame Dressing, '87 153
    Spicy Southwestern Dressing, '94 136
    Spring Garden Dressing, '85 157
    Stay Trim Dressing, '86 40
    Sweet-and-Sour Dressing, '87 305
    Tangy Dressing, '83 9
    Thousand Island Dressing, Special,
        '82 79

Vinaigrette Dressing, '95 231
Wine Vinegar Dressing, '93 126
Yogurt Dressing, '85 59, 215; '88 27
Yogurt Dressing, Sweet-Hot, '86 40
Yogurt-Herb Dressing, '92 96
Yogurt-Honey Poppy Seed Dressing,
    '83 177
Salads
    Ambrosia, Brunch, '83 57
    Apple-Apricot Salad, '88 121
    Apple-Bran Salad, Lemony, '86 223
    Apple Cider Salad Mold, '85 54
    Apple Salad, Spicy, '85 215
    Apple Salad, Triple, '88 122
    Apple Toss, Sesame-, '88 21
    Asparagus, Marinated, '84 67
    Asparagus Salad, '88 121; '94 67
    Asparagus Vinaigrette, Light, '82 50
    Aspic, Light Tomato, '85 83
    Aspic, Three-Layer, '88 120
    Aspic, Tomato-Crab, '85 287
    Aspic with Horseradish Dressing, Crisp
        Vegetable, '87 152
    Barley-Broccoli Salad, '90 135
    Bean-and-Rice Salad, Marinated, '87 152
    Bean Salad, Marinated, '85 137, 296
    Bean Salad, Supreme, '91 202
    Beans with Sprouts, Sweet-and-Sour,
        '86 32
    Beef-and-Broccoli Salad, '87 187
    Beef Fajita Salad, '91 70
    Black Bean-and-Barley Salad, '94 174
    Black Bean Salad, '89 217
    Black-Eyed Pea Salad, '95 203
    Black-Eyed Pea Salad, Marinated,
        '93 190
    Broccoli-Corn Salad, '87 24
    Brown Rice-and-Vegetable Salad, '84 202
    Brown Rice Confetti Salad, '94 174
    Caesar Salad, '92 71
    Cantaloupe, Fruit-Filled, '83 120
    Carrot-and-Seed Salad, Fruity, '86 223
    Carrot-Pineapple Salad, '91 83
    Carrot-Raisin Salad, '84 174
    Cauliflower-Vegetable Salad, '85 158
    Cherry-Apple Salad, '86 31
    Cherry Salad, Fresh, '83 120
    Chicken-and-Walnut Salad, Sunburst,
        '93 91
    Chicken-Fruit Salad, '82 79
    Chicken Noodle Salad, '95 25
    Chicken Pasta Salad, '88 89
    Chicken-Raspberry Salad, Marinated,
        '93 190
    Chicken Salad, Blue Cheese, '94 81
    Chicken Salad, Crunchy, '86 207
    Chicken Salad, Moroccan Grilled,
        '95 231
    Chicken Salad, Special, '85 82
    Chicken Salad, Tarragon, '90 199
    Chicken Salad with Raspberry Dressing,
        Grilled, '95 202
    Chicken Taco Salad, '94 M136
    Chile-Tomato Salad, Spicy, '88 121
    Citrus Salad, Tangy, '89 34
    Coleslaw, Crunchy, '86 295
    Coleslaw, Light and Creamy, '93 318
    Composé, Salad, '93 126
    Corn Salad, '85 236
    Cottage Cheese Salad in Tomatoes,
        '86 208
    Couscous Salad, Basil-and-Tomato,
        '94 175

LIVING LIGHT, Salads *(continued)*

Crab-and-Asparagus Salad, '92 141
Crab-Wild Rice Salad, '86 207
Cucumber Mousse, '88 121
Cucumber Salad, Dilled, '92 72
Cucumber-Yogurt Salad, '87 33
English Pea-and-Apple Salad, '87 24
Fennel and Radicchio with Orange
    Vinaigrette, Grilled, '95 253
Freezer Salad, '94 118
Fruit Cups, Sangría, '89 34
Fruit, Dressed-Up, '82 5
Fruit Salad, Chef's, '86 35
Fruit Salad, Curried, '85 107
Fruit with Mint-Balsamic Tea, Fresh,
    '95 232
Garden-Patch Salad Molds, '86 283
Garden Salad, Summer, '87 153
Gazpacho Molded Salad, '92 323
Grapefruit Salad, '88 122
Grape Salad Mold, '83 120
Green Beans with Creamy Tarragon
    Dressing, '93 191
Green Salad, Mixed, '90 230
Greens, Crimson, '87 153
Greens with Blue Cheese Vinaigrette,
    Mixed, '90 280
Greens with Raspberry Dressing, Peppery,
    '95 254
Hominy-Bean Salad, '88 266
Italian Salad, Cheesy, '84 33
Jicama-Orange Salad, '90 122
Layered Salad, '86 35
Legumes, Marinated, '90 197
Lentils-and-Rice Salad, '90 197
Lettuce, Confetti-Stuffed, '87 24
Lettuces with Mustard Vinaigrette, Baby,
    '93 67
Lima Bean-Tomato Salad, '85 137
Macaroni-Cheese Salad, Dilled, '86 208
Macaroni-Chicken Salad, Dilled, '92 142
Macaroni-Tuna Salad, Whole Wheat,
    '84 193
Mandarin Salad Molds, '85 54
Meal-in-One Salad, '86 43
Melon Ball Bowl with Cucumber-Mint
    Dressing, '87 153
Mushroom-Zucchini Salad, '85 8
New Potato Salad, '84 139
Niçoise, Salad, '86 35
Oriental Salad Bowl, '87 153
Paella Salad, '86 207
Pasta-and-Tomato Salad, Herbed,
    '92 144
Pasta Salad, '84 139; '89 217
Pasta Salad, Garden, '86 188
Peaches in a Garden Nest, '87 154
Pork Salad, Oriental, '92 140
Potato Salad, '90 122
Potato Salad, Hot-and-Light, '93 90
Potato Salad, Pesto, '90 164
Potato Slices, Marinated, '93 98
Rice-and-Vegetable Salad, '86 42
Rice-Shrimp Salad, '92 142
Romaine with Caper Vinaigrette, Hearts
    of, '91 310
Salmon-and-Wild Rice Salad, Oriental,
    '94 173
Seafood Salad Sussex Shores, '93 98
Shrimp-and-Rice Salad, '92 307
Shrimp Salad, Fruited, '86 156

Shrimp Salad, Marinated, '85 82
Slaw, Apple-Carrot, '92 243
Slaw, Cabbage-Pineapple, '92 182
Slaw, Chinese Cabbage, '89 312
Slaw, Green Bean, '95 108
Slaw, Healthy, '92 183
Slaw, Red Cabbage-and-Apple, '87 31
Spinach-Blue Cheese Salad, '82 166
Spinach-Kiwifruit Salad, '87 305
Spinach Salad, Citrus, '90 59
Spinach Salad, Wilted, '93 125
Spinach Salad with Orange Dressing,
    '87 187
Sprout Salad, '90 137
Steak Salad Cups, Pepper, '86 206
Strawberry Salad, Frozen, '94 119
Tabbouleh Salad, '91 70; '94 174
Tofu Salad, '88 27
Tomato-Cucumber Salad, '92 199
Tomato-Cucumber Salad with Yogurt-
    Herb Dressing, '92 96
Tomatoes Stuffed with Sea Slaw, '89 96
Tortellini Salad, '89 237
Tuna-and-Cannellini Bean Salad,
    '86 143
Tuna Chef Salad, '82 78
Tuna-Mac in Tomatoes, '87 188
Tuna-Pasta Salad, '92 141
Tuna Salad, Curried, '86 208
Turkey Waldorf Salad with Yogurt
    Dressing, '88 53
Turnip Salad, '85 235
Vegetable Salad, Crispy Marinated,
    '84 193
Vegetable Salad, Grilled, '94 203
Vegetable Salad, Italian, '82 19
Vegetable Salad, Marinated, '84 13
Vegetable Salad, Minted, '88 23
Vegetable Salad, Tarragon-, '85 288
Vegetable Salad, Winter, '86 42
Vegetables, Zesty Marinated, '82 272
Wheat Berry-and-Roasted Corn Salad,
    '94 175
Wild Rice Salad, '93 191
Sandwiches
    Bagel, Breakfast on a, '94 66
    Breakfast Sandwiches, Open-Faced,
        '92 140
    Chicken Pita, Oriental, '89 216
    Chicken Sandwiches, Marinated,
        '86 M45
    Crab Sandwiches, Open-Faced, '87 106
    Eggplant Sandwiches, Open-Face,
        '95 124
    Garden Sandwiches, Open-Faced,
        '87 105
    Ham Sandwiches, Open-Face, '85 8
    Heroes, Healthy, '90 177
    Lamb Pockets with Dilled Cucumber
        Topping, '87 104
    Open-Face Sandwiches, '84 13
    Pimiento Cheese Sandwiches, '82 278
    Pitas, Acadian Stuffed, '90 177
    Pita Sandwiches, '84 139
    Pita, Stuffed, '89 87
    Pizza Sandwiches, Open-Face, '85 22
    Shrimp Salad Sandwiches, '90 178
    Sloppy Toms, '91 51
    Tofu-Veggie Sandwiches, Open-Face,
        '86 5
    Turkey-in-the-Slaw Sandwich, '90 177
    Turkey-Roasted Pepper Sandwiches,
        Smoked, '94 66

    Vegetable Pockets, '85 215
    Vegetarian Melt, Open-Faced, '87 106
    Vegetarian Pita Sandwiches, '84 193
Sauces and Gravies
    Alfredo Sauce, '94 84
    Barbecue Sauce, Easy, '82 178
    Barbecue Sauce, Special, '82 177
    Basil-Brown Butter Sauce, '93 92
    Champagne Sauce, '90 29
    Cheese Sauce, Guilt-Free, '93 M95
    Creole Sauce, '90 28
    Cucumber-Dill Sauce, '86 5
    Dill Sauce, Creamy, '94 42
    Ginger-Soy Sauce, '91 33
    Ginger Vinaigrette, '95 162
    Gravy, '88 303
    Gravy, Sausage, '94 20
    Greek Sauce, '91 183
    Hollandaise Sauce, Mock, '85 49;
        '93 68
    Horseradish Sauce, '91 183
    Jalapeño Sauce, '93 230
    Lemon-Chive Sauce, '86 249
    Lemon Sauce, '82 290
    Mandarin Sauce, '84 60
    Marinade, Tangy Light, '82 178
    Marinara Sauce, '82 178; '89 239;
        '92 18
    Mediterranean Sauce, '94 83
    Mushroom Sauce, '83 205; '91 221
    Mushroom Sauce, Spicy Sherried,
        '89 239
    Mustard-Hollandaise Sauce, Mock,
        '87 269
    Mustard Sauce, '87 22
    Mustard Sauce, Easy, '94 83
    Mustard Sauce, Light, '82 178
    Mustard Sauce, Tangy, '92 201
    Parmesan Sauce, '92 17
    Parsley Sauce, '86 108
    Pesto, Dried Tomato, '94 249
    Picante Sauce, Processed, '91 257
    Pizza Sauce, '84 33
    Rancheros Sauce, '88 148
    Red Chile Sauce, '94 251
    Red Wine Garlic Sauce, '94 250
    Salsa, '88 147
    Salsa, Black Bean, '93 155
    Salsa, Black Bean-and-Corn, '94 80
    Salsa Cruda, '88 148
    Salsa, Cucumber-Dill, '95 107
    Salsa, Fiesta Onion, '94 82
    Salsa, Hot Kiwifruit, '94 82
    Salsa, Pepper, '88 26
    Salsa, Poblano, '91 135
    Salsa, Tomato-Avocado, '94 83
    Sauerbraten Sauce, '93 16
    Seafood Sauce, '89 239
    Seafood Sauce, Red, '95 107
    Spaghetti Sauce, Lentil, '90 198
    Swiss Sauce, '83 M195
    Tarragon Sauce, '83 56
    Tartar Sauce, '95 107
    Tomato Sauce, '85 193, 244
    Tomato Sauce, Spicy, '88 19
    Vegetable-Cheese Potato Topper, '86 6
    White Sauce, Low-Calorie Medium,
        '87 26
    Zesty Sauce, '94 82
    Zippy Sauce, '86 44
Sausage, Country, '92 242
Sausage, Italian, '92 242
Sorbet, Pink Grapefruit and Tarragon, '95 163

LIVING LIGHT *(continued)*

Soups and Stews
    Asparagus Soup, '84 67
    Bean-and-Hominy Soup, '95 23
    Bean and Pasta Soup, '94 220
    Bean-and-Turkey Soup, '93 319
    Bean Soup, Leafy, '86 223
    Beef-and-Barley Vegetable Soup, '89 31
    Beef Stew, '90 230
    Beef Stew, Quick, '92 71
    Bisque, Squash, '84 280
    Black Bean Soup, '88 266
    Black Bean Soup, Carolina, '92 139
    Borscht, Ruby Red, '83 176
    Bouillon, Tomato, '83 8
    Broccoli Soup, Creamy, '91 307
    Broccoli Soup, Light Cream of, '93 17
    Broccoli Soup, Mock Cream of, '85 288
    Broccoli-Swiss Soup, '86 6
    Cantaloupe Soup, '83 120
    Carrot-Leek Soup, '86 34
    Chicken, Artichoke, and Mushroom
      Soup, '92 324
    Chicken Soup, Curried, '86 34
    Chicken-Vegetable Soup, '88 18
    Chili Vegetable Soup, '94 120
    Chili, Vegetarian, '84 280
    Chowder, Basque Fish, '86 36
    Chowder, Clam, '86 36; '89 95
    Chowder, Corn, '91 132
    Chowder, Potato-Corn, '94 66
    Chowder, Seafood, '92 122
    Corn-and-Crab Soup, Fresh, '92 183
    Crab Soup, Cream of, '88 302
    Cucumber Soup, Cold Minted, '86 34
    Cucumber-Yogurt Soup, '83 205
    Fish-and-Vegetable Stew, '87 220
    French Market Soup, '92 49
    Gazpacho, Chilled, '84 138
    Gazpacho, Tropical, '95 204
    Gumbo, Catfish, '90 278
    Gumbo, Chicken-and-Sausage, '94 20
    Gumbo, Light Seafood-Okra, '86 155
    Ham-and-Bean Soup, Spicy, '94 322
    Hot-and-Sour Soup, '91 50
    Mex-Tex Soup, '90 278
    Minestrone Soup, '86 144; '91 258
    Minestrone Soup Mix, '91 258
    Navy Bean Soup, '84 280
    Okra-and-Shrimp Soup, '94 323
    Peach Soup, '83 120
    Pepper-and-Chicken Soup, Roasted,
      '90 58
    Pepper Soup, Spicy, '93 98
    Plum Soup, '85 107
    Seafood Stew, '84 280
    Spinach Soup, Oriental, '83 151
    Split Pea Soup, '90 198; '94 322
    Sweet Potato-and-Sausage Soup, '95 23
    Tomato Soup, '89 217
    Tomato Soup, Easy, '84 14
    Tomato Soup Plus, '88 170
    Tortilla Soup, '94 136
    Turkey-Tomato Stew, '90 279
    Vegetable-Beef Stew, '94 323
    Vegetable Soup, '86 187; '88 266
    Vegetable Soup, Light, '84 280
    Vegetable Stew, Mixed, '84 13
Sour Cream, Mock, '83 71, 205
Spice Mix, Tex-Mex, '94 135
Spice Rub, Moroccan, '95 231

Spread, Blue Cheese, '95 79
Spread, Cottage Cheese, '87 107
Spread, Hawaiian Ham, '87 106
Spread, Light Strawberry, '85 55
Spread, Low-Calorie Pimiento Cheese,
  '85 215
Spread, Peachy-Raisin, '86 326
Spread, Raisin-Nut, '95 79
Spread, Strawberry, '95 79
Spread, Sugarless Fruit, '84 60
Spread, Tasty Chicken, '84 193
Spread, Vegetable-Egg, '87 106
Syrup, Maple, '93 16
Topping, Apple, '89 107
Topping, Oat Crunch, '89 108
Topping, Yogurt-Cheese, '88 55
Tortellini with Rosemary-Parmesan Sauce,
  '92 284
Tortilla Rollups, '89 87
Vegetables
    Acorn Squash, Fruited, '85 235;
      '90 228
    Acorn Squash with Nutmeg, '85 267
    Artichokes, Shrimp-Stuffed, '84 67
    Artichokes Stuffed with Shrimp and
      Scallops, '84 174
    Asparagus, Company, '85 82
    Asparagus, Stir-Fried, '87 52
    Asparagus Vinaigrette, '90 138
    Barley and Vegetables, '91 81
    Beans, Lemon-Mint, '88 22
    Beans, Texas Ranch, '90 198
    Beets, Ginger-Marmalade Glazed, '93 35
    Beets, Harvard, '83 M195
    Beets, Orange, '91 219
    Beets, Orange-Glazed, '86 187
    Beets, Pickled, '87 163
    Black Bean Terrine with Fresh Tomato
      Coulis and Jalapeño Sauce, '93 230
    Black-Eyed Peas, '93 180
    Black-Eyed Peas, Seasoned, '85 138
    Black-Eyed Peas, Spicy Hot, '90 135
    Broccoli and Walnut Sauté, '95 52
    Broccoli Casserole, '88 265
    Broccoli, Easy Orange, '85 267
    Broccoli, Garlic, '93 35; '95 54
    Broccoli, Lemon, '95 53
    Broccoli, Sesame, '85 8
    Broccoli Toss, '86 294
    Broccoli with Horseradish Sauce, '84 33
    Broccoli with Tangy Chive Sauce,
      Steamed, '83 101
    Brussels Sprouts, Casserole of, '86 294
    Brussels Sprouts, Glorified, '86 282
    Brussels Sprouts in Mustard Sauce,
      '90 228
    Brussels Sprouts, Marinated, '88 265
    Brussels Sprouts Medley, '85 267
    Bundles, Vegetable, '93 181
    Burritos, Vegetable, '90 134; '92 138
    Butterbeans, '90 166
    Butternut-Orange Bake, '86 295
    Cabbage, Skillet, '90 229
    Cabbage, Sweet-and-Sour, '86 295
    Cabbage with Caraway, '93 181
    Carrots and Onions, Herbed, '87 31
    Carrots and Pineapple, Curried, '90 228
    Carrots, Dilled Baby, '92 145
    Carrots, Ginger, '83 9
    Carrots, Glazed, '88 304
    Carrots, Golden, '85 267
    Carrots, Lemon-Dill Steamed, '93 180
    Carrots, Light Glazed, '92 227

    Carrots, Marinated, '86 108
    Carrots Marsala, '83 56
    Carrots, Orange-Spiced, '88 18
    Carrots Polynesian, Spiced, '88 85
    Carrots, Rosemary, '91 219
    Carrot Strips, Orangy, '89 312
    Carrots, Tropical, '84 34
    Cauliflower Sauté, '94 67
    Cauliflower-Snow Pea Medley, '87 305
    Celeriac and Carrots, '91 219
    Celery-Parmesan Toss, '84 34
    Corn Casserole, Chili-, '88 266
    Corn, Creamy Baked, '90 60
    Corn-on-the-Cob, Grilled, '90 166
    Corn Pudding, Fresh, '89 172
    Corn, Roasted Red Pepper, '91 122
    Corn, Southern-Style Creamed, '92 201
    Corn, Spicy Mexican, '93 90
    Crêpes, Vegetable-Filled Bran, '86 44
    Eggplant Casserole, Spicy Hot, '93 92
    Eggplant, Ratatouille-Bran Stuffed,
      '86 44
    English Pea Medley, '85 236
    English Peas, Deluxe, '84 68
    French Fries, Oven, '91 122
    Green Bean Medley, Peppery, '93 181
    Green Beans and Potatoes, '91 221
    Green Beans, Herbed, '83 177
    Green Beans, Indian-Style, '88 265
    Green Beans, Italian, '90 164; '92 183
    Green Beans Italiano, '86 144
    Green Beans, Seasoned, '88 304
    Green Beans with Mushrooms, '93 89
    Green Beans with New Potatoes, '87 164
    Green Beans with Tomatoes, '85 137
    Green Tomatoes, '89 174
    Green Tomatoes, Oven-Fried, '91 122
    Grilled Vegetables, '92 124
    Grilled Vegetables, Marinated, '95 162
    Grilled Vegetables, Italian-Style, '92 143
    Hominy, Mexican, '91 133
    Kabobs, Marinated Vegetable, '83 M195
    Kale with Tomato and Onion, '92 244
    Kidney Bean Casserole, '90 136
    Lima Beans Creole, '85 137
    Marinated Vegetables, '88 170
    Medley, Chinese Vegetable, '84 33
    Mixed Vegetables, '83 M195
    Mushrooms, Flavor-Stuffed, '85 288
    Mushrooms, Grilled Portabello, '95 123
    Mushrooms, Microwave Portabello,
      '95 M123
    Mushrooms, Sautéed Portabello, '95 123
    Mushrooms, Savory Fresh, '85 268
    New Potatoes, Herbed, '83 9
    New Potatoes, Roasted, '90 138
    New Potato Medley, '90 279
    Okra-and-Tomato Bake, '89 173
    Okra, Corn, and Tomatoes, '95 203
    Okra, Oven-Fried, '91 121
    Onion-Potato Bake, '83 M195
    Onion Rings, Crispy Baked, '93 247
    Onions and Wine, Stuffed, '85 268
    Onions, Stuffed Vidalia, '89 172
    Onions Stuffed with Peas, '84 68
    Parsnips, Glazed, '91 220
    Peas-and-Corn Medley, '85 138
    Peas and Ham, Southern, '85 138
    Peas and Peppers, Stir-Fried, '87 51
    Pepper Kabobs, Pretty, '90 166
    Peppers, Stuffed, '84 202
    Pilaf, Barley-Vegetable, '91 33
    Potato-Cheese Dream, '91 307

LIVING LIGHT, Vegetables *(continued)*

Potatoes and Turnips, Scalloped, **'85** 235
Potatoes au Gratin, **'93** 90
Potatoes, Buttermilk-Basil Mashed, **'95** 330
Potatoes, Cottage, **'93** M92
Potatoes, Double-Cheese, **'86** 6
Potatoes, Herbed, **'91** 220
Potatoes, Light Scalloped, **'89** 311
Potatoes, Mexican-Stuffed, **'91** 131
Potatoes, Mushroom-Dill-Topped, **'86** 41
Potatoes, Rosemary-Roasted, **'95** 20
Potatoes, Scalloped, **'92** 48
Potatoes, Stuffed, **'89** 173
Potatoes, Twice Baked Cottage-Style, **'91** 135
Potatoes, Vegetable-Topped Stuffed, **'85** 235
Potato, Twice-Baked, **'90** M295
Potato Wedges, **'94** M119
Potato Wedges, Lemon, **'88** 21
Ragout, Vegetable, **'89** 172
Ratatouille, Microwave, **'95** M232
Red Cabbage-and-Apple Slaw, **'91** 309
Rice Toss, Vegetable-, **'91** 309
Rice, Vegetables and, **'93** 91
Risotto Primavera, **'95** 163
Rutabaga, Honey, **'91** 220
Rutabagas, Mashed, **'86** 295
Sautéed Vegetable Medley, **'83** 101
Sauté, Tossed Vegetable, **'92** 138
Snap Beans, Sweet-and-Sour, **'89** 173
Snow Peas with Red Pepper, **'90** 102
Spinach Quiche, **'85** 49; **'91** 204
Spinach Soufflé, **'86** 108
Squash Casserole, **'87** 163
Squash Stuffed with Spinach Pesto, **'89** M133
Steamed Garden Vegetables, **'93** 155
Steamed Herbed Vegetables, **'93** M303
Steamed Vegetable Medley, **'90** 29
Stir-Fried Vegetables, **'90** 136
Stir-Fried Vegetables with Curry, **'87** 51
Stir-Fry, Almond-Vegetable, **'86** 222
Sugar Snap Peas with Basil and Lemon, **'93** 66
Summer Vegetables, **'91** 136
Summer Vegetables, Cheesy, **'94** 119
Sweet Potato-Apple Bake, **'86** 282
Sweet Potatoes-and-Apple Casserole, **'90** 228
Sweet Potato Puff, **'85** 235
Sweet Potato Puree, **'92** 306
Tomato Coulis, Fresh, **'93** 230
Tomatoes and Okra, **'87** 164
Tomatoes, Bean-Stuffed, **'84** 34
Tomatoes, Cheese Herbed-Topped, **'86** 108
Tomatoes, Cheesy Puff-Top, **'86** 187
Tomatoes, Grilled, **'85** 158
Tomatoes, Parmesan-Stuffed, **'92** 182
Tomatoes, Spinach-Topped, **'88** 265
Tomatoes, Stuffed Scalloped, **'90** 29
Tomato Slices, Herbed, **'89** 173
Torta, Mexican, **'88** 149
Turnips and Carrots Julienne, **'86** 295
Turnips, Braised, **'91** 219
Zucchini-and-Tomato Casserole, **'88** 265
Zucchini and Tomato with Herbs, **'92** 182

Zucchini-Basil Delight, **'85** 267
Zucchini-Basil Scramble, **'87** 34
Zucchini Dressing, **'86** 282
Zucchini Fans, **'91** 33
Zucchini Spears, Oven-Fried, **'91** 121
Zucchini, Stuffed, **'86** 187; **'89** M133
Zucchini with Feta, Greek Grilled, **'95** 190
Zucchini with Pecans, **'87** 31
Vinegar, Raspberry Wine, **'93** 191
Vinegar, Shallot-Tarragon-Garlic, **'93** 191
Waffles, Light, **'91** 139
Waffles, Oat Bran, **'92** 139
Waffles, Oatmeal, **'89** 107
Yogurt Snack, **'88** 55

LOBSTER

Beef Tenderloin, Lobster-Stuffed, **'87** 248
Clambake, Backyard, **'81** 92
Crab-Stuffed Lobster Tails, **'95** 326
Creamy Lobster, **'79** 181
How to Cook Lobster, **'81** 169
Medaillons in Garlic-Chive Butter Sauce, Lobster, **'90** 96
Orange Sauce, Lobster Tails with Spiced, **'86** 155
Salad, Lobster, **'89** 249; **'90** 69
Salad, Lobster and Orange, **'82** 207
Soup, Spicy Thai Lobster, **'94** 102
Taco with Yellow Tomato Salsa and Jicama Salad, Warm Lobster, **'87** 122
Thermidor, Lobster, **'85** 103

MACADAMIA

Beans, Hawaiian-Style Baked, **'86** 210
Brownies, Macadamia-Fudge Designer, **'94** 51
Coffee Cake, Macadamia Ring, **'85** 326
Cookies, Chunky Macadamia Nut White Chocolate, **'92** 207
Cookies, White Chocolate-Macadamia Nut, **'94** 315
Crème Brûlée, White Chocolate-Macadamia Nut, **'95** 323
French Toast, Macadamia, **'86** 96
French Toast, Macadamia Nut, **'95** 282
Grouper Macadamia, **'85** 127
Mahi Mahi, Macadamia, **'88** 164
Oat Snowball, Macadamia, **'92** 274
Pie, Hawaiian Banana Cream, **'90** 105
Pie, Macadamia, **'80** 238
Pie, Pear-Macadamia, **'93** 260
Salad, Macadamia Chicken, **'80** 138
Sauce, Brandy-Macadamia, **'82** 311
MACARONI. *See also* **PASTAS.**
Beef and Macaroni, Skillet, **'82** 130
Beef-Macaroni Bake, **'94** 255
Beef-Macaroni Combo, **'79** 194
Casserole, Chicken-Macaroni, **'85** 219
Casserole, Macaroni, **'84** 220; **'87** 154

Casserole, Macaroni and Chicken, **'80** 260
Casserole, Macaroni-Ham, **'81** M177; **'83** 283
Casserole, Mushroom-Macaroni, **'95** 180
Casserole, Spinach-Beef-Macaroni, **'83** 313
Cheese
    Baked Macaroni and Cheese, **'82** 199
    Blue Cheese, Macaroni and, **'93** 248; **'94** 44
    Casserole, Macaroni-Cheese-Beef, **'95** 125
    Creamy Macaroni and Cheese, **'93** 249; **'94** 45
    Deluxe, Macaroni-and-Cheese, **'79** 84
    Deluxe, Macaroni and Cheese, **'80** 236
    Double Cheese Macaroni, **'82** 224
    Jack-in-the-Macaroni Bake, **'93** 249; **'94** 45
    Macaroni and Cheese, **'83** M7; **'88** M147, M90; **'90** 30
    Mushroom Bake, Cheesy Macaroni-, **'81** 243
    Old-Fashioned Macaroni and Cheese, **'92** 215
    Peppers, Macaroni-and-Cheese-Stuffed, **'80** 65
    Puff, Macaroni and Cheese, **'79** 5
    Soup, Macaroni and Cheese, **'95** 264
    Tasty Macaroni and Cheese, **'83** 288
    Thick-and-Rich Macaroni and Cheese, **'84** 329
    Tomatoes, Macaroni, Cheese, and, **'95** 213
    Wine, Macaroni-and-Cheese with, **'86** 78
Dinner, Sausage Skillet, **'83** 29
Glorious Macaroni, **'84** 76
Ground Beef and Macaroni, **'85** 218
Mexican Luncheon, **'87** 192
Oysters with Macaroni, Scalloped, **'80** 297
Salads
    Acini di Pepe Salad, **'83** 163
    Barbecue Macaroni Salad, **'82** 276
    Chicken Salad, Dilled Macaroni-, **'92** 142
    Chicken Salad, Macaroni-, **'85** 296; **'86** 302
    Confetti Macaroni Salad, **'82** 132; **'85** 297
    Crabmeat Salad, Macaroni-, **'81** 153
    Crunchy Macaroni Salad, **'82** 24
    Dilled Macaroni-Cheese Salad, **'86** 208
    Dilled Macaroni Salad, **'89** 161
    Garden Macaroni Salad, **'84** 290; **'92** 64
    Gourmet Macaroni Salad, **'81** 253
    Ham and Macaroni Salad, **'79** 220
    Ham Salad, Macaroni-, **'85** 218
    Hearty Macaroni Salad, **'84** 90
    Kidney Bean-Salami Pasta Toss, **'85** 165
    Macaroni Salad, **'87** 92
    Olive Clubhouse Salad, **'81** 114
    Overnight Pasta Salad, **'82** 276
    Pineapple Macaroni Salad, **'79** 220
    Refreshing Macaroni Salad, **'80** 177
    Salmon-and-Macaroni Salad, **'81** 114
    Salmon Salad, Macaroni-, **'82** 232
    Shell Macaroni Salad, **'92** 163
    Shell Salad, Macaroni, **'87** 38
    Shrimp Macaroni Salad, **'79** 220
    Shrimp-Macaroni Salad, **'85** 219
    Shrimp Salad, Festive Macaroni-, **'85** 165
    Shrimp Salad, Macaroni-, **'85** 121
    Spiral Macaroni Salad, **'82** 276
    Sweet-and-Sour Macaroni Salad, **'85** 166

MACARONI, Salads (*continued*)

Taco Macaroni Salad, '85 165
Tuna Macaroni Salad, '83 44, 145
Tuna-Macaroni Salad, '84 66
Tuna Salad, Whole Wheat Macaroni-, '84 193
Turkey Macaroni Salad, '83 282
Two, Macaroni Salad for, '81 31
Vegetable Salad, Macaroni-, '86 209
Véronique, Macaroni Salad, '85 164
Supper Supreme, Sunday, '79 76
Tomatoes, Tuna-Mac in, '87 188
Toss, Corkscrew Macaroni, '83 163
Treat, Tuna-Macaroni, '82 131
Whole Wheat Macaroni with Pesto, '89 238

MANGOES
Beef and Rice, Mango-, '88 138
Cake, Mango, '83 150
Chutney, Mango, '89 141
Crêpes, Mango-Pineapple, '86 216
Dessert Tamales, Mango, '94 190
Frappé, Mango, '86 216
Ice Cream, Mango, '86 216
Orange Smoothie, Mango-, '86 216
Pan Dowdy, Mango, '83 150
Pie, Green Mango, '79 137
Pie, Mango-Ginger, '88 138
Preserves, Mango-Pineapple, '79 137
Relish, Mango, '89 198
Salad, Fresh Mango, '84 126
Salad, Mango, '79 137
Salad with Mango, Chicken, '86 215
Salsa, Mango, '91 182; '95 104
Salsa, Seared Scallops with Tomato-Mango, '95 122
Sauce, Mango, '83 120
Sauce, Mango-Spiced Rum, '86 215
Slaw, Mango, '93 31; '94 71
Sorbet, Mango, '86 196
Vinegar, Mango-Cilantro, '95 190

MANICOTTI
Cannelloni, '85 60; '92 17
Cheesy Manicotti, '83 216
Chicken Manicotti, Creamy, '85 60
Chili Manicotti, '89 247
Quick Manicotti, '79 6
Seafood Manicotti, '94 195
Special Manicotti, '88 50
Spinach Manicotti, '82 199
Stuffed Manicotti, '83 M6
Stuffed Manicotti, Saucy, '83 288
Stuffed Manicotti, Spinach-, '88 255
Zucchini Manicotti, '84 194

MARINADES
Beef Marinade, Tangy, '86 113
Cinnamon-Soy Marinade, '93 103
Citrus Marinade, '93 103
Garlic-Basil Marinade, '94 160
Garlic-Honey Marinade, '93 102
Honey-Mustard Marinade, '93 103
Lemon-Soy Marinade, '91 194
Light Marinade, Tangy, '82 178
Marinade, '86 153; '92 283
Minty Marinade, '92 105
Oriental Marinade, '93 102
Southwestern Marinade, '93 102
Sweet-and-Sour Marinade, '86 113
Teriyaki Marinade, '86 114; '93 102
Vegetable Marinade, '92 231

MARSHMALLOWS
Ambrosia, Carrot-Marshmallow, '80 5
Bird's Nests, '95 102
Brownies, Chewy Marshmallow, '83 306
Brownies, Choco-Mallow, '87 198; '90 309
Brownies, No-Bake, '94 330
Cake, No-Egg Chocolate Marshmallow, '87 97
Chocolate, Hot Laced Marshmallow, '93 53
Coffee Mallow, '80 109
Cream, Orange-Mallow, '94 295
Dip, Marshmallow Fruit, '84 171
Frosting, Chocolate-Marshmallow, '83 245
Monster Mouths, '95 274
Parfaits, Mocha-Mallow, '80 219
Popcorn Balls, Marshmallow, '90 226
Pudding, Banana-Mallow, '86 139
Sauce, Marshmallow, '91 91
Squares, Chocolate-Marshmallow, '92 M50

MAYONNAISE
Aioli (Garlic Mayonnaise), '88 221
Anchovy Mayonnaise, '86 179
Citrus Mayonnaise, Creamy, '92 107
Curry Mayonnaise, '95 66
Dill-Garlic Mayonnaise, '92 320
Dip, Artichokes with Herb-Mayonnaise, '84 67
Dip, Seasoned Mayonnaise Artichoke, '80 87
Dressing, Mayonnaise, '86 11
Flavored Mayonnaise, '94 167
Garlic Mayonnaise, '92 56
Herbed Mayonnaise, '82 85, 192
Homemade Mayonnaise, '80 155; '90 81
Homemade Mayonnaise, Easy, '84 12
Italian Herbed Mayonnaise, '92 320
Lemon-Cream Mayonnaise, '85 264
Lemon Mayonnaise, '95 32
Parmesan Mayonnaise, '86 79
Russian Mayonnaise, '80 137
Sauce, Herb-Mayonnaise, '85 73
Tasty Mayonnaise, '82 192
Watercress Mayonnaise, '93 119
Wine Mayonnaise, Hot, '81 83

MEATBALLS
Appetizers
Brandied Meatballs, '83 78
Chafing Dish Meatballs, '81 260
Chestnut Meatballs, '79 110
Flavorful Meatballs, '84 206
German Meatballs, Crisp, '92 326
Ham Balls, '86 256
Ham Balls, Appetizer, '82 39
Hawaiian Meatballs, Tangy, '79 129
Polynesian Meatballs, '80 207
Red Delicious Meatballs, '85 85
Saucy Party Meatballs, '80 149
Sauerkraut Meatballs, '86 257
Spiced Meatballs, '79 284
Sweet-and-Sour Meatballs, '82 247
Sweet-and-Sour Party Meatballs, '79 233
Tamale Balls, Tangy, '89 60
Tamale Meatballs, '80 194
Zesty Meatballs, '80 250
Bacon Meatballs, Burgundy-, '80 283
Bacon-Wrapped Meatballs, '79 81
Beef Balls Heidelberg, '83 164; '84 39
Charleston Press Club Meatballs, '93 129
Chinese Meatballs, '83 116; '87 194
Cocktail Meatballs, '79 63, 207
Creole, Meatball-Okra, '83 156
Creole, Meatballs, '82 233
Español, Meatballs, '82 110
Golden Nugget Meatballs, '82 233

Gravy, Meatballs in, '79 136
Ham Balls, '84 91; '86 256
Hawaiian Meatballs, '85 86
Kabobs, Meatball, '95 192
Lamb Meatballs with Yogurt Sauce, '85 132
Meatballs, '89 237
Mock Meatballs, '81 243
Oven Barbecued Meatballs, '82 233
Pineapple and Peppers, Meatballs with, '90 145
Pizza Meatballs, '85 86
Processor Meatballs, Quick, '87 111
Royal Meatballs, '87 268; '88 102; '89 67
Sandwich, Giant Meatball, '92 196
Saucy Meatballs, '85 68; '90 122
Sauerbraten Meatballs, '85 85
Spaghetti-and-Herb Meatballs, '84 75
Spaghetti with Meatballs, '81 38
Spicy Meatballs and Sausage, '79 163
Stew, Meatball, '79 198
Stroganoff, Meatball, '81 297
Stroganoff, Mushroom-Meatball, '85 85
Swedish Meatballs, '80 80; '86 256
Sweet-and-Sour Meatballs, '82 233, 247; '86 240
Turkey Meatballs, '89 237
Veal Meatballs, European, '85 30
Venison Sausage Balls, '80 42

MEAT LOAF
All-American Meat Loaf, '92 341; '93 46
Barbecued Meat Loaf, '80 60; '81 275; '84 50; '87 216
Basic Meat Loaf, '88 M14
Beef Loaf, Glazed, '86 19
Beef Loaves, Individual Barbecued, '95 242
Beef-Vegetable Loaf, '79 164
Blue Cheese Meat Loaf Roll, '93 247
Cheeseburger Loaf, '81 236, 276
Cheesy Meat Roll, '82 136
Chili Meat Loaf, '81 275
Corny Meat Loaf, '86 68
Crunchy Meat Loaf Oriental, '79 212
Curried Meat Loaf, '86 43
Easy Meat Loaf, '88 M214; '95 125
Elegant Meat Loaf, '89 243
Family-Style Meat Loaf, '93 18
Fennel Meat Loaf, '88 46
German Meat Loaf, '87 216
Ham Loaf, '79 180; '80 272
Ham Loaf, Cranberry-, '82 M77
Ham Loaf, Glazed, '79 187; '90 212
Ham Loaf, Hawaiian, '79 71
Ham Loaf, Pineapple Upside-Down, '79 253
Ham Loaf, Saucy, '86 M328
Ham Loaf, Spicy, '80 110
Ham Loaf, Supreme, '79 242
Ham Loaf, Upside-Down, '82 40
Ham Loaves, '90 235
Ham Loaves, Country, '86 255
Ham Ring, '84 91
Ham Ring, Chili-Sauced, '81 M122
Hurry-Up Meat Loaf, '82 21
Hurry-Up Meat Loaves, '88 15
Individual Meat Loaves, '81 279; '82 24; '83 154; '92 229
Italian Meat Loaf, '79 187
Liver Loaf, Skillet, '80 111
Meat Loaf, '81 170; '89 109
Mexicali Meat Loaf, '81 275
Mexican Meat Loaf, '87 217
Miniature Meat Loaves, '85 24
Mini-Teriyaki Meat Loaf, '90 69

MEAT LOAF (continued)

Mozzarella-Layered Meat Loaf, '79 71
My-Ami's Meat Loaf, '94 229
Oriental Meat Loaf, '81 M122; '83 M194
Parsleyed Meat Loaf, '83 35
Parsley Meat Loaf, '87 22
Pineapple Loaves, Individual, '81 M121
Pizza Meat Loaf, Cheesy, '81 M121
Reuben Loaf, '95 338
Roll, Meat Loaf, '79 129
Saucy Meat Loaves, '79 186
Savory Meat Loaf, '87 216
Southwestern Meat Loaf, '93 248
Special Meat Loaf, '89 70
Spicy Meat Loaf, '79 71
Sprout Meat Loaf, '85 51
Stuffed Beef Log, '79 71
Stuffed Meat Loaf, '79 187
Stuffed Meat Loaf, Rolled, '80 80
Sun-Dried Tomatoes and Herbs, Meat Loaf
  with, '92 192
Supreme, Meat Loaf, '92 33
Swedish Meat Loaf, '81 M121
Tasty Meat Loaf, '83 213
Tex-Mex Meat Loaf for Two, '90 234
Triple Meat Loaf, '79 186
Turkey Loaf, '92 33
Turkey Loaf, Cranberry-Glazed, '86 171
Turkey Loaf, Ground, '86 171
Veal Meat Loaf, '93 292
Vegetable Meat Loaf, '85 M29
Wellington, Meat Loaf, '79 186; '87 284
Wrap, Meat Loaf in a, '89 122

MELONS

Balls and Cherries in Kirsch, Melon, '91 91
Balls, Fiery Sweet Melon, '92 311
Balls, Mellowed-Out Melon, '88 182
Bowl with Cucumber-Mint Dressing, Melon
  Ball, '87 153
Cantaloupe
  Berry-Filled Melon, '86 93
  Compote, Cantaloupe, '81 147
  Compote, Melon Ball, '85 157
  Cream Delight, Cantaloupe, '82 179
  Delight, Cantaloupe, '89 204
  Frozen Cantaloupe Cream, '82 159
  Fruit-Filled Cantaloupe, '83 120
  Fruit Medley, Minted, '80 182
  Grilled Cantaloupe Wedges, '87 162
  Ice Cream, Cantaloupe, '79 177
  Jam, Cantaloupe-Peach, '95 143
  Mold, Double-Grape Cantaloupe,
    '79 173
  Pickled Cantaloupe, Sweet, '89 197
  Pie, Cantaloupe, '86 163
  Pie, Cantaloupe Cream, '79 177
  Pie, Cantaloupe Meringue, '88 182
  Punch, Cantaloupe, '81 147
  Salad, Avocado-Melon, '82 164
  Salad, Cantaloupe, '86 182
  Salad, Cantaloupe-Cheese, '88 184
  Salad, Cantaloupe Cooler, '79 176
  Salad, Cantaloupe Green, '91 126
  Salad, Cantaloupe-Pecan, '86 178
  Salad, Melon-Berry, '90 180
  Salad with Dill Dressing, Melon, '88 182
  Sherbet, Cantaloupe, '88 183
  Sherbet-Cantaloupe Surprise, '91 105
  Sherbet, Frosty Cantaloupe, '82 144
  Soup, Cantaloupe, '83 120; '88 160
  Soup, Chilled Cantaloupe, '81 156

Soup, Fresh Cantaloupe, '84 190
Soup, Melon, '80 182
Southern Plantation Cantaloupe, '82 179
Sundae, Cantaloupe, '89 166
Sweet-and-Hot Melon, '92 163
Wedges with Berry Sauce, Melon,
  '86 178
Whip, Cantaloupe, '89 198
Citrus Mingle, Melon-, '79 177
Cooler, Melon, '81 146
Fruit Bowl, Sparkling Fresh, '80 146
Fruit Cup with Mint Dressing, Fresh, '80 183
Fruit Deluxe, Marinated, '81 146
Honeydew
  Boats, Honeydew Fruit, '81 147
  Bowl, Honeydew Fruit, '84 186
  Cooler, Melon Ball, '86 131
  Cups, Honeydew Fruit, '82 179
  Dessert, Honeydew-Berry, '83 120
  Granita, Honeydew, '87 162
  Grapes, Honeydew Melon with, '91 91
  Salad, Fruited Ham, '81 146
  Salad, Melon-Berry, '90 180
  Salad with Apricot Cream Dressing,
    Honeydew, '84 191
  Salad with Dill Dressing, Melon, '88 182
  Soup, Melon, '80 182
  Wedges with Berry Sauce, Melon,
    '86 178
Julep, Melon-Mint, '86 196
Julep, Rainbow Melon, '80 183
Mélange, Melon, '84 139
Minted Melon Cocktail, '81 146
Mint Sauce, Melons in, '85 164
Salad, Congealed Melon Ball, '84 125
Salad, Georgia Summer, '92 179
Salad, Melon-and-Prosciutto, '92 191
Salad, Summertime Melon, '82 101
Salad with Orange-Raspberry Vinaigrette,
  Grilled Melon, '95 144
Salsa, Hot Melon, '95 144
Soup, Swirled Melon, '87 162
Watermelon
  Balls, Minted Melon, '87 162
  Basket, Watermelon Fruit, '84 161
  Compote, Watermelon-Cherry, '90 180
  Cookies, Watermelon, '92 179
  Cooler, Melon Ball, '86 131
  Daiquiri, Watermelon, '95 143
  Frost, Watermelon, '86 196
  Ice, Watermelon, '91 173
  Mousse, Frozen Watermelon, '91 96;
    '92 130
  Pickles, Watermelon Rind, '81 174
  Pie, Watermelon, '95 144
  Preserves, Watermelon, '79 120
  Punch, Watermelon, '89 204; '92 190
  Salad with Celery-Nut Dressing,
    Watermelon, '80 182
  Sauce, Melon Balls in Watermelon,
    '79 177
  Sherbet, Light Watermelon, '81 147
  Sherbet, Watermelon, '79 155;
    '92 124
  Sherried Watermelon, '92 117
  Slush, Watermelon-Berry, '90 137
  Sorbet, Watermelon, '92 190
  Sparkle, Watermelon, '84 191

MERINGUES

Acorns, Meringue, '93 284
Asparagus Meringue, '88 131
Baked Pear Meringues, '85 232
Bars, Meringue-Chocolate Chip, '84 118

Basket, Summer Berry, '84 158
Cake, Brown Sugar Meringue, '81 70
Cake, Orange Meringue, '86 336; '87 84
Cakes, Spanish Wind, '84 157
Coconut Kisses, '90 106
Coffee Meringues with Butterscotch Mousse,
  '93 254
Cooked Meringue, '86 130
Cooked Meringue, Easy, '82 207; '83 158
Cookies, Forget 'em, '83 256
Cookies, Meringue Kiss, '86 121
Cookies, Meringue Surprise, '86 320
Cran-Apple Mousse Filling, Meringues with,
  '93 254
Cups, Kiwi and Cream in Meringue, '81 279
Cups, Lemon Custard in Meringue, '80 295;
  '81 172
Cups, Lemon Meringue Cream, '84 23
Fingers, Chocolate-Almond Meringue,
  '84 158
Flowers, Meringue, '84 156
Frosting, Brown Sugar Meringue, '81 70
Frosting, Meringue, '86 336; '87 84
Holiday Meringues, '88 280
Meringue, '87 207; '94 208
Orange Meringues, '95 318
Pavlova, '92 101
Peach Melba Meringues, '87 76
Pears with Meringue, Amaretto, '90 58
Pineapple, Meringue-Topped, '84 178
Piping Meringue, '84 156
Shell, Cinnamon Meringue, '82 263
Shells, Fruited Meringue, '87 32
Shells, Fruit-Filled Meringue, '86 151
Strawberry Meringues, '84 188
Torte, Strawberry Meringue, '88 136
Torte, Toffee Meringue, '87 118
Vacherin Moka, '80 55

MICROWAVE. *Includes microwave conversions.*

Appetizers
  Bacon-Chestnut Wraps, '84 M216
  Brie Appetizer, Bit-of-, '88 M8
  Brie, Chutney-Bacon, '90 M292
  Brie, Tropical Breeze, '94 M18
  Canapés, Green Onion, '84 M216
  Cheese Log, Toasted Pecan, '86 M288
  Cheese Sticks, Peppery, '81 M289
  Crab-Zucchini Bites, '84 M216
  Dip, Cheddar-Bacon, '89 M119
  Dip, Chili-and-Cheese, '89 M328
  Dip, Chipped Beef, '88 M8
  Dip, Creamy Crab, '80 M135
  Dip, Hot Artichoke Seafood, '85 M212
  Dip, Mexican Artichoke, '90 M292
  Dip, Nacho, '93 M330
  Dip, Quick Fiesta, '95 M237
  Dip, Shrimp, '88 M261
  Franks, Saucy Appetizer, '84 M12
  Mix, Spicy Party, '81 M138
  Mushrooms, Shrimp-Stuffed, '80 M135
  Mushrooms, Spinach-Stuffed, '88 M261;
    '89 M133
  Mushrooms, Tipsy, '84 M216
  Nachos, Make-Ahead, '80 M135
  Nuts, Sherry-Orange, '86 M289
  Nuts, Spiced, '91 M316
  Pâté, Chicken Liver, '88 M132
  Pecans, Spicy, '81 M289
  Pizzas, Appetizer, '89 M118
  Plantain Chips, '95 M203
  Popcorn, Caramel, '86 M212
  Popcorn, Garlic, '83 M315
  Potato Shell Appetizers, '89 M119

Potato Skins, Cheese, '84 M239
Rumaki, '80 M136
Spread, Artichoke-Parmesan, '92 M95
Spread, Chicken Salad Party, '88 M8
Spread, Hearts of Palm, '90 M293
Spread, Hot Beef, '84 M216
Spread, Seafood, '86 M58
Spread, Spinach-Bacon, '92 M310
Sweet Potato Chips, '95 M203
Apples, Honey-Glazed, '90 M125
Apples, Rosy Cinnamon, '87 M37
Apples, Spicy Poached, '90 M141
Beverages
Café Colombian Royal, '80 M290
Chocolate, Creole Hot, '80 M290
Chocolate, Flaming Brandied, '80 M290
Coffee, Mocha, '85 M329
Hot Chocolate Mix, Deluxe, '80 M290
Mocha, Mexican, '93 M341
Mocha, Spirited Hot, '91 M260
Spoons, Dipped Chocolate-Almond,
'95 M277
Tomato Cocktail, '83 M203
Blanching Chart, Microwave, '80 M181
Breads
Caramel Ring, Easy, '85 M89
Cheese-Herb Bread, '84 M144
Chocolate Loaf Bread, '88 M188
Coffee Cake, Cinnamon, '83 M203
Coffee Cake, Orange, '85 M88
Coffee Cake Ring, '85 M89
Coffee Ring, Sugarplum, '83 M37
English Muffin Bread, '95 M79
French Toast, Easy, '82 M172
Muffins, Apple-Bran, '85 M89
Muffins, Cheesy Cornbread, '88 M275
Muffins, Cinnamon-Nut, '85 M88
Muffins, Corn, '82 M282
Muffins, Cranberry Streusel Cake,
'88 M274
Muffins, Fudge Brownie, '95 M50
Muffins, Lemon, '88 M275
Muffins, Whole Wheat Bran, '88 M274
Pumpkin Bread, Harvest, '90 M215
Rolls, Cherry-Almond, '84 M198
Rolls, Dinner, '93 M326
Rolls, Easy Orange, '89 M131
Whole Wheat-Rye Bread, '83 M37
Butter, Sweet Potato, '95 M290
Chutney, Autumn Fruit, '88 M230
Croutons, '86 M288
Croutons, Microwave, '86 M227
Desserts. *See also* Microwave/Sauces.
Apple Crumble, Whole Wheat-,
'90 M213
Apple Dessert, Honey-Baked,
'90 M213
Apple-Nut Crunch, '82 M238
Apple Rings, Cinnamon, '82 M237
Apples and Cream, Brandied, '82 M237
Apples, Caramel, '89 M231
Apples, Caramel-Peanut, '93 M244
Apples, Easy Baked, '82 M238
Bananas Foster, '83 M114
Bars, Blackberry Jam, '82 M185
Bars, Chewy Peanut, '80 M172
Bars, Date-Oat, '80 M172
Bars, Peanut Butter-and-Fudge, '80 M172
Blueberry Dessert, Easy, '89 M130
Brie, Almond-Raspberry, '94 M89

Brownies, Biscuit Mix, '94 M51
Brownies, Chocolate-Mint, '85 M294
Brownies, Mississippi Mud, '89 M25
Brownies, Nutty Fudge, '80 M171
Brownies, Quick, '87 M302
Cake for Grown-Ups, Ice Cream,
'88 M192
Cake, Fruit and Spice, '87 M97
Cake, Fudge, '94 M293
Cake, German Chocolate, '83 M233
Cake, No-Egg Chocolate Marshmallow,
'87 M97
Cake, Old-Fashioned Carrot, '83 M232
Cake, Peanut Butter, '83 M233
Candies, Turtle, '93 M41
Charlotte Russe, '82 M142
Cheesecake, Chocolate-Amaretto,
'85 M294
Cheesecake, Luscious Lemon, '90 M196
Cheesecake, Pear-Berry, '82 M141
Cherries Jubilee, Quick, '82 M100
Chocolate-Marshmallow Squares,
'92 M50
Chocolate-Mint Parfaits, '90 M15
Chocolate-Peanut Butter Bites, '92 M317
Chocolate Peanutty Swirls, '94 M330
Cobbler, Apple-Pecan, '84 M198
Cookies, Chocolate-Almond Surprise,
'88 M45
Cookies, Doubly-Good Chocolate,
'82 M185
Cookies, Keyboard, '94 M330
Cookies, Nutty Oatmeal-Chocolate Chip,
'82 M185
Cookies, Spice, '87 M278
Cookies, Spider, '93 M166
Cookies, Wedding, '82 M185
Cream, Bavarian, '86 M165
Cream, Vanilla, '83 M115
Crème, Orange-Tapioca, '82 M283
Crust, Chocolate, '90 M15
Crust, Graham Cracker, '88 M45;
'91 M234
Crust, Microwaved Graham Cracker,
'82 M141
Cupcakes, Cinnamon-Chocolate,
'81 M139
Custard, Chocolate-Topped Amaretto,
'87 M37
Divinity, Peanut, '87 M278
Frosting, Buttery Cinnamon, '81 M139
Frosting, Caramel, '81 M289
Frosting, Chocolate, '80 M171;
'83 M233; '87 M97; '89 M25
Frosting, Coconut-Pecan, '83 M233
Frosting, Cream Cheese, '83 M233
Fudge, Double-Good, '79 M263;
'95 M50
Fudge, Double Good, '87 M278
Fudge, Microwave, '91 M92
Fudge, Microwave Chocolate, '92 M50
Fudge, Quick-and-Easy, '88 M190
Glaze, Chocolate, '91 M296
Jam Squares, '81 M289
Jellyrolls, Raspberry, '93 M255
Kahlúa Delight, Make-Ahead, '84 M89
Kahlúa Velvet Dessert, '85 M294
Millionaires, '79 M262
Oatmeal Cherry-Apple Crisp, '90 M16
Oranges, Wine-Poached, '84 M323
Pastry, Basic, '81 M268
Pastry, Basic Microwave, '82 M142;
'85 M113

Pastry, Double-Crust, '82 M298
Peaches, Gingersnap, '85 M329
Peach Melba, '83 M114
Peanut Brittle, '79 M263
Peanut Butter Slice-and-Bakes, '82 M185
Peanut-Fudge Bites, '91 M231; '92 M68
Pears with Dark Chocolate Sauce,
Poached, '90 M141
Pecan Brittle, '91 M272
Pecan-Coconut Clusters, '86 M251
Pie, Best-Ever Chocolate, '88 M45
Pie, Caramel-Banana, '86 M165
Pie, Cranberry-Apple Holiday, '81 M269
Pie, Double Chocolate, '82 M282
Pie, Easy Cherry, '82 M299
Pie, Festive Pumpkin, '81 M269
Pie, Fluffy Eggnog, '81 M269
Pie, Frosty Pumpkin-Praline, '91 M234
Pie, Glazed Strawberry, '82 M142
Pie, Lemon Meringue, '85 M112
Pie, Microwave Chocolate, '90 M15
Pie, Nutty Cranberry, '82 M298
Pie, Old-Fashioned Apple, '82 M299
Pie, Old-Fashioned Pecan, '81 M269
Pie, Quick Pumpkin, '88 M230
Plums, Poached, '90 M141
Pots de Crème, '84 M145
Pots de Crème, Mocha, '88 M45
Pralines, '86 M288
Pralines, Old-Fashioned, '89 M318
Pralines, Southern, '79 M263
Pudding, Bread, '89 M130
Pudding, Brown Sugar-Pecan, '86 M165
Pudding, Butternut Squash, '89 M313;
'90 M19
Pudding, Chocolate-Almond, '82 M142
Pudding, Creamy Banana, '89 M130
Pudding, Mandarin-Almond, '85 M12
Pudding, Pecan-Mocha, '89 M130
Pudding, Pumpkin, '89 M313;
'90 M20
Soufflé, Brandy Alexander, '83 M114
Sundaes, Cocoa-Kahlúa, '83 M58
Sundaes, Hot Strawberry, '81 M5
Sundaes, Spicy Apple Ice Cream,
'86 M195
Tart, Caramel Turtle Truffle, '93 M131
Toffee, Microwave, '92 M317
Toffee, Nutty, '79 M263
Truffles, Yule Street, '90 M242
Eggs and Omelets
Baked Eggs Florentine, '86 M12
Benedict, Easy Eggs, '80 M268
Benedict, Light Eggs, '93 M68
Casserole, Saucy Scrambled Egg,
'89 M213
Cheddar Eggs, '94 M141
Creamed Eggs in Patty Shells, '80 M267
Medley, Cheddary Egg, '81 M176
Olé Omelet, '87 M124
Sausage Omelet, Puffy, '80 M268
Scramble, Bacon-and-Eggs, '80 M267
Scrambled Eggs, Creamy Onion,
'83 M203
Vegetable Omelet, Golden, '82 M123
Frosting. *See* Microwave/Desserts.
Fruit Bake, Cranberry-Mustard, '90 M287
Fruit Compote, Hot, '90 M124
Fruit Mélange, '88 M295
Grits, Quick Cheese, '83 M203
Jam, Freezer Blackberry, '84 M181
Jam, Freezer Peach, '84 M182
Jam, Freezer Plum, '89 M156

Jam, Raspberry Freezer, '84 M181
Jam, Strawberry Freezer, '84 M182
Jelly, Christmas Freezer, '86 M288
Jelly, Quick Grape, '89 M156
Jelly, Red Pepper, '89 M156
Macaroni and Cheese, '83 M7;
  '88 M147, M190
Main Dishes
  Beans and Franks, Jiffy, '91 M172
  Beans-and-Franks, Polynesian, '84 M11
  Beef Casserole, Easy, '86 M58
  Beef Casserole, Layered, '82 M203
  Beef Roast, Easy, '89 M65
  Beef with Pea Pods, Oriental, '86 M328
  Broccoli-Ham au Gratin, '90 M239
  Burgers, Blue Cheese, '89 M66
  Casserole, Mexi, '83 M87
  Casserole, Mexican, '92 M22
  Casserole, Microwave Mexican,
    '90 M231
  Catfish, Microwave, '89 M52
  Catfish, Spicy-Seasoned, '89 M66
  Chicken alla Romano, '83 M58
  Chicken-and-Broccoli Stroganoff,
    '89 M248
  Chicken and Cashews, Ginger, '85 M11
  Chicken and Dumplings with Vegetables,
    '85 M56
  Chicken and Pasta, Pesto, '89 M132
  Chicken and Spinach Rollups, '82 M68
  Chicken-and-Vegetable Platter,
    '88 M52
  Chicken and Vegetables Vermouth,
    '87 M37
  Chicken-Asparagus Rolls, '86 M211
  Chicken, Barbecued, '89 M167
  Chicken Breasts, Breaded, '89 M196
  Chicken Breasts, Herb-Seasoned,
    '93 M325
  Chicken, Crispy Parmesan, '80 M76
  Chicken, Crunchy Spiced, '85 M57
  Chicken Dinner, Hot-and-Spicy, '94 M94
  Chicken Divan, '80 M10; '87 M218
  Chicken Divan Casserole, '82 M203
  Chicken Divan Quiche, '88 M125
  Chicken, Easy, '89 M129
  Chicken, Ginger-Nut, '90 M33
  Chicken in a Bag, '86 M57
  Chicken Kabobs, Marinated, '84 M144
  Chicken Kabobs, Pineapple-, '86 M328
  Chicken Lasagna, '87 M302
  Chicken, Lemon, '81 M138
  Chicken, Lemon-Garlic, '89 M132
  Chicken Mexicana, '91 M127
  Chicken, Orange, '86 M140
  Chicken, Pineapple, '83 M194
  Chicken, Tangy Herbed, '87 M302
  Chicken Teriyaki, '80 M76
  Chicken Tetrazzini, '80 M75
  Chicken Tetrazzini, Cheesy, '83 M87
  Chicken Toss, Quick, '87 M124
  Chicken, Vegetable-Stuffed, '89 M65
  Chicken with Noodles, Sesame,
    '88 M125
  Chicken with Pecan-Rice Dressing,
    '85 M57
  Chicken with Tomato-Basil Pasta, Basil-
    Stuffed, '94 M204
  Chicken with White Barbecue Sauce,
    '89 M84

  Chicken with Wild Rice, Elegant,
    '80 M76
  Chicken, Zesty Barbecued, '80 M76
  Chiles Rellenos with Walnut Cream
    Sauce, Havarti-and-Corn-Stuffed,
    '93 M275
  Chili-Cheese Dogs, '81 M176
  Chili, Microwave, '91 M232
  Chili, Turkey-Bean, '88 M213
  Cornish Hens, Orange-Glazed Stuffed,
    '84 M89
  Crab Imperial, Pineapple-, '84 M286
  Crabmeat and Mushrooms on Toast
    Points, '82 M91
  Crabmeat Imperial, Speedy, '90 M112
  Crab, Shrimp, and Artichoke au Gratin,
    '90 M240
  Crêpes, Sherried Beef, '85 M29
  Dinner, Easy Steamed, '83 M314
  Filet Mignon Patties, Mock, '82 M68
  Fillets, Apple-Carrot Stuffed, '88 M192
  Fillets, Lemon-Coated, '80 M53
  Fillets, Parmesan, '86 M112
  Fillets, Spanish-Style, '86 M112
  Fish Amandine, Fillet of, '80 M54
  Fish-and-Potato Platter, '89 M248
  Fish-and-Vegetable Dinner, '91 M196
  Fish, Creole, '87 M79
  Fish Delight, '86 M212
  Fish, Easy Italian, '86 M112
  Fish, Herb-Coated, '86 M112
  Fish in Creamy Swiss Sauce, Poached,
    '80 M53
  Fish Rolls, Vegetable-Filled, '86 M251
  Fish Steaks, Soy, '86 M112
  Fish, Sweet-and-Sour, '80 M54
  Fish with Greek Sauce, Poached,
    '91 M183
  Flounder Amandine, '89 M196
  Flounder, Baked, '90 M316
  Frankfurters, Barbecued, '84 M12
  Grits, Sausage-Cheese, '90 M238
  Grouper Fillets, Breaded, '89 M36
  Grouper with Confetti Vegetables,
    '88 M189
  Grouper with Sautéed Vegetables,
    '90 M233
  Haddock Fillets with Zucchini Stuffing,
    '88 M191
  Haddock Italiano, '81 M4
  Halibut Steaks Italiano, '88 M191
  Halibut with Swiss Sauce, '83 M195
  Ham and Apples, Baked, '82 M237
  Ham and Chicken, Creamed, '81 M74
  Ham-Asparagus Dinner, '80 M10
  Hamburger Patties, '82 M172
  Ham Casserole, Macaroni-, '81 M177
  Ham Loaf, Cranberry-, '82 M77
  Ham Loaf, Saucy, '86 M328
  Ham, Marmalade-Glazed, '89 M196
  Ham Ring, Chili-Sauced, '81 M122
  Ham Roll Casserole, '91 M127
  Ham Slice, Fruited, '83 M317
  Ham Steak, Glazed, '91 M13
  Ham, Sweet-and-Sour Glazed,
    '88 M15
  Ham Tetrazzini, '82 M77
  Ham Towers, Cheesy, '82 M77
  Ham with Raisin Sauce, '82 M76
  Kabobs, Shish, '85 M112
  Kielbasa and Cabbage, '89 M196
  Lasagna, '83 M6
  Lasagna, Easy, '92 M197; '93 M24

  Lasagna, Lots of Noodles, '91 M127
  Lasagna, One-Step, '89 M129
  Lasagna, Quick 'n Easy, '80 M10
  Lasagna Rolls, Pepper-Topped,
    '89 M36
  Lasagna, Zesty, '87 M188
  Manicotti, Stuffed, '83 M6
  Meat Loaf, Basic, '88 M14
  Meat Loaf, Cheesy Pizza, '81 M121
  Meat Loaf, Easy, '88 M214
  Meat Loaf, Oriental, '81 M122;
    '83 M194
  Meat Loaf, Swedish, '81 M121
  Meat Loaf, Vegetable, '85 M29
  Monkfish, Greek-Style, '87 M79
  Mussels Linguine, '90 M112
  Orange Roughy with Spinach Pesto,
    '88 M192
  Oysters on the Half Shell, Dressed,
    '87 M79
  Paella, Party, '88 M189
  Papillote, Ocean, '84 M287
  Patties, Cracked Pepper, '89 M131
  Peppers, Beef-Stuffed, '91 M127
  Peppers, Hearty Stuffed, '88 M214
  Pie, Country Breakfast, '93 M328
  Pineapple Loaves, Individual, '81 M121
  Pizza Casserole, Microwave, '89 M248
  Pizza, Jiffy Jazzed-Up, '83 M314
  Pizza, Taco, '89 M177
  Pork Casserole, Cheesy, '81 M74
  Pork Chop, Saucy, '86 M140
  Pork Chops, Lemon-Herb, '89 M132
  Pork Chops, Pineapple, '87 M124
  Pork Chops with Apricot Glaze, Stuffed,
    '89 M36
  Pork Loin Roast with Red Currant Sauce,
    '89 M84
  Potatoes, Frank-Filled, '84 M11
  Pot Roast, Basic, '81 M208
  Pot Roast, Company, '88 M14
  Pot Roast with Vegetables, '81 M208
  Pot Roast with Vegetables, Marinated,
    '88 M52
  Quiche, Benedict, '80 M107
  Quiche, Crab, '82 M122
  Quiche Lorraine, '80 M108
  Quiche, Spicy Sausage, '80 M108
  Quiche, Spinach-Mushroom, '81 M74
  Quiche, Vegetable, '87 M219
  Ribs, Sweet-and-Sour, '89 M84
  Round Steak over Rice, Burgundy,
    '90 M33
  Salmon Patties, Open-Faced, '87 M218
  Sausage and Rice Casserole, Oriental,
    '82 M123
  Sausage Casserole, Easy, '87 M189
  Sausage Dinner, Beefy, '80 M9
  Sausage-Egg Casserole, '86 M12
  Sausage Jambalaya Casserole, '82 M203
  Shrimp Creole, '90 M220
  Shrimp, Garlic-Buttered, '86 M226
  Shrimp in Cream Sauce, '84 M286
  Shrimp, Quick Curried, '84 M198
  Shrimp, Sweet-and-Sour, '90 M112
  Sloppy Joes, Pocket, '85 M328
  Snapper Provençal, '91 M170
  Sole, Saucy, '82 M68
  Sole with Cucumber Sauce, '84 M286
  Spaghetti, Easy, '83 M317
  Spaghetti Pie, '81 M32
  Spinach-Tenderloin Pinwheels,
    '89 M118

MICROWAVE, Main Dishes *(continued)*

Steak, Onion-Smothered, '87 M189
Taco Pies, Individual, '82 M282
Tacos, Jiffy, '83 M318
Tacos, Microwave, '88 M213
Tortilla Pie, '85 M211
Trout, Sunshine, '84 M286
Tuna Casserole, Easy, '82 M203
Turkey Breast and Gravy, Savory
   Seasoned, '89 M309
Turkey Casserole, Crunchy, '89 M282
Turkey Divan, Creamy, '90 M34
Turkey-Noodle-Poppyseed Casserole,
   '90 M239
Turkey Scaloppine, Easy, '95 M192
Veal and Carrots in Wine Sauce,
   '86 M139
Veal, Italian Style, '82 M68
Welsh Rarebit with Tomatoes and Bacon,
   '92 M159
Zucchini, Beef-Stuffed, '86 M139
Marmalade, Orange-Pineapple,
   '89 M156
Mustard, Coarse-and-Sweet, '86 M288
Noodles, Cheesy Parmesan, '83 M7
Pastry, Microwaved Quiche, '81 M74;
   '82 M122
Pastry, Quiche, '80 M107
Peaches, Bay Laurel, '90 M124
Peaches with Rum, Ginger, '84 M323
Pears, Gingered, '89 M231
Pears, Marmalade Breakfast, '83 M203
Pears, Spiced Fall, '89 M231
Pineapple, Scalloped, '84 M323
Pizza on a Bagel, '93 M94
Pumpkin, Cooked Fresh, '88 M230
Pumpkin Seeds, Seasoned, '91 M234
Pumpkin Seeds, Toasted, '88 M230
Relish, Cranberry-Orange, '81 M289
Relish, Quick Corn, '90 M13
Relish, Spicy Apple, '84 M323
Relish, Tipsy Cranberry, '92 M310
Rice, Almond, '85 M112
Rice, Basic Long-Grain, '83 M285
Rice, Basic Quick-Cooking, '83 M285
Rice, Chicken-Flavored, '84 M144
Rice, Curry-Spiced, '86 M226
Rice, Herb, '91 M257
Rice, Herbed, '83 M285
Rice, Jiffy Spanish, '90 M176
Rice, Oriental, '85 M12, 146
Rice, Parsleyed, '83 M58
Rice with Almonds, Curried, '83 M285
Salads
   Artichokes with Orzo Salad, '88 M193
   Beef Salad, Tangy, '87 M218
   Chef Salad, Microwave, '90 M146
   Chicken Salad, Special, '88 M193
   Chicken Taco Salad, '94 M136
   Fast-and-Easy Salad, '85 M328
   Fruit Salad with Mint Sauce, '88 M96
   Green Beans-and-Cheese Salad,
      '91 M159
   Pork-and-Spinach Salad, Mandarin,
      '88 M126
   Potato Salad, Chunky, '81 M138
   Potato Salad, German-Style, '88 M194
   Spinach Salad, Sweet-Sour, '85 M112
   Spinach Salad, Wilted, '81 M4
   Taco Salad Cups, '85 M29
   Tuna Salad, Cheese-Sauced, '87 M124

Sandwiches
   Asparagus-and-Ham Melt Sandwiches,
      '88 M96
   Breakfast Pita Pockets, '89 M21
   Breakfast Sandwiches, '82 M123;
      '89 M230
   Brown Bread-Cream Cheese Sandwiches,
      '87 M6
   Burgers, Pizza, '80 M201
   Crabmeat Sandwiches, Deluxe, '81 M74
   Frankfurter Sandwiches, '84 M11
   Fruit-and-Cheese Breakfast Sandwiches,
      '89 M21
   Grilled Cheese Sandwiches, '82 M172
   Hot Brown Sandwiches, '80 M202
   Pita Sandwiches, Denver, '86 M12
   Pita Sandwiches, Hot, '87 M6
   Pizza Sandwiches, Open-Face, '84 M198
   Pork Sandwiches, Party, '88 M273
   Reuben Sandwiches, '80 M201
   Sausage-Cheese Muffin Sandwiches,
      '92 M212
   Tuna Sandwiches, Hot, '86 M194
Sauces
   Almond-Vanilla Custard Sauce,
      '88 M177
   Amaretto-Strawberry Sauce, '87 M165
   Apple Dessert Sauce, '87 M165
   Barbecue Sauce, Lemony, '88 M177
   Béchamel Sauce, '84 M239
   Blueberry Sauce, '89 M130
   Cheese Sauce, '79 M156; '82 M123
   Cheese Sauce, Guilt-Free, '93 M95
   Cheesy Vegetable Sauce, '92 M134
   Cherry Sauce, Elegant, '79 M156
   Chocolate Cherry Sauce, '87 M165
   Chocolate Mint Sauce, Quick, '86 M58
   Chocolate-Peanut Butter Sauce,
      '79 M156
   Chocolate-Praline Sauce, '85 M295
   Chocolate Sauce, Creamy, '88 M177
   Crab Marinara Sauce, Quick, '85 M151
   Cream Sauce, Sherried, '85 M152
   Curry Sauce, '79 M156; '84 M71
   Dill Sauce, '84 M70
   Dill Sauce, Creamy, '79 M156
   Garlic-Cheese Sauce, '84 M70
   Hollandaise Sauce, '80 M107, M268;
      '88 M177
   Horseradish-Mustard Sauce, Creamy,
      '88 M177
   Horseradish Sauce, '88 M273
   Lemon Dessert Sauce, '87 M165
   Mint Sauce, '88 M96
   Mushroom Sauce, '84 M70
   Mustard Sauce, '84 M70
   Orange Sauce, '84 M286
   Orange Sauce, Sweet, '93 M325
   Parsley-Garlic Sauce, '84 M70
   Peach-Berry Sauce, '87 M165
   Peanut Dessert Sauce, '86 M251
   Pineapple Ice Cream Sauce, '81 M289
   Praline Ice Cream Sauce, Southern,
      '86 M227
   Sour Cream Sauce, '82 M68
   Swiss Sauce, '83 M195
   Taco Sauce, '82 M283
   Tomato Sauce, Herbed Fresh, '85 M151
   Tomato Sauce, Italian, '82 M68
   Vegetable-Cheese Sauce, '85 M152
   White Sauce, Basic, '79 M156
Sausage in a Bun, '89 M22
Shortcuts, '89 M134

Soups and Stews
   Bacon-Beer Cheese Soup, '87 M7
   Beef Stew with Parsley Dumplings,
      '85 M246
   Broccoli Soup, '86 M194
   Broccoli Soup, Cream of, '80 M225
   Carrot-Mint Soup, Chilled, '90 M168
   Carrot Soup, Creamy, '92 M218
   Cauliflower Soup, Cream of, '87 M7
   Cheese Soup, Bacon-Topped, '80 M224
   Cheese Soup, Monterey Jack, '85 M211
   Chicken Broth, Easy Microwave,
      '90 M167
   Chicken Soup, Quick, '86 M72
   Chili, Basic, '82 M11
   Chili, Beefy Sausage, '82 M11
   Chili, Cheese-Topped, '82 M11
   Chili, Chunky, '82 M11
   Chili with Rice, '82 M11
   Chowder, Corn, '84 M38
   Chowder, Creamy Ham, '88 M53
   Chowder, Fish, '84 M38
   Chowder, New England Clam,
      '86 M72
   Crab Soup, Creamy, '80 M224
   Cucumber Soup, Dilled, '90 M167
   Egg-Drop Soup, '85 M12
   Garden Harvest Soup, Italian, '90 M167
   Mushroom Soup, '86 M73
   Mushroom Soup, Curried, '84 M89
   Onion Soup, French, '86 M212
   Onion Soup, Shortcut French, '85 M328
   Oyster-and-Artichoke Soup, Louisiana,
      '92 M81
   Pea Soup, Spring, '88 M96
   Potato-Bacon Soup, '84 M38
   Potato Soup, Cream of, '80 M224
   Potato-Yogurt Soup, '92 M217
   Strawberry Soup Supreme, '81 M144
   Tomato-Celery Soup, '83 M58
   Tomato-Vegetable Soup, '81 M177
   Vegetable Soup, Beefy, '84 M38
   Vegetable Soup, Chunky, '89 M283
Spoons, Dipped Chocolate-Almond,
   '95 M277
Spread, Peachy Cream Cheese, '90 M215
Topping, Streusel, '88 M275
Vegetables
   Acorn Rings, Easy Glazed, '81 M231
   Acorn Squash, Cranberry-Filled,
      '81 M231
   Acorn Squash, Sausage-Stuffed,
      '81 M231
   Artichokes, '92 M107
   Artichokes, Stuffed, '91 M117
   Asparagus-Carrot-Squash Toss, '91 M45
   Asparagus in Lemon Butter, '80 M123
   Asparagus, Lemon-Sesame, '91 M31
   Asparagus-Pea Casserole, '88 M294
   Asparagus with Almond Sauce, '91 M117
   Asparagus with Lemon Butter, '87 M151
   Beans, Marinated Italian, '86 M226
   Beets, Harvard, '83 M195
   Beets with Sour Cream Dressing,
      '88 M295
   Black-Eyed Peas, Fresh, '81 M165
   Broccoli au Gratin, '82 M20
   Broccoli Casserole, Cheesy, '95 M191
   Broccoli, Chinese, '85 M12
   Broccoli Goldenrod, Lemon-, '84 M89
   Broccoli, Marinated Fresh, '81 M139
   Broccoli-Swiss Cheese Casserole,
      '85 M211

MICROWAVE, Vegetables (continued)

Butternut Squash Ring, '81 M232
Carrots-and-Celery, Scalloped, '84 M112
Carrots, Orange-Fennel, '92 M133
Carrots, Orange-Glazed, '81 M165;
　'90 M98
Carrots, Peach-Glazed, '90 M13
Carrots, Spice-Glazed, '83 M58
Corn-and-Bean Casserole, '90 M208
Corn Fix-Up, Quick, '81 M4
Corn, Mexi-, '82 M21
Corn on the Cob, Microwaved,
　'80 M122
Corn on the Cob, Parmesan, '88 M187
Corn on the Cob, Spicy, '87 M151
Corn, Parslied, '90 M155
Corn, Seasoned Fresh, '83 M147
Corn, Southern-Style Creamed,
　'81 M165
Eggplant, Easy, '87 M151
Fresh Vegetables, Microwaving,
　'82 M138
Garden Harvest, '85 M142
Green Beans, '87 M151
Green Beans Amandine, '82 M20
Green Beans, Bacon-Topped, '80 M123
Green Beans, Baked, '91 M159
Green Beans, French, '90 M208
Green Beans, Garlic, '91 M159
Green Beans, Herbed, '83 M147;
　'88 M190
Green Beans, Nutty, '88 M187
Green Beans Oriental, '91 M158
Green Beans, Tangy, '85 M142
Green Beans with Marjoram, Fresh,
　'91 M159
Green Peas, Company, '91 M31
Julienne Vegetables with Walnuts,
　'86 M251
Kabobs, Marinated Vegetable, '83 M195
Leeks in Dilled Lemon-Butter, '90 M98
Medley, Garden Vegetable, '91 M45
Medley, Vegetable, '89 M129
Mixed Vegetables, '83 M195
Mushrooms, Microwave Portabello,
　'95 M123
New Potatoes, Herbed, '83 M148
New Potatoes, Seasoned, '87 M151
Okra and Tomatoes, Fresh, '81 M165
Okra, Corn, and Peppers, '87 M151
Okra Medley, '88 M185
Onion-Potato Bake, '83 M195
Onions and Peppers, Sautéed, '83 M148
Onions, Micro-Baked, '82 M32
"Pasta," Garden-Fresh, '94 M134
Peas and Peppers, Minted, '90 M99
Peas in a Potato Nest, '84 M239
Peas with Almonds, Curried, '88 M294
Pepper Cups, Hot Vegetable, '88 M188
Platter, Vegetable, '88 M187
Potato Casserole, Creamy, '84 M113
Potatoes, Basil-Cheese, '90 M316
Potatoes, Blue Cheese Stuffed, '92 M228
Potatoes, Broccoli-Shrimp Stuffed,
　'92 M228
Potatoes, Cheesy Bacon-Stuffed,
　'81 M61
Potatoes, Chili-Cheese, '90 M62
Potatoes, Cottage, '93 M92
Potatoes, Creamy Cheese, '88 M146
Potatoes, Hearty Stuffed, '89 M282

Potatoes, Jalapeño-Ham Stuffed,
　'81 M61
Potatoes, Micro-Baked, '81 M61
Potatoes, Parmesan, '90 M62; '92 M341;
　'93 M46
Potatoes, Quick Baked, '92 M134
Potatoes, Quick Browned, '82 M172
Potatoes, Seafood-Stuffed, '95 M192
Potatoes, Shrimp-Sauced, '81 M61
Potatoes, Soufflé, '90 M14
Potatoes, Summertime, '86 M195
Potatoes, Taco-Topped, '93 M18
Potatoes, Twice-Baked, '91 M185
Potatoes with Béchamel Sauce, Stuffed,
　'84 M239
Potatoes with Chives, '81 M61
Potatoes with Hot Bacon Dressing,
　'88 M294
Potatoes, Zesty Stuffed, '94 M46
Potato Fans, Parmesan, '84 M240
Potato Fans, Parmesan-, '88 M190
Potato, Twice-Baked, '90 M295
Potato Wedges, '94 M119
Potato Wedges, Lemony, '90 M61
Ratatouille, Microwave, '95 M232
Snow Peas and Tomatoes, Basil,
　'88 M185
Spaghetti Squash with Meat Sauce,
　'88 M180
Spinach Casserole, '91 M31
Spinach Delight, '84 M144
Squash-and-Pepper Toss, Crisp,
　'87 M152
Squash, Apple-Stuffed Butternut,
　'81 M232
Squash Bake, Cheddar-, '84 M113
Squash Casserole, Jiffy, '81 M144
Squash, Country Club, '88 M16
Squash Medley, Fresh, '81 M165
Squash Mexican, Stuffed, '90 M200
Squash Stuffed with Spinach Pesto,
　'89 M133
Squash Toss, Simple, '85 M142
Steamed Herbed Vegetables, '93 M303
Stir-Fry, Vegetable, '82 M172
Sweet Potatoes, Applesauce, '91 M292;
　'92 M256
Sweet Potatoes, Cinnamon-Apple,
　'95 M23
Sweet Potatoes, Orange-Baked,
　'88 M294
Tomatoes with Walnut-Rice Stuffing,
　'91 M102
Tomatoes, Zippy Mustard, '86 M226
White Squash, Stuffed, '90 M201
Zucchini and Carrots, Julienne, '90 M14
Zucchini Boats, '85 M143
Zucchini-Egg Casserole, '84 M113
Zucchini, Italian, '83 M147
Zucchini, Stuffed, '89 M133
Vinaigrette Dressing and Croutons,
　'86 M288
Waffles, Honey-Buttered Peanut Butter,
　'94 M206

MINCEMEAT

Apples, Baked Mincemeat-Filled, '80 276
Bars, Mincemeat-Spice, '88 231; '89 22
Cake, Mincemeat Spice, '79 246
Cakes, Mini-Mincemeat Nut, '88 257
Cookies, Mincemeat, '79 51
Cookies, Mincemeat Drop, '79 246
Cookies, Mincemeat Sweetheart, '87 293
Cookies, Pear Mincemeat, '84 264

Homemade Mincemeat, '79 245
Peaches, Mincemeat, '85 178
Peaches with Mincemeat, Brandied, '81 47
Pear Mincemeat, '79 196; '84 264;
　'88 226
Pies
　Apple-Mincemeat Pie, '85 316
　Cheese Pie, Mincemeat-, '80 253
　Chiffon Pie, Mincemeat, '79 245
　Holiday Mincemeat Pie, '80 282;
　　'87 213
　Kentucky Mincemeat Pie, '95 302
　Peach Pie, Mincemeat-, '80 295;
　　'81 188
　Pear Mincemeat Pie, '84 264; '88 226
　Pear-Mince Pie, '81 271
　Spirited Mince Pie, '92 316
Pudding, Steamed Mincemeat, '80 264
Salad, Holiday Mincemeat, '85 263
Salad, Mincemeat, '94 282

MOUSSES. See also CUSTARDS, PUDDINGS.

Amaretto Mousse, '86 188
Apricot Mousse, '82 72; '91 297
Asparagus Mousse Salad, '86 252
Butter Pecan Mousse, '95 286
Butterscotch Mousse, '93 254
Catfish Mousse, '92 327
Caviar Mousse, '82 71; '85 86; '92 83
Chicken Mousse, Curried, '95 328
Chocolate
　Almond Mousse, Chocolate-, '93 316
　Amaretto-Chocolate Mousse, '86 50
　Amaretto-Chocolate Mousse, Elegant,
　　'86 337
　au Grand Marnier, Chocolate Mousse,
　　'91 296
　Baked Alaska Chocolate Mousse, '85 195
　Blender Chocolate Mousse, '82 71
　Blender-Quick Chocolate Mousse,
　　'80 269
　Brandy-Chocolate Mousse, '85 102
　Cake, Chocolate Mousse, '87 264
　Chocolate Mousse, '88 280
　Creamy Chocolate Mousse, '87 133
　Honeyed Chocolate Mousse, '87 223
　Kid-Pleasin' Chocolate Mousse,
　　'90 271
　Orange Mousse, Chocolate-,
　　'81 16, 205
　Parfait, Chocolate Mousse, '94 90
　Pie, Chocolate-Amaretto Mousse,
　　'80 180; '81 30
　Pie, Chocolate Mousse, '81 136
　Quick-as-a-Wink Mousse, '84 311
　Quick Chocolate Mousse, '85 87
　Roll, Chocolate Mousse, '88 280
　Rum Mousse, Chocolate, '86 189
　Truffle Mousse with Raspberry Sauce,
　　Chocolate, '95 327
　White Chocolate Mousse, '91 247;
　　'93 315
Coconut-Pineapple Mousse, '94 198
Coffee Mousse, '84 126
Coffee-Nut Mousse, '86 319
Crabmeat Mousse, '90 190; '91 244;
　'94 159
Crab Mousse, '79 117; '95 327
Cran-Apple Mousse, '93 255
Crème de Menthe Mousse, '80 109
Cucumber Mousse, '79 11; '88 121
Cucumber Mousse with Dill Sauce, '95 216
Ham Mousse Pitas, '95 328
Horseradish Mousse, '84 126

MOUSSES (continued)

Lemon Cloud Mousse, '90 90
Lemon Mousse with Raspberry Sauce, '91 96;
    '92 130
Lime Mousse Freeze, Luscious, '81 173
Mustard Mousse, '84 127; '86 184; '95 328
Orange Mousse, '86 69; '94 198
Oyster Mousse, '81 245
Oyster Mousse, Smoked, '84 320
Peach Macaroon Mousse, '80 153
Peach Mousse, '85 54
Peppermint Candy Mousse, '82 71; '94 198
Peppermint Mousse, '93 315
Pineapple Mousse, Elegant, '79 230
Pumpkin Mousse, '91 96; '92 130
Raspberry Mousse, '81 34
Raspberry Mousse in Chocolate Crinkle Cups,
    '93 270
Rhubarb Mousse, '88 93
Roquefort Mousse, '82 71
Salmon Dill Mousse, '81 21
Salmon Mousse, Irresistible, '79 284
Sherried Mousse, '81 247
Shrimp Mousse, '79 57; '87 196, 251
Strawberry-Lemon Mousse, '82 128
Strawberry Mousse, '81 95
Strawberry Mousse, Fresh, '82 72
Tuna Mousse, '80 275
Watercress Mousse, '88 104
Watermelon Mousse, Frozen, '91 96; '92 130

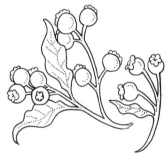

MUFFINS
Almond Muffins, '90 87
Almond Muffins, Peachy-, '86 301
Apple
    Apple Muffins, '83 96; '84 193; '87 23
    Applesauce Muffins, '84 284; '91 141
    Bite-Size Applesauce Muffins, '82 104
    Bran Muffins, Apple-, '85 M89
    Carrot Muffins, Apple-, '91 213
    Cinnamon Oat Bran Muffins, Apple-,
        '89 106
    Fresh Apple Muffins, '84 264
    Oat Muffins, Spicy Apple-, '86 45
    Spiced Apple Muffins, '79 60
    Spice Muffins, Applesauce, '88 236
Bacon-and-Cheese Muffins, '89 205
Banana
    Banana Muffins, '80 88; '84 75
    Bran Muffins, Banana, '83 48
    Chocolate Chip Muffins, Jumbo Banana-,
        '93 339
    Chocolate Muffins, Banana-, '94 197
    Honey-Nut Muffins, Banana-, '88 62
    Nut Muffins, Banana-, '93 140
    Oat Bran-Banana Muffins, '91 18
    Oat Bran Muffins, Banana, '89 106
    Oatmeal Muffins, Banana-, '84 20

    Oat Muffins, Banana-, '87 188
    Orange Muffins, Banana-, '84 148
    Poppyseed Muffins, Banana-, '89 205
    Raisin Muffins, Banana-, '89 218
    Surprise Muffins, Banana, '82 105
Basic Cupcake Muffins, '90 87
Blueberry
    Blueberry Muffins, '80 143;
        '91 140, 203
    Bran Muffins, Blueberry-, '89 23
    Buttermilk Muffins, Blueberry, '80 16
    Cream Cheese Muffins, Blueberry-,
        '86 14
    Easy Blueberry Muffins, '81 197
    Golden Blueberry Muffins, '79 235
    Ice Cream Muffins, Blueberry, '82 143
    Lemon Muffins, Blueberry-, '79 7
    Oat Bran Muffins, Blueberry, '89 106
    Oatmeal Muffins, Blueberry-, '87 24
    Oat Muffins, Blueberry-, '92 119
    Old-Fashioned Blueberry Muffins,
        '86 161
    Speedy Blueberry Muffins, '95 135
    Streusel Muffins, Blueberry, '80 46
    Streusel Topping, Blueberry Muffins
        with, '88 129
Bran
    All-Bran Oat Bran Muffins, '91 134
    Apple-Bran Muffins, '85 M89
    Apple-Cinnamon Oat Bran Muffins,
        '89 106
    Banana Bran Muffins, '83 48
    Banana Oat Bran Muffins, '89 106
    Big Batch Moist Bran Muffins, '95 214
    Blueberry-Bran Muffins, '89 23
    Blueberry Oat Bran Muffins, '89 106
    Bran Muffins, '84 53
    Buttermilk Muffins, Bran-, '85 7
    Cranberry Oat Bran Muffins, '89 107
    Easy Bran Muffins, '83 55
    Ever-Ready Bran Muffins, '81 106
    Fiber Muffins, High-, '85 250
    Freezer Bran Muffins, '91 141
    Honey Bran Muffins, '88 171
    Honey-Bran Muffins, '89 250
    Made of Bran, Muffins, '86 103
    Maple-Bran Muffins, '90 66
    Quick Bran Muffins, '86 85
    Raisin Oat Bran Muffins, '89 106
    Refrigerator Bran Muffins, '79 6
    Sour Cream-Bran Muffins, '87 98
    Spiced Bran Muffins, '84 229
    Two, Bran Muffins for, '84 211
    Whole Wheat Bran Muffins, '88 M274
Breakfast Bites, '86 15
Caraway-Cheese Muffins, '91 213
Carrot-and-Raisin Muffins, '87 24
Carrot-Date-Nut Muffins, '86 262
Carrot-Pineapple Muffins, '81 6
Carrot-Wheat Muffins, '88 9
Cheddar Muffins, '89 15
Cheddar-Raisin Muffins, '91 51
Cheese-and-Pepper Muffin Mix, '89 330
Cheese-and-Pepper Muffins, '84 139
Cheese Muffins, Dilly, '95 245
Cheese Muffins, Marvelous, '83 96
Cherry Muffins, '82 105
Cherry Muffins, Dried, '94 59
Cherry-Nut Muffins, '90 87
Chive Muffins, '91 34
Chocolate Chip Muffins, '90 87
Cinnamon-Nut Muffins, '85 M88
Cinnamon-Pecan Muffins, '84 219

Coconut-Molasses Muffins, '82 210
Coconut Muffins, '95 214
Coffee Cake Muffins, '79 7
Corn
    Blue Corn Muffins, '89 145; '92 52
    Cheesy Cornbread Muffins, '88 M275
    Cornmeal Muffins, '80 90; '88 92;
        '91 19
    Corn Muffins, '82 M282; '84 16
    Jalapeño-Corn Muffins, '93 164
    Miniature Cornmeal Muffins, '93 119
    Oat Muffins, Corn-, '89 108
    Quick Corn Muffins, '88 15
    Sage-Corn Muffins, '83 207
    Sour Cream Corn Muffins, '95 176
    Southern Cornbread Muffins, '85 201
    Southwestern Muffins, '91 34
    Spicy Cornbread Muffins, '90 59
    Tex-Mex Corn Muffins, '92 253; '93 144
    Tomato Corn Muffins, '81 137
    Yeast Muffins, Cornmeal, '92 49
Cranberry Muffins, '81 249
Cranberry Muffins, Miniature, '90 294
Cranberry Oat Bran Muffins, '89 107
Cranberry-Pecan Muffins, '84 269
Cranberry Streusel Cake Muffins, '88 M274
Date Muffins, '79 142
Date Muffins, Surprise, '79 216
Date-Nut Muffins, '84 75
Dino-Mite Muffins, '94 197
Egg Muffins, One-, '83 9
English Muffins, '87 49; '88 76
English Muffins, Raisin, '80 75
Fig Muffins, '86 206
Fudge Brownie Muffins, '95 M50
Gingerbread Muffins, '81 285
Gingerbread Muffins, Last-Minute, '82 105
Grain Muffins, Four-, '80 46
Granola Muffins, '95 78
Ham-and-Cheese Muffins, '92 252; '93 144
Honey Bran Muffins, '88 171
Honey-Bran Muffins, '89 250
Honey-Oatmeal Muffins, '84 229
Honey-Wheat Muffins, '83 96; '88 263
Jam Muffins, '79 7
Jelly-Filled Muffins, '80 16
Key Lime Muffins, '95 50
Kiwifruit Muffins, '87 255
Lemon Muffins, '88 119, M275
Lemon Muffins, Fresh, '79 161
Lemon-Raspberry Muffins, '92 119
Magic Muffins, '79 244
Mayonnaise Muffins, '83 57; '86 16
Merry Muffins, '82 253
Mix, Quick, '94 167
Mix, Quick Bread, '81 90
Monster Muffins, '94 256
Morning Glory Muffins, '93 327
Muffins, '81 90
Nut Crunch Muffins, Best Ever, '82 65;
    '83 106
Nut Muffins, Tasty, '79 208
Nutty Muffins, '86 141
Oat
    All-Bran Oat Bran Muffins, '91 134
    Apple-Cinnamon Oat Bran Muffins,
        '89 106
    Apple-Oat Muffins, Spicy, '86 45
    Banana Muffins, Oat Bran-, '91 18
    Banana Oat Bran Muffins, '89 106
    Banana-Oatmeal Muffins, '84 20
    Banana-Oat Muffins, '87 188
    Best-Ever Oatmeal Muffins, '84 242

MUFFINS, Oat (continued)

Blueberry Oat Bran Muffins, '89 106
Blueberry-Oatmeal Muffins, '87 24
Blueberry-Oat Muffins, '92 119
Bran Muffins, Oatmeal, '81 236
Bran Muffins, Oatmeal-, '91 83
Corn-Oat Muffins, '89 108
Cranberry Oat Bran Muffins, '89 107
Honey Muffins, Oatmeal-, '83 95
Honey-Oatmeal Muffins, '84 229
Oat Bran Muffins, '89 106
Oatmeal Muffins, '82 129, 210;
'84 72, 140; '92 163
Orange-Oatmeal Muffins, '85 202
Raisin Oat Bran Muffins, '89 106
Okra Muffins, Fresh, '93 161
Onion-Dill Muffins, '92 253; '93 144
Orange
Banana-Orange Muffins, '84 148
Date Muffins, Orange-, '92 119
Ginger Muffins, Orange-, '89 41
Honey Muffins, Orange-, '88 284
Honey Spread, Orange Juice Muffins
with, '81 229
Oatmeal Muffins, Orange-, '85 202
Orange Muffins, '79 236; '81 107;
'83 54; '89 205
Pecan Muffins, Orange-, '83 96
Streusel-Topped Orange Muffins, '84 74
Peach Muffins, Special, '84 74
Peanut Butter-Chocolate Chip Muffins,
'94 167
Peanut Butter-Honey Muffins, '82 56
Peanut Butter Muffins, '80 86; '87 158
Peanut Muffins, '91 223
Pear-Ginger Muffins, '91 240
Pecan Muffins, '80 16
Pecan Muffins, Chunky, '88 9
Pecan Muffins, Country, '83 222
Pineapple Muffins, '81 14, 250
Plum Good Muffins, '83 96
Poppy Seed Muffins, '81 63; '91 34
Prune Muffins, Miniature, '85 223
Pumpkin Muffins, '79 206, 275; '81 272
Pumpkin Muffins, Nutty, '86 291
Raisin Muffins, Breakfast, '84 59
Raisin-Nut Muffins, '92 46
Raisin Oat Bran Muffins, '89 106
Raisin-Pecan Ginger Muffins, '88 9
Rum-Nut Muffins, '90 87
Sandwiches, Sausage-Cheese Muffin,
'92 M212
Sausage-Cheese Muffins, '86 213
Sausage Muffins, '88 52; '95 49
Sausage Muffins, Cheesy, '92 252; '93 144
Sesame-Cheese Muffins, '86 16
Sour Cream Muffins, '90 283
Sour Cream Muffins, Mini, '88 283
Squash Muffins, '91 69
Sunshine Muffins, '86 9
Sweet Potato Muffins, '81 224; '85 6;
'87 280; '92 31
Tea Muffins, '82 105
Tropical Muffins, '84 299
Wheat Germ-Prune Muffins, '81 106
Wheat Muffins, Fruited, '79 93
Whole Wheat Bran Muffins, '88 M274
Whole Wheat Raisin Muffins, '85 207
Yam Muffins, '79 7
Yeast Muffins, Quick, '84 69
Yellow Squash Muffins, '81 163

Yogurt-Muesli Muffins, '90 215
Yogurt Muffins, '88 55
Zucchini Muffins, '83 121; '86 146
MUSHROOMS
Appetizers, Chicken-Mushroom, '88 210
Artichokes, Ham-Mushroom-Stuffed, '95 228
Aztec Mushrooms, '82 51
Balls, Cheese and Mushroom, '79 63
Casserole, Mushroom-Macaroni, '95 180
Champignons au Vin, '79 47
Cheesecake, Spinach-Mushroom, '92 326
Creamed Mushrooms on Toast, '81 190
Curried Mushrooms, '84 214
Dip, Hot Mushroom, '89 48
Drunk Mushrooms, '83 174
Filling in a Peel, Mushroom, '84 214
Filling, Mushroom, '81 89; '82 259; '83 51;
'88 84
Filling, Spinach-Mushroom, '80 215
Fluted Mushrooms, '82 280
French-Fried Mushrooms, '82 78
French-Fried Mushrooms with Tartar Sauce,
'86 233
Garlic and Mushrooms, '95 165
Logs, Mushroom, '84 206
Main Dishes
Beef Tenderloin with Mushrooms,
'87 115
Burgers, Brie-Mushroom, '95 128
Burgers, Mushroom, '89 164
Casserole, Crab-and-Mushroom, '89 96
Casserole, Egg-Mushroom, '83 49
Casserole, Sausage-Mushroom Breakfast,
'86 95
Chicken and Mushrooms in Wine Sauce,
'81 109
Chicken Bake, Mushroom-, '89 147
Chicken Livers with Mushrooms, '81 133
Chicken-Mushroom Bundles, '80 157
Chicken-Mushroom Dinner, '81 3
Chicken with Artichokes and
Mushrooms, '90 35
Chicken with Sautéed Peppers and
Mushrooms, Herb-Stuffed, '91 26
Crabmeat and Mushrooms on Toast
Points, '82 M91
Creamed Mushrooms in Wild Rice Ring,
'80 270
Crêpes, Cheese and Mushroom, '81 88
Crêpes, Coquilles St. Jacques, '83 13
Crêpes, Mushroom-Cheese, '87 289;
'88 135
Egg Delight, Mushroom-, '83 14
Eggs, Saucy Mushrooms and, '79 138
Eggs, Sherried Mushroom, '83 49
Flank Steak and Mushrooms, '87 61
Macaroni-Mushroom Bake, Cheesy,
'81 243
Muffin Stacks, Mushroom-Topped,
'80 271
Omelet, Broccoli-Mushroom, '85 45
Omelet, Rolled Mushroom, '82 70
Patty Shells, Mushrooms and Eggs in,
'85 143
Pizza, Cheese-and-Mushroom, '83 226
Pork Chops, Apricot-Mushroom Stuffed,
'95 287
Pork Loin with Apples and Mushrooms,
Roast, '92 218
Pork Loin with Mushrooms and Garlic,
Roasted, '92 301
Pork Tenderloin, Apple-Mushroom,
'95 53

Pot Roast, Mushroom, '79 17
Quail with Mushroom Gravy, Baked,
'89 273
Quail with Mushrooms, '85 138
Quail with Mushrooms, Baked,
'81 259
Quiche, Ham-and-Mushroom, '81 11
Quiche Lorraine, Mushroom-, '86 242
Quiche, Mushroom, '81 244
Quiche, Spinach-Mushroom, '81 M74
Quiche, Zucchini-Mushroom, '79 127
Ragoût of Wild Mushrooms with Creamy
Grits, '92 238
Rice, Baked Mushroom, '92 170
Salmon with Mushrooms and Green
Onions, Fresh, '93 180
Scallops and Mushrooms, Creamy,
'83 144
Shrimp and Mushrooms with Angel Hair
Pasta, '92 34
Shrimp-Mushroom Italienne, Green Pasta
with, '79 170
Spaghetti with Mushrooms, Spicy, '85 2
Spinach and Mushrooms with Bow Tie
Pasta, '95 341
Stir-Fry, Shiitake-Chicken, '89 61
Stroganoff, Mushroom, '81 298
Stroganoff, Mushroom-Meatball, '85 85
Tart, Smoked Portabello Mushroom,
'94 163
Veal-and-Mushrooms Marsala, '89 44
Veal-Cepe Sauté, '89 62
Venison Loin, Mushroom-Crusted,
'94 302
Vermicelli with Mushrooms, '79 195
Marinated
Caps, Marinated Mushroom, '83 128
Easy Marinated Mushrooms, '86 217
Herb Mushrooms, Marinated, '86 327
Marinated Mushrooms, '80 82, 270;
'81 69; '86 135; '91 306; '92 328
Mexican Marinated Mushrooms,
'81 66
Special Marinated Mushrooms, '83 13
Omelet, Golden Cheese-Shiitake, '95 265
Pastry Cups, Mushroom-Almond, '88 210
Pâté de Champignon, '93 171
Pâté in Pastry, Turkey-Mushroom, '92 327
Pâté, Mushroom, '89 157
Patty Shells, Mushrooms and Eggs in,
'85 143; '88 197
Patty Shells, Mushrooms in, '80 283
Phyllo Bites, Sausage-Mushroom-, '89 284
Piroshki, '92 84
Portabello Mushrooms, Grilled, '95 123
Portabello Mushrooms, Microwave, '95 M123
Portabello Mushrooms, Sautéed, '95 123
Rollups, Mushroom, '85 318
Salads
Cheesy-Mushroom Salad, Quick, '89 128
Fabulous Mushroom Salad, '81 190
Fresh Mushroom Salad, '93 65
Marinated Mushroom Salad, '88 215;
'90 181
Pepper Salad, Mushroom-and-, '86 68
Rice Salad with Fresh Mushrooms,
'80 231
Spinach and Mushroom Salad, '80 112
Spinach-Enoki Salad, '89 62
Watercress-and-Mushroom Salad,
'88 104
Zucchini Salad, Mushroom-, '85 8
Sandwiches, Toasted Mushroom, '87 281

Sauces
　Beef Tenderloin with Mushroom Sauce,
　　'88 3
　Chanterelle Brown Sauce, '89 62
　Cheese Sauce, Mushroom-, '83 190;
　　'86 48
　Chicken Florentine with Mushroom
　　Sauce, '87 250
　Dill Sauce, Mushroom-, '80 271
　Eggs Baked in Mushroom Sauce, '93 47
　Filet Mignon with Mushroom Sauce,
　　'94 250
　Ham-and-Mushroom Sauce, Steak with,
　　'83 109
　Madeira Sauce, Filet Mignons with
　　Shiitake, '95 265
　Mushroom Sauce, '81 90, 200; '82 46;
　　'83 71, 205, 212; '84 M70; '85 40;
　　'86 198; '87 36, 186, 284; '91 221
　Onion-Mushroom Sauce, '85 224;
　　'86 84
　Sherried Mushroom Sauce, Green Beans
　　in, '93 206
　Sherried Mushroom Sauce, Spicy,
　　'89 239
　Sherry Sauce, Beef Tenderloin with
　　Mushroom-, '87 306
　Steak with Mushroom Sauce, '83 212
　Supreme on Vermicelli, Mushroom Sauce,
　　'86 158
　Tomatoes with Mushroom Sauce,
　　Broiled, '81 103
　Wine Sauce, Mushroom-, '84 84; '86 24
　Zucchini-Mushroom Sauce, '93 71
Shiitakes, Grilled, '95 265
Side Dishes
　Acorn Squash-Mushroom Puree, '93 305
　à la King, Mushrooms, '89 285
　Asparagus and Mushrooms, '85 108
　Asparagus-and-Mushroom Sauté, '93 115
　au Gratin, Mushrooms, '81 108
　Baked Mushroom Rice, '95 84
　Baked Mushrooms, Creamy, '87 127
　Bake, Windsor Mushroom, '88 132
　Casserole, Mushroom, '95 211
　Casserole, Mushroom-Artichoke, '87 241
　Casserole, Mushroom-Cheese, '83 216
　Casserole, Mushroom-Potato, '84 5
　Creamed Oyster Mushrooms, '89 61
　Dressing, Whole Wheat-Mushroom,
　　'84 283
　Eggplant, Mushroom-Stuffed, '83 136
　Fresh Mushrooms, Savory, '85 268
　Green Beans, Mushroom-Bacon,
　　'91 291; '92 255
　Green Beans with Bacon and Mushrooms,
　　'92 13
　Green Beans with Mushrooms, '82 21;
　　'93 89
　Green Peas with Mushrooms, '80 101
　Heavenly Mushrooms, '87 281
　Herbed Mushrooms, '84 214; '88 176
　Newburg, Mushroom, '88 252
　Noodles and Mushrooms, Cheesy, '79 84
　Panuchos, Mushroom, '83 51
　Peas and Mushrooms, '83 141
　Peas and Mushrooms, Buttered,
　　'82 204
　Peas with Mushrooms, Creamy, '84 196
　Pepper-Mushroom Medley, '90 98

Potatoes, Mushroom-Dill-Topped,
　'86 41
Potatoes, Mushroom Scalloped, '87 191
Quiche, Mushroom, '80 222; '89 285
Quiches, Wild Rice-and-Mushroom,
　'93 237
Rice, Easy Mushroom, '89 286
Sautéed Mushrooms, '84 35
Sautéed Mushrooms, Easy, '81 131
Sautéed Mushroom Spectacular, '83 206
Sauté, Mixed Mushroom, '89 62
Seasoned Mushrooms, '83 291
Sherried Mushrooms, '83 13
Soufflés, Mushroom, '87 282
Sour Cream-Dill Sauce, Mushrooms in,
　'84 215
Sparkling Mushrooms, '94 24
Spinach and Mushrooms with Bow Tie
　Pasta, '95 341
Spinach with Mushrooms, '80 19
Stir-Fried Mushrooms with Bacon,
　'80 123
Supreme, Mushrooms, '84 214
Tarts, Mushroom, '88 161
Tomatoes, Mushroom-Stuffed, '86 218
Turnovers, Tiny Mushroom, '86 24
Vermouth, Mushrooms in, '89 203
Wild Rice and Mushrooms, '83 278
Wild Rice with Morels, '89 62
Wine Sauce, Mushrooms with, '85 292
Yellow Squash, Mushroom-Stuffed,
　'84 154
Zesty Mushrooms, '93 218
Zucchini with Mushrooms, Sautéed,
　'94 135
Soups
　Avocado-Mushroom Soup, Creamy,
　　'85 25
　Bisque, Brisk Mushroom, '81 190
　Chicken, Artichoke, and Mushroom
　　Soup, '92 324
　Chowder, Mushroom, '79 16
　Chowder, Mushroom-Potato, '92 331
　Chunky Mushroom Soup, '88 12
　Consommé aux Champignons, '79 48
　Cream of Mushroom Soup, '84 5;
　　'85 93, 261
　Creamy Mushroom Soup, '79 243;
　　'81 307
　Curried Mushroom Soup, '84 M89
　Elegant Mushroom Soup, '83 99
　Fresh Mushroom Soup, '81 109; '90 190
　Mushroom Soup, '82 286; '86 M73;
　　'94 54
　Onion Soup, Mushroom-, '80 25
　Oyster-and-Mushroom Soup, '87 39
　Rice Soup, Mushroom-, '90 32
　Shiitake Soup, Cream of, '95 265
Spread, Eggplant-Mushroom, '92 156
Spread, Hot Mushroom, '81 190
Stewed Anasazi Beans with Mushrooms,
　'95 226
Stuffed
　Appetizers, Stuffed Mushroom, '88 210
　Black Olive-Stuffed Mushrooms, '86 258
　Canapés, Mushroom, '80 285
　Cheese 'n' Bacon-Stuffed Mushrooms,
　　'86 258
　Cheese-Stuffed Mushrooms, Elegant,
　　'81 57
　Chicken-Stuffed Mushrooms, '80 162
　Crab, Mushrooms Stuffed with, '82 249
　Crab-Stuffed Mushroom Caps, '84 160

Crab-Stuffed Mushrooms, '81 190
Crawfish-Stuffed Mushrooms, '86 258
Delight, Stuffed Mushroom, '87 281
Flavor-Stuffed Mushrooms, '85 288
Florentine, Stuffed Mushrooms, '82 270
Italian Sausage-Stuffed Mushrooms,
　'83 127
Parmesan Stuffed Mushrooms, '83 115
Pâté-Stuffed Mushrooms, '85 118
Pecan-Stuffed Mushrooms, '84 261
Pesto-Stuffed Mushrooms, '86 150
Pistachio-Stuffed Mushrooms, '86 141
Ricotta-Stuffed Mushrooms, '85 20
Samurai 'shrooms, '93 258
Sausage-Stuffed Mushrooms, '80 248;
　'91 164
Seasoned Stuffed Mushrooms, '84 206
Shrimp-Stuffed Mushrooms, '80 M135
Spinach-Stuffed Mushrooms, '86 81;
　'88 131, M261; '89 M133
Stems, Mushrooms with, '86 258
Stuffed Mushrooms, '79 212; '81 239;
　'83 13, 66, 126, 136; '93 172
Vegetable Mushroom Caps, '81 246
Tapas, Majorcan Mushroom, '95 159
Tarts, Hot Sherried Mushroom, '83 78
Tipsy Mushrooms, '84 M216
Turnovers, Hot Mushroom, '89 285
MUSTARD
Bourbon Mustard, '93 240
Brie, Honey-Mustard, '91 252
Brussels Sprouts with Shallots and Mustard,
　'85 258
Chicken, Mustard, '93 239
Coarse-and-Sweet Mustard, '86 M288
Compote, Baked Mustard Fruit, '85 47
Dressing, Dijon-Honey, '89 45
Dressing, Honey-Mustard, '90 55, 111, 146
Dressing, Mustard, '80 112
Dressing, Tangy Mustard, '93 323
Flounder Dijon, '85 95
Fruit Bake, Mustard, '90 291
Glaze, Game Hens with Chutney-Mustard,
　'93 66
Glaze, Roast Chicken with Pineapple-Mustard,
　'89 83
Herbed Mustard, '87 134
Homemade Mustard, '81 77
Homemade Mustard, Zesty, '82 55
Honey Mustard, Hot, '93 240
Honey Mustard, Peppered, '95 312
Horseradish Mustard, '93 240
Horseradish Mustard, Lower Sodium, '86 325
Hot German Mustard, '82 298
Hot Mustard, Chinese, '85 12
Hot Mustard, Really, '95 312
Hot Sweet Mustard, '85 12
Jalapeño Mustard, '93 240; '95 312
Key Lime Mustard, '94 278
Marinade, Honey-Mustard, '93 103
Mousse, Mustard, '84 127; '86 184; '95 328
Pork Tenderloin, Honey-Mustard, '95 52
Raspberry Mustard, '95 313
Sauces
　Asparagus in Mustard Sauce, Chilled,
　　'88 130
　Barbecue Sauce, Mustard, '84 173
　Chutney-Mustard Sauce, '89 242
　Cream Sauce, Chicken in Mustard,
　　'92 181
　Cream Sauce, Mustard, '88 61
　Creamy Mustard Sauce, '80 272;
　　'86 257; '87 232; '93 240

MUSTARD, Sauces (continued)

Creamy Mustard Sauce, Champagne-
    Poached Chicken with, '94 24
Easy Mustard Sauce, '94 83
Extra-Special Mustard Sauce, '79 82
Hamburger Steaks with Mustard Sauce,
    '84 230
Hollandaise Sauce, Mock Mustard-,
    '87 269
Honey-Lemon Mustard Sauce, '84 275
Honey-Mustard Sauce, '85 13
Honey-Mustard Sauce, Smoked Ribs
    with, '92 168
Horseradish-Mustard Sauce, Creamy,
    '88 M177
Hot Mustard Sauce, '93 240
Leg of Lamb with Mustard Sauce, '89 71
Light Mustard Sauce, '82 178
Mild Mustard Sauce, '85 224; '86 84
Mustard Sauce, '80 222, 283;
    '83 21, 321; '84 M70, 289; '85 148;
    '86 185; '87 22; '89 122, 333;
    '90 19, 97; '92 302; '93 118
Sausage Sandwiches with Mustard Sauce,
    '84 250
Scallops with Mustard Sauce, '84 163
Smoked Sausages with Mustard Sauce,
    '81 56
Sour Cream Sauce, Mustard-, '81 68
Stone Crab Mustard Sauce, '80 3
Sweet Mustard Sauce, '85 12
Tangy Mustard Sauce, '92 201
Tarragon-Mustard Sauce, Turkey Cutlets
    with, '93 239
Vinaigrette Sauce, Mustard-, '84 174
Vinegar Sauce, Shrimp with Mustard-,
    '93 240
Spread, Chive-Mustard, '91 12
Spread, Mustard, '86 105
Sweet Cider Mustard, '95 312
Vegetables, Honey-Mustard Marinated,
    '93 236
Vinaigrette, Baby Lettuces with Mustard,
    '93 67
Vinaigrette, Honey-Mustard, '94 249

NECTARINES
Apple Juice, Nectarines in, '83 183
Butter, Nectarine, '79 175
Cocktail, Nectarine, '85 107
Royale, Nectarines, '85 132
Salad, Nectarine Chicken, '79 175
Sherbet, Nectarine, '89 199
NOODLES
Broccoli and Sausage, Pasta with, '87 109
Caraway Buttered Noodles, '87 230
Casserole, Eggplant and Noodle, '82 230
Casserole, Vegetable Noodle, '91 30
Green Noodles, '80 211
Kugel, Apricot Noodle, '92 251
Kugel, Nu Awlins, '94 229
Kugel, Sweet, '90 254
Main Dishes
    Beef and Noodles, Easy, '83 288
    Beef over Rice Noodles, Shredded, '85 74
    Beefy Noodle Dinner, '81 179
    Casserole, Beef-and-Noodles, '84 72
    Casserole, Chicken and Green Noodle,
        '80 32

Casserole, Chicken-Noodle, '94 286
Casserole, Ham and Noodle, '80 300
Casserole, Sausage and Noodle, '82 123
Casserole, Sausage-and-Noodle, '95 255
Casserole, Shrimp-and-Noodle, '90 240
Casserole, Turkey-Noodle-Poppyseed,
    '90 239
Cheesy Noodles and Mushrooms, '79 84
Chicken and Spinach Noodles, '82 19
Chicken with Noodles, Sesame,
    '88 M125
Chili with Noodles, '81 282; '82 57
Chow Mein over Crispy Noodles,
    '85 286
Ham and Swiss on Noodles, '87 108
Hamburger-Noodle Bake, '81 140
Ham-Noodle Skillet, '87 78
Italian Sauce with Noodles, '84 250
Lasagna, Lots of Noodles, '91 M127
Liver and Noodle Dinner, Creamy,
    '80 11
Pork-and-Noodle Bake, '88 98
Pork-and-Noodles Skillet Dinner,
    '88 199
Ring, Noodle, '85 285
Sausage and Mixed Vegetables, Pasta
    with, '87 249
Sausage-Noodle Bake, '81 92
Scallops and Pasta, Fresh, '83 164
Shrimp and Noodles, Creamy, '92 100
Sour Cream-Noodle Bake, '79 55
Stew with Noodles, Hungarian,
    '80 263
Taco Beef-Noodle Bake, '81 141
Turkey Noodle Bake, '93 243
Veal Sauce, Noodles with, '80 236
Orange Noodles, '84 177
Parmesan Noodles, '83 118
Parmesan Noodles, Cheesy, '83 M7
Parslied Noodles, '85 31
Salad, Chicken Noodle, '95 25
Salad, Ham-Noodle, '85 249
Salad, Ramen Noodle, '88 41
Soup, Chicken Noodle, '80 264; '95 45
Soup Mix, Turkey-Noodle, '89 330
Soup, Turkey-Noodle, '91 312
Spinach with Noodles, Creamed, '84 29
White Noodles, '80 211

OATMEAL
Applesauce Oatmeal, '89 108
Bake, Pear-Oatmeal, '89 208
Breads
    Biscuits, Oatmeal, '89 108
    Blueberry-Oatmeal Bread, '83 139
    Buns, Honey Oatmeal, '83 154
    Caraway-Raisin Oat Bread, '86 44
    Dill-Oat Bread, '91 95
    Honey-Oat Bread, '89 107
    Honey Oatmeal Bread, '80 60
    Loaf, Banana-Oat Tea, '87 256
    Loaf, Pumpkin-Oatmeal, '81 49
    Muffins, Banana-Oat, '87 188
    Muffins, Banana-Oatmeal, '84 20
    Muffins, Best-Ever Oatmeal, '84 242
    Muffins, Blueberry-Oat, '92 119
    Muffins, Blueberry-Oatmeal, '87 24
    Muffins, Corn-Oat, '89 108
    Muffins, Honey-Oatmeal, '84 229
    Muffins, Oat Bran, '89 106
    Muffins, Oat Bran-Banana, '91 18

Muffins, Oatmeal, '82 129, 210;
    '84 72, 140; '92 163
Muffins, Oatmeal Bran, '81 236
Muffins, Oatmeal-Bran, '91 83
Muffins, Oatmeal-Honey, '83 95
Muffins, Orange-Oatmeal, '85 202
Muffins, Spicy Apple-Oat, '86 45
Oatmeal Bread, '81 236, 300; '92 212
Oatmeal Raisin Bread, '81 14
Oatmeal-Raisin Bread, '83 59
Oat-Molasses Bread, '82 139
Round Oatmeal Bread, '84 20
Whole Wheat-Oatmeal Bread, '87 85
Breakfast Oatmeal Surprise, '93 178
Breakfast Oatmeal, Swiss Style, '81 49
Brownies, Oat, '89 59
Brownies, Oatmeal, '87 199
Brownies, Oat 'n' Crunch, '91 233
Cake, Applesauce-Oatmeal, '92 119
Cake, Dutch Oatmeal, '83 95
Cake, Golden Apple-Oatmeal, '86 301
Cake, Honey-Oatmeal, '87 222
Cereal, Full-of-Fiber Hot, '89 208
Coffee Cake, Oatmeal-Coconut, '83 312
Cookies
    Apple-Nut Cookies, '80 228
    Apple-Oatmeal Cookies, '85 215;
        '90 218
    Banana Oatmeal Cookies, '79 217
    Bars, Apricot-Oatmeal, '86 216
    Bars, Chocolate-Topped Oatmeal,
        '86 110
    Bars, Date-Oat, '80 M172
    Bars, Layered Oatmeal-Date, '85 10
    Bars, Oatmeal-Caramel, '85 247
    Bars, Yummy Fudge, '87 158
    Breakfast Cookies, Take-Along, '84 59
    Carrot Cookies, Oatmeal-, '94 292
    Chocolate Chip Cookies, Nutty
        Oatmeal-, '82 M185
    Chocolate Chip-Oatmeal Cookies, '84 119
    Chocolate Chippers, Oatmeal-, '90 218
    Chocolate Morsel Cookies, Oatmeal-,
        '95 46
    Chocolate-Oatmeal Cookies, '80 105
    Chocolate-Raisin Oatmeal Cookies,
        '95 136
    Cinnamon Oatmeal Cookies, '84 72
    Coconut Cookies, Oatmeal-, '80 218
    Coconut-Oatmeal Cookies, Crispy,
        '93 80
    Crackers, Oatmeal-Wheat Germ, '84 236
    Crispies, Oat, '83 96
    Crispy Oat Cookies, '88 203; '90 311
    Crispy Oatmeal Cookies, '89 328
    Crunchy Oatmeal Cookies, '85 202
    Date Cookies, Oatmeal-, '82 109
    Date-Filled Oatmeal Cookies, '86 314
    Date Sandwich Cookies, Oatmeal-,
        '83 257
    Easy Oatmeal Cookies, '80 105
    Fibber McGee Cookies, '95 72
    Krispies, Oatmeal, '85 115
    Lace Cookies, '86 8
    Macadamia-Oat Snowballs, '92 274
    Nut Crispies, Oatmeal, '80 208
    Nutty Oatmeal Cookies, '81 130
    Oatmeal Cookies, '92 82
    Old-Fashioned Oatmeal Cookies,
        '80 106; '85 250
    Orange-Glazed Oatmeal Cookies, '80 60
    Peanut Butter Chocolate Chip Cookies,
        Oatmeal-, '92 207

OATMEAL, Cookies (continued)

Peanut Butter Cookies, Oatmeal-, '85 171
Peanut Butter-Oatmeal Cookies, '81 218; '84 72
Peanut Cookies, Oats-and-, '89 60
Peanutty Oatmeal Cookies, '80 106; '83 95
Raisin Cookies, Frosted Oatmeal-, '79 290
Raisin Cookies, Oatmeal-, '87 221; '93 127
Slice-and-Bake Oatmeal Cookies, '80 105
Special Oatmeal Cookies, '81 236
Spice Cookies, Giant Oatmeal-, '80 105
Spicy Oatmeal Cookies, '81 197
Sunshine Cookies, Oatmeal, '89 59
Toasted Oatmeal Cookies, '92 273; '95 136
Toffee Lizzies, Crispy Oatmeal-, '95 136
Crisp, Oatmeal Cherry-Apple, '90 M16
Crust, Nutty Oat, '89 251
Fruited Oatmeal, '88 19
Granola Bars, '83 305
Granola, Crunchy, '81 218; '84 144
Granola, Easy, '81 49
Granola, Fruity, '84 148
Granola, Homemade, '84 58
Granola, Sunny Orange, '84 212
Ice Cream Sandwiches, Oatmeal Crispy, '93 199
Mix, Rolled Oats, '84 72
Muesli, '89 208
Muesli, Homestyle, '91 315
Pancakes, Oat, '89 227
Pancakes, Oatmeal, '80 44; '89 107
Pancakes, Oatmeal-Brown Sugar, '88 203
Pancakes, Whole Wheat-Oat, '93 16
Piecrust, Crisp Cereal, '83 100
Piecrust, Oatmeal, '79 79
Topping, Oat Crunch, '89 108
Topping, Oatmeal Cookie, '95 291
Waffles, Banana-Oatmeal, '94 206
Waffles, Oatmeal, '89 107
Waffles, Oatmeal-Nut, '83 96

OKRA
Bake, Okra-and-Tomato, '89 173
Bake, Okra-Tomato, '80 298; '81 26
Casserole, Okra, '79 160
Chowder, Quick Okra, '80 185
Corn, and Peppers, Okra, '87 M151
Corn, and Tomatoes, Okra, '95 203
Cream, Okra and Corn in, '79 160
Creole, Corn-and-Okra, '89 127
Creole, Meatball-Okra, '83 156
Creole Okra, '81 182
Creole, Okra-Corn, '83 157
Fresh Okra and Tomatoes, '87 89
Fried
Cheese, Okra with, '80 185
Crispy Fried Okra, '86 169
Deep-Fried Okra, '90 154
Fingers, Okra, '85 196
French-Fried Okra, '82 126
Fried Okra, '79 122; '86 211; '87 89; '88 111
Fritter-Fried Okra, '86 218
Fritters, Okra, '79 160; '92 133
Green Tomatoes, Fried Okra and, '93 160

Green Tomatoes, Okra and, '79 160
Old-Time Fried Okra, '80 185
Oven-Fried Okra, '91 121
Potato Fry, Okra-, '81 159
Puffs, Okra, '83 157
Goulash, Okra, '93 160
Gumbo, Deep South Okra, '79 48
Gumbo Freezer Mix, Okra, '86 210
Gumbo, Light Seafood-Okra, '86 155
Gumbo, Okra, '86 210; '91 206
How to Can Okra, '80 127
Medley, Okra, '88 M185
Medley, Okra-Corn-Tomato, '81 159
Muffins, Fresh Okra, '93 161
Pickles, Okra, '81 173
Pilaf, Okra, '80 185; '82 126; '93 160
Plantation Okra, '82 126
Salad, Okra, '90 155
Sautéed Corn and Okra, '84 158
Skillet Okra, '95 179
Soup, Charleston Okra, '87 156
Soup, Okra-and-Shrimp, '94 323
Soup, Sausage and Okra, '80 209
Stewed Okra, Southern, '82 134
Stew, Old-Fashioned Okra, '84 158
Surprise, Okra, '79 160; '84 158
Tomato Combo, Okra-, '83 157
Tomatoes and Okra, '86 170; '87 164
Tomatoes, Fresh Okra and, '81 M165
Tomatoes, Okra and, '80 185; '81 139; '92 215
Tomatoes with Okra, '85 106
Vinaigrette, Okra-Corn-and-Tomato, '90 173

OLIVES
Antipasto, Easy, '85 114
Appetizers, Cheesy Olive, '85 113
Appetizers, Cheesy-Olive, '87 246
Ball, Blue Cheese-Olive, '82 248
Ball, Olive Cheese, '80 258
Black Olives, Shrimp Spaghetti with, '85 13
Black Olive-Stuffed Mushrooms, '86 258
Bread, Olive, '93 78
Bread, Olive-Dill Casserole, '92 16
Butter, Olive, '91 295
Casserole, Turkey-Olive, '87 268
Chalupas, Chicken-Olive, '81 227
Chicken-and-Rice Valencia, '85 113
Filling, Chicken-Olive, '81 227
Ham-and-Swiss Rollups, '85 113
Lemon-Garlic Olives, '94 118
Marinated Olives, Caliente, '95 177
Marinated Olives, Herb-, '92 176
Potatoes, Olive, '80 114
Salad, Doodles Olive, '94 35
Salad, Italian Olive, '94 35
Salad, Mexican Olive, '85 84
Salad Mix, Muffy, '94 34
Salad, Olive Clubhouse, '81 114
Salad, Olive-Potato, '85 114
Salad with Sherry Vinaigrette, Shrimp, Orange, and Olive, '93 177
Snack, Open-Faced Cheese-and-Olive, '89 97
Spread, Antipasto, '81 25
Spread, Cheese-Olive, '79 82
Spread, Cream Cheese-Olive, '82 35
Spread, Creamy Olive, '81 290
Spread, Tomatoes with Olive, '85 114
Stuffed Olives, Almond-, '88 95
Tapenade, '92 194
Toss, Cauliflower-Olive, '85 198; '86 147
Toss, Tomato-Olive Pasta, '86 209

OMELETS
Apple Omelet Stack, '94 50
Baked Omelets, '94 50
Broccoli-Mushroom Omelet, '85 45
Cheese Omelet, Herbed, '93 47
Cheese Omelet, Puffed, '89 227
Cheese Omelet, Zippy, '87 287
Cheese-Shiitake Omelet, Golden, '95 265
Cheesy Picante Omelet, '86 95
Chicken Liver Omelet, '82 44
Country Omelets, '91 128
Creole Sauce, Omelets with, '89 228
Dill-Cheese-Ham Omelet, '95 33
Filling, Greek Omelet, '80 68
Filling, Spanish Omelet, '80 68
Fluffy Omelet, '84 56
George's Omelets, '80 68
Ham and Cheese Omelet, '79 262; '80 123
Mexican Omelet, '79 128; '81 225
Mushroom Omelet, Rolled, '82 70
Mushroom Sauce, Puffy Omelets with, '85 40
Olé Omelet, '87 M124
Olé, Omelet, '94 31
Oyster Omelets, Smoked, '84 96
Potato Omelet, Family-Size, '94 31
Potato-Sprout Omelet, '79 128
Primavera, Omelet, '87 71
Rising Sun Omelet, '82 281; '83 42
Rolled Omelet, '89 228
Sandwich, Omelet, '86 95
Sausage Filling, Omelet with, '81 43
Sausage Omelet, Puffy, '80 M268
Shrimp-and-Cheddar Omelet, '84 57
Shrimp-and-Cheese Omelet, '94 31
Sour Cream-Ham Omelet, '79 261
Spanish Omelet, '81 201; '83 243; '84 101
Spanish-Style Omelets, '83 188
Spinach-Cheese Omelet, '83 119
Strawberry-Sour Cream Omelet, '89 229
Sunrise Omelet, '83 289
Swiss Oven Omelet, '80 189
Tarragon Omelet, '89 144
Tex-Mex Omelet con Carne, '81 209
Vegetable Omelet, Beefy, '83 188
Vegetable Omelet, Cheddar-, '83 205
Vegetable Omelet, Cheesy, '85 49
Vegetable Omelet, Fresh, '84 211
Vegetable Omelet, Golden, '82 M123
Vegetable Omelet, Puffy, '83 188
Vegetarian Omelet, '84 114
White Wine Omelet, '79 103
Yogurt-Avocado Omelet, '81 33
Zucchini Omelet, '81 99

ONIONS
Appetizers, Bacon-Onion, '94 290
Bake, Cheese Onion, '82 32
Baked Onions, Micro-, '82 M32
Baked Onions, Spicy, '84 65
Baked Onions, Sweet-and-Sour, '90 34
Bake, Four Onion, '93 304
Bake, Onion-Potato, '83 M195
Bake, Romano Onion, '90 98
Barbecued Onions, '88 86
Beef and Onions, Smothered, '85 293
Breads
Biscuits, Cheesy Onion, '95 98
Buns, Cheesy Onion, '85 5
Buns, Onion-Cheese, '88 218
Cheese Bread, Onion-, '79 180; '81 8
Cheese Supper Bread, Onion-, '83 112
Cornbread, Onion, '88 283
Cornbread, Onion-Topped, '84 153
Dill Bread, Easy Onion-, '85 5

ONIONS, Breads *(continued)*

Easy Onion Bread, '81 162
Focaccia, Mustard-and-Onion, '90 321; '92 97
Focaccia, Onion, '93 77
French Bread, Onion-Cheese, '89 29
French Onion Bread, '91 90
Herb Bread, Onion-, '90 165
Herb Bread, Toasted Onion-, '83 266
Hush Puppies, Onion, '85 14
Hush Puppies, Tomato-Onion, '91 201
Loaves, Onion Twist, '84 300
Muffins, Onion-Dill, '92 253; '93 144
Parmesan Bread, Onion-, '84 284
Rolls, Onion Twist, '89 288
Rolls, Poppy Seed Onion, '81 63
Sesame Rolls, Onion-and-, '95 292
Burgers, Open-Faced Chicken-Onion, '94 139
Butter, Onion, '86 253
Caramelized Onions, Green Beans with, '95 288
Carrots with Bacon and Onion, Glazed, '87 200
Casserole, Cheesy Onion, '79 101
Cheese Onions, Sherried, '82 32
Chicken, Onion-Crusted, '88 40
Confit, Roasted Shallot-Garlic, '94 303
Crème Brûlée, Onion, '95 324
Crunch Sticks, Onion Crescent, '90 206
Curried Onions, '90 34
Deluxe, Broccoli-Onion, '81 75
Dip, Cheesy Onion, '83 145
Dip, Chunky Onion, '84 257
Dip, Cream Cheese-Onion, '79 236
Dip, Curry-Onion, '93 313
Dip, Swiss-Onion, '95 93
Dressing, Green Pepper-Onion Salad, '84 12
Dressing, Onion-French, '84 283
Fried
Beer-Battered Onion Rings, '92 52
Crisp Fried Onion Rings, '84 65
Crispy Fried Onion Rings, '80 108
Crispy Onion Rings, '86 110
Deluxe Fried Onion Rings, '80 108
Easy Onion Rings, '80 108
Favorite Fried Onion Rings, '81 86
French-Fried Onion Rings, '88 111
French-Fried Onion Rings Supreme, '80 109
Green Onions, Fried, '81 106
Leonard's-Style Onion Rings, '90 120
Rings, Fried Onion, '83 85; '85 69
Glazed Carrots and Onions, '83 25; '87 128
Glazed Onions, '84 104
Gourmet Onions, '81 86
Gravy, Fried Quail with Onion, '82 214
Green Onions. *See also* Onions/Fried, Soups.
Canapés, Green Onion, '84 M216
Cukes and Scallions, '91 168
Dip, Onion, '94 21
Eggs, Creamy Onion Scrambled, '83 M203
Hoecakes, Green Onion, '88 112
Lima Beans and Scallions, Fresh, '82 133
Pork-and-Onions with Bean Sauce, '85 76
Quiche, Cheesy Green Onion, '83 194; '84 42
Relish, Green Onion, '84 65
Salmon with Mushrooms and Green Onions, Fresh, '93 180

Sauce, Onion-Mushroom, '85 224; '86 84
Sautéed Onions and Peppers, '83 M148
Spread, Green Onion-Cheese, '92 24
Teasers, Green Onion, '82 42
Grilled Squash and Onion, '79 150
Herbed Carrots and Onions, '87 31
Herbed Onions, '84 149
Honey Onions, '81 86
Italian Dressing, Tomato, Onion, and Cucumber in, '81 83
Kale with Tomato and Onion, '92 244
Kuchen, Onion, '90 34
Patties, Potato-Onion, '95 269
Pearl Onions, Beef Burgundy with, '81 108
Pearl Onions, Glazed, '85 258
Pearl Onions, Green Beans with Roasted Red Peppers and, '93 260
Pearl Onions, Snap Peas and, '89 280
Peas with Onions, Buttered, '80 242
Pickled Cocktail Onions, '89 197
Pickled Refrigerator Onion Rings, '84 265
Pie, Onion, '82 191
Pudding, Kathy's Onion, '95 318
Quiche, Onion, '83 121
Relish, Pepper-Onion, '84 180
Rice, Seasoned Onion, '82 166
Salad, Lemon-Onion, '85 252
Salad, Roasted Onion, '95 65
Salad, Tomato-Cucumber-Onion, '81 239
Sauce, Brussels Sprouts in Onion, '81 308
Sauce, Onion, '82 72; '87 248
Sauce, Onion Cream, '87 232
Sauce, Onion-Parsley, '85 148
Sauce, Pepper-Onion, '84 125
Sautéed Apples, Onions, and Pears over Spinach, '94 212
Selecting and Storing Onions, '84 65
Shells, Cheese and Limas in Onion, '81 86
Soufflé, Onion, '79 247
Soups
Cheese Onion Soup, Double-, '85 227
Cheese Soup, Onion-, '87 81
Classic Onion Soup, '84 65
Creamy Onion Soup, '90 211
Double Cheese-Topped Onion Soup, '79 49
Easy Onion Soup, '85 226
French Onion-Beef Soup, '87 54
French Onion Soup, '79 49; '80 188; '83 126; '85 226; '86 M212; '90 31; '93 246
French Onion Soup, Shortcut, '85 M328
French Onion Soup, Toasty, '81 306
Green Onion Soup, '84 112
Green Onion Soup, Creamed, '83 82
Mushroom-Onion Soup, '80 25
Oven-Browned Onion Soup, '79 49
Potato Soup, Creamy Onion-and-, '92 51
Rich Onion Soup, '85 226
Superb Onion Soup, '81 86
Vichyssoise, '86 181
Sour Cream, Cucumber and Onion in, '81 69
Spread, Braunschweiger-Onion, '79 82
Squares, Creamy Onion, '79 48
Squares, Sausage-Onion, '83 112
Steak, Onion-Smothered, '87 M189
Stew, Beef-and-Onion, '87 18
Stuffed
Baked Onions, Stuffed, '82 32
Baked Stuffed Onions, '83 135
Broccoli-Stuffed Onions, '84 154
Cheese-Stuffed Onions, '90 34

Peas, Onions Stuffed with, '84 68
Sweet Onions, Stuffed, '91 79
Vidalia Onions, Stuffed, '89 172
Wine, Stuffed Onions and, '85 268
Stuffing, Rice-and-Onion, '88 246
Sweet
Baked Sweet Onions, '91 79
Balsamic Caramelized Florida Sweet Onions, '94 163
Blossom, Onion, '94 226
Butter, Sweet Onion, '93 124
Casserole, French Onion, '95 26
Chutney, Kiwifruit-Onion, '93 125
Creole Onions, '82 32
Grilled Stuffed Onions, '95 180
Honey-Paprika Sweet Onions, '92 52
Hot Onions, Sweet-, '85 139
Jelly, Onion, '93 135
Marinated Bermuda Onions, '92 194
Parmesan Onions, '93 170
Pie, Onion-Cheese, '88 86
Relish, Onion, '91 79
Relish, Purple Onion, '95 253
Relish, Sweet Onion, '93 124
Rings, Crispy Baked Onion, '93 247
Salad Bowl, Spinach-and-Onion, '81 157
Salad, Marinated Orange-Onion, '91 231; '92 68
Salad, Orange-Onion, '89 41
Salsa, Fiesta Onion, '94 82
Shortcake, Onion, '92 51
Tarts, Sweet Onion, '95 229
Vidalia Deep Dish, '89 120
Vidalia Onion Sauté, '89 119
Vidalia Onions with Pecans and Roasted Carrots, Roasted, '92 340
Vidalia Sandwiches on Salt-Rising Bread, '79 145
Vidalias, Marinated, '89 119
Vidalia-Tomato Salad, '84 65
Vinaigrette, Spinach Salad with Apple-Onion, '94 276
Taters, Buck's, '95 72
Turnips and Onions, '83 242
Veal and Onions, Herbed, '79 108
Vinegar Sauce, Whole Onions with Warm, '94 172
ON THE LIGHT SIDE. *See* **LIVING LIGHT.**
ORANGES
Appetizer, Orange-Berry, '85 81
Apples, Orange-Glazed, '82 51
Baked Fruit, Ginger-Orange, '93 313
Baked Oranges, '79 247; '89 41
Baked Orange Slices, '89 88
Baskets, Orange, '93 286
Beverages
Blend, Orange, '95 276
Blush, Orange, '80 51
Breakfast Eye-Opener, '87 199
Champagne with Orange Juice, '91 71
Cider, Apple-Orange, '92 20
Citrus Cooler, '82 160
Cocktail, Orange-Champagne, '79 39
Cocktail, Tomato-Orange Juice, '83 169
Coffee, Viennese Orange, '84 54
Cubes, Florida, '95 201
Flip, Orange-Banana, '82 48
Flips, Orange Blossom, '80 51
Frosty, Orange, '86 101
Frosty Sours, '81 156
Jogger's Sunrise, '93 213
Juicy, Orange, '90 178
Lemonade, Orange-Mint, '88 82

ORANGES, Beverages *(continued)*

Liqueur, Orange, '81 287
Magnolia Blossoms, '87 72
Magnolias, '82 196
Mist, Orange-Lemon, '79 288; '80 35
Nog, Orange Spiced, '82 48
Pick-Me-Up, Orange, '80 232
Pineapple Drink, Orange-, '89 35
Punch, Citrus Party, '83 141
Punch, Orange Blossom, '83 142
Punch, Orange-Lime, '82 160
Punch, Orange-Mint, '82 121
Punch, Orange Sherbet Party, '83 142
Punch, Orange Soda, '87 214
Punch, Pineapple-Orange, '85 236
Punch, Refreshing Orange, '81 39
Refresher, Grapefruit-Orange, '82 174
Sangría, '81 67
Sangría, Easy Citrus, '80 218
Sangría, Orange, '81 237
Shake, Orange Milk, '84 166
Shake, Peachy Orange, '81 156
Shake, Strawberry-Orange Breakfast,
    '87 186
Shake, Tropical, '87 200
Slush, Banana-Orange, '80 48; '81 155
Slush, Orange, '82 49
Slush, Strawberry-Orange, '83 172
Slush, Vodka-Orange, '89 92
Smoothie, Mango-Orange, '86 216
Smoothie, Tropical, '81 50
Soda, Cranberry-Orange, '79 148
Sunshine Fizz, '92 44
Whiskey Sours, Frozen Orange-, '92 67
Breads
Anise-Orange Bread, '83 295
Apricot-Orange Bread, '92 285
Baba au Orange, '86 138
Biscuits, Orange, '88 85
Blueberry-Orange Bread, '87 140
Breakfast Ring, Orange, '81 229
Coffee Cake, Cranberry-Orange, '82 283
Coffee Cake, Nutty Orange, '95 160
Coffee Cake, Orange, '85 M88
Coffee Cake, Orange Butter, '89 229
Coffee Cake, Orange Marmalade Swirl,
    '81 107
Coffee Cake, Orange-Pecan, '86 86
Coffee Ring, Caramel-Orange, '80 45
Cranberry Bread, Orange-, '85 266
Cranberry-Orange Bread, '87 244
Cream Cheese Bread, Orange-, '82 210
French Toast, Orange, '83 292; '84 78;
    '86 329
French Toast with Orange Sauce, '82 47
Muffins, Banana-Orange, '84 148
Muffins, Orange, '79 236; '81 107;
    '83 54; '89 205
Muffins, Orange-Date, '92 119
Muffins, Orange-Ginger, '89 41
Muffins, Orange-Honey, '88 284
Muffins, Orange-Oatmeal, '85 202
Muffins, Orange-Pecan, '83 96
Muffins, Streusel-Topped Orange, '84 74
Muffins with Honey Spread, Orange
    Juice, '81 229
Nut Bread, Blueberry-Orange, '84 141
Nut Bread, Cranberry-Orange, '80 288
Nut Bread, Orange-, '82 75
Nut Loaf, Orange, '80 226
Pecan Bread, Glazed Orange-, '81 250

Pecan Bread, Orange-, '79 148
Pecan Loaves, Orange-, '79 215
Puffs, Upside-Down Orange, '83 57
Pumpkin Bread, Orange-, '87 300
Rolls, Easy Orange, '89 M131
Rolls, Frosted Hot Orange, '80 257
Rolls, Glazed Orange, '90 194
Rolls, Luscious Orange, '86 298
Rolls, Orange, '80 22; '82 17; '88 79
Rolls, Orange Butter, '82 206; '83 33
Rolls, Speedy Orange, '89 287
Rye Bread, Swedish Orange-, '85 111
Scones, Orange-Pecan, '94 215
Tea Bread, Orange, '79 234
Toast, Orange Praline, '79 36
Toast Topper, Orange, '79 36
Whole Wheat Orange Bread, '85 5
Broiled Orange Halves, '85 288
Butter, Honey-Orange, '79 36; '85 19
Butter, Orange, '81 8, 42; '90 323; '92 319;
    '94 115
Butter, Orange-Pecan, '84 75
Butter, Prune-Orange, '92 49
Butter, Tomato-Curry-Orange, '93 159
Candied Orange Peel, '81 286
Chutney, Cranberry-Orange, '79 292
Chutney, Orange-Cranberry, '86 266
Cream Cheese, Orange, '91 177
Cream, Orange, '90 126
Crêpes, Chocolate-Orange, '85 263
Desserts
Alaska, Orange, '83 177
Ambrosia, Pineapple-Orange,
    '88 252
Apples, Orange-Pecan Baked, '85 45
Apples with Cookie Crumbs, Orange
    Baked, '95 271
Apples with Orange Sauce, Baked,
    '84 314
Baked Orange Elegance, '80 13
Balls, Orange, '94 331
Bananas Foster, Orange-Glazed, '91 91
Bananas with Orange Sauce, Baked,
    '79 115
Bars, Pineapple-Orange, '82 129
Baskets, Orange, '81 308
Cake, Chocolate-Orange Pound, '89 94
Cake, Fresh Orange, '83 300
Cake, Fresh Orange Chiffon, '88 179
Cake, General Robert E. Lee Orange-
    Lemon, '88 92
Cake, Mandarin Orange, '83 24
Cake, Mandarin-Rum, '84 150
Cake, Orange, '86 61; '95 320
Cake, Orange Butter, '95 46
Cake, Orange Chiffon, '91 56
Cake, Orange-Coconut Angel Food,
    '94 294
Cake, Orange-Cranberry, '85 314
Cake, Orange-Date, '94 60
Cake, Orange Liqueur, '87 84
Cake, Orange Marmalade, '85 53
Cake, Orange Meringue, '86 336;
    '87 84
Cake, Orange Nut, '80 70
Cake, Orange-Nut Butter, '80 254
Cake, Orange-Pecan Crunch, '83 10
Cake, Orange-Pecan Pound, '93 13
Cake, Orange Pound, '87 84, 221;
    '92 69
Cake, Orange Rum, '79 2
Cake, Orange-Slice, '81 264
Cake, Orange Streusel, '88 10

Cake, Rum-Orange Coconut, '88 224
Cake, Sour Cream-Orange Pecan Pound,
    '89 207
Cake Squares, Apple-Orange, '84 150
Cake Squares, Orange, '81 34
Cake Squares, Orange-Pumpkin, '83 242
Cake, Williamsburg Orange, '81 120;
    '82 23
Candied Orange Zest, '95 320
Champagne Oranges, '93 83
Cheesecake, Orange, '81 84; '85 38
Chiffon Dessert, Orange, '93 295
Chocolate-Orange Delights, '93 52
Chocolate-Orange Roll, '87 21
Cookies, Carrot-Orange, '83 149
Cookies, Frosted Orange, '83 114
Cookies, Orange-Chocolate, '83 113
Cookies, Orange-Glazed Oatmeal, '80 60
Cookies, Orange-Pecan, '88 119
Cookies, Orange Refrigerator, '86 230
Cookies, Orange-Slice, '89 294
Cookies, Orange Sugar, '89 329
Cran-Orange Surprise, '94 143
Cream Dessert, Orange, '80 254;
    '84 165
Cream, Orange, '81 12
Cream, Orange Chantilly, '84 156
Cream, Orange-Coconut, '84 24
Cream, Orange-Mallow, '94 295
Cream, Orange Whipped, '88 83
Crème Brûlée, Orange, '95 323
Crème, Orange-Tapioca, '82 M283
Crêpes, Amaretto-and-Orange, '86 260
Crêpes, Orange Dream, '82 183
Crinkles, Orange, '95 272
Crispies, Orange, '84 205
Crisp, Orange-Apple, '80 295
Dip, Creamy Orange, '84 117
Éclairs, Miniature Orange, '95 92
Filling, Lemon-Orange, '81 71
Filling, Orange, '79 229; '86 336;
    '87 84; '88 224
Fingers, Orange, '87 57
Flambé, Dessert Orange, '85 313
Flan, Orange, '84 95
Frosted Oranges, '83 270
Frosting, Creamy Orange, '83 24, 241
Frosting, Orange, '81 7; '86 61; '88 119
Frosting, Orange Butter, '83 300
Frosting, Orange Buttercream, '80 70
Frosting, Orange Cream, '81 207; '82 14
Frosting, Orange-Cream Cheese, '81 70;
    '82 16; '92 19
Frosting, Orange-Lemon, '88 92
Frozen Orange Dessert, '92 44
Fruit Dessert Orange, '84 314
Fudge, Orange-Walnut, '92 288
Glazed Oranges and Pineapple, '86 318
Grand Marnier, Oranges, '92 82
Grand Marnier, Oranges in, '95 142
Granita, Orange, '88 118
Ice Cream, Orange-Pineapple, '86 117
Ice, Strawberry-Orange, '86 196
Ice, Tart Cranberry-Orange, '86 317
Juice, Strawberries with Brandied Orange,
    '82 160
Kiwi-and-Orange Dessert, '93 295
Meringues, Orange, '95 318
Molded Dessert, Orange, '83 302
Mousse, Chocolate-Orange, '81 16, 205
Mousse, Orange, '86 69; '94 198
Parfaits, Chilled Orange, '80 219
Parfaits, Orange Cream, '94 198

ORANGES, Desserts *(continued)*

Peanut Brittle, Orange, '80 302
Pears Flambé, Orange-Poached, '85 313
Pears in Orange Sauce, Poached, '82 19
Pears, Orange Poached, '80 218
Pie, Coconut-Orange Chess, '89 169
Pie, Florida Orange, '91 43
Pie, Frosty Orange, '90 296
Pie, Lemon-Orange, '85 172
Pie, Orange Ambrosia, '80 237
Pie, Orange Chess, '88 204
Pie, Orange Chiffon, '87 260
Pie, Orange-Coconut, '90 90
Pie, Orange-Coconut Cream, '94 208
Pie, Orange Meringue, '81 12, 309
Pie, Orange-Pecan, '79 282; '83 222
Pie, Sweet Potato-Orange, '88 207
Poached Oranges, Wine-, '84 M323
Pops, Hawaiian Orange-Pineapple, '94 143
Pops, Orange-Banana, '82 129
Pralines, Orange, '92 313; '93 51
Pudding, Mandarin-Almond, '85 M12
Pudding, Orange, '81 85; '82 111;
   '83 153
Pudding, Orange Custard, '88 174
Pumpkin-Orange Delight, '86 321
Rice Cream with Mandarin Oranges,
   '85 317
Roulage, Chocolate-Orange, '94 314
Sherbet Ambrosia Cups, '82 159
Sherbet, Banana-Orange, '83 162
Sherbet, Orange, '79 155
Sherbet with Blackberry Sauce, Orange,
   '94 232
Shortbread Madeleines, Orange, '88 242
Shortbread, Orange, '91 272
Shortcake, Fresh Orange, '80 100
Shortcake, Orange-Strawberry, '95 100
Slices, Burgundy-Spiced Orange, '93 294
Sorbet, Banana-Orange, '88 117
Sorbet, Fresh Orange, '92 143
Soufflé, Chilled Orange, '84 317;
   '86 189
Soufflé, Frozen Orange, '79 211
Soufflé, Grand Marnier, '79 281
Soufflé, Orange Dessert, '83 206
Special, Orange Blossom, '79 48
Squares, Orange-Crunch, '86 136
Squash Brûlée, Orange-, '94 267
Tapioca Fluff, Orange, '87 31
Tarts, Frozen Orange, '80 154
Tarts, Orange Curd, '92 193
Topping, Whipped Orange, '80 254
Truffles, Orange-Pecan, '95 92
Dip, Creamy Orange, '87 247
Dip, Orange Sour Cream, '79 208
Dip, Spicy Orange, '85 230
Doughnuts, Orange Spiced, '79 136
Dressings
Blossom Dressing, Orange, '82 266
Coconut Dressing, Orange-, '80 158
Cranberry-Orange Dressing, '91 287
Curd Dressing, Orange-, '93 22
Mandarin Dressing, '89 137
Marmalade-Fruit Dressing, '84 171
Orange Dressing, '81 141
Poppy Seed Dressing, Orange-, '87 187
Vinaigrette Dressing, Tangy Orange,
   '93 46
Vinaigrette, Honey-Orange, '91 255
Yogurt Dressing, Orange-, '85 304

Filling, Cheese-and-Orange, '93 159
Filling, Orange, '89 287
Filling, Orange-Cheese, '90 47
Fritters, Puffy Orange, '81 169
Granola, Sunny Orange, '84 212
Gravy, Orange, '81 259; '89 323
Grits, Orange, '81 47
Honey Yogurt, Orange Slices with, '91 68
Jelly, Pineapple-Orange Mint, '92 105
Main Dishes
Catfish Amandine, Mandarin, '84 183
Chicken à l'Orange, '84 277
Chicken à l'Orange, Stir-Fry, '83 82
Chicken Breasts with Orange Sauce,
   '79 77
Chicken Breasts with Parslied Rice,
   Orange, '87 242
Chicken, Crispy Mandarin, '86 119
Chicken Drummettes, Orange-Pecan,
   '93 158
Chicken, Grilled Ginger-Orange, '91 26
Chicken in Orange-Almond Sauce,
   '79 219; '80 13
Chicken in Orange Sauce, '83 8
Chicken in Orange Sauce, Skillet, '94 252
Chicken Livers in Orange Sauce, '82 218
Chicken, Orange, '83 278; '86 M140
Chicken, Orange-Avocado, '80 38
Chicken, Orange Barbecued, '88 123
Chicken Stir-Fry, Kyoto Orange-, '87 96
Chicken Stir-Fry, Orange-, '84 68
Chicken with Orange, Lime, and Ginger
   Sauce, '92 123
Chuck Roast, Orange Marinated, '85 179
Cornish Hens à l'Orange, '95 325
Cornish Hens, Orange-Glazed, '83 267
Cornish Hens, Orange-Glazed Grilled,
   '86 250
Cornish Hens, Orange-Glazed Stuffed,
   '84 M89
Cornish Hens with Cranberry-Orange
   Sauce, '86 119
Cornish Hens with Orange Glaze,
   '79 244
Duck, Chafing Dish Orange, '79 226
Duck with Orange Sauce, Grilled,
   '94 305
Fish à l'Orange, Fillet of, '89 180
Halibut with Orange-Curry Sauce, '87 91
Ham, Cranberry-Orange Glazed,
   '81 295
Ham, Orange-Glazed, '89 324
Lamb Chops, Orange, '83 35
Lobster Tails with Spiced Orange Sauce,
   '86 155
Porc à l'Orange, '80 242
Pork Chops, Orange, '84 81
Pork Chops, Orange-Cranberry, '86 335;
   '87 84
Pork Chops, Orange-Glazed, '81 234;
   '82 25; '83 39; '91 84
Pork Tenderloin with Orange Marmalade,
   '91 49
Scampi, Orange, '85 303
Snapper à l'Orange, Baked, '85 181
Snapper, Orangy, '88 23
Spareribs, Orange-Glazed, '84 296
Spareribs with Orange Barbecue Sauce,
   '83 11
Swordfish Steaks, Orange-Ginger
   Marinated, '93 271
Turkey Breast with Orange-Raspberry
   Glaze, '91 253

Turkey-Orange Skillet, Oriental, '86 284
Turkey Slices, Orange-, '90 53
Marmalade, Orange, '81 42
Marmalade, Orange-Pineapple, '82 150;
   '89 M156
Marmalade, Peach-Orange, '82 150
Noodles, Orange, '84 177
Nuts, Sherry-Orange, '86 M289
Pancakes, Orange-Yogurt, '87 225
Pears and Oranges, Spicy, '89 305
Pears, Marmalade Breakfast, '83 M203
Pears, Orange-Glazed, '79 247
Pecans, Orange, '84 299; '87 292
Popcorn, Orange, '86 230
Prunes, Orange-Spiced, '85 224
Relish, Cranberry-Orange, '81 M289; '88 254
Rice à l'Orange, '90 236
Rice, Orange, '79 43; '81 175; '82 200
Rice, Orange-Herb, '89 286
Salads
Ambrosia Supreme, Orange, '79 37
Aspic, Orange-and-Carrot, '86 199
Avocado-Orange Salad, '91 44
Beet Salad, Orange-and-, '88 43
Broccoli-Orange Salad, '94 281
Buttermilk Salad, Orange-, '95 134
Carrot Salad, Orange-, '80 89; '84 325
Carrot-Tangerine Salad, '83 316; '84 16
Cauliflower Salad, Orange-, '82 266
Cherry-Orange Salad, '79 74; '82 56
Chicken-and-Orange Salad, Curried,
   '87 144
Chicken Salad, Persian, '81 12
Congealed Salad, Pineapple-Orange,
   '83 218
Cottage Cheese Salad, Orange-, '79 44
Cranberry-Orange Delight, '90 168
Creamy Orange Salad, '84 124
Cup, Orange Fruit, '91 277
Cups, Citrus Salad in Orange, '85 47
Cups, Orange, '86 92
Cups, Orange Salad, '85 40
Frosted Orange Salad, '81 154; '83 123
Grapefruit-Orange Salad, '91 276
Grapefruit Salad, Orange-, '93 294
Honey-Berry Dressing, Orange Salad
   with, '89 250
Honey Dressing, Orange Salad with,
   '89 14
Jeweled Orange Salad, '83 210
Jicama-and-Orange Salad, '88 246
Jicama-Orange Salad, '86 83; '90 122
Lobster and Orange Salad, '82 207
Mandarin Chicken, Carousel, '79 88
Mandarin Ham-and-Rice Salad,
   '87 145
Mandarin Orange and Pineapple Salad,
   '82 266
Mandarin Orange-Lettuce Salad, '92 79
Mandarin Orange Salad, '81 252;
   '84 161
Mandarin Orange Salad, Congealed,
   '89 327
Mandarin Orange Tossed Salad, '92 303
Mandarin Pork-and-Spinach Salad,
   '88 M126
Mandarin Rice Salad, '88 271
Mandarin Salad, Broccoli-, '93 325
Mandarin Salad Molds, '85 54
Mandarin Spinach Salad, '85 163
Mandarin Tossed Salad, '89 12
Marinated Orange-Onion Salad, '91 231;
   '92 68

ORANGES, Salads *(continued)*

Minted Orange Salad, '92 105
Onion Salad, Orange-, '89 41
Pear Salad, Orange-, '84 164
Quick Orange Salad, '87 80
Red Cabbage Citrus Salad, '94 72
Romaine Salad, Orange-, '84 325;
  '87 239
Sesame-Citrus Green Salad, '86 33
Sherbet Salad, Orange, '81 154
Shrimp-and-Orange Rice Salad, Zesty,
  '87 155
Shrimp, Orange, and Olive Salad with
  Sherry Vinaigrette, '93 177
Shrimp Salad, Orange-, '84 197
Slaw, Cabbage-Orange, '79 135
Spinach-and-Orange Salad, '86 15
Spinach Salad, Orange-, '83 316;
  '84 16
Strawberry Salad with Orange-Curd
  Dressing, Orange-, '93 22
Sunshine Delight, '86 117
Surprise Salad, Orange, '79 12
Tropical Orange Salad, '92 97
Turkey-in-the-Orange Salad, '93 21
Walnut Salad, Orange, '80 246
Sauces and Glazes
  Butter Glaze, Orange, '90 194
  Caramel Sauce, Pears with Orange-,
    '95 281
  Chocolate-Orange Sauce, '86 165;
    '94 314
  Coconut-Orange Sauce, '85 189
  Dessert Sauce, Orange, '86 337;
    '87 58
  Fresh Orange Glaze, '88 179
  Fresh Orange Sauce, '85 209
  Hard Sauce, Orange, '88 225
  Honey-Orange Sauce, '85 108
  Liqueur Sauce, Orange, '86 142
  Mandarin Orange Sauce, '89 204
  Mandarin Sauce, '84 60
  Nutty Orange Glaze, '80 45
  Orange Glaze, '79 2; '80 257;
    '81 34, 107; '82 75, 206;
    '83 33, 114, 140, 267; '84 161;
    '86 298; '92 263; '95 320
  Orange Sauce, '82 47; '83 10, 277;
    '84 M286; '86 294
  Pineapple Glaze, Orange-, '81 60
  Pineapple-Orange Sauce, '84 14
  Raspberry-Orange Sauce, '88 22;
    '92 154
  Sweet Orange Sauce, '93 M325
  Syrup, Orange, '80 228; '89 254
Slices, Spicy Orange, '81 12
Snack Balls, Orange-Almond, '95 214
Soup, Carrot-Orange, '79 172
Special, Orange Blossom, '88 158
Spread, Orange Cheese, '87 292
Spread, Tropical Cheese, '95 46
Vegetables
  Asparagus with Orange Butter Sauce,
    '85 43
  Asparagus with Orange Sauce, '83 46
  Beets, Orange, '91 219
  Beets, Orange-Ginger, '80 137
  Beets, Orange-Glazed, '81 167; '85 289;
    '86 187
  Beets, Spicy Orange, '94 280
  Broccoli, Easy Orange, '85 267

Broccoli with Orange Sauce, '80 243
Brussels Sprouts, Orange, '84 34
Butternut-Orange Bake, '86 295
Carrots and Turnips, Sunset Orange,
  '94 213
Carrots in Orange Sauce, '82 107
Carrots, Orange-Fennel, '92 133
Carrots, Orange-Glazed, '79 12;
  '81 M165; '90 M98
Carrots, Orange-Raisin, '80 24
Carrots, Orange-Spiced, '88 18
Carrot Strips, Orangy, '89 312
Celery in Orange Sauce, '79 70
Green Peas in Orange Sauce, '88 97
Leeks in Orange Sauce, '88 86
Squash à l'Orange, '85 230
Sweet Potatoes, Coconut-Orange,
  '84 252
Sweet Potatoes in Orange Cups,
  '82 272
Sweet Potatoes, Orange, '86 279
Sweet Potatoes, Orange-Baked,
  '88 M294
Sweet Potatoes, Orange-Glazed, '81 223;
  '83 280
Sweet Potato-Orange Bake, '83 226
Sweet Potato-Stuffed Orange Cups,
  '81 223
Vinaigrette, Grilled Fennel and Radicchio with
  Orange, '95 253
Vinaigrette, Orange-Raspberry, '95 144
Vinegar, Orange, '95 31
Whip, Orange-Banana, '95 244
ORZO
Marinara on Beds of Spinach and Orzo,
  '93 320
Primavera, Orzo, '92 192
Salad, Artichokes with Orzo, '88 M193
Salad, Confetti Orzo, '92 173
Salad, Peppers Stuffed with Shrimp-and-Orzo,
  '91 203
Three-Grain Rice, '95 166
OYSTERS
Appetizers
  Annapolis, Oysters, '89 195
  Bacon, Oysters in, '83 211
  Baked Oysters Bienville, '90 27
  Barbecued Oysters, '82 247
  Bienville, Oysters, '93 257
  Casino, Oysters à la, '80 296
  Creamed Oysters, '92 254
  Dip, Smoked Oyster, '79 233
  Dressed Oysters on the Half Shell,
    '87 M79
  Mousse, Oyster, '81 245
  Mousse, Smoked Oyster, '84 320
  Spread, Smoked Oyster, '91 64
  Stuffed Oysters, Crabmeat, '94 328
Baked Oysters, Bacon-, '86 132
Baked Oysters Italiano, '89 97
Baked Oysters on the Half Shell, '93 269
Bake, Oyster-and-Corn, '83 34; '84 44
Bisque, Oyster, '83 252
Brochette, Oysters, '80 56
Casserole, Oyster-and-Spinach, '83 34;
  '84 44
Casserole, Oyster-and-Wild Rice, '83 34;
  '84 44
Chesapeake, Oysters, '92 254
Chowder, Oyster, '83 229
Chowder, Oyster-Corn, '83 211
Eggplant-and-Oyster Louisiane, '95 196
Fresh Oysters, Preparing, '82 127

Fried Oysters, '85 104
Fried Oysters, Delicious, '83 212
Fried Oysters, Southern, '88 111
Fried Raw Oysters, '81 135; '82 14
Fritters, Oyster, '79 31
Grilled Oysters Mornay, '89 195
Gumbo, Chicken and Oyster, '81 198
Gumbo, Duck, Oyster, and Sausage, '79 226
Gumbo, Seafood, '83 90; '87 210
Johnny Reb, Oysters, '82 42
Loaves, Spinach-Oyster, '84 213
Main Dishes
  Baked Oysters over Toast Points,
    '84 214
  Bienville, Oysters, '79 182
  Buccaneer, Oysters, '87 40
  Casserole, Oyster, '79 228
  Casserole, Wild Rice-Oyster, '86 256
  Cornbread, Oysters Casino on, '79 34
  Crabmeat, Creamy Oysters and,
    '83 211
  Creamed Oysters, Pan-Fried Grits with,
    '93 62
  Crêpes, Virginia, '79 264
  Dressing, Oyster, '79 250
  Dressing, Oyster Bread, '82 251
  Fried Oyster Bubbles, '80 296
  Fry, Hangtown, '80 297
  Gino, Oysters à la, '81 126
  Ham, Edwards' Oysters and, '86 253
  Landmark, Oyster, '84 88
  Loaf, Crusty Oyster, '92 254
  Mornay, Seafood, '83 67
  Omelets, Smoked Oyster, '84 96
  Pie, Turkey-and-Oyster, '82 267
  Rockefeller, Southern Oysters, '80 212
  Sandwich, Oyster Submarine, '80 92
  Sautéed Oysters, '86 132
  Sautéed Seafood Platter, '83 89
  Scalloped Oysters, '79 225; '84 213;
    '95 318
  Scalloped Oysters with Macaroni,
    '80 297
  Shrimp Sauce, Oysters in, '87 40
  Smoky Oysters Supreme, '87 60
  Stewed in Cream, Oysters, '93 50
  St. Jacques, Oysters, '80 103
  Stuffing, Roast Turkey with Oyster,
    '80 251
Nachos, Texas Oyster, '87 39
Patty Shells, Oysters in, '83 212; '85 257
Pie, Creole Oyster, '84 214
Poor Boys, Oyster-and-Bacon, '87 40
Scalloped Oysters, '79 225; '84 213; '86 132;
  '90 249; '95 318
Smoked Oysters, Deviled Eggs with, '84 161
Soup, Chicken, Ham, and Oyster, '79 198
Soup, Louisiana Oyster-and-Artichoke,
  '92 81
Soup, Oyster, '79 228; '83 211
Soup, Oyster-and-Mushroom, '87 39
Soup, Oyster-Cheese, '84 213
Soup, Oyster-Turnip, '94 328
Spinach Salad with Oysters and Red Wine
  Vinaigrette, '94 327
Stew, Company Oyster, '80 297
Stew, Golden Oyster, '86 132
Stew, Holiday Oyster, '85 264
Stew, Oyster, '80 221
Stew, Oyster-Broccoli, '89 242
Stew, Oyster-Sausage, '89 242
Stew, Potato-Oyster, '89 243
Wild Rice and Oysters, '92 339

Pancakes

Ambrosia Pancakes with Orange Syrup, '89 254
Apple-Filled Pancake, '86 96
Apple Pancakes with Cider Sauce, Spicy, '87 224
Applesauce Pancakes, '79 114
Apple-Topped Pancakes, '93 339
Apricot Delight, '81 42
Black Bean Pancakes with Gazpacho Butter, '92 86
Blueberry Buttermilk Pancakes, '79 114
Blueberry Pancakes, '85 152; '89 138
Blueberry Pancakes, Sour Cream, '81 164
Blue Cornmeal-Blueberry Pancakes, '94 115
Bran Pancakes with Cinnamon Syrup, '91 315
Buttermilk Griddle Cakes, '81 120; '82 22
Buttermilk Pancakes, '83 243; '84 101
Buttermilk Pancakes with Fruit Topping, '89 50
Cornmeal Batter Cakes, '87 16
Cornmeal Pancakes, Hearty, '88 129
Corn Pancakes, '93 43
Cottage Cheese Pancakes, '79 115
Dessert Pancakes, Luau, '88 154
Easy Pancakes, '92 203
Fluffy Pancakes, '86 137
Fruit Topping, Pancakes with, '81 42
Gingerbread Pancakes, '84 242; '95 282
Ginger Pancakes, Dessert, '88 153
Ham Griddle Cakes, '89 255
Honey Pancakes, '91 139
Island Pancakes, '87 225
Latkes, '90 254
Maple-Bacon Oven Pancake, '89 255
Mix, Quick Bread, '81 90
Oatmeal-Brown Sugar Pancakes, '88 203
Oatmeal Pancakes, '80 44; '89 107
Oat Pancakes, '89 227
Orange-Yogurt Pancakes, '87 225
Oven-Baked Pancake for Two, '89 227
Pancakes, '81 90
Potato Pancake, '85 20
Potato Pancakes, '79 115; '89 144
Potato Pancakes, Moist, '80 36
Pumpkin Pancakes, '80 228
Refrigerator Pancakes, Overnight, '93 196
Rice Pancakes, '85 147
Sauce, Cinnamon-Pecan-Honey Pancake, '88 46
Sauce, Peach-Blueberry Pancake, '82 177
Sausage Rollups, Pancake-, '83 246; '84 42
Sausage Wedges, Pancake-, '93 196
Sour Cream Pancakes, '79 213
Sour Cream Pancakes, Fluffy, '79 209
Sour Cream Pancakes with Fruit Topping, '90 142
Squash Pancakes, Granola-, '94 267
Strawberry Pancakes, '84 219
Supper Pancake, '86 242
Sweet Potato Pancakes, '87 280
Vegetable Pancakes, '88 297
Vegetable-Rice Pancakes, '93 43
Wheat Germ-Banana Pancakes, '79 114
Wheat Germ Pancakes, '86 242
Wheat Pancakes, Shredded, '84 59
Wheat Quick Pancakes, '85 278
Whole Grain Pancakes, '93 123
Whole Wheat-Oat Pancakes, '93 16
Whole Wheat Pancakes, '83 18
Zucchini Pancakes, '93 43

Parsnips

Candied Parsnips, '86 224
Glazed Parsnips, '91 220
Soufflé, Golden Parsnip, '83 266
Sugar-Crusted Parsnips, '88 229

Pastas. See also Couscous, Fettuccine, Linguine, Macaroni, Orzo, Spaghetti.

Angel Hair Pasta, Shrimp and Mushrooms with, '92 34
Angel Hair Pasta with Shrimp and Asparagus, '92 100
Angel Hair Pasta with Tomato Cream Sauce, '93 292
Antipasto, Pasta, '85 286
Asparagus, Tomatoes, and Shrimp, Garlicky Pasta with, '95 82
Bow Tie Pasta, Spinach and Mushrooms with, '95 341
Bow-Tie Pesto, '94 231
Bow-Tie with Marinara, '94 64
Broccoli Pasta, '84 176
Cannelloni, '85 60; '92 17
Casserole, Freezer Eggplant-Sausage-Pasta, '95 197
Catfish and Artichokes, Pasta with, '90 123
Cherry Tomatoes over Pasta, Herbed, '95 229
Chicken-and-Broccoli Pasta, '87 286
Chicken, Bird's-Nest, '88 152
Clam Sauce, Pasta with, '84 291
Collards and Sausage, Pasta with, '94 230
Dressing, Pasta Salad, '86 121
Frittata, Firecracker Pasta, '94 230
Garden-Fresh "Pasta," '94 M134
Garlic Pasta with Marinara Sauce, '92 78
Green Pasta with Shrimp-Mushroom Italienne, '79 170
Greens, Pasta with, '95 211
Late-Night Pasta Chez Frank, '95 228
Mamma Mia Pasta, '95 25
Mediterranean Pasta, '95 341
Minestrone, Dixie, '94 230
Mostaccioli Alfredo, '91 47
Oregano Pasta, '84 176
Peppery Pasta, '94 164
Pesto and Pasta, '92 98
Pie, Broccoli-and-Turkey Pasta, '88 269
Pimiento Pasta, '84 176
Potpourri, Pasta, '94 33
Primavera
    Almost Pasta Primavera, '86 38
    Chicken-Pasta Primavera, '91 72
    Creamy Pasta Primavera, '95 167
    Garden Spiral Primavera, '91 30
    Pasta Primavera, '85 86; '89 105; '93 168
    Tomato-Pasta Primavera, '86 209
    Turkey Pasta Primavera, Smoked, '90 84
Prosciutto, Party Pasta with, '94 176
Provençale, Pasta, '88 90
Ravioli, Homemade, '87 230

Ravioli, Mediterranean, '93 301
Ravioli Pasta, Homemade, '87 231
Ravioli, St. Louis Toasted, '95 117
Ravioli with Creamy Pesto Sauce, '92 79
Rotelle, Chicken and Tomato with, '87 108
Rotelle, Shrimp, '85 165
Rotini Romano, '87 193
Salads
    Acini di Pepe Salad, '83 163
    Artichoke-Pasta Salad, '94 180
    Bean-Pasta Salad, Marinated, '94 167
    Bean Salad, Pasta-, '86 169
    Broccoli-Cauliflower Pasta Salad, '88 269
    Chicken Pasta Salad, '88 89
    Chicken-Pasta Salad, Grilled, '94 64
    Chicken Salad, Tarragon Pasta-, '87 155
    Confetti-Pasta Salad, Easy, '92 220
    Crabmeat-Shrimp Pasta Salad, '86 208
    Crunchy Pasta Salad, '85 166
    Fruited Pasta Salad, '92 108
    Garden Pasta Salad, '86 188
    Ham-and-Pasta Salad, '90 128
    Ham-Dijon Pasta Salad, '92 191
    Ham, Pasta Salad with, '92 108
    Ham-Pecan-Blue Cheese Pasta Salad, '90 62
    Herbed Pasta-and-Tomato Salad, '92 144
    Italian Salad, '87 145
    Luncheon Pasta Salad, '90 191
    Main-Dish Pasta Salad, '82 199
    Oriental Pasta Salad, '90 63
    Overnight Pasta Salad, '82 276
    Pasta Salad, '84 139; '86 120; '87 36; '89 217; '90 62, 91
    Pistachio-Pasta Salad, '86 141
    Presto Pasta Salad, '90 63
    Ratatouille Pasta Salad, '90 74
    Ravioli Salad, Caesar, '95 183
    Rotelle Salad, Crunchy, '86 209
    Rotini Salad, '88 42
    Salmon-Pasta Salad, '87 9
    Salmon Salad Shells, '85 286
    Seafood Pasta Salad, '90 62
    Seashell Salad, '86 209
    Shell Salad, Tossed, '91 256
    Shrimp Salad, Pasta-and-, '83 163
    Southwestern Pasta Salad, '94 278
    Tortellini-Pesto Salad, '92 22
    Tortellini Salad, '89 237
    Tortellini Salad, Chicken, '87 288
    Tortellini Salad, Garden, '91 44
    Tuna-Pasta Salad, '91 43; '92 141
    Tuna Pasta Salad, '92 108
    Turkey 'n' Pasta Salad, Ranch-Style, '94 184
    Vegetable Pasta Salad, '89 256; '91 143
    Vegetable-Pasta Salad, '92 167
    Vegetable Salad, Pasta-, '95 238
    Vermicelli Salad, Shrimp, '88 139
    Vermicelli Vinaigrette Salad, '82 189
    Ziti-Cheddar Salad, '85 165
Scallops and Pasta, Fresh, '83 164
Shells
    Bake, Quick Crab, '87 192
    Bites, Pesto-Cheese Pasta, '87 251
    Casserole, Seashell-Provolone, '80 189
    Cavatini, '94 214
    Garden Pasta Medley, '89 256
    Jumbo Seashells Florentine, '79 6
    Peppers and Broccoli, Pasta with, '91 69
    Seafood and Pasta, '90 234
    Stuffed Shells, Cheesy Beef-, '83 217
    Stuffed Shells, Mexican, '91 87

PASTAS, Shells *(continued)*

Stuffed Shells, Southwestern, '93 234
Stuffed Shells, Spinach-, '85 60; '87 20
Stuffed with Five Cheeses, Pasta, '88 197
Tuna Pasta, Stuffed Tomato with, '88 54
Shrimp and Pasta, '91 207
Shrimp and Pasta, Herbed, '92 329
Shrimp Élégante, '83 48
Shrimp-Pasta Medley, '88 302
Shrimp Scampi, '95 209
Snappy Pasta, '83 164
Soup, Bean and Pasta, '94 220
Spinach-Mustard Twist, '86 209
Spinach Pesto-Pasta, '91 314
Straw and Hay Pasta, '80 211
Toasted Rice and Pasta, '95 57
Tomato-Basil Pasta, '94 204
Tomato-Garlic Pasta, '94 177
Tomato Pasta, Italian, '93 201
Tomato Pasta, Southwestern, '93 201
Tortellini. *See also* Pastas/Salads.
  Carbonara, Tortellini, '91 47
  Kabobs, Antipasto, '94 144
  Parsley-Caper Sauce, Tortellini with, '93 175
  Rosemary-Parmesan Sauce, Tortellini with, '92 284
  Shrimp and Tortellini, '92 34
  Soup with Tortellini, Italian Sausage, '88 46
  Spinach Tortellini with Tomato Sauce, '88 302
  Tomatoes, Quick Pasta and, '92 180
Toss, Pasta-Basil, '87 33
Tricolor Pasta with Clam Sauce, '93 272
Turkey-Basil Pasta, Creamy, '89 216
Vegetables and Pasta, Roasted, '93 184
Vegetable Sauce, Pasta with, '83 163
Vegetables, Pasta and, '89 255
Vegetables, Pasta and Garden, '87 192
Verde, Pasta, '84 201
Vermicelli
  Anchovy-Garlic Sauce over Vermicelli, '86 158
  Chicken and Pasta, Quick, '93 14
  Clam Sauce, Pasta with, '84 291
  Clam Sauce, Vermicelli with, '85 295
  Frittata, Pasta, '85 286
  Garden Pasta, '82 199
  Lemon Vermicelli, '84 329
  Mushroom Sauce Supreme on Vermicelli, '86 158
  Mushrooms, Vermicelli with, '79 195
  Pie, Spinach-Pasta, '85 286
  Platter, Cold Pasta, '88 42
  Red Clam Sauce, Vermicelli and Sprouts with, '86 143
  Salmon-Pesto Vermicelli, '92 200
  Scallop-Vegetable Vermicelli, '87 143
  Shrimp and Feta Cheese on Vermicelli, '87 108
  Soup with Quenelles, Veal-Vermicelli, '94 14
  Spinach Sauce, Vermicelli with Fresh, '89 256
  Tomato Pasta, Caribbean, '93 201
  Tomato Sauce, Vermicelli with, '83 164
Vinaigrette, Italian Pasta, '92 78
Ziti, Baked, '94 65
Ziti with Sausage and Broccoli, '95 340

PÂTÉS
Black-Eyed Pea Pâté, '91 12; '93 97
Braunschweiger Pâté, '83 251
Champignon, Pâté de, '93 171
Cheese Pâté, Four-, '89 284
Cheese Pâté, Layered, '86 105
Cheese Pâté, Sherry, '95 215
Chicken Liver Pâté, '79 153; '81 235; '83 108; '84 205; '88 M132
Chutney-Cheese Pâté, '84 152
Cognac, Pâté with, '86 159
Country Pâté, '86 66
Crab Pâté, '79 233
Cream Cheese Pâté, '80 154
Duck Liver Pâté, '79 227
Duck Pâté, '79 226
en Croûte, Pâté, '86 65
Ham Pâté, '85 279
Lentil Pâté, '92 285
Liver-Cheese Pâté, '85 276
Liver Pâté with Madeira Sauce, '93 323
Maison, Pâté, '84 222
Mock Pâté, '87 251
Mushroom Pâté, '89 157
Pastry, Pâté, '86 65
Pork Pâté with Spinach and Cream, '83 224
Shrimp Pâté with Dill Sauce, '85 39
Spread, Quick Pâté, '84 117
Turkey-Mushroom Pâté in Pastry, '92 327
Vegetable-Chicken Pâté, '86 66
Wine Pâté, '90 36

PEACHES
Alaska, Peachy Melba, '88 266
Ambrosia, Peach, '83 53
Baked Peaches, '92 179
Baked Peaches and Sausage, '82 50
Baked Peaches, Spicy, '86 39
Baked Peaches with Ginger, Oven-, '82 170
Bay Laurel Peaches, '90 124
Beverages
  Bellinis, '88 77
  Bellini Spritzers, '90 110
  Cooler, Peach, '85 198; '86 6
  Cream, Peaches 'n' Almond, '86 229
  Daiquiris, Peach, '90 322
  Frost, Peach, '89 155
  Frosty, Peach, '81 156; '83 318
  Fuzz Buzz, '82 160
  Petals, Peach, '90 104
  Pick-Me-Up, Peach, '89 183
  Refresher, Peach, '86 103
  Shake, Peach Melba Sundae, '93 134
  Shake, Peachy Orange, '81 156
  Shake, Pep, '79 38
  Smash, Peach, '88 161
  Smoothie, Strawberry-Peach, '89 182
Bombe with Raspberry Sauce, Creamy, '89 322
Brandied Peaches with Mincemeat, '81 47
Brandy Peaches, '85 275
Bread, Georgia Peach, '79 161
Bread, Peach, '82 170
Butter, Golden Peach, '91 178
Cake, Fresh Peach, '85 178
Cake, Peach-Almond Pound, '89 86
Cake, Peaches and Cream, '80 142
Cake, Peach Upside-Down, '87 8
Cake, Peachy Almond-Butter, '90 107
Cake, Peachy Picnic, '79 178
Caramel Peaches, '93 134
Cardinale, Peach, '89 155
Champagne, Peaches, '79 146
Charlotte, Peach, '79 68

Cheesecake, Peaches 'n' Cream, '88 137
Chicken Breasts, Peach-Stuffed, '79 177
Chicken Peach Dinner, '79 77
Chicken, Peachy, '90 212
Cobblers
  Blueberry Cobbler, Peachy, '80 143
  Blueberry-Peach Cobbler, No-Dough, '86 177
  Caramel Cobbler, Peach-, '86 300; '87 178
  Cranberry-Peach Cobbler, '92 322
  Crinkle, Peach, '91 20
  Crisp, Peach, '83 113; '92 13; '93 134
  Fresh Peach Cobbler, '82 139; '89 154
  Grenadine-Peach Cobbler, '85 178
  Lattice-Topped Peach Cobbler, '79 154
  Old-Fashioned Peach Cobbler, '82 170
  Peach Cobbler, '83 175; '84 178; '90 219; '95 264
  Praline Biscuits, Peach Cobbler with, '92 180
  Quick Peach Cobbler, '79 215; '81 142
  Spicy Peach Cobbler, '85 178
  Supreme, Peach Cobbler, '81 184; '90 313
Compote, Berry-Peach, '82 133
Compote, Peach-Berry, '89 112
Crabapple Peaches, Broiled Pork Chops with, '81 83
Cream, Bavarian Peach, '82 171
Cream Cheese, Peachy, '92 289
Cream, Honeyed Peaches 'n', '93 134
Cream, Peach Almond, '82 108
Cream, Peaches and, '95 196
Cream, Peachy-Apricot, '86 163
Crêpes, Fresh Peach, '84 186
Crêpes, Peach, '82 184
Crumble, Easy Peach, '83 116
Curried Ham and Peaches, '82 60
Custard Dessert, Fresh Peach, '86 162
Dessert, Layered Peach, '95 196
Dessert, Peach-Blueberry, '92 184
Dessert, Peachy Melt-Away, '87 298
Dessert, Quick Peach, '85 178
Dip, Creole Peach, '80 142
Dip, Peachy, '92 179
Dressing, Peach, '90 180
Dumplings, Peach, '80 143; '85 177
Filling, Peach, '89 154; '90 107
Flambé, Banana-Peach, '85 316
Flambé, Peach Sundaes, '81 88
Flip, Peach, '79 217
Fluff, Peach, '95 176
Foster, Peaches, '86 240
Freeze, Creamy Peach, '82 144
Frost, Peach, '84 164
Ginger Peaches with Rum, '84 M323
Gingersnap Peaches, '85 M329
Ham Roast, Peachy, '86 118
Honey-Lime Whip, Peaches with, '85 108
Ice Cream, Creamy Peach, '85 177
Ice Cream, Deluxe Peach, '80 176; '90 314
Ice Cream, Fresh Peach, '95 195
Ice Cream, Peach, '81 184; '82 171; '83 159; '86 15; '93 135
Ice Cream, Peach-Almond, '89 156
Ice, Peach, '81 178
Ice, Peach-Yogurt, '84 83
Ketchup, Peach, '95 306
Marinated Peaches, '91 91
Melba, Peach, '81 83; '83 M114
Meringues, Peach Melba, '87 76
Mold, Peachy Berry Cream, '83 130

PEACHES *(continued)*

Mousse, Peach, '85 54
Mousse, Peach Macaroon, '80 153
Muffins, Peachy-Almond, '86 301
Muffins, Special Peach, '84 74
Nest, Peaches in a Garden, '87 154
Parfait, Peach, '82 166
Pies
    Blackberry Pie, Peach-and-, '89 136
    Blueberry-Peach Pie, '94 158
    Chiffon Pie, Peach, '89 155
    Cranberry Pie, Peach-, '83 249
    Cream Pie, Peaches-and-, '81 184
    Filling, Fresh Peach Pie, '95 195
    Fresh Peach Pie, '82 170; '95 195
    Fried Peach Pies, '81 272
    Fried Pies, Delicious, '83 84
    Fried Pies, Easy Peach, '85 178
    Little Peach Pies, '86 303
    Luscious Peach Pie, '81 136
    Mincemeat-Peach Pie, '80 295; '81 188
    Praline Pie, Peach, '89 136
    Quick Peach Pie, '89 252
    Rhubarb-Peach Pie, '86 140
Pork Chops, Peachy, '89 310
Pork Steaks, Peachy, '79 166
Preservation
    Butter, Peach, '82 308
    Chutney, Peach, '84 179
    Conserve, Peach, '79 120
    Honey-Sweet Peaches, '85 107
    Jam, Cantaloupe-Peach, '95 143
    Jam, Freezer Peach, '83 182; '84 M182
    Jam, Peach, '93 135
    Jam, Peach-Plum Freezer, '85 130
    Jam, Rosy Peach-Banana, '80 142
    Marmalade, Peach-Orange, '82 150
    Mincemeat Peaches, '85 178
    Pears, Peaches and, '85 106
    Pickled Peaches, Perfect, '85 178
    Pickles, Peach, '85 177
    Preserves, Cream Cheese and Peach, '84 264
    Preserves, Honeyed Peach, '85 130
    Preserves, Old-Fashioned Peach, '82 150
    Preserves, Peach, '81 147; '89 140
    Relish, Peach, '85 136
    Salsa, Peach, '91 183
    Spiced Peaches, Brandy, '80 142
Pudding, Peachy Bread, '88 175
Puffs, Peach Sweet Potato, '87 280
Ring, Spicy Peach-Cranberry, '85 264
Salads
    Cream Salad, Peaches-and-, '83 108
    Easy Peach Salad Supreme, '79 177
    Fluff, Peach, '95 176
    Frosted Peach Salad, '82 145
    Frozen Peach Salad, '82 54
    Fruit Salad, Peachy, '89 206
    Georgia Peach Salad, '80 142
    Kiwi Salad, Peach-and-, '90 180
    Party Salad, Peach, '84 290
    Pickled Peach Salad, '80 104; '85 264
    Pinwheel Salad, Peach, '79 11
    Slaw, Party Peach, '86 250
    Spiced Peach Salad, '94 68
    Summer Salad, Georgia, '92 179
Sauces
    Berry Sauce, Peach-, '87 M165
    Blueberry Pancake Sauce, Peach-, '82 177

Blueberry Sauce, Peach-, '81 170
Creamy Peach Sauce, '85 189
Fresh Peach Sauce, '87 167
Fresh Peach Sauce, Creamy, '79 177
Peach Sauce, '84 144; '92 203
Praline Sauce, Peach-, '85 161
Salsa, Fresh Peach, '95 195
Strawberry-Peach Sauce, '92 154
Sherbet Cooler, Peachy, '91 187
Sherbet, Peach, '90 179
Shortcakes, Spicy Peach, '89 154
Sorbet, Peach, '93 153
Soup, Peach, '83 120, 180
Soup, Peach-Plum, '87 157
Spareribs, Peach-Glazed, '86 14
Spiced Peach Dessert, '83 9
Spiced Peaches, '91 72, 148
Spiced Peaches, Ginger, '86 15
Spiced Peaches with Nutty Dumplings, '87 164
Split, Peach, '85 277
Spread, Peachy Cream Cheese, '90 M215
Spread, Peachy-Raisin, '86 326
Strawberry Sauce, Peaches with, '85 8
Stuffed Peaches, Macaroon-, '79 178
Stuffed Peach Halves, '86 196
Sweet Potatoes and Peaches, '86 11
Tart, Kiwifruit-Peach, '88 20
Tart, Peach Cream, '90 173
Tarts, Peachy Keen, '91 118
Topping, Peach, '94 22
Topping, Raspberry-Peach, '87 126
Torte, Frozen Peach, '93 135
Trifle, Peach, '92 179
Vinegar, Peach-Mint, '95 190
Wine Sauce, Peaches in, '79 184
Yogurt, Frozen Fresh Peach, '90 139

PEANUT BUTTER
Apple, Piggy, '94 194
Bird's Nests, '95 102
Bites, Peanut Butter Elf, '91 275
Bread, Peanut Butter, '86 171; '88 64
Cake, Chocolate-Peanut Butter, '84 240
Cake, Fudgy Peanut Butter, '85 91
Cake, Peanut Butter, '79 51; '83 M233
Cake, Peanut Butter-and-Jelly, '85 34
Cake, Peanut Butter-Banana, '80 87
Cake, Peanut Butter Swirl, '86 109
Candies
    Balls, Chocolate-Peanut Butter, '80 87
    Balls, No-Cook Candy, '85 14
    Balls, Peanut Butter-Chocolate, '80 269
    Chocolate-Peanut Butter Bites, '92 M317
    Chocolate Peanutty Swirls, '94 M330
    Creams, Peanut Butter, '79 273
    Drops, Chocolate-Peanut Butter, '92 322
    Eggs, Peanut Butter Easter, '87 86
    Fudge Bites, Peanut-, '91 M231; '92 M68
    Fudge, Chocolate-Peanut Butter, '87 257; '90 311
    Fudge, Creamy Peanut Butter, '92 240
    Fudge, Diamond, '92 193
    Fudge, Double-Good, '79 M263; '95 M50
    Fudge, Double Peanut, '85 91
    Fudge, Four Chips, '92 318
    Fudge, Marbled Peanut Butter, '88 65
    Fudge, Peanut Butter, '80 302; '89 307; '95 51
    Peanut Butter Candy, '93 166

Pralines, Chocolate-Peanut Butter, '92 313; '93 51
Pralines, Peanut Butter, '92 313; '93 51
Squares, Peanut Butter-Chocolate Candy, '82 56
Tiger Butter, '86 48
Yummies, Peanut Butter, '83 223
Cheese Ball, Peanut Butter-, '86 136
Cheesecake, Peanut Butter, '94 142
Chicken, Peanut Butter-Marmalade, '81 282; '82 30
"Concrete," All Shook Up, '94 114
Cones, Chocolate-Peanut Butter, '85 14
Cookies
    Bars, Peanut Butter, '84 243; '93 166
    Bars, Peanut Butter-and-Fudge, '80 M172
    Bars, Peanut Butter-Jam, '94 291
    Bars, Peanut Butter 'n' Jelly, '83 305
    Brownies, Chocolate Chip-Peanut Butter, '84 73
    Brownies, Chocolate-Peanut Butter Chip, '91 306
    Brownies, Frosted Peanut Butter, '92 272
    Brownies, Peanut Butter, '87 199
    Chocolate Chip Cookies, Freezer Peanut Butter-, '86 230
    Chocolate Chunk Cookies, Peanut Butter and, '94 169
    Chocolate Kiss Cookies, Peanut Butter-, '86 49
    Chocolate-Peanut Butter Cookies, '85 90
    Choco-Peanut Chip Cookies, '92 318
    Choco Surprise Cookies, '80 60
    Cinnamon Cookies, Peanut Butter-, '84 30
    Coconut Cookies, Peanut Butter-, '83 113
    Crisp Peanuttiest Cookies, '88 65
    Crisps, Peanut Butter, '79 50
    Cups, Chocolate-Peanut Butter, '85 14
    Double Chip Cookies, '81 301
    Double-Chip Peanut Butter Cookies, '89 169
    Double Peanut Butter Cookies, '80 209
    Easter Basket and Eggs, '95 101
    Easy Peanut Butter Cookies, '92 272
    Logs, No-Bake Peanut Butter, '84 211
    Macaroons, Chewy Peanut Butter, '95 214
    Miracle Cookies, '83 149
    Monster Cookies, '84 36
    No-Bake Peanut Butter Cookies, '94 197
    Oatmeal Cookies, Peanut Butter-, '81 218; '84 72
    Oatmeal-Peanut Butter Chocolate Chip Cookies, '92 207
    Oatmeal-Peanut Butter Cookies, '85 171
    Peanut Blossom Cookies, '95 245
    Peanut Butter Cookies, '82 56; '87 58
    Quick Peanut Butter Cookies, '86 109
    Shortbread, Peanut Butter, '95 321
    Slice-and-Bakes, Peanut Butter, '82 M185
    Snaps, Peanut Butter, '81 237
    Spooky Eyes, '95 273
    Squares, Chocolate Chip-Peanut Butter, '84 118
    Squares, Peanut Butter, '83 116
    Temptations, Peanut Butter, '84 29
    Truffle Cookies, Peanut, '93 212

PEANUT BUTTER (continued)

Cooler, Peanut Butter, '84 115
Cupcakes, Chocolate Surprise, '85 91
Dessert, Crunchy Peanut-Buttery, '92 204
Dessert, Peanut Butter, '92 164
Dip, Peanut Butter, '86 135
Dip, Peanut Butter-Honey, '85 19
Dip, Peanut Butter Lovers', '93 162
Fingers, Peanut Butter, '79 256
French Toast, Peanut Butter, '93 166
Frosting, Chocolate-Peanut Butter, '84 240;
    '87 222
Frosting, Creamy Peanut, '80 87
Frosting, Peanut Butter, '83 223; '84 153;
    '85 34
Frosting, Peanut Butter-Fudge, '87 184
Frosting, Peanut Butter Swirl, '86 109
Frosts, Peanut Butter, '84 153
Frozen Peanut Butter Delight, '88 137
Granola, Peanut Butter, '82 296
Ice Cream, Chocolate Chunk-Peanut Butter,
    '85 297; '86 120
Ice Cream, Peanut Butter, '81 103;
    '88 64, 203
Ice Cream Sandwiches, Peanut Butter Cookie,
    '93 199
Milkshakes, Peanut Butter, '85 198
Monster Mouths, '95 274
Muffins, Peanut Butter, '80 86; '87 158
Muffins, Peanut Butter-Chocolate Chip,
    '94 167
Muffins, Peanut Butter-Honey, '82 56
Napoleons, Peanut Butter-and-Chocolate,
    '94 121
Parfait, Bodacious Peanut, '95 167
Parfaits, Crunchy Peanut Butter, '79 176;
    '80 6
Pie, Chocolate-Peanut Butter, '85 91
Pie, Chocolate-Peanut Butter Swirl, '87 262
Pie, Fluffy Peanut Butter, '94 246
Pie, Peanut Butter, '85 275; '86 109;
    '89 252
Pie, Peanut Butter Cream, '79 50; '88 65
Pie, Peanut Butter Meringue, '84 30
Pie, Tin Roof, '85 91
Pie, "Working for Peanuts," '93 115
Pinecones, Peanut Butter-Suet, '93 286
Pizza, Peanut Butter-Fruit, '94 60
Pudding, Peanut Butter, '85 95; '88 32
Pudding, Peanut Butter-Banana, '93 340
Sandwiches, Peanut Butter-and-Jelly "Fish,"
    '91 177
Sandwiches, Peanut-Cheese-Raisin, '88 140
Sandwiches, Spider, '93 193
Sandwich, Peanut Butter Breakfast, '82 55
Sauce, Chocolate-Peanut Butter,
    '79 91, M156
Sauce, Pasta with Peanut, '95 252
Sauce, Peanut Butter Barbecue, '81 233
Sauce, Peanut Butter Ice Cream, '84 30
Shake, PBJ, '93 292
Shake, Peanut Butter, '82 48
Snacks, Chocolate-Peanut Butter, '90 226
Soup, Cream of Peanut, '92 193; '93 288
Soup, Cream of Peanut Butter, '84 29
Soup, Creamy Peanut, '79 50
Soup, Peanut Butter, '89 28
Spread, Peanut Butter, '92 21
Tarts, Chocolate-Peanut Butter, '92 277
Waffles, Honey-Buttered Peanut Butter,
    '94 M206

PEANUTS

Apples, Caramel-Peanut, '93 M244
Apples, Peanutty Stuffed, '85 25
Balls, Peanut-Date, '81 92
Bananas, Nutty, '79 251
Bars, Chewy Peanut, '80 M172
Bars, Fruit and Nut Granola, '81 49
Bars, Peanut, '89 307
Beef Stir-Fry, Peanutty, '95 157
Bread, Peanut, '87 184
Bread, Peanut Lover's, '93 211
Cake, Chocolate-Caramel-Nut, '83 23
Cake, Chocolate-Peanut Cluster, '87 184
Cakes, Nutty, '89 50
Cake, Super Peanutty Layer, '83 222
Candied Popcorn and Peanuts, '82 295
Candies
    Brittle, Golden Peanut, '83 223
    Brittle, Never-Fail Peanut, '79 273
    Brittle, Orange Peanut, '80 302
    Brittle, Peanut, '79 M263; '80 87;
        '84 298; '92 240
    Brittle with Crushed Peanuts, '87 184
    Chili Nuts, Hot, '81 254
    Chocolate Nut Teasers, '91 35
    Chocolate-Peanut Crispies, '93 80
    Clusters, Chocolate-Peanut, '81 16
    Clusters, Nut, '81 254
    Clusters, Peanut, '87 184; '92 288
    Clusters, Peanutty, '83 143
    Divinity, Peanut, '85 233; '87 M278
    Filling, Nut, '91 35
    Fudge, Double Peanut, '85 91
    Squares, Caramel-Peanut, '85 247
Chesapeake Nuts, '93 269
Chicken, Ginger-Nut, '90 M33
Chicken with Peanuts, Oriental, '82 236
Cookies, Chocolate-Peanut, '83 223
Cookies, Crisp Peanuttiest, '88 65
Cookies, Fibber McGee, '95 72
Cookies, Oats-and-Peanut, '89 60
Cookies, Peanutty Oatmeal, '80 106; '83 95
Cookies, Salted Peanut, '87 92
Crunchy Munchies, '94 196
Crust, Peanut-Graham Cracker, '79 50
Crust, Sweet Potatoes with Peanut, '93 212
Dessert, Fudge-Peanut Ice Cream, '88 167
Dessert, Peanut-Chocolate, '80 86
Dressing, Peanut-Ginger, '95 177
Dressing, Roast Turkey with Peanut, '79 283
Filling, Peanut, '93 211
Frosting, Creamy Peanut, '80 87
Fruit Dressing, Nutty, '88 68
Granola, Crunchy Peanut, '90 48
Ice Cream, Chocolate-Covered Peanut,
    '88 203
Ice Cream, Peanut, '92 132
Mix, Nutty Snack, '92 22
Muffins, Peanut, '91 223
Pesto and Pasta, Spinach-Peanut, '93 212
Pie, Caramel-Nut Crunch, '94 244
Pie, Caramel-Peanut, '86 259
Pie, Peanut Raisin, '79 85
Pie, Peanutty Ice Cream, '82 56
Pie, "Working for Peanuts," '93 115
Puff Nibbles, '84 191
Salad, Broccoli-Peanut, '92 35
Salad, Green Bean-Peanut, '86 117
Salad, Nutty Cabbage, '87 42
Salad, Nutty Green, '87 168
Salad, Peanut-Apple, '80 5
Sauce, Hot Indonesian Peanut, '93 211
Sauce, Peanut Dessert, '86 M251

Sauce, Peanut Hot, '86 305
Sauce, Pork Chops with Peanut, '83 29
Sauce, Shrimp with Peanut, '93 303
Slaw, Banana-Nut, '86 250
Slaw, Chinese Peanut, '93 212
Slaw, Nutty Cabbage, '88 218
Slaw, Peanut, '85 139
Slaw, Peanutty-Pear, '86 250
Snack, Toasted Cereal, '85 215
Soup, Chilled Peanut, '79 130
Soup, Creamy Peanut, '79 50
Soup, Peanut, '87 184
Spiced Nuts, '91 M316
Spicy Nuts, '82 161
Sugared Peanuts, '82 249

PEARS

Amaretto Pears with Meringue, '90 M58
Baked Pears à la Mode, '95 129
Baked Pears Elegant, '91 48
Baked Pears, Honey-, '93 47
Belle Helene, Pears, '86 164
Bread, Pear, '80 218
Cake, Pear Preserve, '85 52
Cake, Upside-Down Sunburst, '87 9
Cake with Caramel Drizzle, Pear, '86 247
Cheesecake, Pear-Berry, '82 141
Cheesecake, Pear-Glazed, '79 67
Cobbler, Best Ever Pear, '82 194
Coconut Pears, Spicy, '83 207
Cookies, Pear Mincemeat, '84 264
Cream, Pears in Orange, '84 245
Crème Chantilly, Holiday Pears with, '91 297
Crème de Menthe Pears, '94 50
Crisp, Cranberry-Pear, '83 207
Crisp, Raspberry-Pear, '89 109
Crumble, Pear, '85 221
Dressing, Pear, '83 146
en Croûte, Pears, '93 210
Flaming Pears, '84 313
Fritters, Ol' Timey Pear, '86 51
Gingered Pears, '89 M231
Gratin, Pear-Blue Cheese, '93 328
Meringues, Baked Pear, '85 232
Muffins, Pear-Ginger, '91 240
Muscadine Sauce, Pears in, '88 216
Orange-Caramel Sauce, Pears with, '95 281
Pies
    Apple-Pear Pie, '83 249
    Apple Pie, Natural Pear-, '88 226
    Backyard Pear Pie, '93 237
    Crumble Pie, Pear, '83 207
    Deep-Dish Pear Pie, '80 219
    Delicious Pear Pie, '88 226
    Double-Crust Pear Pie, '82 194
    French Pear Pie, '87 213
    Ginger-Pear Pie, '93 48
    Macadamia Pie, Pear-, '93 260
    Mincemeat Pie, Pear, '84 264; '88 226
    Mince Pie, Pear-, '81 271
    Rhubarb-Raspberry Pear Pie, '95 119
    Streusel Pie, Pear, '83 234; '84 244
    Tennessee Pear Pie, '85 230
Poached
    Belle Helene, Pears, '86 164
    Custard, Poached Pears in, '88 20
    Dark Chocolate Sauce, Poached Pears
        with, '90 M141
    Honey-Yogurt Sauce, Poached Pears
        with, '92 306
    Lemon Poached Pears, '82 74
    Orange Poached Pears, '80 218
    Orange-Poached Pears Flambé, '85 313
    Orange Sauce, Poached Pears in, '82 19

PEARS, Poached (continued)

Raspberry-Orange Sauce, Poached Pear Fans with, '88 22
Raspberry Sauce, Poached Pears with, '84 213; '87 69; '88 223
Red Wine, Pears in, '82 254
Red Wine, Pears Poached in, '83 302
Vanilla Poached Pears, '90 57
Wine, Poached Pears in, '82 194
Wine-Poached Pears with Berry Sauce, '86 144
Preservation
Butter, Pear, '85 130
Butter, Spiced Pear, '80 218
Chutney, Pear, '95 251
Chutney, Pear-Apple, '89 141
Honey, Pear, '90 159
Jam, Paradise Pear, '84 300
Marmalade, Pear, '79 196
Mincemeat, Pear, '79 196; '84 264; '88 226
Peaches and Pears, '85 106
Pickles, Mustard Pear, '79 196
Preserves, Pear, '82 195
Relish, Aunt Glennie's Pear, '95 305
Relish, Pear, '79 196
Relish, Peppery Pear, '89 141
Puree, Grapefruit with Pear-Berry, '89 213
Relish, Cranberry-Pear, '85 232
Salads
Blue Cheese-Pear-Apple Salad, '81 224
Celery Salad, Pear-and-, '87 56
Crunchy Pear Salad, '83 234; '84 244
Festive Fruit Salad, '80 16
Golden Pear Salad, '91 58
Lime Salad, Pear-, '84 152
Orange-Pear Salad, '84 164
Pineapple-Pear Delight, '82 54
Royal Pear Salad, '84 265
Sautéed Apples, Onions, and Pears over Spinach, '94 212
Slaw, Peanutty-Pear, '86 250
Slaw, "Think Pink," '94 247
Spinach Salad, Festive Pear-and-, '85 131
Spinach Salad with Sautéed Pears, '94 237
Swiss Cheese Salad, Pear-, '91 237
Sauce, Pear, '92 164
Shake, Strawberry-Pear, '92 139
Side Dishes
Baked Pears, Honey-, '93 47
Bake, Pear-Oatmeal, '89 208
Blue Cheese Sauce, Brunch Pears with, '90 142
Breakfast Pears, Marmalade, '83 M203
Breakfast Treat, Pear, '87 72
Casserole, Pear-Sweet Potato, '86 280
Crème de Menthe Pears, '94 50
Filled Pears, Cheese-, '81 268
Glazed Pears, Orange-, '79 247
Oranges, Spicy Pears and, '89 305
Pineapple-Honey Pears, '86 94
Plate, Pretty Pear, '89 225
Ruby Pears, '81 288
Soda Pop Pears, '95 55
Spiced Fall Pears, '89 M231
Spiced Pears, '89 305
Sugared Pears, Maple-, '81 232
Wine, Pears in Red, '82 254
Sorbet, Pear-Lemon, '88 116
Soup, Pumpkin-Pear, '92 234

Spread, Pear-Cream Cheese, '93 80
Stuffed Pears, Almond-, '83 207
Stuffed with Cheese, Pears, '82 290
Sundaes, Quick Pear, '86 71
Tart, Pear, '82 304; '92 72
Tart with White Caramel Sauce, Pear, '92 195
Whip, Pear, '89 94
Wild Rice, Cranberry-Pear, '83 279
PEAS
Baked Peas, Chinese-Style, '86 305
Black-Eyed
Best Ever Plain Ole Peas, '88 2
Black-Eyed Peas, '93 180
Cajun Peas, '88 3
Casserole, Reunion Pea, '87 11
Caviar, Texas, '86 218
Chinese Peas, '88 3
Creole Black-Eyed Peas, '86 252
Creole Black-Eyes and Rice, '85 6
Delight, Tomato-Pea, '84 196
Dinner, Black-Eyed Pea Skillet, '86 6
Dip, Black-Eyed Pea, '81 8
Dip, Chili-and-Black-Eyed Pea, '92 155
Flips, Pea, '80 7
Fresh Black-Eyed Peas, '81 M165
Gravy, Black-Eyed Pea, '87 12
Ham Hocks, Black-Eyed Peas with, '79 122; '89 16
Hearty Black-Eyed Peas, '85 7
Hopping Good Peas, '80 7
Hopping John, '80 7; '90 12
Hopping John, Skillet, '79 10
Hopping John with Grilled Pork Medaillons, '93 229
Hopping John with Ham, '81 7
Hummus, Black-Eyed Pea, '94 123
Jalapeño Black-Eyed Peas, '88 166
Jambalaya, Black-Eyed Pea, '92 70
Jambalaya, Good Luck, '87 11
Marinated Black-Eyed Peas, '82 156; '88 101
Mexican Black-Eyed Peas, '84 327
Mexicano, Black-Eyed Peas, '79 10
Mexi-Peas, '88 3
Passion Peas, '89 17
Pâté, Black-Eyed Pea, '91 12; '93 97
Pickled Black-Eyed Peas, '79 10
Pinwheels, Black-Eyed Pea, '85 300; '86 18
Potatoes, Black-Eyed Pea-Spinach-Stuffed, '95 22
Relish, Zesty Black-Eyed Pea, '95 56
Rice, Black-Eyed Peas with, '83 12; '90 208; '91 13
Rice with Black-Eyed Peas, '93 66
Salsa, Black-Eyed Pea, '93 164
Sausage, Black-Eyed Peas with, '86 7
Seasoned Black-Eyed Peas, '85 138
Soup, Beefy Black-Eyed, '85 6
Southern-Style Black-Eyed Peas, '82 107
South-of-the-Border Black-Eyed Peas, '86 7
Spaghetti, Black-Eyed Pea, '81 7
Special, Black-Eyed Pea, '86 7
Spicy Black-Eyed Peas, '92 23
Spicy Black-Eyed Peas, Hot-and-, '84 9
Spicy Hot Black-Eyed Peas, '81 8
Spicy-Hot Black-Eyed Peas, '90 135
Spread, Black-Eyed Pea, '86 77
Stew, Ham-and-Black-Eyed Pea, '93 20
Sweet-and-Sour Black-Eyed Peas, '85 290
Sweet-and-Sour Peas, '88 3

Tasty Black-Eyed Peas, '89 68
Vinaigrette, Black-Eyed Pea, '86 7
Casserole, Curry Pea, '87 154
English
Baked Tuna and Peas in Wine Sauce, '83 196
Braised Belgian Endive and Peas, '93 22
Braised Rice and Peas, '79 101
Broil, Tomato-English Pea, '83 192
Buttered Peas and Mushrooms, '82 204
Buttered Peas with Onions, '80 242
Carrots and Peas, Mint-Glazed, '90 291
Casserole, Asparagus-and-English Pea, '86 324
Casserole, Asparagus and Peas, '80 152
Casserole, Asparagus-Pea, '88 M294
Casserole, Cauliflower-Pea, '85 260
Casserole, Cheesy English Pea, '83 216
Casserole, English Pea-Pimiento, '83 207
Casserole, Quick Fresh English Pea, '84 145
Casserole Supreme, Pea, '82 281; '83 32
Cauliflower and Peas with Curried Almonds, '79 221; '80 82
Cauliflower, Peas and, '82 288
Celery, Deluxe Peas and, '81 267
Celery, Peas and, '93 289
Company Green Peas, '91 31
Continental, Peas, '84 254
Country-Style Peas, '80 101
Country Style, Peas, '81 101
Creamed Peas and New Potatoes, '79 102
Creole Peas, Quick, '84 123
Curried Peas with Almonds, '88 M294
Deluxe English Peas, '84 68
Deviled Peas in Toast Cups, '86 280
Dumplings, Green Peas and, '80 102
Glazed English Peas, '83 111
Italian Peas, '81 83
Lettuce Peas, French, '86 62
Medley, English Pea, '85 236
Medley, Spring Pea, '83 141
Minted Peas, '83 141; '87 56
Mushrooms, Creamy Peas with, '84 196
Mushrooms, Green Peas with, '80 101
Mushrooms, Peas and, '83 141
Onions Stuffed with Peas, '84 68
Orange Sauce, Green Peas in, '88 97
Party Peas, '79 102
Perfection, Peas to, '94 321
Pignoli, Peas, '83 190
Potato Nest, Peas in a, '84 M239
Rice, Holiday Peas and, '86 328
Rice, Peas and, '88 97
Rice with Green Peas, '87 45
Sauce, Green Pea, '83 22
Sautéed Peas and Bacon, '89 331
Scallions, Peas and, '80 101
Sherry, Peas with, '80 102
Soup, Chilled Pea, '84 181
Soup, Cold Curried Pea, '91 120
Soup Élégante, Pea, '79 53
Soup, Fresh Pea, '86 181
Soup, Peppery Pea, '82 271
Soup, Potato-Pea, '94 90
Soup, Spring Pea, '88 M96
Special Peas, '88 97; '95 133
Ham, Southern Peas and, '85 138
Medley, Peas-and-Corn, '85 138
Pasta, Peas and, '93 139
Pigeon Peas, Rice with, '92 157

PEAS (continued)

Salads
    Asparagus Salad, Peas-and-, '83 141
    Black-Eyed Pea Salad, '80 112; '86 225;
        '88 92, 221; '90 173; '95 203
    Black-Eyed Pea Salad, Fearrington House
        Goat Cheese and, '95 60
    Black-Eyed Pea Salad, Marinated,
        '93 190
    Black-Eyed Pea Salad, Overnight,
        '81 280
    Black-Eyed Peas, Zesty, '89 147
    Black-Eyed Salad, Hot Bacon and, '85 7
    Cauliflower and Pea Salad, Savory,
        '81 280
    Cauliflower-Pea Salad, '87 231
    Cheddar-Pea Salad, '84 82
    Chicken-Pea Salad, '83 218
    Chilled Dilly Peas, '90 143
    Corn-and-Pea Salad, '90 181
    Creamy Pea Salad, '80 111
    Crunchy Pea Salad, '90 143
    English Pea-and-Apple Salad, '87 24
    English Pea Salad, '81 280; '90 143
    English Pea Salad, Cauliflower-, '95 66
    English Pea Salad, Lettuce-, '91 208
    English Pea Salad, Marinated, '82 54
    Marinated Pea Salad, '81 204
    Mexi-Pea Salad, '81 7
    Minted Pea Salad, '91 119
    Plentiful P's Salad, '87 12
    Rice-Pea Salad, '85 163
    Special Peas, '95 133
    Special Pea Salad, '83 239
    Sugar Snap Pea Salad, '86 115
    Three Pea Salad, '84 290
Snow
    Basil Snow Peas and Tomatoes, '88 M185
    Beef and Snow Peas, Oriental, '79 105
    Beef with Pea Pods, Oriental, '86 M328
    Cashew Pea Pods, '92 343
    Chicken with Snow Peas, '83 137
    Chinese Peas, Easy, '83 206
    Crunchy Snow Peas and Dip, '86 62
    en Papillote, Fish with Snow Peas,
        '86 144
    Medley, Cauliflower-Snow Pea, '87 305
    Peas and Snow Peas, '88 67
    Peppers, Minted Peas and, '90 M99
    Pineapple, Snow Peas and, '91 120
    Piquant, Snow Peas, '79 21
    Red Pepper, Snow Peas with, '90 102
    Sesame Snow Peas and Red Pepper,
        '84 175
    Shrimp Combo, Snow Pea-, '79 57
    Shrimp with Snow Peas, '85 75
    Skillet Snow Peas with Celery, '84 123
    Stir-Fried Peas and Peppers, '87 51
    Stir-Fry, Beef and Pea, '82 98
    Stir-Fry Beef and Pea Pods, '80 19
    Stir-Fry, Beef and Snow Pea, '82 98
    Stir-Fry Beef and Snow Peas, '83 22
    Stir-Fry, Chicken and Snow Pea, '95 157
    Stir-Fry, Potato-Snow Pea, '86 173
    Stuffed Snow Peas, '84 80
    Stuffed Snow Peas, Crab-, '85 288
    Tomatoes, Snow Peas and, '83 111
Soup, Country-Style Pea, '86 267
Soup, Cream Pea, '90 211
Soup, French Market, '94 317
Soup Mix, French Market, '94 317

Soup, Pea-and-Watercress, '93 162
Soup, Split Pea, '88 235; '89 17; '90 198;
    '94 322
Soup, Split Pea and Frankfurter, '79 64
Sugar Snap
    Appetizers, Sugar Snap Pea, '86 115
    Basil and Lemon, Sugar Snap Peas with,
        '93 66
    Creamed Sugar Snaps and Carrots,
        '93 139
    Dip, Sugar Peas with, '86 170
    Dip, Sugar Snap, '88 91
    Pearl Onions, Snap Peas and, '89 280
    Peppers, Sugar Snaps and, '93 139
    Potato Salad with Sugar Snap Peas,
        '91 120
    Vegetable Medley, Spring, '86 115

PECANS. *See also* **PRALINE.**
Acorn Squash with Molasses and Pecans,
    '85 205
Appetizers
    Ball, Date-Nut, '92 326
    Ball, Deviled Pecan, '80 258
    Ball, Party Pecan Cheese, '81 235
    Ball, Pecan Cheese, '83 127
    Balls, Date-Nut, '85 10
    Ball, Tuna-Pecan, '87 94
    Barbecued Pecans, '83 222
    Bites, Cheesy Pecan, '82 248
    Brie, Kahlúa-Pecan, '92 289
    Brown Sugar Pecans, '81 266
    Candied Nuts, '81 261
    Chesapeake Nuts, '93 269
    Chicken Fingers, Buttermilk-Pecan,
        '93 165
    Christmas Eve Pecans, '91 276
    Coffee 'n' Spice Pecans, '88 256
    Curried Nuts, Spicy, '82 250
    Curried Pecans, '91 208
    Deviled Nuts, '93 118
    Glazed Pecans, '81 254; '82 136
    Grapes, Blue Cheese-Pecan, '95 48
    Honeycomb Pecans, '84 300
    Hot-and-Spicy Pecans, '89 161
    Hot Pepper Pecans, '85 4
    Log, Chicken-Pecan, '81 290
    Log, Roquefort Pecan, '89 247
    Log, Toasted Pecan Cheese, '86 M288
    Mushrooms, Pecan-Stuffed, '84 261
    Nippy Nuts, '93 301
    Orange Nuts, Sherry-, '86 M289
    Orange Pecans, '84 299; '87 292
    Pepper Pecans, '87 137; '93 79
    Pesto-Spiced Nuts, '95 173
    Popcorn Balls, Nutty, '88 227
    Salted Pecans, Southern, '80 285
    Savory Southern Pecans, '95 240
    Spiced Nuts, '91 M316
    Spiced Pecans, '79 296; '80 31;
        '81 286
    Spicy Pecans, '81 M289; '93 279
    Spread, Nutty Carrot, '94 123
    Sugar and Spice Pecans, '82 297
    Sugar-and-Spice Pecans, '86 121;
        '94 272
    Sweet-and-Spicy Pecans, '92 321
    Tarts, Toasty Southern Pecan, '95 329
    Toasted Chili Pecans, '85 154
    Toasted Pecans, '84 321; '86 229
    Toasted Pecans, Buttery, '88 77
    Wafers, Pecan-Cheese, '81 119
    Wafers, Sage-Pecan Cheese, '93 12
Apples, Orange-Pecan Baked, '85 45

Breads
    Apple-Nut Bread, '85 281
    Applesauce Nut Bread, '81 305
    Applesauce-Pecan Bread, '90 66
    Apricot-Nut Loaf, Tasty, '82 10
    Banana-Nut Bread, '86 8, 70
    Banana-Nut-Raisin Bread, '81 59
    Biscuits, Nutty Tea, '89 210
    Bourbon-Pecan Bread, '93 308
    Buns, Nutty, '86 290
    Cheddar-Nut Bread, '85 41
    Cherry Nut Bread, '81 306; '82 36
    Cherry-Nut Bread, Quick, '85 55
    Chocolate Date-Nut Bread, '81 284
    Coconut-Pecan Coils, '90 196
    Cornbread, Pecan, '94 169
    Date-Nut Loaf, '85 10
    Kahlúa Fruit-Nut Bread, '79 235
    Lemon-Pecan Bread, '83 54
    Maple-Nut Coffee Twist, '86 290
    Maraschino Cherry Nut Bread, '79 234
    Muffins, Banana-Nut, '93 140
    Muffins, Cherry-Nut, '90 87
    Muffins, Chunky Pecan, '88 9
    Muffins, Cinnamon-Nut, '85 M88
    Muffins, Cinnamon-Pecan, '84 219
    Muffins, Country Pecan, '83 222
    Muffins, Cranberry-Pecan, '84 269
    Muffins, Nutty Pumpkin, '86 291
    Muffins, Orange-Pecan, '83 96
    Muffins, Pecan, '80 16
    Muffins, Raisin-Nut, '92 46
    Muffins, Raisin-Pecan Ginger, '88 9
    Muffins, Rum-Nut, '90 87
    Orange-Nut Bread, '82 75
    Orange Nut Loaf, '80 226
    Orange-Pecan Bread, '79 148
    Orange-Pecan Bread, Glazed, '81 250
    Orange-Pecan Loaves, '79 215
    Persimmon Date-Nut Bread, '82 218
    Pineapple-Nut Bread, '79 215
    Pineapple-Pecan Loaf Bread, '87 256
    Popovers, Giant Pecan, '83 208
    Prune-Nut Bread, '87 255; '91 55
    Pumpkin-Nut Bread, '83 294
    Pumpkin-Pecan Bread, '87 221
    Roll, Banana-Nut, '85 112
    Rolls, Buttered Rum-Nut, '86 291
    Rolls, Caramel-Nut, '86 312
    Rolls, Easy Cinnamon-Pecan, '89 307
    Rolls, Pecan, '81 62
    Scones, Orange-Pecan, '94 215
    Strawberry-Nut Bread, '79 24
    Wine-Date Nut Bread, '82 253
Brittle, Chocolate, '83 315
Brittle, Pecan, '91 272
Broccoli with Lemon Sauce and Pecans,
    '86 71
Buttered Pecans, Green Beans with, **92** 61
Butter, Orange-Pecan, '84 75
Cakes
    Apple-Pecan Cake, '92 167
    Banana-Nut Cake, '92 120
    Bourbon-Pecan Cake, '84 25
    Butter Pecan Cake, '80 229
    Butter Pecan Cake, Caramel-Filled,
        '88 278
    Cheesecake, Butter Pecan, '86 61
    Cheesecake, Chocolate-Caramel-Pecan,
        '91 197
    Cheesecake, Pecan, '85 38
    Cheesecake, Praline, '83 270; '89 93
    Chocolate-Nut Cake, Rich, '86 8

PECANS, Cakes (continued)

Coffee Cake, Apple-Pecan, '84 242
Coffee Cake, Cinnamon-Pecan, '87 69
Coffee Cake, Nutty Orange, '95 160
Coffee Cake, Orange-Pecan, '86 86
Coffee Cake, Pecan-Topped, '81 41
Cupcakes, Apple-Nut, '82 279
Date Nut Cake, '79 176; '80 5
Funnel Cakes, Nutty, '91 233
Kentucky Pecan Cake, '84 263
Orange-Nut Butter Cake, '80 254
Orange Nut Cake, '80 70
Orange-Pecan Crunch Cake, '83 10
Pineapple-Pecan Upside-Down Cake,
'84 25
Pound Cake, Bourbon-Pecan, '91 270
Pound Cake, Butterscotch-Pecan,
'92 153
Pound Cake, Eggnog-Pecan, '95 313
Pound Cake, Marbled Pecan, '93 313
Pound Cake, Orange-Pecan, '93 13
Pound Cake, Praline, '82 88
Pound Cake, Sour Cream-Orange Pecan,
'89 207
Praline Glaze, Pecan Cake with, '82 196
Praline Ice Cream Cake, '80 84
Roulade, Pecan, '87 183
Roulage, Toffee-Pecan, '94 312
Shortcake, Banana-Pecan, '93 43
Candy, Chocolate-Nut Log, '86 335
Caramel Corn, Nutty, '92 317
Carrots and Celery with Pecans, '84 254
Casserole, Carrot-Pecan, '93 44
Catfish Pecan, '85 53
Chicken, Buttermilk-Pecan, '89 166
Chicken Drummettes, Orange-Pecan,
'93 158
Chicken, Nutty Oven-Fried, '85 160
Chicken, Oven-Fried Pecan, '84 288
Chicken, Pecan, '90 54
Chocolate Date-Nut Delight, '88 168
Clusters, Pecan, '81 266
Clusters, Pecan-Coconut, '86 M251
Clusters, Roasted Pecan, '85 233; '90 310
Coating, Salmon Bake with Pecan-Crunch,
'95 209
Cobbler, Apple-Pecan, '84 M198
Coffee, Praline-Flavored, '87 69
Cookies
Bars, Butter Pecan Turtle, '90 70
Bars, Gooey Pecan, '94 133
Bars, Pecan, '82 209
Brownies, Chocolate-Pecan, '81 64
Brownies, Nutty Blonde, '81 64
Brownies, Nutty Cocoa, '81 64
Brownies, Nutty Fudge, '80 M171
Brownies, Praline, '93 243
Brown Sugar-Pecan Cookies, '91 236
Butter Cookies, Pecan-, '83 113
Butter Pecan Cookies, '82 139
Butter Pecan Shortbread Cookies,
'80 282
Butterscotch-Pecan Cookies, '84 36
Cheese Crispies, Pecan-, '87 168
Cherry Nut Nuggets, '81 286
Cherry Pecan Cookies, '82 136
Chocolate-Nut Chews, '81 92
Chocolate-Nut Freezer Cookies,
'88 217
Crescent Cookies, Pecan, '85 324
Easy Pecan Cookies, '80 208

Fudge-Pecan Chewies, Alabama,
'95 143
Lemon Pecan Dainties, '80 208
Oatmeal-Chocolate Chip Cookies, Nutty,
'82 185
Oatmeal Cookies, Nutty, '81 130
Oatmeal Nut Crispies, '80 208
Orange-Pecan Cookies, '88 119
Pie Cookies, Pecan, '92 289
Praline Cookies, '91 271
Praline Shortbread Cookies, '88 242
Praline Thumbprint Cookies, '89 328
Squares, Lemon-Pecan, '89 124
Squares, Pecan, '79 205; '86 13
Squares, Twice-Baked Pecan, '79 291
Sugar Pecan Crisps, '86 230
Sugarplum Sticks, '95 321
Cornmeal Rounds, Pecan-, '95 99
Crunch, Apple-Nut, '82 M238
Crunchy Munchies, '94 196
Crust, Nutty Oat, '89 251
Crust, Pecan, '86 317; '89 291
Crust, Spiced Nut, '87 295
Cupcakes, Apple-Nut, '82 279
Dessert, Maple Nut, '81 84
Dessert, Nutty Fudgy Frozen, '94 28
Dressing, Chicken with Pecan-Rice,
'85 M57
Dressing, Fruit-and-Pecan, '84 252
Dressing, Pecan-Sage, '80 262
Dressing, Watermelon Salad with Celery-Nut,
'80 182
Dumplings, Spiced Peaches with Nutty,
'87 164
Eggs, Pecan-Stuffed, '80 78
Fettuccine, Chicken-Pecan, '86 52
Filling, Fruit-Nut, '80 289
Filling, Nut, '91 35
Fritters, Chocolate-Covered Pecan, '79 205
Frosting, Banana-Nut, '79 115
Frosting, Butter Pecan, '80 229
Frosting, Chocolate Nut, '80 140
Frosting, Coconut-Pecan, '81 296; '83 M233;
'84 43, 322
Frosting, Nutty Coconut, '86 8
Frosting, Nutty Cream Cheese, '85 117
Frosting, Pecan, '86 86
Fruit Compote, Warm Praline, '85 260
Fudge, Cherry Nut, '83 315
Fudge, Creamy Pecan, '84 321
Fudge, Nutty White, '81 253
Fudge, Quick Nut, '83 316
Glazed Nuts, '88 222
Glaze, Honey-Nut, '87 15
Glaze, Praline, '82 196
Goose, Fruit- and Pecan-Stuffed, '83 268
Grahams, Praline, '92 239
Granola, Nutty, '90 95
Green Beans, Nutty, '88 M187
Ham, Praline, '85 302
Ice Cream, Butter Pecan, '80 176; '86 129;
'88 202
Ice Cream, Cherry-Nut, '86 129
Ice Cream, Cherry-Pecan, '88 203
Ice Cream, Praline, '89 318
Ice Cream, Pralines and Cream, '82 184;
'83 159
Ice Cream, Straw-Ba-Nut, '80 177
Ice Cream, Strawberry-Banana-Nut, '88 203
Mousse, Butter Pecan, '95 286
Onions with Pecans and Roasted Carrots,
Roasted Vidalia, '92 340
Orange Pecans, '84 299; '87 292

Pies and Pastries
Bourbon-Pecan Pie, '85 90
Bourbon-Pecan Pie, Frozen, '89 251
Bourbon-Pecan Pumpkin Pie, '87 264
Caramel-Pecan Apple Pie, '85 247
Caramel-Pecan Pie, '88 282
Cherry-Pecan Pie, '92 30
Chocolate-Banana-Pecan Cream Pie,
'94 210
Chocolate-Pecan Chess Pie, '93 251
Chocolate Pecan Pie, '80 237; '83 12;
'90 184
Chocolate-Pecan Pie, '91 272
Chocolate-Praline Pie, '86 259
Choco-Pecan Pie, '82 86
Coconut-Pecan Chess Pie, '81 248
Coconut Pecan Pie, '81 161
Coffee Pecan Pie, '82 74
Cranberry-Pecan Pie, '92 316
Cranberry Pie, Nutty, '82 298
Custard Pecan Pie, '87 184
Date-Pecan Pie, '80 15
Golden Pecan Pie, '81 266
Grandmother's Pecan Pie, '86 269
Holiday Pecan Pie, '81 296
Honey-Pecan Finger Pies, '90 184
Ice Cream Pie, Nutty, '91 180
Individual Pecan Pies, '85 295
Layered Pecan Pie, '83 305
Lemon-Pecan Pie, '93 251
Louisiana Pecan Pie, '92 83
Maple-Pecan Pie, '81 266
Miniature Pecan Pies, '79 205; '86 13
Molasses-Pecan Pie, '86 259
Old-Fashioned Pecan Pie, '81 M269
Orange-Pecan Pie, '79 282; '83 222
Peach Praline Pie, '89 136
Pecan Pie, '79 251; '80 57; '85 255;
'90 312; '92 234
Praline Pastries, '89 318
Pumpkin-Pecan Pie, '85 233, 282
Pumpkin Pie, Nutty, '82 67
Raisin-Pecan Pie, '87 213
Special, Old Pecan Street, '93 251
Spicy Pecan Pie, '84 240
Sweet Potato-Pecan Pie, '83 90
Tarts, Apple-Pecan, '80 282
Tarts, Easy Pecan, '84 313
Tarts, Pecan, '81 266
Tarts, Special Pecan, '87 224
Tart with Caramel Sauce, Chocolate-
Pecan, '93 296; '94 234
Tart with Praline Cream, Pecan, '90 256
Tassies, Teatime, '84 321
Texas Pecan Pie, '83 159
Texas Star Pecan Pie, '90 184
Tiny Pecan Pies, '79 225
Turtle Pecan Pie, '93 250
Popcorn Balls, Nutty, '88 227
Pork Chops with Beer Sauce, Pecan-Breaded,
'95 266
Pork Loin, Apricot-Pecan Stuffed, '94 274
Praline Freeze, '89 60; '90 48
Pudding, Brown Sugar-Pecan, '86 M165
Pudding, Pecan-Mocha, '89 M130
Pudding, with Hot Rum Sauce, Apple-Nut,
'79 86
Quiche, Chicken-Pecan, '91 206
Rice, Nutted, '85 269
Rice, Pecan, '85 53
Rice, Shrimp-and-Scallop Sauté with Pecan,
'90 317
Roll, Date Nut, '79 249

PECANS *(continued)*

Rolls, Pecan, '79 285
Roughy with Brown Butter Sauce, Pecan, '91 64
Roulade, Pecan, '87 183
Salad, Apple-Nut, '80 226
Salad, Beet-Nut, '79 74
Salad, Cantaloupe-Pecan, '86 178
Salad, Creamy Carrot-Nut, '86 331
Salad, Endive, Bacon, and Pecan, '89 12
Salad, Ham-Pecan-Blue Cheese Pasta, '90 62
Salad, Spinach-Pecan, '89 128
Salad, Strawberry-Nut, '94 132
Sauces
    Bourbon Praline Sauce, '81 170
    Butter Pecan Sauce, '91 174
    Butter Sauce, Pecan-, '91 65
    Butterscotch-Pecan Sauce, '82 212
    Chocolate-Praline Sauce, '85 M295
    Cinnamon-Pecan-Honey Pancake Sauce, '88 46
    Date-Nut Sundae Sauce, '82 167
    Éclairs with Pecan Sauce, '83 219
    Peach-Praline Sauce, '85 161
    Pecan Sauce, '83 219
    Praline Ice Cream Sauce, '85 189
    Praline Ice Cream Sauce, Southern, '86 M227
    Praline Sauce, '83 25; '84 143; '89 95; '92 282; '94 206, 312
Spread, Honey-Nut, '87 157
Spread, Nutty Cream Cheese, '89 327
Spread, Raisin-Nut, '95 79
Squares, Butter Pecan Pie, '81 262
Squares, Easy Pecan, '81 230
Squash, Apple-and-Pecan-Filled, '88 228
Stuffing, Chicken Breasts with Pecan-Sausage, '94 212
Stuffing, Pecan, '79 292; '80 32
Stuffing, Wild Duck with Pecan, '85 269
Sugar-and-Honey Pecans, '86 319
Sugared Pecans, '82 167
Sugarplums, Pecan Shortbread, '83 298
Syrup, Chunky Pecan, '85 278
Syrup, Maple-Nut, '80 228
Toast, Orange Praline, '79 36
Toffee, Microwave, '92 M317
Toffee, Nutty, '79 M263
Topping, Apple-Nut, '93 162
Topping, Butter-Pecan, '95 158
Topping, Cinnamon-Pecan, '85 277
Topping, Nutty, '85 256
Topping, Pecan, '94 36
Torte, Carob-Pecan, '85 218
Torte, Chocolate-Pecan, '89 42
Torte, Heavenly Pecan, '81 266
Torte, Mocha-Pecan, '86 26
Turkey Cutlets, Pecan-Crusted, '94 282
Waffles, Pecan, '87 225
Waffles, Pumpkin-Nut, '86 96
Waffles, Southern Chicken-Pecan, '82 231
Wild Rice, Pecan-Lemon, '92 211
Zucchini with Pecans, '87 31

PEPPERMINT

Bavarian, Peppermint, '80 153
Brownies, Chocolate-Peppermint, '88 262
Brownies, Pistachio-Mint, '94 50
Brownies, Southern Chocolate-Mint, '93 216
Cake, Peppermint Candy, '89 254
Cheesecake, Frozen Peppermint, '94 143
Chocolate Mint Freeze, '88 167

Cookies, Peppermint, '95 322
Cookies, Peppermint Candy, '88 286
Cookies, Peppermint Sandwich, '92 277
Crème Brûlée, Peppermint, '95 323
Dessert, Peppermint Wafer, '79 176; '80 7
Dessert, Triple Mint Ice-Cream Angel, '93 86
Filling, Peppermint, '81 119; '89 254
Flip, Hot Peppermint, '86 329
Fondue, Peppermint, '94 332; '95 35
Frosting, Mint Cream, '93 216
Frosting, Pink Peppermint Birthday Cake, '92 269
Hot Cocoa Mix, Minted, '91 316
Ice Cream, Peppermint, '80 176; '86 129
Mints, Party, '79 273; '81 119
Mousse, Peppermint, '93 315
Mousse, Peppermint Candy, '82 71; '94 198
Parfait, Peppermint, '93 315
Parfaits, Chocolate-Peppermint, '88 65
Patties, Peppermint, '86 278
Pie, Peppermint Candy-Ice Cream, '87 260
Pralines, Chocolate-Mint, '92 313; '93 51
Rounds, Peppermint, '94 19
Sauce, Chocolate-Peppermint, '94 205
Snowball Surprises, '93 315
Soufflé, Chocolate Mint, '81 16
Squares, Chocolate-Peppermint, '81 119
Twists, Mint, '86 106
Wreaths, Melt-Away Peppermint, '85 324

PEPPERS

Chile
    Base, Ancho, '95 205
    Casserole, Chile-Cheese, '82 90
    Casserole, Chile 'n' Cheese Breakfast, '88 57
    Casserole, Chiles Rellenos, '79 84; '84 31, 234; '92 18
    Casserole, Chili-Corn, '88 266
    Casserole, Chili-Rice, '79 54
    Casserole, Corn-and-Green Chile, '89 68
    Casserole, Green Chile-and-Fish, '84 32
    Casserole, Mexican Rice, '83 31
    Casserole, Sausage-Chile Rellenos, '88 52
    Cheesecake, Chicken-Chile, '92 42
    Chicken with Salsa, Baked Chile, '88 147
    Chili Verde, '95 14
    Chimichangas (Fried Burritos), '81 196; '85 244
    con Queso, Chile, '80 194
    con Queso Supreme, Chile, '80 265
    Cornbread, Serrano Chile Blue, '94 114
    Cream, Ancho Chile, '87 121
    Cream Sauce, Boneless Pork Chops with Ancho, '95 205
    Dip, Cheese-and-Chile, '83 31
    Dip, Hot Chile, '82 248

    Dip, Hot Chile-Beef, '83 218
    Egg Rolls, Chiles Rellenos, '86 296
    Eggs, Chile, '88 80
    Enchiladas, Green Chile-Sour Cream, '84 234
    Enchiladas, New Mexican Flat, '85 245
    Green Chile-Cornbread Dressing, '93 306
    Grits with Green Chiles, Cheese, '95 208
    Jelly, Chile Piquín, '94 28
    Kabobs, Chile-Beef, '94 251
    Light Chile Verde, '88 148
    Pie, Green Chile-Cheese, '84 234
    Powder, Red Chile, '85 245
    Puerco en Adobo, '88 116
    Quiche, Chile Pepper, '82 224
    Quiche, Green Chile, '83 31
    Quiche, Shrimp, '83 50
    Quiche, Squash-and-Green Chile, '88 143
    Rellenos, Chiles (Stuffed Chiles), '82 220; '83 150; '88 116; '89 226
    Rellenos, Roasted Chiles, '95 64
    Rellenos with Tomatillo Sauce, Roasted Chiles, '94 203
    Rellenos with Walnut Cream Sauce, Havarti-and-Corn-Stuffed Chiles, '93 M275
    Rice and Green Chiles, '83 152
    Rice, Chili-Cheesy, '79 43
    Rice, Hot Pepper, '92 310
    Salad, Spicy Chile-Tomato, '88 121
    Salsa, Double Chile, '91 182
    Salsa, Pepper, '88 26
    Salsa, Roasted Serrano, '95 207
    Salsa with Homemade Tostados, Hot Chile, '88 115
    Sauce, Ancho Chile, '87 122
    Sauce, Green Chile, '82 220
    Sauce, Red Chile, '85 245; '94 251; '95 17
    Sauce, Red Chile Enchilada, '85 245
    Sauce, Verde, '93 275
    Squash, Chile, '84 77
    Squash, Mexican, '83 31
    Squash with Green Chiles, Stuffed, '83 148
    Stuffed Green Chiles, '93 208
    Tacos, Shrimp-and-Pepper Soft, '95 339
    Tamales, Hot, '83 51
    Tamales, Sweet, '83 52
    Turnovers, Chile-Ham, '88 64
    Waffles, Corn-Chile, '94 206
Dip, Pepperoncini-Cream Cheese, '91 252
Firecrackers, Texas, '95 96
Green
    Beef and Green Peppers, '79 104
    Beefed-Up Peppers, '82 186
    Bread, Pepper, '85 156
    Casserole, Peppered Pork Chop, '82 25
    Casserole, Peppery Potato, '95 182
    Chicken Peppers, Devilish, '80 65
    Cups, Potato Salad in Pepper, '79 78
    Deluxe, Peppers, '81 159
    Dressing, Green Pepper-Onion Salad, '84 12
    Fried Pepper Strips, '82 208
    Jelly, Pepper, '79 121
    Jelly, Unusual Green Pepper, '82 132
    Meatballs with Pineapple and Peppers, '90 145
    Medley, Pepper-Mushroom, '90 98
    Mexican Green Peppers, '80 65

PEPPERS, Green (continued)

Muffins, Cheese-and-Pepper, '84 139
Pizza Peppers, '83 135
Potato Salad 'n' Peppers, '83 135
Ratatouille, '85 92
Relish, Pepper, '83 183
Relish, Pepper-Onion, '84 180
Salad, Ruby-and-Emerald, '85 79
Sauce, Pepper-Onion, '84 125
Sauce, Red or Green Pepper, '91 85
Sausage and Peppers, Italian, '84 9
Sautéed Onions and Peppers, '83 M148
Sauté, Tomato-Pepper, '84 142
Soup, Green Pepper, '88 250
Spread, Roasted Pepper, '94 123
Stacks, Pepper-Cheese, '87 80
Steak and Rice, Pepper, '81 17
Steak, Pepper, '81 273; '85 57; '88 113
Steak, Pepper-Beef, '85 21
Stir-Fried Sweet Peppers with Tomatoes,
  '93 207
Stir-Fry Steak, Pepper, '81 240
Stuffed Green Peppers, Beefy, '81 86
Stuffed Green Peppers, Ham-, '80 65
Stuffed Pepper Medley, '82 131
Stuffed Peppers, '81 239; '83 66;
  '84 202
Stuffed Peppers, Beef-, '84 154; '85 146;
  '91 M127
Stuffed Peppers, Corn-, '84 104
Stuffed Peppers, Curried Chicken-,
  '87 19
Stuffed Peppers for Two, '80 84
Stuffed Peppers, Ham-and-Corn, '81 87
Stuffed Peppers, Hearty, '88 M214
Stuffed Peppers, Macaroni-and-Cheese-,
  '80 65
Stuffed Peppers, Rice-, '80 65
Stuffed Peppers, Shrimp-, '80 162;
  '86 131, 197
Stuffed Peppers, Spinach-, '82 180
Stuffed Peppers with Rice and Ham,
  '82 131
Stuffed with Beef, Peppers, '84 72
Taco Peppers, '81 86
Turkey with Peppers, '92 182
Veal and Peppers, Spaghetti with,
  '81 201; '82 14
Jalapeño
  Biscuits, Cornmeal-Jalapeño, '94 214
  Black-Eyed Peas, Jalapeño, '88 166
  Bread, Jalapeño Pepper, '83 121
  Casserole, Jalapeño Corn, '83 256
  Casserole, Jalapeño Rice, '81 66
  Celery, Jalapeño Stuffed, '79 70
  Cheese, Shrimp with Herbed Jalapeño,
    '87 112
  Cheesy Jalapeño Peppers, '80 195
  Chicken, Grilled Jalapeño, '93 213
  Chicken, Grilled Lime-Jalapeño, '91 87
  Chicken Jalapeño, Easy, '92 310
  Chicken Legs, Jalapeño Oven-Fried,
    '94 94
  Chutney, Jeweled Pepper, '94 316
  Cornbread, Beefy Jalapeño, '82 142
  Cornbread, Cheddar-Jalapeño, '85 3
  Cornbread, Jalapeño, '85 200; '94 78
  Cups, Hot Vegetable Pepper, '88 M188
  Grits, Jalapeño Cheese, '85 43
  Heroes, Open-Faced Jalapeño, '90 144
  Hominy, Jalapeño, '82 51

Jelly, Jalapeño, '92 230
Loaf, Jalapeño-Cheese, '84 76
Muffins, Jalapeño-Corn, '93 164
Mustard, Jalapeño, '93 240; '95 312
Pickled Jalapeño Peppers, '93 136
Potatoes, Jalapeño, '84 39
Potatoes, Jalapeño-Ham Stuffed,
  '81 M61
Puffs, Cajun Hot, '94 277
Quesadillas, Bacon-Jalapeño-Tomato,
  '95 240
Quiche, Cheesy Jalapeño, '84 31
Quiche, Jalapeño-Corn, '85 122
Quiche Squares, Cheesy Hot, '79 124
Rice, Hot Pepper, '92 310
Rice, Jalapeño, '79 43
Rice, Jalapeño Hot, '80 126
Salsa, Double Chile, '91 182
Salsa Picante, '84 108
Salsa Picante, Homemade, '81 67
Sauce, Hot Chile, '92 156
Sauce, Jalapeño, '80 193; '93 230
Sauce, Jalapeño-Cranberry, '92 310
Sauce, San Antonio Hot, '84 291
Spread, Jalapeño-Cheese, '82 248
Squares, Jalapeño Cheese, '80 195
Stuffed Jalapeño Peppers, Fried, '95 22
Stuffed Jalapeños, Fiery Fried, '90 118
Stuffed Jalapeños, Shrimp-, '88 115
Tacos, Shrimp-and-Pepper Soft, '95 339
Vinegar, Southwest, '94 200
Pasta with Peppers and Broccoli, '91 69
Red
  Bread, Roasted Red Bell Pepper, '95 241
  Butter, Roasted Red Bell Pepper,
    '95 242
  Cucumber-and-Pepper Combo, '88 176
  Cups, Hot Vegetable Pepper, '88 M188
  Curried Corn and Sweet Red Peppers,
    '95 47
  Jam, Red Bell Pepper, '95 242
  Jelly, Red Pepper, '89 M156
  Okra, Corn, and Peppers, '87 M151
  Peas and Peppers, Minted, '90 M99
  Peas and Peppers, Stir-Fried, '87 51
  Pizza, Roasted Pepper, '94 218
  Potatoes with Sweet Red Peppers,
    '87 192
  Puree, Red Pepper, '93 275
  Roasted Red Peppers and Pearl Onions,
    Green Beans with, '93 260
  Round Steak, Red Pepper, '88 214
  Salad, Broccoli and Red Pepper, '83 224
  Salad, Roasted Red Pepper and
    Watercress, '90 55
  Salad, Tuna-and-Red Pepper, '93 143
  Sandwiches, Smoked Turkey-Roasted
    Pepper, '94 66
  Sauce, Linguine with Red Pepper,
    '93 127
  Sauce, Red or Green Pepper, '91 85
  Sautéed Peppers and Mushrooms, Herb-
    Stuffed Chicken with, '91 26
  Snow Peas and Red Pepper, Sesame,
    '84 175
  Snow Peas with Red Pepper, '90 102
  Soup, Chilled Sweet Red Pepper, '93 69
  Soup, Cream of Roasted Sweet Red
    Pepper, '95 65
  Soup, Spicy Pepper, '93 98
  Squash-and-Pepper Toss, Crisp,
    '87 M152
Salsa, Roasted, '95 130

Sweet
  Chicken Breasts with Curried Peppers,
    '90 227
  Chicken Sauté, Sweet Pepper-, '89 104
  Chicken Scaloppine with Peppers, '85 78
  Chowder, Bell Pepper-Cheese, '95 240
  Flank Steak with Sweet Peppers, Grilled,
    '90 138
  Green Beans and Pepper Strips, '86 170
  Kabobs, Pretty Pepper, '90 166
  Kabobs, Summery Squash-and-Pepper,
    '95 193
  Marinated Roasted Peppers, '92 176
  Medley, Rainbow Pepper, '91 126
  Parmesan Pepper Toss, '93 208
  Pasta, Peppery, '94 164
  Pesto, Pepper, '89 103; '90 97
  Relish, Confetti Pepper, '91 195
  Relish, Sweet Pepper, '95 104
  Roasted Bell Peppers in Olive Oil,
    '95 242
  Roasted Peppers, Marinated, '87 90
  Roasted Peppers with Balsamic
    Vinaigrette, '94 128
  Salad, Chilled Turkey-and-Pepper
    Stir-Fry, '88 140
  Salad, Mixed Pepper, '89 103
  Salad, Mushroom-and-Pepper, '86 68
  Salad, Three-Pepper, '91 162
  Salsa, Mixed Pepper, '91 181
  Salsa, Yellowfin Tuna with Corn, Pepper,
    and Tomato, '94 164
  Sausage and Peppers, '95 165
  Sausage, Sweet Peppery, '95 69
  Sautéed Sweet Peppers, '89 102
  Sauté, Julienne Pepper, '89 104
  Soup, Bell Pepper, '89 103
  Soup, Roasted Pepper-and-Chicken,
    '90 58
  Soup, Sweet Pepper, '93 277
  Spread, Roasted Pepper, '94 123
  Stuffed with Shrimp-and-Orzo Salad,
    Peppers, '91 203
  Sugar Snaps and Peppers, '93 139
  Tacos, Grilled Pepper, '95 340
  Topping, Rainbow Pepper, '90 117
Turkey and Peppers in Cornbread Crust,
  '95 312

PERSIMMONS
Bread, Persimmon, '80 228
Bread, Persimmon Date-Nut, '82 218
Cake, Persimmon, '79 205
Cookies, Persimmon-Raisin, '85 232
Pie, Persimmon, '79 206
Pudding, Persimmon, '79 206
Salad, Persimmon Fruit, '79 206

PESTOS. See also **RELISHES, SALSAS, SAUCES,
  TOPPINGS.**
Bow-Tie Pesto, '94 231
Dip, Pesto, '95 93
Fresh Pesto, '86 150
Garlic Pesto, '84 108
Nuts, Pesto-Spiced, '95 173
Pasta, Asian Pesto, '95 189
Pasta, Pesto and, '92 98
Pepper Pesto, '89 103; '90 97
Pesto, '80 242
Sauce, Pesto, '89 280; '91 94; '95 267
Spinach-Peanut Pesto and Pasta, '93 212
Spinach Pesto-Pasta, '91 314
Spinach Pesto Sauce, '93 59
Tomato Pesto, Dried, '90 204; '94 249
Tomatoes Pesto, '86 150

PHEASANT. *See* **GAME.**

PICKLES
Asparagus, Pickled, '83 46
Beet Pickles, '81 210
Beets, Easy Pickled, '80 137
Beets, Pickled, '81 216
Broccoli, Pickled, '81 308
Cantaloupe, Sweet Pickled, '89 197
Carrots, Pickled, '93 12
Chayote Squash Pickles, '89 197
Cucumber Chips, '85 176
Cucumber Pickles, Sour, '85 176
Cucumber Rounds, Easy Pickled, '90 143
Cucumber Sandwich Pickles, '81 174
Dill Pickles, '81 174
Dill Pickles, Fried, '84 206
Dills, Lazy Wife, '87 149
Eggs, Beet Pickled, '84 287
Eggs, Spiced Pickled, '84 288
Figs, Pickled, '79 140
Fire-and-Ice Pickles, '94 316
Green Tomato Pickles, '87 134
Icicle Pickles, Sweet, '85 176
Jalapeño Peppers, Pickled, '93 136
Mixed Pickles, '81 174
Okra Pickles, '81 173
Onion Rings, Pickled Refrigerator, '84 265
Onions, Pickled Cocktail, '89 197
Peaches, Perfect Pickled, '85 178
Peach Pickles, '85 177
Pear Pickles, Mustard, '79 196
Pineapple, Pickled, '79 24
Problem Chart, Pickle, '85 176
Squash Pickles, '81 174; '87 150
Sweet Pickles, Quick, '87 149
Watermelon Rind Pickles, '81 174; '84 106
Yellow Squash, Pickled, '93 136
Zucchini, Dilled Fresh, '81 174

PIES AND PASTRIES
Almond Pie, Toasted, '86 163
Ambrosia Pie, '79 284
Angel Pie, '79 123; '80 238
Apple
    Amandine Pie, Apple-, '89 215
    American Apple Pie, '91 197
    Autumn Apple Pie, '79 205
    Berry-Apple Pie, '88 251
    Blackberry-Apple Pie, '87 130
    Bourbon Pie, Apple-, '95 302
    Brandy-Apple Pie, '86 301
    Brandy Raisin-Apple Pie, '83 192
    Cake, Apple Pie, '82 226
    Chess Pie, Apple-Lemon, '86 220
    Cider Pie, Apple, '84 227
    Cinnamon Sauce, Apple Pie with Hot,
       '88 210
    Covered Apple Cake, '89 317
    Cran-Apple Pie, '92 304
    Cranberry-Apple Holiday Pie, '81 M269
    Cranberry-Apple Pie, '79 264
    Cream Cheese Pie, Apple-, '81 247
    Custard Pie, Apple, '88 236
    Dutch Apple Pie, '81 105; '82 273
    Easy-Crust Apple Pie, '87 11
    Fresh Apple Pie, '84 178
    Fried Apple Pies, '81 217; '86 302;
       '88 112, 225; '94 61
    Grandmother's Apple Pie, '87 212
    Grated Apple Pie, '83 304
    Holiday Apple Pie, '87 260
    Lemon-Apple Pie, Tart, '80 100
    Mexican Apple Pie, '94 97
    Mincemeat Pie, Apple-, '85 316

No-Crust Apple Pie, '88 204
Old-Fashioned Apple Pie, '82 M299;
    '88 94
Pear-Apple Pie, Natural, '88 226
Pear Pie, Apple-, '83 249
Raisin Brandy Pie, Apple-, '89 58
Red Apple Pie, '79 282
Upside-Down Southern Apple Pie,
    '88 226
Apricot Fried Pies, '86 269
Apricot Pies, Fried, '95 215
Apricot Pies, Special, '94 60
Apricot Pie, Yogurt-, '85 132
Apricot Surprise Pie, '88 99
Banana Cream Pie, '84 48; '87 207
Banana Cream Pie, Hawaiian, '90 105
Banana Pie with Hot Buttered Rum Sauce,
    '88 204
Bavarian Cream Pie, '79 281
Blackberry Cream Pie, '81 132
Blackberry Pie, '84 141; '86 152
Blackberry Pie, Creamy, '88 179
Black Bottom Pie, Weidmann's, '95 118
Blueberry
    Banana Pie, Blueberry-, '93 115
    Chilled Blueberry Pie, '89 136
    Cream Cheese Pie, Blueberry-, '88 154
    Cream Pie, Blueberry, '84 142
    Cream Pie, Fresh Blueberry, '80 144
    Fresh Blueberry Pie, '83 183; '85 152
    Kuchen, Blueberry, '80 143
    Old-Fashioned Blueberry Pie, '89 136
    Peach Pie, Blueberry-, '94 158
    Sour Cream Pie, Blueberry-, '83 183
    Streusel Pie, Fresh Blueberry, '89 137
Boston Cream Pie, '83 220
Bourbon Pie, Kentucky, '84 87
Boysenberry Pie, '82 133
Brownie Pie, Crustless, '82 33
Buttermilk Chess Pie, '92 214
Buttermilk-Lemon Cream Pie, '88 99
Buttermilk Lemon Pie, '81 120; '82 23
Buttermilk-Lemon Pie, '88 297
Buttermilk Pie, '82 53; '83 158; '88 93; '92 95
Buttermilk Pie, Old-Fashioned, '79 72
Butterscotch Cream Pie, '84 48; '87 207
Butterscotch Meringue Pie, '83 158
Cantaloupe Cream Pie, '79 177
Cantaloupe Meringue Pie, '88 182
Cantaloupe Pie, '86 163
Caramel-Banana Pie, '86 M165
Caramel Banana Pie, Luscious, '79 115
Caramel-Nut Crunch Pie, '94 244
Caramel-Peanut Pie, '86 259
Caramel Pie, Burnt, '82 53
Caviar Pie, '79 154
Cheese
    Apple-Cream Cheese Pie, '81 247
    Blueberry-Cream Cheese Pie, '88 154
    Chocolate-Cream Cheese Pie, '80 69
    Chocolate Cream Cheese Pie, '92 240
    Cottage Cheese Pie, '82 85
    Cream Puffs with Chicken Salad, Cheesy,
       '86 260
    Fruited Cheese Pie, '92 228
    Hors d'Oeuvre Pie, Cheesy, '88 91
    Lemon Cheese Pie, '81 136; '82 146
    Lemon-Cottage Cheese Pie, '79 44
    Lemon Cottage Cheese Pie, '81 143
    Make-Ahead Cheesecake Pie, '81 233
    Mincemeat-Cheese Pie, '80 253
    Phyllo Cheesecakes, Little, '87 275
    Yogurt-Cheese Pie, '82 121

Cherry-Berry Pie, '92 316
Cherry Confetti Pie, No-Bake, '93 114
Cherry Cream Pie with Almond Pastry, '92 30
Cherry Pie, Coconut Crumb, '92 30
Cherry Pie, Easy, '82 299
Cherry Pie, Fresh, '88 178
Cherry Pie, Lemony, '92 30
Cherry Pie, Prize-Winning, '82 57
Cherry Pie, Red, '83 192
Cherry Pie, Scrumptious, '83 250
Chess Pie, Brown Sugar, '86 220
Chess Pie, Old-Fashioned, '86 220
Chocolate
    Almond Pie, Creamy Chocolate-,
       '85 102
    Amandine, Chocolate Pie, '83 300
    Amaretto Mousse Pie, Chocolate-,
       '80 180; '81 30
    Banana-Pecan Cream Pie, Chocolate-,
       '94 210
    Bavarian Pie, Chocolate, '89 326
    Berry Pie, Heavenly Chocolate-, '85 102
    Best-Ever Chocolate Pie, '88 M45
    Black Bottom Pie, '82 53
    Bourbon Pie, Chocolate, '88 99
    Cake, Chocolate Pastry, '91 196
    Chess Pie, Chocolate, '81 161; '86 220;
       '92 13
    Chilled Chocolate Pie, '88 99
    Chip Pie, Chocolate, '85 114
    Coffee Cream Pie, '94 209
    Cream Cheese Pie, Chocolate-, '80 69
    Cream Cheese Pie, Chocolate, '92 240
    Cream Pie, Chocolate, '83 192; '84 49;
       '87 208; '94 208
    Creamy Chocolate Pie, '85 298; '86 119
    Double Chocolate Pie, '82 M282
    Easy Chocolate Pie, '83 158
    French Silk Pie, '80 247
    Frozen Chocolate Pie, '80 154
    Frozen Chocolate Pie with Pecan Crust,
       '89 291
    Fudge Pie, '87 168; '89 252
    Fudge Pie, Sweetheart, '86 316; '90 313
    German Chocolate Pie, '93 129
    Heavenly Chocolate Pie, '87 260
    Meringue Pie, Chocolate, '80 238;
       '82 206; '83 158; '92 216
    Meringue Pie, Chocolate-Filled, '86 121
    Microwave Chocolate Pie, '90 M15
    Mocha Crunch Pie, Chocolate-, '81 136
    Mocha Pie, '94 168
    Mousse Pie, Chocolate, '81 136
    Mud Pie, Decadent, '89 252
    Mud Pie, Mississippi, '89 26
    Mud Pie, Tipsy, '80 255
    Peanut Butter Pie, Chocolate-, '85 91
    Peanut Butter Swirl Pie, Chocolate-,
       '87 262
    Pecan Chess Pie, Chocolate-, '93 251
    Pecan Pie, Choco, '82 86
    Pecan Pie, Chocolate, '80 237; '83 12;
       '90 184
    Pecan Pie, Chocolate-, '91 272
    Pecan Pie, Turtle, '93 250
    Praline Pie, Chocolate-, '86 259
    Silk Pie, Chocolate, '88 67
    Strawberry-Chocolate Truffle Pie,
       '89 112
    Whipped Cream Pie, Chocolate, '79 124
    White Chocolate-Banana Cream Pie,
       '94 314
Christmas Pie, White, '88 281; '93 289

PIES AND PASTRIES (continued)

Cobblers
  Apple Cobbler, Easy, '83 174
  Apple Cobbler for Two, '85 261
  Apple Cobbler, New-Fashioned, '91 221
  Apple Crisp, '84 122
  Apple Crisp, Tart, '92 226
  Apple-Pecan Cobbler, '84 M198
  Apple Walnut Cobbler, '79 154
  Apple-Walnut Cobbler, '81 248
  Apricot Cobble Up, '82 138
  Berry-Cherry Cobbler, '83 270
  Berry Crisp, '83 130
  Blackberry-Almond Cobbler, '81 132
  Blackberry Cobbler, '82 139; '83 175
  Blackberry Cobbler, Deep-Dish,
    '80 186
  Blackberry Cobbler, Deluxe, '81 132
  Blackberry Cobbler, Juicy, '89 137
  Blackberry Cobbler, New-Fashioned,
    '87 164
  Blackberry Cobbler, Southern, '81 132
  Blueberry Buckle, '85 30
  Blueberry Cobbler, '83 175
  Blueberry Cobbler, Easy, '83 183
  Blueberry Cobbler, Fresh, '80 144
  Blueberry Cobbler, Peachy, '80 143
  Blueberry Crisp, '84 177
  Blueberry Crunch, Fresh, '82 143
  Blueberry, Huckle-Buckle, '86 151
  Blueberry-Peach Cobbler, No-Dough,
    '86 177
  Blueberry Pinwheel Cobbler, '87 140
  Blueberry Slump, Quick, '91 20
  Boysenberry Cobbler, '82 133
  Cherry Cobbler, '82 91, 139
  Cherry Cobbler, Colossal, '89 137
  Cherry Cobbler, Fresh, '84 178
  Cherry Crisp, '91 20
  Cherry Slump, '83 139
  Cranberry-and-Apple Cobbler, '84 306;
    '90 294
  Cranberry Cobbler, '81 275
  Cranberry Cobbler, Easy, '86 260
  Cranberry Cobbler Roll, '80 288;
    '81 248
  Cranberry-Peach Cobbler, '92 322
  Cranberry-Pear Crisp, '83 207
  Fig Cobbler, '79 140
  Fig Cobbler, Cajun, '94 196
  Fig Cobbler, Super, '86 206
  Fruit Cobbler, Quick, '91 20
  Grenadine-Peach Cobbler, '85 178
  Peach-Caramel Cobbler, '86 300;
    '87 178
  Peach Cobbler, '83 175; '84 178;
    '90 219; '95 264
  Peach Cobbler, Fresh, '82 139; '89 154
  Peach Cobbler, Lattice-Topped, '79 154
  Peach Cobbler, Old-Fashioned, '82 170
  Peach Cobbler, Quick, '79 215; '81 142
  Peach Cobbler, Spicy, '85 178
  Peach Cobbler Supreme, '81 184;
    '90 313
  Peach Cobbler with Praline Biscuits,
    '92 180
  Peach Crinkle, '91 20
  Peach Crisp, '83 113; '92 13; '93 134
  Peach Crumble, Easy, '83 116
  Pear Cobbler, Best Ever, '82 194
  Pear Crumble, '85 221

Pineapple-Apple Betty, '85 46
Plum Cobbler, Crunchy, '88 152
Raspberry-Cherry Cobbler, '93 230
Strawberry-Rhubarb Cobbler, '88 93
Strawberry-Rhubarb Cobbler, Rosy,
  '79 154
Strawberry-Rhubarb Crisp, '95 119
Coconut
  Blender Coconut Pie, '84 236
  Buttermilk-Coconut Pie, '94 246
  Caramel Pies, Coconut-, '87 260
  Cherry Pie, Coconut Crumb, '92 30
  Chess Pie, Coconut, '86 220
  Chess Pie, Coconut-Orange, '89 169
  Chess Pie, Coconut-Pecan, '81 248
  Cloud, Coconut, '80 70
  Coconut Pie, '93 115
  Cream Pie, Coconut, '80 238; '81 136;
    '82 85; '84 49; '87 207; '89 236;
    '90 312
  Cream Pie, Fresh Coconut, '80 289
  Cream Pie, Surprise Coconut, '92 43
  Crunch Pie, Coconut, '90 105
  Custard Pie, Coconut, '82 33
  French Coconut Pie, '90 162
  Macaroon Pie, Coconut, '88 204
  Magic Coconut Pie, '79 53
  Mock Coconut Pie, '86 200
  Orange-Coconut Cream Pie, '94 208
  Orange-Coconut Pie, '90 90
  Pecan Pie, Coconut, '81 161
  Pineapple Pie, Coconut-, '84 256
  Quick Coconut Pie, '83 115
  Toasted Coconut Pie, '90 105
Coffee Cream Pie, '94 209
Cracker Pie, '79 113
Cranberry-Cherry Pie, Tart, '87 299
Cranberry Freezer Pie, Festive, '84 306
Cranberry Pie, Frosty, '79 249
Cranberry Pie, Nutty, '82 M298
Cranberry Pie, Walnut-, '87 259
Cranberry-Raisin Pie, '80 283; '85 316
Cran-Raspberry Pie, '87 244
Cream Pie, Texas, '81 181
Crème de Menthe Pie, Quick, '88 127
Crusts
  Brown Sugar Crust, '92 118
  Butter Crust, '90 173
  Cereal Piecrust, Crisp, '82 209; '83 100
  Cheese Crust, '80 286; '86 264
  Chocolate-Coconut Crust, '87 261
  Chocolate-Coconut Pie Shell, '82 210;
    '83 100
  Chocolate Crumb Crust, '87 261
  Chocolate Crust, '87 264; '90 M15
  Chocolate Cups, '80 207
  Chocolate Wafer Crust, '89 42, 93
  Cinnamon Meringue Shell, '82 263
  Coconut Crust, '89 160
  Cookie Crust, Spicy, '88 7
  Cracker Crust, '88 97
  Crumb Crust, Cheesy, '88 86
  Crust, '89 272
  Decorating Pie Crusts, '83 248
  Deluxe Piecrust, '79 79
  Ginger Snap Crust, '88 138
  Gingersnap Crust, '89 93; '90 296
  Graham Cracker Crust, '79 45; '86 32;
    '87 139, 243; '88 M45, 55, 67;
    '89 93, 326; '90 296;
    '91 197, M234, 308; '94 310
  Graham Cracker Crust, Microwaved,
    '82 M141

Graham Cracker Crust, Peanut-, '79 50
Italian Sweet Crust, Plum Pie with,
  '79 162
Lattice Crust, '90 294
Nut Crust, Spiced, '87 295
Nutty Oat Crust, '89 251
Oatmeal Piecrust, '79 79
Parmesan Crust, '94 304
Pecan Crust, '86 317; '89 291
Perfect Piecrust, Making, '82 234
Pizza Crust, '80 233; '83 226; '86 77
Pizza Crust, Crispy, '87 181
Rice-Cheese Shell, '82 49
Rice Crust, Crispy, '84 43
Spice Crust, '82 298
Sugar Cookie Crust, '93 131
Tart Crust, '84 178; '90 58
Whole Wheat Crust, '82 298
Custard Pie, Old-Fashioned Egg, '82 261
Custard Pie, Perfect, '82 92
Daiquiri Pie, '79 68
Daiquiri Pie, Daring, '92 191
Dream Pie, '80 90
Eggnog Chiffon Pie, '86 281
Eggnog Pie, '80 254; '83 205; '86 317;
  '87 295
Eggnog Pie, Fluffy, '81 M269
Empanadas de Calabaza (Pumpkin
  Empanadas), '94 28
Fried Pies, Delicious, '83 84
Fruitcake Pie, '80 237
Fruit Pie, Crispy-Crust, '88 68
Fruit Pie, Dried, '83 249
Fruit Pie, Japanese, '80 238
Fruit Pies, Baked, '84 7
Grape Juice Pie, '79 123
Grape Pie, '85 212
Grasshopper Freeze, Creamy, '81 180
Grasshopper Pie, '83 145
Ice Cream
  Absolutely Divine Ice Cream Pie, '82 181
  Caramel Ice Cream Pie, '82 181
  Carrot Ice Cream Pie, '86 200
  Chocolate-Ice Cream Pie, '87 224
  Chocolate Ice Cream Pie, '91 56
  Chocolate-Mint Ice Cream Pie, '81 144
  Coffee Ice Cream Pie, '79 231
  Delight, Ice Cream, '80 69
  Double-Delight Ice Cream Pie, '89 72
  Heavenly Ice Cream Pie, '82 181
  Kona Ice Cream Pie, '83 189
  Lemon Ice Cream Pie, '80 70
  Meringue-Pecan Crust, Ice Cream Pie
    with, '88 127
  Nutty Ice Cream Pie, '91 180
  Peanutty Ice Cream Pie, '82 56
  Peppermint Candy-Ice Cream Pie,
    '87 260
  Pumpkin Ice Cream Pie, '81 272
  Pumpkin-Ice Cream Pie, '87 243
  Rum-Fruit Sauce, Ice Cream Pie with,
    '84 312
  Spectacular, Ice-Cream Pie, '90 314
  Sundae Pie, Ice Cream, '94 244
Kahlúa Pie, '83 191
Key Lime Pie, '91 42
Key Lime Pie, Manny and Isa's, '95 118
Key Lime Pies, '95 86
Lemon
  Buttermilk-Lemon Cream Pie, '88 99
  Buttermilk Lemon Pie, '81 120; '82 23
  Buttermilk-Lemon Pie, '88 297
  Buttermilk Pie, Lemon-, '91 272

Cheese Pie, Lemon, '81 136; '82 146
Cherry Pie, Lemony, '92 30
Chess Pie, Apple-Lemon, '86 220
Chess Pie, Lemon, '79 32; '82 196
Cottage Cheese Pie, Lemon-, '79 44
Cottage Cheese Pie, Lemon, '81 143
Cream Pie, Frozen Lemon, '82 86
Fluff Pie, Lemon, '92 342; '93 46
Frozen Lemonade Pie, '92 101
Heavenly Pie, '83 158
Ice Cream Pie, Lemon, '80 70
Lemonade Pie, '91 42
Magnolia Pie, '94 210
Meringue Pie, Best-Ever Lemon, '94 208
Meringue Pie, Deluxe Lemon, '81 172;
   '90 313
Meringue Pie, Lemon, '85 M112;
   '86 130
Orange Pie, Lemon-, '85 172
Parfait Pie, Lemon, '94 310
Pastry Shell, Lemon in, '84 137
Pecan Pie, Lemon-, '93 251
Slice of Lemon Pie, '84 23
Sour Cream Pie, Lemon-, '82 169
Sponge Pie, Lemon, '83 192
Strawberry Pie, Lemon-, '88 127
Tart Lemon-Apple Pie, '80 100
Tart Lemon Pie, '91 275
Twirl Pie, Lemon, '84 94
Whipped Lemon Pie, '79 124
Lime Chiffon Pie, '86 130
Lime Fluff Pie, '84 43
Lime Party Pies, '92 65
Macadamia Pie, '80 238
Main Dish. *See also* Pies and Pastries/Tarts,
   Turnovers.
Artichoke Pie, '79 25
Beef Pies, Carry-Along, '80 224;
   '81 56
Beef Pot Pie, Oriental, '92 253
Beef Pot Pies with Yorkshire Pudding
   Topping, '93 45
Beef Roast Pot Pie, '88 296
Breakfast Pie, '86 242
Breakfast Pie, Country, '93 M328
Broccoli-and-Turkey Pasta Pie, '88 269
Broccoli-Beef Pie, '83 196
Burrito Pie, Mexican, '87 287
Calzones, All-Star Pizza, '95 308
Cheese-Beef Pie, '85 33
Cheeseburger Pie, '89 121
Cheese Pie, Mexican, '82 9; '83 69
Chicken Breasts in Phyllo Pastry, '91 105
Chicken Breasts Wellington, '84 22
Chicken, Company Creamed, '82 84
Chicken Dumpling Pie, '95 245
Chicken in Pastry, '86 122
Chicken in Phyllo, '87 286
Chicken in Puff Pastry, Spinach-Stuffed,
   '92 125
Chicken Phyllo Pie, Greek, '92 328
Chicken Pie, '81 281; '82 31
Chicken Pie, Biscuit-Topped,
   '86 157, 264
Chicken Pie, Cheesy Mexican, '82 142
Chicken Pie, Deluxe, '88 298
Chicken Pie, Double-Crust, '87 111
Chicken Pie, Egg-Stra Special, '86 264
Chicken Pie, Nana's, '90 25
Chicken Pie, Savory Southern, '90 24

Chicken Pot Pie, '81 210; '82 114;
   '84 21; '94 21; '95 54, 256
Chicken Pot Pie, Double-Crust, '90 220
Chicken Pot Pie, Easy, '83 156; '89 218
Chicken Pot Pie, Old-Fashioned, '92 271
Chicken Pot Pie, Thick 'n' Crusty,
   '87 267; '88 102; '89 67
Chicken Pot Pie with Cheese Crust,
   '86 264
Chicken Salad in Cream Puff Bowl,
   '86 232
Chicken-Vegetable Pot Pie, '81 281;
   '82 30
Chili-Tamale Pie, '82 9; '83 68
Cornbread-Sausage-Apple Pie, '87 171
Cornbread-Tamale Pie, '92 123
Corn Burger Pie, '83 156
Country Pie, '83 155
Enchilada Pie, '83 155
Fish in a Crust, '84 294
Game Pot Pie with Parmesan Crust,
   '94 304
Green Chile-Cheese Pie, '84 234
Grits-and-Ham Pie, Crustless, '86 103
Grits Fiesta Pie, '92 43
Ham-and-Cheese Pie, '95 256
Hamburger Pie, '81 92; '84 13
Ham Pie, Golden, '87 78
Ham Pie with Cheese Crust, '80 286
Ham Pot Pie, '90 25
Ham Towers, Cheesy, '82 77
Lamb Pie, '90 26
Meat-and-Potato Pie, '84 23
Meat Loaf in a Wrap, '89 122
Meat Pie, Continental, '95 256
Meat Pie, Italian, '89 109
Meat Pie, Mexicali, '81 194
Meat Pie, Old-Fashioned, '82 110
Meat Pie, Reuben, '80 189
Meat Pies, Cornish, '84 23
Meat Pies, Natchitoches, '84 21; '91 241
Oyster Pie, Creole, '84 214
Pancake, Supper, '86 242
Pea Flips, '80 7
Pineapple-Chicken Salad Pie, '80 138
Sausage-and-Cornbread Pie, '90 25
Sausage Log, Phyllo, '84 294
Sausage Pizza Pie, Link-, '85 33
Seafood Pie, Hot, '80 32
Shepherd Pie, '83 116
Shepherd's Pie, '92 168
Shrimp Puffs, Luncheon, '85 72
Sombrero Pie, '81 140
Spaghetti-Ham Pie, '93 19
Spaghetti Pie, '81 32
Spaghetti Pie, Weeknight, '95 312
Spanakópita, '86 58
Spinach-Pasta Pie, '85 286
Taco Pie, '88 256
Taco Pie, Crescent, '80 80
Taco Pie, Double-Crust, '88 272;
   '89 180
Taco Pies, Individual, '82 M282
Torta Mexican Style, '89 122
Tortilla Pie, '85 M211
Tortilla Pie, Montezuma, '83 199
Tuna Pie with Cheese Roll Crust,
   '80 286
Tuna-Rice Pie, '84 123
Turkey-and-Dressing Pie, '84 326
Turkey-and-Oyster Pie, '82 267
Turkey-Cheese Pie, '88 264
Turkey Pie, '80 285

Turkey Pie, Crumb-Crust Curried,
   '86 265
Turkey Pie, Golden, '79 253
Turkey Pie, Lattice-Topped, '81 277;
   '82 7
Turkey Pie, Potato-Topped, '86 265
Turkey Pot Pie, '86 265; '90 24; '93 45
Vegetable-Beef Pies, '80 286
Zucchini-Ham-Cheese Pie, '80 272
Mango-Ginger Pie, '88 138
Mango Pie, Green, '79 137
Mincemeat Chiffon Pie, '79 245
Mincemeat-Peach Pie, '80 295; '81 188
Mincemeat Pie, Holiday, '80 282; '83 250;
   '87 213
Mincemeat Pie, Kentucky, '95 302
Mincemeat Pie, Pear, '84 264; '88 226
Mince Pie, Spirited, '92 316
Mint Pie, Candy-Crust, '92 191
Mocha Meringue Pie, '80 242; '88 163
Molasses Pie, '86 20
Muscadine Pie, '82 202
Nesselrode Pie, Fluffy, '87 261
Orange Ambrosia Pie, '80 237
Orange Blossom Special, '79 48
Orange Chess Pie, '88 204
Orange Chiffon Pie, '87 260
Orange-Coconut Pie, '90 90
Orange Meringue Pie, '81 12, 309
Orange Pie, Florida, '91 43
Orange Pie, Frosty, '90 296
Papaya Pie, '86 53
Pastries
Almond Combs, '84 136
Almond Pastry, '85 177; '89 317; '92 30
Apple Dumplings, Old-Fashioned,
   '84 226
Apple Flan, '81 309
Apple Foldovers, '84 136
Apple Roll, '82 178
Apple Rolls, Luscious, '88 225
Apple Squares, '92 311
Apple Strudel, '85 259; '89 267; '92 269
Apricot Pastries, '83 297
Apricot Pinwheels, '87 276
Blackberry Roll, '82 178
Blueberry Kuchen, '80 143
Butter Pastry, Golden, '84 22
Calzones, Spinach-and-Cheese, '95 310
Camembert Bars, '86 58
Cannoli, '80 58
Cheddar Cheese Pastry, '80 219; '82 194
Cheddar Pastry, '86 206
Cheese Pastries, Date-Filled, '83 259
Cheese Pastry, '88 56
Cheese Puffs, Mexican, '87 8
Cheese Rolls, '80 286
Chicken Puffs, Appetizer, '85 72
Chocolate Pastry Shell, '87 262
Chocolate-Raspberry Bags, '95 97
Citrus Pastry, Hint-of-, '93 260
Coconut Puffs, '87 277
Cornmeal Pastry, '81 140
Cornmeal Pastry Cups, '90 69
Cornucopia, Pastry, '95 307
Cream Cheese Pastries, '80 250
Cream Cheese Pastry, '82 39; '86 24, 78;
   '89 136
Cream Cheese Pastry Shells, '86 13
Cream Cheese Pastry Shells, Miniature,
   '87 190
Cream Cheese Patty Shells, '81 266;
   '82 249

PIES AND PASTRIES, Pastries *(continued)*

Cream Cheese Shells, '79 2
Cream Horns, '84 137
Cream Puff Pastry, '85 72
Cream Puffs, Captivating, '81 180
Danish Pastry Puffs, '85 311
Double-Crust Pastry, '81 105;
  '82 85, M298; '83 248; '85 191;
  '87 299; '88 94, 178
Double-Crust Pastry, Flaky, '82 57
Éclairs, Pistachio-Cream, '91 296
Éclairs with Pecan Sauce, '83 219
Empanadas, '92 156
Fig Snacks, Sliced, '86 206
Flaky Pastry, '80 224; '81 56, 210;
  '83 156
Fruit Basket Strudel, '87 276
Fruit Puff, Giant, '85 72
German Pastries, '86 78
Guava Puffs, '92 247
Heart Tart Pastry, '87 14
Java Cream Puffs, '81 187
Lemon Cream Puffs, '93 254
Light Pastry, '92 95
Make-Ahead Pastry, '82 209; '83 100
Maple Cream Coffee Treat, '90 50
Mexican Fiesta Confection, '82 223
Microwave Pastry, Basic, '82 M142;
  '85 M113
Mix, Perfect Pastry, '81 142
Mocha Pastry Shell, '81 136
Mushroom-Almond Pastry Cups, '88 210
Napoleons, '84 138
Napoleons, Berry, '94 120
Napoleons, Blueberry-Lemon, '94 122
Napoleons, Coffee, '95 276
Napoleons, Peanut Butter-and-
  Chocolate, '94 121
Napoleons, Strawberry, '81 126
Never Fail Pastry, '79 79
Orange Shortcake, Fresh, '80 100
Palmiers, '87 277
Papaya-Pineapple Roll, '94 18
Paste Pastry, Common, '94 17
Pastry, '82 85, 139, 259;
  '83 84, 91, 175; '84 21, 23;
  '86 24, 25, 242, 259, 303, 326;
  '87 212, 267; '88 103, 198, 225;
  '89 67, 137, 154, 214, 267;
  '91 23, 241; '92 84, 157
Pastry, Basic, '79 282; '81 M268;
  '82 114; '84 48; '89 215; '91 119;
  '94 210
Pâté Pastry, '86 65
Pears en Croûte, '93 210
Phyllo Baskets, Walnut-, '93 210
Phyllo Bowls, '95 58
Phyllo Cheesecakes, Little, '87 275
Phyllo-Cheese Triangles, '87 246
Phyllo Nests, Nutty, '87 277
Phyllo Tartlet Shells, '95 216
Pineapple Phyllo Bundles, '87 277
Piroshki, '92 84
Plum Kuchen, '79 161
Praline Pastries, '89 318
Preserve-Filled Foldovers, '80 7
Processor Pastry, '87 67
Processor Pie Dough, Quick Food,
  '84 219
Profiteroles, '84 208
Puff Pastry, Basic, '84 135

Puff Pastry Baskets, '93 177
Puff Pastry Baskets, Tropical, '93 177
Puff Pastry Bowls, '95 58
Puff Pastry, Quick, '84 207
Puffs, Cocktail, '91 106
Puffs, Sweet, '89 91
Pumpkin Empanadas, '82 223
Quiche Pastry, '80 M107
Quiche Pastry, Microwaved, '81 M74;
  '82 M122
Raisin Pastry Bites, '90 86
Raspberry-Nut Strudel, '83 304
Raspberry Party Puffs, '90 170
Rugelach, '85 276
Samosas, '89 266
Savory Pastry, '90 24
Seasoned Pastry, '79 253
Sesame Pastry Shell, '82 67
Shell, Pastry, '84 31, 127; '87 262;
  '89 236; '93 289; '94 158
Shell, Perfect Pastry, '81 142
Shells, Pastry, '83 93
Shell, Water-Whipped Baked Pastry,
  '95 246
Shortcake Pastry, '80 100
Sopaipillas, '89 268
Spinach-Artichoke-Tomato Puffs,
  '95 284
Spinach Strudels, '93 249
Strawberry Cream Puffs, '81 95
Strawberry-Lemon Cream Puffs, '87 75
Sugar Cookie Pastry, '91 119
Tart Pastry, '89 232; '90 92; '91 118
Tart Shell, '87 77; '88 20
Tart Shells, '82 304; '83 279; '85 300;
  '86 18, 105; '88 4; '90 84; '91 13
Tart Shells, Cheese, '88 88
Tart Shells, Cheese Pastry, '85 216
Tart Shells, Tea, '85 120
Timbale Shells, '82 108
Triple-Crust Pastry, '80 186
Turkey-Mushroom Pâté in Pastry,
  '92 327
Tutti-Frutti Cream Puffs, '79 231
Vegetable Oil Pastry, '91 204
Whole Wheat Pastry, '81 229
Peach
  Blackberry Pie, Peach-and-, '89 136
  Blueberry-Peach Pie, '94 158
  Chiffon Pie, Peach, '89 155
  Cranberry Pie, Peach-, '83 249
  Cream Pie, Dried Peach, '84 146
  Cream Pie, Peaches-and-, '81 184
  Filling, Fresh Peach Pie, '95 195
  Fresh Peach Pie, '82 170; '95 195
  Fried Peach Pies, '81 272
  Fried Pies, Easy Peach, '85 178
  Little Peach Pies, '86 303
  Luscious Peach Pie, '81 136
  Mincemeat-Peach Pie, '80 295; '81 188
  Praline Pie, Peach, '89 136
  Quick Peach Pie, '89 252
  Rhubarb-Peach Pie, '86 140
Peanut Butter Cream Pie, '79 50; '88 65
Peanut Butter Meringue Pie, '84 30
Peanut Butter Pie, '85 275; '86 109; '89 252
Peanut Butter Pie, Fluffy, '94 246
Peanut-Raisin Pie, '79 85
Peanuts" Pie, "Working for, '93 115
Pear Crumble Pie, '83 207
Pear-Macadamia Pie, '93 260
Pear Mincemeat Pie, '84 264; '88 226
Pear-Mince Pie, '81 271

Pear Pie, Backyard, '93 237
Pear Pie, Deep-Dish, '80 219
Pear Pie, Delicious, '88 226
Pear Pie, Double-Crust, '82 194
Pear Pie, French, '87 213
Pear Pie, Ginger-, '93 48
Pear Pie, Tennessee, '85 230
Pear Streusel Pie, '83 234; '84 244
Pecan
  Bourbon Pecan Pie, '85 90
  Bourbon-Pecan Pie, Frozen, '89 251
  Bourbon-Pecan Pumpkin Pie, '87 264
  Butter Pecan Pie Squares, '81 262
  Caramel-Pecan Apple Pie, '85 247
  Caramel-Pecan Pie, '88 282
  Cherry-Pecan Pie, '92 30
  Chocolate-Banana-Pecan Cream Pie,
    '94 210
  Chocolate-Pecan Chess Pie, '93 251
  Chocolate Pecan Pie, '80 237; '83 12;
    '90 184
  Chocolate-Pecan Pie, '91 272
  Choco-Pecan Pie, '82 86
  Coconut-Pecan Chess Pie, '81 248
  Coconut Pecan Pie, '81 161
  Coffee Pecan Pie, '82 74
  Cranberry-Pecan Pie, '92 316
  Custard Pecan Pie, '87 184
  Date-Pecan Pie, '80 15
  Golden Pecan Pie, '81 266
  Grandmother's Pecan Pie, '86 269
  Holiday Pecan Pie, '81 296
  Honey-Pecan Finger Pies, '90 184
  Individual Pecan Pies, '85 295
  Layered Pecan Pie, '83 305
  Lemon-Pecan Pie, '93 251
  Louisiana Pecan Pie, '92 83
  Maple-Pecan Pie, '81 266
  Miniature Pecan Pies, '79 205; '86 13
  Molasses-Pecan Pie, '86 259
  Old-Fashioned Pecan Pie, '81 M269
  Orange-Pecan Pie, '79 282; '83 222
  Pecan Pie, '79 251; '80 57; '85 255;
    '90 312; '92 234
  Pumpkin-Pecan Pie, '85 233, 282
  Pumpkin Pie, Nutty, '82 67
  Raisin-Pecan Pie, '87 213
  Special, Old Pecan Street, '93 251
  Spicy Pecan Pie, '84 240
  Sweet Potato-Pecan Pie, '83 90
  Texas Pecan Pie, '83 159
  Texas Star Pecan Pie, '90 184
  Tiny Pecan Pies, '79 225
  Turtle Pecan Pie, '93 250
Persimmon Pie, '79 206
Pineapple-Coconut Chess Pie, '92 214
Pineapple Pie, '80 237; '89 252
Pineapple Pie, Double-Crust, '82 85
Pineapple Pie, Fresh, '91 178
Pistachio Pie, '80 56
Plum Cream Pie, Easy, '86 174
Plum Pie, Streusel-Topped, '88 153
Plum Pie with Italian Sweet Crust, '79 162
Pumpkin
  Autumn Pumpkin Pie, '87 213
  Bourbon-Pecan Pumpkin Pie, '87 264
  Chiffon Pie, Pumpkin, '84 312
  Festive Pumpkin Pie, '81 M269
  Fluffy Pumpkin Pie, '80 283
  Ice Cream Pie, Pumpkin-, '87 243
  Meringue, Pumpkin Pie with, '92 268
  New-Fashioned Pumpkin Pie, '90 296
  Nutty Pumpkin Pie, '82 67

PIES AND PASTRIES, Pumpkin (*continued*)

Pecan Pie, Pumpkin-, '85 233, 282
Praline Pie, Frosty Pumpkin-, '91 M234
Praline Pie, Pumpkin, '80 244
Quick Pumpkin Pie, '88 M230
Rich Pumpkin Pie, '86 292
Sour Cream-Pumpkin Pie, '84 263
Spiced Nut Crust, Pumpkin Pie in, '87 295
Spicy Pumpkin Pies, '84 322
Supreme, Pumpkin Pie, '82 217
Traditional Pumpkin Pie, '85 256
Raisin Pie, '83 220
Raisin Pie, Spiced, '84 148
Raspberry Cream Pie, '94 209
Rhubarb-Peach Pie, '86 140
Rhubarb-Raisin Pie, '79 112
Rhubarb-Raspberry Pear Pie, '95 119
Rum Bisque Pie, '79 123
Rum Cream Pie, '85 212
Scuppernong Pie, '88 216
Sour Cream Pie, '86 260
Sour Cream Pie, Tropical, '79 176; '80 6
Strawberry Angel Pie, '88 136
Strawberry-Banana Glazed Pie, '81 181
Strawberry-Glaze Pie, '81 141
Strawberry Pie, Chilled, '82 112
Strawberry Pie, Glazed, '82 M142
Strawberry Yogurt Pie, '80 232
Strawberry-Yogurt Pie, '85 122; '86 124
Tarts
Almond Tart, '89 232
Almond Tassies, Lucky, '91 13
Almond Tea Tarts, '85 120
Apple Cream Tart, '84 207
Apple-Pecan Tarts, '80 282
Apple Tart, Creamed, '94 17
Apple Tart, Deluxe, '84 227
Apple Tart with Cheese Pastry, '88 225
Apricot-Apple Crumb Tart, '94 60
Apricot Tarts, '79 282; '88 281
Berry Tartlets, Fresh, '91 98
Berry Tart, Pick-a-, '91 118
Blackberry Pudding Tarts, '93 200
Black Bottom Mocha-Cream Tart, '92 304
Blue Cheese Appetizer Tarts, '85 300; '86 18
Bouilli, Tarte à la, '83 92
Caramel Tarts, '82 43
Caramel Turtle Truffle Tart, '93 M131
Cheese Tart, Herb-, '87 98
Cheese Tartlets, '88 211
Cherry and Blackberry Tart, '83 225
Cherry Tarts, Cheery, '80 238
Chess Tarts, '90 83
Chicken Salad Tarts, '84 257
Chicken Tarts, Deviled, '94 14
Chocolate-Amaretto Heavenly Tarts, '88 4
Chocolate Chess Tarts, '92 214
Chocolate-Peanut Butter Tarts, '92 277
Chocolate-Pecan Tart with Caramel Sauce, '93 296; '94 234
Chocolate Tarts, Bluegrass, '90 84
Cranberry-Cream Cheese Tarts, '80 154
Cranberry Holiday Tarts, '83 279
Cranberry-Nut Tart, '84 305
Cranberry Tartlets, Fresh, '87 244
Cran-Raspberry Meringue Tarts, '92 286

Cream Cheese Tarts, '84 74; '90 312
Derby Tarts, Miniature, '90 92
Dried Tomato-Cheese Tart, '90 203
Eggnog Tarts, Creamy, '79 255
French Silk Tarts, '79 236
Fruit Tart, Fancy, '82 128; '91 119
Fruit Tart, Fresh, '84 178; '90 58
Fruit Tartlets, Fresh, '93 96
Fruit Tart, Open-Face, '84 207
Fruit Tart, Rainbow, '82 304
Fruit Tarts, Bowl-Me-Over Fresh, '93 200
Grape Tart, Green, '87 77
Grasshopper Tarts, '80 220; '89 275
Ham-and-Cheese Tart, '92 332
Ham Tart, Supreme, '84 22
Heart Tarts, '87 14
Kentucky Derby Tarts, '79 102
Key Lime Tart in Coconut Crust, '89 160
Kiwifruit-Peach Tart, '88 20
Kiwifruit Tart, '89 232
Lady Baltimore Tarts, '88 282
Lemon-Cheese Tarts, '79 2
Lemon Ice Cream Tarts, '80 152
Lemon-Sour Cream Tarts, '81 304
Lemon Tarts, '82 156; '83 79
Lemon Tarts, Berry Good, '91 119
Lemon Tarts, Dainty, '82 304
Lemon Tarts, Golden, '85 191
Lemon Tart Shells, '88 195
Lime-Pineapple Tart, '88 6
Little Bits, '79 196
Midnight Delights, '95 278
Milan, Tart, '87 70
Mushroom Tarts, '88 161
Mushroom Tarts, Hot Sherried, '83 78
Orange Curd Tarts, '92 193
Orange Tarts, Frozen, '80 154
Party Tarts, '95 90
Peach Cream Tart, '90 173
Peachy Keen Tarts, '91 118
Pear Tart, '82 304; '92 72
Pear Tart with White Caramel Sauce, '92 195
Pecan Tarts, '81 266
Pecan Tarts, Easy, '84 313
Pecan Tarts, Special, '87 224
Pecan Tarts, Toasty Southern, '95 329
Pecan Tart with Praline Cream, '90 256
Picadillo Tarts, '91 279
Pommes, La Tarte aux, '80 125
Portabello Mushroom Tart, Smoked, '94 163
Prune Tarts, Brandied, '85 223
Puddin' Pies, President Tyler's, '80 43
Pumpkin Tarts, No-Bake, '86 291
Sausage 'n' Cheese Tarts, '88 51
Seafood Tartlets, '87 247
Shrimp Tart, '87 70
Spinach Tarts, '82 249
Strawberry Dream Tart, '92 118
Strawberry-Lemon Tart, '89 111
Strawberry Tart, '84 138; '89 272
Strawberry Tarts, '80 70
Sweet Onion Tarts, '95 229
Teatime Tassies, '84 321
Tomato Tart, Fresh, '95 170
White Chocolate Chess Tart, '95 303
Tin Roof Pie, '85 91
Transparent Pie, '80 238

Turnovers
Apple Turnovers, Baked, '93 338
Apple Turnovers, Delicious, '86 25
Apple Turnovers, Fried, '81 161
Apple Turnovers, Puffy, '87 276
Apricot Turnovers, Fried, '86 24
Cheesy Sesame Seed Turnovers, '91 252
Chicken Liver Turnovers, '79 141
Fruit Turnovers, '79 150
Ham Turnovers, Party, '82 39
Meat Turnovers, '86 326
Mushroom Turnovers, Hot, '89 285
Mushroom Turnovers, Tiny, '86 24
Reuben Turnovers, '94 253
Roast Beef Turnovers, '88 273; '89 180
Salmon-Spinach Turnovers, '83 44
Sausage-Cheese Turnovers, '88 231
Turkey Turnovers, Home-Style, '94 325
Vegetable Turnovers, '86 24
Vanilla Cream Pie, Fruit-Topped, '84 49
Vegetable. *See also* Pies and Pastries/Tarts, Turnovers.
Broccoli-Cheese Pie, '84 235
Butternut Squash Chiffon Pie, '83 296; '84 285
Butternut Squash Pie, '80 40; '87 212
Butternut Squash Pie, Spicy, '80 296
Carrot Custard Pie, '79 45
Carrot Pie, '83 117
Cauliflower-Carrot Pie, '82 191
Corn Pie, Quick and Cheesy, '82 191
Corn Pie with Fresh Tomato Salsa, Buttercrust, '95 181
Florentine Crêpe Pie, '79 34
Green Tomato Pie, '79 195
Mushrooms in Patty Shells, '80 283
Onion-Cheese Pie, '88 86
Onion Pie, '82 191
Pinto Bean Pie, '80 40
Ratatouille Pie, '88 198
Scallopini Pie, '94 133
Spaghetti Squash Pie, '80 186
Spinach Pie, '82 191; '88 56
Spinach Pie, Greek, '85 59
Spinach, Pie Pan, '94 195
Spinach Pie with Muenster Crust, '95 48
Squash Pie, Spicy, '85 9
Sweet Potato Cream Pie, Southern, '87 260
Sweet Potato Meringue Pie, '81 126; '83 225
Sweet Potato-Orange Pie, '88 207
Sweet Potato-Pecan Pie, '83 90
Sweet Potato Pie, '79 207; '85 255, 275; '86 269; '89 289
Sweet Potato Pie, Carolina, '89 295
Sweet Potato Pie, No-Crust, '84 236
Sweet Potato Pie, Old-Fashioned, '79 9
Sweet Potato Pie, Speedy, '90 219
Sweet Potato Pone Pie, '80 288
Tomato Pie, '88 198
Yam Pie, Louisiana, '81 223
Zucchini Pie, Cheesy, '82 191
Zucchini Pie, Italian-Style, '83 43
Watermelon Pie, '95 144
PIMIENTO
Ball, Pimiento Cheese, '80 258
Bread, Pimiento-Cheese, '85 223
Casserole, English Pea-Pimiento, '83 207
Eggs, Pimiento-Deviled, '84 143
Hoagies, Bacon, Pimiento, and Cheese, '90 144
Pasta, Pimiento, '84 176

PIMIENTO (continued)

Popovers, Pimiento, '79 138
Sandwiches, Pimiento Cheese, '82 278
Sauce, Cauliflower with Pimiento, '87 232
Spreads
    Chunky Pimiento Cheese, '86 295
    Creamy Pimiento Cheese, '86 296
    Creamy Pimiento Cheese Spread, '92 159
    Garlic Pimiento Cheese Spread, '79 58
    Ham and Pimiento Spread, '80 285;
        '81 56
    Low-Calorie Pimiento Cheese Spread,
        '85 215
    Pimiento Cheese Spread, '82 35; '83 93;
        '86 127
    Three Cheeses, Pimiento and, '86 296
    West Texas Pimiento Cheese, '84 9
Topping, Pimiento, '83 93

PINEAPPLE

Acorn Squash, Pineapple-Stuffed, '84 255
Appetizer, Shrimp-Pineapple, '85 80
Bacon-Wrapped Pineapple Chunks, '84 25
Baked Pineapple, '83 261; '84 287
Bake, Pineapple, '79 251
Bake, Pineapple-Cheese, '79 106
Ball, Pineapple Cheese, '81 160
Ball, Pineapple-Cheese, '84 26
Beans, Hawaiian-Style Baked, '86 210
Beets with Pineapple, '79 249; '82 204
Betty, Pineapple-Apple, '85 46
Beverages
    Banana-Pineapple Smoothie, Quick,
        '93 195
    Banana Slush, Pineapple-, '90 14
    Blue Woo-Woo, '94 226
    Coconut-Pineapple Drink, '83 172
    Cooler, Pineapple, '90 207
    Float, Pineapple Sherbet, '79 148
    Hot Buttered Pineapple Drink,
        '91 260
    Lemonade, Pineapple, '93 194
    Milk Shake, Banana-Pineapple,
        '84 59
    Milkshake, Pineapple, '87 199
    Milk Shake, Pineapple, '94 113
    Nectar, Hot Pineapple, '90 21
    Nog, Speedy Breakfast, '82 47
    Orange-Pineapple Drink, '89 35
    Piña Coladas, '95 203
    Piña Colada Slush, '95 90
    Punch, False-Kick, '82 121
    Punch, Frosty Pineapple, '91 66
    Punch, Hot Pineapple, '82 264
    Punch, Lime-Pineapple, '83 142
    Punch, Pineapple, '79 174; '80 128
    Punch, Pineapple-Gin, '95 140
    Punch, Pineapple-Mint, '88 209
    Punch, Pineapple-Orange, '85 236
    Punch, Pineapple Sherbet, '95 141
    Punch, Spiced Pineapple, '83 33;
        '92 66
    Sangría, Pineapple, '91 176
    Shake, Pineapple-Banana, '85 215
    Shake, Strawberry-Pineapple, '84 166
    Slush, Pineapple, '88 82
    Soda, Pineapple, '90 179
    Spiced Pineapple Sparkle, '92 322
    Strawberry Slush, Pineapple-, '94 227
    Tea, Pineapple, '93 165
    Wassail, Pineapple-Apricot, '83 275
    Yogurt Whirl, Pineapple-, '91 132

Breads
    Apricot Bread, Pineapple-, '84 7
    Buns, Easy Pineapple, '85 14
    Carrot Bread, Pineapple-, '79 106
    Carrot-Pineapple Bread, '82 210
    Hawaiian Loaf, '80 225
    Muffins, Carrot-Pineapple, '81 6
    Muffins, Morning Glory, '93 327
    Muffins, Pineapple, '81 14, 250
    Muffins, Sunshine, '86 9
    Nut Bread, Pineapple-, '79 215
    Pecan Loaf Bread, Pineapple-, '87 256
    Pineapple Bread, '83 139
    Rolls, Cranberry-Pineapple, '86 275
    Rolls, Pineapple Angel, '89 72
Carrots, Pineapple, '83 198
Citrus, Pineapple and Fresh, '89 206
Coffee Cake, Pineapple-Coconut, '94 49
Curried Carrots and Pineapple, '90 228
Desserts
    Ambrosia, Pineapple-Orange, '88 252
    Baked Pineapple with Natillas Sauce,
        '83 179
    Bars, Pineapple-Orange, '82 129
    Basket, Summer Berry, '84 158
    Cake, Cajun, '87 138
    Cake, Coconut-Pineapple, '89 56
    Cake, Coconut-Pineapple Layer, '80 140
    Cake, Heavenly Pineapple, '83 303
    Cake, Lemon-Pineapple, '86 60, 239
    Cake, Pineapple-Pecan Upside-Down,
        '84 25
    Cake, Pineapple Pound, '79 148
    Cake, Pineapple Upside-Down, '80 102;
        '88 10
    Cake Roll, Coconut-Pineapple, '84 304
    Cake, Skillet Pineapple Upside-Down,
        '85 242
    Cake, Stacked Pineapple Upside-Down,
        '86 239
    Cake, Zucchini-Pineapple, '95 160
    Charlotte, Pineapple, '90 288
    Cheesecake, Pineapple, '81 32
    Cheesecake, Ultimate Pineapple, '85 38
    Chimichangas, Pineapple Dessert, '86 4
    Chocolate-Drizzled Pineapple with
        Raspberry Sauce, '90 57
    Cookies, Pineapple, '79 216
    Cream, Pineapple 'n', '88 202
    Crêpes, Mango-Pineapple, '86 216
    Delight, Fresh Pineapple, '79 111
    Delight, Pineapple-Almond, '85 96
    Filling, Pineapple, '80 140; '83 179;
        '84 153; '89 57
    Frappé, Hawaiian, '81 178
    Fritters, Pineapple, '88 112
    Frosting, Pineapple-Cream Cheese,
        '95 160
    Frozen Tropical Paradise, '89 206
    Glazed Oranges and Pineapple, '86 318
    Glaze, Orange-Pineapple, '81 60
    Glaze, Pineapple, '83 143; '85 38
    Ice Cream, Orange-Pineapple, '86 117
    Ice Cream, Pineapple-Mint, '84 186
    Meringue-Topped Pineapple, '84 178
    Mousse, Coconut-Pineapple, '94 198
    Mousse, Elegant Pineapple, '79 230
    Papaya-Pineapple Roll, '94 18
    Parfait, Pineapple, '84 83
    Pears, Pineapple-Honey, '86 94
    Phyllo Bundles, Pineapple, '87 277
    Pie, Coconut-Pineapple, '84 256
    Pie, Double-Crust Pineapple, '82 85

Pie, Fresh Pineapple, '91 178
Pie, Pineapple, '80 237; '89 252
Pie, Pineapple-Chicken Salad, '80 138
Pie, Pineapple-Coconut Chess, '92 214
Pops, Hawaiian Orange-Pineapple,
    '94 143
Pops, Pineapple-Yogurt, '91 173
Pudding, Pineapple, '80 102
Sauce, Banana-Pineapple, '83 48
Sauce, Pineapple Ice Cream, '81 M289
Sauce, Pineapple-Orange, '84 14
Sauce, Pineapple-Rum, '84 275
Sherbet, Creamy Pineapple, '79 155
Sherbet, Easy Pineapple, '92 199
Sherbet, Pineapple, '81 177; '84 83;
    '89 199
Sopaipillas, Pineapple, '83 179
Soufflé, Pineapple Dessert, '80 153
Spritz, Pineapple, '86 94
Sundaes, Mauna Loa, '80 126
Tart, Lime-Pineapple, '88 6
Topping, Cherry-Pineapple, '87 126
Topping, Lemon-Pineapple, '86 60
Topping, Pineapple, '86 239
Trifle, Pineapple Angel Food, '93 86
Tropical Snow, '86 34
Dip, Cheesy Pineapple, '80 249
Dip, Pineapple-Ginger, '86 104
Doughnuts, Pineapple Drop, '83 95
Dressing, Fruit Salad with Pineapple, '85 207
Dressing, Pineapple Cream, '83 81
Dressing, Pineapple-Poppy Seed, '85 55
Fried Pineapple, '81 232
Glaze, Pineapple, '83 143; '84 26; '85 38
Gratin, Pineapple, '93 328
Ham-Pineapple Nibbles, '95 283
Hawaiian Dream Boats, '86 151
Jam, Pineapple, '81 147
Jelly, Pineapple-Orange Mint, '92 105
Main Dishes
    Beans and Franks, Hawaiian Baked,
        '80 136
    Beefburgers Hawaiian, '86 137
    Beef Kabobs, Pineapple-, '83 212
    Burgers, Pineapple, '82 169
    Chicken and Pineapple, '81 281; '82 30
    Chicken Bake, Pineapple, '82 120
    Chicken, Hawaiian Sesame, '81 106
    Chicken Kabobs, Pineapple-, '86 M328
    Chicken, Oriental Pineapple, '84 288
    Chicken, Piña Colada, '86 21
    Chicken, Pineapple, '83 M194; '85 3
    Chicken Stir-Fry, Pineapple-, '89 176
    Chicken with Pineapple-Mustard Glaze,
        Roast, '89 83
    Chicken with Pineapple, Oriental, '86 42
    Chops, Pineapple-Curry Glazed, '82 106
    Crab Imperial, Pineapple-, '84 M286
    Franks, Hawaiian, '81 202
    Ham, Citrus-and-Spice, '88 40
    Ham Loaf, Pineapple Upside-Down,
        '79 253
    Ham Patties, Pineapple-, '80 110
    Ham, Pineapple-Baked, '86 48
    Ham, Pineapple-Flavored, '87 160
    Ham-Potato-Pineapple Bake, '93 302
    Ham Sandwich Loaf, Pineapple-, '91 167
    Loaves, Individual Pineapple, '81 M121
    Meatballs, Chinese, '87 194
    Meatballs with Pineapple and Peppers,
        '90 145
    Pork and Pineapple, Polynesian, '83 102
    Pork Chops, Hawaiian, '86 212

PINEAPPLE, Main Dishes (continued)

Pork Chops, Pineapple, '87 M124
Pork, Pineapple, '82 60
Pork, Pineapple Sweet-and-Sour, '82 120
Pork Roast, Pineapple, '79 41
Pot Roast, Hawaiian, '81 298
Pot Roast, Polynesian, '80 59
Marmalade, Orange-Pineapple, '82 150; '89 M156
Marmalade, Strawberry-Pineapple, '85 130
Meatballs, Polynesian, '80 207
Pears, Pineapple-Honey, '86 94
Pickled Pineapple, '79 24
Preserves, Mango-Pineapple, '79 137
Rice with Pineapple, Curried, '79 142
Salad Dressing, Pineapple, '81 36
Salads
Boat Aloha, Pineapple, '80 102
Boats Ahoy, Pineapple, '80 148
Buttermilk Salad, Pineapple-, '82 80
Carrot-Pineapple Salad, '91 83
Celery Salad, Pineapple-, '85 95
Chicken Salad, Pineapple-Nut, '83 80
Citrus, Pineapple and Fresh, '89 206
Coleslaw, Curried Pineapple, '88 172
Congealed Salad, Pineapple-Cucumber, '83 118
Congealed Salad, Pineapple-Orange, '83 218
Cranberry-Pineapple Salad, Frozen, '91 237
Cucumber-Pineapple Salad, '84 124
Daiquiri Salad, Pineapple, '84 232
Delight, Pineapple-Pear, '82 54
Fresh Pineapple Boats, '83 153
Frosted Salad, Heavenly, '79 286
Frosty Pineapple Salad, '89 278
Fruit Salad, Icy Pineapple-, '87 9
Lime Salad, Pineapple-, '84 320
Macaroni Salad, Pineapple, '79 220
Mandarin Orange and Pineapple Salad, '82 266
Mold, Minted Pineapple, '85 240
Shrimp Salad, Aloha, '95 46
Slaw, Apple-Pineapple, '79 241
Slaw, Cabbage-Pineapple, '92 182
Slaw, Colorful Pineapple, '86 250
Slaw, Pineapple, '94 49
Slaw, Pineapple-Almond, '92 171
Waldorf Salad, Pineapple, '92 97
Sauce, Banana-Pineapple, '83 48
Sauce, Jezebel, '81 29; '82 55
Sauce, Pineapple, '84 236; '92 203
Sauce, Pineapple-Curry, '79 252
Sauce, Pineapple-Rhubarb, '88 94
Sauce, Raisin-Pineapple, '82 177
Sauce, Sweet-and-Sour Pineapple, '85 66
Scalloped Pineapple, '79 106; '82 254; '84 M323
Skewered Pineapple and Strawberries, '84 251
Slicing Pineapples, Instructions for, '82 94
Snow Peas and Pineapple, '91 120
Spiced Pineapple, '80 102
Spread, Coconut-Pineapple, '93 309
Spread, Hawaiian Cheese, '87 158
Spread, Pineapple-Cheese, '86 126; '91 167
Spread, Pineapple-Cream Cheese, '82 35
Spread, Pineapple Sandwich, '84 166
Spritz, Pineapple, '86 94

PIZZA
Appetizers
Cocktail Pizzas, '79 110
Horns, Pizza, '89 214
Party Pizzettes, '80 192
Pita Pizzas, '89 19
Pizzas, Appetizer, '89 M118
Shellfish Pizza, '91 224
Shrimp Pizza Wedges, '89 158
Slices, Pizza, '84 269
Snacks, Pizza Party, '86 262
Snacks, Tasty Little Pizza, '79 248
Squares, Pizza, '87 168
Turnovers, Little Pizza, '85 327
Zucchini Pizzas, '88 212
Artichoke and Prosciutto, Pizza with, '87 182
Bagel, Pizza on a, '93 M94
Bayou Pizza, The Best of the, '95 268
Beef-and-Sausage Pizza, Double Cheesy, '86 77
Bites, Pizza, '95 244
Blazing Sunset Pizza, '95 267
Bobolis, Easy Cheesy, '92 278
Bread, Pizza Batter, '85 56
Breakfast Pizza, '85 44; '88 288; '90 140, 178
Burger, Pizza, '87 185
Burgers, All-American Pizza, '92 148
Burgers, Easy Pizza, '82 190
Burger Snacks, Pizza-, '84 30
Burgers, Pizza, '80 M201; '81 73; '89 165
Calzone, '85 94
Calzones, All-Star Pizza, '95 308
Casserole, Microwave Pizza, '89 M248
Casserole, Pizza, '88 273; '89 181
Casserole, Quick Pizza, '83 266
Cheese-and-Mushroom Pizza, '83 226
Chicken Pizza, '94 218
Chocolate Pizza, '91 298
Clam Pizza, Baby, '87 182
Cookie, Pizza, '90 49
Crusts
Crispy Pizza Crust, '87 181; '89 64
Parmesan Pizza Crust, '93 58
Pizza Crust, '80 233; '83 226; '85 243; '86 77
Skillet Pizza Crusts, '94 218
Special Pizza Crust, '90 139
Thick Crust, '81 214
Thin Crust, '81 214
Whole Wheat Crust, '94 78
Whole Wheat Pizza Crust, '93 58
Cups, Pizza, '81 215
Deep-Dish Mediterranean Pizza, '80 163
Deep-Dish Pizza Luncheon Pie, '80 286
Deep-Dish Vegetarian Pizza, '85 243
Easy Pizza, '92 181
Eggplant Pizza, '85 221
French Bread, Pizza on, '82 131
Garden Pizza, '89 108
Grilled Pizzas, '93 178
Gruyère-Chicken Pizza, '87 182
Ham-and-Eggs Crescent Pizza, '93 47
Hamburger Pizza, Quick, '85 243
Herb Pizza, Easy, '92 99
Homemade Pizza, Best Ever, '80 233
Hot Dog Pizzas, '93 78
Italian-Style Pizza, Original, '87 182
Jazzed-Up Pizza, Jiffy, '83 M314
King Henry Pizza, The, '95 267
Kiwi-Berry Pizza, '86 198; '87 55
Kiwifruit Pizza, '89 306
Lasagna Pizza, '85 285
Meatballs, Pizza, '85 86

Meat Loaf, Cheesy Pizza, '81 121
Mexican Pizza, '94 218, 327
Pan Pizza, Quick, '86 160
Peanut Butter-Fruit Pizza, '94 60
Pepperoni Pizza, Thick 'n' Crusty, '85 244
Pepper Pizza, Roasted, '94 218
Peppers, Pizza, '83 135
Pesto Pizza, '87 182; '94 218
Phyllo Pizza, '94 91
Pie, Pizza, '91 23
Pita Pizza Snack, '94 193
Pocket Pizzas, Easy, '90 168
Popcorn, Pizza-Flavored, '85 236
Quiche, Pizza, '86 53
Quick Little Pizzas, '88 227
Salad Pizza, '87 182
Sandwiches, Open-Face Pizza, '82 3; '83 85; '84 M198; '85 22
Sandwich, Giant Pizza, '80 93
Sauce, Pizza, '84 33; '85 285
Sauce, Traditional Pizza, '95 267
Sausage-Pepperoni Pizza, Spicy, '83 226
Sausage Pizza Pie, Link-, '85 33
Shellfish Pizza, '91 224
Southern Classic Pizza, '95 268
Southwest Deluxe Pizza, '95 268
Speedy Pizza, '81 214
Strawberry Pizza, '79 94
Sunburst, Pizza, '94 245
Supreme, Pizza, '81 214
Taco Pizza, '89 M177
Tacos, Pizza-Flavored Chicken, '95 340
Tostada Pizza, '81 16; '82 13
Turkey-Vegetable Pizza, '90 139
Two-Way Pizza, '79 93
Upside-Down Pizza, '91 185
Vegetable Pizza, '89 64; '94 218
Vegetarian Pizza, Deep-Dish, '85 243
Vegetarian Processor Pizza, '89 225
Veggie Pizza, '94 78
Veggie Pizza, Southwestern, '95 126
Whole Wheat Pizza, '84 33
Wide-Eyed Pizzas, '90 94

PLUMS
Bread, Sugar Plum, '80 256
Butter, Plum, '88 152
Chutney, Plum, '84 179
Cobbler, Crunchy Plum, '88 152
Crunch, Layered Plum, '86 174
Fajitas, Plum Good, '94 115
Ham, Plum, '80 110
Jam, Freezer Plum, '89 M156
Jam, Peach-Plum Freezer, '85 130
Jam, Plum Refrigerator, '89 139
Jelly, Plum, '82 150
Kuchen, Plum, '79 161
Muffins, Plum Good, '83 96
Pie, Easy Plum Cream, '86 174
Pie, Streusel-Topped Plum, '88 153
Pie with Italian Sweet Crust, Plum, '79 162
Poached Plums, '90 M141
Pudding, Flamed Plum, '84 276
Pudding-Gelatin Mold, Plum, '86 300; '87 178
Pudding, Light Plum, '86 318
Pudding, Old-Fashioned Plum, '80 264
Pudding, Plum, '79 281
Sauce, Chinese Plum, '82 237
Sauce, Fresh Plum, '94 129
Sauce, Gingered Plum, '87 175
Sauce, Plum, '80 249; '82 40; '88 152
Sauce, Quail with Red Plum, '80 48
Sauce, Spicy Plum, '86 11

PLUMS (continued)

Slush, Plum, '84 139
Soup, Chilled Purple Plum, '79 162
Soup, Peach-Plum, '87 157
Soup, Plum, '85 107
POLENTA
Basic Polenta, '95 164
Grilled Polenta with Black Bean Salsa, '93 155
Sausage, Polenta with, '93 32
POPCORN
Bacon-Cheese Popcorn, '86 74
Balls, Marshmallow Popcorn, '90 226
Balls, Nutty Popcorn, '88 227
Cake, Popcorn-Gumdrop, '87 262
Candied Popcorn and Peanuts, '82 295
Caramel
Baked Caramel Corn, '81 218
Candy, Caramel Corn, '84 243
Caramel Corn, '88 64
Caramel Popcorn, '79 219; '86 M212
Crispy Caramel Popcorn, '85 247
Crunch, Caramel, '95 165
Ghoul's Hands, '94 256
Nutty Caramel Corn, '92 317
Oven-Made Caramel Corn, '91 233
Cheesy Barbecue Popcorn, '95 239
Chili Popcorn, '91 17; '95 166
Cinnamon-Popcorn Crunch, '86 136
Garlic Popcorn, '83 M315
Harvest Popcorn, '84 300
Herb-Seasoned Popcorn, '94 122
Honey-and-Spice Crunch, '94 290
Mix, Curried Popcorn, '86 326
Nutty Popcorn, '85 208
Orange Popcorn, '86 230
Oriental Popcorn, '86 74
Pizza-Flavored Popcorn, '85 236
Pizzazz, Popcorn with, '93 245
Pretzel Popcorn, '84 30
Scramble, Popcorn, '87 185
Sesame-Cheese Popcorn, '79 220
Spiced Popcorn Snack, '87 8

PORK. *See also* **BACON, HAM, SAUSAGE.**
Backbones, Smoked Country-Style, '82 162
Bake, Pork-and-Noodle, '88 98
Bake, Pork Spaghetti, '81 11
Barbecue
Bannister's Barbecue, '92 166
Chops, Barbecued Pork, '81 10
Chops, Barbecued Stuffed, '87 229
Chops, Marinated Barbecued Pork, '79 90
Chops, Oven-Barbecued Pork, '81 234; '82 26; '83 40
Home-Style Barbecue, '88 145
Pork, Barbecued, '80 72

Ribs, Apple Barbecued, '80 111
Ribs, Barbecued, '80 111; '85 159; '91 205
Ribs, Barbecued Country-Style, '95 237
Ribs, Country-Style Barbecued, '79 42
Ribs, Herbed Barbecued, '86 185
Ribs, Oven-Barbecued Pork, '88 132
Ribs, Smoky Barbecued, '80 111
Ribs, Tangy Barbecued, '83 160
Ribs with Blender Barbecue Sauce, '90 12
Roast, Barbecued Pork, '82 11
Roast, Barbecued Pork Loin, '93 34
Roast, Barbecue Pork, '82 97; '83 104
Roast, Berry Barbecued Pork, '80 288
Roast, Oven-Barbecued Pork, '91 50
Shoulder, Barbecued Pork, '81 111; '82 11
Spareribs, Apple-Barbecue, '90 160
Spareribs, Barbecued, '81 112; '82 12; '86 232; '95 236
Spareribs, Barbecued Country-Style, '80 73
Spareribs, Easy Barbecued, '82 97; '83 104
Spareribs, Saucy Barbecued, '79 14
Spareribs, Southern Barbecued, '79 90
Spareribs, Spicy Barbecued, '84 93
Spareribs, Tangy Barbecued, '82 106
Spareribs with Orange Barbecue Sauce, '83 11
Spicy Barbecued Pork, '84 296
Bean Sauce, Pork-and-Onions with, '85 76
Brunch Eggs, '85 44
Burgers, Hearty Sauced Pork, '84 125
Burgoo, Five-Meat, '87 3
Burgoo, Harry Young's, '87 3
Burritos, '80 196
Burritos, Meat-and-Bean, '81 194
Calabaza Guisada con Puerco (Pumpkin Cooked with Pork), '80 193
Casserole, Cheesy Pork, '81 M74
Casserole, Pork, '83 116
Chalupa, Bean, '80 223
Chalupas, Pork, '83 160
Chile Verde, Light, '88 148
Chili, Double-Meat, '79 269; '80 12
Chili Verde, '95 14
Chops. *See also* Pork/Barbecue.
Apple-Kraut Pork Chops, '84 50
Apple Pork Chops, '91 198
Apple Pork Chops, Spicy, '87 230
Apricot-Sauced Pork Chops, '85 22
Arlo, Pork, '87 229
Baked Pork Chops and Apples, '81 10
Bake, Fiesta Pork, '79 265
Beans, Pork Chops with Baked, '93 18
Boneless Pork Chops with Ancho Cream Sauce, '95 205
Braised Pork Chops, Bourbon-, '85 89
Broiled Pork Chops, '89 191
Broiled Pork Chops with Crabapple Peaches, '81 83
Carne Adovada, '91 162
Casserole, Peppered Pork Chop, '81 235; '82 25; '83 39
Casserole, Pork Chop, '94 255
Casserole, Pork Chop-Vegetable, '90 208
Cheesy Pork Chops, '83 102
Chili Chops, '87 10
Cider-Sauced Pork Chops, '86 213; '87 81
Company Pork Chops, '85 109

Costillas Rellenos (Stuffed Pork Chops), '82 219
Country Pride Pork Chops, '79 159
Cranberry Pork, '90 293
Cranberry Pork Chops, '80 288; '90 53
Creamy Gravy, Pork Chops and, '81 207
Creole Pork Chops, '83 102
Creole-Style Pork Chops, '91 49
Curried Apricot Pork Chops, '89 191
Dill-Cream Gravy, Pork Chops with, '84 81
Dinner, Pork Chop, '80 84; '81 180; '88 25
Fiesta, Pork Chops, '86 118
Fruited Pork Chops, '87 194
Fruit-Topped Pork Chops, '94 41
Glazed Apple Pork Chops, '86 300
Glazed Chops, Pineapple-Curry, '82 106
Glazed Pork Chops, '86 185
Glazed Pork Chops, Apple-, '84 212; '87 35
Glazed Pork Chops, Orange-, '81 234; '82 25; '83 39; '84 234; '91 84
Glazed Pork Chops with Green Mole Sauce, Tamarind-, '95 266
Glazed Pork Chops with Rice, Fruit-, '82 73
Glazed Pork Steaks, '83 178
Gourmet Pork Chops, '79 180
Gravy, Pork Chops in, '91 137
Grilled Pork Chops, '88 113
Grilled Pork Chops, Hawaiian, '85 159
Grilled Pork Chops, Marinated, '81 110
Hawaiian Pork Chops, '86 212; '87 82
Honey-Lime Pork Chops, '91 33
Italiano, Pork Chops, '80 72
Italian, Pork Chops, '79 47
Jardinière, Pork Chops, '81 112; '82 12
Lemon-Herb Pork Chops, '84 81; '89 M132
Lemony Pork Chops, '88 118
Marinated Pork Chops, '89 249
Meal for Two, Pork Chop, '81 273
Mustard-Apricot Pork Chops, '89 225
Orange-Cranberry Pork Chops, '86 335; '87 84
Orange Pork Chops, '84 81
Oriental Pork Chops, '84 81; '90 212
Parmesan Pork Chops with Apples, '93 338
Peachy Pork Chops, '89 310
Peanut Sauce, Pork Chops with, '83 29
Pecan-Breaded Pork Chops with Beer Sauce, '95 266
Pineapple Pork Chops, '87 M124
Pleasing Pork Chops, '79 125
Polynesian Pork and Pineapple, '83 102
Rice, Pork Chops and Spanish, '83 103; '85 293
Risotti, Pork Chops, '81 234; '82 26
Saucy Company Pork Chops, '83 102
Saucy Pork Chop, '86 M140
Sauerkraut, Pork Chops and, '88 98
Savory Pork Chops, '87 194
Scallop, Pork Chops and Potato, '82 114
Sherry-Apple Pork Chops, '88 40
Sherry, Chops in, '79 125
Skillet Dinner, Pork Chop, '79 125
Skillet Pork Chops, Easy, '79 255
Sour Cream Sauce, Pork Chops with, '83 102
Special, Pork Chop, '79 81

Stuffed Baked Pork Chops, '79 222;
'80 64
Stuffed Pork Chops, '84 195; '86 89
Stuffed Pork Chops, Apple-, '79 125
Stuffed Pork Chops, Apple-Crumb,
'81 234; '82 26; '83 39
Stuffed Pork Chops, Apricot-, '86 76;
'92 219
Stuffed Pork Chops, Apricot-Mushroom,
'95 287
Stuffed Pork Chops, Braised, '87 249
Stuffed Pork Chops, Cheese-, '84 81
Stuffed Pork Chops, Easy, '81 10
Stuffed Pork Chops, Fruit-, '82 136
Stuffed Pork Chops, Fruited, '86 197
Stuffed Pork Chops, Rice-, '83 102
Stuffed Pork Chops with Apricot Glaze,
'89 M36
Stuffed with Prunes, Pork Chops, '84 7
Sweet-and-Sour Pork Chops, '83 160
Vegetable Pork Chops, Skillet, '85 179
Vegetables, Golden Chops with, '89 218
Vegetables, Pork Chops and Garden,
'88 297
Chow Mein, Pork, '80 208; '90 101
Curry, Hurry, '79 103
Cutlets, Apple-Glazed Pork, '92 181
Dinner, Pork-and-Noodles Skillet, '88 199
Egg Rolls, '86 81
Eggrolls, Shrimp and Pork, '82 240; '83 18
Eggs, Tulsa, '87 95
Hominy, Mexican, '86 255
Hot-and-Spicy Pork, '81 228
Kabobs, Spicy Pork, '82 182
Leg of Pork with Cranberry Glaze, '88 244
Loin Stuffed with Wild Rice, Pork, '84 35
Marinated Pork Strips, '92 219
Meatballs in Gravy, '79 136
Meatballs, Sauerkraut, '86 257
Meatballs, Tangy Hawaiian, '79 129
Meat Loaf
Family-Style Meat Loaf, '93 18
Italian Meat Loaf, '79 187
Mozzarella-Layered Meat Loaf, '79 71
Savory Meat Loaf, '87 216
Skillet Liver Loaf, '80 11
Stuffed Meat Loaf, '79 187
Swedish Meat Loaf, '81 M121
Triple Meat Loaf, '79 186
Meat Mixture, Basic, '92 241
Medaillons of Pork with Vegetables, '88 223
Oriental, Pork, '81 212
Paella, Chicken-Pork-Shrimp, '82 245
Pâté, Country, '86 66
Pâté en Croûte, '86 65
Pâté with Spinach and Cream, Pork,
'83 224
Picadillo II, '93 72
Pie, Continental Meat, '95 256
Pies, Natchitoches Meat, '84 21; '91 241
Pie, Sombrero, '81 140
Pilaf, Fruited Pork, '82 246
Pineapple Pork, '82 60
Polynesian Pork, '85 78
Posole, '95 226
Ribs. *See also* Pork/Barbecue.
Adams' Ribs, '95 236
Baby Loin Back Ribs, John Wills's,
'90 120
Baked Ribs, Easy, '86 20

Baked Ribs, Lemon, '81 166
Chinese Spareribs, '81 10
Glazed Spareribs, '88 98
Glazed Spareribs, Honey-, '82 163
Glazed Spareribs, Orange-, '84 296
Glazed Spareribs, Peach-, '86 14
Grilled Ribs, Lemon, '81 154
Lemony Sweet Spareribs, '80 73
Oven Ribs, Smoky, '81 166
Plantation Ribs, '84 217
Puerco en Adobo, '88 116
Saucy Oven Spareribs, '80 207
Saucy-Sweet Ribs, '81 166
Smoked Ribs, '88 169
Smoked Ribs with Honey-Mustard Sauce,
'92 168
Smoky Ribs, '84 172
Spareribs, Southern, '95 116
Spicy Spareribs, '89 168
Stuffed Spareribs, Fruit-, '79 14
Sweet-and-Sour Ribs, '89 M84
Sweet-and-Sour Spareribs, '83 21
Rice, Pork Fried, '89 99
Risotto, Pork, '82 60
Roasts
à l'Orange, Porc, '80 242
Apples and Mushrooms, Roast Pork
Loin with, '92 218
Arista of Pork, '81 260
Braised Pork, Brown Sugar, '84 36
Chinese Roast Pork, '91 308
Crown Pork Flambé, Stuffed, '83 263
Crown Pork Roast, Stuffed, '89 272
Crown Roast of Pork, Royal, '80 252
Crown Roast of Pork, Stuffed, '86 323
Crown Roast of Pork with Cranberry-
Sausage Stuffing, '88 49
Glazed Pork Loin, '87 229
Glazed Pork Roast, Cherry-, '91 84
Grilled Pork, Honey-and-Herb, '90 148
Grilled Pork Loin, Honey-, '92 219
Indonesian Pork Roast, '81 227
Italian Pork Roast, '91 238; '92 27
Loin of Pork, Roast, '84 276
Loin, Roast Pork, '88 221
Loin Roast with Red Currant Sauce,
Pork, '89 M84
Mandarin Pork Roast, '83 47
Marinated Pork Roast, '80 71; '84 260
Pernil (Pork Roast), '92 157
Pineapple Pork Roast, '79 41
Pineapple Sweet-and-Sour Pork, '82 120
Rio Grande Pork Roast, '84 35, 296
Roasted Pork Loin with Mushrooms and
Garlic, '92 301
Smoked Pork Loin Mahogany, '91 148
Smoked Pork Shoulder, '82 225
Spiced Cherry Sauce, Roast Pork with,
'89 324
Stuffed Pork Loin, Apricot-Pecan,
'94 274
Stuffed Pork Loin, Fruitcake-, '95 250
Stuffed Pork Loin Roast, Prune-, '80 29
Stuffed Pork Rib Roast, Sausage-,
'94 240
Stuffed Pork Roast, '81 111; '82 12;
'85 229
Stuffed Pork Shoulder, '81 11
Stuffed Pork, Spinach-and-Herb, '89 193
Tomato Sauce, Pork Roast with, '87 249
Zesty Pork Roast, '85 179
Salad, Mandarin Pork-and-Spinach, '88 M126
Salad, Oriental Pork, '92 140

Salad, "Pig in the Garden," '92 255
Salad, Pork-'n'-Bean, '87 83
Sandwiches, Party Pork, '88 M273
Sausage, Pork, '81 55
Sauté, Plum Delicious Pork, '89 105
Sesame Pork Rounds, '89 122
Sloppy Joes, Pork, '86 294
Soup, Guadalajara, '88 30
Soup, Homemade, '79 198
Steaks, Herbed Pork, '80 72
Steaks, Peachy Pork, '79 166
Stew, Bama Brunswick, '87 4
Stew, Breeden Liles's Brunswick, '91 14
Stew, Brunswick, '80 264
Stew, Dan Dickerson's Brunswick, '91 16
Stew, Easy Brunswick, '92 280
Stew, Georgian Brunswick, '92 35
Stew, Pancho Villa, '94 44
Stew, Sonny Frye's Brunswick, '87 4
Stew, Virginia Ramsey's Favorite Brunswick,
'91 16
Stir-Fried Pork, '87 51
Stir-Fried Pork in Garlic Sauce, '84 141
St. Tammany, Pork, '82 260
Swedish Porkburgers, '79 42
Sweet-and-Pungent Pork, '86 118
Sweet-and-Sour Pork, '79 42; '80 72, 227;
'81 26, 104, 111; '82 12; '84 218;
'85 34, 194; '86 241; '90 317; '92 219
Tamales, '80 195
Tamales, Hot, '83 51
Tempting Twosome, '81 240
Tenderloin
Apple-Ginger Pork Tenderloin, '86 75
Apple-Mushroom Pork Tenderloin,
'95 53
Blue Cheese, Pork Tenderloin with,
'86 76
Cacciatore, Pork, '95 69
Curried Pork Tenderloin, '86 76
Danish Pork Tenderloin, '82 186
Glazed Pork Tenderloin, '90 315
Grilled Marinated Pork Tenderloin,
'91 199
Grilled Pork Medaillons, '93 229
Grilled Pork Tenderloin, '88 98; '91 163;
'94 88
Grilled Pork Tenderloin, Garlic, '90 172
Grilled Pork Tenderloins, '94 158
Grilled Pork Tenderloin with Apples,
Celery, and Potatoes, '95 161
Grilled Pork Tenderloin with Brown
Sauce, '89 32
Grilled Pork with Salsa, '90 128
Grilled Tenderloins, Honey-, '92 199
Honey-Mustard Pork Tenderloin, '95 52
Marinated Pork Tenderloin, '84 175
Marsala, Pork, '90 35
Medaillons in Mustard Sauce, Pork,
'90 96
Medaillons with Chutney Sauce, Pork,
'87 35
Medaillons with Port Wine and Dried
Cranberry Sauce, Pork, '95 330
Mustard Sauce, Pork Tenderloin with,
'92 302
Orange Marmalade, Pork Tenderloin
with, '91 49
Parmigiana, Easy Pork, '94 57
Peking Pork Tenderloin, '93 173
Piccata, Pork, '94 57
Piccata, Pork Tenderloin, '86 76
Pinwheels, Herbed Pork, '92 23

PORK, Tenderloin (continued)

Pinwheels, Spinach-Tenderloin, '89 M118
Platter, Tenderloin, '79 42
Roast Pork Tenderloin, '84 35
Sandwiches, Beef and Pork Tenderloin, '80 175
Scaloppine Marsala, Pork, '94 57
Scaloppine, Olive-Pork, '89 191
Sesame Pork Tenderloin, '95 53
Stuffed Pork Tenderloins, Fruit-, '87 270
Stuffed Pork Tenderloin, Spinach-and-Bacon, '94 81
Sunrise Pork Tenderloin, '79 103
Towers, Pork Tenderloin, '86 75
Terrine, Jeweled Pork, '84 130
Terrine of Pork and Veal, '93 287
Vegetable-Pork Combo, '85 113
Wontons, Crispy Fried, '83 21
POTATOES. *See also* **SWEET POTATOES.**
Appetizers, Potato Shell, '89 M119
Bacon Dressing, Potatoes with Hot, '88 M294
Bake, Chive-Potato, '82 229
Baked. *See also* Potatoes/Stuffed.
Avocado-Topped Potatoes, '83 3
Beef and Chicken-Topped Potatoes, Creamed, '83 210
Broccoli-and-Almond-Topped Potatoes, '83 3
Broccoli-Topped Baked Potatoes, '86 17
Buck's Taters, '95 72
Cheese Potato Skins, '84 M239
Cheese Sauce, Baked Potatoes with, '83 239
Cheesy Frank-Topped Potatoes, '83 3
Cheesy Potato Skins, '82 78
Chili-Topped Potatoes, '83 3
Crabmeat-Topped Potatoes, '83 3; '95 22
Frank-Filled Potatoes, '84 M11
Garden Potato Cups, '83 76
Garden-Topped Potatoes, '83 4
Gumbo Potatoes, '95 22
Mexican-Topped Potatoes, '83 3
Micro-Baked Potatoes, '81 M61
Million Dollar Potatoes, '83 210
Mushroom-Dill-Topped Potatoes, '86 41
Mushroom Filling in a Peel, '84 214
New Potatoes, Baked, '90 90
Oven-Baked Potatoes, Easy, '82 202
Pleated Potatoes, Baked, '93 54
Quick Baked Potatoes, '92 M134
Quick Potatoes, '94 283
Rosemary-Baked Potatoes, '95 23
Rosemary-Roasted Potatoes, '95 20
Salmon-Topped Potatoes, '84 124
Shrimp-Sauced Potatoes, '81 M61
Skins, Baked Potato, '86 81
Sweet-and-Sour-Topped Potatoes, '83 4
Taco-Baked Potatoes, '84 119
Taco-Topped Potatoes, '93 M18
Wedges, Potato, '94 M119
Bake, Ham-Potato-Pineapple, '93 302
Bake, Herbed Fish and Potato, '79 287
Bake, Onion-Potato, '83 M195
Bake, Potato, '83 209
Barbecued Potatoes, '91 311; '92 26
Basil-Cheese Potatoes, '90 M316
Basque-Style Potatoes, '79 46
Beans and Potatoes, Down-Home, '85 254
Beets, Potato-Stuffed, '83 234

Breads
Biscuits, Potato-Bacon, '94 214
Dough, Potato Sourdough Bread, '94 324; '95 77
Lightbread, Potato, '80 225
Loaves, Potato, '86 162
Old-Fashioned Potato Bread, '86 57
Potato Bread, '85 56
Rolls, Easy Potato, '89 287
Rolls, Feathery Light Potato, '81 305; '82 36
Rolls, Homemade Potato, '82 252
Rolls, Potato, '81 300
Rolls, Potato Sourdough, '94 325; '95 77
Rolls, Potato Sourdough Cinnamon, '94 325; '95 77
Rolls, Potato Yeast, '87 53
Rolls, Refrigerated Potato, '83 254
Rolls, Refrigerator Potato, '87 15
Rolls, Southern Potato, '86 299
Rolls, Super Potato, '85 145
Rolls, Supreme Potato, '82 130
Rolls, Whole Wheat Potato, '89 50
Sourdough Bread, Potato, '94 325; '95 77
Starter Food, '94 324; '95 77
Starter, Potato Sourdough, '94 324; '95 77
Toast, Potato-Crusted Texas, '94 142
Yeast, Potato, '87 53
Breakfast, Farmer's, '81 44
Breakfast Potatoes, '91 68
Breakfast Potatoes, Mexican, '81 209
Broiled Marinated Potatoes, '93 54
Browned Potatoes, Quick, '82 M172
Burgers, Potato-Crusted Crab, '94 139
Candy, Potato, '79 273
Caraway Potatoes, '85 85
Caraway Potatoes, Cheesy, '86 17
Casseroles
au Gratin, Potatoes, '93 90, 217
au Gratin, Potatoes and Eggs, '79 107
au Gratin, Potatoes-and-Zucchini, '84 5
au Gratin, Shredded Potatoes, '89 69
Breakfast Casserole, Potato, '80 52
Broccoli-Cheese Bake, Potato-, '80 114
Brunch for a Bunch, '88 57
Cheese Casserole, Potato-, '79 101
Cheese Dream, Potato-, '91 307
Cheese Potatoes, Creamy, '88 M146
Cheese Potatoes, Double-, '86 6
Cheese Potatoes, Two-, '80 114
Cheesy Potato Casserole, '80 244; '83 53; '92 229
Cheesy Potatoes, '82 211
Chicken Livers and Potatoes, '82 218
Chive Potatoes, Cheesy, '79 46
Christmas Potatoes, '88 252
Cottage Potatoes, '89 69
Creamy Potato Bake, '82 201
Creamy Potato Casserole, '84 M113
Creamy Potatoes with Ham Bits, '87 191
Deviled Potatoes, Hot, '84 296; '85 196
Easy Potato Casserole, '80 114
Egg Casserole, Cheesy Potato-, '84 5
Eggplant Casserole, Potato-, '87 166
Fish and Potato Bake, Herbed, '80 34
Fluffy Potato Casserole, '80 268
Gourmet, Potatoes, '80 114
Gruyère Potatoes, '83 193
Ham-and-Potato Casserole, '83 M87

Ham-and-Potato Casserole, Cheesy, '84 326
Hash Brown Cheese Bake, '82 50
Hash Brown Potato Casserole, '81 40
Holiday Potato Casserole, '92 302
Irish Potato Casserole, '81 263
Italian Casserole, '80 81
Italian-Style Potatoes, '89 69
Jalapeño Potatoes, '84 39
Lemon and Nutmeg Potatoes, '80 36
Lorraine, Potatoes, '87 190
Mashed Potato Casserole, '85 296
Missy Potatoes, '85 259
Moussaka, Potatoes, '93 44
Mushroom-Potato Casserole, '84 5
Olive Potatoes, '80 114
Peppery Potato Casserole, '95 182
Potato Casserole, '87 190
Processor Potato Casserole, '86 159
Saucy Potato Casserole, '81 276
Saucy Potatoes for Company, '82 202
Sausage-Potato Casserole, '86 217
Scalloped Potatoes, '82 300; '83 211; '92 48
Scalloped Potatoes and Turnips, '85 235
Scalloped Potatoes, Cheesy, '83 82
Scalloped Potatoes, Light, '89 311
Scalloped Potatoes, Mushroom, '87 191
Scalloped Potatoes, Party, '87 191
Scalloped Potatoes, Skillet, '79 46
Scalloped Potatoes, Special, '88 162
Scalloped Potatoes, Wayside, '79 283
Scalloped Potatoes with Pimiento, '81 75
Scalloped Potatoes with Sweet Marjoram and Parmesan Cheese, '91 246
Scallop, Pork Chops and Potato, '82 114
Shoestring Potato Tuna Bake, '82 211
Sour Cream Potatoes, '84 39
Tomato Bake, Potato-, '86 17
Tomato Casserole, Saucy Potato-, '79 46
Caviar Potatoes, '84 80
Charcoal Potatoes, '88 129
Chili-Cheese Potatoes, '90 M62
Chili, Savory Potato, '83 284
Colcannon, '90 64
Cottage Potatoes, '89 69; '93 M92
Creamed Potatoes, '83 25
Cream-Wine Sauce, Potatoes in, '86 18
Creole Potatoes, '87 138
Croquettes, Parmesan Potato, '84 210
Croquettes, Potato, '87 116
Doughnuts, Chocolate-Glazed Potato, '85 6
Doughnuts, Old-Fashioned Potato, '84 56
Duchess Potatoes, '93 288
Dumplings, Venison Stew with Potato, '87 304
Eggs and Meat, Potatoes with, '91 311; '92 25
Fans, Parmesan Potato, '84 M240
Feta Cheese, Potatoes with, '84 295; '85 196
Fish-and-Potato Platter, '89 M248
Fried
Almond-Fried Potatoes, '82 25
Baskets, Potato, '86 193
Chips, Homemade Potato, '82 25
Herb French Fries, '82 211
Herb-Fried Potatoes, '82 25
Latkes, '84 318; '90 254
Nests with Savory Shavings, Potato, '84 209
Okra-Potato Fry, '81 159
Oven French Fries, '91 122
Oven-Fried Potatoes, '82 25
Oven Fries, Cheesy, '91 187

POTATOES, Fried (continued)

Patties, Fried Potato, '82 25; '93 54
Patties, Potato-Onion, '95 269
(Plantain Chips), Tostones de Plátano, '92 158
Puffs, Potato, '80 36
Shavings, Savory, '84 209
Southern-Fried Potatoes, '82 25
Special Potatoes, '83 169
Wedges, Beer-Batter Potato, '83 211
Frittata, Potato, '89 145
Frittata, Potato-Bacon, '95 269
Garlic-Parsley Potatoes, '90 290
Garlic Potatoes, '84 296; '85 196
Gratin, Dual Potato, '93 328
Green Beans and Potatoes, '91 221
Grilled Herb Potatoes, '84 172
Hash, Beef, '95 24
Hash Brown Bake, '95 281
Hash Brown Potatoes, '81 48
Hash Browns, Company, '79 268; '80 14
Hash Browns, Convenient, '95 135
Hash Browns, Franks and, '80 166
Hash Brown Skillet Breakfast, '82 5
Herb Butter, Potatoes with, '81 276
Herbed Potatoes, '91 220
Herb Potatoes, '88 134
Italiano, Potatoes, '89 174
Mashed
Bake, Creamy Potato, '88 41
Basic Mashed Potatoes, '92 330
Blue Cheese Mashed Potatoes, '92 330
Buttermilk-Basil Mashed Potatoes, '95 330
Casserole, Mashed Potato, '85 296
Celery Potatoes, Whipped, '94 305
Chive-Cream Cheese Mashed Potatoes, '92 330
Dill-Sour Cream Mashed Potatoes, '92 330
Duchesse, Potatoes, '84 210
Feta Mashed Potatoes, '92 330
Fix-Ahead Mashed Potatoes, '89 70
Fluffy Potatoes, '84 296; '85 196
Garlic Mashed Potatoes, '92 330; '93 328
Good Old Mashed Potatoes, '92 215
Herbed Lemon Mashed Potatoes, '93 208
Jazzy Mashed Potatoes, '87 192
Mexican Mashed Potatoes, '92 330
Nest, Peas in a Potato, '84 M239
Nests, Mashed Potato, '94 141
Old-Fashioned Mashed Potatoes, '89 234
Pesto Mashed Potatoes, '92 330
Quick-and-Easy Mashed Potatoes, '93 41
Roasted Garlic Mashed Potatoes, '95 288
Seasoned Potatoes, '87 253
Snow-Capped Potatoes, '84 255
Thunderbolt Potatoes, '94 213
Topping, Mashed Potato, '89 243
Turnips and Potatoes, '79 254
Mexican-Style Potatoes, '91 78
Mustard Greens and Potatoes, '86 224
Mustard Potatoes, '79 32
New Potatoes
Basil Cream Sauce, New Potatoes with, '91 46
Browned New Potatoes, '86 244
Caviar Potatoes, Appetizer, '86 223

Cheese Potatoes, Double-, '86 6
Cheesy New Potatoes, '85 156
Creamed Peas and New Potatoes, '79 102
Creamy Potatoes and Broccoli, '92 61
Garden New Potatoes, '91 80
Garlic New Potatoes, '92 54
Green Beans with New Potatoes, '87 164
Ham-Stuffed New Potatoes, '88 211
Herbed New Potatoes, '81 102; '83 9, M148
Lemon-Buttered New Potatoes, '84 149; '90 268
Lemon Sauce, New Potatoes with, '86 130
Lemony New Potatoes, '82 158
Medley, New Potato, '90 279
Medley, Potato, '92 61
Parsley-Chive Sauce, New Potatoes with, '84 212
Parsley New Potatoes, '79 122
Roasted New Potatoes, '90 138
Seasoned New Potatoes, '87 M151
Skillet, Potato-Vegetable, '92 61
Steamed Potatoes, Lemon-, '86 177
Summertime Potatoes, '86 M195
Omelet, Family-Size Potato, '94 31
Omelet, Potato-Sprout, '79 128
Omelets, Country, '91 128
Oven Potatoes, Crispy, '82 96
Pancake, Potato, '85 20
Pancakes, Moist Potato, '80 36
Pancakes, Potato, '79 115; '89 144
Parmesan Potatoes, '82 270; '90 M62; '92 M341; '93 M46
Parmesan-Potato Fans, '88 M190
Parmesan Potato Wedges, '95 181
Parslied Potatoes, '86 18
Patties, Thunderbolt Potato, '94 213
Peppers, Potatoes with Sweet Red, '87 192
Pie, Country Breakfast, '93 M328
Pie, Meat-and-Potato, '84 23
Pie, Potato-Topped Turkey, '86 265
Pork Tenderloin with Apples, Celery, and Potatoes, Grilled, '95 161
Pudding, Carrot-Potato, '94 279
Puff, Potato-Cheese, '95 269
Puffs, Celeried Potato, '89 279
Quiche, Crustless Potato, '83 49
Roasted Potatoes, Carrots, and Leeks, '94 276
Roasted Potatoes, Garlic-, '95 87, 342
Rosemary, Potatoes Anna with, '84 209
Roses, Potato, '81 246
Sage Potatoes, '94 320
Salads
Any Day Potato Salad, '81 154
Bacon-Topped Potato Salad, '85 59
Basil Potato Salad, '94 178
Bean Salad, Potato-, '82 301
Blue Cheese-Potato Salad, '91 208
Broccoli-Potato Salad, Hot, '85 23
Chunky Potato Salad, '81 M138
Confetti Potato Salad, '80 5; '88 16
Corned Beef-Potato Salad, '85 213
Corned Beef Salad, Potato-, '81 36
Cottage Cheese-Potato Salad, '79 147, 285
Creamy Potato Salad, '80 178; '88 171; '92 241
Deluxe Potato Salad, '80 155
Dill-and-Sour Cream Potato Salad, '93 105; '94 100
Dill Potato Salad, '85 213; '94 179

Dill Potato Salad, Hot, '79 78
Dutch Potato Salad, Hot, '86 297; '87 176
Festive Potato Salad, '89 315
Fish-Potato Salad, Smoked, '84 233
French-Style Potato Salad, '88 171
Fruity Potato Salad, '85 214
Garden Patch Potato Salad, '84 82
German Potato Salad, '82 134, 239; '84 18; '92 169
German Potato Salad, Hot, '79 78; '94 254
German-Style Potato Salad, '83 23; '88 M194
Grecian Potato Salad, '82 55
Green Bean-Potato Salad, '83 80
Ham-and-Egg Potato Salad, '86 84
Ham and Potato Salad, '80 272
Ham-and-Potato Salad, '95 94
Herbed Potato Salad, '87 171; '94 164
Hot-and-Light Potato Salad, '93 90
Hot Potato Salad, '79 78; '81 276; '86 10
Hot Potato Salad Supreme, '79 78
Layered Creamy Potato Salad, '81 23
Marinated Potato Slices, '93 98
Mustard Potato Salad, '86 302
New Potato Salad, '84 120, 139; '94 162
New Potato Salad, Asparagus-and-, '86 69
Olive-Potato Salad, '85 114
Parmesan Potato Salad, Hot, '79 78
Parslied Potato Salad, '85 240
Patio Potato Salad, '90 160
Pepper Cups, Potato Salad in, '79 78
Peppers, Potato Salad 'n', '83 135
Pesto Potato Salad, '90 164
Pickle-Potato Salad, Sweet, '85 213
Pole Bean-Potato Salad, Hot, '79 74
Potato Salad, '90 122; '94 160
Red Potato Salad, '93 119
Salmon-Potato Salad, '87 285
Saucy Potato Salad, '87 123
Savory Potato Salad, '80 30
Sour Cream Potato Salad, '79 104; '80 79
Sour Cream-Potato Salad, '84 149
South-of-the-Border Potato Salad, '94 178
Spring Salad, Mediterranean, '80 148
Sugar Snap Peas, Potato Salad with, '91 120
Sweet and Sour Potato Salad, '80 152
Sweet-and-Sour Potato Salad, '92 106
Tri Club Potato Salad, '92 166
Tuna-Potato Salad, '84 289
Skillet Potatoes, Oregano-and-Lemon, '93 54
Skillet Potatoes, Peppy, '86 110
Skins, Baked Potato, '86 81
Skins, Cheesy Potato, '82 78
Skin Snack, Potato, '91 18
Slims, Potato, '81 276
Soufflé, Cheesy Potato, '89 332
Soufflé Potatoes, '84 295; '85 196; '90 14
Soups
Asparagus-Potato Soup, '85 23
Bacon Soup, Potato-, '84 M38
Baked Potato Soup, '91 311; '92 26
Beet Soup, Potato-, '88 156
Bisque, Spinach-Potato, '86 66
Carrot Soup, Potato-, '88 297
Celery-and-Potato Soup, '84 279

POTATOES, Soups *(continued)*

Cheesy Potato-and-Wild Rice Soup,
'89 16
Chowder, Mushroom-Potato, '92 331
Chowder, Potato-Corn, '94 66
Cream of Potato Soup, '80 M224; '82 21
Cream of Potato Soup, Golden, '86 302
Creamy Potato Soup, '81 19, 98;
'84 112
Cucumber-Potato Soup, Chilled, '85 93
Cucumber Soup, Cold Potato-, '88 160
Easy Potato Soup, '92 17
Holiday Potato Soup, '79 236
Leek-and-Potato Soup, '84 112
Onion-and-Potato Soup, Creamy,
'92 51
Pea Soup, Potato-, '94 90
Potato Soup, '82 278; '83 292; '92 263
Sausage-Potato Soup, '80 25
Special Potato Soup, '82 3
Subtle Potato Potage, '80 78
Three-Potato Soup, '86 16
Vichyssoise, '86 181
Yogurt Soup, Potato-, '92 217
Steak 'n Potatoes, Skillet, '81 18
Stew, Potato-Oyster, '89 243
Stir-Fry, Potato, '93 240
Stir-Fry, Potato-Snow Pea, '86 173
Stuffed
Alfredo, Potatoes, '89 204
Bacon-Stuffed Potatoes, '86 193
Bacon-Stuffed Potatoes, Cheesy, '81 M61
Bacon-Topped Blue Cheese Potatoes,
'79 46
Baked Potatoes, Stuffed, '83 322
Baked Stuffed Potatoes, '84 38
Béchamel Sauce, Stuffed Potatoes with,
'84 M239
Black-Eyed Pea-Spinach-Stuffed Potatoes,
'95 22
Blue Cheese Stuffed Potatoes, '81 276;
'92 M228
Blue Cheese-Stuffed Potatoes, '89 69
Broccoli-Shrimp Stuffed Potatoes,
'92 M228
Caviar Potatoes, Appetizer, '86 223
Cheese Sauce, Stuffed Potatoes with,
'87 192
Chicken-Cheese Stuffed Potatoes, '86 55
Chives, Potatoes with, '81 M61
Chive-Stuffed Baked Potatoes, '79 52
Chive-Stuffed Potatoes, Cheesy, '91 128
Chive-Stuffed Potatoes, Creamy,
'80 268
Crab-Stuffed Potatoes, '91 311; '92 26
Crab-Stuffed Potatoes, Cheesy, '86 17
Creamy Stuffed Baked Potatoes, '86 55
Creamy Stuffed Potatoes, '79 211
Fish-Stuffed Potatoes, '92 306
Fluffy Stuffed Potatoes, '86 223
Franks and Potatoes, Stuffed, '81 202
Ham Stuffed Potatoes, '79 210
Hearty Stuffed Potatoes, '89 M282
Herb Stuffed Potatoes, '79 211
Jalapeño-Ham Stuffed Potatoes, '81 M61
Lemon-Herb Stuffed Potatoes, '83 173
Mexican-Stuffed Potatoes, '91 131
Patchwork Potatoes, '86 54
Potatoes, Stuffed, '89 173
Roquefort, Potatoes, '79 211
Savory Stuffed Potatoes, '81 101

Seafood-Stuffed Potatoes, '95 M192
Shrimp Boats, '79 57
Shrimp-Stuffed Potatoes, Creamy,
'80 36
South-of-the-Border Stuffed Potatoes,
'86 54
Summertime Potatoes, '86 M195
Tuna Stuffed Potatoes, '79 210
Twice Baked Cottage-Style Potatoes,
'91 135
Twice-Baked Potato, '90 M295
Twice-Baked Potatoes, '83 227;
'91 185
Vegetable-Topped Stuffed Potatoes,
'85 235
Yogurt-Stuffed Potatoes, '88 24
Zesty Stuffed Potatoes, '94 M46
Tacos, Breakfast, '91 316
Tortilla Campesina, '89 85
Tortilla Española, '92 175
Vinaigrette, Potato-Broccoli, '85 84
Wedges, Lemon Potato, '88 21
Wedges, Lemony Potato, '90 M61
PRALINE. *See also* CANDIES/PRALINES.
Bananas, Praline, '84 313
Brownies, Praline, '93 243
Buns, Praline, '90 195
Buttercream, Praline, '95 243
Cake, Praline, '81 162
Cake, Praline Ice Cream, '80 84
Cake, Praline Pound, '82 88
Cheesecake, Praline, '83 270; '89 93
Coffee, Praline-Flavored, '87 69
Compote, Warm Praline Fruit, '85 260
Cookies, Praline, '91 271
Cookies, Praline Shortbread, '88 242
Cookies, Praline Thumbprint, '89 328
Filling, Praline, '89 328
Freeze, Praline, '89 60; '90 48
Glaze, Praline, '82 196
Ham, Praline, '85 302
Ice Cream, Praline, '89 318
Ice Cream, Pralines and Cream, '82 184;
'83 159
Pastries, Praline, '89 318
Pie, Chocolate-Praline, '86 259
Pie, Frosty Pumpkin-Praline, '91 M234
Pie, Peach Praline, '89 136
Pie, Pumpkin Praline, '80 244
Powder, Praline, '95 243
Sauce, Bourbon Praline, '81 170
Sauce, Chocolate-Praline, '85 M295
Sauce, Peach-Praline, '85 161
Sauce, Praline, '83 25; '84 143; '89 95;
'92 282; '93 214; '94 206, 312
Sauce, Praline Ice Cream, '85 189
Sauce, Southern Praline Ice Cream, '86 M227
Toast, Orange Praline, '79 36
Torte, Chocolate Praline, '84 165
Torte, Lucy's Apricot Praline, '95 243
PRETZELS
Brownies, Saucepan Pretzel, '85 171
Chocolate-Covered Pretzels, '82 295
Dressing, Pretzel, '86 280
Frosted Pretzels, '92 280
Garlands, Pretzel, '93 286
Herb Pretzels with Lower Sodium Horseradish
Mustard, '86 325
Homemade Pretzels, '84 159; '91 185
Popcorn, Pretzel, '84 30
Soft Pretzels, '83 18
Soft Pretzels, Chewy, '87 159
Whole Wheat Pretzels, '89 20

PRUNES
Bavarian, Prune, '86 223
Bread, Prune-Nut, '87 255; '91 55
Butter, Prune-Orange, '92 49
Cake and Sauce, Prune, '85 118
Cake, Prune, '85 223
Cake, Spicy Prune, '79 136
Compote, Baked Prune, '94 50
Muffins, Miniature Prune, '85 223
Muffins, Wheat Germ-Prune, '81 106
Pork Chops Stuffed with Prunes, '84 7
Pork Loin Roast, Prune-Stuffed, '80 29
Raspberry Prunes, '82 124
Relish, Peppy Prune, '90 227
Spiced Prunes, Orange-, '85 224
Stuffed Prunes, '85 47
Tarts, Brandied Prune, '85 223
Tzimmes, '95 102
PUDDINGS. *See also* CUSTARDS, MOUSSES.
Apple-Nut Pudding with Hot Rum Sauce,
'79 86
Applesauce-Graham Cracker Pudding,
'81 34
Banana
Almost Banana Pudding, '88 174
Banana Pudding, '82 53; '84 94;
'85 255; '88 16, 32
Basic Banana Pudding, '81 59
Creamy Banana Pudding, '89 M130
Delicious Banana Pudding, '80 9
Mallow Pudding, Banana-, '86 139
No-Bake Banana Pudding, '91 172
Old-Fashioned Banana Pudding,
'92 94
Peanut Butter-Banana Pudding,
'93 340
Surprise Banana Pudding, '86 7
Beach, The, '95 168
Blackberry Pudding Tarts, '93 200
Bread
Amish Bread Pudding, '80 8
Apple-Raisin Bread Pudding, '88 175
Apricot Bread Pudding, '85 24
Biscuit Pudding, '79 86; '93 51
Blueberry Bread Pudding, '88 154
Bread Pudding, '89 M130; '90 219
Buttermilk Bread Pudding with Butter-
Rum Sauce, '95 134
Cheesy Bread Pudding, '83 68
Chocolate Biscuit Bread Pudding,
'94 215
Chocolate Bread Pudding, '80 8
French Bread Pudding, '85 231
Lemon Bread Pudding, Old-Fashioned,
'88 95
Old-Fashioned Bread Pudding, '83 213;
'88 175
Old-Fashioned Bread Pudding with
Bourbon Custard Sauce, '95 271
Old-Fashioned Bread Pudding with Rum
Sauce, '88 32
Peachy Bread Pudding, '88 175
Raisin Bread Pudding, '94 215
Spiced Bread Pudding, '93 52
Sweet Potato Bread Pudding, '94 241
Tennessee Bread Pudding with Bourbon
Sauce, '93 51
Whiskey Sauce, Bread Pudding with,
'80 58; '90 230; '92 93
Brownie Pudding, '79 265; '80 295
Brown Sugar-Pecan Pudding, '86 M165
Buttermilk-Lemon Pudding Cake with
Blueberry Sauce, '95 135

PUDDINGS (continued)

Butternut Squash Pudding, '89 M313; '90 M19
Cake, Carrot Pudding, '83 24
Cake, Danish Pudding, '91 269
Cake, Lemon Pudding, '83 106
Cake Pudding, Chocolate, '81 99
Cake Pudding, Hot Fudge Sundae, '88 167
Cake Pudding, Lemon, '92 96
Cake Pudding, Wine, '79 230
Chocolate-Almond Pudding, '82 M142; '88 24
Chocolate Pudding, Creamy, '83 106
Chocolate-Rum Dessert, '81 247
Christmas Pudding, '79 206
Christmas Pudding, Flaming, '85 312
Christmas Pudding with Brandy Sauce, Baked, '88 279
Cranberry Pudding, '84 306
Finger Painting Never Tasted So Good, '95 167
Frozen Ozark Pudding, '88 127
Fruit Pudding Compote, Fresh, '86 151
Hansel Pudding, '80 9
Holland Rusk Pudding, Yia Yia's, '93 124
Hot Fudge Pudding, '81 208
Kugel, Nu Awlins, '94 229
Lemon Fluff Pudding, '85 304
Lemon Pudding, '79 86; '81 99
Lemon Pudding, Layered, '82 128
Mandarin-Almond Pudding, '85 M12
Orange Custard Pudding, '88 174
Orange Pudding, '81 85; '82 111; '83 153
Orange-Tapioca Crème, '82 M283
Peanut Butter-Banana Pudding, '93 340
Peanut Butter Pudding, '85 95; '88 32
Peanut Parfait, Bodacious, '95 167
Pecan-Mocha Pudding, '89 M130
Pineapple Pudding, '80 102
Plum Pudding, '79 281
Plum Pudding, Flamed, '84 276
Plum Pudding-Gelatin Mold, '86 300; '87 178
Plum Pudding, Light, '86 318
Plum Pudding, Old-Fashioned, '80 264
Pumpkin Pudding, '89 M313; '90 M20
Pumpkin Pudding, Baked, '80 244
Raisin-Pumpkin Pudding, '84 315
Raspberry Pudding, '92 92
Rice
    Amaretto Rice Pudding, '86 334
    Apple Rice Pudding, '91 217
    Brown Rice Pudding, '85 77
    Creamy Rice Pudding, '81 51, 205
    Fruited Rice Pudding, '81 205; '86 95
    Fudgy Rice Pudding, '81 205
    Old-Fashioned Rice Pudding, '85 147
    Raisin-Rice Pudding, '87 46
    Velvety Rice Pudding, '81 205
Rum Pudding with Raspberry Sauce, '82 288
Savory
    Carrot-Potato Pudding, '94 279
    Cheese Pudding, Baked, '86 78
    Corn-Cheese Pudding, '80 244
    Corn Pudding, '79 276; '81 128; '86 192; '90 219
    Corn Pudding, Baked, '83 314
    Corn Pudding, Creamy, '81 267
    Corn Pudding, Easy, '83 280
    Corn Pudding, Fresh, '80 157, 165; '89 172

Corn Pudding, Tee's, '95 318
Onion Pudding, Kathy's, '95 318
Persimmon Pudding, '79 206
Squash Pudding, '82 277; '83 15
Sweet Potato Pudding, '79 244; '86 52
Turnip Pudding, '94 213
Yorkshire Pudding, '80 252
Snowflake Pudding, '85 30
Snow White Pudding, '85 77
Steamed Date Pudding, '79 86
Steamed Holiday Pudding, '84 275
Steamed Mincemeat Pudding, '80 264
Tipsy Pudding, Parson's, '80 156
Vanilla Pudding, '88 32
Vanilla Pudding, Creamy, '83 227
Woodford Pudding, '79 86

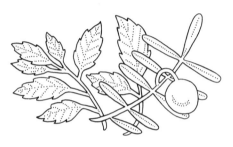

PUMPKIN

Baked Pumpkin, '82 217
Bisque, Spicy Pumpkin, '86 67
Breads
    Coconut Bread, Pumpkin-, '87 255
    Cream Cheese and Preserves, Pumpkin Bread with, '84 264
    Harvest Pumpkin Bread, '90 M215
    Harvest Pumpkin Loaf, '85 232
    Moist Pumpkin Bread, '80 245
    Muffins, Monster, '94 256
    Muffins, Nutty Pumpkin, '86 291
    Muffins, Pumpkin, '79 206, 275; '81 272
    Nut Bread, Pumpkin-, '83 294
    Oatmeal Loaf, Pumpkin-, '81 49
    Orange-Pumpkin Bread, '87 300
    Pecan Bread, Pumpkin-, '87 221
    Pumpkin Bread, '81 8
    Rolls, Pumpkin, '87 254
    Spiced Pumpkin Bread, '91 233
Cake Bars, Pumpkin, '80 245
Cake, Pumpkin, '81 272; '93 303
Cake, Pumpkin Date, '79 251
Cake, Pumpkin Kahlúa, '86 292
Cake, Pumpkin Layer, '80 245
Cake, Pumpkin Pound, '92 235
Cake Squares, Orange-Pumpkin, '83 242
Calabaza Guisada con Puerco (Pumpkin Cooked with Pork), '80 193
Cheesecake, Pumpkin, '80 254; '85 280
Chiffon, Pumpkin, '82 216; '86 283; '88 260
Cooked Fresh Pumpkin, '88 M230
Cookies
    Bars, Pumpkin, '80 40
    Bars, Pumpkin Nut, '82 217
    Chocolate Chip Cookies, Pumpkin-, '93 235
    Drop Cookies, Pumpkin, '79 206
    Great Pumpkin Cookies, '91 234
    Jack-o'-Lantern Cookies, '87 214
    Peppy Pumpkin Cookies, '89 253
    Walnut Cookies, Frosted Pumpkin-, '82 217

Cupcakes, Pumpkin, '85 121
Custard, Pumpkin, '88 279
Delight, Pumpkin-Orange, '86 321
Dessert, Frozen Pumpkin, '88 167
Dessert, Pumpkin Chiffon, '88 128
Doughnut Drops, Pumpkin, '90 323
Empanadas de Calabaza (Pumpkin Empanadas), '94 28
Empanadas, Pumpkin, '82 223
Flan, Pumpkin, '82 217
Gingerbread with Caramel Sauce, Pumpkin, '93 235
Mold, Pumpkin, '82 311
Mousse, Pumpkin, '91 96; '92 130
Pancakes, Pumpkin, '80 228
Pies
    Autumn Pumpkin Pie, '87 213
    Bourbon-Pecan Pumpkin Pie, '87 264
    Chiffon Pie, Pumpkin, '84 312
    Festive Pumpkin Pie, '81 M269
    Fluffy Pumpkin Pie, '80 283
    Ice Cream Pie, Pumpkin, '81 272
    Ice Cream Pie, Pumpkin-, '87 243
    Meringue, Pumpkin Pie with, '92 268
    New-Fashioned Pumpkin Pie, '90 296
    Nutty Pumpkin Pie, '82 67
    Pecan Pie, Pumpkin-, '85 233, 282
    Praline Pie, Frosty Pumpkin-, '91 M234
    Praline Pie, Pumpkin, '80 244
    Quick Pumpkin Pie, '88 M230
    Rich Pumpkin Pie, '86 292
    Sour Cream-Pumpkin Pie, '84 263
    Spiced Nut Crust, Pumpkin Pie in, '87 295
    Spicy Pumpkin Pies, '84 322
    Supreme, Pumpkin Pie, '82 217
    Traditional Pumpkin Pie, '85 256
Pudding, Baked Pumpkin, '80 244
Pudding, Pumpkin, '89 M313; '90 M20
Pudding, Raisin-Pumpkin, '84 315
Roll, Pumpkin, '79 206; '91 297
Sauce, Pumpkin Seed, '88 246
Seeds, Seasoned Pumpkin, '91 234
Seeds, Toasted Pumpkin, '88 M230
Soup, Cream of Pumpkin, '93 234
Soup, Pumpkin, '79 48
Soup, Pumpkin-Pear, '92 234
Soup, Pumpkin-Tomato, '86 291
Soup with Ginger-Lime Cream, Pumpkin-Corn, '95 227
Swirl, Easy Pumpkin, '93 234
Tarts, No-Bake Pumpkin, '86 291
Waffles, Pumpkin, '95 282
Waffles, Pumpkin-Nut, '86 96
Waffles with Mandarin Orange Sauce, Dessert Pumpkin, '89 204

QUAIL. *See* **GAME.**
QUICHES
Artichoke Quiche, '91 71
Asparagus-Tomato Quiche, '88 198
Broccoli Quiche, Easy, '82 34
Broccoli Quiche, Italian, '85 45
Broccoli-Rice Quiche, '81 228
Casserole, Quiche, '95 33
Cauliflower Quiche, '83 86
Cheese
    Bacon-Cheese Quiches, Miniature, '83 93
    Blue Cheese Quiche, '84 52
    Cheddar-Leek Quiche, '88 198

QUICHES, Cheese *(continued)*

Green Onion Quiche, Cheesy, '83 194;
  '84 42
Ham-Cheese Quiche, '79 26
Ham Quiche, Cheesy, '79 127
Jalapeño Quiche, Cheesy, '84 31
Mexican Cheese Pie, '83 69
Miniature Cheese Quiches, '80 150
Sausage-Cheddar Quiche, '79 26
Sealed with a Quiche, '95 135
Spinach Quiche, Cheesy, '81 228
Squares, Cheesy Hot Quiche, '79 124
Squares, Quiche, '84 222
Swiss Alpine Quiche, '90 18
Swiss-Zucchini Quiche, '82 49
Tarragon Cocktail Quiches, '84 127
Vegetable Quiche, Cheese-, '81 228
Zucchini Quiche, Cheesy, '83 312
Chicken Divan Quiche, '88 M125
Chicken-Pecan Quiche, '91 206
Chile Pepper Quiche, '82 224
Clam Quiche, '83 215
Crab Quiche, '82 M122, 243
Crab Quiche, Almond-Topped, '79 127
Crab Quiche, Quick, '84 96
Crab Quiche, Sherried, '83 180
Crab Quiche, Simple, '85 207
Eggless Quiche, '87 220
Fiesta Quiche, '92 47
Green Chile Quiche, '83 31
Jalapeño-Corn Quiche, '85 122
Lorraine, Classic Quiche, '81 131
Lorraine, Mushroom-Quiche, '86 242
Lorraine, Peppery Quiche, '81 228
Lorraine, Perfect Quiche, '79 127
Lorraine, Quiche, '79 40; '80 M108
Meat
  Bacon Quiche, '85 60
  Benedict Quiche, '80 M107
  Ham-and-Grits Crustless Quiche, '94 89
  Ham-and-Mushroom Quiche, '81 11
  Ham-and-Vegetable Quiche, '84 326
  Ham-Cheese Quiche, '79 26
  Ham Quiche, '80 110
  Ham Quiche, Cheesy, '79 127
  Ham Quiche, Country, '87 287
  Ham Quiche, Crustless, '84 235
  Sausage-Apple Quiche, Crustless, '87 70
  Sausage-Cheddar Quiche, '79 26
  Sausage Quiche, Easy, '79 261
  Sausage Quiche, Italian, '81 200
  Sausage Quiche, Spicy, '80 M108
  Sausage Quiche, Zucchini-, '83 122
Mexicali Quiche with Avocado Topping,
  '93 309; '94 96
Miniature
  Bacon-Cheese Quiches, Miniature,
    '83 93
  Cheese Quiches, Miniature, '80 150
  Olive Quiche Appetizers, '86 159
  Shrimp Miniquiches, '87 146
  Spinach Quichelets, '87 67
  Spinach Quiches, Miniature, '82 38
  Squares, Quiche, '84 222
  Tarragon Cocktail Quiches, '84 127
  Wild Rice-and-Mushroom Quiches,
    '93 237
Mushroom Quiche, '80 222; '81 244;
  '89 285
Noël, Quiche, '82 310
Onion Quiche, '83 121

Pastry, Microwaved Quiche, '81 M74;
  '82 M123
Pastry, Quiche, '80 M107
Pizza Quiche, '86 53
Potato Quiche, Crustless, '83 49
Salmon Quiche, '82 87; '87 38
Shrimp Quiche, '83 50
South-of-the-Border Quiche, '93 321
Spinach
  Cheesy Spinach Quiche, '81 228
  Crustless Spinach Quiche, '84 235
  Greek Spinach Quiche, '86 10
  Individual Spinach Quiches, '86 38
  Miniature Spinach Quiches, '82 38
  Mushroom Quiche, Spinach-, '81 M74
  No-Crust Spinach Quiche, '90 142
  Spinach Quiche, '81 44; '85 49;
    '91 204
  Spinach Quichelets, '87 67
Springtime Quiche, '83 122
Squash-and-Green Chile Quiche, '88 143
Tasty Quiche, '82 264
Vegetable Quiche, '87 M219
Zucchini Frittata, '86 103
Zucchini-Mushroom Quiche, '79 127
Zucchini Pie, Italian-Style, '83 43
Zucchini-Sausage Quiche, '83 122

RABBIT. *See* GAME.
RAISINS
Bars, Raisin, '94 228
Breads
  Banana-Nut-Raisin Bread, '81 59
  Biscuits, Buttermilk-Raisin, '92 338
  Biscuits, Cinnamon-Raisin Breakfast,
    '93 159
  Biscuits, Glazed Raisin, '89 210
  Buns, Rum-Raisin, '80 22
  Butternut-Raisin Bread, '79 25
  Caraway-Raisin Oat Bread, '86 44
  Chicken Salad on Raisin Bread, Curried,
    '85 96
  Cinnamon Pull-Aparts, Raisin, '82 205;
    '83 32
  Cinnamon Raisin Bread, '80 22
  Cranberry Bread, Raisin-, '81 305;
    '82 36
  Homemade Raisin Bread, '87 300
  Muffins, Banana-Raisin, '89 218
  Muffins, Breakfast Raisin, '84 59
  Muffins, Carrot-and-Raisin, '87 24
  Muffins, Cheddar-Raisin, '91 51
  Muffins, Raisin English, '80 75
  Muffins, Raisin-Nut, '92 46
  Muffins, Raisin-Pecan Ginger, '88 9
  Muffins, Whole Wheat Raisin, '85 207
  Oatmeal Raisin Bread, '81 14
  Oatmeal-Raisin Bread, '83 59
  Pastry Bites, Raisin, '90 86
  Rolls, Raisin Cinnamon, '81 107
  Rolls, Raisin-Cinnamon, '91 240
  Rollups, Sweet Raisin, '86 290
  Round Raisin Bread, '89 230
  Salt-Free Raisin Batter Bread, '86 33
  Scones, Currant, '84 117; '92 332
  Scones, Lemon-Raisin, '87 69
  Teacakes, Currant, '80 88
  Whole Wheat Bread, Raisin-, '93 77
Bugs in a Rug, '95 178
Butter, Raisin, '81 272
Cake, Spicy Raisin Layer, '79 230

Candy, Mixed Raisin, '84 111
Carrots, Orange-Raisin, '80 24
Chocolate-Bran Raisin Jumbos, '91 142
Coffee Cake, Cinnamon-Raisin, '93 180
Coffee Cake, Spicy Raisin, '88 63
Cookies, Alltime Favorite Raisin, '80 24
Cookies, Chocolate-Raisin Oatmeal,
  '95 136
Cookies, Frosted Oatmeal-Raisin, '79 290
Cookies, Nugget, '79 291
Cookies, Oatmeal-Raisin, '87 221; '93 127
Cookies, Persimmon-Raisin, '85 232
Filling, Raisin, '90 86
Gingersnaps, Raisin, '85 324
Granola Gorp, '89 59
Granola Treats, Raisin-, '92 22
Gravy, Currant, '83 276
Ham, Raisin, '80 124
Mix, Raisin-Nut Party, '83 60
Pie, Apple-Raisin Brandy, '89 58
Pie, Brandy Raisin-Apple, '83 192
Pie, Cranberry-Raisin, '80 283; '85 316
Pie, Peanut-Raisin, '79 85
Pie, Raisin, '83 220
Pie, Raisin-Pecan, '87 213
Pie, Rhubarb-Raisin, '79 112
Pie, Spiced Raisin, '84 148
Pudding, Apple-Raisin Bread, '88 175
Pudding, Raisin Bread, '94 215
Pudding, Raisin-Pumpkin, '84 315
Pudding, Raisin-Rice, '87 46
Relish, Raisin, '92 310
Rice with Curry, Raisin, '85 83
Salad, Carrot-Raisin, '83 117; '84 174;
  '87 10
Salad, Creamy Broccoli-Raisin, '92 106
Salad, Curried Apple-Raisin, '80 24
Sandwiches, Peanut-Cheese-Raisin, '88 140
Sandwich, Raisin Country, '91 168
Sauce, Baked Ham with Cranberry-Raisin,
  '88 244
Sauce, Caramel-Raisin, '88 127
Sauce, Ham with Raisin, '82 M76
Sauce, Raisin, '83 59, 215; '84 91, 275;
  '87 127; '89 58
Sauce, Raisin-Pineapple, '82 177
Sauce, Rum-Raisin, '84 7; '94 295
Shake, Amazin' Raisin, '86 195
Slaw, Sweet Potato-Currant, '93 246
Spread, Creamy Raisin, '90 36
Spread, Peachy-Raisin, '86 326
Spread, Raisin-Nut, '95 79
RASPBERRIES
Appetizer, Orange-Berry, '85 81
Bars, Raspberry, '82 209; '84 212
Bavarian, Raspberry-Strawberry, '89 15
Beverages
  "Concrete," Foxtreat, '94 113
  Cooler, Raspberry, '89 171
  Cubes, Berry-Good, '95 201
  Fizz, Rosy Raspberry, '90 179
  Kir, Raspberry, '86 183
  Milk Shakes, Raspberry, '95 238
  Punch, Raspberry-Rosé, '87 242
  Punch, Raspberry Sherbet, '95 141
  Punch, Raspberry Sparkle, '84 57
  Shake, Peach Melba Sundae, '93 134
  Shake, Raspberry-and-Banana,
    '89 183
  Shrub, Berry, '95 29
  Slush, Watermelon-Berry, '90 137
  Tea, Rasp-Berry Good, '95 200
  Tea, Sangría, '94 131

Raspberries 153

Biscuits, Raspberry-Almond, '93 160
Bisque, Banana-Raspberry, '93 161
Brie, Almond-Raspberry, '94 M89
Brie in Rye, Raspberry, '93 252
Brownies, Raspberry, '92 274
Cake, Chocolate-Raspberry, '92 173
Cake, Lemon-Raspberry, '91 247
Cheesecake, Chocolate-Raspberry Truffle, '91 270
Chocolate Cups, Miniature, '87 132
Chocolate-Raspberry Bags, '95 97
Chocolates, Raspberry Cream, '91 36
Cobbler, Berry-Cherry, '83 270
Cobbler, Raspberry-Cherry, '93 230
Coffee Cake, Raspberry, '83 112
Compote, Berry, '81 275
Compote, Berry-Peach, '82 133
Compote, Spicy Grapefruit-Berry, '91 19
Cookies, Raspberry Swirl, '90 111
Crème Brûlée, Berry, '95 323
Crème Brûlée, Double Raspberry, '95 323
Crêpes, Raspberry, '87 126
Crêpes Suzette, Raspberry, '84 84
Crêpes with Yogurt Filling, Fresh Raspberry, '93 123
Crisp, Raspberry-Pear, '89 109
Custard with Raspberries, Almond Crème, '88 174
Custard with Raspberries, Amaretto, '86 152
Dessert, Frozen Raspberry, '84 192
Dessert, Raspberry-Jellyroll, '85 95
Dessert, Raspberry Sauce, '80 147
Dream, Raspberry, '83 108
Dressing, Bibb Salad with Raspberry-Maple, '91 246
Dressing, Peppery Greens with Raspberry, '95 254
Dressing, Raspberry, '87 153; '95 202
Filling, Raspberry, '90 111
Fluff, Raspberry, '89 198
Glaze, Turkey Breast with Orange-Raspberry, '91 253
Granita, Raspberry Liqueur, '88 117
Ice Cream, Fresh Raspberry, '86 152
Ice Cream, Raspberry, '80 176
Ice, Raspberry, '92 268
Jam, Berry Refrigerator, '89 139
Jam, Raspberry Freezer, '84 M181
Jellyrolls, Raspberry, '93 M255
Lemon Curd with Berries, '90 102
Mousse in Chocolate Crinkle Cups, Raspberry, '93 270
Mousse, Raspberry, '81 34
Muffins, Lemon-Raspberry, '92 119
Mustard, Raspberry, '95 313
Napoleons, Berry, '94 120
Parfait, White Chocolate-Raspberry Swirl, '93 315
Party Puffs, Raspberry, '90 170
Pie, Cherry-Berry, '92 316
Pie, Cran-Raspberry, '87 244
Pie, Raspberry Cream, '94 209
Pie, Rhubarb-Raspberry Pear, '95 119
Prunes, Raspberry, '82 124
Pudding, Raspberry, '92 92
Puree, Fruit Compote with Raspberry, '88 81
Salad Dressing, Raspberry, '94 158

Salads
Chicken-Raspberry Salad, Marinated, '93 190
Frozen Raspberry Salad, '79 287; '80 35
Fruit Mounds, Raspberry, '79 35
Mold, Raspberry Holiday, '84 253
Raspberry Salad, '86 286
Ribbon Salad, Raspberry, '87 236
Walnut Salad, Raspberry-, '94 158
Wine Salad, Raspberry-, '91 256
Sauces
Amaretto Sauce, Raspberry-, '88 130
Berry Sauce, '94 130
Crimson Raspberry Sauce, '79 91; '85 30
Custard Sauce, Fresh Berries with Raspberry, '88 163
Duck Breasts with Raspberry Sauce, '87 240
Flambé, Raspberry Sauce, '84 142
Fresh Raspberry Sauce, '93 120
Melba Sauce, '87 77
Mimosa Sauce, Berry, '90 315
Orange Sauce, Raspberry-, '88 22; '92 154
Peach-Berry Sauce, '87 M165
Poached Pears with Raspberry Sauce, '87 69; '88 223
Raspberry Sauce, '82 289; '83 108; '84 73, 213; '87 69, 117, 183; '88 267; '89 183, 322; '91 96, 180, 270; '92 130; '93 82, 99, 315; '94 295; '95 327
Tea-Berry Sauce, '94 130
Sherbet, Raspberry, '83 162
Shortcake, Chocolate-Raspberry, '95 99
Soufflé, Raspberry, '86 188
Soufflé, Raspberry-Topped, '85 317
Soup, Chilled Raspberry, '81 130
Soup, Sherry-Berry Dessert, '91 180
Spirited Raspberries, '95 142
Strudel, Raspberry-Nut, '83 304
Sweet Potatoes, Raspberry, '87 280
Tartlets, Fresh Berry, '91 98
Tart, Pick-a-Berry, '91 118
Tarts, Berry Good Lemon, '91 119
Tarts, Cran-Raspberry Meringue, '92 286
Tea Cake, Raspberry, '91 271
Topping, Raspberry, '85 317
Topping, Raspberry-Peach, '87 126
Trifle, Raspberry, '88 259
Vinaigrette, Orange-Raspberry, '95 144
Vinaigrette, Raspberry, '94 249
Vinegar, Raspberry-Lemon, '87 134
Vinegar, Raspberry-Thyme, '95 190
Vinegar, Raspberry Wine, '93 191

RELISHES. *See also* **CHUTNEYS, PESTOS, SALSAS, TOPPINGS.**
Antipasto Relish, '86 327
Apple-Celery Relish, '89 141
Apple Relish, Spicy, '84 M323
Avocado Relish, '87 120
Beet Relish, '84 179
Beet Relish, Colorful, '85 136
Black Bean-Tomatillo Relish, '87 121
Black-Eyed Pea Relish, Zesty, '95 56
Cabbage Relish, '83 260
Cabbage Relish, Spanish, '95 270
Chow Chow, '82 196
Chowchow, '87 150
Chowchow, Nannie's, '95 250
Confit, Roasted Shallot-Garlic, '94 303

Corn Relish, '81 129, 175; '83 189; '84 107; '85 136; '87 120, 245; '92 241
Corn Relish, Easy, '83 260
Corn Relish, Quick, '90 13
Corn Relish, Summer, '89 127
Corn Relish, Sweet, '93 119
Corn Relish, Virginia, '79 283
Cran-Apple Relish, '84 300
Cranberry-Nut Relish, '86 275
Cranberry-Orange Relish, '81 M289; '88 254
Cranberry-Pear Relish, '85 232
Cranberry Relish, '81 275; '83 144; '85 258, 264; '86 283; '87 245; '91 257; '92 341; '95 318
Cranberry Relish, Frozen, '95 302
Cranberry Relish, Holiday, '88 304
Cranberry Relish, Lemony, '79 243
Cranberry Relish, Old-Fashioned, '82 297
Cranberry Relish, Tipsy, '92 M310
Cucumber Relish, '85 176
Eggplant Relish, '95 342
Fruit Relish, Fresh, '95 158
Garden Relish, '83 259
Garden Relish, End-of-the-, '80 179
Green Onion Relish, '84 65
Green Tomato Sweet Relish, '93 136
India Relish, '84 179
Jerusalem Artichoke Relish, '89 197
Kraut Relish, '91 232
Mango Relish, '89 198
Onion Relish, '91 79
Onion Relish, Sweet, '93 124
Orange Slices, Spicy, '81 12
Papaya-Basil Relish, '94 82
Peach Relish, '85 136
Pear Relish, '79 196
Pear Relish, Aunt Glennie's, '95 305
Pear Relish, Peppery, '89 141
Pepper-Onion Relish, '84 180
Pepper Relish, '83 183
Pepper Relish, Confetti, '91 195
Prune Relish, Peppy, '90 227
Purple Onion Relish, '95 253
Raisin Relish, '92 310
Salad, Relish, '84 121
Sauerkraut Relish, '85 136
Summer Squash Relish, Pollock with, '92 200
Sweet Pepper Relish, '95 104
Tomato Relish, '85 188
Tomato Relish, Easy, '80 126
Vegetable Relish, '90 147
Vegetable Relish, Eight-, '84 179
White Bean Relish, '93 229
Zucchini Relish, '87 200
Zucchini Relish, Sweet, '95 159

RHUBARB
Ambrosia, Rhubarb, '88 93
Bavarian, Rhubarb-Strawberry, '86 140
Chutney, Rhubarb, '87 245
Cobbler, Rosy Strawberry-Rhubarb, '79 154
Cobbler, Strawberry-Rhubarb, '88 93
Crisp, Rhubarb, '91 146; '92 130
Crisp, Strawberry-Rhubarb, '95 119
Mousse, Rhubarb, '88 93
Pie, Rhubarb-Peach, '86 140
Pie, Rhubarb-Raisin, '79 112
Pie, Rhubarb-Raspberry Pear, '95 119
Salad, Rhubarb, '91 146; '92 129
Salad, Rhubarb Congealed, '86 140
Salad, Tart Rhubarb, '91 146; '92 129

RHUBARB *(continued)*

Sauce, Chilled Rhubarb, '88 94
Sauce, Pineapple-Rhubarb, '88 94
Squares, Rhubarb, '91 146; '92 129
Squares, Rosy Rhubarb, '79 111
Whip, Rhubarb, '79 112

RICE

Almond Rice, '81 195; '85 M112; '89 100; '91 291
à l'Orange, Rice, '90 236
Apple-Cinnamon Rice, '86 249
Arabic Rice, '94 200
Asparagus, Rice and, '93 324
Bacon-Chive Rice, '83 129
Balls, Rice, '81 51
Basic Long-Grain Rice, '83 M285
Basic Molding Rice, '86 221
Basic Quick-Cooking Rice, '83 M285
Basic Rice, '79 64
Beans and Rice. *See also* Rice/Salads.
  Black Beans and Rice, '80 222; '89 178; '91 82; '95 309
  Black Beans and Yellow Rice, '95 126
  Black Beans and Yellow Rice, Easy, '92 308
  Black Beans with Yellow Rice, '82 2
  Cajun Peas, '88 3
  Cajun Red Beans and Rice, '83 26
  Creole Beans and Rice, '80 223
  Easy Red Beans and Rice, '90 220
  Red Beans and Rice, '80 58; '83 89; '84 37; '87 45; '90 27
  Sausage, Beans, and Rice, Texas, '84 296
  South Texas Beans and Rice, '85 252
Black-Eyed Peas, Rice with, '93 66
Black-Eyed Peas with Rice, '83 12; '90 208; '91 13
Black-Eyes and Rice, Creole, '85 6
Braised Rice and Peas, '79 101
Brown Rice
  Brown Rice, '82 275
  Calico Brown Rice, '86 33
  Casserole, Brown Rice, '87 118
  Chicken-Brown Rice Bake, '91 314
  Confetti Rice, '89 146
  Cornish Hens with Brown Rice, '82 275
  Garden Rice, '92 12
  Mix, Fruited Curry-Rice, '86 326
  Pancakes, Vegetable-Rice, '93 43
  Parmesan, Brown Rice, '84 196
  Pecan Rice, '85 53
  Pilaf, Brown Rice, '90 136; '91 82
  Pudding, Brown Rice, '85 77
  Roast Chicken and Brown Rice, '83 268
  Rolls, Crunchy Cabbage-Rice, '85 32
  Spanish Brown Rice, '84 196
  Stew, Lentil-Rice, '82 232
  Stuffing, Tomatoes with Walnut-Rice, '91 102
  Vegetables and Rice, '93 91
Brussels Sprouts and Rice, '79 288; '80 26
Calas, Easy, '92 89
Calico Rice, '85 83
Casseroles. *See also* Rice/Brown Rice, Wild Rice.
  Almond Rice, '91 291
  au Gratin, Rice, '83 129
  au Gratin Supreme, Rice, '86 78
  Baked Rice, '94 270
  Beef and Rice, Spiced, '84 285

Black-Eyed Peas with Rice, '83 12
Broccoli-Rice Casserole, '81 101
Broccoli with Rice, Holiday, '87 252
Chantilly, Rice, '86 82
Cheese-Parslied Rice, '89 99
Chicken and Rice, '95 54
Chicken and Rice Casserole, '80 260
Chicken Casserole, Rice-and-, '87 154
Chicken-Rice Casserole, '86 52
Chiles, Rice-and-Cheese con, '89 99
Chiles, Rice and Green, '83 152
Chili-Cheesy Rice, '79 43
Chili-Rice Casserole, '79 54
Colorful Rice Casserole, '82 199
Cornish Hens-and-Rice Casserole, '92 267
Fiesta Rice, '84 76
French Rice, '83 24
Golden Rice, '79 270
Green Rice Casserole, '95 181
Ham-and-Rice Casserole, '84 75
Ham-Rice-Tomato Bake, '87 78
Jalapeño Rice Casserole, '81 66
Lentils-and-Rice Casserole, '93 301
Mexican Rice Casserole, '83 31
Mushroom Rice, Baked, '95 84
Mushroom Rice, Easy, '89 286
Pepper Rice, Hot, '92 310
Red Rice, Savannah, '95 27
Rice Casserole, '87 45
Sausage-and-Rice Bake, Creole, '88 58
Sausage and Rice Casserole, Oriental, '82 M123
Sausage-Rice Casserole, '82 50; '83 75
Shrimp and Rice Casserole, '79 228
Shrimp-and-Rice Casserole, '94 328
Spanish Rice Casserole, '79 192
Spinach Rice, '85 146
Squash Casserole, Creamy Rice and, '95 26
Strata, Cheese-Rice, '81 176
Zucchini-Rice Casserole Italiano, '89 146
Chicken-Flavored Rice, '84 M144
Consommé Rice, '80 246
Cream with Mandarin Oranges, Rice, '85 317
Creole Rice, '90 183
Cumin Rice, '85 83
Curried Rice, '90 183
Curried Rice, Quick, '86 81
Curried Rice with Almonds, '83 M285
Curried Rice with Pineapple, '79 142
Curry-Spiced Rice, '86 M226
Custard, Baked Rice, '92 308
Dirty Rice, '86 142
Dressing, Rice, '91 217
Fried Rice
  Bacon Fried Rice, '80 115
  Calas, Easy, '92 89
  Easy Fried Rice, '84 76
  Egg Fried Rice, '79 252; '80 19
  Fried Rice, '83 129; '84 197; '88 67
  Pork Fried Rice, '89 99
  Refried Rice, Shrimp and, '89 176
  Sausage, Fried Rice with, '83 12
  Special, Fried Rice, '80 56
  Turkey Fried Rice, '83 282
  Two, Fried Rice for, '81 31
Ginger Rice, Fluffy, '83 102
Glorified Rice, '83 129
Grape Leaves, Stuffed, '94 48
Green Peas, Rice with, '87 45

Green Rice Bake, '79 43
Green Rice, Celebrity, '81 207
Herbed Rice, '83 M285; '93 278
Herb Rice, '91 257
Honey Rice, '85 83
Hopping John, Skillet, '79 10
Lemon Rice, '89 166
Lime-Flavored Rice, '84 175
Lyonnaise, Rice, '83 151
Main Dishes. *See also* Rice/Brown Rice, Pilaf, Wild Rice.
  Beef and Cauliflower over Rice, '93 94
  Beef and Rice, Curried, '88 164
  Beef-and-Rice Dinner, Mexican, '88 199
  Beef and Rice, Mango-, '88 138
  Beef and Rice, Spicy, '83 231
  Beef over Rice Noodles, Shredded, '85 74
  Beef Rollups with Rice, Royal, '79 105
  Beef Tips on Rice, '85 87
  Black-Eyed Peas with Rice, '90 208
  Boudin, Old-Fashioned, '85 250
  Cabbage Rolls, Stuffed, '88 18
  Chicken-and-Rice Cacciatore, Quick, '88 38
  Chicken and Rice, Creole, '92 262
  Chicken and Rice Dressing, '79 288
  Chicken and Rice, Shortcut, '90 220
  Chicken and Rice, Spicy, '88 200
  Chicken-and-Rice Valencia, '85 113
  Chicken Breasts, Celebrity, '95 60
  Chicken Caruso and Rice, '89 177
  Chicken Livers and Rice Dish, '82 218
  Chicken Livers with Rice, '80 200; '81 58; '84 292
  Chicken over Confetti Rice Squares, Creamed, '81 282; '82 31
  Chicken over Rice, Cajun, '88 102; '89 67
  Chicken-Rice Medaillons in Pepper Pesto, '90 97
  Chicken, Rice-Stuffed, '81 4
  Chicken, Rice-Stuffed Roasted, '88 38
  Chicken with Pecan-Rice Dressing, '85 M57
  Chicken with Rice, Roast, '95 261
  Chicken with Rice, Sherry, '81 97
  Chili with Rice, '82 11
  Cornish Hens, Rice-Stuffed, '82 302
  Dirty Rice, Hot, '93 219
  Egg and Rice Bake, '83 119
  Fruited Rice, Far East, '81 175
  Ham Rolls, Rice-Stuffed, '83 190
  Ham with Rice, Curried, '80 111
  Indian Rice, '79 64
  Jollof Rice Dinner, '91 230; '92 325
  Lamb Curry with Rice, '80 83; '81 10
  Lentil-and-Rice Supper, '84 202
  Meatballs Paprikash with Rice, '85 31
  Oriental Rice, '85 146
  Paella, Chicken-Pork-Shrimp, '82 245
  Paella, Seafood, '82 245
  Paella, Spanish, '85 26
  Paella Valenciana, '82 246
  Pancakes, Rice, '85 147
  Peppers, Beef-Stuffed, '85 146
  Peppers, Rice-Stuffed, '80 65
  Pepper Steak and Rice, '81 17
  Peppers with Rice and Ham, Stuffed, '82 131
  Pork Chops, Rice-Stuffed, '83 102
  Red Rice, '92 235

RICE, Main Dishes (continued)

Red Rice Jambalaya, '91 18
Sausage and Rice, Italian, '86 53
Shrimp and Refried Rice, '89 176
Shrimp and Rice, Oriental, '90 183
Shrimp and Sausage Rice, '79 64
Shrimp-and-Scallop Sauté with Pecan
   Rice, '90 317
Shrimp Creole in a Rice Ring, '86 222
Shrimp, Curried Rice and, '83 231
Tuna-Rice Pie, '84 123
Turkey with Rice Dressing, Roast,
   '82 286
Medley, Rice, '79 270
Mélange, Rice, '87 240
Mexican Rice
   Dressing, Mexican Rice, '87 253
   Jalapeño Hot Rice, '80 126
   Jalapeño Rice, '79 43
   Mexican Rice, '83 85; '85 147;
     '91 217
   Mold, Chile-Rice, '86 221
   Spanish Rice, '81 51; '83 209; '90 183;
     '94 27
   Spanish Rice, Jiffy, '90 176
   Spanish Rice, Pork Chops and, '83 103;
     '85 293
   Spanish Rice with Tofu, '88 26
   Spanish-Style Rice, '83 152
   Spicy Mexican Rice, '88 149
Mix, Fruited Rice, '90 267
Mix, Herb-Rice, '91 257
Mold, Curried Rice, '85 36
Mold, Saffron Rice, '86 221
Mushroom Rice, Baked, '92 170
Nutted Rice, '85 269
Orange-Herb Rice, '89 286
Orange Rice, '79 43; '81 175; '82 200
Oriental Rice, '85 M12, 146
Oven Rice, '83 89
Paella, Garden, '82 245
Paella Rice Mix, '94 168
Pancakes, Rice, '85 147
Parsleyed Rice, '83 M58
Parsley Rice, '84 197; '85 95
Parslied Rice, '87 167, 243
Parslied Rice, Creamy, '88 255
Peas and Rice, '88 97
Peas and Rice, Holiday, '86 328
Peppered Rice, '82 4
Pigeon Peas, Rice with, '92 157
Pilaf
   Browned Rice Pilaf, '87 305
   Brown Rice Pilaf, '90 136; '91 82
   Chicken Pilaf, '82 246
   Fruit-and-Vegetable Rice Pilaf,
     '84 196
   Fruited Pork Pilaf, '82 246
   Fruited Rice Pilaf, Chicken Breasts with,
     '92 307
   Ham Pilaf Mold, '86 222
   Lentil Pilaf, Rice-and-, '88 17
   Near-Eastern Pilaf, '82 246
   Okra Pilaf, '80 185; '82 126; '93 160
   Rice Pilaf, '86 82; '87 229; '88 42;
     '89 286
   Savory Pilaf, '83 93
   Shrimp Pilaf, '82 246
   Turkey-Asparagus Pilaf, '88 200
   Turkey-Rice Pilaf, '86 284
   Turkish Pilaf, '79 184

Pudding, Amaretto Rice, '86 334
Pudding, Apple Rice, '91 217
Pudding, Creamy Rice, '81 51, 205
Pudding, Fruited Rice, '81 205; '86 95
Pudding, Fudgy Rice, '81 205
Pudding, Old-Fashioned Rice, '85 147
Pudding, Raisin-Rice, '87 46
Pudding, Velvety Rice, '81 205
Quiche, Broccoli-Rice, '81 228
Raisin Rice with Curry, '85 83
Red Rice, Savannah, '80 119; '89 286
Ring, Oregano Rice, '86 222
Ring, Rice-Carrot, '79 246
Ring with Beets, Rice, '79 225
Risotto, '95 280
Risotto alla Milanese, '85 228
Risotto Primavera, '95 163
Risotto, Seafood, '95 280
Risotto, Southwestern, '92 211
Risotto, Tomato-Basil, '95 269
Saffron Rice, '79 43; '93 282
Saffron Rice Mold, '86 221
Salads. See also Rice/Brown Rice, Wild Rice.
   Artichoke-Chicken-Rice Salad, '94 132
   Artichoke Hearts, Rice Salad with,
     '80 232
   Artichoke-Rice Salad, '80 178; '81 41;
     '85 81
   Avocado Salad, Rice-and-, '89 146
   Bacon, Rice Salad with, '79 52
   Bean-and-Rice Salad, Marinated, '87 152
   Bean Salad, Rice-and-, '85 22
   Beans-and-Rice Salad, '91 44
   Brown Rice-and-Vegetable Salad,
     '84 202
   Brown Rice Confetti Salad, '94 174
   Chicken-and-Rice Salad, Hot, '83 22
   Chicken-Rice Salad, '81 203
   Chicken-Rice Salad, Nutty, '83 157
   Chutneyed Rice Salad, '88 100
   Colorful Rice Salad, '81 253
   Confetti Rice Salad, '80 232
   Crunchy Rice Salad, '82 302
   Curried Chicken-Rice Salad, '92 190
   Curried Rice Salad, '80 84; '85 147, 220
   Curry Rice Salad, '89 146
   Egg-Rice Salad, '84 18; '86 169
   Gazpacho-Rice Salad, Molded, '86 221
   Ham-and-Rice Salad, Colorful, '90 319
   Ham-and-Rice Salad, Mandarin,
     '87 145
   Ham-Rice Toss, '82 40
   Hearty Rice Salad, '82 233
   Lentils-and-Rice Salad, '90 197
   Mandarin Rice Salad, '88 271
   Mardi Gras Rice, '91 217
   Mushrooms, Rice Salad with Fresh,
     '80 231
   Paella Salad, '86 207
   Pea Salad, Rice-, '85 163
   Pebble Salad, '91 27
   Red Rice Salad, Charleston, '79 146
   Rice Salad, '79 74; '81 51
   Salmon-Rice Salad, '84 289
   Shrimp-and-Orange Rice Salad, Zesty,
     '87 155
   Shrimp and Rice Salad, '80 231; '82 207
   Shrimp-and-Rice Salad, '92 307
   Shrimp-Rice Salad, Baked, '83 22
   Shrimp-Rice Salad, Tangy, '84 66
   Shrimp Salad, Rice-, '79 270; '92 142
   Shrimp Salad, Rice-and-, '83 82
   Spinach-Rice Salad, '94 63

Tomatoes and Basil, Rice with, '95 232
Tuna-Rice Salad, '87 202
Vegetable-Rice Salad, '80 148; '83 198;
   '85 87
Vegetable Salad, Rice-and-, '86 42
Zesty Rice Salad, '81 23
Savory Rice, '89 201
Seasoned Onion Rice, '82 166
Seasoned Rice, '79 244; '83 212
Shell, Rice-Cheese, '82 49
Soufflé, Rice-Cheese, '79 270
Soup, Chicken-and-Rice, '88 236
Soup, Mushroom-Rice, '90 32
Soup, Tomato-and-Rice, '85 24
Soup, Turkey-Rice, '90 89
Southern Rice, '90 250
Southwestern Rice, '90 121
Spicy Rice, '83 215; '85 256
Steamed Rice, Oven-, '89 226
Strata, Cheese-Rice, '81 176
Stuffing, Rice, '95 290
Stuffing, Rice-and-Onion, '88 246
Three-Grain Rice, '95 166
Timbales, Rice, '94 32
Timbales, Spinach-Rice, '88 271
Toasted Rice and Pasta, '95 57
Tomatoes and Basil, Rice with, '95 232
Vegetable-Rice Toss, '91 309
Vegetables, Rice with, '79 64; '85 83
Waldorf Rice, '84 281
Wild Rice
   Almond Wild Rice, '86 50
   Belvedere, Wild Rice, '86 82
   Bulgur, Wild Rice, '91 83
   Casserole, Chicken-Wild Rice, '84 241;
     '85 65
   Casserole, Duck and Wild Rice,
     '79 224
   Casserole, Oyster-and-Wild Rice, '83 34;
     '84 44
   Casserole, Sausage and Wild Rice,
     '83 196
   Casserole, Sausage-Wild Rice, '84 250
   Casserole, Veal and Wild Rice, '79 180
   Casserole, Wild Rice, '82 199; '95 176
   Casserole, Wild Rice-Oyster, '86 256
   Chicken and Wild Rice, '79 248
   Chicken-Fried Wild Rice, '89 24;
     '91 132
   Chicken Rollups, '88 38
   Chicken, Wild Rice-Stuffed, '79 219
   Chicken-Wild Rice Supreme, '79 77
   Chicken with Wild Rice, Elegant,
     '80 M76
   Cranberry-Pear Wild Rice, '83 279
   Creole, Wild Rice-and-Shrimp, '84 292
   Dressed-Up Wild Rice, '92 60
   Eggs with Wild Rice, Scrambled,
     '80 42
   Gourmet Wild Rice, '89 271
   Grapes, Wild Rice with, '95 48
   Morels, Wild Rice with, '89 62
   Mushrooms, Wild Rice and, '83 278
   Oysters, Wild Rice and, '92 339
   Pecan-Lemon Wild Rice, '92 211
   Popped Wild Rice, '85 65
   Pork Loin Stuffed with Wild Rice,
     '84 35
   Quiches, Wild Rice-and-Mushroom,
     '93 237
   Ring, Creamed Mushrooms in Wild Rice,
     '80 270
   Ring, Wild Rice, '83 253

RICE, Wild Rice *(continued)*

Salad, Crab and Wild Rice, '79 116
Salad, Crab-Wild Rice, '86 207
Salad, Oriental Salmon-and-Wild Rice,
'94 173
Salad, Springtime Wild Rice, '88 100
Salad, Wild Rice, '85 65; '89 147;
'93 191
Salad, Wild Rice-Chicken, '83 146
Salad, Wild Rice-Green Apple, '92 90
Salad, Wild Tuna, '95 243
Sausage and Wild Rice, '85 65
Sausage, Wild Rice and, '86 268
Scallops and Wild Rice, '90 129
Soup, Cheesy Potato-and-Wild Rice,
'89 16
Stuffing, Cornish Hens with Wild Rice,
'79 222; '80 64; '82 136
Yellow Rice, '91 136
Yellow Rice, Black Beans with, '82 2
Yellow Rice, Easy Black Beans and, '92 308
Yellow Rice with Water Chestnuts, '85 24
ROLLS AND BUNS. *See also* **BREADS.**
Angel's Wing Rolls, '95 329
Apple Pinwheel, Quick, '85 42
Blueberry Pinwheels, '82 205
Broccoli-Cheddar Rolls, '91 21
Buttered Rum-Nut Rolls, '86 291
Butterscotch Pinwheels, '90 49
Caramel-Chocolate Sticky Buns, Easy, '95 36
Caramel Rolls, Easy, '90 195
Centerpiece Rolls, '94 276
Cheese-Apricot Sweet Rolls, '90 195
Cherry-Almond Rolls, '84 M198
Cinnamon
Chocolate-Cinnamon Buns, '85 5
Cinnamon Buns, '91 68
Cinnamon Rolls, '79 80; '88 290;
'92 270
Crisps, Cinnamon, '81 113
Easy Cinnamon Rolls, '85 290
Glazed Cinnamon Rolls, '86 312
Old-Fashioned Cinnamon Rolls, '86 298;
'90 196; '92 226
Pecan Rolls, Easy Cinnamon-, '89 307
Potato Sourdough Cinnamon Rolls,
'94 325; '95 77
Raisin Cinnamon Pull-Aparts, '82 205;
'83 32
Raisin Cinnamon Rolls, '81 107
Raisin-Cinnamon Rolls, '91 240
Spiral Cinnamon Rolls, '82 205;
'83 32
Sticky Buns, Cinnamon, '83 244
Tea Rolls, Cinnamon, '92 263
Twists, Cinnamon, '83 53
Cornmeal Rolls, '79 60; '89 184
Crescent
Almond Crescent Rolls, '90 283
Apricot Crescents, '90 181
Butter Crescent Rolls, '95 292
Butter-Rich Crescent Rolls, '81 211
Buttery Crescent Rolls, '83 180
Crescent Rolls, '84 267; '89 235
Deep South Crescent Rolls, '82 309;
'83 16
Easy Crescent Rolls, '79 60
Festive Crescents, '80 281
French-Style Crescent Rolls, '82 288
Yogurt Crescent Rolls, '91 123
Croissants, Cream Cheese, '92 159

Dinner
Dinner Rolls, '79 251; '89 312;
'93 M326
Fancy Dinner Rolls, '86 299
Freezer Dinner Rolls, '90 251
How to Shape Dinner Rolls, '83 323
Italian Dinner Rolls, '83 254
Italiano Dinner Rolls, '85 32
Refrigerator Dinner Rolls, '81 78
Whole Wheat Dinner Rolls, '91 53
Garlic Rolls, Easy, '86 234
Jam Teasers, '81 8
Lemon Knots, Glazed, '86 290
Mayonnaise Rolls, '90 283
Nutty Buns, '86 290
Onion-and-Sesame Rolls, '95 292
Onion-Cheese Buns, '88 218
Onion Rolls, Poppy Seed, '81 63
Orange
Butter Rolls, Orange, '82 206; '83 33
Easy Orange Rolls, '89 M131
Frosted Hot Orange Rolls, '80 257
Glazed Orange Rolls, '90 194
Luscious Orange Rolls, '86 298
Orange Rolls, '80 22; '82 17; '88 79
Speedy Orange Rolls, '89 287
Parmesan Rolls, '79 181
Parsley-Garlic Rolls, '93 319
Pineapple Buns, Easy, '85 14
Potato
Easy Potato Rolls, '89 287
Feathery Light Potato Rolls, '81 305;
'82 36
Homemade Potato Rolls, '82 252
Potato Rolls, '81 300
Refrigerated Potato Rolls, '83 254
Refrigerator Potato Rolls, '87 15
Sourdough Cinnamon Rolls, Potato,
'94 325; '95 77
Sourdough Rolls, Potato, '94 325;
'95 77
Southern Potato Rolls, '86 299
Super Potato Rolls, '85 145
Supreme Potato Rolls, '82 130
Whole Wheat Potato Rolls, '89 50
Yeast Rolls, Potato, '87 53
Pull-Apart Buns, Easy, '83 100
Pumpkin Rolls, '87 254
Quick Rolls, '95 245
Raisin Rollups, Sweet, '86 290
Refrigerator
Big-Batch Rolls, '88 289
Bran Rolls, '85 145
Buttermilk Refrigerator Rolls, '81 120;
'82 22
Caramel Breakfast Rolls, '79 193
Caramel-Nut Rolls, '86 312
Cloverleaf Refrigerator Rolls, '80 256
Croissants, '83 54
Icebox Rolls, '80 242
Lemon Spirals, French, '81 94
Low-Sodium Refrigerator Rolls, '82 67
Overnight Rolls, '86 233
Parker House Refrigerator Rolls, '82 310;
'83 17
Party Refrigerator Rolls, '79 248
Refrigerator Rolls, '82 287; '91 53
Reuben Buns, '88 298
Sour Cream Rolls, '80 71
Sour Cream Yeast Rolls, '85 259; '90 17;
'93 232
Spoon Rolls, '87 15; '91 275
Sweet Rolls, Yummy, '80 281

Three-Day Refrigerator Rolls, '86 306
Twists, Austrian, '80 45
Yeast Rolls, Refrigerator, '81 296, 307;
'82 309; '83 17, 118; '91 80
Romano Sesame Rolls, '87 144
Rum Rolls, Easy, '79 287; '80 35
Sesame Knots, '89 29
Snack Buns, '87 279
Sweet Rolls, Quick Breakfast, '90 195
Toasted Rolls with Herb Butter, '89 70
Wheat. *See also* Rolls and Buns/Dinner.
Easy Whole Wheat Rolls, '86 286;
'87 74
Feather Rolls, Shredded Wheat, '82 309;
'83 16
Hearty Whole Wheat Bread and Rolls,
'79 92
Honey Wheat Rolls, '83 278
Honey-Wheat Rolls, Dilled, '83 254
Light Wheat Rolls, '87 254
Pan Rolls, Whole Grain, '89 256
Petite Whole Wheat Rolls, '85 146
Wholesome Whole Wheat Rolls, '92 31
Whole Wheat Buns, '86 236
Whole Wheat Rolls, '79 275; '90 111
Yeast. *See also* Rolls and Buns/Cinnamon,
Crescent, Dinner, Potato, Refrigerator,
Wheat.
Anise Rolls, '89 91
Basic Angel Rolls, '89 72
Best-Ever Yeast Rolls, '90 46
Blueberry Buns, Deluxe, '81 164
Bolillos, '88 247
Bran Yeast Rolls, '87 116
Butter-and-Herb Rolls, '86 306
Butterhorn Rolls, '89 288
Butterhorns, '84 267
Buttermilk Rolls, Quick, '83 155
Buttermilk Yeast Rolls, '79 59
Caraway Puffs, '82 174
Cheese Buns, Hurry-Up, '81 300
Cheese Crescents, '82 18
Chocolate Sticky Buns, '81 300;
'82 124
Cloverleaf Rolls, '82 18
Cloverleaf Rolls, Light, '83 290
Coconut-Pecan Coils, '90 196
Cornmeal Yeast Rolls, '86 177
Cottage Cheese Rolls, '81 78
Cranberry-Pineapple Rolls, '86 275
Cream Cheese Pinches, '87 85
Dough, Basic Roll, '82 17
Dough, Sweet Roll, '79 80
Easy Yeast Rolls, '81 78; '86 16
Fantan Rolls, French, '80 276
Finger Rolls, '83 254
Hard Rolls, '86 85, 306
Holiday Sparkle Rolls, '83 296
Honey Oatmeal Buns, '83 154
Honey Rolls, Super, '80 115
Hot Cross Buns, '81 77; '95 100
Hurry-Up Yeast Rolls, '90 90
Jam Kolaches, '85 290
Low-Sodium Yeast Rolls, '84 228
Make-Ahead Yeast Rolls, '95 307
Moravian Feast Buns, '83 295
Onion Buns, Cheesy, '85 5
Onion Twist Rolls, '89 288
Pan Rolls, '88 76
Pan Rolls, Brown-and-Serve, '91 52
Parkerhouse Rolls, Super, '81 78
Pecan Rolls, '81 62
Pepperoni Rolls, Ground-, '83 244

Rolls and Buns 157

ROLLS AND BUNS, Yeast *(continued)*

Pineapple Angel Rolls, '89 72
Pinwheel Rolls, Sweet, '90 46
Praline Buns, '90 195
Quick Yeast Rolls, '84 267; '95 45
Refrigerator Yeast Rolls, '81 296, 307;
 '82 309; '83 17, 118; '91 80
Rounds, Individual Bread, '83 159
Rum Buns, '81 299
Rum-Raisin Buns, '80 22
Saffron Rolls, '83 296
Sesame Buns, '82 17
Sourdough Hot Rolls, '82 201
Special Rolls, Extra-, '88 257
Speedy Yeast Rolls, '82 309; '83 17
Sticky Buns, '80 23
Sweet Potato Rolls, '93 172
Sweet Rolls, Mexican, '81 285
Tasty Rolls, '90 85
Yam Rolls, Golden, '86 299

RUTABAGAS
au Gratin, Rutabaga, '79 254
Bacon, Rutabaga with, '83 243
Boiled Rutabagas, '86 224
Buttered Rutabagas, '81 274
Creamy Rutabaga, '79 254
Glazed Rutabaga, '88 229
Honey Rutabaga, '91 220
Mashed Rutabagas, '86 295
Simple Rutabaga, '83 243
Steamed Rutabagas, '81 274
Whip, Rutabaga, '95 179

S
ALAD DRESSINGS. *See also* **MAYONNAISE.**
Almond Salad Dressing, '81 37
Apple Dressing, '83 181; '92 216
Artichoke Dressing, '84 126
Avocado Cream, '92 158
Avocado Dressing, '80 15; '92 321
Bacon Dressing, Hot, '84 12
Barbecue Salad Dressing, '80 74
Basil-and-Garlic Dressing, '94 55
Basil Dressing, '88 24
B. B.'s Salad Dressing, '91 65
Blender Dressing, '80 78
Buttermilk Dressing, Down-Home,
 '84 114
Buttermilk Salad Dressing, '79 69
Caesar Salad Dressing, '82 94
Celery-Honey Dressing, '80 42
Celery Seed Dressing, '82 265
Celery Seed Salad Dressing, '82 94
Cheese
 Barbecue Salad Dressing, Cheesy-,
  '92 255
 Blue Cheese Dressing, '79 69; '82 166;
  '86 233; '90 286
 Blue Cheese Dressing, Creamy, '81 150;
  '91 307
 Blue Cheese Dressing, Special, '80 30
 Blue Cheese Dressing, Tangy, '87 81
 Blue Cheese Dressing, Zesty, '79 104
 Blue Cheese Salad Dressing, '82 94
 Blue Cheese Salad Dressing, Creamy,
  '86 123
 Dairy Land Salad Dressing, '86 85
 Fluff Dressing, Cheese, '91 256
 Parmesan Dressing, '86 192
 Romano Dressing, '80 174

Roquefort Dressing, '79 85; '80 74;
 '93 128
Roquefort Dressing, Creamy, '84 12
Citrus-Cilantro Dressing, '93 310; '94 97
Citrus Dressing, '85 92
Coconut Dressing, '87 251
Cooked Salad Dressing, '90 231
Cranberry-Orange Dressing, '91 287
Creamy Dressing, '79 159; '83 81; '85 26;
 '92 45, 241; '93 318; '95 66
Creamy Salad Dressing, '83 181
Cucumber-Curry Dressing, '89 179
Cucumber Dressing, '80 74; '90 144
Cucumber-Mint Dressing, '87 153
Cucumber Salad Dressing, Creamy, '82 79
Curried Dressing, '84 115
Curry Dressing, '80 242; '82 78
Date Dressing, '87 57
Delightful Salad Dressing, '83 181
Dijon Dressing, '94 282
Dijon-Honey Dressing, '89 45
Dill Dressing, '88 182
Dill Dressing, Creamy, '91 213
Dilly Dressing, '80 74
Egg Dressing, '86 79
French
 Creamy French Dressing, '81 60;
  '90 286
 French Dressing, '89 46
 Grapefruit French Dressing, '80 101
 Honey French Dressing, '87 81
 Miracle French Dressing, '82 79
 Onion-French Dressing, '84 283
 Piquant French Dressing, '87 202;
  '88 43
 Spicy French Dressing, '81 150;
  '86 123
 Sweet French Dressing, '82 94
 Tangy French Dressing, '84 12
 Tomato-Honey French Dressing,
  '81 105
Fruit
 Avocado Fruit Salad Dressing, '82 93
 Coconut-Fruit Dressing, Tangy, '84 171
 Creamy Fruit Salad Dressing, '82 94
 Dressing for Fruit Salad, '87 81
 Fluffy Fruit Dressing, '79 69
 Fresh Fruit Dressing, '87 134
 Fruit Salad Dressing, '79 69; '93 184
 Lime-Honey Fruit Salad Dressing, '87 81
 Marmalade-Fruit Dressing, '84 171
 Red Fruit Salad Dressing, '83 231
 Salad Dressing for Fruit, '86 40
 Sweet-and-Sour Fruit Dressing, '84 125
 Whipped Cream Fruit Dressing, '79 270
Garden Dew Dressing, '86 50
Garlic-Herb Salad Dressing, Creamy, '84 66
Garlic Salad Dressing, '86 123
Ginger Dressing, '82 194; '88 61; '90 160;
 '93 290
Grapefruit Salad Dressing, '84 262
Greek Goddess Dressing, '81 150
Greek Salad Dressing, '90 286
Green Pepper-Onion Salad Dressing, '84 12
Guacamole Dressing, '92 64
Herb Dressing, '80 122
Herb-Mayonnaise Sauce, '85 73
Herb Salad Dressing, '86 40
Honey Dressing, '79 242; '83 146; '87 129
Honey-Lemon Dressing, '95 133
Honey-Lime Dressing, '83 139; '93 71
Honey-Mustard Dressing, '90 55, 111, 146
Honey-Walnut Dressing, '93 107

Italian
 Cream Dressing, Italian, '89 83
 Creamy Italian-American Salad Dressing,
  '79 69
 Grapefruit Salad Dressing, '84 262
 Italian Dressing, '79 52; '85 261;
  '89 166
 Italian Salad Dressing, '80 82; '84 12
 Sour Cream Italian Dressing, '89 45
 Special Italian Dressing, '79 190
Lemon-and-Herb Dressing, '92 108
Lemon Cream Dressing, '82 170
Lemon Dressing, Creamy, '88 M193
Lemon-Herb Salad Dressing, '82 67
Lemon-Pepper Dressing, '87 55
Lemon Salad Dressing, '79 8
Lime Dressing, '79 2; '83 120
Lime-Honey Dressing, '92 213
Lime-Parsley Dressing, '85 131
Lime Sherbet Dressing, '80 221
Magnificent Seven Salad Dressing, '89 45
Margarita Dressing, '94 107
Mayonnaise Dressing, '86 11
Mayonnaise Dressing, Herbed-, '86 119
Mint Dressing, '80 183
Mint Dressing, Fresh, '84 126
Mustard Dressing, '80 112
Mustard Dressing, Tangy, '93 323
Olive Oil Dressing, '84 266
Olive Oil, Flavored, '89 193
Orange Blossom Dressing, '82 266
Orange-Coconut Dressing, '80 158
Orange Cream, '90 126
Orange-Curd Dressing, '93 22
Orange Dressing, '81 141
Orange-Poppy Seed Dressing, '87 187
Oregano Dressing, '86 141
Oriental Dressing, '91 277
Papaya Seed Dressing, '95 204
Paprika Dressing, '86 191
Pasta Salad Dressing, '86 121
Peach Dressing, '90 180
Peanut-Ginger Dressing, '95 177
Pear Dressing, '83 146
Pepper Dressing, '80 174
Peppery Salad Dressing, '79 69
Pesto Salad Dressing, '86 150
Pineapple Cream Dressing, '83 81
Pineapple-Poppy Seed Dressing, '85 55
Pineapple Salad Dressing, '81 36
Poppy Seed Dressing, '80 152; '81 63, 252;
 '83 153, 316; '84 16; '86 123, 305;
 '88 78; '91 169; '92 191; '93 65, 168
Poppy Seed Dressing, Blender, '79 176
Raspberry Dressing, '87 153; '95 202
Raspberry Salad Dressing, '94 158
Rémoulade Dressing, '86 123
Rosemary Dressing, '81 131
Rum Dressing, '80 139
Russian Dressing, '80 4
Russian Sour Cream Dressing, '79 55
Russian-Style Dressing, '83 181
Russian-Style Salad Dressing, '86 305
Salad Dressing, '90 161
Sesame Seed Dressing, '87 81
Sesame-Soy Dressing, '93 106
Sour Cream Dressing, '82 165; '86 331
Sour Cream Sauce, '87 233
Southwestern Dressing, Spicy, '94 136
Southwestern Salad Dressing, Creamy,
 '94 278
Soy Dressing, '86 191
Soy-Sesame Dressing, '87 153

SALAD DRESSINGS (continued)

Spinach Salad Dressing, '83 181; '93 250
Stay Trim Dressing, '86 40
Strawberry Dressing, Creamy, '84 161
Sweet-and-Sour Dressing, '80 247;
 '84 70, 161; '85 163; '87 305; '89 62;
 '91 126; '94 281
Sweet-Sour Dressing, '80 246
Tangy Dressing, '83 9
Tangy Red Dressing, '86 191
Tangy Salad Dressing, '80 146; '84 115
Tarragon Dressing, '90 55
Thousand Island Dressing, '80 74; '81 104;
 '83 135; '86 123
Thousand Island Dressing, Special, '82 79
Tomato Salad Dressing, Fresh, '83 193
Tossed Salad Dressing, '84 115
Touchdown Salad Dressing, '81 197
Vanilla Oil, '94 243
Vinaigrette
 Balsamic Dressing, '95 281
 Basic Vinaigrette, '94 249
 Basil Vinaigrette, '93 106
 Blue Cheese Vinaigrette, '89 45;
  '90 55, 280
 Caper Vinaigrette, '91 310
 Cilantro-Lime Vinaigrette, '94 77
 Croutons, Vinaigrette Dressing and,
  '86 M288
 Curry Vinaigrette, Warm, '93 107
 Dijon Vinaigrette, '95 301
 Dried Tomato Vinaigrette, '93 272
 Garlic-Blue Cheese Vinaigrette, '92 57
 Garlic-Chive Vinaigrette, '91 44
 Garlic Dressing, '79 269; '80 14
 Garlic-Ginger Vinaigrette Dressing,
  '92 195
 Garlic Vinaigrette, '95 65
 Herbed Salad Dressing, '88 29
 Herbed Vinaigrette, '93 120
 Honey-Mustard Vinaigrette, '94 249
 Honey-Orange Vinaigrette, '91 255
 Lemon-Basil Vinaigrette, '94 205
 Lemon Vinaigrette, '95 31
 Marinara Vinaigrette, '94 64
 Orange-Raspberry Vinaigrette,
  '95 144
 Orange Vinaigrette Dressing, Tangy,
  '92 341; '93 46
 Oregano-Vinaigrette Dressing, '79 113
 Papaya Vinaigrette Dressing, '95 206
 Poppy Seed Vinaigrette, '94 249
 Raspberry Vinaigrette, '94 249
 Red Wine Vinaigrette, '94 327
 Spicy Dressing, '80 55
 Tarragon Vinaigrette, '94 201
 Vanilla Vinaigrette, '94 242
 Versatile Vinaigrette, '93 140
 Vinaigrette, '94 179; '95 61
 Vinaigrette Dressing, '79 171; '87 138;
  '89 12, 220, 256; '90 173; '92 303;
  '93 41; '95 231
 White Wine Vinaigrette, '89 46
 Wine Vinegar Dressing, '92 91; '93 126
Whipped Cream Salad Dressing, '82 145
Wine Dressing, Creamy, '85 20
Yogurt
 Coconut Dressing, '87 251
 Creamy Dressing, '93 318
 Cucumber-Mint Dressing, '87 153
 Dill Dressing, '88 182

Garden Dressing, Spring, '85 157
Ginger-Yogurt Dressing, '81 302
Herb Dressing, Yogurt-, '92 96
Honey-Lime Dressing, '93 71
Honey-Mustard Dressing, '90 111
Honey Poppy Seed Dressing, Yogurt-,
 '83 177
Honey-Yogurt Dressing, '93 172
Horseradish Dressing, '87 152; '91 32
Lemon-Yogurt Dressing, '93 17
Lemon-Yogurt Slaw or Salad Dressing,
 '88 54
Orange-Yogurt Dressing, '85 304
Strawberry Dressing, Creamy, '84 161
Sweet-Hot Yogurt Dressing, '86 40
Yogurt Dressing, '85 59, 215; '88 27
Yogurt Salad Dressing, '79 69
Zesty Salad Dressing, '92 60

SALADS. *See also* **AMBROSIA, ASPIC, SLAWS.**
Acini di Pepe Salad, '83 163
Alfalfa-Celery Salad, Overnight, '82 97
Antipasto, Easy, '85 114
Antipasto, Pasta, '85 286
Antipasto Salad, '84 66; '89 145
Antipasto Salad, Layered, '92 220
Apple. *See also* Salads/Congealed, Rice,
 Waldorf.
 Apple Salad, '87 233
 Beet Salad, Apple-, '91 237
 Blue Cheese Dressing, Apple Salad with,
  '87 103
 Blue Cheese-Pear-Apple Salad, '81 224
 Bran Salad, Lemony Apple-, '86 223
 Carrot Salad, Apple-, '85 22
 Cheesy Apple Salad, '86 301
 Chicken-Apple Salad, '90 216
 Crunchy Apple Salad, '80 138
 Double Apple Salad, '84 227
 English Pea-and-Apple Salad, '87 24
 Fresh Apple Salad, '81 207
 Frozen Apple-Cream Salad, '82 80
 Grapefruit-Apple Salad, '89 41
 Nut Salad, Apple-, '80 226
 Peanut-Apple Salad, '80 5
 Raisin Salad, Curried Apple-, '80 24
 Sesame-Apple Toss, '88 21
 Snow Salad, Apple, '81 224
 Spicy Apple Salad, '85 215
 Stuffed Apple Ring Salad, '91 198
 Stuffed Apple Salad, '92 266
 Summer Apple Salad, '80 149
 Swiss-Apple Salad, '84 81
 Turkey-Apple Salad, '88 123; '90 181
 Wedges with Poppyseed Dressing, Apple,
  '86 131

Apricot Salad, Frosted, '80 248
Artichoke-Pasta Salad, '94 180
Artichoke-Rice Salad, '80 178; '81 41;
 '85 81
Artichoke Salad, '86 333
Artichoke Salad, Marinated, '83 241; '95 66
Artichokes Vinaigrette, '88 101
Artichokes with Orzo Salad, '88 M193
Artichoke-Tomato Salad, '82 239
Asparagus
 Artichoke Salad, Asparagus-, '85 162
 Asparagus Salad, '94 67
 Chicken Salad, Asparagus-, '89 83
 Chicken Salad with Asparagus, Curried,
  '81 36
 Crab-and-Asparagus Salad, '92 141
 Cups, Asparagus Salad, '83 47
 Easy Asparagus Salad, '88 131
 Egg Salad, Asparagus-and-, '86 305
 Horseradish Salad, Asparagus-, '87 80
 Marinated Asparagus, '83 46; '86 92
 Marinated Asparagus Medley, '91 105
 Marinated Asparagus Salad, '79 20
 Peas-and-Asparagus Salad, '83 141
 Tarragon Marinade, Asparagus with,
  '83 47
 Vinaigrette, Asparagus, '80 77;
  '90 138
 Vinaigrette, Asparagus Salad, '88 56
 Vinaigrette, Light Asparagus, '82 50
 Yogurt Dressing, Asparagus with,
  '79 66
Australian Outback Salad, '92 45
Avocado Acapulco, '83 2
Avocado and Zucchini Salad, Creamy,
 '79 208
Avocado Garbanzo Salad, '81 33
Avocado-Grapefruit Salad, '85 26; '93 282
Avocado-Melon Salad, '82 164
Avocado-Orange Salad, '91 44
Avocado Salad, '81 195; '82 9; '83 69;
 '92 246
Avocado Salad, Citrus-, '82 265
Avocado Salad, Spanish, '87 41
Avocados, Salmon-Stuffed, '86 74
Avocados, Shrimp-Filled, '83 2
Avocado with Crabmeat, '86 119
Banana Salad, '87 80
Banana Salad, Frozen, '82 80, 132
Bananas, Nutty, '79 251
Barley-Broccoli Salad, '90 135
Barley Salad, '92 212
Bean
 Black Bean-and-Barley Salad, '94 174
 Black Bean-and-Cheese Salad, '92 217
 Black Bean Salad, '89 217
 Chilled Bean Salad, '80 178
 Cucumber-Bean Salad, '83 81
 Five-Bean Salad, Hot, '81 149
 Four-Bean Salad, '79 20; '84 82
 Full o' Beans Salad, '81 38
 Garbanzo Salad, '82 2
 Garbanzo Salad, Avocado-, '81 33
 Green Bean-and-Tomato Salad,
  '86 180
 Green Bean-Peanut Salad, '86 117
 Green Bean-Potato Salad, '83 80
 Green Bean Salad, '87 90
 Green Bean Salad, Cold, '84 106
 Green Bean Salad, Crispy, '82 154
 Green Bean Salad, German, '92 169
 Green Bean Salad, Hot, '86 298; '87 176
 Green Bean Salad, Lettuce and, '80 79

Green Bean Salad, Molded, '85 252
Green Bean Salad, Paprika-, '86 191
Green Bean Salad, Pickled, '82 239
Green Bean Salad, Speedy, '84 283
Green Beans-and-Cheese Salad,
    '91 159
Green Beans, Marinated, '83 145
Green Beans Vinaigrette, '83 25
Green Beans Vinaigrette, Kentucky
    Wonder, '94 158
Hacienda Salad, '81 67
Hominy-Bean Salad, '88 266
Hot German-Style Bean Salad, '91 314
Kidney Bean-Salami Pasta Toss, '85 165
Lima Beans, Chilly, '81 206
Lima Bean-Tomato Salad, '85 137
Marinated Bean-and-Rice Salad, '87 152
Marinated Bean-Pasta Salad, '94 167
Marinated Bean Salad, '85 137, 296;
    '89 314; '93 312; '94 167
Marinated Bean Salad, Crunchy,
    '84 197
Marinated Corn-Bean Salad, '87 9
Mexican Salad, '81 113; '94 202
Mexican-Style Salad, '83 240
Mexican Tossed Salad, '81 280
Mixed Bean Salad, '83 217
Niçoise, Salad, '86 35
Overnight Fiesta Salad, '83 80
Pasta-Bean Salad, '86 169
Pinto Salad, '86 169
Pole Bean-Potato Salad, Hot, '79 74
Pork-'n'-Bean Salad, '87 83
Potato-Bean Salad, '82 301
Quick Bean Salad, '89 128
Rice-and-Bean Salad, '85 22
Rice Salad, Beans-and-, '91 44
Sandwiches, Bean Salad, '81 243
Saucy Bean Salad, '84 18
Sausage Salad, Bean-and-, '91 313
Six-Bean Salad, Colorful, '87 82
Southwest Salad, '81 113
Sprout Salad, Bean, '82 113
Supreme Bean Salad, '91 202
Sweet-and-Sour Bean Salad, '85 198;
    '86 147
White Beans, Caesar Salad with, '93 30
Beet Salad, Marinated, '83 216
Beets and Cauliflower, Chilled, '80 137
Berry Grapefruit Cup, '79 242
Black Cherry Salad, Frozen, '89 163
Blue Cheese-Pear-Apple Salad, '81 224
Blue Cheese Salad, '88 48
Boats, Salad, '80 93
Broccoli
    Broccoli Salad, '82 24; '85 249; '90 292;
        '95 95
    Cauliflower Pasta Salad, Broccoli-,
        '88 269
    Cauliflower Salad, Broccoli-, '92 97
    Cauliflower Salad, Broccoli and,
        '81 280
    Cauliflower Salad, Broccoli 'n', '90 32
    Cauliflower Salad, Creamy Broccoli and,
        '81 23
    Cauliflower Toss, Crunchy Broccoli and,
        '83 25
    Chilled Broccoli with Lemon Dressing,
        '88 270
    Corn Salad, Broccoli-, '87 24

Creamy Broccoli Salad, '79 143
Crunchy Broccoli Salad, '83 39
Curried Broccoli Salad, '86 225
Fresh Broccoli Salad, '82 34; '87 103
Mandarin Salad, Broccoli-, '93 325
Marinated Broccoli, '81 40
Marinated Broccoli Salad, '83 240
Medley, Broccoli, '81 206
Orange Salad, Broccoli-, '94 281
Peanut Salad, Broccoli-, '92 35
Raisin Salad, Creamy Broccoli-, '92 106
Red Pepper Salad, Broccoli and,
    '83 224
Supreme, Broccoli Salad, '83 260
Warm Broccoli Salad, '92 35
Brussels Sprouts Salad, '87 233
Cabbage and Fruit Salad, '79 286
Cabbage Salad, '87 120, 233
Cabbage Salad, Austrian Hash with,
    '95 262
Cabbage Salad, Chinese, '81 271
Cabbage Salad, Garden, '81 210
Cabbage Salad, Nutty, '87 42
Cabbage Salad, Overnight, '79 83
Cabbage Salad, Tangy, '82 55
Cabbage Salad, Wilted, '94 281
Cabbage, Sweet-Sour Red, '79 5
Caesar Margarita Salad, '94 107
Caesar Salad, Maui, '94 107
Caesar Salad, Oriental, '94 107
Caesar Salad, Southern, '94 106
Caesar Salad, Turkey, '93 320
Caesar Salad with White Beans, '93 30
Cantaloupe-Cheese Salad, '88 184
Cantaloupe Cooler Salad, '79 176
Cantaloupe-Pecan Salad, '86 178
Cantaloupe Salad, '86 182
Carrot
    Apple-Carrot Salad, '85 22
    Caraway Salad, Carrot-, '89 105
    Favorite Carrot Salad, '80 33
    Fruit Toss, Carrot-, '82 235
    Harvest Carrot Salad, '89 128
    Honey-Sweet Carrot Salad, '89 161
    Marinated Carrots, Creamy, '87 200
    Orange-Carrot Salad, '80 89; '84 325
    Raisin Salad, Carrot-, '83 117; '84 174;
        '87 10
    Ring, Festive Carrot, '82 16
    Seed Salad, Fruity Carrot-and-, '86 223
    Shredded Carrot Salad, '80 178
    Simple Carrot Salad, '82 101; '84 152
    Sunshine Carrot Salad, '82 132
    Tangerine Salad, Carrot-, '83 316;
        '84 16
    Turkey-Carrot Salad, '86 283
    Turnip-and-Carrot Salad, '91 212
    Zucchini Salad, Carrot-and-, '83 240
Cauliflower
    Beets and Cauliflower, Chilled,
        '80 137
    Broccoli Crunch, Cauliflower-, '88 216
    Broccoli Salad, Cauliflower-, '79 20
    Broccoli Toss, Cauliflower-, '82 54
    Broccoli Toss, Italian Cauliflower-,
        '88 269
    Brussels Sprouts Salad, Cauliflower-,
        '83 240
    Cauliflower Salad, '79 221; '80 83;
        '81 225; '84 291; '85 240, 279;
        '92 36
    Celery-and-Cauliflower Salad, '83 39
    Corned Beef-Cauliflower Salad, '83 16

Creamy Cauliflower Salad, '82 102
Crunchy Cauliflower Salad, '80 4;
    '82 75
English Pea Salad, Cauliflower-, '95 66
Layered Cauliflower Salad, '83 240
Marinated Cauliflower Salad, '82 303;
    '84 232
Olive Toss, Cauliflower-, '85 198;
    '86 147
Orange-Cauliflower Salad, '82 266
Pea Salad, Cauliflower-, '87 231
Pea Salad, Savory Cauliflower and-,
    '81 280
Sweet-and-Sour Cauliflower Salad,
    '81 2
Vegetable Salad, Cauliflower-, '85 158
Celery Salad, '79 70
Cheesy Italian Salad, '84 33
Chef's
    Bowl, Chef's Salad, '84 66
    Chef's Salad, '86 186
    Combination Chef's Salad, '86 47
    Fruited Chef Salad, '85 222
    Fruit Salad, Chef's, '86 35
    Garden Salad, Chef's, '83 146
    Mexican Chef Salad, '85 84; '92 64
    Microwave Chef Salad, '90 M146
    Vinaigrette Chef's Salad, '81 9
    Zucchini Chef's Salad, '83 143
Cherry-Orange Salad, '79 74; '82 56
Cherry Salad, Delicious Frozen, '81 252
Cherry Salad, Fresh, '83 120
Cherry Salad, Frozen, '79 126
Cherry Salad with Honey-Lime Dressing,
    '83 139
Cherry Salad with Sherry Dressing, '79 165
Chicken
    Almond-Chicken Salad Shanghai,
        '90 160
    Almond Salad, Chicken-, '81 133
    Aloha Chicken Salad, '80 297
    Amandine, Chicken Salad, '81 37
    Ambrosia, Chicken Salad, '85 216
    Apple Salad, Chicken-, '90 216
    Artichoke-Chicken-Rice Salad, '94 132
    Artichokes, Chicken Salad with,
        '86 186
    Asparagus-Chicken Salad, '89 83
    Aspic-Topped Chicken Salad, '88 88
    Avocado-Chicken Salad, '87 107
    Avocado Salad, Chicken-, '80 139
    Avocado Salad, Fruited Chicken, '82 101
    Avocado Salad Platter, Chicken-, '83 2
    Avocado Salad, Tossed Chicken-, '80 4
    Avocados, Chicken Salad in, '85 216
    Baked Chicken Salad, '86 297; '87 176
    Basil-Chicken-Vegetable Salad, '92 162
    BLT Chicken Salad, '87 144
    Blue Cheese Chicken Salad, '94 81
    Broccoli-Chicken Salad, '90 129
    Celery Salad, Chicken-, '81 187
    Chicken Salad, '86 232, 261
    Chop Suey Salad, '81 37
    Chutney-Chicken Salad, '87 74
    Chutney Salad, Chicken, '82 108
    Coleslaw, Chicken, '84 2
    Cream Puff Bowl, Chicken Salad in,
        '86 232
    Crisp Salad, Crunchy, '95 28
    Crunchy Chicken Salad, '86 157, 207
    Curried Chicken-and-Orange Salad,
        '87 144
    Curried Chicken-Rice Salad, '92 190

SALADS, Chicken *(continued)*

Curried Chicken Salad, '79 219; '84 66;
'85 96; '86 131; '89 176
Curried Chicken Salad on Raisin Bread,
'85 96
Curried Chicken Salad with Asparagus,
'81 36
Dilled Chicken Salad, '91 212
Fancy Chicken Salad, '79 55
Filling, Chicken Salad, '87 106
Fried Chicken Ginger Salad, '93 290
Fruit, Chicken Salad with, '82 171
Fruited Chicken Salad, '84 25, 290;
'88 88; '90 318
Fruited Chicken Salad in Avocados,
'87 41
Fruit Salad, Chicken-, '82 79; '90 234
Fruity Chicken Salad, '83 157
Grapes, Chicken Salad with, '86 117
Green Salad with Chicken, Mixed,
'80 54
Grilled Chicken Salad, Moroccan,
'95 231
Hot Chicken Salad, '81 201; '83 196
Hot Chicken Salad, Country Club-Style,
'86 10
Hot Chicken Salad, Crunchy, '80 138
Hot Chicken Salad Pinwheel, '80 139
Italian, Chicken Salad, '89 18
Layered Chicken Salad, '89 162
Lettuce Folds, Thai, '94 47
Macadamia Chicken Salad, '80 138
Macaroni-Chicken Salad, '85 296;
'86 302
Macaroni-Chicken Salad, Dilled,
'92 142
Mama Hudson's Chicken Salad,
'93 238
Mandarin Chicken, Carousel, '79 88
Mango, Chicken Salad with, '86 215
Marinated Chicken-Grape Salad, '85 74
Marinated Chicken-Raspberry Salad,
'93 190
Mexican Chicken Salad, '85 84; '88 272
Minted Chicken Salad, '92 104
Nectarine Chicken Salad, '79 175
Noodle Salad, Chicken, '95 25
Old-Fashioned Chicken Salad, '83 79
Oriental Chicken Salad, '85 216; '88 271
Oriental, Chicken Salad, '90 146
Oriental Chicken Salad, '91 43
Pasta-Chicken Salad, Tarragon, '87 155
Pasta Salad, Chicken, '88 89
Pasta Salad, Grilled Chicken-, '94 64
Pea Salad, Chicken-, '83 218
Persian Chicken Salad, '81 12
Pineapple-Chicken Salad Pie, '80 138
Pineapple-Nut Chicken Salad, '83 80
Pocket, Chicken Salad in a, '88 139
Polynesian Chicken Salad, '88 272
Poulet Rémoulade, '87 144
Rice Salad, Chicken-, '81 203
Rice Salad, Hot Chicken-and-, '83 22
Rice Salad, Nutty Chicken-, '83 157
Roasted Chicken Salad, '93 14
Sandwiches, Chicken-Salad Finger,
'85 119
Southwestern Chicken Salad, '88 88
Spaghetti Salad, Chicken-, '90 146
Special Chicken Salad, '85 82; '87 183;
'88 M193

Spinach Tossed Salad, Chicken-and-,
'83 157
Spread, Chicken Salad Party, '88 M8
Stack-Up Salad, Chicken, '83 80
Summer Chicken Salad, '83 145
Summery Chicken Salad, '95 138
Super Chicken Salad, '82 174
Supreme, Chicken Salad, '79 107, 152;
'89 176
Taco Salad, Chicken, '94 M136
Tahitian Chicken Salad, '84 120
Tarragon Chicken Salad, '90 199
Tarts, Chicken Salad, '84 257
Thai Chicken Salad, '95 177
Tortellini Salad, Chicken, '87 288
Tortilla Salads, Mexican Chicken,
'95 129
Tropical Chicken Boats for Two,
'82 186
Tropical Chicken Salad, '85 216
Twist, Chicken Salad with a, '84 221
Vegetable-Chicken Salad, '91 287
Walnut-Chicken Salad, '89 14
Walnut Salad, Sunburst Chicken-and-,
'93 91
Wild Rice-Chicken Salad, '83 146
Citrus-Blue Cheese Salad, '92 220
Citrus Salad, '87 103
Citrus Salad Bowl, '86 335; '87 83
Citrus Salad in Orange Cups, '85 47
Citrus Salad, Southern-Style, '84 262
Citrus Salad, Tangy, '89 34
Citrus Vinaigrette Salad, '86 192
Congealed
Apple-Apricot Salad, '88 121
Apple Cider Salad, '83 123
Apple Cider Salad Mold, '85 54
Apple Crunch Salad, '84 232; '86 331
Apple Salad, Congealed, '85 252
Apple Salad, Triple, '88 122
Apricot Fruit Salad, '82 132
Apricot Nectar Salad, '83 218;
'87 236
Apricot Salad, '81 251; '83 123
Apricot Salad, Creamy, '85 263
Asheville Salad, '86 199
Asparagus-Cucumber Mold, '85 252
Asparagus Mold, '80 104
Asparagus Mousse Salad, '86 252
Asparagus Salad, '88 121
Asparagus Salad, Congealed, '83 260
Asparagus Salad, Creamy Lemon-,
'93 116
Asparagus Salad, Tart, '81 203
Avocado Crunch Salad, Congealed,
'85 26
Avocado Salad, Congealed, '84 266
Avocado Salads, Congealed, '87 42
Beet-Nut Salad, '79 74
Beet Salad Mold, '82 267
Beet Salad, Pickled, '83 234
Beet Salad, Tangy, '86 199
Berry Salad, Layered, '79 173
Broccoli Salad, Congealed, '84 124
Cantaloupe, Southern Plantation,
'82 179
Carrot-Nut Salad, Creamy, '86 331
Carrot-Pineapple Salad, '91 83
Carrot Salad, '82 137
Cauliflower-Lemon Salad, '81 23
Cheese Molds, Snowcap, '79 242
Cherry-Apple Salad, '86 31
Cherry Cola Salad, '80 104

Cherry-Cola Salad, '91 224; '95 94
Cherry-Salad, Best, '82 302
Cherry Salad, Congealed, '89 278
Cherry Salad, Festive, '84 265
Cherry Salad, Port Wine-, '86 11
Cherry Salad, Sweet, '89 326
Cherry-Wine Salad, Elegant, '82 56
Chicken-Cucumber Mold, '80 175
Chicken Jewel Ring Salad, '83 282
Chicken-Pea Salad, '83 218
Chicken Salad Mold, '83 80; '84 163
Chicken Salad Ring, '90 123
Chile-Tomato Salad, Spicy, '88 121
Christmas Salad, '88 249
Christmas Snow Salad, '82 266
Citrus Mold, Sparkling, '86 331
Citrus Salad Mold, Golden, '85 303
Corned Beef Salad, '80 104
Corned Beef Salad, Molded, '82 86
Crabmeat-and-Asparagus, Congealed
Salad with, '84 86
Cranberry-Apple Mold, '89 277
Cranberry Congealed Salad, '91 296
Cranberry Gelatin Mold, '92 271
Cranberry Mold, '79 250
Cranberry-Orange Delight, '90 168
Cranberry Ring, '90 291
Cranberry Salad, Congealed, '90 124
Cranberry Salad, Festive, '81 264, 296
Cranberry Salad, Frosted, '90 288
Cranberry Salad, Holiday, '82 266, 288;
'95 301
Cranberry Salad, Jellied, '83 279;
'85 281
Cranberry Salad, Layered, '84 322;
'86 325
Cranberry Salad Ring, '80 247
Crème de Menthe Salad, '82 122
Creole Salad, '79 147
Cucumber Mold, Creamy, '84 164
Cucumber Mousse, '88 121
Cucumber-Pineapple Salad, '84 124
Cucumber Salad, Creamy, '86 147;
'92 97
Cucumber Salad Mold, '82 111;
'83 81, 253
Eggnog Christmas Salad, '86 281
Egg Salad, Deviled, '83 124
Emerald Salad, '81 143
Emerald Salad, Snowy, '87 311
Fall Salad with Ginger Dressing,
'82 194
Frosted Salad, Heavenly, '79 286
Fruit, Jeweled Congealed Fresh, '95 89
Fruit Mold, Sherried, '90 124
Fruit Salad, Cherry, '87 236
Fruit Salad, Sparkling, '82 266
Fruit Salad, Spiced Autumn, '87 228
Garden-Patch Salad Molds, '86 283
Garden Salad, Molded, '86 199
Gazpacho Molded Salad, '92 323
Gazpacho Salad Mold, '87 311
Gazpacho Salad, Molded, '79 159
Gazpacho Salad with Avocado Cream,
Congealed, '92 158
Grape-Cantaloupe Mold, Double,
'79 173
Grapefruit Congealed Salad, '83 190
Grapefruit-Orange Salad, '91 276
Grapefruit Salad, '83 124; '84 325;
'88 122
Grapefruit Salad, Congealed, '84 325;
'85 279

SALADS, Congealed *(continued)*

Grape Salad Mold, '83 120
Green Bean Salad, Molded, '85 252
Green Spring Salad, '83 124
Ham Salad, Congealed, '81 36
Holiday Jewel Salad, '81 252
Horseradish Salad, '85 66
Layered Congealed Salad, '81 143
Layered Holiday Salad, '81 252
Layered Salad, Make Ahead, '81 296
Layer Mold, Three-, '82 54
Lemon-Cheese Salad, '85 240
Lemon-Cranberry Congealed Salad,
   '87 311
Lemon-Cream Salad, '88 250
Lemon-Cucumber Mold, '87 90
Lemon Mold, Cheesy, '79 241
Lemon-Onion Salad, '85 252
Lemon-Tomato Salad, Congealed,
   '89 178
Lemon-Vegetable Congealed Salad,
   '85 22
Lime-Carrot Salad, '92 65
Lime-Cheese Salad, Frosted, '79 286
Lime Sherbet Salad, '80 104
Mandarin Orange Salad, Congealed,
   '89 327
Mandarin Salad Molds, '85 54
Melon Ball Salad, Congealed, '84 125
Mincemeat Salad, '94 282
Mincemeat Salad, Holiday, '85 263
Molds, Perfection, '81 153
Mosaic Salad, '89 313
Orange-Buttermilk Salad, '95 134
Orange-Pear Salad, '84 164
Orange Salad, Creamy, '84 124
Orange Salad, Frosted, '81 154;
   '83 123
Orange Salad, Jeweled, '83 210
Orange Sherbet Salad, '81 154
Orange Surprise Salad, '79 12
Peach-Cranberry Ring, Spicy, '85 264
Peaches-and-Cream Salad, '83 108
Peach Fluff, '95 176
Peach Frost, '84 164
Peach Party Salad, '84 290
Peach Pinwheel Salad, '79 11
Peach Salad, Pickled, '80 104; '85 264
Peach Salad, Spiced, '94 68
Peachy Berry Cream Mold, '83 130
Pear-Lime Salad, '84 152
Pear Salad, Royal, '84 265
Pimiento Salad, Sunshine, '84 124
Pineapple-Buttermilk Salad, '82 80
Pineapple-Cucumber Congealed Salad,
   '83 118
Pineapple Daiquiri Salad, '84 232
Pineapple-Lime Salad, '84 320
Pineapple Mold, Minted, '85 240
Pineapple-Orange Congealed Salad,
   '83 218
Pineapple-Pear Delight, '82 54
Raspberry Fruit Mounds, '79 35
Raspberry Holiday Mold, '84 253
Raspberry Ribbon Salad, '87 236
Raspberry Salad, '86 286
Raspberry-Wine Salad, '91 256
Rhubarb Congealed Salad, '86 140
Rhubarb Salad, '91 146; '92 129
Rhubarb Salad, Tart, '91 146;
   '92 129

Roquefort Salad, Creamy, '79 73
Ruby-and-Emerald Salad, '85 79
Salmon Salad, Chilly, '80 104
Sangría Salad, '86 331
Shrimp Salad, '84 221
Strawberry-Nut Salad, '94 132
Strawberry Salad, Hidden Treasure,
   '79 11
Strawberry-Wine Salad Mold, '83 261
Sunshine Delight, '86 117
Tomato Mold, Tangy, '79 74
Tomato Ring, Tangy, '84 164
Tomato Salad, Frozen, '84 52
Tomato-Vegetable Ring, '81 302
Tuna-Cheese Mold, Creamy, '81 135
Tuna Ring, Creamy, '80 275
Tuna Salad, Congealed, '84 163
Tuna Salad, Creamy, '82 87, 208
Tuna Salad, Luncheon, '81 135
Vegetable Congealed Salad, Cheesy-,
   '86 199
Vegetable Congealed Salad, Fresh,
   '91 229
Vegetable Relish Salad, '82 267
Vegetable Salad, Congealed, '79 276
Vegetable Salad, Congealed Fresh,
   '82 240
Waldorf Salad, Congealed, '82 80
Waldorf Salad, Molded, '84 326
Corn-and-Pea Salad, '90 181
Cornbread Salad, '87 172
Cornbread Salad, Mexican, '95 210
Corn-in-the-Shuck Salad, '93 236
Corn Salad, '80 247; '81 139; '85 236;
   '91 27; '95 214
Corn Salad, Chilled, '79 20
Corn Salad, Festive, '92 263
Corn Salad, Fresh, '91 126; '94 162
Corn Salad, Marinated, '89 126
Corn Salad, Shoepeg, '81 23
Corn Salad, Tangy, '88 176
Corn Salad, Tasty, '84 289
Cottage Cheese-Banana Splits, '87 56
Cottage Cheese Salad, Different, '85 328;
   '86 22
Cottage Cheese Salad in Tomatoes, '86 208
Cottage Cheese Salad, Out-of-This-World,
   '79 44
Cottage-Tomato Salad, '85 163
Couscous Salad, Curried, '91 44
Cranberry
   Cheese Ribbon Salad, Cranberry-,
      '79 241
   Christmas Salad, Cranberry, '79 243
   Cloud, Cranberry, '90 287
   Cranberry Salad, '88 250
   Frozen Cranberry-Pineapple Salad,
      '91 237
   Holiday Salad, Cranberry, '89 277
   Oriental, Cranberry, '79 126
   Tart Cranberry Salad, '79 286
   Whipped Cream Salad, Cranberry-,
      '83 261
Crunchy-Creamy Salad, '88 100
Cucumber-Almond Salad, '86 147
Cucumber and Tomato Salad, Dilled,
   '81 153
Cucumber Cooler, Simple, '86 147
Cucumber Mousse, '79 11
Cucumber Mousse with Dill Sauce,
   '95 216
Cucumber Salad, Dilled, '82 229; '92 72;
   '93 65

Cucumber Salad, Marinated, '82 111
Cucumbers and Artichokes, Marinated,
   '82 111
Cucumbers, Cool, '84 152
Cucumbers in Sour Cream, '79 52;
   '80 178
Cucumber-Tomato Salad, '90 144
Cucumber-Vinaigrette Oriental, '85 198;
   '86 147
Cucumber-Yogurt Salad, '87 33
Cukes and Scallions, '91 168
Curry Salad, Hot Indian, '83 23
Eggplant Salad, '90 99
Egg-Rice Salad, '84 18; '86 169
Egg Salad, Bacon-Horseradish, '94 181
Egg Salad, Green Vegetable and, '79 191
Egg Salad Spread, Cottage-, '82 146
Egg Salad Tacos, Mexican, '94 181
Egg Salad, Yolkless, '94 181
Endive, Bacon, and Pecan Salad, '89 12
Endive-Tomato Starburst Salad, '93 323
Escarole-and-Bacon Salad, '84 85
Fennel and Radicchio with Orange
   Vinaigrette, Grilled, '95 253
Fennel Salad, Marinated, '93 56
Fish. *See also* Salads/Seafood.
   Confetti Salad, '80 4
   Crawfish Salad, Dilled, '83 126
   Meal-in-One Salad, '82 232
   Salmon-and-Macaroni Salad, '81 114
   Salmon on Mixed Greens with Creamy
      Dill Dressing, '93 143
   Salmon-Pasta Salad, '87 9
   Salmon-Rice Salad, '84 289
   Salmon Salad, '89 99
   Salmon Salad, Broiled, '92 108
   Salmon Salad, Crunchy, '81 148
   Salmon Salad Shells, '85 286
   Salmon Salad, Simple, '91 23
   Salmon Salad, Summertime, '82 207
   Salmon-Spinach Salad, '87 145
   Salmon-Stuffed Avocados, '86 74
   Tuna-and-Cannellini Bean Salad,
      '86 143
   Tuna-and-Red Pepper Salad, '93 143
   Tuna Chef Salad, '82 78
   Tuna-Egg Salad, '81 135
   Tuna-Macaroni Salad, '83 145; '84 66
   Tuna Macaroni Salad, '83 44
   Tuna-Mac in Tomatoes, '87 188
   Tuna-Pasta Salad, '91 43; '92 141
   Tuna Pasta Salad, '92 108
   Tuna-Potato Salad, '84 289
   Tuna-Rice Salad, '87 202
   Tuna Salad, Cheese-Sauced, '87 M124
   Tuna Salad, Company, '87 201
   Tuna Salad, Crunchy, '87 201
   Tuna Salad, Curried, '86 208
   Tuna Salad, Favorite, '82 208
   Tuna Salad, Flavorful, '81 37
   Tuna Salad, Fresh Greens and, '80 55
   Tuna Salad, Layered, '84 221
   Tuna Salad Rolls, Hot, '84 281
   Tuna Salad, Swiss, '86 186
   Tuna Salad, Whole Wheat Macaroni-,
      '84 193
   Tuna Salad, Wild, '95 243
   Tuna Salad with Grapes, Curried, '87 201
   Tuna-Taco Salad, '87 145
Freezer Salad, '94 118
Fruit. *See also* Salads/Congealed.
   Ambrosia, Mixed Fruit, '83 10
   Avocado Fruit Salad, '87 41

SALADS, Fruit *(continued)*

Avocado-Fruit Salad with Honey-Yogurt Dressing, '93 172
Banana Split Salad, '91 58
Berry-Citrus Twist, '95 100
Cabbage and Fruit Salad, '79 286
Chef Salad, Fruited, '85 222
Chef's Fruit Salad, '86 35
Chicken-Fruit Salad, '82 79; '90 234
Chicken Salad, Fruited, '84 25, 290; '88 88; '90 318
Chicken Salad, Fruity, '83 157
Chicken Salad in Avocados, Fruited, '87 41
Chicken Salad with Fruit, '82 171
Chilled Fruit with Dressing, '85 222
Citrus-Cilantro Dressing, Fruit Salad with, '93 310; '94 97
Citrus Dressing, Fruit Salad with, '88 6
Coconut Fruit Bowl, '83 111
Coconut Salad, Chunky Fruit-and-, '84 24
Colorful Fruit Salad, '82 113
Cottage Cheese-and-Fruit Salad, '86 16
Cottage-Fruit Split, '86 169
Cream Dressing, Fruit Salad with, '89 277
Creamy Fruit Salad, '84 265
Creamy Holiday Fruit Salad, '90 251
Cups, Royal Fruit, '81 146
Cups, Sangría Fruit, '89 34
Cups with Pineapple Cream Dressing, Fruit, '83 81
Curried Fruit Salad, '85 107
Date Dressing, Fruit Salad with, '87 57
Delight, Fruit, '86 131
Dressed-Up Fruit, '82 5
Easy Fruit Salad, '80 221
Easy Patio Fruit Salad, '88 184
Festive Fruit Salad, '80 16
Fresh Fruit Bowl, Sparkling, '80 146
Fresh Fruit Cup with Mint Dressing, '80 183
Fresh Fruit Salad, '82 165
Fresh Fruit Salad with Celery-Honey Dressing, '80 42
Fresh Fruit Salad with Poppy-Seed Dressing, '80 137
Fresh Fruit Salad with Poppy Seed Dressing, '91 168
Fresh Fruit with Lemon Sauce, '82 290
Frisky Fruit Salad, '85 46
Frozen Fruit Salad, '83 110
Frozen Fruit Salad, Dreamy, '79 126
Frozen Fruit Salad, Luscious, '81 204
Frozen Fruit Salad, Summertime, '89 111
Frozen Salad, Christmas Wreath, '79 241
Fruit Salad, '83 209; '89 277
Gingered Fruit Salad, '95 95
Glazed Fruit Salad, '83 48; '84 290
Green Fruit Salad with Honey-Lime Dressing, '93 71
Hawaiian Fruit Dish, '82 112
Heavenly Salad, '81 252
Holiday Fruit Salad, '87 236
Honeydew Fruit Boats, '81 147
Honeydew Fruit Bowl, '84 186
Honey Dressing, Fruit Salad with, '87 129

Honey Fruit Salad, '80 276
Honey-Lemon Dressing, Fruit Salad with, '93 21
Hurry-Up Fruit Salad, '87 236
Jicama-Fruit Salad, '86 83
Layered Fruit Salad, '84 290; '89 277; '91 58
Lemonade Fruit Salad, '84 24
Lemon Freeze, Fruity, '82 145
Lettuce and Fruit Salad with Poppy Seed Dressing, '80 152
Main Dish Fruit Salad, '83 119
Marinated Fruit Bowl, '80 297
Marinated Fruit Deluxe, '81 146
Medley, Chilled Fruit, '84 60
Medley, Fruit Cup, '85 47
Mélange Delight, Fruit, '81 302
Melon Balls in Watermelon Sauce, '79 177
Melon-Citrus Mingle, '79 177
Melon Cocktail, Minted, '81 146
Melon Cooler, '81 146
Melon Mélange, '84 139
Melon Salad, Summertime, '82 101
Melon Salad with Orange-Raspberry Vinaigrette, Grilled, '95 144
Minted Fruit Medley, '80 182
Mint-Gin Fruit Salad, '92 92
Mint Sauce, Fruit Salad with, '88 M96
Mixed Fruit Cup, '87 233
Mixed Fruit Salad, Banana-, '79 270
Multi-Fruit Salad, '93 184
Nut Salad, Cheesy Fruit-'n'-, '87 56
Old-Fashioned Fruit Salad, '82 80
Orange Cream, Fresh Fruit Salad with, '90 126
Orange Fruit Cup, '91 277
Oriental Dressing, Fruit Salad with, '91 277
Party Freeze Salad, '82 145
Pasta Salad, Fruited, '92 108
Peachy Fruit Salad, '89 206
Persimmon Fruit Salad, '79 206
Picks, Fruit on, '80 159
Pineapple Dressing, Fruit Salad with, '85 207
Pineapple-Fruit Salad, Icy, '87 9
Platter, Fresh Fruit Salad, '92 213
Platter, Fruit Salad, '83 261
Poppy Seed Dressing, Fruit Salad with, '88 78
Quick-and-Easy Fruit Salad, '81 99
Refreshing Fruit Salad, '85 92
Rhapsody, Fruit, '80 158
Rum, Fruit Cup with, '83 55
Sherried Fruit Mélange, '80 158
Shrimp Salad, Fruited, '86 156
Sour Cream Fruit Salad, '80 138
Springtime Fruit Salad, '81 96
Summer Fruit Salad, '82 164; '92 171
Summer Salad, Favorite, '80 158
Summer Salad, Georgia, '92 179
Sunny Fruit Salad, '91 58
Sunny Salad, '80 138
Sweet-and-Sour Fruit Salad, '80 13; '84 125
Tossed Fruit Salad, '92 106
Tropical Fruit Salad, '89 306
Tropical Fruit Salad with Fresh Mint Dressing, '84 126
Turkey Salad, Fruit-and-, '89 176
Turkey Salad, Fruit-and-Spice, '94 325
Vanilla Fruit Cup, '80 183

Watermelon Fruit Basket, '84 161
White Wine, Fruit in, '81 48
Winter Fruit Delight, '80 243
Winter Fruit Salad, '80 248; '82 23
Wreath, Della Robbia Fruit, '87 294
Yogurt Fruit Salad, '81 114
Yogurt-Granola Fruit Medley, '91 58
Gazpacho Salad, '91 313
Grapefruit-Apple Salad, '89 41
Grapefruit-Avocado Salad, '83 316; '84 16; '89 41
Grapefruit-Banana Salad with Celery Seed Dressing, '91 237
Grapefruit Combo Salad, '80 50
Grapefruit-Cucumber Salad, '80 100
Grapefruit Winter Salad, '84 24
Greek Salad, '87 103; '93 208; '94 160, 202
Greek-Style Salad, '91 27
Green. *See also* Salads/Spinach.
   Apple and Brie, Salad Greens with, '93 241
   Balsamico, Insalata, '94 46
   B.B.'s Salad Dressing, Green Salad with, '91 65
   Bibb Salad, Tossed, '87 128
   Bibb Salad with Raspberry-Maple Dressing, '91 246
   Boston Lettuce and Watercress Salad, '93 65
   Bouquet, A Salad, '91 44
   Caesar Salad, '80 112; '86 80; '92 71
   Caesar Salad, Easy, '87 116
   Caesar Salad, Flippo, '87 61
   Caesar Salad, Mock, '92 283
   California Green Salad, '81 84
   Cantaloupe Green Salad, '91 126
   Chinese Green Salad, '88 48
   Citrus Green Salad, '85 304
   Citrus Salad, Southern-Style, '84 262
   Combination Salad Bowl, '85 132
   Combo Salad Bowl, '81 9
   Company's Coming Salad, '79 113
   Cranberry-Topped Green Salad, '87 311
   Crimson Greens, '87 153
   Crunchy Green Salad, '89 321
   Endive Salad, Avocado-, '94 88
   Endive-Watercress Salad, '93 22
   Fast-and-Easy Salad, '85 M328
   Fenron Salad, '79 85
   Garden Salad, '85 92; '92 60
   Garden Salad Centerpiece, '83 171
   Garden Salad, Herbed, '85 328; '86 22
   Garden Salad, Summer, '87 153
   Garden Salad Toss, '81 9
   Garden Salad with Rosemary Dressing, Fresh, '81 131
   Garlic-Tarragon Green Salad, '92 79
   Goat Cheese and Greens, '90 54
   Grapefruit Salad, Greens and, '95 301
   Grecian Green Salad, '84 266
   Grecian Tossed Salad, '79 174
   Hill Country Salad, '81 9
   Lemony French Dressing, Green Salad with, '85 67
   Lettuce, Cheesy Stuffed, '79 175
   Lettuce, Confetti-Stuffed, '87 24
   Lettuce, Delicate Garden, '87 62
   Lettuce-English Pea Salad, '91 208
   Lettuce, Garden-Stuffed, '83 135
   Lettuce Salad, Blue Cheese Stuffed, '94 202

SALADS, Green (continued)

Lettuce Salad, French, '84 187
Lettuce Salad, Tennessee-Killed,
  '88 86
Lettuce Salad, Wilted, '82 302
Lettuce Salad, Wilted Bacon-and-,
  '85 69
Lettuces with Mustard Vinaigrette, Baby,
  '93 67
Lettuce Wedges with Pimiento Dressing,
  '84 212
Lettuce, Wilted, '86 269
Lettuce with Sour Cream Dressing
  Deluxe, '88 48
Marinated Cheese Dressing, Green Salad
  with, '93 206
Mediterranean Salad, '90 99
Mesclun with Tarragon Dressing,
  '90 55
Mint-Fresh Green Salad, '92 105
Mixed Green Salad, '90 230
Mixed Green Salad, Wilted, '85 69
Mixed Green Salad with Chicken,
  '80 54
Mixed Greens Salad, '87 62
Mixed Greens with Blue Cheese
  Vinaigrette, '89 274; '90 280
Mixed Greens with Parmesan Walnuts,
  '95 301
Mixed Greens with Tarragon Vinaigrette,
  '95 326
Nutty Green Salad, '87 168
Oriental, Green Salad, '85 92
Peppery Greens with Raspberry Dressing,
  '95 254
Red-and-Green Salad, '90 55
Robust Salad, '90 181
Romaine Salad, Tangy, '80 155
Romaine-Spinach Salad, '89 123
Romaine with Caper Vinaigrette, Hearts
  of, '91 310
Salmagundi Salad, '83 146
Savory Green Salad, '82 74
Sensational Salad, '84 320
Sesame-Citrus Green Salad, '86 33
Shrimp, Green Salad with, '88 49
Simply Good Salad, '85 131
Soy Dressing, Green Salad with, '86 191
Spring Salad, '87 62
Spring Salad, Mediterranean, '80 148
Spring Salad Wedges, '87 62
Summer Salad, Crisp, '85 92
Summertime Salad, '79 143; '84 195
Sweet-and-Sour Green Salad, '94 281
Tangy Wilted Salad, '85 69
Tossed Mixed Green Salad, '84 126
Tossed Salad, Blue Cheese, '84 195
Tossed Salad, Boston, '84 85
Tossed Salad, Colorful, '90 55
Tossed Salad, Radish-Dressed, '79 104
Watercress-and-Mushroom Salad,
  '88 104
Watercress Salad, Roasted Red Pepper
  and, '90 55
Winter Salad, '95 280
Guacamole Salad, '80 14; '87 181
Guacamole-Tomato Salad, '81 302
Hearts of Palm Salad, '81 252; '89 276
Hearts-of-Palm Salad, '87 138
Hearts of Palm Salad with Basil-and-Garlic
  Dressing, '94 55

Herb Salad, '87 90
Honeydew Salad with Apricot Cream
  Dressing, '84 191
Ice Cream Salad, '79 126
Italian Salad, '87 145
Jicama-and-Orange Salad, '88 246
Jicama-Orange Salad, '86 83; '90 122
Jicama Salad, '87 123
Layered Overnight Salad, '90 319
Layered Salad, '86 35, 79
Layered Salad, Cheesy, '81 37
Layered Salad Deluxe, '81 153
Layered Salad, Hearty, '85 79
Layered Salad, Majestic, '86 79
Layered Salad, Make-Ahead, '81 296
Layered Salad, Overnight, '81 188
Legumes, Marinated, '90 197
Lentils-and-Rice Salad, '90 197
Magnolia Blossom Salad, '89 123
Main-Dish Salad, '86 191
Mandarin, Salad, '84 231
Mandarin Spinach Salad, '85 163
Mandarin Tossed Salad, '89 12
Mango Salad, '79 137
Mango Salad, Fresh, '84 126
Meal-in-One Salad, '86 43
Meat
  Beef-and-Broccoli Salad, '87 187
  Beef Fajita Salad, '91 70
  Beef Salad, Gingered, '88 61
  Beef Salad, Peking, '88 60
  Beef Salad, Tangy, '87 M218
  Beef Salad, Western-Style, '93 321
  Beef Salad, Zesty, '79 56
  Beef Vinaigrette Salad, '95 177
  Chili Salad, Spicy, '86 71
  Committee, Salad by, '87 288
  Corned Beef-Cauliflower Salad,
    '83 16
  Corned Beef-Potato Salad, '85 213
  Corned Beef Salad, '80 104
  Corned Beef Salad, Molded, '82 86
  Corned Beef Salad, Potato-, '81 36
  Corned Beef Salad, Vegetable-,
    '80 148
  Dude Ranch Salad, '80 15
  Ham-and-Apple Salad, '88 139
  Ham-and-Cheese Salad, '88 138
  Ham and Cheese Toss, '79 55
  Ham and Macaroni Salad, '79 220
  Ham-and-Pasta Salad, '90 128
  Ham-and-Rice Salad, Colorful,
    '90 319
  Ham-and-Rice Salad, Mandarin,
    '87 145
  Ham-Dijon Pasta Salad, '92 191
  Ham 'n Egg Salad, '81 36
  Ham-Noodle Salad, '85 249
  Ham-Rice Toss, '82 40
  Ham Salad, Congealed, '81 36
  Ham Salad, Crunchy Baked, '83 23
  Ham Salad, Fruited, '81 36, 146
  Ham Salad, Hearty, '82 40
  Ham Salad Sandwich, Tangy, '80 272
  Ham Salad, Spicy Italian, '85 74
  Ham Salad Spread, '87 92
  Ham Salad, Tropical, '89 175
  Ham-Sweet Potato Salad, Hawaiian,
    '82 232
  Mexican Salad in a Shell, '86 4
  Mexican Salad Supper, '82 9; '83 68
  Paella Salad, '86 207
  "Pig in the Garden" Salad, '92 255

  Pork-and-Spinach Salad, Mandarin,
    '88 M126
  Pork Salad, Oriental, '92 140
  Roast Beef Salad, '80 223; '81 56;
    '90 318
  Roast Beef Salad, Cucumber-, '89 162
  Rolls, Hearty Salad, '81 206
  Sirloin Salad, Grilled, '94 129
  Steak Salad Cups, Pepper, '86 206
  Steak Salad, Greek, '92 107
  Taco Salad, '79 56; '83 145; '84 221;
    '85 84; '89 332; '90 20
  Taco Salad Cups, '85 M29
  Taco Salad, Spicy, '87 287
Melon-and-Prosciutto Salad, '92 191
Melon Balls, Minted, '87 162
Melon-Berry Salad, '90 180
Melon Salad with Dill Dressing, '88 182
Mexican Salad with Avocado Dressing,
  '92 321
Middle Eastern Salad, '87 107
Minestrone Salad, '79 220
Mix, Muffy Salad, '94 34
Mozzarella-Tomato-Basil Salad, Fresh,
  '93 131
Mushroom-and-Pepper Salad, '86 68
Mushroom Salad, Fabulous, '81 190
Mushroom Salad, Fresh, '93 65
Mushroom Salad, Marinated, '88 215;
  '90 181
Mushroom Salad, Quick Cheesy-, '89 128
Mushroom-Zucchini Salad, '85 8
Okra-Corn-and-Tomato Vinaigrette,
  '90 173
Okra Salad, '90 155
Olive Clubhouse Salad, '81 114
Olive Salad, Doodles, '94 35
Olive Salad, Italian, '94 35
Olive Salad, Mexican, '85 84
Onion Salad, Roasted, '95 65
Orange-and-Beet Salad, '88 43
Orange and Pineapple Salad, Mandarin,
  '82 266
Orange-Carrot Salad, '80 89; '84 325
Orange-Cauliflower Salad, '82 266
Orange-Cottage Cheese Salad, '79 44
Orange Cups, '86 92
Orange-Grapefruit Salad, '93 294
Orange-Lettuce Salad, Mandarin, '92 79
Orange-Onion Salad, '89 41
Orange-Onion Salad, Marinated, '91 231;
  '92 68
Orange-Romaine Salad, '84 325; '87 239
Orange Salad Cups, '85 40
Orange Salad, Mandarin, '81 252; '84 161
Orange Salad, Quick, '87 80
Orange Salad, Tropical, '92 97
Orange Salad with Honey-Berry Dressing,
  '89 250
Orange Salad with Honey Dressing, '89 14
Orange-Shrimp Salad, '84 197
Orange-Spinach Salad, '83 316; '84 16
Orange-Strawberry Salad with Orange-Curd
  Dressing, '93 22
Orange Tossed Salad, Mandarin, '92 303
Orange Walnut Salad, '80 246
Oriental Salad Bowl, '87 153
Orzo Salad, Confetti, '92 173
Paella Salad, '86 207
Pasta
  Artichoke-Pasta Salad, '94 180
  Bean-Pasta Salad, Marinated, '94 167
  Bean Salad, Pasta-, '86 169

SALADS, Pasta (continued)

Broccoli-Cauliflower Pasta Salad, '88 269
Caesar Salad Pasta, '95 230
Chicken Pasta Salad, '88 89
Chicken-Pasta Salad, Grilled, '94 64
Chicken Salad, Tarragon Pasta-,
'87 155
Cold Pasta Platter, '88 42
Crabmeat-Shrimp Pasta Salad, '86 208
Crunchy Pasta Salad, '85 166
Easy Confetti-Pasta Salad, '92 220
Fruited Pasta Salad, '92 108
Garden Pasta Salad, '86 188
Ham, Pasta Salad with, '92 108
Ham-Pecan-Blue Cheese Pasta Salad,
'90 62
Herbed Pasta-and-Tomato Salad, '92 144
Luncheon Pasta Salad, '90 191
Macaroni-Cheese Salad, Dilled, '86 208
Macaroni-Chicken Salad, '85 296;
'86 302
Macaroni-Chicken Salad, Dilled, '92 142
Macaroni-Crabmeat Salad, '81 153
Macaroni-Ham Salad, '85 218
Macaroni Salad, '87 92
Macaroni Salad, Barbecue, '82 276
Macaroni Salad, Confetti, '82 132;
'85 297
Macaroni Salad, Crunchy, '82 24
Macaroni Salad, Dilled, '89 161
Macaroni Salad for Two, '81 31
Macaroni Salad, Garden, '84 290;
'92 64
Macaroni Salad, Gourmet, '81 253
Macaroni Salad, Hearty, '84 90
Macaroni Salad, Pineapple, '79 220
Macaroni Salad, Refreshing, '80 177
Macaroni Salad, Shell, '92 163
Macaroni Salad, Spiral, '82 276
Macaroni Salad, Sweet-and-Sour,
'85 166
Macaroni Salad, Taco, '85 165
Macaroni Salad Véronique, '85 164
Macaroni-Salmon Salad, '82 232
Macaroni Shell Salad, '87 38
Macaroni-Shrimp Salad, '85 121
Macaroni-Shrimp Salad, Festive, '85 165
Macaroni Toss, Corkscrew, '83 163
Macaroni-Tuna Salad, Whole Wheat,
'84 193
Macaroni-Vegetable Salad, '86 209
Main-Dish Pasta Salad, '82 199
Mediterranean Salad, '95 132
Medley, Garden Pasta, '89 256
Oriental Pasta Salad, '90 63
Overnight Pasta Salad, '82 276
Pasta Salad, '84 139; '86 120; '87 36;
'90 62, 91
Pistachio-Pasta Salad, '86 141
Plentiful P's Salad, '87 12
Presto Pasta Salad, '90 63
Ramen Noodle Salad, '88 41
Ratatouille Pasta Salad, '90 74
Ravioli Salad, Caesar, '95 183
Rotelle Salad, Crunchy, '86 209
Rotini Salad, '88 42
Seafood Pasta Salad, '90 62
Seashell Salad, '86 209
Shell Salad, Tossed, '91 256
Shrimp Salad, Pasta-and-, '83 163
Snappy Pasta, '83 164

Southwestern Pasta Salad, '94 278
Spaghetti Salad, '82 277; '84 205
Spaghetti Salad, Chicken-, '90 146
Spinach-Mustard Twist, '86 209
Tortellini-Pesto Salad, '92 22
Tortellini Salad, '89 237
Tortellini Salad, Chicken, '87 288
Tortellini Salad, Garden, '91 44
Turkey 'n' Pasta Salad, Ranch-Style,
'94 184
Vegetable Salad, Pasta-, '95 238
Vermicelli Vinaigrette Salad, '82 189
Vinaigrette, Italian Pasta, '92 78
Ziti-Cheddar Salad, '85 165
Pea
Asparagus Salad, Peas-and-, '83 141
Black-Eyed Pea Salad, '80 112; '86 225;
'88 92, 221; '90 173; '95 203
Black-Eyed Pea Salad, Fearrington House
Goat Cheese and, '95 60
Black-Eyed Pea Salad, Marinated,
'93 190
Black-Eyed Pea Salad, Overnight,
'81 280
Black-Eyed Peas, Marinated, '82 156
Black-Eyed Peas, Zesty, '89 147
Black-Eyed Pea Vinaigrette, '86 7
Black-Eyed Salad, Hot Bacon and, '85 7
Cauliflower and Pea Salad, Savory,
'81 280
Cauliflower-Pea Salad, '87 231
Cheddar-Pea Salad, '84 82
Chicken-Pea Salad, '83 218
Corn-and-Pea Salad, '90 181
Creamy Pea Salad, '80 111
Crunchy Pea Salad, '90 143
English Pea-and-Apple Salad, '87 24
English Pea Salad, '81 280; '90 143
English Pea Salad, Cauliflower-, '95 66
English Pea Salad, Marinated, '82 54
Marinated Pea Salad, '81 204
Mexi-Pea Salad, '81 7
Minted Pea Salad, '91 119
Plentiful P's Salad, '87 12
Special Peas, '95 133
Special Pea Salad, '83 239
Sugar Snap Pea Salad, '86 115
Three Pea Salad, '84 290
Peach-and-Kiwi Salad, '90 180
Peaches in a Garden Nest, '87 154
Peach Salad, Frosted, '82 145
Peach Salad, Frozen, '82 54
Peach Salad, Georgia, '80 142
Peach Salad Supreme, Easy, '79 177
Peanut-Apple Salad, '80 5
Pear-and-Celery Salad, '87 56
Pear-and-Spinach Salad, Festive, '85 131
Pear Plate, Pretty, '89 225
Pear Salad, Crunchy, '83 234; '84 244
Pear Salad, Golden, '91 58
Pear-Swiss Cheese Salad, '91 237
Pepper-Cheese Stacks, '87 80
Pepperoni-and-Broccoli Salad, '83 216
Pepper Salad, Mixed, '89 103
Pepper Salad, Three-, '91 162
Pineapple Boat Aloha, '80 102
Pineapple Boats Ahoy, '80 148
Pineapple Boats, Fresh, '83 153
Pineapple-Celery Salad, '85 95
Pineapple Salad, Frosty, '89 278
Pineapple Waldorf Salad, '92 97
Pita Salad Sandwiches, '83 134
Pizza, Salad, '87 182

Potato
Any Day Potato Salad, '81 154
Asparagus-and-New Potato Salad,
'86 69
Bacon-Topped Potato Salad, '85 59
Basil Potato Salad, '94 178
Bean Salad, Potato-, '82 301
Blue Cheese-Potato Salad, '91 208
Broccoli-Potato Salad, Hot, '85 23
Chunky Potato Salad, '81 M138
Confetti Potato Salad, '80 5; '88 16
Corned Beef-Potato Salad, '85 213
Corned Beef Salad, Potato-, '81 36
Cottage Cheese-Potato Salad,
'79 147, 285
Creamy Potato Salad, '80 178; '88 171;
'92 241
Deluxe Potato Salad, '80 155
Dill-and-Sour Cream Potato Salad,
'93 105; '94 100
Dill Potato Salad, '85 213; '94 179
Dill Potato Salad, Hot, '79 78
Dutch Potato Salad, Hot, '87 176
Festive Potato Salad, '89 315
Fish-Potato Salad, Smoked, '84 233
French-Style Potato Salad, '88 171
Fruity Potato Salad, '85 214
Garden Patch Potato Salad, '84 82
German Potato Salad, '82 134, 239;
'84 18; '92 169
German Potato Salad, Hot, '79 78;
'94 254
German-Style Potato Salad, '83 23;
'88 M194
Grecian Potato Salad, '82 55
Green Bean-Potato Salad, '83 80
Ham-and-Egg Potato Salad, '86 84
Ham and Potato Salad, '80 272
Ham-and-Potato Salad, '95 94
Herbed Potato Salad, '87 171;
'94 164
Hot-and-Light Potato Salad, '93 90
Hot Dutch Potato Salad, '86 297
Hot Potato Salad, '79 78; '81 276;
'86 10
Hot Potato Salad Supreme, '79 78
Layered Creamy Potato Salad, '81 23
Marinated Potato Slices, '93 98
Mustard Potato Salad, '86 302
New Potato Salad, '84 120, 139;
'94 162
Olive-Potato Salad, '85 114
Parmesan Potato Salad, Hot, '79 78
Parslied Potato Salad, '85 240
Patio Potato Salad, '90 160
Pepper Cups, Potato Salad in, '79 78
Peppers, Potato Salad 'n', '83 135
Pesto Potato Salad, '90 164
Pickle-Potato Salad, Sweet, '85 213
Pole Bean-Potato Salad, Hot, '79 74
Potato Salad, '90 122; '94 160
Red Potato Salad, '93 119
Salmon-Potato Salad, '87 285
Saucy Potato Salad, '87 123
Savory Potato Salad, '80 30
Sour Cream Potato Salad, '79 104;
'80 79
Sour Cream-Potato Salad, '84 149
South-of-the-Border Potato Salad,
'94 178
Spring Salad, Mediterranean, '80 148
Sugar Snap Peas, Potato Salad with,
'91 120

SALADS, Potato (continued)

Sweet and Sour Potato Salad, '80 152
Sweet-and-Sour Potato Salad, '92 106
Sweet Potato Salad, Fresh, '86 226
Tri Club Potato Salad, '92 166
Tuna-Potato Salad, '84 289
Raspberry Salad, Frozen, '79 287; '80 35
Raspberry-Walnut Salad, '94 158
Red Cabbage Citrus Salad, '94 72
Relish Salad, '84 121
Rice. *See also* Salads/Vegetable.
Artichoke Hearts, Rice Salad with, '80 232
Artichoke-Rice Salad, '80 178; '81 41; '85 81
Avocado Salad, Rice-and-, '89 146
Bacon, Rice Salad with, '79 52
Bean-and-Rice Salad, Marinated, '87 152
Bean Salad, Rice-and-, '85 22
Beans-and-Rice Salad, '91 44
Brown Rice-and-Vegetable Salad, '84 202
Brown Rice Confetti Salad, '94 174
Chicken-and-Rice Salad, Hot, '83 22
Chicken-Rice Salad, '81 203
Chicken-Rice Salad, Curried, '92 190
Chicken-Rice Salad, Nutty, '83 157
Chutneyed Rice Salad, '88 100
Colorful Rice Salad, '81 253
Confetti Rice Salad, '80 232
Crunchy Rice Salad, '82 302
Curried Rice Salad, '80 84; '85 147, 220
Curry Rice Salad, '89 146
Egg-Rice Salad, '84 18; '86 169
Hearty Rice Salad, '82 233
Madras Salad, '86 82
Mandarin Rice Salad, '88 271
Mardi Gras Rice, '91 217
Meal-in-One Salad, '86 43
Molded Gazpacho-Rice Salad, '86 221
Mushrooms, Rice Salad with Fresh, '80 231
Paella Salad, '86 207
Pea Salad, Rice-, '85 163
Pebble Salad, '91 27
Red Rice Salad, Charleston, '79 146
Rice Salad, '79 74; '81 51
Ring, Rice-Carrot, '79 246
Shrimp Salad, Rice-, '79 270; '92 142
Shrimp Salad, Rice-and-, '83 82
Spinach-Rice Salad, '94 63
Tomatoes and Basil, Rice with, '95 232
Tuna Salad, Wild, '95 243
Vegetable-Rice Salad, '80 148; '83 198; '85 87
Wild Rice-Chicken Salad, '83 146
Wild Rice-Green Apple Salad, '92 90
Wild Rice Salad, '85 65; '89 147; '93 191
Wild Rice Salad, Crab-, '86 207
Wild Rice Salad, Crab and, '79 116
Wild Rice Salad, Oriental Salmon-and-, '94 173
Wild Rice Salad, Springtime, '88 100
Zesty Rice Salad, '81 23
Sauerkraut Salad, '80 178
Sauerkraut Salad, Crunchy, '87 9
Seafood. *See also* Salads/Fish.
Baked Seafood Salad, '86 10
Crab-and-Asparagus Salad, '92 141

Crab-and-Endive Salad, Marinated, '93 22
Crab and Wild Rice Salad, '79 116
Crab-Avocado Salad, '81 114
Crab Louis, '95 94
Crabmeat, Avocado with, '86 119
Crabmeat Luncheon Salad, '82 207
Crabmeat Salad, '91 169
Crabmeat-Shrimp Pasta Salad, '86 208
Crab Mousse, '79 117
Crab Salad, Chesapeake, '89 195
Crab Salad, Delightful, '87 145
Crab-Wild Rice Salad, '86 207
Hot Seafood Salad, '79 117; '80 164
Lobster and Orange Salad, '82 207
Lobster Salad, '89 249; '90 69
Paella Salad, '86 207
Polynesian Seafood Salad, '79 57
Seafood Salad, '90 88
Shrimp and Avocado Salad, '80 266
Shrimp-and-Black Bean Salad, Caribbean, '93 143
Shrimp-and-Egg Salad Sandwiches, '94 182
Shrimp-and-Orange Rice Salad, Zesty, '87 155
Shrimp-and-Orzo Salad, Peppers Stuffed with, '91 203
Shrimp and Rice Salad, '80 231; '82 207
Shrimp-and-Rice Salad, '92 307
Shrimp Bowl, Mediterranean, '80 174
Shrimp-Egg Salad, Tossed, '80 4
Shrimp-Endive Salad, '85 73
Shrimp-Filled Avocados, '83 2
Shrimp, Green Salad with, '88 49
Shrimp Macaroni Salad, '79 220
Shrimp-Macaroni Salad, '85 219
Shrimp Mousse, '79 57
Shrimp, Orange, and Olive Salad with Sherry Vinaigrette, '93 177
Shrimp Rémoulade, '90 255
Shrimp-Rice Salad, Baked, '83 22
Shrimp-Rice Salad, Tangy, '84 66
Shrimp Rotelle, '85 165
Shrimp Salad, '81 94; '86 186; '93 238
Shrimp Salad, Aloha, '95 46
Shrimp Salad, Avocado Stuffed with, '82 207
Shrimp Salad, Creamy, '79 56
Shrimp Salad Filling, '87 106
Shrimp Salad, Grapefruit-and-, '88 5
Shrimp Salad in Pastry, '86 105
Shrimp Salad, Layered, '88 100
Shrimp Salad, Marinated, '85 82; '93 321
Shrimp Salad on the Half Shell, '86 73
Shrimp Salad, Orange-, '84 197
Shrimp Salad, Oriental, '91 313
Shrimp Salad, Picnic, '95 182
Shrimp Salad Sandwiches, '90 178
Shrimp Salads, Individual, '83 146
Shrimp Salad, Super, '81 37
Shrimp Salad, Vegetable-, '79 190
Shrimp Vermicelli Salad, '88 139
Smoky Seafood Salad, '84 46
Sussex Shores, Seafood Salad, '93 98
Tropical Salad, '85 91
Sesame-Almond Salad, '89 123
Spaghetti Squash Salad, Marinated, '94 134

Spinach
Apple-Onion Vinaigrette, Spinach Salad with, '94 276
Apple Salad, Spinach-, '90 89; '92 13
Apricot Salad, Spinach-, '94 63
Arranged Spinach Salad, '91 210; '92 160
Bacon Salad, Spinach and, '81 143
Beet Salad, Spinach-, '83 227
Blue Cheese Salad, Spinach-, '82 166
Blues, Spinach Salad with the, '95 66
Chili-Lime Dressing, Spinach Salad with, '94 63
Citrus Dressing, Spinach Salad with, '88 133
Citrus Spinach Salad, '90 59
Combination Spinach Salad, '85 327; '86 22
Creamy Dressing, Crisp Spinach Salad with, '83 81
Creamy Spinach Salad, '83 60
Crunchy Spinach Salad, '80 147; '81 225
Curry Spinach Salad, '80 242
Dijon Spinach Salad, '89 282
Dried Tomato Vinaigrette, Spinach Salad with, '93 272
Easy Spinach Salad, '91 249
Enoki Salad, Spinach-, '89 62
Festive Spinach Salad, '80 247
French Spinach Salad, '79 8
Fresh Spinach Salad, '82 73; '83 240; '84 15, 77; '86 130
Fresh Spinach Salad Delight, '80 146
Garlic-Ginger Vinaigrette Dressing, Spinach Salad with, '92 195
Green Spinach Salad, '79 142
Honey Dressing, Spinach Salad with, '90 16
Hot Bacon Dressing, Spinach Salad with, '82 211
Kiwifruit Salad, Spinach-, '87 305
Lamb Salad, Spinach-, '85 58
Layered Spinach Salad, '80 5; '89 163
Lettuce Salad, Layered Spinach-, '84 266
Mandarin Spinach Salad, '85 163
Minted Spinach Salad, '94 63
Mushroom Salad, Spinach and, '80 112
Mustard Twist, Spinach-, '86 209
Onion Salad Bowl, Spinach-and-, '81 157
Orange Dressing, Spinach Salad with, '87 187
Orange Salad, Spinach-and-, '86 15
Orange-Spinach Salad, '83 316; '84 16
Oriental Spinach Salad, '82 23
Oysters and Red Wine Vinaigrette, Spinach Salad with, '94 327
Pear-and-Spinach Salad, Festive, '85 131
Pecan Salad, Spinach-, '89 128
Pickled Spinach, '81 69
Poppy Seed Dressing, Spinach Salad with, '91 210; '92 160
Pork-and-Spinach Salad, Mandarin, '88 M126
Raspberry Cream Dressing, Spinach Salad with, '94 321
Rice Salad, Spinach-, '94 63
Russian Dressing, Spinach Salad with, '79 144
Sesame Salad, Spinach-, '91 211; '92 160

SALADS, Spinach *(continued)*

Sesame Spinach Salad, '90 292
Southern Spinach Salad, '80 55
Special Spinach Salad, '80 78
Spicy Dressing, Fresh Spinach with,
  '80 55
Spinach Salad, '82 102; '86 302; '87 62;
  '88 299; '92 281, 341; '93 46, 65
Springtime Spinach Salad, '81 114
Sprout Salad, Fresh Spinach-, '82 281;
  '83 42
Strawberry-Spinach Salad, '91 169;
  '93 168
Sun-Dried Tomato Salad, Spinach and,
  '93 250
Supreme, Spinach Salad, '79 243
Sweet-Sour Spinach Salad, '85 M112
Tropical Spinach Salad, '90 231
Wilted, Spinach Salad, '81 M4; '89 123;
  '91 210; '92 160; '93 125
Zesty Spinach Salad, '79 88
Sprout Salad, '90 137
Sprout Salad, Spanish, '85 327; '86 22
Strawberry Salad, Frozen, '94 119
Strawberry Yogurt Salad, '80 232
Summer Salad, '93 179
Tabbouleh, '85 148; '93 70
Tabbouleh Salad, '91 70; '92 212; '94 174
Taco Salad, Meatless, '81 204
Tofu Salad, '88 27
Tomato
  Artichoke-Tomato Salad, '82 239
  Asparagus Salad, Tomato-, '92 79
  Avocado Salad, Tomato-, '86 74
  Basil-and-Tomato Couscous Salad,
    '94 175
  Basil-Mozzarella Salad, Tomato-, '95 171
  Cherry Tomato Salad, '87 156
  Cottage Cheese Salad in Tomatoes,
    '86 208
  Cottage-Tomato Salad, '85 163
  Cucumber and Tomato Salad, Dilled,
    '81 153
  Cucumber-Onion Salad, Tomato-,
    '81 239
  Cucumber Salad, Tomato-, '86 218;
    '92 199
  Cucumber Salad with Yogurt-Herb
    Dressing, Tomato-, '92 96
  Cucumber Summer Salad, Tomato-and-,
    '93 141
  Cucumber-Tomato Salad, '90 144
  Endive-Tomato Starburst Salad,
    '93 323
  Feta Salad, Tomato-, '81 246; '91 168
  Flower Salad, Tomato, '89 128
  Guacamole-Tomato Salad, '81 302
  Herbed Tomatoes, '83 173
  Herb Salad, Tomato-, '89 220
  Lima Bean-Tomato Salad, '85 137
  Marinated Salsa Tomatoes, '82 164
  Marinated Tomato and Brie Salad,
    '95 95
  Marinated Tomato-and-Cucumber Salad,
    '92 216
  Marinated Tomatoes, '85 156, 163;
    '89 174, 202
  Marinated Tomato Slices, '83 193
  Mozzarella Salad, Tomato-, '89 220
  Mozzarella-Tomato-Basil Salad, Fresh,
    '93 131

  Okra-Corn-and-Tomato Vinaigrette,
    '90 173
  Onion, and Cucumber in Italian
    Dressing, Tomato, '81 83
  Oregano, Tomatoes, '83 145
  Petal Salad, Tomato, '79 88
  Refresher, Tomato, '81 94
  Relish Salad, Tomato, '83 111
  Slices with Lemon Dressing, Tomato,
    '87 167
  Stuffed Tomatoes, Avocado-, '82 101
  Stuffed Tomatoes, Cold, '80 100
  Stuffed Tomato Salad, Artichoke-,
    '82 101
  Stuffed Tomato Salad, Crab-, '80 148
  Stuffed Tomato Salad, Oriental-,
    '82 101
  Stuffed with Sea Slaw, Tomatoes,
    '89 96
  Summer Tomato Salad, '94 201
  Summer Tomato Treat, '79 143
  Vidalia-Tomato Salad, '84 65
  Vinaigrette, Tomato-Basil, '87 89
  Vinaigrette, Tomatoes, '84 106
  Watercress-Tomato Salad, '85 132
Tossed Salad with Parmesan Dressing,
  '86 192
Turkey-and-Pepper Stir-Fry Salad, Chilled,
  '88 140
Turkey-Carrot Salad, '86 283
Turkey-Fruit Salad, '79 56
Turkey Fruit Salad, '83 233; '84 244
Turkey-in-the-Orange Salad, '93 21
Turkey Macaroni Salad, '83 282
Turkey 'n' Pasta Salad, Ranch-Style,
  '94 184
Turkey Salad, '90 318
Turkey Salad Bake, '79 253
Turkey Salad, Curried, '88 140
Turkey Salad, Fruit-and-Spice, '94 325
Turkey Salad, Fruitful, '84 197
Turkey Salad, Holiday, '84 320
Turkey Salad, Honey-Mustard, '92 309
Turkey Salad, Hot, '86 10, 297; '87 176
Turkey Salad, Layered, '86 332; '92 220
Turkey Salad Pita Sandwiches, '87 202;
  '88 43
Turkey Salad, Polynesian, '87 285
Turkey Salad, Southwestern, '91 313
Turkey Salad with Hot Bacon Dressing,
  '87 285
Turkey Salad with Sautéed Walnuts,
  '86 117
Turkey Taco Salad, '95 25
Turkey Waldorf Salad with Yogurt Dressing,
  '88 53
Turkey-Zucchini Salad, '85 74
Turnip-and-Carrot Salad, '91 212
Turnip Salad, '85 235
Turnip Salad, Irish, '94 178
Vegetable. *See also* Salads/Congealed, Pasta.
  Antipasto, Vegetable, '85 263
  Basil-Chicken-Vegetable Salad, '92 162
  Boats, Salad, '80 93
  Calico Salad, '82 35
  Cauliflower-Vegetable Salad, '85 158
  Chicken Salad, Vegetable-, '91 287
  Chinese Salad, '80 4
  Composée, Salad, '79 171
  Composé, Salad, '93 126
  Corned Beef Salad, Vegetable-, '80 148
  Creamy Vegetable Salad, '79 47
  Creole Salad, '79 147

  Crunchy Vegetable Salad, '79 11;
    '80 217; '83 216
  Different Vegetable Salad, '82 143
  Easy Vegetable Salad, '83 316; '84 16
  Extravaganza, Salad, '87 233
  Garden Marinade, '81 23
  Garden Medley Salad, '80 122
  Garden Salad, '87 62; '89 166
  Garden Salad Bowl, '82 239
  Garden Salad with Tomato-Cream Cheese
    Dressing, '79 173
  Greek Salad, Garden, '86 173
  Green-and-White Vegetable Salad,
    '79 286
  Green Vegetable and Egg Salad,
    '79 191
  Green Vegetable Salad, Overnight,
    '80 5
  Grilled Vegetable Salad, '94 203
  Healthy Salad, '95 133
  Horseradish Dressing, Vegetable Salad
    with, '92 85
  Italian Vegetable Salad, '81 253;
    '82 19
  Luncheon Salad, '84 232
  Marinade, Fresh Vegetable, '83 209
  Marinade, Garden, '81 23
  Marinade, Medley, '79 20
  Marinade, Tossed Vegetable, '84 266
  Marinated Combo Salad, '82 267
  Marinated Garden Vegetables, '87 252
  Marinated Mixed Vegetables, '89 276;
    '92 106
  Marinated Salad, '83 170; '91 186
  Marinated Salad, Eight-Vegetable,
    '80 218
  Marinated Salad, Zesty, '90 90
  Marinated Summer Salad, '81 153
  Marinated Tex-Mex Salad, '93 106
  Marinated Vegetable-Bacon Bowl,
    '79 191
  Marinated Vegetable Patch Salad,
    '84 232
  Marinated Vegetables, '79 146; '81 239;
    '85 67; '88 4, 170
  Marinated Vegetable Salad, '79 106, 143;
    '81 280; '82 163; '83 260; '84 13;
    '87 243; '92 64, 91
  Marinated Vegetable Salad, Crispy,
    '84 193
  Marinated Vegetable Salad, Fresh,
    '86 173
  Marinated Vegetables, Sweet-and-Sour,
    '83 266
  Marinated Vegetables, Zesty, '82 272
  Marinate, Fresh Vegetable, '80 33;
    '81 230
  Meal-in-One Salad, '82 232
  Medley Salad, Vegetable, '88 86
  Mexican Salad, '81 36, 113
  Minted Vegetable Salad, '88 23
  Mixed Vegetable Salad, '80 115;
    '81 302; '82 239; '83 317; '84 16;
    '86 136
  Next-Day Vegetable Salad, '83 81
  Oriental Salad, Make-Ahead, '82 163
  Oriental Vegetable Salad, '84 290
  Overnight Vegetable Salad, '90 33
  Party Vegetable Salad, '86 79
  Pasta and Vegetables, '89 255
  Pasta Salad, Vegetable, '89 256; '91 143
  Pasta Salad, Vegetable-, '92 167
  Pebble Salad, '91 27

SALADS, Vegetable *(continued)*

Pita Bread Salad, '95 86
Primavera Salad, '93 140
Quick Summer Italian Salad, '92 79
Rainbow Vegetable Salad, '83 111
Red, White, and Green Salad, '90 18
Refrigerated Vegetable Salad, '84 120
Rice-and-Vegetable Salad, '86 42
Riviera, Salade, '89 12
Rolls, Picnic Salad, '79 127
Rolls, Vegetable Salad, '82 278
Senator's Salad, '79 191
Seven-Layer Vegetable Salad, '79 88
Spring Vegetable Salad, '88 48
Summer Salad with Citrus Marinade, '92 133
Swedish Vegetable Salad, '82 23
Sweet-and-Sour Vegetable Salad, '81 25
Tangy Vegetable Toss, '79 144
Tarragon-Vegetable Salad, '85 288
Variety Salad, '79 113
Vinaigrette Salad, Vegetable-Chicken, '86 135
Vinaigrette, Vegetables, '82 225, 290
Walnuts, Vegetable Salad with, '86 118
Warm Vegetable Salad, '95 174
Winter Vegetable Salad, '86 42
Waldorf. *See also* Salads/Congealed.
Creamy Waldorf Salad, '87 311
Deluxe Waldorf Salad, '83 81
Frozen Waldorf Salad, '79 126; '82 145
Jiffy Waldorf Salad, '88 100
New Wave Waldorf Salad, '92 36
Old-Fashioned Waldorf Salad, '81 295
Overnight Waldorf Salad, '81 309
Pineapple Waldorf Salad, '92 97
Southern Classic Waldorf Salad, '92 36
Tropical Waldorf Salad, '89 12
Turkey Waldorf Salad with Yogurt Dressing, '88 53
Waldorf Salad, '89 278
Watercress Salad, '79 144
Watercress-Tomato Salad, '85 132
Watermelon Salad with Celery-Nut Dressing, '80 182
Watermelon Sparkle, '84 191
Wheat Berry-and-Roasted Corn Salad, '94 175
Yogurt-Cucumber Salad, '82 122
Yogurt Salad, Frozen, '92 303
Zucchini-Artichoke Salad, '91 229
Zucchini Chef's Salad, '83 143
Zucchini, Marinated, '80 33
Zucchini Salad, '82 104; '87 103; '89 128
Zucchini Salad, Marinated, '82 164; '90 32
Zucchini Salad, Summer, '95 229
SALMON
Bake with Pecan-Crunch Coating, Salmon, '95 209
Ball, Salmon, '80 149; '86 262
Ball, Smoky Salmon Cheese, '82 247
Barbecued Salmon, '81 181
Burgers, Salmon, '89 98; '95 24
Carbonara, Salmon, '83 43
Casserole, Salmon, '81 22
Chilled Salmon with Dill Sauce, '84 285
Croquettes, Baked Salmon, '81 22
Fettuccine, Salmon, '90 123
Fillets with Red Wine Garlic Sauce, Salmon, '94 250

Fillets with Sweet Corn Relish, Salmon, '93 119
Florentine, Salmon, '83 43
Kabobs, Salmon, '81 182
Loaf, Easy Salmon, '80 4
Loaf, Savory Salmon, '92 33
Loaf with Cucumber-Dill Sauce, Salmon, '86 5
Log, Salmon, '81 22
Mousse, Irresistible Salmon, '79 284
Mousse, Salmon, '83 79
Mousse, Salmon Dill, '81 21
Mushrooms and Green Onions, Fresh Salmon with, '93 180
Parchment, Salmon in, '95 311
Patties, Cheesy Salmon, '89 99
Patties, Open-Faced Salmon, '87 M218
Patties, Salmon, '92 215
Patties with Lemon-Cheese Sauce, Salmon, '91 24
Patties with Sauce, Salmon, '88 164
Poached Salmon, '83 35
Poached Salmon with Emerald Sauce, '90 63
Poached Salmon with Horseradish Sauce, '91 183
Potatoes, Salmon-Topped, '84 124
Quesadilla with Cucumber Salsa, Grilled Salmon, '95 131
Quiche, Salmon, '82 87; '87 38
Roll, Salmon Party, '83 127
Salads
Avocados, Salmon-Stuffed, '86 74
Broiled Salmon Salad, '92 108
Chilly Salmon Salad, '80 104
Crunchy Salmon Salad, '81 148
Greens with Creamy Dill Dressing, Salmon on Mixed, '93 143
Macaroni Salad, Salmon-and-, '81 114
Macaroni-Salmon Salad, '82 232
Pasta Salad, Salmon-, '87 9
Potato Salad, Salmon-, '87 285
Rice Salad, Salmon-, '84 289
Salmon Salad, '89 99
Shells, Salmon Salad, '85 286
Simple Salmon Salad, '91 23
Spinach Salad, Salmon-, '87 145
Summertime Salmon Salad, '82 207
Wild Rice Salad, Oriental Salmon-and-, '94 173
Scalloped Salmon, '81 273
Scalloped Salmon for Two, '89 98
Scaloppine with Vegetable Confetti and Pernod Sauce, Salmon, '94 172
Sesame-Crusted Salmon with Ginger Vinaigrette, '95 162
Smoked Salmon, '95 114
Smoked Salmon and Cucumber Tartlets, '95 216
Smoked Salmon, Drizzled, '88 91
Smoked Salmon or Mackerel, '84 46
Soufflé, Fresh Salmon, '81 182
Spread, Salmon, '81 149
Spread, Salmon-and-Horseradish, '87 146
Spread, Smoked Salmon, '84 324
Steaks, Baked Salmon, '85 54
Steaks, Glazed Salmon, '86 256
Steaks, Grilled Herbed Salmon, '93 176
Steaks, Grilled Salmon, '94 278
Steaks, Marinated Salmon, '87 6

Steaks, Oven-Fried Salmon, '81 181
Steaks with Dill Sauce, Salmon, '85 164
Steaks with Tarragon Butter, Salmon, '87 155
Terrine, Layered Salmon-and-Spinach, '84 132
Turnovers, Salmon-Spinach, '83 44
Vermicelli, Salmon-Pesto, '92 200

SALSAS. *See also* **PESTOS, RELISHES, SAUCES, TOPPINGS.**
Avocado-Corn Salsa, '94 201
Avocado Salsa, '91 182
Black Bean-and-Corn Salsa, '94 80
Black Bean Salsa, '93 155; '94 161
Black-Eyed Pea Salsa, '93 164
Chile Salsa, Double, '91 182
Chile Salsa with Homemade Tostados, Hot, '88 115
Chunky Salsa, '86 130; '90 206
Corn, Pepper, and Tomato Salsa, Yellowfin Tuna with, '94 164
Corn Salsa, Spicy, '93 322
Corn Salsa, Sweet, '95 156
Cruda, Salsa, '87 180; '88 148
Cucumber-Dill Salsa, '95 107
Cucumber Salsa, '95 131
Fresh Salsa, '95 42
Fresh Summer Salsa, '87 89
Garden Salsa, '91 182
Green Salsa, Creamy, '91 162
Hot Mexican Salsa, '85 136
Kale with Salsa, Southwest, '94 246
Kiwifruit Salsa, Hot, '94 82
Mango Salsa, '91 182; '95 104
Melon Salsa, Hot, '95 144
Mexi-Corn Salsa, '91 182
One-Minute Salsa, '95 93
Onion Salsa, Fiesta, '94 82
Papaya Salsa, '94 173
Peach Salsa, '91 183
Peach Salsa, Fresh, '95 195
Pepper Salsa, '88 26
Pepper Salsa, Mixed, '91 181
Picante, Homemade Salsa, '81 67
Picante with Shrimp, Salsa, '92 210
Poblano Salsa, '91 135
Red Salsa, '90 172
Roasted Salsa, '95 130
Salsa, '80 196; '87 217; '88 147
Serrano Salsa, Roasted, '95 207
Tomatillo Salsa, '92 245
Tomatillo Salsa, Roasted, '95 64
Tomato-Avocado Salsa, '94 83
Tomato-Mango Salsa, Seared Scallops with, '95 122
Tomato Salsa, '87 120
Tomato Salsa, Fresh, '91 182; '95 181
Tomato Salsa, Roasted, '95 64
Tomato Salsa, Three, '93 138
Tropical Rainbow Salsa, '94 161
Verde, Salsa, '91 182
Yellow Tomato Salsa, '87 122

SANDWICHES
Apple Breakfast Sandwiches, '92 332
Apple-Cinnamon Breakfast Sandwiches, '85 298
Apple Party Sandwiches, '92 234
Apple Sandwiches, '79 164; '80 130
Asparagus Grill Sandwiches, '79 164; '80 130
Asparagus Spear Sandwiches, '84 165
Avocado, Bacon, and Cheese Sandwiches, '87 279
Bacon, Cheese, and Tomato Sandwiches, '84 14
Bacon-Cheese Sandwiches, Grilled, '83 242
Bacon, Pimiento, and Cheese Hoagies, '90 144
Bacon Sandwiches, Open-Faced Cheesy, '80 78
Bagel, Breakfast on a, '94 66
Bagels, Meal-in-One, '88 159
Bar, Super Summer Sandwich, '91 143
Basket of Sandwiches, Bread, '86 126
Beef
    Barbecued Beef Sandwiches, '81 25; '82 31; '83 34
    Beef-Eater Sandwiches, '86 72
    Cheeseburger Biscuits, '79 194
    Corned Beef and Cheese Sandwich, '79 214
    Corned Beef Sandwiches, '83 291; '85 242; '92 23
    Corned Beef Sandwiches, Barbecued, '83 130
    Corned Beef Sandwiches, Grilled, '87 54
    French Beef Slice, '79 125
    Gumbo Joes, '88 158
    Jalapeño Heroes, Open-Faced, '90 144
    Kraut Sandwich, Beef-and-, '91 167
    Loaf, Big Wheel, '84 281
    Meatball Sandwich, Giant, '92 196
    Pizza Sandwiches, Open-Face, '82 3; '83 85; '84 M198; '85 22
    Pork Tenderloin Sandwiches, Beef and, '80 175
    Reuben Sandwiches, '80 M201
    Reuben Sandwiches, Broiled, '81 240; '83 69
    Reuben Sandwiches, Crispy, '85 299
    Reuben Sandwiches, Grilled, '81 206
    Reuben Sandwiches, Open-Face, '91 199
    Reubens, Party, '90 61
    Roast Beef Hero Sandwich, '91 167
    Sloppy Joes, '91 172
    Steak Stroganoff Sandwiches, '85 110
    Taco Joes, '91 167
    Tenderloin Picnic Sandwiches, Beef, '90 91
    Wake-Up Sandwiches, '84 58
BLT Croissants, '93 158
BLT Sandwiches, Curried, '93 158
BLT's, Cheesy, '85 92
Breakfast Sandwiches, '80 52; '82 M123; '89 M230
Breakfast Sandwiches, Cheesy, '90 140
Breakfast Sandwiches, Open-Faced, '92 140
Brown Bread-Cream Cheese Sandwiches, '87 M6
Bunwiches, '80 92
Calla Lily Sandwiches, '91 106
Calzone, '85 94
Cheese Sandwiches, Hot French, '82 3
Cheese Sandwiches, Leafy, '90 56
Cheese Tea Sandwiches, '92 276

Chicken
    Artichokes, Chicken Salad with, '86 186
    Baked Chicken Sandwiches, '79 164; '80 130; '84 165
    Cheese Chicken Sandwich, Ham 'n', '95 153
    Cheese Sandwiches, Toasted Chicken-and-, '85 242
    Cheesy Chicken Sandwiches, '82 190
    Chutney-Chicken Croissants, '92 22
    Club Sandwiches, Chicken, '86 160
    Crispy Chicken Sandwich, '81 114
    Curried Chicken Salad on Raisin Bread, '85 96
    English Muffin Delight, '82 45
    Finger Sandwiches, Chicken-Salad, '85 119
    Hot Chicken Sandwiches, '83 291
    Jamaican Chicken Sandwich, '95 153
    Marinated Chicken in a Sandwich, '86 185
    Marinated Chicken Sandwiches, '86 M45
    Mozzarella Melt, Italian Chicken-, '95 153
    Parmigiana Sandwich, Chicken, '94 65
    Puffed Chicken Sandwiches, '82 35
    Saucy Chick-Wiches, '81 25; '82 31; '83 34
    Spread, Tasty Chicken, '84 193
    Sprout Sandwiches, Polynesian, '85 51
Christmas Tree Sandwiches, '92 279
Club Sandwich Bar, Easy, '91 279
Club Sandwiches, Double-Decker, '91 231; '92 68
Club Sandwiches, Tangy, '80 93
Confetti Sandwiches, '79 236
Crab Burgers, Potato-Crusted, '94 139
Croissant Eggwiches, '91 160
Crostini, Feta-Tomato, '92 159
Cucumber Pinwheel Sandwiches, '85 120
Cucumber Sandwiches, '88 159; '90 81; '94 14
Cucumber Sandwiches, Dainty, '81 119
Curried Tea Sandwiches, '91 314
Date-Nut Lettuce Sandwich, '94 202
Eggplant Sandwiches, Baked, '82 230
Eggplant Sandwiches, Open-Face, '95 124
Egg Sandwiches, Open-Face, '83 292; '84 78; '86 160
Egg Sandwiches, Open-Faced Cheesy, '86 67
Egg Sandwiches, Saucy, '91 160
Eggsclusive Sandwiches, '79 164; '80 130
Eggs-Tra Special Sandwiches, '81 240; '83 69
Fish
    Amberjack Sandwiches, Grilled, '91 195
    Heroes, Neptune, '84 281
    Tuna Burgers, Zippy, '81 135
    Tuna Cheesies, '82 191
    Tuna Club Sandwiches, '83 134
    Tuna Melts, Curried, '95 46
    Tuna Melts, Hot, '95 126
    Tuna Melts, Southwestern, '95 127
    Tuna Melts, Tempting, '88 158
    Tuna Pockets, '88 139
    Tuna Salad Rolls, Hot, '84 281
    Tuna Salad, Swiss, '86 186
    Tuna Sandwich Boats, '91 166
    Tuna Sandwiches, French Toasted, '80 275
    Tuna Sandwiches, Hot, '85 299; '86 M194
    Tuna Waffle-Wich, Hot, '88 272; '89 181

Frankfurter Sandwiches, '84 M11
French Toast Sandwiches, Strawberry-, '91 160
Fruit-and-Cheese Breakfast Sandwiches, '89 M21
Fruit Sandwiches, Glazed Breakfast, '93 178
Garden Sandwiches, Open-Faced, '87 105
Garden, The, '83 134
Grilled Cheese Sandwiches, '82 M172; '94 167
Grilled Cheese Sandwich, Mexican, '92 63
Grilled Sandwiches, Tasty, '84 30
Guacamole Sandwiches, '82 9; '83 68
Guacamole Subs, '84 293
Ham
    Asparagus-and-Ham Melt Sandwiches, '88 M96
    Baked Ham Sandwiches, '81 29
    Basket of Sandwiches, Bread, '86 126
    Blue Cheese-Ham Sandwiches, Creamy, '87 279
    Cheese-and-Ham Striped Tea Sandwiches, Cheshire Claret, '94 16
    Cheese Chicken Sandwich, Ham 'n', '95 153
    Cheese Rolls, Ham-and-, '82 3
    Cheese Sandwiches, Hot Ham-and-, '85 299
    Cheese Sandwich Round, Ham-and-, '94 326
    Cheese Sandwich, Tex-Mex Ham-and-, '86 4
    Country Ham Loaves, '86 255
    Croissant Sandwiches, '89 161
    Deviled Delight, '83 130
    Grinder Sandwich, '85 299
    Hideaways, Ham, '81 29
    Hot Ham Sandwiches, '79 214
    Hot Rods, Ham, '86 136
    Loaf, Big Wheel, '84 281
    Omelet Sandwich, '86 95
    Open-Face Ham Sandwiches, '82 40; '85 8
    Open-Face Sandwiches, '84 13
    Pineapple-Ham Sandwich Loaf, '91 167
    Po-Boy, Pain-Perdu, '93 291
    Salad Boats, '80 93
    Salad Sandwich, Tangy Ham, '80 272
    Sebastian, The, '94 184
    Swiss, Ham and Eggs à la, '88 158
    Swiss Sandwiches, Tangy Ham-and-, '85 164
    Turkey Specials, Cheesy Ham-and-, '84 14
    Virginia Ham Sandwiches, '80 155
    Yummy Sandwiches, '81 229
Hearts of Palm Sandwich, '92 191
Heroes, Healthy, '90 177
Hero, E-Z, '92 63
Hot Brown Sandwiches, '80 M202
Italian Pesto Sandwich, Grilled, '94 170
Meal-in-One Sandwiches, '80 218
Monte Cristo Sandwiches, '83 134
Muffaletta-Style Po-Boys, '83 230
Muffin Stacks, Mushroom-Topped, '80 271
Muffuletta, Doodles, '94 35
Muffuletta, Napoleon House, '94 35
"Muffy" Sandwich, Fertitta's, '94 34
Mushroom Sandwiches, Toasted, '87 281
Open-Faced Sandwiches, '79 214
Orange Blossom Special, '88 158
Party Sandwiches, Double-Filled, '93 159

Peanut Butter-and-Jelly "Fish" Sandwiches, '91 177
Peanut Butter-and-Jelly Sandwiches, Christmas Tree, '85 319
Peanut Butter Breakfast Sandwich, '82 55
Peanut-Cheese-Raisin Sandwiches, '88 140
Pimiento Cheese Sandwiches, '82 278
Pita
    Acadian Stuffed Pitas, '90 177
    Alfalfa Pocket Bread Sandwiches, '82 282; '83 41
    Bavarian Pita Sandwiches, '83 31
    Bean Salad Sandwiches, '81 243
    Beef Pitas, Curried, '85 220
    Beef Pocket Sandwich, Saucy, '80 92
    Beef Salad Pocket Sandwiches, '83 267
    BLT in Pita Pockets, '93 158
    Breakfast Pita Pockets, '89 M21
    Chef's Salad, '86 186
    Chicken-Almond Pocket Sandwiches, '81 240; '83 69
    Chicken Pita, Oriental, '89 216
    Chicken Salad in a Pocket, '88 139
    Denver Pita Sandwiches, '86 M12
    Dried Beef Pita Sandwiches, '86 160
    Ham-and-Cheese Pita Pockets, '90 271
    Ham-and-Cheese Pita Sandwiches, '87 202; '88 44
    Ham and Swiss in the Pocket, '83 31
    Hearty Pocket Sandwiches, '80 93
    Hot Pita Sandwiches, '83 217; '87 M6
    Lamb Pockets with Dilled Cucumber Topping, '87 104
    Oriental Stuffed Pockets, '79 14
    Pita Sandwiches, '84 139
    Salad Sandwiches, Pita, '83 134
    Sloppy Joe Pocket Sandwiches, '81 200
    Spinach-Walnut Pitas, '87 202; '88 43
    Steaks, Greek Pocket, '81 262
    Stuffed Pita, '89 87
    Taco Pitas, '83 31
    Tuna-in-a-Pita Pocket, '87 202
    Turkey-Mozzarella Rounds, '82 3
    Turkey Salad Pita Sandwiches, '87 202; '88 43
    Vegetable Pockets, '85 215
    Vegetarian Pita Sandwiches, '84 193
Pizza Sandwiches, Open-Face, '82 3; '83 85; '84 M198; '85 22
Pizza Sandwich, Giant, '80 93
Pork Sandwiches, Party, '88 M273
Pound Cake Dessert Sandwich, Grilled, '94 171
Raisin Country Sandwich, '91 168
Rarebit, Tangy Welsh, '88 159
Rarebit, Uptown Welsh, '87 279
Rarebit with Tomatoes and Bacon, Welsh, '92 M159
Salad Rolls, Hearty, '81 206
Salami Sandwiches, Open-Faced, '87 279
Sausage and Pepper Loaves, Italian, '83 11
Sausage-Cheese Loaves, '88 235
Sausage-Cheese Muffin Sandwiches, '92 M212
Sausage Sandwiches with Mustard Sauce, '84 250
Sausage Sandwich, Italian, '80 92
Sausage Sloppy Joes, Italian, '86 160
Sausage-Stuffed French Loaf, '90 19

Seafood
    Club Sandwich, South Seas, '84 282
    Crab-and-Cheese Sandwiches, Hot, '87 279
    Crabmeat Sandwiches, '84 285
    Crabmeat Sandwiches, Avocado-, '83 2
    Crabmeat Sandwiches, Deluxe, '81 M74
    Crab Sandwiches, Open-Faced, '87 106
    Crab Sandwiches, Puffy, '83 291
    Crab Tomato Sandwiches, Open-Face, '81 29
    English Muffin Delight, '82 45
    Hot Brown, Seafood, '88 158
    Oyster-and-Bacon Poor Boys, '87 40
    Oyster Loaves, Spinach-, '84 213
    Oyster Submarine Sandwich, '80 92
    Shrimp-and-Egg Salad Sandwiches, '94 182
    Shrimp-Cheese Sandwiches, '85 242
    Shrimp Destin, '82 29
    Shrimp Salad, '86 186
    Shrimp Salad Sandwiches, '90 178
Sloppy Toms, '91 51
Snack Buns, '87 279
Snackwiches, '88 172
Spider Sandwiches, '93 193
Spinach Fondue Sandwich, Grilled, '94 171
Spinach Sandwiches, Fresh, '85 59
Stacking Sandwiches, '86 127
Stromboli, '88 272
Submarine Sandwiches, Superb, '84 250
Tea Sandwiches, Gingered, '84 116
Tempting Twosome, '81 240; '83 69
Tofu-Veggie Sandwiches, Open-Face, '86 5
Tomatillo Sandwiches, Open-Faced, '92 246
Tomatoes with Cheese Sauce over Toast, '88 159
Tomato Sandwich, Floyd's Favorite, '95 172
Tortilla Stack-Ups, '92 196
Turkey-Cheese Puffs, '87 301
Turkey Hero Sandwiches, '92 196
Turkey Hero with Garlic Sauce, '90 145
Turkey-in-the-Slaw Sandwich, '90 177
Turkey Open-Facers, '82 190
Turkey-Roasted Pepper Sandwiches, Smoked, '94 66
Turkey Sandwich, Hot, '93 306
Turkey Sandwich, Waffle-Grilled, '94 170
Vegetable Garden Heroes, '84 14
Vegetable Puff Sandwich, '85 51
Vegetable Salad Rolls, '82 278
Vegetarian Melt, Open-Faced, '87 106
Veggie Sandwich, Big, '92 196
Victoria Sandwiches, '94 16
Vidalia Sandwiches on Salt-Rising Bread, '79 145
Watercress Sandwiches, '90 82
Wreath, Festive Sandwich, '86 333
Zucchini Sandwiches, Open-Faced, '88 159
SAUCES. *See also* DESSERTS/SAUCES; GRAVIES; MARINADES; MUSTARD/SAUCES; PESTOS; SALSAS; TOPPINGS.
Alfredo Sauce, '94 84
Almond Sauce, Asparagus with, '91 117
Ancho Chile Cream, '87 121
Ancho Chile Sauce, '87 122
Anchovy-Garlic Sauce over Vermicelli, '86 158
Avgolemono Sauce, '94 48
Avocado Sauce, '80 198; '83 200
Avocado-Tomatillo Sauce, '95 206
Barbecue
    Bannister's Barbecue Sauce, '92 166
    Barbecue Sauce, '84 172; '86 153; '88 218; '91 16, 205; '93 129; '94 27

Beer Barbecue Sauce, '84 173
Bourbon Barbecue Sauce, '85 90
Dressed-Up Barbecue Sauce, '84 173
Eastern-Style Barbecue Sauce, '88 145
Easy Barbecue Sauce, '79 90; '82 178
John Wills's Barbecue Sauce, '92 255
Lemon Barbecue Sauce, Herbed, '94 154
Lemony Barbecue Sauce, '95 31
Maple Syrup Barbecue Sauce, '94 154
Mustard Barbecue Sauce, '84 173
Oven Barbecue Sauce, '82 233
Paprika Barbecue Sauce, '79 90
Peanut Butter Barbecue Sauce, '81 233
Piquant Barbecue Sauce, '79 159
Savory Barbecue Sauce, '86 153
Southwest Barbecue Sauce, Spicy, '94 154
Special Barbecue Sauce, '82 177
Thick and Robust Barbecue Sauce, '94 95
Thick and Sweet Barbecue Sauce, '94 95
Thin and Tasty Barbecue Sauce, '94 95
Tomato Barbecue Sauce, Fresh, '84 172
Western-Style Barbecue Sauce, '88 145
White Barbecue Sauce, '94 95
White Barbecue Sauce, Chicken with, '89 M84
Zippy Barbecue Sauce, '92 166
Basil and Cream Sauce, '90 118
Basil-Brown Butter Sauce, '93 92
Basil Cream, '89 159
Basil Cream Sauce, New Potatoes with, '91 46
Basil Sauce, '90 85
Basil Sauce, Asparagus with, '86 33
Bean Sauce, Pork-and-Onions with, '85 76
Béarnaise Sauce, '83 138; '85 37; '86 193; '89 201
Béarnaise Sauce, Blender, '81 90
Béarnaise Sauce, Classic, '86 244
Béarnaise Sauce, Quick, '82 84
Béchamel Sauce, '80 190; '83 277; '84 M239; '87 286; '91 94
Beer Sauce, '95 266
Black Bean Sauce, '93 59
Bordelaise Sauce, '83 138, 262
Bouillon Sauce, '80 8
Brandy-Butter Sauce, '79 230
Brandy Sauce, Carrots in, '83 86
Brandy Sauce, Lemony-Butter Steak with, '85 78
Broccoli Sauce, '91 85
Brown Butter Sauce, '91 65
Brown Sauce, '89 32; '94 15, 240
Buttermilk Sauce, '84 6
Butter Sauce, '86 268
Butter Sauce, Vegetable, '86 174
Catsup Sauce, '81 228
Catsup Topping, '81 170
Champagne-Saffron Sauce, Scallops with, '93 177
Champagne Sauce, '90 29
Champagne Sauce, Chicken Breasts with, '86 49
Chanterelle Brown Sauce, '89 62
Cheese
    Blue Cheese Sauce, '90 142; '94 320
    Brussels Sprouts with Cheese Sauce, '79 246
    Cheddar Cheese Sauce, '91 286
    Cheese Sauce, '79 M156; '81 43, 44, 225; '82 M123; '83 49, 138, 188; '84 57; '85 92; '86 241; '88 78, 272; '89 181, 229; '90 235; '93 48

SAUCES, Cheese *(continued)*

Cottage Cheese Sauce, '87 232
Cream Sauce, Cheesy, '82 79
Easy Cheese Sauce, '79 22
Garlic-Cheese Sauce, '84 M70
Guilt-Free Cheese Sauce, '93 M95
Heather Sauce, '84 182
Lemon-Cheese Sauce, '91 24
Lemony Cheese Sauce, '84 183
Monterey Jack Sauce, '84 293
Mornay Sauce, '80 120; '81 90; '83 138;
    '84 295; '89 195
Mushroom-Cheese Sauce, '83 190;
    '86 48
Parmesan Cheese Sauce, '79 165;
    '80 162; '85 143
Parmesan Sauce, '92 17
Rich Cheese Sauce, '81 89
Roquefort Sauce, '89 321
Seafood Cheese Sauce, '89 240
Swiss Cheese Sauce, '79 35; '87 289;
    '88 135
Swiss Sauce, '83 M195
Swiss Sauce, Creamy, '80 M53
Topper, Vegetable-Cheese Potato, '86 6
Turnips in Cheese Sauce, '84 229
Vegetable-Cheese Sauce, '85 M152
Vegetable Sauce, Cheesy, '92 M134
Cherry-Wine Sauce, '95 285
Chervil-and-Savory Sauce, '90 117
Chervil Sauce, '83 128
Chicken Curry Sauce, '90 117
Chicken Sauce, Creamy, '81 91
Chile Sauce, Hot, '92 156
Chili Meat Sauce, '83 4
Chili Sauce, '81 175; '94 287
Chili Sauce, Chunky, '85 188
Chili Sauce, Spicy, '87 127
Chive Sauce, Steamed Broccoli with Tangy,
    '83 101
Chutney-Mustard Sauce, '89 242
Cider Sauce, '87 224
Cilantro Cream, '87 121
Citrus Sauce, Stuffed Flounder Rolls with,
    '85 180
Clam Sauce, Tricolor Pasta with, '93 272
Cocktail Sauce, '87 128; '90 242
Cocktail Sauce, Boiled Shrimp with, '79 151
Cocktail Sauce, Coastal, '92 254
Cocktail Sauce, Delta, '91 147
Cocktail Sauce, French Fried Zucchini with,
    '86 146
Cocktail Sauce, Spicy, '83 258
Country Ham Sauce, '90 117
Cream Sauce, '85 291; '93 157
Cream Sauce, Brandied, '82 70
Cream Sauce, Peppery, '88 206
Cream Sauce, Sherried, '84 210; '85 M152
Cream Sauce, Shrimp in, '84 M286
Cream Sauce, Spicy, '82 45
Cream-Wine Sauce, Potatoes in, '86 18
Creamy Sauce, '79 41
Creolaise Sauce, '83 91, 262
Creole Sauce, '89 228; '90 28; '92 87
Cucumber Cream Sauce, '92 33
Cucumber-Dill Sauce, '86 5; '91 62; '92 51
Cucumber Dipping Sauce, '94 47
Cucumber Sauce, '82 111; '84 M286; '92 41
Cucumber Sauce, Lemony, '89 245
Cumberland Sauce, '92 309
Currant Jelly Sauce, Quail with, '86 94

Currant Sauce, '87 240
Curried Cream Sauce, Turkey Slices with,
    '91 60
Curried Rum Sauce, '91 164
Curried Sour Cream Sauce, '90 174
Curry Sauce, '79 M156; '83 138; '84 M71;
    '94 54; '95 18
Curry Sauce, Asparagus with, '90 17
Custard Sauce, '89 291
Custard Sauce, Bourbon, '95 271
Dill Sauce, '84 M70, 107; '85 39; '88 162;
    '95 216
Dill Sauce, Chilled Salmon with, '84 285
Dill Sauce, Creamy, '79 M156; '94 42
Dill Sauce, Salmon Steaks with, '85 164
Egg Foo Yong Sauce, '86 232
Emerald Sauce, '90 63
Enchilada Sauce, '81 194
Enchilada Sauce, Red Chile, '85 245
Florentine Sauce, '93 48
Foo Yong Sauce, '80 223
French Sauce, Broccoli with, '81 295
Fruit
    Apple-Horseradish Sauce, '82 229
    Apricot Sauce, '87 172
    Apricot-Sauced Pork Chops, '85 22
    Blueberry Sauce, '80 144; '86 248
    Cherry Sauce, '83 276; '84 91; '91 67
    Cherry Sauce, Elegant, '79 M156
    Cherry Sauce, Roast Ducklings with,
        '86 312
    Cherry Sauce, Roast Pork with Spiced,
        '89 324
    Cherry Sauce, Royal, '85 224; '86 83
    Cherry Sauce, Spicy, '83 244
    Cranberry-Apple Sauce, '92 203
    Cranberry-Apricot Sauce, Fresh, '87 243
    Cranberry Juice Sauce, '85 224; '86 83
    Cranberry-Raisin Sauce, Baked Ham
        with, '88 244
    Cranberry Sauce, '92 269
    Cranberry Sauce, Baked, '88 257
    Cranberry Sauce, Cornish Hens with,
        '79 180
    Cranberry Sauce, Fresh, '79 283; '84 275
    Cranberry Sauce, Tart, '83 261
    Cranberry Wine Sauce, '83 276
    Devonshire Cream, Mock, '81 288
    Devonshire Sauce, Processor, '86 337;
        '87 58
    Fruit Sauce, '81 177
    Grand Marnier Fruit Sauce, '90 93
    Grape Sauce, Mahimahi in, '91 218
    Honey-Lime Sauce, '82 85
    Lemon-Butter Sauce, '84 252; '92 337
    Lemon-Celery Sauce, Baked Fillets in,
        '84 91
    Lemon-Cheese Sauce, '91 24
    Lemon Cream Sauce, Braised Chicken
        Breast in, '94 184
    Lemon Garlic Sauce, Shrimp in, '83 67
    Lemon-Herb Sauce, Hot, '91 286
    Lemon Meunière Sauce, '88 222
    Lemon Parsley Sauce, '81 106
    Lemon-Parsley Sauce, '93 48
    Lemon Sauce, '82 290
    Lemon Sauce, Asparagus with, '86 62
    Lemon Sauce, Chicken Scallopini with,
        '86 156
    Lime-Saffron Sauce, '94 71
    Lime Sauce, Sour Cream-, '91 286
    Mandarin-Almond Cream Sauce, '84 183
    Mandarin Sauce, '84 60

Mimosa, Sauce, '88 288
Orange-Almond Sauce, Chicken in,
    '79 219; '80 13
Orange Butter Sauce, Asparagus with,
    '85 43
Orange, Lime, and Ginger Sauce,
    Chicken with, '92 123
Orange Liqueur Sauce, '86 142
Orange Sauce, '82 47; '83 10, 277;
    '84 M286
Orange Sauce, Asparagus with, '83 46
Orange Sauce, Brussels Sprouts in, '86 55
Orange Sauce, Celery in, '79 70
Orange Sauce, Chicken Breasts with,
    '79 77
Orange Sauce, Grilled Duck with,
    '94 305
Orange Sauce, Lobster Tails with Spiced,
    '86 155
Orange Sauce, Sweet, '93 M325
Peach-Blueberry Pancake Sauce, '82 177
Peach-Blueberry Sauce, '81 170
Peach Sauce, '92 203
Peach Sauce, Creamy Fresh, '79 177
Pineapple-Curry Sauce, '79 252
Pineapple-Rhubarb Sauce, '88 94
Pineapple Sauce, '84 236; '92 203
Pineapple Sauce, Raisin-, '82 177
Plum Sauce, '80 249; '82 40; '88 152
Plum Sauce, Chinese, '82 237
Plum Sauce, Gingered, '87 175
Plum Sauce, Red, '80 49
Plum Sauce, Spicy, '86 11
Strawberry-Banana Sauce, '81 41
Tangy Sauce for Fruit, '90 161
White Grape Sauce, '80 38
Garlic Buerre Blanc Sauce, '88 222
Garlic-Butter Sauce, '95 327
Garlic-Chive Butter Sauce, '90 96
Garlic-Ginger Butter Sauce, '94 89
Garlic Sauce, '92 56
Garlic Sauce, Roasted, '95 268
Garlic Sauce, Stir-Fried Pork in, '84 141
Garlic Sauce, Turkey Hero with, '90 145
Ginger-Soy Sauce, '91 33
Ginger Vinaigrette, '95 162
Goat Cheese Sauce, Asparagus with, '93 116
Greek Sauce, '91 183
Green Chile Sauce, '82 220
Green Mole Sauce, '95 267
Green Pea Sauce, '83 22
Green Sauce, Herbed, '86 244
Grill Basting Sauce, '95 236
Guacamole, '89 226
Ham-and-Mushroom Sauce, Steak with,
    '83 109
Herb Butter Sauce, Corn with, '79 150
Herb-Mayonnaise Sauce, '85 73
Herb Sauce, '91 29
Herb Sauce, Green, '83 36
Hollandaise Sauce, '80 M107, M268; '81 90;
    '83 137; '85 295; '86 94; '87 195;
    '88 58, M177, 222; '89 24; '92 93; '95 86
Hollandaise Sauce, Blender, '79 39;
    '82 84, 234
Hollandaise Sauce, Broccoli with,
    '79 244, 276
Hollandaise Sauce, Broccoli with Mock,
    '82 272
Hollandaise Sauce, Classic, '88 53
Hollandaise Sauce, Easy Dilled, '92 107
Hollandaise Sauce, Lime, '93 121
Hollandaise Sauce, Mock, '85 49; '93 68

SAUCES *(continued)*

Hollandaise-Shrimp Sauce, Flounder with, '86 234
Hollandaise, Tangy, '85 148
Honey-Butter Sauce, '85 18
Honey-Lemon Mustard Sauce, '84 275
Honey-Mustard Sauce, '85 13
Honey-Mustard Sauce, Smoked Ribs with, '92 168
Honey-Poppy Seed Sauce, '93 13
Honey Sauce, Chicken in, '89 82
Horseradish-Mustard Sauce, Creamy, '88 M177
Horseradish Sauce, '84 190; '85 224; '86 83; '87 127; '88 207, M273; '91 183; '93 215
Horseradish Sauce and Curried Bananas, Fillets with, '85 230
Horseradish Sauce, Broccoli with, '81 2; '83 206; '84 33
Horseradish Sauce, Carrots and Broccoli with, '91 246
Horseradish Sour Cream, '86 244
Hot Diggity Dog Sauce, '93 198
Hot Sauce, '79 185; '83 74
Hot Sauce, San Antonio, '84 291
Hunter Sauce, '95 317
Italian Sauce, '80 63; '90 67
Italian Sauce, Quick, '82 230
Italian-Style Sauce, '83 250
Jalapeño-Cranberry Sauce, '92 310
Jalapeño Sauce, '80 193
Jezebel Sauce, '81 29; '82 55; '93 331
Juniper Sauce, '93 278
Lemon Basting Sauce, '95 32
Mahogany Sauce, '91 148
Maple-Cider Sauce, '95 288
Marinara Sauce, '82 178; '89 239; '92 18
Mediterranean Sauce, '94 83
Meunière Sauce, '80 57
Mexican Sauce, '80 198
Microwaving Sauces, '84 M70
Mint Sauce, '84 107; '88 M96
Mint Sauce over Vegetables, '92 104
Mushroom-Dill Sauce, '80 271
Mushroom Sauce, '81 90, 200; '82 46; '83 71, 205, 212; '84 M70; '85 40; '86 198; '87 36, 186, 284; '91 221
Mushroom Sauce, Eggs Baked in, '93 47
Mushroom Sauce, Filet Mignon with, '94 250
Mushroom Sauce, Spicy Sherried, '89 239
Mushroom Sauce Supreme on Vermicelli, '86 158
Mushroom-Wine Sauce, '84 84; '86 24
Natillas Sauce, '83 179
Olive-Butter Sauce, Broccoli with, '83 118
Onion Cream Sauce, '87 232
Onion-Mushroom Sauce, '85 224; '86 84
Onion-Parsley Sauce, '85 148
Onion Sauce, '82 72; '87 248
Onion Sauce, Brussels Sprouts in, '81 308
Pancake Sauce, Cinnamon-Pecan-Honey, '88 46
Parsley-Caper Sauce, Tortellini with, '93 175
Parsley-Chive Sauce, '84 212
Parsley-Garlic Sauce, '83 138; '84 M70
Parsley Sauce, '82 248; '86 108
Peanut Hot Sauce, '86 305
Peanut Sauce, Hot Indonesian, '93 211
Peanut Sauce, Shrimp with, '93 303
Pecan-Butter Sauce, '91 65
Pepper-Onion Sauce, '84 125

Pesto Sauce, '89 280; '91 94; '95 267
Port Wine Sauce, '84 252
Pumpkin Seed Sauce, '88 246
Raisin Sauce, '83 59, 215; '84 91, 275; '87 127; '89 58
Raisin Sauce, Ham with, '82 M76
Red Chile Sauce, '94 251; '95 17
Red Chili Sauce, '85 245
Red Hot Sauce, '93 158
Red or Green Pepper Sauce, '91 85
Red Sauce, Zippy, '91 147
Red Wine Garlic Sauce, '94 250
Rémoulade Sauce, '80 58; '81 89; '82 178; '91 147; '93 280; '94 139
Rémoulade Sauce, Shrimp with, '91 29
Rhubarb Sauce, Chilled, '88 94
Rosemary-Parmesan Sauce, Tortellini with, '92 284
Rum Sauce, Mango-Spiced, '86 215
Sauerbraten Sauce, '93 16
Savory Sauce, '84 196
Seafood
    Clam Sauce, Linguine with, '84 124; '88 90; '89 178
    Clam Sauce, Pasta with, '84 291
    Clam Sauce, Vermicelli and Sprouts with Red, '86 143
    Clam Sauce, Vermicelli with, '85 295
    Clam Sauce with Linguine, '84 9
    Crab and Shrimp Sauce Piquante, '83 92
    Crab Marinara Sauce, Quick, '85 M151
    Delight, Seafood Sauce, '82 91
    Linguine with Seafood Sauce, '83 232
    Red Seafood Sauce, '95 107
    Seafood Sauce, '79 3; '82 84; '83 36; '86 304; '89 239
    Shrimp-and-Almond Sauce, '87 282
    Shrimp Sauce, '87 138, 232
    Shrimp Sauce, Broccoli and Cauliflower with, '84 248
    Shrimp Sauce, Flounder Fillets in, '83 227
    Stone Crab Mustard Sauce, '80 3
    Stone Crab Sauce, Tangy, '80 3
Sesame Sauce, Vegetables with, '83 112
Sherry Sauce, '87 96
Shiitake Madeira Sauce, Filet Mignons with, '95 265
Sofrito, '92 158
Sour Cream-Dill Sauce, Mushrooms in, '84 215
Sour Cream-Horseradish Sauce, '88 4
Sour Cream, Mock, '83 71, 205
Sour Cream Sauce, '82 68; '84 132; '87 233; '93 162
Sour Cream Sauce, Broccoli with, '87 127
Soy Sauce, Grilled Trout with Ginger and, '85 228
Spaghetti Sauce, Grisanti, '94 194
Spinach Pasta Sauce, '93 71
Spinach Sauce, Fettuccine with, '84 329
Spinach Sauce, Vermicelli with Fresh, '89 256
Sunshine Sauce, '87 96
Sweet-and-Sour Sauce, '80 20; '85 12, 34; '86 240
Taco Sauce, '82 M283; '93 69
Tarragon-Mustard Sauce, Turkey Cutlets with, '93 239
Tarragon Sauce, '83 56; '84 190; '87 229
Tartar Sauce, '79 184; '81 134; '82 135; '86 233; '91 147; '95 107, 155
Tartar Sauce, Boiled Shrimp with Green Peppercorn, '94 144

Tartar Sauce, Bold-and-Spicy, '86 180
Tartar Sauce, Creamy, '80 164
Tartar Sauce, Lemony, '95 32
Tartar Sauce, Quick, '87 128
Tempura Sauce, Basic, '81 68
Teriyaki Sauce, '93 258
The Sauce, '95 237
Tomatillo Sauce, '94 231; '95 206
Tomatillo Sauce, Roasted Chiles Rellenos with, '94 203
Tomato
    Basil Sauce, Tomato, '91 85
    Basil Sauce, Tomato-, '92 180
    Basil-Tomato Sauce, '92 198; '93 25, 48, 65
    Caper Sauce, Turkey Cutlets with Tomato-, '91 61
    Chunky Tomato Sauce, '95 264
    Cream Sauce, Angel Hair Pasta with Tomato, '93 292
    Cream Sauce, Linguine with Tomato-, '86 158
    Cream, Tomato, '94 70
    Creamy Tomato Sauce, '93 71
    Fish in Tomato Sauce, '85 75
    Fresh Tomato Sauce, '83 224; '87 171
    Fresh Tomato Sauce over Basil Pasta, '93 176
    Green Chiles Tomato Sauce with, '81 196
    Herbed Fresh Tomato Sauce, '85 M151
    Herbed Tomato Sauce, '86 277
    Hot Sauce, Kleberg, '94 28
    Italian-Style Tomato Sauce, '87 182
    Italian Tomato Sauce, '82 M68; '92 57
    Italian Tomato Sauce for Spaghetti, '81 134
    Marinara Sauce, '89 239; '92 18; '94 64
    Meat Sauce, Italian, '83 193
    Picante Sauce, '94 116
    Picante Sauce, Homemade, '90 205
    Picante Sauce, Processed, '91 257
    Pico de Gallo, '79 185; '86 19
    Pizza Sauce, '80 163; '84 33; '85 285
    Pizza Sauce, Traditional, '95 267
    Rancheros Sauce, '88 148
    Red Pepper-Tomato Sauce, '93 59
    Refrigerator Tomato Sauce, '85 188
    Seasoned Tomato Sauce, '83 150
    Spaghetti Meat Sauce for 4, Easy, '92 244
    Spaghetti Meat Sauce for 25, Easy, '92 245
    Spaghetti Sauce, Beer, '85 13
    Spaghetti Sauce, Dried Tomato, '90 202
    Spaghetti Sauce, Herbed, '85 13
    Spaghetti Sauce, Lentil, '90 198
    Spaghetti Sauce, Thick, '84 118
    Spaghetti Sauce, Turkey, '85 13
    Spicy Sauce, '84 77
    Spicy Tomato Sauce, '84 294; '88 19
    Taco Sauce, '94 30
    Tarragon-Tomato Sauce, '84 131
    Tomato Sauce, '85 193, 244; '87 249; '88 116
    Vermicelli with Tomato Sauce, '83 164
Vanilla Wine Sauce, Pan-Fried Grouper with, '94 241
Vegetable Sauce, '89 98
Vegetable Sauce, Greek Fish with, '82 72
Vegetable Sauce, Pasta with, '83 163
Vegetable Sauce, Tangy, '89 280
Velouté Sauce, '84 22
Venison Reduction Sauce, '94 303

SAUCES (continued)

Verde Sauce, '93 275
Vinaigrette, Versatile, '93 141
Vinegar Basting Sauce, '91 205
Walnut Cream Sauce, '93 275
Walnut Sauce, Spaghetti with Parsley and,
'80 30
Watercress Sauce, '91 85
Whiskey Sauce, '80 58
White Butter Sauce, '92 107
White Sauce, '82 269; '83 138, 245;
'87 166
White Sauce, Asparagus, '80 147
White Sauce, Basic, '79 M156; '81 89
White Sauce, Low-Calorie, Medium, '87 26
White Sauce, Medium, '93 48
White Sauce, Thick, '82 42
Wine Reduction Sauce, '94 270
Wine Sauce, Beef Cubes in, '79 264
Wine Sauce, Broccoli with, '84 187
Wine Sauce, Chicken in, '80 8
Wine Sauce, Marsala, '81 77
Wine Sauce, Mushrooms with, '85 292
Wine Sauce, Red Snapper in, '85 138
Wine Sauce, Skillet Steak in Red, '85 21
Wine Sauce, Veal and Carrots in, '86 M139
Wine Sauce, White, '84 132; '89 24; '92 41;
'93 49
Yogurt-Horseradish Sauce, '85 66
Yogurt Sauce, '89 283
Yogurt Sauce, Creamy, '91 238; '92 28
Yogurt Sauce, Lamb Meatballs with, '85 132
Zesty Sauce, '94 82
Zippy Sauce, '86 44
Zucchini-Mushroom Sauce, '93 71
Zucchini Sauce, Spaghetti with, '81 38
SAUERKRAUT
Bratwurst and Sauerkraut, '84 250
Cake, Sauerkraut, '94 254
Franks, Beany Kraut and, '79 64
Homemade Sauerkraut, '81 216
Meatballs, Sauerkraut, '86 257
Pork Chops and Sauerkraut, '88 98
Relish, Kraut, '91 232
Relish, Sauerkraut, '85 136
Salad, Crunchy Sauerkraut, '87 9
Salad, Sauerkraut, '80 178
Sandwich, Beef-and-Kraut, '91 167
Sausage and Kraut, '83 11
SAUSAGE
Acorn Squash, Sausage-Stuffed, '81 231;
'83 296; '84 285
Acorn Squash with Sausage, '85 9
Andouille, '92 242
Appetizers
Balls in Cheese Pastry, Sausage, '80 248
Balls, Sausage-Apple, '90 85
Balls, Venison Sausage, '80 42
Chile con Queso Supreme, '80 265
Cocktail Sausages, Saucy, '87 173
Cocktail Smoky Links, '90 168
Dip, Braunschweiger-and-Beer, '85 69
Dip, Chili con Queso, '86 81
Italian Sausage-Stuffed Mushrooms,
'83 127
Kielbasa, Sweet-and-Sour, '89 327
Meatballs, Chestnut, '79 110
Meatballs, Crisp German, '92 326
Meatballs, Sweet-and-Sour, '82 247
Mushrooms, Sausage-Stuffed, '80 248;
'91 164

Party Rye Appetizers, '86 262
Phyllo Bites, Sausage-Mushroom-,
'89 284
Pizza Snacks, Tasty Little, '79 248
Puffs, Cajun Hot, '94 277
Quesadillas, Sausage, '90 118
Rolls with Sweet-and-Sour Sauce,
Sausage, '83 74
Ryes, Sausage Party, '89 315
Salami Rollups, '90 226
Smoked Sausages with Mustard Sauce,
'81 56
Squares, Chile-Sausage, '86 297
Sticks, Beef, '93 331
Sweet-and-Sour Sausage, '88 296
Turkey Sausage Turnovers, '95 239
Baked Peaches and Sausage, '82 50
Baked Sausage Patties, '90 82
Bake, Sausage Egg, '81 225
Barbecued Sausage, '86 153
Basic Sausage, '88 104
Beans, and Rice, Texas Sausage, '84 296
Beans, Spicy-Hot, '89 17
Black-Eyed Peas Mexicano, '79 10
Black-Eyed Peas with Sausage, '86 7
Boudin, Old-Fashioned, '85 250
Bratwurst, Grilled, '94 253
Bratwurst and Sauerkraut, '84 250
Bratwurst Dinner, Krause's Café, '87 238
Breads
Biscuit Bites, Sausage, '84 95
Biscuits, Cheesy Sausage, '80 78
Biscuits, Pepperoni, '84 95
Biscuits, Southern Sausage and, '82 43
Biscuits with Sausage, Angel Heart,
'87 156
Muffins, Cheesy Sausage, '92 252;
'93 144
Muffins, Sausage, '88 52; '95 49
Muffins, Sausage-Cheese, '86 213
Rolls, Ground-Pepperoni, '83 244
Breakfast Delight, '93 195
Breakfast Dish, Sausage-Apricot, '82 10
Burritos, Breakfast, '84 57; '90 192
Cabbage, Italian Stuffed, '84 294
Cabbage Rolls, Hot-and-Spicy, '84 249
Cabbage, Sausage-Sauced, '81 271
Cabbage, Stuffed, '84 282
Casseroles
Beefy Sausage Dinner, '80 M9
Breakfast Casserole, '91 285
Breakfast Casserole, Sausage, '81 270
Breakfast Casserole, Sausage-Mushroom,
'86 95
Broccoli Casserole, Sausage and, '80 33
Brunch Casserole, '82 124
Brunch for a Bunch, '88 57
Cheese Bake, Sausage-, '88 58
Cheesy Sausage Casserole, '82 124
Chile Rellenos Casserole, Sausage-,
'88 52
Country Sausage Casserole, '79 192
Creole Sausage-and-Rice Bake, '88 58
Crunchy Sausage Casserole, '81 288
Easy Sausage Casserole, '87 M189
Egg Casserole, Sausage-, '86 M12
Egg Casserole, Sausage-and-, '94 284
Eggplant Parmesan, '86 53
Eggplant-Sausage Bake, '85 221
Eggplant-Sausage Casserole, '84 215
Eggplant-Sausage-Pasta Casserole,
Freezer, '95 197
Grits-Sausage Casserole, '84 75; '86 241

Ground Beef and Sausage Casserole,
'80 260
Hawaiian Sausage Casserole, '85 42
Hominy-Sausage Bake, '88 51
Italian Casserole, '90 238
Italian Sausage Brunch, '88 57
Jambalaya Casserole, Sausage, '82 M203
Lasagna Florentine, Creamy, '91 94
Lasagna Maria, '90 191
Lasagna Rollups, Sausage-, '80 236
Lasagna, Sausage, '83 288
Lasagna Sausage Pinwheels, '79 6
Manicotti, Saucy Stuffed, '83 288
Noodle Bake, Sausage-, '81 92
Noodle Casserole, Sausage and, '82 123
Noodle Casserole, Sausage-and-, '95 255
Paella Casserole, '95 254
Potato Casserole, Sausage-, '86 217
Rice Casserole, Oriental Sausage and,
'82 M123
Rice Casserole, Sausage-, '82 50; '83 75
Salami-Corn Casserole, '80 209
Sausage Casserole, '81 112; '82 12
Smoked Sausage-Egg Bake, '85 248
Spanish Rice Casserole, '79 192
Strata, Christmas Morning, '95 282
Swiss Sausage Casserole, '80 209
Venison-Vegetable Bake, '87 304
Wild Rice and Sausage, '86 268
Wild Rice Casserole, Sausage-, '84 250
Wild Rice Casserole, Sausage and,
'83 196
Zucchini and Sausages, Baked, '80 300
Chicken Rolls Élégante, '80 210
Chili, Beefy Sausage, '82 11
Chili, Company, '82 311
Chili con Carne, Beef and Sausage, '83 284
Chili Goes Southwest, Basic, '93 326
Chili, Hearty Kielbasa, '91 28
Chili, Hotto Lotto, '89 316
Chili-I-Cious, '89 315
Chili, Lolly's Pop, '89 316
Chili, Now, Thatsa, '95 16
Chili, Sausage-Beef, '86 232
Chili, Texas-Style, '82 311; '83 30
Chorizo, '92 241
Chorizo and Egg Tortillas, '81 193
Chorizo, Breakfast, '91 77
Chorizo Carbonara, '94 230
Chorizo (Spicy Spanish Sausage), '81 193
Chorizo Substitute, '87 238
Chowder, Clam-and-Sausage, '94 104
Chowder, Sausage-Bean, '83 20
Country Sausage, '88 104; '92 242
Country Sausage, Spiced, '88 104
Crêpes, Cheesy Sausage, '82 240; '83 71
Crêpes, Sausage, '88 295
Crêpes, Sausage-Filled, '79 39
Dinner, Sausage-and-Bean, '95 108
Dinner, Sausage-Vegetable, '84 250
Dressing, Cajun, '82 307
Dressing, Cornbread-and-Sausage, '83 213
Dressing, Cornbread-Sausage, '82 307;
'85 280
Dressing, Harvest Sausage, '88 254
Dressing, Sausage, '86 280
Dressing, Sausage-Apple, '93 305; '94 296
Dressing, Sausage-Cornbread, '95 289
Dressing, Turkey with Sausage-Cornbread,
'83 287
Eggplant, Sausage Stuffed, '81 204
Eggplant, Sausage-Stuffed, '91 211
Eggs Creole, '92 86

SAUSAGE *(continued)*

Eggs, Scotch, '79 261; '83 289
Filling, Omelet with Sausage, '81 43
Garlic Sausage, '88 104
Gravy, Sausage, '92 271; '94 20
Grits and Sausage, Country, '83 54
Grits Italiano, '92 43
Grits, Sausage, '86 92
Grits, Sausage-Cheese, '90 238
Gumbo, Chicken-and-Sausage, '89 275;
  '90 256; '94 20
Gumbo, Dove and Sausage, '81 199
Gumbo, Duck, Oyster, and Sausage,
  '79 226
Gumbo, The Gullah House, '92 237
Gumbo Ya Ya, '87 210
Gumbo z'Herbes, '94 239
Homemade Sausage, Spicy, '84 320
Hominy-Sausage Skillet, '81 29
Italian Meat Sauce, '83 193
Italian Sauce with Noodles, '84 250
Italian Sausage, '88 104; '92 242
Italian Sausage and Peppers, '84 9
Italian Sausage and Rice, '86 53
Italian Sausage Dinner, '91 218
Italian Sausage Quiche, '81 200
Italian Sausage Soup, '84 235
Italian Sausage Soup with Tortellini, '88 46
Italian Sausage Supper, '88 164
Italian Sausage-Zucchini Soup, '84 4
Italian Turkey Sausage, Marinara Sauce with,
  '89 239
Jambalaya, Chicken-and-Sausage, '88 200;
  '91 216
Jambalaya, Creole, '81 51
Jambalaya de Covington, '87 211
Jambalaya, Northshore, '87 45
Jambalaya, Oven, '84 44
Jambalaya, Sausage, '80 210; '84 249
Jambalaya, Trail, '93 179
Kielbasa, '92 242
Kielbasa and Cabbage, '85 67; '89 M196
Kielbasa, Cabbage, '87 42
Kielbasa-Vegetable Dinner, '91 274
Kraut, Sausage and, '83 11
Loaf, Hawaiian Ham, '79 71
Loaf, Skillet Liver, '80 11
Log, Phyllo Sausage, '84 294
Log, Stuffed Beef, '79 71
Main Dish, Sausage-Eggplant, '80 211
Meatballs and Sausage, Spicy, '79 163
Meat Loaf, Mozzarella-Layered, '79 71
Mexican Luncheon, '87 192
Omelet, Puffy Sausage, '80 M268
Onions, Baked Stuffed, '83 135
Pancake-Sausage Wedges, '93 196
Pasta with Broccoli and Sausage, '87 109
Pasta with Collards and Sausage, '94 230
Pasta with Sausage and Mixed Vegetables,
  '84 249
Patties, Apples on Sausage, '82 120
Pepperoni-and-Broccoli Salad, '83 216
Pepperoni Pasta, '83 105
Pepperoni-Squash Toss, '84 127
Peppers, Sausage and, '95 165
Pie, Breakfast, '86 242
Pie, Cornbread-Sausage-Apple, '87 171
Pie, Sausage-and-Cornbread, '90 25
Pintos and Sausage, Hearty, '88 296
Pinwheels, Sausage, '80 209; '93 238
Pizza, Breakfast, '85 44; '88 288

Pizza, Double Cheesy Beef-and-Sausage,
  '86 77
Pizza Luncheon Pie, Deep-Dish, '80 286
Pizza Peppers, '83 135
Pizza Pie, Link-Sausage, '85 33
Pizza, Speedy, '81 214
Pizza, Spicy Sausage-Pepperoni, '83 226
Pizza, The King Henry, '95 267
Pizza, Thick 'n' Crusty Pepperoni, '85 244
Polenta with Sausage, '93 32
Polish Sausage, Cabbage with, '83 104
Pork Rib Roast, Sausage Stuffed, '94 240
Pork Sausage, '81 55
Pork Sausage Ring, '80 49
Potatoes, Mexican-Topped, '83 3
Potatoes with Eggs and Meat, '91 311;
  '92 25
Quiche, Crustless Sausage-Apple, '87 70
Quiche, Easy Sausage, '79 261
Quiche, Pizza, '86 53
Quiche, Sausage-Cheddar, '79 26
Quiche, South-of-the-Border, '93 321
Quiche, Spicy Sausage, '80 M108
Quiche with Avocado Topping, Mexicali,
  '93 309; '94 96
Quiche, Zucchini-Sausage, '83 122
Ratatouille, Sausage, '89 248
Rice, Shrimp and Sausage, '79 64
Rice with Sausage, Fried, '83 12
Rollups, Pancake-Sausage, '83 246; '84 42
Rollups, Sausage-Bacon, '88 51
Roll-Ups, Spicy Egg, '90 140
Salad, Bean-and-Sausage, '91 313
Sandwiches
  Breakfast Pita Pockets, '89 M21
  Breakfast Sandwiches, '80 52
  Bun, Sausage in a, '89 M22
  Burgers, All-American Pizza, '92 148
  Burgers, Sausage, '83 212
  Calzone, '85 94
  Cheese Muffin Sandwiches, Sausage-,
    '92 M212
  Italian Sausage and Pepper Loaves,
    '83 11
  Italian Sausage Sandwich, '80 92
  Italian Sausage Sloppy Joes, '86 160
  Loaf, Sausage-Stuffed French, '90 19
  Loaves, Sausage-Cheese, '88 235
  Mustard Sauce, Sausage Sandwiches with,
    '84 250
  Pepperoni and Cheese Loaf, '82 32
  Pizza Sandwich, Giant, '80 93
  Salami Sandwiches, Open-Faced,
    '87 279
Shrimp and Sausage over Creamy Grits with
  Tasso Gravy, Spicy, '92 236
Skillet Dinner, Sausage, '83 29
Skillet Express, Sausage, '83 117
Skillet, Mexican-Style, '83 12
Skillet Supper, Sausage, '85 293
Smoked Sausage, '86 154
Smoked Sausage, Chicken Gumbo with,
  '81 199
Smoked Sausage Jambalaya, '79 42
Smoked Sausage Stew, '82 231
Soup, Sausage and Okra, '80 209
Soup, Sausage-Bean, '85 88
Soup, Sausage-Potato, '80 25
Soup, Spicy Sausage-Bean, '83 229
Soup, Sweet Potato-and-Sausage, '95 23
Spaghetti Dinner, Sausage, '79 194
Spaghetti, Italian, '81 38
Spaghetti, Italian Zucchini, '85 2

Spaghetti, Real Italian, '81 233
Spaghetti, Sausage, '83 160
Spicy Sausage, Dieters', '85 49
Squares, Chile-Sausage, '86 297
Squares, Sausage-Onion, '83 112
Squash, Harvest, '80 214
Squash, Sausage-Stuffed, '81 183
Stew, Frogmore, '92 236
Stew, Oyster-Sausage, '89 242
Stew, Venison Sausage, '87 238
Stir-Fry, Sausage, '82 236
Stir-Fry Sausage and Vegetables, '86 213;
  '87 82
Strata, Sausage, '83 243; '84 101
Stuffing, Chicken Breasts with Pecan-Sausage,
  '94 212
Stuffing, Crown Roast of Pork with
  Cranberry-Sausage, '88 49
Supper, Cabbage, '89 314
Supper, Sausage-Bean, '86 52
Surprise, Sausage, '83 245; '84 42
Sweet Peppery Sausage, '95 69
Tacos, Breakfast, '80 43; '95 340
Taquitos, Breakfast, '87 237
Tarts, Sausage 'n' Cheese, '88 51
Tomatoes, Sausage-Stuffed, '80 47
Tortilla Campesina, '89 85
Tortillas, Sausage-and-, '83 246; '84 42
Turban Squash, Sausage-Stuffed, '80 214
Turnovers, Sausage-Cheese, '88 231;
  '89 22
Vegetables and Sausage, Spicy, '80 82
Waffles, Sausage, '83 50
Wild Rice, Sausage and, '85 65
Ziti with Sausage and Broccoli, '95 340
Zucchini and Sausage, Sautéed, '83 289

SCALLOPS
Appetizer, Scallop, '86 155
Appetizers, Flaky Scallop, '86 327
Artichokes Stuffed with Shrimp and Scallops,
  '84 174
Bacon-Wrapped Scallops, '87 94
Baked Gruyère Scallops, '92 57
Broiled Scallops, '91 170
Broiled Scallops with Tartar Sauce, '80 164
Broth with Black Beans and Cilantro,
  Southwestern Scallop, '87 123
Casserole, Scallop, '79 228
Ceviche (Marinated Raw Fish), '82 220
Champagne-Saffron Sauce, Scallops with,
  '93 177
Cheese Scallops, Chip and, '80 301
Coquilles Saint Cyrano, '86 90
Creamy Scallops and Mushrooms, '83 144
Crêpes, Coquilles St. Jacques, '83 13
en Brochette with Vegetables, Scallops,
  '80 163
Grilled Orange Scallops with Cilantro-Lime
  Vinaigrette, '94 77
Grilled Scallops, Marinated, '84 171
Kabobs, Grilled Scallop, '83 101
Kabobs, Grilled Shrimp-and-Scallop,
  '92 210
Kabobs, Scallop-Bacon, '81 111
Kabobs, Sea Scallop, '82 162
Mornay, Scallops, '80 164
Mustard Sauce, Scallops with, '84 163
Pasta, Fresh Scallops and, '83 164
Provençal, Scallops, '85 66
Salad, Hot Seafood, '80 164
Sautéed Scallops with Cranberry Relish,
  '83 144
Sauté, Scallop, '88 28

SCALLOPS *(continued)*

Sauté, Shrimp-and-Scallop, '85 103
Sauté with Pecan Rice, Shrimp-and-Scallop, '90 317
Savannah, Scallops, '79 145
Seared Scallops with Tomato-Mango Salsa, '95 122
Sherried Scallops, '83 281
Stir-Fry, Scallop, '94 32
Supreme, Seafood, '82 284
Tostada, Grilled Scallops, '87 120
Vegetable Nests, Scallops in, '91 70
Vegetables, Bay Scallops with, '84 233
Vermicelli, Scallop-Vegetable, '87 143
Véronique, Scallops, '83 144
Wild Rice, Scallops and, '90 129
Wine, Scallops in, '91 48

SEAFOOD. *See also* **CLAMS, CRAB, FISH, LOBSTER, OYSTERS, SALMON, SCALLOPS, SHRIMP, TUNA.**

Appetizer, Layered Seafood, '88 2
Bisque, Seafood, '86 66
Boil, Low Country Seafood, '80 119
Boil, Southern Shellfish, '93 258
Bouillabaisse, Florida, '79 158
Brochette, Seafood, '87 96
Broiled Shellfish, Quick, '79 228
Casserole, Seafood, '87 109; '89 63
Chowder, Curried Seafood, '94 103
Chowder, Seafood, '85 9; '92 122
Chowder, Southern Seafood, '83 20
Cioppino, Gulf Coast, '94 102
Delight, Seafood, '86 208
Dip, Hot Artichoke-Seafood, '80 241
Dip, Hot Artichoke Seafood, '85 M212
Dip, Hot Cheesy Seafood, '84 221
Dip, Seafood, '79 3
Dip, Super Seafood, '90 292
Eggplant, Seafood Stuffed, '79 187
Gumbos
　Cajun Seafood Gumbo, '94 238
　Champion Seafood Gumbo, '86 293
　Chicken-Ham-Seafood Gumbo, '81 6
　Creole Gumbo, '86 228
　Creole Gumbo, Quick, '82 87
　Creole Seafood Gumbo, '82 278
　Ham and Seafood Gumbo, '81 199
　Okra Gumbo, Light Seafood-, '86 155
　Seafood Gumbo, '79 198, 286; '80 34;
　　'81 5; '83 90; '84 87, 92; '87 210;
　　'90 154
　Spicy Seafood Gumbo, '91 207
　Whole Crabs, Seafood Gumbo with, '85 2
Hot Brown, Seafood, '88 158
Imperials, Individual Seafood, '84 162
Jambalaya, Three-Seafood, '82 126
Linguine, Seafood, '79 227
Manicotti, Seafood, '94 195
Mayonnaise, Seafood with Dill, '86 234
Mold, Chilled Seafood, '86 70
Mornay, Seafood, '83 67
Mussels Linguine, '90 M112
Mussel Soup, '93 259
Paella, Chicken-Seafood, '88 68
Paella, Party, '88 M189
Paella, Seafood, '82 245
Papillote, Ocean, '84 M287
Pasta, Seafood and, '90 234
Pie, Hot Seafood, '80 32
Potatoes, Seafood-Stuffed, '95 M192
Risotto, Seafood, '95 280

Salads
　Baked Seafood Salad, '86 10
　Hot Seafood Salad, '79 117; '80 164
　Paella Salad, '86 207
　Pasta Salad, Seafood, '90 62
　Polynesian Seafood Salad, '79 57
　Seafood Salad, '90 88
　Seaside Salad, '86 183
　Slaw, Seafood, '79 56
　Smoky Seafood Salad, '84 46
　Sussex Shores, Seafood Salad, '93 98
Sauce Delight, Seafood, '82 91
Sauce, Linguine with Seafood, '83 232
Sauce, Red Seafood, '95 107
Sauce, Seafood, '79 3; '82 48; '86 304;
　'89 239
Sauce, Seafood Cheese, '89 240
Sautéed Seafood Platter, '83 89
Seasoning Blend, Bay Seafood, '92 121
Seasoning Blend, Fish-and-Seafood, '88 28
Seasoning Rub, Seafood, '93 101
Spread, Seafood, '86 M58; '87 146
Spread, Seafood Sandwich, '82 87
Stew, Seafood, '84 280
Stock, Seafood, '94 238
Supreme, Seafood, '82 284
Tartlets, Seafood, '87 247
Tempura, Basic, '81 68
Tempura, Cornmeal, '81 68

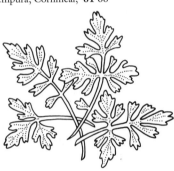

SEASONINGS

Adobo, '92 158
Bay Seafood Seasoning Blend, '92 121
Better-Than-Potpourri Brew, '95 271
Blend, Seasoning, '82 296
Creole Rub, '93 101
Creole Seasoning Blend, '92 121
Fish-and-Seafood Seasoning Blend, '88 28
Five-Spice Powder Blend, '92 121
Garlic, Herbed Roasted, '94 177
Garlic Puree, Roasted, '92 55
Garlic, Roasted, '94 177
Greek Seasoning Blend, '92 121
Gremolata, '95 280
Ground Seasoning Blend, '92 121
Herb Rub, '93 102
Herbs Seasoning Blend, '92 121
Jerk Rub, '93 101
Lemon-Mint Sugar, '95 32
Lemon Squeezers, '95 32
Meat Seasoning Blend, '88 29
Mexican Rub, '93 102
Mix, GOPPS Seasoning, '92 305
Mix, Seasoning, '91 64
Moroccan Spice Rub, '95 231
Olive Oil, Basil-Infused, '95 231
Olive Oil, Lemon-Infused, '95 231
Poultry Seasoning Blend, '88 28
Salt, Gourmet Seasoning, '82 297

Sazon, '92 157
Seafood Seasoning Rub, '93 101
Southwest Seasoning, '95 266
Vanilla Extract, '94 243
Vanilla Oil, '94 243
Vanilla Sugar, '94 243
Vegetable Seasoning Blend, '88 29

SHERBETS. *See also* **ICE CREAMS.**

Ambrosia Cups, Sherbet, '82 159
Apricot Sherbet, '81 177; '92 164
Avocado Sherbet, '83 162
Banana-Orange Sherbet, '83 162
Beverages
　Pineapple Sherbet Float, '79 148
　Punch, Double Sherbet, '79 232
　Punch, Pineapple Sherbet, '95 141
　Punch, Orange Sherbet Party, '83 142
　Punch, Raspberry Sherbet, '95 141
Buttermilk Sherbet, '84 184
Cantaloupe Sherbet, '88 183
Cantaloupe Sherbet, Frosty, '82 144
Cranberry Sherbet, '88 280
Dessert, Layered Sherbet, '87 109
Fruit Punch Sherbet, '86 129
Fruit Sherbet, Freezer, '86 334
Fruit Sherbet, Frozen, '79 155
Fruit Sherbet, Instant, '85 158
Lemon Cream Sherbet, '79 114
Lemon Sherbet, '91 309
Lime Sherbet, '82 159; '89 202
Lime Sherbet, Creamy, '84 165
Macaroon-Sherbet Frozen Dessert, '79 212
Mexican Sherbet, '79 155
Mint Sherbet, Fresh, '88 23
Nectarine Sherbet, '89 199
Orange Sherbet, '79 155
Orange Sherbet Salad, '81 154
Orange Sherbet with Blackberry Sauce, '94 232
Peach Sherbet, '90 179
Pineapple Sherbet, '81 177; '84 83; '89 199
Pineapple Sherbet, Creamy, '79 155
Pineapple Sherbet, Easy, '92 199
Raspberry Sherbet, '83 162
Strawberry Sherbet, '82 112, 160
Watermelon Sherbet, '79 155; '92 124
Watermelon Sherbet, Light, '81 147

SHRIMP

Appetizers
　Artichoke-and-Shrimp Appetizer, '93 271
　Ball, Curried Shrimp Cheese, '86 135
　Balls, Curried Shrimp, '94 180
　Ball, Shrimp-Cheese, '85 208
　Bayou, Shrimp, '88 261
　Boiled Shrimp, Spicy, '83 320; '84 289
　Boiled Shrimp with Cocktail Sauce, '79 151
　Boil, Southern Shellfish, '93 258
　Cajun Shrimp, '89 283
　Canapés, Shrimp, '84 116
　Canapés, Shrimp-and-Cucumber, '93 164
　Cheese, Shrimp with Herbed Jalapeño, '87 112
　Cocktail, Shrimp, '87 173
　Coconut-Beer Shrimp, '85 230; '89 23
　Dilled Shrimp, '88 150
　Dip, Hot Shrimp, '87 190
　Dippers, Shrimp, '84 324
　Dip, Quick Shrimp, '79 153
　Dip, Shrimp, '86 84; '88 M261
　Dip, Zesty Shrimp, '80 150
　Egg Rolls, '86 81

SHRIMP, Appetizers *(continued)*

Eggrolls, Shrimp and Pork, '82 240; '83 18
Filling, Shrimp, '89 320
Fried Marinated Shrimp with Mango Slaw, '93 31
Jalapeños, Shrimp-Stuffed, '88 115
Kabobs, Appetizer Shrimp, '91 251
Kabobs, Shrimp, '80 150
Key West Shrimp, '94 278
Lemon Shrimp, Luscious, '88 150
Manale, Shrimp, '86 268
Marinated Shrimp and Cucumber, '91 166
Marinated Shrimp, Icy, '84 215
Miniquiches, Shrimp, '87 146
Mold, Shrimp, '87 94
Mold with Asparagus, Shrimp, '93 214
Mousse, Shrimp, '79 57; '87 196, 251
Mushrooms, Shrimp-Stuffed, '80 M135
Pâté with Dill Sauce, Shrimp, '85 39
Pickled Shrimp, '94 182
Pickle, Shrimp-in-a-, '86 326
Pineapple Appetizer, Shrimp-, '85 80
Pizza Wedges, Shrimp, '89 158
Puffs, Gouda-Shrimp, '79 234
Rémoulade, Shrimp, '83 173; '90 255
Rock Shrimp Conga, '80 2
Salsa Picante with Shrimp, '92 210
Sesame Shrimp, '95 92
Sherried Garlic Shrimp, '92 175
Soufflé Roll, Shrimp, '89 320
Spread, Chunky Shrimp, '85 300; '86 18
Spread, Curried Shrimp, '87 158
Spread, Shrimp, '81 306; '85 135; '87 111; '93 205
Spread, Shrimp-Cucumber, '79 81
Spread, Tempting Shrimp, '79 57
Spread, Zippy Shrimp, '90 36
Toast, Shrimp, '86 91
Tree, Shrimp, '83 320; '84 288; '85 318
Zucchini-Shrimp Appetizers, '89 311
Ariosto, Shrimp and Chicken, '79 31
Artichokes, Shrimp-Stuffed, '84 67; '87 55
Artichokes, Shrimp Stuffed, '94 62
Artichokes Stuffed with Shrimp and Scallops, '84 174
au Gratin, Crab, Shrimp, and Artichoke, '90 240
au Gratin, Shrimp, '85 79
Avocados, Shrimp-Filled, '83 2
Baked Shrimp, '87 35
Barbecued Shrimp, '82 74; '84 93; '90 28
Barbecued Shrimp, Cajun, '87 95
Boats, Shrimp, '79 57
Boiled Shrimp, '79 3
Boiled Shrimp, Ray Kidd's, '84 87
Boiled Shrimp, Special, '83 36
Boiled Shrimp Supper, '94 200
Boiled Shrimp with Green Peppercorn Tartar Sauce, '94 144
Breakfast Shrimp, Classic Charleston, '93 60
Broiled Shrimp, Beer-, '87 142
Broiled Shrimp, Garlic-, '83 193
Broiled Shrimp, Lemon-Garlic, '82 29; '86 182
Broiled Shrimp Supreme, '79 3
Butter, Shrimp, '92 91
Cajun Shrimp, Fiery, '91 218
Cashew Shrimp Supreme, '83 29
Casserole, Chayotes and Shrimp, '80 230

Casserole, Crab-and-Shrimp, '84 71
Casserole, Miss Hannah's, '92 236
Casserole, Shrimp, '85 240
Casserole, Shrimp-and-Chicken, '91 102
Casserole, Shrimp-and-Noodle, '90 240
Casserole, Shrimp and Rice, '79 228
Casserole, Shrimp-and-Rice, '94 328
Casserole, Turkey-and-Shrimp Florentine, '92 122
Catfish, Crown Room's Shrimp-Stuffed, '84 182
C'est Bon, Shrimp, '94 195
Cheesecake, Shrimp-and-Gruyère, '92 57
Chicken Breasts, Stuffed, '88 50
Chow Mein, Shrimp, '82 30
Creamed Shrimp on Pecan-Cornmeal Rounds, '95 99
Cream Sauce, Shrimp in, '84 M286
Creole, Easy Shrimp, '95 68
Creole in a Rice Ring, Shrimp, '86 222
Creole, Shrimp, '86 256; '87 18; '90 M220; '93 282
Creole, Special Shrimp, '87 172
Creole, Spicy Shrimp, '79 181
Creole, Wild Rice-and-Shrimp, '84 292
Curry
    Charleston-Style Shrimp Curry, '84 109
    Creamy Shrimp Curry, '90 145
    Curried Shrimp, '84 110
    Eggs, Saucy Shrimp-Curried, '84 143
    Polynesian Shrimp Curry, '89 23
    Quick Curried Shrimp, '84 M198
    Rice and Shrimp, Curried, '83 231
    Sauce, Hawaiian Shrimp with Curry, '94 54
    Shrimp Malai Curry, '84 110
    Sour Cream and Shrimp Curry, '81 10
    Sour Cream Shrimp Curry, '80 83
    West Indian Curried Shrimp, '79 227
Dee-Lish, Shrimp, '90 216
de Jonghe, Shrimp, '79 228
Delight, English Muffin, '82 45
Delight, Shrimp, '79 192
Destin, Shrimp, '82 29
Dijonnaise, Shrimp, '87 91
Dilled Sauced Shrimp, '86 88
Dinner, Jollof Rice, '91 230; '92 325
Egg Foo Yong, '80 19; '86 232
Egg Foo Yong, Shrimp, '83 22
Eggplant, Shrimp-Stuffed, '92 99
Eggrolls, Shrimp and Pork, '82 240; '83 18
Eggs, Shrimp and Crab Scrambled, '79 261
Élégante, Shrimp, '83 48
Enchiladas in Tomatillo Sauce, Shrimp, '95 310
en Papillote, Shrimp Cancun, '91 136
en Papillote, Shrimp with Asparagus, '86 145
Étouffée, Crab-and-Shrimp, '89 96
Étouffée, Shrimp, '79 4; '90 229
Fish with Shrimp, Veracruz, '86 130
Flambé, Prawns, '89 24
Florentine, Chicken-and-Shrimp, '89 64
Flounder Stuffed with Shrimp, '88 51
Fondue, Shrimp, '86 244
French-Fried Shrimp, '79 4
French Shrimp, '80 85
Fresh Shrimp, Preparing, '82 127
Fried Marinated Shrimp with Mango Slaw, '93 31
Fried Shrimp, Golden, '82 29
Fried Shrimp, Gulf Coast, '91 29
Fried Shrimp, Puffy, '79 4

Fried Shrimp with Apricot Sauce, '87 172
Garlic-Buttered Shrimp, '86 M226
Garlic Shrimp, '79 268; '80 14
Gin and Ginger, Shrimp with, '95 205
Grilled Shrimp, '85 103
Honeyed Shrimp, Tangy, '94 32
Kabobs, Grilled Shrimp-and-Scallop, '92 210
Kabobs, Marinated Shrimp, '84 276; '85 158
Kabobs, Shrimp, '80 150, 184
Kabobs, Steak-and-Shrimp, '80 184
Lamb Chops with Shrimp, '88 58
Lemon Butter, Shrimp in, '84 163
Lemon Garlic Sauce, Shrimp in, '83 67
Lemon Shrimp, Luscious, '88 150
Marinara, Shrimp, '84 233
Marinated and Grilled Shrimp, '87 141
Marinated Shrimp, Grilled, '87 173
Marinated Shrimp, Zesty, '87 173
Mediterranean Shrimp Bowl, '80 174
Medley, Eggplant-Shrimp, '79 188
Melba, Shrimp, '84 86
Mustard-Vinegar Sauce, Shrimp with, '93 240
Omelet, Shrimp-and-Cheddar, '84 57
Omelet, Shrimp-and-Cheese, '94 31
Oven Shrimp, Vic's, '95 215
Paella Casserole, '95 254
Paella, Chicken-Pork-Shrimp, '82 245
Paella, Party, '88 M189
Paella, Shrimp-and-Chicken, '94 168
Paella, Spanish, '85 26
Paella Valenciana, '82 246
Pasta
    Angel Hair Pasta, Shrimp and Mushrooms with, '92 34
    Angel Hair Pasta with Shrimp and Asparagus, '92 100
    Asparagus, Tomatoes, and Shrimp, Garlicky Pasta with, '95 82
    Fettuccine and Shrimp with Dried Tomato Pesto, '94 249
    Fettuccine, Shrimp, '94 84
    Green Pasta with Shrimp-Mushroom Italienne, '79 170
    Herbed Shrimp and Pasta, '92 329
    Linguine, Artichoke and Shrimp, '95 210
    Linguine, Spicy Shrimp and, '92 34
    Mediterranean Shrimp and Pasta, '95 286
    Medley, Shrimp-Pasta, '88 302
    Noodles, Creamy Shrimp and, '92 100
    Primavera, Shrimp with Pasta, '93 168
    Rotelle, Shrimp, '85 165
    Scampi, Shrimp, '95 209
    Shrimp and Pasta, '91 207
    Spaghetti, Shrimp-and-Vegetable, '91 170
    Spaghetti with Black Olives, Shrimp, '85 13
    Tortellini, Shrimp and, '92 34
    Vermicelli, Shrimp and Feta Cheese on, '87 108
Patties, Shrimp, '92 128
Peanut Sauce, Shrimp with, '93 303
Peppers, Shrimp-Stuffed, '80 162; '86 131, 197
Pickled Shrimp, '79 3
Pickled Shrimp, New Orleans, '79 145
Pilaf, Shrimp, '82 246
Pizza, The Best of the Bayou, '95 268
Polynesian Shrimp, '79 3
Potatoes, Broccoli-Shrimp Stuffed, '92 M228
Potatoes, Creamy Shrimp-Stuffed, '80 36
Potatoes, Shrimp-Sauced, '81 M61

SHRIMP *(continued)*

Puff, Shrimp-Crab, '79 57
Puffs, Luncheon Shrimp, '85 72
Quesadillas with Shrimp and Brie, '94 173
Quiche, Shrimp, '83 50
Rémoulade Sauce, Shrimp with, '91 29
Rice, Oriental Shrimp and, '90 183
Rice, Shrimp and Refried, '89 176
Rice, Shrimp and Sausage, '79 64
Rock Shrimp Tails, Batter-Fried, '80 2
Rock Shrimp Tails, Broiled, '80 3
Rock Shrimp Tails, Sweet-and-Sour, '80 3
Rollups, Shrimp-Stuffed, '82 234
Sailor Shrimp for Two, '82 276
Salads
    Aloha Shrimp Salad, '95 46
    Aspic, Shrimp-Coleslaw, '79 88
    Aspic, Shrimp-Cucumber, '83 108
    Aspic with Shrimp, Tomato, '79 241
    Avocado Salad, Shrimp and, '80 266
    Avocado Stuffed with Shrimp Salad,
      '82 207
    Black Bean Salad, Caribbean Shrimp-and-,
      '93 143
    Boiled Shrimp, '79 3
    Crabmeat-Shrimp Pasta Salad, '86 208
    Creamy Shrimp Salad, '79 56
    Egg Salad Sandwiches, Shrimp-and-,
      '94 182
    Endive Salad, Shrimp-, '85 73
    Filling, Shrimp Salad, '87 106
    Fruited Shrimp Salad, '86 156
    Grapefruit-and-Shrimp Salad, '88 5
    Green Salad with Shrimp, '88 49
    Half Shell, Shrimp Salad on the, '86 73
    Individual Shrimp Salads, '83 146
    Layered Shrimp Salad, '88 100
    Macaroni Salad, Shrimp, '79 220
    Macaroni Salad, Shrimp-, '85 219
    Macaroni-Shrimp Salad, '85 121
    Macaroni-Shrimp Salad, Festive, '85 165
    Marinated Shrimp Salad, '85 82; '93 321
    Orange, and Olive Salad with Sherry
      Vinaigrette, Shrimp, '93 177
    Orange Rice Salad, Zesty Shrimp-and-,
      '87 155
    Orange-Shrimp Salad, '84 197
    Oriental Shrimp Salad, '91 313
    Pasta-and-Shrimp Salad, '83 163
    Pastry, Shrimp Salad in, '86 105
    Peppers Stuffed with Shrimp-and-Orzo
      Salad, '91 203
    Picnic Shrimp Salad, '95 182
    Rice-and-Shrimp Salad, '83 82
    Rice Salad, Baked Shrimp-, '83 22
    Rice Salad, Shrimp and, '80 231; '82 207
    Rice Salad, Shrimp-and-, '92 307
    Rice Salad, Tangy Shrimp-, '84 66
    Rice-Shrimp Salad, '79 270; '92 142
    Sandwiches, Shrimp Salad, '90 178
    Sea Slaw, Tomatoes Stuffed with, '89 96
    Shrimp Salad, '81 94; '84 221; '86 186;
      '93 238
    Super Shrimp Salad, '81 37
    Tossed Shrimp-Egg Salad, '80 4
    Vegetable-Shrimp Salad, '79 190
    Vermicelli Salad, Shrimp, '88 139
    Walnut Salad, Shrimp-, '86 182
Sandwiches, Shrimp-Cheese, '85 242
Sauce, Broccoli and Cauliflower with Shrimp,
  '84 248

Sauce, Flounder Fillets in Shrimp, '83 227
Sauce, Flounder with Hollandaise-Shrimp,
  '86 234
Sauce, Oysters in Shrimp, '87 40
Sauce Piquante, Crab and Shrimp, '83 92
Sauce, Shrimp, '87 138, 232
Sauce, Shrimp-and-Almond, '87 282
Sausage over Creamy Grits with Tasso Gravy,
  Spicy Shrimp and, '92 236
Sautéed Shrimp, '79 3
Sauté, Shrimp-and-Grouper, '87 91
Sauté, Shrimp-and-Scallop, '85 103
Sauté with Pecan Rice, Shrimp-and-Scallop,
  '90 317
Scampi, Easy, '84 291
Scampi, Orange, '85 303
Scampi, Quick, '88 301
Scampi, Shrimp, '84 230; '92 117; '93 70
Sesame Shrimp, '95 92
Shells, Creamy Shrimp, '79 4
Sirloin Supreme, Shrimp and, '81 131
Skillet, Quick Shrimp, '87 50
Smoked Shrimp, Citrus-Marinated, '95 114
Snow Pea-Shrimp Combo, '79 57
Snow Peas, Shrimp with, '85 75
Soups
    Bisque, Shrimp, '95 19
    Bisque, Shrimp-Chile, '94 272
    Bisque, Shrimp-Cucumber, '79 172
    Bisque, Shrimp-Vegetable, '82 313;
      '83 66
    Bisque, Tomato-Shrimp, '86 66
    Chowder, Shrimp, '89 218
    Chowder, Shrimp and Corn, '79 199
    Corn Soup, Shrimp-and-, '84 88
    Enchilada Soup, Shrimp, '94 103
    Gazpacho, Shrimp-Cream Cheese, '94 137
    Gumbo, Crab and Shrimp, '81 200
    Gumbo, Quick Shrimp, '86 71
    Gumbo, Shrimp, '81 199
    Jambalaya, Creole Shrimp, '92 99
    Mushroom Soup, Shrimp-, '85 87
    Okra-and-Shrimp Soup, '94 323
    Stock, Shrimp, '93 60
Spread, Shrimp, '81 306; '85 135; '87 111;
  '93 205
Spread, Shrimp-Cucumber, '79 81
Steak and Shrimp, '88 123
Stew and Grits, Shrimp, '80 118
Stewed Shrimp with Dumplings, '79 31
Stew, Frogmore, '92 236
Stew over Grits, Shrimp, '88 126; '89 47
Stew, Shrimp, '83 4
Stir-Fry, Beef-and-Shrimp, '93 32
Stir-Fry, Cajun Shrimp, '92 127
Stir-Fry Shrimp and Vegetables, '87 91
Stroganoff, Oven-Baked Shrimp, '81 297
Stroganoff, Shrimp, '79 81
Stuffed Shrimp Bundles, Crab-, '81 176
Stuffed Shrimp, Crab-, '84 259
Stuffed Shrimp, Parmesan-, '85 103
Stuffed Shrimp with Hollandaise Sauce, '95 86
Sweet-and-Sour Shrimp, '83 278; '90 M112
Sweet-and-Sour Shrimp and Chicken, '87 267;
  '88 103; '89 66
Szechuan Shrimp, '86 173
Tacos, Shrimp-and-Pepper Soft, '95 339
Tart, Shrimp, '87 70
Topping, Shrimp, '93 291
Tostadas, Shrimp-and-Black Bean, '93 204
Vegetables, Shrimp and, '82 6
Versailles, Shrimp, '90 233
Yellow Squash, Shrimp-Stuffed, '84 194

SLAWS

Apple-Carrot Slaw, '92 243
Apple Coleslaw, '89 315
Apple-Pineapple Slaw, '79 241
Apple Slaw, Fresh, '81 63
Apple Slaw, Nutty, '88 216
Aspic, Shrimp-Coleslaw, '79 88
Bacon Coleslaw, '83 58
Banana-Nut Slaw, '86 250
Blue Cheese Coleslaw, '89 13; '95 270
Broccoli Slaw, Zesty, '93 246
Cabbage-Orange Slaw, '79 135
Cabbage-Pineapple Slaw, '92 182
Cabbage Slaw, Fresh, '85 139
Cabbage Slaw, Nutty, '88 218
Cabbage Slaw, Sweet, '79 76
Cauliflower Slaw, '92 167
Chicken Coleslaw, '84 2
Chili Coleslaw, '80 178
Chinese Cabbage Slaw, '89 312
Coleslaw, '79 152; '82 135
Colorful Coleslaw, '88 166
Confetti Slaw, '89 48
Corn and Cabbage Slaw, '79 135
Cottage Coleslaw, '80 64
Country-Style Coleslaw, '83 59
Creamy Coleslaw, '83 170
Crunchy Coleslaw, '86 295
Cucumber Slaw, Creamy, '89 49
Curried Coleslaw, '85 139
Freezer Coleslaw, '89 49
Freezer Slaw, '81 279; '82 24; '83 154
Frozen Coleslaw, '82 102
Fruit Coleslaw, Three-, '86 250
Fruited Coleslaw, '83 209; '85 139
Grape-Poppy Seed Slaw, '86 225
Grapes and Almonds, Coleslaw with, '83 59
Green Bean Slaw, '95 108
Guacamole Mexican Coleslaw, '82 302
Ham Coleslaw, '84 195
Healthy Slaw, '92 183
Hot-and-Creamy Dutch Slaw, '87 127
Hot-and-Sour Chinese Slaw, '85 139
Hot Slaw, '89 49
Kentucky Coleslaw, '81 216
Layered Coleslaw, '86 180
Layered Slaw, '93 214
Light and Creamy Coleslaw, '93 318
Make-Ahead Coleslaw, '81 155
Mango Slaw, '93 31; '94 71
Marinated Coleslaw, '79 135
Marinated Slaw, '91 229
Memphis Slaw, '91 28
Mexicali Coleslaw, '84 18
Mexican Coleslaw, '89 48
Mustard Slaw, Texas, '88 172
Old-Fashioned Coleslaw, '80 120; '82 225
Old-Fashioned Slaw, '84 149
Old-Fashioned Sweet Coleslaw, '93 128
Overnight Cabbage Slaw, '81 88; '82 7
Overnight Coleslaw, '79 135
Overnight Slaw, '79 5; '92 280
Peach Slaw, Party, '86 250
Peanut Slaw, '85 139
Peanut Slaw, Chinese, '93 212
Pear Slaw, Peanutty-, '86 250
Pineapple-Almond Slaw, '92 171
Pineapple Coleslaw, Curried, '88 172
Pineapple Slaw, '94 49
Pineapple Slaw, Colorful, '86 250
Polka Dot Slaw, '83 59
Red Bean Slaw, '79 247
Red Cabbage-and-Apple Slaw, '87 31; '91 309

SLAWS (continued)

Red Cabbage Slaw, '95 153
Seafood Slaw, '79 56
Sea Slaw, Tomatoes Stuffed with, '89 96
Silks, Slaw, '93 236
Sour Cream Slaw, '87 10
Swedish Slaw, '79 135
Sweet and Crunchy Slaw, '79 104
Sweet-and-Sour Hot Slaw, '92 63
Sweet-and-Sour Slaw, '81 237
Sweet Potato-Currant Slaw, '93 246
Tangy Coleslaw, '83 59
"Think Pink" Slaw, '94 247
Tomatoes, Coleslaw with, '80 34
Turnip Slaw, '89 245
Vegetable Slaw, '81 280
Zesty Slaw, '82 127
Zucchini Coleslaw, Fiesta, '91 168

SOUFFLÉS
Blue Cheese Soufflé, '91 244
Cheese Soufflé, '79 72, 261; '94 116
Cheese Soufflé for Two, '81 226
Cheese Soufflé, Rolled, '89 13
Cheese Soufflé, Three-Egg, '87 234
Chicken-Chestnut Soufflé, '79 107
Crab Soufflé Spread, '85 4
Cups, Hot Soufflé, '85 284
Dessert
    Apricot Soufflé, Baked, '88 267
    au Chocolat Cointreau, Soufflé, '94 56
    Banana Daiquiri Soufflé, '84 317
    Blintz Soufflé, '88 155
    Brandy Alexander Soufflé, '82 173;
        '83 M114
    Bread Pudding Soufflé, Creole, '92 87
    Chocolate Mint Soufflé, '81 16
    Chocolate Soufflé, '84 317; '94 46
    Chocolate Soufflé, Light, '83 278
    Coconut Soufflé, '79 73; '85 212
    Cranberry-Topped Holiday Soufflé,
        '84 306
    Cream Cheese Soufflé, '88 11
    Daiquiri Soufflé, Elegant, '80 69
    Devonshire Soufflé, Chilled, '88 279
    Grand Marnier Soufflé, '79 281
    Grand Marnier Soufflés, '89 290
    Grasshopper Soufflé, '81 248; '86 188
    Kahlúa Soufflé, '82 173
    Lemon-Lime Soufflé, Cold, '84 24
    Lemon Sauce Soufflés, Quick, '88 43
    Lemon Soufflé, '82 170, 252; '94 199
    Lemon Soufflé, Tart, '85 82
    Lemon Soufflé with Raspberry-Amaretto
        Sauce, Frozen, '88 130
    Orange Dessert Soufflé, '83 206
    Orange Soufflé, Chilled, '84 317;
        '86 189
    Orange Soufflé, Frozen, '79 211
    Pineapple Dessert Soufflé, '80 153
    Raspberry Soufflé, '86 188
    Raspberry-Topped Soufflé, '85 317
    Vanilla Soufflé, Frozen, '79 230; '82 173
    Vanilla Soufflés with Vanilla Crème Sauce,
        '94 242
Egg Soufflé Casserole, '83 55
Egg Soufflés, Little, '83 57
Frozen Soufflés, Individual, '80 52
Grits Soufflé, '80 30
Grits Soufflé, Mexican, '79 55
Ham Breakfast Soufflé, Virginia, '93 121
Ham Soufflé with Cucumber Sauce, '92 41

Individual Soufflés, '80 190
Rice-Cheese Soufflé, '79 270
Salmon Soufflé, Fresh, '81 182
Shrimp Soufflé Roll, '89 320
Sour Cream Soufflé, '80 43
Turkey Soufflé, '80 271
Vegetable
    Asparagus Soufflé, '79 66; '83 265;
        '89 89
    Broccoli Soufflé, '81 24
    Broccoli Soufflé, Golden, '84 283
    Butternut Soufflé, '83 266
    Carrot Puff, '89 89
    Carrot Soufflé, '79 73; '83 265
    Cauliflower Soufflé, '82 76; '89 279;
        '90 17
    Corn-and-Cheese Soufflé, '88 122
    Mushroom Soufflés, '87 282
    Onion Soufflé, '79 247
    Parsnip Soufflé, Golden, '83 266
    Potatoes, Soufflé, '84 295; '85 196;
        '90 14
    Potato Soufflé, Cheesy, '89 332
    Spinach Soufflé, '79 73; '81 304; '84 78;
        '85 248; '86 108
    Spinach Soufflé, Cheesy, '81 53
    Spinach Soufflé Deluxe, '79 8
    Spinach Soufflé Roll, '80 215
    Squash Soufflé, '95 215
    Squash Soufflé, Cheesy, '82 146
    Sweet Potato Soufflé, '82 286; '86 121;
        '93 325
    Turnip Soufflé, '79 254
    Yellow Squash Soufflé, '89 89
    Zucchini-and-Corn Soufflé, '83 265
    Zucchini Soufflé, '79 157
SOUPS. See also CHILI, CHOWDERS, JAMBALAYAS,
    GUMBOS, STEWS.
Acorn Squash Soup, '91 294
Acorn Squash Soup, Cream of, '94 268
Almond Soup, '79 48
Artichoke Cream Soup, '94 62
Artichoke Soup, '89 269
Artichoke Soup, Cream of, '82 232
Asparagus Soup, '84 67
Asparagus Soup, Cream of, '84 111
Asparagus Soup, Creamy, '94 225
Avocado-Banana-Yogurt Soup, '80 78
Avocado-Mushroom Soup, Creamy, '85 25
Avocado Soup, '88 160
Avocado Soup, Chilled, '81 34; '87 37;
    '93 108
Avocado Soup, Creamy, '79 107
Avocado Soup, Sherried, '84 181
Bacon, Lettuce, and Tomato Soup, '91 207
Bean
    Bacon Soup, Bean and, '83 26
    Barley Soup, Hearty Bean-and-,
        '86 304
    "Bean Counter" Soup, '92 80
    Beanolla Soup, '94 248
    Bean Soup, '80 25
    Black Beans and Cilantro, Southwestern
        Scallop Broth with, '87 123
    Black Bean Soup, '88 30, 266; '89 28;
        '93 231
    Black Bean Soup, Carolina, '92 139
    Capitol Hill Bean Soup, '80 222
    Chill-Chaser Soup, '87 282
    Drunken Bean Soup, '87 283
    French Market Soup, '85 277; '92 49;
        '94 317
    Green Bean Soup, Cream of, '84 111

Ham-and-Bean Soup, '84 4
Hominy Soup, Bean-and-, '95 23
Leafy Bean Soup, '86 223
Mix, French Market Soup, '85 277;
    '94 317
Navy Bean Soup, '84 280
Navy Bean Soup, Chunky, '83 291
Navy Bean Soup, Savory, '87 282
Pasta Soup, Bean and, '94 220
Sausage-Bean Soup, '85 88
Sausage-Bean Soup, Spicy, '83 229
Three-Bean Soup, '89 17
Three-Bean Soup, Spicy, '91 28
Turkey Soup, Bean-and-, '93 319
White Bean Pot, '86 194
White Bean Soup, '83 229; '90 201
White Bean Soup, Spicy, '94 225
Bell Pepper Soup, '89 103
Bisques
    Banana-Raspberry Bisque, '93 161
    Clam Bisque, '86 228
    Crab-and-Corn Bisque, '87 137
    Crab-and-Leek Bisque, '94 104
    Crab Bisque, '88 251
    Mushroom Bisque, Brisk, '81 190
    Oyster Bisque, '83 252
    Pumpkin Bisque, Spicy, '86 67
    Seafood Bisque, '86 66
    Shrimp Bisque, '95 19
    Shrimp-Chile Bisque, '94 272
    Shrimp-Cucumber Bisque, '79 172
    Shrimp-Vegetable Bisque, '82 313;
        '83 66
    Spinach-Potato Bisque, '86 66
    Squash Bisque, '84 280
    Tomato-Basil Bisque, Make-Ahead,
        '93 322
    Tomato-Shrimp Bisque, '86 66
    Tuna Bisque, '79 76
Black-Eyed Soup, Beefy, '85 6
Black, White, and Red All Over Soup,
    '95 126
Borscht, Crawfish, '92 84
Borscht, Ruby Red, '83 176
Bouillabaisse, Florida, '79 158
Bouillon, Redfish Court, '83 290; '84 93
Bouillon, Tomato, '83 8
Bourbon with Molasses Sauce, Burned,
    '95 17
Broccoli
    Broccoli Soup, '86 161, M194; '87 288
    Cheesy-Broccoli Soup, '86 258
    Chicken Soup, Broccoli-and-, '90 202
    Creamed Broccoli Soup, '85 24
    Cream of Broccoli Soup, '79 130;
        '80 188, M225; '82 314; '83 66;
        '86 259
    Cream-of-Broccoli Soup, '88 56
    Cream of Broccoli Soup, Light, '93 17
    Cream of Broccoli Soup, Mock, '85 288
    Creamy Broccoli Soup, '81 75; '82 13;
        '83 99; '91 307
    Easy Broccoli Soup, '81 307
    Fresh Broccoli Soup, '91 86
    Hot Broccoli Soup, '81 235; '83 44
    Swiss Soup, Broccoli-, '86 6
Butternut-and-Apple Soup, Creamed, '88 228
Butternut Squash Soup, '95 62
Cabbage Soup, '83 291; '85 88
Cabbage Soup, Sweet-and-Sour, '89 314
Cantaloupe Soup, '83 120; '88 160
Cantaloupe Soup, Chilled, '81 156
Cantaloupe Soup, Fresh, '84 190

SOUPS *(continued)*

Carrot
    Carrot Soup, '80 88; '89 146
    Cheesy Carrot Soup, '81 262
    Chilled Carrot-Mint Soup, '90 M168
    Cream of Carrot Soup, '81 307; '88 46;
       '91 69
    Cream Soup, Carrot, '90 210
    Creamy Carrot Soup, '92 218
    Curried Carrot Soup, '82 157
    Leek Soup, Carrot-, '86 34
    Orange Soup, Carrot-, '79 172
    Savory Carrot Soup, '84 107
    Tomato Soup, Cream of Carrot-and-,
       '94 176
Cauliflower and Caraway Soup, '82 264
Cauliflower and Watercress Soup, Cream of,
  '83 126
Cauliflower Soup, '90 211
Cauliflower Soup, Cream of, '87 M7; '88 12
Cauliflower Soup, Creamy, '82 76
Cauliflower Soup, Fresh, '84 279
Celery Soup, Burnet-, '84 107
Celery Soup, Cream of, '79 71; '90 210
Celery Soup, Light Cream-of-, '82 279
Cheese
    Anytime Soup, Cheesy, '81 307; '82 314;
       '83 66
    Bacon-Beer Cheese Soup, '87 M7
    Bacon-Topped Cheese Soup, '80 M224
    Beer-Cheese Soup, '84 246
    Broccoli Soup, Cheese-and-, '89 276
    Cream of Cheese Soup, '83 99
    Favorite Cheese Soup, Uncle Ed's,
       '94 228
    Gazebo Cheese Soup, '90 158
    Hearty Cheese Soup, '84 4
    Monterey Jack Cheese Soup, '81 112;
       '85 M211
    Velvet Soup, Cheese, '80 74; '92 193
    Vichyssoise, Velvety Roquefort, '83 223
Consommé aux Champignons, '79 48
Corn-and-Bourbon Soup, '92 194
Corned Beef Soup, '83 16
Corn Soup, '80 56; '85 243; '87 156
Corn Soup, Cream of, '90 210
Corn Soup, Favorite, '85 155
Corn Soup, Grilled, '87 121
Corn Soup, Pimiento-, '89 126
Cucumber-Buttermilk Soup, Chilled, '95 134
Cucumber Soup, Chilled, '79 144
Cucumber Soup, Cold, '79 130; '81 130
Cucumber Soup, Cold Minted, '86 34
Cucumber Soup, Cream of, '81 98
Cucumber Soup, Creamy, '80 171
Cucumber Soup, Dilled, '90 M167
Cucumber-Yogurt Soup, '82 157; '83 205
Curried Soup, '81 130
Dill Soup, Cold, '84 107
Egg Drop Soup, '83 21; '86 16
Egg-Drop Soup, '85 M12
Egg Flower Soup, '81 307; '82 313; '83 65
Eggplant Soup, Herbed, '90 173
Eggplant Supper Soup, '85 221
Fish Soup with Garlic Mayonnaise, Rich,
  '92 56
Fruit Soup, '87 98
Fruit Soup, Chilled Fresh, '88 160
Fruit Soup, Cold Fresh, '87 157
Fruit Soup Dessert, '79 172
Fruit Soup, Dried, '79 23

Fruit Soup, Swedish, '82 313; '83 65
Fruit Soup, Yogurt, '86 176
Gazpacho
    Blender Gazpacho, '85 93
    Chilled Gazpacho, '84 138
    Classy Gazpacho, '89 220
    Cool Gazpacho, '83 140
    Gazpacho, '79 172; '80 266; '81 98;
       '82 73; '84 112; '85 164; '91 94;
       '92 64; '93 215
    Herbed Gazpacho, '95 175
    Saucy Gazpacho, '82 157
    Secret Gazpacho, '93 161
    Shrimp-Cream Cheese Gazpacho, '94 137
    Spring Gazpacho, '81 112
    Summer Gazpacho, '84 181
    Tropical Gazpacho, '95 204
    Vegetable Gazpacho, Smoked, '93 156
Green Pepper Soup, '88 250
Greens Soup, Cream with, '94 277
Guadalajara Soup, '88 30
Ham-and-Bean Soup, Spicy, '94 322
Hamburger Soup, '80 263
Ham Soup, Hearty, '82 4
Harvest Soup, '79 101
Homemade Soup, '79 198
Hot-and-Sour Soup, '83 68; '91 50
Lemon-Egg Drop Soup, '93 81
Lemon Soup, '85 94
Lentil Soup, '83 292; '86 304; '91 28
Lentil Soup, Beefy, '87 282
Lime Soup, '88 31
Macaroni and Cheese Soup, '95 264
Melon Soup, '80 182
Melon Soup, Swirled, '87 162
Minestrone, '82 4
Minestrone, Dixie, '94 230
Minestrone Soup, '84 202; '86 144; '91 258
Minestrone Soup Mix, '91 258
Mushroom-Onion Soup, '80 25
Mushroom-Rice Soup, '90 32
Mushroom Soup, '82 286; '86 M73; '94 54
Mushroom Soup, Chunky, '88 12
Mushroom Soup, Cream of, '84 5;
  '85 93, 261
Mushroom Soup, Creamy, '79 243; '81 307
Mushroom Soup, Curried, '84 M89
Mushroom Soup, Elegant, '83 99
Mushroom Soup, Fresh, '81 109; '90 190
Mushroom Soup, Shrimp-, '85 87
Mustard Green Soup, Cream of, '93 280
Okra Soup, Charleston, '87 156
Onion
    Cheese Soup, Onion-, '87 81
    Classic Onion Soup, '84 65
    Creamy Onion Soup, '90 211
    Double-Cheese Onion Soup, '85 227
    Double Cheese-Topped Onion Soup,
       '79 49
    Easy Onion Soup, '85 226
    French Onion-Beef Soup, '87 54
    French Onion Soup, '79 49; '80 188;
       '83 126; '85 226; '86 M212; '90 31;
       '93 246
    French Onion Soup, Shortcut, '85 M328
    French Onion Soup, Toasty, '81 306
    Green Onion Soup, '84 112
    Green Onion Soup, Creamed, '83 82
    Mushroom-Onion Soup, '80 25
    Oven-Browned Onion Soup, '79 49
    Potato Soup, Creamy Onion-and-, '92 51
    Rich Onion Soup, '85 226
    Superb Onion Soup, '81 86

Pea-and-Watercress Soup, '93 162
Peach-Plum Soup, '87 157
Peach Soup, '83 120, 180
Peanut Butter Soup, '89 28
Peanut Butter Soup, Cream of, '84 29
Peanut Soup, '87 184
Peanut Soup, Chilled, '79 130
Peanut Soup, Cream of, '92 193; '93 288
Peanut Soup, Creamy, '79 50
Pea Soup, Chilled, '84 181
Pea Soup, Cold Curried, '91 120
Pea Soup, Country-Style, '86 267
Pea Soup, Cream, '90 211
Pea Soup Élégante, '79 53
Pea Soup, Fresh, '86 181
Pea Soup, Peppery, '82 271
Pea Soup, Spring, '88 M96
Pepper Soup, Spicy, '93 98
Pepper Soup, Sweet, '93 277
Plum Soup, '85 107
Plum Soup, Chilled Purple, '79 162
Potato
    Asparagus-Potato Soup, '85 23
    Bacon Soup, Potato-, '84 M38
    Baked Potato Soup, '91 311; '92 26
    Beet Soup, Potato-, '88 156
    Carrot Soup, Potato-, '88 297
    Celery-and-Potato Soup, '84 279
    Chilled Cucumber-Potato Soup, '85 93
    Cold Potato-Cucumber Soup, '88 160
    Cream of Potato Soup, '80 M224;
       '82 21
    Cream of Potato Soup, Golden, '86 302
    Creamy Potato Soup, '81 19, 98;
       '84 112
    Easy Potato Soup, '92 17
    Holiday Potato Soup, '79 236
    Leek-and-Potato Soup, '84 112
    Pea Soup, Potato-, '94 90
    Potato Soup, '82 278; '83 292;
       '92 263
    Sausage-Potato Soup, '80 25
    Special Potato Soup, '82 3
    Subtle Potato Potage, '80 78
    Sweet Potato-and-Sausage Soup,
       '95 23
    Sweet Potato Soup, '88 250
    Sweet Potato Velouté, '94 238
    Three-Potato Soup, '86 16
    Wild Rice Soup, Cheesy Potato-and-,
       '89 16
    Yogurt Soup, Potato-, '92 217
Pot-of-Gold Soup, '86 259
Poultry
    Chicken-Almond Cream Soup, '92 21
    Chicken-and-Rice Soup, '88 236
    Chicken, Artichoke, and Mushroom
      Soup, '92 324
    Chicken Broth, Easy Microwave,
      '90 M167
    Chicken Enchilada Soup, '86 22
    Chicken, Ham, and Oyster Soup,
      '79 198
    Chicken Noodle Soup, '80 264; '95 45
    Chicken-Noodle Soup, Chunky, '88 12
    Chicken Soup, '81 98
    Chicken Soup, Cream of, '85 243
    Chicken Soup, Creamy Asparagus-
      and-, '95 82
    Chicken Soup, Curried, '86 34
    Chicken Soup, Homemade, '82 34
    Chicken Soup, Mexican, '84 234
    Chicken Soup, Quick, '86 M72

Chicken Soup, Roasted Pepper-and-,
'90 58
Chicken-Vegetable Soup, '88 18
Stock, Light Poultry, '90 31
Turkey-Barley Soup, '91 312
Turkey Carcass Soup, '86 284
Turkey-Noodle Soup, '91 312
Turkey-Noodle Soup Mix, '89 330
Turkey-Rice Soup, '90 89
Turkey Soup, Curried, '86 332
Turkey Soup, Williamsburg, '90 287
Turkey-Vegetable Soup, '84 4; '88 264;
'91 312
Pumpkin-Corn Soup with Ginger-Lime
Cream, '95 227
Pumpkin-Pear Soup, '92 234
Pumpkin Soup, '79 48
Pumpkin Soup, Cream of, '93 234
Raspberry Soup, Chilled, '81 130
Red Pepper Soup, Chilled Sweet, '93 69
Sausage and Okra Soup, '80 209
Sausage Soup, Italian, '84 235
Sausage Soup with Tortellini, Italian, '88 46
Sausage-Zucchini Soup, Italian, '84 4
Seafood
Cioppino, Gulf Coast, '94 102
Clam Florentine Soup, '85 23
Crabmeat Soup, '84 123
Crab Soup, Beaufort, '92 238
Crab Soup, Cream of, '88 302
Crab Soup, Creamy, '80 M224
Crab Soup, Elegant, '80 188
Crab Soup, Fresh Corn-and-, '92 183
Crab Soup, Old-Fashioned, '90 71
Crab Soup, Plantation, '92 237
Crab Soup, Quick, '84 279
Crab Soup, Steamboat's Cream of,
'81 127
Lobster Soup, Spicy Thai, '94 102
Mussel Soup, '93 259
Oyster-and-Artichoke Soup, Louisiana,
'92 81
Oyster-and-Mushroom Soup, '87 39
Oyster-Cheese Soup, '84 213
Oyster Soup, '79 228; '83 211
Oyster-Turnip Soup, '94 328
Scallop Broth with Black Beans and
Cilantro, Southwestern, '87 123
She-Crab Soup with Marigold, '79 32
Shrimp-and-Corn Soup, '84 88
Shrimp Enchilada Soup, '94 103
Shrimp Soup, Okra-and-, '94 323
Stock, Seafood, '94 238
Sherry-Berry Dessert Soup, '91 180
Shiitake Soup, Cream of, '95 265
Sopa de Lima, '79 211
Southwest Soup, '86 255
Spinach Soup, Cream of, '82 38; '90 211
Spinach Soup, Hot Cream of, '84 29
Spinach Soup, Oriental, '83 151
Spinach Soup with Meatballs, Italian, '92 331
Split Pea and Frankfurter Soup, '79 64
Split Pea Soup, '88 235; '89 17; '94 322
Squash Soup, '94 134
Squash Soup, Chilled, '92 173
Squash Soup, Cold Cream of, '81 130
Squash Soup, Cream of, '81 246
Squash Soup, Perky, '85 20
Stock, Beef, '95 17
Stock, Brown Meat, '90 31

Stock, Chicken, '95 18
Stock, Fish, '95 19
Stock, Homemade Fish, '92 237
Stock, Light Poultry, '90 31
Stock, Quick Full-Bodied, '95 17
Stock, Seafood, '94 238
Stock, Vegetable, '90 31
Stock, Venison, '94 302
Strawberry-Banana Soup, '86 181
Strawberry Soup, '88 160
Strawberry Soup, Cold, '82 157
Strawberry Soup Supreme, '81 M144
Summer Squash Soup, '83 99; '84 193;
'85 136
Sweet Red Pepper Soup, Cream of Roasted,
'95 65
Taco Soup, '94 225
Tamale Soup, '95 213
Tomatillo Soup with Crunchy Jicama, '92 245
Tomato
Appetizer Tomato Soup, '86 258
Celery Soup, Tomato-, '83 M58
Chilled Tomato Soup, '82 155
Cioppino, Gulf Coast, '94 102
Cold Tomato Soup, '88 160
Consommé, Tomato, '88 250
Cream of Tomato Soup with Parmesan
Cheese, '86 161
Cream Soup, Refreshing Tomato,
'79 172
Creamy Tomato Soup, '83 267; '86 258
Dried Tomato-Cream Soup, '90 203
Easy Tomato Soup, '84 14
Fire Water, '80 188
Fresh Tomato Soup, '83 140
Hot Tomato Juice Soup, '86 302
Iced Tomato Soup, '79 170
Mexican Tomato Soup, Icy-Spicy,
'90 155
Plus, Tomato Soup, '88 170
Pumpkin-Tomato Soup, '86 291
Rice Soup, Tomato-and-, '85 24
Savory Tomato Soup, '94 91
Sour Cream-Topped Tomato Soup,
'80 246
Summer Tomato Soup, '79 130
Tomato Potage, '79 250
Tomato Soup, '81 236; '83 44; '89 217
Vegetable Soup, Tomato-, '81 M177;
'86 9
Tortilla Soup, '88 31, 245; '90 201;
'93 197, 274; '94 136
Tortilla Soup, Spicy, '90 32; '93 108
Turnip Soup, '92 217
Turnip Soup, Creamy, '84 279
Turtle Soup, '92 92
Turtle Soup au Sherry, '80 56
Veal-Vermicelli Soup with Quenelles, '94 14
Vegetable
Bean Soup, Vegetable-, '83 317
Beef-and-Barley Vegetable Soup, '89 31
Beef Soup, Hearty Vegetable-, '84 102
Beef Soup, Spicy Vegetable-, '88 11
Beef Soup, Vegetable-, '88 296
Beefy Vegetable Soup, '79 113; '84 M38
Beefy Vegetable Soup, Quick, '80 25
Broth, Savory Vegetable, '81 230
Burger Soup, Vegetable-, '82 6
Cheese Soup, Creamy Vegetable-,
'81 244
Cheese Soup, Creamy Vegetable, '83 230
Cheese Soup, Vegetable-, '89 15
Cheesy Vegetable Soup, '80 73

Chili Vegetable Soup, '94 120
Chunky Vegetable Soup, '89 M283
Clear Vegetable Soup, '79 130
Cold Garden Vegetable Soup, '84 197
Down-Home Vegetable Soup, '90 32
Garden Harvest Soup, Italian, '90 M167
Garden Soup, '85 241
Garden Vegetable Soup, '83 140;
'86 160
Hearty Vegetable Soup, '80 26
Leek-Vegetable Soup, '86 304
Light Vegetable Soup, '84 280
Marvelous Vegetable Soup, '82 3
Mix, Vegetable Soup, '84 148
Old-Fashioned Vegetable Soup, '86 304
Quick Vegetable Soup, '79 190;
'85 24, 32
Quick Veggie Soup, '91 31
Spicy Vegetable Soup, '79 198; '93 293
Stock, Vegetable, '90 31
Vegetable Soup, '80 128; '84 148;
'85 106; '86 187; '87 83, 123;
'88 266; '93 157
Venison Soup, '82 216
Vichyssoise, '86 181
Vichyssoise, Cucumber, '94 90
Vichyssoise, Velvety Roquefort, '83 223
Watercress-and-Leek Soup, '86 161
Watercress Soup, '79 82; '88 104
Zucchini Soup, '82 104; '84 181; '86 181;
'89 14
Zucchini Soup, Chilled, '87 90
Zucchini Soup, Cold, '85 265; '92 64
Zucchini Soup, Cream of, '83 99
Zucchini Soup, Creamy, '83 140
Zucchini Soup, Dilled, '90 88
Zucchini Soup, Watercress-, '91 72
Zucchini Soup with Cilantro, '93 130
SPAGHETTI
Bacon Spaghetti, '86 213; '87 82
Black Bean Spaghetti, '92 217
Black-Eyed Pea Spaghetti, '81 7
Carbonara, Chorizo, '94 230
Carbonara, Salmon, '83 43
Carbonara, Spaghetti, '85 34; '87 167
Carbonara, Spaghetti alla, '81 38
Casseroles
Asparagus-Spaghetti Casserole, '80 77
Beef Casserole, Spaghetti and, '79 129
Casserole Spaghetti, '95 132
Chicken-Spaghetti Casserole, '84 15
Florentine Bake, Cheesy, '95 131
Ham-and-Turkey Spaghetti, '95 19
Italian Casserole, '90 238
Pork Spaghetti Bake, '81 11
Spaghetti Casserole, '84 241
Tetrazzini, Chicken, '79 268; '80 75;
'83 288
Tetrazzini, Ham, '82 77; '84 241
Tetrazzini, Herbed Turkey, '86 47
Cheese Spaghetti, Three-, '83 105
Chicken Spaghetti, '83 105; '87 221
Chicken-Vegetable Spaghetti, '92 281
Chili-Spaghetti, Herbed, '84 222
Clam Sauce, Pasta with, '84 291
Crawfish Spaghetti, '85 104
Easy Spaghetti, '83 M317; '84 72; '92 66
Etcetera, Spaghetti, '83 105
Ham Spaghetti Skillet, '83 283
Herbal Dressing, Spaghetti with, '86 158
Hot Dog and Spaghetti Skillet, '83 144
Italian Spaghetti, '81 38
Italian Spaghetti, Real, '81 233

SPAGHETTI (continued)

Lemon-Garlic Pasta, '95 181
Meatballs, Spaghetti-and-Herb, '84 75
Meatballs, Spaghetti with, '81 38
Meaty Spaghetti, '82 19
Mushrooms, Spicy Spaghetti with, '85 2
Parmesan Noodles, Cheesy, '83 M7
Parsley and Walnut Sauce, Spaghetti with, '80 30
Parsley, Spaghetti with, '80 236
Peanut Sauce, Pasta with, '95 252
Pepperoni Pasta, '83 105
Pepperoni Spaghetti, Quick, '88 40
Pie, Spaghetti, '81 M32
Pie, Spaghetti-Ham, '93 19
Pie, Weeknight Spaghetti, '95 312
Pizzazz, Spaghetti with, '80 85
Pot Roast with Spaghetti, '80 59
Salad, Chicken-Spaghetti, '90 146
Salad, Mediterranean, '95 132
Salad, Spaghetti, '82 277; '84 205
Sauces
    Beer Spaghetti Sauce, '85 13
    Grisanti Spaghetti Sauce, '94 194
    Herbed Spaghetti Sauce, '85 13
    Italian Tomato Sauce for Spaghetti, '81 134
    Meat Sauce, Quick Spaghetti and, '94 64
    Thick Spaghetti Sauce, '84 118
    Turkey Spaghetti Sauce, '85 13
    Vegetable Sauce, Pasta with, '83 163
    Zucchini Sauce, Spaghetti with, '81 38
Sausage Spaghetti, '83 160
Sausage Spaghetti Dinner, '79 194
Shrimp and Pasta, '91 207
Shrimp-and-Vegetable Spaghetti, '91 170
Shrimp Spaghetti with Black Olives, '85 13
Szechuan Noodle Toss, '91 30
Thick-and-Spicy Spaghetti, '83 287
Tomatoes and Garlic, Spaghetti with, '91 47
Tomato Pasta, Italian, '93 201
Veal and Peppers, Spaghetti with, '81 201; '82 14
Veal Spaghetti, '84 276
Vegetable Sauce, Pasta with, '83 163
Vegetables, Spaghetti with, '85 67
Vegetables with Spaghetti, Fresh, '86 257
Vegetables with Spaghetti, Sautéed, '81 89
Zucchini Spaghetti, '83 160
Zucchini Spaghetti, Italian, '85 2
SPICE. *See also* **SEASONINGS.**
Balls, Decorative Ribbon-Spice, '84 325
Blend, Five-Spice Powder, '92 121
Dry Spices, '90 120
Mix, Mulled Wine Spice, '85 266
Mix, Tex-Mex Spice, '94 135
Rub, Moroccan Spice, '95 231
SPINACH
Appetizers
    Bread, Spinach, '83 121
    Cheese Bites, Spinach-, '94 23
    Cheesecake, Spinach-Mushroom, '92 326
    con Queso, Easy Spinach, '88 101
    Cups, Cottage Cheese-Spinach, '87 190
    Dip, Cheesy Spinach, '82 59
    Dip, Creamy Spinach, '88 132
    Dip, Hot Spinach, '80 249
    Dip, Hot Spinach-Cheese, '89 48
    Dip in Cabbage, Spinach, '82 155
    Dip, Spinach, '80 86; '86 159; '87 25, 214; '93 324

Filling, Spinach, '95 316
Madeleine in Chafing Dish, Spinach, '85 319
Mushrooms, Spinach-Stuffed, '86 81; '88 131, M261; '89 M133
Pâté with Spinach and Cream, Pork, '83 224
Phyllo-Spinach Triangles, '87 53
Phyllo Triangles, Spinach-Filled, '84 52
Phyllo Triangles, Spinach-Ricotta, '88 212
Pinwheels, Spinach-Tenderloin, '89 M118
Puffs, Cheese-and-Spinach, '87 246
Puffs, Spinach, '95 316
Puffs, Spinach-Artichoke-Tomato, '95 284
Quichelets, Spinach, '87 67
Quiche, No-Crust Spinach, '90 142
Quiches, Miniature Spinach, '82 38
Sauce, Herbed Green, '86 244
Spread, Parmesan-Spinach, '93 55
Spread, Savory Spinach, '82 180
Spread, Spinach, '88 132
Spread, Spinach-Bacon, '92 M310
Squares, Spinach, '88 131
Strudels, Spinach, '93 249
Supreme, Layered Spinach, '82 38
Tarts, Spinach, '82 249
Terrine, Layered Salmon-and-Spinach, '84 132
Wontons, Spinach, '83 74
Apples, Onions, and Pears over Spinach, Sautéed, '94 212
Baked Spinach, Gourmet, '82 180
Bisque, Spinach-Potato, '86 66
Bread, Spinach, '83 121; '87 144
Calzones, Spinach-and-Cheese, '95 310
Casseroles
    Artichoke Bake, Spinach-, '95 48
    Artichoke Casserole, Spinach-, '88 252; '93 44
    Artichoke Casserole, Spinach and, '81 103
    Beef Casserole, Spinach and, '79 192
    Beef-Macaroni Casserole, Spinach-, '83 313
    Cannelloni, '85 60; '92 17
    Celery Casserole, Spinach-and-, '84 294
    Cheese Bake, Spinach-, '88 10
    Cheese Casserole, Spinach-, '83 216; '89 64
    Cheesy Florentine Bake, '95 131
    Cheesy Spinach Casserole, '81 263
    Company Spinach, '89 280
    Cottage Cheese-and-Spinach Casserole, '84 77
    Crab and Spinach Casserole, Creamy, '80 3
    Creamy Spinach Bake, '89 68
    Creamy Spinach Casserole, '86 111
    Delight, Spinach, '84 M144
    Egg Casserole, Spinach and, '82 270
    Enchiladas, Chicken-and-Spinach, '91 222
    Enchiladas, Spinach, '83 60; '84 14
    Florentine Casserole, Turkey-and-Shrimp, '92 122
    Florentine, Chicken-and-Shrimp, '89 64
    Florentine, Creamy Lasagna, '91 94
    Florentine, Jumbo Seashells, '79 6
    Florentine, Lasagna, '88 196
    Florentine, Salmon, '83 43

Florentine, Turkey, '88 264
Lasagna, Cheesy Spinach, '80 32; '83 204
Lasagna Florentine, Chicken, '95 158
Lasagna, Spinach, '79 25; '81 243
Lasagna, Spinach-Bean, '92 96
Manicotti, Spinach, '82 199
Manicotti, Spinach-Stuffed, '88 255
Oyster-and-Spinach Casserole, '83 34; '84 44
Parmesan Casserole, Spinach-, '82 281; '83 32
Parmesan, Spinach, '93 72
Puff, Spinach-Cheese, '84 96
Rice Bake, Green, '79 43
Rice, Spinach, '85 146
Ricotta Bake, Spinach-, '88 97
Roll-Ups, Ham and Spinach, '81 143
Scalloped Spinach with Cheese, '79 8
Shells, Spinach-Stuffed, '85 60
Spinach Casserole, '79 265; '91 31
Supreme, Spinach, '84 77
Surprise, Spinach, '82 42
Turkey-Spinach Casserole, '84 71
Cheesecake, Spinach Pesto, '90 175
Cheesy Topped Spinach, '84 85
Chicken Breasts, Fried Spinach-Stuffed, '88 206
Chicken, Garlic-Spinach, '92 56
Chicken in Puff Pastry, Spinach-Stuffed, '92 125
Chicken Rolls, Spinach-Stuffed, '86 248
Chinese Spinach, '79 179; '82 39
Chinese Spinach Sauté, '83 208
Cornbread, Spinach, '95 49
Creamed Spinach, '81 54; '86 110
Creamed Spinach in Pastry Shells, '89 280
Creamed Spinach with Noodles, '84 29
Creamy Spinach, '85 289
Crêpes, Spinach-Ricotta, '81 52
Eggs Sardou, '92 93
Enchiladas, Spinach, '83 60; '84 14
Filling, Spinach, '79 34
Filling, Spinach-Mushroom, '80 215
Filling, Spinach-Ricotta, '81 53
Florentine, Baked Eggs, '86 M12
Florentine, Cheesy Trout, '85 53
Florentine, Chicken, '93 107
Florentine Crêpe Cups, '89 44
Florentine Crêpe Pie, '79 34
Florentine, Crêpes, '80 190
Florentine, Eggs, '79 39; '83 56
Florentine, Fish, '86 35
Florentine in Parchment, Fish, '87 22
Florentine Sauce, '93 48
Florentine, Stuffed Mushrooms, '82 270
Florentine-Style Eggs, '82 38
Florentine with Mushroom Sauce, Chicken, '87 250
Frittata, Spinach, '81 53
Garden, The, '83 134
Greek Sunburst, '94 245
Grits, Garlicky Ham-and-Spinach, '94 177
Lemon Spinach, Creamy, '82 302
Lemon Spinach with Feta, '85 190
Loaves, Spinach-Oyster, '84 213
Marinara on Beds of Spinach and Orzo, '93 320
Mushrooms, Spinach with, '80 19
Nests, Baked Eggs in Spinach, '82 70
Noodles, Chicken and Spinach, '82 19
Omelet, Spinach-Cheese, '83 119
Parmesan Spinach, Savory, '85 68

SPINACH (continued)

Pasta
  Bow Tie Pasta, Spinach and Mushrooms
    with, '95 341
  Cannelloni, '85 60; '92 17
  Fantastic, Spinach, '93 173
  Fettuccine and Spinach, '88 90
  Fettuccine, Easy Chicken with Spinach,
    '88 89
  Fettuccine, Fresh Spinach, '83 60
  Fettuccine, Spinach, '82 179
  Fettuccine with Mustard Greens, Spinach,
    '94 247
  Fettuccine with Spinach Sauce, '84 329
  Green Pasta with Shrimp-Mushroom
    Italienne, '79 170
  Linguine with Spinach, '91 30
  Pesto and Pasta, Spinach-Peanut,
    '93 212
  Pesto-Cheese Pasta Bites, '87 251
  Pesto-Pasta, Spinach, '91 314
  Pie, Spinach-Pasta, '85 286
  Sauce, Spinach Pasta, '93 71
  Shells, Spinach-Stuffed, '87 20
  Tortellini with Tomato Sauce, Spinach,
    '88 302
  Verde, Pasta, '84 201
  Vermicelli with Fresh Spinach Sauce,
    '89 256
Peppers, Spinach-Stuffed, '82 180
Pesto, Orange Roughy with Spinach,
  '88 M192
Pesto, Squash Stuffed with Spinach, '89 M133
Pie, Greek Spinach, '85 59
Pie Pan Spinach, '94 195
Pie, Spinach, '82 191; '88 56
Pie, Spinach-Pasta, '85 286
Pie with Muenster Crust, Spinach, '95 48
Pinwheels, Flank Steak-and-Spinach, '95 56
Pitas, Spinach-Walnut, '87 202; '88 43
Pork, Spinach-and-Herb Stuffed, '89 193
Pork Tenderloin, Spinach-and-Bacon Stuffed,
  '94 81
Potatoes, Black-Eyed Pea-Spinach-Stuffed,
  '95 22
Quiche, Cheesy Spinach, '81 228
Quiche, Crustless Spinach, '84 235
Quiche, Greek Spinach, '86 10
Quiche, No-Crust Spinach, '90 142
Quiches, Individual Spinach, '86 38
Quiche, Spinach, '81 44; '85 49; '91 204
Quiche, Spinach-Mushroom, '81 M74
Ring au Fromage, Spinach, '79 8
Roll, Feta Cheese-Spinach, '91 22
Rolls, Spinach-Ham, '88 78
Rollups, Chicken and Spinach, '80 90;
  '82 M68
Roll-Ups, Ham and Spinach, '81 143
Rollups, Spinach-and-Ham, '86 84
Salad Dressing, Spinach, '83 181; '93 250
Salads
  Apple-Onion Vinaigrette, Spinach Salad
    with, '94 276
  Apple Salad, Spinach-, '90 89; '92 13
  Apricot Salad, Spinach-, '94 63
  Arranged Spinach Salad, '91 210;
    '92 160
  Bacon Dressing, Spinach Salad with Hot,
    '82 211
  Bacon Salad, Spinach and, '81 143
  Beet Salad, Spinach-, '83 227

Blue Cheese Salad, Spinach-, '82 166
Blues, Spinach Salad with the, '95 66
Chicken-and-Spinach Tossed Salad,
  '83 157
Chili-Lime Dressing, Spinach Salad with,
  '94 63
Citrus Dressing, Spinach Salad with,
  '88 133
Citrus Spinach Salad, '90 59
Combination Spinach Salad, '85 327;
  '86 22
Creamy Spinach Salad, '83 60
Crisp Spinach Salad with Creamy
  Dressing, '83 81
Crunchy Spinach Salad, '80 147; '81 225
Curry Spinach Salad, '80 242
Dijon Spinach Salad, '89 282
Dried Tomato Vinaigrette, Spinach Salad
  with, '93 272
Easy Spinach Salad, '91 249
Enoki Salad, Spinach-, '89 62
Festive Spinach Salad, '80 247
French Spinach Salad, '79 8
Fresh Spinach Salad, '82 73; '83 240;
  '84 15, 77; '86 130
Fresh Spinach Salad Delight, '80 146
Fresh Spinach with Spicy Dressing,
  '80 55
Garden Salad Toss, '81 9
Garlic-Ginger Vinaigrette Dressing,
  Spinach Salad with, '92 195
Green Spinach Salad, '79 142
Honey Dressing, Spinach Salad with,
  '90 16
Kiwifruit Salad, Spinach-, '87 305
Lamb Salad, Spinach-, '85 58
Layered Salad, Make-Ahead, '81 296
Layered Spinach-Lettuce Salad, '84 266
Layered Spinach Salad, '80 5; '89 163
Mandarin Spinach Salad, '85 163
Minted Spinach Salad, '94 63
Mushroom Salad, Spinach and, '80 112
Onion Salad Bowl, Spinach-and-,
  '81 157
Orange Dressing, Spinach Salad with,
  '87 187
Orange Salad, Spinach-and-, '86 15
Orange-Spinach Salad, '83 316; '84 16
Oriental Spinach Salad, '82 23
Oysters and Red Wine Vinaigrette,
  Spinach Salad with, '94 327
Pears, Spinach Salad with Sautéed,
  '94 237
Pecan Salad, Spinach-, '89 128
Pickled Spinach, '81 69
Poppy Seed Dressing, Spinach Salad with,
  '91 210; '92 160
Pork-and-Spinach Salad, Mandarin,
  '88 M126
Raspberry Cream Dressing, Spinach Salad
  with, '94 321
Rice Salad, Spinach-, '94 63
Romaine-Spinach Salad, '89 123
Russian Dressing, Spinach Salad with,
  '79 144
Salmon-Spinach Salad, '87 145
Sesame Salad, Spinach-, '91 211; '92 160
Sesame Spinach Salad, '90 292
Southern Spinach Salad, '80 55
Special Spinach Salad, '80 78
Spinach Salad, '82 102; '86 302; '87 62;
  '88 299; '92 281, 341; '93 46, 65
Springtime Spinach Salad, '81 114

Sprout Salad, Fresh Spinach-, '82 281;
  '83 42
Strawberry-Spinach Salad, '91 169;
  '93 168
Sun-Dried Tomato Salad, Spinach and,
  '93 250
Supreme, Spinach Salad, '79 243
Sweet-Sour Spinach Salad, '85 M112
Tropical Spinach Salad, '90 231
Twist, Spinach-Mustard, '86 209
Vinaigrette Spinach, '79 8
Wilted Spinach Salad, '81 M4; '89 123;
  '91 210; '92 160; '93 125
Zesty Spinach Salad, '79 88
Sandwiches, Fresh Spinach, '85 59
Sandwich, Grilled Spinach Fondue, '94 171
Sauce, Emerald, '90 63
Sauce, Fettuccine with Spinach, '84 329
Sauce, Herbed Green, '86 244
Sauce, Spinach Pesto, '93 59
Sautéed Spinach, '93 250
Sauté, Fresh Spinach, '93 55
Soufflé, Cheesy Spinach, '81 53
Soufflé Deluxe, Spinach, '79 8
Soufflé Roll, Spinach, '80 215
Soufflé, Spinach, '79 73; '81 304; '84 78;
  '85 248; '86 108
Soup, Cream of Spinach, '82 38; '90 211
Soup, Cream with Greens, '94 277
Soup, Hot Cream of Spinach, '84 29
Soup, Oriental Spinach, '83 151
Soup with Meatballs, Italian Spinach, '92 331
Spanakópita, '86 58
Squares, Spinach, '95 49
Squash, Spinach-Stuffed, '82 4; '91 14
Stir-Fry Spinach, '81 182
Strudels, Spinach, '93 249
Supreme, Layered Spinach, '82 38
Tart Milan, '87 70
Tenderloin, Spinach-Stuffed, '89 311
Terrine, Layered Salmon-and-Spinach,
  '84 132
Timbales, Spinach, '84 29
Timbales, Spinach-Rice, '88 271
Tomatoes, Baked Spinach, '90 92
Tomatoes, Spinach-Stuffed, '89 203; '93 281
Tomatoes, Spinach-Stuffed Baked, '86 14
Tomatoes, Spinach-Topped, '88 265;
  '94 321
Turnovers, Salmon-Spinach, '83 44
Zucchini Boats with Spinach, '82 252

SPREADS. *See also* **APPETIZERS/SPREADS.**
Aioli, Shortcut, '93 157
Ambrosia Spread, '92 50
Apple-Date Spread, '91 231; '92 67
Beef Spread, Hot, '83 50
Braunschweiger-Onion Spread, '79 82
Bread Spread, Party, '82 161
Caraway Spread, '85 276
Caviar Spread, Creamy, '92 58

SPREADS *(continued)*

Cheese
    Almond Cheese Spread, '87 292
    Aloha Spread, '83 93
    Bacon-Cheese Spread, '83 241
    Beer Cheese Spread, '81 69; '94 123
    Beer-Cheese Spread, '85 69
    Beer Spread, Cheesy, '87 196
    Blue Cheese Spread, '95 79
    Boursin Cheese Spread, Buttery, '94 301
    Boursin Cheese Spread, Garlic, '94 301
    Brie Spread, Apricot, '86 275
    Cheese Spread, '86 135
    Chile-Cheese Spread, '86 297
    Chili Cheese Spread, '93 242
    Chocolate Cheese Spread, '87 292
    Chocolate Chip Cheese Loaves, '91 299;
        '92 264
    Coconut-Cranberry Cheese Spread,
        '92 328
    Confetti Cheese Spread, '84 256
    Cottage Cheese Spread, '87 107
    Cream Cheese-Olive Spread, '82 35
    Cream Cheese Spread, Apricot-, '82 161;
        '87 158
    Cream Cheese Spread, Caviar-, '84 256
    Cream Cheese Spread, Cucumber and,
        '82 140
    Cream Cheese Spread, Deviled, '81 235
    Cream Cheese Spread, Herb-, '83 24
    Cream Cheese Spread, Nutty, '89 327
    Cream Cheese Spread, Peachy, '90 M215
    Cream Cheese Spread, Pear-, '93 80
    Cream Cheese Spread, Pineapple-, '82 35
    Dried Tomato-Cheese Spread, '90 204
    Edam-Sherry Spread, '84 257
    Fruit and Cheese Spread, '81 245
    Fruit-and-Cheese Spread, Nutty, '87 246
    German Cheese Spread, '79 82
    Gouda Cheese Spread, '90 36
    Green Onion-Cheese Spread, '92 24
    Gruyère-Apple Spread, '81 160
    Hawaiian Cheese Spread, '87 158
    Herb-Cheese Spread, '91 124
    Herbed Cheese, '88 152
    Herbed Cheese Spread, '87 247
    Horseradish Spread, Cheese-, '84 222
    Italian Spread, '85 135
    Jalapeño-Cheese Spread, '82 248
    Make-Ahead Cheese Spread, '93 324
    Mexican Cheese Spread, '90 119
    Olive Spread, Cheese-, '79 82
    Orange Cheese Spread, '87 292
    Pimiento Cheese Spread, '82 35; '83 93;
        '86 127
    Pimiento Cheese Spread, Creamy,
        '92 159
    Pimiento Cheese Spread, Garlic, '79 58
    Pimiento Cheese Spread, Low-Calorie,
        '85 215
    Pineapple-Cheese Spread, '86 126;
        '91 167
    Raisin-Nut Spread, '95 79
    Sandwich Spread, Benedictine, '80 299
    Sandwich Spread, Chunky, '82 140
    Sombrero Spread, '87 111
    Strawberry Spread, '95 79
    Sweet Cheese Spread, Creamy, '79 264
    Sweet 'n' Sour Spread, '86 184
    Swiss Cheese Spread, '90 60
    Tipsy Cheese Spread, '80 150

Tomato-Cheese Spread, '81 157
Tomato-Cheese Spread, Fiery, '87 196
Zesty Cheese Spread, '82 140
Zippy Cheese Spread, '85 4
Cherry Spread, '93 309
Chicken Salad Party Spread, '88 M8
Chicken Spread, Festive, '87 158
Chicken Spread, Low-Fat, '82 290
Chicken Spread, Tasty, '84 193
Chive-Mustard Spread, '91 12
Chutney Spread, Curried, '89 283
Coconut-Pineapple Spread, '93 309
Corned Beef Spread, '87 196
Cranberry Salsa with Sweet Potato Chips,
    '93 332
Curry Spread, '93 159
Date Spread, Breakfast, '84 7
Date-Walnut Spread, '87 292
Deviled Delight, '83 130
Egg Salad Spread, '86 127
Egg Salad Spread, Cottage-, '82 146
Egg, Sour Cream, and Caviar Spread, '85 279
Fish Spread, Smoked, '92 305
Fruit Spread, '85 135
Fruit Spread, Sugarless, '84 60
Garlic Puree, Roasted, '92 55
Garlic Spread, '85 111
Ham-and-Egg Spread, '79 59
Ham and Pimiento Spread, '80 285; '81 56
Ham Spread, '86 126
Ham Spread, Buttery, '95 93
Ham Spread, Cold, '82 248
Ham Spread, Country, '87 8
Ham Spread, Deviled, '79 81
Ham Spread, Hawaiian, '87 106
Honey-Nut Spread, '87 157
Honey Spread, '81 229
Horseradish-Ham Spread, '91 167
Horseradish, Homemade, '92 25
Horseradish Spread, '90 243
Liver Spread, '89 161
Liver Spread, Sherried, '80 86
Mustard Spread, '86 105
Olive Spread, Creamy, '81 290
Olive Spread, Tomatoes with, '85 114
Orange Toast Topper, '79 36
Peanut Butter Spread, '92 21
Pineapple Sandwich Spread, '84 166
Raisin Spread, Creamy, '90 36
Raisin Spread, Peachy-, '86 326
Relish Spread, Creamy, '93 217
Salad Dressing Spread, '82 140
Seafood
    Clam Spread, Creamy, '91 274
    Crabmeat-Horseradish Spread, '90 292
    Crabmeat Spread, '79 81
    Crabmeat Spread, Layered, '83 127
    Crab Soufflé Spread, '85 4
    Crab Spread, '93 167
    Crab Spread, Baked, '80 86
    Crab Spread, Superb, '81 255
    Oyster Spread, Smoked, '91 64
    Salmon-and-Horseradish Spread, '87 146
    Salmon Spread, '81 149
    Salmon Spread, Smoked, '84 324
    Sandwich Spread, Seafood, '82 87
    Seafood Spread, '86 M58; '87 146
    Shrimp-Cucumber Spread, '79 81
    Shrimp Spread, '81 306; '85 135;
        '87 111; '93 205
    Shrimp Spread, Chunky, '85 300
    Shrimp Spread, Curried, '87 158
    Shrimp Spread, Tempting, '79 57

    Shrimp Spread, Zippy, '90 36
    Tuna Tapenade, '95 127
Spinach-Bacon Spread, '92 M310
Spinach Spread, '88 132
Spinach Spread, Savory, '82 180
Strawberry Spread, Light, '85 55
Sweet 'n' Sour Spread, '86 184
Trout Spread, Smoked, '84 47
Tuna Spread, '83 174; '91 305
Tuna Spread, Chunky, '89 147
Turkey Party Spread, '83 282
Turkey Spread, Curried, '92 16
Vegetable
    Antipasto Spread, '81 25
    Artichoke-Crab Spread, Hot, '85 81
    Artichoke Hearts with Caviar, '79 142
    Artichoke Spread, Hot, '79 110
    Broccamoli Curry Spread, '88 55
    Carrot Spread, Nutty, '94 123
    Cucumber Spread, '79 295; '80 31;
        '93 158
    Eggplant Spread, '86 278
    Egg Spread, Vegetable-, '87 106
    Garden Spread, '86 135
    Green Onion-Cheese Spread, '92 24
    Green Tomato Sandwich Spread, '95 172
    Guacamole Spread, '90 119
    Hearts of Palm Spread, '90 293
    Mushroom Spread, Hot, '81 190
    Party Spread, Vegetable, '84 166
    Pepper Spread, Roasted, '94 123
    Radish Spread, Fresh, '84 166
    Sandwich Spread, Benedictine, '80 299
    Sandwich Spread, Home-Style, '80 179
    Sandwich Spread, Vegetable, '83 174;
        '85 135
    Tomato Spread, '94 123
    Vegetable Spread, '90 144
    Watercress Spread, '88 103
White Bean Spread, '93 30; '95 279
Whitefish Spread, Smoked, '92 58
SPROUTS
    Beans with Sprouts, Sweet-and-Sour, '86 32
    Beef and Bean Sprouts, '82 281; '83 42
    Meat Loaf, Sprout, '85 51
    Omelet, Potato-Sprout, '79 128
    Omelet, Rising Sun, '82 281
    Patties, Ham-Sprout, '85 51
    Salad, Bean Sprout, '82 113
    Salad, Fresh Spinach-Sprout, '82 281; '83 42
    Salad, Spanish Sprout, '85 327; '86 22
    Salad, Sprout, '90 137
    Sandwiches, Alfalfa Pocket Bread, '82 282;
        '83 41
    Sandwiches, Polynesian Sprout, '85 51
SQUASH. *See also* **CHAYOTES, ZUCCHINI.**
    Acorn. *See also* Squash/Stuffed.
        Bake, Acorn Squash, '83 280
        Baked Sweet Dumpling Squash, '94 266
        Bake, Squash, '82 107
        Bread, Squash, '79 210
        Butter, Acorn Squash-and-Bourbon,
            '94 266
        Delight, Acorn Squash, '81 267
        Orange Squash Brûlée, '94 267
        Pancakes, Granola-Squash, '94 267
        Puppies, Acorn Squash, '94 268
        Puree, Basic Acorn Squash, '94 267
        Rings, Easy Glazed Acorn, '81 M231
        Rings, Glazed Acorn, '80 214
        Sherried Acorn Squash, '85 9
        Soup, Acorn Squash, '91 294
        Soup, Cream of Acorn Squash, '94 268

SQUASH *(continued)*

Baby Squash, '93 118
Butternut. *See also* Squash/Stuffed.
    Bake, Butternut-Orange, '86 295
    Baked Butternut Squash, '85 205
    Bake, Squash and Apple, '79 210
    Bisque, Squash, '84 280
    Bread, Butternut-Raisin, '79 25
    Bread, Squash, '79 210
    Casserole, Butternut, '83 280
    Casserole, Butternut Squash, '79 210
    Casserole, Squash and Apple, '79 209
    Casserole, Sweet Butternut, '83 256
    Pie, Butternut Squash, '80 40; '87 212
    Pie, Butternut Squash Chiffon, '83 296;
      '84 285
    Pie, Spicy Butternut Squash, '80 296
    Pie, Spicy Squash, '85 9
    Pudding, Butternut Squash, '89 M313;
      '90 M19
    Pudding, Squash, '82 277; '83 15
    Puff, Butternut Squash, '85 205
    Ring, Butternut Squash, '81 M232
    Sauté, Savory Butternut, '85 205
    Skillet Butternut and Bacon, '85 9
    Soufflé, Butternut, '83 266
    Soup, Butternut Squash, '95 62
    Soup, Creamed Butternut-and-Apple,
      '88 228
    Stir-Fry, Honey-Butternut, '93 184
    Sunshine Squash, '85 205
    Whipped Butternut Squash, '94 302
    Whipped Squash, Tasty, '82 277;
      '83 15
Cajun Squash, '88 142
Calabacitas, '95 130
Casserole, Calico Squash, '90 290
Casserole, Squash, '87 163; '89 159; '90 161;
    '92 342
Casserole, Two-Squash, '79 101
Chile Squash, '84 77
con Crema, Squash, '89 148
Delight, Squash, '90 236
Dressing, Squash, '95 290
Dressing, Turkey with Squash, '87 248
Greek-Style Squash, '92 26
Hubbard Squash, Tart, '80 214
Kabobs, Summery Squash-and-Pepper,
    '95 193
Marinated Squash Medley, '94 126
Medley, Carrot-Lima-Squash, '80 123
Medley, Fresh Squash, '81 M165
Medley, Sautéed Vegetable, '83 101
Medley, Squash, '81 139; '84 128
Mirliton Balls, '90 217
Muffins, Squash, '91 69
"Pasta," Garden-Fresh, '94 M134
Pattypan-Zucchini Skillet, '82 103
Pickles, Squash, '87 150
Pie, Mock Coconut, '86 200
Pie, Scallopini, '94 133
Puff, Golden Squash, '82 288
Relish, Pollock with Summer Squash,
    '92 200
Rosemary, Summer Squash with, '88 143
Sauté, Squash, '82 67
Scallop, Green-and-Gold, '81 159
Skillet Squash, '82 195
Spaghetti Squash, '92 340
Spaghetti Squash and Chicken Skillet
    Casserole, '94 134

Spaghetti Squash, Asian, '94 268
Spaghetti Squash Lasagna, '84 127
Spaghetti Squash Pie, '80 186
Spaghetti Squash Salad, Marinated, '94 134
Spaghetti Squash, Sautéed Vegetables with,
    '84 128
Spaghetti Squash with Meat Sauce, '88 M180
Spaghetti Squash with Sesame Eggplant,
    '92 252
Stir-Fried Squash Medley, '80 123
Stir-Fry, Squash, '80 184
Stir-Fry, Two-Squash, '86 174
Stuffed
    Acorn Squash, Apple-Stuffed, '83 296;
      '84 285
    Acorn Squash, Baked, '81 24
    Acorn Squash, Cranberry-Filled,
      '81 M231
    Acorn Squash, Custard-Filled, '86 334
    Acorn Squash, Deluxe, '80 215
    Acorn Squash, Fruited, '85 235; '90 228
    Acorn Squash, Fruit-Stuffed, '81 295
    Acorn Squash, Ham-Stuffed, '81 239;
      '83 66
    Acorn Squash-Mushroom Puree, '93 305
    Acorn Squash, Pineapple-Stuffed,
      '84 255
    Acorn Squash, Sausage-Stuffed,
      '81 M231; '83 296; '84 285
    Acorn Squash, Stuffed, '82 277; '83 15
    Acorn Squash with Molasses and Pecans,
      '85 205
    Acorn Squash with Nutmeg, '85 267
    Acorn Squash with Sausage, '85 9
    Apple-and-Pecan-Filled Squash, '88 228
    Apple-Stuffed Squash, '85 206
    Baked Squash, Stuffed, '85 206
    Beef-Stuffed Squash, '83 134
    Butternut Squash, Apple-Stuffed,
      '81 232
    Chayote, Stuffed, '92 247
    Cheesy Stuffed Squash, '82 134
    Crumb-Stuffed Squash, '89 148
    Green Chiles, Stuffed Squash with,
      '83 148
    Harvest Squash, '80 214
    Maple-Flavored Stuffed Squash, '85 205
    Mexican, Stuffed Squash, '90 200
    Mirlitons, Stuffed, '90 217; '93 278
    Parmesan-Stuffed Squash Boats, '79 156
    Pattypan Squash, Stuffed, '82 103;
      '85 136; '88 142
    Plantation Squash, '79 225
    Sausage-Stuffed Squash, '81 183
    Spinach Pesto, Squash Stuffed with,
      '89 M133
    Spinach-Stuffed Squash, '82 4; '91 14
    Turban Chicken Curry, '94 266
    Turban Squash, Sausage-Stuffed, '80 214
    Turban Squash, Stuffed Turks, '88 228
    Vegetable-Stuffed Squash, '84 104
    White Squash, Stuffed, '90 M201
    Yellow Squash, Garden-Stuffed, '84 106
    Yellow Squash, Italian Stuffed, '86 111
    Yellow Squash, Mushroom-Stuffed,
      '84 154
    Yellow Squash, Shrimp-Stuffed, '84 194
    Yellow Squash with Cheese Sauce,
      Stuffed, '80 162
Tomatoes, Squash-Stuffed, '82 102
Tomato Squash, '86 111
Toss, Pepperoni-Squash, '84 127
Turban Squash, Glazed, '81 24

Yellow. *See also* Squash/Stuffed.
    à l'Orange, Squash, '85 230
    Bacon-Flavored Squash, '82 158
    Bake, Cheddar-Squash, '84 M113, 128
    Bake, Cheesy Squash, '80 183
    Bake, Squash and Tomato, '95 180
    Beans, and Tomatoes, Squash, '83 148
    Bread, Spicy Squash, '83 121
    Bread, Yellow Squash, '84 140
    Buttered Summer Squash, '81 84
    Cake, Squash, '86 200
    Casserole, Baked Squash, '83 149
    Casserole, Blender Squash, '81 212
    Casserole, Cheesy Squash, '79 123;
      '82 M21
    Casserole, Chicken-Squash, '95 121
    Casserole, Company Squash, '81 183
    Casserole, Creamy Rice and Squash,
      '95 26
    Casserole, Crunchy Squash, '84 293
    Casserole, Fresh Squash, '82 204
    Casserole, Jiffy Squash, '81 M144
    Casserole, Squash and Egg, '80 146
    Casserole, Squash-Carrot, '81 157
    Casserole, Summer Squash, '81 102, 184
    Casserole, Yellow Squash, '79 179;
      '85 135; '88 166
    Casserole, Zippy Squash, '80 183
    Country Club Squash, '79 158;
      '88 M16
    Croquettes, Squash, '79 157; '83 148;
      '88 142
    Dip, Yellow Squash-Zucchini, '89 48
    Dressing, Squash, '83 315; '86 280
    Fiesta Squash, '82 102
    Fried Yellow Squash, '86 211
    Fritters, Squash, '89 68
    Greek-Style Squash, '91 285
    Grilled Squash and Onion, '79 150
    Grilled Vegetables, '84 172
    Marinated Cucumbers and Squash,
      '86 146
    Medley, Summer Garden, '84 158
    Mexican Squash, '82 103
    Muffins, Yellow Squash, '81 163
    Nicholas, Squash, '94 236
    Nosh, Squash, '90 147
    Pats, Squash, '80 298; '81 25
    Patties, Squash, '79 158
    Patties, Summer Squash, '81 184
    Pickled Yellow Squash, '93 136
    Pickles, Squash, '81 174
    Posh Squash, '81 159
    Puffs, Yellow Squash, '82 103
    Puppies, Squash, '83 170
    Quiche, Squash-and-Green Chile,
      '88 143
    Rings, Asparagus in Squash, '87 68
    Skillet Squash, '92 62
    Skillet Summer Squash, '82 96
    Soufflé, Cheesy Squash, '82 146
    Soufflé, Squash, '95 215
    Soufflé, Yellow Squash, '89 89
    Soup, Chilled Squash, '92 173
    Soup, Cold Cream of Squash, '81 130
    Soup, Cream of Squash, '81 246
    Soup, Perky Squash, '85 20
    Soup, Squash, '94 134
    Soup, Summer Squash, '83 99; '85 136
    South-of-the-Border Squash, '89 148
    Stir-Fried Squash Medley, '80 123
    Summer Squash, '80 127; '85 105
    Toss, Asparagus-Carrot-Squash, '91 45

SQUASH, Yellow (continued)

Toss, Crisp Squash-and-Pepper, '87 M152
Toss, Simple Squash, '85 M142
Vegetable-Herb Trio, '83 172

STEWS. *See also* CHILI, GUMBOS, JAMBALAYAS, SOUPS.
Bean Pot, White, '86 194
Beef-and-Onion Stew, '87 18
Beef and Vegetable Stew, Sweet-and-Sour, '85 87
Beef Stew, '86 51; '90 230
Beef Stew, Burgundy, '88 234
Beef Stew, Company, '83 85
Beef Stew, Oven, '79 222; '80 64
Beef Stew, Quick, '86 302; '92 71
Beef Stew, Spicy, '86 228
Beef Stew with Dumplings, '84 3
Beef Stew with Parsley Dumplings, '81 76; '82 13; '85 M246
Brown Stew, '85 239
Brunswick
    Aunt Willette's Brunswick Stew, '85 320
    Bama Brunswick Stew, '87 4
    Blakely Brunswick Stew, '87 4
    Breeden Liles's Brunswick Stew, '91 14
    Brunswick Stew, '80 264
    Chicken Stew, Brunswick, '87 4
    Dan Dickerson's Brunswick Stew, '91 16
    Easy Brunswick Stew, '92 280
    Family-Size Brunswick Stew, Van Doyle's, '91 14
    Favorite Brunswick Stew, Virginia Ramsey's, '91 16
    Gay Neale's Brunswick Stew, '91 17
    Georgian Brunswick Stew, '92 35
    Jeff Daniel's Brunswick Stew, '91 16
    Sonny Frye's Brunswick Stew, '87 4
    Virginian Brunswick Stew, '92 34
Burgoo, Five-Meat, '87 3
Burgoo, Harry Young's, '87 3
Burgoo, Kentucky, '88 235
Burgoo, Old-Fashioned, '87 3
Burgundy Stew with Drop Dumplings, '83 125
Caldo de Rez (Mexican Beef Stew), '89 276
Catfish Stew, Cajun-Style, '88 12
Chicken Ragout with Cheddar Dumplings, '94 44
Chicken Stew and Dumplings, '84 4
Chicken Stew, Chili-, '90 319
Chili Stew, Red, '95 226
Emerald Isle Stew, '95 71
Fish-and-Vegetable Stew, '87 220
Fisherman's Stew, '81 98
Frogmore Stew, '92 236
Game Pot Pie with Parmesan Crust, '94 304
Ham-and-Black-Eyed Pea Stew, '93 20
Hamburger Oven Stew, '84 4
Hungarian Stew with Noodles, '80 263
Hunter's Stew, '85 270
Irish Stew, '90 64
Lamb Stew, '79 293; '88 58
Lamb Stew-in-a-Loaf, '85 37
Lamb Stew with Popovers, '94 43
Lentil-Rice Stew, '82 232
Meatball Stew, '79 198
Mexican Stew, '82 231
Mexican Stew Olé, '86 296
Minestrone Stew, '93 184
Okra Stew, Old-Fashioned, '84 158

Oyster-Broccoli Stew, '89 242
Oyster-Sausage Stew, '89 242
Oyster Stew, '80 221
Oyster Stew, Company, '80 297
Oyster Stew, Golden, '86 132
Oyster Stew, Holiday, '85 264
Pancho Villa Stew, '94 44
Pollo en Pipián, Mexican, '88 31
Potato-Oyster Stew, '89 243
Rib-Tickling Stew, Campeche Bay, '89 317
Sausage Stew, Smoked, '82 231
Seafood Stew, '84 280
Shrimp Creole, '93 282
Shrimp Creole, Spicy, '79 181
Shrimp Creole, Wild Rice-and-, '84 292
Shrimp Stew, '83 4
Shrimp Stew and Grits, '80 118
Shrimp Stew over Grits, '88 126; '89 47
Strader Stew, '89 28
Turkey Stew, Hearty, '79 252
Turkey-Tomato Stew, '90 279
Tzimmes with Brisket, Mixed Fruit, '93 114
Veal-and-Artichoke Ragout, '94 43
Vegetable-Beef Stew, '94 323
Vegetable-Beef Stew, Shortcut, '89 218
Vegetable Stew, Mixed, '84 13
Venison Sausage Stew, '87 238
Venison Stew, '86 294
Venison Stew with Potato Dumplings, '87 304
White Wine Stew, '82 228

STIR-FRY. *See* WOK COOKING.

STRAWBERRIES
Almond Cream Dip with Strawberries, '92 164
Arnaud, Strawberries, '93 50
Banana-Berry Flip, '88 215; '89 20
Bars, Strawberry, '81 301
Bavarian, Raspberry-Strawberry, '89 15
Bavarian, Rhubarb-Strawberry, '86 140
Beets, Strawberry-Glazed, '83 234
Beverages
    Brandied Orange Juice, Strawberries with, '82 160
    Calypso, Coco-Berry, '89 171
    Coolers, Strawberry, '92 67
    Cooler, Strawberry, '83 56; '84 51
    Cooler, Strawberry-Mint, '84 57
    Cubes, Berry-Good, '95 201
    Daiquiris, Creamy Strawberry, '91 66
    Daiquiris, Strawberry, '90 125
    Daiquiri, Strawberry, '81 156
    Float, Strawberry-Banana, '87 160
    Frost, Banana-Strawberry, '87 199
    Frozen Strawberry Refresher, '93 213
    Ice Mold, Strawberry, '91 278
    Ice Ring, Strawberry, '94 176
    Lemonade, Berry Delicious, '93 205
    Lemonade, Strawberry, '80 160
    Milkshake, Fresh Strawberry, '82 113
    Milk Shake, Strawberry, '94 113
    Mimosa, Sparkling Strawberry, '88 169
    Pineapple-Strawberry Slush, '94 227
    Punch, Berry, '92 67
    Punch, Creamy Strawberry, '86 195
    Punch, Strawberry, '90 273
    Punch, Strawberry Champagne, '90 315
    Punch, Strawberry-Lemonade, '85 116; '91 175
    Sangría, Teaberry, '87 147
    Shake, Strawberry-Banana, '89 35
    Shake, Strawberry-Cheesecake, '92 44

Shake, Strawberry-Orange Breakfast, '87 186
Shake, Strawberry-Pear, '92 139
Shake, Strawberry-Pineapple, '84 166
Shake, Strawberry-Yogurt, '87 199
Shrub, Berry, '95 29
Slurp, Strawberry, '81 96
Slush, Strawberry-Orange, '83 172
Smoothie, Strawberry, '86 183
Smoothie, Strawberry-Banana, '81 59
Smoothie, Strawberry-Peach, '89 182
Smoothie, Tropical, '81 50
Soda, Old-Fashioned Strawberry, '79 149
Soda, Strawberry, '84 115
Spritzer, Strawberry, '90 14
Tea, Sparkling Strawberry, '94 131
Tea, Strawberry, '88 248
Bread, Strawberry, '81 250; '83 140; '84 49
Bread, Strawberry Jam, '79 216
Bread, Strawberry-Nut, '79 24
Butter, Strawberry, '79 36; '81 286; '91 71
Cake Roll, Strawberries 'n Cream Sponge, '81 95
Cake Roll, Strawberry, '79 49; '83 129; '84 305; '85 172
Cake, Strawberry Cream, '86 61
Cake, Strawberry Crunch, '79 288; '80 35
Cake, Strawberry Delight, '85 30
Cake, Strawberry Meringue, '86 240
Cake, Strawberry Yogurt Layer, '94 85
Cake with Strawberries and Chocolate Glaze, White, '87 76
Carousel, Strawberry, '91 247
Cheesecake, Almost Strawberry, '86 32
Cheesecake, Pear-Berry, '82 M141
Cherry-Berry on a Cloud, '79 94
Christmas Strawberries, '87 293; '94 331
Chocolate Combo, Strawberry-, '85 96
Citrus Twist, Berry-, '95 100
Cobbler, Rosy Strawberry-Rhubarb, '79 154
Cobbler, Strawberry-Rhubarb, '88 93
Coffee Cake, Strawberry, '85 46
Compote, Peach-Berry, '89 112
Cookie Tarts, Strawberry, '89 112
Cream, Chocolate Baskets with Berry, '92 118
Cream Dip, Fresh Strawberries with, '90 86
Cream Puffs, Strawberry, '81 95
Cream Puffs, Strawberry-Lemon, '87 75
Cream, Strawberries and, '82 100; '92 132
Cream, Strawberries in, '89 88
Cream, Strawberries 'n', '90 30
Cream, Strawberries 'n Lemon, '85 120
Cream, Strawberries with Chocolate, '85 81
Cream, Strawberries with French, '83 191
Cream, Strawberries with Strawberry, '84 108
Cream, Strawberry, '88 153
Cream with Fresh Strawberries, Almond, '87 93
Crêpes, Nutritious Brunch, '80 44
Crêpes, Strawberry Dessert, '83 122
Crêpes with Fruit Filling, '81 96
Crisp, Strawberry-Rhubarb, '95 119
Deep-Fried Strawberries, '84 109
Delight, Frozen Strawberry, '82 112, 174
Delight, Strawberry, '81 85
Delight, Strawberry Cheese, '79 50
Delight, Strawberry Yogurt, '85 77
Dessert, Chilled Strawberry, '84 164
Dessert, Glazed Strawberry, '84 33
Dessert, Honeydew-Berry, '83 120

STRAWBERRIES *(continued)*

Dessert, Strawberry, '83 123
Dessert, Strawberry-Cream Cheese, '83 123
Dessert, Strawberry-Lemon, '86 162
Dessert, Strawberry-Yogurt, '90 295
Dessert, Summer Strawberry, '92 143
Dessert, Sweet-and-Sour Strawberry, '92 54
Dipped Strawberries, '94 17
Divinity, Strawberry, '91 272
Dressing, Creamy Strawberry, '84 161
French Toast Sandwiches, Strawberry-,
    '91 160
Frosting, Strawberry, '89 184
Frost, Strawberry, '81 279; '82 24; '83 154
Frozen Strawberry Cups, '91 173
Fudge Balls, Strawberry, '93 80
Glaze, Strawberry, '80 35; '83 142
Ham, Strawberry-Glazed, '91 84
Ice Cream Crêpes, Strawberry, '87 290;
    '88 135
Ice Cream, Fresh Strawberry, '89 111
Ice Cream, Homemade Strawberry, '84 184
Ice Cream, Old-Fashioned Strawberry, '79 94
Ice Cream Roll, Strawberry, '84 105
Ice Cream, Straw-Ba-Nut, '80 177
Ice Cream, Strawberry, '80 177
Ice Cream, Strawberry-Banana-Nut, '88 203
Ice Cream Torte, Chocolate-Strawberry, '79 7
Ice Cream, Very Strawberry, '81 155
Ice Milk, Fresh Strawberry, '92 94
Ice, Strawberry, '84 175; '85 108
Ice, Strawberry-Orange, '86 196
Jamaica, Strawberries, '85 161; '93 239
Jam, Christmas, '88 288
Jam, Strawberry, '89 138
Jam, Strawberry Freezer, '84 M182
Jellyroll, Easy, '82 176
Jelly, Strawberry, '81 147
Juliet, Strawberries, '84 82
Lemon Cream, Strawberries with, '90 170
Marmalade, Strawberry-Pineapple, '85 130
Marsala, Strawberries, '88 171
Melon, Berry-Filled, '86 93
Meringues, Strawberry, '84 188
Mousse, Fresh Strawberry, '82 72
Mousse, Strawberry, '81 95
Mousse, Strawberry-Lemon, '82 128
Napoleons, Strawberry, '81 126
Nests, Strawberry Coconut, '88 136
Omelet, Strawberry-Sour Cream, '89 229
Pancakes, Strawberry, '84 219
Parfait, Crunchy Strawberry-Yogurt, '79 124
Parfaits, Frosty Strawberry, '85 213
Parfaits, Strawberry-Lemon, '84 198
Parfait, Strawberry, '79 99
Parfait, Surprise Strawberry, '86 151
Pie, Chilled Strawberry, '82 112
Pie, Glazed Strawberry, '82 M142
Pie, Heavenly Chocolate-Berry, '85 102
Pie, Lemon-Strawberry, '88 127
Pie, Strawberry Angel, '88 136
Pie, Strawberry-Banana Glazed, '81 181
Pie, Strawberry-Chocolate Truffle, '89 112
Pie, Strawberry-Glaze, '81 141
Pie, Strawberry Yogurt, '80 232
Pie, Strawberry-Yogurt, '85 122; '86 124
Pizza, Kiwi-Berry, '86 198; '87 55
Pizza, Strawberry, '79 94
Popsicles, Smoothie Strawberry, '82 112
Preserves Deluxe, Strawberry, '82 150
Preserves, Freezer Strawberry, '82 112

Preserves, Strawberry, '79 120; '81 96
Puff, Strawberry, '82 5
Raspberry Custard Sauce, Fresh Berries with,
    '88 163
Ring, Strawberry-Cheese, '86 14
Rock Cream with Strawberries, Old-
    Fashioned, '90 125
Roll, Heavenly Strawberry, '82 176
Roll, Strawberry, '82 120
Romanoff, Strawberries, '84 108; '88 95;
    '91 126; '94 68
Ruby Strawberries, '82 100
Sabayon, Strawberries, '79 94
Salad, Frozen Strawberry, '94 119
Salad, Hidden Treasure Strawberry, '79 11
Salad Mold, Strawberry-Wine, '83 261
Salad, Strawberry-Nut, '94 132
Salad, Strawberry-Spinach, '91 169; '93 168
Salad, Strawberry Yogurt, '80 232
Salad with Orange-Curd Dressing, Orange-
    Strawberry, '93 22
Sauces
    Amaretto-Strawberry Sauce, '87 M165
    Arnaud Sauce, Strawberries, '93 50
    Banana Sauce, Strawberry-, '81 41
    Berry Sauce, '87 290; '88 135; '95 103
    Brandied Strawberry Sauce, '88 196
    Crunchy Topping, Strawberry Sauce with,
        '81 170
    Dumplings, Strawberry Sauce with,
        '84 314
    Fresh Strawberry Sauce, '82 177
    Melon Wedges with Berry Sauce, '86 178
    Mimosa Sauce, Berry, '90 315
    Old-Fashioned Strawberry Sauce,
        '94 130
    Peaches with Strawberry Sauce, '85 8
    Peach Sauce, Strawberry-, '92 154
    Strawberry Sauce, '84 144; '87 93, 198;
        '92 85; '94 121
Sherbet, Strawberry, '82 112, 160
Shortcake, A Favorite Strawberry, '88 136
Shortcake, Chocolate-Strawberry, '89 216
Shortcake, Elegant Strawberry, '88 37
Shortcake Jubilee, Strawberry, '88 209
Shortcake, Orange-Strawberry, '95 100
Shortcake Shells, Strawberry, '88 196
Shortcake Squares, Strawberry, '86 124
Shortcakes, Strawberry Crispy, '93 42
Shortcake, Strawberry, '81 96; '83 122;
    '92 184; '94 162
Shortcake, Strawberry Pinwheel, '89 112
Skewered Pineapple and Strawberries, '84 251
Sorbet, Strawberry, '88 117; '93 153
Sorbet, Strawberry-Champagne, '83 162;
    '95 20
Sorbet, Strawberry Margarita, '89 111
Sorbet, Very Berry, '90 85
Soup, Cold Strawberry, '82 157
Soup, Sherry-Berry Dessert, '91 180
Soup, Strawberry, '88 160
Soup, Strawberry-Banana, '86 181
Soup Supreme, Strawberry, '81 M144
Spread, Light Strawberry, '85 55
Spread, Strawberry, '95 79
Spumoni and Berries, '91 204
Squares, Strawberry Shortcake, '85 122
Stuffed Strawberries with Walnuts, '85 122;
    '86 124
Sundaes, Hot Strawberry, '81 M5
Supreme, Banana-Berry, '81 205
Swirl, Strawberry, '84 108
Tartlets, Fresh Berry, '91 98

Tarts, Berry Good Lemon, '91 119
Tarts, Strawberry, '80 70
Tart, Strawberry, '84 138; '89 272
Tart, Strawberry Dream, '92 118
Tart, Strawberry-Lemon, '89 111
Topping, Pound Cake with Strawberry-
    Banana, '89 200
Topping, Strawberry, '86 32; '90 142
Topping, Strawberry-Banana, '87 125
Torte, Spring, '91 57
Torte, Strawberry Meringue, '88 136
Treasure, Berried, '89 124
Trifle, Easy Strawberry, '88 201
Whip, Strawberry, '89 198
White Chocolate, Strawberries Dipped in,
    '90 83
Zabaglione, Strawberries, '81 95

STROGANOFF
Beef Burgundy Stroganoff, '85 31
Beef Stroganoff, '79 163; '81 179; '91 134;
    '93 18
Beef Stroganoff, Light, '86 36
Beef Stroganoff, Quick, '92 20
Chicken Livers Stroganoff, '80 200; '81 57
Chicken Livers Supreme, '81 298
Crab Stroganoff, '79 116
Crawfish Stroganoff, '91 89
Ground Beef Stroganoff, '84 71
Hamburger Stroganoff, '82 108, 110
Hamburger Stroganoff, Easy, '79 208
Ham Stroganoff, '82 40
Ham Stroganoff on Cheesy Onion Biscuits,
    '95 98
Liver Stroganoff, '79 54
Meatballs, European Veal, '85 30
Meatballs Paprikash with Rice, '85 31
Meatball Stroganoff, '81 297
Mushroom-Meatball Stroganoff, '85 85
Mushroom Stroganoff, '81 298
Quickie Stroganoff, '81 200
Shrimp Stroganoff, '79 81
Shrimp Stroganoff, Oven-Baked, '81 297
Sirloin Stroganoff, '81 297
Steak Stroganoff Sandwiches, '85 110
Steak Stroganoff with Parslied Noodles,
    '85 31
Tofu, Stroganoff, '84 202
Turkey Stroganoff, '91 61
Veal Stroganoff, '79 108

STUFFINGS. *See also* **DRESSINGS.**
Apple-Crumb Stuffing, '81 234; '82 26;
    '83 39
Apple-Walnut Stuffing, '95 289
Cornbread Stuffing, '94 305
Crabmeat Stuffing, '94 68
Crabmeat Stuffing, Chicken Breasts with,
    '85 302
Cranberry-Sausage Stuffing, Crown Roast of
    Pork with, '88 49
Fruited Stuffing, Cornish Hens with, '90 191
Fruited Stuffing Mix, '89 331
Low-Sodium Stuffing, '82 66
Oyster Stuffing, Roast Turkey with, '80 251
Pecan-Sausage Stuffing, Chicken Breasts with,
    '94 212
Pecan Stuffing, '79 292; '80 32
Pecan Stuffing, Wild Duck with, '85 269
Rice-and-Onion Stuffing, '88 246
Rice Stuffing, '95 290
Tangerine Stuffing, '90 16
Walnut-Rice Stuffing, Tomatoes with, '91 102
Wild Rice Stuffing, Cornish Hens with,
    '79 222; '80 64; '82 136

SWEET-AND-SOUR

Beets, Sweet-and-Sour, '81 167; '82 22; '89 314
Black-Eyed Peas, Sweet-and-Sour, '85 290
Burgers, Sweet-and-Sour, '90 128
Cabbage, Sweet-and-Sour, '86 295; '87 189
Cabbage, Sweet-Sour Red, '79 5
Carrots, Sweet-and-Sour, '82 137
Chicken Nuggets, Sweet-and-Sour, '90 168
Chicken, Sweet-and-Sour, '79 106; '86 217, 240; '90 161; '91 202
Chicken, Sweet-and-Sour Lemon, '84 93
Chicken Wings, Sweet-and-Sour, '90 206
Dessert, Sweet-and-Sour Strawberry, '92 54
Dressing, Sweet-and-Sour, '80 247; '84 70, 161; '85 163; '87 305; '89 62; '91 126; '94 281
Dressing, Sweet-and-Sour Fruit, '84 125
Dressing, Sweet-Sour, '80 246
Fish, Sweet-and-Sour, '80 M54
Green Beans and Carrots, Sweet-and-Sour, '83 6
Green Beans, Sweet-and-Sour, '79 184; '81 158; '82 90; '91 250
Ham, Sweet-and-Sour Glazed, '88 M15
Ham, Sweet-Sour Glazed, '83 311
Kale, Sweet-and-Sour, '80 298
Kielbasa, Sweet-and-Sour, '89 327
Liver, Sweet-and-Sour, '81 277
Marinade, Sweet-and-Sour, '86 113; '87 115
Meatballs, Sweet-and-Sour, '82 233, 247; '86 240
Meatballs, Sweet-and-Sour Party, '79 233
Onions, Sweet-and-Sour Baked, '90 34
Peas, Sweet-and-Sour, '88 3
Pork Chops, Sweet-and-Sour, '83 160
Pork, Pineapple Sweet-and-Sour, '82 120
Pork, Sweet-and-Sour, '79 42; '80 72, 227; '81 26, 104, 111; '82 12; '84 218; '85 34, 194; '86 241; '90 317; '92 219
Potatoes, Sweet-and-Sour-Topped, '83 4
Pot Roast, Sweet-and-Sour, '83 8
Riblets, Sweet-and-Sour, '85 276
Ribs, Sweet-and-Sour, '89 M84
Salads
    Asparagus, Sweet-and-Sour, '89 159
    Bean Salad, Sweet-and-Sour, '85 198; '86 147
    Beans, Sweet-and-Sour, '87 197
    Beans with Sprouts, Sweet-and-Sour, '86 32
    Cauliflower Salad, Sweet-and-Sour, '81 2
    Fruit Salad, Sweet-and-Sour, '80 13; '84 125
    Green Salad, Sweet-and-Sour, '94 281
    Macaroni Salad, Sweet-and-Sour, '85 166
    Potato Salad, Sweet and Sour, '80 152
    Potato Salad, Sweet-and-Sour, '92 106
    Slaw, Sweet-and-Sour, '81 237
    Slaw, Sweet-and-Sour Hot, '92 63
    Spinach Salad, Sweet-Sour, '85 M112
    Vegetable Salad, Sweet-and-Sour, '81 25
Sauce, Sausage Rolls with Sweet-and-Sour, '83 74
Sauce, Sweet-and-Sour, '80 20; '85 12, 34; '86 240
Sauce, Sweet-and-Sour Pineapple, '85 66
Sausage, Sweet-and-Sour, '88 296
Shrimp and Chicken, Sweet-and-Sour, '87 267; '88 103; '89 66
Shrimp, Sweet-and-Sour, '83 278; '90 M112
Shrimp Tails, Sweet-and-Sour Rock, '80 3

Snap Beans, Sweet-and-Sour, '89 173
Soup, Sweet-and-Sour Cabbage, '89 314
Spareribs, Sweet-and-Sour, '83 21
Spread, Sweet 'n' Sour, '86 184
Steaks, Sweet-and-Sour Marinated, '83 110
Stew, Sweet-and-Sour Beef and Vegetable, '85 87
Turkey, Sweet-and-Sour, '79 252
Turnips, Sweet-and-Sour, '81 274
Vegetables, Sweet-and-Sour Marinated, '83 266

SWEET POTATOES

Apple Shells, Sweet Potatoes in, '85 206
Apple-Stuffed Sweet Potatoes, '88 207
Apricot Glaze, Sweet Potatoes with, '89 331
Bake, Southern Sweet Potato, '85 229
Bake, Sweet Potato-Apricot, '85 206
Balls, Sweet Potato, '86 312
Boats, Sweet Potato, '80 287
Boniato Chips, '92 247
Breads
    Biscuits, Sweet Potato, '80 287; '84 140; '89 210
    Biscuits, Sweet Potato Angel, '93 312
    Muffins, Sweet Potato, '81 224; '85 6; '87 280; '92 31
    Muffins, Yam, '79 7
    Rolls, Golden Yams, '86 299
    Rolls, Sweet Potato, '93 172
Broiled Sweet Potatoes, Coconut-, '84 231
Butter, Sweet Potato, '95 M290
Candied Sweet Potatoes, '79 9, 251; '86 111; '88 207
Candied Sweet Potatoes, Nannie's, '95 306
Casseroles
    Apple Bake, Sweet Potato-, '83 25; '86 282
    Apple Casserole, Sweet Potato-and-, '94 280
    Apple Casserole, Sweet Potatoes-and-, '90 228
    Applesauce Sweet Potatoes, '91 292; '92 256
    Apricot Sweet Potatoes, '82 228
    Bake, Sweet Potato, '80 287
    Banana Casserole, Sweet Potato-, '86 276
    Berries Casserole, Sweet Potatoes-and-, '84 231
    Bourbon Sweet Potatoes, '86 324; '87 280
    Candied Sweet Potatoes, '88 207
    Coconut-Orange Sweet Potatoes, '84 252
    Delight, Sweet Potato, '86 335; '87 83
    Eggnog Casserole, Sweet Potato-, '95 291

Festive Sweet Potatoes, '80 244
Glazed Sweet Potato Casserole, '90 250
Glazed Sweet Potatoes, Tropical, '83 226
Holiday Sweet Potato Bake, '90 291
Orange Bake, Sweet Potato-, '83 226
Peaches, Sweet Potatoes and, '86 11
Pear-Sweet Potato Casserole, '86 280
Puree, Carrot-and-Sweet Potato, '94 56
Royale, Sweet Potatoes, '91 250
Rum Casserole, Sweet Potato-, '84 231
Scallop, Yam-and-Apple, '91 199
Sherry and Walnuts, Sweet Potatoes with, '86 286
Surprise, Holiday Sweet Potato, '84 254
Surprise, Sweet Potato, '81 267
Sweet Potato Casserole, '79 289; '80 26; '85 256; '89 279
Yams, Cornwallis, '79 276
Chips, Sweet Potato, '91 138; '93 332; '95 M203
Chips with Blue Cheese, Sweet Potato, '93 290
Cinnamon-Apple Sweet Potatoes, '95 M23
Croquettes, Sweet Potato, '81 223
Cups, Sunshine Sweet Potato, '82 195
Desserts
    Cake, Sweet Potato, '79 207; '89 295
    Cake, Sweet Potato Loaf, '81 224
    Cake, Sweet Potato Pound, '83 85
    Cake, Sweet Potato Surprise, '80 287
    Cheesecake, Sweet Potato, '80 287
    Cheesecake, Yam, '81 224
    Flan, Sweet Potato, '95 291
    Pie, Carolina Sweet Potato, '89 295
    Pie, Louisiana Yam, '81 223
    Pie, No-Crust Sweet Potato, '84 236
    Pie, Old-Fashioned Sweet Potato, '79 9
    Pie, Southern Sweet Potato Cream, '87 260
    Pie, Speedy Sweet Potato, '90 219
    Pie, Sweet Potato, '79 207; '85 255, 275; '86 269; '89 289
    Pie, Sweet Potato Meringue, '81 126; '83 225
    Pie, Sweet Potato-Orange, '88 207
    Pie, Sweet Potato-Pecan, '83 90
    Pie, Sweet Potato Pone, '80 288
    Pudding, Sweet Potato, '80 228; '86 52
    Pudding, Sweet Potato Bread, '94 241
    Roll, Sweet Potato Log, '82 227
French-Fried Sweet Potatoes, '81 223
Fried Sweet Potatoes, '83 226
Fried Sweet Potato Strips, '94 238
Fritters, Golden Sweet Potato, '79 9
Fritters, Sweet Potato, '88 44
Glazed Sweet Potatoes, '85 206; '89 274
Glazed Sweet Potatoes, Apple-, '82 303
Glazed Sweet Potatoes, Apricot-, '81 295
Glazed Sweet Potatoes, Orange-, '81 223; '83 280
Gravy, Roast Duck with Sweet Potato-Eggplant, '83 90
Grilled Sweet Potatoes, '93 213
Hash, Sweet Potato, '92 337
Mashed Sweet Potatoes, '85 25
Orange-Baked Sweet Potatoes, '88 M294
Orange Cups, Sweet Potatoes in, '82 272

SWEET POTATOES *(continued)*

Orange Cups, Sweet Potato-Stuffed,
   '81 223
Orange Sweet Potatoes, '86 279
Oven-Fried Sweet Potatoes with Chutney,
   '93 241
Pancakes, Sweet Potato, '87 280
Peaks, Sweet Potato, '95 291
Peanut Crust, Sweet Potatoes with,
   '93 212
Pudding, Sweet Potato, '79 244; '80 228;
   '86 52
Puffs, Peach Sweet Potato, '87 280
Puffs, Sweet Potato, '87 253
Puff, Sweet Potato, '85 235
Puree, Carrot-Sweet Potato, '92 90
Puree, Sweet Potato, '92 306
Raspberry Sweet Potatoes, '87 280
Salad, Fresh Sweet Potato, '86 226
Salad, Hawaiian Ham-Sweet Potato,
   '82 232
Slaw, Sweet Potato-Currant, '93 246
Soufflé, Sweet Potato, '82 286; '86 121;
   '93 325
Soup, Sweet Potato, '88 250
Soup, Sweet Potato-and-Sausage, '95 23
Stacked Sweet Potato Blues, '95 290
Stuffed Baked Sweet Potatoes, '79 207;
   '84 231
Stuffed Sweet Potatoes, '86 224
Stuffed Sweet Potatoes, Bacon-, '86 224
Stuffed Sweet Potatoes, Coconut-, '82 204
Stuffed Sweet Potatoes, Fluffy, '79 9
Stuffed with Apples, Sweet Potatoes,
   '82 228
Supreme, Sweet Potato, '94 196
Tzimmes, '95 102
Tzimmes, Sweet Potato-Beef, '92 234
Velouté, Sweet Potato, '94 238
Waffles, Sweet Potato, '88 208
Waffles with Orange Butter, Sweet Potato,
   '90 323
Yams, Bourbon, '90 232
Yams, Brandied, '94 273
Yams Cointreau, '92 192
Yams, Rosemary-Garlic, '93 174

SWISS CHARD
Bundles, Swiss Chard, '94 48
Buttered Chard, '83 36
Tomatoes, Swiss Chard with, '83 36

SYRUPS
Almond Syrup, '82 47
Anise Sugar Syrup, '86 248
Apple Syrup, Spiced, '79 114
Apricot Fruit Syrup, '82 10
Barbecue Sauce, Maple Syrup, '94 154
Caramel Syrup, '82 43
Cherry-Lemonade Syrup, '86 214
Cinnamon Syrup, '91 315
Citrus Syrup, Sweet, '86 270
Fruit Syrup, '86 176
Kirsch Syrup, '80 280
Maple-Honey-Cinnamon Syrup, '85 19
Maple-Nut Syrup, '80 228
Maple Syrup, '81 120; '82 23; '93 16
Maple Syrup, Homemade, '79 114
Mint Syrup, '90 89
Orange Syrup, '80 228; '89 254
Pecan Syrup, Chunky, '85 278
Rum Syrup, '95 313
Sugar Syrup, '93 29

TACOS

al Carbón, Tacos, '86 19
al Carbón, Tailgate Tacos, '79 185
Appetizer, Layered Taco, '84 206
Bake, Taco Beef-Noodle, '81 141
Basic Tacos, '83 199
Beef Tacos, Soft, '91 88
Biscuit Bites, Taco, '91 89
Breakfast Tacos, '80 43; '91 316; '95 340
Casserole, Taco, '80 33
Chicken-and-Bean Tacos, '93 293
Chicken Tacos, Pizza-Flavored, '95 340
Corn Chip Tacos, '81 67
Deep-Dish Taco Squares, '91 88
Dip, Hot Taco, '93 238
Egg Salad Tacos, Mexican, '94 181
Fish Tacos, Barbecued, '95 339
Jiffy Tacos, '83 M318
Joes, Taco, '91 167
Lentil Tacos, '88 197
Lobster Taco with Yellow Tomato Salsa and
   Jicama Salad, Warm, '87 122
Microwave Tacos, '88 M213
Navajo Tacos, '84 246
Peppers, Taco, '81 86
Pepper Tacos, Grilled, '95 340
Pie, Crescent Taco, '80 80
Pie, Double-Crust Taco, '88 272; '89 180
Pies, Individual Taco, '82 M282
Pie, Taco, '88 256
Pitas, Taco, '83 31
Pizza, Taco, '89 M177
Potatoes, Taco-Topped, '93 M18
Rolls, Chinese Taco, '95 339
Salad, Chicken Taco, '94 M136
Salad Cups, Taco, '85 M29
Salad, Meatless Taco, '81 204
Salad, Spicy Taco, '87 287
Salad, Taco, '79 56; '83 145; '85 84; '89 332;
   '90 20
Salad, Taco Macaroni, '85 165
Salad, Tuna-Taco, '87 145
Sauce, Taco, '82 M283; '93 69; '94 30
Shrimp-and-Pepper Soft Tacos, '95 339
Soup, Taco, '94 225
Tacos, '80 196
Tassies, Taco, '95 339

TAMALES
Bake, Cornbread Tamale, '79 163
Casserole, Quick Tamale, '94 255
Chicken Tamales, '88 151
Dessert Tamales, Mango, '94 190
Hot Tamales, '83 51
Meatballs, Tamale, '80 194
Miniature Tamales, '85 154
Mozzarella Tamale, '95 70
Pie, Chili-Tamale, '82 9; '83 68
Pie, Cornbread-Tamale, '92 123
Soup, Tamale, '95 213
Sweet Tamales, '83 52
Tamales, '80 195

TEA
Almond-Lemonade Tea, '86 229
Almond Tea, '85 43; '86 329; '89 212
Apple-Cinnamon Tea, Hot, '87 57
Apricot Tea, Hot Spiced, '88 248
Brew, Quilter's, '85 43
Citrus-Mint Tea Cooler, '92 105
Citrus Tea, Hot, '83 275
Citrus Tea, Iced, '85 162
Cranberry-Apple Tea, '88 169
Cranberry Tea, '94 131
Cubes, Frozen Tea, '85 161

Fruited Tea Cooler, '94 131
Fruit Tea, Christmas, '83 275
Fruit Tea, Hot Spiced, '87 242
Ginger-Almond Tea, '94 131
Ginger Tea, '81 100
Granita, Mint Tea, '88 117
Grapefruit Tea, '92 67
Grape Tea, Spiced, '79 174
Hawaiian Tea, '87 57
Honey Tea, '81 105
Iced Tea, Bubbly, '81 168
Johnny Appleseed Tea, '85 23
Lemon-Mint Tea, '85 162
Lemon Tea, '82 156
Lemon Tea Tingler, '95 200
Long Island Iced Tea, Southern, '90 207
Minted Tea, '86 101; '88 163; '92 54
Mint Tea, '87 107; '90 89
Mint Tea, Easy, '91 187
Mint Tea, Fresh, '95 88
Mint Tea, Frosted, '84 161
Mint Tea, Fruited, '88 79; '91 81
Mint Tea, Iced, '83 170
Mix, Deluxe Spiced Tea, '88 257
Mix, Friendship Tea, '83 283
Mix, Spiced Tea, '86 32
Mix, Sugar-Free Spiced Tea, '91 258
Pineapple Tea, '93 165
Punch, Apple-Tea, '85 82
Punch, Bourbon-Tea, '87 57
Punch, Citrus-Tea, '85 116
Punch, Cran-Grape-Tea, '92 209
Punch, Spiked Tea, '86 101
Punch, Tea, '90 143, 207
Rasp-Berry Good Tea, '95 200
Sangría Tea, '94 131
Sangría, Teaberry, '87 147
Sangría Tea, Pink, '95 200
Sauce, Tea-Berry, '94 130
Spiced Iced Tea, '91 209
Spiced Tea Cooler, '83 55
Spiced Tea, Hot, '83 244
Strawberry Tea, '88 248
Strawberry Tea, Sparkling, '94 131
Summer Tea, '85 162
Summertime Tea, '81 167
Sun Tea, Southern, '81 168
Tropical Tea-Ser, '95 200
White Grape Juice Tea, '87 57
Yaupon Tea, '79 31

TEMPURA
Basic Tempura, '81 68
Chicken Tempura Delight, '85 66
Cornmeal Tempura, '81 68
Sauce, Basic Tempura, '81 68
Sauce, Mustard-Sour Cream, '81 68
Vegetable Tempura, '79 112

TERRINES
Black Bean Terrine with Fresh Tomato Coulis
   and Jalapeño Sauce, '93 230
Black Bean Terrine with Goat Cheese,
   '87 120
Cheese Terrine, Italian, '93 64
Chicken-Leek Terrine, Cold, '92 145
Chicken Terrine Ring, '84 132
Chicken-Vegetable Terrine, '84 131
Pork and Veal, Terrine of, '93 287
Pork Terrine, Jeweled, '84 130
Salmon-and-Spinach Terrine, Layered,
   '84 132
Veal Terrine with Mustard Sauce,
   '93 118
Vegetable-Chicken Terrine, '83 224

TIMBALES

Cheesy Mexicali Appetizer, '82 108
Chicken Chutney Salad, '82 108
Corn-and-Zucchini Timbales, '92 100
Grits Timbales, '88 223
Grits Timbales, Chives-, '90 172
Hamburger Stroganoff, '82 108
Peach Almond Cream, '82 108
Rice Timbales, '94 32
Shells, Timbale, '82 108
Spinach-Rice Timbales, '88 271
Spinach Timbales, '84 29

TOFU

Dip, Tofu, '86 109
Drink, Tofruitti Breakfast, '88 26
Lasagna, Tofu, '83 312
Rice with Tofu, Spanish, '88 26
Salad, Tofu, '88 27
Sandwiches, Open-Face Tofu-Veggie, '86 5
Stroganoff Tofu, '84 202

TOMATILLOS

Beef Saltillo (Beef with Tomatillos), '82 219
Fillets Tomatillo, '94 135
Relish, Black Bean-Tomatillo, '87 121
Salsa, Roasted Tomatillo, '95 64
Salsa, Tomatillo, '92 245
Sandwiches, Open-Faced Tomatillo, '92 246
Sauce, Avocado-Tomatillo, '95 206
Sauce, Roasted Chiles Rellenos with Tomatillo, '94 203
Sauce, Shrimp Enchiladas in Tomatillo, '95 310
Sauce, Tomatillo, '94 231; '95 206
Soup with Crunchy Jicama, Tomatillo, '92 245

TOMATOES

Appetizers, Oven-Baked Tomato, '95 172
au Gratin, Zucchini and Tomato, '82 208
Bake, Chicken-Tomato, '83 35
Baked Cheddar Tomatoes, '85 43
Baked Ranch Tomatoes, '94 72
Baked Tomatoes, '83 53; '87 197
Baked Tomato Halves, Zippy, '81 182
Bake, Ham-Rice-Tomato, '87 78
Bake, Okra-and-Tomato, '89 173
Bake, Okra-Tomato, '80 298; '81 26
Bake, Potato-Tomato, '86 17
Bake, Tomato-and-Artichoke Heart, '85 81
Bake, Zucchini and Tomato, '82 158
Basil, and Cheese, Tomato, '95 165
Basil, Zucchini and Tomatoes, '89 147
Bean-and-Tomato Skillet, '90 316
Beans and Tomatoes, Basil, '83 172
Beef with Tomatoes and Artichokes, '92 282
Biscuit Cakes, Tomato-Eggplant, '95 170
Biscuits, Tomato, '86 72
Biscuits, Tomato-Herb, '94 215
Bowl, Tomato, '81 69
Breaded Tomatoes, '95 180
Bread, Herbed Tomato-Cheese, '88 143
Broiled Tomatoes, '80 152
Broiled Tomatoes, Quick, '79 153
Broiled Tomatoes, Romano, '80 42
Broiled Tomatoes with Dill Sauce, '80 161
Broiled Tomatoes with Mushroom Sauce, '81 103
Broil, Tomato-English Pea, '83 192
Butter, Tomato, '86 128
Butter, Tomato-Curry-Orange, '93 159
Cabbage and Tomatoes, '83 104
Cabbage and Tomatoes, Tasty, '86 72

Cacciatore, Chicken, '86 42
Canned Flavored Tomatoes, '95 217
Canning Tomatoes, '80 128; '85 106
Casserole, Corn and Tomato, '81 127
Casserole, Corn-and-Tomato, '84 145
Casserole, Eggplant-and-Tomato, '83 187
Casserole, Saucy Potato-Tomato, '79 46
Casserole, Scalloped Tomato, '88 144
Casserole, Zucchini-and-Tomato, '88 265
Catsup, Spicy Tomato, '83 182
Cheese Herbed-Topped Tomatoes, '86 108
Cheese Sauce over Toast, Tomatoes with, '88 159
Cheese-Topped Tomatoes, '81 160
Cheesy Puff-Top Tomatoes, '86 187
Cherry
Bites, Tomato, '84 80
Brown Butter Sauce, Cherry Tomatoes in, '81 168
Caviar Tomatoes, '91 12
Cheesy Cherry Tomatoes, '83 135
Green Beans with Cherry Tomatoes, '86 177
Herbed Cherry Tomatoes, '82 128
Herbed Cherry Tomatoes over Pasta, '95 229
Rum, Cherry Tomatoes with, '83 192
Salad, Cherry Tomato, '87 156
Sautéed Roma Tomatoes, '92 338
Stuffed Cherry Tomatoes, '84 160; '88 95, 212; '92 25
Stuffed Cherry Tomatoes, Crab-, '82 289; '88 78
Stuffed Cherry Tomatoes, Cucumber-, '88 262
Stuffed Cherry Tomatoes, Tuna-, '89 214
Chicken, Tomato-Baked, '81 281; '82 30
Chutney, Tomato-Apple, '84 180
Cocktail, Tomato, '83 M203
Cocktail, Tomato-Clam, '87 252
Cocktail, Tomato Juice, '79 212; '83 230; '90 12
Cocktail, Tomato-Orange Juice, '83 169
Cocktail, Zesty Tomato Juice, '83 289
Cream, Tomato, '94 70
Creole-Style Tomatoes-and-Corn, '84 142
Croissants, BLT, '93 158
Crostini, Feta-Tomato, '92 159
Delight, Tomato-Pea, '84 196
Dip, Bacon-and-Tomato, '90 147
Dip, Gazpacho, '95 243
Dressing, Fresh Tomato Salad, '83 193
Dressing, Garden Salad with Tomato-Cream Cheese, '79 173
Dressing, Tomato-Honey French, '81 105
Dried
Cheese Balls with Sun-Dried Tomatoes, '94 317
Cherry Tomatoes, Marinated Dried, '93 23
Dip, Cottage Cheese Sun-Dried Tomato, '93 13
Focaccia, Dried Tomato, '94 65
Goat Cheese with Sun-Dried Tomatoes and Rosemary, '93 175
Hummus, Creamy Dried Tomato, '95 284
Meat Loaf with Sun-Dried Tomatoes and Herbs, '92 192
Pesto, Dried Tomato, '90 204; '94 249
Salad, Spinach and Sun-Dried Tomato, '93 250

Sauce, Dried Tomato Spaghetti, '90 202
Soup, Dried Tomato-Cream, '90 203
Spread, Dried Tomato-Cheese, '90 204
Tart, Dried Tomato-Cheese, '90 203
Vinaigrette, Dried Tomato, '93 272
Dumplings, Tomato, '88 144
Eggs Benedict, Bacon-and-Tomato, '87 195
Fire-and-Ice Tomatoes, '87 92
Fried Herb Tomatoes, '88 144
Fried Red Tomatoes, '81 102
Fried Ripe Tomatoes, '81 168
Fried Ripe Tomatoes with Gravy, '82 180
Fried Tomatoes with Bacon, Saucy, '81 210
Fried Tomatoes with Gravy, '86 211
Gazpacho-Stuffed Endive, '95 287
Gratin, Tomato-Zucchini, '95 171
Gravy, Spicy Tomato, '95 172
Gravy, Tomato, '93 18
Green
Baked Green Tomatoes, Herb-, '85 214
Curried Green Tomatoes, '93 138
Fried Green Tomato Cheeseburgers, '94 138
Fried Green Tomatoes, '79 123; '80 178; '81 210; '85 214
"Fried" Green Tomatoes, '89 174
Fried Green Tomatoes, '95 171
Fried Okra and Green Tomatoes, '93 160
Hot Tomatoes, '93 138
Italian-Sauced Green Tomatoes, '85 214
Jam, Green Tomato, '79 121
Okra and Green Tomatoes, '79 160
Oven-Fried Green Tomatoes, '82 107; '91 122
Pickles, Green Tomato, '87 134
Pie, Green Tomato, '79 195
Relish, Green Tomato Sweet, '93 136
Spread, Green Tomato Sandwich, '95 172
Green Beans with Tomatoes, '85 137
Grilled Tomatoes, '85 158
Grilled Tomatoes, Cheesy, '79 150
Grits, Hot Tomato, '95 171
Herbed Tomatoes, '81 102; '82 49; '83 173
Herbed Tomato Slices, '89 173
Hush Puppies, Tomato-Onion, '91 201
Juice, Homemade Tomato, '81 50
Juice, Spicy Tomato, '85 189
Kale with Tomato and Onion, '92 244
Lima and Tomato Combo, Hot, '83 219
Marinade, Bright Tomato, '88 176
Marinara Vinaigrette, '94 64
Marinated Sliced Tomatoes, '92 173
Medley, Okra-Corn-Tomato, '81 159
Medley, Tomato, '81 159
Muffins, Tomato Corn, '81 137
Mustard, Green Beans and Tomatoes with, '87 83
Mustard Tomatoes, Zippy, '86 M226
Okra and Tomatoes, '80 185; '81 139; '92 215
Okra and Tomatoes, Fresh, '81 M165; '87 89
Okra, Corn, and Tomatoes, '95 203
Okra-Tomato Combo, '83 157
Okra, Tomatoes and, '86 170; '87 164
Okra, Tomatoes with, '85 106
Parmesan Tomatoes, '80 161

TOMATOES (continued)

Pasta. See also Tomatoes/Sauces.
  Asparagus, Tomatoes, and Shrimp,
    Garlicky Pasta with, '95 82
  Basil Pasta, Tomato-, '94 204
  Caribbean Tomato Pasta, '93 201
  Fettuccine, Chicken-and-Tomatoes over,
    '90 204
  Garlic Pasta, Tomato-, '94 177
  Italian Tomato Pasta, '93 201
  Late-Night Pasta Chez Frank, '95 228
  Macaroni, Cheese, and Tomatoes,
    '95 213
  Primavera, Tomato-Pasta, '86 209
  Quick Pasta and Tomatoes, '92 180
  Rotelle, Chicken and Tomato with,
    '87 108
  Southwestern Tomato Pasta, '93 201
  Spaghetti with Tomatoes and Garlic,
    '91 47
  Toss, Tomato-Olive Pasta, '86 209
Pesto, Tomatoes, '86 150
Pie, Tomato, '88 198
Pita Pockets, BLT in, '93 158
Provençal, Tomatoes, '82 181
Puffs, Spinach-Artichoke-Tomato, '95 284
Puree, Seasoned Tomato, '83 182
Quesadillas, Bacon-Jalapeño-Tomato,
  '95 240
Quiche, Asparagus-Tomato, '88 198
Refresher, Tomato, '81 94; '83 318
Relish, Easy Tomato, '80 126
Relish, End-of-the-Garden, '80 179
Relish, Tomato, '85 188
Rice, Red, '92 235
Rice with Tomatoes and Basil, '95 232
Risotto, Tomato-Basil, '95 269
Roma Tomatoes, Sautéed, '92 338
Rose, Tomato, '82 51; '85 338
Salads
  Artichoke-Stuffed Tomato Salad,
    '82 101
  Artichoke-Tomato Salad, '82 239
  Asparagus and Tomatoes, Fresh,
    '94 162
  Asparagus Salad, Tomato-, '92 79
  Aspic, Bloody Mary-Tomato, '81 77
  Aspic, Chicken in Tomato, '84 190
  Aspic, Chili Sauce Tomato, '85 252
  Aspic, Classic Tomato, '91 229
  Aspic, Herbed Tomato, '81 73
  Aspic, Layered Tomato, '90 99
  Aspic, Light Tomato, '85 83
  Aspic, Ranch Tomato, '83 218
  Aspic, Spicy Tomato, '81 40; '89 288
  Aspic, Tangy Tomato, '83 124
  Aspic, Tomato-Artichoke, '84 320;
    '86 92
  Aspic, Tomato-Crab, '85 287
  Aspic with Shrimp, Tomato, '79 241
  Avocado Salad, Tomato-, '86 74
  Basil-and-Tomato Couscous Salad,
    '94 175
  Basil-Mozzarella Salad, Tomato-,
    '95 171
  Chile-Tomato Salad, Spicy, '88 121
  Citrus Marinade, Summer Salad with,
    '92 133
  Coleslaw with Tomatoes, '80 34
  Congealed Lemon-Tomato Salad,
    '89 178

Cottage Cheese Salad in Tomatoes,
  '86 208
Cottage-Tomato Salad, '85 163
Crab-Stuffed Tomato Salad, '80 148
Cucumber and Tomato Salad, Dilled,
  '81 153
Cucumber-Onion Salad, Tomato-,
  '81 239
Cucumber on Tomatoes, Dilled,
  '84 142
Cucumber Salad, Tomato-, '86 218;
  '92 199
Cucumber Salad with Yogurt-Herb
  Dressing, Tomato-, '92 96
Cucumber Summer Salad, Tomato-and-,
  '93 141
Cucumber-Tomato Salad, '90 144
Endive-Tomato Starburst Salad,
  '93 323
Feta Salad, Tomato-, '81 246; '91 168
Flower Salad, Tomato, '89 128
Frozen Tomato Salad, '84 52
Guacamole-Tomato Salad, '81 302
Herbed Pasta-and-Tomato Salad,
  '92 144
Herbed Tomatoes, '83 173
Herb Salad, Tomato-, '89 220
Italian Dressing, Tomato, Onion, and
  Cucumber in, '81 83
Italiano, Tomatoes, '88 29
Lemon Dressing, Tomato Slices with,
  '87 167
Lima Bean-Tomato Salad, '85 137
Marinated Salad, '83 170
Marinated Salsa Tomatoes, '82 164
Marinated Tomato and Brie Salad,
  '95 95
Marinated Tomato-and-Cucumber Salad,
  '92 216
Marinated Tomatoes, '85 156, 163;
  '89 174, 202
Marinated Tomato Slices, '82 134;
  '83 193
Mold, Tangy Tomato, '79 74
Mozzarella Salad, Tomato-, '89 220
Mozzarella-Tomato-Basil Salad, Fresh,
  '93 131
Olive Spread, Tomatoes with, '85 114
Oregano Tomatoes, '83 145
Petal Salad, Tomato, '79 88
Red, White, and Green Salad, '90 18
Relish Salad, Tomato, '83 111
Ring, Tangy Tomato, '84 164
Ring, Tomato-Vegetable, '81 302
Ruby-and-Emerald Salad, '85 79
Stuffed Tomato Salad, Oriental-,
  '82 101
Summer Tomato Salad, '94 201
Summer Tomato Treat, '79 143
Vidalia-Tomato Salad, '84 65
Vinaigrette, Marinara, '94 64
Vinaigrette, Okra-Corn-and-Tomato,
  '90 173
Vinaigrette, Tomato-Basil, '87 89
Vinaigrette, Tomatoes, '84 106
Watercress-Tomato Salad, '85 132
Sandwiches, Bacon, Cheese, and Tomato,
  '84 14
Sandwiches, Curried BLT, '93 158
Sandwiches, Open-Face Crab Tomato,
  '81 29
Sandwich, Floyd's Favorite Tomato,
  '95 172

Sauces
  Asparagus with Tomato Sauce, '83 46
  Basil Sauce, Tomato, '91 85
  Basil Sauce, Tomato-, '92 180
  Basil-Tomato Sauce, '92 198;
    '93 25, 48, 65
  Caper Sauce, Turkey Cutlets with
    Tomato-, '91 61
  Chili Sauce, '94 287
  Chunky Tomato Sauce, '95 264
  Coulis, Fresh Tomato, '93 230
  Cream Sauce, Angel Hair Pasta with
    Tomato, '93 292
  Cream Sauce, Linguine with Tomato-,
    '86 158
  Cream, Tomato, '94 70
  Creamy Tomato Sauce, '93 71
  Fish in Tomato Sauce, '85 75
  Fresh Tomato Sauce, '83 224; '87 171
  Fresh Tomato Sauce over Basil Pasta,
    '93 176
  Green Chiles, Tomato Sauce with,
    '81 196
  Hamburgers with Tomato Sauce,
    '81 73
  Herbed Fresh Tomato Sauce, '85 M151
  Hot Sauce, Kleberg, '94 28
  Italian-Style Tomato Sauce, '87 182
  Italian Tomato Sauce, '82 M68; '92 57
  Italian Tomato Sauce for Spaghetti,
    '81 134
  Marinara Sauce, '94 64
  Pesto, Bow-Tie, '94 231
  Pesto, Tomatoes, '86 150
  Pizza Sauce, Traditional, '95 267
  Red Pepper-Tomato Sauce, '93 59
  Refrigerator Tomato Sauce, '85 188
  Salsa, '88 147
  Salsa, Chunky, '86 130; '90 206
  Salsa, Fresh, '95 42
  Salsa, Fresh Tomato, '91 182; '95 181
  Salsa, One-Minute, '95 93
  Salsa, Red, '90 172
  Salsa, Roasted Tomato, '95 64
  Salsa, Seared Scallops with Tomato-
    Mango, '95 122
  Salsa, Three Tomato, '93 138
  Salsa, Tomato, '87 120
  Salsa, Tomato-Avocado, '94 83
  Salsa, Yellowfin Tuna with Corn, Pepper,
    and Tomato, '94 164
  Salsa, Yellow Tomato, '87 122
  Seasoned Tomato Sauce, '83 150
  Spicy Tomato Sauce, '84 294; '88 19
  Spinach Tortellini with Tomato Sauce,
    '88 302
  Tarragon-Tomato Sauce, '84 131
  Tomato Sauce, '85 193, 244; '87 249;
    '88 116
  Vegetable-Tomato Sauce, Turkey Patties
    in, '87 18
  Vermicelli with Tomato Sauce,
    '83 164
Sauté, Tomato-Pepper, '84 142
Scalloped Tomatoes, '84 142
Scalloped Tomato Slices, '81 168
Sesame Tomatoes, '84 142
Sipper, Peppy Tomato, '94 227
Skillet, Cabbage-and-Tomato, '86 110
Skillet Tomatoes, '81 108
Skillet, Zucchini-Tomato, '93 206
Snow Peas and Tomatoes, '83 111
Snow Peas and Tomatoes, Basil, '88 M185

TOMATOES (continued)

Soups
 Appetizer Tomato Soup, '86 258
 Bacon, Lettuce, and Tomato Soup, '91 207
 Bisque, Make-Ahead Tomato-Basil, '93 322
 Bisque, Tomato-Shrimp, '86 66
 Black, White, and Red All Over Soup, '95 126
 Bouillon, New Year's Tomato, '94 24
 Bouillon, Tomato, '83 8
 Carrot-and-Tomato Soup, Cream of, '94 176
 Celery Soup, Tomato-, '83 M58
 Chilled Tomato Soup, '82 155
 Chowder, Tomato-Clam, '84 251
 Cioppino, Gulf Coast, '94 102
 Cold Tomato Soup, '88 160
 Consommé, Tomato, '88 250
 Cream of Tomato Soup with Parmesan Cheese, '86 161
 Cream Soup, Refreshing Tomato, '79 172
 Creamy Tomato Soup, '83 267; '86 258
 Easy Tomato Soup, '84 14
 French Market Soup, '94 317
 Fresh Tomato Soup, '83 140
 Hot Tomato Juice Soup, '86 302
 Iced Tomato Soup, '79 170
 Mexican Tomato Soup, Icy-Spicy, '90 155
 Plus, Tomato Soup, '88 170
 Potage, Tomato, '79 250
 Pumpkin-Tomato Soup, '86 291
 Rice Soup, Tomato-and-, '85 24
 Savory Tomato Soup, '94 91
 Sour Cream-Topped Tomato Soup, '80 246
 Summer Tomato Soup, '79 130
 Tomato Soup, '81 236; '83 44; '89 217
 Vegetable Soup, Tomato-, '81 M177; '86 9
Spicy Tomato Sipper, '86 229
Spicy Tomato Warm-Up, '95 328
Spinach-Topped Tomatoes, '88 265; '94 321
Spread, Fiery Tomato-Cheese, '87 196
Spread, Home-Style Sandwich, '80 179
Spread, Tomato, '94 123
Spread, Tomato-Cheese, '81 157
Squash and Tomato Bake, '95 180
Squash, Beans, and Tomatoes, '83 148
Squash, Tomato, '86 111
Stack-Ups, Jiffy Tomato, '80 161
Stewed Tomatoes, '83 182
Stewed Tomatoes and Greens, '95 234
Stew, Turkey-Tomato, '90 279
Stir-Fried Sweet Peppers with Tomatoes, '93 207
Stir-Fry, Italian, '92 126
Stir-Fry, Tomato-Zucchini, '80 158
Stir-Fry, Zucchini-and-Tomato, '85 108
Strata, Tomato-Cheese, '81 209
Stuffed
 Avocado-Stuffed Tomatoes, '82 101
 Bacon-and-Egg-Stuffed Tomatoes, '80 162
 Baked Spinach Tomatoes, '90 92
 Baked Stuffed Tomatoes, '88 162
 Baked Tangy Tomatoes, '81 168
 Baked Tomatoes with Corn, '80 161
 Bean-Stuffed Tomatoes, '84 34
 Broccoli-Stuffed Tomatoes, '83 136; '93 216
 Buffet Tomatoes, '82 180
 Cheese-Stuffed Tomatoes, '91 69
 Cheesy Stuffed Tomatoes, '80 161
 Chile-Cheese Stuffed Tomatoes, '94 141
 Cold Stuffed Tomatoes, '80 100
 Corn-Stuffed Tomatoes, '82 270
 Crab-and-Avocado Stuffed Tomatoes, '94 141
 Cups, Turkey-Tomato, '84 119
 Delights, Tomato, '81 140
 Easy Stuffed Tomatoes, '82 264
 Eggs-and-Tomato Slices, Stuffed, '84 152
 Herbed Tomatoes, '82 49
 Hot Tomatoes, '93 138
 Maque Choux Stuffed Tomatoes, '87 89
 Mushroom-Stuffed Tomatoes, '86 218
 Parmesan-Stuffed Tomatoes, '92 182
 Puffs, Tomato Cheese, '81 48
 Sausage-Stuffed Tomatoes, '80 47
 Scalloped Tomatoes, Stuffed, '90 29
 Sea Slaw, Tomatoes Stuffed with, '89 96
 Spinach-Stuffed Baked Tomatoes, '86 14
 Spinach-Stuffed Tomatoes, '89 203; '93 281
 Squash-Stuffed Tomatoes, '82 102
 Stuffed Tomatoes, '83 252
 Tuna-Mac in Tomatoes, '87 188
 Tuna Pasta, Stuffed Tomato with, '88 54
 Turkey Stuffed Tomatoes, '94 140
 Vegetable Stuffed Tomatoes, '94 141
 Walnut-Rice Stuffing, Tomatoes with, '91 102
Swiss Chard with Tomatoes, '83 36
Tart, Fresh Tomato, '95 170
Venison and Tomatoes, '85 270
Vinegar, Tomato-Herb, '94 200
Welsh Rarebit with Tomatoes and Bacon, '92 M159
Zucchini and Tomato with Herbs, '92 182

TOPPINGS. *See also* **FROSTINGS, GLAZES, PESTOS, RELISHES, SALSAS, SAUCES.**
Savory
 Almond-Garlic Streusel, '95 159
 Apple Topping, '89 107
 Avocado Topping, '93 309; '94 96
 Biscuit Topping, '86 157, 265
 Blue Cheese Burger Topping, '93 218
 Butter-Pecan Topping, '95 158
 Catsup Topping, '81 170
 Cheese Topping, '86 233
 Chili Topping, '94 22
 Crabmeat Topping, '91 64
 Cream, Mock Devonshire, '81 288
 Eggs and Cheese, '95 165
 Fruit Dressing, Nutty, '88 68
 Fruit Fluff, Tropical, '88 68
 Fruit Topping, '81 42; '87 225; '89 50
 Ginger-Lime Cream, '95 227
 Hazelnut Whipped Cream, '94 16
 Honey Topping, '83 154
 Horseradish Cream, '90 96
 Ketchup, Hoisin, '94 138
 Lemon Curd, '87 139
 Mushrooms, Garlic and, '95 165
 Nutty Topping, '86 16
 Oat Crunch Topping, '89 108
 Oatmeal Cookie Topping, '95 291
 Olive Salad, Doodles, '94 35
 Olive Salad, Italian, '94 35
 Peach Ketchup, '95 306
 Peach Topping, '94 22
 Pecan Topping, '94 36
 Pepper Topping, Rainbow, '90 117
 Pimiento Topping, '83 93
 Potato Topping, Mashed, '89 243
 Red Pepper Puree, '93 275
 Salad Mix, Muffy, '94 34
 Sausage and Peppers, '95 165
 Shrimp Topping, '93 291
 Sour Cream Topping, Spicy, '95 15
 Southwestern Dressing, '91 195
 Strawberry Topping, '90 142
 Streusel, '85 326
 Streusel Topping, '94 280
 Tomato, Basil, and Cheese, '95 165
 Turkey-Vegetable Topping, '94 22
 Vegetable Topping, '79 79
 Yogurt-Cheese Topping, '88 55
Sweet
 Almond Topping, '85 152; '86 200
 Apple-Nut Topping, '93 162
 Bananas Hawaiian, '89 94
 Brown Sugar Topping, '81 162
 Caramel Drizzle, '86 247
 Chantilly Cream, '83 91
 Chocolate Cream, '94 57
 Chocolate-Peanut Topping, '79 222
 Cinnamon-Pecan Topping, '85 277
 Cream Topping, Spicy, '85 177
 Crème Chantilly, '91 297
 Crème Patissière, '83 225
 Crumb Topping, '83 183; '88 216
 Fruit Fluff, Tropical, '88 68
 Fruity Dessert Topping, '82 167
 Ginger Cream Topping, '84 312
 Kahlúa Cream, '91 197
 Lemon-Blueberry Cream, '92 153
 Lemon Cream, '82 237
 Lemon Curd, '94 315
 Lemon-Pineapple Topping, '86 60
 Lime-Rum Cream, '93 169
 Mocha Cream, '94 47
 Nutty Topping, '85 256
 Orange-Mallow Cream, '94 295
 Oranges in Grand Marnier, '95 142
 Orange Topping, Whipped, '80 254
 Paint, Egg Yolk, '86 322
 Papaya Topping, '86 181
 Pear Whip, '89 94
 Pineapple Topping, '86 239
 Raspberries, Spirited, '95 142
 Raspberry Topping, '85 317
 Rum Cream, '88 154
 Rum Cream Topping, '80 255
 Rumtopf, '95 142
 Sour Cream Topping, '85 298; '86 120
 Strawberry Cream, '88 153
 Strawberry Topping, '86 32
 Streusel Topping, '88 154, M275
 Sugars, Colored, '90 21
 Vanilla Cream, '81 248
 Whipped Cream Topping, '87 264; '89 154
 Whipped Topping, Reduced-Calorie, '85 55

TORTILLAS. *See also* **BURRITOS, ENCHILADAS.**
Appetizers, Tex-Mex Tortilla, '86 297
Bake, Cheesy Beef-and-Bean, '82 89
Bake, Chicken Tortilla, '82 89
Bake, Texas Tortilla, '94 285
Baskets, Tortilla, '94 97
Bites, Tortilla, '95 42
Buñuelos, '80 199
Buñuelos, King-Size, '86 5
Burgers, Tortilla, '94 138
Campesina, Tortilla, '89 85
Casserole, Chicken Tortilla, '81 166
Casserole, El Dorado, '81 140
Casserole, Mexican Chicken, '82 143
Chalupas, Bean, '83 313
Chalupas, Chicken, '79 185
Chalupas, Chicken-Olive, '81 227
Chalupas, Texas Turkey, '80 196
Cheese Tortilla Snack, Two-, '90 119
Cheesy Tortillas, '81 62
Chicken Acapulco, '84 32
Chicken-Tortilla Stack, Cheesy, '86 3
Chicken Tostadas, '93 204
Chilaquiles, '82 220
Chilaquiles con Pollo, '81 66
Chimichangas, '86 114
Chimichangas, Apple, '95 43
Chimichangas, Oven-Fried Beef, '92 124
Chimichangas, Pineapple Dessert, '86 4
Chips, Corn Tortilla, '91 17
Chips, Light Tortilla, '90 278; '91 257
Chips, Tortilla, '91 137
Chorizo and Egg Tortillas, '81 193
Dippers, Rolled Tortilla, '86 4
Egg-and-Sausage Tortillas, '83 246;
    '84 42
Eggs Sonora, '80 196
Española, Tortilla, '92 175
Flautas, '83 199
Flautas with Guacamole, Chicken,
    '89 226
Flour Tortillas, '81 303; '95 44
Flour Tortillas, Never-Fail, '80 198
Franks, Mexican, '93 78
Ham Appetillas, '93 63
Huevos Rancheros, '82 197; '91 77
Migas, '94 26
Picadillo, '84 118
Pie, Mexican Cheese, '82 9; '83 69
Pie, Montezuma Tortilla, '83 199
Pie, Tortilla, '85 M211
Quesadillas, Bacon-Jalapeño-Tomato,
    '95 240
Quesadillas, Quick, '89 87
Quesadillas, Sausage, '90 118
Quesadillas, Spicy Chicken, '95 42
Quesadilla with Cucumber Salsa, Grilled
    Salmon, '95 131
Quesadilla with Roasted Salsa, Northern
    New Mexican Vegetable, '95 130
Roll-Ups, Mexican Beef, '90 176
Rollups, Tortilla, '89 87
Salad in a Shell, Mexican, '86 4
Salads, Mexican Chicken Tortilla, '95 129
Sandwiches, Guacamole, '82 9; '83 68
Sandwich, Tex-Mex Ham-and-Cheese,
    '86 4
Snacks, Pesto Tortilla, '89 19
Soup, Spicy Tortilla, '90 32; '93 108
Soup, Tortilla, '88 31, 245; '90 201;
    '93 197, 274; '94 136
Stack-Ups, Tortilla, '92 196
Tacoritos, '90 133
Tostada Compuestas, '81 194
Tostadas, Chicken, '95 122
Tostadas, Crab, '93 203
Tostadas, Crispy, '83 2
Tostadas, Shrimp-and-Black Bean,
    '93 204
Tostadas, Super, '83 199
Triangles, Tortilla, '94 107

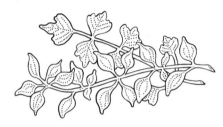

TUNA
Appetizers
    Ball, Tuna-Pecan, '87 94
    Cherry Tomatoes, Tuna-Stuffed, '89 214
    Dip, Low-Cal Tuna, '87 25
    Dip, Tuna-Curry, '84 31
    Mold, Creamy Tuna-Cheese, '81 135
    Mound, Tuna, '80 276
    Mousse, Tuna, '80 275
    Spread, Chunky Tuna, '89 147
    Spread, Tuna, '83 174; '91 305
Baked Tuna and Peas in Wine Sauce,
    '83 196
Bake, Shoestring Potato Tuna, '82 211
Barbecued Tuna, '80 275
Bisque, Tuna, '79 76
Broiled Tuna with Rosemary, '93 127
Burgers, Tuna, '95 128
Burgers, Zippy Tuna, '81 135
Casserole, Biscuit-Topped Tuna, '79 113
Casserole, Easy Tuna, '82 M203
Casserole, Nippy Tuna, '84 241
Casserole, Tangy Tuna-Broccoli, '83 75
Casserole, Tuna, '82 119
Casserole, Tuna Vegetable, '81 135
Casserole with Cheese Swirls, Tuna, '88 256
Cheesies, Tuna, '82 191
Chopsticks, Tuna, '94 255
Creamed Chipped Tuna, '95 127
Croquettes, Tuna-Egg, '80 275
Croquettes with Parsley Sauce, Tuna,
    '86 108
Grilled Florida Tuna, '93 128
Grilled Tuna with Poblano Salsa, '91 135
Jambalaya, Tuna, '83 44
Lasagna, Tuna '83 44; '84 123
Macaroni Treat, Tuna-, '82 131
Melts, Curried Tuna, '95 46
Melts, Hot Tuna, '95 126
Melts, Southwestern Tuna, '95 127
Melts, Tempting Tuna, '88 158
Mustard Sauce, Tuna with Tangy, '92 201
Nachos, Tuna, '95 127
Pie, Tuna-Rice, '84 123
Pie with Cheese Roll Crust, Tuna, '80 286
Pita Pocket, Tuna-in-a-, '87 202
Pockets, Tuna, '88 139
Potatoes, Tuna-Stuffed, '79 210
Salads
    Cannellini Bean Salad, Tuna-and-,
        '86 143
    Cheese-Sauced Tuna Salad, '87 M124
    Chef Salad, Tuna, '82 78
Company Tuna Salad, '87 201
Confetti Salad, '80 4
Congealed Tuna Salad, '84 163
Creamy Tuna Salad, '82 87, 208
Crunchy Tuna Salad, '87 201
Cucumber Tuna Boats, '83 136
Curried Tuna Salad, '86 208
Curried Tuna Salad with Grapes, '87 201
Egg Salad, Tuna-, '81 135
Eggs, Tuna-Stuffed, '83 83
Favorite Tuna Salad, '82 208
Flavorful Tuna Salad, '81 37
Greens and Tuna Salad, Fresh, '80 55
Hot Tuna Salad Rolls, '84 281
Layered Tuna Salad, '84 221
Luncheon Tuna Salad, '81 135
Macaroni Salad, Tuna, '83 44, 145
Macaroni Salad, Tuna-, '84 66
Macaroni-Tuna Salad, Whole Wheat,
    '84 193
Meal-in-One Salad, '82 232
Pasta Salad, Tuna-, '91 43; '92 141
Pasta Salad, Tuna, '92 108
Pasta, Stuffed Tomato with Tuna,
    '88 54
Potato Salad, Tuna-, '84 289
Red Pepper Salad, Tuna-and-, '93 143
Rice Salad, Tuna-, '87 202
Ring, Creamy Tuna, '80 275
Swiss Tuna Salad, '86 186
Taco Salad, Tuna-, '87 145
Tomatoes, Tuna-Mac in, '87 188
Wild Tuna Salad, '95 243
Sandwich Boats, Tuna, '91 166
Sandwiches, French Toasted Tuna, '80 275
Sandwiches, Hot Tuna, '85 299; '86 M194
Sandwiches, Tuna Club, '83 134
Southwestern Tuna Melts, '95 127
Steaks, Grilled Tuna, '90 129
Steaks on Mixed Greens with Lemon-Basil
    Vinaigrette, Seared Tuna, '94 205
Steaks with Tarragon Butter, Tuna, '92 328
Tapenade, Tuna, '95 127
Waffle-Wich, Hot Tuna, '88 272; '89 181
Yellowfin Tuna with Corn, Pepper, and
    Tomato Salsa, '94 164
TURKEY
Appetizers, Turkey, '91 314
Baked Turkey, Cider, '83 263
Bake, Layered Ham and Turkey, '79 252
Barbecue, Turkey, '90 158
Braised Turkey Breast, '84 260
Breast and Gravy, Savory Seasoned Turkey,
    '89 M309
Breast, Citrus-Marinated Turkey, '94 272
Breast, Herb Butter-Basted Turkey, '86 285
Breast, Herbed Turkey, '92 266
Breast, Smoky Turkey, '89 323
Breast with Orange-Raspberry Glaze, Turkey,
    '91 253
Buffet Turkey, '80 29
Cabbage Rolls, Stuffed, '88 18
Casserole, Crunchy Turkey, '89 M282
Casserole, Golden Turkey, '80 271
Casserole, Stuffed Turkey, '88 246
Casserole, Turkey, '84 327
Casserole, Turkey-and-Broccoli, '86 332
Casserole, Turkey-and-Shrimp Florentine,
    '92 122
Casserole, Turkey-Asparagus, '86 284
Casserole, Turkey-Olive, '87 268
Casserole, Turkey-Spinach, '84 71
Casserole, Turkey-Swiss, '86 283

TURKEY (continued)

Chalupas, Texas Turkey, '80 196
Chili, Southwestern, '91 284
Chili Topping, '84 246
Chili, Turkey-Bean, '88 M213
Chowder, Turkey, '85 10; '91 312
Chowder, Turkey-Corn, '81 98
Citrus-Marinated Turkey Breast, '94 272
Cornbread Crust, Turkey and Peppers in, '95 312
Creamed Turkey, Southern, '80 272
Crêpes, Elegant Turkey, '83 282
Crêpes, Turkey, '92 41
Cups, Turkey-Tomato, '84 119
Curried Cream Sauce, Turkey Slices with, '91 60
Cutlets, Oven-Fried Turkey, '91 121
Cutlets, Pecan-Crusted Turkey, '94 282
Cutlets with Pepper Salsa, Spicy Turkey, '88 26
Cutlets with Tarragon-Mustard Sauce, Turkey, '93 239
Cutlets with Tomato-Caper Sauce, Turkey, '91 61
Deep-Fried Turkey, '92 339
Divan, Creamy Turkey, '90 M34
Divan, Quick Turkey, '89 178
Divan, Turkey, '82 268
Dressing, Easy Turkey and, '79 296
Dressing, Turkey, '85 298
Drumsticks, Grilled Turkey, '89 168
Fast-and-Savory Turkey, '87 306
Florentine, Turkey, '88 264
Galantine of Turkey, '85 150
Giblet Dressing and Turkey Gravy, Turkey with, '91 254
Gravy, Savory Turkey and, '94 326
Gravy, Turkey, '91 255; '94 306
Grilled Turkey Breast with Cranberry Salsa, '95 252
Gumbo, Turkey, '82 268; '85 258
Hash, Turkey, '95 262
Herbed Turkey-in-a-Bag, '91 253
Indian Turkey, '85 302
Italiano, Turkey, '91 62
Jambalaya de Covington, '87 211
Kabobs, Turkey-and-Fruit, '88 140
Lazy Day Turkey, '93 93
Loaf, Cranberry-Glazed Turkey, '86 171
Loaf, Ground Turkey, '86 171
Loaf, Turkey, '92 33
Meatballs, Turkey, '89 237
Meat Mixture, Basic, '92 241
Mix, Ground Meat, '89 143
Nachos, Turkey, '90 118
Oriental Turkey, '82 268
Parmesan, Turkey, '82 268
Parmigiana, Turkey, '87 193
Pasta
    Basil Pasta, Creamy Turkey-, '89 216
    Lasagna, Easy, '92 M197; '93 24
    Lasagna, Lean, '86 37
    Lasagna, Turkey, '83 239; '91 130
    Noodle Bake, Turkey, '93 243
    Noodle-Poppyseed Casserole, Turkey-, '90 239
    Noodle Soup Mix, Turkey-, '89 330
    Noodle Soup, Turkey-, '91 312
    Pie, Broccoli-and-Turkey Pasta, '88 269
    Primavera, Smoked Turkey Pasta, '90 84
    Salad, Ranch-Style Turkey 'n' Pasta, '94 184

Spaghetti, Ham-and-Turkey, '95 19
Spaghetti Sauce, Turkey, '85 13
Stroganoff, Turkey, '91 61
Tetrazzini, Herbed Turkey, '86 47
Pâté in Pastry, Turkey-Mushroom, '92 327
Patties in Vegetable-Tomato Sauce, Turkey, '87 18
Patties, Stuffed Ground Turkey, '86 171
Peppers, Turkey with, '92 182
Piccata, Turkey, '91 137
Pie, Crumb-Crust Curried Turkey, '86 265
Pie, Golden Turkey, '79 253
Pie, Italian Meat, '89 109
Pie, Lattice-Topped Turkey, '81 277; '82 7
Pie, Potato-Topped Turkey, '86 265
Pie, Turkey, '80 285
Pie, Turkey-and-Dressing, '84 326
Pie, Turkey-and-Oyster, '82 267
Pie, Turkey-Cheese, '88 264
Pie, Turkey Pot, '86 265; '90 24; '93 45
Pilaf, Turkey-Asparagus, '88 200
Pilaf, Turkey-Rice, '86 284
Pizza, Turkey-Vegetable, '90 139
Puffs, Turkey-Cheese, '87 301
Rice, Turkey Fried, '83 282
Roast Turkey, '79 250; '80 262; '86 47; '88 253; '90 321
Roast Turkey and Cornbread Dressing, '89 324
Roast Turkey and Giblet Gravy, '94 308
Roast Turkey Breast and Gravy, '88 303
Roast Turkey Breast with Special Gravy, '86 282
Roast Turkey, How to, '83 286
Roast Turkey with Grandmother's Dressing, Madeira, '91 254
Roast Turkey with Herbs, '95 305
Roast Turkey with Oyster Stuffing, '80 251
Roast Turkey with Peanut Dressing, '79 283
Roast Turkey with Rice Dressing, '82 286
Rollups, Turkey, '86 198
Salads
    Apple Salad, Turkey-, '88 123; '90 181
    Bake, Turkey Salad, '79 253
    Caesar Salad, Turkey, '93 320
    Carrot Salad, Turkey-, '86 283
    Curried Turkey Salad, '88 140
    Fruit-and-Spice Turkey Salad, '94 325
    Fruit-and-Turkey Salad, '89 176
    Fruitful Turkey Salad, '84 197
    Fruit Salad, Turkey-, '79 56
    Fruit Salad, Turkey, '83 233; '84 244
    Holiday Turkey Salad, '84 320
    Honey-Mustard Turkey Salad, '92 309
    Hot Bacon Dressing, Turkey Salad with, '87 285
    Hot Turkey Salad, '86 10, 297; '87 176
    Layered Turkey Salad, '86 332; '92 220
    Macaroni Salad, Turkey, '83 282
    Meal-in-One Salad, '86 43
    Orange Salad, Turkey-in-the-, '93 21
    Pasta Salad, Ranch-Style Turkey 'n', '94 184
    Polynesian Turkey Salad, '87 285
    Sandwiches, Turkey Salad Pita, '87 202; '88 43
    Sautéed Walnuts, Turkey Salad with, '86 117
    Southwestern Turkey Salad, '91 313
    Stir-Fry Salad, Chilled Turkey-and-Pepper, '88 140
    Taco Salad, Turkey, '95 25

Turkey Salad, '90 318
Waldorf Salad with Yogurt Dressing, Turkey, '88 53
Zucchini Salad, Turkey-, '85 74
Sandwiches
    Burgers, All-American Pizza, '92 148
    Burgers, Grilled Turkey, '91 61
    Burgers, Pizza, '89 165
    Club Sandwiches, Double-Decker, '91 231; '92 68
    Ham-and-Turkey Specials, Cheesy, '84 14
    Hero Sandwiches, Turkey, '92 196
    Hero with Garlic Sauce, Turkey, '90 145
    Hot Brown Sandwiches, '80 M202
    Hot Turkey Sandwich, '93 306
    Meal-in-One Sandwiches, '80 218
    Monte Cristo Sandwiches, '83 134
    Mozzarella Rounds, Turkey-, '82 3
    Open-Faced Sandwiches, '79 214
    Open-Facers, Turkey, '82 190
    Roast Turkey, '90 321
    Slaw Sandwich, Turkey-in-the-, '90 177
    Sloppy Toms, '91 51
    Smoked Turkey-Roasted Pepper Sandwiches, '94 66
    Waffle-Grilled Turkey Sandwich, '94 170
Sausage-Cornbread Dressing, Turkey with, '83 287
Sausage, Marinara Sauce with Italian Turkey, '89 239
Sauté, Creamy Turkey, '93 19
Sauté, Turkey, '89 105
Scaloppine, Easy Turkey, '95 M192
Schnitzel, Turkey, '84 230
Skillet, Oriental Turkey-Orange, '86 284
Skillet Turkey Dinner, '91 61
Slices, Orange-Turkey, '90 53
Smoked Turkey, '79 293; '84 160; '85 258; '90 249
Smoked Turkey Breast, '88 169
Smoked Turkey Medley, '90 128
Soufflé, Turkey, '80 271
Soup, Bean-and-Turkey, '93 319
Soup, Curried Turkey, '86 332
Soup Mix, Turkey-Noodle, '89 330
Soup, Turkey-Barley, '91 312
Soup, Turkey Carcass, '86 284
Soup, Turkey-Noodle, '91 312
Soup, Turkey-Rice, '90 89
Soup, Turkey-Vegetable, '84 4; '88 264; '91 312
Soup, Williamsburg Turkey, '90 287
Spread, Curried Turkey, '92 16
Spread, Turkey Party, '83 282
Squash Dressing, Turkey with, '87 248
Steaks, Grilled Marinated Turkey, '93 170
Stew, Hearty Turkey, '79 252
Stew, Turkey-Tomato, '90 279
Stir-Fry, Italian, '92 126
Stir-Fry, Turkey-Broccoli, '91 62
Stock, Light Poultry, '90 31
Stuffed Turkey Breast, '87 270; '89 322
Stuffed Turkey Breast with Seasoned Dressing, '83 320; '84 128
Sweet-and-Sour Turkey, '79 252
Tarragon Cream, Turkey with, '91 60
Tenderloins, Lime-Buttered Turkey, '92 127
Tomatoes, Turkey Stuffed, '94 140
Topping, Turkey-Vegetable, '94 22
Treats, Turkey, '93 256
Turnovers, Home-Style Turkey, '94 325
Turnovers, Turkey Sausage, '95 239
Wild Turkey, Country-Fried, '94 306

TURNIPS
    au Gratin, Turnip, '79 289
    au Gratin, Turnips, '84 229; '88 229;
      '89 244
    Boiled Turnips, '83 242
    Braised Turnips, '91 219
    Casserole, Baked Turnip, '82 274
    Casserole, Turnip, '83 242; '84 229
    Cheese Sauce, Turnips in, '84 229
    Creamy Cooked Turnips, '86 224
    Dip, Turnip Green, '91 13
    Fried Turnips, Shoestring, '81 274
    Gingered Turnips, '82 274
    Glazed Turnips, '81 274
    Greens and Ham Hock, Southern Turnip,
      '80 119
    Greens, Fresh Turnip, '92 339
    Greens, Old-Fashioned Turnip, '85 255
    Greens, Turnip, '90 13, 232; '95 306
    Greens, Turnip-and-Collard, '92 215
    Greens with Turnips, Turnip, '84 230
    Hash Brown Turnips, '79 254
    Julienne, Turnips and Carrots, '86 295
    Onions, Turnips and, '83 242
    Orange Carrots and Turnips, Sunset,
      '94 213
    Parsleyed Turnips and Carrots, '79 253
    Party Turnips, '84 230
    Potatoes, Turnips and, '79 254
    Pudding, Turnip, '94 213
    Salad, Irish Turnip, '94 178
    Salad, Turnip, '85 235
    Salad, Turnip-and-Carrot, '91 212
    Saucy Turnips, '85 289
    Sauté, Carrot-Turnip, '93 241
    Scalloped Potatoes and Turnips, '85 235
    Scalloped Turnips, '79 254
    Slaw, Turnip, '89 245
    Soufflé, Turnip, '79 254
    Soup, Creamy Turnip, '84 279
    Soup, Oyster-Turnip, '94 328
    Soup, Turnip, '92 217
    Southern Turnips, '87 190
    Supreme, Turnip, '79 254
    Sweet-and-Sour Turnips, '81 274
TURTLE
    Fried Cooter (Soft-Shell Turtle), '80 99
    Soup au Sherry, Turtle, '80 56
    Soup, Turtle, '92 92
TZIMMES
    Fruit Tzimmes with Brisket, Mixed, '93 114
    Sweet Potato-Beef Tzimmes, '92 234
    Tzimmes, '95 102

V

VANILLA
    Almond Crunch, Vanilla, '93 243
    Beach, The, '95 168
    Cake, Vanilla Chiffon, '79 266
    Cheesecake, Creamy Vanilla, '89 93
    Cookies 'n' Cream Dessert, Gold-Dusted,
      '94 271
    Cookies, Vanilla Slice-and-Bake, '85 171
    Cream, Vanilla, '81 248; '83 M115
    Crescents, Vanilla, '82 307
    Cupcakes, Golden Vanilla, '85 121
    Cupcakes, Vanilla, '92 14
    Custard, Baked Vanilla, '82 129
    Dessert, Glorified Vanilla Sherry, '81 85
    Extract, Home-Brewed Vanilla, '83 228
    Extract, Homemade Vanilla, '83 228
    Extract, Vanilla, '94 243

Finger Painting Never Tasted So Good,
    '95 167
Frosting, Vanilla, '84 36; '85 236; '92 14, 274
Frosting, Vanilla Buttercream, '92 239;
    '94 99
Frosting, Vanilla-Rum, '85 324
Frosty, French Vanilla, '79 148
Fruit Cup, Vanilla, '80 183
Glaze, Vanilla, '85 M89; '89 211
Helado, Caramel-Vanilla (Caramel-Vanilla Ice
    Cream), '81 67
Ice Cream, Basic Vanilla, '88 202
Ice Cream, Country Vanilla, '82 143
Ice Cream, Honey-Vanilla, '95 178
Ice Cream Spectacular, Vanilla, '82 166
Ice Cream, Vanilla, '80 176; '86 129;
    '91 174
Ice Cream, Vanilla Custard, '92 148
Oil, Vanilla, '94 243
Parfait, Bodacious Peanut, '95 167
Pears, Vanilla Poached, '90 57
Pie, Fruit-Topped Vanilla Cream, '84 49
Pralines, Vanilla, '92 313; '93 51
Pudding, Creamy Vanilla, '83 227
Pudding, Vanilla, '88 32
Sauce, Almond-Vanilla Custard, '88 M177
Sauce, Pan-Fried Grouper with Vanilla Wine,
    '94 241
Sauce, Vanilla Crème, '94 243
Shortbread, Scottish, '94 242
Soufflé, Frozen Vanilla, '79 230; '82 173
Soufflés with Vanilla Crème Sauce, Vanilla,
    '94 242
Sugar, Vanilla, '94 243
Vinaigrette, Vanilla, '94 242
VEAL
    Amaretto-Lime Veal, '93 54
    Amelio, Veal, '86 142
    au Madeira, Veal, '81 131
    Birds, Veal, '84 260
    Burgoo, Five-Meat, '87 3
    Casserole, Veal and Wild Rice, '79 180
    Casserole, Veal Cutlet, '79 109
    Chops, Apple Veal, '87 220
    Chops Mediterranean, Veal, '79 108
    Company Veal and Carrots, '85 22
    Cordon Bleu, Veal, '87 219
    Cutlets, Stuffed Veal, '92 329
    Delight, Veal, '79 109
    Herbed Veal and Onions, '79 108
    Herbed Veal with Wine, '86 193
    Italian Style, Veal, '82 M68
    Lemon Veal, '93 35
    Lemon Veal Piccata, '86 118
    Lemon Veal with Artichoke Hearts,
      '87 219
    Marsala, Veal, '91 218, 310
    Marsala, Veal-and-Mushrooms, '89 44
    Meatballs, European Veal, '85 30
    Meat Loaf, Italian, '79 187
    Meat Loaf, Savory, '87 216
    Meat Loaf, Triple, '79 186
    Meat Loaf, Veal, '93 292
    New Orleans Veal with Crabmeat, '86 94
    Paprika, Veal, '88 113
    Parmigiana, Veal, '81 227
    Peppercorns, Veal with Green, '87 220
    Picante, Veal, '87 31
    Piccata, Veal, '92 181
    Piccata with Capers, Veal, '87 142
    Ragout, Veal-and-Artichoke, '94 43
    Roast, Best Baked Veal, '87 219
    Roast with Vegetables, Veal, '89 71

Sauce, Noodles with Veal, '80 236
Sauté, Veal-Cepe, '89 62
Savory Veal, '83 281
Scallopini à la Marsala, Veal, '79 109
Scallopini Marsala, Veal, '85 295
Scallopini of Veal al Sorriso, '79 85
Scallopini, Veal, '83 8, 125
Schnitzel, Swiss, '80 189
Skillet Veal, '83 200
Soup with Quenelles, Veal-Vermicelli,
    '94 14
Spaghetti, Veal, '84 276
Spaghetti with Veal and Peppers, '81 201;
    '82 14
Steak, Veal, '82 276
Stock, Brown Meat, '90 31
Stroganoff, Veal, '79 108
Supreme, Veal, '85 109
Sweetbreads, Creamed, '90 82
Swirls, Veal-and-Smithfield Ham, '86 253
Terrine of Pork and Veal, '93 287
Terrine with Mustard Sauce, Veal, '93 118
Wine Sauce, Veal and Carrots in, '81 31;
    '86 M139
VEGETABLES. *See also specific types.*
    à la Grill, Vegetables, '88 130
    Appetizers
        Antipasto, Easy, '92 24
        Antipasto, Vegetable, '85 263
        Bites, Veggie, '91 171
        Canapés, Vegetable, '91 252
        Cocktail, Fresh Vegetable, '82 165
        Dip and Vegetable Platter, Curry,
          '89 327
        Dip, Creamy Vegetable, '83 180
        Dip, Cucumber-Cheese Vegetable,
          '83 128
        Dip, Fresh Vegetable, '80 249
        Dip, Herb Vegetable, '89 269
        Dip, Starburst Vegetable, '82 248
        Dip, Tangy Vegetable, '87 196
        Dip, Vegetable, '79 52; '82 161
        Dip, Vegetable Garden, '85 215
        Dip, Zippy Vegetable, '84 256
        Egg Rolls, Vegetarian, '86 148
        Fresh Vegetable Party Tray, '82 122
        Fresh Vegetables, Parsley-Dill Dip with,
          '85 79
        Hot Vegetable Juice Appetizer,
          '93 324
        Marinated Vegetable Medley, '85 319;
          '95 91
        Marinated Vegetables, '94 183
        Marinated Vegetables Italian, '90 242
        Mushroom Caps, Vegetable, '81 246
        Nachos, Vegetable, '91 17
        Pâté, Vegetable-Chicken, '86 66
        Relish Tree, Christmas, '84 257
        Spread, Garden, '86 135
        Spread, Garden Vegetable, '93 184
        Spread, Vegetable, '90 144
        Spread, Vegetable Party, '84 166
        Tarragon Vegetable Appetizer, '83 277
        Terrine, Chicken-Vegetable, '84 131
        Terrine, Vegetable-Chicken, '83 224
    Bake with Sweet Bacon Dressing, Vegetable-
      Chicken, '93 108
    Barley and Vegetables, '91 81
    Beef and Vegetables, Company, '88 234
    Beef and Vegetables, Savory, '79 163
    Blanching Chart, Microwave, '80 M181
    Bread, Breakaway Vegetable, '82 74
    Bread, Herb-Vegetable-Cheese, '88 172

VEGETABLES *(continued)*

Bundles, Vegetable, '93 181
Buñuelos, '93 29
Burgers, Beef-and-Vegetable, '84 125
Burgers, Vegetable, '89 164
Burritos, Vegetable, '80 197; '90 134;
  '92 138
Burritos, Vegetarian, '93 319
Burritos with Avocado Sauce, Vegetable,
  '83 200
Buttermilk Sauce, Vegetables with, '84 6
Cabbage Rolls, Vegetarian, '91 86
Calabacitas, '95 130
Casseroles
  Beef and Vegetable Chow Mein
    Casserole, '83 313
  Beefy Vegetable Casserole, '79 248
  Cashew Casserole, '95 166
  Cheesy Vegetable Casserole, '81 103
  Curry Casserole, Vegetable-, '91 286;
    '92 27
  Enchiladas, Meatless, '93 106
  Fresh Vegetable Casserole, '82 225
  Garden Casserole, '82 168; '88 122
  Ham Casserole, Vegetable-and-, '84 91
  Lasagna Casserole, Vegetable, '92 198;
    '93 25
  Lasagna, Cheesy Vegetable, '79 84
  Lasagna, Colorful Vegetable, '87 19
  Lasagna, Garden, '83 119
  Lasagna, Vegetable, '84 201; '93 320;
    '95 211
  Layered Vegetable Casserole, '91 286;
    '92 27
  Medley Bake, Vegetable, '81 268
  Medley, Green Vegetable, '79 287;
    '80 34
  Mixed Vegetable Casserole,
    '83 208, 256; '86 327
  Mixed-Vegetable Casserole, '87 154
  Noodle Casserole, Vegetable, '91 30
  Pork Combo, Vegetable-, '85 113
  Scalloped Mixed Vegetables, '83 5
  Swiss Vegetable Medley, '95 26
  Tuna Vegetable Casserole, '81 135
  Veggies Casserole, '88 123
  Wine Sauce Casserole, Vegetables in,
    '95 133
Cheesecake, Layered Vegetable, '91 62;
  '92 51
Chicken and Dumplings with Vegetables,
  '85 M56
Chicken-and-Vegetable Platter, '88 M52
Chicken and Vegetables, '88 165
Chicken and Vegetables, Creamed, '91 90
Chicken and Vegetables, Roast, '81 3
Chicken and Vegetables Vermouth, '87 M37
Chicken and Vegetables with Ginger-Soy
  Sauce, '91 32
Chicken Breast with Turned Vegetables and
  Chive Sauce, Poached, '94 309
Chicken Strips and Vegetables, Marinated,
  '90 110
Chicken, Vegetable-Stuffed, '89 M65
Chicken with Vegetables Vinaigrette, Grilled,
  '91 26
Chicken with Wine-Soaked Vegetables, Baked,
  '84 277
Chili, Bodacious, '95 14
Chili, Mom's, '93 292
Chili, Vegetable, '91 28

Chili, Vegetarian, '84 280, 327; '91 284
Chops with Vegetables, Golden, '89 218
Chowchow, Nannie's, '95 250
Cornish Hens with Vegetables, Tarragon
  Roasted, '94 79
Creamed Spring Vegetables, '87 127
Crêpes, Chicken-Vegetable, '83 70
Crêpes, Vegetable-Filled Bran, '86 44
Croutons, Vegetable-Flavored, '84 148
Dilled Vegetable Sticks, '88 179
Dinner, Jollof Rice, '91 230; '92 325
Egg Rolls, Vegetarian, '86 148
Enchiladas, Meatless, '93 106
Enchiladas, Vegetable-Cheese, '94 42
en Papillote, Chicken and Vegetables, '86 145
Fennel, Braised, '88 46
Fennel, Italian-Style Braised, '93 56
Fennel with Garlic Butter, Steamed, '93 56
Fish-and-Vegetable Dinner, '91 196
Fish and Vegetables, Cheesy, '94 254
Fish and Vegetables, Grilled, '89 179
Fish Rolls, Vegetable-Filled, '86 M251
Fish with Vegetables, Poached, '89 332;
  '90 18
Flounder Rolls, Vegetable-Stuffed, '87 6
Flounder-Vegetable Medley, '85 217
Freezing Chart, Vegetable, '85 185
Fresh Vegetable Potpourri, '79 208
Frittata, Fresh Vegetable, '93 140
Frittata, Vegetable, '92 48; '93 183
Garden Combo, '86 172
Garden Harvest, '85 M142
Garden Surprise, '83 112
Garnishes, '82 280; '85 338, 339
Grilled Vegetables, Marinated, '95 162
Grilled Vegetables, '84 172; '92 124, 231
Grilled Vegetables, Italian-Style, '92 143
Grilled Vegetable Skewers, '94 160
Grouper with Confetti Vegetables, '88 M189
Ham-and-Vegetables, Skillet, '84 90
Hash, Vegetable, '95 262
Herbed-Smoked Vegetables, '85 145
Heroes, Vegetable Garden, '84 14
Juice Delight, Vegetable, '84 58
Julienne Vegetables, '93 31
Julienne Vegetables with Walnuts, '86 M251
Kabobs, Beef-and-Vegetable, '91 148
Kabobs, Fresh Vegetable, '81 158; '92 101
Kabobs, Grilled Vegetable, '93 170
Kabobs, Marinated Vegetable, '83 M195
Kabobs, Tangy Marinated Vegetable, '88 142
Kabobs, Vegetable, '87 116
Kabobs with Vegetables, Beef, '90 148
Kielbasa-Vegetable Dinner, '91 274
Lamb with Vegetables, Fillets of, '85 36
Lemon Vegetables, '93 83
Limping Susan, '90 155
Liver with Vegetables, Calf's, '85 219
Loaf, Beef-Vegetable, '79 164
Loaf, Pureed Vegetable-Cheese, '85 297
Loaf, Vegetable Meat, '85 M29
Marinade, Fresh Vegetable, '83 209
Marinade, Vegetable, '92 231
Marinated Vegetable Medley, '85 319; '89 14;
  '95 91
Marinated Vegetables, '79 146; '81 239;
  '85 67; '86 286
Marinated Vegetables, Honey-Mustard,
  '93 236
Marinated Vegetables, Sweet-and-Sour,
  '83 266
Meatballs and Vegetables with Horseradish
  Dressing, '91 32

Medley, Baked Vegetable, '81 75
Medley, Crunchy Vegetable, '84 254
Medley, Fresh Vegetable, '85 155
Medley, Garden Vegetable, '91 45
Medley, Italian Vegetable, '88 143
Medley, Masala Vegetable, '94 56
Medley, Mixed Vegetable, '82 126
Medley, Sautéed Vegetable, '83 101
Medley, Skillet Vegetable, '81 134
Medley, Spring Vegetable, '86 115
Medley, Summer Garden, '84 158
Medley, Summer Vegetable, '83 208
Medley, Vegetable, '79 102; '83 112; '86 327;
  '89 M129
Microwaving Fresh Vegetables, '82 M138
Mint Sauce over Vegetables, '92 104
Mixed Vegetables, '83 M195
Mushroom Caps, Vegetable, '81 246
Nests, Scallops in Vegetable, '91 70
Olive Butter, Vegetables Tossed in, '91 295
Omelet, Beefy Vegetable, '83 188
Omelet, Cheddar-Vegetable, '83 205
Omelet, Cheesy Vegetable, '85 49
Omelet, Fresh Vegetable, '84 211
Omelet, Golden Vegetable, '82 123
Omelet Primavera, '87 71
Omelet, Puffy Vegetable, '83 188
Omelet, Vegetarian, '84 114
Open-Faced Vegetarian Melt, '87 106
Orange Roughy, Vegetable-Topped, '93 67
Orange Roughy with Vegetables, Basil-,
  '92 98
Paella, Garden, '82 245
Paella, Spanish, '85 26
Pancakes, Vegetable, '88 297
Pancakes, Vegetable-Rice, '93 43
Pasta
  Fettuccine Primavera, '89 238; '94 85
  Fettuccine, Vegetable, '83 312
  Garden Pasta, '82 199
  Garden Vegetables, Pasta and, '87 192
  Linguine with Roasted Vegetables,
    Traveling, '93 178
  Mediterranean Pasta, '95 341
  Mixed Vegetables, Pasta with Sausage
    and, '84 249
  Noodle Ring, Beef and Vegetables in a,
    '85 285
  Orzo Primavera, '92 192
  Potpourri, Pasta, '94 33
  Primavera, Almost Pasta, '86 38
  Primavera, Chicken-Pasta, '91 72
  Primavera, Creamy Pasta, '95 167
  Primavera, Garden Spiral, '91 30
  Primavera, Pasta, '85 86; '89 105;
    '93 168
  Primavera, Smoked Turkey Pasta,
    '90 84
  Roasted Vegetables and Pasta, '93 184
  Sauce, Pasta with Vegetable, '83 163
  Spaghetti, Chicken-Vegetable, '92 281
  Spaghetti, Fresh Vegetables with, '86 257
  Spaghetti, Sautéed Vegetables with,
    '81 89
  Spaghetti, Shrimp-and-Vegetable,
    '91 170
  Spaghetti with Vegetables, '85 67
  Vermicelli, Scallop-Vegetable, '87 143
Pepper Cups, Hot Vegetable, '88 M188
Pie, Chicken-Vegetable Pot, '81 281; '82 30
Pies, Vegetable-Beef, '80 286
Pilaf, Barley-Vegetable, '91 33
Pilaf, Fruit-and-Vegetable Rice, '84 196

VEGETABLES (continued)

Pizza, Blazing Sunset, '95 267
Pizza, Deep-Dish Vegetarian, '85 243
Pizza, Garden, '89 108
Pizza, Southwestern Veggie, '95 126
Pizza, Turkey-Vegetable, '90 139
Pizza, Vegetable, '89 64; '94 218
Pizza, Vegetarian Processor, '89 225
Pizza, Veggie, '94 78
Platter, Fresh Vegetable, '92 60
Platter, Vegetable, '88 M187
Pockets, Vegetable, '85 215
Pork Chops and Garden Vegetables, '88 297
Pork Chops, Skillet Vegetable, '85 179
Pork with Vegetables, Medaillons of, '88 223
Potatoes, Vegetable-Topped Stuffed, '85 235
Pot Roast Medley, Vegetable-, '83 319
Pot Roast with Vegetables, '80 59; '81 M208
Pot Roast with Vegetables, Marinated, '88 M52
Punch, Hot Vegetable, '93 12
Puree, Smoked Vegetable, '93 156
Quesadilla with Roasted Salsa, Northern New Mexican Vegetable, '95 130
Quiche, Cheese-Vegetable, '81 228
Quiche, Ham-and-Vegetable, '84 326
Quiche, Vegetable, '87 M219
Ragoût, Vegetable, '89 172
Ratatouille, '84 105, 243; '85 92; '89 174
Ratatouille-Bran Stuffed Eggplant, '86 44
Ratatouille, Eggplant-Zucchini, '81 205
Ratatouille, Microwave, '95 M232
Ratatouille Niçoise, '81 22
Ratatouille Pie, '88 198
Ratatouille, Quick-and-Easy, '80 212
Ratatouille, Sausage, '89 248
Ratatouille-Stuffed Eggplant, '83 187
Ratatouille Supreme, '86 172
Relish, Eight-Vegetable, '84 179
Relish, Garden, '83 259
Relish, Vegetable, '90 147
Rice, Garden, '92 12
Rice Toss, Vegetable-, '91 309
Rice, Vegetables and, '93 91
Rice with Vegetables, '79 64; '85 83
Risotto Primavera, '95 163
Roasted Vegetables, '95 64
Salads
　　Aspic, Cheesy Vegetable, '81 73
　　Aspic with Horseradish Dressing, Crisp Vegetable, '87 152
　　Boats, Salad, '80 93
　　Brown Rice-and-Vegetable Salad, '84 202
　　Calico Salad, '82 35
　　Cauliflower-Vegetable Salad, '85 158
　　Chicken Salad, Vegetable-, '91 287
　　Chicken-Vegetable Salad, Basil-, '92 162
　　Chicken Vinaigrette Salad, Vegetable-, '86 135
　　Chinese Salad, '80 4
　　Composée, Salad, '79 171
　　Composé, Salad, '93 126
　　Congealed Fresh Vegetable Salad, '82 240
　　Congealed Salad, Cheesy-Vegetable, '86 199
　　Congealed Salad, Fresh Vegetable, '91 229

Congealed Salad, Lemon-Vegetable, '85 22
Congealed Vegetable Salad, '79 276
Corned Beef Salad, Vegetable-, '80 148
Creamy Vegetable Salad, '79 47
Creole Salad, '79 147
Crunchy Vegetable Salad, '79 11; '80 217; '83 216
Different Vegetable Salad, '82 143
Easy Vegetable Salad, '83 316; '84 16
Fennel Salad, Marinated, '93 56
Freezer Salad, '94 118
Garden Medley Salad, '80 122
Garden Salad, '87 62
Garden Salad Bowl, '82 239
Greek Salad, '93 208
Greek Salad, Garden, '86 173
Green-and-White Vegetable Salad, '79 286
Green Vegetable and Egg Salad, '79 191
Green Vegetable Salad, Overnight, '80 5
Grilled Vegetable Salad, '94 203
Healthy Salad, '95 133
Horseradish Dressing, Vegetable Salad with, '92 85
Italian Vegetable Salad, '81 253; '82 19
Luncheon Salad, '84 232
Macaroni-Vegetable Salad, '86 209
Marinade, Garden, '81 23
Marinade, Medley, '79 20
Marinade, Tossed Vegetable, '84 266
Marinated Combo Salad, '82 267
Marinated Garden Vegetables, '87 252
Marinated Mixed Vegetables, '89 276; '92 106
Marinated Salad, '91 186
Marinated Salad, Eight-Vegetable, '80 218
Marinated Summer Salad, '81 153
Marinated Vegetable-Bacon Bowl, '79 191
Marinated Vegetable Medley, '95 91
Marinated Vegetable Patch Salad, '84 232
Marinated Vegetables, '85 67; '86 286; '88 4, 170
Marinated Vegetable Salad, '79 106, 143; '81 280; '82 163; '83 260; '84 13; '87 243; '92 64, 91
Marinated Vegetable Salad, Crispy, '84 193
Marinated Vegetable Salad, Fresh, '86 173
Marinated Vegetables, Honey-Mustard, '93 236
Marinated Vegetables, Zesty, '82 272
Marinated Vegetable Toss, '82 113
Marinated Veggies, '91 46
Marinate, Fresh Vegetable, '80 33; '81 230
Meal-in-One Salad, '82 232
Mediterranean Salad, '95 132
Medley Salad, Vegetable, '88 86
Mexican Salad, '81 113
Minted Vegetable Salad, '88 23
Mixed Vegetable Salad, '80 115; '81 302; '82 239; '83 317; '84 16; '86 136
Next-Day Vegetable Salad, '83 81
Oriental Salad, Make-Ahead, '82 163
Oriental Vegetable Salad, '84 290

Overnight Vegetable Salad, '90 33
Pasta and Vegetables, '89 255
Pasta Salad, Vegetable, '89 256; '91 143
Pasta Salad, Vegetable-, '92 167
Pasta-Vegetable Salad, '95 238
Pebble Salad, '91 27
Pita Bread Salad, '95 86
Primavera Salad, '93 140
Quick Summer Italian Salad, '92 79
Rainbow Vegetable Salad, '83 111
Ratatouille Pasta Salad, '90 74
Refrigerated Vegetable Salad, '84 120
Relish Salad, Vegetable, '82 267
Rice-and-Vegetable Salad, '86 42
Rice Salad, Vegetable-, '80 148; '83 198; '85 87
Ring, Tomato-Vegetable, '81 302
Riviera, Salade, '89 12
Rolls, Vegetable Salad, '82 278
Senator's Salad, '79 191
Seven-Layer Vegetable Salad, '79 88
Shrimp Salad, Vegetable-, '79 190
Slaw, Layered, '93 214
Slaw, Vegetable, '81 280
Spring Vegetable Salad, '88 48
Summertime Salad, '79 143
Swedish Vegetable Salad, '82 23
Sweet-and-Sour Vegetable Salad, '81 25
Tangy Vegetable Toss, '79 144
Tarragon-Vegetable Salad, '85 288
Tortellini Salad, Garden, '91 44
Variety Salad, '79 113
Vinaigrette, Vegetables, '82 225, 290
Walnuts, Vegetable Salad with, '86 118
Warm Vegetable Salad, '95 174
Winter Vegetable Salad, '86 42
Salmon Scaloppine with Vegetable Confetti and Pernod Sauce, '94 172
Salsa, Garden, '91 182
Sandwich, Big Veggie, '92 196
Sandwiches, Open-Face Tofu-Veggie, '86 5
Sandwiches, Vegetarian Pita, '84 193
Sandwich, Vegetable Puff, '85 51
Sauce, Cheesy Vegetable, '92 M134
Sauce, Greek Fish with Vegetable, '82 72
Sauce, Tangy Vegetable, '89 280
Sauce, Turkey Patties in Vegetable-Tomato, '87 18
Sauce, Vegetable, '89 98
Sauce, Vegetable Butter, '86 174
Sauce, Vegetable-Cheese, '85 M152
Sausage, Spicy Vegetables and, '80 82
Sausage Vegetable Dinner, '84 250
Sauté, Cajun Vegetable, '92 62
Sautéed Vegetables, Grouper with, '90 M233
Sautéed Vegetables with Spaghetti Squash, '84 128
Sauté, Garden, '87 90
Sautéing Fresh Vegetables, '82 138
Sauté, Tossed Vegetable, '92 138
Sauté, Vegetarian, '95 69
Scallops en Brochette with Vegetables, '80 163
Scallops with Vegetables, Bay, '84 233
Seasoning Blend, Vegetable, '88 29
Sesame Sauce, Vegetables with, '83 112
Shrimp and Vegetables, '82 6
Skillet Dinner, Fresh Vegetable, '95 229
Skillet, Potato-Vegetable, '92 61
Skillet, Vegetable-Beef, '86 172

VEGETABLES *(continued)*

Soups

Bean Soup, Vegetable-, **'83** 317
Beef-and-Barley Vegetable Soup,
  '89 31
Beef Soup, Hearty Vegetable-, **'84** 102
Beef Soup, Spicy Vegetable-, **'88** 11
Beef Soup, Vegetable-, **'88** 296
Beefy Vegetable Soup, **'79** 113; **'84** M38
Beefy Vegetable Soup, Quick, **'80** 25
Bisque, Shrimp-Vegetable, **'82** 313;
  '83 66
Broth, Savory Vegetable, **'81** 230
Burger Soup, Vegetable-, **'82** 6
Cheese Soup, Creamy Vegetable-,
  '81 244
Cheese Soup, Creamy Vegetable,
  '83 230
Cheese Soup, Vegetable-, **'89** 15
Cheesy Vegetable Soup, **'80** 73
Chicken-Vegetable Soup, **'88** 18
Chili Vegetable Soup, **'94** 120
Chowder, Cheesy Vegetable, **'80** 25;
  '83 20
Chowder, Creamy Chicken-Vegetable,
  '92 20
Chowder, Harvest, **'83** 317
Chowder, Hearty Vegetable, **'88** 56
Chowder, Oven-Roasted Vegetable,
  '95 229
Chunky Vegetable Soup, **'89** M283
Clear Vegetable Soup, **'79** 130
Down-Home Vegetable Soup, **'90** 32
Garden Soup, **'85** 241
Garden Vegetable Soup, **'83** 140;
  '86 160
Garden Vegetable Soup, Cold, **'84** 197
Gazpacho, **'84** 112; **'85** 164
Gazpacho, Chilled, **'84** 138
Gazpacho, Cool, **'83** 140
Gazpacho, Smoked Vegetable, **'93** 156
Gazpacho, Spring, **'81** 112
Gazpacho, Summer, **'84** 181
Harvest Soup, **'79** 101
Hearty Vegetable Soup, **'80** 26
Homemade Soup, **'79** 198
Leek-Vegetable Soup, **'86** 304
Light Vegetable Soup, **'84** 280
Marvelous Vegetable Soup, **'82** 3
Mix, Vegetable Soup, **'84** 148
Old-Fashioned Vegetable Soup, **'86** 304
Quick Vegetable Soup, **'79** 190;
  '85 24, 32
Quick Veggie Soup, **'91** 31
Spicy Vegetable Soup, **'79** 198; **'93** 293
Stock, Vegetable, **'90** 31
Tomato-Vegetable Soup, **'81** 177;
  '86 9
Turkey-Vegetable Soup, **'84** 4; **'88** 264;
  '91 312
Vegetable Soup, **'80** 128; **'84** 148;
  '85 106; **'86** 187; **'87** 83, 123;
  '88 266; **'93** 157
Spread, Vegetable-Egg, **'87** 106
Spread, Vegetable Sandwich, **'83** 174;
  '85 135
Squash, Vegetable-Stuffed, **'84** 104
Steak with Vegetables, Skewered, **'81** 124
Steak with Vegetables, Swiss, **'81** 273
Steamed and Minted Garden Toss, **'83** 173
Steamed Dinner, Easy, **'83** M314

Steamed Fish and Vegetables, **'91** 32
Steamed Garden Vegetables, **'93** 155
Steamed Herbed Vegetables, **'93** M303
Steamed Vegetable Medley, **'86** 50; **'90** 29
Steamed Vegetables with Garlic-Ginger Butter
  Sauce, **'94** 89
Steamed Vegetables with Mustard Sauce,
  '83 208
Steaming Fresh Vegetables, **'82** 138, 183
Stew, Fish-and-Vegetable, **'87** 220
Stew, Minestrone, **'93** 184
Stew, Mixed Vegetable, **'84** 13
Stew, Shortcut Vegetable-Beef, **'89** 218
Stew, Sweet-and-Sour Beef and Vegetable,
  '85 87
Stew, Vegetable-Beef, **'94** 323
Stir-Fry. *See also* Wok Cooking.
  Almond-Vegetable Stir-Fry, **'86** 222
  Beef and Vegetables, Stir-Fried,
    '88 301
  Beef-and-Vegetables, Stir-Fry, **'84** 141
  Beef-and-Vegetable Stir-Fry, **'81** 211;
    '87 22
  Beef with Chinese Vegetables, **'81** 211
  Beef with Oriental Vegetables, **'84** 140
  Chicken and Vegetables, Almond,
    '86 21
  Chicken and Vegetables, Chinese,
    '81 212
  Chicken and Vegetables, Lemon,
    '88 118
  Chicken and Vegetables, Stir-Fry, **'86** 249
  Chicken-and-Vegetables, Stir-Fry,
    '86 68
  Chicken and Vegetable Stir-Fry, **'82** 237
  Chicken and Vegetables, Walnut,
    '85 194
  Chicken, Stir-Fry Vegetables with,
    '84 195
  Chicken-Vegetable Stir-Fry, **'83** 151;
    '84 13, 141
  Chinese Vegetable Pouches, **'94** 34
  Convenient Vegetable Stir-Fry, **'95** 157
  Curried Vegetables, **'89** 219
  Curry, Stir-Fried Vegetables with,
    '87 51
  Medley, Chinese Vegetable, **'84** 33
  Medley, Stir-Fry, **'88** 156
  Medley Stir-Fry, Vegetable, **'85** 109
  Mixed Vegetable Stir-Fry, **'79** 268;
    '80 14
  Orange Roughy-and-Vegetable Stir-Fry,
    '91 50
  Oriental Vegetables, **'84** 26; **'85** 108
  Sausage and Vegetables, Stir-Fry, **'86** 213;
    '87 82
  Shrimp and Vegetables, Stir-Fry, **'87** 91
  Skillet-Fried Vegetables, **'88** 156
  Steak-and-Vegetable Stir-Fry, **'84** 8
  Stir-Fried Vegetables, **'79** 217; **'83** 193;
    '90 136
  Stir-Frying Fresh Vegetables, **'82** 138
  Three-Vegetable Stir-Fry, **'86** 174
  Vegetable Stir-Fry, **'79** 214;
    '82 M172, 208; **'84** 104
Succotash, **'85** 106
Succotash, Easy, **'80** 165
Succotash, Summer, **'86** 170
Summer Vegetables, **'91** 136
Supper, Vegetarian, **'86** 222
Tempura, Basic, **'81** 68
Tempura, Cornmeal, **'81** 68
Tempura, Vegetable, **'79** 112

Terrine, Chicken-Vegetable, **'84** 131
Terrine, Vegetable-Chicken, **'83** 224
Tomatoes, Vegetable Stuffed, **'94** 141
Topper, Vegetable-Cheese Potato, **'86** 6
Topping, Turkey-Vegetable, **'94** 22
Topping, Vegetable, **'79** 79
Torte, Layered Vegetable, **'84** 52
Trio, Vegetable-Herb, **'83** 172
Turnovers, Vegetable, **'86** 24
Tzimmes, **'95** 102
Veal Roast with Vegetables, **'89** 71
Venison-Vegetable Bake, **'87** 304
Yataklete Kilkil, **'95** 71
Yuca Con Mojo, **'93** 29
VENISON. *See* **GAME.**
VINEGARS
Basil Vinegar, **'93** 218
Cranberry Vinegar, **'91** 288
Dill-and-Chive Vinegar, **'84** 300
Garlic-Basil Vinegar, **'85** 124
Herb Vinegar, Five-, **'85** 124
Herb Vinegar, Homemade, **'79** 100
Herb Vinegar, Mixed, **'84** 107
Lemon-Mint Vinegar, **'85** 124
Lemon Vinegar, **'95** 31
Mango-Cilantro Vinegar, **'95** 190
Mint Vinegar, **'92** 104
Orange Vinegar, **'95** 31
Oregano-Lemon Vinegar, Spicy, **'85** 124
Peach-Mint Vinegar, **'95** 190
Raspberry-Lemon Vinegar, **'87** 134
Raspberry-Thyme Vinegar, **'95** 190
Shallot-Tarragon-Garlic Vinegar, **'93** 191
Southwest Vinegar, **'94** 200
Tarragon-Dill Vinegar, **'85** 124
Tarragon Vinegar, **'84** 107; **'89** 194;
  '94 201
Tomato-Herb Vinegar, **'94** 200

Waffles

Banana-Ginger Waffles, **'86** 96
Banana-Oatmeal Waffles, **'94** 206
Banana Split Waffles, **'89** 205
Belgian Waffles, **'94** 206
Brunch Waffles, Crunchy, **'81** 41
Chicken-Pecan Waffles, Southern, **'82** 231
Chocolate Waffles with Strawberry Cream,
  '88 153
Club Soda Waffles, **'94** 206
Cornbread Waffles, **'79** 265; **'91** 90
Corn-Chile Waffles, **'94** 206
Cornmeal Waffles, **'85** 201; **'94** 22
French Toast, Waffled, **'82** 47
French Waffles, **'86** 138
Fudge Waffles, **'94** 205
Gingerbread Waffles, **'91** 68
Ham Waffles, **'80** 44
Light Waffles, **'91** 139
Oat Bran Waffles, **'92** 139
Oatmeal-Nut Waffles, **'83** 96
Oatmeal Waffles, **'89** 107
Peanut Butter Waffles, Honey-Buttered,
  '94 M206
Pecan Waffles, **'87** 225
Pumpkin-Nut Waffles, **'86** 96
Pumpkin Waffles, **'95** 282
Pumpkin Waffles with Mandarin Orange
  Sauce, Dessert, **'89** 204
Quick Bread Mix, **'81** 90
Quick Mix Waffles, **'86** 9
Refrigerator Waffles, Best Ever, **'87** 225

WAFFLES (continued)

Sausage Waffles, '83 50
Sorghum-Ginger Waffles, '85 239
Southern Waffles, '87 225
Sweet Potato Waffles, '88 208
Sweet Potato Waffles with Orange Butter, '90 323
Tuna Waffle-Wich, Hot, '88 272; '89 181
Wacky Waffles, '93 195
Waffles, '81 90
Walnut Waffles, Crunchy, '85 48
Whole Wheat Dessert Waffle, '79 92
Whole Wheat Waffles, '84 228
WALNUTS
Apple-Date-Nut Ring, '90 212
Bonbons, Coconut-Black Walnut, '82 307
Breads
    Apple-Nut Bread, '79 12
    Apple-Nut Bread, Fresh, '87 256
    Applesauce-Honey Nut Bread, '87 300
    Apricot-Nut Bread, '79 24
    Carrot-Walnut Bread, '88 284
    Cherry Nut Bread, '81 306; '82 36
    Chocolate Date-Nut Bread, '81 284
    Cinnamon-Nut Bubble Bread, '80 22
    Cranberry-Orange Nut Bread, '80 288
    Date-Nut Bread, '85 306
    Honey-Walnut Swirl, '80 21
    Loaf, Apricot-Nut, '81 8
    Loaf, Blue Ribbon Date-Walnut, '80 15
    Loaf, Nutty Wheat, '90 65
    Muffins, Carrot-Date-Nut, '86 262
    Muffins, Nutty Pumpkin, '86 291
    Twists, Fruit-Nut, '82 253
    Walnut Bread, '93 77
    Wine-Date Nut Bread, '82 253
Brie, Walnut-Baked, '93 241
Brie, Walnut-Fried, '86 244
Broccoli, English Walnut, '89 68
Brownies, Chocolate-Walnut, '89 325
Brownies, Walnut-Cream Cheese, '84 240
Burgers, Nutty, '87 185
Burgers, Walnut, '89 163
Cake, Apple-Nut, '87 76
Cake, Apple-Walnut, '94 242
Cake, Black Walnut, '80 253; '84 316; '90 308
Cake, Black Walnut Pound, '92 16
Cake, Orange Nut, '80 70
Cake, Orange-Nut Butter, '80 254
Cake Roll, Date-Nut, '89 94
Cakes, Mini-Mincemeat Nut, '88 257
Cake, Yogurt-Lemon-Nut, '89 169
Candied Nuts, '81 261
Carrots with Walnuts, Julienne, '84 188
Cheese, Nutty Date Dessert, '87 299
Chicken and Vegetables, Walnut, '85 194
Chicken Breasts, Walnut-Stuffed, '85 293
Chicken, Crispy Walnut, '90 89
Chicken, Deep-Fried Walnut, '87 175
Chicken, Walnut, '85 194
Chocolate-Nut Chews, '81 92
Cobbler, Apple-Walnut, '79 154; '81 248
Coffee Cake, Cranberry-Nut, '81 250
Coffee Cake, Sour Cream-Walnut, '79 209
Coffee Cake, Walnut, '93 124
Cookies, Apple-Nut, '80 228

Cookies, Frosted Pumpkin-Walnut, '82 217
Cookies, Nutty Oatmeal, '81 130
Cookies, Rich Date-Nut Chocolate Chip, '92 207
Cookies, Simply Walnut, '91 236
Cookies, Walnut, '81 301
Cupcakes, Apple-Nut, '82 279
Cups, Chocolate-Walnut, '85 213
Dressing, Green Beans with Walnut, '94 279
Dressing, Honey-Walnut, '93 107
Fillets, Blue Cheese-Walnut Stuffed, '95 327
Filling, Honey-Walnut, '80 21
Fried Walnuts, Chinese, '81 254
Frosting, Nutty Coconut, '86 8
Fruit, Cheese, and Nuts, '93 324
Fudge, Nutty White, '81 253
Fudge, Orange-Walnut, '92 288
Green Beans, Lemon-Walnut, '93 304
Ice Cream Balls, Nutty, '89 72
Meatballs, Mock, '81 243
Mousse, Coffee-Nut, '86 319
Parmesan Walnuts, Mixed Greens with, '95 301
Phyllo Baskets, Walnut-, '93 210
Pie, Walnut-Cranberry, '87 259
Pitas, Spinach-Walnut, '87 202; '88 43
Salad, Orange Walnut, '80 246
Salad, Raspberry-Walnut, '94 158
Salad, Shrimp-Walnut, '86 182
Salad, Sunburst Chicken-and-Walnut, '93 91
Salad, Walnut-Chicken, '89 14
Salad with Walnuts, Vegetable, '86 118
Sandwich, Date-Nut Lettuce, '94 202
Sauce, Apricot-Walnut Hard, '88 153
Sauce, Spaghetti with Parsley and Walnut, '80 30
Sauce, Walnut Cream, '93 275
Sauté, Broccoli and Walnut, '95 52
Sautéed Walnuts, Turkey Salad with, '86 117
Sherry-Orange Nuts, '86 M289
Slaw, Nutty Apple, '88 216
Spice Kisses, Walnut, '89 295
Spread, Date-Walnut, '87 292
Spread, Nutty Fruit-and-Cheese, '87 246
Strawberries with Walnuts, Stuffed, '85 122; '86 124
Stuffing, Apple-Walnut, '95 289
Stuffing, Tomatoes with Walnut-Rice, '91 102
Sweet Potatoes with Sherry and Walnuts, '86 286
Syrup, Maple-Nut, '80 228
Topping, Nutty, '86 16
Vegetables with Walnuts, Julienne, '86 M251
Waffles, Crunchy Walnut, '85 48
Zucchini with Walnuts, '84 213
WATERMELON. *See* **MELONS.**
WHEAT GERM
Biscuits, Wheat Germ, '86 261
Bread, Banana Wheat, '81 14
Crackers, Oatmeal-Wheat Germ, '84 236
Crisps, Sesame Wheat, '81 106
Muffins, Carrot-Wheat, '88 9
Muffins, Wheat Germ-Prune, '81 106
Pancakes, Wheat Germ, '86 242
Pancakes, Wheat Germ-Banana, '79 114
Squares, Spicy Wheat Germ, '80 44

WILD RICE. *See* **RICE/WILD RICE.**
WOK COOKING
Beef
    Asparagus, Stir-Fry Beef and, '91 124
    Broccoli and Beef, Stir-Fry, '83 110
    Broccoli, Quick Beef and, '91 123
    Broccoli, Stir-Fry Beef and, '79 47
    Broccoli Stir-Fry, Beef-and-, '91 46
    Chinese Beef Stir-Fry, '83 151
    Chinese-Style Beef, '87 50
    Chinese Vegetables, Beef with, '81 211
    Hungarian Stir-Fry, '93 64
    Indian Stir-Fry, '92 126
    Lime-Ginger Beef Stir-Fry, '92 65
    Meatballs, Sweet-and-Sour, '86 240
    Mongolian Beef, '85 2, 75
    Mongolian Beef Stir-Fry, '89 25
    Oriental Beef, '85 20
    Oriental Vegetables, Beef with, '84 140
    Peanutty Beef Stir-Fry, '95 157
    Pea Pods, Stir-Fry Beef and, '80 19
    Shredded Beef over Rice Noodles, '85 74
    Shrimp Stir-Fry, Beef-and-, '93 32
    Snow Peas, Oriental Beef and, '79 105
    Snow Peas, Stir-Fry Beef and, '83 22
    Snow Pea Stir-Fry, Beef and, '82 98
    Steak, Chinese Pepper, '82 236
    Steak, Fast-and-Easy Stir-Fried, '87 50
    Steak, Pepper Stir-Fry, '81 240
    Steak Sukiyaki, Flank, '88 233
    Stew, Beef, '86 51
    Stir-Fried Beef, '84 26
    Teriyaki Stir-Fry, '83 110
    Vegetables, Stir-Fried Beef and, '88 301
    Vegetables, Stir-Fry Beef-and-, '84 141
    Vegetable Stir-Fry, Beef-and-, '81 211; '87 22
    Wontons, Tex-Mex, '87 196
Catfish Stir, '84 184
Cheese Wontons with Hot Sauce, '83 74
Egg Rolls, '86 81
Eggrolls, Shrimp and Pork, '82 240; '83 18
Ham and Zucchini Stir-Fry, '79 47
Ham Stir-Fry, Easy, '86 332
Indian Stir-Fry, '92 126
Orange Roughy-and-Vegetable Stir-Fry, '91 50
Pasta Potpourri, '94 33
Pear Fritters, Ol' Timey, '86 51
Pork-and-Onions with Bean Sauce, '85 76
Pork, Hot-and-Spicy, '81 228
Pork in Garlic Sauce, Stir-Fried, '84 141
Pork Oriental, '81 212
Pork, Stir-Fried, '87 51
Pork, Sweet-and-Sour, '79 42; '80 227; '81 26; '85 34, 194
Pork Tenderloin, Curried, '86 76
Poultry
    Chicken à l'Orange, Stir-Fry, '83 82
    Chicken and Snow Pea Stir-Fry, '95 157
    Chicken and Vegetables, Almond, '86 21
    Chicken and Vegetables, Chinese, '81 212
    Chicken-and-Vegetables, Stir-Fry, '86 68
    Chicken and Vegetable Stir-Fry, '82 237

WOK COOKING, Poultry *(continued)*

Chicken and Vegetables, Walnut, '85 194
Chicken, Braised Bourbon, '86 51
Chicken-Broccoli Stir-Fry, '82 33
Chicken, Cashew, '79 255; '83 21
Chicken Chinese, '94 33
Chicken Curry, Stir-Fried, '87 51
Chicken-in-a-Garden, '80 18
Chicken in Soy and Wine, '84 26
Chicken, Lemon, '86 173
Chicken, Princess, '86 122
Chicken Stir-Fry, Chinese, '90 100
Chicken Stir-Fry, Easy, '91 124
Chicken Stir-Fry, Herb-, '89 177
Chicken Stir-Fry, Hurry-Up, '91 124
Chicken Stir-Fry, Kyoto Orange-, '87 96
Chicken Stir-Fry, Orange-, '84 68
Chicken Stir-Fry, Pineapple-, '89 176
Chicken Stir-Fry, Shiitake-, '89 61
Chicken, Stir-Fry Vegetables with, '84 195
Chicken, Sweet-and-Sour, '86 240
Chicken, Szechwan, '83 85
Chicken Tempura Delight, '85 66
Chicken-Vegetable Stir-Fry, '83 151; '84 13, 141
Chicken, Walnut, '85 126
Chicken with Cashews, '79 207
Chicken with Cashews, Szechwan, '81 212
Chicken with Peanuts, Oriental, '82 236
Chicken with Pineapple, Oriental, '86 42
Chicken with Plum Sauce, '82 236
Chicken, Zesty Stir-Fried, '83 82
Chicken-Zucchini Stir-Fry, '84 50
Chinese-Style Dinner, '84 26
Italian Stir-Fry, '92 126
Mexican Stir-Fry, '92 126
Turkey-Broccoli Stir-Fry, '91 62
Rice, Easy Fried, '84 76
Rice, Egg Fried, '80 19
Rice Special, Fried, '80 56
Rice with Sausage, Fried, '83 12
Sausage Rolls with Sweet-and-Sour Sauce, '83 74
Sausage Stir-Fry, '82 236
Scallop Stir-Fry, '94 32
Shrimp and Refried Rice, '89 176
Shrimp and Sirloin Supreme, '81 131
Shrimp and Vegetables, Stir-Fry, '87 91
Shrimp Skillet, Quick, '87 50
Shrimp Stir-Fry, Cajun, '92 127
Shrimp, Szechuan, '86 173
Shrimp, Tangy Honeyed, '94 32
Shrimp with Snow Peas, '85 75
Sugar Flips, '83 74
Vegetables
Asparagus and Mushrooms, '85 108
Asparagus, Stir-Fried, '87 52
Bok Choy-Broccoli Stir-Fry, '84 2
Broccoli, Jade-Green, '80 12
Broccoli, Stir-Fried, '83 227
Broccoli, Stir-Fry, '80 19
Broccoli with Sesame, '80 13
Broccoli with Sesame Seeds, '82 34
Brussels Sprouts Stir-Fry, '81 308
Cabbage, Lemon-Butter, '88 156

Cabbage, Stir-Fried, '81 75, 271; '85 109
Chinese Vegetable Medley, '84 33
Chinese Vegetable Pouches, '94 34
Convenient Vegetable Stir-Fry, '95 157
Curry, Stir-Fried Vegetables with, '87 51
Egg Rolls, Vegetarian, '86 148
Green Bean Medley, '85 108
Green Beans, Stir-Fried, '85 148
Greens, Stir-Fried, '94 33
Medley, Stir-Fry, '88 156
Medley Stir-Fry, Vegetable, '85 109
Mixed Vegetable Stir-Fry, '79 268; '80 14
Mushrooms with Bacon, Stir-Fried, '80 123
Oriental Vegetables, '84 26; '85 108
Pasta Potpourri, '94 33
Peas and Peppers, Stir-Fried, '87 51
Potato-Snow Pea Stir-Fry, '86 173
Skillet-Fried Vegetables, '88 156
Spinach, Chinese, '79 179
Spinach, Stir-Fry, '81 182
Spinach with Mushrooms, '80 19
Spinach Wontons, '83 74
Squash Medley, '84 128
Squash Medley, Stir-Fried, '80 123
Squash Stir-Fry, '80 184
Squash Stir-Fry, Two-, '86 174
Sweet Potato Pudding, '86 52
Three-Vegetable Stir-Fry, '86 174
Tomato-Zucchini Stir-Fry, '80 158
Vegetables, Stir-Fried, '79 217; '83 193; '90 136
Vegetable Stir-Fry, '82 208; '84 104
Zucchini-and-Tomato Stir-Fry, '85 108
Zucchini, Italian-Style, '80 123
Zucchini Pesto, '84 194
Zucchini Toss, Stir-Fry, '88 156

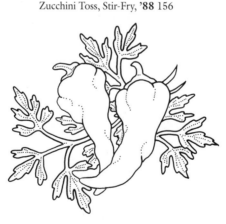

WONTONS
Bowls, Wonton Wrapper, '95 58
Cheese Wontons with Hot Sauce, '83 74
Chicken Wontons, '92 284
Chips, Baked Wonton, '91 138
Chips, Cinnamon-and-Sugar Wonton, '91 138
Chips, Garlic Wonton, '91 138
Chips, Lemon-and-Herb Wonton, '91 138
Chips, Parmesan Cheese Wonton, '91 138
Fried Wonton Envelopes, '95 96
Fried Wontons, Crispy, '83 21
Fruit-Filled Wontons, '85 287
Nibbles, Wonton, '85 287

Preparation Techniques, '83 74
Sausage Rolls with Sweet-and-Sour Sauce, '83 74
Spinach Wontons, '83 74
Sugar Flips, '83 74
Tex-Mex Wontons, '87 196

Y**OGURT**

Apples, Honey-Yogurt, '92 46
Breakfast-in-a-Bowl, '89 87
Carambola-Yogurt Calypso, '90 169
Chicken, Grilled Yogurt-Lemon, '81 111
Chicken, Savory Yogurt, '91 238; '92 28
Chicken, Yogurt-Sesame, '90 216
Desserts
Bars, Lemon Yogurt Wheat, '79 93
Cake, Strawberry Yogurt Layer, '94 85
Cake, Yogurt-Lemon-Nut, '89 169
Cake, Yogurt Pound, '84 10
Chocolate Yogurt, Mocha Sauce with, '92 243
Ice, Apricot Yogurt, '81 177
Ice Milk, Banana Yogurt, '89 199
Ice, Peach-Yogurt, '84 83
Lemon-Chiffon Frozen Yogurt, '85 54
Nectarines Royale, '85 132
Parfait, Crunchy Strawberry-Yogurt, '79 124
Peach Yogurt, Frozen Fresh, '90 139
Pie, Strawberry Yogurt, '80 232
Pie, Strawberry-Yogurt, '85 122; '86 124
Pie, Yogurt-Apricot, '85 132
Pie, Yogurt-Cheese, '82 121
Pops, Pineapple-Yogurt, '91 173
Sauce, Honey-Yogurt, '92 307
Strawberry Yogurt Delight, '85 77
Strawberry-Yogurt Dessert, '90 295
Tortoni, Apricot-Yogurt, '95 124
Vanilla Frozen Yogurt, '87 125
Dip, Curry, '85 132
Dip, Fruited Yogurt, '84 171
Dip, Yogurt, '94 21
Dip, Yogurt Herring, '80 232
Dressing, Asparagus with Yogurt, '79 66
Dressing, Ginger-Yogurt, '81 302
Dressing, Honey-Yogurt, '93 172
Dressing, Lemon-Yogurt, '93 17
Dressing, Orange-Yogurt, '85 304
Dressing, Sweet-Hot Yogurt, '86 40
Dressing, Turkey Waldorf Salad with Yogurt, '88 53
Dressing, Yogurt, '85 59, 215; '88 27
Dressing, Yogurt-Herb, '92 96
Dressing, Yogurt-Honey Poppy Seed, '83 177
Dressing, Yogurt Salad, '79 69
Filling, Fresh Raspberry Crêpes with Yogurt, '93 123
Fruit Medley, Yogurt-Granola, '91 58
Honey Yogurt, Orange Slices with, '91 68
Muffins, Yogurt, '88 55
Muffins, Yogurt-Muesli, '90 215
Omelet, Yogurt-Avocado, '81 33
Pancakes, Orange-Yogurt, '87 225
Pineapple-Yogurt Whirl, '91 132
Potatoes, Yogurt-Stuffed, '88 24
Rolls, Yogurt Crescent, '91 123
Salad, Crème de Menthe, '82 122
Salad, Cucumber-Yogurt, '87 33
Salad, Frozen Yogurt, '92 303
Salad, Strawberry Yogurt, '80 232
Salad, Yogurt-Cucumber, '82 122

YOGURT (continued)

Salad, Yogurt Fruit, '81 114
Sauce, Creamy Yogurt, '91 238; '92 28
Sauce, Lamb Meatballs with Yogurt, '85 132
Sauce, Yogurt, '89 283
Sauce, Yogurt-Horseradish, '85 66
Shake, Strawberry-Yogurt, '87 199
Slaw or Salad Dressing, Lemon-Yogurt, '88 54
Smoothie, Fruited Honey-Yogurt, '88 231;
    '89 23
Snack, Yogurt, '88 55
Soup, Avocado-Banana-Yogurt, '80 78
Soup, Cucumber-Yogurt, '82 157; '83 205
Soup, Potato-Yogurt, '92 217
Soup, Yogurt Fruit, '86 176
Topping, Yogurt-Cheese, '88 55

ZUCCHINI

Appetizers
    Caviar, Zucchini, '88 212
    Crab-Zucchini Bites, '84 M216
    Dip, Yellow Squash-Zucchini, '89 48
    French Fried Zucchini with Cocktail
        Sauce, '86 146
    French Fries, Zucchini, '82 78
    Fries, Zucchini, '90 147
    Hors d'Oeuvres, Zucchini, '80 151
    Pizzas, Zucchini, '88 212
    Scalloped Zucchini Bites, '91 165
    Shrimp Appetizers, Zucchini-, '89 311
Baked Zucchini, '83 209
Baked Zucchini Fans, '87 243
Bars, Zucchini, '85 77
Basil, Zucchini and Tomatoes, '89 147
Boats with Spinach, Zucchini, '82 252
Boats, Zucchini, '85 M143
Breads
    Apple Bread, Zucchini-, '87 255
    Banana-Zucchini Bread, '85 326
    Carrot Bread, Zucchini-, '83 190
    Chocolate-Zucchini Bread, '93 308
    Fritters, Cheesy Zucchini, '88 44
    Fritters, Zucchini, '81 163
    Honey Bread, Zucchini-, '89 143
    Muffins, Zucchini, '83 121; '86 146
    Spiced Zucchini Bread, '79 161; '86 162
    Spicy Zucchini Bread, '81 305; '82 36
    Squares, Zucchini, '82 103
    Zucchini Bread, '85 111; '86 93
Broiled Zucchini, Quick-and-Easy, '86 169
Buttered Zucchini and Carrots, '83 252
Cajun Squash, '88 142
Cake, Chocolate-Zucchini, '85 156
Cake, Zucchini, '79 24
Cake, Zucchini-Carrot, '93 20
Cake, Zucchini-Pineapple, '95 160
Calabaza Guisada con Puerco (Pumpkin
    Cooked with Pork), '80 193
Carrots and Zucchini, '84 262
Carrots, Zucchini with Baby, '88 24
Casseroles
    au Gratin, Potatoes-and-Zucchini, '84 5
    au Gratin, Zucchini and Tomato,
        '82 208
    Beef Bake, Zucchini-, '86 146
    Calabaza Mexicana (Mexican Squash),
        '81 196
    Carrot and Zucchini Casserole, '83 256
    Cheese-Egg-Zucchini Casserole, '84 114

Cheesy Zucchini Casserole, '82 168;
    '84 145
Corn-Zucchini Bake, '79 178
Egg Casserole, Zucchini-, '84 M113
Eggplant and Zucchini, Italian-Style,
    '79 289; '80 26
Italian Squash, '79 158
Italian Zucchini Casserole, '85 59
Jack Casserole, Zucchini-, '85 296
Lasagna, Garden, '83 119
Lasagna, Zucchini, '85 194
Manicotti, Zucchini, '84 194
Mexican Squash, '83 31
Parmesan Zucchini, '81 234
Parmesan, Zucchini, '81 108
Rice Casserole Italiano, Zucchini-,
    '89 146
Sausages Baked Zucchini and, '80 300
Scallop, Green-and-Gold, '81 159
Squash Bake, '82 107
Tomato Bake, Zucchini and, '82 158
Tomato Casserole, Zucchini-and-,
    '88 265
Zucchini Casserole, '79 157; '87 154
Coleslaw, Fiesta Zucchini, '91 168
Corn and Zucchini, '83 190
Corn Combo, Zucchini-, '86 218
Corn, Zucchini and, '86 177
Crab Cakes, Mock, '95 159
Crêpes, Zucchini, '79 157
Crispies, Zucchini, '95 179
Delight, Zucchini-Basil, '85 267
Dilled Fresh Zucchini, '81 174
Dilled Zucchini and Corn, '83 173
Dressing, Zucchini, '86 282
Easy Zucchini, '87 167
Eggplant and Squash, '83 187
Eggplant and Zucchini, Sautéed, '82 96
Fans, Baked Zucchini, '88 246
Fans, Herb Butter Zucchini, '90 201
Fans, Zucchini, '91 33
Fried Zucchini Strips, '81 184
Fries, Parmesan-Zucchini, '95 129
Frittata, Corn-and-Squash, '89 144
Frittata, Zucchini, '86 103
Fritters, Cheesy Zucchini, '88 44
Fritters, Zucchini, '81 163
Fruitcake, Zucchini, '88 284
Fry, Zucchini, '81 102
Gratin, Tomato-Zucchini, '95 171
Green Beans with Zucchini, '84 128
Grilled Zucchini Fans, '89 200
Grilled Zucchini with Feta, Greek, '95 190
Herbed Zucchini, '84 104
Italiano, Zucchini, '81 183
Italian Squash, '79 158
Italian-Style Zucchini, '80 123
Italian Zucchini, '83 M147
Julienne Zucchini and Carrots, '90 M14
Lemon-Garlic Zucchini, '89 226
Marinated Squash Medley, '94 126
Marinated Zucchini, '80 33; '89 102
Medley, Zucchini-and-Corn, '80 298;
    '81 25
Mexican Style, Zucchini, '80 184
Omelet, Zucchini, '81 99
Oven-Fried Zucchini, '86 211
Oven-Fried Zucchini Spears, '91 121
Pancakes, Zucchini, '93 43
Parmesan, Zucchini, '81 108; '82 103
Pecans, Zucchini with, '87 31
Pesto, Zucchini, '84 194
Pie, Cheesy Zucchini, '82 103

Pie, Italian-Style Zucchini, '83 43
Pie, Zucchini-Ham-Cheese, '80 272
Pollo con Calabacita (Mexican Chicken with
    Zucchini), '82 219
Provençal, Zucchini, '86 146
Quiche, Cheesy Zucchini, '83 312
Quiche, Swiss-Zucchini, '82 49
Quiche, Zucchini-Mushroom, '79 127
Quiche, Zucchini-Sausage, '83 122
Ratatouille, Eggplant-Zucchini, '81 205
Relish, Pollock with Summer Squash, '92 200
Relish, Sweet Zucchini, '95 159
Relish, Zucchini, '87 200
Rosemary, Summer Squash with, '88 143
Salad, Carrot-and-Zucchini, '83 240
Salad, Creamy Avocado and Zucchini, '79 208
Salad, Marinated Zucchini, '82 164; '90 32
Salad, Mushroom-Zucchini, '85 8
Salad, Summer Zucchini, '95 229
Salad, Turkey-Zucchini, '85 74
Salad, Zucchini, '82 104; '87 103; '89 128
Salad, Zucchini-Artichoke, '91 229
Salad, Zucchini Chef's, '83 143
Sandwiches, Open-Faced Zucchini, '88 159
Sauce, Spaghetti with Zucchini, '81 38
Sauce, Zucchini-Mushroom, '93 71
Sautéed Zucchini, '83 86; '92 60
Sautéed Zucchini and Carrots, '92 62, 99
Sautéed Zucchini and Sausage, '83 289
Sautéed Zucchini with Mushrooms, '94 135
Sauté, Zucchini, '81 183; '84 35
Scramble, Zucchini-Basil, '87 34
Skillet, Pattypan-Zucchini, '82 103
Skillet, Squash, '82 195
Skillet, Zippy Zucchini, '82 158
Skillet, Zucchini-Tomato, '93 206
Soufflé, Zucchini, '79 157
Soufflé, Zucchini-and-Corn, '83 265
Soups
    Chilled Zucchini Soup, '87 90
    Cilantro, Zucchini Soup with, '93 130
    Cold Zucchini Soup, '85 265; '92 64
    Cream of Zucchini Soup, '83 99
    Creamy Zucchini Soup, '83 140
    Dilled Zucchini Soup, '90 88
    Italian Sausage-Zucchini Soup, '84 4
    Summer Squash Soup, '84 193
    Watercress-Zucchini Soup, '91 72
    Zucchini Soup, '82 104; '84 181;
        '86 181; '89 14
South-of-the-Border Zucchini, '85 135
Spaghetti, Italian Zucchini, '85 2
Spaghetti, Zucchini, '83 160
Stir-Fried Squash Medley, '80 123
Stir-Fry, Chicken-Zucchini, '84 50
Stir-Fry, Ham and Zucchini, '79 47
Stir-Fry, Squash, '80 184
Stir-Fry, Tomato-Zucchini, '80 158
Stir-Fry, Two-Squash, '86 174
Stir-Fry, Zucchini-and-Tomato, '85 108
Stir-Fry Zucchini Toss, '88 156
Stuffed Zucchini, '86 54, 187; '89 M133
Stuffed Zucchini, Beef-, '86 M139
Stuffed Zucchini, Ham and Cheese, '79 157
Stuffed Zucchini, Italian, '84 119
Stuffed Zucchini Main Dish, '79 215
Stuffed Zucchini, Savory, '80 161
Stuffed Zucchini Supreme, '83 136
Stuffing, Haddock Fillets with Zucchini,
    '88 M191
Timbales, Corn-and-Zucchini, '92 100
Tomato with Herbs, Zucchini and, '92 182
Toss, Zucchini, '91 292